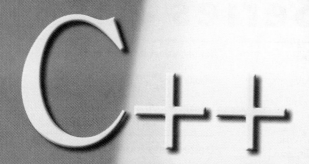

C++

HOW TO PROGRAM

NINTH EDITION

KT-471-294

Deitel Series Page

How To Program Series

Android How to Program
C How to Program, 7/E
C++ How to Program, 9/E
C++ How to Program, Late Objects Version, 7/E
Java™ How to Program, 9/E
Java™ How to Program, Late Objects Version, 8/E
Internet & World Wide Web How to Program, 5/E
Visual Basic® 2012 How to Program
Visual C#® 2012 How to Program, 3/E
Visual C++® 2008 How to Program, 2/E
Small Java™ How to Program, 6/E
Small C++ How to Program, 5/E

Simply Series

Simply C++: An App-Driven Tutorial Approach
Simply Java™ Programming: An App-Driven
    Tutorial Approach
Simply Visual Basic® 2010, 4/E: An App-Driven
    Tutorial Approach

CourseSmart Web Books

www.deitel.com/books/CourseSmart/

C++ How to Program, 7/E, 8/E & 8/E
Simply C++: An App-Driven Tutorial Approach
Java™ How to Program, 7/E, 8/E & 9/E

Simply Visual Basic 2010: An App-Driven
    Approach, 4/E
Visual Basic® 2012 How to Program
Visual Basic® 2010 How to Program
Visual C#® 2012 How to Program, 5/E
Visual C#® 2010 How to Program, 4/E

Deitel Developer Series

C++ for Programmers, 2/E
Android for Programmers: An App-Driven
    Approach
C# 2010 for Programmers, 3/E
Dive Into iOS 6: An App-Driven Approach
iOS 6 for Programmers: An App-Driven Approach
Java™ for Programmers, 2/E
JavaScript for Programmers

LiveLessons Video Learning Products

www.deitel.com/books/LiveLessons/

Android® App Development Fundamentals
C++ Fundamentals
C# Fundamentals
iOS 6 App Development Fundamentals
Java™ Fundamentals
JavaScript Fundamentals
Visual Basic Fundamentals

To receive updates on Deitel publications, Resource Centers, training courses, partner offers and more, please register for the free *Deitel Buzz Online* e-mail newsletter at:

www.deitel.com/newsletter/subscribe.html

and join the Deitel communities on Twitter®

@deitel

Facebook®

facebook.com/DeitelFan

and Google+

gplus.to/deitel

To communicate with the authors, send e-mail to:

deitel@deitel.com

For information on government and corporate *Dive-Into Series* on-site seminars offered by Deitel & Associates, Inc. worldwide, visit:

www.deitel.com/training/

or write to

deitel@deitel.com

For continuing updates on Prentice Hall/Deitel publications visit:

www.deitel.com
www.pearsoninternationaleditions.com/deitel

Visit the Deitel Resource Centers that will help you master programming languages, software development, Android and iPhone/iPad app development, and Internet- and web-related topics:

www.deitel.com/ResourceCenters.html

C++

HOW TO PROGRAM

NINTH EDITION

Paul Deitel
Deitel & Associates, Inc.

Harvey Deitel
Deitel & Associates, Inc.

International Edition contributions by
Soumen Mukherjee
Arup Kumar Bhattacharjee

PEARSON

Boston   Columbus   Indianapolis   New York   San Francisco   Upper Saddle River
Amsterdam   Cape Town   Dubai   London   Madrid   Milan   Munich   Paris   Montréal   Toronto
Delhi   Mexico City   São Paulo   Sydney   Hong Kong   Seoul   Singapore   Taipei   Tokyo

Vice President and Editorial Director: *Marcia J. Horton*
Executive Editor: *Tracy Johnson*
Associate Editor: *Carole Snyder*
Director of Marketing: *Christy Lesko*
Marketing Manager: *Yezan Alayan*
Marketing Assistant: *Jon Bryant*
Director of Production: *Erin Gregg*
Managing Editor: *Scott Disanno*
Associate Managing Editor: *Robert Engelhardt*
Publisher, International Edition: *Angshuman Chakraborty*
Publishing Administrator and Business Analyst, International Edition: *Shokhi Shah Khandelwal*
Acquisitions Editor, International Edition: *Shivangi Ramachandran*
Publishing Administrator, International Edition: *Hema Mehta*
Project Editor, International Edition: *Karthik Subramanian*
Senior Manufacturing Controller, Production, International Edition: *Trudy Kimber*
Operations Specialist: *Lisa McDowell*
Art Director: *Anthony Gemmellaro*
Cover Design: *Jodi Notowitz*
Cover Photo Credit: *lebbid/Shutterstock*
Media Project Manager: *Renata Butera*

Pearson Education Limited
Edinburgh Gate
Harlow
Essex CM20 2JE
England

and Associated Companies throughout the world

Visit us on the World Wide Web at:
www.pearsoninternationaleditions.com

© Pearson Education Limited 2014

The rights of Paul Deitel and Harvey Deitel to be identified as authors of this work have been asserted by them in accordance with the Copyright, Designs and Patents Act 1988.

Authorized adaptation from the United States edition, entitled C++ How to Program, Ninth Edition, ISBN 978-0-13-337871-9, *by Paul Deitel and Harvey Deitel, published by Pearson Education © 2014.*

All rights reserved. No part of this publication may be reproduced, stored in a retrieval system, or transmitted in any form or by any means, electronic, mechanical, photocopying, recording or otherwise, without either the prior written permission of the publisher or a license permitting restricted copying in the United Kingdom issued by the Copyright Licensing Agency Ltd, Saffron House, 6-10 Kirby Street, London EC1N 8TS.

All trademarks used herein are the property of their respective owners. The use of any trademark in this text does not vest in the author or publisher any trademark ownership rights in such trademarks, nor does the use of such trademarks imply any affiliation with or endorsement of this book by such owners.

Microsoft and/or its respective suppliers make no representations about the suitability of the information contained in the documents and related graphics published as part of the services for any purpose. All such documents and related graphics are provided "as is" without warranty of any kind. Microsoft and/or its respective suppliers hereby disclaim all warranties and conditions with regard to this information, including all warranties and conditions of merchantability, whether express, implied or statutory, fitness for a particular purpose, title and non-infringement. In no event shall Microsoft and/or its respective suppliers be liable for any special, indirect or consequential damages or any damages whatsoever resulting from loss of use, data or profits, whether in an action of contract, negligence or other tortious action, arising out of or in connection with the use or performance of information available from the services.

The documents and related graphics contained herein could include technical inaccuracies or typographical errors. Changes are periodically added to the information herein. Microsoft and/or its respective suppliers may make improvements and/or changes in the product(s) and/or the program(s) described herein at any time. Partial screen shots may be viewed in full within the software version specified.

Microsoft® and Windows® are registered trademarks of the Microsoft Corporation in the U.S.A. and other countries. This book is not sponsored or endorsed by or affiliated with the Microsoft Corporation.

ISBN 10: 0-273-79329-2
ISBN 13: 978-0-273-79329-8

British Library Cataloguing-in-Publication Data
A catalogue record for this book is available from the British Library

10 9 8 7 6 5 4 3 2 1
14 13

Typeset in AGaramond Regular by GEX Publishing Services

Printed and bound by Courier Westford in The United States of America
The publisher's policy is to use paper manufactured from sustainable forests.

In memory of Dennis Ritchie,
creator of the C programming language—
one of the key languages that inspired C++.

Paul and Harvey Deitel

Trademarks

Carnegie Mellon Software Engineering Institute[TM] is a trademark of Carnegie Mellon University.

CERT® is registered in the U.S. Patent and Trademark Office by Carnegie Mellon University.

Microsoft® and Windows® are registered trademarks of the Microsoft Corporation in the U.S.A. and other countries. Screen shots and icons reprinted with permission from the Microsoft Corporation. This book is not sponsored or endorsed by or affiliated with the Microsoft Corporation.

UNIX is a registered trademark of The Open Group.

Throughout this book, trademarks are used. Rather than put a trademark symbol in every occurrence of a trademarked name, we state that we are using the names in an editorial fashion only and to the benefit of the trademark owner, with no intention of infringement of the trademark.

Contents

Chapters 24–26 and Appendices F–K are PDF documents posted online at the book's Companion Website, which is accessible from www.pearsoninternationaleditions.com/deitel.

8   Pointers   368

9   Classes: A Deeper Look; Throwing Exceptions   411

10 Operator Overloading; Class string   467

11 Object-Oriented Programming: Inheritance   516

12 Object-Oriented Programming: Polymorphism 551

17 Exception Handling: A Deeper Look 774

18 Introduction to Custom Templates 799

19 Custom Templatized Data Structures 811

Online Chapters and Appendices

Chapters 24–26 and Appendices F–K are PDF documents posted online at the book's Companion Website, which is accessible from www.pearsoninternationaleditions.com/deitel.

F   C Legacy Code Topics   F-1

G   UML 2: Additional Diagram Types   G-1

H   Using the Visual Studio Debugger   H-1

20   Contents

[*Note:* The test drives for Windows and Linux are in Chapter 1.]

Preface

"The chief merit of language is clearness ... "
—Galen

Welcome to the C++ computer programming language and *C++ How to Program, Ninth Edition*. This book presents leading-edge computing technologies. It's appropriate for introductory course sequences based on the curriculum recommendations of two key professional organizations—the ACM and the IEEE. If you haven't already done so, please read the back cover and inside back cover—these capture the essence of the book concisely. In this Preface we provide more detail for students, instructors and professionals.

At the heart of the book is the Deitel signature *live-code approach*—we present concepts in the context of complete working programs followed by sample executions, rather than in code snippets. Read the online Before You Begin section (www.deitel.com/books/cpphtp9/cpphtp9_BYB.pdf) to learn how to set up your Linux-based, Windows-based or Apple OS X-based computer to run the hundreds of code examples. All the source code is available at www.deitel.com/books/cpphtp9 and www.pearsoninternational-editions.com/deitel. Use the source code we provide to *run each program* as you study it.

We believe that this book and its support materials will give you an informative, challenging and entertaining introduction to C++. As you read the book, if you have questions, we're easy to reach at deitel@deitel.com—we'll respond promptly. For book updates, visit www.deitel.com/books/cpphtp9, join our social media communities on Facebook (www.deitel.com/DeitelFan), Twitter (@deitel), Google+ (gplus.to/deitel) and LinkedIn (bit.ly/DeitelLinkedIn), and subscribe to the *Deitel Buzz Online* newsletter (www.deitel.com/newsletter/subscribe.html).

C++11 Standard

The new C++11 standard, published in 2011, motivated us to write *C++ How to Program, 9/e*. Throughout the book, each new C++11 feature is marked with the "11" icon you see here in the margin. These are some of the key C++11 features of this new edition:

- *Conforms to the new C++11 standard.* Extensive coverage of the new C++11 features (Fig. 1).

- *Code thoroughly tested on three popular industrial-strength C++11 compilers.* We tested the code examples on GNU™ C++ 4.7, Microsoft® Visual C++® 2012 and Apple® LLVM in Xcode® 4.5.

- *Smart pointers.* Smart pointers help you avoid dynamic memory management errors by providing additional functionality beyond that of built-in pointers. We discuss unique_ptr in Chapter 17, and shared_ptr and weak_ptr in Chapter 24.

C++11 features in C++ *How to Program, 9/e*		
all_of algorithm	Inheriting base-class constructors	Non-deterministic random
any_of algorithm	insert container member func-	number generation
array container	tions return iterators	none_of algorithm
auto for type inference	is_heap algorithm	Numeric conversion
begin/end functions	is_heap_until algorithm	functions
cbegin/cend container member	Keywords new in C++11	nullptr
functions	Lambda expressions	override keyword
Compiler fix for >> in template	List initialization of key–value	Range-based for statement
types	pairs	Regular expressions
copy_if algorithm	List initialization of pair objects	Rvalue references
copy_n algorithm	List initialization of return values	Scoped enums
crbegin/crend container mem-	List initializing a dynamically	shared_ptr smart pointer
ber functions	allocated array	shrink_to_fit vector/deque
decltype	List initializing a vector	member function
Default type arguments in func-	List initializers in constructor	Specifying the type of an
tion templates	calls	enum's constants
defaulted member functions	long long int type	static_assert objects for
Delegating constructors	min and max algorithms with	file names
deleted member functions	initializer_list parameters	string objects for file names
explicit conversion operators	minmax algorithm	swap non-member function
final classes	minmax_element algorithm	Trailing return types for
final member functions	move algorithm	functions
find_if_not algorithm	Move assignment operators	tuple variadic template
forward_list container	move_backward algorithm	unique_ptr smart pointer
Immutable keys in associative	Move constructors	Unsigned long long int
containers	noexcept	weak_ptr smart pointer
In-class initializers		

Fig. 1 | A sampling of C++11 features in C++ *How to Program, 9/e.*

- *Earlier coverage of Standard Library containers, iterators and algorithms, enhanced with C++11 capabilities.* We moved the treatment of Standard Library containers, iterators and algorithms from Chapter 22 in the previous edition to Chapters 15 and 16 and enhanced it with additional C++11 features. The vast majority of your data structure needs can be fulfilled by *reusing* these Standard Library capabilities. We'll show you how to build your own *custom* data structures in Chapter 19.

- *Online Chapter 24, C++11: Additional Topics.* In this chapter, we present additional C++11 topics. The new C++11 standard has been available since 2011, but not all C++ compilers have fully implemented the features. If all three of our key compilers already implemented a particular C++11 feature at the time we wrote this book, we generally integrated a discussion of that feature into the text with a live-code example. If any of these compilers had *not* implemented that feature, we included a bold italic heading followed by a brief discussion of the feature. Many of those discussions are expanded in online Chapter 24 as the features are implemented. This chapter includes discussions of regular expressions, `shared_ptr` and `weak_ptr` smart pointers, move semantics and more.

- ***Random Number generation, simulation and game playing.*** To help make programs more secure, we've added a treatment of C++11's new non-deterministic random-number generation capabilities.

Object-Oriented Programming

- ***Early-objects approach.*** The book introduces the basic concepts and terminology of object technology in Chapter 1. You'll develop your first customized classes and objects in Chapter 3. Presenting objects and classes early gets you "thinking about objects" immediately and mastering these concepts more thoroughly.[1]

- ***C++ Standard Library*** `string`. C++ offers *two* types of strings—`string` class objects (which we begin using in Chapter 3) and C strings. We've replaced most occurrences of C strings with instances of C++ class `string` to make programs more robust and eliminate many of the security problems of C strings. We continue to discuss C strings later in the book to prepare you for working with the legacy code that you'll encounter in industry. In new development, you should favor `string` objects.

- ***C++ Standard Library*** `array`. Our primary treatment of arrays now uses the Standard Library's `array` class template instead of built-in, C-style, pointer-based arrays. We still cover built-in arrays because they remain useful in C++ and so that you'll be able to read legacy code. C++ offers *three* types of arrays—`array`s and `vector`s (which we start using in Chapter 7) and C-style, pointer-based arrays which we discuss in Chapter 8. As appropriate, we use class template `array` instead of C arrays throughout the book. In new development, you should favor class template `array` objects.

- ***Crafting valuable classes.*** A key goal of this book is to prepare you to build valuable classes. In the Chapter 10 case study, you'll build your own custom `Array` class, then in the Chapter 18 exercises you'll convert it to a class template. You'll truly appreciate the class concept. Chapter 10 begins with a test-drive of class template `string` so you can see an elegant use of operator overloading before you implement your own customized class with overloaded operators.

- ***Case studies in object-oriented programming.*** We provide case studies that span multiple sections and chapters and cover the software development lifecycle. These include the `GradeBook` class in Chapters 3–7, the `Time` class in Chapter 9 and the `Employee` class in Chapters 11–12. Chapter 12 contains a detailed diagram and explanation of how C++ can implement polymorphism, `virtual` functions and dynamic binding "under the hood."

- ***Optional case study: Using the UML to develop an object-oriented design and C++ implementation of an ATM.*** The UML™ (Unified Modeling Language™) is the

1. For courses that require a late-objects approach, consider *C++ How to Program, Late Objects Version*, which begins with six chapters on programming fundamentals (including two on control statements) and continues with seven chapters that gradually introduce object-oriented programming concepts.

industry-standard graphical language for modeling object-oriented systems. We introduce the UML in the early chapters. Online Chapters 25 and 26 include an *optional* case study on object-oriented design using the UML. We design and implement the software for a simple automated teller machine (ATM). We analyze a typical requirements document that specifies the system to be built. We determine the classes needed to implement that system, the attributes the classes need to have, the behaviors the classes need to exhibit and we specify how the classes must interact with one another to meet the system requirements. From the design we produce a complete C++ implementation. Students often report that the case study helps them "tie it all together" and truly understand object orientation.

- *Exception handling.* We integrate basic exception handling *early* in the book. Instructors can easily pull more detailed material forward from Chapter 17, Exception Handling: A Deeper Look.

- *Custom template-based data structures.* We provide a rich multi-chapter treatment of data structures—see the Data Structures module in the chapter dependency chart (Fig. 6).

- *Three programming paradigms.* We discuss *structured programming, object-oriented programming* and *generic programming.*

Pedagogic Features

- *Rich coverage of C++ fundamentals.* We include a clear two-chapter treatment of control statements and algorithm development.

- *Chapter 2 provides a simple introduction to C++ programming.*

- *Examples.* We include a broad range of example programs selected from computer science, business, simulation, game playing and other topics (Fig. 2).

Examples	
Array class case study	Craps dice game simulation
Author class	Credit inquiry program
Bank account program	Date class
Bar chart printing program	Downcasting and runtime type information
BasePlusCommissionEmployee class	Employee class
Binary tree creation and traversal	explicit constructor
BinarySearch test program	fibonacci function
Card shuffling and dealing	fill algorithms
ClientData class	Function-template specializations of function
CommissionEmployee class	template printArray
Comparing strings	generate algorithms
Compilation and linking process	GradeBook Class
Compound interest calculations with for	Initializing an array in a declaration
Converting string objects to C strings	Input from an istringstream object
Counter-controlled repetition	Iterative factorial solution

Fig. 2 | A sampling of the book's examples. (Part 1 of 2.)

Examples

Lambda expressions	SalesPerson class
Linked list manipulation	Searching and sorting algorithms of the Standard Library
map class template	
Mathematical algorithms of the Standard Library	Sequential files
maximum function template	set class template
Merge sort program	shared_ptr program
multiset class template	stack adapter class
new throwing bad_alloc on failure	Stack class
PhoneNumber class	Stack unwinding
Poll analysis program	Standard Library string class program
Polymorphism demonstration	Stream manipulator showbase
Preincrementing and postincrementing	string assignment and concatenation
priority_queue adapter class	string member function substr
queue adapter class	Summing integers with the for statement
Random-access files	Time class
Random number generation	unique_ptr object managing dynamically allocated memory
Recursive function factorial	
Rolling a six-sided die 6,000,000 times	Validating user input with regular expressions
SalariedEmployee class	vector class template

Fig. 2 | A sampling of the book's examples. (Part 2 of 2.)

- *Audience.* The examples are accessible to computer science, information technology, software engineering and business students in novice-level and intermediate-level C++ courses. The book is also used by professional programmers.

- *Self-Review Exercises and Answers.* Extensive self-review exercises *and* answers are included for self-study.

- *Interesting, entertaining and challenging exercises.* Each chapter concludes with a substantial set of exercises, including simple recall of important terminology and concepts, identifying the errors in code samples, writing individual program statements, writing small portions of C++ classes and member and non-member functions, writing complete programs and implementing major projects. Figure 3 lists a sampling of the book's exercises, including our *Making a Difference* exercises, which encourage you to use computers and the Internet to research and solve significant social problems. We hope you'll approach these exercises with *your own* values, politics and beliefs.

Exercises

Airline Reservations System	Bubble Sort	Calculating Salaries
Advanced String-Manipulation Exercises	Build Your Own Compiler	CarbonFootprint Abstract Class: Polymorphism
	Build Your Own Computer	

Fig. 3 | A sampling of the book's exercises. (Part I of 2.)

Exercises

Card Shuffling and Dealing
Computer-Assisted Instruction
Computer-Assisted Instruction: Difficulty Levels
Computer-Assisted Instruction: Monitoring Student Performance
Computer-Assisted Instruction: Reducing Student Fatigue
Computer-Assisted Instruction: Varying the Types of Problems
Cooking with Healthier Ingredients
Craps Game Modification
Credit Limits
Crossword Puzzle Generator
Cryptograms
De Morgan's Laws
Dice Rolling

Eight Queens
Emergency Response
Enforcing Privacy with Cryptography
Facebook User Base Growth
Fibonacci Series
Gas Mileage
Global Warming Facts Quiz
Guess the Number Game
Hangman Game
Health Records Knight's Tour
Limericks
Maze Traversal: Generating Mazes Randomly
Morse Code
Payroll System Modification
Peter Minuit Problem
Phishing Scanner
Pig Latin
Polymorphic Banking Program Using Account Hierarchy

Pythagorean Triples
Salary Calculator
Sieve of Eratosthenes
Simple Decryption
Simple Encryption
SMS Language
Spam Scanner
Spelling Checker
Target-Heart-Rate Calculator
Tax Plan Alternatives; The "Fair Tax"
Telephone number word generator
"The Twelve Days of Christmas" Song
Tortoise and the Hare Simulation
Towers of Hanoi
World Population Growth

Fig. 3 | A sampling of the book's exercises. (Part 2 of 2.)

- *Illustrations and figures.* Abundant tables, line drawings, UML diagrams, programs and program outputs are included. A sampling of the book's drawings and diagrams is shown in (Fig. 4).

Drawings and diagrams

Main text drawings and diagrams

Data hierarchy
Compilation and linking process for multiple source file programs
Order in which a second-degree polynomial is evaluated
GradeBook class diagrams
if single-selection statement activity diagram
if...else double-selection statement activity diagram

while repetition statement UML activity diagram
for repetition statement UML activity diagram
do...while repetition statement UML activity diagram
switch multiple-selection statement activity diagram
C++'s single-entry/single-exit sequence, selection and repetition statements

Pass-by-value and pass-by-reference analysis of a program
Inheritance hierarchy diagrams
Function-call stack and activation records
Recursive calls to function fibonacci
Pointer arithmetic diagrams
CommunityMember Inheritance hierarchy
Shape inheritance hierarchy

Fig. 4 | A sampling of the book's drawings and diagrams. (Part I of 2.)

Drawings and diagrams		
`public`, `protected` and `private` inheritance `Employee` hierarchy UML class diagram How `virtual` function calls work Stream-I/O template hierarchy Two self-referential class objects linked together	Graphical representation of a list Operation `insertAtFront` represented graphically Operation `insertAtBack` represented graphically Operation `removeFromFront` represented graphically	Operation `removeFromBack` represented graphically Circular, singly linked list Doubly linked list Circular, doubly linked list Graphical representation of a binary tree

ATM Case Study drawings and diagrams

Use case diagram for the ATM system from the User's perspective Class diagram showing an association among classes Class diagram showing composition relationships Class diagram for the ATM system model Classes with attributes State diagram for the ATM Activity diagram for a `BalanceInquiry` transaction Activity diagram for a `Withdrawal` transaction	Classes in the ATM system with attributes and operations Communication diagram of the ATM executing a balance inquiry Communication diagram for executing a balance inquiry Sequence diagram that models a `Withdrawal` executing Use case diagram for a modified version of our ATM system that also allows users to transfer money between accounts	Class diagram showing composition relationships of a class `Car` Class diagram for the ATM system model including class `Deposit` Activity diagram for a `Deposit` transaction Sequence diagram that models a `Deposit` executing

Fig. 4 | A sampling of the book's drawings and diagrams. (Part 2 of 2.)

- *VideoNotes.* The Companion Website includes many hours of *VideoNotes* in which co-author Paul Deitel explains in detail key programs in the core chapters. We've created a jump table that maps each VideoNote to the corresponding figures in the book (www.deitel.com/books/cpphtp9/jump_table.pdf).

Other Features

- *Pointers.* We provide thorough coverage of the built-in pointer capabilities and the intimate relationship among built-in pointers, C strings and built-in arrays.

- *Visual presentation of searching and sorting, with a simple explanation of Big O.*

- *Printed book contains core content; additional content is online.* A few online chapters and appendices are included. These are available in searchable PDF format on the book's password-protected Companion Website—see the access card information on the inside front cover.

- *Debugger appendices.* We provide three debugger appendices on the book's Companion Website—Appendix H, Using the Visual Studio Debugger, Appendix I, Using the GNU C++ Debugger and Appendix J, Using the Xcode Debugger.

Secure C++ Programming

It's difficult to build industrial-strength systems that stand up to attacks from viruses, worms, and other forms of "malware." Today, via the Internet, such attacks can be instantaneous and global in scope. Building security into software from the beginning of the development cycle can greatly reduce vulnerabilities.

The CERT® Coordination Center (www.cert.org) was created to analyze and respond promptly to attacks. CERT—the Computer Emergency Response Team—is a government-funded organization within the Carnegie Mellon University Software Engineering Institute™. CERT publishes and promotes secure coding standards for various popular programming languages to help software developers implement industrial-strength systems that avoid the programming practices that leave systems open to attacks.

We'd like to thank Robert C. Seacord, Secure Coding Manager at CERT and an adjunct professor in the Carnegie Mellon University School of Computer Science. Mr. Seacord was a technical reviewer for our book, *C How to Program, 7/e*, where he scrutinized our C programs from a security standpoint, recommending that we adhere to the *CERT C Secure Coding Standard*.

We've done the same for *C++ How to Program, 9/e*, adhering to the *CERT C++ Secure Coding Standard*, which you can find at:

```
www.securecoding.cert.org
```

We were pleased to discover that we've already been recommending many of these coding practices in our books. We upgraded our code and discussions to conform to these practices, as appropriate for an introductory/intermediate-level textbook. If you'll be building industrial-strength C++ systems, consider reading *Secure Coding in C and C++, Second Edition* (Robert Seacord, Addison-Wesley Professional).

Online Content

The book's Companion Website, which is accessible at

```
www.pearsoninternationaleditions.com/deitel
```

(see the inside front cover of the book for an access code) contains the following chapters and appendices in searchable PDF format:

- Chapter 24, C++11 Additional Topics
- Chapter 25, ATM Case Study, Part 1: Object-Oriented Design with the UML
- Chapter 26, ATM Case Study, Part 2: Implementing an Object-Oriented Design
- Appendix F, C Legacy Code Topics
- Appendix G, UML 2: Additional Diagram Types
- Appendix H, Using the Visual Studio Debugger
- Appendix I, Using the GNU C++ Debugger
- Appendix J, Using the Xcode Debugger
- Appendix K, Test Driving a C++ Program on Mac OS X. (The test drives for Windows and Linux are in Chapter 1.)

The Companion Website also includes:

- Extensive *VideoNotes*—watch and listen as co-author Paul Deitel discusses key code examples in the core chapters of the book.
- Building Your Own Compiler exercise descriptions from Chapter 19 (posted at the Companion Website and at `www.deitel.com/books/cpphtp9`).
- Chapter 1 test-drive for Mac OS X.

Dependency Chart

The chart in Fig. 6 shows the dependencies among the chapters to help instructors plan their syllabi. *C++ How to Program, 9/e* is appropriate for CS1 and many CS2 courses. The chart shows the book's modular organization.

Teaching Approach

C++ How to Program, 9/e, contains a rich collection of examples. We stress program clarity and concentrate on building well-engineered software.

Live-code approach. The book is loaded with "live-code" examples—most new concepts are presented in *complete working C++ applications*, followed by one or more executions showing program inputs and outputs. In the few cases where we use a code snippet, to ensure that it's correct we tested it in a complete working program, then copied and pasted it into the book.

Syntax coloring. For readability, we syntax color all the C++ code, similar to the way most C++ integrated-development environments and code editors syntax color code. Our coloring conventions are as follows:

```
comments appear like this
keywords appear like this
constants and literal values appear like this
all other code appears in black
```

Code highlighting. We place light-blue shaded rectangles around key code segments.

Using fonts for emphasis. We color the defining occurrence of each key term in **bold blue** text for easy reference. We emphasize on-screen components in the **bold Helvetica** font (e.g., the **File** menu) and C++ program text in the `Lucida` font (for example, `int x = 5;`).

Objectives. The opening quotes are followed by a list of chapter objectives.

Programming tips. We include programming tips to help you focus on key aspects of program development. These tips and practices represent the best we've gleaned from a combined seven decades of teaching and industry experience.

Good Programming Practices
The Good Programming Practices *call attention to techniques that will help you produce programs that are clearer, more understandable and more maintainable.*

Common Programming Errors
Pointing out these Common Programming Errors *reduces the likelihood that you'll make them.*

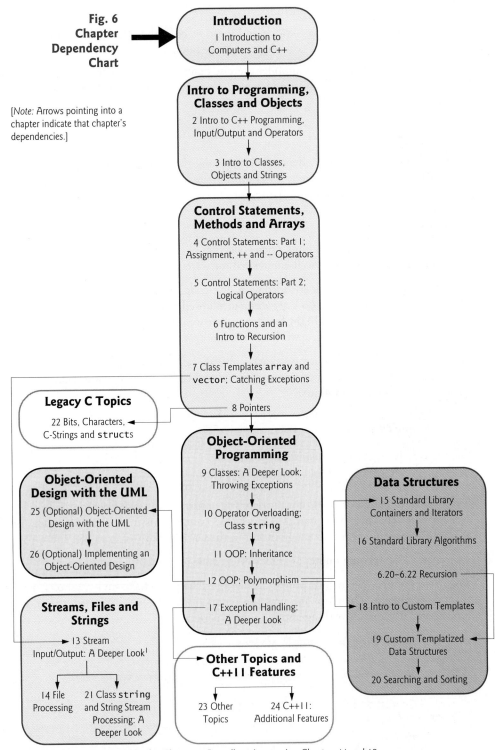

Fig. 6 Chapter Dependency Chart

[*Note:* Arrows pointing into a chapter indicate that chapter's dependencies.]

Introduction

1 Introduction to Computers and C++

Intro to Programming, Classes and Objects

2 Intro to C++ Programming, Input/Output and Operators

3 Intro to Classes, Objects and Strings

Control Statements, Methods and Arrays

4 Control Statements: Part 1; Assignment, ++ and -- Operators

5 Control Statements: Part 2; Logical Operators

6 Functions and an Intro to Recursion

7 Class Templates `array` and `vector`; Catching Exceptions

8 Pointers

Legacy C Topics

22 Bits, Characters, C-Strings and `struct`s

Object-Oriented Programming

9 Classes: A Deeper Look; Throwing Exceptions

10 Operator Overloading; Class `string`

11 OOP: Inheritance

12 OOP: Polymorphism

17 Exception Handling: A Deeper Look

Object-Oriented Design with the UML

25 (Optional) Object-Oriented Design with the UML

26 (Optional) Implementing an Object-Oriented Design

Streams, Files and Strings

13 Stream Input/Output: A Deeper Look[1]

14 File Processing

21 Class `string` and String Stream Processing: A Deeper Look

Other Topics and C++11 Features

23 Other Topics

24 C++11: Additional Features

Data Structures

15 Standard Library Containers and Iterators

16 Standard Library Algorithms

6.20–6.22 Recursion

18 Intro to Custom Templates

19 Custom Templatized Data Structures

20 Searching and Sorting

1. Most of Chapter 13 is readable after Chapter 7. A small portion requires Chapters 11 and 18.

Error-Prevention Tips

These tips contain suggestions for exposing and removing bugs from your programs; many describe aspects of C++ that prevent bugs from getting into programs in the first place.

Performance Tips

These tips highlight opportunities for making your programs run faster or minimizing the amount of memory that they occupy.

Portability Tips

The Portability Tips *help you write code that will run on a variety of platforms.*

Software Engineering Observations

The Software Engineering Observations *highlight architectural and design issues that affect the construction of software systems, especially large-scale systems.*

Summary Bullets. We present a section-by-section, bullet-list summary of the chapter. We include the page number of each term's defining occurrence in the chapter for easy reference.

Index. We've included an extensive index, with defining occurrences of key terms highlighted with a **bold blue** page number.

Obtaining the Software Used in C++ *How to Program, 9/e*

We wrote the code examples in *C++ How to Program, 9/e* using the following C++ development tools:

- Microsoft's free Visual Studio Express 2012 for Windows Desktop, which includes Visual C++ and other Microsoft development tools. This runs on Windows 7 and 8 and is available for download at

```
www.microsoft.com/visualstudio/eng/downloads#
d-express-windows-desktop
```

- GNU's free GNU C++ (gcc.gnu.org/install/binaries.html), which is already installed on most Linux systems and can also be installed on Mac OS X and Windows systems.

- Apple's free Xcode, which OS X users can download from the Mac App Store.

Instructor Supplements

The following supplements are available to *qualified instructors only* through Pearson Education's Instructor Resource Center (www.pearsoninternationaleditions.com/deitel):

- *Solutions Manual* contains solutions to *most* of the end-of-chapter exercises. We've added many *Making a Difference* exercises, most with solutions. **Please do not write to us requesting access to the Pearson Instructor's Resource Center. Access is restricted to college instructors teaching from the book.** Instructors may obtain access only through their Pearson representatives. If you're not a registered faculty member, contact your Pearson representative. Exercise Solutions are *not* provided for "project" exercises. Check out our Programming Projects Resource Center for lots of additional exercise and project possibilities

```
www.deitel.com/ProgrammingProjects
```

- *Test Item File* of multiple-choice questions (approximately two per book section)
- *Customizable PowerPoint® slides* containing all the code and figures in the text, plus bulleted items that summarize the key points in the text

Online Practice and Assessment with MyProgrammingLab™

MyProgrammingLab™ helps students fully grasp the logic, semantics, and syntax of programming. Through practice exercises and immediate, personalized feedback, MyProgrammingLab improves the programming competence of beginning students who often struggle with the basic concepts and paradigms of popular high-level programming languages.

A self-study and homework tool, a MyProgrammingLab course consists of hundreds of small practice problems organized around the structure of this textbook. For students, the system automatically detects errors in the logic and syntax of their code submissions and offers targeted hints that enable students to figure out what went wrong—and why. For instructors, a comprehensive gradebook tracks correct and incorrect answers and stores the code inputted by students for review.

For a full demonstration, to see feedback from instructors and students or to get started using MyProgrammingLab in your course, visit www.myprogramminglab.com.

Acknowledgments

We'd like to thank Abbey Deitel and Barbara Deitel of Deitel & Associates, Inc. for long hours devoted to this project. Abbey co-authored Chapter 1 and she and Barbara painstakingly researched the new capabilities of C++11.

We're fortunate to have worked with the dedicated team of publishing professionals at Pearson Higher Education. We appreciate the guidance, wisdom and energy of Tracy Johnson, Executive Editor, Computer Science. Carole Snyder did an extraordinary job recruiting the book's reviewers and managing the review process. Bob Engelhardt did a wonderful job bringing the book to publication.

Reviewers
We wish to acknowledge the efforts of our reviewers. The book was scrutinized by current and former members of the C++ standards committee that developed C++11, academics teaching C++ courses and industry experts. They provided countless suggestions for improving the presentation. Any remaining flaws in the book are our own.

Ninth Edition reviewers: Dean Michael Berris (Google, Member ISO C++ Committee), Danny Kalev (C++ expert, certified system analyst and former member of the C++ Standards Committee), Linda M. Krause (Elmhurst College), James P. McNellis (Microsoft Corporation), Robert C. Seacord (Secure Coding Manager at SEI/CERT, author of *Secure Coding in C and C++*) and José Antonio González Seco (Parliament of Andalusia).

Other recent edition reviewers: Virginia Bailey (Jackson State University), Thomas J. Borrelli (Rochester Institute of Technology), Ed Brey (Kohler Co.), Chris Cox (Adobe

Systems), Gregory Dai (eBay), Peter J. DePasquale (The College of New Jersey), John Dibling (SpryWare), Susan Gauch (University of Arkansas), Doug Gregor (Apple, Inc.), Jack Hagemeister (Washington State University), Williams M. Higdon (University of Indiana), Anne B. Horton (Lockheed Martin), Terrell Hull (Logicalis Integration Solutions), Ed James-Beckham (Borland), Wing-Ning Li (University of Arkansas), Dean Mathias (Utah State University), Robert A. McLain (Tidewater Community College), Robert Myers (Florida State University), Gavin Osborne (Saskatchewan Inst. of App. Sci. and Tech.), Amar Raheja (California State Polytechnic University, Pomona), April Reagan (Microsoft), Raymond Stephenson (Microsoft), Dave Topham (Ohlone College), Anthony Williams (author and C++ Standards Committee member) and Chad Willwerth (University Washington, Tacoma).

As you read the book, we'd sincerely appreciate your comments, criticisms and suggestions for improving the text. Please address all correspondence to:

```
deitel@deitel.com
```

We'll respond promptly. We enjoyed writing C++ *How to Program, Ninth Edition.* We hope you enjoy reading it!

Paul Deitel
Harvey Deitel

About the Authors

Paul Deitel, CEO and Chief Technical Officer of Deitel & Associates, Inc., is a graduate of MIT, where he studied Information Technology. Through Deitel & Associates, Inc., he has delivered hundreds of programming courses to industry clients, including Cisco, IBM, Siemens, Sun Microsystems, Dell, Fidelity, NASA at the Kennedy Space Center, the National Severe Storm Laboratory, White Sands Missile Range, Rogue Wave Software, Boeing, SunGard Higher Education, Nortel Networks, Puma, iRobot, Invensys and many more. He and his co-author, Dr. Harvey M. Deitel, are the world's best-selling programming-language textbook/professional book/video authors.

Dr. Harvey Deitel, Chairman and Chief Strategy Officer of Deitel & Associates, Inc., has 50 years of experience in the computer field. Dr. Deitel earned B.S. and M.S. degrees in Electrical Engineering from MIT and a Ph.D. in Mathematics from Boston University. He has extensive college teaching experience, including earning tenure and serving as the Chairman of the Computer Science Department at Boston College before founding Deitel & Associates, Inc., in 1991 with his son, Paul Deitel. The Deitels' publications have earned international recognition, with translations published in Chinese, Korean, Japanese, German, Russian, Spanish, French, Polish, Italian, Portuguese, Greek, Urdu and Turkish. Dr. Deitel has delivered hundreds of programming courses to corporate, academic, government and military clients.

Corporate Training from Deitel & Associates, Inc.

Deitel & Associates, Inc., founded by Paul Deitel and Harvey Deitel, is an internationally recognized authoring and corporate training organization, specializing in computer programming languages, object technology, mobile app development and Internet and web software technology. The company's clients include many of the world's largest companies, government agencies, branches of the military, and academic institutions. The company offers instructor-led training courses delivered at client sites worldwide on major programming languages and platforms, including C++, Visual C++®, C, Java™, Visual C#®, Visual Basic®, XML®, Python®, object technology, Internet and web programming, Android app development, Objective-C and iPhone app development and a growing list of additional programming and software development courses.

Through its 36-year publishing partnership with Prentice Hall/Pearson, Deitel & Associates, Inc., publishes leading-edge programming college textbooks, professional books and *LiveLessons* video courses. Deitel & Associates, Inc. and the authors can be reached at:

```
deitel@deitel.com
```

To learn more about Deitel's *Dive-Into Series* Corporate Training curriculum, visit:

```
www.deitel.com/training
```

To request a proposal for worldwide on-site, instructor-led training at your organization, e-mail deitel@deitel.com.

Individuals wishing to purchase Deitel books and *LiveLessons* video training can do so through www.deitel.com. Bulk orders by corporations, the government, the military and academic institutions should be placed directly with Pearson.

Introduction to Computers and C++

Man is still the most extraordinary computer of all.
—John F. Kennedy

Good design is good business.
—Thomas J. Watson, Founder of IBM

How wonderful it is that nobody need wait a single moment before starting to improve the world.
—Anne Frank

Objectives

In this chapter you'll learn:

- Exciting recent developments in the computer field.

- Computer hardware, software and networking basics.

- The data hierarchy.

- The different types of programming languages.

- Basic object-technology concepts.

- Some basics of the Internet and the World Wide Web.

- A typical C++ program-development environment.

- To test-drive a C++ application.

- Some key recent software technologies.

- How computers can help you make a difference.

Outline

1.1 Introduction

Welcome to C++—a powerful computer programming language that's appropriate for technically oriented people with little or no programming experience, and for experienced programmers to use in building substantial information systems. You're already familiar with the powerful tasks computers perform. Using this textbook, you'll write instructions commanding computers to perform those kinds of tasks. *Software* (i.e., the instructions you write) controls *hardware* (i.e., computers).

You'll learn *object-oriented programming*—today's key programming methodology. You'll create many *software objects* that model *things* in the real-world.

C++ is one of today's most popular software development languages. This text provides an introduction to programming in C++11—the latest version standardized through the International Organization for Standardization (ISO) and the International Electrotechnical Commission (IEC).

In use today are more than a billion general-purpose computers and billions more cell phones, smartphones and handheld devices (such as tablet computers). According to a study by eMarketer, the number of mobile Internet users will reach approximately 134 million by 2013.[1] Smartphone sales surpassed personal computer sales in 2011.[2] Tablet sales are expected to account for over 20% of all personal computer sales by 2015.[3] By 2014, the smartphone applications market is expected to exceed $40 billion.[4] This explosive growth is creating significant opportunities for programming mobile applications.

1.2 Computers and the Internet in Industry and Research

These are exciting times in the computer field. Many of the most influential and successful businesses of the last two decades are technology companies, including Apple, IBM, Hew-

---

1.   www.circleid.com/posts/mobile_internet_users_to_reach_134_million_by_2013/.
2.   www.mashable.com/2012/02/03/smartphone-sales-overtake-pcs/.
3.   www.forrester.com/ER/Press/Release/0,1769,1340,00.html.
4.   *Inc.*, December 2010/January 2011, pages 116–123.

lett Packard, Dell, Intel, Motorola, Cisco, Microsoft, Google, Amazon, Facebook, Twitter, Groupon, Foursquare, Yahoo!, eBay and many more. These companies are major employers of people who study computer science, computer engineering, information systems or related disciplines. At the time of this writing, Apple was the most valuable company in the world. Figure 1.1 provides a few examples of the ways in which computers are improving people's lives in research, industry and society.

Name	Description
Electronic health records	These might include a patient's medical history, prescriptions, immunizations, lab results, allergies, insurance information and more. Making this information available to health care providers across a secure network improves patient care, reduces the probability of error and increases overall efficiency of the health care system.
Human Genome Project	The Human Genome Project was founded to identify and analyze the 20,000+ genes in human DNA. The project used computer programs to analyze complex genetic data, determine the sequences of the billions of chemical base pairs that make up human DNA and store the information in databases which have been made available over the Internet to researchers in many fields.
AMBER™ Alert	The AMBER (America's Missing: Broadcast Emergency Response) Alert System is used to find abducted children. Law enforcement notifies TV and radio broadcasters and state transportation officials, who then broadcast alerts on TV, radio, computerized highway signs, the Internet and wireless devices. AMBER Alert recently partnered with Facebook, whose users can "Like" AMBER Alert pages by location to receive alerts in their news feeds.
World Community Grid	People worldwide can donate their unused computer processing power by installing a free secure software program that allows the World Community Grid (www.worldcommunitygrid.org) to harness unused capacity. This computing power, accessed over the Internet, is used in place of expensive supercomputers to conduct scientific research projects that are making a difference—providing clean water to third-world countries, fighting cancer, growing more nutritious rice for regions fighting hunger and more.
Cloud computing	Cloud computing allows you to use software, hardware and information stored in the "cloud"—i.e., accessed on remote computers via the Internet and available on demand—rather than having it stored on your personal computer. These services allow you to increase or decrease resources to meet your needs at any given time, so they can be more cost effective than purchasing expensive hardware to ensure that you have enough storage and processing power to meet your needs at their peak levels. Using cloud computing services shifts the burden of managing these applications from the business to the service provider, saving businesses money.

Fig. 1.1 | A few uses for computers. (Part 1 of 3.)

Name	Description
Medical imaging	X-ray computed tomography (CT) scans, also called CAT (computerized axial tomography) scans, take X-rays of the body from hundreds of different angles. Computers are used to adjust the intensity of the X-rays, optimizing the scan for each type of tissue, then to combine all of the information to create a 3D image. MRI scanners use a technique called magnetic resonance imaging, also to produce internal images non-invasively.
GPS	Global Positioning System (GPS) devices use a network of satellites to retrieve location-based information. Multiple satellites send time-stamped signals to the GPS device, which calculates the distance to each satellite based on the time the signal left the satellite and the time the signal arrived. This information is used to determine the exact location of the device. GPS devices can provide step-by-step directions and help you locate nearby businesses (restaurants, gas stations, etc.) and points of interest. GPS is used in numerous location-based Internet services such as check-in apps to help you find your friends (e.g., Foursquare and Facebook), exercise apps such as RunKeeper that track the time, distance and average speed of your outdoor jog, dating apps that help you find a match nearby and apps that dynamically update changing traffic conditions.
Robots	Robots can be used for day-to-day tasks (e.g., iRobot's Roomba vacuuming robot), entertainment (e.g., robotic pets), military combat, deep sea and space exploration (e.g., NASA's Mars rover Curiosity) and more. RoboEarth (www.roboearth.org) is "a World Wide Web for robots." It allows robots to learn from each other by sharing information and thus improving their abilities to perform tasks, navigate, recognize objects and more.
E-mail, Instant Messaging, Video Chat and FTP	Internet-based servers support all of your online messaging. E-mail messages go through a mail server that also stores the messages. Instant Messaging (IM) and Video Chat apps, such as AIM, Skype, Yahoo! Messenger, Google Talk, Trillian, Microsoft's Messenger and others allow you to communicate with others in real time by sending your messages and live video through servers. FTP (file transfer protocol) allows you to exchange files between multiple computers (e.g., a client computer such as your desktop and a file server) over the Internet.
Internet TV	Internet TV set-top boxes (such as Apple TV, Google TV and TiVo) allow you to access an enormous amount of content on demand, such as games, news, movies, television shows and more, and they help ensure that the content is streamed to your TV smoothly.
Streaming music services	Streaming music services (such as Pandora, Spotify, Last.fm and more) allow you listen to large catalogues of music over the web, create customized "radio stations" and discover new music based on your feedback.

Fig. 1.1 | A few uses for computers. (Part 2 of 3.)

Name	Description
Game programming	Analysts expect global video game revenues to reach $91 billion by 2015 (www.vg247.com/2009/06/23/global-industry-analysts-predicts-gaming-market-to-reach-91-billion-by-2015/). The most sophisticated games can cost as much as $100 million to develop. Activision's *Call of Duty: Black Ops*—one of the best-selling games of all time—earned $360 million in just one day (www.forbes.com/sites/insertcoin/2011/03/11/call-of-duty-black-ops-now-the-best-selling-video-game-of-all-time/)! Online *social gaming*, which enables users worldwide to compete with one another over the Internet, is growing rapidly. Zynga—creator of popular online games such as *Words with Friends*, *CityVille* and others—was founded in 2007 and already has over 300 million monthly users. To accommodate the growth in traffic, Zynga is adding nearly 1,000 servers each week (techcrunch.com/2010/09/22/zynga-moves-1-petabyte-of-data-daily-adds-1000-servers-a-week/)!

Fig. 1.1 | A few uses for computers. (Part 3 of 3.)

1.3 Hardware and Software

Computers can perform calculations and make logical decisions phenomenally faster than human beings can. Many of today's personal computers can perform billions of calculations in one second—more than a human can perform in a lifetime. *Supercomputers* are already performing *thousands of trillions (quadrillions) of instructions per second!* IBM's Sequoia supercomputer can perform over 16 quadrillion calculations per second (16.32 *petaflops*)![5] To put that in perspective, *the IBM Sequoia supercomputer can perform in one second about 1.5 million calculations for every person on the planet!* And—these "upper limits" are growing quickly!

Computers process data under the control of sequences of instructions called computer programs. These programs guide the computer through ordered actions specified by people called computer programmers. The programs that run on a computer are referred to as software. In this book, you'll learn a key programming methodology that's enhancing programmer productivity, thereby reducing software development costs—*object-oriented programming*.

A computer consists of various devices referred to as hardware (e.g., the keyboard, screen, mouse, hard disks, memory, DVD drives and processing units). Computing costs are *dropping dramatically*, owing to rapid developments in hardware and software technologies. Computers that might have filled large rooms and cost millions of dollars decades ago are now inscribed on silicon chips smaller than a fingernail, costing perhaps a few dollars each. Ironically, silicon is one of the most abundant materials on Earth—it's an ingredient in common sand. Silicon-chip technology has made computing so economical that computers have become a commodity.

---

5. www.top500.org/.

1.3.1 Moore's Law

Every year, you probably expect to pay at least a little more for most products and services. The opposite has been the case in the computer and communications fields, especially with regard to the costs of hardware supporting these technologies. For many decades, hardware costs have fallen rapidly. Every year or two, the capacities of computers have approximately *doubled* inexpensively. This remarkable trend often is called Moore's Law, named for the person who identified it in the 1960s, Gordon Moore, co-founder of Intel—the leading manufacturer of the processors in today's computers and embedded systems. Moore's Law and related observations apply especially to the amount of memory that computers have for programs, the amount of secondary storage (such as disk storage) they have to hold programs and data over longer periods of time, and their processor speeds—the speeds at which computers execute their programs (i.e., do their work). Similar growth has occurred in the communications field, in which costs have plummeted as enormous demand for communications bandwidth (i.e., information-carrying capacity) has attracted intense competition. We know of no other fields in which technology improves so quickly and costs fall so rapidly. Such phenomenal improvement is truly fostering the *Information Revolution*.

1.3.2 Computer Organization

Regardless of differences in *physical* appearance, computers can be envisioned as divided into various logical units or sections (Fig. 1.2).

Logical unit	Description
Input unit	This "receiving" section obtains information (data and computer programs) from input devices and places it at the disposal of the other units for processing. Most information is entered into computers through keyboards, touch screens and mouse devices. Other forms of input include receiving voice commands, scanning images and barcodes, reading from secondary storage devices (such as hard drives, DVD drives, Blu-ray Disc™ drives and USB flash drives—also called "thumb drives" or "memory sticks"), receiving video from a webcam and having your computer receive information from the Internet (such as when you stream videos from YouTube™ or download e-books from Amazon). Newer forms of input include position data from a GPS device, and motion and orientation information from an accelerometer in a smartphone or game controller (such as Microsoft® Kinect™, Wii™ Remote and Sony's PlayStation® Move).
Output unit	This "shipping" section takes information that the computer has processed and places it on various output devices to make it available for use outside the computer. Most information that's output from computers today is displayed on screens, printed on paper ("going green" discourages this), played as audio or video on PCs and media players (such as Apple's popular iPods) and giant screens in sports stadiums, transmitted over the Internet or used to control other devices, such as robots and "intelligent" appliances.

Fig. 1.2 | Logical units of a computer. (Part 1 of 2.)

Logical unit	Description
Memory unit	This rapid-access, relatively low-capacity "warehouse" section retains information that has been entered through the input unit, making it immediately available for processing when needed. The memory unit also retains processed information until it can be placed on output devices by the output unit. Information in the memory unit is *volatile*—it's typically lost when the computer's power is turned off. The memory unit is often called either memory or primary memory. Main memories on desktop and notebook computers commonly contain as much as 16 GB (GB stands for gigabytes; a gigabyte is approximately one billion bytes).
Arithmetic and logic unit (ALU)	This "manufacturing" section performs *calculations*, such as addition, subtraction, multiplication and division. It also contains the *decision* mechanisms that allow the computer, for example, to compare two items from the memory unit to determine whether they're equal. In today's systems, the ALU is usually implemented as part of the next logical unit, the CPU.
Central processing unit (CPU)	This "administrative" section coordinates and supervises the operation of the other sections. The CPU tells the input unit when information should be read into the memory unit, tells the ALU when information from the memory unit should be used in calculations and tells the output unit when to send information from the memory unit to certain output devices. Many of today's computers have multiple CPUs and, hence, can perform many operations simultaneously. A multi-core processor implements multiple processors on a single integrated-circuit chip—a *dual-core processor* has two CPUs and a *quad-core processor* has four CPUs. Today's desktop computers have processors that can execute billions of instructions per second.
Secondary storage unit	This is the long-term, high-capacity "warehousing" section. Programs or data not actively being used by the other units normally are placed on secondary storage devices (e.g., your *hard drive*) until they're again needed, possibly hours, days, months or even years later. Information on secondary storage devices is *persistent*—it's preserved even when the computer's power is turned off. Secondary storage information takes much longer to access than information in primary memory, but the cost per unit of secondary storage is much less than that of primary memory. Examples of secondary storage devices include CD drives, DVD drives and flash drives, some of which can hold up to 768 GB. Typical hard drives on desktop and notebook computers can hold up to 2 TB (TB stands for terabytes; a terabyte is approximately one trillion bytes).

Fig. 1.2 | Logical units of a computer. (Part 2 of 2.)

1.4 Data Hierarchy

Data items processed by computers form a data hierarchy that becomes larger and more complex in structure as we progress from bits to characters to fields, and so on. Figure 1.3 illustrates a portion of the data hierarchy. Figure 1.4 summarizes the data hierarchy's levels.

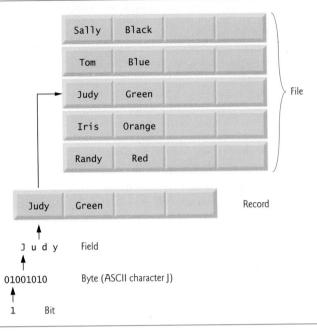

Fig. 1.3 | Data hierarchy.

Level	Description
Bits	The smallest data item in a computer can assume the value 0 or the value 1. Such a data item is called a bit (short for "binary digit"—a digit that can assume one of two values). It's remarkable that the impressive functions performed by computers involve only the simplest manipulations of 0s and 1s—*examining a bit's value, setting a bit's value* and *reversing a bit's value* (from 1 to 0 or from 0 to 1).
Characters	It's tedious for people to work with data in the low-level form of bits. Instead, they prefer to work with *decimal digits* (0–9), *letters* (A–Z and a–z), and *special symbols* (e.g., $, @, %, &, *, (,), –, +, ", :, ? and /). Digits, letters and special symbols are known as characters. The computer's character set is the set of all the characters used to write programs and represent data items. Computers process only 1s and 0s, so every character is represented as a pattern of 1s and 0s. The Unicode® character set contains characters for many of the world's languages. C++ supports several character sets, including 16-bit Unicode® characters that are composed of two bytes, each composed of eight bits. See Appendix B for more information on the ASCII (American Standard Code for Information Interchange) character set—the popular subset of Unicode that represents uppercase and lowercase letters, digits and some common special characters.
Fields	Just as characters are composed of bits, fields are composed of characters or bytes. A field is a group of characters or bytes that conveys meaning. For example, a field consisting of uppercase and lowercase letters could be used to represent a person's name, and a field consisting of decimal digits could represent a person's age.

Fig. 1.4 | Levels of the data hierarchy. (Part 1 of 2.)

Level	Description
Records	Several related fields can be used to compose a record. In a payroll system, for example, the record for an employee might consist of the following fields (possible types for these fields are shown in parentheses): <ul><li>Employee identification number (a whole number)</li><li>Name (a string of characters)</li><li>Address (a string of characters)</li><li>Hourly pay rate (a number with a decimal point)</li><li>Year-to-date earnings (a number with a decimal point)</li><li>Amount of taxes withheld (a number with a decimal point)</li></ul> Thus, a record is a group of related fields. In the preceding example, all the fields belong to the same employee. A company might have many employees and a payroll record for each one.
Files	A file is a group of related records. [*Note:* More generally, a file contains arbitrary data in arbitrary formats. In some operating systems, a file is viewed simply as a *sequence of bytes*—any organization of the bytes in a file, such as organizing the data into records, is a view created by the application programmer.] It's not unusual for an organization to have many files, some containing billions, or even trillions, of characters of information.
Database	A database is an electronic collection of data that's organized for easy access and manipulation. The most popular database model is the relational database in which data is stored in simple *tables*. A table includes *records* and *fields*. For example, a table of students might include first name, last name, major, year, student ID number and grade point average. The data for each student is a record, and the individual pieces of information in each record are the fields. You can search, sort and manipulate the data based on its relationship to multiple tables or databases. For example, a university might use data from the student database in combination with databases of courses, on-campus housing, meal plans, etc.

Fig. 1.4 | Levels of the data hierarchy. (Part 2 of 2.)

1.5 Machine Languages, Assembly Languages and High-Level Languages

Programmers write instructions in various programming languages, some directly understandable by computers and others requiring intermediate *translation* steps.

Machine Languages

Any computer can directly understand only its own **machine language** (also called *machine code*), defined by its hardware architecture. Machine languages generally consist of numbers (ultimately reduced to 1s and 0s). Such languages are cumbersome for humans.

Assembly Languages

Programming in machine language was simply too slow and tedious for most programmers. Instead, they began using English-like *abbreviations* to represent elementary operations. These abbreviations formed the basis of **assembly languages**. *Translator programs* called **assemblers** were developed to convert assembly-language programs to machine language. Although assembly-language code is clearer to humans, it's incomprehensible to computers until translated to machine language.

High-Level Languages

To speed up the programming process further, **high-level languages** were developed in which single statements could be written to accomplish substantial tasks. High-level languages, such as C++, Java, C# and Visual Basic, allow you to write instructions that look more like everyday English and contain commonly used mathematical expressions. Translator programs called **compilers** convert high-level language programs into machine language.

The process of compiling a large high-level language program into machine language can take a considerable amount of computer time. **Interpreter** programs were developed to execute high-level language programs directly (without the need for compilation), although more slowly than compiled programs. **Scripting languages** such as the popular web languages JavaScript and PHP are processed by interpreters.

Performance Tip 1.1

Interpreters have an advantage over compilers in Internet scripting. An interpreted program can begin executing as soon as it's downloaded to the client's machine, without needing to be compiled before it can execute. On the downside, interpreted scripts generally run slower than compiled code.

1.6 C++

C++ evolved from C, which was developed by Dennis Ritchie at Bell Laboratories. C is available for most computers and is hardware independent. With careful design, it's possible to write C programs that are **portable** to most computers.

The widespread use of C with various kinds of computers (sometimes called **hardware platforms**) unfortunately led to many variations. A standard version of C was needed. The American National Standards Institute (ANSI) cooperated with the International Organization for Standardization (ISO) to standardize C worldwide; the joint standard document was published in 1990 and is referred to as *ANSI/ISO 9899: 1990*.

C11 is the latest ANSI standard for the C programming language. It was developed to evolve the C language to keep pace with increasingly powerful hardware and ever more demanding user requirements. C11 also makes C more consistent with C++. For more information on C and C11, see our book *C How to Program, 7/e* and our C Resource Center (located at www.deitel.com/C).

C++, an extension of C, was developed by Bjarne Stroustrup in 1979 at Bell Laboratories. Originally called "C with Classes", it was renamed to C++ in the early 1980s. C++ provides a number of features that "spruce up" the C language, but more importantly, it provides capabilities for object-oriented programming.

You'll begin developing customized, reusable classes and objects in Chapter 3, Introduction to Classes, Objects and Strings. The book is object oriented, where appropriate, from the start and throughout the text.

We also provide an *optional* automated teller machine (ATM) case study in Chapters 25–26, which contains a complete C++ implementation. The case study presents a carefully paced introduction to object-oriented design using the UML—an industry standard graphical modeling language for developing object-oriented systems. We guide you through a friendly design experience intended for the novice.

C++ Standard Library

C++ programs consist of pieces called **classes** and **functions**. You can program each piece yourself, but most C++ programmers take advantage of the rich collections of classes and functions in the C++ Standard Library. Thus, there are really two parts to learning the C++ "world." The first is learning the C++ language itself; the second is learning how to use the classes and functions in the C++ Standard Library. We discuss many of these classes and functions. P. J. Plauger's book, *The Standard C Library* (Upper Saddle River, NJ: Prentice Hall PTR, 1992), is a must read for programmers who need a deep understanding of the ANSI C library functions included in C++. Many special-purpose class libraries are supplied by independent software vendors.

Software Engineering Observation 1.1

Use a "building-block" approach to create programs. Avoid reinventing the wheel. Use existing pieces wherever possible. Called software reuse, this practice is central to object-oriented programming.

Software Engineering Observation 1.2

When programming in C++, you typically will use the following building blocks: classes and functions from the C++ Standard Library, classes and functions you and your colleagues create and classes and functions from various popular third-party libraries.

The advantage of creating your own functions and classes is that you'll know exactly how they work. You'll be able to examine the C++ code. The disadvantage is the time-consuming and complex effort that goes into designing, developing and maintaining new functions and classes that are correct and that operate efficiently.

Performance Tip 1.2

Using C++ Standard Library functions and classes instead of writing your own versions can improve program performance, because they're written carefully to perform efficiently. This technique also shortens program development time.

Portability Tip 1.1

Using C++ Standard Library functions and classes instead of writing your own improves program portability, because they're included in every C++ implementation.

1.7 Programming Languages

In this section, we provide brief comments on several popular programming languages (Fig. 1.5).

Programming language	Description
Fortran	Fortran (FORmula TRANslator) was developed by IBM Corporation in the mid-1950s to be used for scientific and engineering applications that require complex mathematical computations. It's still widely used and its latest versions support object-oriented programming.
COBOL	COBOL (COmmon Business Oriented Language) was developed in the late 1950s by computer manufacturers, the U.S. government and industrial computer users based on a language developed by Grace Hopper, a career U.S. Navy officer and computer scientist. COBOL is still widely used for commercial applications that require precise and efficient manipulation of large amounts of data. Its latest version supports object-oriented programming.
Pascal	Research in the 1960s resulted in *structured programming*—a disciplined approach to writing programs that are clearer, easier to test and debug and easier to modify than large programs produced with previous techniques. One of the more tangible results of this research was the development of Pascal by Professor Niklaus Wirth in 1971. It was designed for teaching structured programming and was popular in college courses for several decades.
Ada	Ada, based on Pascal, was developed under the sponsorship of the U.S. Department of Defense (DOD) during the 1970s and early 1980s. The DOD wanted a single language that would fill most of its needs. The Pascal-based language was named after Lady Ada Lovelace, daughter of the poet Lord Byron. She's credited with writing the world's first computer program in the early 1800s (for the Analytical Engine mechanical computing device designed by Charles Babbage). Ada also supports object-oriented programming.
Basic	Basic was developed in the 1960s at Dartmouth College to familiarize novices with programming techniques. Many of its latest versions are object oriented.
C	C was implemented in 1972 by Dennis Ritchie at Bell Laboratories. It initially became widely known as the UNIX operating system's development language. Today, most of the code for general-purpose operating systems is written in C or C++.
Objective-C	Objective-C is an object-oriented language based on C. It was developed in the early 1980s and later acquired by NeXT, which in turn was acquired by Apple. It has become the key programming language for the OS X operating system and all iOS-powered devices (such as iPods, iPhones and iPads).

Fig. 1.5 | Some other programming languages. (Part 1 of 3.)

Programming language	Description
Java	Sun Microsystems in 1991 funded an internal corporate research project led by James Gosling, which resulted in the C++-based object-oriented programming language called Java. A key goal of Java is to be able to write programs that will run on a great variety of computer systems and computer-control devices. This is sometimes called "write once, run anywhere." Java is used to develop large-scale enterprise applications, to enhance the functionality of web servers (the computers that provide the content we see in our web browsers), to provide applications for consumer devices (e.g., smartphones, tablets, television set-top boxes, appliances, automobiles and more) and for many other purposes. Java is also the key language for developing Android smartphone and tablet apps.
Visual Basic	Microsoft's Visual Basic language was introduced in the early 1990s to simplify the development of Microsoft Windows applications. Its latest versions support object-oriented programming.
C#	Microsoft's three object-oriented primary programming languages are Visual Basic (based on the original Basic), Visual C++ (based on C++) and C# (based on C++ and Java, and developed for integrating the Internet and the web into computer applications).
PHP	PHP is an object-oriented, "open-source" (see Section 1.11.2) "scripting" language supported by a community of users and developers and is used by numerous websites including Wikipedia and Facebook. PHP is platform independent—implementations exist for all major UNIX, Linux, Mac and Windows operating systems. PHP also supports many databases, including MySQL.
Perl	Perl (Practical Extraction and Report Language), one of the most widely used object-oriented scripting languages for web programming, was developed in 1987 by Larry Wall. It features rich text-processing capabilities and flexibility.
Python	Python, another object-oriented scripting language, was released publicly in 1991. Developed by Guido van Rossum of the National Research Institute for Mathematics and Computer Science in Amsterdam (CWI), Python draws heavily from Modula-3—a systems programming language. Python is "extensible"—it can be extended through classes and programming interfaces.
JavaScript	JavaScript is the most widely used scripting language. It's primarily used to add programmability to web pages—for example, animations and interactivity with the user. It's provided with all major web browsers.

Fig. 1.5 | Some other programming languages. (Part 2 of 3.)

Programming language	Description
Ruby on Rails	Ruby—created in the mid-1990s by Yukihiro Matsumoto—is an open-source, object-oriented programming language with a simple syntax that's similar to Perl and Python. Ruby on Rails combines the scripting language Ruby with the Rails web application framework developed by 37Signals. Their book, *Getting Real* (available free at gettingreal.37signals.com/toc.php), is a must read for web developers. Many Ruby on Rails developers have reported productivity gains over other languages when developing database-intensive web applications. Ruby on Rails was used to build Twitter's user interface.
Scala	Scala (www.scala-lang.org/node/273)—short for "scalable language"—was designed by Martin Odersky, a professor at École Polytechnique Fédérale de Lausanne (EPFL) in Switzerland. Released in 2003, Scala uses both the object-oriented programming and functional programming paradigms and is designed to integrate with Java. Programming in Scala can reduce the amount of code in your applications significantly. Twitter and Foursquare use Scala.

Fig. 1.5 | Some other programming languages. (Part 3 of 3.)

1.8 Introduction to Object Technology

Building software quickly, correctly and economically remains an elusive goal at a time when demands for new and more powerful software are soaring. *Objects*, or more precisely—as we'll see in Chapter 3—the *classes* objects come from, are essentially *reusable* software components. There are date objects, time objects, audio objects, video objects, automobile objects, people objects, etc. Almost any *noun* can be reasonably represented as a software object in terms of *attributes* (e.g., name, color and size) and *behaviors* (e.g., calculating, moving and communicating). Software developers have discovered that using a modular, object-oriented design-and-implementation approach can make software-development groups much more productive than was possible with earlier techniques—object-oriented programs are often easier to understand, correct and modify.

The Automobile as an Object

Let's begin with a simple analogy. Suppose you want to *drive a car and make it go faster by pressing its accelerator pedal*. What must happen before you can do this? Well, before you can drive a car, someone has to *design* it. A car typically begins as engineering drawings, similar to the *blueprints* that describe the design of a house. These drawings include the design for an accelerator pedal. The pedal *hides* from the driver the complex mechanisms that actually make the car go faster, just as the brake pedal hides the mechanisms that slow the car, and the steering wheel *hides* the mechanisms that turn the car. This enables people with little or no knowledge of how engines, braking and steering mechanisms work to drive a car easily.

Before you can drive a car, it must be *built* from the engineering drawings that describe it. A completed car has an *actual* accelerator pedal to make the car go faster, but even that's not enough—the car won't accelerate on its own (hopefully!), so the driver must *press* the pedal to accelerate the car.

Member Functions and Classes

Let's use our car example to introduce some key object-oriented programming concepts. Performing a task in a program requires a **member function**. The member function houses the program statements that actually perform its task. It hides these statements from its user, just as the accelerator pedal of a car hides from the driver the mechanisms of making the car go faster. In C++, we create a program unit called a **class** to house the set of member functions that perform the class's tasks. For example, a class that represents a bank account might contain one member function to *deposit* money to an account, another to *withdraw* money from an account and a third to *inquire* what the account's current balance is. A class is similar in concept to a car's engineering drawings, which house the design of an accelerator pedal, steering wheel, and so on.

Instantiation

Just as someone has to *build a car* from its engineering drawings before you can actually drive a car, you must *build an object* from a class before a program can perform the tasks that the class's methods define. The process of doing this is called *instantiation*. An object is then referred to as an **instance** of its class.

Reuse

Just as a car's engineering drawings can be *reused* many times to build many cars, you can *reuse* a class many times to build many objects. Reuse of existing classes when building new classes and programs saves time and effort. Reuse also helps you build more reliable and effective systems, because existing classes and components often have gone through extensive *testing, debugging* and *performance tuning*. Just as the notion of *interchangeable parts* was crucial to the Industrial Revolution, reusable classes are crucial to the software revolution that has been spurred by object technology.

Messages and Member Function Calls

When you drive a car, pressing its gas pedal sends a *message* to the car to perform a task—that is, to go faster. Similarly, you *send messages to an object*. Each message is implemented as a **member function call** that tells a member function of the object to perform its task. For example, a program might call a particular bank account object's *deposit* member function to increase the account's balance.

Attributes and Data Members

A car, besides having capabilities to accomplish tasks, also has *attributes*, such as its color, its number of doors, the amount of gas in its tank, its current speed and its record of total miles driven (i.e., its odometer reading). Like its capabilities, the car's attributes are represented as part of its design in its engineering diagrams (which, for example, include an odometer and a fuel gauge). As you drive an actual car, these attributes are carried along with the car. Every car maintains its *own* attributes. For example, each car knows how much gas is in its own gas tank, but *not* how much is in the tanks of *other* cars.

An object, similarly, has attributes that it carries along as it's used in a program. These attributes are specified as part of the object's class. For example, a bank account object has a *balance attribute* that represents the amount of money in the account. Each bank account object knows the balance in the account it represents, but *not* the balances of the *other* accounts in the bank. Attributes are specified by the class's **data members**.

Encapsulation
Classes **encapsulate** (i.e., wrap) attributes and member functions into objects—an object's attributes and member functions are intimately related. Objects may communicate with one another, but they're normally not allowed to know how other objects are implemented—implementation details are *hidden* within the objects themselves. This **information hiding**, as we'll see, is crucial to good software engineering.

Inheritance
A new class of objects can be created quickly and conveniently by **inheritance**—the new class absorbs the characteristics of an existing class, possibly customizing them and adding unique characteristics of its own. In our car analogy, an object of class "convertible" certainly *is an* object of the more *general* class "automobile," but more *specifically*, the roof can be raised or lowered.

Object-Oriented Analysis and Design (OOAD)
Soon you'll be writing programs in C++. How will you create the **code** (i.e., the program instructions) for your programs? Perhaps, like many programmers, you'll simply turn on your computer and start typing. This approach may work for small programs (like the ones we present in the early chapters of the book), but what if you were asked to create a software system to control thousands of automated teller machines for a major bank? Or suppose you were asked to work on a team of thousands of software developers building the next U.S. air traffic control system? For projects so large and complex, you should not simply sit down and start writing programs.

To create the best solutions, you should follow a detailed **analysis** process for determining your project's **requirements** (i.e., defining *what* the system is supposed to do) and developing a **design** that satisfies them (i.e., deciding *how* the system should do it). Ideally, you'd go through this process and carefully review the design (and have your design reviewed by other software professionals) before writing any code. If this process involves analyzing and designing your system from an object-oriented point of view, it's called an **object-oriented analysis and design (OOAD) process**. Languages like C++ are object oriented. Programming in such a language, called **object-oriented programming (OOP)**, allows you to implement an object-oriented design as a working system.

The UML (Unified Modeling Language)
Although many different OOAD processes exist, a single graphical language for communicating the results of *any* OOAD process has come into wide use. This language, known as the Unified Modeling Language (UML), is now the most widely used graphical scheme for modeling object-oriented systems. We present our first UML diagrams in Chapters 3 and 4, then use them in our deeper treatment of object-oriented programming through Chapter 12. In our *optional* ATM Software Engineering Case Study in Chapters 25–26 we present a simple subset of the UML's features as we guide you through an object-oriented design experience.

1.9 Typical C++ Development Environment

C++ systems generally consist of three parts: a program development environment, the language and the C++ Standard Library. C++ programs typically go through six phases: edit, preprocess, compile, link, load and execute. The following discussion explains a typical C++ program development environment.

Phase 1: Editing a Program

Phase 1 consists of editing a file with an *editor program*, normally known simply as an *editor* (Fig. 1.6). You type a C++ program (typically referred to as **source code**) using the editor, make any necessary corrections and save the program on a secondary storage device, such as your hard drive. C++ source code filenames often end with the .cpp, .cxx, .cc or .C extensions (note that C is in uppercase) which indicate that a file contains C++ source code. See the documentation for your C++ compiler for more information on file-name extensions.

Phase 1:
Programmer creates program in the editor and stores it on disk

Fig. 1.6 | Typical C++ development environment—editing phase.

Two editors widely used on Linux systems are vi and emacs. C++ software packages for Microsoft Windows such as Microsoft Visual C++ (microsoft.com/express) have editors integrated into the programming environment. You can also use a simple text editor, such as Notepad in Windows, to write your C++ code.

For organizations that develop substantial information systems, **integrated development environments** (IDEs) are available from many major software suppliers. IDEs provide tools that support the software-development process, including editors for writing and editing programs and debuggers for locating **logic errors**—errors that cause programs to execute incorrectly. Popular IDEs include Microsoft® Visual Studio 2012 Express Edition, Dev C++, NetBeans, Eclipse, Apple's Xcode and CodeLite.

Phase 2: Preprocessing a C++ Program

In Phase 2, you give the command to **compile** the program (Fig. 1.7). In a C++ system, a **preprocessor** program executes automatically before the compiler's translation phase begins (so we call preprocessing Phase 2 and compiling Phase 3). The C++ preprocessor obeys commands called **preprocessing directives**, which indicate that certain manipulations are to be performed on the program before compilation. These manipulations usually include other text files to be compiled, and perform various text replacements. The most common preprocessing directives are discussed in the early chapters; a detailed discussion of preprocessor features appears in Appendix E, Preprocessor.

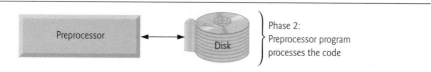

Phase 2:
Preprocessor program processes the code

Fig. 1.7 | Typical C++ development environment—preprocessor phase.

Phase 3: Compiling a C++ Program

In Phase 3, the compiler translates the C++ program into machine-language code—also referred to as object code (Fig. 1.8).

Fig. 1.8 | Typical C++ development environment—compilation phase.

Phase 4: Linking

Phase 4 is called **linking**. C++ programs typically contain references to functions and data defined elsewhere, such as in the standard libraries or in the private libraries of groups of programmers working on a particular project (Fig. 1.9). The object code produced by the C++ compiler typically contains "holes" due to these missing parts. A **linker** links the object code with the code for the missing functions to produce an **executable program** (with no missing pieces). If the program compiles and links correctly, an executable image is produced.

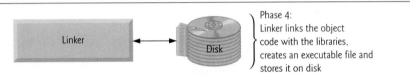

Fig. 1.9 | Typical C++ development environment—linking phase.

Phase 5: Loading

Phase 5 is called **loading**. Before a program can be executed, it must first be placed in memory (Fig. 1.10). This is done by the **loader**, which takes the executable image from disk and transfers it to memory. Additional components from shared libraries that support the program are also loaded.

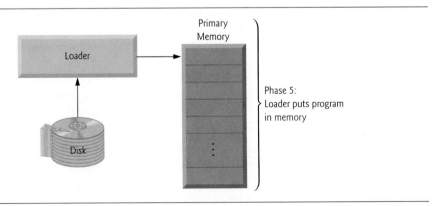

Fig. 1.10 | Typical C++ development environment—loading phase.

Phase 6: Execution

Finally, the computer, under the control of its CPU, **executes** the program one instruction at a time (Fig. 1.11). Some modern computer architectures can execute several instructions in parallel.

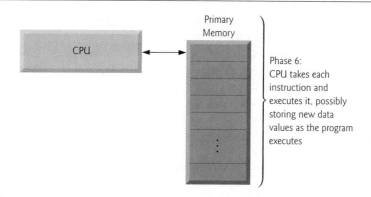

Fig. 1.11 | Typical C++ development environment—execution phase.

Problems That May Occur at Execution Time

Programs might not work on the first try. Each of the preceding phases can fail because of various errors that we'll discuss throughout this book. For example, an executing program might try to divide by zero (an illegal operation for integer arithmetic in C++). This would cause the C++ program to display an error message. If this occurred, you'd have to return to the edit phase, make the necessary corrections and proceed through the remaining phases again to determine that the corrections fixed the problem(s). [*Note:* Most programs in C++ input or output data. Certain C++ functions take their input from cin (the **standard input stream**; pronounced "see-in"), which is normally the keyboard, but cin can be redirected to another device. Data is often output to cout (the **standard output stream**; pronounced "see-out"), which is normally the computer screen, but cout can be redirected to another device. When we say that a program prints a result, we normally mean that the result is displayed on a screen. Data may be output to other devices, such as disks and hardcopy printers. There is also a **standard error stream** referred to as **cerr**. The cerr stream (normally connected to the screen) is used for displaying error messages.

Common Programming Error 1.1

Errors such as division by zero occur as a program runs, so they're called runtime errors or execution-time errors. Fatal runtime errors cause programs to terminate immediately without having successfully performed their jobs. Nonfatal runtime errors allow programs to run to completion, often producing incorrect results.

1.10 Test-Driving a C++ Application

In this section, you'll run and interact with your first C++ application. You'll begin by running an entertaining guess-the-number game, which picks a number from 1 to 1000 and prompts you to guess it. If your guess is correct, the game ends. If your guess is not correct, the application indicates whether your guess is higher or lower than the correct number. There is no limit on the number of guesses you can make. [*Note:* For this test drive only, we've modified this application from the exercise you'll be asked to create in Chapter 6, Functions and an Introduction to Recursion. Normally this application randomly selects the correct answer as you execute the program. The modified application uses the same correct answer every time the program executes (though this may vary by compiler), so you can use the *same* guesses we use in this section and see the *same* results as we walk you through interacting with your first C++ application.]

We'll demonstrate running a C++ application using the Windows **Command Prompt** and a shell on Linux. The application runs similarly on both platforms. Many development environments are available in which you can compile, build and run C++ applications, such as GNU C++, Microsoft Visual C++, Apple Xcode, Dev C++, CodeLite, NetBeans, Eclipse etc. Consult your instructor for information on your specific development environment.

In the following steps, you'll run the application and enter various numbers to guess the correct number. The elements and functionality that you see in this application are typical of those you'll learn to program in this book. We use fonts to distinguish between features you see on the screen (e.g., the **Command Prompt**) and elements that are not directly related to the screen. We emphasize screen features like titles and menus (e.g., the **File** menu) in a semibold **sans-serif Helvetica** font and emphasize filenames, text displayed by an application and values you should enter into an application (e.g., GuessNumber or 500) in a sans-serif Lucida font. As you've noticed, the **defining occurrence** of each term is set in blue, bold type. For the figures in this section, we point out significant parts of the application. To make these features more visible, we've modified the background color of the **Command Prompt** window (for the Windows test drive only). To modify the **Command Prompt** colors on your system, open a **Command Prompt** by selecting **Start > All Programs > Accessories > Command Prompt**, then right click the title bar and select **Properties**. In the **"Command Prompt" Properties** dialog box that appears, click the **Colors** tab, and select your preferred text and background colors.

Running a C++ Application from the Windows Command Prompt

1. *Checking your setup.* It's important to read the Before You Begin section at www.deitel.com/books/cpphtp9/ to make sure that you've copied the book's examples to your hard drive correctly.

2. *Locating the completed application.* Open a **Command Prompt** window. To change to the directory for the completed **GuessNumber** application, type cd C:\examples\ch01\GuessNumber\Windows, then press *Enter* (Fig. 1.12). The command cd is used to change directories.

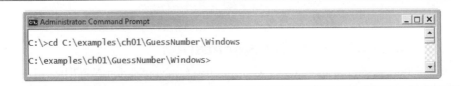

Fig. 1.12 | Opening a **Command Prompt** window and changing the directory.

3. *Running the GuessNumber application.* Now that you are in the directory that contains the **GuessNumber** application, type the command **GuessNumber** (Fig. 1.13) and press *Enter*. [*Note:* GuessNumber.exe is the actual name of the application; however, Windows assumes the .exe extension by default.]

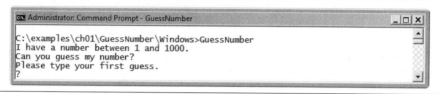

Fig. 1.13 | Running the **GuessNumber** application.

4. *Entering your first guess.* The application displays "Please type your first guess.", then displays a question mark (?) as a prompt on the next line (Fig. 1.13). At the prompt, enter **500** (Fig. 1.14).

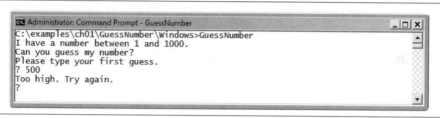

Fig. 1.14 | Entering your first guess.

5. *Entering another guess.* The application displays "Too high. Try again.", meaning that the value you entered is greater than the number the application chose as the correct guess. So, you should enter a lower number for your next guess. At the prompt, enter **250** (Fig. 1.15). The application again displays "Too high. Try again.", because the value you entered is still greater than the number that the application chose as the correct guess.

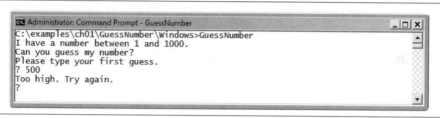

Fig. 1.15 | Entering a second guess and receiving feedback.

6. *Entering additional guesses.* Continue to play the game by entering values until you guess the correct number. The application will display "Excellent! You guessed the number!" (Fig. 1.16).

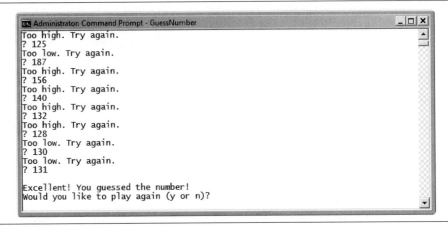

Fig. 1.16 | Entering additional guesses and guessing the correct number.

7. *Playing the game again or exiting the application.* After you guess correctly, the application asks if you'd like to play another game (Fig. 1.16). At the "Would you like to play again (y or n)?" prompt, entering the one character **y** causes the application to choose a new number and displays the message "Please type your first guess." followed by a question mark prompt (Fig. 1.17) so you can make your first guess in the new game. Entering the character **n** ends the application and returns you to the application's directory at the **Command Prompt** (Fig. 1.18). Each time you execute this application from the beginning (i.e., *Step 3*), it will choose the same numbers for you to guess.

8. *Close the* **Command Prompt** *window.*

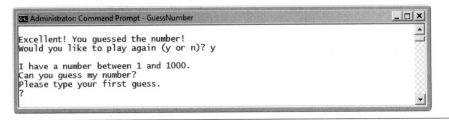

Fig. 1.17 | Playing the game again.

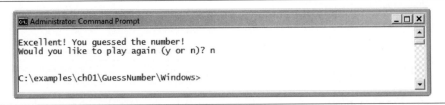

Fig. 1.18 | Exiting the game.

Running a C++ Application Using GNU C++ with Linux

For this test drive, we assume that you know how to copy the examples into your home directory. Please see your instructor if you have any questions regarding copying the files to your Linux system. Also, for the figures in this section, we use a bold highlight to point out the user input required by each step. The prompt in the shell on our system uses the tilde (~) character to represent the home directory, and each prompt ends with the dollar sign ($) character. The prompt will vary among Linux systems.

1. **Locating the completed application.** From a Linux shell, change to the completed **GuessNumber** application directory (Fig. 1.19) by typing

```
cd Examples/ch01/GuessNumber/GNU_Linux
```

then pressing *Enter*. The command cd is used to change directories.

```
~$ cd examples/ch01/GuessNumber/GNU_Linux
~/examples/ch01/GuessNumber/GNU_Linux$
```

Fig. 1.19 | Changing to the **GuessNumber** application's directory.

2. **Compiling the GuessNumber application.** To run an application on the GNU C++ compiler, you must first compile it by typing

```
g++ GuessNumber.cpp -o GuessNumber
```

as in Fig. 1.20. This command compiles the application and produces an executable file called GuessNumber.

```
~/examples/ch01/GuessNumber/GNU_Linux$ g++ GuessNumber.cpp -o GuessNumber
~/examples/ch01/GuessNumber/GNU_Linux$
```

Fig. 1.20 | Compiling the **GuessNumber** application using the g++ command.

3. **Running the GuessNumber application.** To run the executable file GuessNumber, type ./GuessNumber at the next prompt, then press *Enter* (Fig. 1.21).

```
~/examples/ch01/GuessNumber/GNU_Linux$ ./GuessNumber
I have a number between 1 and 1000.
Can you guess my number?
Please type your first guess.
?
```

Fig. 1.21 | Running the **GuessNumber** application.

4. **Entering your first guess.** The application displays "Please type your first guess.", then displays a question mark (?) as a prompt on the next line (Fig. 1.21). At the prompt, enter **500** (Fig. 1.22). [*Note:* This is the same application that we modified and test-drove for Windows, but the outputs could vary based on the compiler being used.]

5. *Entering another guess.* The application displays "Too high. Try again.", meaning that the value you entered is greater than the number the application chose as the correct guess (Fig. 1.22). At the next prompt, enter **250** (Fig. 1.23). This time the application displays "Too low. Try again.", because the value you entered is less than the correct guess.

6. *Entering additional guesses.* Continue to play the game (Fig. 1.24) by entering values until you guess the correct number. When you guess correctly, the application displays "Excellent! You guessed the number."

```
~/examples/ch01/GuessNumber/GNU_Linux$ ./GuessNumber
I have a number between 1 and 1000.
Can you guess my number?
Please type your first guess.
? 500
Too high. Try again.
?
```

Fig. 1.22 | Entering an initial guess.

```
~/examples/ch01/GuessNumber/GNU_Linux$ ./GuessNumber
I have a number between 1 and 1000.
Can you guess my number?
Please type your first guess.
? 500
Too high. Try again.
? 250
Too low. Try again.
?
```

Fig. 1.23 | Entering a second guess and receiving feedback.

```
Too low. Try again.
? 375
Too low. Try again.
? 437
Too high. Try again.
? 406
Too high. Try again.
? 391
Too high. Try again.
? 383
Too low. Try again.
? 387
Too high. Try again.
? 385
Too high. Try again.
? 384
Excellent! You guessed the number.
Would you like to play again (y or n)?
```

Fig. 1.24 | Entering additional guesses and guessing the correct number.

7. *Playing the game again or exiting the application.* After you guess the correct number, the application asks if you'd like to play another game. At the "Would you like to play again (y or n)?" prompt, entering the one character **y** causes the application to choose a new number and displays the message "Please type your first guess." followed by a question mark prompt (Fig. 1.25) so you can make your first guess in the new game. Entering the character **n** ends the application and returns you to the application's directory in the shell (Fig. 1.26). Each time you execute this application from the beginning (i.e., *Step 3*), it will choose the same numbers for you to guess.

```
Excellent! You guessed the number.
Would you like to play again (y or n)? y

I have a number between 1 and 1000.
Can you guess my number?
Please type your first guess.
?
```

Fig. 1.25 | Playing the game again.

```
Excellent! You guessed the number.
Would you like to play again (y or n)? n

~/examples/ch01/GuessNumber/GNU_Linux$
```

Fig. 1.26 | Exiting the game.

1.11 Operating Systems

Operating systems are software systems that make using computers more convenient for users, application developers and system administrators. They provide services that allow each application to execute safely, efficiently and *concurrently* (i.e., in parallel) with other applications. The software that contains the core components of the operating system is called the **kernel**. Popular desktop operating systems include Linux, Windows and OS X (formerly called Mac OS X)—we used all three in developing this book. Popular mobile operating systems used in smartphones and tablets include Google's Android, Apple's iOS (for iPhone, iPad and iPod Touch devices), BlackBerry OS and Windows Phone. You can develop applications in C++ for all of the following key operating systems, including several of the latest mobile operating systems.

1.11.1 Windows—A Proprietary Operating System

In the mid-1980s, Microsoft developed the **Windows operating system**, consisting of a graphical user interface built on top of DOS—an enormously popular personal-computer operating system that users interacted with by *typing* commands. Windows borrowed from many concepts (such as icons, menus and windows) developed by Xerox PARC and popularized by early Apple Macintosh operating systems. Windows 8 is Microsoft's latest operating system—its features include enhancements to the user interface, faster startup times, further refinement of security features, touch-screen and multitouch support, and more. Windows is a *proprietary* operating system—it's controlled by Microsoft exclusively. Windows is by far the world's most widely used desktop operating system.

1.11.2 Linux—An Open-Source Operating System

The Linux operating system is perhaps the greatest success of the *open-source* movement. Open-source software departs from the *proprietary* software development style that dominated software's early years. With open-source development, individuals and companies *contribute* their efforts in developing, maintaining and evolving software in exchange for the right to use that software for their own purposes, typically at *no charge*. Open-source code is often scrutinized by a much larger audience than proprietary software, so errors often get removed faster. Open source also encourages innovation. Enterprise systems companies, such as IBM, Oracle and many others, have made significant investments in Linux open-source development.

Some key organizations in the open-source community are the Eclipse Foundation (the Eclipse Integrated Development Environment helps programmers conveniently develop software), the Mozilla Foundation (creators of the Firefox web browser), the Apache Software Foundation (creators of the Apache web server used to develop web-based applications) and SourceForge (which provides tools for managing open-source projects—it has hundreds of thousands of them under development). Rapid improvements to computing and communications, decreasing costs and open-source software have made it much easier and more economical to create a software-based business now than just a decade ago. A great example is Facebook, which was launched from a college dorm room and built with open-source software.

The Linux kernel is the core of the most popular open-source, freely distributed, full-featured operating system. It's developed by a loosely organized team of volunteers and is popular in servers, personal computers and embedded systems. Unlike that of proprietary operating systems like Microsoft's Windows and Apple's OS X, Linux source code (the program code) is available to the public for examination and modification and is free to download and install. As a result, Linux users benefit from a community of developers actively debugging and improving the kernel, and the ability to customize the operating system to meet specific needs.

A variety of issues—such as Microsoft's market power, the small number of user-friendly Linux applications and the diversity of Linux distributions, such as Red Hat Linux, Ubuntu Linux and many others—have prevented widespread Linux use on desktop computers. Linux has become extremely popular on servers and in embedded systems, such as Google's Android-based smartphones.

1.11.3 Apple's OS X; Apple's iOS for iPhone®, iPad® and iPod Touch® Devices

Apple, founded in 1976 by Steve Jobs and Steve Wozniak, quickly became a leader in personal computing. In 1979, Jobs and several Apple employees visited Xerox PARC (Palo Alto Research Center) to learn about Xerox's desktop computer that featured a graphical user interface (GUI). That GUI served as the inspiration for the Apple Macintosh, launched with much fanfare in a memorable Super Bowl ad in 1984.

The Objective-C programming language, created by Brad Cox and Tom Love at Stepstone in the early 1980s, added capabilities for object-oriented programming (OOP) to the C programming language. At the time of this writing, Objective-C was comparable in popularity to C++.[6] Steve Jobs left Apple in 1985 and founded NeXT Inc. In 1988, NeXT licensed Objective-C from StepStone and developed an Objective-C compiler and libraries which were used as the platform for the NeXTSTEP operating system's user interface and Interface Builder—used to construct graphical user interfaces.

Jobs returned to Apple in 1996 when Apple bought NeXT. Apple's OS X operating system is a descendant of NeXTSTEP. Apple's proprietary operating system, iOS, is derived from Apple's OS X and is used in the iPhone, iPad and iPod Touch devices.

1.11.4 Google's Android

Android—the fastest growing mobile and smartphone operating system—is based on the Linux kernel and Java. Experienced Java programmers can quickly dive into Android development. One benefit of developing Android apps is the openness of the platform. The operating system is open source and free.

The Android operating system was developed by Android, Inc., which was acquired by Google in 2005. In 2007, the Open Handset Alliance™—a consortium of 34 companies initially and 84 by 2011—was formed to continue developing Android. As of June 2012, more than 900,000 Android devices were being activated each day![7] Android smartphones are now outselling iPhones in the United States.[8] The Android operating system is used in numerous smartphones (such as the Motorola Droid, HTC One S, Samsung Galaxy Nexus and many more), e-reader devices (such as the Kindle Fire and Barnes and Noble Nook™), tablet computers (such as the Dell Streak and the Samsung Galaxy Tab), in-store touch-screen kiosks, cars, robots, multimedia players and more.

1.12 The Internet and World Wide Web

The Internet—a global network of computers—was made possible by the *convergence of computing and communications technologies.* In the late 1960s, ARPA (the Advanced Research Projects Agency) rolled out blueprints for networking the main computer systems of about a dozen ARPA-funded universities and research institutions. Academic research was about to take a giant leap forward. ARPA proceeded to implement the **ARPANET**, which eventually evolved into today's **Internet**. It rapidly became clear that communicating quickly and easily via electronic mail was the key early benefit of the ARPANET. This is true even today on the Internet, which facilitates communications of all kinds among the world's Internet users.

Packet Switching

A primary goal for ARPANET was to allow *multiple* users to send and receive information simultaneously over the *same* communications paths (e.g., phone lines). The network operated with a technique called **packet switching**, in which digital data was sent in small bundles called **packets**. The packets contained *address, error-control* and *sequencing* infor-

---

6.   www.tiobe.com/index.php/content/paperinfo/tpci/index.html.
7.   mashable.com/2012/06/11/900000-android-devices/.
8.   www.pcworld.com/article/196035/android_outsells_the_iphone_no_big_surprise.html.

mation. The address information allowed packets to be *routed* to their destinations. The sequencing information helped in *reassembling* the packets—which, because of complex routing mechanisms, could arrive out of order—into their original order for presentation to the recipient. Packets from different senders were intermixed on the *same* lines to efficiently use the available bandwidth. This packet-switching technique greatly reduced transmission costs, as compared with the cost of *dedicated* communications lines.

The network was designed to operate without centralized control. If a portion of the network failed, the remaining working portions would still route packets from senders to receivers over alternative paths for reliability.

TCP/IP

The protocol (i.e., set of rules) for communicating over the ARPANET became known as TCP—the **Transmission Control Protocol**. TCP ensured that messages were properly routed from sender to receiver and that they arrived intact.

As the Internet evolved, organizations worldwide were implementing their own networks. One challenge was to get these different networks to communicate. ARPA accomplished this with the development of **IP**—the **Internet Protocol**, truly creating a network of networks, the current architecture of the Internet. The combined set of protocols is now commonly called TCP/IP.

World Wide Web, HTML, HTTP

The **World Wide Web** allows you to locate and view multimedia-based documents on almost any subject over the Internet. The web is a relatively recent creation. In 1989, Tim Berners-Lee of CERN (the European Organization for Nuclear Research) began to develop a technology for sharing information via hyperlinked text documents. Berners-Lee called his invention the **HyperText Markup Language** (HTML). He also wrote communication protocols to form the backbone of his new information system, which he called the World Wide Web. In particular, he wrote the **Hypertext Transfer Protocol** (**HTTP**)—a communications protocol used to send information over the web. The URL (**Uniform Resource Locator**) specifies the address (i.e., location) of the web page displayed in the browser window. Each web page on the Internet is associated with a unique URL. **Hypertext Transfer Protocol Secure** (HTTPS) is the standard for transferring encrypted data on the web.

Mosaic, Netscape, Emergence of Web 2.0

Web use exploded with the availability in 1993 of the Mosaic browser, which featured a user-friendly graphical interface. Marc Andreessen, whose team at the National Center for Supercomputing Applications developed Mosaic, went on to found Netscape, the company that many people credit with igniting the explosive Internet economy of the late 1990s.

In 2003 there was a noticeable shift in how people and businesses were using the web and developing web-based applications. The term **Web 2.0** was coined by Dale Dougherty of O'Reilly Media[9] in 2003 to describe this trend. Generally, Web 2.0 companies use the web as a platform to create collaborative, community-based sites (e.g., social networking sites, blogs, wikis).

---

9. T. O'Reilly, "What is Web 2.0: Design Patterns and Business Models for the Next Generation of Software." September 2005 <http://www.oreillynet.com/pub/a/oreilly/tim/news/2005/09/30/what-is-web-20.html?page=1>.

Companies with Web 2.0 characteristics are Google (web search), YouTube (video sharing), Facebook (social networking), Twitter (microblogging), Groupon (social commerce), Foursquare (mobile check-in), Salesforce (business software offered as online services "in the cloud"), Craigslist (mostly free classified listings), Flickr (photo sharing), Skype (Internet telephony and video calling and conferencing) and Wikipedia (a free online encyclopedia).

Web 2.0 *involves* the users—not only do they create content, but they help organize it, share it, remix it, critique it, update it, etc. Web 2.0 is a *conversation*, with everyone having the opportunity to speak and share views. Companies that understand Web 2.0 realize that their products and services are conversations as well.

Architecture of Participation

Web 2.0 embraces an **architecture of participation**—a design that encourages user interaction and community contributions. You, the user, are the most important aspect of Web 2.0—so important, in fact, that in 2006, *TIME* magazine's "Person of the Year" was "You."[10] The article recognized the social phenomenon of Web 2.0—the shift away from a *powerful few* to an *empowered many*. Popular blogs now compete with traditional media powerhouses, and many Web 2.0 companies are built almost entirely on user-generated content. For websites like Facebook, Twitter, YouTube, eBay and Wikipedia users create the content, while the companies provide the *platforms* on which to enter, manipulate and share the information.

1.13 Some Key Software Development Terminology

Figure 1.27 lists a number of buzzwords that you'll hear in the software development community. We've created Resource Centers on most of these topics, with more on the way.

Technology	Description
Ajax	Ajax is one of the premier Web 2.0 software technologies. Ajax helps Internet-based applications perform like desktop applications—a difficult task, given that such applications suffer transmission delays as data is shuttled back and forth between your computer and servers on the Internet.
Agile software development	Agile software development is a set of methodologies that try to get software implemented faster and using fewer resources than previous methodologies. Check out the Agile Alliance (www.agilealliance.org) and the Agile Manifesto (www.agilemanifesto.org).
Refactoring	Refactoring involves reworking programs to make them clearer and easier to maintain while preserving their correctness and functionality. It's widely employed with agile development methodologies. Many IDEs include *refactoring tools* to do major portions of the reworking automatically.

Fig. 1.27 | Software technologies. (Part 1 of 2.)

---

10. www.time.com/time/magazine/article/0,9171,1570810,00.html.

Technology	Description
Design patterns	Design patterns are proven architectures for constructing flexible and maintainable object-oriented software. The field of design patterns tries to enumerate those recurring patterns, encouraging software designers to *reuse* them to develop better-quality software using less time, money and effort.
LAMP	LAMP is an acronym for the set of open-source technologies that many developers use to build web applications—it stands for Linux, Apache, MySQL and PHP (or Perl or Python—two other languages used for similar purposes). MySQL is an open-source database management system. PHP is the most popular open-source server-side Internet "scripting" language for developing Internet-based applications.
Software as a Service (SaaS)	Software has generally been viewed as a product; most software still is offered this way. If you want to run an application, you buy a software package from a software vendor—often a CD, DVD or web download. You then install that software on your computer and run it as needed. As new versions of the software appear, you upgrade your software, often requiring significant time and at considerable expense. This process can become cumbersome for organizations with tens of thousands of systems that must be maintained on a diverse array of computer equipment. With Software as a Service (SaaS), the software runs on servers elsewhere on the Internet. When that server is updated, all clients worldwide see the new capabilities—no local installation is needed. You access the service through a browser. Browsers are quite portable, so you can run the same applications on a wide variety of computers from anywhere in the world. Salesforce.com, Google, and Microsoft's Office Live and Windows Live all offer SaaS. SaaS is a capability of cloud computing.
Platform as a Service (PaaS)	Platform as a Service (PaaS), another capability of cloud computing, provides a computing platform for developing and running applications as a service over the web, rather than installing the tools on your computer. PaaS providers include Google App Engine, Amazon EC2, Bungee Labs and more.
Software Development Kit (SDK)	Software Development Kits (SDKs) include the tools and documentation developers use to program applications.

Fig. 1.27 | Software technologies. (Part 2 of 2.)

Figure 1.28 describes software product-release categories.

Version	Description
Alpha	An *alpha* version is the earliest release of a software product that's still under active development. Alpha versions are often buggy, incomplete and unstable and are released to a relatively small number of developers for testing new features, getting early feedback, etc.

Fig. 1.28 | Software product-release terminology. (Part 1 of 2.)

Version	Description
Beta	*Beta* versions are released to a larger number of developers later in the development process after most major bugs have been fixed and new features are nearly complete. Beta software is more stable, but still subject to change.
Release candidates	*Release candidates* are generally *feature complete* and (supposedly) bug free and ready for use by the community, which provides a diverse testing environment—the software is used on different systems, with varying constraints and for a variety of purposes. Any bugs that appear are corrected, and eventually the final product is released to the general public. Software companies often distribute incremental updates over the Internet.
Continuous beta	Software that's developed using this approach generally does not have version numbers (for example, Google search or Gmail). The software, which is hosted in the cloud (not installed on your computer), is constantly evolving so that users always have the latest version.

Fig. 1.28 | Software product-release terminology. (Part 2 of 2.)

1.14 C++11 and the Open Source Boost Libraries

C++11 (formerly called C++0x)—the latest C++ programming language standard—was published by ISO/IEC in 2011. Bjarne Stroustrup, the creator of C++, expressed his vision for the future of the language—the main goals were to make C++ easier to learn, improve library building capabilities and increase compatibility with the C programming language. The new standard extends the C++ Standard Library and includes several features and enhancements to improve performance and security. The major C++ compiler vendors have already implemented many of the new C++11 features (Fig. 1.29). Throughout the book, we discuss various key features of C++11. For more information, visit the C++ Standards Committee website at www.open-std.org/jtc1/sc22/wg21/ and isocpp.org. Copies of the C++11 language specification (ISO/IEC 14882:2011) can be purchased at:

```
http://bit.ly/CPlusPlus11Standard
```

C++ Compiler	URL of C++11 feature descriptions
C++11 features implemented in each of the major C++ compilers.	wiki.apache.org/stdcxx/C%2B%2B0xCompilerSupport
Microsoft® Visual C++	msdn.microsoft.com/en-us/library/hh567368.aspx
GNU Compiler Collection (g++)	gcc.gnu.org/projects/cxx0x.html
Intel® C++ Compiler	software.intel.com/en-us/articles/c0x-features-supported-by-intel-c-compiler/

Fig. 1.29 | C++ compilers that have implemented major portions of C++11.

C++ Compiler	URL of C++11 feature descriptions
IBM® XL C/C++	www.ibm.com/developerworks/mydeveloperworks/ blogs/5894415f-be62-4bc0-81c5-3956e82276f3/ entry/xlc_compiler_s_c_11_support50?lang=en
Clang	clang.llvm.org/cxx_status.html
EDG ecpp	www.edg.com/docs/edg_cpp.pdf

Fig. 1.29 | C++ compilers that have implemented major portions of C++11.

Boost C++ Libraries

The Boost C++ Libraries are free, open-source libraries created by members of the C++ community. They are peer reviewed and portable across many compilers and platforms. Boost has grown to over 100 libraries, with more being added regularly. Today there are thousands of programmers in the Boost open source community. Boost provides C++ programmers with useful libraries that work well with the existing C++ Standard Library. The Boost libraries can be used by C++ programmers working on a wide variety of platforms with many different compilers. Some of the new C++11 Standard Library features were derived from corresponding Boost libraries. We overview the libraries and provide code examples for the "regular expression" and "smart pointer" libraries, among others.

Regular expressions are used to match specific character patterns in text. They can be used to validate data to ensure that it's in a particular format, to replace parts of one string with another, or to split a string.

Many common bugs in C and C++ code are related to pointers, a powerful programming capability that C++ absorbed from C. As you'll see, **smart pointers** help you avoid errors associated with traditional pointers.

1.15 Keeping Up to Date with Information Technologies

Figure 1.30 lists key technical and business publications that will help you stay up to date with the latest news and trends and technology. You can also find a growing list of Internet- and web-related Resource Centers at www.deitel.com/resourcecenters.html.

Publication	URL
ACM TechNews	technews.acm.org/
ACM Transactions on Accessible Computing	www.gccis.rit.edu/taccess/index.html
ACM Transactions on Internet Technology	toit.acm.org/
Bloomberg BusinessWeek	www.businessweek.com
CNET	news.cnet.com
Communications of the ACM	cacm.acm.org/

Fig. 1.30 | Technical and business publications. (Part 1 of 2.)

Publication	URL
Computerworld	`www.computerworld.com`
Engadget	`www.engadget.com`
eWeek	`www.eweek.com`
Fast Company	`www.fastcompany.com/`
Fortune	`money.cnn.com/magazines/fortune/`
IEEE Computer	`www.computer.org/portal/web/computer`
IEEE Internet Computing	`www.computer.org/portal/web/internet/home`
InfoWorld	`www.infoworld.com`
Mashable	`mashable.com`
PCWorld	`www.pcworld.com`
SD Times	`www.sdtimes.com`
Slashdot	`slashdot.org/`
Smarter Technology	`www.smartertechnology.com`
Technology Review	`technologyreview.com`
Techcrunch	`techcrunch.com`
Wired	`www.wired.com`

Fig. 1.30 | Technical and business publications. (Part 2 of 2.)

1.16 Web Resources

This section provides links to our C++ and related Resource Centers that will be useful to you as you learn C++. These include blogs, articles, whitepapers, compilers, development tools, downloads, FAQs, tutorials, webcasts, wikis and links to C++ game programming resources. For updates on Deitel publications, Resource Centers, training courses, partner offers and more, follow us on Facebook® at `www.facebook.com/deitelfan/`, Twitter® @deitel, Google+ at `gplus.to/deitel` and LinkedIn at `bit.ly/DeitelLinkedIn`.

Deitel & Associates Websites

`www.deitel.com/books/cpphtp9/`
The Deitel & Associates *C++ How to Program, 9/e* site. Here you'll find links to the book's examples and other resources.

`www.deitel.com/cplusplus/`
`www.deitel.com/visualcplusplus/`
`www.deitel.com/codesearchengines/`
`www.deitel.com/programmingprojects/`
Check these Resource Centers for compilers, code downloads, tutorials, documentation, books, e-books, articles, blogs, RSS feeds and more that will help you develop C++ applications.

`www.deitel.com`
Check this site for updates, corrections and additional resources for all Deitel publications.

`www.deitel.com/newsletter/subscribe.html`
Subscribe here to the *Deitel® Buzz Online* e-mail newsletter to follow the Deitel & Associates publishing program, including updates and errata to *C++ How to Program, 9/e*.

Self-Review Exercises

1.1   Fill in the blanks in each of the following statements:
   a) _____ devices use a network of satellites to retrieve location-based information.
   b) Every year or two, the capacities of computers have approximately doubled inexpensively. This statement is known as _____.
   c) A _____ is an electronic collection of data that's organized for easy access and manipulation.
   d) Any computer can directly understand only its own _____.
   e) Translator programs called _____ convert high-level language programs into machine language.
   f) _____ allow you listen to large catalogues of music over the web, create customized "radio stations" and discover new music based on your feedback.
   g) _____ are dropping dramatically, owing to rapid developments in hardware and software technologies.

1.2   Fill in the blanks in each of the following sentences about the C++ environment.
   a) C++ source code filenames often end with the _____, _____, _____ or _____ extensions.
   b) C++ offers software packages for Microsoft Windows such as _____.
   c) In a C++ system, a(n) _____ program executes automatically before the compiler's translation phase begins.
   d) There is also a standard error stream referred to as _____.

1.3   Fill in the blanks in each of the following statements (based on Section 1.8):
   a) Objects have the property of _____—although objects may know how to communicate with one another across well-defined interfaces, they normally are not allowed to know how other objects are implemented.
   b) C++ programmers concentrate on creating _____, which contain data members and the member functions that manipulate those data members and provide services to clients.
   c) The process of analyzing and designing a system from an object-oriented point of view is called _____.
   d) With _____, new classes of objects are derived by absorbing characteristics of existing classes, then adding unique characteristics of their own.
   e) _____ is a graphical language that allows people who design software systems to use an industry-standard notation to represent them.
   f) The size, shape, color and weight of an object are considered _____ of the object's class.

Answers to Self-Review Exercises

1.1   a) Global Positioning System (GPS). b) Moore's Law. c) database. d) machine language. e) compilers. f) Streaming music services. g) Computing costs.

1.2   a) `.cpp`, `.cxx`, `.cc`, `.C` b) Microsoft Visual C++ c) pre-processor d) `cerr`.

1.3   a) information hiding. b) classes. c) object-oriented analysis and design (OOAD). d) inheritance. e) The Unified Modeling Language (UML). f) attributes.

Exercises

1.4   Fill in the blanks in each of the following statements:
   a) The logical unit of the computer that receives information from outside the computer for use by the computer is the _____.

b) The process of instructing the computer to solve a problem is called _____.
c) _____ is a type of computer language that uses English-like abbreviations for machine-language instructions.
d) _____ is a logical unit of the computer that sends information which has already been processed by the computer to various devices so that it may be used outside the computer.
e) _____ and _____ are logical units of the computer that retain information.
f) _____ is a logical unit of the computer that performs calculations.
g) _____ is a logical unit of the computer that makes logical decisions.
h) _____ languages are most convenient to the programmer for writing programs quickly and easily.
i) The only language a computer can directly understand is that computer's _____.
j) _____ is a logical unit of the computer that coordinates the activities of all the other logical units.

1.5 Fill in the blanks in each of the following statements:
a) _____ are used to match specific character patterns in text.
b) _____ (formerly called C++0x)—the latest C++ programming language standard—was published by ISO/IEC in 2011.

1.6 Fill in the blanks in each of the following statements:
a) Software product-release categories are _____, _____, _____ are _____.
b) _____ involves reworking programs to make them clearer and easier to maintain while preserving their correctness and functionality.

1.7 You're probably used one of the world's most common types of objects—a pen. Discuss how each of the following terms and concepts applies to the notion of a pen: object, attributes, behaviors, class, inheritance (consider, for example, a fountain pen), modeling, messages, encapsulation, interface and information hiding.

Making a Difference

Throughout the book we've included Making a Difference exercises in which you'll be asked to work on problems that really matter to individuals, communities, countries and the world. For more information about worldwide organizations working to make a difference, and for related programming project ideas, visit our Making a Difference Resource Center at www.deitel.com/makingadifference.

1.8 *(Test Drive: Carbon Footprint Calculator)* Some scientists believe that carbon emissions, especially from the burning of fossil fuels, contribute significantly to global warming and that this can be combatted if individuals take steps to limit their use of carbon-based fuels. Various organizations and individuals are increasingly concerned about their "carbon footprints." Websites such as TerraPass

    www.terrapass.com/corbon-footprint-calculator/

and Carbon Footprint

    www.carbonfootprint.com/calculator.aspx

provide carbon footprint calculators. Test drive these calculators to determine your carbon footprint. Exercises in later chapters will ask you to program your own carbon footprint calculator. To prepare for this, research the formulas for calculating carbon footprints.

1.9   *(Test Drive: Body Mass Index Calculator)* By recent estimates, two-thirds of the people in the United States are overweight and about half of those are obese. This causes significant increases in illnesses such as diabetes and heart disease. To determine whether a person is overweight or obese, you can use a measure called the body mass index (BMI). The United States Department of Health and Human Services provides a BMI calculator at www.nhlbisupport.com/bmi/. Use it to calculate your own BMI. An exercise in Chapter 2 will ask you to program your own BMI calculator. To prepare for this, research the formulas for calculating BMI.

1.10   *(Attributes of Hybrid Vehicles)* In this chapter you learned the basics of classes. Now you'll begin "fleshing out" aspects of a class called "Hybrid Vehicle." Hybrid vehicles are becoming increasingly popular, because they often get much better mileage than purely gasoline-powered vehicles. Browse the web and study the features of four or five of today's popular hybrid cars, then list as many of their hybrid-related attributes as you can. For example, common attributes include city-miles-per-gallon and highway-miles-per-gallon. Also list the attributes of the batteries (type, weight, etc.).

1.11   *(Gender Neutrality)* Some people want to eliminate sexism in all forms of communication. You've been asked to create a program that can process a paragraph of text and replace gender-specific words with gender-neutral ones. Assuming that you've been given a list of gender-specific words and their gender-neutral replacements (e.g., replace "wife" by "spouse," "man" by "person," "daughter" by "child" and so on), explain the procedure you'd use to read through a paragraph of text and manually perform these replacements. How might your procedure generate a strange term like "woperchild," which is actually listed in the Urban Dictionary (www.urbandictionary.com)? In Chapter 4, you'll learn that a more formal term for "procedure" is "algorithm," and that an algorithm specifies the steps to be performed and the order in which to perform them.

1.12   *(Authentication)* Suppose an authentication server used for email services to post all of the email correspondences for millions of people, including yours, on the Internet is being hacked by a group of disgruntled employees of the sever maintenance company. Discuss the issues.

1.13   *(Programmer Responsibility and Liability)* As a programmer, you may develop software that could affect people's social life and security. Suppose a software bug in one of your programs were to cause religious extremism and terrorism. Discuss the issues.

1.14   *(2010 "Flash Crash")* An example of the consequences of our dependency on computers was the so-called "flash crash" which occurred on May 6, 2010, when the U.S. stock market fell precipitously in a matter of minutes, wiping out trillions of dollars of investments, and then recovered within minutes. Use the Internet to investigate the causes of this crash and discuss the issues it raises.

Making a Difference Resources

The *Microsoft Image Cup* is a global competition in which students use technology to try to solve some of the world's most difficult problems, such as environmental sustainability, ending hunger, emergency response, literacy, combating HIV/AIDS and more. For more information about the competition and to learn about previous winners' projects, visit www.imaginecup.com/about. You can also find several project ideas submitted by worldwide charitable organizations.

For additional ideas for programming projects that can make a difference, search the web for "making a difference" and visit the following websites:

   www.un.org/millenniumgoals

The United Nations Millennium Project seeks solutions to major worldwide issues such as environmental sustainability, gender equality, child and maternal health, universal education and more.

`www.ibm.com/smarterplanet/`

The IBM® Smarter Planet website discusses how IBM is using technology to solve issues related to business, cloud computing, education, sustainability and more.

`www.gatesfoundation.org/Pages/home.aspx`

The Bill and Melinda Gates Foundation provides grants to organizations that work to alleviate hunger, poverty and disease in developing countries. In the U.S., the foundation focusses on improving public education, particularly for people with few resources.

`www.nethope.org/`

NetHope is a collaboration of humanitarian organizations worldwide working to solve technology problems such as connectivity, emergency response and more.

`www.rainforestfoundation.org/home`

The Rainforest Foundation works to preserve rainforests and to protect the rights of the indigenous people who call the rainforests home. The site includes a list of things you can do to help.

`www.undp.org/`

The United Nations Development Programme (UNDP) seeks solutions to global challenges such as crisis prevention and recovery, energy and the environment, democratic governance and more.

`www.unido.org`

The United Nations Industrial Development Organization (UNIDO) seeks to reduce poverty, give developing countries the opportunity to participate in global trade, and promote energy efficiency and sustainability.

`www.usaid.gov/`

USAID promotes global democracy, health, economic growth, conflict prevention, humanitarian aid and more.

`www.toyota.com/ideas-for-good/`

Toyota's Ideas for Good website describes several Toyota technologies that are making a difference—including their Advanced Parking Guidance System, Hybrid Synergy Drive®, Solar Powered Ventilation System, T.H.U.M.S. (Total Human Model for Safety) and Touch Tracer Display. You can participate in the Ideas for Good challenge by submitting a short essay or video describing how these technologies can be used for other good purposes.

2

Introduction to C++ Programming, Input/Output and Operators

What's in a name? that which we call a rose By any other name would smell as sweet.
—William Shakespeare

High thoughts must have high language.
—Aristophanes

One person can make a difference and every person should try.
—John F. Kennedy

Objectives

In this chapter you'll learn:

- To write simple computer programs in C++.

- To write simple input and output statements.

- To use fundamental types.

- Basic computer memory concepts.

- To use arithmetic operators.

- The precedence of arithmetic operators.

- To write simple decision-making statements.

2.1 Introduction

We now introduce C++ programming, which facilitates a disciplined approach to program development. Most of the C++ programs you'll study in this book process data and display results. In this chapter, we present five examples that demonstrate how your programs can display messages and obtain data from the user for processing. The first three examples simply display messages on the screen. The next obtains two numbers from a user, calculates their sum and displays the result. The accompanying discussion shows you how to perform *arithmetic calculations* and save their results for later use. The fifth example demonstrates *decision-making* by showing you how to *compare* two numbers, then display messages based on the comparison results. We analyze each program one line at a time to help you ease your way into C++ programming.

Compiling and Running Programs

At www.deitel.com/books/cpphtp9, we've posted videos that demonstrate compiling and running programs in Microsoft Visual C++, GNU C++ and Xcode.

2.2 First Program in C++: Printing a Line of Text

Consider a simple program that prints a line of text (Fig. 2.1). This program illustrates several important features of the C++ language. The text in lines 1–11 is the program's *source code* (or *code*). The line numbers are not part of the source code.

```
1   // Fig. 2.1: fig02_01.cpp
2   // Text-printing program.
3   #include <iostream> // allows program to output data to the screen
4
5   // function main begins program execution
6   int main()
7   {
8      std::cout << "Welcome to C++!\n"; // display message
9
10      return 0; // indicate that program ended successfully
11   } // end function main
```

```
Welcome to C++!
```

Fig. 2.1 | Text-printing program.

Comments
Lines 1 and 2

```
// Fig. 2.1: fig02_01.cpp
// Text-printing program.
```

each begin with //, indicating that the remainder of each line is a comment. You insert comments to *document* your programs and to help other people read and understand them. Comments do not cause the computer to perform any action when the program is run—they're *ignored* by the C++ compiler and do *not* cause any machine-language object code to be generated. The comment Text-printing program describes the purpose of the program. A comment beginning with // is called a single-line comment because it terminates at the end of the current line. [*Note:* You also may use comments containing one or more lines enclosed in /* and */.]

Good Programming Practice 2.1
Every program should begin with a comment that describes the purpose of the program.

#include Preprocessing Directive
Line 3

```
#include <iostream> // allows program to output data to the screen
```

is a preprocessing directive, which is a message to the C++ preprocessor (introduced in Section 1.9). Lines that begin with # are processed by the preprocessor *before* the program is compiled. This line notifies the preprocessor to include in the program the contents of the input/output stream header <iostream>. This header is a file containing information used by the compiler when compiling any program that outputs data to the screen or inputs data from the keyboard using C++'s stream input/output. The program in Fig. 2.1 outputs data to the screen, as we'll soon see. We discuss headers in more detail in Chapter 6 and explain the contents of <iostream> in Chapter 13.

Common Programming Error 2.1
Forgetting to include the <iostream> header in a program that inputs data from the keyboard or outputs data to the screen causes the compiler to issue an error message.

Blank Lines and White Space
Line 4 is simply a *blank line*. You use blank lines, *space characters* and *tab characters* (i.e., "tabs") to make programs easier to read. Together, these characters are known as white space. White-space characters are normally *ignored* by the compiler.

The main Function
Line 5

```
// function main begins program execution
```

is another single-line comment indicating that program execution begins at the next line.
Line 6

```
int main()
```

is a part of every C++ program. The parentheses after `main` indicate that `main` is a program building block called a function. C++ programs typically consist of one or more functions and classes (as you'll learn in Chapter 3). Exactly *one* function in every program *must* be named `main`. Figure 2.1 contains only one function. C++ programs begin executing at function `main`, even if `main` is *not* the first function defined in the program. The keyword `int` to the left of `main` indicates that `main` "returns" an integer (whole number) value. A keyword is a word in code that is reserved by C++ for a specific use. The complete list of C++ keywords can be found in Fig. 4.3. We'll explain what it means for a function to "return a value" when we demonstrate how to create your own functions in Section 3.3. For now, simply include the keyword `int` to the left of `main` in each of your programs.

The left brace, {, (line 7) must *begin* the body of every function. A corresponding right brace, }, (line 11) must *end* each function's body.

An Output Statement
Line 8

```
std::cout << "Welcome to C++!\n"; // display message
```

instructs the computer to **perform an action**—namely, to print the characters contained between the double quotation marks. Together, the quotation marks and the characters between them are called a **string**, a **character string** or a **string literal**. In this book, we refer to characters between double quotation marks simply as strings. White-space characters in strings are not ignored by the compiler.

The entire line 8, including `std::cout`, the `<<` operator, the string `"Welcome to C++!\n"` and the semicolon (;), is called a **statement**. Most C++ statements end with a semicolon, also known as the **statement terminator** (we'll see some exceptions to this soon). Preprocessing directives (like `#include`) do not end with a semicolon. Typically, output and input in C++ are accomplished with **streams** of characters. Thus, when the preceding statement is executed, it sends the stream of characters `Welcome to C++!\n` to the standard output stream object—`std::cout`—which is normally "connected" to the screen.

Common Programming Error 2.2
Omitting the semicolon at the end of a C++ statement is a syntax error. The syntax of a programming language specifies the rules for creating proper programs in that language. A syntax error occurs when the compiler encounters code that violates C++'s language rules (i.e., its syntax). The compiler normally issues an error message to help you locate and fix the incorrect code. Syntax errors are also called compiler errors, compile-time errors or compilation errors, because the compiler detects them during the compilation phase. You cannot execute your program until you correct all the syntax errors in it. As you'll see, some compilation errors are not syntax errors.

Good Programming Practice 2.2
Indent the body of each function one level within the braces that delimit the function's body. This makes a program's functional structure stand out and makes the program easier to read.

Good Programming Practice 2.3
Set a convention for the size of indent you prefer, then apply it uniformly. The tab key may be used to create indents, but tab stops may vary. We prefer three spaces per level of indent.

The std Namespace

The std:: before cout is required when we use names that we've brought into the program by the preprocessing directive #include <iostream>. The notation std::cout specifies that we are using a name, in this case cout, that belongs to namespace std. The names cin (the standard input stream) and cerr (the standard error stream)—introduced in Chapter 1—also belong to namespace std. Namespaces are an advanced C++ feature that we discuss in depth in Chapter 23, Other Topics. For now, you should simply remember to include std:: before each mention of cout, cin and cerr in a program. This can be cumbersome—the next example introduces using declarations and the using directive, which will enable you to omit std:: before each use of a name in the std namespace.

The Stream Insertion Operator and Escape Sequences

In the context of an output statement, the << operator is referred to as the **stream insertion operator**. When this program executes, the value to the operator's right, the right **operand**, is inserted in the output stream. Notice that the operator points in the direction of where the data goes. A string literal's characters *normally* print exactly as they appear between the double quotes. However, the characters \n are *not* printed on the screen (Fig. 2.1). The backslash (\) is called an **escape character**. It indicates that a "special" character is to be output. When a backslash is encountered in a string of characters, the next character is combined with the backslash to form an **escape sequence**. The escape sequence \n means **newline**. It causes the **cursor** (i.e., the current screen-position indicator) to move to the beginning of the next line on the screen. Some common escape sequences are listed in Fig. 2.2.

Escape sequence	Description
\n	Newline. Position the screen cursor to the beginning of the next line.
\t	Horizontal tab. Move the screen cursor to the next tab stop.
\r	Carriage return. Position the screen cursor to the beginning of the current line; do not advance to the next line.
\a	Alert. Sound the system bell.
\\	Backslash. Used to print a backslash character.
\'	Single quote. Used to print a single quote character.
\"	Double quote. Used to print a double quote character.

Fig. 2.2 | Escape sequences.

The return Statement
Line 10

```
return 0; // indicate that program ended successfully
```

is one of several means we'll use to exit a function. When the **return** statement is used at the end of main, as shown here, the value 0 indicates that the program has *terminated successfully*. The right brace, }, (line 11) indicates the end of function main. According to the

C++ standard, if program execution reaches the end of `main` without encountering a return statement, it's assumed that the program terminated successfully—exactly as when the last statement in main is a `return` statement with the value 0. For that reason, we *omit* the `return` statement at the end of main in subsequent programs.

A Note About Comments

As you write a new program or modify an existing one, you should *keep your comments up-to-date* with the program's code. You'll *often* need to make changes to existing programs—for example, to fix errors (commonly called *bugs*) that prevent a program from working correctly or to enhance a program. Updating your comments as you make code changes helps ensure that the comments accurately reflect what the code does. This will make your programs easier to understand and modify in the future.

2.3 Modifying Our First C++ Program

We now present two examples that modify the program of Fig. 2.1 to print text on one line by using multiple statements and to print text on several lines by using a single statement.

Printing a Single Line of Text with Multiple Statements

`Welcome to C++!` can be printed several ways. For example, Fig. 2.3 performs stream insertion in multiple statements (lines 8–9), yet produces the same output as the program of Fig. 2.1. [*Note:* From this point forward, we use a *light blue background* to highlight the key features each program introduces.] Each stream insertion resumes printing where the previous one stopped. The first stream insertion (line 8) prints `Welcome` followed by a space, and because this string did not end with \n, the second stream insertion (line 9) begins printing on the *same* line immediately following the space.

```
1   // Fig. 2.3: fig02_03.cpp
2   // Printing a line of text with multiple statements.
3   #include <iostream> // allows program to output data to the screen
4
5   // function main begins program execution
6   int main()
7   {
8      std::cout << "Welcome ";
9      std::cout << "to C++!\n";
10  } // end function main
```

```
Welcome to C++!
```

Fig. 2.3 | Printing a line of text with multiple statements.

Printing Multiple Lines of Text with a Single Statement

A single statement can print multiple lines by using newline characters, as in line 8 of Fig. 2.4. Each time the \n (newline) escape sequence is encountered in the output stream, the screen cursor is positioned to the beginning of the next line. To get a blank line in your output, place two newline characters back to back, as in line 8.

```
1   // Fig. 2.4: fig02_04.cpp
2   // Printing multiple lines of text with a single statement.
3   #include <iostream> // allows program to output data to the screen
4
5   // function main begins program execution
6   int main()
7   {
8      std::cout << "Welcome\nto\n\nC++!\n";
9   } // end function main
```

```
Welcome
to

C++!
```

Fig. 2.4 | Printing multiple lines of text with a single statement.

2.4 Another C++ Program: Adding Integers

Our next program obtains two integers typed by a user at the keyboard, computes the sum of these values and outputs the result using std::cout. Figure 2.5 shows the program and sample inputs and outputs. In the sample execution, we highlight the user's input in bold. The program begins execution with function main (line 6). The left brace (line 7) begins main's body and the corresponding right brace (line 22) ends it.

```
1   // Fig. 2.5: fig02_05.cpp
2   // Addition program that displays the sum of two integers.
3   #include <iostream> // allows program to perform input and output
4
5   // function main begins program execution
6   int main()
7   {
8      // variable declarations
9      int number1 = 0; // first integer to add (initialized to 0)
10     int number2 = 0; // second integer to add (initialized to 0)
11     int sum = 0; // sum of number1 and number2 (initialized to 0)
12
13     std::cout << "Enter first integer: "; // prompt user for data
14     std::cin >> number1; // read first integer from user into number1
15
16     std::cout << "Enter second integer: "; // prompt user for data
17     std::cin >> number2; // read second integer from user into number2
18
19     sum = number1 + number2; // add the numbers; store result in sum
20
21     std::cout << "Sum is " << sum << std::endl; // display sum; end line
22  } // end function main
```

```
Enter first integer: 45
Enter second integer: 72
Sum is 117
```

Fig. 2.5 | Addition program that displays the sum of two integers.

Variable Declarations
Lines 9–11

```
int number1 = 0; // first integer to add (initialized to 0)
int number2 = 0; // second integer to add (initialized to 0)
int sum = 0; // sum of number1 and number2 (initialized to 0)
```

are declarations. The identifiers number1, number2 and sum are the names of variables. A variable is a location in the computer's memory where a value can be stored for use by a program. These declarations specify that the variables number1, number2 and sum are data of type int, meaning that these variables will hold integer values, i.e., whole numbers such as 7, –11, 0 and 31914. The declarations also initialize each of these variables to 0.

Error-Prevention Tip 2.1

Although it's not always necessary to initialize every variable explicitly, doing so will help you avoid many kinds of problems.

All variables *must* be declared with a *name* and a *data type before* they can be used in a program. Several variables of the same type may be declared in one declaration or in multiple declarations. We could have declared all three variables in one declaration by using a comma-separated list as follows:

```
int number1 = 0, number2 = 0, sum = 0;
```

This makes the program less readable and prevents us from providing comments that describe each variable's purpose.

Good Programming Practice 2.4

Declare only one variable in each declaration and provide a comment that explains the variable's purpose in the program.

Fundamental Types
We'll soon discuss the type double for specifying *real numbers*, and the type char for specifying *character data*. Real numbers are numbers with decimal points, such as 3.4, 0.0 and –11.19. A char variable may hold only a single lowercase letter, a single uppercase letter, a single digit or a single special character (e.g., $ or *). Types such as int, double and char are called fundamental types. Fundamental-type names consist of one or more *keywords* and therefore *must* appear in all lowercase letters. Appendix C contains the complete list of fundamental types.

Identifiers
A variable name (such as number1) is any valid identifier that is *not* a keyword. An identifier is a series of characters consisting of letters, digits and underscores (_) that does *not* begin with a digit. C++ is case sensitive—uppercase and lowercase letters are *different*, so a1 and A1 are *different* identifiers.

Portability Tip 2.1

C++ allows identifiers of any length, but your C++ implementation may restrict identifier lengths. Use identifiers of 31 characters or fewer to ensure portability.

Good Programming Practice 2.5
Choosing meaningful identifiers makes a program self-documenting—a person can understand the program simply by reading it rather than having to refer to program comments or documentation.

Good Programming Practice 2.6
Avoid using abbreviations in identifiers. This improves program readability.

Good Programming Practice 2.7
Do not use identifiers that begin with underscores and double underscores, because C++ compilers may use names like that for their own purposes internally. This will prevent the names you choose from being confused with names the compilers choose.

Placement of Variable Declarations
Declarations of variables can be placed almost anywhere in a program, but they *must* appear *before* their corresponding variables are used in the program. For example, in the program of Fig. 2.5, the declaration in line 9

```
int number1 = 0; // first integer to add (initialized to 0)
```

could have been placed immediately before line 14

```
std::cin >> number1; // read first integer from user into number1
```

the declaration in line 10

```
int number2 = 0; // second integer to add (initialized to 0)
```

could have been placed immediately before line 17

```
std::cin >> number2; // read second integer from user into number2
```

and the declaration in line 11

```
int sum = 0; // sum of number1 and number2 (initialized to 0)
```

could have been placed immediately before line 19

```
sum = number1 + number2; // add the numbers; store result in sum
```

Obtaining the First Value from the User
Line 13

```
std::cout << "Enter first integer: "; // prompt user for data
```

displays Enter first integer: followed by a space. This message is called a **prompt** because it directs the user to take a specific action. We like to pronounce the preceding statement as "std::cout *gets* the string "Enter first integer: "." Line 14

```
std::cin >> number1; // read first integer from user into number1
```

uses the **standard input stream object cin** (of namespace std) and the **stream extraction operator, >>**, to obtain a value from the keyboard. Using the stream extraction operator with std::cin takes character input from the standard input stream, which is usually the keyboard. We like to pronounce the preceding statement as, "std::cin *gives* a value to number1" or simply "std::cin *gives* number1."

When the computer executes the preceding statement, it waits for the user to enter a value for variable number1. The user responds by typing an integer (as characters), then pressing the *Enter* key (sometimes called the *Return* key) to send the characters to the computer. The computer converts the character representation of the number to an integer and assigns (i.e., copies) this number (or **value**) to the variable number1. Any subsequent references to number1 in this program will use this same value.

The std::cout and std::cin stream objects facilitate interaction between the user and the computer.

Users can, of course, enter *invalid* data from the keyboard. For example, when your program is expecting the user to enter an integer, the user could enter alphabetic characters, special symbols (like # or @) or a number with a decimal point (like 73.5), among others. In these early programs, we assume that the user enters *valid* data. As you progress through the book, you'll learn various techniques for dealing with the broad range of possible data-entry problems.

Obtaining the Second Value from the User
Line 16

```
std::cout << "Enter second integer: "; // prompt user for data
```

prints Enter second integer: on the screen, prompting the user to take action. Line 17

```
std::cin >> number2; // read second integer from user into number2
```

obtains a value for variable number2 from the user.

Calculating the Sum of the Values Input by the User
The assignment statement in line 19

```
sum = number1 + number2; // add the numbers; store result in sum
```

adds the values of variables number1 and number2 and assigns the result to variable sum using the **assignment operator** =. We like to read this statement as, "sum *gets* the value of number1 + number2." Most calculations are performed in assignment statements. The = operator and the + operator are called **binary operators** because each has *two* operands. In the case of the + operator, the two operands are number1 and number2. In the case of the preceding = operator, the two operands are sum and the value of the expression number1 + number2.

Good Programming Practice 2.8

Place spaces on either side of a binary operator. This makes the operator stand out and makes the program more readable.

Displaying the Result
Line 21

```
std::cout << "Sum is " << sum << std::endl; // display sum; end line
```

displays the character string Sum is followed by the numerical value of variable sum followed by std::endl—a so-called **stream manipulator**. The name endl is an abbreviation for "end line" and belongs to namespace std. The std::endl stream manipulator outputs a newline, then "flushes the output buffer." This simply means that, on some systems where outputs accumulate in the machine until there are enough to "make it worthwhile" to display them on the screen, std::endl forces any accumulated outputs to be displayed at that moment. This can be important when the outputs are prompting the user for an action, such as entering data.

The preceding statement outputs multiple values of different types. The stream insertion operator "knows" how to output each type of data. Using multiple stream insertion operators (<<) in a single statement is referred to as **concatenating, chaining or cascading stream insertion operations**.

Calculations can also be performed in output statements. We could have combined the statements in lines 19 and 21 into the statement

```
std::cout << "Sum is " << number1 + number2 << std::endl;
```

thus eliminating the need for the variable sum.

A powerful feature of C++ is that you can create your own data types called classes (we introduce this capability in Chapter 3 and explore it in depth in Chapter 9). You can then "teach" C++ how to input and output values of these new data types using the >> and << operators (this is called **operator overloading**—a topic we explore in Chapter 10).

2.5 Memory Concepts

Variable names such as number1, number2 and sum actually correspond to *locations* in the computer's memory. Every variable has a *name*, a *type*, a *size* and a *value*.

In the addition program of Fig. 2.5, when the statement in line 14

```
std::cin >> number1; // read first integer from user into number1
```

is executed, the integer typed by the user is placed into a memory location to which the name number1 has been assigned by the compiler. Suppose the user enters 45 for number1. The computer will place 45 into the location number1, as shown in Fig. 2.6. When a value is placed in a memory location, the value *overwrites* the previous value in that location; thus, placing a new value into a memory location is said to be a **destructive operation**.

number1   45

Fig. 2.6 | Memory location showing the name and value of variable number1.

Returning to our addition program, suppose the user enters 72 when the statement

```
std::cin >> number2; // read second integer from user into number2
```

is executed. This value is placed into the location number2, and memory appears as in Fig. 2.7. The variables' locations are not necessarily adjacent in memory.

Once the program has obtained values for number1 and number2, it adds these values and places the total into the variable sum. The statement

```
sum = number1 + number2; // add the numbers; store result in sum
```

Fig. 2.7 | Memory locations after storing values in the variables for number1 and number2.

replaces whatever value was stored in sum. The calculated sum of number1 and number2 is placed into variable sum without regard to what value may already be in sum—that value is *lost*). After sum is calculated, memory appears as in Fig. 2.8. The values of number1 and number2 appear exactly as they did before the calculation. These values were used, but *not* destroyed, as the computer performed the calculation. Thus, when a value is read *out* of a memory location, the operation is **nondestructive**.

number1	45
number2	72
sum	117

Fig. 2.8 | Memory locations after calculating and storing the sum of number1 and number2.

2.6 Arithmetic

Most programs perform arithmetic calculations. Figure 2.9 summarizes the C++ arithmetic operators. Note the use of various special symbols not used in algebra. The **asterisk** (*) indicates *multiplication* and the **percent sign** (%) is the *modulus operator* that will be discussed shortly. The arithmetic operators in Fig. 2.9 are all *binary* operators, i.e., operators that take two operands. For example, the expression number1 + number2 contains the binary operator + and the two operands number1 and number2.

Integer division (i.e., where both the numerator and the denominator are integers) yields an integer quotient; for example, the expression 7 / 4 evaluates to 1 and the expres-

C++ operation	C++ arithmetic operator	Algebraic expression	C++ expression
Addition	+	$f + 7$	f + 7
Subtraction	–	$p - c$	p – c
Multiplication	*	bm or $b \cdot m$	b * m
Division	/	x / y or $\frac{x}{y}$ or $x \div y$	x / y
Modulus	%	$r \bmod s$	r % s

Fig. 2.9 | Arithmetic operators.

sion 17 / 5 evaluates to 3. *Any fractional part in integer division is truncated (i.e., discarded)—no rounding occurs.*

C++ provides the **modulus operator**, %, that yields the *remainder after integer division*. The modulus operator can be used *only* with integer operands. The expression x % y yields the *remainder* after x is divided by y. Thus, 7 % 4 yields 3 and 17 % 5 yields 2. In later chapters, we discuss many interesting applications of the modulus operator, such as determining whether one number is a *multiple* of another (a special case of this is determining whether a number is *odd* or *even*).

Arithmetic Expressions in Straight-Line Form

Arithmetic expressions in C++ must be entered into the computer in **straight-line form**. Thus, expressions such as "a divided by b" must be written as a / b, so that all constants, variables and operators appear in a straight line. The algebraic notation

$$\frac{a}{b}$$

is generally *not* acceptable to compilers, although some special-purpose software packages do support more natural notation for complex mathematical expressions.

Parentheses for Grouping Subexpressions

Parentheses are used in C++ expressions in the same manner as in algebraic expressions. For example, to multiply a times the quantity b + c we write a * (b + c).

Rules of Operator Precedence

C++ applies the operators in arithmetic expressions in a precise order determined by the following **rules of operator precedence**, which are generally the same as those in algebra:

1. Operators in expressions contained within pairs of *parentheses* are evaluated first. Parentheses are said to be at the "highest level of precedence." In cases of **nested**, or **embedded**, **parentheses**, such as

```
( a * ( b + c ) )
```

   the operators in the *innermost* pair of parentheses are applied first.

2. Multiplication, division and modulus operations are applied next. If an expression contains several multiplication, division and modulus operations, operators are applied from *left to right*. Multiplication, division and modulus are said to be on the *same* level of precedence.

3. Addition and subtraction operations are applied last. If an expression contains several addition and subtraction operations, operators are applied from *left to right*. Addition and subtraction also have the *same* level of precedence.

The rules of operator precedence define the order in which C++ applies operators. When we say that certain operators are applied from left to right, we are referring to the **associativity** of the operators. For example, the addition operators (+) in the expression

```
a + b + c
```

associate from left to right, so a + b is calculated first, then c is added to that sum to determine the whole expression's value. We'll see that some operators associate from *right to left*. Figure 2.10 summarizes these rules of operator precedence. We expand this table as we introduce additional C++ operators. Appendix A contains the complete precedence chart.

Operator(s)	Operation(s)	Order of evaluation (precedence)
( )	Parentheses	Evaluated first. If the parentheses are *nested*, such as in the expression a * (b + c / d + e)), the expression in the *innermost* pair is evaluated first. [*Caution:* If you have an expression such as (a + b) * (c - d) in which two sets of parentheses are not nested, but appear "on the same level," the C++ Standard does *not* specify the order in which these parenthesized subexpressions will be evaluated.]
* / %	Multiplication Division Modulus	Evaluated second. If there are several, they're evaluated left to right.
+ -	Addition Subtraction	Evaluated last. If there are several, they're evaluated left to right.

Fig. 2.10 | Precedence of arithmetic operators.

Sample Algebraic and C++ Expressions

Now consider several expressions in light of the rules of operator precedence. Each example lists an algebraic expression and its C++ equivalent. The following is an example of an arithmetic mean (average) of five terms:

Algebra: $m = \dfrac{a + b + c + d + e}{5}$

C++: m = (a + b + c + d + e) / 5;

The parentheses are required because division has *higher* precedence than addition. The *entire* quantity (a + b + c + d + e) is to be divided by 5. If the parentheses are erroneously omitted, we obtain a + b + c + d + e / 5, which evaluates incorrectly as

$a + b + c + d + \dfrac{e}{5}$

The following is an example of the equation of a straight line:

Algebra: $y = mx + b$

C++: y = m * x + b;

No parentheses are required. The multiplication is applied first because multiplication has a *higher* precedence than addition.

The following example contains modulus (%), multiplication, division, addition, subtraction and assignment operations:

Algebra: $z = pr \% q + w/x - y$

C++:

The circled numbers under the statement indicate the order in which C++ applies the operators. The multiplication, modulus and division are evaluated *first* in left-to-right order (i.e., they associate from left to right) because they have *higher precedence* than addition and subtraction. The addition and subtraction are applied next. These are also applied left to right. The assignment operator is applied *last* because its precedence is *lower* than that of any of the arithmetic operators.

Evaluation of a Second-Degree Polynomial

To develop a better understanding of the rules of operator precedence, consider the evaluation of a second-degree polynomial $y = ax^2 + bx + c$:

```
y  =  a  *  x  *  x  +  b  *  x  +  c;
     6     1     2     4     3     5
```

The circled numbers under the statement indicate the order in which C++ applies the operators. *There is no arithmetic operator for exponentiation in C++, so we've represented x^2* as x * x. In Chapter 5, we'll discuss the standard library function pow ("power") that performs exponentiation.

Suppose variables a, b, c and x in the preceding second-degree polynomial are initialized as follows: a = 2, b = 3, c = 7 and x = 5. Figure 2.11 illustrates the order in which the operators are applied and the final value of the expression.

Step 1.   y = 2 * 5 * 5 + 3 * 5 + 7;   *(Leftmost multiplication)*

2 * 5 is 10

Step 2.   y = 10 * 5 + 3 * 5 + 7;   *(Leftmost multiplication)*

10 * 5 is 50

Step 3.   y = 50 + 3 * 5 + 7;   *(Multiplication before addition)*

3 * 5 is 15

Step 4.   y = 50 + 15 + 7;   *(Leftmost addition)*

50 + 15 is 65

Step 5.   y = 65 + 7;   *(Last addition)*

65 + 7 is 72

Step 6.   y = 72   *(Last operation—place 72 in y)*

Fig. 2.11 | Order in which a second-degree polynomial is evaluated.

Redundant Parentheses

As in algebra, it's acceptable to place *unnecessary* parentheses in an expression to make the expression clearer. These are called redundant parentheses. For example, the preceding assignment statement could be parenthesized as follows:

```
y = ( a * x * x ) + ( b * x ) + c;
```

2.7 Decision Making: Equality and Relational Operators

We now introduce a simple version of C++'s if statement that allows a program to take alternative action based on whether a condition is true or false. If the condition is *true*, the statement in the body of the if statement *is* executed. If the condition is *false*, the body statement *is not* executed. We'll see an example shortly.

Conditions in if statements can be formed by using the relational operators and equality operators summarized in Fig. 2.12. The relational operators all have the same level of precedence and associate left to right. The equality operators both have the same level of precedence, which is *lower* than that of the relational operators, and associate left to right.

Algebraic relational or equality operator	C++ relational or equality operator	Sample C++ condition	Meaning of C++ condition
Relational operators			
>	>	x > y	x is greater than y
<	<	x < y	x is less than y
≥	>=	x >= y	x is greater than or equal to y
≤	<=	x <= y	x is less than or equal to y
Equality operators			
=	==	x == y	x is equal to y
≠	!=	x != y	x is not equal to y

Fig. 2.12 | Relational and equality operators.

Common Programming Error 2.3

Reversing the order of the pair of symbols in the operators !=, >= and <= (by writing them as =!, => and =<, respectively) is normally a syntax error. In some cases, writing != as =! will not be a syntax error, but almost certainly will be a logic error that has an effect at execution time. You'll understand why when you learn about logical operators in Chapter 5. A fatal logic error causes a program to fail and terminate prematurely. A nonfatal logic error allows a program to continue executing, but usually produces incorrect results.

Common Programming Error 2.4

Confusing the equality operator == with the assignment operator = results in logic errors. We like to read the equality operator as "is equal to" or "double equals," and the assignment operator as "gets" or "gets the value of" or "is assigned the value of." As you'll see in Section 5.9, confusing these operators may not necessarily cause an easy-to-recognize syntax error, but may cause subtle logic errors.

Using the **if** *Statement*

The following example (Fig. 2.13) uses six if statements to compare two numbers input by the user. If the condition in any of these if statements is satisfied, the output statement associated with that if statement is executed.

```cpp
1  // Fig. 2.13: fig02_13.cpp
2  // Comparing integers using if statements, relational operators
3  // and equality operators.
4  #include <iostream> // allows program to perform input and output
5
6  using std::cout; // program uses cout
7  using std::cin; // program uses cin
8  using std::endl; // program uses endl
9
10 // function main begins program execution
11 int main()
12 {
13    int number1 = 0; // first integer to compare (initialized to 0)
14    int number2 = 0; // second integer to compare (initialized to 0)
15
16    cout << "Enter two integers to compare: "; // prompt user for data
17    cin >> number1 >> number2; // read two integers from user
18
19    if ( number1 == number2 )
20       cout << number1 << " == " << number2 << endl;
21
22    if ( number1 != number2 )
23       cout << number1 << " != " << number2 << endl;
24
25    if ( number1 < number2 )
26       cout << number1 << " < " << number2 << endl;
27
28    if ( number1 > number2 )
29       cout << number1 << " > " << number2 << endl;
30
31    if ( number1 <= number2 )
32       cout << number1 << " <= " << number2 << endl;
33
34    if ( number1 >= number2 )
35       cout << number1 << " >= " << number2 << endl;
36 } // end function main
```

```
Enter two integers to compare: 3 7
3 != 7
3 < 7
3 <= 7
```

```
Enter two integers to compare: 22 12
22 != 12
22 > 12
22 >= 12
```

Fig. 2.13 | Comparing integers using if statements, relational operators and equality operators. (Part 1 of 2.)

```
Enter two integers to compare: 7 7
7 == 7
7 <= 7
7 >= 7
```

Fig. 2.13 | Comparing integers using if statements, relational operators and equality operators. (Part 2 of 2.)

using *Declarations*
Lines 6–8

```
using std::cout; // program uses cout
using std::cin; // program uses cin
using std::endl; // program uses endl
```

are **using** declarations that eliminate the need to repeat the std:: prefix as we did in earlier programs. We can now write cout instead of std::cout, cin instead of std::cin and endl instead of std::endl, respectively, in the remainder of the program.

In place of lines 6–8, many programmers prefer to provide the **using** directive

```
using namespace std;
```

which enables a program to use *all* the names in any standard C++ header (such as <iostream>) that a program might include. From this point forward in the book, we'll use the preceding directive in our programs.[1]

Variable Declarations and Reading the Inputs from the User
Lines 13–14

```
int number1 = 0; // first integer to compare (initialized to 0)
int number2 = 0; // second integer to compare (initialized to 0)
```

declare the variables used in the program and initializes them to 0.

The program uses cascaded stream extraction operations (line 17) to input two integers. Remember that we're allowed to write cin (instead of std::cin) because of line 7. First a value is read into variable number1, then a value is read into variable number2.

Comparing Numbers
The if statement in lines 19–20

```
if ( number1 == number2 )
    cout << number1 << " == " << number2 << endl;
```

compares the values of variables number1 and number2 to test for equality. If the values are equal, the statement in line 20 displays a line of text indicating that the numbers are equal. If the conditions are true in one or more of the if statements starting in lines 22, 25, 28, 31 and 34, the corresponding body statement displays an appropriate line of text.

Each if statement in Fig. 2.13 has a single statement in its body and each body statement is indented. In Chapter 4 we show how to specify if statements with multiple-statement bodies (by enclosing the body statements in a pair of braces, { }, creating what's called a **compound statement** or a **block**).

---

1. In Chapter 23, Other Topics, we'll discuss some issues with using directives in large-scale systems.

Good Programming Practice 2.9

Indent the statement(s) in the body of an if *statement to enhance readability.*

Common Programming Error 2.5

Placing a semicolon immediately after the right parenthesis after the condition in an if *statement is often a logic error (although not a syntax error). The semicolon causes the body of the* if *statement to be empty, so the* if *statement performs no action, regardless of whether or not its condition is true. Worse yet, the original body statement of the* if *statement now becomes a statement* in sequence *with the* if *statement and always* executes, *often causing the program to produce incorrect results.*

White Space

Note the use of white space in Fig. 2.13. Recall that white-space characters, such as tabs, newlines and spaces, are normally ignored by the compiler. So, statements may be split over several lines and may be spaced according to your preferences. It's a syntax error to split identifiers, strings (such as `"hello"`) and constants (such as the number 1000) over several lines.

Good Programming Practice 2.10

A lengthy statement may be spread over several lines. If a single statement must be split across lines, choose meaningful breaking points, such as after a comma in a comma-separated list, or after an operator in a lengthy expression. If a statement is split across two or more lines, indent all subsequent lines and left-align the group of indented lines.

Operator Precedence

Figure 2.14 shows the precedence and associativity of the operators introduced in this chapter. The operators are shown top to bottom in decreasing order of precedence. All these operators, with the exception of the assignment operator =, associate from left to right. Addition is left-associative, so an expression like x + y + z is evaluated as if it had been written (x + y) + z. The assignment operator = associates from *right to left*, so an expression such as x = y = 0 is evaluated as if it had been written x = (y = 0), which, as we'll soon see, first assigns 0 to y, then assigns the *result* of that assignment—0—to x.

Operators				Associativity	Type
( )				*[See caution in Fig. 2.10]*	grouping parentheses
*	/	%		left to right	multiplicative
+	-			left to right	additive
<<	>>			left to right	stream insertion/extraction
<	<=	>	>=	left to right	relational
==	!=			left to right	equality
=				right to left	assignment

Fig. 2.14 | Precedence and associativity of the operators discussed so far.

Good Programming Practice 2.11

Refer to the operator precedence and associativity chart (Appendix A) when writing expressions containing many operators. Confirm that the operators in the expression are performed in the order you expect. If you're uncertain about the order of evaluation in a complex expression, break the expression into smaller statements or use parentheses to force the order of evaluation, exactly as you'd do in an algebraic expression. Be sure to observe that some operators such as assignment (=) associate right to left rather than left to right.

2.8 Wrap-Up

You learned many important basic features of C++ in this chapter, including displaying data on the screen, inputting data from the keyboard and declaring variables of fundamental types. In particular, you learned to use the output stream object `cout` and the input stream object `cin` to build simple interactive programs. We explained how variables are stored in and retrieved from memory. You also learned how to use arithmetic operators to perform calculations. We discussed the order in which C++ applies operators (i.e., the rules of operator precedence), as well as the associativity of the operators. You also learned how C++'s `if` statement allows a program to make decisions. Finally, we introduced the equality and relational operators, which you use to form conditions in `if` statements.

The non-object-oriented applications presented here introduced you to basic programming concepts. As you'll see in Chapter 3, C++ applications typically contain just a few lines of code in function `main`—these statements normally create the objects that perform the work of the application, then the objects "take over from there." In Chapter 3, you'll learn how to implement your own classes and use objects of those classes in applications.

Summary

Section 2.2 First Program in C++: Printing a Line of Text

- Single-line comments (p. 74) begin with //. You insert comments to document your programs and improve their readability.

- Comments do not cause the computer to perform any action (p. 75) when the program is run—they're ignored by the compiler and do not cause any machine-language object code to be generated.

- A preprocessing directive (p. 74) begins with # and is a message to the C++ preprocessor. Preprocessing directives are processed before the program is compiled.

- The line `#include <iostream>` (p. 74) tells the C++ preprocessor to include the contents of the input/output stream header, which contains information necessary to compile programs that use `std::cin` (p. 80) and `std::cout` (p. 75) and the stream insertion (<<, p. 76) and stream extraction (>>, p. 80) operators.

- White space (i.e., blank lines, space characters and tab characters, p. 74) makes programs easier to read. White-space characters outside of string literals are ignored by the compiler.

- C++ programs begin executing at `main` (p. 75), even if `main` does not appear first in the program.

- The keyword `int` to the left of `main` indicates that `main` "returns" an integer value.

- The body (p. 75) of every function must be contained in braces ({ and }).

- A string (p. 75) in double quotes is sometimes referred to as a character string, message or string literal. White-space characters in strings are *not* ignored by the compiler.

- Most C++ statements (p. 75) end with a semicolon, also known as the statement terminator (we'll see some exceptions to this soon).

- Output and input in C++ are accomplished with streams (p. 75) of characters.

- The output stream object std::cout—normally connected to the screen—is used to output data. Multiple data items can be output by concatenating stream insertion (<<) operators.

- The input stream object std::cin—normally connected to the keyboard—is used to input data. Multiple data items can be input by concatenating stream extraction (>>) operators.

- The notation std::cout specifies that we are using cout from "namespace" std.

- When a backslash (i.e., an escape character) is encountered in a string of characters, the next character is combined with the backslash to form an escape sequence (p. 76).

- The newline escape sequence \n (p. 76) moves the cursor to the beginning of the next line on the screen.

- A message that directs the user to take a specific action is known as a prompt (p. 80).

- C++ keyword return (p. 76) is one of several means to exit a function.

Section 2.4 Another C++ Program: Adding Integers

- All variables (p. 79) in a C++ program must be declared before they can be used.

- A variable name is any valid identifier (p. 79) that is not a keyword. An identifier is a series of characters consisting of letters, digits and underscores (_). Identifiers cannot start with a digit. Identifiers can be any length, but some systems or C++ implementations may impose length restrictions.

- C++ is case sensitive (p. 79).

- Most calculations are performed in assignment statements (p. 81).

- A variable is a location in memory (p. 82) where a value can be stored for use by a program.

- Variables of type int (p. 79) hold integer values, i.e., whole numbers such as 7, –11, 0, 31914.

Section 2.5 Memory Concepts

- Every variable stored in the computer's memory has a name, a value, a type and a size.

- Whenever a new value is placed in a memory location, the process is destructive (p. 82); i.e., the new value replaces the previous value in that location. The previous value is lost.

- When a value is read from memory, the process is nondestructive (p. 83); i.e., a copy of the value is read, leaving the original value undisturbed in the memory location.

- The std::endl stream manipulator (p. 81) outputs a newline, then "flushes the output buffer."

Section 2.6 Arithmetic

- C++ evaluates arithmetic expressions (p. 83) in a precise sequence determined by the rules of operator precedence (p. 84) and associativity (p. 84).

- Parentheses may be used to group expressions.

- Integer division (p. 83) yields an integer quotient. Any fractional part in integer division is truncated.

- The modulus operator, % (p. 84), yields the remainder after integer division.

Section 2.7 Decision Making: Equality and Relational Operators

- The `if` statement (p. 87) allows a program to take alternative action based on whether a condition is met. The format for an `if` statement is

      if (*condition*)
          statement;

If the condition is true, the statement in the body of the `if` is executed. If the condition is not met, i.e., the condition is false, the body statement is skipped.

- Conditions in `if` statements are commonly formed by using equality and relational operators (p. 87). The result of using these operators is always the value true or false.
- The `using` declaration (p. 89)

      using std::cout;

informs the compiler where to find `cout` (namespace `std`) and eliminates the need to repeat the `std::` prefix. The `using` directive (p. 89)

      using namespace std;

enables the program to use all the names in any included C++ standard library header.

Self-Review Exercises

2.1   Fill in the blanks in each of the following.
  a) Every C++ program begins execution at the function _____.
  b) A(n) _____ begins the body of every function and a(n) _____ ends the body.
  c) Most C++ statements end with a(n) _____.
  d) The escape sequence \n represents the _____ character, which causes the cursor to position to the beginning of the next line on the screen.
  e) The _____ statement is used to make decisions.

2.2   State whether each of the following is *true* or *false*. If *false*, explain why. Assume the statement using std::cout; is used.
  a) Comments cause the computer to print the text after the // on the screen when the program is executed.
  b) The escape sequence \n, when output with cout and the stream insertion operator, causes the cursor to position to the beginning of the next line on the screen.
  c) All variables must be declared before they're used.
  d) All variables must be given a type when they're declared.
  e) C++ considers the variables number and NuMbEr to be identical.
  f) Declarations can appear almost anywhere in the body of a C++ function.
  g) The modulus operator (%) can be used only with integer operands.
  h) The arithmetic operators *, /, %, + and – all have the same level of precedence.
  i) A C++ program that prints three lines of output must contain three statements using cout and the stream insertion operator.

2.3   Write a single C++ statement to accomplish each of the following (assume that neither using declarations nor a using directive have been used):
  a) Declare the variables c, thisIsAVariable, q76354 and number to be of type int (in one statement).
  b) Prompt the user to enter an integer. End your prompting message with a colon (:) followed by a space and leave the cursor positioned after the space.
  c) Read an integer from the user at the keyboard and store it in integer variable age.
  d) If the variable number is not equal to 7, print "The variable number is not equal to 7".

e) Print the message "This is a C++ program" on one line.

f) Print the message "This is a C++ program" on two lines. End the first line with C++.

g) Print the message "This is a C++ program" with each word on a separate line.

h) Print the message "This is a C++ program". Separate each word from the next by a tab.

2.4 Write a statement (or comment) to accomplish each of the following (assume that using declarations have been used for cin, cout and endl):

a) State that a program calculates the product of three integers.

b) Declare the variables x, y, z and result to be of type int (in separate statements) and initalize each to 0.

c) Prompt the user to enter three integers.

d) Read three integers from the keyboard and store them in the variables x, y and z.

e) Compute the product of the three integers contained in variables x, y and z, and assign the result to the variable result.

f) Print "The product is " followed by the value of the variable result.

g) Return a value from main indicating that the program terminated successfully.

2.5 Similar to the concept mentioned in Exercise 2.4, write a complete program that calculates and displays the sum of three integers. Add comments to the code where appropriate. [*Note:* You'll need to write the necessary using declarations or directive.]

2.6 Identify and correct the errors in each of the following statements (assume that the statement using std::cout; is used):

a) if (c < 7
    cout << "c is less than 7\n";

b) if (c =! 7)
    cout << "c is equal to or greater than 7\n";

Answers to Self-Review Exercises

2.1 a) main. b) left brace ({), right brace (}). c) semicolon. d) newline. e) if.

2.2 a) False. Comments do not cause any action to be performed when the program is executed. They're used to document programs and improve their readability.

b) True.

c) True.

d) True.

e) False. C++ is case sensitive, so these variables are different.

f) True.

g) True.

h) False. The operators *, / and % have the same precedence, and the operators + and - have a lower precedence.

i) False. One statement with cout and multiple \n escape sequences can print several lines.

2.3 a) int c, thisIsAVariable, q76354, number;

b) std::cout << "Enter an integer: ";

c) std::cin >> age;

d) if (number != 7)
    std::cout << "The variable number is not equal to 7\n";

e) std::cout << "This is a C++ program\n";

f) std::cout << "This is a C++\nprogram\n";

g) std::cout << "This\nis\na\nC++\nprogram\n";

h) std::cout << "This\tis\ta\tC++\tprogram\n";

2.4   a) `// Calculate the product of three integers`
      b) `int x = 0;`
          `int y = 0;`
          `int z = 0;`
          `int result = 0;`
      c) `cout << "Enter three integers: ";`
      d) `cin >> x >> y >> z;`
      e) `result = x * y * z;`
      f) `cout << "The product is " << result << endl;`
      g) `return 0;`

2.5   (See program below.)

```
1   // Calculate the sum of three integers
2   #include <iostream> // allows program to perform input and output
3   using namespace std; // program uses names from the std namespace
4
5   // function main begins program execution
6   int main()
7   {
8      int x = 0; // first integer to add
9      int y = 0; // second integer to add
10     int z = 0; // third integer to add
11     int result = 0; // the sum of the three integers
12
13     cout << "Enter three integers: "; // prompt user for data
14     cin >> x >> y >> z; // read three integers from user
15     result = x + y + z; // sum the three integers; store result
16     cout << "The sum is " << result << endl; // print result; end line
17  } // end function main
```

2.6   a) *Error* Right parenthesis of the condition in the `if` statement is missing.
              Correction: Add a right parenthesis at the end of the condition i.e. after 7.
      b) *Error:* The relational operator =!.
              Correction: Change =! to != .

Exercises

2.7   Discuss the meaning of each of the following terms/ operators:
      a) `#include <iostream>`
      b) Insertion (`<<`) operator

2.8   Fill in the blanks in each of the following:
      a) _____ are used to document a program and improve its readability.
      b) The object used to print information on the screen is _____.
      c) A C++ statement that makes a decision is _____.
      d) Most calculations are normally performed by _____ statements.
      e) The _____ object inputs values from the keyboard.

2.9   Write a single C++ statement or line that accomplishes each of the following:
      a) Print the message `"Welcome to the world of C++"`.

b) Assign the sum of variables b and c to variable a.
c) State that a program calculates the simple interest (i.e., use text that helps to document a program).
d) Output three integer variables a, b and c to the screen.

2.10 State which of the following are *true* and which are *false*. If *false*, explain your answers.
a) C++ is a case sensitive language.
b) The following are all valid variable names: findSum2, _findSum2, find_Sum2, _2findSum, 2_findSum, hello, abcOne, var1.xyz.
c) The statement cout >> " Hello World"; is a typical example of output to a screen.
d) Parentheses may be used to group expressions.
e) The following are all invalid variable names: _1a., 1_a, a_1, $1a.

2.11 Fill in the blanks in each of the following:
a) What arithmetic operations are on the same level of precedence as addition? _____ .
b) When an arithmetic expression contains minus and multiplication operator, which will be operated first? _____ .
c) Whenever a new value is placed in a memory location, the process is _____.

2.12 What, if anything, prints when each of the following C++ statements is performed? If nothing prints, then answer "nothing." Assume x = 10 and y = 20.
a) cout << y << " " <<x;
b) cout << (x + y);
c) cout << "x is equal to" << x;
d) cout << "y = " << y;
e) z = x * y;
f) z = x - y;
g) cout<< x << "\\" << y;
h) // cout << x << y;
i) cout << x<<"\n"<<y;

2.13 Which of the following C++ statements contain variables whose values are replaced?
a) cout<< x << y;
b) i = i + j;
c) cout << "x";
d) cin>> x;

2.14 Given the algebraic equation $y = abx^2 + 7$, which of the following, if any, are correct C++ statements for this equation?
a) y = a * b * x * x + 7;
b) y = a * b * x * (x + 7);
c) y = (a * x) * b * (x + 7);
d) y = (a * x) * b * x + 7;
e) y = a * (x * x * b) + 7;
f) y = a * b * (x * x + 7);

2.15 *(Order of Evaluation)* State the order of evaluation of the operators in each of the following C++ statements and show the value of x after each statement is performed.
a) x = 3 + 3 * 4 / 2 - 2;
b) x = 4 % 2 + 2 * 4 - 2 / 2;
c) x = (2 * 4 * 2 + (9 * 3 / 3));

2.16   *(Arithmetic)* Write a program that asks the user to enter three numbers, obtains the two numbers from the user and prints the sum, product of the three numbers.

2.17   *(Printing)* Write a program that prints the numbers 1 to 6 with two numbers in one line separated by a tab. Do this several ways:
   a) Using one statement with one stream insertion operator.
   b) Using one statement with six stream insertion operators.
   c) Using six statements.

2.18   *(Comparing Integers)* Write a program that asks the user to enter two integers, obtains the numbers from the user, then prints the smaller number followed by the words "is smaller." If the numbers are equal, it prints the message "These numbers are equal."

2.19   *(Arithmetic, Smallest and Largest)* Write a program that inputs three integers from the keyboard and prints the sum, average, product, smallest and largest of these numbers. The screen dialog should appear as follows:

```
Input three different integers: 13 27 14
Sum is 54
Average is 18
Product is 4914
Smallest is 13
Largest is 27
```

2.20   *(Volume and Surface Area of a Cylinder)* Write a program that reads in the radius and height of a Cylinder as an integer and prints the cylinder's volume and surface area. Use the constant value 3.14159 for π. Do all calculations in output statements. [*Note:* In this chapter, we've discussed only integer constants and variables. In Chapter 4 we discuss floating-point numbers, i.e., values that can have decimal points.]

2.21   *(Displaying Shapes with Asterisks)* Write a program that prints a box, an oval, an arrow and a diamond as follows:

```
*********          ***              *                 *
*       *         *   *            ***               * *
*       *        *     *          *****              *   *
*       *        *     *            *               *     *
*       *        *     *            *              *       *
*       *        *     *            *               *     *
*       *        *     *            *               *     *
*       *         *   *             *                * *
*********          ***              *                 *
```

2.22   What does the following code print?

```
cout << "*****\n*****\n***\n **\n*\n " << endl;
```

2.23   *(Largest and Smallest Integers)* Write a program that reads in three integers and determines and prints the largest and the smallest integers in the group. Use only the programming techniques you learned in this chapter.

2.24   *(Divisible by 3)* Write a program that reads an integer and determines and prints whether it's divisible by 3 or not. [*Hint:* Use the modulus operator. Any multiple of three leaves a remainder of zero when divided by 3.]

2.25 *(Factor)* Write a program that reads in two integers and determines and prints if the first is a factor of the second. [*Hint:* Use the modulus operator.]

2.26 *(Checkerboard Pattern)* Display the following checkerboard pattern with eight output statements, then display the same pattern using as few statements as possible.

```
* * * * * * * *
 * * * * * * * *
* * * * * * * *
 * * * * * * * *
* * * * * * * *
 * * * * * * * *
* * * * * * * *
 * * * * * * * *
```

2.27 *(Integer Equivalent of a Character)* Here is a peek ahead. In this chapter you learned about integers and the type int. C++ can also represent uppercase letters, lowercase letters and a considerable variety of special symbols. C++ uses small integers internally to represent each different character. The set of characters a computer uses and the corresponding integer representations for those characters are called that computer's **character set**. You can print a character by enclosing that character in single quotes, as with

```
cout << 'A'; // print an uppercase A
```

You can print the integer equivalent of a character using static_cast as follows:

```
cout << static_cast< int >( 'A' ); // print 'A' as an integer
```

This is called a **cast** operation (we formally introduce casts in Chapter 4). When the preceding statement executes, it prints the value 65 (on systems that use the **ASCII character set**). Write a program that prints the integer equivalent of a character typed at the keyboard. Store the input in a variable of type char. Test your program several times using uppercase letters, lowercase letters, digits and special characters (like $).

2.28 *(Digits of an Integer)* Write a program that inputs a five-digit integer, separates the integer into its digits and prints them separated by three spaces each. [*Hint:* Use the integer division and modulus operators.] For example, if the user types in 42339, the program should print:

```
4   2   3   3   9
```

2.29 *(Table)* Using the techniques of this chapter, write a program that calculates the squares and cubes of the integers from 0 to 10. Use tabs to print the following neatly formatted table of values:

```
integer square  cube
0        0       0
1        1       1
2        4       8
3        9       27
4        16      64
5        25      125
6        36      216
7        49      343
8        64      512
9        81      729
10       100     1000
```

Making a Difference

2.30 *(Body Mass Index Calculator)* We introduced the body mass index (BMI) calculator in Exercise 1.9. The formulas for calculating BMI are

$$BMI = \frac{weightInPounds \times 703}{heightInInches \times heightInInches}$$

or

$$BMI = \frac{weightInKilograms}{heightInMeters \times heightInMeters}$$

Create a BMI calculator application that reads the user's weight in pounds and height in inches (or, if you prefer, the user's weight in kilograms and height in meters), then calculates and displays the user's body mass index. Also, the application should display the following information from the Department of Health and Human Services/National Institutes of Health so the user can evaluate his/her BMI:

```
BMI VALUES
Underweight:  less than 18.5
Normal:       between 18.5 and 24.9
Overweight:   between 25 and 29.9
Obese:        30 or greater
```

[*Note:* In this chapter, you learned to use the int type to represent whole numbers. The BMI calculations when done with int values will both produce whole-number results. In Chapter 4 you'll learn to use the double type to represent numbers with decimal points. When the BMI calculations are performed with doubles, they'll both produce numbers with decimal points—these are called "floating-point" numbers.]

2.31 *(Car-Pool Savings Calculator)* Research several car-pooling websites. Create an application that calculates your daily driving cost, so that you can estimate how much money could be saved by car pooling, which also has other advantages such as reducing carbon emissions and reducing traffic congestion. The application should input the following information and display the user's cost per day of driving to work:

  a) Total miles driven per day.
  b) Cost per gallon of gasoline.
  c) Average miles per gallon.
  d) Parking fees per day.
  e) Tolls per day.

3

Introduction to Classes, Objects and Strings

Nothing can have value without being an object of utility.
—Karl Marx

Your public servants serve you right.
—Adlai E. Stevenson

Knowing how to answer one who speaks,
To reply to one who sends a message.
—Amenemopel

Objectives

In this chapter you'll learn:

- How to define a class and use it to create an object.

- How to implement a class's behaviors as member functions.

- How to implement a class's attributes as data members.

- How to call a member function of an object to perform a task.

- The differences between data members of a class and local variables of a function.

- How to use a constructor to initialize an object's data when the object is created.

- How to engineer a class to separate its interface from its implementation and encourage reuse.

- How to use objects of class `string`.

3.1 Introduction

In Chapter 2, you created simple programs that displayed messages to the user, obtained information from the user, performed calculations and made decisions. In this chapter, you'll begin writing programs that employ the basic concepts of *object-oriented programming* that we introduced in Section 1.8. One common feature of every program in Chapter 2 was that all the statements that performed tasks were located in function main. Typically, the programs you develop in this book will consist of function main and one or more *classes*, each containing *data members* and *member functions*. If you become part of a development team in industry, you might work on software systems that contain hundreds, or even thousands, of classes. In this chapter, we develop a simple, well-engineered framework for organizing object-oriented programs in C++.

We present a carefully paced sequence of complete working programs to demonstrate creating and using your own classes. These examples begin our integrated case study on developing a grade-book class that instructors can use to maintain student test scores. We also introduce the C++ standard library class string.

3.2 Defining a Class with a Member Function

We begin with an example (Fig. 3.1) that consists of class GradeBook (lines 8–16)—which, when it's fully developed in Chapter 7, will represent a grade book that an instructor can use to maintain student test scores—and a main function (lines 19–23) that creates a GradeBook object. Function main uses this object and its displayMessage member function (lines 12–15) to display a message on the screen welcoming the instructor to the grade-book program.

```
1   // Fig. 3.1: fig03_01.cpp
2   // Define class GradeBook with a member function displayMessage,
3   // create a GradeBook object, and call its displayMessage function.
4   #include <iostream>
5   using namespace std;
```

Fig. 3.1 | Define class GradeBook with a member function displayMessage, create a GradeBook object and call its displayMessage function. (Part 1 of 2.)

```
 6
 7    // GradeBook class definition
 8    class GradeBook
 9    {
10    public:
11       // function that displays a welcome message to the GradeBook user
12       void displayMessage() const
13       {
14          cout << "Welcome to the Grade Book!" << endl;
15       } // end function displayMessage
16    }; // end class GradeBook
17
18    // function main begins program execution
19    int main()
20    {
21       GradeBook myGradeBook; // create a GradeBook object named myGradeBook
22       myGradeBook.displayMessage(); // call object's displayMessage function
23    } // end main
```

```
Welcome to the Grade Book!
```

Fig. 3.1 | Define class GradeBook with a member function displayMessage, create a GradeBook object and call its displayMessage function. (Part 2 of 2.)

Class *GradeBook*

Before function main (lines 19–23) can create a GradeBook object, we must tell the compiler what member functions and data members belong to the class. The GradeBook **class definition** (lines 8–16) contains a member function called displayMessage (lines 12–15) that displays a message on the screen (line 14). We need to make an object of class Grade-Book (line 21) and call its displayMessage member function (line 22) to get line 14 to execute and display the welcome message. We'll soon explain lines 21–22 in detail.

The class definition begins in line 8 with the keyword class followed by the class name GradeBook. By convention, the name of a user-defined class begins with a capital letter, and for readability, each subsequent word in the class name begins with a capital letter. This capitalization style is often referred to as **Pascal case**, because the convention was widely used in the Pascal programming language. The occasional uppercase letters resemble a camel's humps. More generally, **camel case** capitalization style allows the first letter to be either lowercase or uppercase (e.g., myGradeBook in line 21).

Every class's **body** is enclosed in a pair of left and right braces ({ and }), as in lines 9 and 16. The class definition terminates with a semicolon (line 16).

Common Programming Error 3.1

Forgetting the semicolon at the end of a class definition is a syntax error.

Recall that the function main is always called automatically when you execute a program. Most functions do *not* get called automatically. As you'll soon see, you must call member function displayMessage *explicitly* to tell it to perform its task.

Line 10 contains the keyword **public**, which is an **access specifier**. Lines 12–15 define member function displayMessage. This member function appears *after* access specifier public: to indicate that the function is "available to the public"—that is, it can be called by other functions in the program (such as main), and by member functions of other classes (if there are any). Access specifiers are always followed by a colon (:). For the remainder of the text, when we refer to the access specifier public in the text, we'll omit the colon as we did in this sentence. Section 3.4 introduces the access specifier private. Later in the book we'll study the access specifier protected.

Each function in a program performs a task and may *return a value* when it completes its task—for example, a function might perform a calculation, then return the result of that calculation. When you define a function, you must specify a **return type** to indicate the type of the value returned by the function when it completes its task. In line 12, keyword **void** to the left of the function name displayMessage is the function's return type. Return type void indicates that displayMessage will *not* return any data to its **calling function** (in this example, line 22 of main, as we'll see in a moment) when it completes its task. In Fig. 3.5, you'll see an example of a function that *does* return a value.

The name of the member function, displayMessage, follows the return type (line 12). By convention, our function names use the *camel case* style with a lowercase first letter. The parentheses after the member function name indicate that this is a *function*. An empty set of parentheses, as shown in line 12, indicates that this member function does *not* require additional data to perform its task. You'll see an example of a member function that *does* require additional data in Section 3.3.

We declared member function displayMessage **const** in line 12 because in the process of displaying "Welcome to the Grade Book!" the function *does not*, and *should not*, modify the GradeBook object on which it's called. Declaring displayMessage const tells the compiler, "this function should *not* modify the object on which it's called—if it does, please issue a compilation error." This can help you locate errors if you accidentally insert code in displayMessage that *would* modify the object. Line 12 is commonly referred to as a **function header**.

Every function's *body* is delimited by left and right braces ({ and }), as in lines 13 and 15. The *function body* contains statements that perform the function's task. In this case, member function displayMessage contains one statement (line 14) that displays the message "Welcome to the Grade Book!". After this statement executes, the function has completed its task.

Testing Class **GradeBook**

Next, we'd like to use class GradeBook in a program. As you saw in Chapter 2, the function main (lines 19–23) begins the execution of every program.

In this program, we'd like to call class GradeBook's displayMessage member function to display the welcome message. Typically, you cannot call a member function of a class until you *create an object* of that class. (As you'll learn in Section 9.14, static member functions are an exception.) Line 21 creates an object of class GradeBook called myGradeBook. The variable's type is GradeBook—the class we defined in lines 8–16. When we declare variables of type int, as we did in Chapter 2, the compiler knows what int is—it's a *fundamental type* that's "built into" C++. In line 21, however, the compiler does *not* automatically know what type GradeBook is—it's a **user-defined type**. We tell the compiler what GradeBook is by including the *class definition* (lines 8–16). If we omitted these lines, the compiler would issue an error message. Each class you create becomes a new *type* that can be used to create objects. You can define new class types as needed; this is one reason why C++ is known as an **extensible programming language**.

Line 22 *calls* the member function displayMessage using variable myGradeBook followed by the **dot operator** (.), the function name displayMessage and an empty set of parentheses. This call causes the displayMessage function to perform its task. At the beginning of line 22, "myGradeBook." indicates that main should use the GradeBook object that was created in line 21. The *empty parentheses* in line 12 indicate that member function displayMessage does *not* require additional data to perform its task, which is why we called this function with empty parentheses in line 22. (In Section 3.3, you'll see how to pass data to a function.) When displayMessage completes its task, the program reaches the end of main (line 23) and terminates.

UML Class Diagram for Class GradeBook
Recall from Section 1.8 that the UML is a standardized graphical language used by software developers to represent their object-oriented systems. In the UML, each class is modeled in a **UML class diagram** as a *rectangle* with three *compartments*. Figure 3.2 presents a class diagram for class GradeBook (Fig. 3.1). The *top compartment* contains the class's name centered horizontally and in boldface type. The *middle compartment* contains the class's attributes, which correspond to data members in C++. This compartment is currently empty, because class GradeBook does not yet have any attributes. (Section 3.4 presents a version of class GradeBook with an attribute.) The *bottom compartment* contains the class's operations, which correspond to member functions in C++. The UML models operations by listing the operation name followed by a set of parentheses. Class GradeBook has only one member function, displayMessage, so the bottom compartment of Fig. 3.2 lists one operation with this name. Member function displayMessage does *not* require additional information to perform its tasks, so the parentheses following displayMessage in the class diagram are *empty*, just as they are in the member function's header in line 12 of Fig. 3.1. The *plus sign (+)* in front of the operation name indicates that displayMessage is a *public* operation in the UML (i.e., a public member function in C++).

Fig. 3.2 | UML class diagram indicating that class GradeBook has a public displayMessage operation.

3.3 Defining a Member Function with a Parameter

In our car analogy from Section 1.8, we mentioned that pressing a car's gas pedal sends a *message* to the car to perform a task—make the car go faster. But *how fast* should the car accelerate? As you know, the farther down you press the pedal, the faster the car accelerates. So the message to the car includes *both* the *task to perform* and *additional information that helps the car perform the task*. This additional information is known as a **parameter**—the *value* of the parameter helps the car determine how fast to accelerate. Similarly, a member function can require one or more parameters that represent additional data it needs to perform its task. A function call supplies values—called **arguments**—for each of the function's parameters. For example, to make a deposit into a bank account, suppose a deposit member function of an Account class specifies a parameter that represents the *deposit amount*. When the deposit member function is called, an argument value representing the deposit amount is copied to the member function's parameter. The member function then adds that amount to the account balance.

Defining and Testing Class GradeBook

Our next example (Fig. 3.3) redefines class GradeBook (lines 9–18) with a display-Message member function (lines 13–17) that displays the course name as part of the welcome message. The new version of displayMessage requires a *parameter* (courseName in line 13) that represents the course name to output.

```
1   // Fig. 3.3: fig03_03.cpp
2   // Define class GradeBook with a member function that takes a parameter,
3   // create a GradeBook object and call its displayMessage function.
4   #include <iostream>
5   #include <string> // program uses C++ standard string class
6   using namespace std;
7
8   // GradeBook class definition
9   class GradeBook
10  {
11  public:
12     // function that displays a welcome message to the GradeBook user
13     void displayMessage( string courseName ) const
14     {
15        cout << "Welcome to the grade book for\n" << courseName << "!"
16           << endl;
17     } // end function displayMessage
18  }; // end class GradeBook
19
20  // function main begins program execution
21  int main()
22  {
23     string nameOfCourse; // string of characters to store the course name
24     GradeBook myGradeBook; // create a GradeBook object named myGradeBook
25
26     // prompt for and input course name
27     cout << "Please enter the course name:" << endl;
28     getline( cin, nameOfCourse ); // read a course name with blanks
29     cout << endl; // output a blank line
30
31     // call myGradeBook's displayMessage function
32     // and pass nameOfCourse as an argument
33     myGradeBook.displayMessage( nameOfCourse );
34  } // end main
```

Fig. 3.3 | Define class GradeBook with a member function that takes a parameter, create a GradeBook object and call its displayMessage function. (Part 1 of 2.)

```
Please enter the course name:
CS101 Introduction to C++ Programming

Welcome to the grade book for
CS101 Introduction to C++ Programming!
```

Fig. 3.3 | Define class GradeBook with a member function that takes a parameter, create a GradeBook object and call its displayMessage function. (Part 2 of 2.)

Before discussing the new features of class GradeBook, let's see how the new class is used in main (lines 21–34). Line 23 creates a variable of type **string** called nameOfCourse that will be used to store the course name entered by the user. A variable of type string represents a string of characters such as "CS101 Introduction to C++ Programming". A string is actually an *object* of the C++ Standard Library class string. This class is defined in **header <string>**, and the name string, like cout, belongs to namespace std. To enable lines 13 and 23 to compile, line 5 *includes* the <string> header. The using directive in line 6 allows us to simply write string in line 23 rather than std::string. For now, you can think of string variables like variables of other types such as int. You'll learn additional string capabilities in Section 3.8 and in Chapter 21.

Line 24 creates an object of class GradeBook named myGradeBook. Line 27 prompts the user to enter a course name. Line 28 reads the name from the user and assigns it to the nameOfCourse variable, using the library function **getline** to perform the input. Before we explain this line of code, let's explain why we cannot simply write

```
cin >> nameOfCourse;
```

to obtain the course name.

In our sample program execution, we use the course name "CS101 Introduction to C++ Programming," which contains multiple words *separated by blanks*. (Recall that we highlight user-entered data in bold.) When reading a string with the stream extraction operator, cin reads characters *until the first white-space character is reached*. Thus, only "CS101" would be read by the preceding statement. The rest of the course name would have to be read by subsequent input operations.

In this example, we'd like the user to type the complete course name and press *Enter* to submit it to the program, and we'd like to store the *entire* course name in the string variable nameOfCourse. The function call getline(cin, nameOfCourse) in line 28 reads characters (*including* the space characters that separate the words in the input) from the standard input stream object cin (i.e., the keyboard) until the *newline* character is encountered, places the characters in the string variable nameOfCourse and *discards* the newline character. When you press *Enter* while entering data, a newline is inserted in the input stream. The <string> header must be included in the program to use function getline, which belongs to namespace std.

Line 33 calls myGradeBook's displayMessage member function. The nameOfCourse variable in parentheses is the *argument* that's passed to member function displayMessage so that it can perform its task. The value of variable nameOfCourse in main is *copied* to member function displayMessage's parameter courseName in line 13. When you execute this program, member function displayMessage outputs as part of the welcome message the course name you type (in our sample execution, CS101 Introduction to C++ Programming).

More on Arguments and Parameters

To specify in a function definition that the function requires data to perform its task, you place additional information in the function's **parameter list**, which is located in the parentheses following the function name. The parameter list may contain *any* number of parameters, including *none at all* (represented by empty parentheses as in Fig. 3.1, line 12) to indicate that a function does *not* require any parameters. The displayMessage member function's parameter list (Fig. 3.3, line 13) declares that the function requires one parameter. Each parameter specifies a *type* and an *identifier*. The type string and the identifier courseName indicate that member function displayMessage requires a string to perform its task. The member function body uses the parameter courseName to access the value that's passed to the function in the function call (line 33 in main). Lines 15–16 display parameter courseName's value as part of the welcome message. The parameter variable's name (courseName in line 13) can be the *same* as or *different* from the argument variable's name (nameOfCourse in line 33)—you'll learn why in Chapter 6.

A function can specify multiple parameters by separating each from the next with a comma. The number and order of arguments in a function call *must match* the number and order of parameters in the parameter list of the called member function's header. Also, the argument types in the function call must be consistent with the types of the corresponding parameters in the function header. (As you'll learn in subsequent chapters, an argument's type and its corresponding parameter's type need not always be *identical*, but they must be "consistent.") In our example, the one string argument in the function call (i.e., nameOfCourse) *exactly matches* the one string parameter in the member-function definition (i.e., courseName).

*Updated UML Class Diagram for Class **GradeBook***

The UML class diagram of Fig. 3.4 models class GradeBook of Fig. 3.3. Like the class GradeBook defined in Fig. 3.1, this GradeBook class contains public member function displayMessage. However, this version of displayMessage has a *parameter*. The UML models a parameter by listing the parameter name, followed by a colon and the parameter type in the parentheses following the operation name. The UML has its *own* data types similar to those of C++. The UML is *language independent*—it's used with many different programming languages—so its terminology does not exactly match that of C++. For example, the UML type String corresponds to the C++ type string. Member function displayMessage of class GradeBook (Fig. 3.3, lines 13–17) has a string parameter named courseName, so Fig. 3.4 lists courseName : String between the parentheses following the operation name displayMessage. This version of the GradeBook class still does *not* have any data members.

Fig. 3.4 | UML class diagram indicating that class GradeBook has a public displayMessage operation with a courseName parameter of UML type String.

3.4 Data Members, *set* Member Functions and *get* Member Functions

In Chapter 2, we declared all of a program's variables in its main function. Variables declared in a function definition's body are known as **local variables** and can be used *only* from the line of their declaration in the function to the closing right brace (}) of the block in which they're declared. A local variable must be declared *before* it can be used in a function. A local variable cannot be accessed *outside* the function in which it's declared. *When a function terminates, the values of its local variables are lost.* (You'll see an exception to this in Chapter 6 when we discuss static local variables.)

A class normally consists of one or more member functions that manipulate the attributes that belong to a particular object of the class. Attributes are represented as variables in a class definition. Such variables are called **data members** and are declared *inside* a class definition but *outside* the bodies of the class's member-function definitions. Each object of a class maintains its own attributes in memory. These attributes exist throughout the life of the object. The example in this section demonstrates a GradeBook class that contains a courseName data member to represent a particular GradeBook object's course name. If you create more than one GradeBook object, each will have its own courseName data member, and these can contain *different* values.

GradeBook Class with a Data Member, and set *and* get *Member Functions*

In our next example, class GradeBook (Fig. 3.5) maintains the course name as a *data member* so that it can be *used* or *modified* throughout a program's execution. The class contains member functions setCourseName, getCourseName and displayMessage. Member function setCourseName *stores* a course name in a GradeBook data member. Member function getCourseName *obtains* the course name from that data member. Member function displayMessage—which now specifies *no parameters*—still displays a welcome message that includes the course name. However, as you'll see, the function now *obtains* the course name by calling another function in the same class—getCourseName.

```
1   // Fig. 3.5: fig03_05.cpp
2   // Define class GradeBook that contains a courseName data member
3   // and member functions to set and get its value;
4   // Create and manipulate a GradeBook object with these functions.
5   #include <iostream>
6   #include <string> // program uses C++ standard string class
7   using namespace std;
8
9   // GradeBook class definition
10  class GradeBook
11  {
12  public:
13     // function that sets the course name
14     void setCourseName( string name )
15     {
16        courseName = name; // store the course name in the object
17     } // end function setCourseName
```

Fig. 3.5 | Defining and testing class GradeBook with a data member and *set* and *get* member functions. (Part 1 of 2.)

```
18
19       // function that gets the course name
20       string getCourseName() const
21       {
22          return courseName; // return the object's courseName
23       } // end function getCourseName
24
25       // function that displays a welcome message
26       void displayMessage() const
27       {
28          // this statement calls getCourseName to get the
29          // name of the course this GradeBook represents
30          cout << "Welcome to the grade book for\n" << getCourseName() << "!"
31             << endl;
32       } // end function displayMessage
33    private:
34       string courseName; // course name for this GradeBook
35    }; // end class GradeBook
36
37    // function main begins program execution
38    int main()
39    {
40       string nameOfCourse; // string of characters to store the course name
41       GradeBook myGradeBook; // create a GradeBook object named myGradeBook
42
43       // display initial value of courseName
44       cout << "Initial course name is: " << myGradeBook.getCourseName()
45          << endl;
46
47       // prompt for, input and set course name
48       cout << "\nPlease enter the course name:" << endl;
49       getline( cin, nameOfCourse ); // read a course name with blanks
50       myGradeBook.setCourseName( nameOfCourse ); // set the course name
51
52       cout << endl; // outputs a blank line
53       myGradeBook.displayMessage(); // display message with new course name
54    } // end main
```

```
Initial course name is:

Please enter the course name:
CS101 Introduction to C++ Programming

Welcome to the grade book for
CS101 Introduction to C++ Programming!
```

Fig. 3.5 | Defining and testing class GradeBook with a data member and *set* and *get* member functions. (Part 2 of 2.)

A typical instructor teaches *several* courses, each with its own course name. Line 34 declares that courseName is a variable of type string. Because the variable is declared in the class definition (lines 10–35) but outside the bodies of the class's member-function definitions (lines 14–17, 20–23 and 26–32), the variable is a *data member*. Every instance (i.e., object) of class GradeBook contains each of the class's data members—if there are two GradeBook objects, each has its *own* courseName (one per object), as you'll see in the example of Fig. 3.7. A benefit of making courseName a data member is that *all* the member functions of the class can manipulate any data members that appear in the class definition (in this case, courseName).

Access Specifiers *public* and *private*

Most data-member declarations appear after the **private** access specifier. Variables or functions declared after access specifier private (and *before* the next access specifier if there is one) are accessible only to member functions of the class for which they're declared (or to "friends" of the class, as you'll see in Chapter 9). Thus, data member courseName can be used *only* in member functions setCourseName, getCourseName and displayMessage of class GradeBook (or to "friends" of the class, if there are any).

Error-Prevention Tip 3.1

Making the data members of a class private and the member functions of the class public facilitates debugging because problems with data manipulations are localized to either the class's member functions or the friends of the class.

Common Programming Error 3.2

An attempt by a function, which is not a member of a particular class (or a friend of that class) to access a private member of that class is a compilation error.

The *default access* for class members is private so all members *after* the class header and *before* the first access specifier (if there are any) are private. The access specifiers public and private may be repeated, but this is unnecessary and can be confusing.

Declaring data members with access specifier private is known as **data hiding**. When a program creates a GradeBook object, data member courseName is *encapsulated* (hidden) in the object and can be accessed only by member functions of the object's class. In class GradeBook, member functions setCourseName and getCourseName manipulate the data member courseName directly.

Member Functions *setCourseName* and *getCourseName*

Member function setCourseName (lines 14–17) does not *return* any data when it completes its task, so its return type is void. The member function *receives* one parameter—name—which represents the course name that will be passed to it as an argument (as we'll see in line 50 of main). Line 16 assigns name to data member courseName, thus *modifying* the object—for this reason, we do *not* declare setCourseName const. In this example, setCourseName does not *validate* the course name—i.e., the function does *not* check that the course name adheres to any particular format or follows any other rules regarding what a "valid" course name looks like. Suppose, for instance, that a university can print student transcripts containing course names of only 25 characters or fewer. In this case, we might want class GradeBook to ensure that its data member courseName never contains more than 25 characters. We discuss validation in Section 3.8.

Member function getCourseName (lines 20–23) *returns* a particular GradeBook object's courseName, *without* modifying the object—for this reason, we declare getCourseName const. The member function has an *empty parameter list*, so it does *not* require additional data to perform its task. The function specifies that it returns a `string`. When a function that specifies a return type other than `void` is called and completes its task, the function uses a **return statement** (as in line 22) to *return a result* to its calling function. For example, when you go to an automated teller machine (ATM) and request your account balance, you expect the ATM to give you a value that represents your balance. Similarly, when a statement calls member function `getCourseName` on a `GradeBook` object, the statement expects to receive the `GradeBook`'s course name (in this case, a `string`, as specified by the function's return type).

If you have a function `square` that returns the square of its argument, the statement

```
result = square( 2 );
```

returns 4 from function `square` and assigns to variable `result` the value 4. If you have a function `maximum` that returns the largest of three integer arguments, the statement

```
biggest = maximum( 27, 114, 51 );
```

returns 114 from function `maximum` and assigns this value to variable `biggest`.

The statements in lines 16 and 22 each use variable `courseName` (line 34) even though it was *not* declared in any of the member functions. We can do this because `courseName` is a *data member* of the class and data members are accessible from a class's member functions.

Member Function *displayMessage*
Member function `displayMessage` (lines 26–32) does *not* return any data when it completes its task, so its return type is `void`. The function does *not* receive parameters, so its parameter list is empty. Lines 30–31 output a welcome message that includes the value of data member `courseName`. Line 30 calls member function `getCourseName` to obtain the value of `courseName`. Member function `displayMessage` could also access data member `courseName` directly, just as member functions `setCourseName` and `getCourseName` do. We explain shortly why it's preferable from a software engineering perspective to call member function `getCourseName` to obtain the value of `courseName`.

Testing Class *GradeBook*
The `main` function (lines 38–54) creates one object of class `GradeBook` and uses each of its member functions. Line 41 creates a `GradeBook` object named `myGradeBook`. Lines 44–45 display the initial course name by calling the object's `getCourseName` member function. The first line of the output does not show a course name, because the object's `courseName` data member (i.e., a `string`) is initially empty—by default, the initial value of a `string` is the so-called **empty string**, i.e., a string that does not contain any characters. Nothing appears on the screen when an empty string is displayed.

Line 48 prompts the user to enter a course name. Local `string` variable `nameOfCourse` (declared in line 40) is set to the course name entered by the user, which is obtained by the call to the `getline` function (line 49). Line 50 calls object `myGradeBook`'s `setCourseName` member function and supplies `nameOfCourse` as the function's argument. When the function is called, the argument's value is copied to parameter `name` (line 14) of member function `setCourseName`. Then the parameter's value is assigned to data member `courseName` (line 16). Line 52 skips a line; then line 53 calls object `myGradeBook`'s `displayMessage` member function to display the welcome message containing the course name.

Software Engineering with Set *and* Get *Functions*

A class's `private` data members can be manipulated *only* by member functions of that class (and by "friends" of the class as you'll see in Chapter 9). So a **client of an object**—that is, any statement that calls the object's member functions from *outside* the object—calls the class's `public` member functions to request the class's services for particular objects of the class. This is why the statements in function `main` call member functions `setCourseName`, `getCourseName` and `displayMessage` on a `GradeBook` object. Classes often provide `public` member functions to allow clients of the class to *set* (i.e., assign values to) or *get* (i.e., obtain the values of) `private` data members. These member function names need not begin with `set` or `get`, but this naming convention is common. In this example, the member function that *sets* the `courseName` data member is called `setCourseName`, and the member function that *gets* the value of the `courseName` data member is called `getCourseName`. *Set* functions are sometimes called **mutators** (because they mutate, or change, values), and *get* functions are also called **accessors** (because they access values).

Recall that declaring data members with access specifier `private` enforces data hiding. Providing `public` *set* and *get* functions allows clients of a class to access the hidden data, but only *indirectly*. The client knows that it's attempting to modify or obtain an object's data, but the client does *not* know *how* the object performs these operations. In some cases, a class may *internally* represent a piece of data one way, but expose that data to clients in a different way. For example, suppose a `Clock` class represents the time of day as a `private` `int` data member `time` that stores the number of seconds since midnight. However, when a client calls a `Clock` object's `getTime` member function, the object could return the time with hours, minutes and seconds in a `string` in the format `"HH:MM:SS"`. Similarly, suppose the `Clock` class provides a *set* function named `setTime` that takes a `string` parameter in the `"HH:MM:SS"` format. Using `string` capabilities presented in Chapter 21, the `setTime` function could convert this `string` to a number of seconds, which the function stores in its `private` data member. The *set* function could also check that the value it receives represents a valid time (e.g., `"12:30:45"` is valid but `"42:85:70"` is not). The *set* and *get* functions allow a client to interact with an object, but the object's `private` data remains safely *encapsulated* (i.e., hidden) in the object itself.

The *set* and *get* functions of a class also should be used by other member functions *within* the class to manipulate the class's `private` data, even though these member functions *can* access the `private` data directly. In Fig. 3.5, member functions `setCourseName` and `getCourseName` are `public` member functions, so they're accessible to clients of the class, as well as to the class itself. Member function `displayMessage` calls member function `getCourseName` to obtain the value of data member `courseName` for display purposes, even though `displayMessage` can access `courseName` directly—accessing a data member via its *get* function creates a better, more robust class (i.e., a class that's easier to maintain and less likely to malfunction). If we decide to change the data member `courseName` in some way, the `displayMessage` definition will *not* require modification—only the bodies of the *get* and *set* functions that directly manipulate the data member will need to change. For example, suppose we want to represent the course name as two separate data members—`courseNumber` (e.g., `"CS101"`) and `courseTitle` (e.g., `"Introduction to C++ Programming"`). Member function `displayMessage` can still issue a single call to member function `getCourseName` to obtain the full course name to display as part of the welcome message. In this case, `getCourseName` would need to build and return a `string` containing the courseNumber followed by the courseTitle. Member function displayMessage could continue to display the complete course title "CS101 Introduction to C++ Programming." The benefits of calling a *set* function from another member function of the same class will become clearer when we discuss validation in Section 3.8.

Good Programming Practice 3.1
Always try to localize *the effects of changes to a class's data members by accessing and manipulating the data members through their corresponding* get *and set functions.*

Software Engineering Observation 3.1
Write programs that are clear and easy to maintain. Change is the rule rather than the exception. You should anticipate that your code will be modified, and possibly often.

GradeBook's UML Class Diagram with a Data Member and* set *and* get *Functions
Figure 3.6 contains an updated UML class diagram for the version of class GradeBook in Fig. 3.5. This diagram models GradeBook's data member courseName as an attribute in the middle compartment. The UML represents data members as attributes by listing the attribute name, followed by a colon and the attribute type. The UML type of attribute courseName is String, which corresponds to string in C++. Data member courseName is private in C++, so the class diagram lists a *minus sign (–)* in front of the corresponding attribute's name. Class GradeBook contains three public member functions, so the class diagram lists three operations in the third compartment. Operation setCourseName has a String parameter called name. The UML indicates the *return type* of an operation by placing a colon and the return type after the parentheses following the operation name. Member function getCourseName of class GradeBook has a string return type in C++, so the class diagram shows a String return type in the UML. Operations setCourseName and displayMessage do not return values (i.e., they return void in C++), so the UML class diagram does not specify a return type after the parentheses of these operations.

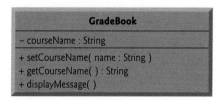

Fig. 3.6 | UML class diagram for class GradeBook with a private courseName attribute and public operations setCourseName, getCourseName and displayMessage.

3.5 Initializing Objects with Constructors

As mentioned in Section 3.4, when an object of class GradeBook (Fig. 3.5) is created, its data member courseName is initialized to the empty string by default. What if you want to provide a course name when you *create* a GradeBook object? Each class you declare can provide one or more **constructors** that can be used to initialize an object of the class when the object is created. A constructor is a special member function that must be defined with the *same* *name as the class*, so that the compiler can distinguish it from the class's other member functions. An important difference between constructors and other functions is that *constructors cannot return values*, so they *cannot* specify a return type (not even void). Normally, constructors are declared public. In the early chapters, our classes will generally have one constructor—in later chapters, you'll see how to create classes with more that one constructor using the technique of *function overloading*, which we introduce in Section 6.18.

C++ automatically calls a constructor for each object that's created, which helps ensure that objects are initialized properly before they're used in a program. The constructor call occurs when the object is created. If a class does not *explicitly* include constructors, the compiler provides a **default constructor** with *no* parameters. For example, when line 41 of Fig. 3.5 creates a GradeBook object, the default constructor is called. The default constructor provided by the compiler creates a GradeBook object without giving any initial values to the object's fundamental type data members. For data members that are objects of other classes, the default constructor implicitly calls each data member's default constructor to ensure that the data member is initialized properly. This is why the string data member courseName (in Fig. 3.5) was initialized to the empty string—the default constructor for class string sets the string's value to the empty string.

In the example of Fig. 3.7, we specify a course name for a GradeBook object when the object is created (e.g., line 47). In this case, the argument "CS101 Introduction to C++ Programming" is passed to the GradeBook object's constructor (lines 14–18) and used to initialize the courseName. Figure 3.7 defines a modified GradeBook class containing a constructor with a string parameter that receives the initial course name.

```
1   // Fig. 3.7: fig03_07.cpp
2   // Instantiating multiple objects of the GradeBook class and using
3   // the GradeBook constructor to specify the course name
4   // when each GradeBook object is created.
5   #include <iostream>
6   #include <string> // program uses C++ standard string class
7   using namespace std;
8
9   // GradeBook class definition
10  class GradeBook
11  {
12  public:
13     // constructor initializes courseName with string supplied as argument
14     explicit GradeBook( string name )
15        : courseName( name ) // member initializer to initialize courseName
16     {
17        // empty body
18     } // end GradeBook constructor
19
20     // function to set the course name
21     void setCourseName( string name )
22     {
23        courseName = name; // store the course name in the object
24     } // end function setCourseName
```

Fig. 3.7 | Instantiating multiple objects of the GradeBook class and using the GradeBook constructor to specify the course name when each GradeBook object is created. (Part 1 of 2.)

```
25
26      // function to get the course name
27      string getCourseName() const
28      {
29         return courseName; // return object's courseName
30      } // end function getCourseName
31
32      // display a welcome message to the GradeBook user
33      void displayMessage() const
34      {
35         // call getCourseName to get the courseName
36         cout << "Welcome to the grade book for\n" << getCourseName()
37            << "!" << endl;
38      } // end function displayMessage
39   private:
40      string courseName; // course name for this GradeBook
41   }; // end class GradeBook
42
43   // function main begins program execution
44   int main()
45   {
46      // create two GradeBook objects
47      GradeBook gradeBook1( "CS101 Introduction to C++ Programming" );
48      GradeBook gradeBook2( "CS102 Data Structures in C++" );
49
50      // display initial value of courseName for each GradeBook
51      cout << "gradeBook1 created for course: " << gradeBook1.getCourseName()
52         << "\ngradeBook2 created for course: " << gradeBook2.getCourseName()
53         << endl;
54   } // end main
```

```
gradeBook1 created for course: CS101 Introduction to C++ Programming
gradeBook2 created for course: CS102 Data Structures in C++
```

Fig. 3.7 | Instantiating multiple objects of the GradeBook class and using the GradeBook constructor to specify the course name when each GradeBook object is created. (Part 2 of 2.)

Defining a Constructor

Lines 14–18 of Fig. 3.7 define a constructor for class GradeBook. The constructor has the *same* name as its class, GradeBook. A constructor specifies in its parameter list the data it requires to perform its task. When you create a new object, you place this data in the parentheses that follow the object name (as we did in lines 47–48). Line 14 indicates that class GradeBook's constructor has a string parameter called name. We declared this constructor **explicit**, because it takes a *single* parameter—this is important for subtle reasons that you'll learn in Section 10.13. For now, just declare *all* single-parameter constructors explicit. Line 14 does *not* specify a return type, because constructors *cannot* return values (or even void). Also, constructors cannot be declared const (because initializing an object modifies it).

The constructor uses a **member-initializer list** (line 15) to initialize the courseName data member with the value of the constructor's parameter name. *Member initializers* appear between a constructor's parameter list and the left brace that begins the constructor's body. The member initializer list is separated from the parameter list with a *colon (:)*. A member initializer consists of a data member's *variable name* followed by parentheses containing the member's *initial value*. In this example, courseName is initialized with the value of the parameter name. If a class contains more than one data member, each data member's initializer is separated from the next by a comma. The member initializer list executes *before* the body of the constructor executes. You can perform initialization in the constructor's body, but you'll learn later in the book that it's more efficient to do it with member initializers, and some types of data members must be initialized this way.

Notice that both the constructor (line 14) and the setCourseName function (line 21) use a parameter called name. You can use the *same* parameter names in *different* functions because the parameters are *local* to each function—they do *not* interfere with one another.

Testing Class GradeBook

Lines 44–54 of Fig. 3.7 define the main function that tests class GradeBook and demonstrates initializing GradeBook objects using a constructor. Line 47 creates and initializes GradeBook object gradeBook1. When this line executes, the GradeBook constructor (lines 14–18) is called with the argument "CS101 Introduction to C++ Programming" to initialize gradeBook1's course name. Line 48 repeats this process for GradeBook object gradeBook2, this time passing the argument "CS102 Data Structures in C++" to initialize gradeBook2's course name. Lines 51–52 use each object's getCourseName member function to obtain the course names and show that they were indeed initialized when the objects were created. The output confirms that each GradeBook object maintains its *own* data member courseName.

Ways to Provide a Default Constructor for a Class

Any constructor that takes *no* arguments is called a default constructor. A class can get a default constructor in one of several ways:

1. The compiler *implicitly* creates a default constructor in every class that does *not* have any user-defined constructors. The default constructor does *not* initialize the class's data members, but *does* call the default constructor for each data member that's an object of another class. An uninitialized variable contains an undefined ("garbage") value.

2. You *explicitly* define a constructor that takes no arguments. Such a default constructor will call the default constructor for each data member that's an object of another class and will perform additional initialization specified by you.

3. *If you define any constructors with arguments, C++ will not implicitly create a default constructor for that class.* We'll show later that C++11 allows you to force the compiler to create the default constructor even if you've defined non-default constructors.

For each version of class GradeBook in Fig. 3.1, Fig. 3.3 and Fig. 3.5 the compiler *implicitly* defined a default constructor.

> **Error-Prevention Tip 3.2**
> *Unless no initialization of your class's data members is necessary (almost never), provide constructors to ensure that your class's data members are initialized with meaningful values when each new object of your class is created.*

Software Engineering Observation 3.2

Data members can be initialized in a constructor, or their values may be set *later after the object is created. However, it's a good software engineering practice to ensure that an object is fully initialized* before *the client code invokes the object's member functions. You should not rely on the client code to ensure that an object gets initialized properly.*

Adding the Constructor to Class **GradeBook's** *UML Class Diagram*

The UML class diagram of Fig. 3.8 models the GradeBook class of Fig. 3.7, which has a constructor with a name parameter of type string (represented by type String in the UML). Like operations, the UML models constructors in the third compartment of a class in a class diagram. To distinguish a constructor from a class's operations, the UML places the word "constructor" between guillemets (« and ») before the constructor's name. By convention, you list the class's constructor *before* other operations in the third compartment.

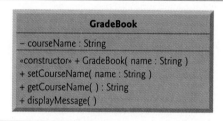

Fig. 3.8 | UML class diagram indicating that class GradeBook has a constructor with a name parameter of UML type String.

3.6 Placing a Class in a Separate File for Reusability

One of the benefits of creating class definitions is that, when packaged properly, your classes can be *reused* by other programmers. For example, you can *reuse* C++ Standard Library type string in any C++ program by including the header <string> (and, as you'll see, by being able to link to the library's object code).

Programmers who wish to use our GradeBook class cannot simply include the file from Fig. 3.7 in another program. As you learned in Chapter 2, function main begins the execution of every program, and every program must have *exactly one* main function. If other programmers include the code from Fig. 3.7, they get extra "baggage"—our main function—and their programs will then have two main functions. Attempting to compile a program with two main functions produces an error. So, placing main in the same file with a class definition *prevents that class from being reused* by other programs. In this section, we demonstrate how to make class GradeBook reusable by *separating it into another file* from the main function.

Headers

Each of the previous examples in the chapter consists of a single .cpp file, also known as a **source-code file**, that contains a GradeBook class definition and a main function. When building an object-oriented C++ program, it's customary to define *reusable* source code (such as a class) in a file that by convention has a .h filename extension—known as a **header**. Programs use #include preprocessing directives to include headers and take advantage of reusable software components, such as type `string` provided in the C++ Standard Library and user-defined types like class `GradeBook`.

Our next example separates the code from Fig. 3.7 into two files—`GradeBook.h` (Fig. 3.9) and `fig03_10.cpp` (Fig. 3.10). As you look at the header in Fig. 3.9, notice that it contains only the `GradeBook` class definition (lines 7–38) and the headers on which the class depends. The `main` function that *uses* class `GradeBook` is defined in the source-code file `fig03_10.cpp` (Fig. 3.10) in lines 8–18. To help you prepare for the larger programs you'll encounter later in this book and in industry, we often use a separate source-code file containing function `main` to test our classes (this is called a **driver program**). You'll soon learn how a source-code file with `main` can use the class definition found in a header to create objects of a class.

```
 1   // Fig. 3.9: GradeBook.h
 2   // GradeBook class definition in a separate file from main.
 3   #include <iostream>
 4   #include <string> // class GradeBook uses C++ standard string class
 5
 6   // GradeBook class definition
 7   class GradeBook
 8   {
 9   public:
10      // constructor initializes courseName with string supplied as argument
11      explicit GradeBook( std::string name )
12         : courseName( name ) // member initializer to initialize courseName
13      {
14         // empty body
15      } // end GradeBook constructor
16
17      // function to set the course name
18      void setCourseName( std::string name )
19      {
20         courseName = name; // store the course name in the object
21      } // end function setCourseName
22
23      // function to get the course name
24      std::string getCourseName() const
25      {
26         return courseName; // return object's courseName
27      } // end function getCourseName
28
29      // display a welcome message to the GradeBook user
30      void displayMessage() const
31      {
32         // call getCourseName to get the courseName
33         std::cout << "Welcome to the grade book for\n" << getCourseName()
34            << "!" << std::endl;
35      } // end function displayMessage
36   private:
37      std::string courseName; // course name for this GradeBook
38   }; // end class GradeBook
```

Fig. 3.9 | GradeBook class definition in a separate file from `main`.

```
1   // Fig. 3.10: fig03_10.cpp
2   // Including class GradeBook from file GradeBook.h for use in main.
3   #include <iostream>
4   #include "GradeBook.h" // include definition of class GradeBook
5   using namespace std;
6
7   // function main begins program execution
8   int main()
9   {
10     // create two GradeBook objects
11     GradeBook gradeBook1( "CS101 Introduction to C++ Programming" );
12     GradeBook gradeBook2( "CS102 Data Structures in C++" );
13
14     // display initial value of courseName for each GradeBook
15     cout << "gradeBook1 created for course: " << gradeBook1.getCourseName()
16        << "\ngradeBook2 created for course: " << gradeBook2.getCourseName()
17        << endl;
18  } // end main
```

```
gradeBook1 created for course: CS101 Introduction to C++ Programming
gradeBook2 created for course: CS102 Data Structures in C++
```

Fig. 3.10 | Including class GradeBook from file GradeBook.h for use in main.

Use std:: with Standard Library Components in Headers

Throughout the header (Fig. 3.9), we use std:: when referring to string (lines 11, 18, 24 and 37), cout (line 33) and endl (line 34). For subtle reasons that we'll explain in a later chapter, headers should *never* contain using directives or using declarations (Section 2.7).

Including a Header That Contains a User-Defined Class

A header such as GradeBook.h (Fig. 3.9) cannot be used as a complete program, because it does not contain a main function. To test class GradeBook (defined in Fig. 3.9), you must write a separate source-code file containing a main function (such as Fig. 3.10) that instantiates and uses objects of the class.

The compiler doesn't know what a GradeBook is because it's a user-defined type. In fact, the compiler doesn't even know the classes in the C++ Standard Library. To help it understand how to use a class, we must explicitly provide the compiler with the class's definition—that's why, for example, to use type string, a program must include the <string> header. This enables the compiler to determine the amount of memory that it must reserve for each string object and ensure that a program calls a string's member functions correctly.

To create GradeBook objects gradeBook1 and gradeBook2 in lines 11–12 of Fig. 3.10, the compiler must know the *size* of a GradeBook object. While objects conceptually contain data members and member functions, C++ objects actually contain *only* data. The compiler creates only *one* copy of the class's member functions and *shares* that copy among all the class's objects. Each object, of course, needs its own data members, because their contents can vary among objects (such as two different BankAccount objects having two different balances). The member-function code, however, is *not modifiable*, so it can be shared among all objects of the class. Therefore, the size of an object depends on the amount of memory required to store the class's data members. By including GradeBook.h in line 4, we give the compiler access to the information it needs (Fig. 3.9, line 37) to determine the size of a GradeBook object and to determine whether objects of the class are used correctly (in lines 11–12 and 15–16 of Fig. 3.10).

Line 4 instructs the C++ preprocessor to replace the directive with a copy of the contents of GradeBook.h (i.e., the GradeBook class definition) *before* the program is compiled. When the source-code file fig03_10.cpp is compiled, it now contains the GradeBook class definition (because of the #include), and the compiler is able to determine how to create GradeBook objects and see that their member functions are called correctly. Now that the class definition is in a header (without a main function), we can include that header in *any* program that needs to reuse our GradeBook class.

How Headers Are Located

Notice that the name of the GradeBook.h header in line 4 of Fig. 3.10 is enclosed in quotes (" ") rather than angle brackets (< >). Normally, a program's source-code files and user-defined headers are placed in the *same* directory. When the preprocessor encounters a header name in quotes, it attempts to locate the header in the same directory as the file in which the #include directive appears. If the preprocessor cannot find the header in that directory, it searches for it in the same location(s) as the C++ Standard Library headers. When the preprocessor encounters a header name in angle brackets (e.g., <iostream>), it assumes that the header is part of the C++ Standard Library and does *not* look in the directory of the program that's being preprocessed.

Error-Prevention Tip 3.3

To ensure that the preprocessor can locate headers correctly, #include preprocessing directives should place user-defined headers names in quotes (e.g., "GradeBook.h") and place C++ Standard Library headers names in angle brackets (e.g., <iostream>).

Additional Software Engineering Issues

Now that class GradeBook is defined in a header, the class is *reusable*. Unfortunately, placing a class definition in a header as in Fig. 3.9 still *reveals the entire implementation of the class to the class's clients*—GradeBook.h is simply a text file that anyone can open and read. Conventional software engineering wisdom says that to use an object of a class, the client code needs to know only what member functions to call, what arguments to provide to each member function and what return type to expect from each member function. *The client code does not need to know how those functions are implemented.*

If client code *does* know how a class is implemented, the programmer might write client code based on the class's implementation details. Ideally, if that implementation changes, the class's clients should not have to change. *Hiding the class's implementation details makes it easier to change the class's implementation while minimizing, and hopefully eliminating, changes to client code.*

In Section 3.7, we show how to break up the GradeBook class into two files so that

1. the class is *reusable*,

2. the clients of the class know what member functions the class provides, how to call them and what return types to expect, and

3. the clients do *not* know how the class's member functions are implemented.

3.7 Separating Interface from Implementation

In the preceding section, we showed how to promote software reusability by separating a class definition from the client code (e.g., function main) that uses the class. We now introduce another fundamental principle of good software engineering—**separating interface from implementation**.

Interface of a Class

Interfaces define and standardize the ways in which things such as people and systems interact with one another. For example, a radio's controls serve as an interface between the radio's users and its internal components. The controls allow users to perform a limited set of operations (such as changing the station, adjusting the volume, and choosing between AM and FM stations). Various radios may implement these operations differently—some provide push buttons, some provide dials and some support voice commands. The interface specifies *what* operations a radio permits users to perform but does not specify *how* the operations are implemented inside the radio.

Similarly, the **interface of a class** describes *what* services a class's clients can use and how to *request* those services, but not *how* the class carries out the services. A class's public interface consists of the class's public member functions (also known as the class's **public services**). For example, class GradeBook's interface (Fig. 3.9) contains a constructor and member functions setCourseName, getCourseName and displayMessage. GradeBook's clients (e.g., main in Fig. 3.10) *use* these functions to request the class's services. As you'll soon see, you can specify a class's interface by writing a class definition that lists *only* the member-function names, return types and parameter types.

Separating the Interface from the Implementation

In our prior examples, each class definition contained the complete definitions of the class's public member functions and the declarations of its private data members. However, it's better software engineering to define member functions *outside* the class definition, so that their implementation details can be *hidden* from the client code. This practice *ensures* that you do not write client code that depends on the class's implementation details.

The program of Figs. 3.11–3.13 separates class GradeBook's interface from its implementation by splitting the class definition of Fig. 3.9 into two files—the header GradeBook.h (Fig. 3.11) in which class GradeBook is defined, and the source-code file GradeBook.cpp (Fig. 3.12) in which GradeBook's member functions are defined. By convention, member-function definitions are placed in a source-code file of the same base name (e.g., GradeBook) as the class's header but with a .cpp filename extension. The source-code file fig03_13.cpp (Fig. 3.13) defines function main (the client code). The code and output of Fig. 3.13 are identical to that of Fig. 3.10. Figure 3.14 shows how this three-file program is compiled from the perspectives of the GradeBook class programmer and the client-code programmer—we'll explain this figure in detail.

GradeBook.h: Defining a Class's Interface with Function Prototypes

Header GradeBook.h (Fig. 3.11) contains another version of GradeBook's class definition (lines 8–17). This version is similar to the one in Fig. 3.9, but the function definitions in Fig. 3.9 are replaced here with **function prototypes** (lines 11–14) that *describe the class's* *public interface without revealing the class's member-function implementations.* A function prototype is a *declaration* of a function that tells the compiler the function's name, its return type and the types of its parameters. Also, the header still specifies the class's private data member (line 16) as well. Again, the compiler *must* know the data members of the class to determine how much memory to reserve for each object of the class. Including the header GradeBook.h in the client code (line 5 of Fig. 3.13) provides the compiler with the information it needs to ensure that the client code calls the member functions of class GradeBook correctly.

```
1   // Fig. 3.11: GradeBook.h
2   // GradeBook class definition. This file presents GradeBook's public
3   // interface without revealing the implementations of GradeBook's member
4   // functions, which are defined in GradeBook.cpp.
5   #include <string> // class GradeBook uses C++ standard string class
6
7   // GradeBook class definition
8   class GradeBook
9   {
10  public:
11     explicit GradeBook( std::string ); // constructor initialize courseName
12     void setCourseName( std::string ); // sets the course name
13     std::string getCourseName() const; // gets the course name
14     void displayMessage() const; // displays a welcome message
15  private:
16     std::string courseName; // course name for this GradeBook
17  }; // end class GradeBook
```

Fig. 3.11 | GradeBook class definition containing function prototypes that specify the interface of the class.

The function prototype in line 11 (Fig. 3.11) indicates that the constructor requires one string parameter. Recall that constructors don't have return types, so no return type appears in the function prototype. Member function setCourseName's function prototype indicates that setCourseName requires a string parameter and does not return a value (i.e., its return type is void). Member function getCourseName's function prototype indicates that the function does not require parameters and returns a string. Finally, member function displayMessage's function prototype (line 14) specifies that displayMessage does not require parameters and does not return a value. These function prototypes are the same as the first lines of the corresponding function definitions in Fig. 3.9, except that the parameter names (which are *optional* in prototypes) are not included and each function prototype *must* end with a semicolon.

Good Programming Practice 3.2

Although parameter names in function prototypes are optional (they're ignored by the compiler), many programmers use these names for documentation purposes.

GradeBook.cpp: *Defining Member Functions in a Separate Source-Code File*
Source-code file GradeBook.cpp (Fig. 3.12) *defines* class GradeBook's member functions, which were *declared* in lines 11–14 of Fig. 3.11. The definitions appear in lines 9–33 and

are nearly identical to the member-function definitions in lines 11–35 of Fig. 3.9. Note that the const keyword *must* appear in *both* the function prototypes (Fig. 3.11, lines13–14) and the function definitions for functions getCourseName and display-Message (lines 22 and 28).

```cpp
// Fig. 3.12: GradeBook.cpp
// GradeBook member-function definitions. This file contains
// implementations of the member functions prototyped in GradeBook.h.
#include <iostream>
#include "GradeBook.h" // include definition of class GradeBook
using namespace std;

// constructor initializes courseName with string supplied as argument
GradeBook::GradeBook( string name )
   : courseName( name ) // member initializer to initialize courseName
{
   // empty body
} // end GradeBook constructor

// function to set the course name
void GradeBook::setCourseName( string name )
{
   courseName = name; // store the course name in the object
} // end function setCourseName

// function to get the course name
string GradeBook::getCourseName() const
{
   return courseName; // return object's courseName
} // end function getCourseName

// display a welcome message to the GradeBook user
void GradeBook::displayMessage() const
{
   // call getCourseName to get the courseName
   cout << "Welcome to the grade book for\n" << getCourseName()
      << "!" << endl;
} // end function displayMessage
```

Fig. 3.12 | GradeBook member-function definitions represent the implementation of class GradeBook.

Each member-function name (lines 9, 16, 22 and 28) is preceded by the class name and ::, which is known as the **scope resolution operator**. This "ties" each member function to the (now separate) GradeBook class definition (Fig. 3.11), which declares the class's member functions and data members. Without "GradeBook::" preceding each function name, these functions would *not* be recognized by the compiler as member functions of class Grade-Book—the compiler would consider them "free" or "loose" functions, like main. These are also called *global functions*. Such functions cannot access GradeBook's private data or call the class's member functions, without specifying an object. So, the compiler would *not* be able to compile these functions. For example, lines 18 and 24 in Fig. 3.12 that access variable courseName would cause compilation errors because courseName is not declared as a local variable in each function—the compiler would not know that `courseName` is already declared as a data member of class `GradeBook`.

 Common Programming Error 3.3

When defining a class's member functions outside that class, omitting the class name and scope resolution operator (::) preceding the function names causes errors.

To indicate that the member functions in `GradeBook.cpp` are part of class `GradeBook`, we must first include the `GradeBook.h` header (line 5 of Fig. 3.12). This allows us to access the class name `GradeBook` in the `GradeBook.cpp` file. When compiling `GradeBook.cpp`, the compiler uses the information in `GradeBook.h` to ensure that

1. the first line of each member function (lines 9, 16, 22 and 28) matches its prototype in the `GradeBook.h` file—for example, the compiler ensures that `getCourseName` accepts no parameters and returns a `string`, and that

2. each member function knows about the class's data members and other member functions—for example, lines 18 and 24 can access variable `courseName` because it's declared in `GradeBook.h` as a data member of class `GradeBook`, and line 31 can call function `getCourseName`, because it's declared as a member function of the class in `GradeBook.h` (and because the call conforms with the corresponding prototype).

Testing Class GradeBook

Figure 3.13 performs the same `GradeBook` object manipulations as Fig. 3.10. Separating `GradeBook`'s interface from the implementation of its member functions does *not* affect the way that this client code uses the class. It affects only how the program is compiled and linked, which we discuss in detail shortly.

```
1   // Fig. 3.13: fig03_13.cpp
2   // GradeBook class demonstration after separating
3   // its interface from its implementation.
4   #include <iostream>
5   #include "GradeBook.h" // include definition of class GradeBook
6   using namespace std;
7
8   // function main begins program execution
9   int main()
10  {
11     // create two GradeBook objects
12     GradeBook gradeBook1( "CS101 Introduction to C++ Programming" );
13     GradeBook gradeBook2( "CS102 Data Structures in C++" );
14
15     // display initial value of courseName for each GradeBook
16     cout << "gradeBook1 created for course: " << gradeBook1.getCourseName()
17        << "\ngradeBook2 created for course: " << gradeBook2.getCourseName()
18        << endl;
19  } // end main
```

Fig. 3.13 | GradeBook class demonstration after separating its interface from its implementation. (Part 1 of 2.)

```
gradeBook1 created for course: CS101 Introduction to C++ Programming
gradeBook2 created for course: CS102 Data Structures in C++
```

Fig. 3.13 | GradeBook class demonstration after separating its interface from its implementation. (Part 2 of 2.)

As in Fig. 3.10, line 5 of Fig. 3.13 includes the GradeBook.h header so that the compiler can ensure that GradeBook objects are created and manipulated correctly in the client code. Before executing this program, the source-code files in Fig. 3.12 and Fig. 3.13 must both be compiled, then linked together—that is, the member-function calls in the client code need to be tied to the implementations of the class's member functions—a job performed by the linker.

The Compilation and Linking Process

The diagram in Fig. 3.14 shows the compilation and linking process that results in an executable GradeBook application that can be used by instructors. Often a class's interface and implementation will be created and compiled by one programmer and used by a separate programmer who implements the client code that uses the class. So, the diagram shows what's required by both the class-implementation programmer and the client-code programmer. The dashed lines in the diagram show the pieces required by the class-implementation programmer, the client-code programmer and the GradeBook application user, respectively. [*Note:* Figure 3.14 is *not* a UML diagram.]

A class-implementation programmer responsible for creating a reusable GradeBook class creates the header GradeBook.h and the source-code file GradeBook.cpp that #includes the header, then compiles the source-code file to create GradeBook's object code. To hide the class's member-function implementation details, the class-implementation programmer would provide the client-code programmer with the header GradeBook.h (which specifies the class's interface and data members) and the GradeBook object code (i.e., the machine code instructions that represent GradeBook's member functions). The client-code programmer is *not* given GradeBook.cpp, so the client remains unaware of how GradeBook's member functions are implemented.

The client code programmer needs to know only GradeBook's interface to use the class and must be able to link its object code. Since the interface of the class is part of the class definition in the GradeBook.h header, the client-code programmer must have access to this file and must #include it in the client's source-code file. When the client code is compiled, the compiler uses the class definition in GradeBook.h to ensure that the main function creates and manipulates objects of class GradeBook correctly.

To create the executable GradeBook application, the last step is to link

1. the object code for the main function (i.e., the client code),

2. the object code for class GradeBook's member-function implementations and

3. the C++ Standard Library object code for the C++ classes (e.g., string) used by the class-implementation programmer and the client-code programmer.

The linker's output is the *executable* GradeBook application that instructors can use to manage their students' grades. Compilers and IDEs typically invoke the linker for you after compiling your code.

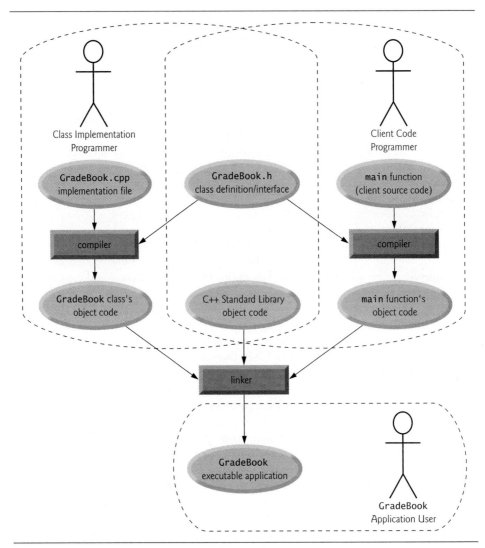

Fig. 3.14 | Compilation and linking process that produces an executable application.

For further information on compiling multiple-source-file programs, see your compiler's documentation. We provide links to various C++ compilers in our C++ Resource Center at www.deitel.com/cplusplus/.

3.8 Validating Data with *set* Functions

In Section 3.4, we introduced *set* functions for allowing clients of a class to modify the value of a private data member. In Fig. 3.5, class GradeBook defines member function set-CourseName to simply assign a value received in its parameter name to data member courseName. This member function does not ensure that the course name adheres to any particular format or follows any other rules regarding what a "valid" course name looks like. Suppose that a university can print student transcripts containing course names of only 25 characters or less. If the university uses a system containing GradeBook objects to generate the transcripts, we might want class GradeBook to ensure that its data member courseName never contains more than 25 characters. The program of Figs. 3.15–3.17 enhances class GradeBook's member function setCourseName to perform this **validation** (also known as **validity checking**).

GradeBook *Class Definition*

GradeBook's class definition (Fig. 3.15)—and hence, its interface—is identical to that of Fig. 3.11. Since the interface remains unchanged, clients of this class need not be changed when the definition of member function setCourseName is modified. This enables clients to take advantage of the improved GradeBook class simply by linking the client code to the updated GradeBook's object code.

```
 1   // Fig. 3.15: GradeBook.h
 2   // GradeBook class definition presents the public interface of
 3   // the class. Member-function definitions appear in GradeBook.cpp.
 4   #include <string> // program uses C++ standard string class
 5
 6   // GradeBook class definition
 7   class GradeBook
 8   {
 9   public:
10      explicit GradeBook( std::string ); // constructor initialize courseName
11      void setCourseName( std::string ); // sets the course name
12      std::string getCourseName() const; // gets the course name
13      void displayMessage() const; // displays a welcome message
14   private:
15      std::string courseName; // course name for this GradeBook
16   }; // end class GradeBook
```

Fig. 3.15 | GradeBook class definition presents the `public` interface of the class.

Validating the Course Name with GradeBook *Member Function* setCourseName

The changes to class GradeBook are in the definitions of the constructor (Fig. 3.16, lines 9–12) and setCourseName (lines 16–29). Rather than using a member initializer, the constructor now calls setCourseName. In general, *all* data members should be initialized with *member initializers*. However, sometimes a constructor must also *validate* its argument(s)—often, this is handled in the constructor's body (line 11). The call to setCourse-Name *validates* the constructor's argument and *sets* the data member courseName. Initially, courseName's value will be set to the empty string *before* the constructor's body executes, then setCourseName will *modify* courseName's value.

In setCourseName, the if statement in lines 18–19 determines whether parameter name contains a *valid* course name (i.e., a string of 25 or fewer characters). If the course name is valid, line 19 stores it in data member courseName. Note the expression name.size() in line 18. This is a member-function call just like myGradeBook.display-Message(). The C++ Standard Library's string class defines a member function **size** that returns the number of characters in a string object. Parameter name is a string object, so the call `name.size()` returns the number of characters in `name`. If this value is less than or equal to 25, `name` is valid and line 19 executes.

```cpp
1   // Fig. 3.16: GradeBook.cpp
2   // Implementations of the GradeBook member-function definitions.
3   // The setCourseName function performs validation.
4   #include <iostream>
5   #include "GradeBook.h" // include definition of class GradeBook
6   using namespace std;
7
8   // constructor initializes courseName with string supplied as argument
9   GradeBook::GradeBook( string name )
10  {
11     setCourseName( name ); // validate and store courseName
12  } // end GradeBook constructor
13
14  // function that sets the course name;
15  // ensures that the course name has at most 25 characters
16  void GradeBook::setCourseName( string name )
17  {
18     if ( name.size() <= 25 ) // if name has 25 or fewer characters
19        courseName = name; // store the course name in the object
20
21     if ( name.size() > 25 ) // if name has more than 25 characters
22     {
23        // set courseName to first 25 characters of parameter name
24        courseName = name.substr( 0, 25 ); // start at 0, length of 25
25
26        cerr << "Name \"" << name << "\" exceeds maximum length (25).\n"
27           << "Limiting courseName to first 25 characters.\n" << endl;
28     } // end if
29  } // end function setCourseName
30
31  // function to get the course name
32  string GradeBook::getCourseName() const
33  {
34     return courseName; // return object's courseName
35  } // end function getCourseName
36
37  // display a welcome message to the GradeBook user
38  void GradeBook::displayMessage() const
39  {
40     // call getCourseName to get the courseName
41     cout << "Welcome to the grade book for\n" << getCourseName()
42        << "!" << endl;
43  } // end function displayMessage
```

Fig. 3.16 | Member-function definitions for class `GradeBook` with a *set* function that validates the length of data member `courseName`.

The `if` statement in lines 21–28 handles the case in which `setCourseName` receives an *invalid* course name (i.e., a name that is more than 25 characters long). Even if parameter name is too long, we still want to leave the `GradeBook` object in a **consistent state**—that is, a state in which the object's data member courseName contains a valid value (i.e., a string of 25 characters or less). Thus, we truncate the specified course name and assign the first 25 characters of name to the courseName data member (unfortunately, this could truncate the course name awkwardly). Standard class string provides member function **substr** (short for "substring") that returns a new string object created by copying part of an existing string object. The call in line 24 (i.e., name.substr(0, 25)) passes two integers (0 and 25) to name's member function substr. These arguments indicate the portion of the string name that substr should return. The first argument specifies the *starting position* in the original string from which characters are copied—the first character in every string is considered to be at position 0. The second argument specifies the *number of characters to copy*. Therefore, the call in line 24 returns a 25-character substring of name starting at position 0 (that is, the first 25 characters in name). For example, if name holds the value "CS101 Introduction to Programming in C++", substr returns "CS101 Introduction to Pro". After the call to substr, line 24 assigns the substring returned by substr to data member courseName. In this way, setCourseName ensures that courseName is always assigned a string containing 25 or fewer characters. If the member function has to truncate the course name to make it valid, lines 26–27 display a warning message using cerr, as mentioned in Chapter 1.

The if statement in lines 21–28 contains two body statements—one to set the courseName to the first 25 characters of parameter name and one to print an accompanying message to the user. Both statements should execute when name is too long, so we place them in a pair of braces, { }. Recall from Chapter 2 that this creates a *block*. You'll learn more about placing multiple statements in a control statement's body in Chapter 4.

The statement in lines 26–27 could also appear without a stream insertion operator at the start of the second line of the statement, as in:

```
cerr << "Name \"" << name << "\" exceeds maximum length (25).\n"
        "Limiting courseName to first 25 characters.\n" << endl;
```

The C++ compiler combines adjacent string literals, even if they appear on separate lines of a program. Thus, in the statement above, the C++ compiler would combine the string literals "\" exceeds maximum length (25).\n" and "Limiting courseName to first 25 characters.\n" into a single string literal that produces output identical to that of lines 26–27 in Fig. 3.16. This behavior allows you to print lengthy strings by breaking them across lines in your program without including additional stream insertion operations.

Testing Class *GradeBook*

Figure 3.17 demonstrates the modified version of class GradeBook (Figs. 3.15–3.16) featuring validation. Line 12 creates a GradeBook object named gradeBook1. Recall that the GradeBook constructor calls setCourseName to initialize data member courseName. In previous versions of the class, the benefit of calling setCourseName in the constructor was not evident. Now, however, *the constructor takes advantage of the validation* provided by setCourseName. The constructor simply calls setCourseName, *rather than duplicating* its validation code. When line 12 of Fig. 3.17 passes an initial course name of "CS101 Introduction to Programming in C++" to the GradeBook constructor, the constructor passes this value to setCourseName, where the actual initialization occurs. Because this course name contains more than 25 characters, the body of the second if statement executes, causing courseName to be initialized to the truncated 25-character course name "CS101 Introduction to Pro" (the truncated part is highlighted in line 12). The output in Fig. 3.17 contains the warning message output by lines 26–27 of Fig. 3.16 in member function setCourseName. Line 13 creates another GradeBook object called gradeBook2—the valid course name passed to the constructor is exactly 25 characters.

```
1   // Fig. 3.17: fig03_17.cpp
2   // Create and manipulate a GradeBook object; illustrate validation.
3   #include <iostream>
4   #include "GradeBook.h" // include definition of class GradeBook
5   using namespace std;
6
7   // function main begins program execution
8   int main()
9   {
10      // create two GradeBook objects;
11      // initial course name of gradeBook1 is too long
12      GradeBook gradeBook1( "CS101 Introduction to Programming in C++" );
13      GradeBook gradeBook2( "CS102 C++ Data Structures" );
14
15      // display each GradeBook's courseName
16      cout << "gradeBook1's initial course name is: "
17         << gradeBook1.getCourseName()
18         << "\ngradeBook2's initial course name is: "
19         << gradeBook2.getCourseName() << endl;
20
21      // modify gradeBook1's courseName (with a valid-length string)
22      gradeBook1.setCourseName( "CS101 C++ Programming" );
23
24      // display each GradeBook's courseName
25      cout << "\ngradeBook1's course name is: "
26         << gradeBook1.getCourseName()
27         << "\ngradeBook2's course name is: "
28         << gradeBook2.getCourseName() << endl;
29   } // end main
```

```
Name "CS101 Introduction to Programming in C++" exceeds maximum length (25).
Limiting courseName to first 25 characters.

gradeBook1's initial course name is: CS101 Introduction to Pro
gradeBook2's initial course name is: CS102 C++ Data Structures

gradeBook1's course name is: CS101 C++ Programming
gradeBook2's course name is: CS102 C++ Data Structures
```

Fig. 3.17 | Creating and manipulating a GradeBook object in which the course name is limited to 25 characters in length.

Lines 16–19 of Fig. 3.17 display the truncated course name for gradeBook1 (we highlight this in blue in the program output) and the course name for gradeBook2. Line 22 calls gradeBook1's setCourseName member function directly, to change the course name in the `GradeBook` object to a shorter name that does not need to be truncated. Then, lines 25–28 output the course names for the `GradeBook` objects again.

Additional Notes on Set *Functions*

A `public` *set* function such as `setCourseName` should carefully scrutinize any attempt to modify the value of a data member (e.g., `courseName`) to ensure that the new value is appropriate for that data item. For example, an attempt to *set* the day of the month to 37 should be rejected, an attempt to *set* a person's weight to zero or a negative value should be rejected, an attempt to *set* a grade on an exam to 185 (when the proper range is zero to 100) should be rejected, and so on.

Software Engineering Observation 3.3

Making data members `private` *and controlling access, especially write access, to those data members through* `public` *member functions helps ensure data integrity.*

Error-Prevention Tip 3.4

The benefits of data integrity are not automatic simply because data members are made `private`*—you must provide appropriate validity checking and report the errors.*

A *set* function could return a value indicating that an attempt was made to assign invalid data to an object of the class. A client could then test the return value of the *set* function to determine whether the attempt to modify the object was successful and to take appropriate action if not. We will do that in later chapters after we introduce a bit more programming technology. In C++, clients of objects also can be notified of problems via the *exception-handling mechanism*, which we begin discussing in Chapter 7 and present in-depth in Chapter 17.

3.9 Wrap-Up

In this chapter, you created user-defined classes, and created and used objects of those classes. We declared data members of a class to maintain data for each object of the class. We also defined member functions that operate on that data. You learned that member functions that do not modify a class's data should be declared `const`. We showed how to call an object's member functions to request the services the object provides and how to pass data to those member functions as arguments. We discussed the difference between a local variable of a member function and a data member of a class. We also showed how to use a constructor and a member-initializer list to ensure that every object is initialized properly. You learned that a single-parameter constructor should be declared `explicit`, and that a constructor cannot be declared `const` because it modifies the object being initialized. We demonstrated how to separate the interface of a class from its implementation to promote good software engineering. You learned that `using` directives and `using` declarations should never be placed in headers. We presented a diagram that shows the files that class-implementation programmers and client-code programmers need to compile the code they write. We demonstrated how *set* functions can be used to validate an object's data and ensure that objects are maintained in a consistent state. UML class diagrams were used to model classes and their constructors, member functions and data members. In the next chapter, we begin our introduction to control statements, which specify the order in which a function's actions are performed.

Summary

Section 3.2 Defining a Class with a Member Function

- A class definition (p. 102) contains the data members and member functions that define the class's attributes and behaviors, respectively.

- A class definition begins with the keyword class followed immediately by the class name.

- By convention, the name of a user-defined class (p. 103) begins with a capital letter and, for readability, each subsequent word in the class name begins with a capital letter.

- Every class's body (p. 102) is enclosed in a pair of braces ({ and }) and ends with a semicolon.

- Member functions that appear after access specifier public (p. 102) can be called by other functions in a program and by member functions of other classes.

- Access specifiers are always followed by a colon (:).

- Keyword void (p. 103) is a special return type which indicates that a function will perform a task but will not return any data to its calling function when it completes its task.

- By convention, function names (p. 103) begin with a lowercase first letter and all subsequent words in the name begin with a capital letter.

- An empty set of parentheses after a function name indicates that the function does not require additional data to perform its task.

- A function that does not, and should not, modify the object on which it's called should be declared const.

- Typically, you cannot call a member function until you create an object of its class.

- Each new class you create becomes a new type in C++.

- In the UML, each class is modeled in a class diagram (p. 104) as a rectangle with three compartments, which (top to bottom) contain the class's name, attributes and operations, respectively.

- The UML models operations as the operation name followed by parentheses. A plus sign (+) preceding the name indicates a public operation (i.e., a public member function in C++).

Section 3.3 Defining a Member Function with a Parameter

- A member function can require one or more parameters (p. 104) that represent additional data it needs to perform its task. A function call supplies an argument (p. 105) for each function parameter.

- A member function is called by following the object name with a dot (.) operator (p. 104), the function name and a set of parentheses containing the function's arguments.

- A variable of C++ Standard Library class string (p. 106) represents a string of characters. This class is defined in header <string>, and the name string belongs to namespace std.

- Function getline (from header <string>, p. 106) reads characters from its first argument until a newline character is encountered, then places the characters (not including the newline) in the string variable specified as its second argument. The newline character is discarded.

- A parameter list (p. 107) may contain any number of parameters, including none at all (represented by empty parentheses) to indicate that a function does not require any parameters.

- The number of arguments in a function call must match the number of parameters in the parameter list of the called member function's header. Also, the argument types in the function call must be consistent with the types of the corresponding parameters in the function header.

- The UML models a parameter of an operation by listing the parameter name, followed by a colon and the parameter type between the parentheses following the operation name.

- The UML has its own data types. Not all the UML data types have the same names as the corresponding C++ types. The UML type String corresponds to the C++ type string.

Section 3.4 Data Members, set Member Functions and get Member Functions

- Variables declared in a function's body are local variables (p. 108) and can be used only from the point of their declaration to the closing right brace (}) of the block in which they are declared.

- A local variable must be declared before it can be used in a function. A local variable cannot be accessed outside the function in which it's declared.

- Data members (p. 108) normally are private (p. 110). Variables or functions declared private are accessible only to member functions of the class in which they're declared, or to friends of the class.

- When a program creates (instantiates) an object, its private data members are encapsulated (hidden, p. 110) in the object and can be accessed only by member functions of the object's class (or by "friends" of the class, as you'll see in Chapter 9).

- When a function that specifies a return type other than void is called and completes its task, the function returns a result to its calling function.

- By default, the initial value of a string is the empty string (p. 111)—i.e., a string that does not contain any characters. Nothing appears on the screen when an empty string is displayed.

- A class often provides public member functions to allow the class's clients to *set* or *get* (p. 112) private data members. The names of these member functions normally begin with *set* or *get*.

- *Set* and *get* functions allow clients of a class to indirectly access the hidden data. The client does not know how the object performs these operations.

- A class's *set* and *get* functions should be used by other member functions of the class to manipulate the class's private data. If the class's data representation is changed, member functions that access the data only via the *set* and *get* functions will not require modification.

- A public *set* function should carefully scrutinize any attempt to modify the value of a data member to ensure that the new value is appropriate for that data item.

- The UML represents data members as attributes by listing the attribute name, followed by a colon and the attribute type. Private attributes are preceded by a minus sign (-) in the UML.

- The UML indicates the return type of an operation by placing a colon and the return type after the parentheses following the operation name.

- UML class diagrams do not specify return types for operations that do not return values.

Section 3.5 Initializing Objects with Constructors

- Each class should provide one or more constructors (p. 113) to initialize an object of the class when the object is created. A constructor must be defined with the same name as the class.

- A difference between constructors and functions is that constructors cannot return values, so they cannot specify a return type (not even void). Normally, constructors are declared public.

- C++ automatically calls a constructor for each object that's created, which helps ensure that objects are initialized properly before they're used in a program.

- A constructor with no parameters is a default constructor (p. 114). If you do not provide a constructor, the compiler provides a default constructor. You can also define a default constructor explicitly. If you define any constructors for a class, C++ will not create a default constructor.

- A single-parameter constructor should be declared explicit.

- A constructor uses a member initializer list to initialize a class's data members. Member initializers appear between a constructor's parameter list and the left brace that begins the constructor's body. The member initializer list is separated from the parameter list with a colon (:). A member initializer consists of a data member's variable name followed by parentheses containing the member's initial value. You can perform initialization in the constructor's body, but you'll learn later in the book that it's more efficient to do it with member initializers, and some types of data members must be initialized this way.

- The UML models constructors as operations in a class diagram's third compartment with the word "constructor" between guillemets (« and ») before the constructor's name.

Section 3.6 Placing a Class in a Separate File for Reusability

- Class definitions, when packaged properly, can be reused by programmers worldwide.
- It's customary to define a class in a header (p. 117) that has a .h filename extension.

Section 3.7 Separating Interface from Implementation

- If the class's implementation changes, the class's clients should not be required to change.
- Interfaces define and standardize the ways in which things such as people and systems interact.
- A class's public interface (p. 121) describes the public member functions that are made available to the class's clients. The interface describes *what* services (p. 121) clients can use and how to *request* those services, but does not specify *how* the class carries out the services.
- Separating interface from implementation (p. 121) makes programs easier to modify. Changes in the class's implementation do not affect the client as long as the class's interface remains unchanged.
- You should never place using directives and using declarations in headers.
- A function prototype (p. 121) contains a function's name, its return type and the number, types and order of the parameters the function expects to receive.
- Once a class is defined and its member functions are declared (via function prototypes), the member functions should be defined in a separate source-code file.
- For each member function defined outside of its corresponding class definition, the function name must be preceded by the class name and the scope resolution operator (::, p. 123).

Section 3.8 Validating Data with set Functions

- Class string's size member function (p. 127) returns the number of characters in a string.
- Class string's member function substr (p. 129) returns a new string containing a copy of part of an existing string. The first argument specifies the starting position in the original string. The second specifies the number of characters to copy.

Self-Review Exercises

3.1 Fill in the blanks in each of the following:
   a) A _____ variable must be declared before it can be used in a function.
   b) Function _____ reads characters from its first argument until a newline character is encountered.
   c) The UML models constructors as operations in a class diagram's third compartment with the word "_____" between guillemets (« and ») before the constructor's name.
   d) A _____ *set* function should carefully scrutinize any attempt to modify the value of a data member to ensure that the new value is appropriate for that data item.
   e) You should never place using directives and using declarations in _____.
   f) An _____ after a function name indicates that the function does not require additional data to perform its task.
   g) _____ define and standardize the ways in which things such as people and systems interact.
   h) A constructor with no parameters is a _____ constructor. If you do not provide a constructor, the compiler provides a _____.

i) A function _____ contains a function's name, its return type and the number, types and order of the parameters the function expects to receive.

3.2   State whether each of the following is *true* or *false*. If *false*, explain why.
  a) By convention, class names begin with a capital letter and all subsequent words in the name begin with a capital letter.
  b) A class definition begins with the keyword class followed immediately by the class name.
  c) A function that does not, and should not, modify the object on which it's called should be declared const.
  d) A class often provides public member functions to allow the class's clients to *set* or *get* private data members.
  e) UML class diagrams do specify return types for operations that do not return values.
  f) A single-parameter constructor should be declared implicit.
  g) Class string's size member function returns the number of characters in a string.

3.3   What is the use of a function parameter list?

3.4   Explain the purpose of local variables.

Answers to Self-Review Exercises

3.1   a) local. b) getline. c) constructor. d) public. e) headers. f) empty set of parentheses. g) Interfaces. h) default, default constructor i) prototype.

3.2   a) True. b) True. c) True. d) True. e) False, UML class diagrams do not specify return types for operations that do not return values. f) False, A single-parameter constructor should be declared explicit. g) True.

3.3   To specify in a function definition that the function requires data to perform its task, you place additional information in the function's parameter list, which is located in the parentheses following the function name. The parameter list may contain any number of parameters, including none at all to indicate that a function does not require any parameters.

3.4   Variables declared in a function definition's body are known as local variables and can be used only from the line of their declaration in the function to the closing right brace (}) of the block in which they're declared.

Exercises

3.5   *(Private Access Specifier)* What are the different uses of private access specifiers?

3.6   *(Mutators and Accessors)* Explain what is meant by the client of an object. What are mutators and accessors?

3.7   *(Data Hiding)* Explain the purpose of data hiding.

3.8   *(Scope Resolution Operator)* What is a scope resolution operator? Briefly explain the various uses of these operators.

3.9   *(Using a Class Without a using Directive)* Explain how a program could use class string without inserting a using directive.

3.10   *(Driver Program)* What is the use of a driver program?

3.11   *(Modifying Class GradeBook)* Modify class GradeBook (Figs. 3.11–3.12) as follows:
   a) Include a second string data member that represents the course instructor's name.
   b) Provide a *set* function to change the instructor's name and a *get* function to retrieve it.
   c) Modify the constructor to specify course name and instructor name parameters.
   d) Modify function displayMessage to output the welcome message and course name, then the string "This course is presented by: " followed by the instructor's name.

Use your modified class in a test program that demonstrates the class's new capabilities.

3.12   *(Account Class)* Create an Account class that a bank might use to represent customers' bank accounts. Include a data member of type int to represent the account balance. [*Note:* In subsequent chapters, we'll use numbers that contain decimal points (e.g., 2.75)—called floating-point values—to represent dollar amounts.] Provide a constructor that receives an initial balance and uses it to initialize the data member. The constructor should validate the initial balance to ensure that it's greater than or equal to 0. If not, set the balance to 0 and display an error message indicating that the initial balance was invalid. Provide three member functions. Member function credit should add an amount to the current balance. Member function debit should withdraw money from the Account and ensure that the debit amount does not exceed the Account's balance. If it does, the balance should be left unchanged and the function should print a message indicating "Debit amount exceeded account balance." Member function getBalance should return the current balance. Create a program that creates two Account objects and tests the member functions of class Account.

3.13   *(Invoice Class)* Create a class called Invoice that a hardware store might use to represent an invoice for an item sold at the store. An Invoice should include four data members—a part number (type string), a part description (type string), a quantity of the item being purchased (type int) and a price per item (type int). [*Note:* In subsequent chapters, we'll use numbers that contain decimal points (e.g., 2.75)—called floating-point values—to represent dollar amounts.] Your class should have a constructor that initializes the four data members. A constructor that receives multiple arguments is defined with the form:

   ClassName(TypeName1 parameterName1, TypeName2 parameterName2, ...)

Provide a *set* and a *get* function for each data member. In addition, provide a member function named getInvoiceAmount that calculates the invoice amount (i.e., multiplies the quantity by the price per item), then returns the amount as an int value. If the quantity is not positive, it should be set to 0. If the price per item is not positive, it should be set to 0. Write a test program that demonstrates class Invoice's capabilities.

3.14   *(Employee Class)* Create a class called Employee that includes three pieces of information as data members—a first name (type string), a last name (type string) and a monthly salary (type int). [*Note:* In subsequent chapters, we'll use numbers that contain decimal points (e.g., 2.75)—called floating-point values—to represent dollar amounts.] Your class should have a constructor that initializes the three data members. Provide a *set* and a *get* function for each data member. If the monthly salary is not positive, set it to 0. Write a test program that demonstrates class Employee's capabilities. Create two Employee objects and display each object's *yearly* salary. Then give each Employee a 10 percent raise and display each Employee's yearly salary again.

3.15   *(Date Class)* Create a class called Date that includes three pieces of information as data members—a month (type int), a day (type int) and a year (type int). Your class should have a constructor with three parameters that uses the parameters to initialize the three data members. For the purpose of this exercise, assume that the values provided for the year and day are correct, but ensure that the month value is in the range 1–12; if it isn't, set the month to 1. Provide a *set* and a *get* function for each data member. Provide a member function displayDate that displays the month, day and year separated by forward slashes (/). Write a test program that demonstrates class `Date`'s capabilities.

Making a Difference

3.16   *(Target-Heart-Rate Calculator)* While exercising, you can use a heart-rate monitor to see that your heart rate stays within a safe range suggested by your trainers and doctors. According to the American Heart Association (AHA) (`www.americanheart.org/presenter.jhtml?identifier=4736`), the formula for calculating your *maximum heart rate* in beats per minute is 220 minus your age in years. Your *target heart rate* is a range that is 50–85% of your maximum heart rate. [Note: *These formulas are estimates provided by the AHA. Maximum and target heart rates may vary based on the health, fitness and gender of the individual. Always consult a physician or qualified health care professional before beginning or modifying an exercise program.*] Create a class called `HeartRates`. The class attributes should include the person's first name, last name and date of birth (consisting of separate attributes for the month, day and year of birth). Your class should have a constructor that receives this data as parameters. For each attribute provide *set* and *get* functions. The class also should include a function `getAge` that calculates and returns the person's age (in years), a function `getMaxiumumHeartRate` that calculates and returns the person's maximum heart rate and a function `getTargetHeartRate` that calculates and returns the person's target heart rate. Since you do not yet know how to obtain the current date from the computer, function `getAge` should prompt the user to enter the current month, day and year before calculating the person's age. Write an application that prompts for the person's information, instantiates an object of class `HeartRates` and prints the information from that object—including the person's first name, last name and date of birth—then calculates and prints the person's age in (years), maximum heart rate and target-heart-rate range.

3.17   *(Computerization of Health Records)* A health care issue that has been in the news lately is the computerization of health records. This possibility is being approached cautiously because of sensitive privacy and security concerns, among others. [We address such concerns in later exercises.] Computerizing health records could make it easier for patients to share their health profiles and histories among their various health care professionals. This could improve the quality of health care, help avoid drug conflicts and erroneous drug prescriptions, reduce costs and in emergencies, could save lives. In this exercise, you'll design a "starter" `HealthProfile` class for a person. The class attributes should include the person's first name, last name, gender, date of birth (consisting of separate attributes for the month, day and year of birth), height (in inches) and weight (in pounds). Your class should have a constructor that receives this data. For each attribute, provide *set* and *get* functions. The class also should include functions that calculate and return the user's age in years, maximum heart rate and target-heart-rate range (see Exercise 3.16), and body mass index (BMI; see Exercise 2.30). Write an application that prompts for the person's information, instantiates an object of class `HealthProfile` for that person and prints the information from that object—including the person's first name, last name, gender, date of birth, height and weight—then calculates and prints the person's age in years, BMI, maximum heart rate and target-heart-rate range. It should also display the "BMI values" chart from Exercise 2.30. Use the same technique as Exercise 3.16 to calculate the person's age.

4

Control Statements: Part 1; Assignment, ++ and -- Operators

Let's all move one place on.
—Lewis Carroll

The wheel is come full circle.
—William Shakespeare

All the evolution we know of proceeds from the vague to the definite.
—Charles Sanders Peirce

Objectives

In this chapter you'll learn:

- Basic problem-solving techniques.

- To develop algorithms through the process of top-down, stepwise refinement.

- To use the `if` and `if...else` selection statements to choose among alternative actions.

- To use the `while` repetition statement to execute statements in a program repeatedly.

- Counter-controlled repetition and sentinel-controlled repetition.

- To use the increment, decrement and assignment operators.

4.1 Introduction

Before writing a program to solve a problem, we must have a thorough understanding of the problem and a carefully planned approach to solving it. When writing a program, we must also understand the available building blocks and employ proven program construction techniques. In this chapter and in Chapter 5, Control Statements: Part 2; Logical Operators, we discuss these issues as we present the theory and principles of *structured programming*. The concepts presented here are crucial to building effective classes and manipulating objects.

In this chapter, we introduce C++'s if, if...else and while statements, three of the building blocks that allow you to specify the logic required for member functions to perform their tasks. We devote a portion of this chapter (and Chapters 5–7) to further developing the GradeBook class. In particular, we add a member function to the GradeBook class that uses control statements to calculate the average of a set of student grades. Another example demonstrates additional ways to combine control statements. We introduce C++'s assignment, increment and decrement operators. These additional operators abbreviate and simplify many program statements.

4.2 Algorithms

Any solvable computing problem can be solved by executing a series of actions in a specific order. A **procedure** for solving a problem in terms of

1. the **actions** to execute and
2. the **order** in which the actions execute

is called an **algorithm**. The following example demonstrates that correctly specifying the order in which the actions execute is important.

Consider the "rise-and-shine algorithm" followed by one junior executive for getting out of bed and going to work: (1) Get out of bed, (2) take off pajamas, (3) take a shower, (4) get dressed, (5) eat breakfast, (6) carpool to work. This routine gets the executive to work prepared to make critical decisions. Suppose the same steps are performed in a different order: (1) Get out of bed, (2) take off pajamas, (3) get dressed, (4) take a shower, (5) eat breakfast, (6) carpool to work. In this case, our junior executive shows up for work soaking wet. Specifying the order in which statements (actions) execute is called **program control**. This chapter investigates program control using C++'s **control statements**.

4.3 Pseudocode

Pseudocode (or "fake" code) is an artificial and informal language that helps you develop algorithms without having to worry about the details of C++ language syntax. The pseudocode we present is helpful for developing algorithms that will be converted to structured C++ programs. Pseudocode is similar to everyday English; it's convenient and user friendly, although it isn't an actual computer programming language.

Pseudocode does *not* execute on computers. Rather, it helps you "think out" a program before attempting to write it in a programming language, such as C++.

The style of pseudocode we present consists purely of characters, so you can type pseudocode conveniently, using any editor program. A carefully prepared pseudocode program can easily be converted to a corresponding C++ program. In many cases, this simply requires replacing pseudocode statements with C++ equivalents.

Pseudocode normally describes only **executable statements**, which cause specific actions to occur after you convert a program from pseudocode to C++ and the program is compiled and run on a computer. Declarations (that do not have initializers or do not involve constructor calls) are *not* executable statements. For example, the declaration

```
int counter;
```

tells the compiler the type of variable `counter` and instructs the compiler to reserve space in memory for the variable. This declaration does *not* cause any action—such as input, output or a calculation—to occur when the program executes. We typically do not include variable declarations in our pseudocode. Some programmers choose to list variables and mention their purposes at the beginning of pseudocode programs.

Let's look at an example of pseudocode that may be written to help a programmer create the addition program of Fig. 2.5. This pseudocode (Fig. 4.1) corresponds to the algorithm that inputs two integers from the user, adds these integers and displays their sum. We show the complete pseudocode listing here—we'll show how to *create pseudocode from a problem statement* later in the chapter.

Lines 1–2 correspond to the statements in lines 13–14 of Fig. 2.5. Notice that the pseudocode statements are simply English statements that convey what task is to be performed in C++. Likewise, lines 4–5 correspond to the statements in lines 16–17 of Fig. 2.5 and lines 7–8 correspond to the statements in lines 19 and 21 of Fig. 2.5.

---

1   *Prompt the user to enter the first integer*
2   *Input the first integer*
3
4   *Prompt the user to enter the second integer*
5   *Input the second integer*
6
7   *Add first integer and second integer, store result*
8   *Display result*

Fig. 4.1 | Pseudocode for the addition program of Fig. 2.5.

4.4 **Control Structures**

Normally, statements in a program execute one after the other in the order in which they're written. This is called **sequential execution**. Various C++ statements we'll soon discuss enable you to specify that *the next statement to execute may be other than the next one in sequence*. This is called **transfer of control**.

During the 1960s, it became clear that the indiscriminate use of transfers of control was the root of much difficulty experienced by software development groups. Blame was pointed at the **goto statement**, which allows you to specify a transfer of control to one of a wide range of possible destinations in a program (creating what's often called "spaghetti code"). The notion of so-called **structured programming** became almost synonymous with "**goto elimination**."

The research of Böhm and Jacopini[1] demonstrated that programs could be written *without* any goto statements. It became the challenge of the era for programmers to shift their styles to "goto-less programming." It was not until the 1970s that programmers started taking structured programming seriously. The results have been impressive, as software development groups have reported reduced development times, more frequent on-time delivery of systems and more frequent within-budget completion of software projects. The key to these successes is that structured programs are clearer, easier to debug, test and modify and more likely to be bug-free in the first place.

Böhm and Jacopini's work demonstrated that all programs could be written in terms of only three **control structures**, namely, the **sequence structure**, the **selection structure** and the **repetition structure**. The term "control structures" comes from the field of computer science. When we introduce C++'s implementations of control structures, we'll refer to them in the terminology of the C++ standard document as "control statements."

Sequence Structure in C++
The *sequence structure* is built into C++. Unless directed otherwise, the computer executes C++ statements one after the other in the order in which they're written—that is, in sequence. The UML **activity diagram** of Fig. 4.2 illustrates a typical sequence structure in

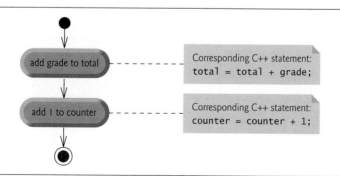

Fig. 4.2 | Sequence-structure activity diagram.

---

1. Böhm, C., and G. Jacopini, "Flow Diagrams, Turing Machines, and Languages with Only Two Formation Rules," *Communications of the ACM*, Vol. 9, No. 5, May 1966, pp. 366–371.

which two calculations are performed in order. C++ allows you to have as many actions as you want in a sequence structure. As you'll soon see, anywhere a *single action* may be placed, you may place *several actions in sequence*.

In this figure, the two statements add a grade to a `total` variable and add the value 1 to a `counter` variable. Such statements might appear in a program that *averages* several student grades. To calculate an average, the *total of the grades* being averaged is divided by the *number of grades*. A counter variable would be used to keep track of the number of values being averaged. You'll see similar statements in the program of Section 4.8.

An activity diagram models the **workflow** (also called the **activity**) of a portion of a software system. Such workflows may include a portion of an algorithm, such as the sequence structure in Fig. 4.2. Activity diagrams are composed of special-purpose symbols, such as **action state symbols** (a rectangle with its left and right sides replaced with arcs curving outward), **diamonds** and **small circles**; these symbols are connected by **transition arrows**, which represent the flow of the activity.

Activity diagrams clearly show how control structures operate. Consider the sequence-structure activity diagram of Fig. 4.2. It contains two **action states** that represent actions to perform. Each action state contains an **action expression**—e.g., "add grade to total" or "add 1 to counter"—that specifies a particular action to perform. Other actions might include calculations or input/output operations. The arrows in the activity diagram are called **transition arrows**. These arrows represent **transitions**, which indicate the *order* in which the actions represented by the action states occur—the program that implements the activities illustrated by the activity diagram in Fig. 4.2 first adds `grade` to `total`, then adds `1` to `counter`.

The **solid circle** at the top of the diagram represents the activity's **initial state**—the *beginning* of the workflow *before* the program performs the modeled activities. The solid circle surrounded by a hollow circle that appears at the bottom of the activity diagram represents the **final state**—the *end* of the workflow *after* the program performs its activities.

Figure 4.2 also includes rectangles with the upper-right corners folded over. These are called **notes** in the UML—explanatory remarks that describe the purpose of symbols in the diagram. Figure 4.2 uses UML notes to show the C++ code associated with each action state in the activity diagram. A **dotted line** connects each note with the element that the note describes. Activity diagrams normally do not show the C++ code that implements the activity. We use notes for this purpose here to illustrate how the diagram relates to C++ code. For more information on the UML, see our optional (but strongly recommended) case study, which appears in Chapters 25–26, and visit our UML Resource Center at www.deitel.com/UML/.

Selection Statements in C++

C++ provides three types of selection statements (discussed in this chapter and Chapter 5). The `if` selection statement either performs (selects) an action if a condition is true or skips the action if the condition is false. The `if...else` selection statement performs an action if a condition is true or performs a different action if the condition is false. The `switch` selection statement (Chapter 5) performs one of *many* different actions, depending on the value of an integer expression.

The `if` selection statement is a **single-selection statement** because it selects or ignores a *single action* (or, as you'll soon see, a *single group of actions*). The `if...else` statement is called a **double-selection statement** because it selects between two different actions (or groups of actions). The `switch` selection statement is called a **multiple-selection statement** because it selects among many different actions (or groups of actions).

Repetition Statements in C++

C++ provides three types of repetition statements (also called **looping statements** or **loops**) for performing statements repeatedly while a condition (called the **loop-continuation condition**) remains true. These are the `while`, `do…while` and `for` statements. (Chapter 5 presents the do…while and for statements, and Chapter 7 presents a specialized version of the for statement that's used with so-called arrays and containers.) The while and for statements perform the action (or group of actions) in their bodies zero or more times— if the loop-continuation condition is initially false, the action (or group of actions) will *not* execute. The do…while statement performs the action (or group of actions) in its body *at least once*.

Each of the words `if`, `else`, `switch`, `while`, `do` and `for` is a C++ keyword. Keywords *cannot* be used as identifiers, such as variable names, and must be spelled with only lower-case letters. Figure 4.3 provides a complete list of C++ keywords.

C++ Keywords

Keywords common to the C and C++ programming languages

auto	break	case	char	const
continue	default	do	double	else
enum	extern	float	for	goto
if	int	long	register	return
short	signed	sizeof	static	struct
switch	typedef	union	unsigned	void
volatile	while			

C++-only keywords

and	and_eq	asm	bitand	bitor
bool	catch	class	compl	const_cast
delete	dynamic_cast	explicit	export	false
friend	inline	mutable	namespace	new
not	not_eq	operator	or	or_eq
private	protected	public	reinterpret_cast	static_cast
template	this	throw	true	try
typeid	typename	using	virtual	wchar_t
xor	xor_eq			

C++11 keywords

alignas	alignof	char16_t	char32_t	constexpr
decltype	noexcept	nullptr	static_assert	thread_local

Fig. 4.3 | C++ keywords.

Summary of Control Statements in C++

C++ has only three kinds of control structures, which from this point forward we refer to as control statements: the sequence statement, selection statements (three types—if, if...else and switch) and repetition statements (three types—while, for and do...while). Each program combines as many of each of these control statements as appropriate for the algorithm the program implements. We can model each control statement as an activity diagram with initial and final states representing that control statement's entry and exit points, respectively. These **single-entry/single-exit control statements** make it easy to build programs—control statements are attached to one another by connecting the exit point of one to the entry point of the next. This is similar to the way a child stacks building blocks, so we call this **control-statement stacking.** You'll see that there's only one other way to connect control statements—called **control-statement nesting**, in which one control statement is contained *inside* another.

Software Engineering Observation 4.1

Any C++ program can be constructed from only seven different types of control statements (sequence, if, if...else, switch, while, do...while and for) combined in only two ways (control-statement stacking and control-statement nesting).

4.5 if Selection Statement

Programs use selection statements to choose among alternative courses of action. For example, suppose the passing grade on an exam is 60. The pseudocode statement

> *If student's grade is greater than or equal to 60*
>   *Print "Passed"*

determines whether the condition "student's grade is greater than or equal to 60" is true or false. If the condition is true, "Passed" is printed and the next pseudocode statement in order is "performed" (remember that pseudocode is not a real programming language). If the condition is false, the print statement is ignored and the next pseudocode statement in order is performed. The indentation of the second line is optional, but it's recommended because it emphasizes the inherent structure of structured programs.

The preceding pseudocode *If* statement can be written in C++ as

```
if ( grade >= 60 )
    cout << "Passed";
```

The C++ code corresponds closely to the pseudocode. This is one of the properties of pseudocode that make it such a useful program development tool.

It's important to note here that we're casually assuming that grade contains a valid value—an integer in the range 0 to 100. Throughout the book, we'll introduce many important validation techniques.

Error-Prevention Tip 4.1

In industrial-strength code, always validate all inputs.

Figure 4.4 illustrates the single-selection if statement. It contains what is perhaps *the* most important symbol in an activity diagram—the diamond or **decision symbol**, which indicates that a *decision* is to be made. A decision symbol indicates that the workflow will continue along a path determined by the symbol's associated **guard conditions**, which can be true or false. Each transition arrow emerging from a decision symbol has a guard condition specified in *square brackets* above or next to the transition arrow. If a particular guard condition is true, the workflow enters the action state to which that transition arrow points. In Fig. 4.4, if the grade is greater than or equal to 60, the program prints "Passed" to the screen, then transitions to the final state of this activity. If the grade is less than 60, the program immediately transitions to the final state without displaying a message.

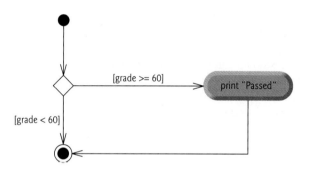

Fig. 4.4 | if single-selection statement activity diagram.

You saw in Chapter 2 that decisions can be based on conditions containing relational or equality operators. Actually, in C++, a decision can be based on *any* expression—if the expression evaluates to *zero*, it's treated as *false*; if the expression evaluates to *nonzero*, it's treated as true. C++ provides the data type **bool** for variables that can hold only the values **true** and **false**—each of these is a C++ keyword.

Portability Tip 4.1

For compatibility with earlier versions of C, which used integers for Boolean values, the bool *value* true *also can be represented by any* nonzero *value (compilers typically use 1) and the* bool *value* false *also can be represented as the value* zero.

The if statement is a *single-entry/single-exit* statement. We'll see that the activity diagrams for the remaining control statements also contain initial states, transition arrows, action states that indicate actions to perform, decision symbols (with associated guard conditions) that indicate decisions to be made and final states.

Envision seven bins, each containing only empty UML activity diagrams of one of the seven types of control statements. Your task, then, is assembling a program from the activity diagrams of as many of each type of control statement as the algorithm demands, combining the activity diagrams in only two possible ways (stacking or nesting), then filling in the action states and decisions with action expressions and guard conditions in a manner appropriate to form a structured implementation for the algorithm. We'll continue discussing the variety of ways in which actions and decisions may be written.

4.6 if...else Double-Selection Statement

The if single-selection statement performs an indicated action only when the condition is true; otherwise the action is skipped. The if...else double-selection statement allows you to specify an action to perform when the condition is true and a *different* action to perform when the condition is false. For example, the pseudocode statement

If student's grade is greater than or equal to 60
 Print "Passed"
Else
  Print "Failed"

prints "Passed" if the student's grade is greater than or equal to 60, but prints "Failed" if the student's grade is less than 60. In either case, after printing occurs, the next pseudocode statement in sequence is "performed."

The preceding pseudocode *If...Else* statement can be written in C++ as

```
if ( grade >= 60 )
   cout << "Passed";
else
   cout << "Failed";
```

The body of the else is also indented.

Good Programming Practice 4.1

If there are several levels of indentation, each level should be indented the same additional amount of space to promote readability and maintainability.

Figure 4.5 illustrates the the if...else statement's flow of control.

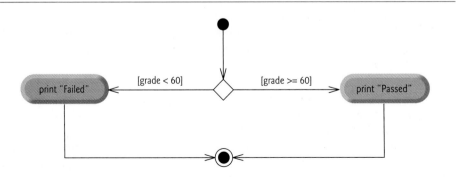

Fig. 4.5 | if...else double-selection statement activity diagram.

Conditional Operator (?:)

C++ provides the **conditional operator (?:)**, which is closely related to the if…else statement. The conditional operator is C++'s only **ternary operator**—it takes three operands. The operands, together with the conditional operator, form a **conditional expression**. The first operand is a condition, the second operand is the value for the entire conditional expression if the condition is true and the third operand is the value for the entire conditional expression if the condition is false. For example, the output statement

```
cout << ( grade >= 60 ? "Passed" : "Failed" );
```

contains a conditional expression, grade >= 60 ? "Passed" : "Failed", that evaluates to the string "Passed" if the condition grade >= 60 is true, but evaluates to "Failed" if the condition is false. Thus, the statement with the conditional operator performs essentially the same as the preceding if…else statement. As we'll see, the precedence of the conditional operator is low, so the parentheses in the preceding expression are required.

Error-Prevention Tip 4.2

To avoid precedence problems (and for clarity), place conditional expressions (that appear in larger expressions) in parentheses.

The values in a conditional expression also can be actions to execute. For example, the following conditional expression also prints "Passed" or "Failed":

```
grade >= 60 ? cout << "Passed" : cout << "Failed";
```

The preceding conditional expression is read, "If grade is greater than or equal to 60, then cout << "Passed"; otherwise, cout << "Failed"." This, too, is comparable to the preceding if…else statement. Conditional expressions can appear in some program locations where if…else statements cannot.

Nested if…else Statements

Nested if…else statements test for multiple cases by placing if…else selection statements *inside* other if…else selection statements. For example, the following pseudocode if…else statement prints A for exam grades greater than or equal to 90, B for grades in the range 80 to 89, C for grades in the range 70 to 79, D for grades in the range 60 to 69 and F for all other grades:

> *If student's grade is greater than or equal to 90*
>> *Print "A"*
> *Else*
>> *If student's grade is greater than or equal to 80*
>>> *Print "B"*
>> *Else*
>>> *If student's grade is greater than or equal to 70*
>>>> *Print "C"*
>>> *Else*
>>>> *If student's grade is greater than or equal to 60*
>>>>> *Print "D"*
>>>> *Else*
>>>>> *Print "F"*

This pseudocode can be written in C++ as

```
if ( studentGrade >= 90 ) // 90 and above gets "A"
   cout << "A";
else
   if ( studentGrade >= 80 ) // 80-89 gets "B"
      cout << "B";
   else
      if ( studentGrade >= 70 ) // 70-79 gets "C"
         cout << "C";
      else
         if ( studentGrade >= 60 ) // 60-69 gets "D"
            cout << "D";
         else // less than 60 gets "F"
            cout << "F";
```

If studentGrade is greater than or equal to 90, the first four conditions are true, but only the statement after the first test executes. Then, the program skips the else-part of the "outermost" if...else statement. Most programmers write the preceding statement as

```
if ( studentGrade >= 90 ) // 90 and above gets "A"
   cout << "A";
else if ( studentGrade >= 80 ) // 80-89 gets "B"
   cout << "B";
else if ( studentGrade >= 70 ) // 70-79 gets "C"
   cout << "C";
else if ( studentGrade >= 60 ) // 60-69 gets "D"
   cout << "D";
else // less than 60 gets "F"
   cout << "F";
```

The two forms are identical except for the spacing and indentation, which the compiler ignores. The latter form is popular because it avoids deep indentation of the code to the right, which can force lines to wrap.

Performance Tip 4.1

A nested if...else statement can perform much faster than a series of single-selection if statements because of the possibility of early exit after one of the conditions is satisfied.

Performance Tip 4.2

In a nested if...else statement, test the conditions that are more likely to be true at the beginning of the nested statement. This will enable the nested if...else statement to run faster by exiting earlier than if infrequently occurring cases were tested first.

Dangling-else Problem

The C++ compiler always associates an else with the *immediately preceding* if unless told to do otherwise by the placement of braces ({ and }). This behavior can lead to what's referred to as the **dangling-else** problem. For example,

```
if ( x > 5 )
   if ( y > 5 )
      cout << "x and y are > 5";
else
   cout << "x is <= 5";
```

appears to indicate that if x is greater than 5, the nested if statement determines whether y is also greater than 5. If so, "x and y are > 5" is output. Otherwise, it appears that if x is not greater than 5, the else part of the if...else outputs "x is <= 5".

Beware! This nested if...else statement does not execute as it appears. The compiler actually interprets the statement as

```
if ( x > 5 )
    if ( y > 5 )
        cout << "x and y are > 5";
    else
        cout << "x is <= 5";
```

in which the body of the first if is a nested if...else. The outer if statement tests whether x is greater than 5. If so, execution continues by testing whether y is also greater than 5. If the second condition is true, the proper string—"x and y are > 5"—is displayed. However, if the second condition is false, the string "x is <= 5" is displayed, even though we know that x is greater than 5.

To force the nested if...else statement to execute as originally intended, we can write it as follows:

```
if ( x > 5 )
{
    if ( y > 5 )
        cout << "x and y are > 5";
}
else
    cout << "x is <= 5";
```

The braces ({}) indicate to the compiler that the second if statement is in the body of the first if and that the else is associated with the first if. Exercises 4.23–4.24 further investigate the dangling-else problem.

Blocks

The if selection statement expects *only one* statement in its body. Similarly, the if and else parts of an if...else statement each expect *only one* body statement. To include *several* statements in the body of an if or in either part of an if...else, enclose the statements in braces ({ and }). A set of statements contained within a pair of braces is called a **compound statement** or a **block**. We use the term "block" from this point forward.

Software Engineering Observation 4.2

A block can be placed anywhere in a program that a single statement can be placed.

The following example includes a block in the else part of an if...else statement.

```
if ( studentGrade >= 60 )
    cout << "Passed.\n";
else
{
    cout << "Failed.\n";
    cout << "You must take this course again.\n";
}
```

In this case, if `studentGrade` is less than 60, the program executes *both* statements in the body of the `else` and prints

```
    Failed.
    You must take this course again.
```

Notice the braces surrounding the two statements in the `else` clause. These braces are important. Without the braces, the statement

```
    cout << "You must take this course again.\n";
```

would be *outside* the body of the `else` part of the `if` and would execute regardless of whether the grade was less than 60. This is a logic error.

Just as a block can be placed anywhere a single statement can be placed, it's also possible to have no statement at all, which is called a **null statement** or an **empty statement**. The null statement is represented by placing a semicolon (;) where a statement would normally be.

Common Programming Error 4.1

Placing a semicolon after the condition in an `if` statement leads to a logic error in single-selection `if` statements and a syntax error in double-selection `if…else` statements (when the `if` part contains an actual body statement).

4.7 `while` Repetition Statement

A **repetition statement** specifies that a program should repeat an action while some condition remains true. The pseudocode statement

> *While there are more items on my shopping list*
> *Purchase next item and cross it off my list*

describes the repetition that occurs during a shopping trip. The *condition*, "there are more items on my shopping list" is either true or false. If it's true, then the action, "Purchase next item and cross it off my list" is performed. This action will be performed repeatedly while the condition remains true. The statement contained in the *While* repetition statement constitutes the body of the *While*, which can be a single statement or a block. Eventually, the condition will become false (when the last item on the shopping list has been purchased and crossed off the list). At this point, the repetition terminates, and the first pseudocode statement after the repetition statement executes.

As an example of C++'s `while` repetition statement, consider a program segment designed to find the first power of 3 larger than 100. Suppose the integer variable `product` has been initialized to 3. When the following `while` repetition statement finishes executing, `product` contains the result:

```
    int product = 3;

    while ( product <= 100 )
        product = 3 * product;
```

When the `while` statement begins execution, `product`'s value is 3. Each repetition multiplies `product` by 3, so `product` takes on the values 9, 27, 81 and 243 successively. When `product` becomes 243, the `while` statement condition (`product <= 100`) becomes `false`.

This terminates the repetition, so the final value of product is 243. At this point, program execution continues with the next statement after the while statement.

Common Programming Error 4.2

A logic error called an **infinite loop**, *in which the repetition statement never terminates, occurs if you do not provide an action in a while statement's body that eventually causes the condition in the while to become false normally. This can make a program appear to "hang" or "freeze" if the loop body does not contain statements that interact with the user.*

The UML activity diagram of Fig. 4.6 illustrates the flow of control that corresponds to the preceding while statement. Once again, the symbols in the diagram (besides the initial state, transition arrows, a final state and three notes) represent an action state and a decision. This diagram also introduces the UML's **merge symbol**, which joins two flows of activity into one flow of activity. The UML represents *both* the merge symbol and the decision symbol as diamonds. In this diagram, the merge symbol joins the transitions from the initial state and from the action state, so they *both* flow into the decision that determines whether the loop should begin (or continue) executing. The decision and merge symbols can be distinguished by the number of "incoming" and "outgoing" transition arrows. A decision symbol has one transition arrow pointing *to* the diamond and two or more transition arrows pointing out *from* the diamond to indicate possible transitions from that point. In addition, each transition arrow pointing out of a decision symbol has a guard condition next to it. A merge symbol has two or more transition arrows pointing *to* the diamond and only one transition arrow pointing *from* the diamond, to indicate multiple activity flows merging to continue the activity. Unlike the decision symbol, the merge symbol does *not* have a counterpart in C++ code.

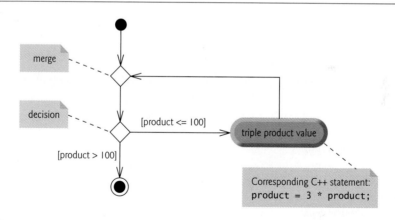

Fig. 4.6 | while repetition statement UML activity diagram.

The diagram of Fig. 4.6 clearly shows the repetition of the while statement discussed earlier in this section. The transition arrow emerging from the action state points to the merge, which transitions back to the decision that's tested each time through the loop until the guard condition product > 100 becomes true. Then the while statement exits (reaches its final state) and control passes to the next statement in sequence in the program.

Performance Tip 4.3
A small performance improvement for code that executes many times in a loop can result in substantial overall performance improvement.

4.8 Formulating Algorithms: Counter-Controlled Repetition

To illustrate how programmers develop algorithms, this section and Section 4.9 solve two variations of a class average problem. Consider the following problem statement:

A class of ten students took a quiz. The grades (0 to 100) for this quiz are available to you. Calculate and display the total of the grades and the class average.

The class average is equal to the sum of the grades divided by the number of students. The algorithm for solving this problem on a computer must input each of the grades, calculate the average and print the result.

Pseudocode Algorithm with Counter-Controlled Repetition

Let's use pseudocode to list the *actions* to execute and specify the *order* in which these actions should occur. We use **counter-controlled repetition** to input the grades one at a time. This technique uses a variable called a **counter** to control the number of times a group of statements will execute (also known as the number of **iterations** of the loop).

Counter-controlled repetition is often called **definite repetition** because the number of repetitions is known *before* the loop begins executing. In this example, repetition terminates when the counter exceeds 10. This section presents a fully developed pseudocode algorithm (Fig. 4.7) and a version of class GradeBook (Figs. 4.8–4.9) that implements the algorithm in a C++ member function. The section then presents an application (Fig. 4.10) that demonstrates the algorithm in action. In Section 4.9 we demonstrate how to use pseudocode to develop such an algorithm from scratch.

Software Engineering Observation 4.3
The most difficult part of solving a problem on a computer is developing the algorithm. Producing a working C++ program from the algorithm is typically straightforward.

```
1   Set total to zero
2   Set grade counter to one
3
4   While grade counter is less than or equal to ten
5       Prompt the user to enter the next grade
6       Input the next grade
7       Add the grade into the total
8       Add one to the grade counter
9
10  Set the class average to the total divided by ten
11  Print the total of the grades for all students in the class
12  Print the class average
```

Fig. 4.7 | Pseudocode for solving the class average problem with counter-controlled repetition.

Note the references in the pseudocode algorithm of Fig. 4.7 to a *total* and a *counter*. A **total** is a variable used to accumulate the sum of several values. A **counter** is a variable used to count—in this case, the grade counter indicates which of the 10 grades is about to be entered by the user. Variables that are used to store totals are normally initialized to zero before being used in a program; otherwise, the sum would include the previous value stored in the total's memory location. Recall from Chapter 2 that all variables should be initialized.

Enhancing *GradeBook* Validation

Let's consider an enhancement we made to class GradeBook. In Fig. 3.16, our setCourse-Name member function validated the course name by testing whether the course name's length was less than or equal to 25 characters, using an if statement. If this was true, the course name would be set. This code was followed by an if statement that tested whether the course name's length was larger than 25 characters (in which case the course name would be shortened). The second if statement's condition is the exact opposite of the first if statement's condition. If one condition evaluates to true, the other must evaluate to false. Such a situation is ideal for an if...else statement, so we've modified our code, replacing the two if statements with one if...else statement, as shown in lines 18–25 of Fig. 4.9).

Implementing *Counter-Controlled Repetition in Class* **GradeBook**

Class GradeBook (Figs. 4.8–4.9) contains a constructor (declared in line 10 of Fig. 4.8 and defined in lines 9–12 of Fig. 4.9) that assigns a value to the class's data member course-Name (declared in line 16 of Fig. 4.8). Lines 16–26, 29–32 and 35–39 of Fig. 4.9 define member functions setCourseName, getCourseName and displayMessage, respectively. Lines 42–64 define member function determineClassAverage, which implements the class average algorithm described by the pseudocode in Fig. 4.7.

```
 1   // Fig. 4.8: GradeBook.h
 2   // Definition of class GradeBook that determines a class average.
 3   // Member functions are defined in GradeBook.cpp
 4   #include <string> // program uses C++ standard string class
 5
 6   // GradeBook class definition
 7   class GradeBook
 8   {
 9   public:
10      explicit GradeBook( std::string ); // initializes course name
11      void setCourseName( std::string ); // set the course name
12      std::string getCourseName() const; // retrieve the course name
13      void displayMessage() const; // display a welcome message
14      void determineClassAverage() const; // averages user-entered grades
15   private:
16      std::string courseName; // course name for this GradeBook
17   }; // end class GradeBook
```

Fig. 4.8 | Class average problem using counter-controlled repetition: GradeBook header.

```cpp
1   // Fig. 4.9: GradeBook.cpp
2   // Member-function definitions for class GradeBook that solves the
3   // class average program with counter-controlled repetition.
4   #include <iostream>
5   #include "GradeBook.h" // include definition of class GradeBook
6   using namespace std;
7
8   // constructor initializes courseName with string supplied as argument
9   GradeBook::GradeBook( string name )
10  {
11     setCourseName( name ); // validate and store courseName
12  } // end GradeBook constructor
13
14  // function to set the course name;
15  // ensures that the course name has at most 25 characters
16  void GradeBook::setCourseName( string name )
17  {
18     if ( name.size() <= 25 ) // if name has 25 or fewer characters
19        courseName = name; // store the course name in the object
20     else // if name is longer than 25 characters
21     { // set courseName to first 25 characters of parameter name
22        courseName = name.substr( 0, 25 ); // select first 25 characters
23        cerr << "Name \"" << name << "\" exceeds maximum length (25).\n"
24           << "Limiting courseName to first 25 characters.\n" << endl;
25     } // end if...else
26  } // end function setCourseName
27
28  // function to retrieve the course name
29  string GradeBook::getCourseName() const
30  {
31     return courseName;
32  } // end function getCourseName
33
34  // display a welcome message to the GradeBook user
35  void GradeBook::displayMessage() const
36  {
37     cout << "Welcome to the grade book for\n" << getCourseName() << "!\n"
38        << endl;
39  } // end function displayMessage
40
41  // determine class average based on 10 grades entered by user
42  void GradeBook::determineClassAverage() const
43  {
44     // initialization phase
45     int total = 0; // sum of grades entered by user
46     unsigned int gradeCounter = 1; // number of grade to be entered next
47
48     // processing phase
49     while ( gradeCounter <= 10 ) // loop 10 times
50     {
51        cout << "Enter grade: "; // prompt for input
```

Fig. 4.9 | Class average problem using counter-controlled repetition: GradeBook source code file. (Part 1 of 2.)

```
52        int grade = 0; // grade value entered by user
53        cin >> grade; // input next grade
54        total = total + grade; // add grade to total
55        gradeCounter = gradeCounter + 1; // increment counter by 1
56    } // end while
57
58    // termination phase
59    int average = total / 10; // ok to mix declaration and calculation
60
61    // display total and average of grades
62    cout << "\nTotal of all 10 grades is " << total << endl;
63    cout << "Class average is " << average << endl;
64 } // end function determineClassAverage
```

Fig. 4.9 | Class average problem using counter-controlled repetition: GradeBook source code file. (Part 2 of 2.)

Because the gradeCounter variable (Fig. 4.9, line 46) is used to count from 1 to 10 in this program (all positive values), we declared the variable as an **unsigned int**, which can store only *non-negative* values (that is, 0 and higher). Local variables total (Fig. 4.9, line 45), grade (line 52) and average (line 59) to be of type int. Variable grade stores the user input. Notice that the preceding declarations appear in the body of member function determineClassAverage. Also, variable grade is declared in the while statement's body because it's used *only* in the loop—in general, variables should be declared just before they're used. We initialize grade to 0 (line 52) as a good practice, even though a new value is immediately input for grade in line 53.

Good Programming Practice 4.2
Declare each variable on a separate line with its own comment for readability.

In this chapter's versions of class GradeBook, we simply read and process a set of grades. The averaging calculation is performed in member function determineClass-Average using *local variables*—we do not preserve any information about student grades in the class's data members. In Chapter 7, we modify class GradeBook to maintain the grades in memory using a data member that refers to a data structure known as an *array*. This allows a GradeBook object to perform various calculations on a set of grades without requiring the user to enter the grades multiple times.

Lines 45–46 initialize total to 0 and gradeCounter to 1 before they're used in calculations. You'll normally initialize counter variables to zero or one, depending on how they are used in an algorithm. An uninitialized variable contains a "garbage" value (also called an **undefined value**)—the value last stored in the memory location reserved for that variable.

Error-Prevention Tip 4.3
Always initialize variables when they're declared. This helps you avoid logic errors that occur when you perform calculations with uninitialized variables.

Error-Prevention Tip 4.4
In some cases, compilers issue a warning *if you attempt to use an uninitialized variable's* value. You should always get a *clean compile* by resolving *all* errors and warnings.*

Line 49 indicates that the while statement should continue looping (also called iterating) as long as gradeCounter's value is less than or equal to 10. While this condition remains true, the while statement repeatedly executes the statements between the braces that delimit its body (lines 49–56).

Line 51 displays the prompt "Enter grade: ". This line corresponds to the pseudocode statement *"Prompt the user to enter the next grade."* Line 53 reads the grade entered by the user and assigns it to variable grade. This line corresponds to the pseudocode statement *"Input the next grade."* Line 54 adds the new grade entered by the user to the total and assigns the result to total, which *replaces* its previous value.

Line 55 adds 1 to gradeCounter to indicate that the program has processed the current grade and is ready to input the next grade from the user. Incrementing gradeCounter eventually causes gradeCounter to exceed 10. At that point the while loop terminates because its condition (line 49) becomes false.

When the loop terminates, line 59 performs the averaging calculation and assigns its result to the variable average. Line 62 displays the text "Total of all 10 grades is " followed by variable total's value. Line 63 then displays the text "Class average is " followed by variable average's value. Member function determineClassAverage then returns control to the calling function (i.e., main in Fig. 4.10).

Demonstrating Class **GradeBook**
Figure 4.10 contains this application's main function, which creates an object of class GradeBook and demonstrates its capabilities. Line 9 of Fig. 4.10 creates a new GradeBook object called myGradeBook. The string in line 9 is passed to the GradeBook constructor (lines 9–12 of Fig. 4.9). Line 11 of Fig. 4.10 calls myGradeBook's displayMessage member function to display a welcome message to the user. Line 12 then calls myGradeBook's determineClassAverage member function to allow the user to enter 10 grades, for which the member function then calculates and prints the average—the member function performs the algorithm shown in the pseudocode of Fig. 4.7.

```
1   // Fig. 4.10: fig04_10.cpp
2   // Create GradeBook object and invoke its determineClassAverage function.
3   #include "GradeBook.h" // include definition of class GradeBook
4
5   int main()
6   {
7      // create GradeBook object myGradeBook and
8      // pass course name to constructor
9      GradeBook myGradeBook( "CS101 C++ Programming" );
10
11     myGradeBook.displayMessage(); // display welcome message
12     myGradeBook.determineClassAverage(); // find average of 10 grades
13  } // end main
```

```
Welcome to the grade book for
CS101 C++ Programming
```

Fig. 4.10 | Class average problem using counter-controlled repetition: Creating a GradeBook object (Fig. 4.8–Fig. 4.9) and invoking its determineClassAverage member function. (Part 1 of 2.)

```
Enter grade: 67
Enter grade: 78
Enter grade: 89
Enter grade: 67
Enter grade: 87
Enter grade: 98
Enter grade: 93
Enter grade: 85
Enter grade: 82
Enter grade: 100

Total of all 10 grades is 846
Class average is 84
```

Fig. 4.10 | Class average problem using counter-controlled repetition: Creating a GradeBook object (Fig. 4.8–Fig. 4.9) and invoking its determineClassAverage member function. (Part 2 of 2.)

Notes on Integer Division and Truncation

The averaging calculation performed in response to the function call in line 12 of Fig. 4.10 produces an integer result. The sample execution indicates that the sum of the grade values is 846, which, when divided by 10, should yield 84.6—a number with a decimal point. However, the result of the calculation total / 10 (line 59 of Fig. 4.9) is the integer 84, because total and 10 are both integers. Dividing two integers results in integer division—any fractional part of the calculation is truncated (i.e., discarded). We'll see how to obtain a result that includes a decimal point from the averaging calculation in the next section.

Common Programming Error 4.3

Assuming that integer division rounds (rather than truncates) can lead to incorrect results. For example, 7 ÷ 4, yields 1.75 in conventional arithmetic, but truncates the floating-point part (.75) in integer arithmetic. So the result is 1. Similarly, −7 ÷ 4, yields −1.

In Fig. 4.9, if line 59 used gradeCounter rather than 10, the output for this program would display an incorrect value, 76. This would occur because in the final iteration of the while statement, gradeCounter was incremented to the value 11 in line 55.

Common Programming Error 4.4

Using a loop's counter control variable in a calculation after the loop often causes a common logic error called an off-by-one error. In a counter-controlled loop that counts up by one each time through the loop, the loop terminates when the counter's value is one higher than its last legitimate value (i.e., 11 in the case of counting from 1 to 10).

A Note About Arithmetic Overflow

In Fig. 4.9, line 54

```
total = total + grade; // add grade to total
```

added each grade entered by the user to the total. Even this simple statement has a *potential* problem—adding the integers could result in a value that's *too large* to store in an int variable. This is known as **arithmetic overflow** and causes *undefined behavior*, which can lead to unintended results (en.wikipedia.org/wiki/Integer_overflow#Security_ramifications). Figure 2.5's addition program had the same issue in line 19, which calculated the sum of two int values entered by the user:

```
sum = number1 + number2; // add the numbers; store result in sum
```

The maximum and minimum values that can be stored in an int variable are represented by the constants INT_MAX and INT_MIN, respectively, which are defined in the header <climits>. There are similar constants for the other integral types and for floating-point types. You can see your platform's values for these constants by opening the headers <climits> and <cfloat> in a text editor (you can search your file system for these files).

It's considered a good practice to ensure that *before* you perform arithmetic calculations like the ones in line 54 of Fig. 4.9 and line 19 of Fig. 2.5, they will *not* overflow. The code for doing this is shown on the CERT website www.securecoding.cert.org—just search for guideline "INT32-CPP." The code uses the && (logical AND) and || (logical OR) operators, which are introduced in Chapter 5. In industrial-strength code, you should perform checks like these for *all* calculations.

A Deeper Look at Receiving User Input

Any time a program receives input from the user various problems might occur. For example, in line 53 of Fig. 4.9

```
cin >> grade; // input next grade
```

we assume that the user will enter an integer grade in the range 0 to 100. However, the person entering a grade could enter, an integer less than 0, an integer greater than 100, an integer outside the range of values that can be stored in an int variable, a number containing a decimal point or a value containing letters or special symbols that's not even an integer.

To ensure that the user's input is valid, industrial-strength programs must test for all possible erroneous cases. As you progress through the book, you'll learn various techniques for dealing with the broad range of possible input problems.

4.9 Formulating Algorithms: Sentinel-Controlled Repetition

Let's generalize the class average problem. Consider the following problem:

> Develop a class average program that processes grades for an arbitrary *number of students each time it's run.*

In the previous example, the problem statement specified the number of students, so the number of grades (10) was known in advance. In this example, no indication is given of how many grades the user will enter during the program's execution. The program must process an *arbitrary* number of grades. How can the program determine when to stop the input of grades? How will it know when to calculate and print the class average?

To solve this problem, we can use a special value called a sentinel value (also called a signal value, a dummy value or a flag value) to indicate "end of data entry." After typing the legitimate grades, the user types the sentinel value to indicate that the last grade has been entered. Sentinel-controlled repetition is often called **indefinite repetition** because the number of repetitions is *not* known before the loop begins executing.

The sentinel value must be chosen so that it's not confused with an acceptable input value. Grades are normally nonnegative integers, so –1 is an acceptable sentinel value. Thus, a run of the program might process inputs such as 95, 96, 75, 74, 89 and –1. The program would then compute and print the class average for the grades 95, 96, 75, 74 and 89. Since –1 is the sentinel value, it should not enter into the averaging calculation.

Developing the Pseudocode Algorithm with Top-Down, Stepwise Refinement: The Top and First Refinement

We approach the class average program with a technique called **top-down, stepwise refinement**, a technique that's helpful to the development of well-structured programs. We begin with a pseudocode representation of the top—a single statement that conveys the overall function of the program:

> *Determine the class average for the quiz for an arbitrary number of students*

The top is, in effect, a *complete* representation of a program. Unfortunately, the top (as in this case) rarely conveys sufficient detail from which to write a program. So we now begin the refinement process. We divide the top into a series of smaller tasks and list these in the order in which they need to be performed. This results in the following **first refinement**.

> *Initialize variables*
> *Input, sum and count the quiz grades*
> *Calculate and print the total of all student grades and the class average*

This refinement uses only the sequence structure—these steps execute in order.

Software Engineering Observation 4.4
Each refinement, as well as the top itself, is a complete *specification of the algorithm; only the level of detail varies.*

Software Engineering Observation 4.5
Many programs can be divided logically into three phases: an initialization phase *that initializes the program variables, a* processing phase *that inputs data values and adjusts program variables (such as counters and totals) accordingly, and a* termination phase *that calculates and outputs the final results.*

Proceeding to the Second Refinement

The preceding *Software Engineering Observation* is often all you need for the first refinement in the top-down process. In the **second refinement**, we commit to specific variables. In this example, we need a running total of the numbers, a count of how many numbers have been processed, a variable to receive the value of each grade as it's entered by the user and a variable to hold the calculated average. The pseudocode statement

> *Initialize variables*

can be refined as follows:

> *Initialize total to zero*
> *Initialize counter to zero*

The pseudocode statement

> *Input, sum and count the quiz grades*

requires a repetition statement (i.e., a loop) that successively inputs each grade. We don't know in advance how many grades are to be processed, so we'll use **sentinel-controlled repetition**. The user enters legitimate grades one at a time. After entering the last legitimate grade, the user enters the sentinel value. The program tests for the sentinel value after each grade is input and terminates the loop when the user enters the sentinel value. The second refinement of the preceding pseudocode statement is then

> *Prompt the user to enter the first grade*
> *Input the first grade (possibly the sentinel)*
>
> *While the user has not yet entered the sentinel*
>   *Add this grade into the running total*
>   *Add one to the grade counter*
>   *Prompt the user to enter the next grade*
>   *Input the next grade (possibly the sentinel)*

In pseudocode, we do *not* use braces around the statements that form the body of the *While* structure. We simply *indent* the statements under the *While* to show that they belong to the *While*. Again, pseudocode is only an informal program development aid.

The pseudocode statement

> *Calculate and print the total of all student grades and the class average*

can be refined as follows:

> *If the counter is not equal to zero*
>   *Set the average to the total divided by the counter*
>   *Print the total of the grades for all students in the class*
>   *Print the class average*
> *else*
>   *Print "No grades were entered"*

We test for the possibility of *division by zero*—normally a **fatal logic error** that, if undetected, would cause the program to fail (often called "**crashing**"). The complete second refinement of the pseudocode for the class average problem is shown in Fig. 4.11.

 Common Programming Error 4.5
Dividing by zero cuases undefined behavior and normally causes a fatal runtime error.

---

1   *Initialize total to zero*
2   *Initialize counter to zero*
3
4   *Prompt the user to enter the first grade*
5   *Input the first grade (possibly the sentinel)*

Fig. 4.11 | Sentinel-controlled class average problem pseudocode algorithm.

```
 6
 7   While the user has not yet entered the sentinel
 8       Add this grade into the running total
 9       Add one to the grade counter
10       Prompt the user to enter the next grade
11       Input the next grade (possibly the sentinel)
12
13   If the counter is not equal to zero
14       Set the average to the total divided by the counter
15       Print the total of the grades for all students in the class
16       Print the class average
17   else
18       Print "No grades were entered"
```

Fig. 4.11 | Sentinel-controlled class average problem pseudocode algorithm.

Error-Prevention Tip 4.5

When performing division by an expression whose value could be zero, explicitly test for this possibility and handle it appropriately in your program (such as by printing an error message) rather than allowing the fatal error to occur. We'll say more about dealing with these kinds of errors when we discuss exception handling (Chapters 7, 9 and 17).

The pseudocode in Fig. 4.11 solves the more general class average problem. This algorithm required only two levels of refinement. Sometimes more levels are necessary.

Software Engineering Observation 4.6

Terminate the top-down, stepwise refinement process when the pseudocode algorithm is specified in sufficient detail for you to convert the pseudocode to C++. Typically, implementing the C++ program is then straightforward.

Software Engineering Observation 4.7

Many experienced programmers write programs without ever using program development tools like pseudocode. These programmers feel that their ultimate goal is to solve the problem on a computer and that using program development tools like pseudocode merely delays the production of final outputs. Although this method might work for simple and familiar problems, it can lead to serious difficulties in large, complex projects.

Implementing Sentinel-Controlled Repetition in Class *GradeBook*

Figures 4.12–4.13 show class GradeBook containing member function determineClass-Average that implements the pseudocode algorithm of Fig. 4.11 (this class is demonstrated in Fig. 4.14). Although each grade entered is an integer, the averaging calculation is likely to produce a number with a decimal point—in other words, a real number or floating-point number (e.g., 7.33, 0.0975 or 1000.12345). The type int cannot represent such a number, so this class must use another type to do so. C++ provides several data types for storing floating-point numbers in memory, including float and double. The primary difference between these types is that, compared to float variables, double variables can typically store numbers with larger magnitude and finer detail (i.e., more digits to the right of the decimal point—also known as the number's **precision**). This program introduces a special operator called a **cast operator** to *force* the averaging calculation to produce a floating-point numeric result.

```
1   // Fig. 4.12: GradeBook.h
2   // Definition of class GradeBook that determines a class average.
3   // Member functions are defined in GradeBook.cpp
4   #include <string> // program uses C++ standard string class
5
6   // GradeBook class definition
7   class GradeBook
8   {
9   public:
10     explicit GradeBook( std::string ); // initializes course name
11     void setCourseName( std::string ); // set the course name
12     std::string getCourseName() const; // retrieve the course name
13     void displayMessage() const; // display a welcome message
14     void determineClassAverage() const; // averages user-entered grades
15  private:
16     std::string courseName; // course name for this GradeBook
17  }; // end class GradeBook
```

Fig. 4.12 | Class average problem using sentinel-controlled repetition: GradeBook header.

```
1   // Fig. 4.13: GradeBook.cpp
2   // Member-function definitions for class GradeBook that solves the
3   // class average program with sentinel-controlled repetition.
4   #include <iostream>
5   #include <iomanip> // parameterized stream manipulators
6   #include "GradeBook.h" // include definition of class GradeBook
7   using namespace std;
8
9   // constructor initializes courseName with string supplied as argument
10  GradeBook::GradeBook( string name )
11  {
12     setCourseName( name ); // validate and store courseName
13  } // end GradeBook constructor
14
15  // function to set the course name;
16  // ensures that the course name has at most 25 characters
17  void GradeBook::setCourseName( string name )
18  {
19     if ( name.size() <= 25 ) // if name has 25 or fewer characters
20        courseName = name; // store the course name in the object
21     else // if name is longer than 25 characters
22     { // set courseName to first 25 characters of parameter name
23        courseName = name.substr( 0, 25 ); // select first 25 characters
24        cerr << "Name \"" << name << "\" exceeds maximum length (25).\n"
25           << "Limiting courseName to first 25 characters.\n" << endl;
26     } // end if...else
27  } // end function setCourseName
```

Fig. 4.13 | Class average problem using sentinel-controlled repetition: GradeBook source code file. (Part 1 of 3.)

```
28
29   // function to retrieve the course name
30   string GradeBook::getCourseName() const
31   {
32      return courseName;
33   } // end function getCourseName
34
35   // display a welcome message to the GradeBook user
36   void GradeBook::displayMessage() const
37   {
38      cout << "Welcome to the grade book for\n" << getCourseName() << "!\n"
39         << endl;
40   } // end function displayMessage
41
42   // determine class average based on 10 grades entered by user
43   void GradeBook::determineClassAverage() const
44   {
45      // initialization phase
46      int total = 0; // sum of grades entered by user
47      unsigned int gradeCounter = 0; // number of grades entered
48
49      // processing phase
50      // prompt for input and read grade from user
51      cout << "Enter grade or -1 to quit: ";
52      int grade = 0; // grade value
53      cin >> grade; // input grade or sentinel value
54
55      // loop until sentinel value read from user
56      while ( grade != -1 ) // while grade is not -1
57      {
58         total = total + grade; // add grade to total
59         gradeCounter = gradeCounter + 1; // increment counter
60
61         // prompt for input and read next grade from user
62         cout << "Enter grade or -1 to quit: ";
63         cin >> grade; // input grade or sentinel value
64      } // end while
65
66      // termination phase
67      if ( gradeCounter != 0 ) // if user entered at least one grade...
68      {
69         // calculate average of all grades entered
70         double average = static_cast< double >( total ) / gradeCounter;
71
72         // display total and average (with two digits of precision)
73         cout << "\nTotal of all " << gradeCounter << " grades entered is "
74            << total << endl;
75         cout << setprecision( 2 ) << fixed;
76         cout << "Class average is " << average << endl;
77      } // end if
```

Fig. 4.13 | Class average problem using sentinel-controlled repetition: GradeBook source code file. (Part 2 of 3.)

```
78          else // no grades were entered, so output appropriate message
79             cout << "No grades were entered" << endl;
80    } // end function determineClassAverage
```

Fig. 4.13 | Class average problem using sentinel-controlled repetition: GradeBook source code file. (Part 3 of 3.)

```
 1    // Fig. 4.14: fig04_14.cpp
 2    // Create GradeBook object and invoke its determineClassAverage function.
 3    #include "GradeBook.h" // include definition of class GradeBook
 4
 5    int main()
 6    {
 7       // create GradeBook object myGradeBook and
 8       // pass course name to constructor
 9       GradeBook myGradeBook( "CS101 C++ Programming" );
10
11       myGradeBook.displayMessage(); // display welcome message
12       myGradeBook.determineClassAverage(); // find average of 10 grades
13    } // end main
```

```
Welcome to the grade book for
CS101 C++ Programming

Enter grade or -1 to quit: 97
Enter grade or -1 to quit: 88
Enter grade or -1 to quit: 72
Enter grade or -1 to quit: -1

Total of all 3 grades entered is 257
Class average is 85.67
```

Fig. 4.14 | Class average problem using sentinel-controlled repetition: Creating a GradeBook object and invoking its determineClassAverage member function.

This example stacks control statements on top of one another—the while statement (lines 56–64 of Fig. 4.13) is immediately followed by an if...else statement (lines 67–79) in sequence. Much of the code in this program is identical to the code in Fig. 4.9, so we concentrate on the new features and issues.

Lines 46–47 initialize variables total and gradeCounter to 0, because no grades have been entered yet. Remember that this program uses sentinel-controlled repetition. To keep an accurate record of the number of grades entered, the program increments variable gradeCounter *only* when the user enters a grade value that is *not* the sentinel value and the program completes the processing of the grade. We declared and initialized variables grade (line 52) and average (line 70) where they are used. Notice that line 70 declares the variable average as type double. Recall that we used an int variable in the preceding example to store the class average. Using type double in the current example allows us to store the class average calculation's result as a floating-point number. Finally, notice that both input statements (lines 53 and 63) are preceded by an output statement that prompts the user for input.

Good Programming Practice 4.3

Prompt the user for each keyboard input. The prompt should indicate the form of the input and any special input values. In a sentinel-controlled loop, the prompts requesting data entry should explicitly remind the user what the sentinel value is.

Program Logic for Sentinel-Controlled Repetition vs. Counter-Controlled Repetition
Compare the program logic for sentinel-controlled repetition with that for counter-controlled repetition in Fig. 4.9. In counter-controlled repetition, each iteration of the `while` statement (lines 49–56 of Fig. 4.9) reads a value from the user, for the specified number of iterations. In sentinel-controlled repetition, the program reads the first value (lines 51–53 of Fig. 4.13) before reaching the `while`. This value determines whether the program's flow of control should enter the body of the `while`. If the condition is false, the user entered the sentinel value, so the body does not execute (i.e., no grades were entered). If, on the other hand, the condition is true, the body begins execution, and the loop adds the `grade` value to the `total` (line 58) and increments `gradeCounter` (line 59). Then lines 62–63 in the loop's body prompt for and input the next value from the user. Next, program control reaches the closing right brace (`}`) of the `while`'s body in line 64, so execution continues with the test of the `while`'s condition (line 56). The condition uses the most recent `grade` input by the user to determine whether the loop's body should execute again. The value of variable `grade` is always input from the user immediately before the program tests the `while` condition. This allows the program to determine whether the value *just input* is the sentinel value *before* the program processes that value (i.e., adds it to the `total` and increments `gradeCounter`). If the sentinel value is input, the loop terminates, and the program does not add the value –1 to the `total`.

After the loop terminates, the `if...else` statement (lines 67–79) executes. The condition in line 67 determines whether any grades were entered. If none were, the `else` part (lines 78–79) of the `if...else` statement executes and displays the message `"No grades were entered"` and the member function returns control to the calling function.

Notice the block in the `while` loop in Fig. 4.13. Without the braces, the last three statements in the body of the loop would fall outside the loop, causing the computer to interpret this code incorrectly, as follows:

```
// loop until sentinel value read from user
while ( grade != -1 )
   total = total + grade; // add grade to total
gradeCounter = gradeCounter + 1; // increment counter

// prompt for input and read next grade from user
cout << "Enter grade or -1 to quit: ";
cin >> grade;
```

This would cause an infinite loop in the program if the user did not input –1 for the first grade (in line 53).

Common Programming Error 4.6

Omitting the braces that delimit a block can lead to logic errors, such as infinite loops. To prevent this problem, some programmers enclose the body of every control statement in braces, even if the body contains only a single statement.

Floating-Point Number Precision and Memory Requirements
Variables of type `float` represent single-precision floating-point numbers and have approximately seven significant digits on most of today's systems. Variables of type `double` represent double-precision floating-point numbers. These require twice as much memory as `float` variables and provide approximately 15 significant digits on most of today's systems—approximately double the precision of `float` variables. Most programmers represent floating-point numbers with type `double`. In fact, C++ treats all floating-point numbers you type in a program's source code (such as 7.33 and 0.0975) as `double` values by default. Such values in the source code are known as *floating-point literals*. See Appendix C, Fundamental Types, for the ranges of values for `float`s and `double`s.

In conventional arithmetic, floating-point numbers often arise as a result of division—when we divide 10 by 3, the result is 3.3333333..., with the sequence of 3s repeating infinitely. The computer allocates only a *fixed* amount of space to hold such a value, so clearly the stored floating-point value can be only an *approximation*.

Common Programming Error 4.7
Using floating-point numbers in a manner that assumes they're represented exactly (e.g., using them in comparisons for equality) can lead to incorrect results. Floating-point numbers are represented only approximately.

Although floating-point numbers are not always 100 percent precise, they have numerous applications. For example, when we speak of a "normal" body temperature of 98.6 degrees Fahrenheit, we do not need to be precise to a large number of digits. When we read the temperature on a thermometer as 98.6, it may actually be 98.5999473210643. Calling this number simply 98.6 is fine for most applications involving body temperatures. Due to the imprecise nature of floating-point numbers, type `double` is preferred over type `float`, because `double` variables can represent floating-point numbers more accurately. For this reason, we use type `double` throughout the book.

Converting Between Fundamental Types Explicitly and Implicitly
The variable `average` is declared to be of type `double` (line 70 of Fig. 4.13) to capture the fractional result of our calculation. However, `total` and `gradeCounter` are both integer variables. Recall that dividing two integers results in integer division, in which any fractional part of the calculation is lost truncated). In the following statement:

```
double average = total / gradeCounter;
```

the division occurs *first*—the result's fractional part is lost *before* it's assigned to `average`. To perform a floating-point calculation with integers, we must create *temporary* floating-point values. C++ provides the **static_cast** operator to accomplish this task. Line 70 uses the cast operator `static_cast<double>(total)` to create a *temporary* floating-point copy of its operand in parentheses—`total`. Using a cast operator in this manner is called **explicit conversion**. The value stored in `total` is still an integer.

The calculation now consists of a floating-point value (the temporary `double` version of `total`) divided by the integer `gradeCounter`. The compiler knows how to evaluate *only* expressions in which the operand types are *identical*. To ensure that the operands are of the same type, the compiler performs an operation called **promotion** (also called **implicit conversion**) on selected operands. For example, in an expression containing values of data types `int` and `double`, C++ promotes `int` operands to `double` values. In our example, we are treating total as a double (by using the static_cast operator), so the compiler promotes gradeCounter to double, allowing the calculation to be performed—the result of the floating-point division is assigned to average. In Chapter 6, Functions and an Introduction to Recursion, we discuss all the fundamental data types and their order of promotion.

Cast operators are available for use with every data type and with class types as well. The static_cast operator is formed by following keyword static_cast with angle brackets (< and >) around a data-type name. The static_cast operator is a unary operator—an operator that takes only one operand. In Chapter 2, we studied the binary arithmetic operators. C++ also supports unary versions of the plus (+) and minus (-) operators, so that you can write such expressions as -7 or +5. Cast operators have higher precedence than other unary operators, such as unary + and unary -. This precedence is higher than that of the multiplicative operators *, / and %, and lower than that of parentheses. We indicate the cast operator with the notation static_cast<*type*>() in our precedence charts.

Formatting for Floating-Point Numbers

The formatting capabilities in Fig. 4.13 are discussed here briefly and explained in depth in Chapter 13, Stream Input/Output: A Deeper Look. The call to setprecision in line 75 (with an argument of 2) indicates that double variable average should be printed with *two* digits of precision to the right of the decimal point (e.g., 92.37). This call is referred to as a parameterized stream manipulator (because of the 2 in parentheses). Programs that use these calls must contain the preprocessing directive (line 5)

```
#include <iomanip>
```

The manipulator endl is a nonparameterized stream manipulator (because it isn't followed by a value or expression in parentheses) and does *not* require the <iomanip> header. If the precision is not specified, floating-point values are normally output with *six* digits of precision (i.e., the default precision on most of today's systems), although we'll see an exception to this in a moment.

The stream manipulator fixed (line 75) indicates that floating-point values should be output in so-called fixed-point format, as opposed to scientific notation. Scientific notation is a way of displaying a number as a floating-point number between the values of 1.0 and 10.0, multiplied by a power of 10. For instance, the value 3,100.0 would be displayed in scientific notation as 3.1×10^3. Scientific notation is useful when displaying values that are very large or very small. Formatting using scientific notation is discussed further in Chapter 13. Fixed-point formatting, on the other hand, is used to force a floating-point number to display a specific number of digits. Specifying fixed-point formatting also forces the decimal point and trailing zeros to print, even if the value is a whole number amount, such as 88.00. Without the fixed-point formatting option, such a value prints in C++ as 88 *without* the trailing zeros and *without* the decimal point. When the stream manipulators fixed and setprecision are used in a program, the *printed* value is rounded to the number of decimal positions indicated by the value passed to setprecision (e.g., the value 2 in line 75), although the value in memory remains unaltered. For example, the values 87.946 and 67.543 are output as 87.95 and 67.54, respectively. It's also possible to *force* a decimal point to appear by using stream manipulator showpoint. If showpoint is specified without fixed, then trailing zeros will not print. Like endl, stream manipulators fixed and showpoint do not use parameters, nor do they require the <iomanip> header. Both can be found in header <iostream>.

Lines 75 and 76 of Fig. 4.13 output the class average *rounded* to the nearest hundredth and with *exactly* two digits to the right of the decimal point. The parameterized stream manipulator (line 75) indicates that variable average's value should be displayed with *two* digits of precision to the right of the decimal point—as indicated by setprecision(2). The three grades entered during the execution of the program in Fig. 4.14 total 257, which yields the average 85.666... and prints with rounding as 85.67.

A Note About Unsigned Integers

In Fig. 4.9, line 46 declared the variable gradeCounter as an unsigned int because it can assume only the values from 1 through 11 (11 terminates the loop), which are all positive values. In general, counters that should store only non-negative values should be declared with unsigned types. Variables of unsigned integer types can represent values from 0 to approximately *twice the positive range* of the corresponding signed integer types. You can determine your platform's maximum unsigned int value with the constant UINT_MAX from <climits>.

Figure 4.9 could have also declared as unsigned int the variables grade, total and average. Grades are normally values from 0 to 100, so the total and average should each be greater than or equal to 0. We declared those variables as ints because we can't control what the user actually enters—the user could enter *negative* values. Worse yet, the user could enter a value that's not even a number. (We'll show how to deal with such erroneous inputs later in the book.)

Sometimes sentinel-controlled loops use *intentionally* invalid values to terminate a loop. For example, in line 56 of Fig. 4.13, we terminate the loop when the user enters the sentinel -1 (an invalid grade), so it would be improper to declare variable grade as an unsigned int. As you'll see, the end-of-file (EOF) indicator—which is introduced in the next chapter and is often used to terminate sentinel-controlled loops—is also normally implemented internally in the compiler as a negative number.

4.10 Formulating Algorithms: Nested Control Statements

For the next example, we once again formulate an algorithm by using pseudocode and top-down, stepwise refinement, and write a corresponding C++ program. We've seen that control statements can be *stacked* on top of one another (in sequence). Here, we examine the only other structured way control statements can be connected, namely, by nesting one control statement within another. Consider the following problem statement:

> *A college offers a course that prepares students for the state licensing exam for real estate brokers. Last year, ten of the students who completed this course took the exam. The college wants to know how well its students did on the exam. You've been asked to write a program to summarize the results. You've been given a list of these 10 students. Next to each name is written a 1 if the student passed the exam or a 2 if the student failed.*
>
> *Your program should analyze the results of the exam as follows:*
>
>   *1. Input each test result (i.e., a 1 or a 2). Display the prompting message "Enter result" each time the program requests another test result.*
>
>   *2. Count the number of test results of each type.*

   3. Display a summary of the test results indicating the number of students who passed and the number who failed.

   4. If more than eight students passed the exam, print the message "Bonus to instructor!"

After reading the problem statement carefully, we make the following observations:

1. The program must process test results for 10 students. A *counter-controlled loop* can be used because the number of test results is known in advance.

2. Each test result is a number—either a 1 or a 2. Each time the program reads a test result, the program must determine whether the number is a 1 or a 2. For simplicity, we test only for a 1 in our algorithm. If the number is not a 1, we assume that it's a 2. (Please be sure to do Exercise 4.20, which considers the consequences of this assumption.)

3. Two counters are used to keep track of the exam results—one to count the number of students who passed the exam and one to count the number of students who failed the exam.

4. After the program has processed all the results, it must decide whether more than eight students passed the exam.

Let's proceed with top-down, stepwise refinement. We begin with a pseudocode representation of the top:

> *Analyze exam results and decide whether a bonus should be paid*

Once again, it's important to emphasize that the top is a *complete* representation of the program, but several refinements are likely to be needed before the pseudocode evolves naturally into a C++ program.

Our first refinement is

> *Initialize variables*
> *Input the 10 exam results, and count passes and failures*
> *Display a summary of the exam results and decide whether a bonus should be paid*

Here, too, even though we have a *complete* representation of the entire program, further refinement is necessary. We now commit to specific variables. Counters are needed to record the passes and failures, a counter will be used to control the looping process and a variable is needed to store the user input.

The pseudocode statement

> *Initialize variables*

can be refined as follows:

> *Initialize passes to zero*
> *Initialize failures to zero*
> *Initialize student counter to one*

Notice that only the counters are initialized at the start of the algorithm.

The pseudocode statement

> *Input the 10 exam results, and count passes and failures*

requires a loop that successively inputs the result of each exam. Here it's known in advance that there are precisely 10 exam results, so counter-controlled looping is appropriate. Inside the loop (i.e., **nested** within the loop), an `if...else` statement will determine whether each exam result is a pass or a failure and will increment the appropriate counter. The refinement of the preceding pseudocode statement is then

> *While student counter is less than or equal to 10*
>   *Prompt the user to enter the next exam result*
>   *Input the next exam result*
>
>   *If the student passed*
>   *Add one to passes*
>   *Else*
>   *Add one to failures*
>
>   *Add one to student counter*

We use blank lines to isolate the *If...Else* control structure, which improves readability. The pseudocode statement

> *Display a summary of the exam results and decide whether a bonus should be paid*

can be refined as follows:

> *Display the number of passes*
> *Display the number of failures*
>
> *If more than eight students passed*
>   *Display "Bonus to instructor!"*

The complete second refinement appears in Fig. 4.15. Blank lines set off the *While* structure for readability. This pseudocode is now sufficiently refined for conversion to C++.

```
1   Initialize passes to zero
2   Initialize failures to zero
3   Initialize student counter to one
4
5   While student counter is less than or equal to 10
6       Prompt the user to enter the next exam result
7       Input the next exam result
8
9       If the student passed
10          Add one to passes
11      Else
12          Add one to failures
13
14      Add one to student counter
15
16  Display the number of passes
17  Display the number of failures
```

Fig. 4.15 | Pseudocode for examination-results problem. (Part 1 of 2.)

18	
19	*If more than eight students passed*
20	*Display "Bonus to instructor!"*

Fig. 4.15 | Pseudocode for examination-results problem. (Part 2 of 2.)

Conversion to Class Analysis

The program that implements the pseudocode algorithm is shown in Fig. 4.16. This example does not contain a class—it contains just a source code file with function main performing all the application's work. In this chapter and in Chapter 3, you've seen examples consisting of one class (including the header and source code files for this class), as well as another source code file testing the class. This source code file contained function main, which created an object of the class and called its member functions. Occasionally, when it does not make sense to try to create a *reusable* class to demonstrate a concept, we'll use an example contained entirely within the main function of a *single* source code file.

Lines 9–11 and 18 declare and initialize the variables used to process the examination results. Looping programs sometimes require initialization at the beginning of *each* repetition; such reinitialization would be performed by assignment statements rather than in declarations or by moving the declarations inside the loop bodies.

```
1   // Fig. 4.16: fig04_16.cpp
2   // Examination-results problem: Nested control statements.
3   #include <iostream>
4   using namespace std;
5
6   int main()
7   {
8      // initializing variables in declarations
9      unsigned int passes = 0; // number of passes
10     unsigned int failures = 0; // number of failures
11     unsigned int studentCounter = 1; // student counter
12
13     // process 10 students using counter-controlled loop
14     while ( studentCounter <= 10 )
15     {
16        // prompt user for input and obtain value from user
17        cout << "Enter result (1 = pass, 2 = fail): ";
18        int result = 0; // one exam result (1 = pass, 2 = fail)
19        cin >> result; // input result
20
21        // if...else nested in while
22        if ( result == 1 )          // if result is 1,
23           passes = passes + 1;     // increment passes;
24        else                        // else result is not 1, so
25           failures = failures + 1; // increment failures
26
27        // increment studentCounter so loop eventually terminates
28        studentCounter = studentCounter + 1;
29     } // end while
```

Fig. 4.16 | Examination-results problem: Nested control statements. (Part 1 of 2.)

```
30
31      // termination phase; display number of passes and failures
32      cout << "Passed " << passes << "\nFailed " << failures << endl;
33
34      // determine whether more than eight students passed
35      if ( passes > 8 )
36         cout << "Bonus to instructor!" << endl;
37   } // end main
```

```
Enter result (1 = pass, 2 = fail): 1
Enter result (1 = pass, 2 = fail): 2
Enter result (1 = pass, 2 = fail): 2
Enter result (1 = pass, 2 = fail): 1
Enter result (1 = pass, 2 = fail): 1
Enter result (1 = pass, 2 = fail): 1
Enter result (1 = pass, 2 = fail): 2
Enter result (1 = pass, 2 = fail): 1
Enter result (1 = pass, 2 = fail): 1
Enter result (1 = pass, 2 = fail): 2
Passed 6
Failed 4
```

```
Enter result (1 = pass, 2 = fail): 1
Enter result (1 = pass, 2 = fail): 1
Enter result (1 = pass, 2 = fail): 1
Enter result (1 = pass, 2 = fail): 1
Enter result (1 = pass, 2 = fail): 2
Enter result (1 = pass, 2 = fail): 1
Enter result (1 = pass, 2 = fail): 1
Enter result (1 = pass, 2 = fail): 1
Enter result (1 = pass, 2 = fail): 1
Enter result (1 = pass, 2 = fail): 1
Passed 9
Failed 1
Bonus to instructor!
```

Fig. 4.16 | Examination-results problem: Nested control statements. (Part 2 of 2.)

The while statement (lines 14–29) loops 10 times. Each iteration inputs and processes one exam result. The if...else statement (lines 22–25) for processing each result is nested in the while statement. If the result is 1, the if...else statement increments passes; otherwise, it assumes the result is 2 and increments failures. Line 28 increments studentCounter before the loop condition is tested again in line 15. After 10 values have been input, the loop terminates and line 32 displays the number of passes and the number of failures. The if statement in lines 35–36 determines whether more than eight students passed the exam and, if so, outputs the message "Bonus to instructor!".

Figure 4.16 shows the input and output from two sample executions of the program. At the end of the second sample execution, the condition in line 35 is true—more than eight students passed the exam, so the program outputs a message indicating that the instructor should receive a bonus.

C++11 List Initialization

C++11 introduces a new variable initialization syntax. List initialization (also called uniform initialization) enables you to use one syntax to initialize a variable of *any* type. Consider line 11 of Fig. 4.16

```
unsigned int studentCounter = 1;
```

In C++11, you can write this as

```
unsigned int studentCounter = { 1 };
```

or

```
unsigned int studentCounter{ 1 };
```

The braces ({ and }) represent the *list initializer*. For a fundamental-type variable, you place only one value in the list initializer. For an object, the list initializer can be a *comma-separated list* of values that are passed to the object's constructor. For example, Exercise 3.14 asked you to create an Employee class that could represent an employee's first name, last name and salary. Assuming the class defines a constructor that receives strings for the first and last names and a double for the salary, you could initialize Employee objects as follows:

```
Employee employee1{ "Bob", "Blue", 1234.56 };
Employee employee2 = { "Sue", "Green", 2143.65 };
```

For fundamental-type variables, list-initialization syntax also *prevents* so-called narrowing conversions that could result in *data loss*. For example, previously you could write

```
int x = 12.7;
```

which attempts to assign the double value 12.7 to the int variable x. A double value is converted to an int, by *truncating* the floating-point part (.7), which results in a *loss of information*—a *narrowing conversion*. The actual value assigned to x is 12. Many compilers generate a *warning* for this statement, but still allow it to compile. However, using list initialization, as in

```
int x = { 12.7 };
```

or

```
int x{ 12.7 };
```

yields a *compilation error*, thus helping you avoid a potentially subtle logic error. For example, Apple's Xcode LLVM compiler gives the error

```
Type 'double' cannot be narrowed to 'int' in initializer list
```

We'll discuss additional list-initializer features in later chapters.

4.11 Assignment Operators

C++ provides several assignment operators for abbreviating assignment expressions. For example, the statement

```
c = c + 3;
```

can be abbreviated with the addition assignment operator += as

```
c += 3;
```

which adds the value of the expression on the operator's right to the value of the variable on the operator's left and stores the result in the left-side variable. Any statement of the form

> *variable = variable operator expression*;

in which the same *variable* appears on both sides of the assignment operator and *operator* is one of the binary operators +, -, *, /, or % (or a few others we'll discuss later in the text), can be written in the form

> *variable operator= expression*;

Thus the assignment c += 3 adds 3 to c. Figure 4.17 shows the arithmetic assignment operators, sample expressions using these operators and explanations.

Assignment operator	Sample expression	Explanation	Assigns
Assume: int c = 3, d = 5, e = 4, f = 6, g = 12;			
+=	c += 7	c = c + 7	10 to c
-=	d -= 4	d = d - 4	1 to d
*=	e *= 5	e = e * 5	20 to e
/=	f /= 3	f = f / 3	2 to f
%=	g %= 9	g = g % 9	3 to g

Fig. 4.17 | Arithmetic assignment operators.

4.12 Increment and Decrement Operators

In addition to the arithmetic assignment operators, C++ also provides two unary operators for adding 1 to or subtracting 1 from the value of a numeric variable. These are the unary increment operator, ++, and the unary decrement operator, --, which are summarized in Fig. 4.18. A program can increment by 1 the value of a variable called c using the increment operator, ++, rather than the expression c = c + 1 or c += 1. An increment or decrement operator that's prefixed to (placed *before*) a variable is referred to as the prefix increment or prefix decrement operator, respectively. An increment or decrement operator that's postfixed to (placed *after*) a variable is referred to as the postfix increment or postfix decrement operator, respectively.

Operator	Called	Sample expression	Explanation
++	preincrement	++a	Increment a by 1, then use the new value of a in the expression in which a resides.
++	postincrement	a++	Use the current value of a in the expression in which a resides, then increment a by 1.

Fig. 4.18 | Increment and decrement operators. (Part 1 of 2.)

Operator	Called	Sample expression	Explanation
--	predecrement	--b	Decrement b by 1, then use the new value of b in the expression in which b resides.
--	postdecrement	b--	Use the current value of b in the expression in which b resides, then decrement b by 1.

Fig. 4.18 | Increment and decrement operators. (Part 2 of 2.)

Using the prefix increment (or decrement) operator to add (or subtract) 1 from a variable is known as **preincrementing** (or **predecrementing**) the variable. Preincrementing (or predecrementing) causes the variable to be incremented (decremented) by 1, then the new value of the variable is used in the expression in which it appears. Using the postfix increment (or decrement) operator to add (or subtract) 1 from a variable is known as **postincrementing** (or **postdecrementing**) the variable. Postincrementing (or postdecrementing) causes the *current* value of the variable to be used in the expression in which it appears, then the variable's value is incremented (decremented) by 1.

Good Programming Practice 4.4

Unlike binary operators, the unary increment and decrement operators should be placed next to their operands, with no intervening spaces.

Figure 4.19 demonstrates the difference between the prefix increment and postfix increment versions of the ++ increment operator. The decrement operator (--) works similarly.

```cpp
1   // Fig. 4.19: fig04_19.cpp
2   // Preincrementing and postincrementing.
3   #include <iostream>
4   using namespace std;
5
6   int main()
7   {
8      // demonstrate postincrement
9      int c = 5; // assign 5 to c
10     cout << c << endl; // print 5
11     cout << c++ << endl; // print 5 then postincrement
12     cout << c << endl; // print 6
13
14     cout << endl; // skip a line
15
16     // demonstrate preincrement
17     c = 5; // assign 5 to c
18     cout << c << endl; // print 5
19     cout << ++c << endl; // preincrement then print 6
20     cout << c << endl; // print 6
21  } // end main
```

Fig. 4.19 | Preincrementing and postincrementing. (Part 1 of 2.)

```
5
5
6

5
6
6
```

Fig. 4.19 | Preincrementing and postincrementing. (Part 2 of 2.)

Line 9 initializes c to 5, and line 10 outputs c's initial value. Line 11 outputs the value of the expression c++. This postincrements the variable c, so c's original value (5) is output, then c's value is incremented. Thus, line 11 outputs c's initial value (5) again. Line 12 outputs c's new value (6) to prove that the variable's value was incremented in line 11.

Line 17 resets c's value to 5, and line 18 outputs that value. Line 19 outputs the value of the expression ++c. This expression preincrements c, so its value is incremented, then the new value (6) is output. Line 20 outputs c's value again to show that the value of c is still 6 after line 19 executes.

The arithmetic assignment operators and the increment and decrement operators can be used to simplify program statements. The three assignment statements in Fig. 4.16

```
passes = passes + 1;
failures = failures + 1;
studentCounter = studentCounter + 1;
```

can be written more concisely with assignment operators as

```
passes += 1;
failures += 1;
studentCounter += 1;
```

with prefix increment operators as

```
++passes;
++failures;
++studentCounter;
```

or with postfix increment operators as

```
passes++;
failures++;
studentCounter++;
```

When you increment (++) or decrement (−−) an integer variable in a statement by itself, the preincrement and postincrement forms have the same logical effect, and the predecrement and postdecrement forms have the same logical effect. It's only when a variable appears in the context of a larger expression that preincrementing the variable and postincrementing the variable have different effects (and similarly for predecrementing and postdecrementing).

Common Programming Error 4.8

Attempting to use the increment or decrement operator on an expression other than a modifiable variable name, e.g., writing ++(x + 1), is a syntax error.

Figure 4.20 shows the precedence and associativity of the operators introduced to this point. The operators are shown top-to-bottom in decreasing order of precedence. The second column indicates the associativity of the operators at each level of precedence. Notice that the conditional operator (?:), the unary operators preincrement (++), predecrement (--), plus (+) and minus (-), and the assignment operators =, +=, -=, *=, /= and %= associate from *right to left*. All other operators in Fig. 4.20 associate from *left to right*. The third column names the various groups of operators.

Operators	Associativity	Type
:: ()	left to right *[See caution in Fig. 2.10 regarding grouping parentheses.]*	primary
++ -- static_cast<*type*>()	left to right	postfix
++ -- + -	right to left	unary (prefix)
* / %	left to right	multiplicative
+ -	left to right	additive
<< >>	left to right	insertion/extraction
< <= > >=	left to right	relational
== !=	left to right	equality
?:	right to left	conditional
= += -= *= /= %=	right to left	assignment

Fig. 4.20 | Operator precedence for the operators encountered so far in the text.

4.13 Wrap-Up

This chapter presented basic problem-solving techniques that you use in building classes and developing member functions for these classes. We demonstrated how to construct an algorithm (i.e., an approach to solving a problem) in pseudocode, then how to refine the algorithm through pseudocode development, resulting in C++ code that can be executed as part of a function. You learned how to use top-down, stepwise refinement to plan out the actions that a function must perform and the order in which it must perform them.

You learned that only three types of control structures—sequence, selection and repetition—are needed to develop any algorithm. We demonstrated two of C++'s selection statements—the if single-selection statement and the if...else double-selection statement. The if statement is used to execute a set of statements based on a condition—if the condition is true, the statements execute; if it isn't, the statements are skipped. The if...else double-selection statement is used to execute one set of statements if a condition is true, and another set of statements if the condition is false. We then discussed the while repetition statement, where a set of statements are executed repeatedly as long as a condition is true. We used control-statement stacking to total and compute the average of a set of student grades with counter- and sentinel-controlled repetition, and we used control-statement nesting to analyze and make decisions based on a set of exam results. We introduced assignment operators, which can be used for abbreviating statements. We presented the increment and decrement operators, which can be used to add or subtract the value 1 from a variable. In the next chapter, we continue our discussion of control statements, introducing the for, do...while and switch statements.

Summary

Section 4.2 Algorithms
- An algorithm (p. 139) is a procedure for solving a problem in terms of the actions to execute and the order in which to execute them.
- Specifying the order in which statements execute in a program is called program control (p. 140).

Section 4.3 Pseudocode
- Pseudocode (p. 140) helps you think out a program before writing it in a programming language.

Section 4.4 Control Structures
- An activity diagram models the workflow (also called the activity, p. 142) of a software system.
- Activity diagrams (p. 141) are composed of symbols, such as action state symbols, diamonds and small circles, that are connected by transition arrows representing the flow of the activity.
- Like pseudocode, activity diagrams help you develop and represent algorithms.
- An action state is represented as a rectangle with its left and right sides replaced with arcs curving outward. The action expression (p. 142) appears inside the action state.
- The arrows in an activity diagram represent transitions (p. 142), which indicate the order in which the actions represented by action states occur.
- The solid circle in an activity diagram represents the initial state (p. 142)—the beginning of the workflow before the program performs the modeled actions.
- The solid circle surrounded by a hollow circle that appears at the bottom of the activity diagram represents the final state (p. 142)—the end of the workflow after the program performs its actions.
- Rectangles with the upper-right corners folded over are called notes (p. 142) in the UML. A dotted line (p. 142) connects each note with the element that the note describes.
- There are three types of control structures (p. 141)—sequence, selection and repetition.
- The sequence structure is built in—by default, statements execute in the order they appear.
- A selection structure chooses among alternative courses of action.

Section 4.5 if Selection Statement
- The if single-selection statement (p. 144) either performs (selects) an action if a condition is true, or skips the action if the condition is false.
- A decision symbol (p. 145) in an activity diagram indicates that a decision is to be made. The workflow follows a path determined by the associated guard conditions. Each transition arrow emerging from a decision symbol has a guard condition. If a guard condition is true, the workflow enters the action state to which the transition arrow points.

Section 4.6 if...else Double-Selection Statement
- The if...else double-selection statement (p. 146) performs (selects) an action if a condition is true and performs a different action if the condition is false.

- To include several statements in an if's body (or the body of an else for an if...else statement), enclose the statements in braces ({ and }). A set of statements contained in braces is called a block (p. 149). A block can be placed anywhere in a program that a single statement can be placed.
- A null statement (p. 150), indicating that no action is to be taken, is indicated by a semicolon (;).

Section 4.7 *while Repetition Statement*
- A repetition statement (p. 150) repeats an action while some condition remains true.
- A UML merge symbol (p. 151) has two or more transition arrows pointing to the diamond and only one pointing from it, to indicate multiple activity flows merging to continue the activity.

Section 4.8 *Formulating Algorithms: Counter-Controlled Repetition*
- Counter-controlled repetition (p. 152) is used when the number of repetitions is known before a loop begins executing, i.e., when there is definite repetition.
- Adding integers can result in a value that's too large to store in an int variable. This is known as arithmetic overflow and causes unpredictable runtime behavior.
- The maximum and minimum values that can be stored in an int variable are represented by the constants INT_MAX and INT_MIN, respectively, from the header <climits>.
- It's considered a good practice to ensure that arithmetic calculations will not overflow before you perform the calculation. In industrial-strength code, you should perform checks for all calculations that can result on overflow or underflow.

Section 4.9 *Formulating Algorithms: Sentinel-Controlled Repetition*
- Top-down, stepwise refinement (p. 159) is a process for refining pseudocode by maintaining a complete representation of the program during each refinement.
- Sentinel-controlled repetition (p. 160) is used when the number of repetitions is not known before a loop begins executing, i.e., when there is indefinite repetition.
- A value that contains a fractional part is referred to as a floating-point number and is represented approximately by data types such as float and double (p. 161).
- The cast operator static_cast<double> (p. 166) can be used to create a temporary floating-point copy of its operand.
- Unary operators (p. 167) take only one operand; binary operators take two.
- The parameterized stream manipulator setprecision (p. 167) indicates the number of digits of precision that should be displayed to the right of the decimal point.
- The stream manipulator fixed (p. 167) indicates that floating-point values should be output in so-called fixed-point format, as opposed to scientific notation.
- In general, any integer variable that should store only non-negative values should be declared with unsigned before the integer type. Variables of unsigned types can represent values from 0 to approximately double the positive range of the corresponding signed integer type.
- You can determine your platform's maximum unsigned int value with the constant UINT_MAX from <climits>.

Section 4.10 *Formulating Algorithms: Nested Control Statements*
- A nested control statement (p. 168) appears in the body of another control statement.
- C++11 introduces the new list initialization for initializing variables in their declarations, as in

```
int studentCounter = { 1 };
```

or

```
int studentCounter{ 1 };
```

- The braces ({ and }) represent the list initializer. For a fundamental-type variable, you place only one value in the list initializer. For an object, the list initializer can be a comma-separated list of values that are passed to the object's constructor.

- For fundamental-type variables, list-initialization syntax also prevents so-called narrowing conversions that could result in data loss.

Section 4.11 Assignment Operators
- The arithmetic operators +=, -=, *=, /= and %= abbreviate assignment expressions (p. 174).

Section 4.12 Increment and Decrement Operators
- The increment (++) and decrement (--) operators (p. 174) increment or decrement a variable by 1, respectively. If the operator is prefixed to the variable, the variable is incremented or decremented by 1 first, then its new value is used in the expression in which it appears. If the operator is postfixed to the variable, the variable is first used in the expression in which it appears, then the variable's value is incremented or decremented by 1.

Self-Review Exercises

4.1   Answer each of the following questions.
   a) _____ repetition is used when the number of repetitions is not known before a loop begins executing.
   b) The cast operator _____ can be used to create a temporary floating point copy of its operand.
   c) A null statement is indicated by a _____.
   d) A/An _____ is a procedure for solving a problem in terms of the actions to execute and the order in which to execute them.

4.2   Write four different C++ statements that each subtract 1 from an integer variable x.

4.3   Write C++ statements to accomplish each of the following:
   a) In one statement, assign the product of the current value of x and y to z and post-decrement the value of x.
   b) Determine whether the value of the variable count is less than 10. If it is, print "Count is less than 10."
   c) Preincrement the variable x by 1, then add it from the variable total.
   d) Calculate the quotient after q is divided by divisor and assign the result to q. Write this statement two different ways.

4.4   Write C++ statements to accomplish each of the following tasks.
   a) Declare variable var to be of type long and initialize it to 10.
   b) Declare variable x to be of type long and initialize it to 0.
   c) Subtract variable x from the variable var and assign the result to variable var.
   d) Print the value of variable var.

4.5   Combine the statements that you wrote in Exercise 4.4 into a program that prints all the numbers from 10 to 0. Use the while statement to loop through the calculation and decrement statements. The loop should terminate when the value of x becomes 11.

4.6   State the values of each of these unsigned int variables after the calculation is performed. Assume that, when each statement begins executing, all variables have the integer value 2.
   a) sum += x++;
   b) sub -= ++x;

4.7   Write single C++ statements or portions of statements that do the following:
   a) Input unsigned int variable lb with cin and >>.

b) Input unsigned int variable ub with cin and >>.
c) Declare unsigned int variable i and initialize it to lb.
d) Declare unsigned int variable sum and initialize it to 0.
e) Add variable i with sum and assign the result to sum.
f) Preincrement variable i by 1.
g) Determine whether i is less than or equal to ub.
h) Output integer variable sum with cout and <<.

4.8 Write a C++ program that uses the statements in Exercise 4.7 to calculate the sum of all numbers in a given range. The program should have a while repetition statement.

4.9 Identify and correct the errors in each of the following:

a)
```
while ( c <= 5 )
(
    product *= c;
    ++c;
)
```
b) `cout >> value;`
c)
```
if ( i == 1 )
    cout << "A" << endl;
    cout << "B" << endl;
else
    cout << "C" << endl;
```

4.10 What's wrong with the following while repetition statement?
```
while ( i <= 10 )
    product *= i;
```

Answers to Self-Review Exercises

4.1 a) Sentinel-controlled. b) static_cast<double>. c) Semicolon (;) d) Algorithm.

4.2
```
x = x - 1;
x -= 1;
--x;
x--;
```

4.3
a) `z = x-- + y;`
b)
```
if ( count < 10 )
    cout << "Count is less than 10" << endl;
```
c) `total += ++x;`
d)
```
q /= divisor;
q = q / divisor;
```

4.4
a) `long var = 10;`
b) `long x = 0;`
c)
```
var -= x;
```
or
```
var = var - x;
```
d) `cout << var << endl;`

4.5 See the following code:

```
1   // Exercise 4.5 Solution
2   // Display all the integers from 10 to 0.
3   #include <iostream>
```

```
4   using namespace std;
5
6   int main()
7   {
8      long var = 10;
9      long x = 0; // counter
10
11     while ( x <= 10 ) // loop 10 times
12     {
13        var -= x;
14        ++x; // increment x
15     cout <<  var << endl;
16     } // end while
17  } // end main
```

4.6   a) sum = 4, x = 3.
          b) sub = -1, x = 3.

4.7   a) cin>> lb;
          b) cin >> ub;
          c) unsigned int i = lb;
          d) unsigned int sum = 0;
          e) sum += i;
          f) ++i;
          g) if (i <= ub)
          h) cout<< sum << endl;

4.8   See the following code:

```
1   // Exercise 4.8 Solution
2   // Sum of all numbers in a given range
3   #include <iostream>
4   using namespace std;
5
6   int main()
7   {
8      unsigned int i;
9      unsigned int sum = 0;
10
11     cout << "Enter the lower bound: ";
12     unsigned int lb;
13     cin >> lb;
14
15     cout << "Enter the upper bound: ";
16     unsigned int ub;
17     cin >> ub;
18
19     i = lb;
20
21     while ( i <= ub )
22     {
23        sum += i;
24        ++i;
25     } // end while
```

```
26
27      cout << sum << endl; // display result
28    } // end main
```

4.9 a) *Error:* Use of ( ) for representing the body of the while loop.
Correction: Replace ( ) with { } to represent the body of the while loop;.

b) *Error:* Used stream extraction instead of stream insertion.
Correction: Change >> to <<.

c) *Error:* Missing { } to represent the body of the if condition as it contains multiple statements.
Correction: Add { before the first output statement and add } after the second output statement.

4.10 The value of the variable i is never changed in the while statement. Therefore, if the loop continuation condition (i<= 10) is initially true, an infinite loop is created. To prevent the infinite loop, i must be increment so that it eventually becomes greater than 10.

Exercises

4.11 *(Correct the Code Errors)* Identify and correct the error(s) in each of the following:

a)
```
if ( age >= 65 );
   cout << "Age is greater than or equal to 65" << endl;
else
   cout << "Age is less than 65 << endl";
```

b)
```
if ( age >= 65 )
   cout << "Age is greater than or equal to 65" << endl;
else;
   cout << "Age is less than 65 << endl";
```

c)
```
unsigned int x = 1;
unsigned int total;

while ( x <= 10 )
{
   total += x;
   ++x;
}
```

d)
```
While ( x <= 100 )
   total += x;
   ++x;
```

e)
```
while ( y > 0 )
{
   cout << y << endl;
   ++y;
}
```

4.12 *(What Does this Program Do?)* What does the following program print?

```
1   // Exercise 4.12: ex04_12.cpp
2   // What does this program print?
3   #include <iostream>
4   using namespace std;
5
6   int main()
7   {
```

```
 8      unsigned int y = 0; // declare and initialize y
 9      unsigned int x = 1; // declare and initialize x
10      unsigned int total = 0; // declare and initialize total
11
12      while ( x <= 10 ) // loop 10 times
13      {
14         y = x * x; // perform calculation
15         cout << y << endl; // output result
16         total += y; // add y to total
17         ++x; // increment counter x
18      } // end while
19
20      cout << "Total is " << total << endl; // display result
21   } // end main
```

For Exercises 4.13–4.16, perform each of these steps:

a) Read the problem statement.
b) Formulate the algorithm using pseudocode and top-down, stepwise refinement.
c) Write a C++ program.
d) Test, debug and execute the C++ program.

4.13   *(Gas Mileage)* Drivers are concerned with the mileage obtained by their automobiles. One driver has kept track of several trips by recording miles driven and gallons used for each trip. Develop a C++ program that uses a while statement to input the miles driven and gallons used for each trip. The program should calculate and display the miles per gallon obtained for each trip and print the combined miles per gallon obtained for all tankfuls up to this point.

```
Enter miles driven (-1 to quit): 287
Enter gallons used: 13
MPG this trip: 22.076923
Total MPG: 22.076923

Enter miles driven (-1 to quit): 200
Enter gallons used: 10
MPG this trip: 20.000000
Total MPG: 21.173913

Enter the miles driven (-1 to quit): 120
Enter gallons used: 5
MPG this trip: 24.000000
Total MPG: 21.678571

Enter the miles used (-1 to quit): -1
```

4.14   *(Credit Limits)* Develop a C++ program that will determine whether a department-store customer has exceeded the credit limit on a charge account. For each customer, the following facts are available:

a) Account number (an integer)
b) Balance at the beginning of the month
c) Total of all items charged by this customer this month
d) Total of all credits applied to this customer's account this month
e) Allowed credit limit

The program should use a while statement to input each of these facts, calculate the new balance (= beginning balance + charges – credits) and determine whether the new balance exceeds the customer's credit limit. For those customers whose credit limit is exceeded, the program should display the customer's account number, credit limit, new balance and the message "Credit Limit Exceeded."

```
Enter account number (or -1 to quit): 100
Enter beginning balance: 5394.78
Enter total charges: 1000.00
Enter total credits: 500.00
Enter credit limit: 5500.00
New balance is 5894.78
Account:      100
Credit limit: 5500.00
Balance:      5894.78
Credit Limit Exceeded.

Enter Account Number (or -1 to quit): 200
Enter beginning balance: 1000.00
Enter total charges: 123.45
Enter total credits: 321.00
Enter credit limit: 1500.00
New balance is 802.45

Enter Account Number (or -1 to quit): -1
```

4.15   *(Sales Commission Calculator)* A large company pays its salespeople on a commission basis. The salespeople each receive $200 per week plus 9% of their gross sales for that week. For example, a salesperson who sells $5000 worth of chemicals in a week receives $200 plus 9% of $5000, or a total of $650. Develop a C++ program that uses a while statement to input each salesperson's gross sales for last week and calculates and displays that salesperson's earnings. Process one salesperson's figures at a time.

```
Enter sales in dollars (-1 to end): 5000.00
Salary is: $650.00

Enter sales in dollars (-1 to end): 6000.00
Salary is: $740.00

Enter sales in dollars (-1 to end): 7000.00
Salary is: $830.00

Enter sales in dollars (-1 to end): -1
```

4.16   *(Salary Calculator)* Develop a C++ program that uses a while statement to determine the gross pay for each of several employees. The company pays "straight time" for the first 40 hours worked by each employee and pays "time-and-a-half" for all hours worked in excess of 40 hours. You are given a list of the employees of the company, the number of hours each employee worked last week and the hourly rate of each employee. Your program should input this information for each employee and should determine and display the employee's gross pay.

```
Enter hours worked (-1 to end): 39
Enter hourly rate of the employee ($00.00): 10.00
Salary is $390.00

Enter hours worked (-1 to end): 40
Enter hourly rate of the employee ($00.00): 10.00
Salary is $400.00

Enter hours worked (-1 to end): 41
Enter hourly rate of the employee ($00.00): 10.00
Salary is $415.00

Enter hours worked (-1 to end): -1
```

4.17   *(Find the Largest)* The process of finding the largest number (i.e., the maximum of a group of numbers) is used frequently in computer applications. For example, a program that determines the winner of a sales contest inputs the number of units sold by each salesperson. The salesperson who sells the most units wins the contest. Write a C++ program that uses a while statement to determine and print the largest number of 10 numbers input by the user. Your program should use three variables, as follows:

> counter: A counter to count to 10 (i.e., to keep track of how many numbers have been input and to determine when all 10 numbers have been processed).
> number: The current number input to the program.
> largest: The largest number found so far.

4.18   *(Tabular Output)* Write a C++ program that uses a while statement and the tab escape sequence \t to print the following table of values:

N	10*N	100*N	1000*N
1	10	100	1000
2	20	200	2000
3	30	300	3000
4	40	400	4000
5	50	500	5000

4.19   *(Find the largest and the smallest Number)* Find the largest and the smallest value among 10 numbers. [*Note:* You must input each number only once.]

4.20   *(Validating User Input)* The examination-results program of Fig. 4.16 assumes that any value input by the user that's not a 1 must be a 2. Modify the application to validate its inputs. On any input, if the value entered is other than 1 or 2, keep looping until the user enters a correct value.

4.21   *(What Does this Program Do?)* What does the following program print?

```
1    // Exercise 4.21: ex04_21.cpp
2    // What does this program print?
3    #include <iostream>
4    using namespace std;
5
6    int main()
7    {
8       unsigned int count = 1; // initialize count
9
10      while ( count <= 10 ) // loop 10 times
11      {
12         // output line of text
13         cout << ( count % 2 ? "*****" : "++++++++" ) << endl;
14         ++count; // increment count
15      } // end while
16   } // end main
```

4.22   *(What Does this Program Do?)* What does the following program print?

```
1    // Exercise 4.22: ex04_22.cpp
2    // What does this program print?
3    #include <iostream>
4    using namespace std;
5
6    int main()
7    {
```

```
8      unsigned int row = 10; // initialize row
9
10     while ( row >= 1 ) // loop until row < 1
11     {
12        unsigned int column = 1; // set column to 1 as iteration begins
13
14        while ( column <= 10 ) // loop 10 times
15        {
16           cout << ( row % 2 ? "<" : ">" ); // output
17           ++column; // increment column
18        } // end inner while
19
20        --row; // decrement row
21        cout << endl; // begin new output line
22     } // end outer while
23  } // end main
```

4.23 *(Dangling-else Problem)* State the output for each of the following when x is 9 and y is 11 and when x is 11 and y is 9. The compiler ignores the indentation in a C++ program. The C++ compiler always associates an else with the previous if unless told to do otherwise by the placement of braces {}. On first glance, you may not be sure which if and else match, so this is referred to as the "dangling-else" problem. We eliminated the indentation from the following code to make the problem more challenging. [*Hint:* Apply indentation conventions you've learned.]

a)
```
if ( x < 10 )
if ( y > 10 )
cout << "*****" << endl;
else
cout << "#####" << endl;
cout << "$$$$$" << endl;
```

b)
```
if ( x < 10 )
{
if ( y > 10 )
cout << "*****" << endl;
}
else
{
cout << "#####" << endl;
cout << "$$$$$" << endl;
}
```

4.24 *(Another Dangling-else Problem)* Modify the following code to produce the output shown. Use proper indentation techniques. You must not make any changes other than inserting braces. The compiler ignores indentation in a C++ program. We eliminated the indentation from the following code to make the problem more challenging. [*Note:* It's possible that no modification is necessary.]

```
if ( y == 8 )
if ( x == 5 )
cout << "@@@@@" << endl;
else
cout << "#####" << endl;
cout << "$$$$$" << endl;
cout << "&&&&&" << endl;
```

a) Assuming x = 5 and y = 8, the following output is produced.

```
@@@@@
$$$$$
&&&&&
```

b) Assuming x = 5 and y = 8, the following output is produced.

```
@@@@@
```

c) Assuming x = 5 and y = 8, the following output is produced.

```
@@@@@
&&&&&
```

d) Assuming x = 5 and y = 7, the following output is produced. [*Note:* The last three output statements after the else are all part of a block.]

```
#####
$$$$$
&&&&&
```

4.25 *(Square of Asterisks)* Write a program that reads in the size of the side of a square then prints a hollow square of that size out of asterisks and blanks. Your program should work for squares of all side sizes between 1 and 20. For example, if your program reads a size of 5, it should print

```
*****
*   *
*   *
*   *
*****
```

4.26 *(Palindromes)* A palindrome is a number or a text phrase that reads the same backward as forward. For example, each of the following five-digit integers is a palindrome: 12321, 55555, 45554 and 11611. Write a program that reads in a five-digit integer and determines whether it's a palindrome. [*Hint:* Use the division and modulus operators to separate the number into its individual digits.]

4.27 *(Printing the Decimal Equivalent of a Binary Number)* Input an integer containing only 0s and 1s (i.e., a "binary" integer) and print its decimal equivalent. Use the modulus and division operators to pick off the "binary" number's digits one at a time from right to left. Much as in the decimal number system, where the rightmost digit has a positional value of 1, the next digit left has a positional value of 10, then 100, then 1000, and so on, in the binary number system the rightmost digit has a positional value of 1, the next digit left has a positional value of 2, then 4, then 8, and so on. Thus the decimal number 234 can be interpreted as 2 * 100 + 3 * 10 + 4 * 1. The decimal equivalent of binary 1101 is 1 * 1 + 0 * 2 + 1 * 4 + 1 * 8 or 1 + 0 + 4 + 8, or 13. [*Note:* To learn more about binary numbers, refer to Appendix D.]

4.28 *(Checkerboard Pattern of Asterisks)* Write a program that displays the following checkerboard pattern. Your program must use only three output statements, one of each of the following forms:

```
cout << "* ";
cout << ' ';
cout << endl;
```

4.29   *(Multiples of 3 with an Infinite Loop)* Write a program that prints the powers of the integer 3, namely 3, 9, 27, 81, etc. Your while loop should not terminate (i.e., you should create an infinite loop). To do this, simply use the keyword true as the expression for the while statement. What happens when you run this program?

4.30   *(Calculating a Square's Perimeter and Area)* Write a program that reads the side of a square (as a double value) and computes and prints the perimeter and the area.

4.31   What's wrong with the following statement? Provide the correct statement to accomplish what the programmer was probably trying to do.

```
cout << ( x + y + z )++;
```

4.32   *(Sides of a Triangle)* Write a program that reads three nonzero double values and determines and prints whether they could represent the sides of a triangle.

4.33   *(Area of a Right Triangle)* Write a program that reads the base and height of a right triangle and determines and prints its area.

4.34   *(Factorial)* The factorial of a nonnegative integer n is written $n!$ (pronounced "n factorial") and is defined as follows:

$n! = n \cdot (n-1) \cdot (n-2) \cdot \ldots \cdot 1$ (for values of n greater than 1)

and

$n! = 1$ (for $n = 0$ or $n = 1$).

For example, $5! = 5 \cdot 4 \cdot 3 \cdot 2 \cdot 1$, which is 120. Use while statements in each of the following:

   a) Write a program that reads a nonnegative integer and computes and prints its factorial.
   b) Write a program that estimates the value of the mathematical constant e by using the formula:

$$e = 1 + \frac{1}{1!} + \frac{1}{2!} + \frac{1}{3!} + \ldots$$

   Prompt the user for the desired accuracy of e (i.e., the number of terms in the summation).
   c) Write a program that computes the value of e^x by using the formula

$$e^x = 1 + \frac{x}{1!} + \frac{x^2}{2!} + \frac{x^3}{3!} + \ldots$$

   Prompt the user for the desired accuracy of e (i.e., the number of terms in the summation).

4.35   *(C++11 List Initializers)* Write statements that use C++11 list initialization to perform each of the following tasks:

   a) Initialize the unsigned int variable studentCounter to 0.
   b) Initialize the double variable initialBalance to 1000.0.

c) Initialize an object of class Account which provides a constructor that receives an unsigned int, two strings and a double to initialize the object's accountNumber, first-Name, lastName and balance data members.

Making a Difference

4.36   *(Enforcing Privacy with Cryptography)* The explosive growth of Internet communications and data storage on Internet-connected computers has greatly increased privacy concerns. The field of cryptography is concerned with coding data to make it difficult (and hopefully—with the most advanced schemes—impossible) for unauthorized users to read. In this exercise you'll investigate a simple scheme for encrypting and decrypting data. A company that wants to send data over the Internet has asked you to write a program that will encrypt it so that it may be transmitted more securely. All the data is transmitted as four-digit integers. Your application should read a four-digit integer entered by the user and encrypt it as follows: Replace each digit with the result of adding 7 to the digit and getting the remainder after dividing the new value by 10. Then swap the first digit with the third, and swap the second digit with the fourth. Then print the encrypted integer. Write a separate application that inputs an encrypted four-digit integer and decrypts it (by reversing the encryption scheme) to form the original number. [*Optional reading project:* Research "public key cryptography" in general and the PGP (Pretty Good Privacy) specific public key scheme. You may also want to investigate the RSA scheme, which is widely used in industrial-strength applications.]

4.37   *(World Population Growth)* World population has grown considerably over the centuries. Continued growth could eventually challenge the limits of breathable air, drinkable water, arable cropland and other precious resources. There is evidence that growth has been slowing in recent years and that world population could peak some time this century, then start to decline.

For this exercise, research world population growth issues online. *Be sure to investigate various viewpoints.* Get estimates for the current world population and its growth rate (the percentage by which it is likely to increase this year). Write a program that calculates world population growth each year for the next 75 years, *using the simplifying assumption that the current growth rate will stay constant.* Print the results in a table. The first column should display the year from year 1 to year 75. The second column should display the anticipated world population at the end of that year. The third column should display the numerical increase in the world population that would occur that year. Using your results, determine the year in which the population would be double what it is today, if this year's growth rate were to persist.

Control Statements: Part 2; Logical Operators

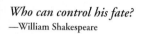

5

Who can control his fate?
—William Shakespeare

The used key is always bright.
—Benjamin Franklin

Objectives

In this chapter you'll learn:

- The essentials of counter-controlled repetition.

- To use **for** and **do...while** to execute statements in a program repeatedly.

- To implement multiple selection using the **switch** selection statement.

- How **break** and **continue** alter the flow of control.

- To use the logical operators to form complex conditional expressions in control statements.

- To avoid the consequences of confusing the equality and assignment operators.

5.1 Introduction

In this chapter, we continue our presentation of structured programming by introducing C++'s remaining control statements. The control statements we study here and those you learned in Chapter 4 will help you build and manipulate objects. We continue our early emphasis on object-oriented programming that began with a discussion of basic concepts in Chapter 1 and extensive object-oriented code examples and exercises in Chapters 3–4.

In this chapter, we demonstrate the for, do...while and switch statements. Through short examples using while and for, we explore counter-controlled repetition. We expand the GradeBook class to use a switch statement to count the number of A, B, C, D and F grades in a set of letter grades entered by the user. We introduce the break and continue program control statements. We discuss the logical operators, which enable you to use more powerful conditional expressions. We also examine the common error of confusing the equality (==) and assignment (=) operators, and how to avoid it.

5.2 Essentials of Counter-Controlled Repetition

This section uses the while repetition statement to formalize the elements required to perform counter-controlled repetition:

1. the name of a control variable (or loop counter)
2. the initial value of the control variable
3. the loop-continuation condition that tests for the final value of the control variable (i.e., whether looping should continue)
4. the increment (or decrement) by which the control variable is modified each time through the loop.

The program in Fig. 5.1 prints the numbers from 1 to 10. The declaration in line 8 *names* the control variable (counter), declares it to be an unsigned int, reserves space for it in memory and sets it to an *initial value* of 1. Declarations that require initialization are *executable* statements. In C++, it's more precise to call a variable declaration that also reserves memory a **definition**. Because definitions are declarations, too, we'll use the term "declaration" except when the distinction is important.

Line 13 *increments* the loop counter by 1 each time the loop's body is performed. The loop-continuation condition (line 10) in the while statement determines whether the value of the control variable is less than or equal to 10 (the final value for which the

```
 1   // Fig. 5.1: fig05_01.cpp
 2   // Counter-controlled repetition.
 3   #include <iostream>
 4   using namespace std;
 5
 6   int main()
 7   {
 8      unsigned int counter = 1; // declare and initialize control variable
 9
10      while ( counter <= 10 ) // loop-continuation condition
11      {
12         cout << counter << " ";
13         ++counter; // increment control variable by 1
14      } // end while
15
16      cout << endl; // output a newline
17   } // end main
```

```
1 2 3 4 5 6 7 8 9 10
```

Fig. 5.1 | Counter-controlled repetition.

condition is true). The body of this while executes even when the control variable is 10. The loop terminates when the control variable is greater than 10 (i.e., when counter is 11).

Figure 5.1 can be made more concise by initializing counter to 0 and by replacing the while statement with

```
counter = 0;

while ( ++counter <= 10 ) // loop-continuation condition
   cout << counter << " ";
```

This code saves a statement, because the incrementing is done in the while condition *before* the condition is tested. Also, the code eliminates the braces around the body of the while, because the while now contains only *one* statement. Coding in such a condensed fashion can lead to programs that are more difficult to read, debug, modify and maintain.

Error-Prevention Tip 5.1

Floating-point values are approximate, so controlling counting loops with floating-point variables can result in imprecise counter values and inaccurate tests for termination. Control counting loops with integer values. Separately, ++ and -- can be used only with integer operands.

5.3 for Repetition Statement

In addition to while, C++ provides the **for repetition** statement, which specifies the counter-controlled repetition details in a single line of code. To illustrate the power of for, let's rewrite the program of Fig. 5.1. The result is shown in Fig. 5.2.

When the for statement (lines 10–11) begins executing, the control variable counter is declared and initialized to 1. Then, the loop-continuation condition (line 10 between the semicolons) counter <= 10 is checked. The initial value of counter is 1, so the condi-

```
 1   // Fig. 5.2: fig05_02.cpp
 2   // Counter-controlled repetition with the for statement.
 3   #include <iostream>
 4   using namespace std;
 5
 6   int main()
 7   {
 8      // for statement header includes initialization,
 9      // loop-continuation condition and increment.
10      for ( unsigned int counter = 1; counter <= 10; ++counter )
11         cout << counter << " ";
12
13      cout << endl; // output a newline
14   } // end main
```

```
1 2 3 4 5 6 7 8 9 10
```

Fig. 5.2 | Counter-controlled repetition with the for statement.

tion is satisfied and the body statement (line 11) prints the value of counter, namely 1. Then, the expression ++counter increments control variable counter and the loop begins again with the loop-continuation test. The control variable is now 2, so the final value is not exceeded and the program performs the body statement again. This process continues until the loop body has executed 10 times and the control variable counter is incremented to 11—this causes the loop-continuation test to fail, so repetition terminates. The program continues by performing the first statement after the for statement (in this case, the output statement in line 13).

for Statement Header Components
Figure 5.3 takes a closer look at the for statement header (line 10) of Fig. 5.2. Notice that the for statement header "does it all"—it specifies each of the items needed for counter-controlled repetition with a control variable. If there's more than one statement in the body of the for, braces are required to enclose the body of the loop. Typically, for statements are used for counter-controlled repetition and while statements are used for sentinel-controlled repetition.

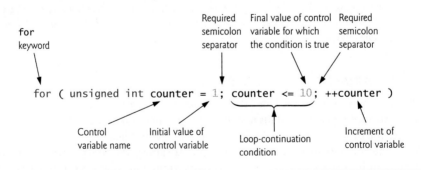

Fig. 5.3 | for statement header components.

Off-By-One Errors

If you incorrectly wrote counter < 10 as the loop-continuation condition in Fig. 5.2, then the loop would execute only 9 times. This is a common off-by-one error.

Common Programming Error 5.1

Using an incorrect relational operator or using an incorrect final value of a loop counter in the condition of a while or for statement can cause off-by-one errors.

Good Programming Practice 5.1

Using the final value in the condition of a while or for statement and using the <= relational operator will help avoid off-by-one errors. For a loop used to print the values 1 to 10, for example, the loop-continuation condition should be counter <= 10 rather than counter < 10 (which is an off-by-one error) or counter < 11 (which is nevertheless correct). Many programmers prefer so-called zero-based counting, in which, to count 10 times through the loop, counter would be initialized to zero and the loop-continuation test would be counter < 10.

*General Format of a **for** Statement*

The general form of the for statement is

for (*initialization*; *loopContinuationCondition*; *increment*)
    statement

where the *initialization* expression initializes the loop's control variable, *loopContinuationCondition* determines whether the loop should continue executing and *increment* increments the control variable. In most cases, the for statement can be represented by an equivalent while statement, as follows:

initialization;

while (*loopContinuationCondition*)
{
    statement
    increment;
}

There's an exception to this rule, which we'll discuss in Section 5.7.

If the *initialization* expression declares the control variable (i.e., its type is specified before its name), the control variable can be used *only* in the body of the for statement—the control variable will be unknown *outside* the for statement. This restricted use of the control variable name is known as the variable's scope. The scope of a variable specifies *where* it can be used in a program. Scope is discussed in detail in Chapter 6.

Comma-Separated Lists of Expressions

The *initialization* and *increment* expressions can be comma-separated lists of expressions. The commas, as used in these expressions, are **comma operators**, which guarantee that lists of expressions evaluate from left to right. The comma operator has the lowest precedence of all C++ operators. *The value and type of a comma-separated list of expressions is the value and type of the rightmost expression.* The comma operator is often used in for statements. Its primary application is to enable you to use *multiple initialization expressions* and/or *mul-*

tiple increment expressions. For example, there may be several control variables in a single for statement that must be initialized and incremented.

Good Programming Practice 5.2
Place only expressions involving the control variables in the initialization and increment sections of a for statement.

Expressions in the **for** Statement's Header Are Optional

The three expressions in the for statement header are optional (but the two semicolon separators are *required*). If the *loopContinuationCondition* is omitted, C++ assumes that the condition is true, thus creating an *infinite loop*. One might omit the *initialization* expression if the control variable is initialized earlier in the program. One might omit the *increment* expression if the increment is calculated by statements in the body of the for or if no increment is needed.

Increment Expression Acts Like a Standalone Statement

The increment expression in the for statement acts like a standalone statement at the end of for statement's body. Therefore, for integer counters, the expressions

```
counter = counter + 1
counter += 1
++counter
counter++
```

are all equivalent in the *increment* expression (when no other code appears there). The integer variable being incremented here does not appear in a larger expression, so both preincrementing and postincrementing actually have the *same* effect.

Common Programming Error 5.2
Placing a semicolon immediately to the right of the right parenthesis of a for header makes the body of that for statement an empty statement. This is usually a logic error.

for Statement: Notes and Observations

The initialization, loop-continuation condition and increment expressions of a for statement can contain arithmetic expressions. For example, if x = 2 and y = 10, and x and y are not modified in the loop body, the for header

```
for ( unsigned int j = x; j <= 4 * x * y; j += y / x )
```

is equivalent to

```
for ( unsigned int j = 2; j <= 80; j += 5 )
```

The "increment" of a for statement can be negative, in which case it's really a *decrement* and the loop actually counts *downward* (as shown in Section 5.4).

If the loop-continuation condition is *initially false*, the body of the for statement is not performed. Instead, execution proceeds with the statement following the for.

Frequently, the control variable is printed or used in calculations in the body of a for statement, but this is not required. It's common to use the control variable for controlling repetition while never mentioning it in the body of the for statement.

> ### Error-Prevention Tip 5.2
> *Although the value of the control variable can be changed in the body of a for statement, avoid doing so, because this can lead to subtle logic errors.*

for *Statement UML Activity Diagram*

The for repetition statement's UML activity diagram is similar to that of the while statement (Fig. 4.6). Figure 5.4 shows the activity diagram of the for statement in Fig. 5.2. The diagram makes it clear that initialization occurs once *before* the loop-continuation test is evaluated the first time, and that incrementing occurs *each time* through the loop *after* the body statement executes. Note that (besides an initial state, transition arrows, a merge, a final state and several notes) the diagram contains only *action states* and a *decision*.

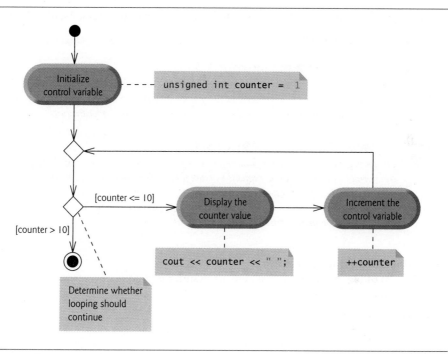

Fig. 5.4 | UML activity diagram for the for statement in Fig. 5.2.

5.4 Examples Using the for Statement

The following examples show methods of varying the control variable in a for statement. In each case, we write the appropriate for statement header. Note the change in the relational operator for loops that *decrement* the control variable.

a) Vary the control variable from 1 to 100 in increments of 1.

```
for ( unsigned int i = 1; i <= 100; ++i )
```

b) Vary the control variable from 100 down to 0 in decrements of 1. Notice that we used type int for the control variable in this for header. The condition does not become false until control variable i contains -1, so the control variable must be able to store both positive and negative numbers.

```
for ( int i = 100; i >= 0; --i )
```

c) Vary the control variable from 7 to 77 in steps of 7.

```
for ( unsigned int i = 7; i <= 77; i += 7 )
```

d) Vary the control variable from 20 down to 2 in steps of -2.

```
for ( unsigned int i = 20; i >= 2; i -= 2 )
```

e) Vary the control variable over the following sequence of values: 2, 5, 8, 11, 14, 17.

```
for ( unsigned int i = 2; i <= 17; i += 3 )
```

f) Vary the control variable over the following sequence of values: 99, 88, 77, 66, 55.

```
for ( unsigned int i = 99; i >= 55; i -= 11 )
```

 Common Programming Error 5.3

Not using the proper relational operator in the loop-continuation condition of a loop that counts downward (such as incorrectly using i <= 1 instead of i >= 1 in a loop counting down to 1) is a logic error that yields incorrect results when the program runs.

 Common Programming Error 5.4

Do not use equality operators (!= or ==) in a loop-continuation condition if the loop's control variable increments or decrements by more than 1. For example consider the for statement header for (unsigned int counter = 1; counter != 10; counter += 2). The loop-continuation test counter != 10 never becomes false (resulting in an infinite loop) because counter increments by 2 after each iteration.

Application: Summing the Even Integers from 2 to 20
The program of Fig. 5.5 uses a for statement to sum the even integers from 2 to 20. Each iteration of the loop (lines 11–12) adds control variable number's value to variable total.

```
1   // Fig. 5.5: fig05_05.cpp
2   // Summing integers with the for statement.
3   #include <iostream>
4   using namespace std;
5
6   int main()
7   {
8      unsigned int total = 0; // initialize total
9
10     // total even integers from 2 through 20
11     for ( unsigned int number = 2; number <= 20; number += 2 )
12        total += number;
13
14     cout << "Sum is " << total << endl; // display results
15  } // end main
```

Fig. 5.5 | Summing integers with the for statement. (Part 1 of 2.)

```
Sum is 110
```

Fig. 5.5 | Summing integers with the for statement. (Part 2 of 2.)

The body of the for statement in Fig. 5.5 actually could be merged into the increment portion of the for header by using the *comma operator* as follows:

```
for ( unsigned int number = 2; // initialization
      number <= 20; // loop continuation condition
      total += number, number += 2 ) // total and increment
  ; // empty body
```

Good Programming Practice 5.3

Although statements preceding a for and statements in the body of a for often can be merged into the for header, doing so can make the program more difficult to read, maintain, modify and debug.

Application: Compound Interest Calculations

Consider the following problem statement:

> *A person invests $1000.00 in a savings account yielding 5 percent interest. Assuming that all interest is left on deposit in the account, calculate and print the amount of money in the account at the end of each year for 10 years. Use the following formula for determining these amounts:*
>
> $$a = p\,(1 + r)^n$$
>
> *where*
> p *is the original amount invested (i.e., the principal),*
> r *is the annual interest rate,*
> n *is the number of years and*
> a *is the amount on deposit at the end of the* n^{th} *year.*

The for statement (Fig. 5.6, lines 21–28) performs the indicated calculation for each of the 10 years the money remains on deposit, varying a control variable from 1 to 10 in increments of 1. C++ does *not* include an exponentiation operator, so we use the **standard library function pow** (line 24). The function pow(x, y) calculates the value of x raised to the yth power. In this example, the algebraic expression $(1 + r)^n$ is written as pow(1.0 + rate, year), where variable rate represents *r* and variable year represents *n*. Function pow takes two arguments of type double and returns a double value.

```
1   // Fig. 5.6: fig05_06.cpp
2   // Compound interest calculations with for.
3   #include <iostream>
4   #include <iomanip>
5   #include <cmath> // standard math library
6   using namespace std;
7
8   int main()
9   {
```

Fig. 5.6 | Compound interest calculations with for. (Part I of 2.)

```
10      double amount; // amount on deposit at end of each year
11      double principal = 1000.0; // initial amount before interest
12      double rate = .05; // annual interest rate
13
14      // display headers
15      cout << "Year" << setw( 21 ) << "Amount on deposit" << endl;
16
17      // set floating-point number format
18      cout << fixed << setprecision( 2 );
19
20      // calculate amount on deposit for each of ten years
21      for ( unsigned int year = 1; year <= 10; ++year )
22      {
23         // calculate new amount for specified year
24         amount = principal * pow( 1.0 + rate, year );
25
26         // display the year and the amount
27         cout << setw( 4 ) << year << setw( 21 ) << amount << endl;
28      } // end for
29   } // end main
```

```
Year     Amount on deposit
   1              1050.00
   2              1102.50
   3              1157.63
   4              1215.51
   5              1276.28
   6              1340.10
   7              1407.10
   8              1477.46
   9              1551.33
  10              1628.89
```

Fig. 5.6 | Compound interest calculations with for. (Part 2 of 2.)

This program will not compile without including header <cmath> (line 5). Function pow requires two double arguments. Variable year is an integer. Header <cmath> includes information that tells the compiler to convert the value of year to a temporary double representation before calling the function. This information is contained in pow's function prototype. Chapter 6 summarizes other math library functions.

Common Programming Error 5.5

Forgetting to include the appropriate header when using standard library functions (e.g., <cmath> in a program that uses math library functions) is a compilation error.

A Caution about Using Type **float** or **double** for Monetary Amounts

Lines 10–12 declare the double variables amount, principal and rate. We did this for simplicity because we're dealing with fractional parts of dollars, and we need a type that allows decimal points in its values. Unfortunately, this can cause trouble. Here's a simple explanation of what can go wrong when using float or double to represent dollar amounts (assuming `setprecision(2)` is used to specify two digits of precision when printing): Two dollar amounts stored in the machine could be 14.234 (which prints as 14.23) and 18.673 (which prints as 18.67). When these amounts are added, they produce the internal sum 32.907, which prints as 32.91. Thus your printout could appear as

```
   14.23
 + 18.67
 -------
   32.91
```

but a person adding the individual numbers as printed would expect the sum 32.90! You've been warned! In the exercises, we explore the use of integers to perform monetary calculations. [*Note:* Some third-party vendors sell C++ class libraries that perform precise monetary calculations.]

Using Stream Manipulators to Format Numeric Output

The output statement in line 18 before the `for` loop and the output statement in line 27 in the `for` loop combine to print the values of the variables `year` and `amount` with the formatting specified by the parameterized stream manipulators `setprecision` and `setw` and the nonparameterized stream manipulator `fixed`. The stream manipulator `setw(4)` specifies that the next value output should appear in a field width of 4—i.e., `cout` prints the value with *at least* 4 character positions. If the value to be output is *less* than 4 character positions wide, the value is right justified in the field by default. If the value to be output is *more* than 4 character positions wide, the field width is extended *rightward* to accommodate the entire value. To indicate that values should be output left justified, simply output nonparameterized stream manipulator `left` (found in header `<iostream>`). Right justification can be restored by outputting nonparameterized stream manipulator `right`.

The other formatting in the output statements indicates that variable `amount` is printed as a fixed-point value with a decimal point (specified in line 18 with the stream manipulator `fixed`) right justified in a field of 21 character positions (specified in line 27 with `setw(21)`) and two digits of precision to the right of the decimal point (specified in line 18 with manipulator `setprecision(2)`). We applied the stream manipulators `fixed` and `setprecision` to the output stream (i.e., `cout`) before the `for` loop because these format settings remain in effect until they're changed—such settings are called sticky settings and they do *not* need to be applied during each iteration of the loop. However, the field width specified with `setw` applies *only* to the *next* value output. We discuss C++'s powerful input/output formatting capabilities in Chapter 13, Stream Input/Output: A Deeper Look.

The calculation `1.0 + rate`, which appears as an argument to the `pow` function, is contained in the body of the `for` statement. In fact, this calculation produces the *same* result during each iteration of the loop, so repeating it is wasteful—it should be performed once before the loop.

Be sure to try our Peter Minuit problem in Exercise 5.29. This problem demonstrates the wonders of compound interest.

Performance Tip 5.1

Avoid placing expressions whose values do not change inside loops. Even if you do, many of today's sophisticated optimizing compilers will automatically place such expressions outside the loops in the generated machine code.

> **Performance Tip 5.2**
>
> *Many compilers contain optimization features that improve the performance of the code you write, but it's still better to write good code from the start.*

5.5 do...while Repetition Statement

The do...while repetition statement is similar to the while statement. In the while statement, the loop-continuation condition test occurs at the beginning of the loop *before* the body of the loop executes. The do...while statement tests the loop-continuation condition *after* the loop body executes; therefore, *the loop body always executes at least once.*

Figure 5.7 uses a do...while statement to print the numbers 1–10. Upon entering the do...while statement, line 12 outputs counter's value and line 13 increments counter. Then the program evaluates the loop-continuation test at the bottom of the loop (line 14). If the condition is true, the loop continues from the first body statement in the do...while (line 12). If the condition is false, the loop terminates and the program continues with the next statement after the loop (line 16).

```cpp
1   // Fig. 5.7: fig05_07.cpp
2   // do...while repetition statement.
3   #include <iostream>
4   using namespace std;
5
6   int main()
7   {
8      unsigned int counter = 1; // initialize counter
9
10     do
11     {
12        cout << counter << " "; // display counter
13        ++counter; // increment counter
14     } while ( counter <= 10 ); // end do...while
15
16     cout << endl; // output a newline
17  } // end main
```

```
1 2 3 4 5 6 7 8 9 10
```

Fig. 5.7 | do...while repetition statement.

do...while *Statement UML Activity Diagram*

Figure 5.8 contains the do...while statement's UML activity diagram, which makes it clear that the loop-continuation condition is not evaluated until *after* the loop performs its body at least once. Compare this activity diagram with that of the while statement (Fig. 4.6).

Braces in a do...while *Statement*

It's not necessary to use braces in the do...while statement if there's only one statement in the body; however, most programmers include the braces to avoid confusion between the while and do...while statements. For example,

```cpp
while ( condition )
```

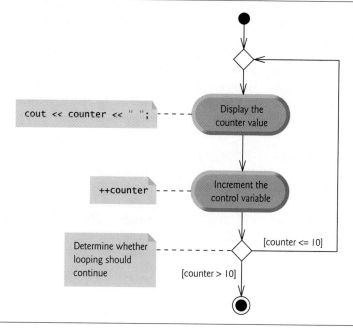

Fig. 5.8 | UML activity diagram for the do...while repetition statement of Fig. 5.7.

normally is regarded as the header of a while statement. A do...while with no braces around the single statement body appears as

```
do
    statement
while ( condition );
```

which can be confusing. You might misinterpret the last line—while(*condition*);—as a while statement containing as its body an empty statement. Thus, the do...while with one statement often is written as follows to avoid confusion:

```
do
{
    statement
} while ( condition );
```

5.6 switch Multiple-Selection Statement

C++ provides the switch multiple-selection statement to perform many different actions based on the possible values of a variable or expression. Each action is associated with the value of an integral constant expression (i.e., any combination of character and integer constants that evaluates to a constant integer value).

GradeBook Class with switch Statement to Count A, B, C, D and F Grades
This next version of the GradeBook class asks the user to enter a set of letter grades, then displays a summary of the number of students who received each grade. The class uses a

switch to determine whether each grade entered is an A, B, C, D or F and to increment
the appropriate grade counter. Class GradeBook is defined in Fig. 5.9, and its member-
function definitions appear in Fig. 5.10. Figure 5.11 shows sample inputs and outputs of
the main program that uses class GradeBook to process a set of grades.

Like earlier versions of the class definition, the GradeBook class definition (Fig. 5.9)
contains function prototypes for member functions setCourseName (line 11), getCourse-
Name (line 12) and displayMessage (line 13), as well as the class's constructor (line 10).
The class definition also declares private data member courseName (line 17).

GradeBook Class Header
Class GradeBook (Fig. 5.9) now contains five additional private data members (lines
18–22)—counter variables for each grade category (i.e., A, B, C, D and F). The class also contains two additional public member functions—inputGrades and displayGradeReport.
Member function inputGrades (declared in line 14) reads an arbitrary number of letter grades
from the user using sentinel-controlled repetition and updates the appropriate grade counter
for each grade entered. Member function displayGradeReport (declared in line 15) outputs
a report containing the number of students who received each letter grade.

```
1   // Fig. 5.9: GradeBook.h
2   // GradeBook class definition that counts letter grades.
3   // Member functions are defined in GradeBook.cpp
4   #include <string> // program uses C++ standard string class
5
6   // GradeBook class definition
7   class GradeBook
8   {
9   public:
10      explicit GradeBook( std::string ); // initialize course name
11      void setCourseName( std::string ); // set the course name
12      std::string getCourseName() const; // retrieve the course name
13      void displayMessage() const; // display a welcome message
14      void inputGrades(); // input arbitrary number of grades from user
15      void displayGradeReport() const; // display report based on user input
16   private:
17      std::string courseName; // course name for this GradeBook
18      unsigned int aCount; // count of A grades
19      unsigned int bCount; // count of B grades
20      unsigned int cCount; // count of C grades
21      unsigned int dCount; // count of D grades
22      unsigned int fCount; // count of F grades
23   }; // end class GradeBook
```

Fig. 5.9 | GradeBook class definition that counts letter grades.

GradeBook Class Source-Code File
Source-code file GradeBook.cpp (Fig. 5.10) contains the member-function definitions for
class GradeBook. Lines 11–15 in the constructor initialize the five grade counters to
0—when a GradeBook object is first created, no grades have been entered yet. These counters
will be incremented in member function inputGrades as the user enters grades. The def-

initions of member functions setCourseName, getCourseName and displayMessage are
identical to those in the earlier versions of class GradeBook.

```cpp
 1   // Fig. 5.10: GradeBook.cpp
 2   // Member-function definitions for class GradeBook that
 3   // uses a switch statement to count A, B, C, D and F grades.
 4   #include <iostream>
 5   #include "GradeBook.h" // include definition of class GradeBook
 6   using namespace std;
 7
 8   // constructor initializes courseName with string supplied as argument;
 9   // initializes counter data members to 0
10   GradeBook::GradeBook( string name )
11      : aCount( 0 ), // initialize count of A grades to 0
12        bCount( 0 ), // initialize count of B grades to 0
13        cCount( 0 ), // initialize count of C grades to 0
14        dCount( 0 ), // initialize count of D grades to 0
15        fCount( 0 )  // initialize count of F grades to 0
16   {
17      setCourseName( name );
18   } // end GradeBook constructor
19
20   // function to set the course name; limits name to 25 or fewer characters
21   void GradeBook::setCourseName( string name )
22   {
23      if ( name.size() <= 25 ) // if name has 25 or fewer characters
24         courseName = name; // store the course name in the object
25      else // if name is longer than 25 characters
26      { // set courseName to first 25 characters of parameter name
27         courseName = name.substr( 0, 25 ); // select first 25 characters
28         cerr << "Name \"" << name << "\" exceeds maximum length (25).\n"
29            << "Limiting courseName to first 25 characters.\n" << endl;
30      } // end if...else
31   } // end function setCourseName
32
33   // function to retrieve the course name
34   string GradeBook::getCourseName() const
35   {
36      return courseName;
37   } // end function getCourseName
38
39   // display a welcome message to the GradeBook user
40   void GradeBook::displayMessage() const
41   {
42      // this statement calls getCourseName to get the
43      // name of the course this GradeBook represents
44      cout << "Welcome to the grade book for\n" << getCourseName() << "!\n"
45         << endl;
46   } // end function displayMessage
47
48   // input arbitrary number of grades from user; update grade counter
49   void GradeBook::inputGrades()
50   {
```

Fig. 5.10 | GradeBook class uses switch statement to count letter grades. (Part 1 of 3.)

```
51      int grade; // grade entered by user
52
53      cout << "Enter the letter grades." << endl
54         << "Enter the EOF character to end input." << endl;
55
56      // loop until user types end-of-file key sequence
57      while ( ( grade = cin.get() ) != EOF )
58      {
59         // determine which grade was entered
60         switch ( grade ) // switch statement nested in while
61         {
62            case 'A': // grade was uppercase A
63            case 'a': // or lowercase a
64               ++aCount; // increment aCount
65               break; // necessary to exit switch
66
67            case 'B': // grade was uppercase B
68            case 'b': // or lowercase b
69               ++bCount; // increment bCount
70               break; // exit switch
71
72            case 'C': // grade was uppercase C
73            case 'c': // or lowercase c
74               ++cCount; // increment cCount
75               break; // exit switch
76
77            case 'D': // grade was uppercase D
78            case 'd': // or lowercase d
79               ++dCount; // increment dCount
80               break; // exit switch
81
82            case 'F': // grade was uppercase F
83            case 'f': // or lowercase f
84               ++fCount; // increment fCount
85               break; // exit switch
86
87            case '\n': // ignore newlines,
88            case '\t': // tabs,
89            case ' ': // and spaces in input
90               break; // exit switch
91
92            default: // catch all other characters
93               cout << "Incorrect letter grade entered."
94                  << " Enter a new grade." << endl;
95               break; // optional; will exit switch anyway
96         } // end switch
97      } // end while
98   } // end function inputGrades
99
100  // display a report based on the grades entered by user
101  void GradeBook::displayGradeReport() const
102  {
```

Fig. 5.10 | GradeBook class uses switch statement to count letter grades. (Part 2 of 3.)

```
103      // output summary of results
104      cout << "\n\nNumber of students who received each letter grade:"
105         << "\nA: " << aCount // display number of A grades
106         << "\nB: " << bCount // display number of B grades
107         << "\nC: " << cCount // display number of C grades
108         << "\nD: " << dCount // display number of D grades
109         << "\nF: " << fCount // display number of F grades
110         << endl;
111   } // end function displayGradeReport
```

Fig. 5.10 | GradeBook class uses switch statement to count letter grades. (Part 3 of 3.)

Reading Character Input

The user enters letter grades for a course in member function inputGrades (lines 49–98). In the while header, in line 57, the parenthesized assignment (grade = cin.get()) executes first. The cin.get() function reads one character from the keyboard and stores that character in integer variable grade (declared in line 51). Normally, characters are stored in variables of type char; however, characters can be stored in any integer data type, because types short, int, long and long long are guaranteed to be at least as big as type char. Thus, we can treat a character either as an integer or as a character, depending on its use. For example, the statement

```
cout << "The character (" << 'a' << ") has the value "
     << static_cast< int > ( 'a' ) << endl;
```

prints the character a and its integer value as follows:

```
The character (a) has the value 97
```

The integer 97 is the character's numerical representation in the computer. Appendix B shows the characters and decimal equivalents from the ASCII (American Standard Code for Information Interchange) character set.

Generally, assignment statements have the value that's assigned to the variable on the left side of the =. Thus, the value of the assignment expression grade = cin.get() is the same as the value returned by cin.get() and assigned to the variable grade.

The fact that assignment expressions have values can be useful for assigning the same value to *several* variables. For example,

```
a = b = c = 0;
```

first evaluates c = 0 (because the = operator associates from right to left). The variable b is then assigned the value of c = 0 (which is 0). Then, a is assigned the value of b = (c = 0) (which is also 0). In the program, the value of grade = cin.get() is compared with the value of EOF (a symbol whose acronym stands for "end-of-file"). We use EOF (which normally has the value –1) as the sentinel value. *However, you do not type the value –1, nor do you type the letters EOF as the sentinel value.* Rather, you type a *system-dependent keystroke combination* that means "end-of-file" to indicate that you have no more data to enter. EOF is a symbolic integer constant that is included into the program via the <iostream> header.[1] If the value assigned

---

1.   To compile this program, some compilers require the header <cstdio> which defines EOF.

to grade is equal to EOF, the while loop (lines 57–97) terminates. We've chosen to represent the characters entered into this program as ints, because EOF has type int.

Entering the EOF Indicator
On OS X/Linux/UNIX systems and many others, end-of-file is entered by typing

> *\<Ctrl> d*

on a line by itself. This notation means to press and hold down the *Ctrl* key, then press the *d* key. On other systems such as Microsoft Windows, end-of-file can be entered by typing

> *\<Ctrl> z*

[*Note:* In some cases, you must press *Enter* after the preceding key sequence. Also, the characters ^Z sometimes appear on the screen to represent end-of-file, as shown in Fig. 5.11.]

Portability Tip 5.1
The keystroke combinations for entering end-of-file are system dependent.

Portability Tip 5.2
Testing for the symbolic constant EOF rather than –1 makes programs more portable. The C standard, from which C++ adopts the definition of EOF, states that EOF is a negative integral value, so EOF could have different values on different systems.

In this program, the user enters grades at the keyboard. When the user presses the *Enter* (or the *Return*) key, the characters are read by the cin.get() function, one character at a time. If the character entered is not end-of-file, the flow of control enters the switch statement (Fig. 5.10, lines 60–96), which increments the appropriate letter-grade counter.

switch Statement Details
The switch statement consists of a series of **case** labels and an optional **default** case. These are used in this example to determine which counter to increment, based on a grade. When the flow of control reaches the switch, the program evaluates the expression in the parentheses (i.e., grade) following keyword switch (line 60). This is called the **controlling expression**. The switch statement compares the value of the controlling expression with each case label. Assume the user enters the letter C as a grade. The program compares C to each case in the switch. If a match occurs (case 'C': in line 72), the program executes the statements for that case. For the letter C, line 74 increments cCount by 1. The break statement (line 75) causes program control to proceed with the first statement after the switch—in this program, control transfers to line 97. This line marks the end of the body of the while loop that inputs grades (lines 57–97), so control flows to the while's condition (line 57) to determine whether the loop should continue executing.

The cases in our switch explicitly test for the lowercase and uppercase versions of the letters A, B, C, D and F. Note the cases in lines 62–63 that test for the values 'A' and 'a' (both of which represent the grade A). Listing cases consecutively with no statements between them enables the cases to perform the same set of statements—when the controlling expression evaluates to either 'A' or 'a', the statements in lines 64–65 will execute. Each case can have multiple statements. The switch selection statement does not require braces around multiple statements in each case.

Without break statements, each time a match occurs in the switch, the statements for that case *and* subsequent cases execute until a break statement or the end of the switch is encountered. This feature is perfect for writing a concise program that displays the iterative song "The Twelve Days of Christmas" in Exercise 5.28.

Common Programming Error 5.6
Forgetting a break *statement when one is needed in a* switch *statement is a logic error.*

Common Programming Error 5.7
Omitting the space between the word case *and the integral value tested in a* switch *statement—e.g., writing* case3: *instead of* case 3:—*is a logic error. The* switch *statement will not perform the appropriate actions when the controlling expression has a value of 3.*

Providing a default *Case*
If *no* match occurs between the controlling expression's value and a case label, the default case (lines 92–95) executes. We use the default case in this example to process all controlling-expression values that are neither valid grades nor newline, tab or space characters. If no match occurs, the default case executes, and lines 93–94 print an error message indicating that an incorrect letter grade was entered. If no match occurs in a switch statement that does not contain a default case, program control continues with the first statement after the switch.

Error-Prevention Tip 5.3
Provide a default *case in* switch *statements. Cases not explicitly tested in a* switch *statement without a* default *case are ignored. Including a* default *case focuses you on the need to process exceptional conditions. There are situations in which no* default *processing is needed. Although the* case *clauses and the* default *case clause in a* switch *statement can occur in* any *order, it's common practice to place the* default *clause last.*

Good Programming Practice 5.4
The last case *in a* switch *statement does not require a* break *statement. Nevertheless, include this* break *for clarity and for symmetry with other cases.*

Ignoring Newline, Tab and Blank Characters in Input
Lines 87–90 in the switch statement of Fig. 5.10 cause the program to skip newline, tab and blank characters. Reading characters one at a time can cause problems. To have the program read the characters, we must send them to the computer by pressing the *Enter* key. This places a newline character in the input after the character we wish to process. Often, this newline character must be specially processed. By including these cases in our switch statement, we prevent the error message in the default case from being printed each time a newline, tab or space is encountered in the input.

Testing Class *GradeBook*
Figure 5.11 creates a GradeBook object (line 8). Line 10 invokes its displayMessage member function to output a welcome message to the user. Line 11 invokes member function inputGrades to read a set of grades from the user and keep track of how many students received each grade. The output window in Fig. 5.11 shows an error message displayed in

response to entering an invalid grade (i.e., E). Line 12 invokes GradeBook member function displayGradeReport (defined in lines 101–111 of Fig. 5.10), which outputs a report based on the grades entered (as in the output in Fig. 5.11).

```
 1   // Fig. 5.11: fig05_11.cpp
 2   // Creating a GradeBook object and calling its member functions.
 3   #include "GradeBook.h" // include definition of class GradeBook
 4
 5   int main()
 6   {
 7      // create GradeBook object
 8      GradeBook myGradeBook( "CS101 C++ Programming" );
 9
10      myGradeBook.displayMessage(); // display welcome message
11      myGradeBook.inputGrades(); // read grades from user
12      myGradeBook.displayGradeReport(); // display report based on grades
13   } // end main
```

```
Welcome to the grade book for
CS101 C++ Programming!

Enter the letter grades.
Enter the EOF character to end input.
a
B
c
C
A
d
f
C
E
Incorrect letter grade entered. Enter a new grade.
D
A
b
^Z


Number of students who received each letter grade:
A: 3
B: 2
C: 3
D: 2
F: 1
```

Fig. 5.11 | Creating a GradeBook object and calling its member functions.

switch Statement UML Activity Diagram

Figure 5.12 shows the UML activity diagram for the general switch multiple-selection statement. Most switch statements use a break in each case to terminate the switch statement after processing the case. Figure 5.12 emphasizes this by including break statements in the activity diagram. Without the break statement, control would not transfer to the first statement after the switch statement after a case is processed. Instead, control would transfer to the next case's actions.

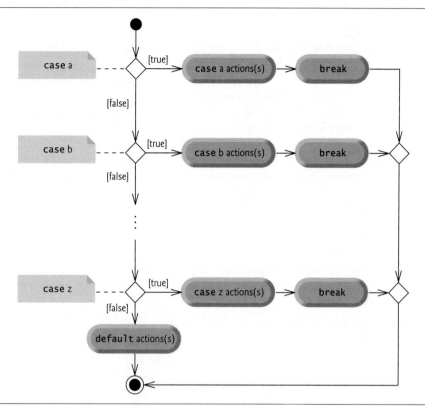

Fig. 5.12 | switch multiple-selection statement UML activity diagram with break statements.

The diagram makes it clear that the break statement at the end of a case causes control to exit the switch statement immediately. Again, note that (besides an initial state, transition arrows, a final state and several notes) the diagram contains action states and decisions. Also, the diagram uses merge symbols to merge the transitions from the break statements to the final state.

When using the switch statement, remember that each case can be used to test only an integral *constant* expression—any combination of character constants and integer constants that evaluates to a constant integer value. A character constant is represented as the specific character in single quotes, such as 'A'. An integer constant is simply an integer value. Also, each case label can specify only one integral constant expression.

Common Programming Error 5.8
Specifying a nonconstant integral expression in a switch's case label is a syntax error.

Common Programming Error 5.9
Providing case labels with identical values in a switch statement is a compilation error.

In Chapter 12, we present a more elegant way to implement switch logic. We'll use a technique called *polymorphism* to create programs that are often clearer, more concise, easier to maintain and easier to extend than programs that use switch logic.

Notes on Data Types

C++ has *flexible data type sizes* (see Appendix C, Fundamental Types). Different applications, for example, might need integers of different sizes. C++ provides several integer types. The range of integer values for each type is platform dependent. In addition to the types int and char, C++ provides the types short (an abbreviation of short int), long (an abbreviation of long int) and long long (an abbreviation of long long int). The minimum range of values for short integers is –32,767 to 32,767. For the vast majority of integer calculations, long integers are sufficient. The minimum range of values for long integers is –2,147,483,647 to 2,147,483,647. On most computers, ints are equivalent either to short or to long. The range of values for an int is at least the same as that for short integers and no larger than that for long integers. The data type char can be used to represent any of the characters in the computer's character set. It also can be used to represent small integers.

C++11 In-Class Initializers

C++11 allows you to provide a default value for a data member when you declare it in the class declaration. For example, lines 19–23 of Fig. 5.9 could have initialized data members aCount, bCount, cCount, dCount and fCount to 0 as follows:

```
unsigned int aCount = 0; // count of A grades
unsigned int bCount = 0; // count of B grades
unsigned int cCount = 0; // count of C grades
unsigned int dCount = 0; // count of D grades
unsigned int fCount = 0; // count of F grades
```

rather than initializing them in the class's constructor (Fig. 5.10, lines 10–18). In later chapters, we'll continue discussing in-class initializers and show how they enable you to perform certain data member initializations that were not possible in earlier C++ versions.

5.7 break and continue Statements

C++ also provides statements break and continue to alter the flow of control. The preceding section showed how break can be used to terminate a switch statement's execution. This section discusses how to use break in a repetition statement.

break Statement

The **break** statement, when executed in a while, for, do...while or switch statement, causes immediate exit from that statement. Program execution continues with the next statement. Common uses of the break statement are to escape early from a loop or to skip the remainder of a switch statement. Figure 5.13 demonstrates the break statement (line 13) exiting a for repetition statement.

When the if statement detects that count is 5, the break statement executes. This terminates the for statement, and the program proceeds to line 18 (immediately after the for statement), which displays a message indicating the control variable value that terminated the loop. The for statement fully executes its body only four times instead of 10. The

```
 1   // Fig. 5.13: fig05_13.cpp
 2   // break statement exiting a for statement.
 3   #include <iostream>
 4   using namespace std;
 5
 6   int main()
 7   {
 8      unsigned int count; // control variable also used after loop terminates
 9
10      for ( count = 1; count <= 10; ++count ) // loop 10 times
11      {
12         if ( count == 5 )
13            break; // break loop only if count is 5
14
15         cout << count << " ";
16      } // end for
17
18      cout << "\nBroke out of loop at count = " << count << endl;
19   } // end main
```

```
1 2 3 4
Broke out of loop at count = 5
```

Fig. 5.13 | break statement exiting a for statement.

control variable count is defined outside the for statement header, so that we can use the control variable both *in* the loop's body and *after* the loop completes its execution.

continue *Statement*

The **continue statement**, when executed in a while, for or do...while statement, skips the remaining statements in the body of that statement and proceeds with the next iteration of the loop. In while and do...while statements, the loop-continuation test evaluates immediately after the continue statement executes. In the for statement, the increment expression executes, then the loop-continuation test evaluates.

Figure 5.14 uses the continue statement (line 11) in a for statement to skip the output statement (line 13) when the nested if (lines 10–11) determines that the value of count is 5. When the continue statement executes, program control continues with the increment of the control variable in the for header (line 8) and loops five more times.

```
 1   // Fig. 5.14: fig05_14.cpp
 2   // continue statement terminating an iteration of a for statement.
 3   #include <iostream>
 4   using namespace std;
 5
 6   int main()
 7   {
 8      for ( unsigned int count = 1; count <= 10; ++count ) // loop 10 times
 9      {
```

Fig. 5.14 | continue statement terminating an iteration of a for statement. (Part 1 of 2.)

```
10          if ( count == 5 ) // if count is 5,
11              continue;        // skip remaining code in loop
12
13          cout << count << " ";
14      } // end for
15
16      cout << "\nUsed continue to skip printing 5" << endl;
17  } // end main
```

```
1 2 3 4 6 7 8 9 10
Used continue to skip printing 5
```

Fig. 5.14 | `continue` statement terminating an iteration of a `for` statement. (Part 2 of 2.)

In Section 5.3, we stated that the `while` statement could be used in most cases to represent the `for` statement. The one exception occurs when the increment expression in the `while` statement follows the `continue` statement. In this case, the increment does not execute before the program tests the loop-continuation condition, and the `while` does not execute in the same manner as the `for`.

Good Programming Practice 5.5

Some programmers feel that break *and* continue *violate structured programming. The effects of these statements can be achieved by structured programming techniques we soon will learn, so these programmers do not use* break *and* continue. *Most programmers consider the use of* break *in* switch *statements acceptable.*

Software Engineering Observation 5.1

There's a tension between achieving quality software engineering and achieving the best-performing software. Often, one of these goals is achieved at the expense of the other. For all but the most performance-intensive situations, apply the following guidelines: First, make your code simple and correct; then make it fast and small, but only if necessary.

5.8 Logical Operators

So far we've studied only simple conditions, such as `counter <= 10`, `total > 1000` and `number != sentinelValue`. We expressed these conditions in terms of the relational operators `>`, `<`, `>=` and `<=`, and the equality operators `==` and `!=`. Each decision tested precisely one condition. To test multiple conditions while making a decision, we performed these tests in separate statements or in nested `if` or `if...else` statements.

C++ provides **logical operators** that are used to form more complex conditions by combining simple conditions. The logical operators are **&&** (logical AND), **||** (logical OR) and **!** (logical NOT, also called logical negation).

Logical AND (&&) Operator

Suppose that we wish to ensure that two conditions are *both* `true` before we choose a certain path of execution. In this case, we can use the **&&** (logical AND) operator, as follows:

```
if ( gender == FEMALE && age >= 65 )
    ++seniorFemales;
```

This `if` statement contains two simple conditions. The condition `gender == FEMALE` is used here to determine whether a person is a female. The condition `age >= 65` determines whether a person is a senior citizen. The simple condition to the left of the `&&` operator evaluates first. If necessary, the simple condition to the right of the `&&` operator evaluates next. As we'll discuss shortly, the right side of a logical AND expression is evaluated *only* if the left side is `true`. The `if` statement then considers the combined condition

```
gender == FEMALE && age >= 65
```

This condition is `true` if and only if *both* of the simple conditions are `true`. Finally, if this combined condition is indeed `true`, the statement in the `if` statement's body increments the count of `seniorFemales`. If either (or both) of the simple conditions are `false`, then the program skips the incrementing and proceeds to the statement following the `if`. The preceding combined condition can be made more readable by adding redundant parentheses:

```
( gender == FEMALE ) && ( age >= 65 )
```

Common Programming Error 5.10
Although 3 < x < 7 is a mathematically correct condition, it does not evaluate as you might expect in C++. Use (3 < x && x < 7) to get the proper evaluation in C++.

Figure 5.15 summarizes the `&&` operator. The table shows all four possible combinations of `false` and `true` values for *expression1* and *expression2*. Such tables are often called truth tables. C++ evaluates to `false` or `true` all expressions that include relational operators, equality operators and/or logical operators.

expression1	expression2	expression1 && expression2
false	false	false
false	true	false
true	false	false
true	true	true

Fig. 5.15 | `&&` (logical AND) operator truth table.

Logical OR (||) Operator
Now let's consider the `||` (logical OR) operator. Suppose we wish to ensure that either *or* both of two conditions are `true` before we choose a certain path of execution. In this case, we use the `||` operator, as in the following program segment:

```
if ( ( semesterAverage >= 90 ) || ( finalExam >= 90 ) )
    cout << "Student grade is A" << endl;
```

This preceding condition contains two simple conditions. The simple condition `semesterAverage >= 90` evaluates to determine whether the student deserves an "A" in the course because of a solid performance throughout the semester. The simple condition finalExam >= 90 evaluates to determine whether the student deserves an "A" in the course because of an outstanding performance on the final exam. The if statement then considers the combined condition

```
( semesterAverage >= 90 ) || ( finalExam >= 90 )
```

and awards the student an "A" if *either or both* of the simple conditions are true. The message "Student grade is A" prints unless *both* of the simple conditions are false. Figure 5.16 is a truth table for the logical OR operator (||).

expression1	expression2	expression1 || expression2
false	false	false
false	true	true
true	false	true
true	true	true

Fig. 5.16 | || (logical OR) operator truth table.

The && operator has a higher precedence than the || operator. Both operators associate from left to right. An expression containing && or || operators evaluates only until the truth or falsehood of the expression is known. Thus, evaluation of the expression

```
( gender == FEMALE ) && ( age >= 65 )
```

stops immediately if gender is not equal to FEMALE (i.e., the entire expression is false) and continues if gender is equal to FEMALE (i.e., the entire expression could still be true if the condition age >= 65 is true). This performance feature for the evaluation of logical AND and logical OR expressions is called **short-circuit evaluation**.

Performance Tip 5.3

In expressions using operator &&, if the separate conditions are independent of one another, make the condition most likely to be false the leftmost condition. In expressions using operator ||, make the condition most likely to be true the leftmost condition. This use of short-circuit evaluation can reduce a program's execution time.

Logical Negation (!) Operator
C++ provides the ! (logical NOT, also called logical negation) operator to "reverse" a condition's meaning. The unary logical negation operator has only a single condition as an operand. The unary logical negation operator is placed *before* a condition when we are interested in choosing a path of execution if the original condition (without the logical negation operator) is false, such as in the following program segment:

```
if ( !( grade == sentinelValue ) )
    cout << "The next grade is " << grade << endl;
```

The parentheses around the condition grade == sentinelValue are needed because the logical negation operator has a higher precedence than the equality operator.

You can often avoid the ! operator by using an appropriate relational or equality operator. For example, the preceding if statement also can be written as follows:

```
if ( grade != sentinelValue )
    cout << "The next grade is " << grade << endl;
```

This flexibility often can help you express a condition in a more "natural" or convenient manner. Figure 5.17 is a truth table for the logical negation operator (!).

expression	!expression
false	true
true	false

Fig. 5.17 | ! (logical negation) operator truth table.

Logical Operators Example

Figure 5.18 demonstrates the logical operators by producing their truth tables. The output shows each expression that's evaluated and its bool result. By default, bool values true and false are displayed by cout and the stream insertion operator as 1 and 0, respectively. We use **stream manipulator boolalpha** (a *sticky* manipulator) in line 9 to specify that the value of each bool expression should be displayed as either the word "true" or the word "false." For example, the result of the expression false && false in line 10 is false, so the second line of output includes the word "false." Lines 9–13 produce the truth table for &&. Lines 16–20 produce the truth table for ||. Lines 23–25 produce the truth table for !.

```
1   // Fig. 5.18: fig05_18.cpp
2   // Logical operators.
3   #include <iostream>
4   using namespace std;
5
6   int main()
7   {
8      // create truth table for && (logical AND) operator
9      cout << boolalpha << "Logical AND (&&)"
10        << "\nfalse && false: " << ( false && false )
11        << "\nfalse && true: " << ( false && true )
12        << "\ntrue && false: " << ( true && false )
13        << "\ntrue && true: " << ( true && true ) << "\n\n";
14
15     // create truth table for || (logical OR) operator
16     cout << "Logical OR (||)"
17        << "\nfalse || false: " << ( false || false )
18        << "\nfalse || true: " << ( false || true )
19        << "\ntrue || false: " << ( true || false )
20        << "\ntrue || true: " << ( true || true ) << "\n\n";
```

Fig. 5.18 | Logical operators. (Part 1 of 2.)

```
21
22      // create truth table for ! (logical negation) operator
23      cout << "Logical NOT (!)"
24          << "\n!false: " << ( !false )
25          << "\n!true: " << ( !true ) << endl;
26   } // end main
```

```
Logical AND (&&)
false && false: false
false && true: false
true && false: false
true && true: true

Logical OR (||)
false || false: false
false || true: true
true || false: true
true || true: true

Logical NOT (!)
!false: true
!true: false
```

Fig. 5.18 | Logical operators. (Part 2 of 2.)

Summary of Operator Precedence and Associativity

Figure 5.19 adds the logical and comma operators to the operator precedence and associativity chart. The operators are shown from top to bottom, in decreasing order of precedence.

Operators						Associativity	Type
::	()					left to right	primary
						[See caution in Fig. 2.10 regarding grouping parentheses.]	
++	--	static_cast< *type* >()				left to right	postfix
++	--	+	-	!		right to left	unary (prefix)
*	/	%				left to right	multiplicative
+	-					left to right	additive
<<	>>					left to right	insertion/extraction
<	<=	>	>=			left to right	relational
==	!=					left to right	equality
&&						left to right	logical AND
||						left to right	logical OR
?:						right to left	conditional
=	+=	-=	*=	/=	%=	right to left	assignment
,						left to right	comma

Fig. 5.19 | Operator precedence and associativity.

5.9 Confusing the Equality (==) and Assignment (=) Operators

There's one error that C++ programmers, no matter how experienced, tend to make so frequently that we feel it requires a separate section. That error is accidentally swapping the operators == (equality) and = (assignment). What makes this so damaging is that it ordinarily does *not* cause *syntax errors*—statements with these errors tend to compile correctly and the programs run to completion, often generating incorrect results through *runtime logic errors*. Some compilers issue a *warning* when = is used in a context where == is expected.

Two aspects of C++ contribute to these problems. One is that *any expression that produces a value can be used in the decision portion of any control statement.* If the value of the expression is zero, it's treated as the value `false`, and if the value is nonzero, it's treated as the value `true`. The second is that assignments produce a value—namely, the value assigned to the variable on the left side of the assignment operator. For example, suppose we intend to write

```
if ( payCode == 4 ) // good
    cout << "You get a bonus!" << endl;
```

but we accidentally write

```
if ( payCode = 4 ) // bad
    cout << "You get a bonus!" << endl;
```

The first `if` statement properly awards a bonus to the person whose `payCode` is equal to 4. The second one—which contains the error—evaluates the assignment expression in the `if` condition to the constant 4. *Any nonzero value is interpreted as `true`*, so this condition always evaluates as `true` and the person *always* receives a bonus regardless of what the actual paycode is! Even worse, the paycode has been *modified* when it was only supposed to be *examined!*

Common Programming Error 5.11

Using operator == for assignment and using operator = for equality are logic errors.

Error-Prevention Tip 5.4

Programmers normally write conditions such as x == 7 with the variable name on the left and the constant on the right. By placing the constant on the left, as in 7 == x, you'll be protected by the compiler if you accidentally replace the == operator with =. The compiler treats this as a compilation error, because you can't change the value of a constant. This will prevent the potential devastation of a runtime logic error.

lvalues *and* rvalues

Variable names are said to be *lvalues* (for "left values") because they can be used on the *left* side of an assignment operator. Constants are said to be *rvalues* (for "right values") because they can be used on only the *right* side of an assignment operator. *Lvalues* can also be used as *rvalues*, but not vice versa.

There's another equally unpleasant situation. Suppose you want to assign a value to a variable with a simple statement like

```
x = 1;
```

but instead write

```
x == 1;
```

Here, too, this is *not* a syntax error. Rather, the compiler simply evaluates the conditional expression. If x is equal to 1, the condition is `true` and the expression evaluates to the value `true`. If x is not equal to 1, the condition is `false` and the expression evaluates to the value `false`. Regardless of the expression's value, there's no assignment operator, so the value simply is lost. The value of x remains unaltered, probably causing an execution-time logic error. Unfortunately, we do not have a handy trick to help you with this problem!

Error-Prevention Tip 5.5

Use your text editor to search for all occurrences of = in your program and check that you have the correct assignment operator or logical operator in each place.

5.10 Structured Programming Summary

Just as architects design buildings by employing the collective wisdom of their profession, so should programmers design programs. Our field is younger than architecture is, and our collective wisdom is sparser. We've learned that structured programming produces programs that are easier than unstructured programs to understand, test, debug, modify, and even prove correct in a mathematical sense.

Figure 5.20 uses activity diagrams to summarize C++'s control statements. The initial and final states indicate the *single entry point* and the *single exit point* of each control statement. Arbitrarily connecting individual symbols in an activity diagram can lead to unstructured programs. Therefore, the programming profession uses only a limited set of control statements that can be combined in only two simple ways to build structured programs.

For simplicity, only *single-entry/single-exit control statements* are used—there's only one way to enter and only one way to exit each control statement. Connecting control statements in sequence to form structured programs is simple—the final state of one control statement is connected to the initial state of the next—that is, they're placed one after another in a program. We've called this control-statement *stacking*. The rules for forming structured programs also allow for control statements to be *nested*.

Figure 5.21 shows the rules for forming structured programs. The rules assume that action states may be used to indicate any action. The rules also assume that we begin with the so-called *simplest activity diagram* (Fig. 5.22), consisting of only an initial state, an action state, a final state and transition arrows.

Applying the rules of Fig. 5.21 always results in an activity diagram with a neat, building-block appearance. For example, repeatedly applying Rule 2 to the simplest activity diagram results in an activity diagram containing many action states in sequence (Fig. 5.23). Rule 2 generates a stack of control statements, so let's call Rule 2 the **stacking rule**. The vertical dashed lines in Fig. 5.23 are not part of the UML—we use them to separate the four activity diagrams that demonstrate Rule 2 of Fig. 5.21 being applied.

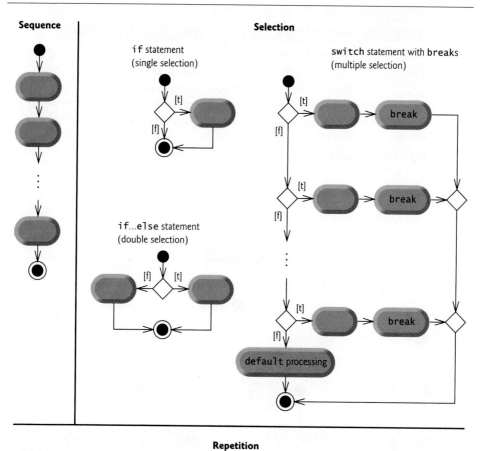

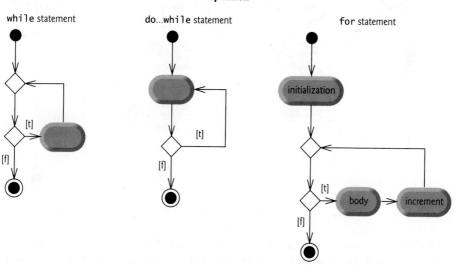

Fig. 5.20 | C++'s single-entry/single-exit sequence, selection and repetition statements.

Rules for forming structured programs
1)   Begin with the "simplest activity diagram" (Fig. 5.22).
2)   Any action state can be replaced by two action states in sequence.
3)   Any action state can be replaced by any control statement (sequence, if, if...else, switch, while, do...while or for).
4)   Rules 2 and 3 can be applied as often as you like and in any order.

Fig. 5.21 | Rules for forming structured programs.

Fig. 5.22 | Simplest activity diagram.

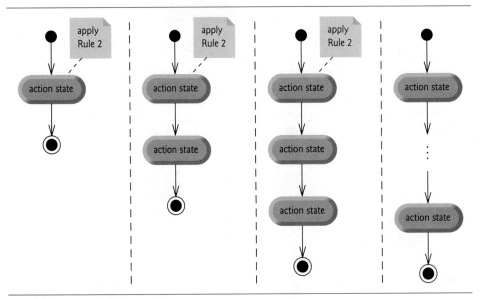

Fig. 5.23 | Repeatedly applying Rule 2 of Fig. 5.21 to the simplest activity diagram.

Rule 3 is the **nesting rule**. Repeatedly applying Rule 3 to the simplest activity diagram results in one with neatly nested control statements. For example, in Fig. 5.24, the action state in the simplest activity diagram is replaced with a double-selection (if...else) statement. Then Rule 3 is applied again to the action states in the double-selection statement, replacing each with a double-selection statement. The dashed action-state symbols around each of the double-selection statements represent an action state that was replaced in the preceding activity diagram. [*Note:* The dashed arrows and dashed action state symbols shown in Fig. 5.24 are not part of the UML. They're used here as pedagogic devices to illustrate that any action state may be replaced with a control statement.]

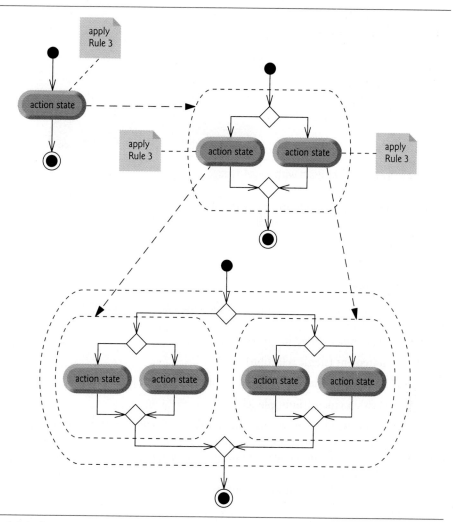

Fig. 5.24 | Applying Rule 3 of Fig. 5.21 to the simplest activity diagram several times.

Rule 4 generates larger, more involved and more deeply *nested* statements. The diagrams that emerge from applying the rules in Fig. 5.21 constitute the set of all possible activity diagrams and hence the set of all possible structured programs. The beauty of the structured approach is that we use only *seven* simple single-entry/single-exit control statements and assemble them in only *two* simple ways.

If the rules in Fig. 5.21 are followed, an activity diagram with illegal syntax (such as that in Fig. 5.25) cannot be created. If you're uncertain about whether a particular diagram is legal, apply the rules of Fig. 5.21 in reverse to try to reduce the diagram to the simplest activity diagram. If it's reducible to the simplest activity diagram, the original diagram is structured; otherwise, it isn't.

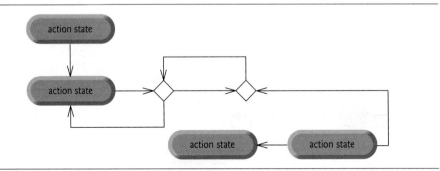

Fig. 5.25 | Activity diagram with illegal syntax.

Structured programming promotes simplicity. Böhm and Jacopini have given us the result that only *three* forms of control are needed:

- Sequence
- Selection
- Repetition

The sequence structure is trivial. Simply list the statements to execute in the order in which they should execute.

Selection is implemented in one of three ways:

- `if` statement (single selection)
- `if...else` statement (double selection)
- `switch` statement (multiple selection)

It's straightforward to prove that the *simple if statement is sufficient* to provide *any* form of selection—everything that can be done with the `if...else` statement and the `switch` statement can be implemented (although perhaps not as clearly and efficiently) by combining `if` statements.

Repetition is implemented in one of three ways:

- `while` statement
- `do...while` statement
- `for` statement

It's straightforward to prove that the *while statement is sufficient* to provide any form of repetition. Everything that can be done with the `do...while` statement and the `for` statement can be done (although perhaps not as smoothly) with the `while` statement.

Combining these results illustrates that *any* form of control ever needed in a C++ program can be expressed in terms of the following:

- sequence
- `if` statement (selection)
- `while` statement (repetition)

and that these control statements can be combined in only *two* ways—stacking and nesting. Indeed, structured programming promotes simplicity.

5.11 Wrap-Up

We've now completed our introduction to control statements, which enable you to control the flow of execution in programs. Chapter 4 discussed the `if`, `if...else` and `while` statements. This chapter demonstrated the `for`, `do...while` and `switch` statements. We showed that any algorithm can be developed using combinations of the sequence structure, the three types of selection statements—`if`, `if...else` and `switch`—and the three types of repetition statements—`while`, `do...while` and `for`. We discussed how you can combine these building blocks to utilize proven program construction and problem-solving techniques. You used the `break` and `continue` statements to alter a repetition statement's flow of control. We also introduced logical operators, which enable you to use more complex conditional expressions in control statements. Finally, we examined the common errors of confusing the equality and assignment operators and provided suggestions for avoiding these errors. In Chapter 6, we examine functions in greater depth.

Summary

Section 5.2 Essentials of Counter-Controlled Repetition
- In C++, it's more precise to call a variable declaration that also reserves memory a definition (p. 192).

Section 5.3 **for** Repetition Statement
- The `for` repetition statement (p. 193) handles all the details of counter-controlled repetition.
- The general format of the `for` statement is

      for (*initialization*; *loopContinuationCondition*; *increment*)
          statement

  where *initialization* initializes the control variable, *loopContinuationCondition* determines whether the loop should continue executing and *increment* increments or decrements the control variable.
- Typically, `for` statements are used for counter-controlled repetition and `while` statements are used for sentinel-controlled repetition.
- The scope of a variable (p. 195) specifies where it can be used in a program.
- The comma operator (p. 195) has the lowest precedence of all C++ operators. The value and type of a comma-separated list of expressions is the value and type of the rightmost expression in the list.
- The initialization, loop-continuation condition and increment expressions of a `for` statement can contain arithmetic expressions. Also, the increment of a `for` statement can be negative.
- If the loop-continuation condition in a `for` header is initially `false`, the body of the `for` statement is not performed. Instead, execution proceeds with the statement following the `for`.

Section 5.4 Examples Using the **for** Statement

- Standard library function pow(x, y) (p. 199) calculates the value of x raised to the yth power. Function pow takes two arguments of type double and returns a double value.

- Parameterized stream manipulator setw (p. 201) specifies the field width in which the next value output should appear, right justified by default. If the value is larger than the field width, the field width is extended to accommodate the entire value. Stream manipulator left (p. 201) causes a value to be left justified and right (p. 201) can be used to restore right justification.

- Sticky output-formatting settings settings (p. 201) remain in effect until they're changed.

Section 5.5 **do...while** Repetition Statement

- The do...while repetition statement tests the loop-continuation condition at the end of the loop, so the body of the loop will be executed at least once. The format for the do...while statement is

```
do
{
    statement
} while ( condition );
```

Section 5.6 **switch** Multiple-Selection Statement

- The switch multiple-selection statement (p. 203) performs different actions based on its controlling expression's value.

- Function cin.get() reads one character from the keyboard. Characters normally are stored in variables of type char (p. 207). A character can be treated either as an integer or as a character.

- A switch statement consists of a series of case labels (p. 208) and an optional default case (p. 208).

- The expression in the parentheses following switch is called the controlling expression (p. 208). The switch statement compares the value of the controlling expression with each case label.

- Consecutive cases with no statements between them perform the same set of statements.

- Each case label can specify only one integral constant expression.

- Each case can have multiple statements. The switch selection statement differs from other control statements in that it does not require braces around multiple statements in each case.

- C++ provides several data types to represent integers—int, char, short, long and long long. The range of integer values for each type is platform dependent.

- C++11 allows you to provide a default value for a data member when you declare it in the class declaration.

Section 5.7 **break** and **continue** Statements

- The break statement (p. 212), when executed in one of the repetition statements (for, while and do...while), causes immediate exit from the statement.

- The continue statement (p. 213), when executed in a repetition statement, skips any remaining statements in the loop's body and proceeds with the next iteration of the loop. In a while or do...while statement, execution continues with the next evaluation of the condition. In a for statement, execution continues with the increment expression in the for statement header.

Section 5.8 Logical Operators

- Logical operators (p. 214) enable you to form complex conditions by combining simple conditions. The logical operators are && (logical AND), || (logical OR) and ! (logical negation).

- The && (logical AND, p. 214) operator ensures that two conditions are *both* true.

- The || (logical OR, p. 215) operator ensures that either *or* both of two conditions are true.
- An expression containing && or || operators evaluates only until the truth or falsehood of the expression is known. This performance feature for the evaluation of logical AND and logical OR expressions is called short-circuit evaluation (p. 216).
- The ! (logical NOT, also called logical negation; p. 216) operator enables a programmer to "reverse" the meaning of a condition. The unary logical negation operator is placed before a condition to choose a path of execution if the original condition (without the logical negation operator) is false. In most cases, you can avoid using logical negation by expressing the condition with an appropriate relational or equality operator.
- When used as a condition, any nonzero value implicitly converts to true; 0 (zero) implicitly converts to false.
- By default, bool values true and false are displayed by cout as 1 and 0, respectively. Stream manipulator boolalpha (p. 217) specifies that the value of each bool expression should be displayed as either the word "true" or the word "false."

Section 5.9 Confusing the Equality (==) and Assignment (=) Operators
- Any expression that produces a value can be used in the decision portion of any control statement. If the value of the expression is zero, it's treated as false, and if the value is nonzero, it's treated as true.
- An assignment produces a value—namely, the value assigned to the variable on the left side of the assignment operator.

Section 5.10 Structured Programming Summary
- Any form of control can be expressed in terms of sequence, selection and repetition statements, and these can be combined in only two ways—stacking and nesting.

Self-Review Exercises

5.1 State whether the following are *true* or *false*. If the answer is *false*, explain why.
  a) Each case label can specify only one integral constant expression.
  b) The switch selection statement differs from other control statements in that it does not require braces around multiple statements in each case.
  c) The expression (x > y || a < b) is true if either the expression x > y is true or the expression a < b is true.
  d) An expression containing the && operator is true if either or both of its operands are true.

5.2 Write a C++ statement or a set of C++ statements to accomplish each of the following:
  a) Sum the even integers between 2 and 999 using a for statement. Use the unsigned int variables sum and count.
  b) Print the value 345.796372 in a 15-character field with precisions of 1, 2 and 3. Print each number on the same line. Left-justify each number in its field.
  c) Calculate the value of 3.5 raised to the power 4 using function pow. Print the result with a precision of 3 in a field width of 20 positions.
  d) Print the integers from 1 to 30 using a while loop and the unsigned int counter variable x. Print only 7 integers per line. [*Hint:* When x % 7 is 0, print a newline character; otherwise, print a tab character.]
  e) Repeat Exercise 5.2(d) using a for statement.

5.3   Find the errors in each of the following code segments and explain how to correct them.

a)
```
unsigned int x = 11;
while ( x <= 10 )
    ++x;
}
```

b)
```
for ( char y = 'a'; y != 'z'; y += 1 )
    cout << y << endl;
```

c)
```
switch ( n )
{
    case 1:
        cout << "The number is 1" << endl;
        break;
    case 2:
        cout << "The number is 2" << endl;
        break;
}
```

d) The following code should print the values 1 to 10.
```
unsigned int n = 1;
while ( n <= 11 )
    cout << n++ << endl;
```

Answers to Self-Review Exercises

5.1   a) True.
b) True.
c) True.
d) False, An expression containing the && operator is true if both of its operands are true.

5.2   a)
```
unsigned int sum = 0;
for ( unsigned int count = 2; count <= 999; count += 2 )
    sum += count;
```
b)
```
cout << fixed << left
    << setprecision( 1 ) << setw( 15 ) << 345.796372
    << setprecision( 2 ) << setw( 15 ) << 345.796372
    << setprecision( 3 ) << setw( 15 ) << 345.796372
    << endl;
```
c)
```
cout << fixed << setprecision( 3 ) << setw( 20 ) << pow( 3.5, 4 ) << endl;
```
d)
```
unsigned int x = 1;
while ( x <= 30 )
{
```

```
         if ( x % 7 == 0 )
            cout << x << endl;
         else
            cout << x << '\t';
         ++x;
      }
   e) for ( unsigned int x = 1; x <= 30; ++x )
      {
         if ( x % 7 == 0 )
            cout << x << endl;
         else
            cout << x << '\t';
      }
```

5.3   a) *Error:* The program does not enter into the while loop.
   Correction: The while statement condition must be lesser or greater than the initial value.
   b) *Error:* Using a character to control a for repetition statement.
   Correction: Use an unsigned int and perform the proper calculation to get the values you desire.

```
      for ( unsigned int y = 1; y != 10; ++y )
         cout << ( static_cast< double >( y ) / 10 ) << endl;
```

   c) *Error:* Missing default statement.
   Correction: Add a default statement at the end of the switch case statement. This is not an error if you are only providing a specific value.
   d) *Error:* Improper relational operator used in the loop-continuation condition.
   Correction: Use < rather than <=, or change 11 to 10.

Exercises

5.4   *(Find the Code Errors)* Find the error(s), if any, in each of the following:
   a)
```
For ( unsigned int x = 100, x >= 1, ++x )
   cout << x << endl;
```
   b) The following code should print whether integer value is odd or even:
```
switch ( value % 2 )
{
   case 0:
      cout << "Even integer" << endl;
   case 1:
      cout << "Odd integer" << endl;
}
```
   c) The following code should output the odd integers from 19 to 1:
```
for ( unsigned int x = 19; x >= 1; x += 2 )
   cout << x << endl;
```
   d) The following code should output the even integers from 2 to 100:
```
unsigned int counter = 2;

do
{
   cout << counter << endl;
   counter += 2;
} While ( counter < 100 );
```

5.5 *(Product Integers)* Write a program that uses a for statement to multiply a sequence of integers. Assume that the first integer read specifies the number of values remaining to be entered. Your program should read only one value per input statement. A typical input sequence might be

    5 1 2 3 4 5

where the 5 indicates that the subsequent 5 values are to be multiplied.

5.6 *(Averaging Integers)* Write a program that uses a for statement to calculate the average of several integers. Assume the last value read is the sentinel 9999. For example, the sequence 10 8 11 7 9 9999 indicates that the program should calculate the average of all the values preceding 9999.

5.7 *(What Does This Program Do?)* What does the following program do?

```cpp
1   // Exercise 5.7: ex05_07.cpp
2   // What does this program do?
3   #include <iostream>
4   using namespace std;
5
6   int main()
7   {
8      unsigned int x; // declare x
9      unsigned int y; // declare y
10
11     // prompt user for input
12     cout << "Enter two integers in the range 1-20: ";
13     cin >> x >> y;  // read values for x and y
14
15     for ( unsigned int i = 1; i <= y; ++i ) // count from 1 to y
16     {
17        for ( unsigned int j = 1; j <= x; ++j ) // count from 1 to x
18           cout << '@'; // output @
19
20        cout << endl; // begin new line
21     } // end outer for
22  } // end main
```

5.8 *(Find the Largest Integer)* Write a program that uses a for statement to find the largest of several integers. Assume that the first value read specifies the number of values remaining.

5.9 *(Product of Even Integers)* Write a program that uses a for statement to calculate and print the product of the even integers from 1 to 15.

5.10 *(Factorials)* The factorial function is used frequently in probability problems. Using the definition of factorial in Exercise 4.34, write a program that uses a for statement to evaluate the factorials of the integers from 1 to 7. Print the results in tabular format. What difficulty might prevent you from calculating the factorial of 25?

5.11 *(Compound Interest)* Modify the compound interest program of Section 5.4 to repeat its steps for the interest rates 11%, 12%, 13%, 14%, 15% and 16%. Use a for statement to vary the interest rate.

5.12 *(Drawing Patterns with Nested for Loops)* Write a program that uses for statements to print the following patterns separately, one below the other. Use for loops to generate the patterns. All asterisks (*) should be printed by a single statement of the form cout << '*'; (this causes the asterisks to print side by side). [*Hint:* The last two patterns require that each line begin with an appropriate number of blanks. *Extra credit:* Combine your code from the four separate problems into a single program that prints all four patterns side by side by making clever use of nested for loops.]

```
(a)              (b)                  (c)                 (d)
*                **********           **********              *
**               *********            *********              **
***              ********             ********               ***
****             *******              *******                ****
*****            ******               ******                 *****
******           *****                *****                  ******
*******          ****                 ****                   *******
********         ***                  ***                    ********
*********        **                   **                     *********
**********       *                    *                      **********
```

5.13 *(Bar Chart)* One interesting application of computers is drawing graphs and bar charts. Write a program that reads five numbers (each between 1 and 30). Assume that the user enters only valid values. For each number that is read, your program should print a line containing that number of adjacent asterisks. For example, if your program reads the number 7, it should print *******.

5.14 *(Calculating Total Sales)* A mail order house sells five different products whose retail prices are: product 1 — $2.98, product 2—$4.50, product 3—$9.98, product 4—$4.49 and product 5—$6.87. Write a program that reads a series of pairs of numbers as follows:
   a) product number
   b) quantity sold

Your program should use a switch statement to determine the retail price for each product. Your program should calculate and display the total retail value of all products sold. Use a sentinel-controlled loop to determine when the program should stop looping and display the final results.

5.15 *(GradeBook Modification)* Modify the GradeBook program of Figs. 5.9–5.11 to calculate the grade-point average. A grade of A is worth 5 points, B is worth 4 points, and so on.

5.16 *(Compound Interest Calculation)* Modify Fig. 5.6 so it uses only integers to calculate the compound interest. [*Hint:* Treat all monetary amounts as numbers of pennies. Then "break" the result into its dollar and cents portions by using the division and modulus operations. Insert a period.]

5.17 *(What Prints?)* Assume i = 2, j = 3, k = 4 and m = 3. What does each statement print?
   a) cout << (i == 1) << endl;
   b) cout << (j == 3) << endl;
   c) cout << (i >= 1 && j < 4) << endl;
   d) cout << (m <= 99 && k < m) << endl;
   e) cout << (j >= i || k == m) << endl;
   f) cout << (k + m < j || 3 - j >= k) << endl;
   g) cout << (!m) << endl;
   h) cout << (!(j - m)) << endl;
   i) cout << (!(k > m)) << endl;

5.18 *(Number Systems Table)* Write a program that prints a table of the binary, octal and hexadecimal equivalents of the decimal numbers in the range 1–256. If you are not familiar with these number systems, read Appendix D. [*Hint:* You can use the stream manipulators dec, oct and hex to display integers in decimal, octal and hexadecimal formats, respectively.]

5.19 *(Calculating π)* Calculate the value of π from the infinite series

$$\pi = 4 - \frac{4}{3} + \frac{4}{5} - \frac{4}{7} + \frac{4}{9} - \frac{4}{11} + \cdots$$

Print a table that shows the approximate value of π after each of the first 1000 terms of this series.

5.20 *(Pythagorean Triples)* A right triangle can have sides that are all integers. A set of three integer values for the sides of a right triangle is called a Pythagorean triple. These three sides must satisfy the relationship that the sum of the squares of two of the sides is equal to the square of the hypotenuse. Find all Pythagorean triples for side1, side2 and hypotenuse all no larger than 500. Use a triple-nested for loop that tries all possibilities. This is an example of **brute force** computing. You'll learn in more advanced computer science courses that there are many interesting problems for which there's no known algorithmic approach other than sheer brute force.

5.21 *(Calculating Salaries)* A company pays its employees as managers (who receive a fixed weekly salary), hourly workers (who receive a fixed hourly wage for up to the first 40 hours they work and "time-and-a-half"—1.5 times their hourly wage—for overtime hours worked), commission workers (who receive $250 plus 5.7 percent of their gross weekly sales), or pieceworkers (who receive a fixed amount of money per item for each of the items they produce—each pieceworker in this company works on only one type of item). Write a program to compute the weekly pay for each employee. You do not know the number of employees in advance. Each type of employee has its own pay code: Managers have code 1, hourly workers have code 2, commission workers have code 3 and pieceworkers have code 4. Use a switch to compute each employee's pay according to that employee's paycode. Within the switch, prompt the user (i.e., the payroll clerk) to enter the appropriate facts your program needs to calculate each employee's pay according to that employee's paycode.

5.22 *(De Morgan's Laws)* In this chapter, we discussed the logical operators &&, || and !. De Morgan's laws can sometimes make it more convenient for us to express a logical expression. These laws state that the expression !(*condition1* && *condition2*) is logically equivalent to the expression (!*condition1* || !*condition2*). Also, the expression !(*condition1* || *condition2*) is logically equivalent to the expression (!*condition1* && !*condition2*). Use De Morgan's laws to write equivalent expressions for each of the following, then write a program to show that the original expression and the new expression in each case are equivalent:

  a) !(x < 5) && !(y >= 7)
  b) !(a == b) || !(g != 5)
  c) !((x <= 8) && (y > 4))
  d) !((i > 4) || (j <= 6))

5.23 *(Diamond of Asterisks)* Write a program that prints the following diamond shape. You may use output statements that print a single asterisk (*), a single blank or a single newline. Maximize your use of repetition (with nested for statements) and minimize the number of output statements.

```
      *
     ***
    *****
   *******
  *********
   *******
    *****
     ***
      *
```

5.24 *(Diamond of Asterisks Modification)* Modify Exercise 5.23 to read an even number in the range 1 to 19 to specify the number of rows in the diamond, then display a diamond of the appropriate size.

5.25 *(Removing break and continue)* A criticism of the break and continue statements is that each is unstructured. These statements can always be replaced by structured statements. Describe in general how you'd remove any break statement from a loop in a program and replace it with some structured equivalent. [*Hint:* The break statement leaves a loop from within the body of the loop. Another way to leave is by failing the loop-continuation test. Consider using in the loop-continuation test a second test that indicates "early exit because of a 'break' condition."] Use the technique you developed here to remove the break statement from the program of Fig. 5.13.

5.26   *(What Does This Code Do?)* What does the following program segment do?

```
 1   for ( unsigned int i = 2; i <= 6; ++i )
 2   {
 3      for ( unsigned int j = 2; j <= 8; ++j )
 4      {
 5         for ( unsigned int k = 2; k <= 7; ++k )
 6            cout << '*';
 7
 8         cout << endl;
 9      } // end inner for
10
11      cout << endl;
12   } // end outer for
```

5.27   *(Removing the continue Statement)* Describe in general how you'd remove any continue statement from a loop in a program and replace it with some structured equivalent. Use the technique you developed here to remove the continue statement from the program of Fig. 5.14.

5.28   *("The Twelve Days of Christmas" Song)* Write a program that uses repetition and switch statements to print the song "The Twelve Days of Christmas." One switch statement should be used to print the day (i.e., "first," "second," etc.). A separate switch statement should be used to print the remainder of each verse. Visit the website www.12days.com/library/carols/12daysofxmas.htm for the complete lyrics to the song.

5.29   *(Peter Minuit Problem)* Legend has it that, in 1626, Peter Minuit purchased Manhattan Island for $24.00 in barter. Did he make a good investment? To answer this question, modify the compound interest program of Fig. 5.6 to begin with a principal of $24.00 and to calculate the amount of interest on deposit if that money had been kept on deposit until this year (e.g., 387 years through 2013). Place the for loop that performs the compound interest calculation in an outer for loop that varies the interest rate from 5% to 10% to observe the wonders of compound interest.

Making a Difference

5.30   *(Global Warming Facts Quiz)* The controversial issue of global warming has been widely publicized by the film *An Inconvenient Truth*, featuring former Vice President Al Gore. Mr. Gore and a U.N. network of scientists, the Intergovernmental Panel on Climate Change, shared the 2007 Nobel Peace Prize in recognition of "their efforts to build up and disseminate greater knowledge about man-made climate change." Research *both* sides of the global warming issue online (you might want to search for phrases like "global warming skeptics"). Create a five-question multiple-choice quiz on global warming, each question having four possible answers (numbered 1–4). Be objective and try to fairly represent both sides of the issue. Next, write an application that administers the quiz, calculates the number of correct answers (zero through five) and returns a message to the user. If the user correctly answers five questions, print "Excellent"; if four, print "Very good"; if three or fewer, print "Time to brush up on your knowledge of global warming," and include a list of the websites where you found your facts.

5.31   *(Tax Plan Alternatives; The "FairTax")* There are many proposals to make taxation fairer. Check out the FairTax initiative in the United States at

     www.fairtax.org/site/PageServer?pagename=calculator

Research how the proposed FairTax works. One suggestion is to eliminate income taxes and most other taxes in favor of a 23% consumption tax on all products and services that you buy. Some FairTax opponents question the 23% figure and say that because of the way the tax is calculated, it would be more accurate to say the rate is 30%—check this carefully. Write a program that prompts the user to enter expenses in various expense categories they have (e.g., housing, food, clothing, transportation, education, health care, vacations), then prints the estimated FairTax that person would pay.

5.32 *(Facebook User Base Growth)* There are approximately 2.5 billion people on the Internet as of January 2013. Facebook reached one billion users in October of 2012. In this exercise, you'll write a program to determine when Facebook will reach 2.5 billion people if it were to grow at fixed monthly percentage rates of 2%, 3%, 4% or 5%. Use the techniques you learned in Fig. 5.6.

Functions and an Introduction to Recursion

Form ever follows function.
—Louis Henri Sullivan

E pluribus unum.
(One composed of many.)
—Virgil

O! call back yesterday, bid time return.
—William Shakespeare

Answer me in one word.
—William Shakespeare

There is a point at which methods devour themselves.
—Frantz Fanon

Objectives

In this chapter you'll learn:

- To construct programs modularly from functions.

- To use common math library functions.

- The mechanisms for passing data to functions and returning results.

- How the function call/return mechanism is supported by the function call stack and activation records.

- To use random number generation to implement game-playing applications.

- How the visibility of identifiers is limited to specific regions of programs.

- To write and use recursive functions.

6.1 Introduction

Most computer programs that solve real-world problems are much larger than the programs presented in the first few chapters of this book. Experience has shown that the best way to develop and maintain a large program is to construct it from small, simple pieces, or components. This technique is called **divide and conquer**.

We'll overview a portion of the C++ Standard Library's math functions. Next, you'll learn how to declare a function with more than one parameter. We'll also present additional information about function prototypes and how the compiler uses them to convert the type of an argument in a function call to the type specified in a function's parameter list, if necessary.

Next, we'll take a brief diversion into simulation techniques with random number generation and develop a version of a popular casino dice game that uses most of the programming techniques you've learned.

We then present C++'s storage-class specifiers and scope rules. These determine the period during which an object exists in memory and where its identifier can be referenced in a program. You'll learn how C++ keeps track of which function is currently executing, how parameters and other local variables of functions are maintained in memory and how a function knows where to return after it completes execution. We discuss topics that help improve program performance—inline functions that can eliminate the overhead of a function call and reference parameters that can be used to pass large data items to functions efficiently.

Many of the applications you develop will have more than one function of the same name. This technique, called function overloading, is used to implement functions that perform similar tasks for arguments of different types or possibly for different numbers of arguments. We consider function templates—a mechanism for defining a family of overloaded functions. The chapter concludes with a discussion of functions that call themselves, either directly, or indirectly (through another function)—a topic called recursion.

6.2 Program Components in C++

As you've seen, C++ programs are typically written by combining new functions and classes you write with "prepackaged" functions and classes available in the C++ Standard Library which provides a rich collection of functions for common mathematical calculations, string manipulations, character manipulations, input/output, error checking and many other useful operations.

Functions allow you to modularize a program by separating its tasks into self-contained units. You've used a combination of library functions and your own functions in every program you've written. Functions you write are referred to as **user-defined functions**. The statements in function bodies are written only once, are reused from perhaps several locations in a program and are hidden from other functions.

There are several motivations for modularizing a program with functions:

- One is the divide-and-conquer approach.

- Another is software reuse. For example, in earlier programs, we did not have to define how to read a line of text from the keyboard—C++ provides this capability via the `getline` function of the `<string>` header.

- A third motivation is to avoid repeating code.

- Also, dividing a program into meaningful functions makes the program easier to debug and maintain.

Software Engineering Observation 6.1

To promote software reusability, every function should be limited to performing a single, well-defined task, and the name of the function should express that task effectively.

As you know, a function is invoked by a function call, and when the called function completes its task, it either returns a *result* or simply returns *control* to the caller. An analogy to this program structure is the hierarchical form of management (Figure 6.1). A boss (similar to the calling function) asks a worker (similar to the called function) to perform a task and report back (i.e., return) the results after completing the task. The boss function does *not* know how the worker function performs its designated tasks. The worker may also call other worker functions, unbeknownst to the boss. This *hiding of implementation details* promotes good software engineering. Figure 6.1 shows the boss

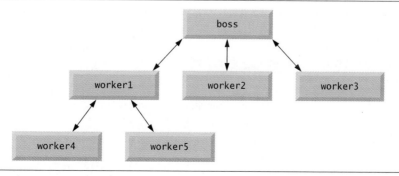

Fig. 6.1 | Hierarchical boss function/worker function relationship.

function communicating with several worker functions. The boss function divides the responsibilities among the worker functions, and worker1 acts as a "boss function" to worker4 and worker5.

6.3 Math Library Functions

Sometimes functions, such as main, are *not* members of a class. Such functions are called **global functions**. Like a class's member functions, the function prototypes for global functions are placed in headers, so that the global functions can be reused in any program that includes the header and that can link to the function's object code. For example, recall that we used function pow of the <cmath> header to raise a value to a power in Figure 5.6. We introduce various functions from the <cmath> header here to present the concept of global functions that do not belong to a particular class.

The <cmath> header provides a collection of functions that enable you to perform common mathematical calculations. For example, you can calculate the square root of 900.0 with the function call

```
sqrt( 900.0 )
```

The preceding expression evaluates to 30.0. Function sqrt takes an argument of type double and returns a double result. There's no need to create any objects before calling function sqrt. Also, *all* functions in the <cmath> header are *global* functions—therefore, each is called simply by specifying the name of the function followed by parentheses containing the function's arguments. If you call sqrt with a negative argument, the function sets a global variable named errno to the constant value EDOM. The variable errno and the constant EDOM are defined in the <cerrno> header. We'll discuss global variables in Section 6.10.

 Error-Prevention Tip 6.1
Do not call sqrt with a negative argument. For industrial-strength code, always check that the arguments you pass to math functions are valid.

Function arguments may be constants, variables or more complex expressions. If c = 13.0, d = 3.0 and f = 4.0, then the statement

```
cout << sqrt( c + d * f ) << endl;
```

displays the square root of 13.0 + 3.0 * 4.0 = 25.0—namely, 5.0. Some math library functions are summarized in Fig. 6.2. In the figure, the variables x and y are of type double.

Function	Description	Example
ceil(x)	rounds x to the smallest integer not less than x	ceil(9.2) is 10.0 ceil(-9.8) is -9.0
cos(x)	trigonometric cosine of x (x in radians)	cos(0.0) is 1.0

Fig. 6.2 | Math library functions. (Part 1 of 2.)

Function	Description	Example
exp(x)	exponential function e^x	exp(1.0) is 2.718282 exp(2.0) is 7.389056
fabs(x)	absolute value of x	fabs(5.1) is 5.1 fabs(0.0) is 0.0 fabs(-8.76) is 8.76
floor(x)	rounds x to the largest integer not greater than x	floor(9.2) is 9.0 floor(-9.8) is -10.0
fmod(x, y)	remainder of x/y as a floating-point number	fmod(2.6, 1.2) is 0.2
log(x)	natural logarithm of x (base e)	log(2.718282) is 1.0 log(7.389056) is 2.0
log10(x)	logarithm of x (base 10)	log10(10.0) is 1.0 log10(100.0) is 2.0
pow(x, y)	x raised to power y (x^y)	pow(2, 7) is 128 pow(9, .5) is 3
sin(x)	trigonometric sine of x (x in radians)	sin(0.0) is 0
sqrt(x)	square root of x (where x is a nonnegative value)	sqrt(9.0) is 3.0
tan(x)	trigonometric tangent of x (x in radians)	tan(0.0) is 0

Fig. 6.2 | Math library functions. (Part 2 of 2.)

6.4 Function Definitions with Multiple Parameters

Let's consider functions with *multiple* parameters. Figures 6.3–6.5 modify class GradeBook by including a user-defined function called maximum that determines and returns the largest of three int grades. When the application executes, the main function (lines 5–13 of Fig. 6.5) creates one GradeBook object (line 8) and calls its inputGrades member function (line 11) to read three integer grades from the user. In class GradeBook's implementation file (Fig. 6.4), lines 52–53 of member function inputGrades prompt the user to enter three integer values and read them from the user. Line 56 calls member function maximum (defined in lines 60–73). Function maximum determines the largest value, then the return statement (line 72) returns that value to the point at which function inputGrades invoked maximum (line 56). Member function inputGrades then stores maximum's return value in data member maximumGrade. This value is then output by calling function display-GradeReport (line 12 of Fig. 6.5). [*Note:* We named this function displayGradeReport because subsequent versions of class GradeBook will use this function to display a complete grade report, including the maximum and minimum grades.] In Chapter 7, we'll enhance class GradeBook to process sets of grades.

```
1   // Fig. 6.3: GradeBook.h
2   // Definition of class GradeBook that finds the maximum of three grades.
3   // Member functions are defined in GradeBook.cpp
4   #include <string> // program uses C++ standard string class
5
6   // GradeBook class definition
7   class GradeBook
8   {
9   public:
10     explicit GradeBook( std::string ); // initializes course name
11     void setCourseName( std::string ); // set the course name
12     std::string getCourseName() const; //retrieve the course name
13     void displayMessage() const; // display a welcome message
14     void inputGrades(); // input three grades from user
15     void displayGradeReport() const; // display report based on the grades
16     int maximum( int, int, int ) const; // determine max of 3 values
17   private:
18     std::string courseName; // course name for this GradeBook
19     int maximumGrade; // maximum of three grades
20   }; // end class GradeBook
```

Fig. 6.3 | Definition of class GradeBook that finds the maximum of three grades.

```
1   // Fig. 6.4: GradeBook.cpp
2   // Member-function definitions for class GradeBook that
3   // determines the maximum of three grades.
4   #include <iostream>
5   using namespace std;
6
7   #include "GradeBook.h" // include definition of class GradeBook
8
9   // constructor initializes courseName with string supplied as argument;
10  // initializes maximumGrade to 0
11  GradeBook::GradeBook( string name )
12     : maximumGrade( 0 ) // this value will be replaced by the maximum grade
13  {
14     setCourseName( name ); // validate and store courseName
15  } // end GradeBook constructor
16
17  // function to set the course name; limits name to 25 or fewer characters
18  void GradeBook::setCourseName( string name )
19  {
20     if ( name.size() <= 25 ) // if name has 25 or fewer characters
21        courseName = name; // store the course name in the object
22     else // if name is longer than 25 characters
23     { // set courseName to first 25 characters of parameter name
24        courseName = name.substr( 0, 25 ); // select first 25 characters
25        cerr << "Name \"" << name << "\" exceeds maximum length (25).\n"
26           << "Limiting courseName to first 25 characters.\n" << endl;
27     } // end if...else
28  } // end function setCourseName
```

Fig. 6.4 | Member-function definitions for class GradeBook that determines the maximum of three grades. (Part 1 of 2.)

```
29
30    // function to retrieve the course name
31    string GradeBook::getCourseName() const
32    {
33       return courseName;
34    } // end function getCourseName
35
36    // display a welcome message to the GradeBook user
37    void GradeBook::displayMessage() const
38    {
39       // this statement calls getCourseName to get the
40       // name of the course this GradeBook represents
41       cout << "Welcome to the grade book for\n" << getCourseName() << "!\n"
42          << endl;
43    } // end function displayMessage
44
45    // input three grades from user; determine maximum
46    void GradeBook::inputGrades()
47    {
48       int grade1; // first grade entered by user
49       int grade2; // second grade entered by user
50       int grade3; // third grade entered by user
51
52       cout << "Enter three integer grades: ";
53       cin >> grade1 >> grade2 >> grade3;
54
55       // store maximum in member maximumGrade
56       maximumGrade = maximum( grade1, grade2, grade3 );
57    } // end function inputGrades
58
59    // returns the maximum of its three integer parameters
60    int GradeBook::maximum( int x, int y, int z ) const
61    {
62       int maximumValue = x; // assume x is the largest to start
63
64       // determine whether y is greater than maximumValue
65       if ( y > maximumValue )
66          maximumValue = y; // make y the new maximumValue
67
68       // determine whether z is greater than maximumValue
69       if ( z > maximumValue )
70          maximumValue = z; // make z the new maximumValue
71
72       return maximumValue;
73    } // end function maximum
74
75    // display a report based on the grades entered by user
76    void GradeBook::displayGradeReport() const
77    {
78       // output maximum of grades entered
79       cout << "Maximum of grades entered: " << maximumGrade << endl;
80    } // end function displayGradeReport
```

Fig. 6.4 | Member-function definitions for class GradeBook that determines the maximum of three grades. (Part 2 of 2.)

```
1   // Fig. 6.5: fig06_05.cpp
2   // Create GradeBook object, input grades and display grade report.
3   #include "GradeBook.h" // include definition of class GradeBook
4
5   int main()
6   {
7      // create GradeBook object
8      GradeBook myGradeBook( "CS101 C++ Programming" );
9
10     myGradeBook.displayMessage(); // display welcome message
11     myGradeBook.inputGrades(); // read grades from user
12     myGradeBook.displayGradeReport(); // display report based on grades
13  } // end main
```

```
Welcome to the grade book for
CS101 C++ Programming!

Enter three integer grades: 86 67 75
Maximum of grades entered: 86
```

```
Welcome to the grade book for
CS101 C++ Programming!

Enter three integer grades: 67 86 75
Maximum of grades entered: 86
```

```
Welcome to the grade book for
CS101 C++ Programming!

Enter three integer grades: 67 75 86
Maximum of grades entered: 86
```

Fig. 6.5 | Create GradeBook object, input grades and display grade report.

Software Engineering Observation 6.2

The commas used in line 56 of Fig. 6.4 to separate the arguments to function maximum are not comma operators as discussed in Section 5.3. The comma operator guarantees that its operands are evaluated left to right. The order of evaluation of a function's arguments, however, is not specified by the C++ standard. Thus, different compilers can evaluate function arguments in different orders. The C++ standard does guarantee that all arguments in a function call are evaluated before the called function executes.

Portability Tip 6.1

Sometimes when a function's arguments are expressions, such as those with calls to other functions, the order in which the compiler evaluates the arguments could affect the values of one or more of the arguments. If the evaluation order changes between compilers, the argument values passed to the function could vary, causing subtle logic errors.

Error-Prevention Tip 6.2
If you have doubts about the order of evaluation of a function's arguments and whether the order would affect the values passed to the function, evaluate the arguments in separate assignment statements before the function call, assign the result of each expression to a local variable, then pass those variables as arguments to the function.

Function Prototype for maximum

Member function maximum's prototype (Fig. 6.3, line 16) indicates that the function returns an integer value, has the name maximum and requires three integer parameters to perform its task. The function's first line (Fig. 6.4, line 60) matches the function prototype and indicates that the parameter names are x, y and z. When maximum is called (Fig. 6.4, line 56), the parameter x is initialized with the value of the argument grade1, the parameter y is initialized with the value of the argument grade2 and the parameter z is initialized with the value of the argument grade3. There must be one argument in the function call for each parameter (also called a **formal parameter**) in the function definition.

Notice that multiple parameters are specified in both the function prototype and the function header as a comma-separated list. The compiler refers to the function prototype to check that calls to maximum contain the correct number and types of arguments and that the types of the arguments are in the correct order. In addition, the compiler uses the prototype to ensure that the value returned by the function can be used correctly in the expression that called the function (e.g., a function call that returns void *cannot* be used as the right side of an assignment statement). Each argument must be *consistent* with the type of the corresponding parameter. For example, a parameter of type double can receive values like 7.35, 22 or –0.03456, but not a string like "hello". If the arguments passed to a function do *not* match the types specified in the function's prototype, the compiler attempts to convert the arguments to those types. Section 6.5 discusses this conversion.

Common Programming Error 6.1
Declaring function parameters of the same type as double x, y instead of double x, double y is a syntax error—a type is required for each parameter in the parameter list.

Common Programming Error 6.2
Compilation errors occur if the function prototype, header and calls do not all agree in the number, type and order of arguments and parameters, and in the return type. Linker errors and other types of errors can occur as well as you'll see later in the book.

Software Engineering Observation 6.3
A function that has many parameters may be performing too many tasks. Consider dividing the function into smaller functions that perform the separate tasks. Limit the function header to one line if possible.

Logic of Function maximum

To determine the maximum value (lines 60–73 of Fig. 6.4), we begin with the assumption that parameter x contains the largest value, so line 62 of function maximum declares local variable maximumValue and initializes it with the value of parameter x. Of course, it's possible that parameter y or z contains the actual largest value, so we must compare each of these values with maximumValue. The if statement in lines 65–66 determines whether y is greater than maximumValue and, if so, assigns y to maximumValue. The if statement in lines 69–70 determines whether z is greater than maximumValue and, if so, assigns z to maximumValue. At this point the largest of the three values is in maximumValue, so line 72 returns that value to the call in line 56. When program control returns to the point in the program where maximum was called, maximum's parameters x, y and z are no longer accessible to the program.

Returning Control from a Function to Its Caller

There are several ways to return control to the point at which a function was invoked. If the function does *not* return a result (i.e., it has a void return type), control returns when the program reaches the function-ending right brace, or by execution of the statement

```
return;
```

If the function *does* return a result, the statement

```
return expression;
```

evaluates *expression* and returns the value of *expression* to the caller. Some compilers issue errors and others issue warnings if you do *not* provide an appropriate return statement in a function that's supposed to return a result.

6.5 Function Prototypes and Argument Coercion

A function prototype (also called a function declaration) tells the compiler the name of a function, the type of data it returns, the number of parameters it expects to receive, the types of those parameters and the order in which the parameters of those types are expected.

Software Engineering Observation 6.4
Function prototypes are required unless the function is defined before it is used. Use #include preprocessing directives to obtain function prototypes for the C++ Standard Library functions from the headers of the appropriate libraries (e.g., the prototype for sqrt is in header <cmath>; a partial list of C++ Standard Library headers appears in Section 6.6). Also use #include to obtain headers containing function prototypes written by you or other programmers.

Common Programming Error 6.3
If a function is defined before it's invoked, then its definition also serves as the function's prototype, so a separate prototype is unnecessary. If a function is invoked before it's defined, and that function does not have a function prototype, a compilation error occurs.

Software Engineering Observation 6.5
Always provide function prototypes, even though it's possible to omit them when functions are defined before they're used. Providing the prototypes avoids tying the code to the order in which functions are defined (which can easily change as a program evolves).

Function Signatures

The portion of a function prototype that includes the *name of the function* and the *types of its arguments* is called the **function signature** or simply the **signature**. The function signature does not specify the function's return type. *Functions in the same scope must have unique signatures.* The scope of a function is the region of a program in which the function is known and accessible. We'll say more about scope in Section 6.11.

In Fig. 6.3, if the function prototype in line 16 had been written

```
void maximum( int, int, int );
```

the compiler would report an error, because the void return type in the function prototype would differ from the int return type in the function header. Similarly, such a prototype would cause the statement

```
cout << maximum( 6, 7, 0 );
```

to generate a compilation error, because that statement depends on maximum to return a value to be displayed.

Argument Coercion

An important feature of function prototypes is **argument coercion**—i.e., forcing arguments to the appropriate types specified by the parameter declarations. For example, a program can call a function with an integer argument, even though the function prototype specifies a double argument—the function will still work correctly.

Argument Promotion Rules and Implicit Conversions[1]

Sometimes, argument values that do not correspond precisely to the parameter types in the function prototype can be converted by the compiler to the proper type before the function is called. These conversions occur as specified by C++'s **promotion rules**. The promotion rules indicate the *implicit conversions* that the compiler can perform between fundamental types. An int can be converted to a double. A double can also be converted to an int but the fractional part of the double value is *truncated*. Keep in mind that double variables can hold numbers of much greater magnitude than int variables, so the loss of data may be considerable. Values may also be modified when converting large integer types to small integer types (e.g., long to short), signed to unsigned or unsigned to signed. Unsigned integers range from 0 to approximately twice the positive range of the corresponding signed type.

The promotion rules apply to expressions containing values of two or more data types; such expressions are also referred to as **mixed-type expressions**. The type of each value in a mixed-type expression is promoted to the "highest" type in the expression (actually a *temporary* version of each value is created and used for the expression—the original values remain unchanged). Promotion also occurs when the type of a function argument does *not* match the parameter type specified in the function definition or prototype. Figure 6.6 lists the arithmetic data types in order from "highest type" to "lowest type."

---

1.   Promotions and conversions are complex topics discussed in Section 4 and the beginning of Section 5 of the C++ standard. You can purchase a copy of the standard at bit.ly/CPlusPlus11Standard.

Data types	
long double	
double	
float	
unsigned long long int	(synonymous with unsigned long long)
long long int	(synonymous with long long)
unsigned long int	(synonymous with unsigned long)
long int	(synonymous with long)
unsigned int	(synonymous with unsigned)
int	
unsigned short int	(synonymous with unsigned short)
short int	(synonymous with short)
unsigned char	
char and signed char	
bool	

Fig. 6.6 | Promotion hierarchy for arithmetic arithmetic data types.

Conversions Can Result in Incorrect Values

Converting values to *lower* fundamental types can result in incorrect values. Therefore, a value can be converted to a lower fundamental type only by *explicitly* assigning the value to a variable of lower type (some compilers will issue a warning in this case) or by using a *cast operator* (see Section 4.9). Function argument values are converted to the parameter types in a function prototype as if they were being assigned directly to variables of those types. If a square function that uses an integer parameter is called with a floating-point argument, the argument is converted to int (a lower type), and square could return an incorrect value. For example, square(4.5) returns 16, not 20.25.

Common Programming Error 6.4

It's a compilation error if the arguments in a function call do not match the number and types of the parameters declared in the corresponding function prototype. It's also an error if the number of arguments in the call matches, but the arguments cannot be implicitly converted to the expected types.

6.6 C++ Standard Library Headers

The C++ Standard Library is divided into many portions, each with its own header. The headers contain the function prototypes for the related functions that form each portion of the library. The headers also contain definitions of various class types and functions, as well as constants needed by those functions. A header "instructs" the compiler on how to interface with library and user-written components.

Figure 6.7 lists some common C++ Standard Library headers, most of which are discussed later in the book. The term "macro" that's used several times in Fig. 6.7 is discussed in detail in Appendix E, Preprocessor.

Standard Library header	Explanation
`<iostream>`	Contains function prototypes for the C++ standard input and output functions, introduced in Chapter 2, and is covered in more detail in Chapter 13, Stream Input/Output: A Deeper Look.
`<iomanip>`	Contains function prototypes for stream manipulators that format streams of data. This header is first used in Section 4.9 and is discussed in more detail in Chapter 13, Stream Input/Output: A Deeper Look.
`<cmath>`	Contains function prototypes for math library functions (Section 6.3).
`<cstdlib>`	Contains function prototypes for conversions of numbers to text, text to numbers, memory allocation, random numbers and various other utility functions. Portions of the header are covered in Section 6.7; Chapter 11, Operator Overloading; Class `string`; Chapter 17, Exception Handling: A Deeper Look; Chapter 22, Bits, Characters, C Strings and `struct`s; and Appendix F, C Legacy Code Topics.
`<ctime>`	Contains function prototypes and types for manipulating the time and date. This header is used in Section 6.7.
`<array>`, `<vector>`, `<list>`, `<forward_list>`, `<deque>`, `<queue>`, `<stack>`, `<map>`, `<unordered_map>`, `<unordered_set>`, `<set>`, `<bitset>`	These headers contain classes that implement the C++ Standard Library containers. Containers store data during a program's execution. The `<vector>` header is first introduced in Chapter 7, Class Templates `array` and `vector`; Catching Exceptions. We discuss all these headers in Chapter 15, Standard Library Containers and Iterators.
`<cctype>`	Contains function prototypes for functions that test characters for certain properties (such as whether the character is a digit or a punctuation), and function prototypes for functions that can be used to convert lowercase letters to uppercase letters and vice versa. These topics are discussed in Chapter 22, Bits, Characters, C Strings and `struct`s.
`<cstring>`	Contains function prototypes for C-style string-processing functions. This header is used in Chapter 10, Operator Overloading; Class `string`.
`<typeinfo>`	Contains classes for runtime type identification (determining data types at execution time). This header is discussed in Section 12.8.
`<exception>`, `<stdexcept>`	These headers contain classes that are used for exception handling (discussed in Chapter 17, Exception Handling: A Deeper Look).
`<memory>`	Contains classes and functions used by the C++ Standard Library to allocate memory to the C++ Standard Library containers. This header is used in Chapter 17, Exception Handling: A Deeper Look.
`<fstream>`	Contains function prototypes for functions that perform input from and output to files on disk (discussed in Chapter 14, File Processing).
`<string>`	Contains the definition of class `string` from the C++ Standard Library (discussed in Chapter 21, Class `string` and String Stream Processing).

Fig. 6.7 | C++ Standard Library headers. (Part 1 of 2.)

Standard Library header	Explanation
`<sstream>`	Contains function prototypes for functions that perform input from strings in memory and output to strings in memory (discussed in Chapter 21, Class `string` and String Stream Processing).
`<functional>`	Contains classes and functions used by C++ Standard Library algorithms. This header is used in Chapter 15.
`<iterator>`	Contains classes for accessing data in the C++ Standard Library containers. This header is used in Chapter 15.
`<algorithm>`	Contains functions for manipulating data in C++ Standard Library containers. This header is used in Chapter 15.
`<cassert>`	Contains macros for adding diagnostics that aid program debugging. This header is used in Appendix E, Preprocessor.
`<cfloat>`	Contains the floating-point size limits of the system.
`<climits>`	Contains the integral size limits of the system.
`<cstdio>`	Contains function prototypes for the C-style standard input/output library functions.
`<locale>`	Contains classes and functions normally used by stream processing to process data in the natural form for different languages (e.g., monetary formats, sorting strings, character presentation, etc.).
`<limits>`	Contains classes for defining the numerical data type limits on each computer platform.
`<utility>`	Contains classes and functions that are used by many C++ Standard Library headers.

Fig. 6.7 | C++ Standard Library headers. (Part 2 of 2.)

6.7 Case Study: Random Number Generation

[*Note:* The random-number generation techniques shown in this section and Section 6.8 are included for readers who are not yet using C++11 compilers. In Section 6.9, we'll present C++11's improved random-number capabilities.]

We now take a brief and hopefully entertaining diversion into a popular programming application, namely simulation and game playing. In this and the next section, we develop a game-playing program that includes multiple functions.

The element of chance can be introduced into computer applications by using the C++ Standard Library function **rand**. Consider the following statement:

```
i = rand();
```

The function `rand` generates an unsigned integer between 0 and RAND_MAX (a symbolic constant defined in the <cstdlib> header). You can determine the value of RAND_MAX for your system simply by displaying the constant. If `rand` truly produces integers at random, every number between 0 and RAND_MAX has an equal *chance* (or probability) of being chosen each time `rand` is called.

The range of values produced directly by the function rand often is different than what a specific application requires. For example, a program that simulates coin tossing might require only 0 for "heads" and 1 for "tails." A program that simulates rolling a six-sided die would require random integers in the range 1 to 6. A program that randomly predicts the next type of spaceship (out of four possibilities) that will fly across the horizon in a video game might require random integers in the range 1 through 4.

Rolling a Six-Sided Die

To demonstrate rand, Fig. 6.8 simulates 20 rolls of a six-sided die and displays the value of each roll. The function prototype for the rand function is in <cstdlib>. To produce integers in the range 0 to 5, we use the modulus operator (%) with rand as follows:

```
rand() % 6
```

This is called **scaling**. The number 6 is called the **scaling factor**. We then **shift** the range of numbers produced by adding 1 to our previous result. Figure 6.8 confirms that the results are in the range 1 to 6. If you execute this program more than once, you'll see that it produces the same "random" values each time. We'll show how to fix this in Figure 6.10.

```cpp
1   // Fig. 6.8: fig06_08.cpp
2   // Shifted, scaled integers produced by 1 + rand() % 6.
3   #include <iostream>
4   #include <iomanip>
5   #include <cstdlib> // contains function prototype for rand
6   using namespace std;
7
8   int main()
9   {
10     // loop 20 times
11     for ( unsigned int counter = 1; counter <= 20; ++counter )
12     {
13        // pick random number from 1 to 6 and output it
14        cout << setw( 10 ) << ( 1 + rand() % 6 );
15
16        // if counter is divisible by 5, start a new line of output
17        if ( counter % 5 == 0 )
18           cout << endl;
19     } // end for
20  } // end main
```

```
6         6         5         5         6
5         1         1         5         3
6         6         2         4         2
6         2         3         4         1
```

Fig. 6.8 | Shifted, scaled integers produced by 1 + rand() % 6.

Rolling a Six-Sided Die 6,000,000 Times

To show that the numbers produced by rand occur with approximately equal likelihood, Fig. 6.9 simulates 6,000,000 rolls of a die. Each integer in the range 1 to 6 should appear approximately 1,000,000 times. This is confirmed by the program's output.

```
1   // Fig. 6.9: fig06_09.cpp
2   // Rolling a six-sided die 6,000,000 times.
3   #include <iostream>
4   #include <iomanip>
5   #include <cstdlib> // contains function prototype for rand
6   using namespace std;
7
8   int main()
9   {
10     unsigned int frequency1 = 0; // count of 1s rolled
11     unsigned int frequency2 = 0; // count of 2s rolled
12     unsigned int frequency3 = 0; // count of 3s rolled
13     unsigned int frequency4 = 0; // count of 4s rolled
14     unsigned int frequency5 = 0; // count of 5s rolled
15     unsigned int frequency6 = 0; // count of 6s rolled
16
17     // summarize results of 6,000,000 rolls of a die
18     for ( unsigned int roll = 1; roll <= 6000000; ++roll )
19     {
20        unsigned int face = 1 + rand() % 6; // random number from 1 to 6
21
22        // determine roll value 1-6 and increment appropriate counter
23        switch ( face )
24        {
25           case 1:
26              ++frequency1; // increment the 1s counter
27              break;
28           case 2:
29              ++frequency2; // increment the 2s counter
30              break;
31           case 3:
32              ++frequency3; // increment the 3s counter
33              break;
34           case 4:
35              ++frequency4; // increment the 4s counter
36              break;
37           case 5:
38              ++frequency5; // increment the 5s counter
39              break;
40           case 6:
41              ++frequency6; // increment the 6s counter
42              break;
43           default: // invalid value
44              cout << "Program should never get here!";
45        } // end switch
46     } // end for
47
48     cout << "Face" << setw( 13 ) << "Frequency" << endl; // output headers
49     cout << "   1" << setw( 13 ) << frequency1
50        << "\n   2" << setw( 13 ) << frequency2
51        << "\n   3" << setw( 13 ) << frequency3
52        << "\n   4" << setw( 13 ) << frequency4
```

Fig. 6.9 | Rolling a six-sided die 6,000,000 times. (Part 1 of 2.)

```
53          << "\n  5" << setw( 13 ) << frequency5
54          << "\n  6" << setw( 13 ) << frequency6 << endl;
55  } // end main
```

Face	Frequency
1	999702
2	1000823
3	999378
4	998898
5	1000777
6	1000422

Fig. 6.9 | Rolling a six-sided die 6,000,000 times. (Part 2 of 2.)

As the output shows, we can simulate the rolling of a six-sided die by scaling and shifting the values produced by rand. The program should *never* get to the default case (lines 43–44) in the switch structure, because the switch's controlling expression (face) *always* has values in the range 1–6; however, we provide the default case as a matter of good practice. After we study arrays in Chapter 7, we show how to replace the entire switch structure in Fig. 6.9 elegantly with a single-line statement.

Error-Prevention Tip 6.3

Provide a default case in a switch to catch errors even if you are absolutely, positively certain that you have no bugs!

Randomizing the Random Number Generator

Executing the program of Fig. 6.8 again produces

6	6	5	5	6
5	1	1	5	3
6	6	2	4	2
6	2	3	4	1

The program prints exactly the *same* sequence of values shown in Fig. 6.8. How can these be random numbers? *When debugging a simulation program, this repeatability is essential for proving that corrections to the program work properly.*

Function rand actually generates **pseudorandom numbers**. Repeatedly calling rand produces a sequence of numbers that appears to be random. However, the sequence *repeats* itself each time the program executes. Once a program has been thoroughly debugged, it can be conditioned to produce a *different* sequence of random numbers for each execution. This is called **randomizing** and is accomplished with the C++ Standard Library function **srand**. Function srand takes an unsigned integer argument and seeds the rand function to produce a different sequence of random numbers for each execution. C++11 provides additional random number capabilities that can produce **nondeterministic random numbers**—a set of random numbers that can't be predicted. Such random number generators are used in simulations and security scenarios where predictability is undesirable. Section 6.9 introduces C++11 random-number generation capabilities.

Good Programming Practice 6.1

Ensure that your program seeds the random number generator differently (and only once) each time the program executes; otherwise, an attacker would easily be able to determine the sequence of pseudorandom numbers that would be produced.

Seeding the Random Number Generator with srand

Figure 6.10 demonstrates function srand. The program uses the data type unsigned int. An int is represented by at least two bytes, is typically four bytes on 32-bit systems and can be as much as eight bytes on 64-bit systems. An int can have positive and negative values. A variable of type unsigned int is also stored in at least two bytes of memory. A four-byte unsigned int can have only *nonnegative* values in the range 0–4294967295. Function srand takes an unsigned int value as an argument. The function prototype for the srand function is in header <cstdlib>.

```
1   // Fig. 6.10: fig06_10.cpp
2   // Randomizing the die-rolling program.
3   #include <iostream>
4   #include <iomanip>
5   #include <cstdlib> // contains prototypes for functions srand and rand
6   using namespace std;
7
8   int main()
9   {
10     unsigned int seed = 0; // stores the seed entered by the user
11
12     cout << "Enter seed: ";
13     cin >> seed;
14     srand( seed ); // seed random number generator
15
16     // loop 10 times
17     for ( unsigned int counter = 1; counter <= 10; ++counter )
18     {
19        // pick random number from 1 to 6 and output it
20        cout << setw( 10 ) << ( 1 + rand() % 6 );
21
22        // if counter is divisible by 5, start a new line of output
23        if ( counter % 5 == 0 )
24           cout << endl;
25     } // end for
26  } // end main
```

```
Enter seed: 67
         6         1         4         6         2
         1         6         1         6         4
```

```
Enter seed: 432
         4         6         3         1         6
         3         1         5         4         2
```

Fig. 6.10 | Randomizing the die-rolling program. (Part 1 of 2.)

```
Enter seed: 67
        6        1        4        6        2
        1        6        1        6        4
```

Fig. 6.10 | Randomizing the die-rolling program. (Part 2 of 2.)

The program produces a *different* sequence of random numbers each time it executes, provided that the user enters a *different* seed. We used the *same* seed in the first and third sample outputs, so the *same* series of 10 numbers is displayed in each of those outputs.

Seeding the Random Number Generator with the Current Time

To randomize *without* having to enter a seed each time, we may use a statement like

```
srand( static_cast<unsigned int>( time( 0 ) ) );
```

This causes the computer to read its *clock* to obtain the value for the seed. Function `time` (with the argument 0 as written in the preceding statement) typically returns the current time as the number of seconds since January 1, 1970, at midnight Greenwich Mean Time (GMT). This value (which is of type `time_t`) is converted to an `unsigned int` and used as the seed to the random number generator—the `static_cast` in the preceding statement eliminates a compiler warning that's issued if you pass a `time_t` value to a function that expects an `unsigned int`. The function prototype for `time` is in `<ctime>`.

Scaling and Shifting Random Numbers

Previously, we simulated the rolling of a six-sided die with the statement

```
face = 1 + rand() % 6;
```

which always assigns an integer (at random) to variable `face` in the range $1 \leq$ `face` ≤ 6. The width of this range (i.e., the number of consecutive integers in the range) is 6 and the starting number in the range is 1. Referring to the preceding statement, we see that the width of the range is determined by the number used to scale `rand` with the modulus operator (i.e., 6), and the starting number of the range is equal to the number (i.e., 1) that is added to the expression `rand % 6`. We can generalize this result as

```
number = shiftingValue + rand() % scalingFactor;
```

where *shiftingValue* is equal to the *first number* in the desired range of consecutive integers and *scalingFactor* is equal to the *width* of the desired range of consecutive integers.

6.8 Case Study: Game of Chance; Introducing enum

One of the most popular games of chance is a dice game known as "craps," which is played in casinos and back alleys worldwide. The rules of the game are straightforward:

> *A player rolls two dice. Each die has six faces. These faces contain 1, 2, 3, 4, 5 and 6 spots. After the dice have come to rest, the sum of the spots on the two upward faces is calculated. If the sum is 7 or 11 on the first roll, the player wins. If the sum is 2, 3 or 12 on the first roll (called "craps"), the player loses (i.e., the "house" wins). If the sum is 4, 5, 6, 8, 9 or 10 on the first roll, then that sum becomes the player's "point." To win, you must continue rolling the dice until you "make your point." The player loses by rolling a 7 before making the point.*

The program in Fig. 6.11 simulates the game. In the rules, notice that the player must roll two dice on the first roll and on all subsequent rolls. We define function rollDice (lines 62–74) to roll the dice and compute and print their sum. The function is defined once, but called from lines 20 and 44. The function takes no arguments and returns the sum of the two dice, so empty parentheses and the return type unsigned int are indicated in the function prototype (line 8) and function header (line 62).

```cpp
// Fig. 6.11: fig06_11.cpp
// Craps simulation.
#include <iostream>
#include <cstdlib> // contains prototypes for functions srand and rand
#include <ctime> // contains prototype for function time
using namespace std;

unsigned int rollDice(); // rolls dice, calculates and displays sum

int main()
{
   // enumeration with constants that represent the game status
   enum Status { CONTINUE, WON, LOST }; // all caps in constants

   // randomize random number generator using current time
   srand( static_cast<unsigned int>( time( 0 ) ) );

   unsigned int myPoint = 0; // point if no win or loss on first roll
   Status gameStatus = CONTINUE; // can contain CONTINUE, WON or LOST
   unsigned int sumOfDice = rollDice(); // first roll of the dice

   // determine game status and point (if needed) based on first roll
   switch ( sumOfDice )
   {
      case 7: // win with 7 on first roll
      case 11: // win with 11 on first roll
         gameStatus = WON;
         break;
      case 2: // lose with 2 on first roll
      case 3: // lose with 3 on first roll
      case 12: // lose with 12 on first roll
         gameStatus = LOST;
         break;
      default: // did not win or lose, so remember point
         gameStatus = CONTINUE; // game is not over
         myPoint = sumOfDice; // remember the point
         cout << "Point is " << myPoint << endl;
         break; // optional at end of switch
   } // end switch

   // while game is not complete
   while ( CONTINUE == gameStatus ) // not WON or LOST
   {
```

Fig. 6.11 | Craps simulation. (Part 1 of 3.)

```cpp
44          sumOfDice = rollDice(); // roll dice again
45
46          // determine game status
47          if ( sumOfDice == myPoint ) // win by making point
48              gameStatus = WON;
49          else
50              if ( sumOfDice == 7 ) // lose by rolling 7 before point
51                  gameStatus = LOST;
52      } // end while
53
54      // display won or lost message
55      if ( WON == gameStatus )
56          cout << "Player wins" << endl;
57      else
58          cout << "Player loses" << endl;
59  } // end main
60
61  // roll dice, calculate sum and display results
62  unsigned int rollDice()
63  {
64      // pick random die values
65      unsigned int die1 = 1 + rand() % 6; // first die roll
66      unsigned int die2 = 1 + rand() % 6; // second die roll
67
68      unsigned int sum = die1 + die2; // compute sum of die values
69
70      // display results of this roll
71      cout << "Player rolled " << die1 << " + " << die2
72          << " = " << sum << endl;
73      return sum; // end function rollDice
74  } // end function rollDice
```

```
Player rolled 2 + 5 = 7
Player wins
```

```
Player rolled 6 + 6 = 12
Player loses
```

```
Player rolled 1 + 3 = 4
Point is 4
Player rolled 4 + 6 = 10
Player rolled 2 + 4 = 6
Player rolled 6 + 4 = 10
Player rolled 2 + 3 = 5
Player rolled 2 + 4 = 6
Player rolled 1 + 1 = 2
Player rolled 4 + 4 = 8
Player rolled 4 + 3 = 7
Player loses
```

Fig. 6.11 | Craps simulation. (Part 2 of 3.)

```
Player rolled 3 + 3 = 6
Point is 6
Player rolled 5 + 3 = 8
Player rolled 4 + 5 = 9
Player rolled 2 + 1 = 3
Player rolled 1 + 5 = 6
Player wins
```

Fig. 6.11 | Craps simulation. (Part 3 of 3.)

enum *Type* Status

The player may win or lose on the first roll or on any subsequent roll. The program uses variable gameStatus to keep track of this. Variable gameStatus is declared to be of new type Status. Line 13 declares a user-defined type called an **enumeration** that's introduced by the keyword **enum** and followed by a type name (in this case, Status) and a set of integer constants represented by identifiers. The values of these **enumeration constants** start at 0, unless specified otherwise, and increment by 1. In the preceding enumeration, the constant CONTINUE has the value 0, WON has the value 1 and LOST has the value 2. The identifiers in an enum must be *unique*, but separate enumeration constants *can* have the same integer value.

Good Programming Practice 6.2

Capitalize the first letter of an identifier used as a user-defined type name.

Good Programming Practice 6.3

Use only uppercase letters in enumeration constant names. This makes these constants stand out in a program and reminds you that enumeration constants are not variables.

Variables of user-defined type Status can be assigned only one of the three values declared in the enumeration. When the game is won, the program sets variable gameStatus to WON (lines 27 and 48). When the game is lost, the program sets variable gameStatus to LOST (lines 32 and 51). Otherwise, the program sets variable gameStatus to CONTINUE (line 35) to indicate that the dice must be rolled again.

Common Programming Error 6.5

Assigning the integer equivalent of an enumeration constant (rather than the enumeration constant, itself) to a variable of the enumeration type is a compilation error.

Another popular enumeration is

```
enum Months { JAN = 1, FEB, MAR, APR, MAY, JUN, JUL, AUG,
    SEP, OCT, NOV, DEC };
```

which creates user-defined type Months with enumeration constants representing the months of the year. The first value in the preceding enumeration is explicitly set to 1, so the remaining values increment from 1, resulting in the values 1 through 12. Any enumeration constant can be assigned an integer value in the enumeration definition, and subsequent enumeration constants each have a value 1 higher than the preceding constant in the list until the next explicit setting.

> ### Error-Prevention Tip 6.4
> *Use unique values for an enum's constants to help prevent hard-to-find logic errors.*

Winning or Losing on the First Roll

After the first roll, if the game is won or lost, the program skips the body of the while statement (lines 42–52) because gameStatus is not equal to CONTINUE. The program proceeds to the if...else statement in lines 55–58, which prints "Player wins" if gameStatus is equal to WON and "Player loses" if gameStatus is equal to LOST.

Continuing to Roll

After the first roll, if the game is not over, the program saves the sum in myPoint (line 36). Execution proceeds with the while statement, because gameStatus is equal to CONTINUE. During each iteration of the while, the program calls rollDice to produce a new sum. If sum matches myPoint, the program sets gameStatus to WON (line 48), the while-test fails, the if...else statement prints "Player wins" and execution terminates. If sum is equal to 7, the program sets gameStatus to LOST (line 51), the while-test fails, the if...else statement prints "Player loses" and execution terminates.

The craps program uses two functions—main and rollDice—and the switch, while, if...else, nested if...else and nested if statements. In the exercises, we further investigate of the game of craps.

C++11—Scoped *enums*

In Fig. 6.11, we introduced enums. One problem with enums (also called *unscoped* enums) is that multiple enums may contain the *same* identifiers. Using such enums in the same program can lead to naming collisions and logic errors. To eliminate these problems, C++11 introduces so-called scoped enums, which are declared with the keywords **enum class** (or the synonym **enum struct**). For example, we can define the Status enum of Fig. 6.11 as:

```
enum class Status { CONTINUE, WON, LOST };
```

To reference a scoped enum constant, you *must* qualify the constant with the scoped enum's type name (Status) and the scope-resolution operator (::), as in Status::CONTINUE. This *explicitly identifies* CONTINUE as a constant in the *scope* of enum class Status. Thus, if another scoped enum contains the same identifier for one of its constants, it's always clear which version of the constant is being used.

> ### Error-Prevention Tip 6.5
> *Use scoped enums to avoid potential naming conflicts and logic errors from unscoped enums that contain the same identifiers.*

C++11—Specifying the Type of an *enum's* Constants

The constants in an enum are represented as integers. By default, an unscoped enum's underlying integral type depends on its constants' values—the type is guaranteed to be large enough to store the constant values specified. By default, a scoped enum's underlying integral type is int. C++11 allows you to specify an enum's underlying integral type by following the enum's type name with a colon (:) and the integral type. For example, we can specify that the constants in the enum class Status should have type unsigned int, as in

```
enum class Status : unsigned int { CONTINUE, WON, LOST };
```

Common Programming Error 6.6

A compilation error occurs if an enum constant's value is outside the range that can be represented by the enum's underlying type.

6.9 C++11 Random Numbers

According to CERT, function rand does not have "good statistical properties" and can be predictable, which makes programs that use rand less secure (CERT guideline MSC30-CPP). As we mentioned in Section 6.7, C++11 provides a new, *more secure* library of random-number capabilities that can produce nondeterministic random numbers for simulations and security scenarios where predictability is undesirable. These new capabilities are located in the C++ Standard Library's <random> header.

Random-number generation is a mathematically sophisticated topic for which mathematicians have developed many random-number generation algorithms with different statistical properties. For flexibility based on how random numbers are used in programs, C++11 provides many classes that represent various random-number generation *engines* and *distributions*. An engine implements a random-number generation algorithm that produce pseudorandom numbers. A distribution controls the range of values produced by an engine, the types of those values (e.g., int, double, etc.) and the statistical properties of the values. In this section, we'll use the default random-number generation engine—default_random_engine—and a uniform_int_distribution, which *evenly* distributes pseudorandom integers over a specified range of values. The default range is from 0 to the maximum value of an int on your platform.

Rolling a Six-Sided Die

Figure 6.12 uses the default_random_engine and the uniform_int_distribution to roll a six-sided die. Line 14 creates a default_random_engine object named engine. Its constructor argument *seeds* the random-number generation engine with the current time. If you don't pass a value to the constructor, the default seed will be used and the program will produce the *same* sequence of numbers each time it executes. Line 15 creates randomInt—a uniform_int_distribution object that produces unsigned int values (as specified by <unsigned int>) in the range 1 to 6 (as specified by the constructor arguments). The expression randomInt(engine) (line 21) returns one unsigned int value in the range 1 to 6.

```
1   // Fig. 6.12: fig06_12.cpp
2   // Using a C++11 random-number generation engine and distribution
3   // to roll a six-sided die.
4   #include <iostream>
5   #include <iomanip>
6   #include <random> // contains C++11 random number generation features
7   #include <ctime>
8   using namespace std;
9
10  int main()
11  {
```

Fig. 6.12 | Using a C++11 random-number generation engine and distribution to roll a six-sided die. (Part 1 of 2.)

```
12        // use the default random-number generation engine to
13        // produce uniformly distributed pseudorandom int values from 1 to 6
14        default_random_engine engine( static_cast<unsigned int>( time(0) ) );
15        uniform_int_distribution<unsigned int> randomInt( 1, 6 );
16
17        // loop 10 times
18        for ( unsigned int counter = 1; counter <= 10; ++counter )
19        {
20           // pick random number from 1 to 6 and output it
21           cout << setw( 10 ) << randomInt( engine );
22
23           // if counter is divisible by 5, start a new line of output
24           if ( counter % 5 == 0 )
25              cout << endl;
26        } // end for
27  } // end main
```

2	1	2	3	5
6	1	5	6	4

Fig. 6.12 | Using a C++11 random-number generation engine and distribution to roll a six-sided die. (Part 2 of 2.)

The notation <unsigned int> in line 15 indicates that uniform_int_distribution is a *class template.* In this case, any integer type can be specified in the angle brackets (< and >). In Chapter 18, we discuss how to create class templates and various other chapters show how to use existing class templates from the C++ Standard Library. For now, you should feel comfortable using class template uniform_int_distribution by mimicking the syntax shown in the example.

6.10 Storage Classes and Storage Duration

The programs you've seen so far use identifiers for variable names and functions. The attributes of variables include *name, type, size* and *value.* Each identifier in a program also has other attributes, including **storage duration**, scope and **linkage**.

C++ provides five **storage-class specifiers** that determine a variable's storage duration: **register, extern, mutable** and **static**. This section discusses storage-class specifiers **register, extern** and **static**. Storage-class specifier **mutable** is used exclusively with classes and **thread_local** is used in multithreaded applications—these are discussed in Chapters 23 and 24, respectively.

Storage Duration
An identifier's *storage duration* determines the period during which that identifier *exists in memory.* Some exist briefly, some are repeatedly created and destroyed and others exist for a program's entire execution. First we discuss the storage durations **static** and **automatic**.

Scope
An identifier's *scope* is where *the identifier can be referenced* in a program. Some identifiers can be referenced throughout a program; others can be referenced from only limited portions of a program. Section 6.11 discusses the scope of identifiers.

Linkage

An identifier's *linkage* determines whether it's known only in the *source file where it's declared* or *across multiple files that are compiled, then linked together*. An identifier's *storage-class specifier* helps determine its storage duration and linkage.

Storage Duration

The storage-class specifiers can be split into four storage durations: *automatic, static, dynamic* and *thread*. Automatic and static storage duration are discussed below. In Chapter 10, you'll learn that you can request additional memory in your program during the program's execution—so-called *dynamic memory allocation*. Variables allocated dynamically have *dynamic storage duration*. Chapter 24 discusses *thread storage duration*.

Local Variables and Automatic Storage Duration

Variables with *automatic storage duration* include:

- local variables declared in functions
- function parameters
- local variables or function parameters declared with `register`

Such variables are created when program execution enters the block in which they're defined, they exist while the block is active and they're destroyed when the program exits the block. An automatic variable exists only in the *nearest enclosing pair of curly braces* within the body of the function in which the definition appears, or for the entire function body in the case of a function parameter. Local variables are of automatic storage duration by *default*. For the remainder of the text, we refer to variables of automatic storage duration simply as *automatic variables*.

Performance Tip 6.1

Automatic storage is a means of conserving memory, because automatic storage duration variables exist in memory only when the block in which they're defined is executing.

Software Engineering Observation 6.6

Automatic storage is an example of the principle of least privilege. In the context of an application, the principle states that code should be granted only the amount of privilege and access that it needs to accomplish its designated task, but no more. Why should we have variables stored in memory and accessible when they're not needed?

Good Programming Practice 6.4

Declare variables as close to where they're first used as possible.

Register Variables

Data in the machine-language version of a program is normally loaded into registers for calculations and other processing.

The compiler might ignore `register` declarations. For example, there might not be a sufficient number of registers available. The following definition *suggests* that the `unsigned int` variable `counter` be placed in one of the computer's registers; regardless of whether the compiler does this, `counter` is initialized to 1:

```
register unsigned int counter = 1;
```

The `register` keyword can be used *only* with local variables and function parameters.

Performance Tip 6.2

The storage-class specifier `register` *can be placed before an automatic variable declaration to suggest that the compiler maintain the variable in one of the computer's high-speed hardware registers rather than in memory. If intensely used variables such as counters or totals are kept in hardware registers, the overhead of repeatedly loading the variables from memory into the registers and storing the results back into memory is eliminated.*

Performance Tip 6.3

Often, `register` *is unnecessary. Today's optimizing compilers can recognize frequently used variables and may place them in registers without needing a* `register` *declaration.*

Static Storage Duration

Keywords `extern` and `static` declare identifiers for variables with *static storage duration* and for functions. Variables with static storage duration exist in memory from the point at which the program begins execution and until the program terminates. Such a variable is *initialized once when its declaration is encountered*. For functions, the name of the function exists when the program begins execution. Even though function names and static-storage-duration variables exist from the start of program execution, their identifiers cannot necessarily be used throughout the program. Storage duration and scope (where a name can be used) are separate issues, as we'll see in Section 6.11.

Identifiers with Static Storage Duration

There are two types of identifiers with *static storage duration*—external identifiers (such as global variables) and local variables declared with the storage-class specifier `static`. Global variables are created by placing variable declarations *outside* any class or function definition. Global variables retain their values throughout a program's execution. Global variables and global functions can be referenced by any function that follows their declarations or definitions in the source file.

Software Engineering Observation 6.7

Declaring a variable as global rather than local allows unintended side effects *to occur when a function that does not need access to the variable accidentally or maliciously modifies it. This is another example of the principle of least privilege—in general, except for truly global resources such as* cin *and* cout*, the use of global variables should be avoided unless there are unique performance requirements.*

Software Engineering Observation 6.8

Variables used only in a particular function should be declared as local variables in that function rather than as global variables.

static Local Variables

Local variables declared `static` are still known only in the function in which they're declared, but, unlike automatic variables, *static local variables retain their values when the function returns to its caller*. The next time the function is called, the `static` local variables contain the values they had when the function last completed execution. The following statement declares local variable count to be static and to be initialized to 1:

```
static unsigned int count = 1;
```

All numeric variables of static storage duration are *initialized to zero by default*, but it's nevertheless a good practice to explicitly initialize all variables.

Storage-class specifiers extern and static have special meaning when they're applied explicitly to external identifiers such as global variables and global function names. In Appendix F, C Legacy Code Topics, we discuss using extern and static with external identifiers and multiple-source-file programs.

6.11 Scope Rules

The portion of the program where an identifier can be used is known as its *scope*. For example, when we declare a local variable in a block, it can be referenced only in that block and in blocks nested within that block. This section discusses **block scope**, **function scope**, **global namespace scope** and **function-prototype scope**. Later we'll see two other scopes—**class scope** (Chapter 9) and **namespace scope** (Chapter 23).

Block Scope
Identifiers declared *inside* a block have *block scope*, which begins at the identifier's declaration and ends at the terminating right brace (}) of the block in which the identifier is declared. Local variables have block scope, as do function parameters. Any block can contain variable declarations. When blocks are nested and an identifier in an outer block has the same name as an identifier in an inner block, the identifier in the outer block is "hidden" until the inner block terminates. The inner block "sees" its own local identifier's value and not that of the enclosing block's identically named identifier. Local variables declared static still have block scope, even though they exist from the time the program begins execution. Storage duration does *not* affect an identifier's scope.

Common Programming Error 6.7
Accidentally using the same name for an identifier in an inner block that's used for an identifier in an outer block, when in fact you want the identifier in the outer block to be active for the duration of the inner block, is typically a logic error.

Error-Prevention Tip 6.6
Avoid variable names that hide names in outer scopes.

Function Scope
Labels (identifiers followed by a colon such as start: or a case label in a switch statement) are the only identifiers with *function scope*. Labels can be used *anywhere* in the function in which they appear, but cannot be referenced *outside* the function body.

Global Namespace Scope
An identifier declared *outside* any function or class has *global namespace scope*. Such an identifier is "known" in all functions from the point at which it's declared until the end of

the file. Global variables, function definitions and function prototypes placed outside a function all have global namespace scope.

Function-Prototype Scope

The only identifiers with *function-prototype scope* are those used in the parameter list of a function prototype. As mentioned previously, function prototypes do *not* require names in the parameter list—only types are required. Names appearing in the parameter list of a function prototype are *ignored* by the compiler. Identifiers used in a function prototype can be reused elsewhere in the program without ambiguity.

Scope Demonstration

The program of Fig. 6.13 demonstrates scoping issues with global variables, automatic local variables and static local variables. Line 10 declares and initializes global variable x to 1. This global variable is hidden in any block (or function) that declares a variable named x. In main, line 14 displays the value of global variable x. Line 16 declares a local variable x and initializes it to 5. Line 18 outputs this variable to show that the global x is hidden in main. Next, lines 20–24 define a new block in main in which another local variable x is initialized to 7 (line 21). Line 23 outputs this variable to show that it *hides* x in the outer block of main as well as the global x. When the block exits, the variable x with value 7 is destroyed automatically. Next, line 26 outputs the local variable x in the outer block of main to show that it's *no longer hidden*.

```cpp
1   // Fig. 6.13: fig06_13.cpp
2   // Scoping example.
3   #include <iostream>
4   using namespace std;
5
6   void useLocal(); // function prototype
7   void useStaticLocal(); // function prototype
8   void useGlobal(); // function prototype
9
10  int x = 1; // global variable
11
12  int main()
13  {
14     cout << "global x in main is " << x << endl;
15
16     int x = 5; // local variable to main
17
18     cout << "local x in main's outer scope is " << x << endl;
19
20     { // start new scope
21        int x = 7; // hides both x in outer scope and global x
22
23        cout << "local x in main's inner scope is " << x << endl;
24     } // end new scope
```

Fig. 6.13 | Scoping example. (Part 1 of 3.)

```
25
26      cout << "local x in main's outer scope is " << x << endl;
27
28      useLocal(); // useLocal has local x
29      useStaticLocal(); // useStaticLocal has static local x
30      useGlobal(); // useGlobal uses global x
31      useLocal(); // useLocal reinitializes its local x
32      useStaticLocal(); // static local x retains its prior value
33      useGlobal(); // global x also retains its prior value
34
35      cout << "\nlocal x in main is " << x << endl;
36   } // end main
37
38   // useLocal reinitializes local variable x during each call
39   void useLocal()
40   {
41      int x = 25; // initialized each time useLocal is called
42
43      cout << "\nlocal x is " << x << " on entering useLocal" << endl;
44      ++x;
45      cout << "local x is " << x << " on exiting useLocal" << endl;
46   } // end function useLocal
47
48   // useStaticLocal initializes static local variable x only the
49   // first time the function is called; value of x is saved
50   // between calls to this function
51   void useStaticLocal()
52   {
53      static int x = 50; // initialized first time useStaticLocal is called
54
55      cout << "\nlocal static x is " << x << " on entering useStaticLocal"
56         << endl;
57      ++x;
58      cout << "local static x is " << x << " on exiting useStaticLocal"
59         << endl;
60   } // end function useStaticLocal
61
62   // useGlobal modifies global variable x during each call
63   void useGlobal()
64   {
65      cout << "\nglobal x is " << x << " on entering useGlobal" << endl;
66      x *= 10;
67      cout << "global x is " << x << " on exiting useGlobal" << endl;
68   } // end function useGlobal
```

```
global x in main is 1
local x in main's outer scope is 5
local x in main's inner scope is 7
local x in main's outer scope is 5

local x is 25 on entering useLocal
local x is 26 on exiting useLocal
```

Fig. 6.13 | Scoping example. (Part 2 of 3.)

```
local static x is 50 on entering useStaticLocal
local static x is 51 on exiting useStaticLocal

global x is 1 on entering useGlobal
global x is 10 on exiting useGlobal

local x is 25 on entering useLocal
local x is 26 on exiting useLocal

local static x is 51 on entering useStaticLocal
local static x is 52 on exiting useStaticLocal

global x is 10 on entering useGlobal
global x is 100 on exiting useGlobal

local x in main is 5
```

Fig. 6.13 | Scoping example. (Part 3 of 3.)

To demonstrate other scopes, the program defines three functions, each of which takes no arguments and returns nothing. Function useLocal (lines 39–46) declares automatic variable x (line 41) and initializes it to 25. When the program calls useLocal, the function prints the variable, increments it and prints it again before the function returns program control to its caller. Each time the program calls this function, the function *recreates* automatic variable x and *reinitializes* it to 25.

Function useStaticLocal (lines 51–60) declares static variable x and initializes it to 50. Local variables declared as static retain their values even when they're out of scope (i.e., the function in which they're declared is not executing). When the program calls useStaticLocal, the function prints x, increments it and prints it again before the function returns program control to its caller. In the next call to this function, static local variable x contains the value 51. The *initialization* in line 53 *occurs only once*—the first time useStaticLocal is called.

Function useGlobal (lines 63–68) does not declare any variables. Therefore, when it refers to variable x, the global x (line 10, preceding main) is used. When the program calls useGlobal, the function prints the global variable x, multiplies it by 10 and prints it again before the function returns program control to its caller. The next time the program calls useGlobal, the global variable has its modified value, 10. After executing functions useLocal, useStaticLocal and useGlobal twice each, the program prints the local variable x in main again to show that none of the function calls modified the value of x in main, because the functions all referred to variables in other scopes.

6.12 Function Call Stack and Activation Records

To understand how C++ performs function calls, we first need to consider a data structure (i.e., collection of related data items) known as a stack. Think of a stack as analogous to a pile of dishes. When a dish is placed on the pile, it's normally placed at the *top*—referred to as pushing the dish onto the stack. Similarly, when a dish is removed from the pile, it's normally removed from the top—referred to as popping the dish off the stack. Stacks are known as **last-in, first-out (LIFO)** data structures—the last item pushed (inserted) on the stack is the first item popped (removed) from the stack.

Function-Call Stack

One of the most important mechanisms for computer science students to understand is the **function call stack** (sometimes referred to as the **program execution stack**). This data structure—working "behind the scenes"—supports the function call/return mechanism. It also supports the creation, maintenance and destruction of each called function's automatic variables. As we'll see in Figs. 6.15–6.17, last-in, first-out (LIFO) behavior is *exactly* what a function needs in order to return to the function that called it.

Stack Frames

As each function is called, it may, in turn, call other functions, which may, in turn, call other functions—all *before* any of the functions return. Each function eventually must return control to the function that called it. So, somehow, we must keep track of the *return addresses* that each function needs to return control to the function that called it. The function call stack is the perfect data structure for handling this information. Each time a function calls another function, an entry is *pushed* onto the stack. This entry, called a **stack frame** or an **activation record**, contains the *return address* that the called function needs in order to return to the calling function. It also contains some additional information we'll soon discuss. If the called function returns, instead of calling another function before returning, the stack frame for the function call is *popped*, and control transfers to the return address in the popped stack frame.

The beauty of the call stack is that each called function always finds the information it needs to return to its caller at the *top* of the call stack. And, if a function makes a call to another function, a stack frame for the new function call is simply *pushed* onto the call stack. Thus, the return address required by the newly called function to return to its caller is now located at the *top* of the stack.

Automatic Variables and Stack Frames

The stack frames have another important responsibility. Most functions have automatic variables—parameters and any local variables the function declares. Automatic variables need to exist while a function is executing. They need to remain active if the function makes calls to other functions. But when a called function returns to its caller, the called function's automatic variables need to "go away." The called function's stack frame is a perfect place to reserve the memory for the called function's automatic variables. That stack frame exists as long as the called function is active. When that function returns—and no longer needs its local automatic variables—its stack frame is *popped* from the stack, and those local automatic variables are no longer known to the program.

Stack Overflow

Of course, the amount of memory in a computer is finite, so only a certain amount of memory can be used to store activation records on the function call stack. If more function calls occur than can have their activation records stored on the function call stack, a fatal error known as **stack overflow** occurs.

Function Call Stack in Action

Now let's consider how the call stack supports the operation of a square function called by main (lines 9–14 of Fig. 6.14). First the operating system calls main—this pushes an activation record onto the stack (shown in Fig. 6.15). The activation record tells main how to return to the operating system (i.e., transfer to return address R1) and contains the space for main's automatic variable (i.e., a, which is initialized to 10).

```cpp
1   // Fig. 6.14: fig06_14.cpp
2   // square function used to demonstrate the function
3   // call stack and activation records.
4   #include <iostream>
5   using namespace std;
6
7   int square( int ); // prototype for function square
8
9   int main()
10  {
11     int a = 10; // value to square (local automatic variable in main)
12
13     cout << a << " squared: " << square( a ) << endl; // display a squared
14  } // end main
15
16  // returns the square of an integer
17  int square( int x ) // x is a local variable
18  {
19     return x * x; // calculate square and return result
20  } // end function square
```

```
10 squared: 100
```

Fig. 6.14 | square function used to demonstrate the function call stack and activation records.

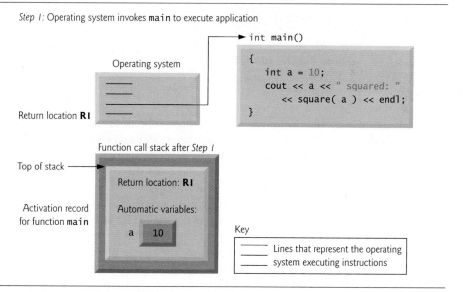

Step 1: Operating system invokes main to execute application

Fig. 6.15 | Function call stack after the operating system invokes main to execute the program.

Function `main`—before returning to the operating system—now calls function `square` in line 13 of Fig. 6.14. This causes a stack frame for `square` (lines 17–20) to be pushed onto the function call stack (Fig. 6.16). This stack frame contains the return address that `square` needs to return to `main` (i.e., R2) and the memory for `square`'s automatic variable (i.e., `x`).

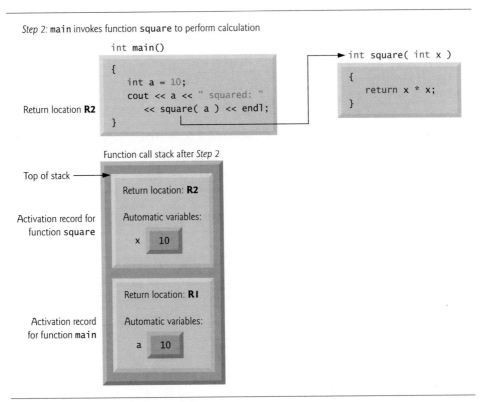

Fig. 6.16 | Function call stack after `main` invokes `square` to perform the calculation.

After `square` calculates the square of its argument, it needs to return to `main`—and no longer needs the memory for its automatic variable x. So `square`'s stack frame is *popped* from the stack—giving `square` the return location in `main` (i.e., R2) and losing `square`'s automatic variable. Figure 6.17 shows the function call stack *after* `square`'s activation record has been popped.

Function `main` now displays the result of calling `square` (Fig. 6.14, line 13). Reaching the closing right brace of `main` causes its stack frame to be *popped* from the stack, gives `main` the address it needs to return to the operating system (i.e., R1 in Fig. 6.15)—at this point, `main`'s automatic variable (i.e., a) no longer exists.

You've now seen how valuable the stack data structure is in implementing a key mechanism that supports program execution. Data structures have many important applications in computer science. We discuss stacks, queues, lists, trees and other data structures in Chapter 15, Standard Library Containers and Iterators, and Chapter 19, Custom Templatized Data Structures.

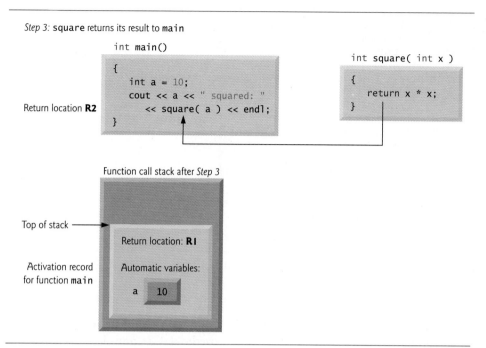

Step 3: `square` returns its result to `main`

Fig. 6.17 | Function call stack after function `square` returns to `main`.

6.13 Functions with Empty Parameter Lists

In C++, an *empty parameter list* is specified by writing either `void` or nothing at all in parentheses. The prototype

```
void print();
```

specifies that function `print` does *not* take arguments and does *not* return a value. Figure 6.18 shows both ways to declare and use functions with empty parameter lists.

```cpp
1   // Fig. 6.18: fig06_18.cpp
2   // Functions that take no arguments.
3   #include <iostream>
4   using namespace std;
5
6   void function1(); // function that takes no arguments
7   void function2( void ); // function that takes no arguments
8
9   int main()
10  {
11     function1(); // call function1 with no arguments
12     function2(); // call function2 with no arguments
13  } // end main
14
```

Fig. 6.18 | Functions that take no arguments. (Part 1 of 2.)

```
15   // function1 uses an empty parameter list to specify that
16   // the function receives no arguments
17   void function1()
18   {
19      cout << "function1 takes no arguments" << endl;
20   } // end function1
21
22   // function2 uses a void parameter list to specify that
23   // the function receives no arguments
24   void function2( void )
25   {
26      cout << "function2 also takes no arguments" << endl;
27   } // end function2
```

```
function1 takes no arguments
function2 also takes no arguments
```

Fig. 6.18 | Functions that take no arguments. (Part 2 of 2.)

6.14 Inline Functions

Implementing a program as a set of functions is good from a software engineering standpoint, but function calls involve execution-time overhead. C++ provides **inline functions** to help reduce function call overhead. Placing the qualifier `inline` before a function's return type in the function definition *advises* the compiler to generate a copy of the function's body code in *every* place where the function is called (when appropriate) to avoid a function call. This often makes the program *larger*. The compiler can *ignore* the `inline` qualifier and generally does so for all but the *smallest* functions. Reusable `inline` functions are typically placed in headers, so that their definitions can be included in each source file that uses them.

Software Engineering Observation 6.9

If you change the definition of an `inline` *function, you should recompile all of that function's clients.*

Performance Tip 6.4

Compilers can inline code for which you have not explicitly used the `inline` *keyword. Today's optimizing compilers are so sophisticated that it's best to leave inlining decisions to the compiler.*

Figure 6.19 uses `inline` function cube (lines 9–12) to calculate the volume of a cube. Keyword **const** in function cube's parameter list (line 9) tells the compiler that the function does *not* modify variable `side`. This ensures that `side`'s value is *not* changed by the function during the calculation. (Keyword const is discussed in detail in Chapters 7–9.)

Software Engineering Observation 6.10

The const *qualifier should be used to enforce the principle of least privilege. Using the principle of least privilege to properly design software can greatly reduce debugging time and improper side effects and can make a program easier to modify and maintain.*

```
 1   // Fig. 6.19: fig06_19.cpp
 2   // inline function that calculates the volume of a cube.
 3   #include <iostream>
 4   using namespace std;
 5
 6   // Definition of inline function cube. Definition of function appears
 7   // before function is called, so a function prototype is not required.
 8   // First line of function definition acts as the prototype.
 9   inline double cube( const double side )
10   {
11      return side * side * side; // calculate cube
12   } // end function cube
13
14   int main()
15   {
16      double sideValue; // stores value entered by user
17      cout << "Enter the side length of your cube: ";
18      cin >> sideValue; // read value from user
19
20      // calculate cube of sideValue and display result
21      cout << "Volume of cube with side "
22         << sideValue << " is " << cube( sideValue ) << endl;
23   } // end main
```

```
Enter the side length of your cube: 3.5
Volume of cube with side 3.5 is 42.875
```

Fig. 6.19 | inline function that calculates the volume of a cube.

6.15 References and Reference Parameters

Two ways to pass arguments to functions in many programming languages are pass-by-value and pass-by-reference. When an argument is passed by value, a *copy* of the argument's value is made and passed (on the function call stack) to the called function. Changes to the copy do *not* affect the original variable's value in the caller. This prevents the *accidental side effects* that so greatly hinder the development of correct and reliable software systems. So far, each argument in the book has been passed by value.

Performance Tip 6.5

One disadvantage of pass-by-value is that, if a large data item is being passed, copying that data can take a considerable amount of execution time and memory space.

Reference Parameters

This section introduces reference parameters—the first of the two means C++ provides for performing pass-by-reference. With *pass-by-reference*, the caller gives the called function the ability to *access the caller's data directly*, and to *modify* that data.

Performance Tip 6.6

Pass-by-reference is good for performance reasons, because it can eliminate the pass-by-value overhead of copying large amounts of data.

Software Engineering Observation 6.11

Pass-by-reference can weaken security; the called function can corrupt the caller's data.

Later, we'll show how to achieve the performance advantage of pass-by-reference while *simultaneously* achieving the software engineering advantage of protecting the caller's data from corruption.

A reference parameter is an *alias* for its corresponding argument in a function call. To indicate that a function parameter is passed by reference, simply follow the parameter's type in the function prototype by an *ampersand (&)*; use the same convention when listing the parameter's type in the function header. For example, the following declaration in a function header

```
int &count
```

when read from *right to left* is pronounced "count is a reference to an int." In the function call, simply mention the variable by name to pass it by reference. Then, mentioning the variable by its parameter name in the body of the called function actually refers to the *original variable* in the calling function, and the original variable can be *modified* directly by the called function. As always, the function prototype and header must agree.

Passing Arguments by Value and by Reference

Figure 6.20 compares pass-by-value and pass-by-reference with reference parameters. The "styles" of the arguments in the calls to function squareByValue and function squareByReference are identical—both variables are simply mentioned by name in the function calls. *Without checking the function prototypes or function definitions, it isn't possible to tell from the calls alone whether either function can modify its arguments.* Because function prototypes are mandatory, the compiler has no trouble resolving the ambiguity.

Common Programming Error 6.8

Because reference parameters are mentioned only by name in the body of the called function, you might inadvertently treat reference parameters as pass-by-value parameters. This can cause unexpected side effects if the original variables are changed by the function.

```
1   // Fig. 6.20: fig06_20.cpp
2   // Passing arguments by value and by reference.
3   #include <iostream>
4   using namespace std;
5
6   int squareByValue( int ); // function prototype (value pass)
7   void squareByReference( int & ); // function prototype (reference pass)
8
9   int main()
10  {
11      int x = 2; // value to square using squareByValue
12      int z = 4; // value to square using squareByReference
13
```

Fig. 6.20 | Passing arguments by value and by reference. (Part 1 of 2.)

```
14      // demonstrate squareByValue
15      cout << "x = " << x << " before squareByValue\n";
16      cout << "Value returned by squareByValue: "
17         << squareByValue( x ) << endl;
18      cout << "x = " << x << " after squareByValue\n" << endl;
19
20      // demonstrate squareByReference
21      cout << "z = " << z << " before squareByReference" << endl;
22      squareByReference( z );
23      cout << "z = " << z << " after squareByReference" << endl;
24   } // end main
25
26   // squareByValue multiplies number by itself, stores the
27   // result in number and returns the new value of number
28   int squareByValue( int number )
29   {
30      return number *= number; // caller's argument not modified
31   } // end function squareByValue
32
33   // squareByReference multiplies numberRef by itself and stores the result
34   // in the variable to which numberRef refers in function main
35   void squareByReference( int &numberRef )
36   {
37      numberRef *= numberRef; // caller's argument modified
38   } // end function squareByReference
```

```
x = 2 before squareByValue
Value returned by squareByValue: 4
x = 2 after squareByValue

z = 4 before squareByReference
z = 16 after squareByReference
```

Fig. 6.20 | Passing arguments by value and by reference. (Part 2 of 2.)

Chapter 8 discusses *pointers*; pointers enable an alternate form of pass-by-reference in which the style of the call clearly indicates pass-by-reference (and the potential for modifying the caller's arguments).

Performance Tip 6.7

For passing large objects, use a constant *reference parameter to simulate the appearance and security of pass-by-value and avoid the overhead of passing a copy of the large object.*

To specify that a reference should not be allowed to modify the argument, place the const qualifier *before* the type specifier in the parameter declaration. Note the placement of & in function squareByReference's parameter list (line 35, Fig. 6.20). Some C++ programmers prefer to write the equivalent form int& numberRef.

References as Aliases within a Function
References can also be used as aliases for other variables *within* a function (although they typically are used with functions as shown in Fig. 6.20). For example, the code

```
int count = 1; // declare integer variable count
int &cRef = count; // create cRef as an alias for count
++cRef; // increment count (using its alias cRef)
```

increments variable count by using its alias cRef. Reference variables *must* be initialized in their declarations and cannot be reassigned as *aliases* to other variables. Once a reference is *declared* as an alias for another variable, all operations supposedly performed on the *alias* (i.e., the reference) are actually performed on the *original* variable. The alias is simply another name for the original variable. Unless it's a reference to a constant, a reference argument must be an *lvalue* (e.g., a variable name), not a constant or *rvalue* expression (e.g., the result of a calculation).

Returning a Reference from a Function
Functions can return references, but this can be dangerous. When returning a reference to a variable declared in the called function, unless that variable is declared static, the reference refers to an automatic variable that's *discarded* when the function terminates. An attempt to access such a variable yields *undefined behavior*. References to undefined variables are called **dangling references**.

Common Programming Error 6.9

Returning a reference to an automatic variable in a called function is a logic error. Compilers typically issue a warning when this occurs. For industrial-strength code, always *eliminate all compilation warnings before producing executable code.*

6.16 Default Arguments

It's common for a program to invoke a function repeatedly with the *same* argument value for a particular parameter. In such cases, you can specify that such a parameter has a **default argument**, i.e., a default value to be passed to that parameter. When a program *omits* an argument for a parameter with a default argument in a function call, the compiler rewrites the function call and inserts the default value of that argument.

Default arguments *must* be the rightmost (trailing) arguments in a function's parameter list. When calling a function with two or more default arguments, if an omitted argument is *not* the rightmost argument in the argument list, then all arguments to the right of that argument also *must* be omitted. Default arguments must be specified with the *first* occurrence of the function name—typically, in the function prototype. If the function prototype is omitted because the function definition also serves as the prototype, then the default arguments should be specified in the function header. Default values can be any expression, including constants, global variables or function calls. Default arguments also can be used with inline functions.

Figure 6.21 demonstrates using default arguments to calculate a box's volume. The function prototype for boxVolume (line 7) specifies that all three parameters have been given default values of 1. We provided variable names in the function prototype for readability. As always, variable names are *not* required in function prototypes.

The first call to boxVolume (line 13) specifies no arguments, thus using all three default values of 1. The second call (line 17) passes only a length argument, thus using default values of 1 for the width and height arguments. The third call (line 21) passes arguments for only length and width, thus using a default value of 1 for the height argu-

```cpp
 1   // Fig. 6.21: fig06_21.cpp
 2   // Using default arguments.
 3   #include <iostream>
 4   using namespace std;
 5
 6   // function prototype that specifies default arguments
 7   unsigned int boxVolume( unsigned int length = 1, unsigned int width = 1,
 8      unsigned int height = 1 );
 9
10   int main()
11   {
12      // no arguments--use default values for all dimensions
13      cout << "The default box volume is: " << boxVolume();
14
15      // specify length; default width and height
16      cout << "\n\nThe volume of a box with length 10,\n"
17         << "width 1 and height 1 is: " << boxVolume( 10 );
18
19      // specify length and width; default height
20      cout << "\n\nThe volume of a box with length 10,\n"
21         << "width 5 and height 1 is: " << boxVolume( 10, 5 );
22
23      // specify all arguments
24      cout << "\n\nThe volume of a box with length 10,\n"
25         << "width 5 and height 2 is: " << boxVolume( 10, 5, 2 )
26         << endl;
27   } // end main
28
29   // function boxVolume calculates the volume of a box
30   unsigned int boxVolume( unsigned int length, unsigned int width,
31      unsigned int height )
32   {
33      return length * width * height;
34   } // end function boxVolume
```

```
The default box volume is: 1

The volume of a box with length 10,
width 1 and height 1 is: 10

The volume of a box with length 10,
width 5 and height 1 is: 50

The volume of a box with length 10,
width 5 and height 2 is: 100
```

Fig. 6.21 | Using default arguments.

ment. The last call (line 25) passes arguments for length, width and height, thus using no default values. Any arguments passed to the function explicitly are assigned to the function's parameters from left to right. Therefore, when boxVolume receives one argument, the function assigns the value of that argument to its length parameter (i.e., the leftmost parameter in the parameter list). When boxVolume receives two arguments, the function assigns the values of those arguments to its `length` and `width` parameters in that order. Finally, when `boxVolume` receives all three arguments, the function assigns the values of those arguments to its `length`, `width` and `height` parameters, respectively.

Good Programming Practice 6.5
Using default arguments can simplify writing function calls. However, some programmers feel that explicitly specifying all arguments is clearer.

6.17 Unary Scope Resolution Operator

It's possible to declare local and global variables of the same name. C++ provides the **unary scope resolution operator** (`::`) to access a global variable when a local variable of the same name is in scope. The unary scope resolution operator cannot be used to access a *local* variable of the same name in an outer block. A global variable can be accessed directly without the unary scope resolution operator if the name of the global variable is not the same as that of a local variable in scope.

Figure 6.22 shows the unary scope resolution operator with local and global variables of the same name (lines 6 and 10). To emphasize that the local and global versions of variable `number` are distinct, the program declares one variable `int` and the other `double`.

```
1   // Fig. 6.22: fig06_22.cpp
2   // Unary scope resolution operator.
3   #include <iostream>
4   using namespace std;
5
6   int number = 7; // global variable named number
7
8   int main()
9   {
10      double number = 10.5; // local variable named number
11
12      // display values of local and global variables
13      cout << "Local double value of number = " << number
14          << "\nGlobal int value of number = " << ::number << endl;
15  } // end main
```

```
Local double value of number = 10.5
Global int value of number = 7
```

Fig. 6.22 | Unary scope resolution operator.

Good Programming Practice 6.6
Always using the unary scope resolution operator (`::`) to refer to global variables makes it clear that you're intending to access a global variable rather than a nonglobal variable.

Software Engineering Observation 6.12
Always using the unary scope resolution operator (`::`) to refer to global variables makes programs easier to modify by reducing the risk of name collisions with nonglobal variables.

Error-Prevention Tip 6.7

Always using the unary scope resolution operator (::) to refer to a global variable eliminates logic errors that might occur if a nonglobal variable hides the global variable.

Error-Prevention Tip 6.8

Avoid using variables of the same name for different purposes in a program. Although this is allowed in various circumstances, it can lead to errors.

6.18 Function Overloading

C++ enables several functions of the same name to be defined, as long as they have different signatures. This is called **function overloading**. The C++ compiler selects the proper function to call by examining the number, types and order of the arguments in the call. Function overloading is used to create several functions of the *same* name that perform similar tasks, but on *different* data types. For example, many functions in the math library are overloaded for different numeric types—the C++ standard requires `float`, `double` and `long double` overloaded versions of the math library functions discussed in Section 6.3.

Good Programming Practice 6.7

Overloading functions that perform closely related tasks can make programs more readable and understandable.

Overloaded **square** *Functions*

Figure 6.23 uses overloaded `square` functions to calculate the square of an `int` (lines 7–11) and the square of a `double` (lines 14–18). Line 22 invokes the `int` version of function `square` by passing the literal value 7. C++ treats whole number literal values as type `int`. Similarly, line 24 invokes the `double` version of function `square` by passing the literal value 7.5, which C++ treats as a `double`. In each case the compiler chooses the proper function to call, based on the type of the argument. The last two lines of the output window confirm that the proper function was called in each case.

```cpp
1   // Fig. 6.23: fig06_23.cpp
2   // Overloaded square functions.
3   #include <iostream>
4   using namespace std;
5
6   // function square for int values
7   int square( int x )
8   {
9      cout << "square of integer " << x << " is ";
10     return x * x;
11  } // end function square with int argument
12
```

Fig. 6.23 | Overloaded `square` functions. (Part 1 of 2.)

```
13   // function square for double values
14   double square( double y )
15   {
16      cout << "square of double " << y << " is ";
17      return y * y;
18   } // end function square with double argument
19
20   int main()
21   {
22      cout << square( 7 ); // calls int version
23      cout << endl;
24      cout << square( 7.5 ); // calls double version
25      cout << endl;
26   } // end main
```

```
square of integer 7 is 49
square of double 7.5 is 56.25
```

Fig. 6.23 | Overloaded `square` functions. (Part 2 of 2.)

How the Compiler Differentiates Among Overloaded Functions

Overloaded functions are distinguished by their *signatures*. A signature is a combination of a function's name and its parameter types (in order). The compiler encodes each function identifier with the types of its parameters (sometimes referred to as **name mangling** or **name decoration**) to enable **type-safe linkage**. Type-safe linkage ensures that the proper overloaded function is called and that the types of the arguments conform to the types of the parameters.

Figure 6.24 was compiled with GNU C++. Rather than showing the execution output of the program (as we normally would), we show the mangled function names produced in assembly language by GNU C++. Each mangled name (other than `main`) begins with two underscores (__) followed by the letter Z, a number and the function name. The number that follows Z specifies how many characters are in the function's name. For example, function `square` has 6 characters in its name, so its mangled name is prefixed with __Z6. The function name is then followed by an encoding of its parameter list. In the parameter list for function `nothing2` (line 25; see the fourth output line), c represents a char, i represents an int, Rf represents a `float` & (i.e., a reference to a `float`) and Rd represents a `double` & (i.e., a reference to a `double`). In the parameter list for function `nothing1`, i represents an int, f represents a float, c represents a char and Ri represents an int &. The two `square` functions are distinguished by their parameter lists; one specifies d for `double` and the other specifies i for `int`. The return types of the functions are *not* specified in the mangled names. *Overloaded functions can have different return types, but if they do, they must also have different parameter lists.* Again, you *cannot* have two functions with the *same* signature and *different* return types. Function-name mangling is compiler specific. Also, function `main` is *not* mangled, because it *cannot* be overloaded.

Common Programming Error 6.10

Creating overloaded functions with identical parameter lists and different return types is a compilation error.

```
 1    // Fig. 6.24: fig06_24.cpp
 2    // Name mangling to enable type-safe linkage.
 3
 4    // function square for int values
 5    int square( int x )
 6    {
 7       return x * x;
 8    } // end function square
 9
10    // function square for double values
11    double square( double y )
12    {
13       return y * y;
14    } // end function square
15
16    // function that receives arguments of types
17    // int, float, char and int &
18    void nothing1( int a, float b, char c, int &d )
19    {
20       // empty function body
21    } // end function nothing1
22
23    // function that receives arguments of types
24    // char, int, float & and double &
25    int nothing2( char a, int b, float &c, double &d )
26    {
27       return 0;
28    } // end function nothing2
29
30    int main()
31    {
32    } // end main
```

```
__Z6squarei
__Z6squared
__Z8nothing1ifcRi
__Z8nothing2ciRfRd
main
```

Fig. 6.24 | Name mangling to enable type-safe linkage.

The compiler uses only the parameter lists to distinguish between overloaded functions. Such functions need *not* have the same number of parameters. Use caution when overloading functions with default parameters, because this may cause ambiguity.

Common Programming Error 6.11

A function with default arguments omitted might be called identically to another overloaded function; this is a compilation error. For example, having a program that contains both a function that explicitly takes no arguments and a function of the same name that contains all default arguments results in a compilation error when an attempt is made to use that function name in a call passing no arguments. The compiler cannot determine which version of the function to choose.

Overloaded Operators

In Chapter 10, we discuss how to overload *operators* to define how they should operate on objects of user-defined data types. (In fact, we've been using many overloaded operators to this point, including the stream insertion << and the stream extraction >> operators, which are overloaded for *all* the fundamental types. We say more about overloading << and >> to be able to handle objects of user-defined types in Chapter 10.)

6.19 Function Templates

Overloaded functions are normally used to perform similar operations that involve different program logic on different data types. If the program logic and operations are *identical* for each data type, overloading may be performed more compactly and conveniently by using function templates. You write a single function template definition. Given the argument types provided in calls to this function, C++ automatically generates separate function template specializations to handle each type of call appropriately. Thus, defining a single function template essentially defines a whole family of overloaded functions.

Figure 6.25 defines a maximum function template (lines 3–17) that determines the largest of three values. All function template definitions begin with the **template** keyword (line 3) followed by a template parameter list to the function template enclosed in angle brackets (< and >). Every parameter in the template parameter list (often referred to as a formal type parameter) is preceded by keyword typename or keyword class (they are synonyms in this context). The formal type parameters are placeholders for fundamental types or user-defined types. These placeholders, in this case, T, are used to specify the types of the function's parameters (line 4), to specify the function's return type (line 4) and to declare variables within the body of the function definition (line 6). A function template is defined like any other function, but uses the formal type parameters as placeholders for actual data types.

```
1   // Fig. 6.25: maximum.h
2   // Function template maximum header.
3   template < typename T >  // or template< class T >
4   T maximum( T value1, T value2, T value3 )
5   {
6      T maximumValue = value1; // assume value1 is maximum
7
8      // determine whether value2 is greater than maximumValue
9      if ( value2 > maximumValue )
10        maximumValue = value2;
11
12     // determine whether value3 is greater than maximumValue
13     if ( value3 > maximumValue )
14        maximumValue = value3;
15
16     return maximumValue;
17  } // end function template maximum
```

Fig. 6.25 | Function template maximum header.

The function template declares a single formal type parameter T (line 3) as a placeholder for the type of the data to be tested by function maximum. The name of a type parameter must be unique in the template parameter list for a particular template definition. When the compiler detects a maximum invocation in the program source code, the *type of* the data passed to maximum is substituted for T throughout the template definition, and C++ creates a complete function for determining the maximum of three values of the specified data type—all three must have the same type, since we use only one type parameter in this example. Then the newly created function is compiled—templates are a means of *code generation.*

Figure 6.26 uses the maximum function template to determine the largest of three int values, three double values and three char values, respectively (lines 17, 27 and 37). Separate functions are created as a result of the calls in lines 17, 27 and 37—expecting three int values, three double values and three char values, respectively.

```cpp
1   // Fig. 6.26: fig06_26.cpp
2   // Function template maximum test program.
3   #include <iostream>
4   #include "maximum.h" // include definition of function template maximum
5   using namespace std;
6
7   int main()
8   {
9      // demonstrate maximum with int values
10     int int1, int2, int3;
11
12     cout << "Input three integer values: ";
13     cin >> int1 >> int2 >> int3;
14
15     // invoke int version of maximum
16     cout << "The maximum integer value is: "
17        << maximum( int1, int2, int3 );
18
19     // demonstrate maximum with double values
20     double double1, double2, double3;
21
22     cout << "\n\nInput three double values: ";
23     cin >> double1 >> double2 >> double3;
24
25     // invoke double version of maximum
26     cout << "The maximum double value is: "
27        << maximum( double1, double2, double3 );
28
29     // demonstrate maximum with char values
30     char char1, char2, char3;
31
32     cout << "\n\nInput three characters: ";
33     cin >> char1 >> char2 >> char3;
34
35     // invoke char version of maximum
36     cout << "The maximum character value is: "
37        << maximum( char1, char2, char3 ) << endl;
38  } // end main
```

Fig. 6.26 | Function template maximum test program. (Part 1 of 2.)

```
Input three integer values: 1 2 3
The maximum integer value is: 3

Input three double values: 3.3 2.2 1.1
The maximum double value is: 3.3

Input three characters: A C B
The maximum character value is: C
```

Fig. 6.26 | Function template maximum test program. (Part 2 of 2.)

The function template specialization created for type int replaces each occurrence of T with int as follows:

```
int maximum( int value1, int value2, int value3 )
{
   int maximumValue = value1; // assume value1 is maximum

   // determine whether value2 is greater than maximumValue
   if ( value2 > maximumValue )
      maximumValue = value2;

   // determine whether value3 is greater than maximumValue
   if ( value3 > maximumValue )
      maximumValue = value3;

   return maximumValue;
} // end function template maximum
```

C++11—Trailing Return Types for Functions

C++11 introduces **trailing return types** for functions. To specify a trailing return type you place the keyword auto before the function name, then follow the function's parameter list with -> and the return type. For example, to specify a trailing return type for function template maximum (Fig. 6.25), you'd write

```
template < typename T >
auto maximum( T x, T y, T z ) -> T
```

As you build more complex function templates, there are cases for which only trailing return types are allowed. Such complex function templates are beyond this book's scope.

6.20 Recursion

For some problems, it's useful to have functions *call themselves*. A **recursive function** is a function that calls itself, either directly, or indirectly (through another function). [*Note:* The C++ standard document indicates that main should not be called within a program or recursively. Its sole purpose is to be the starting point for program execution.] This section and the next present simple examples of recursion. Recursion is discussed at length in upper-level computer-science courses. Figure 6.32 (at the end of Section 6.22) summarizes the extensive recursion examples and exercises in the book.

Recursion Concepts

We first consider recursion conceptually, then examine programs containing recursive functions. Recursive problem-solving approaches have a number of elements in common.

A recursive function is called to solve a problem. The function knows how to solve only the *simplest case(s)*, or so-called **base case(s)**. If the function is called with a base case, the function simply returns a result. If the function is called with a more complex problem, it typically divides the problem into two conceptual pieces—a piece that the function knows how to do and a piece that it does not know how to do. To make recursion feasible, the latter piece *must* resemble the original problem, but be a slightly simpler or smaller version. This new problem looks like the original, so the function calls a copy of itself to work on the smaller problem—this is referred to as a **recursive call** and is also called the **recursion step**. The recursion step often includes the keyword `return`, because its result will be combined with the portion of the problem the function knew how to solve to form the result passed back to the original caller, possibly `main`.

Common Programming Error 6.12

Omitting the base case or writing the recursion step incorrectly so that it does not converge on the base case causes an infinite recursion error, typically causing a stack overflow. This is analogous to the problem of an infinite loop in an iterative (nonrecursive) solution.

The recursion step executes while the original call to the function is still "open," i.e., it has not yet finished executing. The recursion step can result in many more such recursive calls, as the function keeps dividing each new subproblem with which the function is called into two conceptual pieces. In order for the recursion to eventually terminate, each time the function calls itself with a slightly simpler version of the original problem, this sequence of smaller and smaller problems must eventually *converge* on the base case. At that point, the function recognizes the base case and returns a result to the previous copy of the function, and a sequence of returns ensues up the line until the original call eventually returns the final result to `main`. This sounds quite exotic compared to the kind of problem solving we've been using to this point. As an example of these concepts at work, let's write a recursive program to perform a popular mathematical calculation.

Factorial

The factorial of a nonnegative integer *n*, written *n*! (and pronounced "*n* factorial"), is the product

$$n \cdot (n-1) \cdot (n-2) \cdot \ldots \cdot 1$$

with 1! equal to 1, and 0! defined to be 1. For example, 5! is the product $5 \cdot 4 \cdot 3 \cdot 2 \cdot 1$, which is equal to 120.

Iterative Factorial

The factorial of an integer, `number`, greater than or equal to 0, can be calculated **iteratively** (nonrecursively) by using a `for` statement as follows:

```
factorial = 1;

for ( unsigned int counter = number; counter >= 1; --counter )
    factorial *= counter;
```

Recursive Factorial

A *recursive* definition of the factorial function is arrived at by observing the following algebraic relationship:

$$n! = n \cdot (n-1)!$$

For example, 5! is clearly equal to 5 * 4! as is shown by the following:

$$5! = 5 \cdot 4 \cdot 3 \cdot 2 \cdot 1$$
$$5! = 5 \cdot (4 \cdot 3 \cdot 2 \cdot 1)$$
$$5! = 5 \cdot (4!)$$

Evaluating 5!
The evaluation of 5! would proceed as shown in Fig. 6.27, which illustrates how the succession of recursive calls proceeds until 1! is evaluated to be 1, terminating the recursion. Figure 6.27(b) shows the values returned from each recursive call to its caller until the final value is calculated and returned.

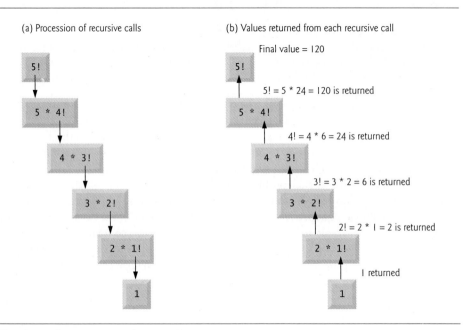

Fig. 6.27 | Recursive evaluation of 5!.

*Using a Recursive **factorial** Function to Calculate Factorials*
Figure 6.28 uses recursion to calculate and print the factorials of the integers 0–10. (The choice of the data type unsigned long is explained momentarily.) The recursive function factorial (lines 18–24) first determines whether the terminating condition number <= 1 (line 20) is true. If number is less than or equal to 1, the factorial function returns 1 (line 21), no further recursion is necessary and the function terminates. If number is greater than 1, line 23 expresses the problem as the product of number and a recursive call to factorial evaluating the factorial of number - 1, which is a slightly simpler problem than the original calculation factorial(number).

*Why We Chose Type **unsigned long** in This Example*
Function factorial has been declared to receive a parameter of type unsigned long and return a result of type unsigned long. This is shorthand notation for unsigned long int. The C++ standard requires that a variable of type unsigned long int be *at least as big as* an int.

```cpp
1   // Fig. 6.28: fig06_28.cpp
2   // Recursive function factorial.
3   #include <iostream>
4   #include <iomanip>
5   using namespace std;
6
7   unsigned long factorial( unsigned long ); // function prototype
8
9   int main()
10  {
11     // calculate the factorials of 0 through 10
12     for ( unsigned int counter = 0; counter <= 10; ++counter )
13        cout << setw( 2 ) << counter << "! = " << factorial( counter )
14           << endl;
15  } // end main
16
17  // recursive definition of function factorial
18  unsigned long factorial( unsigned long number )
19  {
20     if ( number <= 1 ) // test for base case
21        return 1; // base cases: 0! = 1 and 1! = 1
22     else // recursion step
23        return number * factorial( number - 1 );
24  } // end function factorial
```

```
 0! = 1
 1! = 1
 2! = 2
 3! = 6
 4! = 24
 5! = 120
 6! = 720
 7! = 5040
 8! = 40320
 9! = 362880
10! = 3628800
```

Fig. 6.28 | Recursive function `factorial`.

Typically, an `unsigned long int` is stored in at least four bytes (32 bits); such a variable can hold a value in the range 0 to at least 4,294,967,295. (The data type `long int` is also typically stored in at least four bytes and can hold a value at least in the range –2,147,483,647 to 2,147,483,647.) As can be seen in Fig. 6.28, factorial values become large quickly. We chose the data type `unsigned long` so that the program can calculate factorials greater than 7! on computers with small (such as two-byte) integers. Unfortunately, the function `factorial` produces large values so quickly that even `unsigned long` does not help us compute many factorial values before even the size of an `unsigned long` variable is exceeded.

C++11 Type `unsigned long long int`

C++11's new `unsigned long long int` type (which can be abbreviated as `unsigned long long`) on some systems enables you to store values in 8 bytes (64 bits) which can hold numbers as large as 18,446,744,073,709,551,615.

Representing Even Larger Numbers
Variables of type `double` could be used to calculate factorials of larger numbers. This points to a weakness in many programming languages, namely, that the languages are not easily extended to handle the unique requirements of various applications. As we'll see when we discuss object-oriented programming in more depth, C++ is an *extensible* language that allows us to create classes that can represent arbitrarily large integers if we wish. Such classes already are available in popular class libraries, and we work on similar classes of our own in Exercise 9.14 and Exercise 10.9.

6.21 Example Using Recursion: Fibonacci Series

The Fibonacci series

> 0, 1, 1, 2, 3, 5, 8, 13, 21, …

begins with 0 and 1 and has the property that each subsequent Fibonacci number is the sum of the previous two Fibonacci numbers.

The series occurs in nature and, in particular, describes a form of spiral. The ratio of successive Fibonacci numbers converges on a constant value of 1.618…. This number frequently occurs in nature and has been called the **golden ratio** or the **golden mean**. Humans tend to find the golden mean aesthetically pleasing. Architects often design windows, rooms and buildings whose length and width are in the ratio of the golden mean. Postcards are often designed with a golden mean length/width ratio.

Recursive Fibonacci Definition
The Fibonacci series can be defined recursively as follows:

> fibonacci(0) = 0
> fibonacci(1) = 1
> fibonacci(n) = fibonacci($n - 1$) + fibonacci($n - 2$)

The program of Fig. 6.29 calculates the nth Fibonacci number recursively by using function `fibonacci`. Fibonacci numbers tend to become large quickly, although slower than factorials do. Therefore, we chose the data type `unsigned long` for the parameter type and the return type in function `fibonacci`. Figure 6.29 shows the execution of the program, which displays the Fibonacci values for several numbers.

The application begins with a `for` statement that calculates and displays the Fibonacci values for the integers 0–10 and is followed by three calls to calculate the Fibonacci values of the integers 20, 30 and 35 (lines 16–18). The calls to `fibonacci` (lines 13 and 16–18) from `main` are *not* recursive calls, but the calls from line 27 of `fibonacci` are recursive. Each time the program invokes `fibonacci` (lines 22–28), the function immediately tests the base case to determine whether `number` is equal to 0 or 1 (line 24). If this is true, line 25 returns `number`. Interestingly, if `number` is greater than 1, the recursion step (line 27) generates *two* recursive calls, each for a slightly smaller problem than the original call to `fibonacci`.

```
1   // Fig. 6.29: fig06_29.cpp
2   // Recursive function fibonacci.
3   #include <iostream>
```

Fig. 6.29 | Recursive function `fibonacci`. (Part 1 of 2.)

```
 4   using namespace std;
 5
 6   unsigned long fibonacci( unsigned long ); // function prototype
 7
 8   int main()
 9   {
10      // calculate the fibonacci values of 0 through 10
11      for ( unsigned int counter = 0; counter <= 10; ++counter )
12         cout << "fibonacci( " << counter << " ) = "
13            << fibonacci( counter ) << endl;
14
15      // display higher fibonacci values
16      cout << "\nfibonacci( 20 ) = " << fibonacci( 20 ) << endl;
17      cout << "fibonacci( 30 ) = " << fibonacci( 30 ) << endl;
18      cout << "fibonacci( 35 ) = " << fibonacci( 35 ) << endl;
19   } // end main
20
21   // recursive function fibonacci
22   unsigned long fibonacci( unsigned long number )
23   {
24      if ( ( 0 == number ) || ( 1 == number ) ) // base cases
25         return number;
26      else // recursion step
27         return fibonacci( number - 1 ) + fibonacci( number - 2 );
28   } // end function fibonacci
```

```
fibonacci( 0 ) = 0
fibonacci( 1 ) = 1
fibonacci( 2 ) = 1
fibonacci( 3 ) = 2
fibonacci( 4 ) = 3
fibonacci( 5 ) = 5
fibonacci( 6 ) = 8
fibonacci( 7 ) = 13
fibonacci( 8 ) = 21
fibonacci( 9 ) = 34
fibonacci( 10 ) = 55

fibonacci( 20 ) = 6765
fibonacci( 30 ) = 832040
fibonacci( 35 ) = 9227465
```

Fig. 6.29 | Recursive function fibonacci. (Part 2 of 2.)

Evaluating fibonacci(3)

Figure 6.30 shows how function fibonacci would evaluate fibonacci(3). This figure raises some interesting issues about the *order* in which C++ compilers evaluate the operands of operators. This is a *separate* issue from the order in which operators are applied to their operands, namely, the order dictated by the rules of operator precedence and associativity. Figure 6.30 shows that evaluating fibonacci(3) causes two recursive calls, namely, fibonacci(2) and fibonacci(1). In what order are these calls made?

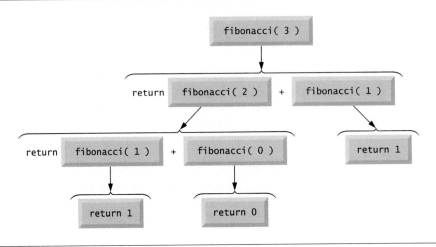

Fig. 6.30 | Set of recursive calls to function `fibonacci`.

Order of Evaluation of Operands

Most programmers simply assume that the operands are evaluated left to right. C++ does *not* specify the order in which the operands of most operators (including +) are to be evaluated. Therefore, you must make no assumption about the order in which these calls execute. The calls could in fact execute `fibonacci(2)` first, then `fibonacci(1)`, or they could execute in the reverse order: `fibonacci(1)`, then `fibonacci(2)`. In this program and in most others, it turns out that the final result would be the same. However, in some programs the evaluation of an operand can have **side effects** (changes to data values) that could affect the final result of the expression.

C++ specifies the order of evaluation of the operands of only *four* operators—&&, ||, comma (,) and ?:. The first three are binary operators whose two operands are guaranteed to be evaluated left to right. The last operator is C++'s only *ternary* operator—its leftmost operand is always evaluated first; if it evaluates to *true*, the middle operand evaluates next and the last operand is ignored; if the leftmost operand evaluates to *false*, the third operand evaluates next and the middle operand is ignored.

 Portability Tip 6.2
Programs that depend on the order of evaluation of the operands of operators other than && , || , ?: and the comma (,) operator can function differently with different compilers and can lead to logic errors.

 Common Programming Error 6.13
Writing programs that depend on the order of evaluation of the operands of operators other than && , || , ?: and the comma (,) operator can lead to logic errors.

 Error-Prevention Tip 6.9
Do not depend on the order in which operands are evaluated. To ensure that side effects are applied in the correct order, break complex expressions into separate statements.

Common Programming Error 6.14

Recall that the && and || operators use short-circuit evaluation. Placing an expression with a side effect on the right side of a && or || operator is a logic error if that expression should always be evaluated.

Exponential Complexity

A word of caution is in order about recursive programs like the one we use here to generate Fibonacci numbers. Each level of recursion in function fibonacci has a *doubling* effect on the number of function calls; i.e., the number of recursive calls that are required to calculate the nth Fibonacci number is on the order of 2^n. This rapidly gets out of hand. Calculating only the 20th Fibonacci number would require on the order of 2^{20} or about a million calls, calculating the 30th Fibonacci number would require on the order of 2^{30} or about a billion calls, and so on. Computer scientists refer to this as exponential complexity. Problems of this nature humble even the world's most powerful computers! Complexity issues in general, and exponential complexity in particular, are discussed in detail in the upper-level computer science course generally called "Algorithms."

Performance Tip 6.8

Avoid Fibonacci-style recursive programs that result in an exponential "explosion" of calls.

6.22 Recursion vs. Iteration

In the two previous sections, we studied two recursive functions that can also be implemented with simple iterative programs. This section compares the two approaches and discusses why you might choose one approach over the other in a particular situation.

- Both iteration and recursion are *based on a control statement*: Iteration uses a *repetition structure*; recursion uses a *selection structure*.

- Both iteration and recursion involve *repetition*: Iteration explicitly uses a *repetition structure*; recursion achieves repetition through *repeated function calls*.

- Iteration and recursion each involve a *termination test*: Iteration terminates when the *loop-continuation condition fails*; recursion terminates when a *base case is recognized*.

- Iteration with counter-controlled repetition and recursion each *gradually approach termination*: Iteration *modifies a counter* until the counter assumes a value that makes the loop-continuation condition fail; recursion produces *simpler versions of the original problem* until the base case is reached.

- Both iteration and recursion *can occur infinitely*: An *infinite loop* occurs with iteration if the loop-continuation test never becomes false; *infinite recursion* occurs if the recursion step does not reduce the problem during each recursive call in a manner that converges on the base case.

Iterative Factorial Implementation

To illustrate the differences between iteration and recursion, let's examine an iterative solution to the factorial problem (Fig. 6.31). A repetition statement is used (lines 23–24 of

Fig. 6.31) rather than the selection statement of the recursive solution (lines 20–23 of Fig. 6.28). Both solutions use a termination test. In the recursive solution, line 20 (Fig. 6.28) tests for the base case. In the iterative solution, line 23 (Fig. 6.31) tests the loop-continuation condition—if the test fails, the loop terminates. Finally, instead of producing simpler versions of the original problem, the iterative solution uses a counter that is modified until the loop-continuation condition becomes false.

```cpp
1   // Fig. 6.31: fig06_31.cpp
2   // Iterative function factorial.
3   #include <iostream>
4   #include <iomanip>
5   using namespace std;
6
7   unsigned long factorial( unsigned int ); // function prototype
8
9   int main()
10  {
11      // calculate the factorials of 0 through 10
12      for ( unsigned int counter = 0; counter <= 10; ++counter )
13          cout << setw( 2 ) << counter << "! = " << factorial( counter )
14              << endl;
15  } // end main
16
17  // iterative function factorial
18  unsigned long factorial( unsigned int number )
19  {
20      unsigned long result = 1;
21
22      // iterative factorial calculation
23      for ( unsigned int i = number; i >= 1; --i )
24          result *= i;
25
26      return result;
27  } // end function factorial
```

```
 0! = 1
 1! = 1
 2! = 2
 3! = 6
 4! = 24
 5! = 120
 6! = 720
 7! = 5040
 8! = 40320
 9! = 362880
10! = 3628800
```

Fig. 6.31 | Iterative function `factorial`.

Negatives of Recursion

Recursion has negatives. It repeatedly invokes the mechanism, and consequently the *overhead, of function calls.* This can be expensive in both processor time and memory space. Each recursive call causes *another copy of the function variables* to be created; this can consume considerable memory. Iteration normally occurs within a function, so the overhead of repeated function calls and extra memory assignment is omitted. So why choose recursion?

Software Engineering Observation 6.13

Any problem that can be solved recursively can also be solved iteratively (nonrecursively). A recursive approach is normally chosen when the recursive approach more naturally mirrors the problem and results in a program that's easier to understand and debug. Another reason to choose a recursive solution is that an iterative solution is not apparent.

Performance Tip 6.9

Avoid using recursion in performance situations. Recursive calls take time and consume additional memory.

Common Programming Error 6.15

Accidentally having a nonrecursive function call itself, either directly or indirectly (through another function), is a logic error.

Summary of Recursion Examples and Exercises in This Book

Figure 6.32 summarizes the recursion examples and exercises in the text.

Location in text	Recursion examples and exercises
Chapter 6	
Section 6.20, Fig. 6.28	Factorial function
Section 6.21, Fig. 6.29	Fibonacci function
Exercise 6.36	Recursive exponentiation
Exercise 6.38	Towers of Hanoi
Exercise 6.40	Visualizing recursion
Exercise 6.41	Greatest common divisor
Exercise 6.44, Exercise 6.45	"What does this program do?" exercise
Chapter 7	
Exercise 7.17	"What does this program do?" exercise
Exercise 7.20	"What does this program do?" exercise
Exercise 7.28	Determine whether a string is a palindrome
Exercise 7.29	Eight Queens
Exercise 7.30	Print an array
Exercise 7.31	Print a string backward
Exercise 7.32	Minimum value in an array
Exercise 7.33	Maze traversal
Exercise 7.34	Generating mazes randomly

Fig. 6.32 | Summary of recursion examples and exercises in the text. (Part 1 of 2.)

Location in text	Recursion examples and exercises
Chapter 19	
Section 19.6, Figs. 19.20–19.22	Binary tree insert
Section 19.6, Figs. 19.20–19.22	Preorder traversal of a binary tree
Section 19.6, Figs. 19.20–19.22	Inorder traversal of a binary tree
Section 19.6, Figs. 19.20–19.22	Postorder traversal of a binary tree
Exercise 19.20	Print a linked list backward
Exercise 19.21	Search a linked list
Exercise 19.22	Binary tree delete
Exercise 19.23	Binary tree search
Exercise 19.24	Level order traversal of a binary tree
Exercise 19.25	Printing tree
Chapter 20	
Section 20.3.3, Fig. 20.6	Mergesort
Exercise 20.8	Linear search
Exercise 20.9	Binary search
Exercise 20.10	Quicksort

Fig. 6.32 | Summary of recursion examples and exercises in the text. (Part 2 of 2.)

6.23 Wrap-Up

In this chapter, you learned more about function declarations, including function proto-types, function signatures, function headers and function bodies. We overviewed the math library functions. You learned about argument coercion, or the forcing of arguments to the appropriate types specified by the parameter declarations of a function. We demonstrated how to use functions rand and srand to generate sets of random numbers that can be used for simulations. We showed how to define sets of constants with enums. You also learned about the scope of variables, storage-class specifiers and storage duration. Two different ways to pass arguments to functions were covered—pass-by-value and pass-by-reference. For pass-by-reference, references are used as an alias to a variable. We showed how to implement inline functions and functions that receive default arguments. You learned that multiple functions in one class can be overloaded by providing functions with the same name and different signatures. Such functions can be used to perform the same or similar tasks, using different types or different numbers of parameters. We demonstrated a simpler way of overloading functions using function templates, where a function is defined once but can be used for several different types. You then studied recursion, where a function calls itself to solve a problem.

In Chapter 7, you'll learn how to maintain lists and tables of data in arrays and object-oriented vectors. You'll see a more elegant array-based implementation of the dice-rolling application and two enhanced versions of the GradeBook case study we presented in Chapters 3–6 that will use arrays to store the actual grades entered.

Summary

Section 6.1 Introduction
- Experience has shown that the best way to develop and maintain a large program is to construct it from small, simple pieces, or components. This technique is called divide and conquer (p. 236).

Section 6.2 Program Components in C++
- C++ programs are typically written by combining new functions and classes you write with "pre-packaged" functions and classes available in the C++ Standard Library.
- Functions allow you to modularize a program by separating its tasks into self-contained units.
- The statements in the function bodies are written only once, are reused from perhaps several locations in a program and are hidden from other functions.

Section 6.3 Math Library Functions
- Sometimes functions are not members of a class. These are called global functions (p. 238).
- The prototypes for global functions are often placed in headers, so that they can be reused in any program that includes the header and that can link to the function's object code.

Section 6.4 Function Definitions with Multiple Parameters
- The compiler refers to the function prototype to check that calls to a function contain the correct number and types of arguments, that the types of the arguments are in the correct order and that the value returned by the function can be used correctly in the expression that called the function.
- If a function does not return a result, control returns when the program reaches the function-ending right brace, or by execution of the statement

      return;

  If a function does return a result, the statement

      return expression;

  evaluates expression and returns the value of expression to the caller.

Section 6.5 Function Prototypes and Argument Coercion
- The portion of a function prototype that includes the name of the function and the types of its arguments is called the function signature (p. 245) or simply the signature.
- An important feature of function prototypes is argument coercion (p. 245)—i.e., forcing arguments to the appropriate types specified by the parameter declarations.
- Arguments can be converted by the compiler to the parameter types as specified by C++'s promotion rules (p. 245). The promotion rules indicate the implicit conversions that the compiler can perform between fundamental types.

Section 6.6 C++ Standard Library Headers
- The C++ Standard Library is divided into many portions, each with its own header. The headers also contain definitions of various class types, functions and constants.
- A header "instructs" the compiler on how to interface with library components.

Section 6.7 Case Study: Random Number Generation
- Calling rand (p. 248) repeatedly produces a sequence of pseudorandom numbers (p. 251). The sequence repeats itself each time the program executes.

- To randomize the numbers produced by rand pass an unsigned integer argument (typically from function time; p. 253) to function srand (p. 251), which seeds the rand function.

- Random numbers in a range can be generated with

    number = *shiftingValue* + rand() % *scalingFactor*;

    where *shiftingValue* (p. 253) is equal to the first number in the desired range of consecutive integers and *scalingFactor* (p. 253) is equal to the width of the desired range of consecutive integers.

Section 6.8 Case Study: Game of Chance; Introducing **enum**
- An enumeration, introduced by the keyword enum and followed by a type name (p. 256), is a set of named integer constants (p. 256) that start at 0, unless specified otherwise, and increment by 1.

- Unscoped enums can lead to naming collisions and logic errors. To eliminate these problems, C++11 introduces scoped enums (p. 257), which are declared with the keywords enum class (or the synonym enum struct).

- To reference a scoped enum constant, you must qualify the constant with the scoped enum's type name and the scope-resolution operator (::). If another scoped enum contains the same identifier for one of its constants, it's always clear which version of the constant is being used.

- The constants in an enum are represented as integers.

- An unscoped enum's underlying integral type depends on its constants' values—the type is guaranteed to be large enough to store the constant values specified.

- A scoped enum's underlying integral type is int by default.

- C++11 allows you to specify an enum's underlying integral type by following the enum's type name with a colon (:) and the integral type.

- A compilation error occurs if an enum constant's value is outside the range that can be represented by the enum's underlying type.

Section 6.9 C++11 Random Numbers
- According to CERT, function rand does not have "good statistical properties" and can be predictable, which makes programs that use rand less secure

- C++11 provides a new, more secure library of random-number capabilities that can produce nondeterministic random numbers for simulations and security scenarios where predictability is undesirable. These new capabilities are located in the C++ Standard Library's <random> header.

- For flexibility based on how random numbers are used in programs, C++11 provides many classes that represent various random-number generation engines and distributions. An engine implements a random-number generation algorithm that produce pseudorandom numbers. A distribution controls the range of values produced by an engine, the types of those values and the statistical properties of the values.

- The type default_random_engine (p. 258) represents the default random-number generation engine.

- The uniform_int_distribution (p. 258) evenly distributes pseudorandom integers over a specified range of values. The default range is from 0 to the maximum value of an int on your platform.

Section 6.10 Storage Classes and Storage Duration
- An identifier's storage duration (p. 259) determines the period during which it exists in memory.

- An identifier's scope is where the identifier can be referenced in a program.

- An identifier's linkage (p. 259) determines whether it's known only in the source file where it's declared or across multiple files that are compiled, then linked together.

- Variables with automatic storage duration include: local variables declared in functions, function parameters and local variables or function parameters declared with `register` (p. 259). Such variables are created when program execution enters the block in which they're defined, exist while the block is active and are destroyed when the program exits the block.

- Keywords `extern` (p. 259) and `static` declare identifiers for variables of the static storage duration (p. 259) and for functions. Static-storage-duration variables exist from the point at which the program begins execution until the program terminates.

- A static-storage-duration variable's storage is allocated when the program begins execution. Such a variable is initialized once when its declaration is encountered. For functions, the name of the function exists when the program begins execution as for all other functions.

- External identifiers (such as global variables) and local variables declared with the storage class-specifier `static` have static storage duration (p. 259).

- Global variables (p. 261) declarations are placed outside any class or function definition. Global variables retain their values throughout the program's execution. Global variables and functions can be referenced by any function that follows their declarations or definitions.

- Unlike automatic variables, `static` local variables retain their values when the function in which they're declared returns to its caller.

Section 6.11 Scope Rules
- An identifier declared outside any function or class has global namespace scope (p. 262).
- Identifiers declared inside a block have block scope (p. 262), which begins at the identifier's declaration and ends at the terminating right brace (}) of the block in which the identifier is declared.
- Labels are the only identifiers with function scope (p. 262). Labels can be used anywhere in the function in which they appear, but cannot be referenced outside the function body.
- An identifier declared outside any function or class has global namespace scope. Such an identifier is "known" in all functions from the point at which it's declared until the end of the file.
- Identifiers in the parameter list of a function prototype have function-prototype scope (p. 262).

Section 6.12 Function Call Stack and Activation Records
- Stacks (p. 265) are known as last-in, first-out (LIFO) data structures—the last item pushed (inserted; p. 265) on the stack is the first item popped (removed; p. 265) from the stack.
- The function call stack (p. 266) supports the function call/return mechanism and the creation, maintenance and destruction of each called function's automatic variables.
- Each time a function calls another function, a stack frame or an activation record (p. 266) is pushed onto the stack containing the return address that the called function needs to return to the calling function, and the function call's automatic variables and parameters.
- The stack frame (p. 266) exists as long as the called function is active. When the called function returns, its stack frame is popped from the stack, and its local automatic variables no longer exist.

Section 6.13 Functions with Empty Parameter Lists
- In C++, an empty parameter list is specified by writing either `void` or nothing in parentheses.

Section 6.14 Inline Functions
- C++ provides inline functions (p. 270) to help reduce function call overhead—especially for small functions. Placing the qualifier `inline` (p. 270) before a function's return type in the function definition advises the compiler to generate a copy of the function's code in every place that the function is called to avoid a function call.

- Compilers can inline code for which you have not explicitly used the `inline` keyword. Today's optimizing compilers are so sophisticated that it's best to leave inlining decisions to the compiler.

Section 6.15 References and Reference Parameters

- When an argument is passed by value (p. 271), a *copy* of the argument's value is made and passed to the called function. Changes to the copy do not affect the original variable's value in the caller.

- With pass-by-reference (p. 271), the caller gives the called function the ability to access the caller's data directly and to modify it if the called function chooses to do so.

- A reference parameter (p. 272) is an alias for its corresponding argument in a function call.

- To indicate that a function parameter is passed by reference, follow the parameter's type in the function prototype and header by an ampersand (&).

- All operations performed on a reference are actually performed on the original variable.

Section 6.16 Default Arguments

- When a function is called repeatedly with the same argument for a particular parameter, you can specify that such a parameter has a default argument (p. 274).

- When a program omits an argument for a parameter with a default argument, the compiler inserts the default value of that argument to be passed to the function call.

- Default arguments must be the rightmost (trailing) arguments in a function's parameter list.

- Default arguments are specified in the function prototype.

Section 6.17 Unary Scope Resolution Operator

- C++ provides the unary scope resolution operator (p. 276), `::`, to access a global variable when a local variable of the same name is in scope.

Section 6.18 Function Overloading

- C++ enables several functions of the same name to be defined, as long as these functions have different sets of parameters. This capability is called function overloading (p. 277).

- When an overloaded function is called, the C++ compiler selects the proper function by examining the number, types and order of the arguments in the call.

- Overloaded functions are distinguished by their signatures.

- The compiler encodes each function identifier with the types of its parameters to enable type-safe linkage (p. 278). Type-safe linkage ensures that the proper overloaded function is called and that the types of the arguments conform to the types of the parameters.

Section 6.19 Function Templates

- Overloaded functions typically perform similar operations that involve different program logic on different data types. If the program logic and operations are identical for each data type, overloading may be performed more compactly and conveniently using function templates (p. 280).

- Given the argument types provided in calls to a function template, C++ automatically generates separate function template specializations (p. 280) to handle each type of call appropriately.

- All function template definitions begin with the `template` keyword (p. 280) followed by a template parameter list (p. 280) to the function template enclosed in angle brackets (< and >).

- The formal type parameters (p. 280) are preceded by keyword `typename` (or `class`) and are placeholders for fundamental types or user-defined types. These placeholders are used to specify the types of the function's parameters, to specify the function's return type and to declare variables within the body of the function definition.

- C++11 introduces trailing return types for functions. To specify a trailing return type place auto before the function name, then follow the function's parameter list with -> and the return type.

Section 6.20 Recursion
- A recursive function (p. 282) calls itself, either directly or indirectly.
- A recursive function knows how to solve only the simplest case(s), or so-called base case(s). If the function is called with a base case (p. 283), the function simply returns a result.
- If the function is called with a more complex problem, the function typically divides the problem into two conceptual pieces—a piece that the function knows how to do and a piece that it does not know how to do. To make recursion feasible, the latter piece must resemble the original problem, but be a slightly simpler or slightly smaller version of it.
- For recursion to terminate, the sequence of recursive calls (p. 283) must converge on the base case.
- C++11's new unsigned long long int type (which can be abbreviated as unsigned long long) on some systems enables you to store values in 8 bytes (64 bits) which can hold numbers as large as 18,446,744,073,709,551,615.

Section 6.21 Example Using Recursion: Fibonacci Series
- The ratio of successive Fibonacci numbers converges on a constant value of 1.618.... This number frequently occurs in nature and has been called the golden ratio or the golden mean (p. 286).

Section 6.22 Recursion vs. Iteration
- Iteration (p. 283) and recursion are similar: both are based on a control statement, involve repetition, involve a termination test, gradually approach termination and can occur infinitely.
- Recursion repeatedly invokes the mechanism, and overhead, of function calls. This can be expensive in both processor time and memory space. Each recursive call (p. 283) causes another copy of the function's variables to be created; this can consume considerable memory.

Self-Review Exercises

6.1   Answer each of the following:
  a) Program components in C++ are called _____ and_____.
  b) A function is invoked with a(n) _____.
  c) A variable known only within the function in which it's defined is called a(n) _____.
  d) The _____ statement in a called function passes the value of an expression back to the calling function.
  e) The keyword _____ is used in a function header to indicate that a function does not return a value or to indicate that a function contains no parameters.
  f) An identifier's _____ is the portion of the program in which the identifier can be used.
  g) The three ways to return control from a called function to a caller are _____, _____ and _____.
  h) A(n) _____ allows the compiler to check the number, types and order of the arguments passed to a function.
  i) Function _____ is used to produce random numbers.
  j) Function _____ is used to set the random number seed to randomize the number sequence generated by function rand.
  k) Storage-class specifier _____ is a recommendation to the compiler to store a variable in one of the computer's registers.
  l) A variable declared outside any block or function is a(n) _____ variable.
  m) For a local variable in a function to retain its value between calls to the function, it must be declared with the _____ storage-class specifier.

n) A function that calls itself either directly or indirectly (i.e., through another function) is a(n) _____ function.

o) A recursive function typically has two components—one that provides a means for the recursion to terminate by testing for a(n) _____ case and one that expresses the problem as a recursive call for a slightly simpler problem than the original call.

p) It's possible to have various functions with the same name that operate on different types or numbers of arguments. This is called function _____.

q) The _____ enables access to a global variable with the same name as a variable in the current scope.

r) The _____ qualifier is used to declare read-only variables.

s) A function _____ enables a single function to be defined to perform a task on many different data types.

6.2   For the program in Fig. 6.33, state the scope (either function scope, global namespace scope, block scope or function-prototype scope) of each of the following elements:

a) The variable x in main.
b) The variable y in cube.
c) The function cube.
d) The function main.
e) The function prototype for cube.
f) The identifier y in the function prototype for cube.

```
1   // Exercise 6.2: Ex06_02.cpp
2   #include <iostream>
3   using namespace std;
4
5   int cube( int y ); // function prototype
6
7   int main()
8   {
9      int x = 0;
10
11     for ( x = 1; x <= 10; x++ ) // loop 10 times
12        cout << cube( x ) << endl; // calculate cube of x and output results
13  } // end main
14
15  // definition of function cube
16  int cube( int y )
17  {
18     return y * y * y;
19  } // end function cube
```

Fig. 6.33 | Program for Exercise 6.2.

6.3   Write a program that tests whether the examples of the math library function calls shown in Fig. 6.2 actually produce the indicated results.

6.4   Give the function header for each of the following functions:

a) Function sum that takes three double-precision, floating-point arguments, x, y and z, and returns a double-precision, floating-point result.

b) Function largest that takes two integers, x and y, and returns an integer.

c) Function display that receive one double-precision, floating-point arguments x and does not return a value. [*Note:* Such functions are commonly used to display the parameter to a user.]

d) Function doubleToInt that takes a double-precision, floating-point argument, number, and returns an integer result.

6.5   Give the function prototype (without parameter names) for each of the following:
    a) Function sum that takes two integers, x and y, and returns an integer.
    b) Function product that takes two integers, x and y, and returns an integer.
    c) Function sum that takes three integers, x, y and z, and returns an integer.
    d) Function sum that takes three integers, x, y and z, and does not return a value.

6.6   Write a declaration for each of the following:
    a) Character type variable ch that should be maintained in a register. Initialize ch to a.
    b) Integer variable var that is to retain its value between calls to the function in which it's defined.

6.7   Find the error(s) in each of the following program segments, and explain how the error(s) can be corrected (see also Exercise 6.47):
    a)
```
int g()
{
    cout << "Inside function g" << endl;
    int h()
    {
        cout << "Inside function h" << endl;
    }
}
```
    b)
```
int sum( int x, int y )
{
    int result = 0;

    result = x + y;
}
```
    c)
```
int sum( int n )
{
    if ( 0 == n )
        return 0;
    else
        n + sum( n - 1 );
}
```
    d)
```
void f( double a );
{
    float a;
    cout << a << endl;
}
```
    e)
```
void product()
{
    int a = 0;
    int b = 0;
    int c = 0;
    cout << "Enter three integers: ";
    cin >> a >> b >> c;
    int result = a * b * c;
    cout << "Result is " << result;
    return result;
}
```

6.8   What is the difference between a parameter type declaration int & and int?

6.9   (True/False) Overloaded functions are distinguished by their signatures.

6.10   Write a complete program that prompts the user for the radius and height of a cylinder, and calculates and prints the volume of that cylinder. Use an inline function `cylinderVolume` that returns the result of the following expression: `(3.14159 * pow(radius, 2) * height)`.

Answers to Self-Review Exercises

6.1   a) functions, classes. b) function call. c) local variable. d) return. e) void. f) scope. g) return;, return *expression*; or encounter the closing right brace of a function. h) function prototype. i) rand. j) srand. k) register. l) global. m) static. n) recursive. o) base. p) overloading. q) unary scope resolution operator (::). r) const. s) template.

6.2   a) block scope. b) block scope. c) global namespace scope. d) global namespace scope. e) global namespace scope. f) function-prototype scope.

6.3   See the following program:

```
 1    // Exercise 6.3: Ex06_03.cpp
 2    // Testing the math library functions.
 3    #include <iostream>
 4    #include <iomanip>
 5    #include <cmath>
 6    using namespace std;
 7
 8    int main()
 9    {
10       cout << fixed << setprecision( 1 );
11
12       cout << "sqrt(" << 9.0 << ") = " << sqrt( 9.0 );
13       cout << "\nexp(" << 1.0 << ") = " << setprecision( 6 )
14          << exp( 1.0 ) << "\nexp(" << setprecision( 1 ) << 2.0
15          << ") = " << setprecision( 6 ) << exp( 2.0 );
16       cout << "\nlog(" << 2.718282 << ") = " << setprecision( 1 )
17          << log( 2.718282 )
18          << "\nlog(" << setprecision( 6 ) << 7.389056 << ") = "
19          << setprecision( 1 ) << log( 7.389056 );
20       cout << "\nlog10(" << 10.0 << ") = " << log10( 10.0 )
21          << "\nlog10(" << 100.0 << ") = " << log10( 100.0 ) ;
22       cout << "\nfabs(" << 5.1 << ") = " << fabs( 5.1 )
23          << "\nfabs(" << 0.0 << ") = " << fabs( 0.0 )
24          << "\nfabs(" << -8.76 << ") = " << fabs( -8.76 );
25       cout << "\nceil(" << 9.2 << ") = " << ceil( 9.2 )
26          << "\nceil(" << -9.8 << ") = " << ceil( -9.8 );
27       cout << "\nfloor(" << 9.2 << ") = " << floor( 9.2 )
28          << "\nfloor(" << -9.8 << ") = " << floor( -9.8 );
29       cout << "\npow(" << 2.0 << ", " << 7.0 << ") = "
30          << pow( 2.0, 7.0 ) << "\npow(" << 9.0 << ", "
31          << 0.5 << ") = " << pow( 9.0, 0.5 );
32       cout << setprecision( 3 ) << "\nfmod("
33          << 2.6 << ", " << 1.2 << ") = "
34          << fmod( 2.6, 1.2 ) << setprecision( 1 );
35       cout << "\nsin(" << 0.0 << ") = " << sin( 0.0 );
36       cout << "\ncos(" << 0.0 << ") = " << cos( 0.0 );
37       cout << "\ntan(" << 0.0 << ") = " << tan( 0.0 ) << endl;
38    } // end main
```

```
sqrt(9.0) = 3.0
exp(1.0) = 2.718282
exp(2.0) = 7.389056
log(2.718282) = 1.0
log(7.389056) = 2.0
log10(10.0) = 1.0
log10(100.0) = 2.0
fabs(5.1) = 5.1
fabs(0.0) = 0.0
fabs(-8.8) = 8.8
ceil(9.2) = 10.0
ceil(-9.8) = -9.0
floor(9.2) = 9.0
floor(-9.8) = -10.0
pow(2.0, 7.0) = 128.0
pow(9.0, 0.5) = 3.0
fmod(2.600, 1.200) = 0.200
sin(0.0) = 0.0
cos(0.0) = 1.0
tan(0.0) = 0.0
```

6.4 a) `double sum( double x, double y, double z)`
b) `int largest( int x, int y )`
c) `void display(double x)`
d) `int doubleToInt(double number )`

6.5 a) `int sum( int , int )`
b) `int product( int , int )`
c) `int sum( int , int, int )`
d) `void sum( int , int, int )`

6.6 a) `register char ch = 'a';`
b) `static int var;`

6.7 a) *Error:* Function h is defined in function g.
Correction: Move the definition of h out of the definition of g.
b) *Error:* The function is supposed to return an integer, but does not.
Correction: Place a `return result;` statement at the end of the function's body or delete variable `result` and place the following statement in the function:

   `return x + y;`

c) *Error:* The result of `n + sum( n - 1 )` is not returned; sum returns an improper result.
Correction: Rewrite the statement in the `else` clause as

   `return n + sum( n - 1 );`

d) *Errors:* Semicolon after the right parenthesis that encloses the parameter list, and redefining the parameter a in the function definition.
Corrections: Delete the semicolon after the right parenthesis of the parameter list, and delete the declaration `float a;`.
e) *Error:* The function returns a value when it isn't supposed to.
Correction: Eliminate the `return` statement or change the return type.

6.8 A reference parameter of type "reference to int" enables the function to modify the original variable in the calling function where as a parameter of type "int" does not allow the function to modify the original variable.

6.9 True.

6.10 See the following program:

```
 1   // Exercise 6.10 Solution
 2   // Inline function that calculates the volume of a cylinder.
 3   #include <iostream>
 4   #include <cmath>
 5   using namespace std;
 6
 7   const double PI = 3.14159; // define global constant PI
 8
 9   // calculates volume of a cylinder
10   inline double cylinderVolume( const double radius, const double height )
11   {
12      return PI * pow( radius, 3 ) * height;
13   } // end inline function sphereVolume
14
15   int main()
16   {
17      double radiusValue = 0;
18      double heightValue = 0;
19      // prompt user for radius and height
20      cout << "Enter the length of the radius  and height of your sphere: ";
21      cin >> radiusValue; // input radius
22      cin >> heightValue; // input height
23      // use radiusValue and heightValue to calculate volume of cylinder and display
            result
24      cout << "Volume of cylinder with radius " << radiusValue << " and height  "
            << heightValue
25         << " is " << sphereVolume( radiusValue, heightValue ) << endl;
26   } // end main
```

Exercises

6.11 Show the value of x after each of the following statements is performed:

a) x = fabs(-2.0)
b) x = fabs(2.0)
c) x = log(7.389056)
d) x = sqrt(16.0)
e) x = log10(1000.0)
f) x = sqrt(36 .0)
g) x = pow(2, 3)

6.12 *(Parking Charges)* A parking garage charges a $2.00 minimum fee to park for up to three hours. The garage charges an additional $0.50 per hour for each hour *or part thereof* in excess of three hours. The maximum charge for any given 24-hour period is $10.00. Assume that no car parks for longer than 24 hours at a time. Write a program that calculates and prints the parking charges for each of three customers who parked their cars in this garage yesterday. You should enter the hours parked for each customer. Your program should print the results in a neat tabular format and should calculate and print the total of yesterday's receipts. The program should use the function calculateCharges to determine the charge for each customer. Your outputs should appear in the following format:

Car	Hours	Charge
1	1.5	2.00
2	4.0	2.50
3	24.0	10.00
TOTAL	29.5	14.50

6.13 *(Rounding Numbers)* An application of function `floor` is rounding a value to the nearest integer. The statement

```
y = floor( x + 0.5 );
```

rounds the number x to the nearest integer and assigns the result to y. Write a program that reads several numbers and uses the preceding statement to round each of these numbers to the nearest integer. For each number processed, print both the original number and the rounded number.

6.14 *(Rounding Numbers)* Function `floor` can be used to round a number to a specific decimal place. The statement

```
y = floor( x * 10 + 0.5 ) / 10;
```

rounds x to the tenths position (the first position to the right of the decimal point). The statement

```
y = floor( x * 100 + 0.5 ) / 100;
```

rounds x to the hundredths position (the second position to the right of the decimal point). Write a program that defines four functions to round a number x in various ways:
a) `roundToInteger( number )`
b) `roundToTenths( number )`
c) `roundToHundredths( number )`
d) `roundToThousandths( number )`

For each value read, your program should print the original value, the number rounded to the nearest integer, the number rounded to the nearest tenth, the number rounded to the nearest hundredth and the number rounded to the nearest thousandth.

6.15 *(Short Answer Questions)* Answer each of the following questions:
a) What is the use of the header?
b) What is the default start value of the named integer constants in enum?
c) What does `default_random_engine` represent?
d) How is an empty parameter list specified in C++?
e) Why do recursions have more overheads than iterations?

6.16 *(Random Numbers)* Write statements that assign random integers to the variable n in the following ranges:
a) $1 \le n \le 2$
b) $1 \le n \le 100$
c) $0 \le n \le 9$
d) $1000 \le n \le 1112$
e) $-1 \le n \le 1$
f) $-3 \le n \le 11$

6.17 *(Random Numbers)* Write a single statement that prints a number at random from each of the following sets:
a) 2, 4, 6, 8, 10.
b) 3, 5, 7, 9, 11.
c) 6, 10, 14, 18, 22.

6.18 *(Exponentiation)* Write a function `integerPower(`*base*`, `*exponent*`)` that returns the value of $base^{exponent}$

For example, `integerPower(3, 4)` = 3 * 3 * 3 * 3. Assume that *exponent* is a positive, nonzero integer and that *base* is an integer. Do not use any math library functions.

6.19 *(Hypotenuse Calculations)* Define a function `hypotenuse` that calculates the hypotenuse of a right triangle when the other two sides are given. The function should take two `double` arguments and return the hypotenuse as a `double`. Use this function in a program to determine the hypotenuse for each of the triangles shown below.

Triangle	Side 1	Side 2
1	3.0	4.0
2	5.0	12.0
3	8.0	15.0

6.20 *(Factor)* Write a function `multiple` that determines for a pair of integers whether the second is a factor of the first. The function should take two integer arguments and return true if the second is a factor of the first, false otherwise. Use this function in a program that inputs a series of pairs of integers.

6.21 *(Odd Numbers)* Write a program that inputs a series of integers and passes them one at a time to function `isOdd`, which uses the modulus operator to determine whether an integer is odd. The function should take an integer argument and return true if the integer is odd and false otherwise.

6.22 *(Square of Asterisks)* Write a function that displays at the left margin of the screen a solid square of asterisks whose side is specified in integer parameter `side`. For example, if `side` is 4, the function displays the following:

```
****
****
****
****
```

6.23 *(Square of Any Character)* Modify the function created in Exercise 6.22 to form the square out of whatever character is contained in character parameter `fillCharacter`. Thus, if `side` is 5 and `fillCharacter` is #, then this function should print the following:

```
#####
#####
#####
#####
#####
```

6.24 *(Separating Digits)* Write program segments that accomplish each of the following:
a) Calculate the integer part of the quotient when integer a is divided by integer b.
b) Calculate the integer remainder when integer a is divided by integer b.
c) Use the program pieces developed in (a) and (b) to write a function that inputs an integer between 1 and 32767 and prints it as a series of digits, each pair of which is separated by two spaces. For example, the integer 4562 should print as follows:

```
4  5  6  2
```

6.25 *(Calculating Number of Seconds)* Write a function that takes the time as three integer arguments (hours, minutes and seconds) and returns the number of seconds since the last time the clock "struck 12." Use this function to calculate the amount of time in seconds between two times, both of which are within one 12-hour cycle of the clock.

6.26   *(Celsius and Fahrenheit Temperatures)* Implement the following integer functions:
a)   Function `celsius` returns the Celsius equivalent of a Fahrenheit temperature.
b)   Function `fahrenheit` returns the Fahrenheit equivalent of a Celsius temperature.
c)   Use these functions to write a program that prints charts showing the Fahrenheit equivalents of all Celsius temperatures from 0 to 100 degrees, and the Celsius equivalents of all Fahrenheit temperatures from 32 to 212 degrees. Print the outputs in a neat tabular format that minimizes the number of lines of output while remaining readable.

6.27   *(Find the Maximum)* Write a program that inputs three double-precision, floating-point numbers and passes them to a function that returns the largest number.

6.28   *(Perfect Numbers)* An integer is said to be a *perfect number* if the sum of its divisors, including 1 (but not the number itself), is equal to the number. For example, 6 is a perfect number, because $6 = 1 + 2 + 3$. Write a function `isPerfect` that determines whether parameter `number` is a perfect number. Use this function in a program that determines and prints all the perfect numbers between 1 and 1000. Print the divisors of each perfect number to confirm that the number is indeed perfect. Challenge the power of your computer by testing numbers much larger than 1000.

6.29   *(Prime Numbers)* An integer is said to be *prime* if it's divisible by only 1 and itself. For example, 2, 3, 5 and 7 are prime, but 4, 6, 8 and 9 are not.
a)   Write a function that determines whether a number is prime.
b)   Use this function in a program that determines and prints all the prime numbers between 2 and 10,000. How many of these numbers do you really have to test before being sure that you've found all the primes?
c)   Initially, you might think that $n/2$ is the upper limit for which you must test to see whether a number is prime, but you need only go as high as the square root of n. Why? Rewrite the program, and run it both ways. Estimate the performance improvement.

6.30   *(Sum of the Digits)* Write a function that takes an integer value and returns the reverse of the number. For example, given the number 7631, the function should return 1367.

6.31   *(Least Common Multiple)* The *least common multiple (LCM)* of two integers is the smallest integer that evenly divided by each of the numbers. Write a function `lcm` that returns the least common multiple of two integers.

6.32   *(Division for Average Marks)* Write a function `generateDivision` that inputs a student's average and returns "First" if a student's average is 60-100, "Second" if the average is 59-45, "Third" if the average is 44-35 and "Fail" if the average is less than 35.

6.33   *(Coin Tossing)* Write a program that simulates coin tossing. For each toss of the coin, the program should print `Heads` or `Tails`. Let the program toss the coin 100 times and count the number of times each side of the coin appears. Print the results. The program should call a separate function `flip` that takes no arguments and returns 0 for tails and 1 for heads. [*Note:* If the program realistically simulates the coin tossing, then each side of the coin should appear approximately half the time.]

6.34   *(Guess-the-Number Game)* Write a program that plays the game of "guess the number" as follows: Your program chooses the number to be guessed by selecting an integer at random in the range 1 to 1000. The program then displays the following:

```
I have a number between 1 and 1000.
Can you guess my number?
Please type your first guess.
```

The player then types a first guess. The program responds with one of the following:

```
1. Excellent! You guessed the number!
   Would you like to play again (y or n)?
2. Too low. Try again.
3. Too high. Try again.
```

If the player's guess is incorrect, your program should loop until the player finally gets the number right. Your program should keep telling the player Too high or Too low to help the player "zero in" on the correct answer.

6.35 *(Guess-the-Number Game Modification)* Modify the program of Exercise 6.34 to count the number of guesses the player makes. If the number is 10 or fewer, print "Either you know the secret or you got lucky!" If the player guesses the number in 10 tries, then print "Ahah! You know the secret!" If the player makes more than 10 guesses, then print "You should be able to do better!" Why should it take no more than 10 guesses? Well, with each "good guess" the player should be able to eliminate half of the numbers. Now show why any number from 1 to 1000 can be guessed in 10 or fewer tries.

6.36 *(Recursive Exponentiation)* Write a recursive function power(base, exponent) that, when invoked, returns

$$base^{exponent}$$

For example, power(3, 4) = 3 * 3 * 3 * 3. Assume that exponent is an integer greater than or equal to 1. *Hint:* The recursion step would use the relationship

$$base^{exponent} = base \cdot base^{exponent - 1}$$

and the terminating condition occurs when exponent is equal to 1, because

$$base^1 = base$$

6.37 *(Least Common Multiple: Recursive Solution)* Write a *recursive* version of the function lcm from Fig. 6.29. Compare this version with the iterative version developed in Exercise 6.31.

6.38 *(Towers of Hanoi)* In this chapter, you studied functions that can be easily implemented both recursively and iteratively. In this exercise, we present a problem whose recursive solution demonstrates the elegance of recursion, and whose iterative solution may not be as apparent.

The **Towers of Hanoi** is one of the most famous classic problems every budding computer scientist must grapple with. Legend has it that in a temple in the Far East, priests are attempting to move a stack of golden disks from one diamond peg to another (Fig. 6.34). The initial stack has 64 disks threaded onto one peg and arranged from bottom to top by decreasing size. The priests are attempting to move the stack from one peg to another under the constraints that exactly one disk is moved at a time and at no time may a larger disk be placed above a smaller disk. Three pegs are provided, one being used for temporarily holding disks. Supposedly, the world will end when the priests complete their task, so there is little incentive for us to facilitate their efforts.

Let's assume that the priests are attempting to move the disks from peg 1 to peg 3. We wish to develop an algorithm that prints the precise sequence of peg-to-peg disk transfers.

If we were to approach this problem with conventional methods, we would rapidly find ourselves hopelessly knotted up in managing the disks. Instead, attacking this problem with recursion in mind allows the steps to be simple. Moving *n* disks can be viewed in terms of moving only *n* – 1 disks (hence, the recursion), as follows:

a) Move *n* – 1 disks from peg 1 to peg 2, using peg 3 as a temporary holding area.
b) Move the last disk (the largest) from peg 1 to peg 3.
c) Move the *n* – 1 disks from peg 2 to peg 3, using peg 1 as a temporary holding area.

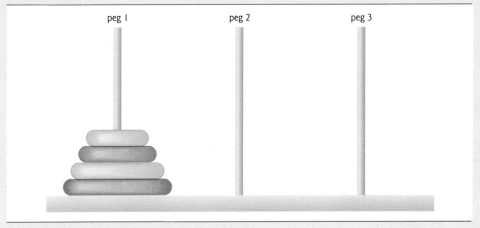

Fig. 6.34 | Towers of Hanoi for the case with four disks.

The process ends when the last task involves moving $n = 1$ disk (i.e., the base case). This task is accomplished by simply moving the disk, without the need for a temporary holding area. Write a program to solve the Towers of Hanoi problem. Use a recursive function with four parameters:

a) The number of disks to be moved
b) The peg on which these disks are initially threaded
c) The peg to which this stack of disks is to be moved
d) The peg to be used as a temporary holding area

Display the precise instructions for moving the disks from the starting peg to the destination peg. To move a stack of three disks from peg 1 to peg 3, the program displays the following moves:

$1 \rightarrow 3$ (This means move one disk from peg 1 to peg 3.)
$1 \rightarrow 2$
$3 \rightarrow 2$
$1 \rightarrow 3$
$2 \rightarrow 1$
$2 \rightarrow 3$
$1 \rightarrow 3$

6.39 *(Towers of Hanoi: Iterative Version)* Any program that can be implemented recursively can be implemented iteratively, although sometimes with more difficulty and less clarity. Try writing an iterative version of the Towers of Hanoi. If you succeed, compare your iterative version with the recursive version developed in Exercise 6.38. Investigate issues of performance, clarity and your ability to demonstrate the correctness of the programs.

6.40 *(Visualizing Recursion)* It's interesting to watch recursion "in action." Modify the factorial function of Fig. 6.28 to print its local variable and recursive call parameter. For each recursive call, display the outputs on a separate line and add a level of indentation. Do your utmost to make the outputs clear, interesting and meaningful. Your goal here is to design and implement an output format that helps a person understand recursion better. You may want to add such display capabilities to the many other recursion examples and exercises throughout the text.

6.41 *(Recursive Greatest Common Divisor)* The greatest common divisor of integers x and y is the largest integer that evenly divides both x and y. Write a recursive function gcd that returns the greatest common divisor of x and y, defined recursively as follows: If y is equal to 0, then gcd(x, y) is x; otherwise, gcd(x, y) is gcd(y, x % y), where % is the modulus operator. [*Note:* For this algorithm, x must be larger than y.]

6.42 *(Distance Between Points)* Write function distance that calculates the distance between two points (x1, y1, z1) and (x2, y2, z2) *in 3 Dimensions*. All numbers and return values should be of type double. [Hint : Distance = SquareRoot(x1*x2 + y1*y2 + z1*z2)].

6.43 What's wrong with the following program?

```
1   // Exercise 6.43: ex06_43.cpp
2   // What is wrong with this program?
3   #include <iostream>
4   using namespace std;
5
6   int main()
7   {
8      int c = 0;
9
10     if ( ( c = cin.get() ) != EOF )
11     {
12        fun1();
13        cout << c;
14     } // end if
15  } // end main
```

6.44 What does the following program do?

```
1   // Exercise 6.44: ex06_44.cpp
2   // What does this program do?
3   #include <iostream>
4   using namespace std;
5
6   int mystery( int );
7
8   int main()
9      int n,s;
10
11     cout << "Enter the number: ";
12     cin >> n;
13
14     s = mystery (n);
15     cout << "Result is "<< s;
16  }
17
18  int mystery (int a) {
19
20     if ( a == 0 )
21        return 0;
22
23        return ( (a% 10 ) + mystery ( a/10 ) );
24  }
```

6.45 After you determine what the program of Exercise 6.44 does, modify the program to write its equivalent iterative code.

6.46 *(Checking Data Types)* Write a program that tests as many of the data types mentioned in Fig. 6.2 as you can. Test each of these data types by having your program taking input and print out these variables.

6.47 *(Find the Error)* Find the error in each of the following program segments and explain how to correct it:

```
a)  float cube( float ); // function prototype

    cube( float number ) // function definition
    {
        return number * number * number;
    }
b)  int randomNumber = srand();
c)  float y = 123.45678;
    int x;

    x = y;
    cout << static_cast< float >( x ) << endl;
d)  double square( double number )
    {
        double number = 0;
        return number * number;
    }
e)  int sum( int n )
    {
        if ( 0 == n )
            return 0;
        else
            return n + sum( n );
    }
```

6.48   *(Craps Game Modification)* Modify the craps program of Fig. 6.11 to allow wagering. Package as a function the portion of the program that runs one game of craps. Initialize variable bankBalance to 1000 dollars. Prompt the player to enter a wager. Use a while loop to check that wager is less than or equal to bankBalance and, if not, prompt the user to reenter wager until a valid wager is entered. After a correct wager is entered, run one game of craps. If the player wins, increase bankBalance by wager and print the new bankBalance. If the player loses, decrease bankBalance by wager, print the new bankBalance, check on whether bankBalance has become zero and, if so, print the message "Sorry. You busted!" As the game progresses, print various messages to create some "chatter" such as "Oh, you're going for broke, huh?", "Aw cmon, take a chance!" or "You're up big. Now's the time to cash in your chips!".

6.49   *(Square Area)* Write a C++ program that prompts the user for the side of a square, then calls inline function squareArea to calculate the area of that square.

6.50   *(Pass-by-Value vs. Pass-by-Reference)* Write a complete C++ program with the two alternate functions specified below, each of which simply triples the variable count defined in main. Then compare and contrast the two approaches. These two functions are
   a) function tripleByValue that passes a copy of count by value, triples the copy and returns the new value and
   b) function tripleByReference that passes count by reference via a reference parameter and triples the original value of count through its alias (i.e., the reference parameter).

6.51   What's the purpose of the default argument in a function? What constraint is attached with the position of the default argument in a function's parameter list?

6.52   *(Function Template sum)* Write a program that uses a function template called sum to determine the sum of two arguments. Test the program using integer, long, and floating-point number arguments.

6.53 *(Function Template product)* Write a program that uses a function template called product to determine the product of two arguments. Test the program using integer, long, and floating-point number arguments.

6.54 *(Find the Error)* Determine whether the following program segments contain errors. For each error, explain how it can be corrected. [*Note:* For a particular program segment, it's possible that no errors are present in the segment.]

a)
```
template < class A >
int sum( int num1, int num2, int num3 )
{
    return num1 + num2 + num3;
}
```

b)
```
void printResults( int x, int y )
{
    cout << "The sum is " << x + y << '\n';
    return x + y;
}
```

c)
```
template < A >
A product( A num1, A num2, A num3 )
{
    return num1 * num2 * num3;
}
```

d)
```
double cube( int );
int cube( int );
```

6.55 *(C++11 Random Numbers: Modified Craps Game)* Modify the program of Fig. 6.11 to use the new C++11 random-number generation features shown in Section 6.9.

6.56 *(C++11 Scoped enum)* Create a scoped enum named Days containing constants named MON, TUES, WED, THU, FRI, SAT and SUN.

Making a Difference

As computer costs decline, it becomes feasible for every student, regardless of economic circumstance, to have a computer and use it in school. This creates exciting possibilities for improving the educational experience of all students worldwide as suggested by the next five exercises. [*Note:* Check out initiatives such as the One Laptop Per Child Project (www.laptop.org). Also, research "green" laptops—and note the key "going green" characteristics of these devices. Look into the Electronic Product Environmental Assessment Tool (www.epeat.net) which can help you assess the "greenness" of desktops, notebooks and monitors to help you decide which products to purchase.]

6.57 *(Computer-Assisted Instruction)* The use of computers in education is referred to as *computer-assisted instruction* (*CAI*). Write a program that will help an elementary school student learn multiplication. Use the rand function to produce two positive one-digit integers. The program should then prompt the user with a question, such as

```
How much is 6 times 7?
```

The student then inputs the answer. Next, the program checks the student's answer. If it's correct, display the message "Very good!" and ask another multiplication question. If the answer is wrong, display the message "No. Please try again." and let the student try the same question repeatedly until the student finally gets it right. A separate function should be used to generate each new question. This function should be called once when the application begins execution and each time the user answers the question correctly.

6.58   *(Computer-Assisted Instruction: Reducing Student Fatigue)* One problem in CAI environments is student fatigue. This can be reduced by varying the computer's responses to hold the student's attention. Modify the program of Exercise 6.57 so that various comments are displayed for each answer as follows:

Possible responses to a correct answer:

```
Very good!
Excellent!
Nice work!
Keep up the good work!
```

Possible responses to an incorrect answer:

```
No. Please try again.
Wrong. Try once more.
Don't give up!
No. Keep trying.
```

Use random-number generation to choose a number from 1 to 4 that will be used to select one of the four appropriate responses to each correct or incorrect answer. Use a `switch` statement to issue the responses.

6.59   *(Computer-Assisted Instruction: Monitoring Student Performance)* More sophisticated computer-assisted instruction systems monitor the student's performance over a period of time. The decision to begin a new topic is often based on the student's success with previous topics. Modify the program of Exercise 6.58 to count the number of correct and incorrect responses typed by the student. After the student types 10 answers, your program should calculate the percentage that are correct. If the percentage is lower than 75%, display `"Please ask your teacher for extra help."`, then reset the program so another student can try it. If the percentage is 75% or higher, display `"Congratulations, you are ready to go to the next level!"`, then reset the program so another student can try it.

6.60   *(Computer-Assisted Instruction: Difficulty Levels)* Exercises 6.57–6.59 developed a computer-assisted instruction program to help teach an elementary school student multiplication. Modify the program to allow the user to enter a difficulty level. At a difficulty level of 1, the program should use only single-digit numbers in the problems; at a difficulty level of 2, numbers as large as two digits, and so on.

6.61   *(Computer-Assisted Instruction: Varying the Types of Problems)* Modify the program of Exercise 6.60 to allow the user to pick a type of arithmetic problem to study. An option of 1 means addition problems only, 2 means subtraction problems only, 3 means multiplication problems only, 4 means division problems only and 5 means a random mixture of all these types.

7

Class Templates **array** and **vector**; Catching Exceptions

*Now go, write it
before them in a table,
and note it in a book.*
—Isaiah 30:8

*Begin at the beginning, ... and
go on till you come to the end:
then stop.*
—Lewis Carroll

*To go beyond is as
wrong as to fall short.*
—Confucius

Objectives

In this chapter you'll:

■ Use C++ Standard Library class template **array**—a fixed-size collection of related data items.

■ Use **array**s to store, sort and search lists and tables of values.

■ Declare **array**s, initialize **array**s and refer to the elements of **array**s.

■ Use the range-based **for** statement.

■ Pass **array**s to functions.

■ Declare and manipulate multidimensional **array**s.

■ Use C++ Standard Library class template **vector**—a variable-size collection of related data items.

7.1 Introduction

This chapter introduces the topic of **data structures**—*collections* of related data items. We discuss **arrays**, which are *fixed-size* collections consisting of data items of the *same* type, and **vectors** which are collections (also of data items of the *same* type) that can grow and shrink *dynamically* at execution time. Both array and vector are C++ standard library class templates. To use them, you must include the <array> and <vector> headers respectively.

After discussing how arrays are declared, created and initialized, we present examples that demonstrate several common array manipulations. We show how to *search* arrays to find particular elements and *sort* arrays to put their data in *order*.

We enhance the GradeBook class by using both one- and two-dimensional arrays to maintain a set of grades in memory and analyze the grades from multiple exams. We introduce the *exception-handling* mechanism and use it to allow a program to continue executing when the program attempts to access an array or vector element that does not exist.

7.2 arrays

An array is a *contiguous* group of memory locations that all have the *same* type. To refer to a particular location or element in the array, we specify the name of the array and the **position number** of the particular element in the array.

Figure 7.1 shows an integer array called c that contains 12 elements. You refer to any one of these elements by giving the array name followed by the particular element's position number in square brackets ([]). The position number is more formally called a **subscript** or **index** (this number specifies the number of elements from the beginning of the array). The first element has **subscript** 0 (zero) and is sometimes called the **zeroth element**. Thus, the elements of array c are c[0] (pronounced "c sub zero"), c[1], c[2] and so on. The highest subscript in array c is 11, which is 1 less than the number of elements in the array (12). array names follow the same conventions as other variable names.

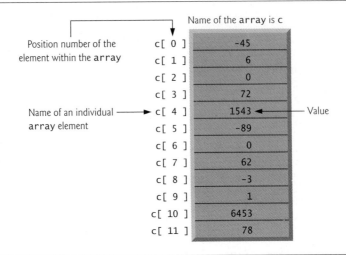

Fig. 7.1 | `array` of 12 elements.

A subscript must be an integer or integer expression (using any integral type). If a program uses an expression as a subscript, then the program evaluates the expression to determine the subscript. For example, if we assume that variable a is equal to 5 and that variable b is equal to 6, then the statement

```
c[ a + b ] += 2;
```

adds 2 to array element c[11]. A subscripted `array` name is an *lvalue*—it can be used on the left side of an assignment, just as non-`array` variable names can.

Let's examine `array` c in Fig. 7.1 more closely. The **name** of the entire `array` is c. Each `array` *knows its own size*, which can be determined by calling its **size** member function as in c.size(). Its 12 elements are referred to as c[0] to c[11]. The value of c[0] is -45, the value of c[7] is 62 and the value of c[11] is 78. To print the sum of the values contained in the first three elements of `array` c, we'd write

```
cout << c[ 0 ] + c[ 1 ] + c[ 2 ] << endl;
```

To divide the value of c[6] by 2 and assign the result to the variable x, we would write

```
x = c[ 6 ] / 2;
```

 Common Programming Error 7.1

Note the difference between the "seventh element of the array" and "array element 7." Subscripts begin at 0, so the "seventh element of the array" has a subscript of 6, while "array element 7" has a subscript of 7 and is actually the eighth element of the array. This distinction is a frequent source of off-by-one errors. To avoid such errors, we refer to specific array elements explicitly by their array name and subscript number (e.g., c[6] or c[7]).

The brackets that enclose a subscript are actually an *operator* that has the same precedence as parentheses. Figure 7.2 shows the precedence and associativity of the operators introduced so far. The operators are shown top to bottom in decreasing order of precedence with their associativity and type.

Operators	Associativity	Type
:: ()	left to right *[See caution in Fig. 2.10 regarding grouping parentheses.]*	primary
() [] ++ -- static_cast<*type*>(*operand*)	left to right	postfix
++ -- + - !	right to left	unary (prefix)
* / %	left to right	multiplicative
+ -	left to right	additive
<< >>	left to right	insertion/extraction
< <= > >=	left to right	relational
== !=	left to right	equality
&&	left to right	logical AND
||	left to right	logical OR
?:	right to left	conditional
= += -= *= /= %=	right to left	assignment
,	left to right	comma

Fig. 7.2 | Precedence and associativity of the operators introduced to this point.

7.3 Declaring arrays

arrays occupy space in memory. To specify the type of the elements and the number of elements required by an array use a declaration of the form:

```
array< type, arraySize > arrayName;
```

The notation <*type, arraySize*> indicates that array is a class template. The compiler reserves the appropriate amount of memory based on the *type* of the elements and the *arraySize*. (Recall that a declaration which reserves memory is more properly known as a *definition*.) The *arraySize* must be an unsigned integer. To tell the compiler to reserve 12 elements for integer array c, use the declaration

```
array< int, 12 > c; // c is an array of 12 int values
```

arrays can be declared to contain values of most data types. For example, an array of type string can be used to store character strings.

7.4 Examples Using arrays

The following examples demonstrate how to declare, initialize and manipulate arrays.

7.4.1 Declaring an array and Using a Loop to Initialize the array's Elements

The program in Fig. 7.3 declares five-element integer array n (line 10). Line 5 includes the <array> header, which contains the definition of class template array. Lines 13–14 use a for statement to initialize the array elements to zeros. Like other automatic variables, automatic arrays are *not* implicitly initialized to zero although static arrays are. The first output statement (line 16) displays the column headings for the columns printed in the subsequent for statement (lines 19–20), which prints the array in tabular format. Remember that setw specifies the field width in which only the *next* value is to be output.

```
1   // Fig. 7.3: fig07_03.cpp
2   // Initializing an array's elements to zeros and printing the array.
3   #include <iostream>
4   #include <iomanip>
5   #include <array>
6   using namespace std;
7
8   int main()
9   {
10      array< int, 5 > n; // n is an array of 5 int values
11
12      // initialize elements of array n to 0
13      for ( size_t i = 0; i < n.size(); ++i )
14         n[ i ] = 0; // set element at location i to 0
15
16      cout << "Element" << setw( 13 ) << "Value" << endl;
17
18      // output each array element's value
19      for ( size_t j = 0; j < n.size(); ++j )
20         cout << setw( 7 ) << j << setw( 13 ) << n[ j ] << endl;
21   } // end main
```

```
Element        Value
      0            0
      1            0
      2            0
      3            0
      4            0
```

Fig. 7.3 | Initializing an array's elements to zeros and printing the array.

In this program, the control variables i (line 13) and j (line 19) that specify array subscripts are declared to be of type **size_t**. According to the C++ standard size_t represents an unsigned integral type. This type is recommended for any variable that represents an array's size or an array's subscripts. Type size_t is defined in the std namespace and is in header <cstddef>, which is included by various other headers. If you attempt to compile a program that uses type size_t and receive errors indicating that it's not defined, simply include <cstddef> in your program.

7.4.2 Initializing an array in a Declaration with an Initializer List

The elements of an array also can be initialized in the array declaration by following the array name with an equals sign and a brace-delimited comma-separated list of **initializers**. The program in Fig. 7.4 uses an **initializer list** to initialize an integer array with five values (line 11) and prints the array in tabular format (lines 13–17).

```
1   // Fig. 7.4: fig07_04.cpp
2   // Initializing an array in a declaration.
3   #include <iostream>
4   #include <iomanip>
5   #include <array>
6   using namespace std;
7
8   int main()
9   {
10      // use list initializer to initialize array n
11      array< int, 5 > n = { 32, 27, 64, 18, 95 };
12
13      cout << "Element" << setw( 13 ) << "Value" << endl;
14
15      // output each array element's value
16      for ( size_t i = 0; i < n.size(); ++i )
17         cout << setw( 7 ) << i << setw( 13 ) << n[ i ] << endl;
18   } // end main
```

```
Element        Value
      0           32
      1           27
      2           64
      3           18
      4           95
```

Fig. 7.4 | Initializing an array in a declaration.

If there are *fewer* initializers than array elements, the remaining array elements are initialized to zero. For example, the elements of array n in Fig. 7.3 could have been initialized to zero with the declaration

```
array< int, 5 > n = {}; // initialize elements of array n to 0
```

which initializes the elements to zero, because there are fewer initializers (none in this case) than array elements. This technique can be used only in the array's declaration, whereas the initialization technique shown in Fig. 7.3 can be used repeatedly during program execution to "reinitialize" an array's elements.

If the array size and an initializer list are specified in an array declaration, the number of initializers must be less than or equal to the array size. The array declaration

```
array< int, 5 > n = { 32, 27, 64, 18, 95, 14 };
```

causes a compilation error, because there are six initializers and only five array elements.

7.4.3 Specifying an array's Size with a Constant Variable and Setting array Elements with Calculations

Figure 7.5 sets the elements of a 5-element array s to the even integers 2, 4, 6, 8 and 10 (lines 15–16) and prints the array in tabular format (lines 18–22). These numbers are generated (line 16) by multiplying each successive value of the loop counter by 2 and adding 2.

Line 11 uses the **const** qualifier to declare a constant variable arraySize with the value 5. A constant variable that's used to specify array's size *must* be initialized with a constant

```
 1   // Fig. 7.5: fig07_05.cpp
 2   // Set array s to the even integers from 2 to 10.
 3   #include <iostream>
 4   #include <iomanip>
 5   #include <array>
 6   using namespace std;
 7
 8   int main()
 9   {
10      // constant variable can be used to specify array size
11      const size_t arraySize = 5; // must initialize in declaration
12
13      array< int, arraySize > s; // array s has 5 elements
14
15      for ( size_t i = 0; i < s.size(); ++i ) // set the values
16         s[ i ] = 2 + 2 * i;
17
18      cout << "Element" << setw( 13 ) << "Value" << endl;
19
20      // output contents of array s in tabular format
21      for ( size_t j = 0; j < s.size(); ++j )
22         cout << setw( 7 ) << j << setw( 13 ) << s[ j ] << endl;
23   } // end main
```

```
Element        Value
      0            2
      1            4
      2            6
      3            8
      4           10
```

Fig. 7.5 | Set array s to the even integers from 2 to 10.

expression when it's declared and *cannot* be modified thereafter (as shown in Fig. 7.6 and Fig. 7.7). Constant variables are also called named constants or read-only variables.

Common Programming Error 7.2
Not initializing a constant variable when it's declared is a compilation error.

Common Programming Error 7.3
Assigning a value to a constant variable in an executable statement is a compilation error.

```
 1   // Fig. 7.6: fig07_06.cpp
 2   // Using a properly initialized constant variable.
 3   #include <iostream>
 4   using namespace std;
 5
 6   int main()
 7   {
```

Fig. 7.6 | Using a properly initialized constant variable. (Part 1 of 2.)

```
8       const int x = 7; // initialized constant variable
9
10      cout << "The value of constant variable x is: " << x << endl;
11   } // end main
```

```
The value of constant variable x is: 7
```

Fig. 7.6 | Using a properly initialized constant variable. (Part 2 of 2.)

```
1    // Fig. 7.7: fig07_07.cpp
2    // A const variable must be initialized.
3
4    int main()
5    {
6       const int x; // Error: x must be initialized
7
8       x = 7; // Error: cannot modify a const variable
9    } // end main
```

Microsoft Visual C++ compiler error message:

```
error C2734: 'x' : const object must be initialized if not extern
error C3892: 'x' : you cannot assign to a variable that is const
```

GNU C++ compiler error message:

```
fig07_07.cpp:6:14: error: uninitialized const 'x' [-fpermissive]
fig07_07.cpp:8:8: error: assignment of read-only variable 'x'
```

LLVM compiler error message:

```
Default initialization of an object of const type 'const int'
```

Fig. 7.7 | A const variable must be initialized.

In Fig. 7.7, the compilation error produced by Microsoft Visual C++ refers to the int variable x as a "const object." The C++ standard defines an "object" as any "region of storage." Like class objects, fundamental-type variables also occupy space in memory, so they're often referred to as "objects."

Constant variables can be placed anywhere a constant expression is expected. In Fig. 7.5, constant variable arraySize specifies the size of array s in line 13.

Good Programming Practice 7.1

Defining the size of an array as a constant variable instead of a literal constant makes programs clearer. This technique eliminates so-called magic numbers—numeric values that are not explained. Using a constant variable allows you to provide a name for a literal constant and can help explain the purpose of the value in the program.

7.4.4 Summing the Elements of an array

Often, the elements of an `array` represent a series of values to be used in a calculation. For example, if the elements of an `array` represent exam grades, a professor may wish to total the elements of the `array` and use that sum to calculate the class average for the exam.

The program in Fig. 7.8 sums the values contained in the four-element integer `array` a. The program declares, creates and initializes the `array` in line 10. The `for` statement (lines 14–15) performs the calculations. The values being supplied as initializers for `array` a also could be read into the program from the user at the keyboard, or from a file on disk (see Chapter 14, File Processing). For example, the `for` statement

```
for ( size_t j = 0; j < a.size(); ++j )
   cin >> a[ j ];
```

reads one value at a time from the keyboard and stores the value in element a[j].

```
1    // Fig. 7.8: fig07_08.cpp
2    // Compute the sum of the elements of an array.
3    #include <iostream>
4    #include <array>
5    using namespace std;
6
7    int main()
8    {
9       const size_t arraySize = 4; // specifies size of array
10      array< int, arraySize > a = { 10, 20, 30, 40 };
11      int total = 0;
12
13      // sum contents of array a
14      for ( size_t i = 0; i < a.size(); ++i )
15         total += a[ i ];
16
17      cout << "Total of array elements: " << total << endl;
18   } // end main
```

```
Total of array elements: 100
```

Fig. 7.8 | Computing the sum of the elements of an `array`.

7.4.5 Using Bar Charts to Display array Data Graphically

Many programs present data to users in a graphical manner. For example, numeric values are often displayed as bars in a bar chart. In such a chart, longer bars represent proportionally larger numeric values. One simple way to display numeric data graphically is with a bar chart that shows each numeric value as a bar of asterisks (*).

Professors often like to examine grade distributions on an exam. A professor might graph the number of grades in each of several categories to visualize the grade distribution. Suppose the grades were 87, 68, 94, 100, 83, 78, 85, 91, 76 and 87. There was one grade of 100, two grades in the 90s, four grades in the 80s, two grades in the 70s, one grade in the 60s and no grades below 60. Our next program (Fig. 7.9) stores this data in an `array` of 11 elements, each corresponding to a grade category. For example, n[0] indicates the number of grades in the range 0–9, n[7] indicates the number of grades in the range 70–79 and

```
 1   // Fig. 7.9: fig07_09.cpp
 2   // Bar chart printing program.
 3   #include <iostream>
 4   #include <iomanip>
 5   #include <array>
 6   using namespace std;
 7
 8   int main()
 9   {
10      const size_t arraySize = 11;
11      array< unsigned int, arraySize > n =
12         { 0, 0, 0, 0, 0, 0, 1, 2, 4, 2, 1 };
13
14      cout << "Grade distribution:" << endl;
15
16      // for each element of array n, output a bar of the chart
17      for ( size_t i = 0; i < n.size(); ++i )
18      {
19         // output bar labels ("0-9:", ..., "90-99:", "100:" )
20         if ( 0 == i )
21            cout << "  0-9: ";
22         else if ( 10 == i )
23            cout << "  100: ";
24         else
25            cout << i * 10 << "-" << ( i * 10 ) + 9 << ": ";
26
27         // print bar of asterisks
28         for ( unsigned int stars = 0; stars < n[ i ]; ++stars )
29            cout << '*';
30
31         cout << endl; // start a new line of output
32      } // end outer for
33   } // end main
```

```
Grade distribution:
  0-9:
10-19:
20-29:
30-39:
40-49:
50-59:
60-69: *
70-79: **
80-89: ****
90-99: **
  100: *
```

Fig. 7.9 | Bar chart printing program.

n[10] indicates the number of grades of 100. The GradeBook versions in Figs. 7.15–7.16 and Figs. 7.22–7.23 contain code that calculates these grade frequencies based on a set of grades. For now, we manually create the array by looking at the set of grades.

The program reads the numbers from the array and graphs the information as a bar chart, displaying each grade range followed by a bar of asterisks indicating the number of grades in that range. To label each bar, lines 20–25 output a grade range (e.g., "70-79: ") based on the current value of counter variable i. The *nested* for statement (lines 28–29) outputs the bars. Note the loop-continuation condition in line 28 (stars < n[i]). Each time the program reaches the *inner* for, the loop counts from 0 up to n[i], thus using a value in array n to determine the number of asterisks to display. In this example, n[0]–n[5] contain zeros because no students received a grade below 60. Thus, the program displays no asterisks next to the first six grade ranges.

7.4.6 Using the Elements of an array as Counters

Sometimes, programs use counter variables to summarize data, such as the results of a survey. In Fig. 6.9, we used separate counters in our die-rolling program to track the number of occurrences of each side of a die as the program rolled the die 6,000,000 times. An array version of this program is shown in Fig. 7.10. This version also uses the new C++11 random-number generation capabilities that were introduced in Section 6.9.

Figure 7.10 uses the array frequency (line 18) to count the occurrences of each side of the die. *The single statement in line 22 of this program replaces the switch statement in lines 23–45 of Fig. 6.9.* Line 22 uses a random value to determine which frequency element to

```cpp
1   // Fig. 7.10: fig07_10.cpp
2   // Die-rolling program using an array instead of switch.
3   #include <iostream>
4   #include <iomanip>
5   #include <array>
6   #include <random>
7   #include <ctime>
8   using namespace std;
9
10  int main()
11  {
12     // use the default random-number generation engine to
13     // produce uniformly distributed pseudorandom int values from 1 to 6
14     default_random_engine engine( static_cast< unsigned int >( time(0) ) );
15     uniform_int_distribution< unsigned int > randomInt( 1, 6 );
16
17     const size_t arraySize = 7; // ignore element zero
18     array< unsigned int, arraySize > frequency = {}; // initialize to 0s
19
20     // roll die 6,000,000 times; use die value as frequency index
21     for ( unsigned int roll = 1; roll <= 6000000; ++roll )
22        ++frequency[ randomInt( engine ) ];
23
24     cout << "Face" << setw( 13 ) << "Frequency" << endl;
25
26     // output each array element's value
27     for ( size_t face = 1; face < frequency.size(); ++face )
28        cout << setw( 4 ) << face << setw( 13 ) << frequency[ face ]
29           << endl;
30  } // end main
```

Fig. 7.10 | Die-rolling program using an array instead of switch. (Part 1 of 2.)

Face	Frequency
1	1000167
2	1000149
3	1000152
4	998748
5	999626
6	1001158

Fig. 7.10 | Die-rolling program using an `array` instead of `switch`. (Part 2 of 2.)

increment during each iteration of the loop. The calculation in line 22 produces a random subscript from 1 to 6, so array `frequency` must be large enough to store six counters. However, we use a seven-element `array` in which we ignore `frequency[0]`—it's clearer to have the die face value 1 increment `frequency[1]` than `frequency[0]`. Thus, each face value is used directly as a subscript for array `frequency`. We also replace lines 49–54 of Fig. 6.9 by looping through array `frequency` to output the results (Fig. 7.10, lines 27–29).

7.4.7 Using arrays to Summarize Survey Results

Our next example uses arrays to summarize the results of data collected in a survey. Consider the following problem statement:

> *Twenty students were asked to rate on a scale of 1 to 5 the quality of the food in the student cafeteria, with 1 being "awful" and 5 being "excellent." Place the 20 responses in an integer array and determine the frequency of each rating.*

This is a popular type of array-processing application (Fig. 7.11). We wish to summarize the number of responses of each type (that is, 1–5). The array `responses` (lines 15–16) is a 20-element integer array of the students' responses to the survey. The array `responses` is declared `const`, as its values do not (and should not) change. We use a six-element array `frequency` (line 19) to count the number of occurrences of each response. Each element of the array is used as a counter for one of the survey responses and is initialized to zero. As in Fig. 7.10, we ignore `frequency[0]`.

```
1   // Fig. 7.11: fig07_11.cpp
2   // Poll analysis program.
3   #include <iostream>
4   #include <iomanip>
5   #include <array>
6   using namespace std;
7
8   int main()
9   {
10     // define array sizes
11     const size_t responseSize = 20; // size of array responses
12     const size_t frequencySize = 6; // size of array frequency
13
14     // place survey responses in array responses
15     const array< unsigned int, responseSize > responses =
16        { 1, 2, 5, 4, 3, 5, 2, 1, 3, 1, 4, 3, 3, 3, 2, 3, 3, 2, 2, 5 };
```

Fig. 7.11 | Poll analysis program. (Part 1 of 2.)

```
17
18      // initialize frequency counters to 0
19      array< unsigned int, frequencySize > frequency = {};
20
21      // for each answer, select responses element and use that value
22      // as frequency subscript to determine element to increment
23      for ( size_t answer = 0; answer < responses.size(); ++answer )
24         ++frequency[ responses[ answer ] ];
25
26      cout << "Rating" << setw( 17 ) << "Frequency" << endl;
27
28      // output each array element's value
29      for ( size_t rating = 1; rating < frequency.size(); ++rating )
30         cout << setw( 6 ) << rating << setw( 17 ) << frequency[ rating ]
31            << endl;
32   } // end main
```

Rating	Frequency
1	3
2	5
3	7
4	2
5	3

Fig. 7.11 | Poll analysis program. (Part 2 of 2.)

The first for statement (lines 23–24) takes the responses one at a time from the array responses and increments one of the five counters in the frequency array (frequency[1] to frequency[5]). The key statement in the loop is line 24, which increments the appropriate frequency counter, depending on the value of responses[answer].

Let's consider several iterations of the for loop. When control variable answer is 0, the value of responses[answer] is the value of responses[0] (i.e., 1 in line 16), so the program interprets ++frequency[responses[answer]] as

```
++frequency[ 1 ]
```

which increments the value in array element 1. To evaluate the expression, start with the value in the *innermost* set of square brackets (answer). Once you know answer's value (which is the value of the loop control variable in line 23), plug it into the expression and evaluate the expression in the next outer set of square brackets (i.e., responses[answer], which is a value selected from the responses array in lines 15–16). Then use the resulting value as the subscript for the frequency array to specify which counter to increment.

When answer is 1, responses[answer] is the value of responses[1], which is 2, so the program interprets ++frequency[responses[answer]] as

```
++frequency[ 2 ]
```

which increments array element 2.

When answer is 2, responses[answer] is the value of responses[2], which is 5, so the program interprets ++frequency[responses[answer]] as

```
++frequency[ 5 ]
```

which increments `array` element 5, and so on. Regardless of the number of responses processed in the survey, the program requires *only* a six-element `array` (ignoring element zero) to summarize the results, because all the response values are between 1 and 5 and the subscript values for an six-element `array` are 0 through 5.

Bounds Checking for `array` *Subscripts*

If the data in `responses` contained an invalid value, such as 13, the program would have attempted to add 1 to `frequency[13]`, which is *outside* the bounds of the array. *When you use the* `[]` *operator to access an array element, C++ provides no automatic* `array` *bounds checking to prevent you from referring to an element that does not exist.* Thus, an executing program can "walk off" either end of an `array` without warning. In Section 7.10, we demonstrate the class template `vector`'s `at` function, which performs bounds checking for you. Class template `array` also has an `at` function.

It's important to ensure that every subscript you use to access an `array` element is within the `array`'s bounds—that is, greater than or equal to 0 and less than the number of `array` elements.

Allowing programs to read from or write to `array` elements outside the bounds of arrays are common *security flaws*. Reading from out-of-bounds `array` elements can cause a program to crash or even appear to execute correctly while using bad data. Writing to an out-of-bounds element (known as a *buffer overflow*) can corrupt a program's data in memory, crash a program and allow attackers to exploit the system and execute their own code. For more information on buffer overflows, see `en.wikipedia.org/wiki/Buffer_overflow`.

Common Programming Error 7.4
Referring to an element outside the `array` *bounds is an* execution-time *logic error. It isn't a syntax error.*

Error-Prevention Tip 7.1
When looping through an array, the index should never go below 0 and should always be less than the total number of array *elements (one less than the size of the* array*). Make sure that the loop-termination condition prevents accessing elements outside this range. In Chapters 15–16, you'll learn about iterators, which can help prevent accessing elements outside an array's (or other container's) bounds.*

7.4.8 Static Local `arrays` and Automatic Local `arrays`

Chapter 6 discussed the storage-class specifier `static`. A `static` local variable in a function definition exists for the program's duration but is visible *only* in the function's body.

Performance Tip 7.1
We can apply `static` *to a local* array *declaration so that it's* not *created and initialized each time the program calls the function and is* not *destroyed each time the function terminates. This can improve performance, especially when using large* arrays*.*

A program initializes `static` local arrays when their declarations are first encountered. If a `static` array is not initialized explicitly by you, each element of that `array` is initialized to *zero* by the compiler when the array is created. Recall that C++ does *not* perform such default initialization for automatic variables.

Figure 7.12 demonstrates function `staticArrayInit` (lines 24–40) with a static local array (line 27) and function `automaticArrayInit` (lines 43–59) with an automatic local array (line 46).

```cpp
1  // Fig. 7.12: fig07_12.cpp
2  // static array initialization and automatic array initialization.
3  #include <iostream>
4  #include <array>
5  using namespace std;
6
7  void staticArrayInit(); // function prototype
8  void automaticArrayInit(); // function prototype
9  const size_t arraySize = 3;
10
11 int main()
12 {
13    cout << "First call to each function:\n";
14    staticArrayInit();
15    automaticArrayInit();
16
17    cout << "\n\nSecond call to each function:\n";
18    staticArrayInit();
19    automaticArrayInit();
20    cout << endl;
21 } // end main
22
23 // function to demonstrate a static local array
24 void staticArrayInit( void )
25 {
26    // initializes elements to 0 first time function is called
27    static array< int, arraySize > array1; // static local array
28
29    cout << "\nValues on entering staticArrayInit:\n";
30
31    // output contents of array1
32    for ( size_t i = 0; i < array1.size(); ++i )
33       cout << "array1[" << i << "] = " << array1[ i ] << "  ";
34
35    cout << "\nValues on exiting staticArrayInit:\n";
36
37    // modify and output contents of array1
38    for ( size_t j = 0; j < array1.size(); ++j )
39       cout << "array1[" << j << "] = " << ( array1[ j ] += 5 ) << "  ";
40 } // end function staticArrayInit
41
42 // function to demonstrate an automatic local array
43 void automaticArrayInit( void )
44 {
45    // initializes elements each time function is called
46    array< int, arraySize > array2 = { 1, 2, 3 }; // automatic local array
47
48    cout << "\n\nValues on entering automaticArrayInit:\n";
```

Fig. 7.12 | static array initialization and automatic array initialization. (Part 1 of 2.)

```
49
50      // output contents of array2
51      for ( size_t i = 0; i < array2.size(); ++i )
52         cout << "array2[" << i << "] = " << array2[ i ] << "  ";
53
54      cout << "\nValues on exiting automaticArrayInit:\n";
55
56      // modify and output contents of array2
57      for ( size_t j = 0; j < array2.size(); ++j )
58         cout << "array2[" << j << "] = " << ( array2[ j ] += 5 ) << "  ";
59   } // end function automaticArrayInit
```

```
First call to each function:

Values on entering staticArrayInit:
array1[0] = 0   array1[1] = 0   array1[2] = 0
Values on exiting staticArrayInit:
array1[0] = 5   array1[1] = 5   array1[2] = 5

Values on entering automaticArrayInit:
array2[0] = 1   array2[1] = 2   array2[2] = 3
Values on exiting automaticArrayInit:
array2[0] = 6   array2[1] = 7   array2[2] = 8

Second call to each function:

Values on entering staticArrayInit:
array1[0] = 5   array1[1] = 5   array1[2] = 5
Values on exiting staticArrayInit:
array1[0] = 10   array1[1] = 10   array1[2] = 10

Values on entering automaticArrayInit:
array2[0] = 1   array2[1] = 2   array2[2] = 3
Values on exiting automaticArrayInit:
array2[0] = 6   array2[1] = 7   array2[2] = 8
```

Fig. 7.12 | static array initialization and automatic array initialization. (Part 2 of 2.)

Function staticArrayInit is called twice (lines 14 and 18). The static local array1 is *initialized to zero* by the compiler the first time the function is called. The function prints the array, adds 5 to each element and prints the array again. The second time the function is called, the static array contains the *modified* values stored during the first function call.

Function automaticArrayInit also is called twice (lines 15 and 19). Automatic local array2's elements are initialized (line 46) with the values 1, 2 and 3. The function prints the array, adds 5 to each element and prints the array again. The second time the function is called, the array elements are *reinitialized* to 1, 2 and 3. The array has *automatic storage duration*, so the array is recreated and reinitialized during each call to automaticArrayInit.

7.5 Range-Based for Statement

As we've shown, it's common to process *all* the elements of an array. The new C++11 range-based **for** statement allows you to do this *without using a counter*, thus avoiding the possibility of "stepping outside" the array and eliminating the need for you to implement your own bounds checking.

Error-Prevention Tip 7.2

When processing all elements of an array, if you don't need access to an array element's subscript, use the range-based for statement.

The syntax of a range-based for statement is:

```
for ( rangeVariableDeclaration : expression )
    statement
```

where *rangeVariableDeclaration* has a type and an identifier (e.g., `int item`), and *expression* is the array through which to iterate. The type in the *rangeVariableDeclaration* must be *consistent* with the type of the array's elements. The identifier represents successive `array` element values on successive iterations of the loop. You can use the range-based `for` statement with most of the C++ Standard Library's prebuilt data structures (commonly called *containers*), including classes `array` and `vector`.

Figure 7.13 uses the range-based `for` to display an array's contents (lines 13–14 and 22–23) and to multiply each of the array's element values by 2 (lines 17–18).

```cpp
 1    // Fig. 7.13: fig07_13.cpp
 2    // Using range-based for to multiply an array's elements by 2.
 3    #include <iostream>
 4    #include <array>
 5    using namespace std;
 6
 7    int main()
 8    {
 9       array< int, 5 > items = { 1, 2, 3, 4, 5 };
10
11       // display items before modification
12       cout << "items before modification: ";
13       for ( int item : items )
14          cout << item << " ";
15
16       // multiply the elements of items by 2
17       for ( int &itemRef : items )
18          itemRef *= 2;
19
20       // display items after modification
21       cout << "\nitems after modification: ";
22       for ( int item : items )
23          cout << item << " ";
24
25       cout << endl;
26    } // end main
```

```
items before modification: 1 2 3 4 5
items after modification: 2 4 6 8 10
```

Fig. 7.13 | Using range-based `for` to multiply an `array`'s elements by 2.

Using the Range-Based *for* to Display an *array's* Contents

The range-based `for` statement simplifies the code for iterating through an `array`. Line 13 can be read as "for each iteration, assign the next element of `items` to `int` variable `item`, then execute the following statement." Thus, for each iteration, identifier item represents one element in items. Lines 13–14 are equivalent to the following counter-controlled repetition:

```
for ( int counter = 0; counter < items.size(); ++counter )
    cout << items[ counter ] << " ";
```

Using the Range-Based for to Modify an array's Contents
Lines 17–18 use a range-based for statement to multiply each element of items by 2. In line 17, the *rangeVariableDeclaration* indicates that itemRef is an int *reference* (&). Recall that a reference is an alias for another variable in memory—in this case, one of the array's elements. We use an int reference because items contains int values and we want to *modify* each element's value—because itemRef is declared as a *reference*, any change you make to itemRef *changes* the corresponding element value in the array.

Using an Element's Subscript
The range-based for statement can be used in place of the counter-controlled for statement whenever code looping through an array does *not* require access to the element's subscript. For example, totaling the integers in an array (as in Fig. 7.8) requires access only to the element values—the elements' subscripts are irrelevant. However, if a program must use subscripts for some reason other than simply to loop through an array (e.g., to print a subscript number next to each array element value, as in the examples early in this chapter), you should use the counter-controlled for statement.

7.6 Case Study: Class GradeBook Using an array to Store Grades

This section further evolves class GradeBook, introduced in Chapter 3 and expanded in Chapters 4–6. Recall that this class represents a grade book used by a professor to store and analyze student grades. Previous versions of the class process grades entered by the user, but *do not* maintain the individual grade values in the class's data members. Thus, repeat calculations require the user to reenter the grades. One way to solve this problem would be to store each grade entered in an individual data member of the class. For example, we could create data members grade1, grade2, ..., grade10 in class GradeBook to store 10 student grades. However, the code to total the grades and determine the class average would be cumbersome. In this section, we solve this problem by storing grades in an array.

Storing Student Grades in an array in Class GradeBook
Figure 7.14 shows the output that summarizes the 10 grades we store in an object of the next version of class GradeBook (Figs. 7.15–7.16), which uses an array of integers to store the grades of 10 students for a single exam. This eliminates the need to repeatedly input the same set of grades. array grades is declared as a data member in line 28 of Fig. 7.15—therefore, each GradeBook object maintains its own set of grades.

```
Welcome to the grade book for
CS101 Introduction to C++ Programming!
```

Fig. 7.14 | Output of the GradeBook example that stores grades in an array. (Part I of 2.)

```
The grades are:

Student  1:  87
Student  2:  68
Student  3:  94
Student  4: 100
Student  5:  83
Student  6:  78
Student  7:  85
Student  8:  91
Student  9:  76
Student 10:  87

Class average is 84.90
Lowest grade is 68
Highest grade is 100

Grade distribution:
   0-9:
  10-19:
  20-29:
  30-39:
  40-49:
  50-59:
  60-69: *
  70-79: **
  80-89: ****
  90-99: **
    100: *
```

Fig. 7.14 | Output of the GradeBook example that stores grades in an `array`. (Part 2 of 2.)

```cpp
 1   // Fig. 7.15: GradeBook.h
 2   // Definition of class GradeBook that uses an array to store test grades.
 3   // Member functions are defined in GradeBook.cpp
 4   #include <string>
 5   #include <array>
 6
 7   // GradeBook class definition
 8   class GradeBook
 9   {
10   public:
11      // constant -- number of students who took the test
12      static const size_t students = 10; // note public data
13
14      // constructor initializes course name and array of grades
15      GradeBook( const std::string &, const std::array< int, students > & );
16
17      void setCourseName( const std::string & ); // set the course name
18      string getCourseName() const; // retrieve the course name
19      void displayMessage() const; // display a welcome message
20      void processGrades() const; // perform operations on the grade data
21      int getMinimum() const; // find the minimum grade for the test
22      int getMaximum() const; // find the maximum grade for the test
```

Fig. 7.15 | Definition of class GradeBook that uses an array to store test grades. (Part 1 of 2.)

```cpp
23        double getAverage() const; // determine the average grade for the test
24        void outputBarChart() const; // output bar chart of grade distribution
25        void outputGrades() const; // output the contents of the grades array
26     private:
27        std::string courseName; // course name for this grade book
28        std::array< int, students > grades; // array of student grades
29     }; // end class GradeBook
```

Fig. 7.15 | Definition of class GradeBook that uses an array to store test grades. (Part 2 of 2.)

```cpp
 1    // Fig. 7.16: GradeBook.cpp
 2    // GradeBook class member functions manipulating
 3    // an array of grades.
 4    #include <iostream>
 5    #include <iomanip>
 6    #include "GradeBook.h" // GradeBook class definition
 7    using namespace std;
 8
 9    // constructor initializes courseName and grades array
10    GradeBook::GradeBook( const string &name,
11       const array< int, students > &gradesArray )
12       : courseName( name ), grades( gradesArray )
13    {
14    } // end GradeBook constructor
15
16    // function to set the course name
17    void GradeBook::setCourseName( const string &name )
18    {
19       courseName = name; // store the course name
20    } // end function setCourseName
21
22    // function to retrieve the course name
23    string GradeBook::getCourseName() const
24    {
25       return courseName;
26    } // end function getCourseName
27
28    // display a welcome message to the GradeBook user
29    void GradeBook::displayMessage() const
30    {
31       // this statement calls getCourseName to get the
32       // name of the course this GradeBook represents
33       cout << "Welcome to the grade book for\n" << getCourseName() << "!"
34          << endl;
35    } // end function displayMessage
36
37    // perform various operations on the data
38    void GradeBook::processGrades() const
39    {
40       // output grades array
41       outputGrades();
42
```

Fig. 7.16 | GradeBook class member functions manipulating an array of grades. (Part 1 of 3.)

```cpp
43      // call function getAverage to calculate the average grade
44      cout << setprecision( 2 ) << fixed;
45      cout << "\nClass average is " << getAverage() << endl;
46
47      // call functions getMinimum and getMaximum
48      cout << "Lowest grade is " << getMinimum() << "\nHighest grade is "
49         << getMaximum() << endl;
50
51      // call function outputBarChart to print grade distribution chart
52      outputBarChart();
53   } // end function processGrades
54
55   // find minimum grade
56   int GradeBook::getMinimum() const
57   {
58      int lowGrade = 100; // assume lowest grade is 100
59
60      // loop through grades array
61      for ( int grade : grades )
62      {
63         // if current grade lower than lowGrade, assign it to lowGrade
64         if ( grade < lowGrade )
65            lowGrade = grade; // new lowest grade
66      } // end for
67
68      return lowGrade; // return lowest grade
69   } // end function getMinimum
70
71   // find maximum grade
72   int GradeBook::getMaximum() const
73   {
74      int highGrade = 0; // assume highest grade is 0
75
76      // loop through grades array
77      for ( int grade : grades )
78      {
79         // if current grade higher than highGrade, assign it to highGrade
80         if ( grade > highGrade )
81            highGrade = grade; // new highest grade
82      } // end for
83
84      return highGrade; // return highest grade
85   } // end function getMaximum
86
87   // determine average grade for test
88   double GradeBook::getAverage() const
89   {
90      int total = 0; // initialize total
91
92      // sum grades in array
93      for ( int grade : grades )
94         total += grade;
95
```

Fig. 7.16 | GradeBook class member functions manipulating an array of grades. (Part 2 of 3.)

```
96      // return average of grades
97      return static_cast< double >( total ) / grades.size();
98   } // end function getAverage
99
100  // output bar chart displaying grade distribution
101  void GradeBook::outputBarChart() const
102  {
103     cout << "\nGrade distribution:" << endl;
104
105     // stores frequency of grades in each range of 10 grades
106     const size_t frequencySize = 11;
107     array< unsigned int, frequencySize > frequency = {}; // init to 0s
108
109     // for each grade, increment the appropriate frequency
110     for ( int grade : grades )
111        ++frequency[ grade / 10 ];
112
113     // for each grade frequency, print bar in chart
114     for ( size_t count = 0; count < frequencySize; ++count )
115     {
116        // output bar labels ("0-9:", ..., "90-99:", "100:" )
117        if ( 0 == count )
118           cout << "  0-9: ";
119        else if ( 10 == count )
120           cout << "  100: ";
121        else
122           cout << count * 10 << "-" << ( count * 10 ) + 9 << ": ";
123
124        // print bar of asterisks
125        for ( unsigned int stars = 0; stars < frequency[ count ]; ++stars )
126           cout << '*';
127
128        cout << endl; // start a new line of output
129     } // end outer for
130  } // end function outputBarChart
131
132  // output the contents of the grades array
133  void GradeBook::outputGrades() const
134  {
135     cout << "\nThe grades are:\n\n";
136
137     // output each student's grade
138     for ( size_t student = 0; student < grades.size(); ++student )
139        cout << "Student " << setw( 2 ) << student + 1 << ": " << setw( 3 )
140           << grades[ student ] << endl;
141  } // end function outputGrades
```

Fig. 7.16 | GradeBook class member functions manipulating an array of grades. (Part 3 of 3.)

The size of the array in line 28 of Fig. 7.15 is specified by public static const data member students (declared in line 12), which is public so that it's accessible to the class's clients. We'll soon see an example of a client program using this constant. Declaring students with the const qualifier indicates that this data member is constant—its value cannot be changed after being initialized. Keyword static in this variable declaration indicates that the data member is *shared by all objects of the class*—so in this particular implementation of class `GradeBook`, all `GradeBook` objects store grades for the same number of students. Recall from Section 3.4 that when each object of a class maintains its own copy of an attribute, the variable that represents the attribute is known as a data member—each object (instance) of the class has a *separate copy* of the variable in memory. There are variables for which each object of a class does *not* have a separate copy. That is the case with **static data members**, which are also known as **class variables**. When objects of a class containing `static` data members are created, all the objects share one copy of the class's `static` data members. A `static` data member can be accessed within the class definition and the member-function definitions like any other data member. As you'll soon see, a `public` `static` data member can also be accessed outside of the class, *even when no objects of the class exist*, using the class name followed by the scope resolution operator (`::`) and the name of the data member. You'll learn more about `static` data members in Chapter 9.

Constructor
The class's constructor (declared in line 15 of Fig. 7.15 and defined in lines 10–14 of Fig. 7.16) has two parameters—the course name and a reference to an `array` of grades. When a program creates a `GradeBook` object (e.g., line 15 of Fig. 7.17), the program passes an existing `int` array to the constructor, which copies the array's values into the data member grades (line 12 of Fig. 7.16). The grade values in the passed `array` could have been input from a user or read from a file on disk (as we discuss in Chapter 14, File Processing). In our test program, we simply initialize an `array` with a set of grade values (Fig. 7.17, lines 11–12). Once the grades are stored in data member grades of class `GradeBook`, all the class's member functions can access the grades array as needed to perform various calculations. Note that the constructor receives both the `string` and the array by reference—this is more efficient than receiving copies of the original `string` and array. The constructor does not need to modify either the original `string` or array, so we also declared each parameter as `const` to ensure that the constructor does not accidentally modify the originald data in the caller. We also modified function `setCourseName` to receives its `string` argument by reference.

Member Function `processGrades`
Member function `processGrades` (declared in line 20 of Fig. 7.15 and defined in lines 38–53 of Fig. 7.16) contains a series of member function calls that output a report summarizing the grades. Line 41 calls member function `outputGrades` to print the contents of the array grades. Lines 138–140 in member function `outputGrades` use a `for` statement to output each student's grade. Although array indices start at 0, a professor would typically number students starting at 1. Thus, lines 139–140 output `student + 1` as the student number to produce grade labels `"Student 1: "`, `"Student 2: "`, and so on.

Member Function `getAverage`
Member function `processGrades` next calls member function `getAverage` (line 45) to obtain the average of the grades. Member function `getAverage` (declared in line 23 of Fig. 7.15 and defined in lines 88–98 of Fig. 7.16) totals the values in array grades before calculating the average. The averaging calculation in line 97 uses `grades.size()` to determine the number of grades being averaged.

Member Functions *getMinimum and getMaximum*
Lines 48–49 in processGrades call member functions getMinimum and getMaximum to determine the lowest and highest grades of any student on the exam, respectively. Let's examine how member function getMinimum finds the *lowest* grade. Because the highest grade allowed is 100, we begin by assuming that 100 is the lowest grade (line 58). Then, we compare each of the elements in the array to the lowest grade, looking for smaller values. Lines 61–66 in member function getMinimum loop through the array, and line 64 compares each grade to lowGrade. If a grade is less than lowGrade, lowGrade is set to that grade. When line 68 executes, lowGrade contains the lowest grade in the array. Member function getMaximum (lines 72–85) works similarly to member function getMinimum.

Member Function *outputBarChart*
Finally, line 52 in member function processGrades calls member function outputBarChart to print a distribution chart of the grade data using a technique similar to that in Fig. 7.9. In that example, we manually calculated the number of grades in each category (i.e., 0–9, 10–19, ..., 90–99 and 100) by simply looking at a set of grades. In this example, lines 110–111 use a technique similar to that in Fig. 7.10 and Fig. 7.11 to calculate the frequency of grades in each category. Line 107 declares and creates array frequency of 11 unsigned ints to store the frequency of grades in each grade category. For each grade in array grades, lines 110–111 increment the appropriate element of the frequency array. To determine which element to increment, line 111 divides the current grade by 10 using integer division. For example, if grade is 85, line 111 increments frequency[8] to update the count of grades in the range 80–89. Lines 114–129 next print the bar chart (see Fig. 7.17) based on the values in array frequency. Like lines 28–29 of Fig. 7.9, lines 125–126 of Fig. 7.16 use a value in array frequency to determine the number of asterisks to display in each bar.

Testing Class *GradeBook*
The program of Fig. 7.17 creates an object of class GradeBook (Figs. 7.15–7.16) using the int array grades (declared and initialized in lines 11–12). The scope resolution operator (::) is used in the expression "GradeBook::students" (line 11) to access class GradeBook's static constant students. We use this constant here to create an array that is the same size as the array stored as a data member in class GradeBook. Line 13 declares a string representing the course name. Line 15 passes the course name and the array of grades to the GradeBook constructor. Line 16 displays a welcome message, and line 17 invokes the GradeBook object's processGrades member function.

```
1   // Fig. 7.17: fig07_17.cpp
2   // Creates GradeBook object using an array of grades.
3   #include <array>
4   #include "GradeBook.h" // GradeBook class definition
5   using namespace std;
6
7   // function main begins program execution
8   int main()
9   {
```

Fig. 7.17 | Creates a GradeBook object' using an array of grades, then invokes member function processGrades to analyze them. (Part 1 of 2.)

```
10    // array of student grades
11    const array< int, GradeBook::students > grades =
12       { 87, 68, 94, 100, 83, 78, 85, 91, 76, 87 };
13    string courseName = "CS101 Introduction to C++ Programming";
14
15    GradeBook myGradeBook( courseName, grades );
16    myGradeBook.displayMessage();
17    myGradeBook.processGrades();
18 } // end main
```

Fig. 7.17 | Creates a `GradeBook` object' using an `array` of grades, then invokes member function `processGrades` to analyze them. (Part 2 of 2.)

7.7 Sorting and Searching arrays

In this section, we use the built-in C++ Standard Library **sort** function to arrange the elements in an `array` into ascending order and the built-in **binary_search** function to determine whether a value is in the `array`.

Sorting

Sorting data—placing it into ascending or descending order—is one of the most important computing applications. A bank sorts all checks by account number so that it can prepare individual bank statements at the end of each month. Telephone companies sort their phone directories by last name; and within all entries with the *same* last name, sorting those by first name to make it easy to find phone numbers. Virtually every organization must sort some data and, in many cases, massive amounts of it. Sorting data is an intriguing problem that has attracted some of the most intense research efforts in the field of computer science. In Chapter 20, we investigate and implement several sorting schemes, discuss their performance and introduce Big O (pronounced "Big Oh") notation for characterizing how hard each scheme works to accomplish its task.

Searching

Often it may be necessary to determine whether an `array` contains a value that matches a certain **key value**. The process of finding a particular element of an `array` is called **searching**. In Chapter 20, we investigate and implement two search algorithms—the simple but slow *linear search* for searching an *unordered* `array` and the more complex but much faster *binary search* for searching an *ordered* `array`.

Demonstrating Functions **sort** *and* **binary_search**

Figure 7.18 begins by creating an unsorted `array` of `string`s (lines 13–14) and displaying the contents of the `array` (lines 17–19). Next, line 21 uses C++ Standard Library function `sort` to sort the elements of the `array` colors into ascending order. The `sort` function's arguments specify the range of elements that should be sorted—in this case, the entire array. We'll discuss the complete details of class template `array`'s `begin` and `end` functions in later chapters. As you'll see, function `sort` can be used to sort the elements of several different types of data structures. Lines 24–26 display the contents of the sorted `array`.

Lines 29 and 34 demonstrate use `binary_search` to determine whether a value is in the array. The sequence of values must be sorted in ascending order first—`binary_search` does *not* verify this for you. The function's first two arguments represent the range of elements to search and the third is the *search key*—the value to locate in the array. The function returns a bool indicating whether the value was found. In Chapter 16, we'll use a C++ Standard function find to obtain the location of the search key in an array.

```
1   // Fig. 7.18: fig07_18.cpp
2   // Sorting and searching arrays.
3   #include <iostream>
4   #include <iomanip>
5   #include <array>
6   #include <string>
7   #include <algorithm> // contains sort and binary_search
8   using namespace std;
9
10  int main()
11  {
12     const size_t arraySize = 7; // size of array colors
13     array< string, arraySize > colors = { "red", "orange", "yellow",
14        "green", "blue", "indigo", "violet" };
15
16     // output original array
17     cout << "Unsorted array:\n";
18     for ( string color : colors )
19        cout << color << " ";
20
21     sort( colors.begin(), colors.end() ); // sort contents of colors
22
23     // output sorted array
24     cout << "\nSorted array:\n";
25     for ( string item : colors )
26        cout << item << " ";
27
28     // search for "indigo" in colors
29     bool found = binary_search( colors.begin(), colors.end(), "indigo" );
30     cout << "\n\n\"indigo\" " << ( found ? "was" : "was not" )
31        << " found in colors" << endl;
32
33     // search for "cyan" in colors
34     found = binary_search( colors.begin(), colors.end(), "cyan" );
35     cout << "\"cyan\" " << ( found ? "was" : "was not" )
36        << " found in colors" << endl;
37  } // end main
```

```
Unsorted array:
red orange yellow green blue indigo violet
Sorted array:
blue green indigo orange red violet yellow

"indigo" was found in colors
"cyan" was not found in colors
```

Fig. 7.18 | Sorting and searching arrays.

7.8 Multidimensional arrays

You can use arrays with two dimensions (i.e., subscripts) to represent tables of values consisting of information arranged in **rows** and **columns**. To identify a particular table element, we must specify two subscripts—by convention, the first identifies the element's *row* and the second identifies the element's *column*. arrays that require two subscripts to identify a particular element are called **two-dimensional arrays** or **2-D arrays**. arrays with two or more dimensions are known as **multidimensional arrays** and can have more than two dimensions. Figure 7.19 illustrates a two-dimensional array, a. The array contains three rows and four columns, so it's said to be a 3-by-4 array. In general, an array with *m* rows and *n* columns is called an *m*-by-*n* **array**.

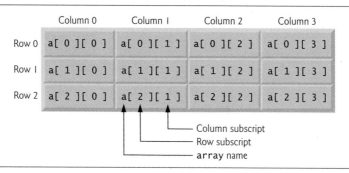

Fig. 7.19 | Two-dimensional array with three rows and four columns.

Every element in array a is identified in Fig. 7.19 by an element name of the form a[i][j], where a is the name of the array, and i and j are the subscripts that uniquely identify each element in a. Notice that the names of the elements in row 0 all have a first subscript of 0; the names of the elements in column 3 all have a second subscript of 3.

Common Programming Error 7.5

Referencing a two-dimensional array element a[x][y] incorrectly as a[x, y] is an error. Actually, a[x, y] is treated as a[y], because C++ evaluates the expression x, y (containing a comma operator) simply as y (the last of the comma-separated expressions).

Figure 7.20 demonstrates initializing two-dimensional arrays in declarations. Lines 13–14 each declare an arrays of arrays with two rows and three columns. Notice the nested array type declaration. In each array, the type of its elements is specified as

```
array< int, columns >
```

indicating that each array contains as its elements three-element arrays of int values—the constant columns has the value 3.

```
1   // Fig. 7.20: fig07_20.cpp
2   // Initializing multidimensional arrays.
3   #include <iostream>
```

Fig. 7.20 | Initializing multidimensional arrays. (Part 1 of 2.)

```
4   #include <array>
5   using namespace std;
6
7   const size_t rows = 2;
8   const size_t columns = 3;
9   void printArray( const array< array< int, columns >, rows> & );
10
11  int main()
12  {
13     array< array< int, columns >, rows > array1 = { 1, 2, 3, 4, 5, 6 };
14     array< array< int, columns >, rows > array2 = { 1, 2, 3, 4, 5 };
15
16     cout << "Values in array1 by row are:" << endl;
17     printArray( array1 );
18
19     cout << "\nValues in array2 by row are:" << endl;
20     printArray( array2 );
21  } // end main
22
23  // output array with two rows and three columns
24  void printArray( const array< array< int, columns >, rows> & a )
25  {
26     // loop through array's rows
27     for ( auto const &row : a )
28     {
29        // loop through columns of current row
30        for ( auto const &element : row )
31           cout << element << ' ';
32
33        cout << endl; // start new line of output
34     } // end outer for
35  } // end function printArray
```

```
Values in array1 by row are:
1 2 3
4 5 6

Values in array2 by row are:
1 2 3
4 5 0
```

Fig. 7.20 | Initializing multidimensional arrays. (Part 2 of 2.)

The declaration of array1 (line 13) provides six initializers. The compiler initializes the elements of row 0 followed by the elements of row 1. So, the first three values initialize row 0's elements to 1, 2 and 3, and the last three initialize row 1's elements to 4, 5 and 6. The declaration of array2 (line 14) provides only five initializers. The initializers are assigned to row 0, then row 1. Any elements that do not have an explicit initializer are initialized to *zero*, so array2[1][2] is 0.

The program calls function printArray to output each array's elements. Notice that the function prototype (line 9) and definition (lines 24–35) specify that the function receives a two row and three column array. The parameter receives the array by reference and is declared const because the function does not modify they array's elements.

Nested Range-Based **for** Statements

To process the elements of a two-dimensional `array`, we use a nested loop in which the *outer* loop iterates through the *rows* and the *inner* loop iterates through the *columns* of a given row. Function `printArray`'s nested loop is implemented with range-based `for` statements. Lines 27 and 30 introduce the C++11 **auto** keyword, which tells the compiler to infer (determine) a variable's data type based on the variable's initializer value. The outer loop's range variable row is initialized with an element from the parameter a. Looking at the `array`'s declaration, you can see that the `array` contains elements of type

```
array< int, columns >
```

so the compiler infers that row refers to a three-element `array` of `int` values (again, columns is 3). The const & in row's declaration indicates that the reference *cannot* be used to modify the rows and prevents each row from being *copied* into the range variable. The inner loop's range variable element is initialized with one element of the `array` represented by row, so the compiler infers that element refers to an `int` because each row contains three `int` values. In an IDE, you can typically hover your mouse over a variable declared with auto and the IDE will display the variable's inferred type. Line 31 displays the value from a given row and column.

Nested Counter-Controlled **for** Statements

We could have implemented the nested loop with counter-controlled repetition as follows:

```
for ( size_t row = 0; row < a.size(); ++row )
{
    for ( size_t column = 0; column < a[ row ].size(); ++column )
        cout << a[ row ][ column ] << ' ';

    cout << endl;
} // end outer for
```

Other Common **array** Manipulations

Many common `array` manipulations use `for` statements. For example, the following `for` statement sets all the elements in row 2 of array a in Fig. 7.19 to zero:

```
for ( size_t column = 0; column < 4; ++column )
    a[ 2 ][ column ] = 0;
```

The `for` statement varies only the second subscript (i.e., the column subscript). The preceding `for` statement is equivalent to the following assignment statements:

```
a[ 2 ][ 0 ] = 0;
a[ 2 ][ 1 ] = 0;
a[ 2 ][ 2 ] = 0;
a[ 2 ][ 3 ] = 0;
```

The following nested counter-controlled `for` statement determines the total of *all* the elements in array a in Fig. 7.19:

```
total = 0;

for ( size_t row = 0; row < a.size(); ++row )
    for ( size_t column = 0; column < a[ row ].size(); ++column )
        total += a[ row ][ column ];
```

The for statement totals the elements of the array one row at a time. The outer for statement begins by setting row (i.e., the row subscript) to 0, so the elements of row 0 may be totaled by the inner for statement. The outer for statement then increments row to 1, so the elements of row 1 can be totaled. Then, the outer for statement increments row to 2, so the elements of row 2 can be totaled. When the nested for statement terminates, total contains the sum of all the array elements. This nested loop can be implemented with range-based for statements as:

```
total = 0;

for ( auto row : a ) // for each row
    for ( auto column : row ) // for each column in row
        total += column;
```

7.9 Case Study: Class GradeBook Using a Two-Dimensional array

In Section 7.6, we presented class GradeBook (Figs. 7.15–7.16), which used a one-dimensional array to store student grades on a single exam. In most semesters, students take several exams. Professors are likely to want to analyze grades across the entire semester, both for a single student and for the class as a whole.

Storing Student Grades in a Two-Dimensional *array* in Class *GradeBook*
Figure 7.21 shows the output that summarizes 10 students grades on three exams. We store the grades as a two-dimensional array in an object of the next version of class Grade-Book Figures 7.22–7.23. Each row of the array represents a single student's grades for the entire course, and each column represents all the grades the students earned for one particular exam. A client program, such as Fig. 7.24, passes the array as an argument to the GradeBook constructor. Since there are 10 students and three exams, we use a ten-by-three array to store the grades.

```
Welcome to the grade book for
CS101 Introduction to C++ Programming!

The grades are:
            Test 1  Test 2  Test 3  Average
Student  1     87      96      70    84.33
Student  2     68      87      90    81.67
Student  3     94     100      90    94.67
Student  4    100      81      82    87.67
Student  5     83      65      85    77.67
Student  6     78      87      65    76.67
Student  7     85      75      83    81.00
Student  8     91      94     100    95.00
Student  9     76      72      84    77.33
Student 10     87      93      73    84.33
```

Fig. 7.21 | Output of GradeBook that uses two-dimensional arrays. (Part 1 of 2.)

```
Lowest grade in the grade book is 65
Highest grade in the grade book is 100

Overall grade distribution:
   0-9:
  10-19:
  20-29:
  30-39:
  40-49:
  50-59:
  60-69: ***
  70-79: ******
  80-89: ************
  90-99: *******
   100: ***
```

Fig. 7.21 | Output of GradeBook that uses two-dimensional arrays. (Part 2 of 2.)

```cpp
1   // Fig. 7.22: GradeBook.h
2   // Definition of class GradeBook that uses a
3   // two-dimensional array to store test grades.
4   // Member functions are defined in GradeBook.cpp
5   #include <array>
6   #include <string>
7
8   // GradeBook class definition
9   class GradeBook
10  {
11  public:
12     // constants
13     static const size_t students = 10; // number of students
14     static const size_t tests = 3; // number of tests
15
16     // constructor initializes course name and array of grades
17     GradeBook( const std::string &,
18        std::array< std::array< int, tests >, students > & );
19
20     void setCourseName( const std::string & ); // set the course name
21     std::string getCourseName() const; // retrieve the course name
22     void displayMessage() const; // display a welcome message
23     void processGrades() const; // perform operations on the grade data
24     int getMinimum() const; // find the minimum grade in the grade book
25     int getMaximum() const; // find the maximum grade in the grade book
26     double getAverage( const std::array< int, tests > & ) const;
27     void outputBarChart() const; // output bar chart of grade distribution
28     void outputGrades() const; // output the contents of the grades array
29  private:
30     std::string courseName; // course name for this grade book
31     std::array< std::array< int, tests >, students > grades; // 2D array
32  }; // end class GradeBook
```

Fig. 7.22 | Definition of class GradeBook that uses a two-dimensional array to store test grades.

```cpp
1   // Fig. 7.23: GradeBook.cpp
2   // Member-function definitions for class GradeBook that
3   // uses a two-dimensional array to store grades.
4   #include <iostream>
5   #include <iomanip> // parameterized stream manipulators
6   using namespace std;
7
8   // include definition of class GradeBook from GradeBook.h
9   #include "GradeBook.h" // GradeBook class definition
10
11  // two-argument constructor initializes courseName and grades array
12  GradeBook::GradeBook( const string &name,
13     std::array< std::array< int, tests >, students > &gradesArray )
14     : courseName( name ), grades( gradesArray )
15  {
16  } // end two-argument GradeBook constructor
17
18  // function to set the course name
19  void GradeBook::setCourseName( const string &name )
20  {
21     courseName = name; // store the course name
22  } // end function setCourseName
23
24  // function to retrieve the course name
25  string GradeBook::getCourseName() const
26  {
27     return courseName;
28  } // end function getCourseName
29
30  // display a welcome message to the GradeBook user
31  void GradeBook::displayMessage() const
32  {
33     // this statement calls getCourseName to get the
34     // name of the course this GradeBook represents
35     cout << "Welcome to the grade book for\n" << getCourseName() << "!"
36        << endl;
37  } // end function displayMessage
38
39  // perform various operations on the data
40  void GradeBook::processGrades() const
41  {
42     // output grades array
43     outputGrades();
44
45     // call functions getMinimum and getMaximum
46     cout << "\nLowest grade in the grade book is " << getMinimum()
47        << "\nHighest grade in the grade book is " << getMaximum() << endl;
48
49     // output grade distribution chart of all grades on all tests
50     outputBarChart();
51  } // end function processGrades
```

Fig. 7.23 | Member-function definitions for class GradeBook that uses a two-dimensional array to store grades. (Part 1 of 4.)

```
52
53   // find minimum grade in the entire gradebook
54   int GradeBook::getMinimum() const
55   {
56      int lowGrade = 100; // assume lowest grade is 100
57
58      // loop through rows of grades array
59      for ( auto const &student : grades )
60      {
61         // loop through columns of current row
62         for ( auto const &grade : student )
63         {
64            // if current grade less than lowGrade, assign it to lowGrade
65            if ( grade < lowGrade )
66               lowGrade = grade; // new lowest grade
67         } // end inner for
68      } // end outer for
69
70      return lowGrade; // return lowest grade
71   } // end function getMinimum
72
73   // find maximum grade in the entire gradebook
74   int GradeBook::getMaximum() const
75   {
76      int highGrade = 0; // assume highest grade is 0
77
78      // loop through rows of grades array
79      for ( auto const &student : grades )
80      {
81         // loop through columns of current row
82         for ( auto const &grade : student )
83         {
84            // if current grade greater than highGrade, assign to highGrade
85            if ( grade > highGrade )
86               highGrade = grade; // new highest grade
87         } // end inner for
88      } // end outer for
89
90      return highGrade; // return highest grade
91   } // end function getMaximum
92
93   // determine average grade for particular set of grades
94   double GradeBook::getAverage( const array<int, tests> &setOfGrades ) const
95   {
96      int total = 0; // initialize total
97
98      // sum grades in array
99      for ( int grade : setOfGrades )
100        total += grade;
101
```

Fig. 7.23 | Member-function definitions for class GradeBook that uses a two-dimensional array to store grades. (Part 2 of 4.)

```
102      // return average of grades
103      return static_cast< double >( total ) / setOfGrades.size();
104   } // end function getAverage
105
106   // output bar chart displaying grade distribution
107   void GradeBook::outputBarChart() const
108   {
109      cout << "\nOverall grade distribution:" << endl;
110
111      // stores frequency of grades in each range of 10 grades
112      const size_t frequencySize = 11;
113      array< unsigned int, frequencySize > frequency = {}; // init to 0s
114
115      // for each grade, increment the appropriate frequency
116      for ( auto const &student : grades )
117         for ( auto const &test : student )
118            ++frequency[ test / 10 ];
119
120      // for each grade frequency, print bar in chart
121      for ( size_t count = 0; count < frequencySize; ++count )
122      {
123         // output bar label ("0-9:", ..., "90-99:", "100:" )
124         if ( 0 == count )
125            cout << "  0-9: ";
126         else if ( 10 == count )
127            cout << "  100: ";
128         else
129            cout << count * 10 << "-" << ( count * 10 ) + 9 << ": ";
130
131         // print bar of asterisks
132         for ( unsigned int stars = 0; stars < frequency[ count ]; ++stars )
133            cout << '*';
134
135         cout << endl; // start a new line of output
136      } // end outer for
137   } // end function outputBarChart
138
139   // output the contents of the grades array
140   void GradeBook::outputGrades() const
141   {
142      cout << "\nThe grades are:\n\n";
143      cout << "                "; // align column heads
144
145      // create a column heading for each of the tests
146      for ( size_t test = 0; test < tests; ++test )
147         cout << "Test " << test + 1 << "  ";
148
149      cout << "Average" << endl; // student average column heading
150
```

Fig. 7.23 | Member-function definitions for class GradeBook that uses a two-dimensional array to store grades. (Part 3 of 4.)

```
151    // create rows/columns of text representing array grades
152    for ( size_t student = 0; student < grades.size(); ++student )
153    {
154       cout << "Student " << setw( 2 ) << student + 1;
155
156       // output student's grades
157       for ( size_t test = 0; test < grades[ student ].size(); ++test )
158          cout << setw( 8 ) << grades[ student ][ test ];
159
160       // call member function getAverage to calculate student's average;
161       // pass row of grades as the argument
162       double average = getAverage( grades[ student ] );
163       cout << setw( 9 ) << setprecision( 2 ) << fixed << average << endl;
164    } // end outer for
165 } // end function outputGrades
```

Fig. 7.23 | Member-function definitions for class GradeBook that uses a two-dimensional array to store grades. (Part 4 of 4.)

Overview of Class *GradeBook's* Functions

Five member functions (declared in lines 24–28 of Fig. 7.22) perform array manipulations to process the grades. Each of these member functions is similar to its counterpart in the earlier one-dimensional array version of class GradeBook (Figs. 7.15–7.16). Member function getMinimum (defined in lines 54–71 of Fig. 7.23) determines the lowest grade of all students for the semester. Member function getMaximum (defined in lines 74–91 of Fig. 7.23) determines the highest grade of all students for the semester. Member function getAverage (lines 94–104 of Fig. 7.23) determines a particular student's semester average. Member function outputBarChart (lines 107–137 of Fig. 7.23) outputs a bar chart of the distribution of all student grades for the semester. Member function outputGrades (lines 140–165 of Fig. 7.23) outputs the two-dimensional array in a tabular format, along with each student's semester average.

Functions *getMinimum and getMaximum*

Member functions getMinimum, getMaximum, outputBarChart and outputGrades each loop through array grades by using nested range-based for or counter-controlled for statements. For example, consider the nested for statement (lines 59–68) in member function getMinimum. The outer for statement loops through the rows that represent each student and the inner for loops through the grades of a student. Each grade is compared with variable lowGrade in the body of the inner for statement. If a grade is less than lowGrade, lowGrade is set to that grade. This repeats until all rows and columns of grades have been traversed. When execution of the nested statement is complete, lowGrade contains the smallest grade in the two-dimensional array. Member function getMaximum works similarly to member function getMinimum.

Function *outputBarChart*

Member function outputBarChart in Fig. 7.23 is nearly identical to the one in Fig. 7.16. However, to output the overall grade distribution for a whole semester, the function uses a nested for statement (lines 116–118) to increment the elements of the one-dimensional array frequency based on all the grades in the two-dimensional array. The rest of the code in each of the two outputBarChart member functions that displays the chart is identical.

Function *outputGrades*

Member function outputGrades (lines 140–165) uses nested counter-controlled for statements to output values of the array grades, in addition to each student's semester average. The output in Fig. 7.21 shows the result, which resembles the tabular format of a professor's physical grade book. Lines 146–147 print the column headings for each test. We use a counter-controlled for statement so that we can identify each test with a number. Similarly, the for statement in lines 152–164 first outputs a row label using a counter variable to identify each student (line 154). Although array indices start at 0, lines 147 and 154 output test + 1 and student + 1, respectively, to produce test and student numbers starting at 1 (see Fig. 7.21). The inner for statement in lines 157–158 uses the outer for statement's counter variable student to loop through a specific row of array grades and output each student's test grade. Finally, line 162 obtains each student's semester average by passing the current row of grades (i.e., grades[student]) to member function getAverage.

Function *getAverage*

Member function getAverage (lines 94–104) takes as an argument a one-dimensional array of test results for a particular student. When line 162 calls getAverage, the first argument is grades[student], which specifies that a particular row of the two-dimensional array grades should be passed to getAverage. For example, based on the array created in Fig. 7.24, the argument grades[1] represents the three values (a one-dimensional array of grades) stored in row 1 of the two-dimensional array grades. A two-dimensional array's elements are one-dimensional arrays. Member function getAverage calculates the sum of the array elements, divides the total by the number of test results and returns the floating-point result as a double value (line 103).

Testing Class *GradeBook*

The program in Fig. 7.24 creates an object of class GradeBook (Figs. 7.22–7.23) using the two-dimensional array of ints named grades (declared and initialized in lines 11–21). Line 11 accesses class GradeBook's static constants students and tests to indicate the size of each dimension of array grades. Lines 23–24 pass a course name and grades to the GradeBook constructor. Lines 25–26 then invoke myGradeBook's displayMessage and processGrades member functions to display a welcome message and obtain a report summarizing the students' grades for the semester, respectively.

```
1   // Fig. 7.24: fig07_24.cpp
2   // Creates GradeBook object using a two-dimensional array of grades.
3   #include <array>
4   #include "GradeBook.h" // GradeBook class definition
5   using namespace std;
6
```

Fig. 7.24 | Creates a GradeBook object using a two-dimensional array of grades, then invokes member function processGrades to analyze them. (Part 1 of 2.)

```
7   // function main begins program execution
8   int main()
9   {
10     // two-dimensional array of student grades
11     array< array< int, GradeBook::tests >, GradeBook::students > grades =
12        { 87, 96, 70,
13          68, 87, 90,
14          94, 100, 90,
15          100, 81, 82,
16          83, 65, 85,
17          78, 87, 65,
18          85, 75, 83,
19          91, 94, 100,
20          76, 72, 84,
21          87, 93, 73 };
22
23     GradeBook myGradeBook(
24        "CS101 Introduction to C++ Programming", grades );
25     myGradeBook.displayMessage();
26     myGradeBook.processGrades();
27  } // end main
```

Fig. 7.24 | Creates a GradeBook object using a two-dimensional array of grades, then invokes member function processGrades to analyze them. (Part 2 of 2.)

7.10 Introduction to C++ Standard Library Class Template vector

We now introduce C++ Standard Library class template **vector**, which is similar to class template array, but also supports dynamic resizing. Except for the features that modify a vector, the other features shown in Fig. 7.25 also work for arrays. Standard class template vector is defined in header <vector> (line 5) and belongs to namespace std. Chapter 15 discusses the full functionality of vector. At the end of this section, we'll demonstrate class vector's bounds checking capabilities and introduce C++'s exception-handling mechanism, which can be used to detect and handle an out-of-bounds vector index.

```
1   // Fig. 7.25: fig07_25.cpp
2   // Demonstrating C++ Standard Library class template vector.
3   #include <iostream>
4   #include <iomanip>
5   #include <vector>
6   #include <stdexcept>
7   using namespace std;
8
9   void outputVector( const vector< int > & ); // display the vector
10  void inputVector( vector< int > & ); // input values into the vector
11
12  int main()
13  {
```

Fig. 7.25 | Demonstrating C++ Standard Library class template vector. (Part 1 of 4.)

```
14    vector< int > integers1( 7 ); // 7-element vector< int >
15    vector< int > integers2( 10 ); // 10-element vector< int >
16
17    // print integers1 size and contents
18    cout << "Size of vector integers1 is " << integers1.size()
19       << "\nvector after initialization:" << endl;
20    outputVector( integers1 );
21
22    // print integers2 size and contents
23    cout << "\nSize of vector integers2 is " << integers2.size()
24       << "\nvector after initialization:" << endl;
25    outputVector( integers2 );
26
27    // input and print integers1 and integers2
28    cout << "\nEnter 17 integers:" << endl;
29    inputVector( integers1 );
30    inputVector( integers2 );
31
32    cout << "\nAfter input, the vectors contain:\n"
33       << "integers1:" << endl;
34    outputVector( integers1 );
35    cout << "integers2:" << endl;
36    outputVector( integers2 );
37
38    // use inequality (!=) operator with vector objects
39    cout << "\nEvaluating: integers1 != integers2" << endl;
40
41    if ( integers1 != integers2 )
42       cout << "integers1 and integers2 are not equal" << endl;
43
44    // create vector integers3 using integers1 as an
45    // initializer; print size and contents
46    vector< int > integers3( integers1 ); // copy constructor
47
48    cout << "\nSize of vector integers3 is " << integers3.size()
49       << "\nvector after initialization:" << endl;
50    outputVector( integers3 );
51
52    // use overloaded assignment (=) operator
53    cout << "\nAssigning integers2 to integers1:" << endl;
54    integers1 = integers2; // assign integers2 to integers1
55
56    cout << "integers1:" << endl;
57    outputVector( integers1 );
58    cout << "integers2:" << endl;
59    outputVector( integers2 );
60
61    // use equality (==) operator with vector objects
62    cout << "\nEvaluating: integers1 == integers2" << endl;
63
64    if ( integers1 == integers2 )
65       cout << "integers1 and integers2 are equal" << endl;
66
```

Fig. 7.25 | Demonstrating C++ Standard Library class template vector. (Part 2 of 4.)

```
67      // use square brackets to use the value at location 5 as an rvalue
68      cout << "\nintegers1[5] is " << integers1[ 5 ];
69
70      // use square brackets to create lvalue
71      cout << "\n\nAssigning 1000 to integers1[5]" << endl;
72      integers1[ 5 ] = 1000;
73      cout << "integers1:" << endl;
74      outputVector( integers1 );
75
76      // attempt to use out-of-range subscript
77      try
78      {
79         cout << "\nAttempt to display integers1.at( 15 )" << endl;
80         cout << integers1.at( 15 ) << endl; // ERROR: out of range
81      } // end try
82      catch ( out_of_range &ex )
83      {
84         cerr << "An exception occurred: " << ex.what() << endl;
85      } // end catch
86
87      // changing the size of a vector
88      cout << "\nCurrent integers3 size is: " << integers3.size() << endl;
89      integers3.push_back( 1000 ); // add 1000 to the end of the vector
90      cout << "New integers3 size is: " << integers3.size() << endl;
91      cout << "integers3 now contains: ";
92      outputVector( integers3 );
93   } // end main
94
95   // output vector contents
96   void outputVector( const vector< int > &array )
97   {
98      for ( int item : items )
99         cout << item << " ";
100
101     cout << endl;
102  } // end function outputVector
103
104  // input vector contents
105  void inputVector( vector< int > &array )
106  {
107     for ( int &item : items )
108        cin >> item;
109  } // end function inputVector
```

```
Size of vector integers1 is 7
vector after initialization:
0 0 0 0 0 0 0

Size of vector integers2 is 10
vector after initialization:
0 0 0 0 0 0 0 0 0 0
```

Fig. 7.25 | Demonstrating C++ Standard Library class template `vector`. (Part 3 of 4.)

```
Enter 17 integers:
1 2 3 4 5 6 7 8 9 10 11 12 13 14 15 16 17

After input, the vectors contain:
integers1:
1 2 3 4 5 6 7
integers2:
8 9 10 11 12 13 14 15 16 17

Evaluating: integers1 != integers2
integers1 and integers2 are not equal

Size of vector integers3 is 7
vector after initialization:
1 2 3 4 5 6 7

Assigning integers2 to integers1:
integers1:
8 9 10 11 12 13 14 15 16 17
integers2:
8 9 10 11 12 13 14 15 16 17

Evaluating: integers1 == integers2
integers1 and integers2 are equal

integers1[5] is 13

Assigning 1000 to integers1[5]
integers1:
8 9 10 11 12 1000 14 15 16 17

Attempt to display integers1.at( 15 )
An exception occurred: invalid vector<T> subscript

Current integers3 size is: 7
New integers3 size is: 8
integers3 now contains: 1 2 3 4 5 6 7 1000
```

Fig. 7.25 | Demonstrating C++ Standard Library class template `vector`. (Part 4 of 4.)

Creating *vector* Objects
Lines 14–15 create two `vector` objects that store values of type `int`—`integers1` contains seven elements, and `integers2` contains 10 elements. By default, all the elements of each vector object are set to 0. Like arrays, vectors can be defined to store most data types, by replacing `int` in `vector<int>` with the appropriate type.

vector Member Function *size*; Function *outputVector*
Line 18 uses `vector` member function **size** to obtain the size (i.e., the number of elements) of `integers1`. Line 20 passes `integers1` to function `outputVector` (lines 96–102), which uses a range-based `for` statement to obtain the value in each element of the `vector` for output. As with class template `array`, you can also do this using a counter-controlled loop and the subscript (`[]`) operator. Lines 23 and 25 perform the same tasks for `integers2`.

Function `inputVector`
Lines 29–30 pass `integers1` and `integers2` to function `inputVector` (lines 105–109) to read values for each `vector`'s elements from the user. The function uses a range-based `for` statement with a range variable that is a reference to an `int` to form *lvalues* that are used to store the input values in each `vector` element.

Comparing `vector` Objects for Inequality
Line 41 demonstrates that `vector` objects can be compared with one another using the `!=` operator. If the contents of two `vector`s are not equal, the operator returns `true`; otherwise, it returns `false`.

Initializing One `vector` with the Contents of Another
The C++ Standard Library class template `vector` allows you to create a new `vector` object that's initialized with the contents of an existing `vector`. Line 46 creates a `vector` object `integers3` and initializes it with a copy of `integers1`. This invokes `vector`'s so-called *copy constructor* to perform the copy operation. You'll learn about copy constructors in detail in Chapter 10. Lines 48–50 output the size and contents of `integers3` to demonstrate that it was initialized correctly.

Assigning `vector`s and Comparing `vector`s for Equality
Line 54 assigns `integers2` to `integers1`, demonstrating that the assignment (=) operator can be used with `vector` objects. Lines 56–59 output the contents of both objects to show that they now contain identical values. Line 64 then compares `integers1` to `integers2` with the equality (==) operator to determine whether the contents of the two objects are equal after the assignment in line 54 (which they are).

Using the `[]` Operator to Access and Modify `vector` Elements
Lines 68 and 70 use square brackets (`[]`) to obtain a `vector` element and use it as an *rvalue* and as an *lvalue*, respectively. Recall from Section 5.9 that an *rvalue* cannot be modified, but an *lvalue* can. As is the case with `array`s, *C++ is not required to perform bounds checking when vector elements are accessed with square brackets.*[1] Therefore, you must ensure that operations using `[]` do not accidentally attempt to manipulate elements outside the bounds of the vector. Standard class template `vector` does, however, provide bounds checking in its member function `at` (as does class template `array`), which we use at line 80 and discuss shortly.

Exception Handling: Processing an Out-of-Range Subscript
An **exception** indicates a problem that occurs while a program executes. The name "exception" suggests that the problem occurs infrequently—if the "rule" is that a statement normally executes correctly, then the problem represents the "exception to the rule." **Exception handling** enables you to create **fault-tolerant programs** that can resolve (or handle) exceptions. In many cases, this allows a program to continue executing as if no problems were encountered. For example, Fig. 7.25 still runs to completion, even though an attempt was made to access an out-of-range subscript. More severe problems might prevent a program from continuing normal execution, instead requiring the program to notify the user of the problem, then terminate. When a function detects a problem, such as

---

1. Some compilers have options for bounds checking to help prevent buffer overflows.

an invalid `array` subscript or an invalid argument, it throws an exception—that is, an exception occurs. Here we introduce exception handling briefly. We'll discuss it in detail in Chapter 17, Exception Handling: A Deeper Look.

The *try* Statement

To handle an exception, place any code that might throw an exception in a `try` statement (lines 77–85). The try block (lines 77–81) contains the code that might *throw* an exception, and the catch block (lines 82–85) contains the code that *handles* the exception if one occurs. As you'll see in Chapter 17, you can have many `catch` blocks to handle different types of exceptions that might be thrown in the corresponding `try` block. If the code in the `try` block executes successfully, lines 82–85 are ignored. The braces that delimit `try` and `catch` blocks' bodies are required.

The `vector` member function `at` provides bounds checking and throws an exception if its argument is an invalid subscript. By default, this causes a C++ program to terminate. If the subscript is valid, function `at` returns the element at the specified location as a modifiable *lvalue* or a nonmodifiable *lvalue*. A nonmodifiable *lvalue* is an expression that identifies an object in memory (such as an element in a `vector`), but cannot be used to modify that object. If `at` is called on a `const` array or via a reference that's declared `const`, the function returns a nonmodifiable *lvalue*.

Executing the *catch* Block

When the program calls `vector` member function at with the argument 15 (line 80), the function attempts to access the element at location 15, which is *outside* the `vector`'s bounds—integers1 has only 10 elements at this point. Because bounds checking is performed at execution time, `vector` member function at generates an exception—specifically line 80 throws an out_of_range exception (from header <stdexcept>) to notify the program of this problem. At this point, the `try` block terminates immediately and the `catch` block begins executing—if you declared any variables in the `try` block, they're now out of scope and are not accessible in the `catch` block.

The `catch` block declares a type (out_of_range) and an exception parameter (ex) that it receives as a reference. The `catch` block can handle exceptions of the specified type. Inside the block, you can use the parameter's identifier to interact with a caught exception object.

what Member Function of the Exception Parameter

When lines 82–85 *catch* the exception, the program displays a message indicating the problem that occurred. Line 84 calls the exception object's what member function to get the error message that is stored in the exception object and display it. Once the message is displayed in this example, the exception is considered handled and the program continues with the next statement after the `catch` block's closing brace. In this example, lines 88–92 execute next. We use exception handling again in Chapters 9–12 and Chapter 17 presents a deeper look at exception handling.

Changing the Size of a *vector*

One of the key differences between a `vector` and an `array` is that a `vector` can dynamically grow to accommodate more elements. To demonstrate this, line 88 shows the current size of integers3, line 89 calls the `vector`'s push_back member function to add a new element containing 1000 to the end of the `vector` and line 90 shows the new size of integers3. Line 92 then displays integers3's new contents.

*C++11: List Initializing a **vector***
Many of the `array` examples in this chapter used list initializers to specify the initial `array` element values. C++11 also allows this for `vector`s (and other C++ Standard Library data structures). At the time of this writing, list initializers were not yet supported for `vector`s in Visual C++.

7.11 Wrap-Up

This chapter began our introduction to data structures, exploring the use of C++ Standard Library class templates `array` and `vector` to store data in and retrieve data from lists and tables of values. The chapter examples demonstrated how to declare an `array`, initialize an `array` and refer to individual elements of an `array`. We passed `array`s to functions by reference and used the `const` qualifier to prevent the called function from modifying the `array`'s elements, thus enforcing the principle of least privilege. You learned how to use C++11's new range-based `for` statement to manipulate all the elements of an `array`. We also showed how to use C++ Standard Library functions `sort` and `binary_search` to sort and search an `array`, respectively. You learned how to declare and manipulate multidimensional `array`s of `array`s. We used nested counter-controlled and nested range-based `for` statements to iterate through all the rows and columns of a two-dimensional `array`. We also showed how to use `auto` to infer a variable's type based on its initializer value. Finally, we demonstrated the capabilities of C++ Standard Library class template `vector`. In that example, we discussed how to access `array` and `vector` elements with bounds checking and demonstrated basic exception-handling concepts. In later chapters, we'll continue our coverage of data structures.

We've now introduced the basic concepts of classes, objects, control statements, functions and array objects. In Chapter 8, we present one of C++'s most powerful features—the pointer. Pointers keep track of where data and functions are stored in memory, which allows us to manipulate those items in interesting ways. As you'll see, C++ also provides a language element called an array (different from the class template `array`) that is closely related to pointers. In contemporary C++ code, its considered better practice to use C++11's array class template rather than traditional arrays.

Summary

Section 7.1 Introduction
- Data structures (p. 313) are collections of related data items. arrays (p. 313) are data structures consisting of related data items of the same type. arrays are "static" entities in that they remain the same size throughout their lifetimes.

Section 7.2 arrays
- An array is a consecutive group of memory locations that share the same type.
- Each array knows its own size, which can be determined by calling its `size` member function (p. 314).
- To refer to a particular location or element in an array, we specify the name of the array (p. 314) and the position number of the particular element in the array.

- A program refers to any one of an array's elements by giving the name of the array followed by the index (p. 313) of the particular element in square brackets ([]).
- The first element in every array has index zero (p. 313) and is sometimes called the zeroth element.
- An index must be an integer or integer expression (using any integral type).
- The brackets used to enclose the index are an operator with the same precedence as parentheses.

Section 7.3 Declaring arrays
- arrays occupy space in memory. You specify the type of each element and the number of elements required by an array as follows:

      array< *type*, *arraySize* > *arrayName*;

  and the compiler reserves the appropriate amount of memory.
- arrays can be declared to contain almost any data type. For example, an array of type char can be used to store a character string.

Section 7.4 Examples Using arrays
- The elements of an array can be initialized in the array declaration by following the array name with an equals sign and an initializer list (p. 316)—a comma-separated list (enclosed in braces) of initializers (p. 316).
- When initializing an array with an initializer list, if there are fewer initializers than elements in the array, the remaining elements are initialized to zero. The number of initializers must be less than or equal to the array size.
- A constant variable that's used to specify an array's size must be initialized with a constant expression when it's declared and cannot be modified thereafter.
- C++ has no array bounds checking (p. 325). You should ensure that all array references remain within the bounds of the array.
- A static local variable in a function definition exists for the duration of the program but is visible only in the function body.
- A program initializes static local arrays when their declarations are first encountered. If a static array is not initialized explicitly by you, each element of that array is initialized to zero by the compiler when the array is created.

Section 7.5 Range-Based for Statement
- The new C++11 range-based for statement (p. 327) allows to manipulate all the elements of an array without using a counter, thus avoiding the possibility of "stepping outside" the array and eliminating the need for you to implement your own bounds checking.
- The syntax of a range-based for statement is:

      for (*rangeVariableDeclaration* : *expression*)
          statement

  where *rangeVariableDeclaration* has a type and an identifier, and *expression* is the array through which to iterate. The type in the *rangeVariableDeclaration* must be consistent with the type of the array's elements. The identifier represents successive array elements on successive iterations of the loop. You can use the range-based for statement with most of the C++ Standard Library's prebuilt data structures (commonly called containers), including classes array and vector.
- You can use a range-based for statement to modify each element by making the *rangeVariableDeclaration* a reference.
- The range-based for statement can be used in place of the counter-controlled for statement whenever code looping through an array does not require access to the element's subscript.

Section 7.6 Case Study: Class **GradeBook** Using an **array** to Store Grades

- Class variables (`static` data members; p. 334) are shared by all objects of the class in which the variables are declared.

- A `static` data member can be accessed within the class definition and the member-function definitions like any other data member.

- A `public` `static` data member can also be accessed outside of the class, even when no objects of the class exist, using the class name followed by the scope resolution operator (`::`) and the name of the data member.

Section 7.7 Sorting and Searching **arrays**

- Sorting data—placing it into ascending or descending order—is one of the most important computing applications.

- The process of finding a particular element of an `array` is called searching.

- C++ Standard Library function `sort` sorts an `array`'s elements into ascending order. The function's arguments specify the range of elements that should be sorted. You'll see that function `sort` can be used on other types of containers too.

- C++ Standard Library function `binary_search` determines whether a value is in an `array`. The sequence of values must be sorted in ascending order first. The function's first two arguments represent the range of elements to search and the third is the search key—the value to locate. The function returns a `bool` indicating whether the value was found.

Section 7.8 Multidimensional **arrays**

- Multidimensional `arrays` (p. 338) with two dimensions are often used to represent tables of values (p. 338) consisting of information arranged in rows and columns.

- `arrays` that require two subscripts to identify a particular element are called two-dimensional arrays (p. 338). An array with *m* rows and *n* columns is called an *m*-by-*n* array (p. 338).

Section 7.9 Case Study: Class **GradeBook** Using a Two-Dimensional **array**

- In a variable declaration, the keyword `auto` (p. 340) can be used in place of a type name to infer the variable's type based on the variable's initializer value.

Section 7.10 Introduction to C++ Standard Library Class Template **vector**

- C++ Standard Library class template `vector` (p. 348) represents a more robust alternative to arrays featuring many capabilities that are not provided for C-style pointer-based `arrays`.

- By default, all the elements of an integer `vector` object are set to 0.

- A `vector` can be defined to store any data type using a declaration of the form

      vector< *type* > *name*(*size*);

- Member function `size` (p. 351) of class template `vector` returns the number of elements in the vector on which it's invoked.

- The value of an element of a `vector` can be accessed or modified using square brackets (`[]`).

- Objects of standard class template `vector` can be compared directly with the equality (`==`) and inequality (`!=`) operators. The assignment (`=`) operator can also be used with `vector` objects.

- A nonmodifiable *lvalue* is an expression that identifies an object in memory (such as an element in a vector), but cannot be used to modify that object. A modifiable *lvalue* also identifies an object in memory, but can be used to modify the object.

- An exception (p. 352) indicates a problem that occurs while a program executes. The name "exception" suggests that the problem occurs infrequently—if the "rule" is that a statement normally executes correctly, then the problem represents the "exception to the rule."

- Exception handling (p. 352) enables you to create fault-tolerant programs (p. 352) that can resolve exceptions.

- To handle an exception, place any code that might throw an exception (p. 353) in a try statement.

- The try block (p. 353) contains the code that might throw an exception, and the catch block (p. 353) contains the code that handles the exception if one occurs.

- When a try block terminates, any variables declared in the try block go out of scope.

- A catch block declares a type and an exception parameter. Inside the catch block, you can use the parameter's identifier to interact with a caught exception object.

- An exception object's what method (p. 353) returns the exception's error message.

Self-Review Exercises

7.1   *(Fill in the Blanks)* Answer each of the following:
a) _____ are collections of related data items.
b) An index must be an integer or _____.
c) _____ are shared by all objects of the class in which the variables are declared.
d) A _____ local variable in a function definition exists for the duration of the program but is visible only in the function body.
e) _____ with two dimensions are often used to represent tables of values consisting of information arranged in rows and columns.
f) _____ enables you to create fault-tolerant programs that can resolve exceptions.
g) By default, all the elements of an integer vector object are set to _____.

7.2   *(True or False)* State whether the following are *true* or *false*. If the answer is *false*, explain why.
a) An array is a consecutive group of memory locations that share the same type.
b) You can use a range-based for statement to modify each element by making the *range-Variable-Declaration* a reference.
c) A static local variable in a function definition exists for the duration of the program but not visible in the function body.
d) The brackets used to enclose the index are an operator with the different precedence as parentheses.

7.3   *(Write C++ Statements)* Write one or more statements that perform the following tasks for an array called fractions:
a) Define a constant variable arraySize to represent the size of an array and initialize it to 8.
b) Declare an array with arraySize elements of type double, and initialize the elements to 1.0.
c) Name the third element of the array.
d) Refer to array element 3.
e) Assign the value 1.667 to array element 7.
f) Assign the value 3.333 to the sixth element of the array.
g) Display array elements 5 and 7 with one digits of precision to the right of the decimal point, and show the output that is actually displayed on the screen.
h) Display all the array elements using a counter-controlled for statement. Define the integer variable j as a control variable for the loop. Show the output.
i) Display all the array elements separated by "-" using a range-based for statement.

7.4   *(Two-Dimensional array Questions)* Answer the following questions regarding an array called table:
a) Declare the array to store int values and to have 4 rows and 4 columns. Assume that the constant variable arraySize has been defined to be 4.

b) How many elements does the array contain?

c) Use a counter-controlled for statement to initialize each element of the array to the product of its subscripts.

d) Write a nested for statement that displays the values of each element of array table in tabular format with 4 rows and 4 columns. Each row and column should be labelled with the row or column number. Assume that the array was initialized with an initialize list containing the values from 1 through 16 in order. Show the output.

7.5   *(Find the Error)* Find the error in each of the following programsegments and correct the error:

a) `$include <iostream>`

b) `arraySize = 12; // array size arraySize was declared const`

c) Assume that `array< int, 10 > b = {};`

```
    for ( size_t i = 0; i <= b.size(); ++i );
        b[ i ] = 1;
```

d) Assume that a is a two-dimensional array of int values with two rows and two columns:

`a[ 2; 2 ] = 10;`

Answers to Self-Review Exercises

7.1   a) Data structures. b) integer expression. c) Class variables. d) `static`. e) Multidimensional arrays. f) Exception handling. g) 0.

7.2   a) True. b) True. c) False, A `static` local variable in a function definition exists for the duration of the program but is visible only in the function body. d) False, The brackets used to enclose the index are an operator with the same precedence as parentheses.

7.3
a) `const size_t arraySize = 8;`

b) `array< double, arraySize > fractions = { 1.0 };`

c) `fractions[ 2 ]`

d) `fractions[ 3 ]`

e) `fractions[ 7 ] = 1.667;`

f) `fractions[ 5 ] = 3.333;`

g) `cout << fixed << setprecision( 1 );`
    `cout << fractions[ 6 ] << ' ' << fractions[ 9 ] << endl;`
    Output: 3.3 1.7

h) `for ( size_t j = 0; j < fractions.size(); ++j )`
        `cout << "fractions[" << j << "] = " << fractions[ j ] << endl;`
    Output:
```
fractions[ 0 ] = 1.0
fractions[ 1 ] = 1.0
fractions[ 2 ] = 1.0
fractions[ 3 ] = 1.0
fractions[ 4 ] = 1.0
fractions[ 5 ] = 3.333
fractions[ 6 ] = 1.0
fractions[ 7 ] = 1.667
```

i) `for ( double element : fractions )`
        `cout << element << '-';`

7.4   a) `array< array< int, arraySize >, arraySize > table;`

b) Sixteen.
c)
```
for ( size_t row = 0; row < table.size(); ++row )
    for ( size_t column = 0; column < table[ row ].size(); ++column )
        table[ row ][ column ] = row * column;
```
d)
```
cout << " [0]  [1]  [2]  [3]" << endl;
for ( size_t i = 0; i < arraySize; ++i ) {
    cout << '[' << i << "] ";
    for ( size_t j = 0; j < arraySize; ++j )
        cout << setw( 3 ) << table[ i ][ j ] << "  ";
    cout << endl;
}
```
Output:
```
     [0]  [1]  [2]  [3]
[0]   1    2    3    4
[1]   5    6    7    8
[2]   9   10   11   12
[3]  13   14   15   16
```

7.5 a) *Error:* $ before include preprocessing directive.
Correction: Change $ by #.
b) *Error:* Assigning a value to a constant variable using an assignment statement.
Correction: Initialize the constant variable in a const size_t arraySize declaration.
c) *Error:* For loop go infinitely.
Correction: Delete the; after the for loop.
d) *Error:* array subscripting done incorrectly.
Correction: Change the statement to a[2][2] = 10;

Exercises

7.6 *(Fill in the Blanks)* Fill in the blanks in each of the following:
a) When a try block terminates, any variables declared in the try block _____.
b) If a _____ is not initialized explicitly by you, each element of that array is initialized to zero by the compiler when the array is created.
c) The elements of an array also can be initialized in the array declaration by following the array name with an equals sign and a brace-delimited comma-separated _____.
d) A *p*-by-q array contains _____ elements.
e) The name of the element in row 4 and column 4 of array d is _____.

7.7 *(True or False)* Determine whether each of the following is *true* or *false*. If *false*, explain why.
a) The vector member function at provides bounds checking and throws an exception if its argument is an invalid subscript.
b) The value of an element of a vector can be accessed or modified using curly brackets ({}).
c) To indicate reserve 50 locations for integer array p, you write

   p[50];

d) A for statement must be used to initialize the elements of a 25-element array to one.
e) Two nested for statements must be used to total the elements of a three-dimensional array.

7.8 *(Write C++ Statements)* Write C++ statements to accomplish each of the following:
a) Display the value of element 5 of character array f.

    b) Input a value into element 3 of one-dimensional floating-point array `b`.

    c) Initialize each of the 4 elements of one-dimensional integer array `g` to 7.

    d) Total and display the elements of floating-point array `c` of 200 elements.

    e) Copy `array a` into the first portion of `array b`. Assume that both `array`s contain `double`s and that `array`s a and b have 17 and 41 elements, respectively.

    f) Determine and display the smallest and largest values contained in 999-element floatingpoint array `w`.

7.9   *(Two-Dimensional* **array** *Questions)* Consider a 2-by-3 integer array `t`.

    a) Write a declaration for `t`.

    b) How many rows does `t` have?

    c) How many columns does `t` have?

    d) How many elements does `t` have?

    e) Write the names of all the elements in row 1 of `t`.

    f) Write the names of all the elements in column 2 of `t`.

    g) Write a statement that sets the element of `t` in the first row and second column to zero.

    h) Write a series of statements that initialize each element of `t` to zero. Do not use a loop.

    i) Write a nested counter-controlled `for` statement that initializes each element of `t` to zero.

    j) Write a nested range-based `for` statement that initializes each element of `t` to zero.

    k) Write a statement that inputs the values for the elements of `t` from the keyboard.

    l) Write a series of statements that determine and display the smallest value in `array t`.

    m) Write a statement that displays the elements in row 0 of `t`.

    n) Write a statement that totals the elements in column 2 of `t`.

    o) Write a series of statements that prints the `array t` in neat, tabular format. List the column subscripts as headings across the top and list the row subscripts at the left of each row.

7.10   *(Salesperson Salary Ranges)* Use a one-dimensional `array` to solve the following problem. A company pays its salespeople on a commission basis. The salespeople each receive $200 per week plus 9 percent of their gross sales for that week. For example, a salesperson who grosses $5000 in sales in a week receives $200 plus 9 percent of $5000, or a total of $650. Write a program (using an array of counters) that determines how many of the salespeople earned salaries in each of the following ranges (assume that each salesperson's salary is truncated to an integer amount):

    a) $200–299

    b) $300–399

    c) $400–499

    d) $500–599

    e) $600–699

    f) $700–799

    g) $800–899

    h) $900–999

    i) $1000 and over

7.11   *(One-Dimensional* **array** *Questions)* Write single statements that perform the following one-dimensional array operations:

    a) Initialize the 20 elements of integer array `increment` to zero.

    b) Add 2 to each of the 25 elements of integer array `bonus`.

    c) Read 14 values for the `array` of `double`s named `monthlyTemperatures` from the keyboard.

    d) Print the 7 values of integer array `bestScores` in column format.

7.12   *(Find the Errors)* Find the error(s) in each of the following statements:

    a) Assume that a is an array of three `int`s.

```
cout << a[ 1 ] << " " << a[ 2 ] << " " << a[ 3 ] << endl;
```

  b) `array< double, 3 > f = { 1.1, 10.01, 100.001, 1000.0001 };`
  c) Assume that d is an `array` of `double`s with two rows and 10 columns.
     `d[ 1, 9 ] = 2.345;`

7.13   *(Duplicate Elimination with* **array***)* Use a one-dimensional array to solve the following problem. Read in 20 numbers, each of which is between 10 and 100, inclusive. As each number is read, validate it and store it in the `array` only if it isn't a duplicate of a number already read. After reading all the values, display only the unique values that the user entered. Provide for the "worst case" in which all 20 numbers are different. Use the smallest possible `array` to solve this problem.

7.14   *(Duplicate Elimination with* **vector***)* Reimplement Exercise 7.13 using a `vector`. Begin with an empty `vector` and use its `push_back` function to add each unique value to the `vector`.

7.15   *(Two-Dimensional* **array** *Initialization)* Label the elements of a 2-by-3 two-dimensional array tax to indicate the order in which they're set to one by the following program segment:

```
for ( size_t row = 0; row < tax.size(); ++row )
   for ( size_t column = 0; column < tax[ row ].size(); ++column )
      tax[ row ][ column ] = 1;
```

Ans:
```
tax[ 0 ][ 0 ], tax[ 0 ][ 1 ], tax[ 0 ][ 2 ],
tax[ 1 ][ 0 ], tax[ 1 ][ 1 ], tax[ 1 ][ 2 ]
```

7.16   *(Dice Rolling)* Write a program that simulates the rolling of two dice. The sum of the two values should then be calculated. [*Note:* Each die can show an integer value from 1 to 6, so the sum of the two values will vary from 2 to 12, with 7 being the most frequent sum and 2 and 12 being the least frequent sums.] Figure 7.26 shows the 36 possible combinations of the two dice. Your program should roll the two dice 36,000 times. Use a one-dimensional `array` to tally the numbers of times each possible sum appears. Print the results in a tabular format. Also, determine if the totals are reasonable (i.e., there are six ways to roll a 7, so approximately one-sixth of all the rolls should be 7).

	1	2	3	4	5	6
1	2	3	4	5	6	7
2	3	4	5	6	7	8
3	4	5	6	7	8	9
4	5	6	7	8	9	10
5	6	7	8	9	10	11
6	7	8	9	10	11	12

Fig. 7.26 | The 36 possible outcomes of rolling two dice.

7.17   *(What Does This Code Do?)* What does the following program do?

```
1   // Ex. 7.17: Ex07_17.cpp
2   // What does this program do?
3   #include <iostream>
4   #include <array>
5   using namespace std;
6
7   const size_t arraySize = 10;
8   int whatIsThis( const array< int, arraySize > &, size_t ); // prototype
9
10  int main()
11  {
12     array< int, arraySize > a = { 1, 2, 3, 4, 5, 6, 7, 8, 9, 10 };
```

```
13
14      int result = whatIsThis( a, arraySize );
15
16      cout << "Result is " << result << endl;
17   } // end main
18
19   // What does this function do?
20   int whatIsThis( const array< int, arraySize > &b, size_t size )
21   {
22      if ( size == 1 ) // base case
23         return b[ 0 ];
24      else // recursive step
25         return b[ size - 1 ] + whatIsThis( b, size - 1 );
26   } // end function whatIsThis
```

7.18   *(Craps Game Modification)* Modify the program of Fig. 6.11 to play 1000 games of craps. The program should keep track of the statistics and answer the following questions:

a) How many games are won on the 1st roll, 2nd roll, ..., 20th roll, and after the 20th roll?
b) How many games are lost on the 1st roll, 2nd roll, ..., 20th roll, and after the 20th roll?
c) What are the chances of winning at craps? [*Note:* You should discover that craps is one of the fairest casino games. What do you suppose this means?]
d) What's the average length of a game of craps?
e) Do the chances of winning improve with the length of the game?

7.19   *(Converting vector Example of Section 7.10 to array)* Convert the vector example of Fig. 7.26 to use arrays. Eliminate any vector-only features.

7.20   *(What Does This Code Do?)* What does the following program do?

```
1    // Ex. 7.20: Ex07_20.cpp
2    // What does this program do?
3    #include <iostream>
4    #include <array>
5    using namespace std;
6
7    const size_t arraySize = 10;
8    void someFunction( const array< int, arraySize > &, size_t ); // prototype
9
10   int main()
11   {
12      array< int, arraySize > a = { 1, 2, 3, 4, 5, 6, 7, 8, 9, 10 };
13
14      cout << "The values in the array are:" << endl;
15      someFunction( a, 0 );
16      cout << endl;
17   } // end main
18
19   // What does this function do?
20   void someFunction( const array< int, arraySize > &b, size_t current )
21   {
22      if ( current < b.size() )
23      {
24         someFunction( b, current + 1 );
25         cout << b[ current ] << "  ";
26      } // end if
27   } // end function someFunction
```

7.21 *(Sales Summary)* Use a two-dimensional `array` to solve the following problem. A company has four salespeople (1 to 4) who sell five different products (1 to 5). Once a day, each salesperson passes in a slip for each different type of product sold. Each slip contains the following:

a) The salesperson number
b) The product number
c) The total dollar value of that product sold that day

Thus, each salesperson passes in between 0 and 5 sales slips per day. Assume that the information from all of the slips for last month is available. Write a program that will read all this information for last month's sales (one salesperson's data at a time) and summarize the total sales by salesperson by product. All totals should be stored in the two-dimensional `array sales`. After processing all the information for last month, print the results in tabular format with each of the columns representing a particular salesperson and each of the rows representing a particular product. Cross total each row to get the total sales of each product for last month; cross total each column to get the total sales by salesperson for last month. Your tabular printout should include these cross totals to the right of the totaled rows and to the bottom of the totaled columns.

7.22 *(Knight's Tour)* One of the more interesting puzzlers for chess buffs is the Knight's Tour problem. The question is this: Can the chess piece called the knight move around an empty chessboard and touch each of the 64 squares once and only once? We study this intriguing problem in depth in this exercise.

The knight makes L-shaped moves (over two in one direction then over one in a perpendicular direction). Thus, from a square in the middle of an empty chessboard, the knight can make eight different moves (numbered 0 through 7) as shown in Fig. 7.27.

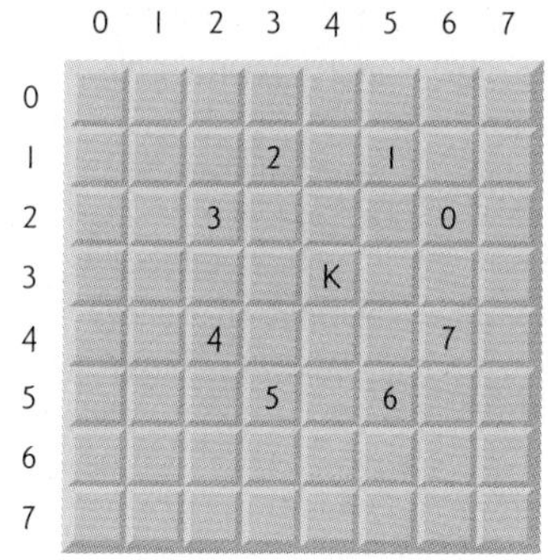

Fig. 7.27 | The eight possible moves of the knight.

a) Draw an 8-by-8 chessboard on a sheet of paper and attempt a Knight's Tour by hand. Put a 1 in the first square you move to, a 2 in the second square, a 3 in the third, etc. Before starting the tour, estimate how far you think you'll get, remembering that a full tour consists of 64 moves. How far did you get? Was this close to your estimate?

b) Now let's develop a program that will move the knight around a chessboard. The board is represented by an 8-by-8 two-dimensional `array board`. Each of the squares is initialized to zero. We describe each of the eight possible moves in terms of both their horizontal and vertical components. For example, a move of type 0, as shown in Fig. 7.27, consists of moving two squares horizontally to the right and one square vertically upward. Move 2 consists of moving one square horizontally to the left and two squares vertically upward. Horizontal moves to the left and vertical moves upward are indicated with negative numbers. The eight moves may be described by two one-dimensional arrays, horizontal and vertical, as follows:

```
horizontal[ 0 ] = 2      vertical[ 0 ] = -1
horizontal[ 1 ] = 1      vertical[ 1 ] = -2
horizontal[ 2 ] = -1     vertical[ 2 ] = -2
horizontal[ 3 ] = -2     vertical[ 3 ] = -1
horizontal[ 4 ] = -2     vertical[ 4 ] = 1
horizontal[ 5 ] = -1     vertical[ 5 ] = 2
horizontal[ 6 ] = 1      vertical[ 6 ] = 2
horizontal[ 7 ] = 2      vertical[ 7 ] = 1
```

Let the variables currentRow and currentColumn indicate the row and column of the knight's current position. To make a move of type moveNumber, where moveNumber is between 0 and 7, your program uses the statements

```
currentRow += vertical[ moveNumber ];
currentColumn += horizontal[ moveNumber ];
```

Keep a counter that varies from 1 to 64. Record the latest count in each square the knight moves to. Remember to test each potential move to see if the knight has already visited that square, and, of course, test every potential move to make sure that the knight does not land off the chessboard. Now write a program to move the knight around the chessboard. Run the program. How many moves did the knight make?

c) After attempting to write and run a Knight's Tour program, you've probably developed some valuable insights. We'll use these to develop a **heuristic** (or strategy) for moving the knight. Heuristics do not guarantee success, but a carefully developed heuristic greatly improves the chance of success. You may have observed that the outer squares are more troublesome than the squares nearer the center of the board. In fact, the most troublesome, or inaccessible, squares are the four corners.

Intuition may suggest that you should attempt to move the knight to the most troublesome squares first and leave open those that are easiest to get to, so when the board gets congested near the end of the tour, there will be a greater chance of success.

We may develop an "accessibility heuristic" by classifying each square according to how accessible it's then always moving the knight to the square (within the knight's L-shaped moves, of course) that is most inaccessible. We label a two-dimensional array accessibility with numbers indicating from how many squares each particular square is accessible. On a blank chessboard, each center square is rated as 8, each corner square is rated as 2 and the other squares have accessibility numbers of 3, 4 or 6 as follows:

```
2  3  4  4  4  4  3  2
3  4  6  6  6  6  4  3
4  6  8  8  8  8  6  4
4  6  8  8  8  8  6  4
4  6  8  8  8  8  6  4
4  6  8  8  8  8  6  4
3  4  6  6  6  6  4  3
2  3  4  4  4  4  3  2
```

Now write a version of the Knight's Tour program using the accessibility heuristic. At any time, the knight should move to the square with the lowest accessibility number. In case of a tie, the knight may move to any of the tied squares. Therefore, the tour may begin in any of the four corners. [*Note:* As the knight moves around the chessboard, your program should reduce the accessibility numbers as more and more squares become occupied. In this way, at any given time during the tour, each available square's accessibility number will remain equal to precisely the number of squares from which that square may be reached.] Run this version of your program. Did you get a full tour? Now modify the program to run 64 tours, one starting from each square of the chessboard. How many full tours did you get?

    d) Write a version of the Knight's Tour program which, when encountering a tie between two or more squares, decides what square to choose by looking ahead to those squares reachable from the "tied" squares. Your program should move to the square for which the next move would arrive at a square with the lowest accessibility number.

7.23   (*Knight's Tour: Brute Force Approaches*) In Exercise 7.22, we developed a solution to the Knight's Tour problem. The approach used, called the "accessibility heuristic," generates many solutions and executes efficiently.

As computers continue increasing in power, we'll be able to solve more problems with sheer computer power and relatively unsophisticated algorithms. This is the "brute force" approach to problem solving.

    a) Use random number generation to enable the knight to walk around the chessboard (in its legitimate L-shaped moves, of course) at random. Your program should run one tour and print the final chessboard. How far did the knight get?

    b) Most likely, the preceding program produced a relatively short tour. Now modify your program to attempt 1000 tours. Use a one-dimensional array to keep track of the number of tours of each length. When your program finishes attempting the 1000 tours, it should print this information in neat tabular format. What was the best result?

    c) Most likely, the preceding program gave you some "respectable" tours, but no full tours. Now "pull all the stops out" and simply let your program run until it produces a full tour. [*Caution:* This version of the program could run for hours on a powerful computer.] Once again, keep a table of the number of tours of each length, and print this table when the first full tour is found. How many tours did your program attempt before producing a full tour? How much time did it take?

    d) Compare the brute force version of the Knight's Tour with the accessibility heuristic version. Which required a more careful study of the problem? Which algorithm was more difficult to develop? Which required more computer power? Could we be certain (in advance) of obtaining a full tour with the accessibility heuristic approach? Could we be certain (in advance) of obtaining a full tour with the brute force approach? Argue the pros and cons of brute force problem solving in general.

7.24   (*Eight Queens*) Another puzzler for chess buffs is the Eight Queens problem. Simply stated: Is it possible to place eight queens on an empty chessboard so that no queen is "attacking" any other, i.e., no two queens are in the same row, the same column, or along the same diagonal? Use the thinking developed in Exercise 7.22 to formulate a heuristic for solving the Eight Queens problem. Run your program. [*Hint:* It's possible to assign a value to each square of the chessboard indicating how many squares of an empty chessboard are "eliminated" if a queen is placed in that square. Each of the corners would be assigned the value 22, as in Fig. 7.28. Once these "elimination numbers" are placed in all 64 squares, an appropriate heuristic might be: Place the next queen in the square with the smallest elimination number. Why is this strategy intuitively appealing?]

7.25   (*Eight Queens: Brute Force Approaches*) In this exercise, you'll develop several brute-force approaches to solving the Eight Queens problem introduced in Exercise 7.24.

    a) Solve the Eight Queens exercise, using the random brute force technique developed in Exercise 7.23.

    b) Use an exhaustive technique, i.e., try all possible combinations of eight queens on the chessboard.

    c) Why do you suppose the exhaustive brute force approach may not be appropriate for solving the Knight's Tour problem?

    d) Compare and contrast the random and exhaustive brute force approaches in general.

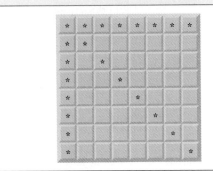

Fig. 7.28 | The 22 squares eliminated by placing a queen in the upper-left corner.

7.26 (*Knight's Tour: Closed-Tour Test*) In the Knight's Tour, a full tour occurs when the knight makes 64 moves, touching each square of the board once and only once. A closed tour occurs when the 64th move is one move away from the location in which the knight started the tour. Modify the Knight's Tour program you wrote in Exercise 7.22 to test for a closed tour if a full tour has occurred.

7.27 (*The Sieve of Eratosthenes*) A prime integer is any integer that is evenly divisible only by itself and 1. The Sieve of Eratosthenes is a method of finding prime numbers. It operates as follows:

a) Create an `array` with all elements initialized to 1 (true). `array` elements with prime subscripts will remain 1. All other `array` elements will eventually be set to zero. You'll ignore elements 0 and 1 in this exercise.

b) Starting with `array` subscript 2, every time an `array` element is found whose value is 1, loop through the remainder of the `array` and set to zero every element whose subscript is a multiple of the subscript for the element with value 1. For `array` subscript 2, all elements beyond 2 in the `array` that are multiples of 2 will be set to zero (subscripts 4, 6, 8, 10, etc.); for `array` subscript 3, all elements beyond 3 in the `array` that are multiples of 3 will be set to zero (subscripts 6, 9, 12, 15, etc.); and so on.

When this process is complete, the `array` elements that are still set to one indicate that the subscript is a prime number. These can then be printed. Write a program that uses an `array` of 1000 elements to determine and print the prime numbers between 2 and 999. Ignore element 0 of the array.

Recursion Exercises

7.28 (*Palindromes*) A palindrome is a string that is spelled the same way forward and backward. Examples of palindromes include "radar" and "able was i ere i saw elba." Write a recursive function `testPalindrome` that returns `true` if a `string` is a palindrome, and `false` otherwise. Note that like an `array`, the square brackets (`[]`) operator can be used to iterate through the characters in a `string`.

7.29 (*Eight Queens*) Modify the Eight Queens program you created in Exercise 7.24 to solve the problem recursively.

7.30 (*Print an* **array**) Write a recursive function `printArray` that takes an array, a starting subscript and an ending subscript as arguments, returns nothing and prints the array. The function should stop processing and return when the starting subscript equals the ending subscript.

7.31 (*Print a String Backward*) Write a recursive function `stringReverse` that takes a `string` and a starting subscript as arguments, prints the string backward and returns nothing. The function should stop processing and return when the end of the string is encountered. Note that like an `array` the square brackets (`[]`) operator can be used to iterate through the characters in a `string`.

7.32 (*Find the Minimum Value in an* **array**) Write a recursive function `recursiveMinimum` that takes an integer array, a starting subscript and an ending subscript as arguments, and returns the smallest element of the array. The function should stop processing and return when the starting subscript equals the ending subscript.

7.33 (*Maze Traversal*) The grid of hashes (#) and dots (.) in Fig. 7.29 is a two-dimensional built-in array representation of a maze. In the two-dimensional built-in array, the hashes represent the walls of the maze and the dots represent squares in the possible paths through the maze. Moves can be made only to a location in the built-in array that contains a dot.

There is a simple algorithm for walking through a maze that guarantees finding the exit (assuming that there is an exit). If there is not an exit, you'll arrive at the starting location again. Place your right hand on the wall to your right and begin walking forward. Never remove your hand from the wall. If the maze turns to the right, you follow the wall to the right. As long as you do not remove your hand from the wall, eventually you'll arrive at the exit of the maze. There may be a shorter path than the one you've taken, but you are guaranteed to get out of the maze if you follow the algorithm.

Fig. 7.29 | Two-dimensional built-in array representation of a maze.

Write recursive function `mazeTraverse` to walk through the maze. The function should receive arguments that include a 12-by-12 built-in array of `char`s representing the maze and the starting location of the maze. As `mazeTraverse` attempts to locate the exit from the maze, it should place the character X in each square in the path. The function should display the maze after each move, so the user can watch as the maze is solved.

7.34 (*Generating Mazes Randomly*) Write a function `mazeGenerator` that randomly produces a maze. The function should take as arguments a two-dimensional 12-by-12 built-in array of `char`s and pointers to the `int` variables that represent the row and column of the maze's entry point. Try your function `mazeTraverse` from Exercise 7.33, using several randomly generated mazes.

Making a Difference

7.35 (*Polling*) The Internet and the web enable people to network, join a cause, and so on. The presidential candidates in 2012 used the Internet to get out their messages and raise money. In this exercise, you'll write a polling program that allows users to rate five social-consciousness issues from 1 to 10 (most important). Pick five causes (e.g., political issues, global environmental issues). Use a one-dimensional `string array` topics to store the causes. To summarize the survey responses, use a 5-row, 10-column two-dimensional array responses (of type `int`), each row corresponding to an element in the topics array. When the program runs, it should ask the user to rate each issue. Have your friends and family respond to the survey. Then have the program display a summary of the results, including:

a) A tabular report with the five topics down the left side and the 10 ratings across the top, listing in each column the number of ratings received for each topic.

b) To the right of each row, show the average of the ratings for that issue.

c) Which issue received the highest point total? Display both the issue and the point total.

d) Which issue received the lowest point total? Display both the issue and the point total.

8

Pointers

*Addresses are given to us to
conceal our whereabouts.*
—Saki (H. H. Munro)

*By indirection find direction
out.*
—William Shakespeare

*Many things, having full
reference
To one consent, may work
contrariously.*
—William Shakespeare

*You will find it a very good
practice always to verify your
references, sir!*
—Dr. Routh

Objectives

In this chapter you'll:

- Learn what pointers are.

- Learn the similarities and
  differences between pointers
  and references.

- Use pointers to pass
  arguments to functions by
  reference.

- Understand the close
  relationships between
  pointers and built-in arrays.

- Use pointer-based strings.

- Use built-in arrays.

- Use C++11 capabilities,
  including `nullptr` and
  Standard Library functions
  `begin` and `end`.

8.1 Introduction

This chapter discusses *pointers*—one of the most powerful, yet challenging to use, C++ capabilities. Our goals here are to help you determine when it's appropriate to use pointers, and show how to use them *correctly* and *responsibly*.

In Chapter 6, we saw that references can be used to perform pass-by-reference. Pointers also enable pass-by-reference and can be used to create and manipulate dynamic data structures that can grow and shrink, such as linked lists, queues, stacks and trees. This chapter explains basic pointer concepts. Chapter 19 presents examples of creating and using dynamic data structures that are implemented with pointers.

We also show the intimate relationship among *built-in arrays* and pointers. C++ inherited built-in arrays from the C programming language. As we saw in Chapter 7, the C++ Standard Library classes array and vector provide implementations of arrays as full-fledged objects—in fact, array and vector each store their elements in built-in arrays. *In new software development projects, you should favor* array *and* vector *objects to built-in arrays.*

Similarly, C++ actually offers two types of strings—string class objects (which we've been using since Chapter 3) and *C-style, pointer-based strings* (*C strings*). This chapter briefly introduces C strings to deepen your knowledge of pointers and built-in arrays. C strings were widely used in older C and C++ software. We discuss C strings in depth in Appendix F. *In new software development projects, you should favor* string *class objects.*

We'll examine the use of pointers with class objects in Chapter 12, where we'll see that the so-called "polymorphic processing" associated with object-oriented programming is performed with pointers and references.

8.2 Pointer Variable Declarations and Initialization

Indirection
Pointer variables contain *memory addresses* as their values. Normally, a variable *directly* contains a specific value. A pointer contains the *memory address* of a variable that, in turn, contains a specific value. In this sense, a variable name directly references a value, and a pointer indirectly references a value (Fig. 8.1). Referencing a value through a pointer is

called **indirection**. Diagrams typically represent a pointer as an *arrow* from the *variable that contains an address* to the *variable located at that address* in memory.

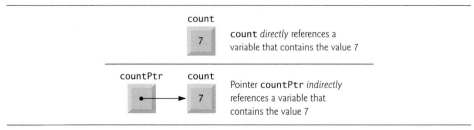

Fig. 8.1 | Directly and indirectly referencing a variable.

Declaring Pointers

Pointers, like any other variables, must be declared *before* they can be used. For example, for the pointer countPtr in Fig. 8.1, the declaration

```
int *countPtr, count;
```

declares the variable countPtr to be of type int * (i.e., a pointer to an int value) and is read (*right to left*), "countPtr is a pointer to int." Also, variable count in the preceding declaration is declared to be an int, *not* a pointer to an int. The * in the declaration applies *only* to countPtr. Each variable being declared as a pointer *must* be preceded by an asterisk (*). For example, the declaration

```
double *xPtr, *yPtr;
```

indicates that both xPtr and yPtr are pointers to double values. When * appears in a declaration, it's *not* an operator; rather, it indicates that the variable being declared is a pointer. Pointers can be declared to point to objects of *any* data type.

Common Programming Error 8.1

*Assuming that the * used to declare a pointer distributes to all names in a declaration's comma-separated list of variables can lead to errors. Each pointer must be declared with the * prefixed to the name (with or without spaces in between). Declaring only one variable per declaration helps avoid these types of errors and improves program readability.*

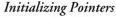

Good Programming Practice 8.1

Although it's not a requirement, including the letters Ptr in a pointer variable name makes it clear that the variable is a pointer and that it must be handled accordingly.

Initializing Pointers

Pointers should be initialized to **nullptr** (new in C++11) or an address of the corresponding type either when they're declared or in an assignment. A pointer with the value nullptr "points to nothing" and is known as a **null pointer**. From this point forward, when we refer to a "null pointer" we mean a pointer with the value nullptr.

Error-Prevention Tip 8.1

Initialize all pointers to prevent pointing to unknown or uninitialized areas of memory.

Null Pointers Prior to C++11

In earlier versions of C++, the value specified for a null pointer was 0 or NULL. NULL is defined in several standard library headers to represent the value 0. Initializing a pointer to NULL is equivalent to initializing a pointer to 0, but prior to C++11, 0 was used by convention. The value 0 is the *only* integer value that can be assigned directly to a pointer variable without first *casting* the integer to a pointer type.

8.3 Pointer Operators

Address (&) Operator

The address operator (&) is a unary operator that *obtains the memory address of its operand.* For example, assuming the declarations

```
int y = 5; // declare variable y
int *yPtr = nullptr; // declare pointer variable yPtr
```

the statement

```
yPtr = &y; // assign address of y to yPtr
```

assigns the address of the variable y to pointer variable yPtr. Then variable yPtr is said to "point to" y. Now, yPtr *indirectly* references variable y's value. The use of the & in the preceding statement is *not* the same as the use of the & in a *reference variable declaration*, which is *always* preceded by a data-type name. When declaring a reference, the & is part of the type. In an expression like &y, the & is the *address operator.*

Figure 8.2 shows a representation of memory after the preceding assignment. The "pointing relationship" is indicated by drawing an arrow from the box that represents the pointer yPtr in memory to the box that represents the variable y in memory.

Figure 8.3 shows another pointer representation in memory with integer variable y stored at memory location 600000 and pointer variable yPtr stored at location 500000. The operand of the address operator must be an *lvalue*—the address operator *cannot* be applied to constants or to expressions that result in temporary values (like the results of calculations).

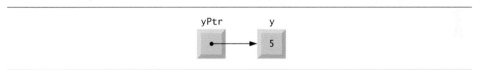

Fig. 8.2 | Graphical representation of a pointer pointing to a variable in memory.

Fig. 8.3 | Representation of y and yPtr in memory.

Indirection (*) Operator

The unary * operator—commonly referred to as the indirection operator or dereferencing operator—*returns an lvalue representing the object to which its pointer operand points.* For example (referring again to Fig. 8.2), the statement

```
        cout << *yPtr << endl;
```

displays the value of variable y, namely, 5, just as the statement

```
        cout << y << endl;
```

would. Using * in this manner is called **dereferencing a pointer**. A *dereferenced pointer* may also be used on the *left* side of an assignment statement, as in

```
        *yPtr = 9;
```

which would assign 9 to y in Fig. 8.3. The *dereferenced pointer* may also be used to receive an input value as in

```
        cin >> *yPtr;
```

which places the input value in y.

Common Programming Error 8.2

Dereferencing an uninitialized pointer results in undefined behavior that could cause a fatal execution-time error. This could also lead to accidentally modifying important data, allowing the program to run to completion, possibly with incorrect results.

Error-Prevention Tip 8.2

Dereferencing a null pointer results in undefined behavior and typically is a fatal execution-time error, so you should ensure that a pointer is not null before dereferencing it.

Using the Address (&) and Indirection (*) Operators

The program in Fig. 8.4 demonstrates the & and * pointer operators. Memory locations are output by << in this example as *hexadecimal* (i.e., base-16) integers. (See Appendix D, Number Systems, for more information on hexadecimal integers.) The memory addresses output by this program are *platform dependent*, so you may get different results when you run the program. The address of a (line 11) and the value of aPtr (line 12) are identical in the output, confirming that the address of a is indeed assigned to the pointer variable aPtr.

```
 1   // Fig. 8.4: fig08_04.cpp
 2   // Pointer operators & and *.
 3   #include <iostream>
 4   using namespace std;
 5
 6   int main()
 7   {
 8      int a = 7; // assigned 7 to a
 9      int *aPtr = &a; // initialize aPtr with the address of int variable a
10
11      cout << "The address of a is " << &a
12         << "\nThe value of aPtr is " << aPtr;
13      cout << "\n\nThe value of a is " << a
14         << "\nThe value of *aPtr is " << *aPtr << endl;
15   } // end main
```

Fig. 8.4 | Pointer operators & and *. (Part 1 of 2.)

```
The address of a is 002DFD80
The value of aPtr is 002DFD80

The value of a is 7
The value of *aPtr is 7
```

Fig. 8.4 | Pointer operators & and *. (Part 2 of 2.)

Precedence and Associativity of the Operators Discussed So Far
Figure 8.5 lists the precedence and associativity of the operators introduced to this point. The address (&) and dereferencing operator (*) are *unary operators* on the fourth level.

Operators	Associativity	Type
:: ()	left to right *[See caution in Fig. 2.10 regarding grouping parentheses.]*	primary
() [] ++ -- static_cast<*type*>(*operand*)	left to right	postfix
++ -- + - ! & *	right to left	unary (prefix)
* / %	left to right	multiplicative
+ -	left to right	additive
<< >>	left to right	insertion/extraction
< <= > >=	left to right	relational
== !=	left to right	equality
&&	left to right	logical AND
||	left to right	logical OR
?:	right to left	conditional
= += -= *= /= %=	right to left	assignment
,	left to right	comma

Fig. 8.5 | Operator precedence and associativity of the operators discussed so far.

8.4 Pass-by-Reference with Pointers

There are three ways in C++ to pass arguments to a function—pass-by-value, pass-by-reference with reference arguments and **pass-by-reference with pointer arguments**. Chapter 6 compared and contrasted pass-by-reference with reference arguments and pass-by-value. Here, we explain pass-by-reference with pointer arguments.

Chapter 6 showed that return can return *one value* from a called function or simply return *control*. You also learned that arguments can be passed to a function using reference parameters, which enable the called function to *modify the original values of the arguments in the caller*. Reference parameters also enable programs to pass *large data objects* to a function and avoid the overhead of passing the objects by value (which, of course, copies the object). Pointers, like references, also can be used to modify one or more variables in the caller or to pass pointers to large data objects to avoid the overhead of passing the objects by value.

You can use pointers and the indirection operator (*) to accomplish pass-by-reference (exactly as pass-by-reference is done in C programs—C does not have references). When calling a function with an argument that should be modified, the *address* of the argument is passed. This is normally accomplished by applying the address operator (&) to the name of the variable whose value will be modified.

An Example of Pass-By-Value

Figure 8.6 and Fig. 8.7 present two versions of a function that cubes an integer. Figure 8.6 passes variable number *by value* (line 14) to function cubeByValue (lines 19–22), which cubes its argument and passes the new value back to main using a return statement (line 21). The new value is assigned to number (line 14) in main. The calling function has the opportunity to examine the function call's result *before* modifying variable number's value. For example, we could have stored the result of cubeByValue in another variable, examined its value and assigned the result to number only after determining that the returned value was reasonable.

```cpp
 1   // Fig. 8.6: fig08_06.cpp
 2   // Pass-by-value used to cube a variable's value.
 3   #include <iostream>
 4   using namespace std;
 5
 6   int cubeByValue( int ); // prototype
 7
 8   int main()
 9   {
10      int number = 5;
11
12      cout << "The original value of number is " << number;
13
14      number = cubeByValue( number ); // pass number by value to cubeByValue
15      cout << "\nThe new value of number is " << number << endl;
16   } // end main
17
18   // calculate and return cube of integer argument
19   int cubeByValue( int n )
20   {
21      return n * n * n; // cube local variable n and return result
22   } // end function cubeByValue
```

```
The original value of number is 5
The new value of number is 125
```

Fig. 8.6 | Pass-by-value used to cube a variable's value.

An Example of Pass-By-Reference with Pointers

Figure 8.7 passes the variable number to function cubeByReference using *pass-by-reference with a pointer argument* (line 15)—the *address* of number is passed to the function. Function cubeByReference (lines 21–24) specifies parameter nPtr (a pointer to int) to receive its argument. The function *uses the dereferenced pointer* to cube the value to which nPtr points (line 23). This *directly* changes the value of number in main (line 11). Line 23 is equivalent to

```cpp
*nPtr = (*nPtr) * (*nPtr) * (*nPtr); // cube *nPtr
```

```
 1   // Fig. 8.7: fig08_07.cpp
 2   // Pass-by-reference with a pointer argument used to cube a
 3   // variable's value.
 4   #include <iostream>
 5   using namespace std;
 6
 7   void cubeByReference( int * ); // prototype
 8
 9   int main()
10   {
11      int number = 5;
12
13      cout << "The original value of number is " << number;
14
15      cubeByReference( &number ); // pass number address to cubeByReference
16
17      cout << "\nThe new value of number is " << number << endl;
18   } // end main
19
20   // calculate cube of *nPtr; modifies variable number in main
21   void cubeByReference( int *nPtr )
22   {
23      *nPtr = *nPtr * *nPtr * *nPtr; // cube *nPtr
24   } // end function cubeByReference
```

```
The original value of number is 5
The new value of number is 125
```

Fig. 8.7 | Pass-by-reference with a pointer argument used to cube a variable's value.

A function receiving an *address* as an argument must define a *pointer parameter* to *receive* the address. For example, the header for function cubeByReference (line 21) specifies that cubeByReference receives the address of an int variable (i.e., a pointer to an int) as an argument, stores the address in nPtr and does *not* return a value.

Function cubeByReference's prototype (line 7) contains int * in parentheses. As with other types, it isn't necessary to include the *names* of pointer parameters in prototypes. Parameter names included for documentation purposes are *ignored* by the compiler.

Insight: All Arguments Are Passed By Value

In C++, *all* arguments are *always* passed by value. Passing a variable by reference with a pointer *does not actually pass anything by reference*—a pointer to that variable is *passed by value* and is *copied* into the function's corresponding pointer parameter. The called function can then access that variable in the caller simply by dereferencing the pointer, thus accomplishing *pass-by-reference*.

Graphical Analysis of Pass-By-Value and Pass-By-Reference

Figures 8.8–8.9 analyze graphically the execution of Fig. 8.6 and Fig. 8.7, respectively. In the diagrams, the values in blue rectangles above a given expression or variable represent the value of that expression or variable. Each diagram's right column shows functions cubeByValue (Fig. 8.6) and cubeByReference (Fig. 8.7) *only* when they're executing.

376   Chapter 8   Pointers

Step 1: Before `main` calls `cubeByValue`:

```
int main()                         number
{
   int number = 5;                    5

   number = cubeByValue( number );
}
```

Step 2: After `cubeByValue` receives the call:

```
int main()              number      int cubeByValue( int n )
{                                    {
   int number = 5;         5            return n * n * n;
                                     }
   number = cubeByValue( number );                        n
}                                                          5
```

Step 3: After `cubeByValue` cubes parameter n and before `cubeByValue` returns to `main`:

```
int main()              number      int cubeByValue( int n )
{                                    {          125
   int number = 5;         5            return n * n * n;
                                     }
   number = cubeByValue( number );                        n
}                                                          5
```

Step 4: After `cubeByValue` returns to `main` and before assigning the result to `number`:

```
int main()                         number
{
   int number = 5;                    5
                         125
   number = cubeByValue( number );
}
```

Step 5: After `main` completes the assignment to `number`:

```
int main()                         number
{
   int number = 5;                   125
        125
   number = cubeByValue( number );
}
```

Fig. 8.8 | Pass-by-value analysis of the program of Fig. 8.6.

Step 1: Before `main` calls `cubeByReference`:

```
int main()                          number
{
    int number = 5;                   5

    cubeByReference( &number );
}
```

Step 2: After `cubeByReference` receives the call and before `*nPtr` is cubed:

```
int main()                  number      void cubeByReference( int *nPtr )
{                                        {
    int number = 5;           5              *nPtr = *nPtr * *nPtr * *nPtr;
                                         }
    cubeByReference( &number );                                    nPtr
}
                                         call establishes this pointer
```

Step 3: Before `*nPtr` is assigned the result of the calculation 5 * 5 * 5:

```
int main()                  number      void cubeByReference( int *nPtr )
{                                        {                    125
    int number = 5;           5              *nPtr = *nPtr * *nPtr * *nPtr;
                                         }
    cubeByReference( &number );                                    nPtr
}
```

Step 4: After `*nPtr` is assigned 125 and before program control returns to `main`:

```
int main()                  number      void cubeByReference( int *nPtr )
{                                        {  125
    int number = 5;          125             *nPtr = *nPtr * *nPtr * *nPtr;
                                         }
    cubeByReference( &number );          called function modifies caller's   nPtr
}                                        variable
```

Step 5: After `cubeByReference` returns to `main`:

```
int main()                  number
{
    int number = 5;          125

    cubeByReference( &number );
}
```

Fig. 8.9 | Pass-by-reference analysis (with a pointer argument) of the program of Fig. 8.7.

8.5 Built-In Arrays

In Chapter 7, we used the array class template to represent *fixed-size* lists and tables of values. We also used the vector class template, which is similar to array, but can also grow (or shrink as you'll see in Chapter 15) dynamically to accommodate more or fewer elements. Here we present *built-in arrays*, which are also *fixed-size* data structures.

Declaring a Built-In Array
To specify the type of the elements and the number of elements required by a built-in array, use a declaration of the form:

```
type arrayName[ arraySize ];
```

The compiler reserves the appropriate amount of memory. The *arraySize* must be an integer constant greater than zero. For example, to tell the compiler to reserve 12 elements for built-in array of ints named c, use the declaration

```
int c[ 12 ]; // c is a built-in array of 12 integers
```

Accessing a Built-In Array's Elements
As with array objects, you use the subscript ([]) operator to access the individual elements of a built-in array. Recall from Chapter 7 that the subscript ([]) operator does *not* provide bounds checking for array objects—this is also true for built-in arrays.

Initializing Built-In Arrays
You can initialize the elements of a built-in array using an *initializer list*. For example,

```
int n[ 5 ] = { 50, 20, 30, 10, 40 };
```

creates a built-in array of five ints and initializes them to the values in the initializer list. If you provide fewer initializers than the number of elements, the remaining elements are *value initialized*—fundamental numeric types are set to 0, bools are set to false, pointers are set to nullptr and class objects are initialized by their default constructors. If you provide too many initializers a compilation error occurs. The new C++11 list-initialization syntax that we introduced in Chapter 4 is based on the built-in array initializer-list syntax.

If a built-in array's size is *omitted* from a declaration with an initializer list, the compiler sizes the built-in array to the number of elements in the initializer list. For example,

```
int n[] = { 50, 20, 30, 10, 40 };
```

creates a five-element array.

Error-Prevention Tip 8.3
Always specify a built-in array's size, even when providing an initializer list. This enables the compiler to ensure that you do not provide too many initializers.

Passing Built-In Arrays to Functions
The value of a built-in array's name is implicitly convertible to the address of the built-in array's first element. So arrayName is implicitly convertible to &arrayName[0]. For this reason,

you don't need to take the address (&) of a built-in array to pass it to a function—you simply pass the built-in array's name. As you saw in Section 8.4, a function that receives a pointer to a variable in the caller can *modify* that variable in the caller. For built-in arrays, this means that the called function can modify *all* the elements of a built-in array in the caller—unless the function precedes the corresponding built-in array parameter with const to indicate that the elements should *not* be modified.

Software Engineering Observation 8.1

Applying the const type qualifier to a built-in array parameter in a function definition to prevent the original built-in array from being modified in the function body is another example of the principle of least privilege. Functions should not be given the capability to modify a built-in array unless it's absolutely necessary.

Declaring Built-In Array Parameters

You can declare a built-in array parameter in a function header, as follows:

```
int sumElements( const int values[], const size_t numberOfElements )
```

which indicates that the function's first argument should be a one-dimensional built-in array of ints that should *not* be modified by the function. Unlike array objects, built-in arrays don't know their own size, so a function that processes a built-in array should have parameters to receive both the built-in array *and* its size.

The preceding header can also be written as:

```
int sumElements( const int *values, const size_t numberOfElements )
```

The compiler does not differentiate between a function that receives a pointer and a function that receives a built-in array. This, of course, means that the function must "know" when it's receiving a built-in array or simply a single variable that's being passed by reference. When the compiler encounters a function parameter for a one-dimensional built-in array of the form const int values[], the compiler converts the parameter to the pointer notation const int *values (that is, "values is a pointer to an integer constant"). These forms of declaring a one-dimensional built-in array parameter are interchangeable—for *clarity* you should use the [] notation when the function expects a built-in array argument.

C++11: Standard Library Functions **begin** *and* **end**

In Section 7.7, we showed how to sort an array object with the C++ Standard Library function sort. We sorted an array of strings called colors as follows:

```
sort( colors.begin(), colors.end() ); // sort contents of colors
```

The array class's begin and end functions specified that the entire array should be sorted. Function sort (and many other C++ Standard Library functions) can also be applied to built-in arrays. For example, to sort the built-in array n shown earlier in this section, you can write:

```
sort( begin( n ), end( n ) ); // sort contents of built-in array n
```

C++11's new **begin** and **end** functions (from header <iterator>) each receive a built-in array as an argument and return a pointer that can be used to represent ranges of elements to process in C++ Standard Library functions like sort.

Built-In Array Limitations

Built-in arrays have several limitations:

- They *cannot be compared* using the relational and equality operators—you must use a loop to compare two built-in arrays element by element.

- They *cannot be assigned* to one another.

- They *don't know their own size*—a function that processes a built-in array typically receives *both* the built-in array's *name* and its *size* as arguments.

- They *don't provide automatic bounds checking*—you must ensure that array-access expressions use subscripts that are within the built-in array's bounds.

Objects of class templates `array` and `vector` are safer, more robust and provide more capabilities than built-in arrays.

Sometimes Built-In Arrays Are Required

In contemporary C++ code, you should use the more robust `array` (or `vector`) objects to represent lists and tables of values. However, there are cases in which built-in arrays *must* be used, such as processing a program's **command-line arguments**. You supply command-line arguments to a program by placing them after the program's name when executing it from the command line. Such arguments typically pass options to a program. For example, on a Windows computer, the command

```
dir /p
```

uses the /p argument to list the contents of the current directory, pausing after each screen of information. Similarly, on Linux or OS X, the following command uses the -la argument to list the contents of the current directory with details about each file and directory:

```
ls -la
```

Command-line arguments are passed to `main` as a built-in array of pointer-based strings (Section 8.10). Appendix F shows how to process command-line arguments.

8.6 Using `const` with Pointers

Recall that `const` enables you to inform the compiler that the value of a particular variable should *not* be modified. Many possibilities exist for using (or *not* using) `const` with function parameters, so how do you choose the most appropriate? Let the *principle of least privilege* be your guide. Always give a function *enough* access to the data in its parameters to accomplish its specified task, *but no more*. This section discusses how to combine `const` with pointer declarations to enforce the principle of least privilege.

Chapter 6 explained that when an argument is passed by value, a *copy* of the argument is passed to the function. If the copy is *modified* in the *called* function, the original value in the caller *does not change*. In some instances, even the copy of the argument's value should *not* be altered in the called function.

Consider a function that takes a pointer to the initial element of a built-in array and the array's size as arguments and subsequently displays the built-in array's elements. Such a function should loop through the elements and output each individually. The built-in array's size is used in the function's body to determine the highest subscript so the loop can terminate when the displaying completes. The size does not need to change in the function body, so it should be declared const to *ensure* that it will not change. Because the built-in array is only being displayed, it, too, should be declared const. This is especially important because built-in arrays are *always* passed by reference and could easily be changed in the called function. An attempt to modify a const value is a *compilation* error.

Software Engineering Observation 8.2
If a value does not (or should not) change in the body of a function to which it's passed, the parameter should be declared const.

Error-Prevention Tip 8.4
Before using a function, check its function prototype to determine the parameters that it can and cannot modify.

There are four ways to pass a pointer to a function: a *nonconstant pointer to nonconstant data*, a *nonconstant pointer to constant data* (Fig. 8.10), a *constant pointer to nonconstant data* (Fig. 8.11) and a *constant pointer to constant data* (Fig. 8.12). Each combination provides a different level of access privilege.

8.6.1 Nonconstant Pointer to Nonconstant Data

The highest access is granted by a **nonconstant pointer to nonconstant data**—the *data can be modified* through the dereferenced pointer, and the *pointer can be modified* to point to other data. Such a pointer's declaration (e.g., int *countPtr) does *not* include const.

8.6.2 Nonconstant Pointer to Constant Data

A **nonconstant pointer to constant data** is a pointer that can be modified to point to *any* data item of the appropriate type, but the data to which it points *cannot* be modified through that pointer. Such a pointer might be used to *receive* a built-in array argument to a function that should be allowed to read the elements, but *not* modify them. Any attempt to modify the data in the function results in a compilation error. The declaration for such a pointer places const to the *left* of the pointer's type, as in

```
const int *countPtr;
```

The declaration is read from *right to left* as "countPtr is a pointer to an integer *constant*" or more precisely, "countPtr is a *non-constant* pointer to an integer *constant.*"

Figure 8.10 demonstrates GNU C++'s compilation error message produced when attempting to compile a function that receives a *nonconstant pointer* to *constant data*, then tries to use that pointer to modify the data.

```
1   // Fig. 8.10: fig08_10.cpp
2   // Attempting to modify data through a
3   // nonconstant pointer to constant data.
4
5   void f( const int * ); // prototype
6
7   int main()
8   {
```

Fig. 8.10 | Attempting to modify data through a nonconstant pointer to const data. (Part 1 of 2.)

```
9      int y = 0;
10
11     f( &y ); // f will attempt an illegal modification
12  } // end main
13
14  // constant variable cannot be modified through xPtr
15  void f( const int *xPtr )
16  {
17     *xPtr = 100; // error: cannot modify a const object
18  } // end function f
```

GNU C++ compiler error message:

```
fig08_10.cpp: In function 'void f(const int*)':
fig08_10.cpp:17:12: error: assignment of read-only location '* xPtr'
```

Fig. 8.10 | Attempting to modify data through a nonconstant pointer to const data. (Part 2 of 2.)

When a function is called with a built-in array as an argument, its contents are effectively passed by reference because the built-in array's name is implicitly convertible to the address of the built-in array's first element. However, *by default, objects such as arrays and vectors are passed by value—a copy of the entire object is passed*. This requires the execution-time overhead of making a *copy* of each data item in the object and storing it on the function call stack. When a pointer to an object is passed, only a copy of the *address* of the object must be made—the *object itself is not copied*.

Performance Tip 8.1
If they do not need to be modified by the called function, pass large objects using pointers to constant data or references to constant data, to obtain the performance benefits of pass-by-reference and avoid the copy overhead of pass-by-value.

Software Engineering Observation 8.3
Passing large objects using pointers to constant data, or references to constant data offers the security of pass-by-value.

Software Engineering Observation 8.4
Use pass-by-value to pass fundamental-type arguments (e.g., ints, doubles, etc.) to a function unless the caller explicitly *requires that the called function be able to directly modify the value in the caller. This is another example of the principle of least privilege.*

8.6.3 Constant Pointer to Nonconstant Data

A constant pointer to nonconstant data is a pointer that always points to the same memory location, and the data at that location *can* be modified through the pointer. Pointers that are declared const *must be initialized when they're declared*, but if the pointer is a function parameter, it's *initialized with the pointer that's passed to the function*.

The program of Fig. 8.11 attempts to modify a constant pointer. Line 11 declares pointer ptr to be of type int * const. The declaration is read from *right to left* as "ptr is a constant pointer to a nonconstant integer." The pointer is *initialized* with the address of integer variable x. Line 14 attempts to *assign* the address of y to ptr, but the compiler generates an error message. No error occurs when line 13 assigns the value 7 to *ptr—the nonconstant value to which ptr points *can* be modified using the dereferenced ptr, even though ptr itself has been declared const.

```
1   // Fig. 8.11: fig08_11.cpp
2   // Attempting to modify a constant pointer to nonconstant data.
3
4   int main()
5   {
6      int x, y;
7
8      // ptr is a constant pointer to an integer that can
9      // be modified through ptr, but ptr always points to the
10     // same memory location.
11     int * const ptr = &x; // const pointer must be initialized
12
13     *ptr = 7; // allowed: *ptr is not const
14     ptr = &y; // error: ptr is const; cannot assign to it a new address
15  } // end main
```

Microsoft Visual C++ compiler error message:

```
you cannot assign to a variable that is const
```

Fig. 8.11 | Attempting to modify a constant pointer to nonconstant data.

8.6.4 Constant Pointer to Constant Data

The *minimum* access privilege is granted by a **constant pointer to constant data**. Such a pointer *always* points to the *same* memory location, and the data at that location *cannot* be modified via the pointer. This is how a built-in array should be passed to a function that *only reads* from the built-in array, using array subscript notation, and *does not modify* the built-in array. The program of Fig. 8.12 declares pointer variable ptr to be of type const int * const (line 13). This declaration is read from *right to left* as "ptr is a *constant pointer to an integer constant*." The figure shows the Xcode LLVM compiler's error messages that are generated when an attempt is made to modify the data to which ptr points (line 17) and when an attempt is made to modify the address stored in the pointer variable (line 18)—these show up on the lines of code with the errors in the Xcode text editor. In line 15, no errors occur when the program attempts to dereference ptr, or when the program attempts to output the value to which ptr points, because *neither* the pointer *nor* the data it points to is being modified in this statement.

```
1   // Fig. 8.12: fig08_12.cpp
2   // Attempting to modify a constant pointer to constant data.
3   #include <iostream>
```

Fig. 8.12 | Attempting to modify a constant pointer to constant data. (Part 1 of 2.)

```
 4    using namespace std;
 5
 6    int main()
 7    {
 8       int x = 5, y;
 9
10       // ptr is a constant pointer to a constant integer.
11       // ptr always points to the same location; the integer
12       // at that location cannot be modified.
13       const int *const ptr = &x;
14
15       cout << *ptr << endl;
16
17       *ptr = 7; // error: *ptr is const; cannot assign new value
18       ptr = &y; // error: ptr is const; cannot assign new address
19    } // end main
```

Xcode LLVM compiler error message:

```
Read-only variable is not assignable
Read-only variable is not assignable
```

Fig. 8.12 | Attempting to modify a constant pointer to constant data. (Part 2 of 2.)

8.7 sizeof Operator

The *compile time* unary operator `sizeof` determines the size in bytes of a built-in array or of any other data type, variable or constant *during program compilation*. When applied to a built-in array's *name*, as in Fig. 8.13 (line 13), the `sizeof` operator returns the *total number of bytes in the built-in array* as a value of type `size_t`. The computer we used to compile this program stores variables of type `double` in 8 bytes of memory, and `numbers` is declared to have 20 elements (line 11), so it uses 160 bytes in memory. When applied to a *pointer parameter* (line 22) in a function that *receives a built-in array as an argument*, the `sizeof` operator returns the size of the *pointer* in bytes (4 on the system we used)—*not* the built-in array's size.

Common Programming Error 8.3

Using the `sizeof` operator in a function to find the size in bytes of a built-in array parameter results in the size in bytes of a pointer, not the size in bytes of the built-in array.

```
1    // Fig. 8.13: fig08_13.cpp
2    // Sizeof operator when used on a built-in array's name
3    // returns the number of bytes in the built-in array.
4    #include <iostream>
5    using namespace std;
6
```

Fig. 8.13 | `sizeof` operator when applied to a built-in array's name returns the number of bytes in the built-in array. (Part 1 of 2.)

```
 7   size_t getSize( double * ); // prototype
 8
 9   int main()
10   {
11      double numbers[ 20 ]; // 20 doubles; occupies 160 bytes on our system
12
13      cout << "The number of bytes in the array is " << sizeof( numbers );
14
15      cout << "\nThe number of bytes returned by getSize is "
16         << getSize( numbers ) << endl;
17   } // end main
18
19   // return size of ptr
20   size_t getSize( double *ptr )
21   {
22      return sizeof( ptr );
23   } // end function getSize
```

```
The number of bytes in the array is 160
The number of bytes returned by getSize is 4
```

Fig. 8.13 | sizeof operator when applied to a built-in array's name returns the number of bytes in the built-in array. (Part 2 of 2.)

The number of *elements* in a built-in array can be determined using the results of two sizeof operations. For example, to determine the number of elements in the built-in array numbers, use the following expression (which is evaluated at *compile time*):

```
sizeof numbers / sizeof( numbers[ 0 ] )
```

The expression divides the number of bytes in numbers (160, assuming 8 byte doubles) by the number of bytes in the built-in array's zeroth element (8)—resulting in the number of elements in numbers (20).

Determining the Sizes of the Fundamental Types, a Built-In Array and a Pointer
Figure 8.14 uses sizeof to calculate the number of bytes used to store many of the standard data types. The output was produced using the default settings in Visual C++ 2012 on a Windows 7 computer. Type sizes are *platform dependent*. On another system, for example, double and long double may be of different sizes.

```
 1   // Fig. 8.14: fig08_14.cpp
 2   // sizeof operator used to determine standard data type sizes.
 3   #include <iostream>
 4   using namespace std;
 5
 6   int main()
 7   {
 8      char c; // variable of type char
 9      short s; // variable of type short
```

Fig. 8.14 | sizeof operator used to determine standard data type sizes. (Part 1 of 2.)

```
10      int i; // variable of type int
11      long l; // variable of type long
12      long ll; // variable of type long long
13      float f; // variable of type float
14      double d; // variable of type double
15      long double ld; // variable of type long double
16      int array[ 20 ]; // built-in array of int
17      int *ptr = array; // variable of type int *
18
19      cout << "sizeof c = " << sizeof c
20         << "\tsizeof(char) = " << sizeof( char )
21         << "\nsizeof s = " << sizeof s
22         << "\tsizeof(short) = " << sizeof( short )
23         << "\nsizeof i = " << sizeof i
24         << "\tsizeof(int) = " << sizeof( int )
25         << "\nsizeof l = " << sizeof l
26         << "\tsizeof(long) = " << sizeof( long )
27         << "\nsizeof ll = " << sizeof ll
28         << "\tsizeof(long long) = " << sizeof( long long )
29         << "\nsizeof f = " << sizeof f
30         << "\tsizeof(float) = " << sizeof( float )
31         << "\nsizeof d = " << sizeof d
32         << "\tsizeof(double) = " << sizeof( double )
33         << "\nsizeof ld = " << sizeof ld
34         << "\tsizeof(long double) = " << sizeof( long double )
35         << "\nsizeof array = " << sizeof array
36         << "\nsizeof ptr = " << sizeof ptr << endl;
37   } // end main
```

```
sizeof c = 1       sizeof(char) = 1
sizeof s = 2       sizeof(short) = 2
sizeof i = 4       sizeof(int) = 4
sizeof l = 4       sizeof(long) = 4
sizeof ll = 8      sizeof(long long) = 8
sizeof f = 4       sizeof(float) = 4
sizeof d = 8       sizeof(double) = 8
sizeof ld = 8      sizeof(long double) = 8
sizeof array = 80
sizeof ptr = 4
```

Fig. 8.14 | `sizeof` operator used to determine standard data type sizes. (Part 2 of 2.)

 Portability Tip 8.1
The number of bytes used to store a particular data type may vary among systems. When writing programs that depend on data type sizes, always use `sizeof` to determine the number of bytes used to store the data types.

Operator `sizeof` can be applied to any expression or type name. When `sizeof` is applied to a variable name (which is not a built-in array's name) or other expression, the number of bytes used to store the specific type of the expression is returned. The parentheses used with `sizeof` are required *only* if a type name (e.g., `int`) is supplied as its operand. The parentheses used with `sizeof` are *not* required when `sizeof`'s operand is an expression. Remember that `sizeof` is a *compile-time* operator, so `sizeof`'s operand is not evaluated.

8.8 Pointer Expressions and Pointer Arithmetic

This section describes the operators that can have *pointers* as operands and how these operators are used with pointers. C++ enables **pointer arithmetic**—a few arithmetic operations may be performed on pointers. *Pointer arithmetic is appropriate only for pointers that point to built-in array elements.*

A pointer may be incremented (++) or decremented (--), an integer may be added to a pointer (+ or +=) or subtracted from a pointer (- or -=), or one pointer may be subtracted from another of the same type—this particular operation is appropriate only for two pointers that point to elements of the *same* built-in array.

Portability Tip 8.2

Most computers today have four-byte or eight-byte integers. Because the results of pointer arithmetic depend on the size of the objects a pointer points to, pointer arithmetic is machine dependent.

Assume that int v[5] has been declared and that its first element is at memory location 3000. Assume that pointer vPtr has been initialized to point to v[0] (i.e., the value of vPtr is 3000). Figure 8.15 diagrams this situation for a machine with four-byte integers. Variable vPtr can be initialized to point to v with either of the following statements (because a built-in array's name evaluates to the address of its zeroth element):

```
int *vPtr = v;
int *vPtr = &v[ 0 ];
```

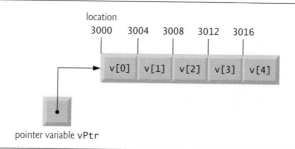

Fig. 8.15 | Built-in array v and a pointer variable int *vPtr that points to v.

Adding Integers to and Subtracting Integers from Pointers
In conventional arithmetic, the addition 3000 + 2 yields the value 3002. This is normally *not* the case with pointer arithmetic. When an integer is added to, or subtracted from, a pointer, the pointer is *not* simply incremented or decremented by that integer, but by that integer *times the size of the object to which the pointer refers.* The number of bytes depends on the object's data type. For example, the statement

```
vPtr += 2;
```

would produce 3008 (from the calculation 3000 + 2 * 4), assuming that an int is stored in four bytes of memory. In the built-in array v, vPtr would now point to v[2] (Fig. 8.16). If an integer is stored in eight bytes of memory, then the preceding calculation would result in memory location 3016 (3000 + 2 * 8).

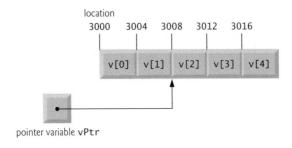

Fig. 8.16 | Pointer vPtr after pointer arithmetic.

If vPtr had been incremented to 3016, which points to v[4], the statement

```
vPtr -= 4;
```

would set vPtr back to 3000—the beginning of the built-in array. If a pointer is being incremented or decremented by one, the increment (++) and decrement (--) operators can be used. Each of the statements

```
++vPtr;
vPtr++;
```

increments the pointer to point to the built-in array's *next* element. Each of the statements

```
--vPtr;
vPtr--;
```

decrements the pointer to point to the built-in array's *previous* element.

 Error-Prevention Tip 8.5

There's no bounds checking on pointer arithmetic. You must ensure that every pointer arithmetic operation that adds an integer to or subtracts an integer from a pointer results in a pointer that references an element within the built-in array's bounds.

Subtracting Pointers
Pointer variables pointing to the *same* built-in array may be subtracted from one another. For example, if vPtr contains the address 3000 and v2Ptr contains the address 3008, the statement

```
x = v2Ptr - vPtr;
```

would assign to x the *number of built-in array elements* from vPtr to v2Ptr—in this case, 2. *Pointer arithmetic is meaningful only on a pointer that points to a built-in array.* We cannot assume that two variables of the same type are stored contiguously in memory unless they're adjacent elements of a built-in array.

 Common Programming Error 8.4

Subtracting or comparing two pointers that do not refer to elements of the same *built-in array is a logic error.*

Pointer Assignment

A pointer can be assigned to another pointer if both pointers are of the *same* type. Otherwise, a cast operator (normally a `reinterpret_cast`; discussed in Section 14.7) must be used to convert the value of the pointer on the right of the assignment to the pointer type on the left of the assignment. The exception to this rule is the **pointer to void** (i.e., **void ***), which is a generic pointer capable of representing *any* pointer type. *Any pointer to a fundamental type or class type can be assigned to a pointer of type* void * *without casting.* However, a pointer of type void * *cannot* be assigned directly to a pointer of another type—the pointer of type void * must first be *cast* to the proper pointer type.

Cannot Dereference a **void ***

A void * pointer *cannot* be dereferenced. For example, the compiler "knows" that a pointer to int refers to four bytes of memory on a machine with four-byte integers, but a pointer to void simply contains a memory address for an *unknown* data type—the compiler does *not* know the precise number of bytes to which the pointer refers and the data type. The compiler must know the data type to determine the number of bytes to dereference for a particular pointer—for a pointer to void, this number of bytes *cannot* be determined.

Common Programming Error 8.5

Assigning a pointer of one type to a pointer of another (other than void *) *without using a cast (normally a* `reinterpret_cast`) *is a compilation error.*

Common Programming Error 8.6

The allowed operations on void * *pointers are: comparing* void * *pointers with other pointers, casting* void * *pointers to other pointer types and assigning addresses to* void * *pointers. All other operations on* void * *pointers are compilation errors.*

Comparing Pointers

Pointers can be compared using equality and relational operators. Comparisons using relational operators are meaningless unless the pointers point to elements of the *same* built-in array. Pointer comparisons compare the *addresses* stored in the pointers. A comparison of two pointers pointing to the same built-in array could show, for example, that one pointer points to a higher numbered element of the built-in array than the other pointer does. A common use of pointer comparison is determining whether a pointer has the value nullptr, 0 or NULL (i.e., the pointer does not point to anything).

8.9 Relationship Between Pointers and Built-In Arrays

Built-in arrays and pointers are intimately related in C++ and may be used *almost* interchangeably. Pointers can be used to do any operation involving array subscripting.

Assume the following declarations

```
int b[ 5 ]; // create 5-element int array b; b is a const pointer
int *bPtr; // create int pointer bPtr, which isn't a const pointer
```

We can set bPtr to the address of the first element in the built-in array b with the statement

```
bPtr = b; // assign address of built-in array b to bPtr
```

This is equivalent to assigning the address of the first element as follows:

```
bPtr = &b[ 0 ]; // also assigns address of built-in array b to bPtr
```

Pointer/Offset Notation

Built-in array element b[3] can alternatively be referenced with the pointer expression

```
*( bPtr + 3 )
```

The 3 in the preceding expression is the **offset** to the pointer. When the pointer points to the beginning of a built-in array, the offset indicates which built-in array element should be referenced, and the offset value is identical to the subscript. This notation is referred to as **pointer/offset notation**. The parentheses are necessary, because the precedence of * is higher than that of +. Without the parentheses, the preceding expression would add 3 to a copy of *bPtr's value (i.e., 3 would be added to b[0], assuming that bPtr points to the beginning of the built-in array).

Just as the built-in array element can be referenced with a pointer expression, the *address*

```
&b[ 3 ]
```

can be written with the pointer expression

```
bPtr + 3
```

Pointer/Offset Notation with the Built-In Array's Name as the Pointer

The built-in array name can be treated as a pointer and used in pointer arithmetic. For example, the expression

```
*( b + 3 )
```

also refers to the element b[3]. In general, all subscripted built-in array expressions can be written with a pointer and an offset. In this case, pointer/offset notation was used with the built-in array's name as a pointer. The preceding expression does *not* modify the built-in array's name; b still points to the built-in array's first element.

Pointer/Subscript Notation

Pointers can be subscripted exactly as built-in arrays can. For example, the expression

```
bPtr[ 1 ]
```

refers to b[1]; this expression uses **pointer/subscript notation**.

The Name of a Built-In Array Is Not Modifiable

The expression

```
b += 3
```

causes a compilation error, because it attempts to *modify* the value of the built-in array's name with pointer arithmetic.

Good Programming Practice 8.2

For clarity, use built-in array notation instead of pointer notation when manipulating built-in arrays.

Demonstrating the Relationship Between Pointers and Built-In Arrays
Figure 8.17 uses the four notations discussed in this section for referring to built-in array elements—*array subscript notation, pointer/offset notation with the built-in array's name as a pointer, pointer subscript notation* and *pointer/offset notation with a pointer*—to accomplish the same task, namely displaying the four elements of the built-in array of ints named b.

```cpp
 1   // Fig. 8.17: fig08_17.cpp
 2   // Using subscripting and pointer notations with built-in arrays.
 3   #include <iostream>
 4   using namespace std;
 5
 6   int main()
 7   {
 8      int b[] = { 10, 20, 30, 40 }; // create 4-element built-in array b
 9      int *bPtr = b; // set bPtr to point to built-in array b
10
11      // output built-in array b using array subscript notation
12      cout << "Array b displayed with:\n\nArray subscript notation\n";
13
14      for ( size_t i = 0; i < 4; ++i )
15         cout << "b[" << i << "] = " << b[ i ] << '\n';
16
17      // output built-in array b using array name and pointer/offset notation
18      cout << "\nPointer/offset notation where "
19         << "the pointer is the array name\n";
20
21      for ( size_t offset1 = 0; offset1 < 4; ++offset1 )
22         cout << "*(b + " << offset1 << ") = " << *( b + offset1 ) << '\n';
23
24      // output built-in array b using bPtr and array subscript notation
25      cout << "\nPointer subscript notation\n";
26
27      for ( size_t j = 0; j < 4; ++j )
28         cout << "bPtr[" << j << "] = " << bPtr[ j ] << '\n';
29
30      cout << "\nPointer/offset notation\n";
31
32      // output built-in array b using bPtr and pointer/offset notation
33      for ( size_t offset2 = 0; offset2 < 4; ++offset2 )
34         cout << "*(bPtr + " << offset2 << ") = "
35            << *( bPtr + offset2 ) << '\n';
36   } // end main
```

```
Array b displayed with:

Array subscript notation
b[0] = 10
b[1] = 20
b[2] = 30
b[3] = 40
```

Fig. 8.17 | Using subscripting and pointer notations with built-in arrays. (Part 1 of 2.)

```
Pointer/offset notation where the pointer is the array name
*(b + 0) = 10
*(b + 1) = 20
*(b + 2) = 30
*(b + 3) = 40

Pointer subscript notation
bPtr[0] = 10
bPtr[1] = 20
bPtr[2] = 30
bPtr[3] = 40

Pointer/offset notation
*(bPtr + 0) = 10
*(bPtr + 1) = 20
*(bPtr + 2) = 30
*(bPtr + 3) = 40
```

Fig. 8.17 | Using subscripting and pointer notations with built-in arrays. (Part 2 of 2.)

8.10 Pointer-Based Strings

We've already used the C++ Standard Library string class to represent strings as full-fledged objects. For example, the GradeBook class case study in Chapters 3–7 represents a course name using a string object. Chapter 21 presents class string in detail. This section introduces C-style, pointer-based strings (as defined by the C programming language), which we'll simply call C strings. *C++'s string class is preferred for use in new programs, because it eliminates many of the security problems and bugs that can be caused by manipulating C strings.* We cover C strings here for a deeper understanding of pointers and built-in arrays. Also, if you work with legacy C and C++ programs, you're likely to encounter pointer-based strings. We cover C strings in detail in Appendix F.

Characters and Character Constants

Characters are the fundamental building blocks of C++ source programs. Every program is composed of a sequence of characters that—when grouped together meaningfully—is interpreted by the compiler as instructions used to accomplish a task. A program may contain character constants. A character constant is an integer value represented as a character in single quotes. The *value* of a character constant is the integer value of the character in the machine's character set. For example, 'z' represents the integer value of z (122 in the ASCII character set; see Appendix B), and '\n' represents the integer value of newline (10 in the ASCII character set).

Strings

A string is a series of characters treated as a single unit. A string may include letters, digits and various special characters such as +, -, *, /and $. String literals, or string constants, in C++ are written in double quotation marks as follows:

```
"John Q. Doe"              (a name)
"9999 Main Street"         (a street address)
"Maynard, Massachusetts"   (a city and state)
"(201) 555-1212"           (a telephone number)
```

Pointer-Based Strings

A pointer-based string is a built-in array of characters ending with a null character ('\0'), which marks where the string terminates in memory. A string is accessed via a pointer to its first character. The sizeof a string literal is the length of the string *including* the terminating null character. Pointer-based strings are like built-in arrays—a built-in array name is also a pointer to its first element.

String Literals as Initializers

A string literal may be used as an initializer in the declaration of either a built-in array of chars or a variable of type const char *. The declarations

```
char color[] = "blue";
const char *colorPtr = "blue";
```

each initialize a variable to the string "blue". The first declaration creates a *five-element* built-in array color containing the characters 'b', 'l', 'u', 'e' *and* '\0'. The second declaration creates pointer variable colorPtr that points to the letter b in the string "blue" (which ends in '\0') somewhere in memory. String literals have *static storage duration* (they exist for the duration of the program) and may or may not be *shared* if the same string literal is referenced from multiple locations in a program.

Error-Prevention Tip 8.6
If you need to modify the contents of a string literal, store it in a built-in array of chars first.

Character Constants as Initializers

The declaration char color[] = "blue"; could also be written

```
char color[] = { 'b', 'l', 'u', 'e', '\0' };
```

which uses character constants in single quotes (') as initializers for each element of the built-in array. When declaring a built-in array of chars to contain a string, the built-in array must be large enough to store the string *and* its terminating null character. The compiler determines the size of the built-in array in the preceding declaration, based on the *number of initializers in the initializer list.*

Common Programming Error 8.7
Not allocating sufficient space in a built-in array of chars to store the null character that terminates a string is a logic error.

Common Programming Error 8.8
Creating or using a C string that does not contain a terminating null character can lead to logic errors.

Error-Prevention Tip 8.7
When storing a string of characters in a built-in array of chars, be sure that the built-in array is large enough to hold the largest string that will be stored. C++ allows strings of any length. If a string is longer than the built-in array of chars in which it's to be stored, characters beyond the end of the built-in array will overwrite data in memory following the built-in array, leading to logic errors and potential security breaches.

394 Chapter 8 Pointers

Accessing Characters in a C String

Because a C string is a built-in array of characters, we can access individual characters in a string directly with array subscript notation. For example, in the preceding declaration, `color[0]` is the character `'b'`, `color[2]` is `'u'` and `color[4]` is the null character.

Reading Strings into char Built-In Arrays with cin

A string can be read into a built-in array of `char`s using stream extraction with `cin`. For example, the following statement reads a string into the built-in 20-element array of `char`s named `word`:

```
cin >> word;
```

The string entered by the user is stored in `word`. The preceding statement reads characters until a white-space character or end-of-file indicator is encountered. The string should be no longer than 19 characters to leave room for the terminating null character. The `setw` stream manipulator can be used to *ensure* that the string read into word *does not exceed the size of the built-in array*. For example, the statement

```
cin >> setw( 20 ) >> word;
```

specifies that `cin` should read a maximum of 19 characters into word and save the 20th location to store the terminating null character for the string. The `setw` stream manipulator is not a sticky setting—it applies *only* to the next value being input. If more than 19 characters are entered, the remaining characters are not saved in word, *but they will be in the input stream and can be read by the next input operation.*[1] Of course, any input operation can also fail. We show how to detect input failures in Section 13.8.

Reading Lines of Text into char Built-In Arrays with cin.getline

In some cases, it's desirable to input an *entire line of text* into a built-in array of `char`s. For this purpose, the `cin` object provides the member function **getline**, which takes three arguments—a *built-in array of chars* in which the line of text will be stored, a *length* and a *delimiter character*. For example, the statements

```
char sentence[ 80 ];
cin.getline( sentence, 80, '\n' );
```

declare `sentence` as a built-in array of 80 characters and read a line of text from the keyboard into the built-in array. The function stops reading characters when the delimiter character `'\n'` is encountered, when the *end-of-file indicator* is entered or when the number of characters read so far is one less than the length specified in the second argument. The last character in the built-in array is reserved for the *terminating null character*. If the delimiter character is encountered, it's read and *discarded*. The third argument to `cin.getline` has `'\n'` as a default value, so the preceding function call could have been written as:

```
cin.getline( sentence, 80 );
```

Chapter 13, Stream Input/Output: A Deeper Look, provides a detailed discussion of `cin.getline` and other input/output functions.

---

1. To learn how to ignore extra characters in the input steam, see the article at: www.daniweb.com/software-development/cpp/threads/90228/flushing-the-input-stream.

Displaying C Strings

A built-in array of chars representing a null-terminated string can be output with cout and
<<. The statement

```
cout << sentence;
```

displays the built-in array sentence. Like cin, cout does not care how large the built-in
array of chars is. The characters are output until a *terminating null character* is encountered; the null character is *not* displayed. [*Note:* cin and cout assume that built-in array of
chars should be processed as strings terminated by null characters; cin and cout do not
provide similar input and output processing capabilities for other built-in array types.]

8.11 Wrap-Up

In this chapter we provided a detailed introduction to pointers—variables that contain memory addresses as their values. We began by demonstrating how to declare and initialize pointers. You saw how to use the address operator (&) to assign the address of a variable to a pointer
and the indirection operator (*) to access the data stored in the variable indirectly referenced
by a pointer. We discussed passing arguments by reference using pointer arguments.

We discussed how to declare and use built-in arrays, which C++ inherited from the C
programming language. You learned how to use const with pointers to enforce the principle of least privilege. We demonstrated using nonconstant pointers to nonconstant data,
nonconstant pointers to constant data, constant pointers to nonconstant data, and constant pointers to constant data. We discussed the compile-time sizeof operator, which
can be used to determine the sizes of data types and variables in bytes at compile time.

We discussed how to use pointers in arithmetic and comparison expressions. You saw
that pointer arithmetic can be used to move from one element of a built-in array to
another. We briefly introduced pointer-based strings.

In the next chapter, we begin our deeper treatment of classes. You'll learn about the
scope of a class's members and how to keep objects in a consistent state. You'll also learn
about using special member functions called constructors and destructors, which execute
when an object is created and destroyed, respectively, and we'll discuss when constructors
and destructors are called. In addition, we'll demonstrate using default arguments with
constructors and using default memberwise assignment to assign one object of a class to
another object of the same class. We'll also discuss the danger of returning a reference to
a private data member of a class.

Summary

Section 8.2 Pointer Variable Declarations and Initialization
- Pointers are variables that contain as their values memory addresses of other variables.
- The declaration

```
int *ptr;
```

declares ptr to be a pointer to a variable of type int and is read, "ptr is a pointer to int." The *
as used here in a declaration indicates that the variable is a pointer.

- You can initialize a pointer with an address of an object of the same type or with `nullptr` (p. 370).
- The only integer that can be assigned to a pointer without casting is 0.

Section 8.3 Pointer Operators
- The & (address) operator (p. 371) obtains the memory address of its operand.
- The operand of the address operator must be a variable name (or another *lvalue*); the address operator cannot be applied to constants or to expressions that result in temporary values (like the results of calculations).
- The * indirection (or dereferencing) operator (p. 371) returns a synonym for the name of the object that its operand points to in memory. This is called dereferencing the pointer (p. 372).

Section 8.4 Pass-by-Reference with Pointers
- When calling a function with an argument that the caller wants the called function to modify, the address of the argument may be passed. The called function then uses the indirection operator (*) to dereference the pointer and modify the value of the argument in the calling function.
- A function receiving an address as an argument must have a pointer as its corresponding parameter.

Section 8.5 Built-In Arrays
- Built-in arrays—like `array` objects—are fixed-size data structures.
- To specify the type of the elements and the number of elements required by a built-in array, use a declaration of the form:

  type arrayName[*arraySize*] ;

  The compiler reserves the appropriate amount of memory. The *arraySize* must be an integer constant greater than zero.
- As with `array` objects, you use the subscript (`[]`) operator to access the individual elements of a built-in array.
- The subscript (`[]`) operator does not provide bounds checking for `array` objects or built-in arrays.
- You can initialize the elements of a built-in array using an initializer list. If you provide fewer initializers than the number of built-in array elements, the remaining elements are initialized to 0. If you provide too many initializers a compilation error occurs.
- If the built-in array's size is omitted from a declaration with an initializer list, the compiler sizes the built-in array to the number of elements in the initializer list.
- The value of a built-in array's name is implicitly convertible to the address in memory of the built-in array's first element.
- To pass a built-in array to a function simply pass the built-in array's name. The called function can modify all the elements of a built-in array in the caller—unless the function precedes the corresponding built-in array parameter with `const` to indicate that the built-in array's elements should not be modified.
- Built-in arrays don't know their own size, so a function that processes a built-in array should have parameters to receive both the built-in array and its size.
- The compiler does not differentiate between a function that receives a pointer and a function that receives a one-dimensional built-in array. A function must "know" when it's receiving a built-in array or simply a single variable that's being passed by reference.
- The compiler converts a function parameter for a one-dimensional built-in array like `const int values[]` to the pointer notation `const int *values`. These forms are interchangeable—for clarity you should use the `[]` when the function expects a built-in array argument.

- Function sort (and many other library functions) can also be applied to built-in arrays.
- C++11's new begin and end functions (from header <iterator>; p. 379) each receive a built-in array as an argument and return a pointer that can be used with C++ Standard Library functions like sort to represent the range of built-in array elements to process.
- Built-in arrays cannot be compared to one another using the relational and equality operators.
- Built-in arrays cannot be assigned to one another—built-in array names are const pointers.
- Built-in arrays don't know their own size.
- Built-in arrays don't provide automatic bounds checking.
- In contemporary C++ code, you should use objects of the more robust array and vector class templates to represent lists and tables of values.

Section 8.6 Using const with Pointers
- The const qualifier enables you to inform the compiler that the value of a particular variable cannot be modified through the specified identifier.
- There are four ways to pass a pointer to a function—a nonconstant pointer to nonconstant data (p. 381), a nonconstant pointer to constant data (p. 381), a constant pointer to nonconstant data (p. 382), and a constant pointer to constant data (p. 383).
- To pass a single built-in array element by reference using pointers, pass the element's address.

Section 8.7 sizeof Operator
- sizeof (p. 384) determines the size in bytes of a type, variable or constant at compile time.
- When applied to a built-in array name, sizeof returns the total number of bytes in the built-in array. When applied to a built-in array parameter, sizeof returns the size of a pointer.

Section 8.8 Pointer Expressions and Pointer Arithmetic
- C++ enables pointer arithmetic (p. 387)—arithmetic operations that may be performed on pointers.
- Pointer arithmetic is appropriate only for pointers that point to built-in array elements.
- The arithmetic operations that may be performed on pointers are incrementing (++) a pointer, decrementing (--) a pointer, adding (+ or +=) an integer to a pointer, subtracting (- or -=) an integer from a pointer and subtracting one pointer from another—this particular operation is appropriate only for two pointers that point to elements of the same built-in array.
- When an integer is added or subtracted from a pointer, the pointer is incremented or decremented by that integer times the size of the object to which the pointer refers.
- Pointers can be assigned to one another if they are of the same type. Otherwise, a cast must be used. The exception to this is a void * pointer, which is a generic pointer type that can hold pointer values of any type.
- The only valid operations on a void * pointer are comparing void * pointers with other pointers, assigning addresses to void * pointers and casting void * pointers to valid pointer types.
- Pointers can be compared using the equality and relational operators. Comparisons using relational operators are meaningful only if the pointers point to members of the same built-in array.

Section 8.9 Relationship Between Pointers and Built-In Arrays
- Pointers that point to built-in arrays can be subscripted exactly as built-in array names can.
- In pointer/offset notation (p. 390), if the pointer points to the first element of a built-in array, the offset is the same as an array subscript.

- All subscripted array expressions can be written with a pointer and an offset (p. 390), using either the built-in array's name as a pointer or using a separate pointer that points to the built-in array.

Section 8.10 Pointer-Based Strings

- A character constant (p. 392) is an integer value represented as a character in single quotes. The value of a character constant is the integer value of the character in the machine's character set.

- A string is a series of characters treated as a single unit. A string may include letters, digits and various special characters such as +, -, *, /and $.

- String literals, or string constants, in C++ are written in double quotation marks (p. 392).

- A pointer-based string is a built-in array of chars ending with a null character ('\0'; p. 393), which marks where the string terminates in memory. A string is accessed via a pointer to its first character.

- The sizeof a string literal is the length of the string including the terminating null character.

- A string literal may be used as an initializer for a built-in array of chars or a variable of type const char *.

- String literals have static storage duration and may or may not be shared if the same string literal is referenced from multiple locations in a program.

- The effect of modifying a string literal is undefined; thus, you should always declare a pointer to a string literal as const char *.

- When declaring a built-in array of chars to contain a string, the built-in array must be large enough to store the string and its terminating null character.

- If a string is longer than the built-in array of chars in which it's to be stored, characters beyond the end of the built-in array will overwrite data in memory following the built-in array, leading to logic errors.

- You can access individual characters in a string directly with array subscript notation.

- A string can be read into a built-in array of chars using stream extraction with cin. Characters are read until a whitespace character or end-of-file indicator is encountered.

- The setw stream manipulator can be used to ensure that the string read into a built-in array of chars does not exceed the size of the built-in array.

- The cin object provides the member function getline (p. 394) to input an entire line of text into a built-in array of chars. The function takes three arguments—a built-in array of chars in which the line of text will be stored, a length and a delimiter character. The third argument has '\n' as a default value.

- A built-in array of chars representing a null-terminated string can be output with cout and <<. The characters of the string are output until a terminating null character is encountered.

Self-Review Exercises

8.1   Answer each of the following:
   a)   Built-in array names are _____ pointers.
   b)   A pointer-based string is a built-in array of chars ending with a _____ character.
   c)   _____ determines the size in bytes of a type, variable or constant at compile time.

8.2   State whether the following are *true* or *false*. If the answer is *false*, explain why.
   a)   The & operator returns a synonym for the name of the object that its operand points to in memory.
   b)   As with array objects, use the * indirection operator to access the individual elements of a built-in array.
   c)   Arithmetic operations cannot be performed on pointers.

8.3   For each of the following, write C++ statements that perform the specified task. Assume that double-precision, floating-point numbers are stored in eight bytes and that the starting address of the built-in array is at location 1002500 in memory. Each part of the exercise should use the results of previous parts where appropriate.

a) Declare a built-in array of type double called numbers with 10 elements, and initialize the elements to the values 0.0, 1.1, 2.2, ..., 9.9. Assume that the constant size has been defined as 10.

b) Declare a pointer nPtr that points to a variable of type double.

c) Use a for statement to display the elements of built-in array numbers using array subscript notation. Display each number with one digit to the right of the decimal point.

d) Write two separate statements that each assign the starting address of built-in array numbers to the pointer variable nPtr.

e) Use a for statement to display the elements of built-in array numbers using pointer/offset notation with pointer nPtr.

f) Use a for statement to display the elements of built-in array numbers using pointer/offset notation with the built-in array's name as the pointer.

g) Use a for statement to display the elements of built-in array numbers using pointer/subscript notation with pointer nPtr.

h) Refer to the fourth element of built-in array numbers using array subscript notation, pointer/offset notation with the built-in array's name as the pointer, pointer subscript notation with nPtr and pointer/offset notation with nPtr.

i) Assuming that nPtr points to the beginning of built-in array numbers, what address is referenced by nPtr + 8? What value is stored at that location?

j) Assuming that nPtr points to numbers[5], what address is referenced by nPtr after nPtr -= 4 is executed? What's the value stored at that location?

8.4   For each of the following, write a single statement that performs the specified task. Assume that integer variables var1 and var2 have been declared and that var2 has been initialized to 10.

a) Declare the variable iPtr to be a pointer to an object of type int and initialize the pointer to nullptr.

b) Assign the address of variable var2 to pointer variable iPtr.

c) Display the value of the object pointed to by iPtr.

d) Assign twice the value of the object pointed to by iPtr to variable var1.

e) Display the value of var1.

f) Display the address of var2.

g) Display the address stored in iPtr. Is the address displayed the same as that of var2?

8.5   Perform the task specified by each of the following statements:

a) Write the function header for a function called update that takes three pointers to integer numbers x, y and z as parameters and does not return a value.

b) Write the function prototype for the function in part (a).

c) Write statement that initializes a built-in array of integers named arr with the values 10, 20, ..., 100.

8.6   Find the error in each of the following program segments. Assume the following declarations and statements:

```
int *zPtr; // zPtr will reference built-in array z
void *sPtr = nullptr;
int number;
int z[ 6 ] = { 10, 20, 30, 40, 50, 60 };
```

a) zPtr = zPtr + 2;

b) // use pointer to get second value of a built-in array
   number = zPtr + 2;

c) // assign built-in array element 3 (the value 40) to number
```
number = *zPtr( 3 );
```
d) // display entire built-in array z in reverse order
```
for ( size_t i = 6; i > 0; --i )
   cout << zPtr[ i ] << endl;
```
e) // assign the value pointed to by sPtr to first element of z
```
z[0] = *sPtr;
```
f) z++;

Answers to Self-Review Exercises

8.1 a) const. b) null c) sizeof.

8.2 a) False. The * indirection (or dereferencing) operator returns a synonym for the name of the object that its operand points to in memory.

b) False. As with array objects, use the subscript ([]) operator to access the individual elements of a built-in array.

c) False. Arithmetic operations that may be performed on pointers.

8.3 a) **double** numbers[size] = { 0.0, 1.1, 2.2, 3.3, 4.4, 5.5, 6.6, 7.7, 8.8, 9.9 };
b) **double** *nPtr;
c) cout << fixed << showpoint << setprecision(1);
```
for ( size_t i = 0; i < size; ++i )
    cout << numbers[ i ] << ' ';
```
d) nPtr = numbers;
```
nPtr = &numbers[ 0 ];
```
e) cout << fixed << showpoint << setprecision(1);
```
for ( size_t j = 0; j < size; ++j )
   cout << *( nPtr + j ) << ' ';
```
f) cout << fixed << showpoint << setprecision(1);
```
for ( size_t k = 0; k < size; ++k )
   cout << *( numbers + k ) << ' ';
```
g) cout << fixed << showpoint << setprecision(1);
```
for ( size_t m = 0; m < size; ++m )
   cout << nPtr[ m ] << ' ';
```
h) numbers[3]
```
*( numbers + 3 )
nPtr[ 3 ]
*( nPtr + 3 )
```
i) The address is 1002500 + 8 * 8 = 1002564. The value is 8.8.
j) The address of numbers[5] is 1002500 + 5 * 8 = 1002540.
The address of nPtr -= 4 is 1002540 - 4 * 8 = 1002508.
The value at that location is 1.1.

8.4 a) int *iPtr = nullptr;
b) iPtr = &var2;
c) cout << "The value of *iPtr is " << *iPtr << endl;
d) var1 = *iPtr * 2;
e) cout << "The value of var1 is " << var1 << endl;
f) cout << "The address of var2 is " << &var2 << endl;

g) `cout << "The address stored in iPtr is " << iPtr << endl;`
   Yes, the value is the same.

8.5   a) `void update( int *x, int *y, int *z )`
   b) `void update( int *, int *, int * );`
   c) `int arr[] = { 10, 20, 30, 40, 50, 60, 70, 80, 90, 100 };`

8.6   a) *Error:* zPtr has not been initialized.
   Correction: Initialize zPtr with zPtr = z;
   b) *Error:* The pointer is not dereferenced.
   Correction: Change the statement to number = *(zPtr + 2);
   c) *Error:* zPtr(3) is not a pointer and should not be dereferenced. Also use [ ] to represent subscript instead of ( ).
   Correction: Change *zPtr(3) to zPtr[3]].
   d) *Error:* Referring to a built-in array element outside the built-in array's bounds with pointer subscripting.
   Correction: To prevent this, change the for loop to
```
for ( size_t i = 5; i >= 0; --i )
    cout << zPtr[ i ] << endl;
```
   e) *Error:* Dereferencing a void pointer.
   Correction: To dereference the void pointer, it must first be cast to an integer pointer. Change the statement to z[0] = *static_cast< int * >(sPtr);
   f) *Error:* Trying to modify a built-in array's name with pointer arithmetic.
   Correction: Use a pointer variable instead of the built-in array's name to accomplish pointer arithmetic, or subscript the built-in array's name to refer to a specific element.

Exercises

8.7   *(True or False)* State whether the following are *true* or *false*. If *false*, explain why.
   a) Pointer arithmetic is appropriate only for pointers that point to built-in array elements.
   b) The only valid operations on a void * pointer are comparing void * pointers with other pointers and casting void * pointers to valid pointer types.

8.8   *(Write C++ Statements)* For each of the following, write C++ statements that perform the specified task. Assume that unsigned integers are stored in two bytes and that the starting address of the built-in array is at location 1002500 in memory.
   a) Declare a built-in array of type `unsigned int` called values with five elements, and initialize the elements to the even integers from 2 to 10. Assume that the constant SIZE has been defined as 5.
   b) Declare a pointer vPtr that points to an object of type `unsigned int`.
   c) Use a `for` statement to display the elements of built-in array values using array subscript notation.
   d) Write two separate statements that assign the starting address of built-in array values to pointer variable vPtr.
   e) Use a `for` statement to display the elements of built-in array values using pointer/offset notation.
   f) Use a `for` statement to display the elements of built-in array values using pointer/offset notation with the built-in array's name as the pointer.
   g) Use a `for` statement to display the elements of built-in array values by subscripting the pointer to the built-in array.
   h) Refer to the fifth element of values using array subscript notation, pointer/offset notation with the built-in array name's as the pointer, pointer subscript notation and pointer/offset notation.

i) What address is referenced by vPtr + 3? What value is stored at that location?

j) Assuming that vPtr points to values[4], what address is referenced by vPtr -= 4? What value is stored at that location?

8.9 *(Write C++ Statements)* For each of the following, write a single statement that performs the specified task. Assume that char variables var1 and var2 have been declared and var2 has been initialized to 'a'.

a) Declare the variable charPtr to be a pointer to an object of type char.

b) Assign the address of variable var2 to pointer variable charPtr.

c) Display the value of the object pointed to by charPtr.

d) Assign the value of the object pointed to by charPtr to variable var1.

e) Display the value of var1.

f) Display the address of var2.

g) Display the address stored in intPtr. Is the address displayed the same as var1's?

8.10 *(Function Headers and Prototypes)* Perform the task in each of the following statements:

a) Write the function header for function check that takes two long integer built-in array parameter bigIntegers1, bigIntegers2 and return an integer value.

b) Write the function prototype for the function in part (a).

c) Write the function header for function max that takes an long built-in array parameter arr and returns an integer.

d) Write the function prototype for the function described in part (c)?

8.11 *(Find the Code Errors)* Find the error in each of the following segments. If the error can be corrected, explain how.

a) `int *number;`
   `cout << number << endl;`

b) `double *realPtr;`
   `long *integerPtr;`
   `integerPtr = realPtr;`

c) `int * x, y;`
   `x = y;`

d) `char s[] = "this is a character array";`
   `for ( ; *s != '\0'; ++s)`
   `    cout << *s << ' ';`

e) `short *numPtr, result;`
   `void *genericPtr = numPtr;`
   `result = *genericPtr + 7;`

f) `double x = 19.34;`
   `double xPtr = &x;`
   `cout << xPtr << endl;`

8.12 *(Simulation: The Tortoise and the Hare)* In this exercise, you'll re-create the classic race of the tortoise and the hare. You'll use random number generation to develop a simulation of this memorable event.

Our contenders begin the race at "square 1" of 70 squares. Each square represents a possible position along the race course. The finish line is at square 70. The first contender to reach or pass square 70 is rewarded with a pail of fresh carrots and lettuce. The course weaves its way up the side of a slippery mountain, so occasionally the contenders lose ground.

There is a clock that ticks once per second. With each tick of the clock, your program should use function moveTortoise and moveHare to adjust the position of the animals according to the rules in Fig. 8.18. These functions should use pointer-based pass-by-reference to modify the position of the tortoise and the hare.

Use variables to keep track of the positions of the animals (i.e., position numbers are 1–70). Start each animal at position 1 (i.e., the "starting gate"). If an animal slips left before square 1, move the animal back to square 1.

Generate the percentages in the preceding table by producing a random integer i in the range $1 \leq i \leq 10$. For the tortoise, perform a "fast plod" when $1 \leq i \leq 5$, a "slip" when $6 \leq i \leq 7$ or a "slow plod" when $8 \leq i \leq 10$. Use a similar technique to move the hare.

Begin the race by displaying

```
BANG !!!!!
AND THEY'RE OFF !!!!!
```

For each tick of the clock (i.e., each repetition of a loop), display a 70-position line showing the letter T in the tortoise's position and the letter H in the hare's position. Occasionally, the contenders land on the same square. In this case, the tortoise bites the hare and your program should display OUCH!!! beginning at that position. All positions other than the T, the H or the OUCH!!! (in case of a tie) should be blank.

After displaying each line, test whether either animal has reached or passed square 70. If so, display the winner and terminate the simulation. If the tortoise wins, display TORTOISE WINS!!! YAY!!! If the hare wins, display Hare wins. Yuch. If both animals win on the same clock tick, you may want to favor the tortoise (the "underdog"), or you may want to display It's a tie. If neither animal wins, perform the loop again to simulate the next tick of the clock.

Animal	Move type	Percentage of the time	Actual move
Tortoise	Fast plod	50%	3 squares to the right
	Slip	20%	6 squares to the left
	Slow plod	30%	1 square to the right
Hare	Sleep	20%	No move at all
	Big hop	20%	9 squares to the right
	Big slip	10%	12 squares to the left
	Small hop	30%	1 square to the right
	Small slip	20%	2 squares to the left

Fig. 8.18 | Rules for moving the tortoise and the hare.

8.13 *(What Does This Code Do?)* What does this program do?

```cpp
// Ex. 8.13: ex08_13.cpp
// What does this program do?
#include <iostream>
using namespace std;

void mystery1( char *, const char * ); // prototype

int main()
{
   char string1[ 80 ];
   char string2[ 80 ];
```

```
13      cout << "Enter two strings: ";
14      cin >> string1 >> string2;
15      mystery1( string1, string2 );
16      cout << string1 << endl;
17   } // end main
18
19   // What does this function do?
20   void mystery1( char *s1, const char *s2 )
21   {
22      while ( *s1 != '\0' )
23         ++s1;
24
25      for ( ; ( *s1 = *s2 ); ++s1, ++s2 )
26         ; // empty statement
27   } // end function mystery1
```

8.14   *(What Does This Code Do?)* Is the program correct? If yes, what does this program do?

```
 1   // Ex. 8.14: ex08_14.cpp
 2   // What does this program do?
 3   #include <iostream>
 4   #include <string>
 5   using namespace std;
 6   void mystery2( const char *, int); // prototype
 7
 8   int main()
 9   {
10      char string1[ 80 ];
11
12      cout << "Enter a string: ";
13      cin >> string1;
14      mystery2( string1,  strlen(string1)) ;
15   } // end main
16
17   // What does this function do?
18   void mystery2( const char *s, int n )
19   {
20      unsigned int x;
21
22      for ( x = n - 1; x >= 0; --x )
23         cout<< s[x];
24
25
26   } // end function mystery2
```

Special Section: Building Your Own Computer

In the next several problems, we take a temporary diversion away from the world of high-level-language programming. We "peel open" a computer and look at its internal structure. We introduce machine-language programming and write several machine-language programs. To make this an especially valuable experience, we then build a computer (using software-based *simulation*) on which you can execute your machine-language programs!

8.15   *(Machine-Language Programming)* Let's create a computer we'll call the Simpletron. As its name implies, it's a simple machine, but, as we'll soon see, it's a powerful one as well. The Simpletron runs programs written in the only language it directly understands, that is, Simpletron Machine Language, or SML for short.

The Simpletron contains an *accumulator*—a "special register" in which information is put before the Simpletron uses that information in calculations or examines it in various ways. All information in the Simpletron is handled in terms of *words*. A word is a signed four-digit decimal number, such as +3364, -1293, +0007, -0001, etc. The Simpletron is equipped with a 100-word memory, and these words are referenced by their location numbers 00, 01, ..., 99.

Before running an SML program, we must *load*, or place, the program into memory. The first instruction (or statement) of every SML program is always placed in location 00. The simulator will start executing at this location.

Each instruction written in SML occupies one word of the Simpletron's memory; thus, instructions are signed four-digit decimal numbers. Assume that the sign of an SML instruction is always plus, but the sign of a data word may be either plus or minus. Each location in the Simpletron's memory may contain an instruction, a data value used by a program or an unused (and hence undefined) area of memory. The first two digits of each SML instruction are the *operation code* that specifies the operation to be performed. SML operation codes are shown in Fig. 8.19.

Operation code	Meaning
Input/output operations	
`const int read = 10;`	Read a word from the keyboard into a specific location in memory.
`const int write = 11;`	Write a word from a specific location in memory to the screen.
Load and store operations	
`const int load = 20;`	Load a word from a specific location in memory into the accumulator.
`const int store = 21;`	Store a word from the accumulator into a specific location in memory.
Arithmetic operations	
`const int add = 30;`	Add a word from a specific location in memory to the word in the accumulator (leave result in accumulator).
`const int subtract = 31;`	Subtract a word from a specific location in memory from the word in the accumulator (leave result in accumulator).
`const int divide = 32;`	Divide a word from a specific location in memory into the word in the accumulator (leave result in accumulator).
`const int multiply = 33;`	Multiply a word from a specific location in memory by the word in the accumulator (leave result in accumulator).
Transfer-of-control operations	
`const int branch = 40;`	Branch to a specific location in memory.
`const int branchneg = 41;`	Branch to a specific location in memory if the accumulator is negative.
`const int branchzero = 42;`	Branch to a specific location in memory if the accumulator is zero.
`const int halt = 43;`	Halt—the program has completed its task.

Fig. 8.19 | Simpletron Machine Language (SML) operation codes.

The last two digits of an SML instruction are the *operand*—the address of the memory location containing the word to which the operation applies.

Now let's consider two simple SML programs. The first (Fig. 8.20) reads two numbers from the keyboard and computes and displays their sum. The instruction +1007 reads the first number from the keyboard and places it into location 07 (which has been initialized to zero). Instruction +1008 reads the next number into location 08. The *load* instruction, +2007, places (copies) the first number into the accumulator, and the *add* instruction, +3008, adds the second number to the number in the accumulator. *All SML arithmetic instructions leave their results in the accumulator.* The *store* instruction, +2109, places (copies) the result back into memory location 09. Then the *write* instruction, +1109, takes the number and displays it (as a signed four-digit decimal number). The *halt* instruction, +4300, terminates execution.

Location	Number	Instruction
00	+1007	(Read A)
01	+1008	(Read B)
02	+2007	(Load A)
03	+3008	(Add B)
04	+2109	(Store C)
05	+1109	(Write C)
06	+4300	(Halt)
07	+0000	(Variable A)
08	+0000	(Variable B)
09	+0000	(Result C)

Fig. 8.20 | SML Example 1.

The SML program in Fig. 8.21 reads two numbers from the keyboard, then determines and displays the larger value. Note the use of the instruction +4107 as a conditional transfer of control, much the same as C++'s if statement.

Location	Number	Instruction
00	+1009	(Read A)
01	+1010	(Read B)
02	+2009	(Load A)
03	+3110	(Subtract B)
04	+4107	(Branch negative to 07)
05	+1109	(Write A)
06	+4300	(Halt)
07	+1110	(Write B)
08	+4300	(Halt)
09	+0000	(Variable A)
10	+0000	(Variable B)

Fig. 8.21 | SML Example 2.

Now write SML programs to accomplish each of the following tasks:
 a)   Use a sentinel-controlled loop to read positive numbers and compute and display their sum. Terminate input when a negative number is entered.
 b)   Use a counter-controlled loop to read seven numbers, some positive and some negative, and compute and display their average.
 c)   Read a series of numbers, and determine and display the largest number. The first number read indicates how many numbers should be processed.

8.16   (*Computer Simulator*) It may at first seem outrageous, but in this problem you are going to build your own computer. No, you won't be soldering components together. Rather, you'll use the powerful technique of *software-based simulation* to create a *software model* of the Simpletron. Your Simpletron simulator will turn the computer you are using into a Simpletron, and you actually will be able to run, test and debug the SML programs you wrote in Exercise 8.15.

When you run your Simpletron simulator, it should begin by displaying

```
*** Welcome to Simpletron! ***

*** Please enter your program one instruction ***
*** (or data word) at a time. I will type the ***
*** location number and a question mark (?).  ***
*** You then type the word for that location. ***
*** Type the sentinel -99999 to stop entering ***
*** your program. ***
```

Your program should simulate the Simpletron's memory with a single-subscripted, 100-element built-in array memory. Now assume that the simulator is running, and let's examine the dialog as we enter the program of the second example of Exercise 8.15:

```
00 ? +1009
01 ? +1010
02 ? +2009
03 ? +3110
04 ? +4107
05 ? +1109
06 ? +4300
07 ? +1110
08 ? +4300
09 ? +0000
10 ? +0000
11 ? -99999

*** Program loading completed ***
*** Program execution begins  ***
```

The numbers to the right of each ? in the preceding dialog represent the SML program instructions input by the user.

The SML program has now been placed (or loaded) into built-in array memory. Now the Simpletron executes your SML program. Execution begins with the instruction in location 00 and, like C++, continues sequentially, unless directed to another part of the program by a transfer of control.

Use variable accumulator to represent the accumulator register. Use variable instructionCounter to keep track of the location in memory that contains the instruction being performed. Use variable operationCode to indicate the operation currently being performed (i.e., the left two digits of the instruction word). Use variable operand to indicate the memory location on which the current instruction operates. Thus, operand is the rightmost two digits of the instruction currently being performed. Do not execute instructions directly from memory. Rather, transfer the next instruction to be performed from memory to a variable called instructionRegister. Then "pick off" the left two digits and place them in operationCode, and "pick off" the right two digits and place them in operand. When Simpletron begins execution, the special registers are all initialized to zero.

Now let's "walk through" the execution of the first SML instruction, +1009 in memory location 00. This is called an *instruction execution cycle.*

The `instructionCounter` tells us the location of the next instruction to be performed. We *fetch* the contents of that location from `memory` by using the C++ statement

```
instructionRegister = memory[ instructionCounter ];
```

The operation code and operand are extracted from the instruction register by the statements

```
operationCode = instructionRegister / 100;
operand = instructionRegister % 100;
```

Now, the Simpletron must determine that the operation code is actually a *read* (versus a *write*, a *load*, etc.). A `switch` differentiates among the 12 operations of SML. In the `switch` statement, the behavior of various SML instructions is simulated as shown in Fig. 8.22 (we leave the others to you).

read:	`cin >> memory[ operand ];`
load:	`accumulator = memory[ operand ];`
add:	`accumulator += memory[ operand ];`
branch:	We'll discuss the branch instructions shortly.
halt:	This instruction displays the message `*** Simpletron execution terminated ***`

Fig. 8.22 | Behavior of SML instructions.

The *halt* instruction also causes the Simpletron to display the name and contents of each register, as well as the complete contents of memory. Such a printout is often called a *register and memory dump.* To help you program your dump function, a sample dump format is shown in Fig. 8.23. Note that a dump after executing a Simpletron program would show the actual values of instructions and data values at the moment execution terminated. To format numbers with their sign as shown in the dump, use stream manipulator `showpos`. To disable the display of the sign, use stream manipulator `noshowpos`. For numbers that have fewer than four digits, you can format numbers with leading zeros between the sign and the value by using the following statement before outputting the value:

```
cout << setfill( '0' ) << internal;
```

```
REGISTERS:
accumulator          +0000
instructionCounter      00
instructionRegister  +0000
operationCode           00
operand                 00

MEMORY:
          0      1      2      3      4      5      6      7      8      9
 0    +0000  +0000  +0000  +0000  +0000  +0000  +0000  +0000  +0000  +0000
10    +0000  +0000  +0000  +0000  +0000  +0000  +0000  +0000  +0000  +0000
20    +0000  +0000  +0000  +0000  +0000  +0000  +0000  +0000  +0000  +0000
30    +0000  +0000  +0000  +0000  +0000  +0000  +0000  +0000  +0000  +0000
40    +0000  +0000  +0000  +0000  +0000  +0000  +0000  +0000  +0000  +0000
50    +0000  +0000  +0000  +0000  +0000  +0000  +0000  +0000  +0000  +0000
60    +0000  +0000  +0000  +0000  +0000  +0000  +0000  +0000  +0000  +0000
70    +0000  +0000  +0000  +0000  +0000  +0000  +0000  +0000  +0000  +0000
80    +0000  +0000  +0000  +0000  +0000  +0000  +0000  +0000  +0000  +0000
90    +0000  +0000  +0000  +0000  +0000  +0000  +0000  +0000  +0000  +0000
```

Fig. 8.23 | A sample register and memory dump.

Parameterized stream manipulator setfill (from header <iomanip>) specifies the fill character that will appear between the sign and the value when a number is displayed with a field width of five characters but does not have four digits. (One position in the field width is reserved for the sign.) Stream manipulator internal indicates that the fill characters should appear between the sign and the numeric value .

Let's proceed with the execution of our program's first instruction—+1009 in location 00. As we've indicated, the switch statement simulates this by performing the C++ statement

```
cin >> memory[ operand ];
```

A question mark (?) should be displayed on the screen before the cin statement executes to prompt the user for input. The Simpletron waits for the user to type a value and press the *Enter* key. The value is then read into location 09.

At this point, simulation of the first instruction is complete. All that remains is to prepare the Simpletron to execute the next instruction. The instruction just performed was not a transfer of control, so we need merely increment the instruction counter register as follows:

```
++instructionCounter;
```

This completes the simulated execution of the first instruction. The entire process (i.e., the instruction execution cycle) begins anew with the fetch of the next instruction to execute.

Now let's consider how to simulate the branching instructions (i.e., the transfers of control). All we need to do is adjust the value in the instructionCounter appropriately. Therefore, the unconditional branch instruction (40) is simulated in the switch as

```
instructionCounter = operand;
```

The conditional "branch if accumulator is zero" instruction is simulated as

```
if ( 0 == accumulator )
    instructionCounter = operand;
```

At this point, you should implement your Simpletron simulator and run each of the SML programs you wrote in Exercise 8.15. The variables that represent the Simpletron simulator's memory and registers should be defined in main and passed to other functions by value or by reference as appropriate.

Your simulator should check for various types of errors. During the program loading phase, for example, each number the user types into the Simpletron's memory must be in the range -9999 to +9999. Your simulator should use a while loop to test that each number entered is in this range and, if not, keep prompting the user to reenter the number until the user enters a correct number.

During the execution phase, your simulator should check for various serious errors, such as attempts to divide by zero, attempts to execute invalid operation codes, accumulator overflows (i.e., arithmetic operations resulting in values larger than +9999 or smaller than -9999) and the like. Such serious errors are called fatal errors. When a fatal error is detected, your simulator should display an error message such as

```
*** Attempt to divide by zero ***
*** Simpletron execution abnormally terminated ***
```

and should display a full register and memory dump in the format we've discussed previously. This will help the user locate the error in the program.

8.17 (*Project: Modifications to the Simpletron Simulator*) In Exercise 8.16, you wrote a software simulation of a computer that executes programs written in Simpletron Machine Language (SML). In this exercise, we propose several modifications and enhancements to the Simpletron Simulator. In Exercises 18.31–18.35, we propose building a compiler that converts programs written in a high-level programming language (a variation of BASIC) to SML. Some of the following modifications and enhancements may be required to execute the programs produced by the compiler. [*Note:* Some modifications may conflict with others and therefore must be done separately.]

a) Extend the Simpletron Simulator's memory to contain 1000 memory locations to enable the Simpletron to handle larger programs.

b) Allow the simulator to perform modulus calculations. This requires an additional Simpletron Machine Language instruction.

c) Allow the simulator to perform exponentiation calculations. This requires an additional Simpletron Machine Language instruction.

d) Modify the simulator to use hexadecimal values rather than integer values to represent Simpletron Machine Language instructions.

e) Modify the simulator to allow output of a newline. This requires an additional Simpletron Machine Language instruction.

f) Modify the simulator to process floating-point values in addition to integer values.

g) Modify the simulator to handle string input. [*Hint:* Each Simpletron word can be divided into two groups, each holding a two-digit integer. Each two-digit integer represents the ASCII decimal equivalent of a character. Add a machine-language instruction that inputs a string and store the string beginning at a specific Simpletron memory location. The first half of the word at that location will be a count of the number of characters in the string (i.e., the length of the string). Each succeeding half-word contains one ASCII character expressed as two decimal digits. The machine-language instruction converts each character into its ASCII equivalent and assigns it to a half-word.]

h) Modify the simulator to handle output of strings stored in the format of part (g). [*Hint:* Add a machine-language instruction that will display a string beginning at a certain Simpletron memory location. The first half of the word at that location is a count of the number of characters in the string (i.e., the length of the string). Each succeeding half-word contains one ASCII character expressed as two decimal digits. The machine-language instruction checks the length and displays the string by translating each two-digit number into its equivalent character.]

i) Modify the simulator to include instruction SML_DEBUG that displays a memory dump after each instruction executes. Give SML_DEBUG an operation code of 44. The word +4401 turns on debug mode, and +4400 turns off debug mode.

Classes: A Deeper Look; Throwing Exceptions

9

My object all sublime
I shall achieve in time.
—W. S. Gilbert

Is it a world to hide virtues in?
—William Shakespeare

Have no friends not equal to
yourself.
—Confucius

Objectives

In this chapter you'll:

- Use an include guard.
- Access class members via an object's name, a reference or a pointer.
- Use destructors to perform "termination housekeeping."
- Learn the order of constructor and destructor calls.
- Learn about the dangers of returning a reference to private data.
- Assign the data members of one object to those of another object.
- Create objects composed of other objects.
- Use friend functions and friend classes.
- Use the this pointer in a member function to access a non-static class member.
- Use static data members and member functions.

Outline

9.1 Introduction

This chapter takes a deeper look at classes. We use an integrated Time class case study and other examples to demonstrate several class construction capabilities. We begin with a Time class that reviews several of the features presented in preceding chapters. The example also demonstrates using an *include guard* in headers to prevent header code from being included in the same source code file more than once.

We demonstrate how client code can access a class's public members via the name of an object, a reference to an object or a pointer to an object. As you'll see, object names and references can be used with the dot (.) member selection operator to access a public member, and pointers can be used with the arrow (->) member selection operator.

We discuss access functions that can read or write an object's data members. A common use of access functions is to test the truth or falsity of conditions—such functions are known as *predicate functions*. We also demonstrate the notion of a utility function (also called a *helper function*)—a private member function that supports the operation of the class's public member functions, but is *not* intended for use by clients of the class.

We show how to pass arguments to constructors and show how default arguments can be used in constructors to enable client code to initialize objects using a variety of arguments. Next, we discuss a special member function called a *destructor* that's part of every class and is used to perform "termination housekeeping" on an object before it's destroyed. We demonstrate the *order* in which constructors and destructors are called.

We show that returning a reference or pointer to private data *breaks the encapsulation of a class*, allowing client code to directly access an object's data. We use default memberwise assignment to assign an object of a class to another object of the same class.

We use const objects and const member functions to prevent modifications of objects and enforce the principle of least privilege. We discuss *composition*—a form of reuse in which a class can have objects of other classes as members. Next, we use *friendship* to specify that a nonmember function can also access a class's non-public members—a technique that's often used in operator overloading (Chapter 10) for performance reasons. We discuss the this pointer, which is an *implicit* argument in all calls to a class's non-static member functions, allowing them to access the correct object's data members and non-static member functions. We motivate the need for static class members and show how to use them in your own classes.

9.2 Time Class Case Study

Our first example creates class Time and tests the class. We demonstrate an important C++ software engineering concept—using an include guard in headers to prevent the code in the header from being included into the same source code file more than once. Since a class can be defined only once, using such preprocessing directives prevents multiple-definition errors.

Time Class Definition

The class definition (Fig. 9.1) contains prototypes (lines 13–16) for member functions Time, setTime, printUniversal and printStandard, and includes private unsigned int members hour, minute and second (lines 18–20). Class Time's private data members can be accessed *only* by its member functions. Chapter 11 introduces a third access specifier, protected, as we study inheritance and the part it plays in object-oriented programming.

Good Programming Practice 9.1
For clarity and readability, use each access specifier only once in a class definition. Place public members first, where they're easy to locate.

Software Engineering Observation 9.1
Each member of a class should have private visibility unless it can be proven that the element needs public visibility. This is another example of the principle of least privilege.

```
1   // Fig. 9.1: Time.h
2   // Time class definition.
3   // Member functions are defined in Time.cpp
4
5   // prevent multiple inclusions of header
6   #ifndef TIME_H
7   #define TIME_H
8
9   // Time class definition
10  class Time
11  {
12  public:
13     Time(); // constructor
14     void setTime( int, int, int ); // set hour, minute and second
15     void printUniversal() const; // print time in universal-time format
16     void printStandard() const; // print time in standard-time format
17  private:
18     unsigned int hour; // 0 - 23 (24-hour clock format)
19     unsigned int minute; // 0 - 59
20     unsigned int second; // 0 - 59
21  }; // end class Time
22
23  #endif
```

Fig. 9.1 | Time class definition.

In Fig. 9.1, the class definition is enclosed in the following **include guard** (lines 6, 7 and 23):

```
// prevent multiple inclusions of header
#ifndef TIME_H
#define TIME_H
   ...
#endif
```

When we build larger programs, other definitions and declarations will also be placed in headers. The preceding include guard prevents the code between `#ifndef` (which means "if not defined") and `#endif` from being included if the name `TIME_H` has been defined. If the header has *not* been included previously in a file, the name `TIME_H` is defined by the `#define` directive and the header statements *are* included. If the header has been included previously, `TIME_H` *is defined* already and the header is *not* included again. Attempts to include a header multiple times (inadvertently) typically occur in large programs with many headers that may themselves include other headers.

Error-Prevention Tip 9.1

Use `#ifndef`, `#define` and `#endif` preprocessing directives to form an include guard that prevents headers from being included more than once in a source-code file.

Good Programming Practice 9.2

By convention, use the name of the header in uppercase with the period replaced by an underscore in the `#ifndef` and `#define` preprocessing directives of a header.

Time Class Member Functions

In Fig. 9.2, the `Time` constructor (lines 11–14) initializes the data members to 0—the universal-time equivalent of 12 AM. Invalid values cannot be stored in the data members of a `Time` object, because the constructor is called when the `Time` object is created, and all subsequent attempts by a client to modify the data members are scrutinized by function `set-Time` (discussed shortly). Finally, it's important to note that you can define *overloaded constructors* for a class—we studied overloaded functions in Section 6.18.

```cpp
 1   // Fig. 9.2: Time.cpp
 2   // Time class member-function definitions.
 3   #include <iostream>
 4   #include <iomanip>
 5   #include <stdexcept> // for invalid_argument exception class
 6   #include "Time.h" // include definition of class Time from Time.h
 7
 8   using namespace std;
 9
10   // Time constructor initializes each data member to zero.
11   Time::Time()
12      : hour( 0 ), minute( 0 ), second( 0 )
13   {
14   } // end Time constructor
```

Fig. 9.2 | Time class member-function definitions. (Part 1 of 2.)

```
15
16   // set new Time value using universal time
17   void Time::setTime( int h, int m, int s )
18   {
19      // validate hour, minute and second
20      if ( ( h >= 0 && h < 24 ) && ( m >= 0 && m < 60 ) &&
21           ( s >= 0 && s < 60 ) )
22      {
23         hour = h;
24         minute = m;
25         second = s;
26      } // end if
27      else
28         throw invalid_argument(
29            "hour, minute and/or second was out of range" );
30   } // end function setTime
31
32   // print Time in universal-time format (HH:MM:SS)
33   void Time::printUniversal() const
34   {
35      cout << setfill( '0' ) << setw( 2 ) << hour << ":"
36         << setw( 2 ) << minute << ":" << setw( 2 ) << second;
37   } // end function printUniversal
38
39   // print Time in standard-time format (HH:MM:SS AM or PM)
40   void Time::printStandard() const
41   {
42      cout << ( ( hour == 0 || hour == 12 ) ? 12 : hour % 12 ) << ":"
43         << setfill( '0' ) << setw( 2 ) << minute << ":" << setw( 2 )
44         << second << ( hour < 12 ? " AM" : " PM" );
45   } // end function printStandard
```

Fig. 9.2 | Time class member-function definitions. (Part 2 of 2.)

Before C++11, only static const int data members (which you saw in Chapter 7) could be initialized where they were declared in the class body. For this reason, data members typically should be initialized by the class's constructor as *there is no default initialization for fundamental-type data members*. As of C++11, you can now use an *in-class initializer* to initialize any data member where it's declared in the class definition.

Time Class Member Function *setTime* and Throwing Exceptions

Function setTime (lines 17–30) is a public function that declares three int parameters and uses them to set the time. Lines 20–21 test each argument to determine whether the value is in range, and, if so, lines 23–25 assign the values to the hour, minute and second data members. The hour value must be greater than or equal to 0 and less than 24, because universal-time format represents hours as integers from 0 to 23 (e.g., 1 PM is hour 13 and 11 PM is hour 23; midnight is hour 0 and noon is hour 12). Similarly, both minute and second must be greater than or equal to 0 and less than 60. For values outside these ranges, setTime throws an exception (lines 28–29) of type **invalid_argument** (from header <stdexcept>), which notifies the client code that an invalid argument was received. As you learned in Section 7.10, you can use try...catch to catch exceptions and attempt to recover from them, which we'll do in Fig. 9.3. The **throw statement** (lines 28–29) creates a new object of type invalid_argument. The parentheses following the class name indicate a call to the invalid_argument constructor that allows us to specify a custom error message string. After the exception object is created, the throw statement immediately terminates function setTime and the exception is returned to the code that attempted to set the time.

Time Class Member Function printUniversal

Function printUniversal (lines 33–37 of Fig. 9.2) takes no arguments and outputs the time in universal-time format, consisting of three colon-separated pairs of digits. If the time were 1:30:07 PM, function printUniversal would return 13:30:07. Line 35 uses parameterized stream manipulator **setfill** to specify the **fill character** that's displayed when an integer is output in a field *wider* than the number of digits in the value. The fill characters appear to the *left* of the digits in the number, because the number is *right aligned* by default—for *left aligned* values, the fill characters would appear to the right. In this example, if the minute value is 2, it will be displayed as 02, because the fill character is set to zero ('0'). If the number being output fills the specified field, the fill character will *not* be displayed. Once the fill character is specified with setfill, it applies for *all* subsequent values that are displayed in fields wider than the value being displayed—setfill is a "sticky" setting. This is in contrast to setw, which applies *only* to the next value displayed—setw is a "nonsticky" setting.

Error-Prevention Tip 9.2

Each sticky setting (such as a fill character or floating-point precision) should be restored to its previous setting when it's no longer needed. Failure to do so may result in incorrectly formatted output later in a program. Chapter 13, Stream Input/Output: A Deeper Look, discusses how to reset the fill character and precision.

Time Class Member Function printStandard

Function printStandard (lines 40–45) takes no arguments and outputs the date in standard-time format, consisting of the hour, minute and second values separated by colons and followed by an AM or PM indicator (e.g., 1:27:06 PM). Like function printUniversal, function printStandard uses setfill('0') to format the minute and second as two digit values with leading zeros if necessary. Line 42 uses the conditional operator (?:) to determine the value of hour to be displayed—if the hour is 0 or 12 (AM or PM), it appears as 12; otherwise, the hour appears as a value from 1 to 11. The conditional operator in line 44 determines whether AM or PM will be displayed.

Defining Member Functions Outside the Class Definition; Class Scope

Even though a member function declared in a class definition may be defined outside that class definition (and "tied" to the class via the *scope resolution operator*), that member function is still within that **class's scope**—that is, its name is known to other class members referred to via an object of the class, a reference to an object of the class, a pointer to an object of the class or the scope resolution operator. We'll say more about class scope shortly.

If a member function is defined in a class's body, the member function is implicitly declared *inline*. Remember that the compiler reserves the right not to inline any function.

Performance Tip 9.1

Defining a member function inside the class definition inlines the member function (if the compiler chooses to do so). This can improve performance.

Software Engineering Observation 9.2

Only the simplest and most stable member functions (i.e., whose implementations are unlikely to change) should be defined in the class header.

Member Functions vs. Global Functions (Also Called Free Functions)

The `printUniversal` and `printStandard` member functions take no arguments, because these member functions implicitly know that they're to print the data members of the particular `Time` object on which they're invoked. This can make member function calls more concise than conventional function calls in procedural programming.

Software Engineering Observation 9.3

Using an object-oriented programming approach often simplifies function calls by reducing the number of parameters. This benefit derives from the fact that encapsulating data members and member functions within a class gives the member functions the right to access the data members.

Software Engineering Observation 9.4

Member functions are usually shorter than functions in non-object-oriented programs, because the data stored in data members have ideally been validated by a constructor or by member functions that store new data. Because the data is already in the object, the member-function calls often have no arguments or fewer arguments than function calls in non-object-oriented languages. Thus, the calls, the function definitions and the function prototypes are shorter. This improves many aspects of program development.

Error-Prevention Tip 9.3

The fact that member function calls generally take either no arguments or substantially fewer arguments than conventional function calls in non-object-oriented languages reduces the likelihood of passing the wrong arguments, the wrong types of arguments or the wrong number of arguments.

Using Class Time

Once defined, `Time` can be used as a type in declarations as follows:

```
Time sunset; // object of type Time
array< Time, 5 > arrayOfTimes; // array of 5 Time objects
Time &dinnerTime = sunset; // reference to a Time object
Time *timePtr = &dinnerTime; // pointer to a Time object
```

Figure 9.3 uses class `Time`. Line 11 instantiates a single object of class `Time` called `t`. When the object is instantiated, the `Time` constructor is called to initialize each `private` data member to 0. Then, lines 15 and 17 print the time in universal and standard formats, respectively, to confirm that the members were initialized properly. Line 19 sets a new time by calling member function `setTime`, and lines 23 and 25 print the time again in both formats.

```
1   // Fig. 9.3: fig09_03.cpp
2   // Program to test class Time.
3   // NOTE: This file must be compiled with Time.cpp.
4   #include <iostream>
5   #include <stdexcept> // for invalid_argument exception class
6   #include "Time.h" // include definition of class Time from Time.h
7   using namespace std;
8
9   int main()
10  {
11     Time t; // instantiate object t of class Time
12
13     // output Time object t's initial values
14     cout << "The initial universal time is ";
15     t.printUniversal(); // 00:00:00
16     cout << "\nThe initial standard time is ";
17     t.printStandard(); // 12:00:00 AM
18
19     t.setTime( 13, 27, 6 ); // change time
20
21     // output Time object t's new values
22     cout << "\n\nUniversal time after setTime is ";
23     t.printUniversal(); // 13:27:06
24     cout << "\nStandard time after setTime is ";
25     t.printStandard(); // 1:27:06 PM
26
27     // attempt to set the time with invalid values
28     try
29     {
30        t.setTime( 99, 99, 99 ); // all values out of range
31     } // end try
32     catch ( invalid_argument &e )
33     {
34        cout << "Exception: " << e.what() << endl;
35     } // end catch
36
37     // output t's values after specifying invalid values
38     cout << "\n\nAfter attempting invalid settings:"
39        << "\nUniversal time: ";
40     t.printUniversal(); // 13:27:06
41     cout << "\nStandard time: ";
42     t.printStandard(); // 1:27:06 PM
43     cout << endl;
44  } // end main
```

```
The initial universal time is 00:00:00
The initial standard time is 12:00:00 AM

Universal time after setTime is 13:27:06
Standard time after setTime is 1:27:06 PM

Exception: hour, minute and/or second was out of range
```

Fig. 9.3 | Program to test class Time. (Part I of 2.)

```
After attempting invalid settings:
Universal time: 13:27:06
Standard time: 1:27:06 PM
```

Fig. 9.3 | Program to test class `Time`. (Part 2 of 2.)

Calling `setTime` with Invalid Values
To illustrate that method `setTime` validates its arguments, line 30 calls `setTime` with invalid arguments of 99 for the `hour`, `minute` and `second`. This statement is placed in a `try` block (lines 28–31) in case `setTime` throws an `invalid_argument` exception, which it will do since the arguments are all invalid. When this occurs, the exception is caught at lines 32–35 and line 34 displays the exception's error message by calling its `what` member function. Lines 38–42 output the time again in both formats to confirm that `setTime` did not change the time when invalid arguments were supplied.

Looking Ahead to Composition and Inheritance
Often, classes do not have to be created "from scratch." Rather, they can *include objects of other classes as members* or they may be **derived** from other classes that provide attributes and behaviors the new classes can use. Such software reuse can greatly enhance productivity and simplify code maintenance. Including class objects as members of other classes is called **composition** (or **aggregation**) and is discussed in Section 9.11. Deriving new classes from existing classes is called **inheritance** and is discussed in Chapter 11.

Object Size
People new to object-oriented programming often suppose that objects must be quite large because they contain data members and member functions. *Logically*, this is true—you may think of objects as containing data and functions (and our discussion has certainly encouraged this view); *physically*, however, this is *not* true.

Performance Tip 9.2
Objects contain only data, so objects are much smaller than if they also contained member functions. The compiler creates one copy (only) of the member functions separate from all objects of the class. All objects of the class share *this one copy. Each object, of course, needs its own copy of the class's data, because the data can vary among the objects. The function code is nonmodifiable and, hence, can be shared among all objects of one class.*

9.3 Class Scope and Accessing Class Members

A class's data members and member functions belong to that class's scope. Nonmember functions are defined at *global namespace scope*, by default. (We discuss namespaces in more detail in Section 23.4.)

Within a class's scope, class members are immediately accessible by all of that class's member functions and can be referenced by name. Outside a class's scope, `public` class members are referenced through one of the **handles** on an object—an *object name*, a *reference* to an object or a *pointer* to an object. The type of the object, reference or pointer specifies the interface (e.g., the member functions) accessible to the client. [We'll see in Section 9.13 that an *implicit handle* is inserted by the compiler on every reference to a data member or member function from within an object.]

Class Scope and Block Scope

Variables declared in a member function have *block scope* and are known only to that function. If a member function defines a variable with the same name as a variable with class scope, the class-scope variable is *hidden* in the function by the block-scope variable. Such a hidden variable can be accessed by preceding the variable name with the class name followed by the scope resolution operator (::). Hidden global variables can be accessed with the scope resolution operator (see Chapter 6).

Dot (.) and Arrow (->) Member Selection Operators

The dot member selection operator (.) is preceded by an object's name or with a reference to an object to access the object's members. The **arrow member selection operator** (->) is preceded by a pointer to an object to access the object's members.

Accessing `public` Class Members Through Objects, References and Pointers

Consider an Account class that has a `public setBalance` member function. Given the following declarations:

```
Account account; // an Account object

// accountRef refers to an Account object
Account &accountRef = account;

// accountPtr points to an Account object
Account *accountPtr = &account;
```

You can invoke member function setBalance using the dot (.) and arrow (->) member selection operators as follows:

```
// call setBalance via the Account object
account.setBalance( 123.45 );

// call setBalance via a reference to the Account object
accountRef.setBalance( 123.45 );

// call setBalance via a pointer to the Account object
accountPtr->setBalance( 123.45 );
```

9.4 Access Functions and Utility Functions

Access Functions

Access functions can read or display data. Another common use for access functions is to test the truth or falsity of conditions—such functions are often called predicate functions. An example of a predicate function would be an isEmpty function for any container class—a class capable of holding many objects, like a vector. A program might test isEmpty before attempting to read another item from the container object. An isFull predicate function might test a container-class object to determine whether it has no additional room. Useful predicate functions for our Time class might be isAM and isPM.

Utility Functions

A **utility function** (also called a **helper function**) is a `private` member function that supports the operation of a class's other member functions. Utility functions are declared private because they're not intended for use by the class's clients. A common use of a utility function would be to place in a function some common code that would otherwise be duplicated in several other member functions.

9.5 Time Class Case Study: Constructors with Default Arguments

The program of Figs. 9.4–9.6 enhances class Time to demonstrate how arguments are implicitly passed to a constructor. The constructor defined in Fig. 9.2 initialized hour, minute and second to 0 (i.e., midnight in universal time). Like other functions, constructors can specify *default arguments*. Line 13 of Fig. 9.4 declares the Time constructor to include default arguments, specifying a default value of zero for each argument passed to the constructor. The constructor is declared explicit because it can be called with one argument. We discuss explicit constructors in detail in Section 10.13.

```
1   // Fig. 9.4: Time.h
2   // Time class containing a constructor with default arguments.
3   // Member functions defined in Time.cpp.
4
5   // prevent multiple inclusions of header
6   #ifndef TIME_H
7   #define TIME_H
8
9   // Time class definition
10  class Time
11  {
12  public:
13     explicit Time( int = 0, int = 0, int = 0 ); // default constructor
14
15     // set functions
16     void setTime( int, int, int ); // set hour, minute, second
17     void setHour( int ); // set hour (after validation)
18     void setMinute( int ); // set minute (after validation)
19     void setSecond( int ); // set second (after validation)
20
21     // get functions
22     unsigned int getHour() const; // return hour
23     unsigned int getMinute() const; // return minute
24     unsigned int getSecond() const; // return second
25
26     void printUniversal() const; // output time in universal-time format
27     void printStandard() const; // output time in standard-time format
28  private:
29     unsigned int hour; // 0 - 23 (24-hour clock format)
30     unsigned int minute; // 0 - 59
31     unsigned int second; // 0 - 59
32  }; // end class Time
33
34  #endif
```

Fig. 9.4 | Time class containing a constructor with default arguments.

In Fig. 9.5, lines 10–13 define the new version of the Time constructor that receives values for parameters hour, minute and second that will be used to initialize private data members hour, minute and second, respectively. The default arguments to the constructor ensure that, even if no values are provided in a constructor call, the constructor still initializes the data members. *A constructor that defaults all its arguments is also a default constructor—that is, a constructor that can be invoked with no arguments. There can be at most one default constructor per class.* The version of class Time in this example provides *set* and *get* functions for each data member. The Time constructor now calls setTime, which calls the setHour, setMinute and setSecond functions to validate and assign values to the data members.

Software Engineering Observation 9.5

Any change to the default argument values of a function requires the client code to be recompiled (to ensure that the program still functions correctly).

```cpp
1   // Fig. 9.5: Time.cpp
2   // Member-function definitions for class Time.
3   #include <iostream>
4   #include <iomanip>
5   #include <stdexcept>
6   #include "Time.h" // include definition of class Time from Time.h
7   using namespace std;
8
9   // Time constructor initializes each data member
10  Time::Time( int hour, int minute, int second )
11  {
12     setTime( hour, minute, second ); // validate and set time
13  } // end Time constructor
14
15  // set new Time value using universal time
16  void Time::setTime( int h, int m, int s )
17  {
18     setHour( h ); // set private field hour
19     setMinute( m ); // set private field minute
20     setSecond( s ); // set private field second
21  } // end function setTime
22
23  // set hour value
24  void Time::setHour( int h )
25  {
26     if ( h >= 0 && h < 24 )
27        hour = h;
28     else
29        throw invalid_argument( "hour must be 0-23" );
30  } // end function setHour
31
32  // set minute value
33  void Time::setMinute( int m )
34  {
35     if ( m >= 0 && m < 60 )
36        minute = m;
37     else
38        throw invalid_argument( "minute must be 0-59" );
39  } // end function setMinute
```

Fig. 9.5 | Member-function definitions for class Time. (Part 1 of 2.)

```
40
41   // set second value
42   void Time::setSecond( int s )
43   {
44      if ( s >= 0 && s < 60 )
45         second = s;
46      else
47         throw invalid_argument( "second must be 0-59" );
48   } // end function setSecond
49
50   // return hour value
51   unsigned int Time::getHour() const
52   {
53      return hour;
54   } // end function getHour
55
56   // return minute value
57   unsigned Time::getMinute() const
58   {
59      return minute;
60   } // end function getMinute
61
62   // return second value
63   unsigned Time::getSecond() const
64   {
65      return second;
66   } // end function getSecond
67
68   // print Time in universal-time format (HH:MM:SS)
69   void Time::printUniversal() const
70   {
71      cout << setfill( '0' ) << setw( 2 ) << getHour() << ":"
72         << setw( 2 ) << getMinute() << ":" << setw( 2 ) << getSecond();
73   } // end function printUniversal
74
75   // print Time in standard-time format (HH:MM:SS AM or PM)
76   void Time::printStandard() const
77   {
78      cout << ( ( getHour() == 0 || getHour() == 12 ) ? 12 : getHour() % 12 )
79         << ":" << setfill( '0' ) << setw( 2 ) << getMinute()
80         << ":" << setw( 2 ) << getSecond() << ( hour < 12 ? " AM" : " PM" );
81   } // end function printStandard
```

Fig. 9.5 | Member-function definitions for class Time. (Part 2 of 2.)

In Fig. 9.5, line 12 of the constructor calls member function setTime with the values passed to the constructor (or the default values). Function setTime calls setHour to ensure that the value supplied for hour is in the range 0–23, then calls setMinute and setSecond to ensure that the values for minute and second are each in the range 0–59. Functions setHour (lines 24–30), setMinute (lines 33–39) and setSecond (lines 42–48) each throw an exception if an out-of-range argument is received.

Function main in Fig. 9.6 initializes five Time objects—one with all three arguments defaulted in the implicit constructor call (line 10), one with one argument specified (line 11), one with two arguments specified (line 12), one with three arguments specified (line 13) and one with three invalid arguments specified (line 38). The program displays each object in universal-time and standard-time formats. For Time object t5 (line 38), the program displays an error message because the constructor arguments are out of range.

```cpp
1   // Fig. 9.6: fig09_06.cpp
2   // Constructor with default arguments.
3   #include <iostream>
4   #include <stdexcept>
5   #include "Time.h" // include definition of class Time from Time.h
6   using namespace std;
7
8   int main()
9   {
10      Time t1; // all arguments defaulted
11      Time t2( 2 ); // hour specified; minute and second defaulted
12      Time t3( 21, 34 ); // hour and minute specified; second defaulted
13      Time t4( 12, 25, 42 ); // hour, minute and second specified
14
15      cout << "Constructed with:\n\nt1: all arguments defaulted\n   ";
16      t1.printUniversal(); // 00:00:00
17      cout << "\n   ";
18      t1.printStandard(); // 12:00:00 AM
19
20      cout << "\n\nt2: hour specified; minute and second defaulted\n   ";
21      t2.printUniversal(); // 02:00:00
22      cout << "\n   ";
23      t2.printStandard(); // 2:00:00 AM
24
25      cout << "\n\nt3: hour and minute specified; second defaulted\n   ";
26      t3.printUniversal(); // 21:34:00
27      cout << "\n   ";
28      t3.printStandard(); // 9:34:00 PM
29
30      cout << "\n\nt4: hour, minute and second specified\n   ";
31      t4.printUniversal(); // 12:25:42
32      cout << "\n   ";
33      t4.printStandard(); // 12:25:42 PM
34
35      // attempt to initialize t6 with invalid values
36      try
37      {
38         Time t5( 27, 74, 99 ); // all bad values specified
39      } // end try
40      catch ( invalid_argument &e )
41      {
42         cerr << "\n\nException while initializing t5: " << e.what() << endl;
43      } // end catch
44   } // end main
```

Fig. 9.6 | Constructor with default arguments. (Part 1 of 2.)

```
Constructed with:

t1: all arguments defaulted
  00:00:00
  12:00:00 AM

t2: hour specified; minute and second defaulted
  02:00:00
  2:00:00 AM

t3: hour and minute specified; second defaulted
  21:34:00
  9:34:00 PM

t4: hour, minute and second specified
  12:25:42
  12:25:42 PM

Exception while initializing t5: hour must be 0-23
```

Fig. 9.6 | Constructor with default arguments. (Part 2 of 2.)

Notes Regarding Class *Time's* Set *and* Get *Functions and Constructor*

Time's *set* and *get* functions are called throughout the class's body. In particular, function setTime (lines 16–21 of Fig. 9.5) calls functions setHour, setMinute and setSecond, and functions printUniversal and printStandard call functions getHour, getMinute and getSecond in line 71–72 and lines 78–80. In each case, these functions could have accessed the class's private data directly. However, consider changing the representation of the time from three int values (requiring 12 bytes of memory on systems with four-byte ints) to a single int value representing the total number of seconds that have elapsed since midnight (requiring only four bytes of memory). If we made such a change, only the bodies of the functions that access the private data directly would need to change—in particular, the individual *set* and *get* functions for the hour, minute and second. There would be no need to modify the bodies of functions setTime, printUniversal or printStandard, because they do *not* access the data directly. Designing the class in this manner reduces the likelihood of programming errors when altering the class's implementation.

Similarly, the Time constructor could be written to include a copy of the appropriate statements from function setTime. Doing so may be slightly more efficient, because the extra call to setTime is eliminated. However, duplicating statements in multiple functions or constructors makes changing the class's internal data representation more difficult. Having the Time constructor call setTime and having setTime call setHour, setMinute and setSecond enables us to limit the changes to code that validates the hour, minute or second to the corresponding *set* function. This reduces the likelihood of errors when altering the class's implementation.

Software Engineering Observation 9.6

If a member function of a class already provides all or part of the functionality required by a constructor (or other member function) of the class, call that member function from the constructor (or other member function). This simplifies the maintenance of the code and reduces the likelihood of an error if the implementation of the code is modified. As a general rule: Avoid repeating code.

Common Programming Error 9.1

A constructor can call other member functions of the class, such as set or get functions, but because the constructor is initializing the object, the data members may not yet be initialized. Using data members before they have been properly initialized can cause logic errors.

C++11: Using List Initializers to Call Constructors

Recall from Section 4.10 that C++11 now provides a uniform initialization syntax called list initializers that can be used to initialize any variable. Lines 11–13 of Fig. 9.6 can be written using list initializers as follows:

```
Time t2{ 2 }; // hour specified; minute and second defaulted
Time t3{ 21, 34 }; // hour and minute specified; second defaulted
Time t4{ 12, 25, 42 }; // hour, minute and second specified
```

or

```
Time t2 = { 2 }; // hour specified; minute and second defaulted
Time t3 = { 21, 34 }; // hour and minute specified; second defaulted
Time t4 = { 12, 25, 42 }; // hour, minute and second specified
```

The form without the = is preferred.

C++11: Overloaded Constructors and Delegating Constructors

Section 6.18 showed how to overload functions. A class's constructors and member functions can also be overloaded. Overloaded constructors typically allow objects to be initialized with different types and/or numbers of arguments. To overload a constructor, provide in the class definition a prototype for each version of the constructor, and provide a separate constructor definition for each overloaded version. This also applies to the class's member functions.

In Figs. 9.4–9.6, the Time constructor with three parameters had a default argument for each parameter. We could have defined that constructor instead as four overloaded constructors with the following prototypes:

```
Time(); // default hour, minute and second to 0
Time( int ); // initialize hour; default minute and second to 0
Time( int, int ); // initialize hour and minute; default second to 0
Time( int, int, int ); // initialize hour, minute and second
```

Just as a constructor can call a class's other member functions to perform tasks, C++11 now allows constructors to call other constructors in the same class. The calling constructor is known as a **delegating constructor**—it *delegates* its work to another constructor. This is useful when overloaded constructors have common code that previously would have been defined in a private utility function and called by all the constructors.

The first three of the four Time constructors declared above can delegate work to one with three int arguments, passing 0 as the default value for the extra parameters. To do so, you use a member initializer with the name of the class as follows:

```
Time::Time()
   : Time( 0, 0, 0 ) // delegate to Time( int, int, int )
{
} // end constructor with no arguments
```

```
Time::Time( int hour )
   : Time( hour, 0, 0 ) // delegate to Time( int, int, int )
{
} // end constructor with one argument
Time::Time( int hour, int minute )
   : Time( hour, minute, 0 ) // delegate to Time( int, int, int )
{
} // end constructor with two arguments
```

9.6 Destructors

A **destructor** is another type of special member function. The name of the destructor for a class is the **tilde character** (~) followed by the class name. This naming convention has intuitive appeal, because as we'll see in a later chapter, the tilde operator is the bitwise complement operator, and, in a sense, the destructor is the complement of the constructor. A destructor may not specify parameters or a return type.

A class's destructor is called *implicitly* when an object is destroyed. This occurs, for example, as an object is destroyed when program execution leaves the scope in which that object was instantiated. *The destructor itself does not actually release the object's memory*—it performs **termination housekeeping** before the object's memory is reclaimed, so the memory may be reused to hold new objects.

Even though destructors have not been defined for the classes presented so far, *every class has one destructor*. If you do not *explicitly* define a destructor, the compiler defines an "empty" destructor. [*Note:* We'll see that such an *implicitly* created destructor does, in fact, perform important operations on class-type objects that are created through composition (Section 9.11) and inheritance (Chapter 11).] In Chapter 10, we'll build destructors appropriate for classes whose objects contain dynamically allocated memory (e.g., for arrays and strings) or use other system resources (e.g., files on disk, which we study in Chapter 14). We discuss how to dynamically allocate and deallocate memory in Chapter 10.

9.7 When Constructors and Destructors Are Called

Constructors and destructors are called *implicitly* by the compiler. The order in which these function calls occur depends on the order in which execution enters and leaves the scopes where the objects are instantiated. Generally, destructor calls are made in the *reverse order* of the corresponding constructor calls, but as we'll see in Figs. 9.7–9.9, the storage classes of objects can alter the order in which destructors are called.

Constructors and Destructors for Objects in Global Scope

Constructors are called for objects defined in global scope (also called global namespace scope) *before* any other function (including main) in that program begins execution (although the order of execution of global object constructors between files is *not* guaranteed). The corresponding destructors are called when main terminates. Function **exit** forces a program to terminate immediately and does *not* execute the destructors of local objects. The exit function often is used to terminate a program when a fatal unrecoverable error occurs. Function **abort** performs similarly to function exit but forces the program to terminate *immediately*, without allowing the destructors of any objects to be called. Function abort is usually used to indicate an *abnormal termination* of the program. (See Appendix F for more information on functions exit and abort.)

Constructors and Destructors for Local Objects

The constructor for an local object is called when execution reaches the point where that object is defined—the corresponding destructor is called when execution leaves the object's scope (i.e., the block in which that object is defined has finished executing). Constructors and destructors for local objects are called each time execution enters and leaves the scope of the object. Destructors are not called for local objects if the program terminates with a call to function exit or function abort.

Constructors and Destructors for static Local Objects

The constructor for a static local object is called only *once*, when execution first reaches the point where the object is defined—the corresponding destructor is called when main terminates or the program calls function exit. Global and static objects are destroyed in the *reverse* order of their creation. Destructors are *not* called for static objects if the program terminates with a call to function abort.

Demonstrating When Constructors and Destructors Are Called

The program of Figs. 9.7–9.9 demonstrates the order in which constructors and destructors are called for objects of class CreateAndDestroy (Fig. 9.7 and Fig. 9.8) of various storage classes in several scopes. Each object of class CreateAndDestroy contains an integer (objectID) and a string (message) that are used in the program's output to identify the object (Fig. 9.7, lines 16–17). This mechanical example is purely for pedagogic purposes. For this reason, line 19 of the destructor in Fig. 9.8 determines whether the object being destroyed has an objectID value 1 or 6 (line 19) and, if so, outputs a newline character. This line makes the program's output easier to follow.

```
 1   // Fig. 9.7: CreateAndDestroy.h
 2   // CreateAndDestroy class definition.
 3   // Member functions defined in CreateAndDestroy.cpp.
 4   #include <string>
 5   using namespace std;
 6
 7   #ifndef CREATE_H
 8   #define CREATE_H
 9
10   class CreateAndDestroy
11   {
12   public:
13      CreateAndDestroy( int, string ); // constructor
14      ~CreateAndDestroy(); // destructor
15   private:
16      int objectID; // ID number for object
17      string message; // message describing object
18   }; // end class CreateAndDestroy
19
20   #endif
```

Fig. 9.7 | CreateAndDestroy class definition.

```
 1   // Fig. 9.8: CreateAndDestroy.cpp
 2   // CreateAndDestroy class member-function definitions.
 3   #include <iostream>
 4   #include "CreateAndDestroy.h"// include CreateAndDestroy class definition
 5   using namespace std;
 6
 7   // constructor sets object's ID number and descriptive message
 8   CreateAndDestroy::CreateAndDestroy( int ID, string messageString )
 9      : objectID( ID ), message( messageString )
10   {
11      cout << "Object " << objectID << "   constructor runs   "
12         << message << endl;
13   } // end CreateAndDestroy constructor
14
15   // destructor
16   CreateAndDestroy::~CreateAndDestroy()
17   {
18      // output newline for certain objects; helps readability
19      cout << ( objectID == 1 || objectID == 6 ? "\n" : "" );
20
21      cout << "Object " << objectID << "   destructor runs   "
22         << message << endl;
23   } // end ~CreateAndDestroy destructor
```

Fig. 9.8 | CreateAndDestroy class member-function definitions.

Figure 9.9 defines object first (line 10) in global scope. Its constructor is actually called *before* any statements in main execute and its destructor is called at program termination *after* the destructors for all objects with automatic storage duration have run.

```
 1   // Fig. 9.9: fig09_09.cpp
 2   // Order in which constructors and
 3   // destructors are called.
 4   #include <iostream>
 5   #include "CreateAndDestroy.h" // include CreateAndDestroy class definition
 6   using namespace std;
 7
 8   void create( void ); // prototype
 9
10   CreateAndDestroy first( 1, "(global before main)" ); // global object
11
12   int main()
13   {
14      cout << "\nMAIN FUNCTION: EXECUTION BEGINS" << endl;
15      CreateAndDestroy second( 2, "(local automatic in main)" );
16      static CreateAndDestroy third( 3, "(local static in main)" );
17
18      create(); // call function to create objects
19
20      cout << "\nMAIN FUNCTION: EXECUTION RESUMES" << endl;
21      CreateAndDestroy fourth( 4, "(local automatic in main)" );
```

Fig. 9.9 | Order in which constructors and destructors are called. (Part 1 of 2.)

```
22         cout << "\nMAIN FUNCTION: EXECUTION ENDS" << endl;
23     } // end main
24
25     // function to create objects
26     void create( void )
27     {
28         cout << "\nCREATE FUNCTION: EXECUTION BEGINS" << endl;
29         CreateAndDestroy fifth( 5, "(local automatic in create)" );
30         static CreateAndDestroy sixth( 6, "(local static in create)" );
31         CreateAndDestroy seventh( 7, "(local automatic in create)" );
32         cout << "\nCREATE FUNCTION: EXECUTION ENDS" << endl;
33     } // end function create
```

```
Object 1   constructor runs    (global before main)

MAIN FUNCTION: EXECUTION BEGINS
Object 2   constructor runs    (local automatic in main)
Object 3   constructor runs    (local static in main)

CREATE FUNCTION: EXECUTION BEGINS
Object 5   constructor runs    (local automatic in create)
Object 6   constructor runs    (local static in create)
Object 7   constructor runs    (local automatic in create)

CREATE FUNCTION: EXECUTION ENDS
Object 7   destructor runs     (local automatic in create)
Object 5   destructor runs     (local automatic in create)

MAIN FUNCTION: EXECUTION RESUMES
Object 4   constructor runs    (local automatic in main)

MAIN FUNCTION: EXECUTION ENDS
Object 4   destructor runs     (local automatic in main)
Object 2   destructor runs     (local automatic in main)

Object 6   destructor runs     (local static in create)
Object 3   destructor runs     (local static in main)

Object 1   destructor runs     (global before main)
```

Fig. 9.9 | Order in which constructors and destructors are called. (Part 2 of 2.)

Function main (lines 12–23) declares three objects. Objects second (line 15) and fourth (line 21) are local objects, and object third (line 16) is a static local object. The constructor for each of these objects is called when execution reaches the point where that object is declared. The destructors for objects fourth then second are called—in the *reverse* of the order in which their constructors were called—when execution reaches the end of main. Because object third is static, it exists until program termination. The destructor for object third is called *before* the destructor for global object first, but *after* all other objects are destroyed.

Function create (lines 26–33) declares three objects—fifth (line 29) and seventh (line 31) as local automatic objects, and sixth (line 30) as a static local object. The destructors for objects seventh then fifth are called—the *reverse* of the order in which their constructors were called—when create terminates. Because sixth is static, it exists until program termination. The destructor for sixth is called *before* the destructors for third and first, but *after* all other objects are destroyed.

9.8 Time Class Case Study: A Subtle Trap— Returning a Reference or a Pointer to a private Data Member

A reference to an object is an alias for the name of the object and, hence, may be used on the left side of an assignment statement. In this context, the reference makes a perfectly acceptable *lvalue* that can receive a value. One way to use this capability is to have a public member function of a class return a reference to a private data member of that class. If a function returns a reference that is declared const, the reference is a non-modifiable *lvalue* and cannot be used to modify the data.

The program of Figs. 9.10–9.12 uses a simplified Time class (Fig. 9.10 and Fig. 9.11) to demonstrate returning a reference to a private data member with member function badSetHour (declared in Fig. 9.10 in line 15 and defined in Fig. 9.11 in lines 37–45). Such a reference return actually makes a call to member function badSetHour an alias for private data member hour! The function call can be used in any way that the private data member can be used, including as an *lvalue* in an assignment statement, thus *enabling clients of the class to clobber the class's private data at will!* A similar problem would occur if a pointer to the private data were to be returned by the function.

```
1    // Fig. 9.10: Time.h
2    // Time class declaration.
3    // Member functions defined in Time.cpp
4
5    // prevent multiple inclusions of header
6    #ifndef TIME_H
7    #define TIME_H
8
9    class Time
10   {
11   public:
12      explicit Time( int = 0, int = 0, int = 0 );
13      void setTime( int, int, int );
14      unsigned int getHour() const;
15      unsigned int &badSetHour( int ); // dangerous reference return
16   private:
17      unsigned int hour;
18      unsigned int minute;
19      unsigned int second;
20   }; // end class Time
21
22   #endif
```

Fig. 9.10 | Time class declaration.

```
 1   // Fig. 9.11: Time.cpp
 2   // Time class member-function definitions.
 3   #include <stdexcept>
 4   #include "Time.h" // include definition of class Time
 5   using namespace std;
 6
 7   // constructor function to initialize private data; calls member function
 8   // setTime to set variables; default values are 0 (see class definition)
 9   Time::Time( int hr, int min, int sec )
10   {
11      setTime( hr, min, sec );
12   } // end Time constructor
13
14   // set values of hour, minute and second
15   void Time::setTime( int h, int m, int s )
16   {
17      // validate hour, minute and second
18      if ( ( h >= 0 && h < 24 ) && ( m >= 0 && m < 60 ) &&
19        ( s >= 0 && s < 60 ) )
20      {
21        hour = h;
22        minute = m;
23        second = s;
24      } // end if
25      else
26        throw invalid_argument(
27          "hour, minute and/or second was out of range" );
28   } // end function setTime
29
30   // return hour value
31   unsigned int Time::getHour()
32   {
33      return hour;
34   } // end function getHour
35
36   // poor practice: returning a reference to a private data member.
37   unsigned int &Time::badSetHour( int hh )
38   {
39      if ( hh >= 0 && hh < 24 )
40        hour = hh;
41      else
42        throw invalid_argument( "hour must be 0-23" );
43
44      return hour; // dangerous reference return
45   } // end function badSetHour
```

Fig. 9.11 | Time class member-function definitions.

Figure 9.12 declares Time object t (line 10) and reference hourRef (line 13), which is initialized with the reference returned by the call t.badSetHour(20). Line 15 displays the value of the alias hourRef. This shows how hourRef *breaks the encapsulation of the class*—statements in main should not have access to the private data of the class. Next, line 16 uses the alias to set the value of hour to 30 (an invalid value) and line 17 displays the value returned by function getHour to show that assigning a value to hourRef actually modifies the `private` data in the Time object t. Finally, line 21 uses the badSetHour function call itself as an *lvalue* and assigns 74 (another invalid value) to the reference returned by the function. Line 26 again displays the value returned by function getHour to show that assigning a value to the result of the function call in line 21 modifies the `private` data in the Time object t.

 Software Engineering Observation 9.7

Returning a reference or a pointer to a `private` data member breaks the encapsulation of the class and makes the client code dependent on the representation of the class's data. There are cases where doing this is appropriate—we'll show an example of this when we build our custom Array class in Section 10.10.

```cpp
1   // Fig. 9.12: fig09_12.cpp
2   // Demonstrating a public member function that
3   // returns a reference to a private data member.
4   #include <iostream>
5   #include "Time.h" // include definition of class Time
6   using namespace std;
7
8   int main()
9   {
10      Time t; // create Time object
11
12      // initialize hourRef with the reference returned by badSetHour
13      int &hourRef = t.badSetHour( 20 ); // 20 is a valid hour
14
15      cout << "Valid hour before modification: " << hourRef;
16      hourRef = 30; // use hourRef to set invalid value in Time object t
17      cout << "\nInvalid hour after modification: " << t.getHour();
18
19      // Dangerous: Function call that returns
20      // a reference can be used as an lvalue!
21      t.badSetHour( 12 ) = 74; // assign another invalid value to hour
22
23      cout << "\n\n*************************************************\n"
24         << "POOR PROGRAMMING PRACTICE!!!!!!!!\n"
25         << "t.badSetHour( 12 ) as an lvalue, invalid hour: "
26         << t.getHour()
27         << "\n*************************************************" << endl;
28   } // end main
```

```
Valid hour before modification: 20
Invalid hour after modification: 30

*************************************************
POOR PROGRAMMING PRACTICE!!!!!!!!
t.badSetHour( 12 ) as an lvalue, invalid hour: 74
*************************************************
```

Fig. 9.12 | `public` member function that returns a reference to a `private` data member.

9.9 Default Memberwise Assignment

The assignment operator (=) can be used to assign an object to another object of the
same class. By default, such assignment is performed by memberwise assignment (also
called copy assignment)—each data member of the object on the *right* of the assignment
operator is assigned individually to the *same* data member in the object on the *left* of the
assignment operator. Figures 9.13–9.14 define a Date class. Line 18 of Fig. 9.15 uses default memberwise assignment to assign the data members of Date object date1 to the
corresponding data members of Date object date2. In this case, the month member of
date1 is assigned to the month member of date2, the day member of date1 is assigned
to the day member of date2 and the year member of date1 is assigned to the year member of date2. [*Caution:* Memberwise assignment can cause serious problems when used
with a class whose data members contain pointers to dynamically allocated memory; we
discuss these problems in Chapter 10 and show how to deal with them.]

```cpp
1   // Fig. 9.13: Date.h
2   // Date class declaration.  Member functions are defined in Date.cpp.
3
4   // prevent multiple inclusions of header
5   #ifndef DATE_H
6   #define DATE_H
7
8   // class Date definition
9   class Date
10  {
11  public:
12     explicit Date( int = 1, int = 1, int = 2000 ); // default constructor
13     void print();
14  private:
15     unsigned int month;
16     unsigned int day;
17     unsigned int year;
18  }; // end class Date
19
20  #endif
```

Fig. 9.13 | Date class declaration.

```cpp
1   // Fig. 9.14: Date.cpp
2   // Date class member-function definitions.
3   #include <iostream>
4   #include "Date.h" // include definition of class Date from Date.h
5   using namespace std;
6
7   // Date constructor (should do range checking)
8   Date::Date( int m, int d, int y )
9      : month( m ), day( d ), year( y )
10  {
11  } // end constructor Date
```

Fig. 9.14 | Date class member-function definitions. (Part 1 of 2.)

```
12
13   // print Date in the format mm/dd/yyyy
14   void Date::print()
15   {
16      cout << month << '/' << day << '/' << year;
17   } // end function print
```

Fig. 9.14 | Date class member-function definitions. (Part 2 of 2.)

```
1    // Fig. 9.15: fig09_15.cpp
2    // Demonstrating that class objects can be assigned
3    // to each other using default memberwise assignment.
4    #include <iostream>
5    #include "Date.h" // include definition of class Date from Date.h
6    using namespace std;
7
8    int main()
9    {
10      Date date1( 7, 4, 2004 );
11      Date date2; // date2 defaults to 1/1/2000
12
13      cout << "date1 = ";
14      date1.print();
15      cout << "\ndate2 = ";
16      date2.print();
17
18      date2 = date1; // default memberwise assignment
19
20      cout << "\n\nAfter default memberwise assignment, date2 = ";
21      date2.print();
22      cout << endl;
23   } // end main
```

```
date1 = 7/4/2004
date2 = 1/1/2000

After default memberwise assignment, date2 = 7/4/2004
```

Fig. 9.15 | Class objects can be assigned to each other using default memberwise assignment.

Objects may be passed as function arguments and may be returned from functions. Such passing and returning is performed using pass-by-value by default—a *copy* of the object is passed or returned. In such cases, C++ creates a new object and uses a **copy constructor** to copy the original object's values into the new object. For each class, the compiler provides a default copy constructor that copies each member of the original object into the corresponding member of the new object. Like memberwise assignment, copy constructors can cause serious problems when used with a class whose data members contain pointers to dynamically allocated memory. Chapter 10 discusses how to define customized copy constructors that properly copy objects containing pointers to dynamically allocated memory.

9.10 const Objects and const Member Functions

Let's see how the principle of least privilege applies to objects. Some objects need to be modifiable and some do not. You may use keyword const to specify that an object *is not* modifiable and that any attempt to modify the object should result in a compilation error. The statement

```
const Time noon( 12, 0, 0 );
```

declares a const object noon of class Time and initializes it to 12 noon. It's possible to instantiate const and non-const objects of the same class.

Software Engineering Observation 9.8

Attempts to modify a const object are caught at compile time rather than causing execution-time errors.

Performance Tip 9.3

Declaring variables and objects const when appropriate can improve performance—compilers can perform optimizations on constants that cannot be performed on non-const variables.

C++ disallows member function calls for const objects unless the member functions themselves are also declared const. This is true even for get member functions that do not modify the object. This is also a key reason that we've declared as const all member-functions that do not modify the objects on which they're called.

As you saw starting with class GradeBook in Chapter 3, a member function is specified as const *both* in its prototype by inserting the keyword const *after* the function's parameter list and, in the case of the function definition, before the left brace that begins the function *body.*

Common Programming Error 9.2

Defining as const a member function that modifies a data member of the object is a compilation error.

Common Programming Error 9.3

Defining as const a member function that calls a non-const member function of the class on the same object is a compilation error.

Common Programming Error 9.4

Invoking a non-const member function on a const object is a compilation error.

An interesting problem arises for constructors and destructors, each of which typically modifies objects. A constructor *must* be allowed to modify an object so that the object can be initialized properly. A destructor must be able to perform its termination housekeeping chores before an object's memory is reclaimed by the system. Attempting to declare a constructor or destructor const is a compilation error. The "constness" of a const object is enforced from the time the constructor *completes* initialization of the object until that object's destructor is called.

Using const and Non-const Member Functions

The program of Fig. 9.16 uses class Time from Figs. 9.4–9.5, but removes const from function printStandard's prototype and definition so that we can show a compilation error. We instantiate two Time objects—non-const object wakeUp (line 7) and const object noon (line 8). The program attempts to invoke non-const member functions setHour (line 13) and printStandard (line 20) on the const object noon. In each case, the compiler generates an error message. The program also illustrates the three other member-function-call combinations on objects—a non-const member function on a non-const object (line 11), a const member function on a non-const object (line 15) and a const member function on a const object (lines 17–18). The error messages generated for non-const member functions called on a const object are shown in the output window.

```cpp
1   // Fig. 9.16: fig09_16.cpp
2   // const objects and const member functions.
3   #include "Time.h" // include Time class definition
4
5   int main()
6   {
7      Time wakeUp( 6, 45, 0 ); // non-constant object
8      const Time noon( 12, 0, 0 ); // constant object
9
10                            // OBJECT       MEMBER FUNCTION
11     wakeUp.setHour( 18 );  // non-const    non-const
12
13     noon.setHour( 12 );    // const        non-const
14
15     wakeUp.getHour();      // non-const    const
16
17     noon.getMinute();      // const        const
18     noon.printUniversal(); // const        const
19
20     noon.printStandard();  // const        non-const
21  } // end main
```

Microsoft Visual C++ compiler error messages:

```
C:\examples\ch09\Fig09_16_18\fig09_18.cpp(13) : error C2662:
   'Time::setHour' : cannot convert 'this' pointer from 'const Time' to
   'Time &'
         Conversion loses qualifiers
C:\examples\ch09\Fig09_16_18\fig09_18.cpp(20) : error C2662:
   'Time::printStandard' : cannot convert 'this' pointer from 'const Time' to
   'Time &'
         Conversion loses qualifiers
```

Fig. 9.16 | const objects and const member functions.

A constructor must be a non-const member function, but it can still be used to initialize a const object (Fig. 9.16, line 8). Recall from Fig. 9.5 that the Time constructor's definition calls another non-const member function—setTime—to perform the initialization of a Time object. Invoking a non-const member function from the constructor call as part of the initialization of a const object is allowed.

Line 20 in Fig. 9.16 generates a compilation error even though member function printStandard of class Time *does not* modify the object on which it's invoked. The fact that a member function does not modify an object is *not* sufficient—the function must *explicitly* be declared const.

9.11 Composition: Objects as Members of Classes

An AlarmClock object needs to know when it's supposed to sound its alarm, so why not include a Time object as a member of the AlarmClock class? Such a capability is called **composition** and is sometimes referred to as a *has-a relationship—a class can have objects of other classes as members.*

Software Engineering Observation 9.9

A common form of software reusability is composition, in which a class has objects of other types as members.

Previously, we saw how to pass arguments to the constructor of an object we created in main. Now we show how *an class's constructor can pass arguments to member-object constructors via member initializers.*

Software Engineering Observation 9.10

Data members are constructed in the order in which they're declared in the class definition (not in the order they're listed in the constructor's member initializer list) and before their enclosing class objects (sometimes called host objects) are constructed.

The next program uses classes Date (Figs. 9.17–9.18) and Employee (Figs. 9.19–9.20) to demonstrate composition. Class Employee's definition (Fig. 9.19) contains private data members firstName, lastName, birthDate and hireDate. Members birthDate and hireDate are const objects of class Date, which contains private data members month, day and year. The Employee constructor's header (Fig. 9.20, lines 10–11) specifies that the constructor has four parameters (first, last, dateOfBirth and dateOfHire). The first two parameters are passed via member initializers to the string class constructor for the firstName and lastName data members. The last two are passed via member initializers to the Date class constructor for the birthDate and hireDate data members..

```
 1   // Fig. 9.17: Date.h
 2   // Date class definition; Member functions defined in Date.cpp
 3   #ifndef DATE_H
 4   #define DATE_H
 5
 6   class Date
 7   {
 8   public:
 9      static const unsigned int monthsPerYear = 12; // months in a year
10      explicit Date( int = 1, int = 1, int = 1900 ); // default constructor
11      void print() const; // print date in month/day/year format
12      ~Date(); // provided to confirm destruction order
```

Fig. 9.17 | Date class definition. (Part 1 of 2.)

```
13  private:
14     unsigned int month; // 1-12 (January-December)
15     unsigned int day; // 1-31 based on month
16     unsigned int year; // any year
17
18     // utility function to check if day is proper for month and year
19     unsigned int checkDay( int ) const;
20  }; // end class Date
21
22  #endif
```

Fig. 9.17 | Date class definition. (Part 2 of 2.)

```
1   // Fig. 9.18: Date.cpp
2   // Date class member-function definitions.
3   #include <array>
4   #include <iostream>
5   #include <stdexcept>
6   #include "Date.h" // include Date class definition
7   using namespace std;
8
9   // constructor confirms proper value for month; calls
10  // utility function checkDay to confirm proper value for day
11  Date::Date( int mn, int dy, int yr )
12  {
13     if ( mn > 0 && mn <= monthsPerYear ) // validate the month
14        month = mn;
15     else
16        throw invalid_argument( "month must be 1-12" );
17
18     year = yr; // could validate yr
19     day = checkDay( dy ); // validate the day
20
21     // output Date object to show when its constructor is called
22     cout << "Date object constructor for date ";
23     print();
24     cout << endl;
25  } // end Date constructor
26
27  // print Date object in form month/day/year
28  void Date::print() const
29  {
30     cout << month << '/' << day << '/' << year;
31  } // end function print
32
33  // output Date object to show when its destructor is called
34  Date::~Date()
35  {
36     cout << "Date object destructor for date ";
37     print();
38     cout << endl;
39  } // end ~Date destructor
```

Fig. 9.18 | Date class member-function definitions. (Part 1 of 2.)

```
40
41   // utility function to confirm proper day value based on
42   // month and year; handles leap years, too
43   unsigned int Date::checkDay( int testDay ) const
44   {
45      static const array< int, monthsPerYear + 1 > daysPerMonth =
46         { 0, 31, 28, 31, 30, 31, 30, 31, 31, 30, 31, 30, 31 };
47
48      // determine whether testDay is valid for specified month
49      if ( testDay > 0 && testDay <= daysPerMonth[ month ] )
50         return testDay;
51
52      // February 29 check for leap year
53      if ( month == 2 && testDay == 29 && ( year % 400 == 0 ||
54         ( year % 4 == 0 && year % 100 != 0 ) ) )
55         return testDay;
56
57      throw invalid_argument( "Invalid day for current month and year" );
58   } // end function checkDay
```

Fig. 9.18 | Date class member-function definitions. (Part 2 of 2.)

```
1   // Fig. 9.19: Employee.h
2   // Employee class definition showing composition.
3   // Member functions defined in Employee.cpp.
4   #ifndef EMPLOYEE_H
5   #define EMPLOYEE_H
6
7   #include <string>
8   #include "Date.h" // include Date class definition
9
10  class Employee
11  {
12  public:
13     Employee( const std::string &, const std::string &,
14        const Date &, const Date & );
15     void print() const;
16     ~Employee(); // provided to confirm destruction order
17  private:
18     std::string firstName; // composition: member object
19     std::string lastName; // composition: member object
20     const Date birthDate; // composition: member object
21     const Date hireDate; // composition: member object
22  }; // end class Employee
23
24  #endif
```

Fig. 9.19 | Employee class definition showing composition.

```
 1    // Fig. 9.20: Employee.cpp
 2    // Employee class member-function definitions.
 3    #include <iostream>
 4    #include "Employee.h" // Employee class definition
 5    #include "Date.h" // Date class definition
 6    using namespace std;
 7
 8    // constructor uses member initializer list to pass initializer
 9    // values to constructors of member objects
10    Employee::Employee( const string &first, const string &last,
11       const Date &dateOfBirth, const Date &dateOfHire )
12       : firstName( first ), // initialize firstName
13         lastName( last ), // initialize lastName
14         birthDate( dateOfBirth ), // initialize birthDate
15         hireDate( dateOfHire ) // initialize hireDate
16    {
17       // output Employee object to show when constructor is called
18       cout << "Employee object constructor: "
19          << firstName << ' ' << lastName << endl;
20    } // end Employee constructor
21
22    // print Employee object
23    void Employee::print() const
24    {
25       cout << lastName << ", " << firstName << "  Hired: ";
26       hireDate.print();
27       cout << "  Birthday: ";
28       birthDate.print();
29       cout << endl;
30    } // end function print
31
32    // output Employee object to show when its destructor is called
33    Employee::~Employee()
34    {
35       cout << "Employee object destructor: "
36          << lastName << ", " << firstName << endl;
37    } // end ~Employee destructor
```

Fig. 9.20 | Employee class member-function definitions.

Employee Constructor's Member Initializer List

The *colon (:)* following the constructor's header (Fig. 9.20, line 12) begins the *member initializer list*. The member initializers specify the Employee constructor parameters being passed to the constructors of the string and Date data members. Parameters first, last, dateOfBirth and dateOfHire are passed to the constructors for objects firstName (line 12), lastName (line 13), birthDate (line 14) and hireDate (line 15), respectively. Again, member initializers are separated by commas. The order of the member initializers does not matter. They're executed in the order that the member objects are declared in class Employee.

Good Programming Practice 9.3

For clarity, list member initializers in the order that the class's data members are declared.

Date Class's Default Copy Constructor

As you study class Date (Fig. 9.17), notice that the class does *not* provide a constructor that receives a parameter of type Date. So, why can the Employee constructor's member initializer list initialize the birthDate and hireDate objects by passing Date objects to their Date constructors? As we mentioned in Section 9.9, the compiler provides each class with a *default copy constructor* that copies each data member of the constructor's argument object into the corresponding member of the object being initialized. Chapter 10 discusses how you can define *customized* copy constructors.

Testing Classes Date and Employee

Figure 9.21 creates two Date objects (lines 10–11) and passes them as arguments to the constructor of the Employee object created in line 12. Line 15 outputs the Employee object's data. When each Date object is created in lines 10–11, the Date constructor defined in lines 11–25 of Fig. 9.18 displays a line of output to show that the constructor was called (see the first two lines of the sample output). [*Note:* Line 12 of Fig. 9.21 causes two additional Date constructor calls that do not appear in the program's output. When each of the Employee's Date member objects is initialized in the Employee constructor's member-initializer list (Fig. 9.20, lines 14–15), the default copy constructor for class Date is called. Since this constructor is defined implicitly by the compiler, it does not contain any output statements to demonstrate when it's called.]

```
1   // Fig. 9.21: fig09_21.cpp
2   // Demonstrating composition--an object with member objects.
3   #include <iostream>
4   #include "Date.h" // Date class definition
5   #include "Employee.h" // Employee class definition
6   using namespace std;
7
8   int main()
9   {
10     Date birth( 7, 24, 1949 );
11     Date hire( 3, 12, 1988 );
12     Employee manager( "Bob", "Blue", birth, hire );
13
14     cout << endl;
15     manager.print();
16  } // end main
```

```
Date object constructor for date 7/24/1949
Date object constructor for date 3/12/1988
Employee object constructor: Bob Blue

Blue, Bob  Hired: 3/12/1988  Birthday: 7/24/1949
Employee object destructor: Blue, Bob
Date object destructor for date 3/12/1988
Date object destructor for date 7/24/1949
Date object destructor for date 3/12/1988
Date object destructor for date 7/24/1949
```

There are actually five constructor calls when an Employee is constructed—two calls to the string class's constructor (lines 12–13 of Fig. 9.20), two calls to the Date class's default copy constructor (lines 14–15 of Fig. 9.20) and the call to the Employee class's constructor.

Fig. 9.21 | Demonstrating composition—an object with member objects.

Class `Date` and class `Employee` each include a destructor (lines 34–39 of Fig. 9.18 and lines 33–37 of Fig. 9.20, respectively) that prints a message when an object of its class is destructed. This enables us to confirm in the program output that objects are constructed from the *inside out* and destroyed in the *reverse* order, from the *outside in* (i.e., the `Date` *member* objects are destroyed after the `Employee` object that *contains* them).

Notice the last four lines in the output of Fig. 9.21. The last two lines are the outputs of the `Date` destructor running on `Date` objects `hire` (Fig. 9.21, line 11) and `birth` (Fig. 9.21, line 10), respectively. These outputs confirm that the three objects created in `main` are destructed in the *reverse* of the order in which they were constructed. The `Employee` destructor output is five lines from the bottom. The fourth and third lines from the bottom of the output window show the destructors running for the `Employee`'s member objects `hireDate` (Fig. 9.19, line 21) and `birthDate` (Fig. 9.19, line 20). The last two lines of the output correspond to the `Date` objects created in lines 11 and 10 of Fig. 9.21.

These outputs confirm that the `Employee` object is destructed from the *outside in*—i.e., the `Employee` destructor runs first (output shown five lines from the bottom of the output window), then the member objects are destructed in the *reverse order* from which they were constructed. Class `string`'s destructor does not contain output statements, so we do *not* see the `firstName` and `lastName` objects being destructed. Again, Fig. 9.21's output did not show the constructors running for member objects `birthDate` and `hireDate`, because these objects were initialized with the *default* `Date` class copy constructors provided by the compiler.

What Happens When You Do Not Use the Member Initializer List?

If a member object is *not* initialized through a member initializer, the member object's *default constructor* will be called *implicitly*. Values, if any, established by the default constructor can be overridden by *set* functions. However, for complex initialization, this approach may require significant additional work and time.

Common Programming Error 9.5

A compilation error occurs if a member object is not initialized with a member initializer and the member object's class does not provide a default constructor (i.e., the member object's class defines one or more constructors, but none is a default constructor).

Performance Tip 9.4

Initialize member objects explicitly through member initializers. This eliminates the overhead of "doubly initializing" member objects—once when the member object's default constructor is called and again when set *functions are called in the constructor body (or later) to initialize the member object.*

Software Engineering Observation 9.11

If a data member is an object of another class, making that member object public *does not violate the encapsulation and hiding of that member object's* private *members. But, it does violate the encapsulation and hiding of the containing class's implementation, so member objects of class types should still be* private*.*

9.12 friend Functions and friend Classes

A **friend** function of a class is a non-member function that has the right to access the public *and* non-public class members. Standalone functions, entire classes or member functions of other classes may be declared to be *friends* of another class.

This section presents a mechanical example of how a friend function works. In Chapter 10 we'll show friend functions that overload operators for use with class objects—as you'll see, sometimes a member function cannot be used for certain overloaded operators.

Declaring a friend

To declare a function as a friend of a class, precede the function prototype in the class definition with keyword friend. To declare all member functions of class ClassTwo as friends of class ClassOne, place a declaration of the form

```
friend class ClassTwo;
```

in the definition of class ClassOne.

Friendship is *granted, not taken*—for class B to be a friend of class A, class A must *explicitly* declare that class B is its friend. Friendship is not *symmetric*—if class A is a friend of class B, you cannot infer that class B is a friend of class A. Friendship is not *transitive*—if class A is a friend of class B and class B is a friend of class C, you cannot infer that class A is a friend of class C.

Modifying a Class's private Data with a Friend Function

Figure 9.22 is a mechanical example in which we define friend function setX to set the private data member x of class Count. As a convention, we place the friend declaration (line 9) *first* in the class definition, even before public member functions are declared. Again, this friend declaration can appear *anywhere* in the class.

Function setX (lines 29–32) is a stand-alone (global) function—it isn't a member function of class Count. For this reason, when setX is invoked for object counter, line 41 passes counter as an argument to setX rather than using a handle (such as the name of the object) to call the function, as in

```
counter.setX( 8 ); // error: setX not a member function
```

If you remove the friend declaration in line 9, you'll receive error messages indicating that function setX cannot modify class Count's private data member x.

```
1   //Fig. 9.22: fig09_22.cpp
2   // Friends can access private members of a class.
3   #include <iostream>
4   using namespace std;
5
6   // Count class definition
7   class Count
8   {
9      friend void setX( Count &, int ); // friend declaration
```

Fig. 9.22 | Friends can access private members of a class. (Part 1 of 2.)

```
10   public:
11      // constructor
12      Count()
13         : x( 0 ) // initialize x to 0
14      {
15         // empty body
16      } // end constructor Count
17
18      // output x
19      void print() const
20      {
21         cout << x << endl;
22      } // end function print
23   private:
24      int x; // data member
25   }; // end class Count
26
27   // function setX can modify private data of Count
28   // because setX is declared as a friend of Count (line 9)
29   void setX( Count &c, int val )
30   {
31      c.x = val; // allowed because setX is a friend of Count
32   } // end function setX
33
34   int main()
35   {
36      Count counter; // create Count object
37
38      cout << "counter.x after instantiation: ";
39      counter.print();
40
41      setX( counter, 8 ); // set x using a friend function
42      cout << "counter.x after call to setX friend function: ";
43      counter.print();
44   } // end main
```

```
counter.x after instantiation: 0
counter.x after call to setX friend function: 8
```

Fig. 9.22 | Friends can access private members of a class. (Part 2 of 2.)

As we mentioned, Fig. 9.22 is a mechanical example of using the friend construct. It would normally be appropriate to define function setX as a member function of class Count. It would also normally be appropriate to separate the program of Fig. 9.22 into three files:

1. A header (e.g., Count.h) containing the Count class definition, which in turn contains the prototype of friend function setX

2. An implementation file (e.g., Count.cpp) containing the definitions of class Count's member functions and the definition of friend function setX

3. A test program (e.g., fig09_22.cpp) with main.

*Overloaded **friend** Functions*

It's possible to specify overloaded functions as friends of a class. Each function intended to be a friend must be explicitly declared in the class definition as a friend of the class.

> **Software Engineering Observation 9.12**
>
> *Even though the prototypes for friend functions appear in the class definition, friends are not member functions.*

> **Software Engineering Observation 9.13**
>
> *Member access notions of private, protected and public are not relevant to friend declarations, so friend declarations can be placed anywhere in a class definition.*

> **Good Programming Practice 9.4**
>
> *Place all friendship declarations first inside the class definition's body and do not precede them with any access specifier.*

9.13 Using the this Pointer

We've seen that an object's member functions can manipulate the object's data. There can be *many* objects of a class, so how do member functions know *which* object's data members to manipulate? Every object has access to its own address through a pointer called **this** (a C++ keyword). The this pointer is *not* part of the object itself—i.e., the memory occupied by the this pointer is not reflected in the result of a sizeof operation on the object. Rather, the this pointer is passed (by the compiler) as an *implicit* argument to each of the object's non-static member functions. Section 9.14 introduces static class members and explains why the this pointer is *not* implicitly passed to static member functions.

*Using the **this** Pointer to Avoid Naming Collisions*

Member functions use the this pointer *implicitly* (as we've done so far) or *explicitly* to reference an object's data members and other member functions. A common *explicit* use of the this pointer is to avoid *naming conflicts* between a class's data members and member-function parameters (or other local variables). Consider the Time class's hour data member and setHour member function in Figs. 9.4–9.5. We could have defined setHour as:

```
// set hour value
void Time::setHour( int hour )
{
   if ( hour >= 0 && hour < 24 )
      this->hour = hour; // use this pointer to access data member
   else
      throw invalid_argument( "hour must be 0-23" );
} // end function setHour
```

In this function definition, setHour's parameter has the *same name* as the data member hour. In setHour's scope, the parameter hour *hides* the data member. However, you can still access the data member hour by qualifying its name with this->. So the following statement assigns the hour parameter's value to the data member hour

```
this->hour = hour; // use this pointer to access data member
```

> **Error-Prevention Tip 9.4**
> *To make your code clearer and more maintainable, and to avoid errors, never hide data members with local variable names.*

Type of the *this* Pointer

The type of the this pointer depends on the type of the object and whether the member function in which this is used is declared const. For example, in a non-const member function of class Employee, the this pointer has the type Employee *. In a const member function, the this pointer has the type const Employee *.

Implicitly and Explicitly Using the *this* Pointer to Access an Object's Data Members

Figure 9.23 demonstrates the implicit and explicit use of the this pointer to enable a member function of class Test to print the private data x of a Test object. In the next example and in Chapter 10, we show some substantial and subtle examples of using this.

```cpp
1  // Fig. 9.23: fig09_23.cpp
2  // Using the this pointer to refer to object members.
3  #include <iostream>
4  using namespace std;
5
6  class Test
7  {
8  public:
9     explicit Test( int = 0 ); // default constructor
10    void print() const;
11 private:
12    int x;
13 }; // end class Test
14
15 // constructor
16 Test::Test( int value )
17    : x( value ) // initialize x to value
18 {
19    // empty body
20 } // end constructor Test
21
22 // print x using implicit and explicit this pointers;
23 // the parentheses around *this are required
24 void Test::print() const
25 {
26    // implicitly use the this pointer to access the member x
27    cout << "        x = " << x;
28
29    // explicitly use the this pointer and the arrow operator
30    // to access the member x
31    cout << "\n  this->x = " << this->x;
32
```

Fig. 9.23 | using the this pointer to refer to object members. (Part 1 of 2.)

```
33        // explicitly use the dereferenced this pointer and
34        // the dot operator to access the member x
35        cout << "\n(*this).x = " << ( *this ).x << endl;
36     } // end function print
37
38     int main()
39     {
40        Test testObject( 12 ); // instantiate and initialize testObject
41
42        testObject.print();
43     } // end main
```

```
      x = 12
  this->x = 12
(*this).x = 12
```

Fig. 9.23 | using the this pointer to refer to object members. (Part 2 of 2.)

For illustration purposes, member function print (lines 24–36) first prints x by using the this pointer *implicitly* (line 27)—only the name of the data member is specified. Then print uses two different notations to access x through the this pointer—the arrow operator (->) off the this pointer (line 31) and the dot operator (.) off the dereferenced this pointer (line 35). Note the parentheses around *this (line 35) when used with the dot member selection operator (.). The parentheses are required because the dot operator has *higher* precedence than the * operator. Without the parentheses, the expression *this.x would be evaluated as if it were parenthesized as *(this.x), which is a *compilation error*, because the dot operator cannot be used with a pointer.

One interesting use of the this pointer is to prevent an object from being assigned to itself. As we'll see in Chapter 10, *self-assignment* can cause serious errors when the object contains pointers to dynamically allocated storage.

Using the **this** Pointer to Enable Cascaded Function Calls

Another use of the this pointer is to enable cascaded member-function calls—that is, invoking multiple functions in the same statement (as in line 12 of Fig. 9.26). The program of Figs. 9.24–9.26 modifies class Time's *set* functions setTime, setHour, setMinute and setSecond such that each returns a reference to a Time object to enable cascaded member-function calls. Notice in Fig. 9.25 that the last statement in the body of each of these member functions returns *this (lines 23, 34, 45 and 56) into a return type of Time &.

The program of Fig. 9.26 creates Time object t (line 9), then uses it in *cascaded member-function calls* (lines 12 and 24). Why does the technique of returning *this as a reference work? The dot operator (.) associates from left to right, so line 12 first evaluates t.setHour(18), then returns a reference to object t as the value of this function call. The remaining expression is then interpreted as

```
    t.setMinute( 30 ).setSecond( 22 );
```

The t.setMinute(30) call executes and returns a reference to the object t. The remaining expression is interpreted as

```
    t.setSecond( 22 );
```

```
1    // Fig. 9.24: Time.h
2    // Cascading member function calls.
3
4    // Time class definition.
5    // Member functions defined in Time.cpp.
6    #ifndef TIME_H
7    #define TIME_H
8
9    class Time
10   {
11   public:
12      explicit Time( int = 0, int = 0, int = 0 ); // default constructor
13
14      // set functions (the Time & return types enable cascading)
15      Time &setTime( int, int, int ); // set hour, minute, second
16      Time &setHour( int ); // set hour
17      Time &setMinute( int ); // set minute
18      Time &setSecond( int ); // set second
19
20      // get functions (normally declared const)
21      unsigned int getHour() const; // return hour
22      unsigned int getMinute() const; // return minute
23      unsigned int getSecond() const; // return second
24
25      // print functions (normally declared const)
26      void printUniversal() const; // print universal time
27      void printStandard() const; // print standard time
28   private:
29      unsigned int hour; // 0 - 23 (24-hour clock format)
30      unsigned int minute; // 0 - 59
31      unsigned int second; // 0 - 59
32   }; // end class Time
33
34   #endif
```

Fig. 9.24 | Time class modified to enable cascaded member-function calls.

```
1    // Fig. 9.25: Time.cpp
2    // Time class member-function definitions.
3    #include <iostream>
4    #include <iomanip>
5    #include <stdexcept>
6    #include "Time.h" // Time class definition
7    using namespace std;
8
9    // constructor function to initialize private data;
10   // calls member function setTime to set variables;
11   // default values are 0 (see class definition)
12   Time::Time( int hr, int min, int sec )
13   {
```

Fig. 9.25 | Time class member-function definitions modified to enable cascaded member-function calls. (Part 1 of 3.)

```
14        setTime( hr, min, sec );
15    } // end Time constructor
16
17    // set values of hour, minute, and second
18    Time &Time::setTime( int h, int m, int s ) // note Time & return
19    {
20        setHour( h );
21        setMinute( m );
22        setSecond( s );
23        return *this; // enables cascading
24    } // end function setTime
25
26    // set hour value
27    Time &Time::setHour( int h ) // note Time & return
28    {
29        if ( h >= 0 && h < 24 )
30            hour = h;
31        else
32            throw invalid_argument( "hour must be 0-23" );
33
34        return *this; // enables cascading
35    } // end function setHour
36
37    // set minute value
38    Time &Time::setMinute( int m ) // note Time & return
39    {
40        if ( m >= 0 && m < 60 )
41            minute = m;
42        else
43            throw invalid_argument( "minute must be 0-59" );
44
45        return *this; // enables cascading
46    } // end function setMinute
47
48    // set second value
49    Time &Time::setSecond( int s ) // note Time & return
50    {
51        if ( s >= 0 && s < 60 )
52            second = s;
53        else
54            throw invalid_argument( "second must be 0-59" );
55
56        return *this; // enables cascading
57    } // end function setSecond
58
59    // get hour value
60    unsigned int Time::getHour() const
61    {
62        return hour;
63    } // end function getHour
64
```

Fig. 9.25 | Time class member-function definitions modified to enable cascaded member-function calls. (Part 2 of 3.)

```
65    // get minute value
66    unsigned int Time::getMinute() const
67    {
68       return minute;
69    } // end function getMinute
70
71    // get second value
72    unsigned int Time::getSecond() const
73    {
74       return second;
75    } // end function getSecond
76
77    // print Time in universal-time format (HH:MM:SS)
78    void Time::printUniversal() const
79    {
80       cout << setfill( '0' ) << setw( 2 ) << hour << ":"
81          << setw( 2 ) << minute << ":" << setw( 2 ) << second;
82    } // end function printUniversal
83
84    // print Time in standard-time format (HH:MM:SS AM or PM)
85    void Time::printStandard() const
86    {
87       cout << ( ( hour == 0 || hour == 12 ) ? 12 : hour % 12 )
88          << ":" << setfill( '0' ) << setw( 2 ) << minute
89          << ":" << setw( 2 ) << second << ( hour < 12 ? " AM" : " PM" );
90    } // end function printStandard
```

Fig. 9.25 | Time class member-function definitions modified to enable cascaded member-function calls. (Part 3 of 3.)

Line 24 (Fig. 9.26) also uses cascading. Note that we cannot chain another member-function call after printStandard here, because printStandard does *not* return a reference to t. Placing the call to printStandard before the call to setTime in line 24 results in a compilation error. Chapter 10 presents several practical examples of using cascaded function calls. One such example uses multiple << operators with cout to output multiple values in a single statement.

```
1     // Fig. 9.26: fig09_26.cpp
2     // Cascading member-function calls with the this pointer.
3     #include <iostream>
4     #include "Time.h" // Time class definition
5     using namespace std;
6
7     int main()
8     {
9        Time t; // create Time object
10
11       // cascaded function calls
12       t.setHour( 18 ).setMinute( 30 ).setSecond( 22 );
13
```

Fig. 9.26 | Cascading member-function calls with the this pointer. (Part 1 of 2.)

```
14      // output time in universal and standard formats
15      cout << "Universal time: ";
16      t.printUniversal();
17
18      cout << "\nStandard time: ";
19      t.printStandard();
20
21      cout << "\n\nNew standard time: ";
22
23      // cascaded function calls
24      t.setTime( 20, 20, 20 ).printStandard();
25      cout << endl;
26  } // end main
```

```
Universal time: 18:30:22
Standard time: 6:30:22 PM

New standard time: 8:20:20 PM
```

Fig. 9.26 | Cascading member-function calls with the this pointer. (Part 2 of 2.)

9.14 static Class Members

There is an important exception to the rule that each object of a class has its own copy of all the data members of the class. In certain cases, only *one* copy of a variable should be *shared* by *all* objects of a class. A **static data member** is used for these and other reasons. Such a variable represents "class-wide" information, i.e., data that is shared by *all* instances and is *not* specific to any one object of the class. Recall, for example, that the versions of class GradeBook in Chapter 7 use static data members to store constants representing the number of grades that all GradeBook objects can hold.

Motivating Class-Wide Data
Let's further motivate the need for static class-wide data with an example. Suppose that we have a video game with Martians and other space creatures. Each Martian tends to be brave and willing to attack other space creatures when the Martian is aware that there are at least five Martians present. If fewer than five are present, each Martian becomes cowardly. So each Martian needs to know the martianCount. We could endow each instance of class Martian with martianCount as a data member. If we do, every Martian will have a *separate* copy of the data member. Every time we create a new Martian, we'll have to update the data member martianCount in all Martian objects. Doing this would require every Martian object to have, or have access to, handles to all other Martian objects in memory. This wastes space with the redundant copies of the martianCount and wastes time in updating the separate copies. Instead, we declare martianCount to be static. This makes martianCount class-wide data. Every Martian can access martianCount as if it were a data member of the Martian, but only *one* copy of the static variable martianCount is maintained in the program. This saves space. We save time by having the Martian constructor increment static variable martianCount and having the Martian destructor decrement martianCount. Because there's only one copy, we do not have to increment or decrement separate copies of martianCount for each Martian object.

Performance Tip 9.5

Use static data members to save storage when a single copy of the data for all objects of a class will suffice.

Scope and Initialization of static Data Members

A class's static data members have *class scope*. A static data member *must* be initialized *exactly* once. Fundamental-type static data members are initialized by default to 0. Prior to C++11, a static const data member of int or enum type could be initialized in its declaration in the class definition and all other static data members had to be defined and intialized *at global namespace scope* (i.e., outside the body of the class definition). Again, C++11's in-class initializers also allow you to initialize these variables where they're declared in the class definition. If a static data member is an object of a class that provides a default constructor, the static data member need not be initialized because its default constructor will be called.

Accessing static Data Members

A class's private and protected static members are normally accessed through the class's public member functions or friends. *A class's static members exist even when no objects of that class exist.* To access a public static class member when no objects of the class exist, simply prefix the class name and the scope resolution operator (::) to the name of the data member. For example, if our preceding variable martianCount is public, it can be accessed with the expression Martian::martianCount, even when there are no Martian objects. (Of course, using public data is discouraged.)

To access a private or protected static class member when *no* objects of the class exist, provide a public **static** member function and call the function by prefixing its name with the class name and scope resolution operator. A static member function is a service of the *class*, *not* of a specific *object* of the class.

Software Engineering Observation 9.14

A class's static data members and static member functions exist and can be used even if no objects of that class have been instantiated.

Demonstrating static Data Members

The program of Figs. 9.27–9.29 demonstrates a private static data member called count (Fig. 9.27, line 24) and a public static member function called getCount (Fig. 9.27, line 18). In Fig. 9.28, line 8 defines and initializes the data member count to zero *at global namespace scope* and lines 12–15 define static member function getCount. Notice that neither line 8 nor line 12 includes keyword static, yet both lines define static class members. The static keyword cannot be applied to a member definition that appears outside the class definition. Data member count maintains a count of the number of objects of class Employee that have been instantiated. When objects of class Employee exist, member count can be referenced through *any* member function of an Employee object—in Fig. 9.28, count is referenced by both line 22 in the constructor and line 32 in the destructor.

```
1   // Fig. 9.27: Employee.h
2   // Employee class definition with a static data member to
3   // track the number of Employee objects in memory
4   #ifndef EMPLOYEE_H
5   #define EMPLOYEE_H
6
7   #include <string>
8
9   class Employee
10  {
11  public:
12     Employee( const std::string &, const std::string & ); // constructor
13     ~Employee(); // destructor
14     std::string getFirstName() const; // return first name
15     std::string getLastName() const; // return last name
16
17     // static member function
18     static unsigned int getCount(); // return # of objects instantiated
19  private:
20     std::string firstName;
21     std::string lastName;
22
23     // static data
24     static unsigned int count; // number of objects instantiated
25  }; // end class Employee
26
27  #endif
```

Fig. 9.27 | Employee class definition with a static data member to track the number of Employee objects in memory.

```
1   // Fig. 9.28: Employee.cpp
2   // Employee class member-function definitions.
3   #include <iostream>
4   #include "Employee.h" // Employee class definition
5   using namespace std;
6
7   // define and initialize static data member at global namespace scope
8   unsigned int Employee::count = 0; // cannot include keyword static
9
10  // define static member function that returns number of
11  // Employee objects instantiated (declared static in Employee.h)
12  unsigned int Employee::getCount()
13  {
14     return count;
15  } // end static function getCount
16
17  // constructor initializes non-static data members and
18  // increments static data member count
19  Employee::Employee( const string &first, const string &last )
20     : firstName( first ), lastName( last )
21  {
```

Fig. 9.28 | Employee class member-function definitions. (Part 1 of 2.)

```
22        ++count; // increment static count of employees
23        cout << "Employee constructor for " << firstName
24           << ' ' << lastName << " called." << endl;
25     } // end Employee constructor
26
27     // destructor deallocates dynamically allocated memory
28     Employee::~Employee()
29     {
30        cout << "~Employee() called for " << firstName
31           << ' ' << lastName << endl;
32        --count; // decrement static count of employees
33     } // end ~Employee destructor
34
35     // return first name of employee
36     string Employee::getFirstName() const
37     {
38        return firstName; // return copy of first name
39     } // end function getFirstName
40
41     // return last name of employee
42     string Employee::getLastName() const
43     {
44        return lastName; // return copy of last name
45     } // end function getLastName
```

Fig. 9.28 | Employee class member-function definitions. (Part 2 of 2.)

Figure 9.29 uses static member function getCount to determine the number of Employee objects in memory at various points in the program. The program calls Employee::getCount() before any Employee objects have been created (line 12), after two Employee objects have been created (line 23) and after those Employee objects have been destroyed (line 34). Lines 16–29 in main define a *nested scope*. Recall that local variables exist until the scope in which they're defined terminates. In this example, we create two Employee objects in lines 17–18 inside the nested scope. As each constructor executes, it increments class Employee's static data member count. These Employee objects are destroyed when the program reaches line 29. At that point, each object's destructor executes and decrements class Employee's static data member count.

```
1     // Fig. 9.29: fig09_29.cpp
2     // static data member tracking the number of objects of a class.
3     #include <iostream>
4     #include "Employee.h" // Employee class definition
5     using namespace std;
6
7     int main()
8     {
9        // no objects exist; use class name and binary scope resolution
10       // operator to access static member function getCount
11       cout << "Number of employees before instantiation of any objects is "
12          << Employee::getCount() << endl; // use class name
```

Fig. 9.29 | static data member tracking the number of objects of a class. (Part 1 of 2.)

```
13
14    // the following scope creates and destroys
15    // Employee objects before main terminates
16    {
17        Employee e1( "Susan", "Baker" );
18        Employee e2( "Robert", "Jones" );
19
20        // two objects exist; call static member function getCount again
21        // using the class name and the scope resolution operator
22        cout << "Number of employees after objects are instantiated is "
23            << Employee::getCount();
24
25        cout << "\n\nEmployee 1: "
26            << e1.getFirstName() << " " << e1.getLastName()
27            << "\nEmployee 2: "
28            << e2.getFirstName() << " " << e2.getLastName() << "\n\n";
29    } // end nested scope in main
30
31    // no objects exist, so call static member function getCount again
32    // using the class name and the scope resolution operator
33    cout << "\nNumber of employees after objects are deleted is "
34        << Employee::getCount() << endl;
35 } // end main
```

```
Number of employees before instantiation of any objects is 0
Employee constructor for Susan Baker called.
Employee constructor for Robert Jones called.
Number of employees after objects are instantiated is 2

Employee 1: Susan Baker
Employee 2: Robert Jones

~Employee() called for Robert Jones
~Employee() called for Susan Baker

Number of employees after objects are deleted is 0
```

Fig. 9.29 | static data member tracking the number of objects of a class. (Part 2 of 2.)

A member function should be declared static if it does *not* access non-static data members or non-static member functions of the class. Unlike non-static member functions, *a static member function does not have a this pointer*, because static *data members and static member functions exist independently of any objects of a class.* The this pointer *must* refer to a specific *object* of the class, and when a static member function is called, there might *not* be any objects of its class in memory.

Common Programming Error 9.6

Using the this pointer in a static member function is a compilation error.

Common Programming Error 9.7

Declaring a static member function const is a compilation error. The const qualifier indicates that a function cannot modify the contents of the object on which it operates, but static member functions exist and operate independently of any objects of the class.

9.15 Wrap-Up

This chapter deepened our coverage of classes, using a `Time` class case study to introduce several new features. We used an include guard to prevent the code in a header (`.h`) file from being included multiple times in the same source code (`.cpp`) file. You learned how to use the arrow operator to access an object's members via a pointer of the object's class type. You learned that member functions have class scope—the member function's name is known only to the class's other members unless referred to by a client of the class via an object name, a reference to an object of the class, a pointer to an object of the class or the scope resolution operator. We also discussed access functions (commonly used to retrieve the values of data members or to test the truth or falsity of conditions) and utility functions (`private` member functions that support the operation of the class's `public` member functions).

You learned that a constructor can specify default arguments that enable it to be called in a variety of ways. You also learned that any constructor that can be called with no arguments is a default constructor and that there can be at most one default constructor per class. We discussed destructors for performing termination housekeeping on an object of a class before that object is destroyed, and demonstrated the order in which an object's constructors and destructors are called.

We demonstrated the problems that can occur when a member function returns a reference or a pointer to a `private` data member, which breaks the encapsulation of the class. We also showed that objects of the same type can be assigned to one another using default memberwise assignment—in Chapter 10, we'll discuss how this can cause problems when an object contains pointer members.

You learned how to specify `const` objects and `const` member functions to prevent modifications to objects, thus enforcing the principle of least privilege. You also learned that, through composition, a class can have objects of other classes as members. We demonstrated how to use `friend` functions.

You learned that the `this` pointer is passed as an implicit argument to each of a class's non-`static` member functions, allowing them to access the correct object's data members and other non-`static` member functions. We used the `this` pointer explicitly to access the class's members and to enable cascaded member-function calls. We motivated the notion of `static` data members and member functions and demonstrated how to declare and use them in your own classes.

In Chapter 10, we continue our study of classes and objects by showing how to enable C++'s operators to work with *class-type objects*—a process called *operator overloading*. For example, you'll see how to overload the `<<` operator so it can be used to output a complete array without explicitly using a repetition statement.

Summary

Section 9.2 *Time Class Case Study*

- Preprocessing directives `#ifndef` (which means "if not defined"; p. 414) and `#endif` (p. 414) are used to prevent multiple inclusions of a header. If the code between these directives has not previously been included in an application, `#define` (p. 414) defines a name that can be used to prevent future inclusions, and the code is included in the source code file.

- Before C++11, only `static const int` data members could be initialized where they were declared in the class body. For this reason, data members typically should be initialized by the class's constructor. As of C++11, you can now use an in-class initializer to initialize any data member where it's declared in the class definition.

• A class's functions can throw (p. 415) exceptions (such as `invalid_argument`; p. 415) to indicate invalid data.

• Stream manipulator `setfill` (p. 416) specifies the fill character (p. 416) that's displayed when an integer is output in a field that's wider than the number of digits in the value.

• If a member function defines a variable with the same name as a variable with class scope (p. 416), the class-scope variable is hidden in the function by the block-scope variable.

• By default, the fill characters appear before the digits in the number.

• Stream manipulator `setfill` is a "sticky" setting, meaning that once the fill character is set, it applies for all subsequent fields being printed.

• Even though a member function declared in a class definition may be defined outside that class definition (and "tied" to the class via the scope resolution operator), that member function is still within that class's scope.

• If a member function is defined in the body of a class definition, the member function is implicitly declared inline.

• Classes can include objects of other classes as members or they may be derived (p. 419) from other classes that provide attributes and behaviors the new classes can use.

Section 9.3 Class Scope and Accessing Class Members
• A class's data members and member functions belong to that class's scope.

• Nonmember functions are defined at global namespace scope.

• Within a class's scope, class members are immediately accessible by all of that class's member functions and can be referenced by name.

• Outside a class's scope, class members are referenced through one of the handles on an object—an object name, a reference to an object or a pointer to an object.

• Variables declared in a member function have block scope and are known only to that function.

• The dot member selection operator (`.`) is preceded by an object's name or by a reference to an object to access the object's `public` members.

• The arrow member selection operator (`->`; p. 420) is preceded by a pointer to an object to access that object's `public` members.

Section 9.4 Access Functions and Utility Functions
• Access functions (p. 420) read or display data. They can also be used to test the truth or falsity of conditions—such functions are often called predicate functions.

• A utility function (p. 420) is a `private` member function that supports the operation of the class's `public` member functions. Utility functions are not intended to be used by clients of a class.

Section 9.5 Time Class Case Study: Constructors with Default Arguments
• Like other functions, constructors can specify default arguments.

Section 9.6 Destructors
• A class's destructor (p. 427) is called implicitly when an object of the class is destroyed.

• The name of the destructor for a class is the tilde (~) character followed by the class name.

• A destructor does not release an object's storage—it performs termination housekeeping (p. 427) before the system reclaims an object's memory, so the memory may be reused to hold new objects.

- A destructor receives no parameters and returns no value. A class may have only one destructor.
- If you do not explicitly provide a destructor, the compiler creates an "empty" destructor, so every class has exactly one destructor.

Section 9.7 When Constructors and Destructors Are Called

- The order in which constructors and destructors are called depends on the order in which execution enters and leaves the scopes where the objects are instantiated.
- Generally, destructor calls are made in the reverse order of the corresponding constructor calls, but the storage classes of objects can alter the order in which destructors are called.

Section 9.8 Time Class Case Study: A Subtle Trap—Returning a Reference or a Pointer to a private Data Member

- A reference to an object is an alias for the name of the object and, hence, may be used on the left side of an assignment statement. In this context, the reference makes a perfectly acceptable *lvalue* that can receive a value.
- If the function returns a reference to const data, then the reference cannot be used as a modifiable *lvalue*.

Section 9.9 Default Memberwise Assignment

- The assignment operator (=) can be used to assign an object to another object of the same type. By default, such assignment is performed by memberwise assignment (p. 434).
- Objects may be passed by value to or returned by value from functions. C++ creates a new object and uses a copy constructor (p. 435) to copy the original object's values into the new object.
- For each class, the compiler provides a default copy constructor that copies each member of the original object into the corresponding member of the new object.

Section 9.10 const Objects and const Member Functions

- The keyword const can be used to specify that an object is not modifiable and that any attempt to modify the object should result in a compilation error.
- C++ compilers disallow non-const member function calls on const objects.
- An attempt by a const member function to modify an object of its class is a compilation error.
- A member function is specified as const both in its prototype and in its definition.
- A const object must be initialized.
- Constructors and destructors cannot be declared const.

Section 9.11 Composition: Objects as Members of Classes

- A class can have objects of other classes as members—this concept is called composition.
- Member objects are constructed in the order in which they're declared in the class definition and before their enclosing class objects are constructed.
- If a member initializer is not provided for a member object, the member object's default constructor (p. 438) will be called implicitly.

Section 9.12 friend Functions and friend Classes

- A friend function (p. 444) of a class is defined outside that class's scope, yet has the right to access all of the class's members. Stand-alone functions or entire classes may be declared to be friends.
- A friend declaration can appear anywhere in the class.
- The friendship relation is neither symmetric nor transitive.

Section 9.13 Using the **this** Pointer

- Every object has access to its own address through the this pointer (p. 446).

- An object's this pointer is not part of the object itself—i.e., the size of the memory occupied by the this pointer is not reflected in the result of a sizeof operation on the object.

- The this pointer is passed as an implicit argument to each non-static member function.

- Objects use the this pointer implicitly (as we've done to this point) or explicitly to reference their data members and member functions.

- The this pointer enables cascaded member-function calls (p. 448) in which multiple functions are invoked in the same statement.

Section 9.14 **static** Class Members

- A static data member (p. 452) represents "class-wide" information (i.e., a property of the class shared by all instances, not a property of a specific object of the class).

- static data members have class scope and can be declared public, private or protected.

- A class's static members exist even when no objects of that class exist.

- To access a public static class member when no objects of the class exist, simply prefix the class name and the scope resolution operator (::) to the name of the data member.

- The static keyword cannot be applied to a member definition that appears outside the class definition.

- A member function should be declared static (p. 453) if it does not access non-static data members or non-static member functions of the class. Unlike non-static member functions, a static member function does not have a this pointer, because static data members and static member functions exist independently of any objects of a class.

Self-Review Exercises

9.1   Fill in the blanks in each of the following:
- a) Class members are accessed via the _____ operator in conjunction with the name of an object (or reference to an object) of the class or via the _____ operator in conjunction with a pointer to an object of the class.
- b) Class members specified as _____ are accessible only to member functions of the class and friends of the class.
- c) _____ class members are accessible anywhere an object of the class is in scope.
- d) _____ can be used to assign an object of a class to another object of the same class.
- e) A nonmember function must be declared as a(n) _____ of a class to have access to that class's private data members.
- f) A constant object must be _____; it cannot be modified after it's created.
- g) A(n) _____ data member represents class-wide information.
- h) An object's non-static member functions have access to a "self pointer" to the object called the _____ pointer.
- i) Keyword _____ specifies that an object or variable is not modifiable.
- j) If a member initializer is not provided for a member object of a class, the object's _____ is called.
- k) A member function should be static if it does not access _____ class members.
- l) Member objects are constructed _____ their enclosing class object.

9.2   Find the error(s) in each of the following and explain how to correct it (them):
- a) Assume the following prototype is declared in class Time:

```
void ~Time( int );
```

b) Assume the following prototype is declared in class `Employee`:

```
int Employee( string, string );
```

c) The following is a definition of class `Example`:

```
class Example
{
public:
    Example( int y = 10 )
        : data( y )
    {
        // empty body
    } // end Example constructor

    int getIncrementedData() const
    {
        return ++data;
    } // end function getIncrementedData

    static int getCount()
    {
        cout << "Data is " << data << endl;
        return count;
    } // end function getCount
private:
    int data;
    static int count;
}; // end class Example
```

Answers to Self-Review Exercises

9.1   a) dot (.), arrow (->). b) `private`. c) `public`. d) Default memberwise assignment (performed by the assignment operator). e) `friend`. f) initialized. g) `static`. h) `this`. i) `const`. j) default constructor. k) non-`static`. l) before.

9.2   a) *Error:* Destructors are not allowed to return values (or even specify a return type) or take arguments.
   Correction: Remove the return type `void` and the parameter `int` from the declaration.
   b) *Error:* Constructors are not allowed to return values.
   Correction: Remove the return type `int` from the declaration.
   c) *Error:* The class definition for `Example` has two errors. The first occurs in function `get-IncrementedData`. The function is declared `const`, but it modifies the object.
   Correction: To correct the first error, remove the `const` keyword from the definition of `getIncrementedData`. [*Note:* It would also be appropriate to rename this member function as *get* functions are typically `const` member functions.]
   Error: The second error occurs in function `getCount`. This function is declared `static`, so it's not allowed to access any non-`static` class member (i.e., data).
   Correction: To correct the second error, remove the output line from the `getCount` definition.

Exercises

9.3   *(Scope Resolution Operator)* What is the purpose of the member selection operators?

9.4   *(Enhancing Class* `Time`*)* Provide a constructor that's capable of using the current time from the `time` and `localtime` functions—declared in the C++ Standard Library header `<ctime>`—to initialize an object of the `Time` class.

9.5 *(Complex Class)* Create a class called Complex for performing arithmetic with complex numbers. Write a program to test your class. Complex numbers have the form

> realPart + imaginaryPart * *i*

where *i* is

$$\sqrt{-1}$$

Use double variables to represent the private data of the class. Provide a constructor that enables an object of this class to be initialized when it's declared. The constructor should contain default values in case no initializers are provided. Provide public member functions that perform the following tasks:

a) Adding two Complex numbers: The real parts are added together and the imaginary parts are added together.

b) Subtracting two Complex numbers: The real part of the right operand is subtracted from the real part of the left operand, and the imaginary part of the right operand is subtracted from the imaginary part of the left operand.

c) Printing Complex numbers in the form (a, b), where a is the real part and b is the imaginary part.

9.6 *(Rational Class)* Create a class called Rational for performing arithmetic with fractions. Write a program to test your class. Use integer variables to represent the private data of the class—the numerator and the denominator. Provide a constructor that enables an object of this class to be initialized when it's declared. The constructor should contain default values in case no initializers are provided and should store the fraction in reduced form. For example, the fraction

$$\frac{2}{4}$$

would be stored in the object as 1 in the numerator and 2 in the denominator. Provide public member functions that perform each of the following tasks:

a) Adding two Rational numbers. The result should be stored in reduced form.

b) Subtracting two Rational numbers. The result should be stored in reduced form.

c) Multiplying two Rational numbers. The result should be stored in reduced form.

d) Dividing two Rational numbers. The result should be stored in reduced form.

e) Printing Rational numbers in the form a/b, where a is the numerator and b is the denominator.

f) Printing Rational numbers in floating-point format.

9.7 *(Enhancing Class Time)* Modify the Time class of Figs. 9.4–9.5 to include a tick member function that increments the time stored in a Time object by one second. Write a program that tests the tick member function in a loop that prints the time in standard format during each iteration of the loop to illustrate that the tick member function works correctly. Be sure to test the following cases:

a) Incrementing into the next minute.

b) Incrementing into the next hour.

c) Incrementing into the next day (i.e., 11:59:59 PM to 12:00:00 AM).

9.8 *(Enhancing Class Date)* Modify the Date class of Figs. 9.13–9.14 to perform error checking on the initializer values for data members month, day and year. Also, provide a member function nextDay to increment the day by one. Write a program that tests function nextDay in a loop that prints the date during each iteration to illustrate that nextDay works correctly. Be sure to test the following cases:

a) Incrementing into the next month.

b) Incrementing into the next year.

9.9   *(Combining Class Time and Class Date)* Combine the modified Time class of Exercise 9.7 and the modified Date class of Exercise 9.8 into one class called DateAndTime. (In Chapter 11, we'll discuss inheritance, which will enable us to accomplish this task quickly without modifying the existing class definitions.) Modify the tick function to call the nextDay function if the time increments into the next day. Modify functions printStandard and printUniversal to output the date and time. Write a program to test the new class DateAndTime. Specifically, test incrementing the time into the next day.

9.10   *(Returning Error Indicators from Class Time's set Functions)* Modify the *set* functions in the Time class of Figs. 9.4–9.5 to return appropriate error values if an attempt is made to *set* a data member of an object of class Time to an invalid value. Write a program that tests your new version of class Time. Display error messages when *set* functions return error values.

9.11   *(Rectangle Class)* Create a class Rectangle with attributes length and width, each of which defaults to 1. Provide member functions that calculate the perimeter and the area of the rectangle. Also, provide *set* and *get* functions for the length and width attributes. The *set* functions should verify that length and width are each floating-point numbers larger than 0.0 and less than 20.0.

9.12   *(Enhancing Class Rectangle)* Create a more sophisticated Rectangle class than the one you created in Exercise 9.11. This class stores only the Cartesian coordinates of the four corners of the rectangle. The constructor calls a *set* function that accepts four sets of coordinates and verifies that each of these is in the first quadrant with no single *x*- or *y*-coordinate larger than 20.0. The *set* function also verifies that the supplied coordinates do, in fact, specify a rectangle. Provide member functions that calculate the length, width, perimeter and area. The length is the larger of the two dimensions. Include a predicate function square that determines whether the rectangle is a square.

9.13   *(Enhancing Class Rectangle)* Modify class Rectangle from Exercise 9.12 to include a draw function that displays the rectangle inside a 25-by-25 box enclosing the portion of the first quadrant in which the rectangle resides. Include a setFillCharacter function to specify the character out of which the body of the rectangle will be drawn. Include a setPerimeterCharacter function to specify the character that will be used to draw the border of the rectangle. If you feel ambitious, you might include functions to scale the size of the rectangle, rotate it, and move it around within the designated portion of the first quadrant.

9.14   *(HugeInteger Class)* Create a class HugeInteger that uses a 40-element array of digits to store integers as large as 40 digits each. Provide member functions input, output, add and subtract. For comparing HugeInteger objects, provide functions isEqualTo, isNotEqualTo, isGreaterThan, isLessThan, isGreaterThanOrEqualTo and isLessThanOrEqualTo—each of these is a "predicate" function that simply returns true if the relationship holds between the two HugeIntegers and returns false if the relationship does not hold. Also, provide a predicate function isZero. If you feel ambitious, provide member functions multiply, divide and modulus.

9.15   *(TicTacToe Class)* Create a class TicTacToe that will enable you to write a complete program to play the game of tic-tac-toe. The class contains as private data a 3-by-3 two-dimensional array of integers. The constructor should initialize the empty board to all zeros. Allow two human players. Wherever the first player moves, place a 1 in the specified square. Place a 2 wherever the second player moves. Each move must be to an empty square. After each move, determine whether the game has been won or is a draw. If you feel ambitious, modify your program so that the computer makes the moves for one of the players. Also, allow the player to specify whether he or she wants to go first or second. If you feel exceptionally ambitious, develop a program that will play three-dimensional tic-tac-toe on a 4-by-4-by-4 board. [*Caution:* This is an extremely challenging project that could take many weeks of effort!]

9.16   *(this pointer)* Explain the notion of the this pointer. Explain the aspects of using sizeof operator for this pointer as described in the text.

9.17   *(Constructor Overloading)* Can a `Time` class definition that includes *both* of the following constructors:

```
Time( int h = 0, int m = 0, int s = 0 );
Time();
```

be used to default construct a `Time` object? If not, explain why.

9.18   *(Copy Constructors)* What happens when a reference of the object of the class is passed to the constructor?

9.19   *(Date Class Modification)* Modify class `Date` in Fig. 9.17 to have the following capabilities:

a) Output the date in multiple formats such as

```
DDD YYYY
MM/DD/YY
June 14, 1992
```

b) Use overloaded constructors to create `Date` objects initialized with dates of the formats in part (a).

c) Create a `Date` constructor that reads the system date using the standard library functions of the `<ctime>` header and sets the `Date` members. See your compiler's reference documentation or `en.cppreference.com/w/cpp/chrono/c` for information on the functions in header `<ctime>`. You might also want to check out C++11's new `chrono` library at `en.cppreference.com/w/cpp/chrono`.

In Chapter 10, we'll be able to create operators for testing the equality of two dates and for comparing dates to determine whether one date is prior to, or after, another.

9.20   *(SavingsAccount Class)* Create a `SavingsAccount` class. Use a `static` data member `annualInterestRate` to store the annual interest rate for each of the savers. Each member of the class contains a `private` data member `savingsBalance` indicating the amount the saver currently has on deposit. Provide member function `calculateMonthlyInterest` that calculates the monthly interest by multiplying the `savingsBalance` by `annualInterestRate` divided by 12; this interest should be added to `savingsBalance`. Provide a `static` member function `modifyInterestRate` that sets the `static` `annualInterestRate` to a new value. Write a driver program to test class `SavingsAccount`. Instantiate two different objects of class `SavingsAccount`, `saver1` and `saver2`, with balances of $2000.00 and $3000.00, respectively. Set the `annualInterestRate` to 3 percent. Then calculate the monthly interest and print the new balances for each of the savers. Then set the `annualInterestRate` to 4 percent, calculate the next month's interest and print the new balances for each of the savers.

9.21   *(IntegerSet Class)* Create class `IntegerSet` for which each object can hold integers in the range 0 through 100. Represent the set internally as a `vector` of `bool` values. Element a[i] is `true` if integer i is in the set. Element a[j] is `false` if integer j is not in the set. The default constructor initializes a set to the so-called "empty set," i.e., a set for which all elements contain `false`.

a) Provide member functions for the common set operations. For example, provide a `unionOfSets` member function that creates a third set that is the set-theoretic union of two existing sets (i.e., an element of the result is set to `true` if that element is `true` in either or both of the existing sets, and an element of the result is set to `false` if that element is `false` in each of the existing sets).

b) Provide an `intersectionOfSets` member function which creates a third set which is the set-theoretic intersection of two existing sets (i.e., an element of the result is set to `false` if that element is `false` in either or both of the existing sets, and an element of the result is set to `true` if that element is `true` in each of the existing sets).

c) Provide an `insertElement` member function that places a new integer k into a set by setting a[k] to `true`. Provide a `deleteElement` member function that deletes integer m by setting a[m] to `false`.

d) Provide a `printSet` member function that prints a set as a list of numbers separated by spaces. Print only those elements that are present in the set (i.e., their position in the vector has a value of `true`). Print `---` for an empty set.

e) Provide an `isEqualTo` member function that determines whether two sets are equal.

f) Provide an additional constructor that receives an array of integers and the size of that array and uses the array to initialize a set object.

Now write a driver program to test your `IntegerSet` class. Instantiate several `IntegerSet` objects. Test that all your member functions work properly.

9.22 *(`Time` Class Modification)* It would be perfectly reasonable for the `Time` class of Figs. 9.4–9.5 to represent the time internally as the number of seconds since midnight rather than the three integer values `hour`, `minute` and `second`. Clients could use the same `public` methods and get the same results. Modify the `Time` class of Fig. 9.4 to implement the time as the number of seconds since midnight and show that there is no visible change in functionality to the clients of the class. [*Note:* This exercise nicely demonstrates the virtues of implementation hiding.]

9.23 *(Card Shuffling and Dealing)* Create a program to shuffle and deal a deck of cards. The program should consist of class `Card`, class `DeckOfCards` and a driver program. Class `Card` should provide:

a) Data members `face` and `suit` of type `int`.

b) A constructor that receives two `int`s representing the face and suit and uses them to initialize the data members.

c) Two `static` arrays of `string`s representing the faces and suits.

d) A `toString` function that returns the `Card` as a `string` in the form *"face of suit."* You can use the `+` operator to concatenate `string`s.

Class `DeckOfCards` should contain:

a) An array of `Card`s named `deck` to store the `Card`s.

b) An integer `currentCard` representing the next card to deal.

c) A default constructor that initializes the `Card`s in the deck.

d) A `shuffle` function that shuffles the `Card`s in the deck. The shuffle algorithm should iterate through the array of `Card`s. For each `Card`, randomly select another `Card` in the deck and swap the two `Card`s.

e) A `dealCard` function that returns the next `Card` object from the deck.

f) A `moreCards` function that returns a `bool` value indicating whether there are more `Card`s to deal.

The driver program should create a `DeckOfCards` object, shuffle the cards, then deal the 52 cards.

9.24 *(Card Shuffling and Dealing)* Modify the program you developed in Exercise 9.23 so that it deals a five-card poker hand. Then write functions to accomplish each of the following:

a) Determine whether the hand contains a pair.

b) Determine whether the hand contains two pairs.

c) Determine whether the hand contains three of a kind (e.g., three jacks).

d) Determine whether the hand contains four of a kind (e.g., four aces).

e) Determine whether the hand contains a flush (i.e., all five cards of the same suit).

f) Determine whether the hand contains a straight (i.e., five cards of consecutive face values).

9.25 *(Project: Card Shuffling and Dealing)* Use the functions from Exercise 9.24 to write a program that deals two five-card poker hands, evaluates each hand and determines which is the better hand.

9.26 *(Project: Card Shuffling and Dealing)* Modify the program you developed in Exercise 9.25 so that it can simulate the dealer. The dealer's five-card hand is dealt "face down" so the player cannot see it. The program should then evaluate the dealer's hand, and, based on the quality of the hand, the dealer should draw one, two or three more cards to replace the corresponding number of unneeded cards in the original hand. The program should then reevaluate the dealer's hand.

9.27 *(Project: Card Shuffling and Dealing)* Modify the program you developed in Exercise 9.26 so that it handles the dealer's hand, but the player is allowed to decide which cards of the player's hand to replace. The program should then evaluate both hands and determine who wins. Now use this new program to play 20 games against the computer. Who wins more games, you or the computer? Have one of your friends play 20 games against the computer. Who wins more games? Based on the results of these games, make appropriate modifications to refine your poker-playing program. Play 20 more games. Does your modified program play a better game?

Making a Difference

9.28 *(Project: Emergency Response Class)* The North American emergency response service, *9-1-1*, connects callers to a *local* Public Service Answering Point (PSAP). Traditionally, the PSAP would ask the caller for identification information—including the caller's address, phone number and the nature of the emergency, then dispatch the appropriate emergency responders (such as the police, an ambulance or the fire department). *Enhanced 9-1-1 (or E9-1-1)* uses computers and databases to determine the caller's physical address, directs the call to the nearest PSAP, and displays the caller's phone number and address to the call taker. *Wireless Enhanced 9-1-1* provides call takers with identification information for wireless calls. Rolled out in two phases, the first phase required carriers to provide the wireless phone number and the location of the cell site or base station transmitting the call. The second phase required carriers to provide the location of the caller (using technologies such as GPS). To learn more about 9-1-1, visit www.fcc.gov/pshs/services/911-services/Welcome.html and people.howstuffworks.com/9-1-1.htm.

An important part of creating a class is determining the class's attributes (instance variables). For this class design exercise, research 9-1-1 services on the Internet. Then, design a class called Emergency that might be used in an object-oriented 9-1-1 emergency response system. List the attributes that an object of this class might use to represent the emergency. For example, the class might include information on who reported the emergency (including their phone number), the location of the emergency, the time of the report, the nature of the emergency, the type of response and the status of the response. The class attributes should completely describe the nature of the problem and what's happening to resolve that problem.

Operator Overloading; Class string

There are two men inside the artist, the poet and the craftsman. One is born a poet. One becomes a craftsman.
—Emile Zola

A thing of beauty is a joy forever.
—John Keats

Objectives

In this chapter you'll:

- Learn how operator overloading can help you craft valuable classes.
- Overload unary and binary operators.
- Convert objects from one class to another class.
- Use overloaded operators and additional features of the string class.
- Create PhoneNumber, Date and Array classes that provide overloaded operators.
- Perform dynamic memory allocation with new and delete.
- Use keyword explicit to indicate that a constructor cannot be used for implicit conversions.
- Experience a "light-bulb moment" when you'll truly appreciate the elegance and beauty of the class concept.

10.1 Introduction

This chapter shows how to enable C++'s operators to work with class objects—a process called **operator overloading**. One example of an overloaded operator built into C++ is <<, which is used *both* as the stream insertion operator *and* as the bitwise left-shift operator (which is discussed in Chapter 22). Similarly, >> also is overloaded; it's used both as the stream extraction operator and the bitwise right-shift operator. Both of these operators are overloaded in the C++ Standard Library. You've been using overloaded operators since early in the book. The overloads are built into the base C++ language itself. For example, C++ overloads the addition operator (+) and the subtraction operator (-) to perform differently, depending on their context in integer, floating-point and pointer arithmetic with data of fundamental types.

You can overload *most* operators to be used with class objects—the compiler generates the appropriate code based on the *types* of the operands. The jobs performed by overloaded operators also can be performed by explicit function calls, but operator notation is often more natural.

Our examples start by demonstrating the C++ Standard Library's class `string`, which has lots of overloaded operators. This enables you to see overloaded operators in use before implementing your own overloaded operators. Next, we create a `PhoneNumber` class that enables us to use overloaded operators << and >> to conveniently output and input fully formatted, 10-digit phone numbers. We then present a `Date` class that overloads the prefix and postfix increment (++) operators to add one day to the value of a `Date`. The class also overloads the += operator to allow a program to increment a `Date` by the number of days specified on the right side of the operator.

Next, we present a capstone case study—an `Array` class that uses overloaded operators and other capabilities to solve various problems with pointer-based arrays. This is one of the most important case studies in the book. Many of our students have indicated that the `Array` case study is their "light bulb moment" in truly understanding what classes and object technology are all about. As part of this class, we'll overload stream insertion, stream extraction, assignment, equality, relational and subscript operators. Once you master this

Array class, you'll indeed understand the essence of object technology—crafting, using and reusing valuable classes.

The chapter concludes with discussions of how you can convert between types (incuding class types), problems with certain implicit conversions and how to prevent those problems.

10.2 Using the Overloaded Operators of Standard Library Class `string`

Figure 10.1 demonstrates many of class `string`'s overloaded operators and several other useful member functions, including `empty`, `substr` and `at`. Function `empty` determines whether a `string` is empty, function `substr` returns a `string` that represents a portion of an existing `string` and function `at` returns the character at a specific index in a `string` (after checking that the index is in range). Chapter 21 presents class `string` in detail.

```
1   // Fig. 10.1: fig10_01.cpp
2   // Standard Library string class test program.
3   #include <iostream>
4   #include <string>
5   using namespace std;
6
7   int main()
8   {
9      string s1( "happy" );
10     string s2( " birthday" );
11     string s3;
12
13     // test overloaded equality and relational operators
14     cout << "s1 is \"" << s1 << "\"; s2 is \"" << s2
15        << "\"; s3 is \"" << s3 << '\"'
16        << "\n\nThe results of comparing s2 and s1:"
17        << "\ns2 == s1 yields " << ( s2 == s1 ? "true" : "false" )
18        << "\ns2 != s1 yields " << ( s2 != s1 ? "true" : "false" )
19        << "\ns2 >  s1 yields " << ( s2 > s1 ? "true" : "false" )
20        << "\ns2 <  s1 yields " << ( s2 < s1 ? "true" : "false" )
21        << "\ns2 >= s1 yields " << ( s2 >= s1 ? "true" : "false" )
22        << "\ns2 <= s1 yields " << ( s2 <= s1 ? "true" : "false" );
23
24     // test string member-function empty
25     cout << "\n\nTesting s3.empty():" << endl;
26
27     if ( s3.empty() )
28     {
29        cout << "s3 is empty; assigning s1 to s3;" << endl;
30        s3 = s1; // assign s1 to s3
31        cout << "s3 is \"" << s3 << "\"";
32     } // end if
33
34     // test overloaded string concatenation operator
35     cout << "\n\ns1 += s2 yields s1 = ";
```

Fig. 10.1 | Standard Library `string` class test program. (Part 1 of 3.)

```
36      s1 += s2; // test overloaded concatenation
37      cout << s1;
38
39      // test overloaded string concatenation operator with a C string
40      cout << "\n\ns1 += \" to you\" yields" << endl;
41      s1 += " to you";
42      cout << "s1 = " << s1 << "\n\n";
43
44      // test string member function substr
45      cout << "The substring of s1 starting at location 0 for\n"
46         << "14 characters, s1.substr(0, 14), is:\n"
47         << s1.substr( 0, 14 ) << "\n\n";
48
49      // test substr "to-end-of-string" option
50      cout << "The substring of s1 starting at\n"
51         << "location 15, s1.substr(15), is:\n"
52         << s1.substr( 15 ) << endl;
53
54      // test copy constructor
55      string s4( s1 );
56      cout << "\ns4 = " << s4 << "\n\n";
57
58      // test overloaded copy assignment (=) operator with self-assignment
59      cout << "assigning s4 to s4" << endl;
60      s4 = s4;
61      cout << "s4 = " << s4 << endl;
62
63      // test using overloaded subscript operator to create lvalue
64      s1[ 0 ] = 'H';
65      s1[ 6 ] = 'B';
66      cout << "\ns1 after s1[0] = 'H' and s1[6] = 'B' is: "
67         << s1 << "\n\n";
68
69      // test subscript out of range with string member function "at"
70      try
71      {
72         cout << "Attempt to assign 'd' to s1.at( 30 ) yields:" << endl;
73         s1.at( 30 ) = 'd'; // ERROR: subscript out of range
74      } // end try
75      catch ( out_of_range &ex )
76      {
77         cout << "An exception occurred: " << ex.what() << endl;
78      } // end catch
79   } // end main
```

```
s1 is "happy"; s2 is " birthday"; s3 is ""

The results of comparing s2 and s1:
s2 == s1 yields false
s2 != s1 yields true
s2 >  s1 yields false
s2 <  s1 yields true
```

Fig. 10.1 | Standard Library `string` class test program. (Part 2 of 3.)

```
s2 >= s1 yields false
s2 <= s1 yields true

Testing s3.empty():
s3 is empty; assigning s1 to s3;
s3 is "happy"

s1 += s2 yields s1 = happy birthday

s1 += " to you" yields
s1 = happy birthday to you

The substring of s1 starting at location 0 for
14 characters, s1.substr(0, 14), is:
happy birthday

The substring of s1 starting at
location 15, s1.substr(15), is:
to you

s4 = happy birthday to you

assigning s4 to s4
s4 = happy birthday to you

s1 after s1[0] = 'H' and s1[6] = 'B' is: Happy Birthday to you

Attempt to assign 'd' to s1.at( 30 ) yields:
An exception occurred: invalid string position
```

Fig. 10.1 | Standard Library string class test program. (Part 3 of 3.)

Lines 9–11 create three string objects—s1 is initialized with the literal "happy", s2 is initialized with the literal " birthday" and s3 uses the default string constructor to create an empty string. Lines 14–15 output these three objects, using cout and operator <<, which the string class designers overloaded to handle string objects. Then lines 16–22 show the results of comparing s2 to s1 by using class string's overloaded equality and relational operators, which perform lexicographical comparisons (i.e., like a dictionary ordering) using the numerical values of the characters (see Appendix B, ASCII Character Set) in each string.

Class string provides member function **empty** to determine whether a string is empty, which we demonstrate in line 27. Member function empty returns true if the string is empty; otherwise, it returns false.

Line 30 demonstrates class string's overloaded copy assignment operator by assigning s1 to s3. Line 31 outputs s3 to demonstrate that the assignment worked correctly.

Line 36 demonstrates class string's overloaded += operator for *string concatenation*. In this case, the contents of s2 are appended to s1. Then line 37 outputs the resulting string that's stored in s1. Line 41 demonstrates that a string literal can be appended to a string object by using operator +=. Line 42 displays the result.

Class string provides member function **substr** (lines 47 and 52) to return a *portion* of a string as a string object. The call to substr in line 47 obtains a 14-character substring (specified by the second argument) of s1 starting at position 0 (specified by the first argument).The call to `substr` in line 52 obtains a substring starting from position 15 of `s1`. When the second argument is not specified, `substr` returns the *remainder* of the `string` on which it's called.

Line 55 creates `string` object `s4` and initializes it with a copy of `s1`. This results in a call to class `string`'s *copy constructor*. Line 60 uses class `string`'s overloaded copy assignment (=) operator to demonstrate that it handles *self-assignment* properly—we'll see when we build class `Array` later in the chapter that self-assignment can be dangerous and we'll show how to deal with the issues.

Lines 64–65 use class `string`'s overloaded `[]` operator to create *lvalues* that enable new characters to replace existing characters in `s1`. Line 67 outputs the new value of `s1`. *Class `string`'s overloaded `[]` operator does not perform any bounds checking.* Therefore, *you must ensure that operations using standard class `string`'s overloaded `[]` operator do not accidentally manipulate elements outside the bounds of the `string`.* Class `string` *does* provide bounds checking in its member function `at`, which throws an exception if its argument is an *invalid* subscript. If the subscript is valid, function `at` returns the character at the specified location as a modifiable *lvalue* or an nonmodifiable *lvalue* (e.g., a `const` reference), depending on the context in which the call appears. Line 73 demonstrates a call to function `at` with an invalid subscript; this throws an `out_of_range` exception.

10.3 Fundamentals of Operator Overloading

As you saw in Fig. 10.1, operators provide a concise notation for manipulating `string` objects. You can use operators with your own user-defined types as well. Although C++ does *not* allow *new* operators to be created, it *does* allow most existing operators to be overloaded so that, when they're used with objects, they have meaning appropriate to those objects.

Operator overloading is *not* automatic—you must write operator-overloading functions to perform the desired operations. An operator is overloaded by writing a non-`static` member function definition or non-member function definition as you normally would, except that the function name starts with the keyword `operator` followed by the symbol for the operator being overloaded. For example, the function name `operator+` would be used to overload the addition operator (+) for use with objects of a particular class (or enum). When operators are overloaded as member functions, they must be non-`static`, because *they must be called on an object of the class* and operate on that object.

To use an operator on an object of a class, you must define overloaded operator functions for that class—with three exceptions:

- The *assignment operator (=)* may be used with *most* classes to perform *memberwise assignment* of the data members—each data member is assigned from the assignment's "source" object (on the right) to the "target" object (on the left). *Memberwise assignment is dangerous for classes with pointer members,* so we'll explicitly overload the assignment operator for such classes.

- The *address (&) operator* returns a pointer to the object; this operator also can be overloaded.

- The *comma operator* evaluates the expression to its left then the expression to its right, and returns the value of the latter expression. This operator also can be overloaded.

Operators That Cannot Be Overloaded

Most of C++'s operators can be overloaded. Figure 10.2 shows the operators that cannot be overloaded.[1]

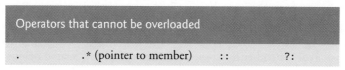

Operators that cannot be overloaded

.	.* (pointer to member)	::	?:

Fig. 10.2 | Operators that cannot be overloaded.

Rules and Restrictions on Operator Overloading

As you prepare to overload operators for your own classes, there are several rules and restrictions you should keep in mind:

- *The precedence of an operator cannot be changed by overloading.* However, parentheses can be used to *force* the order of evaluation of overloaded operators in an expression.

- *The associativity of an operator cannot be changed by overloading*—if an operator normally associates from left to right, then so do all of its overloaded versions.

- *You cannot change the "arity" of an operator* (that is, the number of operands an operator takes)—overloaded unary operators remain unary operators; overloaded binary operators remain binary operators. Operators &, *, + and - all have both unary and binary versions; these unary and binary versions can be separately overloaded.

- *You cannot create new operators; only existing operators can be overloaded.*

- The meaning of how an operator works on values of fundamental types *cannot* be changed by operator overloading. For example, you cannot make the + operator subtract two ints. Operator overloading works only with *objects of user-defined types or with a mixture of an object of a user-defined type and an object of a fundamental type.*

- Related operators, like + and +=, must be overloaded separately.

- When overloading (), [], -> or any of the assignment operators, the operator overloading function *must* be declared as a class member. For all other overloadable operators, the operator overloading functions can be member functions or non-member functions.

Software Engineering Observation 10.1

Overload operators for class types so they work as closely as possible to the way built-in operators work on fundamental types.

10.4 Overloading Binary Operators

A binary operator can be overloaded as a non-static member function with one parameter or as a non-member function with two parameters (one of those parameters must be either a class

---

1. Although it's possible to overload the address (&), comma (,), && and || operators, you should avoid doing so to avoid subtle errors. For insights on this, see CERT guideline DCL10-CPP.

object or a reference to a class object). A non-member operator function is often declared as `friend` of a class for performance reasons.

Binary Overloaded Operators as Member Functions

Consider using < to compare two objects of a `String` class that you define. When overloading binary operator < as a non-`static` member function of a `String` class, if y and z are `String`-class objects, then y < z is treated as if y.`operator<(z)` had been written, invoking the `operator<` member function with one argument declared below:

```
class String
{
public:
   bool operator<( const String & ) const;
   ...
}; // end class String
```

Overloaded operator functions for binary operators can be member functions *only* when the *left* operand is an object of the class in which the function is a member.

Binary Overloaded Operators as Non-Member Functions

As a non-member function, binary operator < *must* take *two* arguments—*one* of which *must* be an object (or a reference to an object) of the class that the overloaded operator is associated with. If y and z are `String`-class objects or references to `String`-class objects, then y < z is treated as if the call `operator<(y, z)` had been written in the program, invoking function `operator<` which is declared as follows:

```
bool operator<( const String &, const String & );
```

10.5 Overloading the Binary Stream Insertion and Stream Extraction Operators

You can input and output fundamental-type data using the stream extraction operator >> and the stream insertion operator <<. The C++ class libraries overload these binary operators for each fundamental type, including pointers and char * strings. You can also overload these operators to perform input and output for your own types. The program of Figs. 10.3–10.5 overloads these operators to input and output PhoneNumber objects in the format "(000) 000-0000." The program assumes telephone numbers are input correctly.

```
 1   // Fig. 10.3: PhoneNumber.h
 2   // PhoneNumber class definition
 3   #ifndef PHONENUMBER_H
 4   #define PHONENUMBER_H
 5
 6   #include <iostream>
 7   #include <string>
 8
 9   class PhoneNumber
10   {
```

Fig. 10.3 | PhoneNumber class with overloaded stream insertion and stream extraction operators as `friend` functions. (Part 1 of 2.)

```
11      friend std::ostream &operator<<( std::ostream &, const PhoneNumber & );
12      friend std::istream &operator>>( std::istream &, PhoneNumber & );
13   private:
14      std::string areaCode; // 3-digit area code
15      std::string exchange; // 3-digit exchange
16      std::string line; // 4-digit line
17   }; // end class PhoneNumber
18
19   #endif
```

Fig. 10.3 | PhoneNumber class with overloaded stream insertion and stream extraction operators as friend functions. (Part 2 of 2.)

```
1    // Fig. 10.4: PhoneNumber.cpp
2    // Overloaded stream insertion and stream extraction operators
3    // for class PhoneNumber.
4    #include <iomanip>
5    #include "PhoneNumber.h"
6    using namespace std;
7
8    // overloaded stream insertion operator; cannot be
9    // a member function if we would like to invoke it with
10   // cout << somePhoneNumber;
11   ostream &operator<<( ostream &output, const PhoneNumber &number )
12   {
13      output << "(" << number.areaCode << ") "
14         << number.exchange << "-" << number.line;
15      return output; // enables cout << a << b << c;
16   } // end function operator<<
17
18   // overloaded stream extraction operator; cannot be
19   // a member function if we would like to invoke it with
20   // cin >> somePhoneNumber;
21   istream &operator>>( istream &input, PhoneNumber &number )
22   {
23      input.ignore(); // skip (
24      input >> setw( 3 ) >> number.areaCode; // input area code
25      input.ignore( 2 ); // skip ) and space
26      input >> setw( 3 ) >> number.exchange; // input exchange
27      input.ignore(); // skip dash (-)
28      input >> setw( 4 ) >> number.line; // input line
29      return input; // enables cin >> a >> b >> c;
30   } // end function operator>>
```

Fig. 10.4 | Overloaded stream insertion and stream extraction operators for class PhoneNumber.

```
1    // Fig. 10.5: fig10_05.cpp
2    // Demonstrating class PhoneNumber's overloaded stream insertion
3    // and stream extraction operators.
4    #include <iostream>
```

Fig. 10.5 | Overloaded stream insertion and stream extraction operators. (Part 1 of 2.)

```
 5   #include "PhoneNumber.h"
 6   using namespace std;
 7
 8   int main()
 9   {
10       PhoneNumber phone; // create object phone
11
12       cout << "Enter phone number in the form (123) 456-7890:" << endl;
13
14       // cin >> phone invokes operator>> by implicitly issuing
15       // the non-member function call operator>>( cin, phone )
16       cin >> phone;
17
18       cout << "The phone number entered was: ";
19
20       // cout << phone invokes operator<< by implicitly issuing
21       // the non-member function call operator<<( cout, phone )
22       cout << phone << endl;
23   } // end main
```

```
Enter phone number in the form (123) 456-7890:
(800) 555-1212
The phone number entered was: (800) 555-1212
```

Fig. 10.5 | Overloaded stream insertion and stream extraction operators. (Part 2 of 2.)

Overloading the Stream Extraction (>>) Operator

The stream extraction operator function operator>> (Fig. 10.4, lines 21–30) takes the istream reference input and the PhoneNumber reference number as arguments and returns an istream reference. Operator function operator>> inputs phone numbers of the form

```
(800) 555-1212
```

into objects of class PhoneNumber. When the compiler sees the expression

```
cin >> phone
```

in line 16 of Fig. 10.5, the compiler generates the *non-member function call*

```
operator>>( cin, phone );
```

When this call executes, reference parameter input (Fig. 10.4, line 21) becomes an alias for cin and reference parameter number becomes an alias for phone. The operator function reads as strings the three parts of the telephone number into the areaCode (line 24), exchange (line 26) and line (line 28) members of the PhoneNumber object referenced by parameter number. Stream manipulator setw limits the number of characters read into each string. *When used with cin and strings, setw restricts the number of characters read to the number of characters specified by its argument* (i.e., setw(3) allows three characters to be read). The parentheses, space and dash characters are skipped by calling istream member function ignore (Fig. 10.4, lines 23, 25 and 27), which discards the specified number of characters in the input stream (one character by default). Function operator>> returns istream reference input (i.e., cin). This enables input operations on PhoneNumber objects to be *cascaded* with input operations on other PhoneNumber objects or other data types. For example, a program can input two PhoneNumber objects in one statement as follows:

```
cin >> phone1 >> phone2;
```

First, the expression cin >> phone1 executes by making the non-member function call

```
operator>>( cin, phone1 );
```

This call then returns a reference to cin as the value of cin >> phone1, so the remaining portion of the expression is interpreted simply as cin >> phone2. This executes by making the *non-member function call*

```
operator>>( cin, phone2 );
```

Good Programming Practice 10.1
Overloaded operators should mimic the functionality of their built-in counterparts—e.g., the + operator should perform addition, not subtraction. Avoid excessive or inconsistent use of operator overloading, as this can make a program cryptic and difficult to read.

Overloading the Stream Insertion (<<) Operator
The stream insertion operator function (Fig. 10.4, lines 11–16) takes an ostream reference (output) and a const PhoneNumber reference (number) as arguments and returns an ostream reference. Function operator<< displays objects of type PhoneNumber. When the compiler sees the expression

```
cout << phone
```

in line 22 of Fig. 10.5, the compiler generates the *non-member function call*

```
operator<<( cout, phone );
```

Function operator<< displays the parts of the telephone number as strings, because they're stored as string objects.

Overloaded Operators as Non-Member *friend* Functions
The functions operator>> and operator<< are declared in PhoneNumber as *non-member, friend functions* (Fig. 10.3, lines 11–12). They're *non-member functions* because the object of class PhoneNumber must be the operator's *right* operand. If these were to be PhoneNumber *member functions*, the following awkward statements would have to be used to output and input a PhoneNumber:

```
phone << cout;
phone >> cin;
```

Such statements would be confusing to most C++ programmers, who are familiar with cout and cin appearing as the *left* operands of << and >>, respectively.

Overloaded operator functions for binary operators can be member functions only when the *left* operand is an object of the class in which the function is a member. *Overloaded input and output operators are declared as friends if they need to access non-public class members directly or because the class may not offer appropriate get functions.* Also, the PhoneNumber reference in function operator<<'s parameter list (Fig. 10.4, line 11) is const, because the PhoneNumber will simply be output, and the PhoneNumber reference in function `operator>>`'s parameter list (line 21) is non-`const`, because the `PhoneNumber` object must be modified to store the input telephone number in the object.

> ### Software Engineering Observation 10.2
> *New input/output capabilities for user-defined types are added to C++ without modifying standard input/output library classes. This is another example of C++'s extensibility.*

Why Overloaded Stream Insertion and Stream Extraction Operators Are Overloaded as Non-Member Functions

The overloaded stream insertion operator (`<<`) is used in an expression in which the left operand has type `ostream &`, as in `cout << classObject`. To use the operator in this manner where the *right* operand is an object of a user-defined class, it must be overloaded as a *non-member function*. To be a member function, operator `<<` would have to be a member of class `ostream`. This is *not* possible for user-defined classes, since we are *not allowed to modify C++ Standard Library classes*. Similarly, the overloaded stream extraction operator (`>>`) is used in an expression in which the *left* operand has the type `istream &`, as in `cin >> classObject`, and the *right* operand is an object of a user-defined class, so it, too, must be a *non-member function*. Also, each of these overloaded operator functions may require access to the `private` data members of the class object being output or input, so these overloaded operator functions can be made `friend` functions of the class for performance reasons.

10.6 Overloading Unary Operators

A unary operator for a class can be overloaded as a non-`static` member function with no arguments or as a non-member function with one argument that must be an object (or a reference to an object) of the class. Member functions that implement overloaded operators must be non-`static` so that they can access the non-`static` data in each object of the class.

Unary Overloaded Operators as Member Functions

Consider overloading unary operator `!` to test whether an object of your own `String` class is empty. Such a function would return a `bool` result. When a unary operator such as `!` is overloaded as a member function with no arguments and the compiler sees the expression `!s` (in which `s` is an object of class `String`), the compiler generates the function call `s.operator!()`. The operand `s` is the `String` object for which the `String` class member function `operator!` is being invoked. The function is declared as follows:

```
class String
{
public:
    bool operator!() const;
    ...
}; // end class String
```

Unary Overloaded Operators as Non-Member Functions

A unary operator such as `!` may be overloaded as a *non-member function* with one parameter. If `s` is a `String` class object (or a reference to a `String` class object), then `!s` is treated as if the call `operator!(s)` had been written, invoking the *non-member* `operator!` function that's declared as follows:

```
bool operator!( const String & );
```

10.7 Overloading the Unary Prefix and Postfix ++ and -- Operators

The prefix and postfix versions of the increment and decrement operators can all be overloaded. We'll see how the compiler distinguishes between the prefix version and the postfix version of an increment or decrement operator.

To overload the prefix and postfix increment operators, each overloaded operator function must have a distinct signature, so that the compiler will be able to determine which version of ++ is intended. The prefix versions are overloaded exactly as any other prefix unary operator would be. Everything stated in this section for overloading prefix and postfix increment operators applies to overloading predecrement and postdecrement operators. In the next section, we examine a `Date` class with overloaded prefix and postfix increment operators.

Overloading the Prefix Increment Operator

Suppose that we want to add 1 to the day in `Date` object `d1`. When the compiler sees the preincrementing expression ++d1, the compiler generates the *member-function call*

```
d1.operator++()
```

The prototype for this operator member function would be

```
Date &operator++();
```

If the prefix increment operator is implemented as a *non-member function*, then, when the compiler sees the expression ++d1, the compiler generates the function call

```
operator++( d1 )
```

The prototype for this non-member operator function would be declared as

```
Date &operator++( Date & );
```

Overloading the Postfix Increment Operator

Overloading the postfix increment operator presents a challenge, because the compiler must be able to distinguish between the signatures of the overloaded prefix and postfix increment operator functions. The *convention* that has been adopted is that, when the compiler sees the postincrementing expression d1++, it generates the *member-function call*

```
d1.operator++( 0 )
```

The prototype for this operator member function is

```
Date operator++( int )
```

The argument 0 is strictly a *dummy value* that enables the compiler to distinguish between the prefix and postfix increment operator functions. The same syntax is used to differentiate between the prefix and postfix decrement operator functions.

If the postfix increment is implemented as a *non-member function*, then, when the compiler sees the expression d1++, the compiler generates the function call

```
operator++( d1, 0 )
```

The prototype for this function would be

```
Date operator++( Date &, int );
```

Once again, the 0 argument is used by the compiler to distinguish between the prefix and postfix increment operators implemented as non-member functions. Note that the *postfix increment operator* returns `Date` objects *by value*, whereas the prefix increment operator returns `Date` objects *by reference*—the postfix increment operator typically returns a temporary object that contains the original value of the object before the increment occurred. C++ treats such objects as *rvalues*, which *cannot be used on the left side of an assignment*. The prefix increment operator returns the actual incremented object with its new value. Such an object *can* be used as an *lvalue* in a continuing expression.

> **Performance Tip 10.1**
>
> *The extra object that's created by the* postfix *increment (or decrement) operator can result in a performance problem—especially when the operator is used in a loop. For this reason, you should prefer the overloaded* prefix *increment and decrement operators.*

10.8 Case Study: A Date Class

The program of Figs. 10.6–10.8 demonstrates a `Date` class, which uses overloaded prefix and postfix increment operators to add 1 to the day in a `Date` object, while causing appropriate increments to the month and year if necessary. The `Date` header (Fig. 10.6) specifies that `Date`'s `public` interface includes an overloaded stream insertion operator (line 11), a default constructor (line 13), a `setDate` function (line 14), an overloaded prefix increment operator (line 15), an overloaded postfix increment operator (line 16), an overloaded `+=` addition assignment operator (line 17), a function to test for leap years (line 18) and a function to determine whether a day is the last day of the month (line 19).

```cpp
1   // Fig. 10.6: Date.h
2   // Date class definition with overloaded increment operators.
3   #ifndef DATE_H
4   #define DATE_H
5
6   #include <array>
7   #include <iostream>
8
9   class Date
10  {
11     friend std::ostream &operator<<( std::ostream &, const Date & );
12  public:
13     Date( int m = 1, int d = 1, int y = 1900 ); // default constructor
14     void setDate( int, int, int ); // set month, day, year
15     Date &operator++(); // prefix increment operator
16     Date operator++( int ); // postfix increment operator
17     Date &operator+=( unsigned int ); // add days, modify object
18     static bool leapYear( int ); // is date in a leap year?
19     bool endOfMonth( int ) const; // is date at the end of month?
20  private:
21     unsigned int month;
22     unsigned int day;
23     unsigned int year;
```

Fig. 10.6 | Date class definition with overloaded increment operators. (Part 1 of 2.)

```
24
25     static const std::array< unsigned int, 13 > days; // days per month
26     void helpIncrement(); // utility function for incrementing date
27  }; // end class Date
28
29  #endif
```

Fig. 10.6 | Date class definition with overloaded increment operators. (Part 2 of 2.)

```
 1   // Fig. 10.7: Date.cpp
 2   // Date class member- and friend-function definitions.
 3   #include <iostream>
 4   #include <string>
 5   #include "Date.h"
 6   using namespace std;
 7
 8   // initialize static member; one classwide copy
 9   const array< unsigned int, 13 > Date::days =
10      { 0, 31, 28, 31, 30, 31, 30, 31, 31, 30, 31, 30, 31 };
11
12   // Date constructor
13   Date::Date( int month, int day, int year )
14   {
15      setDate( month, day, year );
16   } // end Date constructor
17
18   // set month, day and year
19   void Date::setDate( int mm, int dd, int yy )
20   {
21      if ( mm >= 1 && mm <= 12 )
22         month = mm;
23      else
24         throw invalid_argument( "Month must be 1-12" );
25
26      if ( yy >= 1900 && yy <= 2100 )
27         year = yy;
28      else
29         throw invalid_argument( "Year must be >= 1900 and <= 2100" );
30
31      // test for a leap year
32      if ( ( month == 2 && leapYear( year ) && dd >= 1 && dd <= 29 ) ||
33         ( dd >= 1 && dd <= days[ month ] ) )
34         day = dd;
35      else
36         throw invalid_argument(
37            "Day is out of range for current month and year" );
38   } // end function setDate
39
40   // overloaded prefix increment operator
41   Date &Date::operator++()
42   {
```

Fig. 10.7 | Date class member- and friend-function definitions. (Part 1 of 3.)

```
43        helpIncrement(); // increment date
44        return *this; // reference return to create an lvalue
45    } // end function operator++
46
47    // overloaded postfix increment operator; note that the
48    // dummy integer parameter does not have a parameter name
49    Date Date::operator++( int )
50    {
51        Date temp = *this; // hold current state of object
52        helpIncrement();
53
54        // return unincremented, saved, temporary object
55        return temp; // value return; not a reference return
56    } // end function operator++
57
58    // add specified number of days to date
59    Date &Date::operator+=( unsigned int additionalDays )
60    {
61        for ( int i = 0; i < additionalDays; ++i )
62            helpIncrement();
63
64        return *this; // enables cascading
65    } // end function operator+=
66
67    // if the year is a leap year, return true; otherwise, return false
68    bool Date::leapYear( int testYear )
69    {
70        if ( testYear % 400 == 0 ||
71            ( testYear % 100 != 0 && testYear % 4 == 0 ) )
72            return true; // a leap year
73        else
74            return false; // not a leap year
75    } // end function leapYear
76
77    // determine whether the day is the last day of the month
78    bool Date::endOfMonth( int testDay ) const
79    {
80        if ( month == 2 && leapYear( year ) )
81            return testDay == 29; // last day of Feb. in leap year
82        else
83            return testDay == days[ month ];
84    } // end function endOfMonth
85
86    // function to help increment the date
87    void Date::helpIncrement()
88    {
89        // day is not end of month
90        if ( !endOfMonth( day ) )
91            ++day; // increment day
92        else
93            if ( month < 12 ) // day is end of month and month < 12
94            {
95                ++month; // increment month
```

Fig. 10.7 | Date class member- and friend-function definitions. (Part 2 of 3.)

```
96              day = 1; // first day of new month
97          } // end if
98          else // last day of year
99          {
100             ++year; // increment year
101             month = 1; // first month of new year
102             day = 1; // first day of new month
103         } // end else
104  } // end function helpIncrement
105
106  // overloaded output operator
107  ostream &operator<<( ostream &output, const Date &d )
108  {
109     static string monthName[ 13 ] = { "", "January", "February",
110        "March", "April", "May", "June", "July", "August",
111        "September", "October", "November", "December" };
112     output << monthName[ d.month ] << ' ' << d.day << ", " << d.year;
113     return output; // enables cascading
114  } // end function operator<<
```

Fig. 10.7 | Date class member- and friend-function definitions. (Part 3 of 3.)

```
1   // Fig. 10.8: fig10_08.cpp
2   // Date class test program.
3   #include <iostream>
4   #include "Date.h" // Date class definition
5   using namespace std;
6
7   int main()
8   {
9      Date d1( 12, 27, 2010 ); // December 27, 2010
10     Date d2; // defaults to January 1, 1900
11
12     cout << "d1 is " << d1 << "\nd2 is " << d2;
13     cout << "\n\nd1 += 7 is " << ( d1 += 7 );
14
15     d2.setDate( 2, 28, 2008 );
16     cout << "\n\n  d2 is " << d2;
17     cout << "\n++d2 is " << ++d2 << " (leap year allows 29th)";
18
19     Date d3( 7, 13, 2010 );
20
21     cout << "\n\nTesting the prefix increment operator:\n"
22        << "  d3 is " << d3 << endl;
23     cout << "++d3 is " << ++d3 << endl;
24     cout << "  d3 is " << d3;
25
26     cout << "\n\nTesting the postfix increment operator:\n"
27        << "  d3 is " << d3 << endl;
28     cout << "d3++ is " << d3++ << endl;
29     cout << "  d3 is " << d3 << endl;
30  } // end main
```

Fig. 10.8 | Date class test program. (Part 1 of 2.)

```
d1 is December 27, 2010
d2 is January 1, 1900

d1 += 7 is January 3, 2011

  d2 is February 28, 2008
++d2 is February 29, 2008 (leap year allows 29th)

Testing the prefix increment operator:
  d3 is July 13, 2010
++d3 is July 14, 2010
  d3 is July 14, 2010

Testing the postfix increment operator:
  d3 is July 14, 2010
d3++ is July 14, 2010
  d3 is July 15, 2010
```

Fig. 10.8 | Date class test program. (Part 2 of 2.)

Function `main` (Fig. 10.8) creates two `Date` objects (lines 9–10)—d1 is initialized to December 27, 2010 and d2 is initialized by default to January 1, 1900. The `Date` constructor (defined in Fig. 10.7, lines 13–16) calls `setDate` (defined in Fig. 10.7, lines 19–38) to validate the month, day and year specified. Invalid values for the month, day or year result in `invalid_argument` exceptions.

Line 12 of `main` (Fig. 10.8) outputs each of the `Date` objects, using the overloaded stream insertion operator (defined in Fig. 10.7, lines 107–114). Line 13 of `main` uses the overloaded operator += (defined in Fig. 10.7, lines 59–65) to add seven days to d1. Line 15 in Fig. 10.8 uses function `setDate` to set d2 to February 28, 2008, which is a leap year. Then, line 17 preincrements d2 to show that the date increments properly to February 29. Next, line 19 creates a `Date` object, d3, which is initialized with the date July 13, 2010. Then line 23 increments d3 by 1 with the overloaded prefix increment operator. Lines 21–24 output d3 before and after the preincrement operation to confirm that it worked correctly. Finally, line 28 increments d3 with the overloaded postfix increment operator. Lines 26–29 output d3 before and after the postincrement operation to confirm that it worked correctly.

Date Class Prefix Increment Operator
Overloading the prefix increment operator is straightforward. The prefix increment operator (defined in Fig. 10.7, lines 41–45) calls utility function `helpIncrement` (defined in Fig. 10.7, lines 87–104) to increment the date. This function deals with "wraparounds" or "carries" that occur when we increment the last day of the month. These carries require incrementing the month. If the month is already 12, then the year must also be incremented and the month must be set to 1. Function `helpIncrement` uses function `endOfMonth` to determine whether the end of a month has been reached and increment the day correctly.

The overloaded prefix increment operator returns a reference to the current `Date` object (i.e., the one that was just incremented). This occurs because the current object, `*this`, is returned as a `Date &`. This enables a preincremented `Date` object to be used as an *lvalue*, which is how the built-in prefix increment operator works for fundamental types.

Date Class Postfix Increment Operator

Overloading the postfix increment operator (defined in Fig. 10.7, lines 49–56) is trickier. To emulate the effect of the postincrement, we must return an *unincremented copy* of the Date object. For example, if int variable x has the value 7, the statement

```
cout << x++ << endl;
```

outputs the *original* value of variable x. So we'd like our postfix increment operator to operate the same way on a Date object. On entry to operator++, we save the current object (*this) in temp (line 51). Next, we call helpIncrement to increment the current Date object. Then, line 55 returns the *unincremented copy* of the object previously stored in temp. This function *cannot* return a reference to the local Date object temp, because a local variable is destroyed when the function in which it's declared exits. Thus, declaring the return type to this function as Date & would return a reference to an object that no longer exists.

Common Programming Error 10.1

Returning a reference (or a pointer) to a local variable is a common error for which most compilers will issue a warning.

10.9 Dynamic Memory Management

You can control the *allocation* and *deallocation* of memory in a program for objects and for arrays of any built-in or user-defined type. This is known as dynamic memory management and is performed with the operators new and delete. We'll use these capabilities to implement our Array class in the next section.

You can use the new operator to dynamically allocate (i.e., reserve) the exact amount of memory required to hold an object or built-in array at execution time. The object or built-in array is created in the free store (also called the heap)—*a region of memory assigned to each program for storing dynamically allocated objects.*[2] Once memory is allocated in the free store, you can access it via the pointer that operator new returns. When you no longer need the memory, you can *return* it to the free store by using the delete operator to deallocate (i.e., *release*) the memory, which can then be *reused* by future new operations.[3]

Obtaining Dynamic Memory with **new**

Consider the following statement:

```
Time *timePtr = new Time();
```

The new operator allocates storage of the proper size for an object of type Time, calls the default constructor to initialize the object and returns a pointer to the type specified to the right of the new operator (i.e., a Time *). If new is unable to find sufficient space in memory for the object, it indicates that an error occurred by throwing an exception.

---

2. Operator new could fail to obtain the needed memory, in which case a bad_alloc exception will occur. Chapter 17 shows how to deal with failures when using new.
3. Operators new and delete *can* be overloaded, but this is beyond the scope of the book. If you do overload new, then you should overload delete in the *same scope* to avoid subtle dynamic memory management errors.

Releasing Dynamic Memory with **delete**
To destroy a dynamically allocated object and free the space for the object, use the `delete` operator as follows:

```
delete timePtr;
```

This statement first *calls the destructor for the object to which* `timePtr` *points, then deallocates the memory associated with the object, returning the memory to the free store.*

Common Programming Error 10.2
Not releasing dynamically allocated memory when it's no longer needed can cause the system to run out of memory prematurely. This is sometimes called a "memory leak."

Error-Prevention Tip 10.1
Do not delete memory that was not allocated by new. *Doing so results in undefined behavior.*

Error-Prevention Tip 10.2
After you delete a block of dynamically allocated memory be sure not to delete the same block again. One way to guard against this is to immediately set the pointer to `nullptr`. *Deleting a* `nullptr` *has no effect.*

Initializing Dynamic Memory
You can provide an initializer for a newly created fundamental-type variable, as in

```
double *ptr = new double( 3.14159 );
```

which initializes a newly created `double` to `3.14159` and assigns the resulting pointer to `ptr`. The same syntax can be used to specify a comma-separated list of arguments to the constructor of an object. For example,

```
Time *timePtr = new Time( 12, 45, 0 );
```

initializes a new `Time` object to 12:45 PM and assigns the resulting pointer to `timePtr`.

Dynamically Allocating Built-In Arrays with **new []**
You can also use the `new` operator to allocate built-in arrays dynamically. For example, a 10-element integer array can be allocated and assigned to `gradesArray` as follows:

```
int *gradesArray = new int[ 10 ]();
```

which declares `int` pointer `gradesArray` and assigns to it a pointer to the first element of a dynamically allocated 10-element array of `int`s. The parentheses following new int[10] value initialize the array's elements—fundamental numeric types are set to 0, `bool`s are set to `false`, pointers are set to `nullptr` and class objects are initialized by their default constructors. The size of an array created at compile time must be specified using an integral constant expression; however, a dynamically allocated array's size can be specified using *any* non-negative integral expression that can be evaluated at execution time.

C++11: Using a List Initializer with a Dynamically Allocated Built-In Array
Prior to C++11, when allocating a built-in array of objects dynamically, you *could not* pass arguments to each object's constructor—each object was initialized by its *default* construc-

tor. In C++11, you can use a list initializer to initialize the elements of a dynamically allocated built-in array, as in

```
int *gradesArray = new int[ 10 ]{};
```

The empty set of braces as shown here indicates that *default initialization* should be used for each element—for fundamental types each element is set to 0. The braces may also contain a comma-separated list of initializers for the array's elements.

Releasing Dynamically Allocated Built-In Arrays with `delete []`
To deallocate the memory to which `gradesArray` points, use the statement

```
delete [] gradesArray;
```

If the pointer points to a built-in array of objects, the statement first calls the destructor for every object in the array, then deallocates the memory. If the preceding statement did *not* include the square brackets (`[]`) and `gradesArray` pointed to a built-in array of objects, the result is *undefined—some compilers call the destructor only for the first object in the array. Using* `delete` *or* `delete []` *on a* `nullptr` *has no effect.*

Common Programming Error 10.3
Using `delete` *instead of* `delete []` *for built-in arrays of objects can lead to runtime logic errors. To ensure that every object in the array receives a destructor call, always delete memory allocated as an array with operator* `delete []`*. Similarly, always delete memory allocated as an individual element with operator* `delete`*—the result of deleting a single object with operator* `delete []` *is undefined.*

C++11: Managing Dynamically Allocated Memory with `unique_ptr`
C++11's new `unique_ptr` is a "smart pointer" for managing dynamically allocated memory. When a `unique_ptr` goes out of scope, its destructor *automatically* returns the managed memory to the free store. In Chapter 17, we introduce `unique_ptr` and show how to use it to manage dynamically allocated objects or a dynamically allocated built-in arrays.

10.10 Case Study: Array Class
We discussed built-in arrays in Chapter 8. Pointer-based arrays have many problems, including:

- A program can easily "walk off" either end of a built-in array, because C++ *does not check whether subscripts fall outside the range of the array* (though you can still do this explicitly).

- Built-in arrays of size *n* must number their elements 0, ..., *n* − 1; alternate subscript ranges are *not* allowed.

- An entire built-in array cannot be input or output at once; each element must be read or written individually (unless the array is a null-terminated C string).

- Two built-in arrays cannot be meaningfully compared with equality or relational operators (because the array names are simply pointers to where the arrays begin in memory and two arrays will always be at different memory locations).

- When a built-in array is passed to a general-purpose function designed to handle arrays of any size, the array's *size* must be passed as an additional argument.

- One built-in array cannot be *assigned* to another with the assignment operator(s).

Class development is an interesting, creative and intellectually challenging activity—always with the goal of *crafting valuable classes*. With C++, you can implement more robust array capabilities via classes and operator overloading as has been done with class templates `array` and `vector` in the C++ Standard Library. In this section, we'll develop our own custom array class that's preferable to built-in arrays. When we refer to "arrays" in this case study, we mean built-in arrays.

In this example, we create a powerful `Array` class that performs range checking to ensure that subscripts remain within the bounds of the `Array`. The class allows one `Array` object to be assigned to another with the assignment operator. `Array` objects know their size, so the size does not need to be passed separately to functions that receive `Array` parameters. Entire `Array`s can be input or output with the stream extraction and stream insertion operators, respectively. You can compare `Array`s with the equality operators `==` and `!=`.

10.10.1 Using the Array Class

The program of Figs. 10.9–10.11 demonstrates class `Array` and its overloaded operators. First we walk through `main` (Fig. 10.9) and the program's output, then we consider the class definition (Fig. 10.10) and each of its member-function definitions (Fig. 10.11).

```cpp
 1   // Fig. 10.9: fig10_09.cpp
 2   // Array class test program.
 3   #include <iostream>
 4   #include <stdexcept>
 5   #include "Array.h"
 6   using namespace std;
 7
 8   int main()
 9   {
10      Array integers1( 7 ); // seven-element Array
11      Array integers2; // 10-element Array by default
12
13      // print integers1 size and contents
14      cout << "Size of Array integers1 is "
15         << integers1.getSize()
16         << "\nArray after initialization:\n" << integers1;
17
18      // print integers2 size and contents
19      cout << "\nSize of Array integers2 is "
20         << integers2.getSize()
21         << "\nArray after initialization:\n" << integers2;
22
23      // input and print integers1 and integers2
24      cout << "\nEnter 17 integers:" << endl;
25      cin >> integers1 >> integers2;
```

Fig. 10.9 | Array class test program. (Part 1 of 3.)

```
26
27      cout << "\nAfter input, the Arrays contain:\n"
28          << "integers1:\n" << integers1
29          << "integers2:\n" << integers2;
30
31      // use overloaded inequality (!=) operator
32      cout << "\nEvaluating: integers1 != integers2" << endl;
33
34      if ( integers1 != integers2 )
35          cout << "integers1 and integers2 are not equal" << endl;
36
37      // create Array integers3 using integers1 as an
38      // initializer; print size and contents
39      Array integers3( integers1 ); // invokes copy constructor
40
41      cout << "\nSize of Array integers3 is "
42          << integers3.getSize()
43          << "\nArray after initialization:\n" << integers3;
44
45      // use overloaded assignment (=) operator
46      cout << "\nAssigning integers2 to integers1:" << endl;
47      integers1 = integers2; // note target Array is smaller
48
49      cout << "integers1:\n" << integers1
50          << "integers2:\n" << integers2;
51
52      // use overloaded equality (==) operator
53      cout << "\nEvaluating: integers1 == integers2" << endl;
54
55      if ( integers1 == integers2 )
56          cout << "integers1 and integers2 are equal" << endl;
57
58      // use overloaded subscript operator to create rvalue
59      cout << "\nintegers1[5] is " << integers1[ 5 ];
60
61      // use overloaded subscript operator to create lvalue
62      cout << "\n\nAssigning 1000 to integers1[5]" << endl;
63      integers1[ 5 ] = 1000;
64      cout << "integers1:\n" << integers1;
65
66      // attempt to use out-of-range subscript
67      try
68      {
69          cout << "\nAttempt to assign 1000 to integers1[15]" << endl;
70          integers1[ 15 ] = 1000; // ERROR: subscript out of range
71      } // end try
72      catch ( out_of_range &ex )
73      {
74          cout << "An exception occurred: " << ex.what() << endl;
75      } // end catch
76  } // end main
```

Fig. 10.9 | Array class test program. (Part 2 of 3.)

```
Size of Array integers1 is 7
Array after initialization:
          0             0             0             0
          0             0             0

Size of Array integers2 is 10
Array after initialization:
          0             0             0             0
          0             0             0             0
          0             0

Enter 17 integers:
1 2 3 4 5 6 7 8 9 10 11 12 13 14 15 16 17

After input, the Arrays contain:
integers1:
          1             2             3             4
          5             6             7
integers2:
          8             9            10            11
         12            13            14            15
         16            17

Evaluating: integers1 != integers2
integers1 and integers2 are not equal

Size of Array integers3 is 7
Array after initialization:
          1             2             3             4
          5             6             7

Assigning integers2 to integers1:
integers1:
          8             9            10            11
         12            13            14            15
         16            17

integers2:
          8             9            10            11
         12            13            14            15
         16            17

Evaluating: integers1 == integers2
integers1 and integers2 are equal

integers1[5] is 13

Assigning 1000 to integers1[5]
integers1:
          8             9            10            11
         12          1000            14            15
         16            17

Attempt to assign 1000 to integers1[15]
An exception occurred: Subscript out of range
```

Fig. 10.9 | Array class test program. (Part 3 of 3.)

Creating **Arrays**, Outputting Their Size and Displaying Their Contents

The program begins by instantiating two objects of class Array—integers1 (Fig. 10.9, line 10) with seven elements, and integers2 (line 11) with the default Array size—10 elements (specified by the Array default constructor's prototype in Fig. 10.10, line 14). Lines 14–16 in Fig. 10.9 use member function getSize to determine the size of integers1 then output integers1's contents, using the Array overloaded stream insertion operator. The sample output confirms that the Array elements were set correctly to zeros by the constructor. Next, lines 19–21 output the size of Array integers2 then output integers2's contents, using the Array overloaded stream insertion operator.

Using the Overloaded Stream Insertion Operator to Fill an **Array**

Line 24 prompts the user to input 17 integers. Line 25 uses the Array overloaded stream extraction operator to read the first seven values into integers1 and the remaining 10 values into integers2. Lines 27–29 output the two arrays with the overloaded Array stream insertion operator to confirm that the input was performed correctly.

Using the Overloaded Inequality Operator

Line 34 tests the overloaded inequality operator by evaluating the condition

```
integers1 != integers2
```

The program output shows that the Arrays are not equal.

Initializing a New **Array** with a Copy of an Existing **Array's** Contents

Line 39 instantiates a third Array called integers3 and initializes it with a copy of Array integers1. This invokes class Array's copy constructor to copy the elements of integers1 into integers3. We discuss the details of the copy constructor shortly. The copy constructor can also be invoked by writing line 39 as follows:

```
Array integers3 = integers1;
```

The equal sign in the preceding statement is *not* the assignment operator. When an equal sign appears in the declaration of an object, it invokes a constructor for that object. This form can be used to pass only a single argument to a constructor—specifically, the value on the right side of the = symbol.

Lines 41–43 output the size of integers3 then output integers3's contents, using the Array overloaded stream insertion operator to confirm that integers3's elements were set correctly by the copy constructor.

Using the Overloaded Assignment Operator

Line 47 tests the overloaded assignment operator (=) by assigning integers2 to integers1. Lines 49–50 display both Array objects' contents to confirm that the assignment was successful. Array integers1 originally held 7 integers, but was resized to hold a copy of the 10 elements in integers2. As we'll see, the overloaded assignment operator performs this resizing operation in a manner that's transparent to the client code.

Using the Overloaded Equality Operator

Line 55 uses the overloaded equality operator (==) to confirm that objects integers1 and integers2 are indeed *identical* after the assignment in line 47.

Using the Overloaded Subscript Operator

Line 59 uses the overloaded subscript operator to refer to `integers1[5]`—an in-range element of `integers1`. This subscripted name is used as an *rvalue* to print the value stored in `integers1[5]`. Line 63 uses `integers1[5]` as a modifiable *lvalue* on the left side of an assignment statement to assign a new value, 1000, to element 5 of `integers1`. We'll see that `operator[]` returns a reference to use as the modifiable *lvalue* after the operator confirms that 5 is a valid subscript for `integers1`.

Line 70 attempts to assign the value 1000 to `integers1[15]`—an *out-of-range* element. In this example, `operator[]` determines that the subscript is out of range and throws an `out_of_range` exception.

Interestingly, *the array subscript operator [] is not restricted for use only with arrays*; it also can be used, for example, to select elements from other kinds of *container classes*, such as `strings` and dictionaries. Also, when overloaded `operator[]` functions are defined, *subscripts no longer have to be integers*—characters, strings or even objects of user-defined classes also could be used. In Chapter 15, we discuss the Standard Library `map` class that allows `string` subscripts.

10.10.2 Array Class Definition

Now that we've seen how this program operates, let's walk through the class header (Fig. 10.10). As we refer to each member function in the header, we discuss that function's implementation in Fig. 10.11. In Fig. 10.10, lines 34–35 represent the `private` data members of class `Array`. Each `Array` object consists of a `size` member indicating the number of elements in the `Array` and an `int` pointer—`ptr`—that points to the dynamically allocated pointer-based array of integers managed by the `Array` object.

```
1   // Fig. 10.10: Array.h
2   // Array class definition with overloaded operators.
3   #ifndef ARRAY_H
4   #define ARRAY_H
5
6   #include <iostream>
7
8   class Array
9   {
10     friend std::ostream &operator<<( std::ostream &, const Array & );
11     friend std::istream &operator>>( std::istream &, Array & );
12
13  public:
14     explicit Array( int = 10 ); // default constructor
15     Array( const Array & ); // copy constructor
16     ~Array(); // destructor
17     size_t getSize() const; // return size
18
19     const Array &operator=( const Array & ); // assignment operator
20     bool operator==( const Array & ) const; // equality operator
21
```

Fig. 10.10 | Array class definition with overloaded operators. (Part 1 of 2.)

```
22     // inequality operator; returns opposite of == operator
23     bool operator!=( const Array &right ) const
24     {
25        return ! ( *this == right ); // invokes Array::operator==
26     } // end function operator!=
27
28     // subscript operator for non-const objects returns modifiable lvalue
29     int &operator[]( int );
30
31     // subscript operator for const objects returns rvalue
32     int operator[]( int ) const;
33   private:
34     size_t size; // pointer-based array size
35     int *ptr; // pointer to first element of pointer-based array
36   }; // end class Array
37
38   #endif
```

Fig. 10.10 | Array class definition with overloaded operators. (Part 2 of 2.)

```
 1   // Fig. 10.11: Array.cpp
 2   // Array class member- and friend-function definitions.
 3   #include <iostream>
 4   #include <iomanip>
 5   #include <stdexcept>
 6
 7   #include "Array.h" // Array class definition
 8   using namespace std;
 9
10   // default constructor for class Array (default size 10)
11   Array::Array( int arraySize )
12      : size( arraySize > 0 ? arraySize :
13           throw invalid_argument( "Array size must be greater than 0" ) ),
14        ptr( new int[ size ] )
15   {
16      for ( size_t i = 0; i < size; ++i )
17         ptr[ i ] = 0; // set pointer-based array element
18   } // end Array default constructor
19
20   // copy constructor for class Array;
21   // must receive a reference to an Array
22   Array::Array( const Array &arrayToCopy )
23      : size( arrayToCopy.size ),
24        ptr( new int[ size ] )
25   {
26      for ( size_t i = 0; i < size; ++i )
27         ptr[ i ] = arrayToCopy.ptr[ i ]; // copy into object
28   } // end Array copy constructor
29
30   // destructor for class Array
31   Array::~Array()
32   {
```

Fig. 10.11 | Array class member- and friend-function definitions. (Part 1 of 3.)

```
33        delete [] ptr; // release pointer-based array space
34    } // end destructor
35
36    // return number of elements of Array
37    size_t Array::getSize() const
38    {
39        return size; // number of elements in Array
40    } // end function getSize
41
42    // overloaded assignment operator;
43    // const return avoids: ( a1 = a2 ) = a3
44    const Array &Array::operator=( const Array &right )
45    {
46        if ( &right != this ) // avoid self-assignment
47        {
48            // for Arrays of different sizes, deallocate original
49            // left-side Array, then allocate new left-side Array
50            if ( size != right.size )
51            {
52                delete [] ptr; // release space
53                size = right.size; // resize this object
54                ptr = new int[ size ]; // create space for Array copy
55            } // end inner if
56
57            for ( size_t i = 0; i < size; ++i )
58                ptr[ i ] = right.ptr[ i ]; // copy array into object
59        } // end outer if
60
61        return *this; // enables x = y = z, for example
62    } // end function operator=
63
64    // determine if two Arrays are equal and
65    // return true, otherwise return false
66    bool Array::operator==( const Array &right ) const
67    {
68        if ( size != right.size )
69            return false; // arrays of different number of elements
70
71        for ( size_t i = 0; i < size; ++i )
72            if ( ptr[ i ] != right.ptr[ i ] )
73                return false; // Array contents are not equal
74
75        return true; // Arrays are equal
76    } // end function operator==
77
78    // overloaded subscript operator for non-const Arrays;
79    // reference return creates a modifiable lvalue
80    int &Array::operator[]( int subscript )
81    {
82        // check for subscript out-of-range error
83        if ( subscript < 0 || subscript >= size )
84            throw out_of_range( "Subscript out of range" );
85
```

Fig. 10.11 | Array class member- and friend-function definitions. (Part 2 of 3.)

```
86      return ptr[ subscript ]; // reference return
87   } // end function operator[]
88
89   // overloaded subscript operator for const Arrays
90   // const reference return creates an rvalue
91   int Array::operator[]( int subscript ) const
92   {
93      // check for subscript out-of-range error
94      if ( subscript < 0 || subscript >= size )
95         throw out_of_range( "Subscript out of range" );
96
97      return ptr[ subscript ]; // returns copy of this element
98   } // end function operator[]
99
100  // overloaded input operator for class Array;
101  // inputs values for entire Array
102  istream &operator>>( istream &input, Array &a )
103  {
104     for ( size_t i = 0; i < a.size; ++i )
105        input >> a.ptr[ i ];
106
107     return input; // enables cin >> x >> y;
108  } // end function
109
110  // overloaded output operator for class Array
111  ostream &operator<<( ostream &output, const Array &a )
112  {
113     // output private ptr-based array
114     for ( size_t i = 0; i < a.size; ++i )
115     {
116        output << setw( 12 ) << a.ptr[ i ];
117
118        if ( ( i + 1 ) % 4 == 0 ) // 4 numbers per row of output
119           output << endl;
120     } // end for
121
122     if ( a.size % 4 != 0 ) // end last line of output
123        output << endl;
124
125     return output; // enables cout << x << y;
126  } // end function operator<<
```

Fig. 10.11 | Array class member- and friend-function definitions. (Part 3 of 3.)

*Overloading the Stream Insertion and Stream Extraction Operators as **friend**s*
Lines 10–11 of Fig. 10.10 declare the overloaded stream insertion operator and the overloaded stream extraction operator as friends of class Array. When the compiler sees an expression like cout << arrayObject, it invokes *non-member function* operator<< with the call

```
operator<<( cout, arrayObject )
```

When the compiler sees an expression like cin >> arrayObject, it invokes *non-member function* operator>> with the call

```
operator>>( cin, arrayObject )
```

Again, these stream insertion and stream extraction operator functions *cannot* be members of class Array, because the Array object is always mentioned on the *right* side of the stream insertion or stream extraction operator.

Function operator<< (defined in Fig. 10.11, lines 111–126) prints the number of elements indicated by size from the integer array to which ptr points. Function operator>> (defined in Fig. 10.11, lines 102–108) inputs directly into the array to which ptr points. Each of these operator functions returns an appropriate reference to enable *cascaded* output or input statements, respectively. These functions have access to an Array's private data because they're declared as friends of class Array. We could have used class Array's getSize and operator[] functions in the bodies of operator<< and operator>>, in which case these operator functions would not need to be friends of class Array.

 You might be tempted to replace the counter-controlled for statement in lines 104–105 and many of the other for statements in class Array's implementation with the C++11 range-based for statement. Unfortunately, range-based for does *not* work with dynamically allocated built-in arrays.

Array Default Constructor

Line 14 of Fig. 10.10 declares the *default constructor* for the class and specifies a default size of 10 elements. When the compiler sees a declaration like line 11 in Fig. 10.9, it invokes class Array's default constructor to set the size of the Array to 10 elements. The default constructor (defined in Fig. 10.11, lines 11–18) validates and assigns the argument to data member size, uses new to obtain the memory for the *internal pointer-based representation* of this Array and assigns the pointer returned by new to data member ptr. Then the constructor uses a for statement to set all the elements of the array to zero. It's possible to have an Array class that does not initialize its members if, for example, these members are to be read at some later time; but this is considered to be a poor programming practice. Arrays, and *objects in general, should be properly initialized as they're created.*

Array Copy Constructor

Line 15 of Fig. 10.10 declares a *copy constructor* (defined in Fig. 10.11, lines 22–28) that initializes an Array by making a copy of an existing Array object. *Such copying must be done carefully to avoid the pitfall of leaving both Array objects pointing to the same dynamically allocated memory.* This is exactly the problem that would occur with *default memberwise copying*, if the compiler is allowed to define a default copy constructor for this class. Copy constructors are invoked whenever a copy of an object is needed, such as in

- passing an object by value to a function,
- returning an object by value from a function or
- initializing an object with a copy of another object of the same class.

The copy constructor is called in a declaration when an object of class Array is instantiated and initialized with another object of class Array, as in the declaration in line 39 of Fig. 10.9.

The copy constructor for Array copies the size of the initializer Array into data member size, uses new to obtain the memory for the internal pointer-based representation of this Array and assigns the pointer returned by new to data member ptr. Then the copy constructor uses a for statement to copy all the elements of the initializer Array into the new Array object. An object of a class can look at the private data of any other object of that class (using a handle that indicates which object to access).

Software Engineering Observation 10.3
The argument to a copy constructor should be a const reference to allow a const object to be copied.

Common Programming Error 10.4
If the copy constructor simply copied the pointer in the source object to the target object's pointer, then both would point to the same *dynamically allocated memory. The first destructor to execute would delete the dynamically allocated memory, and the other object's* ptr *would point to memory that's no longer allocated, a situation called a* dangling pointer*—this would likely result in a serious runtime error (such as early program termination) when the pointer was used.*

Array Destructor
Line 16 of Fig. 10.10 declares the class's destructor (defined in Fig. 10.11, lines 31–34). The destructor is invoked when an object of class Array goes out of scope. The destructor uses delete [] to release the memory allocated dynamically by new in the constructor.

Error-Prevention Tip 10.3
If after deleting dynamically allocated memory, the pointer will continue to exist *in memory, set the pointer's value to* nullptr *to indicate that the pointer no longer points to memory in the free store. By setting the pointer to* nullptr*, the program loses access to that free-store space, which could be reallocated for a different purpose. If you do not set the pointer to* nullptr*, your code could* inadvertently access the reallocated memory, causing subtle, nonrepeatable logic errors. We did not set ptr to nullptr in line 33 of Fig. 10.11 because after the destructor executes, the Array object no longer exists in memory.*

getSize Member Function
Line 17 of Fig. 10.10 declares function getSize (defined in Fig. 10.11, lines 37–40) that returns the number of elements in the Array.

Overloaded Assignment Operator
Line 19 of Fig. 10.10 declares the overloaded assignment operator function for the class. When the compiler sees the expression integers1 = integers2 in line 47 of Fig. 10.9, the compiler invokes member function operator= with the call

```
integers1.operator=( integers2 )
```

Member function operator='s implementation (Fig. 10.11, lines 44–62) tests for self-assignment (line 46) in which an Array object is being assigned to itself. When this is equal to the right operand's address, a *self-assignment* is being attempted, so the assignment is skipped (i.e., the object already is itself; in a moment we'll see why self-assignment is dangerous). If it isn't a self-assignment, then the function determines whether the sizes of the two Arrays are identical (line 50); in that case, the original array of integers in the left-side Array object is *not* reallocated. Otherwise, operator= uses delete [] (line 52) to release the memory originally allocated to the target Array, copies the size of the source Array to the size of the target Array (line 53), uses new to allocate the memory for the target Array and places the pointer returned by new into the Array's ptr member. Then the for statement in lines 57–58 copies the elements from the source Array to the target Array.

Regardless of whether this is a self-assignment, the member function returns the current object (i.e., `*this` in line 61) as a constant reference; this enables cascaded `Array` assignments such as x = y = z, but prevents ones like (x = y) = z because z cannot be assigned to the `const Array` reference that's returned by (x = y). If self-assignment occurs, and function `operator=` did not test for this case, `operator=` would unnecessarily copy the elements of the `Array` into itself.

Software Engineering Observation 10.4

A copy constructor, a destructor and an overloaded assignment operator are usually provided as a group for any class that uses dynamically allocated memory. With the addition of move semantics in C++11, other functions should also be provided, as you'll see in Chapter 24.

Common Programming Error 10.5

Not providing a copy constructor and overloaded assignment operator for a class when objects of that class contain pointers to dynamically allocated memory is a potential logic error.

C++11: Move Constructor and Move Assignment Operator
C++11 adds the notions of a *move constructor* and a *move assignment operator*. We defer a discussion of these new functions until Chapter 24, C++11: Additional Features. This discussion will affect the two preceding tips.

C++11: Deleting Unwanted Member Functions from Your Class
Prior to C++11, you could prevent class objects from being *copied* or *assigned* by declaring as `private` the class's copy constructor and overloaded assignment operator. As of C++11, you can simply *delete* these functions from your class. To do so in class `Array`, replace the prototypes in lines 15 and 19 of Fig. 10.10 with:

```
Array( const Array & ) = delete;
const Array &operator=( const Array & ) = delete;
```

Though you can delete *any* member function, it's most commonly used with member functions that the compiler can *auto-generate*—the default constructor, copy constructor, assignment operator, and in C++ 11, the move constructor and move assignment operator.

Overloaded Equality and Inequality Operators
Line 20 of Fig. 10.10 declares the overloaded equality operator (==) for the class. When the compiler sees the expression integers1 == integers2 in line 55 of Fig. 10.9, the compiler invokes member function `operator==` with the call

```
integers1.operator==( integers2 )
```

Member function `operator==` (defined in Fig. 10.11, lines 66–76) immediately returns `false` if the `size` members of the `Array`s are not equal. Otherwise, `operator==` compares each pair of elements. If they're all equal, the function returns `true`. The first pair of elements to differ causes the function to return `false` immediately.

Lines 23–26 of Fig. 10.9 define the overloaded inequality operator (!=) for the class. Member function `operator!=` uses the overloaded `operator==` function to determine whether one `Array` is *equal* to another, then returns the *opposite* of that result. Writing `operator!=` in this manner enables you to *reuse* `operator==`, which *reduces the amount of code that must be written in the class.* Also, the full function definition for `operator!=` is in the `Array` header. This allows the compiler to *inline* the definition of `operator!=`.

Overloaded Subscript Operators

Lines 29 and 32 of Fig. 10.10 declare two overloaded subscript operators (defined in Fig. 10.11 in lines 80–87 and 91–98, respectively). When the compiler sees the expression `integers1[5]` (Fig. 10.9, line 59), it invokes the appropriate overloaded `operator[]` member function by generating the call

```
integers1.operator[]( 5 )
```

The compiler creates a call to the `const` version of `operator[]` (Fig. 10.11, lines 91–98) when the subscript operator is used on a `const Array` object. For example, if you pass an `Array` to a function that receives the `Array` as a `const Array &` named z, then the `const` version of `operator[]` is required to execute a statement such as

```
cout << z[ 3 ] << endl;
```

Remember, a program can invoke only the `const` member functions of a `const` object.

Each definition of `operator[]` determines whether the subscript it receives as an argument is *in range* and—if not, each throws an `out_of_range` exception. If the subscript is in range, the non-`const` version of `operator[]` returns the appropriate `Array` element as a reference so that it may be used as a modifiable *lvalue* (e.g., on the *left* side of an assignment statement). If the subscript is in range, the `const` version of `operator[]` returns a copy of the appropriate element of the `Array`.

C++11: Managing Dynamically Allocated Memory with `unique_ptr`

In this case study, class `Array`'s destructor used `delete []` to return the dynamically allocated built-in array to the free store. As you recall, C++11 enables you to use `unique_ptr` to ensure that this dynamically allocated memory is deleted when the `Array` object goes out of scope. In Chapter 17, we introduce `unique_ptr` and show how to use it to manage a dynamically allocated objects or dynamically allocated built-in arrays.

C++11: Passing a List Initializer to a Constructor

In Fig. 7.4, we showed how to initialize an `array` object with a comma-separated list of initializers in braces, as in

```
array< int, 5 > n = { 32, 27, 64, 18, 95 };
```

Recall from Section 4.10 that C++11 now allows *any* object to be initialized with a *list initializer* and that the preceding statement can also be written without the =, as in

```
array< int, 5 > n{ 32, 27, 64, 18, 95 };
```

C++11 also allows you to use list initializers when you declare objects of your own classes. For example, you can now provide an `Array` constructor that would enabled the following declarations:

```
Array integers = { 1, 2, 3, 4, 5 };
```

or

```
Array integers{ 1, 2, 3, 4, 5 };
```

each of which creates an `Array` object with five elements containing the integers from 1 to 5.

To support list initialization, you can define a constructor that receives an *object* of the class template `initializer_list`. For class `Array`, you'd include the `<initializer_list>` header. Then, you'd define a constructor with the first line:

```
Array::Array( initializer_list< int > list )
```

You can determine the number of elements in the `list` parameter by calling its `size` member function. To obtain each initializer and copy it into the `Array` object's dynamically allocated built-in array, you can use a range-based `for` as follows:

```
size_t i = 0;

for ( int item : list )
   ptr[ i++ ] = item;
```

10.11 Operators as Member vs. Non-Member Functions

Whether an operator function is implemented as a *member function* or as a *non-member function*, the operator is still used the same way in expressions. So which is best?

When an operator function is implemented as a *member function*, the *leftmost* (or only) operand must be an object (or a reference to an object) of the operator's class. If the left operand *must* be an object of a different class or a fundamental type, this operator function *must* be implemented as a *non-member function* (as we did in Section 10.5 when overloading << and >> as the stream insertion and stream extraction operators, respectively). A *non-member operator function* can be made a `friend` of a class if that function must access `private` or `protected` members of that class directly.

Operator member functions of a specific class are called (*implicitly* by the compiler) only when the *left* operand of a binary operator is specifically an object of that class, or when the *single operand of a unary operator* is an object of that class.

Commutative Operators
Another reason why you might choose a non-member function to overload an operator is to enable the operator to be *commutative*. For example, suppose we have a *fundamental type variable*, number, of type `long int`, and an *object* `bigInteger1`, of class `HugeInt` (a class in which integers may be arbitrarily large rather than being limited by the machine word size of the underlying hardware; class `HugeInt` is developed in the chapter exercises). The addition operator (+) produces a *temporary* `HugeInt` object as the sum of a `HugeInt` and a `long int` (as in the expression `bigInteger1 + number`), *or* as the sum of a `long int` and a `HugeInt` (as in the expression `number + bigInteger1`). Thus, we require the addition operator to be *commutative* (exactly as it is with two fundamental-type operands). The problem is that the class object *must* appear on the *left* of the addition operator if that operator is to be overloaded as a *member function*. So, we *also* overload the operator as a *non-member function* to allow the `HugeInt` to appear on the *right* of the addition. The `operator+` function that deals with the `HugeInt` on the *left* can still be a *member function*. The *non-member function* can simply swap its arguments and call the *member function*.

10.12 Converting Between Types

Most programs process information of many types. Sometimes all the operations "stay within a type." For example, adding an `int` to an `int` produces an `int`. It's often necessary, however, to convert data of one type to data of another type. This can happen in assignments, in calculations, in passing values to functions and in returning values from functions. The compiler knows how to perform certain conversions among fundamental types. You can use *cast operators* to *force* conversions among fundamental types.

But what about user-defined types? The compiler cannot know in advance how to convert among user-defined types, and between user-defined types and fundamental types, so you must specify how to do this. Such conversions can be performed with conversion constructors—constructors that can be called with a single argument (we'll refer to these as *single-argument constructors*). Such constructors can turn objects of other types (including fundamental types) into objects of a particular class.

Conversion Operators

A conversion operator (also called a *cast operator*) can be used to convert an object of one class to another type. Such a conversion operator must be a *non-static member function*. The function prototype

```
MyClass::operator char *() const;
```

declares an overloaded cast operator function for converting an object of class `MyClass` into a temporary `char *` object. The operator function is declared `const` because it does *not* modify the original object. The return type of an overloaded **cast operator function** is implicitly the type to which the object is being converted. If `s` is a class object, when the compiler sees the expression `static_cast<char *>(s)`, the compiler generates the call

```
s.operator char *()
```

to convert the operand `s` to a `char *`.

Overloaded Cast Operator Functions

Overloaded cast operator functions can be defined to convert objects of user-defined types into fundamental types or into objects of other user-defined types. The prototypes

```
MyClass::operator int() const;
MyClass::operator OtherClass() const;
```

declare *overloaded cast operator functions* that can convert an object of user-defined type `MyClass` into an integer or into an object of user-defined type `OtherClass`, respectively.

Implicit Calls to Cast Operators and Conversion Constructors

One of the nice features of cast operators and conversion constructors is that, when necessary, the compiler can call these functions *implicitly* to create *temporary* objects. For example, if an object `s` of a user-defined `String` class appears in a program at a location where an ordinary `char *` is expected, such as

```
cout << s;
```

the compiler can call the overloaded cast-operator function `operator char *` to convert the object into a `char *` and use the resulting `char *` in the expression. With this cast operator provided for a `String` class, the stream insertion operator does *not* have to be overloaded to output a `String` using `cout`.

Software Engineering Observation 10.5

When a conversion constructor or conversion operator is used to perform an implicit *conversion, C++ can apply only one* implicit constructor or operator function call *(i.e., a single user-defined conversion) to try to match the needs of another overloaded operator. The compiler will not satisfy an overloaded operator's needs by performing a series of implicit, user-defined conversions.*

10.13 `explicit` Constructors and Conversion Operators

Recall that we've been declaring as `explicit` every constructor that can be called with one argument. With the exception of copy constructors, any constructor that can be called with a *single argument* and is *not* declared `explicit` can be used by the compiler to perform an *implicit conversion*. The constructor's argument is converted to an object of the class in which the constructor is defined. The conversion is automatic and you need not use a cast operator. *In some situations, implicit conversions are undesirable or error-prone.* For example, our `Array` class in Fig. 10.10 defines a constructor that takes a single `int` argument. The intent of this constructor is to create an `Array` object containing the number of elements specified by the `int` argument. However, if this constructor were not declared `explicit` it could be misused by the compiler to perform an *implicit conversion*.

Common Programming Error 10.6

Unfortunately, the compiler might use implicit conversions in cases that you do not expect, resulting in ambiguous expressions that generate compilation errors or result in execution-time logic errors.

Accidentally Using a Single-Argument Constructor as a Conversion Constructor
The program (Fig. 10.12) uses the `Array` class of Figs. 10.10–10.11 to demonstrate an improper implicit conversion. To allow this implicit conversion, we removed the explicit keyword from line 14 in `Array.h` (Fig. 10.10).

Line 11 in `main` (Fig. 10.12) instantiates `Array` object `integers1` and calls the *single-argument constructor* with the `int` value 7 to specify the number of elements in the `Array`. Recall from Fig. 10.11 that the `Array` constructor that receives an `int` argument initializes all the `Array` elements to 0. Line 12 calls function `outputArray` (defined in lines 17–21), which receives as its argument a `const Array &` to an `Array`. The function outputs the number of elements in its `Array` argument and the contents of the `Array`. In this case, the size of the `Array` is 7, so seven 0s are output.

Line 13 calls function `outputArray` with the `int` value 3 as an argument. However, this program does *not* contain a function called `outputArray` that takes an `int` argument. So, the compiler determines whether class `Array` provides a *conversion constructor* that can convert an `int` into an `Array`. Since the `Array` constructor receives one `int` argument, the compiler assumes that the constructor is a conversion constructor that can be used to convert the argument 3 into a temporary `Array` object containing three elements. Then, the compiler passes the temporary `Array` object to function `outputArray` to output the `Array`'s contents. Thus, even though we do not *explicitly* provide an `outputArray` function that receives an `int` argument, the compiler is able to compile line 13. The output shows the contents of the three-element `Array` containing 0s.

```
1   // Fig. 10.12: fig10_12.cpp
2   // Single-argument constructors and implicit conversions.
3   #include <iostream>
4   #include "Array.h"
5   using namespace std;
6
7   void outputArray( const Array & ); // prototype
8
9   int main()
10  {
11     Array integers1( 7 ); // 7-element Array
12     outputArray( integers1 ); // output Array integers1
13     outputArray( 3 ); // convert 3 to an Array and output Array's contents
14  } // end main
15
16  // print Array contents
17  void outputArray( const Array &arrayToOutput )
18  {
19     cout << "The Array received has " << arrayToOutput.getSize()
20        << " elements. The contents are:\n" << arrayToOutput << endl;
21  } // end outputArray
```

```
The Array received has 7 elements. The contents are:
        0            0            0            0
        0            0            0
The Array received has 3 elements. The contents are:
        0            0            0
```

Fig. 10.12 | Single-argument constructors and implicit conversions.

Preventing Implicit Conversions with Single-Argument Constructors

The reason we've been declaring every single-argument contructor preceded by the keyword explicit is to *suppress implicit conversions via conversion constructors when such conversions should not be allowed*. A constructor that's declared explicit *cannot* be used in an *implicit* conversion. In the example of Figure 10.13, we use the original version of Array.h from Fig. 10.10, which included the keyword explicit in the declaration of the *single-argument constructor* in line 14

```
explicit Array( int = 10 ); // default constructor
```

Figure 10.13 presents a slightly modified version of the program in Fig. 10.12. When this program in Fig. 10.13 is compiled, the compiler produces an error message indicating that the integer value passed to outputArray in line 13 *cannot* be converted to a const Array &. The compiler error message (from Visual C++) is shown in the output window. Line 14 demonstrates how the explicit constructor can be used to create a temporary Array of 3 elements and pass it to function outputArray.

 Error-Prevention Tip 10.4

Always use the explicit *keyword on single-argument constructors unless they're intended to be used as conversion constructors.*

```
1  // Fig. 10.13: fig10_13.cpp
2  // Demonstrating an explicit constructor.
3  #include <iostream>
4  #include "Array.h"
5  using namespace std;
6
7  void outputArray( const Array & ); // prototype
8
9  int main()
10 {
11    Array integers1( 7 ); // 7-element Array
12    outputArray( integers1 ); // output Array integers1
13    outputArray( 3 ); // convert 3 to an Array and output Array's contents
14    outputArray( Array( 3 ) ); // explicit single-argument constructor call
15 } // end main
16
17 // print Array contents
18 void outputArray( const Array &arrayToOutput )
19 {
20    cout << "The Array received has " << arrayToOutput.getSize()
21       << " elements. The contents are:\n" << arrayToOutput << endl;
22 } // end outputArray
```

```
c:\books\2012\cpphtp9\examples\ch10\fig10_13\fig10_13.cpp(13): error C2664:
'outputArray' : cannot convert parameter 1 from 'int' to 'const Array &'
        Reason: cannot convert from 'int' to 'const Array'
        Constructor for class 'Array' is declared 'explicit'
```

Fig. 10.13 | Demonstrating an `explicit` constructor.

C++11: explicit Conversion Operators

As of C++11, similar to declaring single-argument constructors `explicit`, you can declare conversion operators `explicit` to prevent the compiler from using them to perform implicit conversions. For example, the prototype:

```
explicit MyClass::operator char *() const;
```

declares `MyClass`'s `char *` cast operator `explicit`.

10.14 Overloading the Function Call Operator ()

Overloading the function call operator () is powerful, because functions can take an *arbitrary* number of comma-separated parameters. In a *customized* `String` class, for example, you could overload this operator to select a substring from a `String`—the operator's two integer parameters could specify the *start location* and the *length of the substring to be selected*. The `operator()` function could check for such errors as a *start location out of range* or a *negative substring length*.

The overloaded function call operator must be a *non-static* member function and could be defined with the first line:

```
String String::operator()( size_t index, size_t length ) const
```

Section 10.5 Overloading the Binary Stream Insertion and Stream Extraction Operators

- The overloaded stream insertion operator (<<) is used in an expression in which the left operand has type ostream &. For this reason, it must be overloaded as a non-member function. Similarly, the overloaded stream extraction operator (>>) must be a non-member function.

- Another reason to choose a non-member function to overload an operator is to enable the operator to be commutative.

- When used with cin, setw restricts the number of characters read to the number of characters specified by its argument.

- istream member function ignore discards the specified number of characters in the input stream (one character by default).

- Overloaded input and output operators are declared as friends if they need to access non-public class members directly for performance reasons.

Section 10.6 Overloading Unary Operators

- A unary operator for a class can be overloaded as a non-static member function with no arguments or as a non-member function with one argument; that argument must be either an object of the class or a reference to an object of the class.

- Member functions that implement overloaded operators must be non-static so that they can access the non-static data in each object of the class.

Section 10.7 Overloading the Unary Prefix and Postfix ++ and -- Operators

- The prefix and postfix increment and decrement operators can all be overloaded.

- To overload the pre- and post-increment operators, each overloaded operator function must have a distinct signature. The prefix versions are overloaded like any other unary operator. The postfix increment operator's unique signature is accomplished by providing a second argument, which must be of type int. This argument is not supplied in the client code. It's used implicitly by the compiler to distinguish between the prefix and postfix versions of the increment operator. The same syntax is used to differentiate between the prefix and postfix decrement operator functions.

Section 10.9 Dynamic Memory Management

- Dynamic memory management (p. 485) enables you to control the allocation and deallocation of memory in a program for any built-in or user-defined type.

- The free store (sometimes called the heap; p. 485) is a region of memory assigned to each program for storing objects dynamically allocated at execution time.

- The new operator (p. 485) allocates storage of the proper size for an object, runs the object's constructor and returns a pointer of the correct type. If new is unable to find space in memory for the object, it indicates that an error occurred by "throwing" an "exception." This usually causes the program to terminate immediately, unless the exception is handled.

- To destroy a dynamically allocated object and free its space, use the delete operator (p. 485).

- A built-in array of objects can be allocated dynamically with new as in

```
int *ptr = new int[ 100 ]();
```

which allocates a built-in array of 100 integers, initializes each to 0 with value initialization and assigns the built-in array's starting location to ptr. The preceding built-in array is deleted (p. 487) with the statement

```
delete [] ptr;
```

Section 10.10 Case Study: *Array Class*

- A copy constructor initializes a new object of a class by copying the members of an existing one. Classes that contain dynamically allocated memory typically provide a copy constructor, a destructor and an overloaded assignment operator.

- The implementation of member function `operator=` should test for self-assignment (p. 497), in which an object is being assigned to itself.

- The compiler calls the `const` version of `operator[]` when the subscript operator is used on a `const` object and calls the non-`const` version of the operator when it's used on a non-`const` object.

- The subscript operator (`[]`) can be used to select elements from other types of containers. Also, with overloading, the index values no longer need to be integers.

Section 10.11 *Operators as Member vs. Non-Member Functions*

- Operator functions can be member functions or non-member functions—non-member functions are often made `friend`s for performance reasons. Member functions use the `this` pointer implicitly to obtain one of their class object arguments (the left operand for binary operators). Arguments for both operands of a binary operator must be explicitly listed in a non-member function call.

- When an operator function is implemented as a member function, the leftmost (or only) operand must be an object (or a reference to an object) of the operator's class.

- If the left operand must be an object of a different class or a fundamental type, this operator function must be implemented as a non-member function.

- A non-member operator function can be made a `friend` of a class if that function must access `private` or `protected` members of that class directly.

Section 10.12 *Converting Between Types*

- The compiler cannot know in advance how to convert among user-defined types, and between user-defined types and fundamental types, so you must specify how to do this. Such conversions can be performed with conversion constructors (p. 501)—single-argument constructors that turn objects of other types (including fundamental types) into objects of a particular class.

- A constructor that can be called with a single argument can be used as a conversion constructor.

- A conversion operator (p. 501) must be a non-`static` member function. Overloaded cast-operator functions (p. 501) can be defined for converting objects of user-defined types into fundamental types or into objects of other user-defined types.

- An overloaded cast operator function does not specify a return type—the return type is the type to which the object is being converted.

- When necessary, the compiler can call cast operators and conversion constructors implicitly.

Section 10.13 `explicit` *Constructors and Conversion Operators*

- A constructor that's declared `explicit` (p. 503) cannot be used in an implicit conversion.

Section 10.14 *Overloading the Function Call Operator* ()

- Overloading the function call operator () (p. 504) is powerful, because functions can have an arbitrary number of parameters.

Self-Review Exercises

10.1   Fill in the blanks in each of the following:
- a) When operators are overloaded as member functions, they must be _____, because they must be called on an object of the class and operate on that object.

b) A constructor that's declared _____ cannot be used in an implicit conversion.

c) Standard class string is defined in header <string> and belongs to namespace _____.

d) The istream member function _____ discards the specified number of characters in the input stream.

e) A conversion operator must be a _____ member function.

f) You cannot change the _____ of an operator.

g) A constructor that can be called with a single argument can be used as a _____ constructor.

10.2 Explain the use of the operators new and delete.

10.3 In what context might an operator be used as non-member function?

10.4 (True/False) A constructor that can be called with a single argument can be used as a conversion constructor.

10.5 How does the "arity" of an overloaded operator compared with the "arity" of the original operator?

Answers to Self-Review Exercises

10.1 a) non-static. b) explicit. c) std. d) ignore. e) non-static. f) "arity". g) conversion.

10.2 You can control the *allocation* and *deallocation* of memory in a program for objects and for arrays of any built-in or user-defined type. This is known as dynamic memory management and is performed with the operators new and delete.

10.3 If the left operand *must* be an object of a different class or a fundamental type, this operator function *must* be implemented as a *non-member function*. A *non-member operator function* can be made a friend of a class if that function must access private or protected members of that class directly.

10.4 True.

10.5 You cannot change the "arity" of an operator (that is, the number of operands an operator takes)-overloaded unary operators remain unary operators; overloaded binary operators remain binary operators.

Exercises

10.6 *(Memory Allocation and Deallocation Operators)* Compare and contrast operators as member vs. non-member functions.

10.7 *(Overloading the Parentheses Operator)* One nice example of overloading the function call operator () is to allow another form of double-array subscripting popular in some programming languages. Instead of saying

```
chessBoard[ row ][ column ]
```

for an array of objects, overload the function call operator to allow the alternate form

```
chessBoard( row, column )
```

Create a class DoubleSubscriptedArray that has similar features to class Array in Figs. 10.10–10.11. At construction time, the class should be able to create a DoubleSubscriptedArray of any number of rows and columns. The class should supply operator() to perform double-subscripting operations. For example, in a 3-by-5 DoubleSubscriptedArray called chessBoard, the user could write chessBoard(1, 3) to access the element at row 1 and column 3. Remember that operator() can receive *any* number of arguments. The underlying representation of the DoubleSubscriptedArray could be a single-subscripted array of integers with *rows* * *columns* number of elements. Function operator() should perform the proper pointer arithmetic to access each element of the underlying array. There should be *two* versions of operator()—one that returns int & (so that an element of a

`DoubleSubscriptedArray` can be used as an *lvalue*) and one that returns `int`. The class should also provide the following operators: `==`, `!=`, `=`, `<<` (for outputting the `DoubleSubscriptedArray` in row and column format) and `>>` (for inputting the entire `DoubleSubscriptedArray` contents).

10.8   *(Complex Class)* Consider class `Complex` shown in Figs. 10.14–10.16. The class enables operations on so-called *complex numbers*. These are numbers of the form `realPart + imaginaryPart * i`, where *i* has the value

$$\sqrt{-1}$$

a) Modify the class to enable input and output of complex numbers via overloaded `>>` and `<<` operators, respectively (you should remove the `print` function from the class).

b) Overload the multiplication operator to enable multiplication of two complex numbers as in algebra.

c) Overload the `==` and `!=` operators to allow comparisons of complex numbers.

After doing this exercise, you might want to read about the Standard Library's `complex` class (from header `<complex>`).

```
 1    // Fig. 10.14: Complex.h
 2    // Complex class definition.
 3    #ifndef COMPLEX_H
 4    #define COMPLEX_H
 5
 6    class Complex
 7    {
 8    public:
 9       explicit Complex( double = 0.0, double = 0.0 ); // constructor
10       Complex operator+( const Complex & ) const; // addition
11       Complex operator-( const Complex & ) const; // subtraction
12       void print() const; // output
13    private:
14       double real; // real part
15       double imaginary; // imaginary part
16    }; // end class Complex
17
18    #endif
```

Fig. 10.14 | Complex class definition.

```
 1    // Fig. 10.15: Complex.cpp
 2    // Complex class member-function definitions.
 3    #include <iostream>
 4    #include "Complex.h" // Complex class definition
 5    using namespace std;
 6
 7    // Constructor
 8    Complex::Complex( double realPart, double imaginaryPart )
 9       : real( realPart ),
10         imaginary( imaginaryPart )
11    {
12       // empty body
13    } // end Complex constructor
14
```

Fig. 10.15 | Complex class member-function definitions. (Part 1 of 2.)

```
15    // addition operator
16    Complex Complex::operator+( const Complex &operand2 ) const
17    {
18       return Complex( real + operand2.real,
19          imaginary + operand2.imaginary );
20    } // end function operator+
21
22    // subtraction operator
23    Complex Complex::operator-( const Complex &operand2 ) const
24    {
25       return Complex( real - operand2.real,
26          imaginary - operand2.imaginary );
27    } // end function operator-
28
29    // display a Complex object in the form: (a, b)
30    void Complex::print() const
31    {
32       cout << '(' << real << ", " << imaginary << ')';
33    } // end function print
```

Fig. 10.15 | Complex class member-function definitions. (Part 2 of 2.)

```
34    // Fig. 10.16: fig10_16.cpp
35    // Complex class test program.
36    #include <iostream>
37    #include "Complex.h"
38    using namespace std;
39
40    int main()
41    {
42       Complex x;
43       Complex y( 4.3, 8.2 );
44       Complex z( 3.3, 1.1 );
45
46       cout << "x: ";
47       x.print();
48       cout << "\ny: ";
49       y.print();
50       cout << "\nz: ";
51       z.print();
52
53       x = y + z;
54       cout << "\n\nx = y + z:" << endl;
55       x.print();
56       cout << " = ";
57       y.print();
58       cout << " + ";
59       z.print();
60
61       x = y - z;
62       cout << "\n\nx = y - z:" << endl;
63       x.print();
64       cout << " = ";
65       y.print();
66       cout << " - ";
67       z.print();
68       cout << endl;
69    } // end main
```

Fig. 10.16 | Complex class test program. (Part 1 of 2.)

```
x: (0, 0)
y: (4.3, 8.2)
z: (3.3, 1.1)

x = y + z:
(7.6, 9.3) = (4.3, 8.2) + (3.3, 1.1)

x = y - z:
(1, 7.1) = (4.3, 8.2) - (3.3, 1.1)
```

Fig. 10.16 | Complex class test program. (Part 2 of 2.)

10.9   *(HugeInt Class)* A machine with 32-bit integers can represent integers in the range of approximately –2 billion to +2 billion. This fixed-size restriction is rarely troublesome, but there are applications in which we would like to be able to use a much wider range of integers. This is what C++ was built to do, namely, create powerful new data types. Consider class `HugeInt` of Figs. 10.17–10.19. Study the class carefully, then answer the following:

   a) Describe precisely how it operates.
   b) What restrictions does the class have?
   c) Overload the * multiplication operator.
   d) Overload the / division operator.
   e) Overload all the relational and equality operators.

[*Note:* We do not show an assignment operator or copy constructor for class `HugeInt`, because the assignment operator and copy constructor provided by the compiler are capable of copying the entire array data member properly.]

```
1   // Fig. 10.17: Hugeint.h
2   // HugeInt class definition.
3   #ifndef HUGEINT_H
4   #define HUGEINT_H
5
6   #include <array>
7   #include <iostream>
8   #include <string>
9
10  class HugeInt
11  {
12     friend std::ostream &operator<<( std::ostream &, const HugeInt & );
13  public:
14     static const int digits = 30; // maximum digits in a HugeInt
15
16     HugeInt( long = 0 ); // conversion/default constructor
17     HugeInt( const std::string & ); // conversion constructor
18
19     // addition operator; HugeInt + HugeInt
20     HugeInt operator+( const HugeInt & ) const;
21
22     // addition operator; HugeInt + int
23     HugeInt operator+( int ) const;
24
25     // addition operator;
26     // HugeInt + string that represents large integer value
27     HugeInt operator+( const std::string & ) const;
```

Fig. 10.17 | HugeInt class definition. (Part 1 of 2.)

```
28    private:
29       std::array< short, digits > integer;
30    }; // end class HugetInt
31
32    #endif
```

Fig. 10.17 | HugeInt class definition. (Part 2 of 2.)

```
 1    // Fig. 10.18: Hugeint.cpp
 2    // HugeInt member-function and friend-function definitions.
 3    #include <cctype> // isdigit function prototype
 4    #include "Hugeint.h" // HugeInt class definition
 5    using namespace std;
 6
 7    // default constructor; conversion constructor that converts
 8    // a long integer into a HugeInt object
 9    HugeInt::HugeInt( long value )
10    {
11       // initialize array to zero
12       for ( short &element : integer )
13          element = 0;
14
15       // place digits of argument into array
16       for ( size_t j = digits - 1; value != 0 && j >= 0; j-- )
17       {
18          integer[ j ] = value % 10;
19          value /= 10;
20       } // end for
21    } // end HugeInt default/conversion constructor
22
23    // conversion constructor that converts a character string
24    // representing a large integer into a HugeInt object
25    HugeInt::HugeInt( const string &number )
26    {
27       // initialize array to zero
28       for ( short &element : integer )
29          element = 0;
30
31       // place digits of argument into array
32       size_t length = number.size();
33
34       for ( size_t j = digits - length, k = 0; j < digits; ++j, ++k )
35          if ( isdigit( number[ k ] ) ) // ensure that character is a digit
36             integer[ j ] = number[ k ] - '0';
37    } // end HugeInt conversion constructor
38
39    // addition operator; HugeInt + HugeInt
40    HugeInt HugeInt::operator+( const HugeInt &op2 ) const
41    {
42       HugeInt temp; // temporary result
43       int carry = 0;
44
45       for ( int i = digits - 1; i >= 0; i-- )
46       {
47          temp.integer[ i ] = integer[ i ] + op2.integer[ i ] + carry;
48
```

Fig. 10.18 | HugeInt member-function and friend-function definitions. (Part 1 of 2.)

```
49        // determine whether to carry a 1
50        if ( temp.integer[ i ] > 9 )
51        {
52           temp.integer[ i ] %= 10;  // reduce to 0-9
53           carry = 1;
54        } // end if
55        else // no carry
56           carry = 0;
57     } // end for
58
59     return temp; // return copy of temporary object
60  } // end function operator+
61
62  // addition operator; HugeInt + int
63  HugeInt HugeInt::operator+( int op2 ) const
64  {
65     // convert op2 to a HugeInt, then invoke
66     // operator+ for two HugeInt objects
67     return *this + HugeInt( op2 );
68  } // end function operator+
69
70  // addition operator;
71  // HugeInt + string that represents large integer value
72  HugeInt HugeInt::operator+( const string &op2 ) const
73  {
74     // convert op2 to a HugeInt, then invoke
75     // operator+ for two HugeInt objects
76     return *this + HugeInt( op2 );
77  } // end operator+
78
79  // overloaded output operator
80  ostream& operator<<( ostream &output, const HugeInt &num )
81  {
82     int i;
83
84     for ( i = 0; ( i < HugeInt::digits ) && ( 0 == num.integer[ i ] ); ++i )
85        ; // skip leading zeros
86
87     if ( i == HugeInt::digits )
88        output << 0;
89     else
90        for ( ; i < HugeInt::digits; ++i )
91           output << num.integer[ i ];
92
93     return output;
94  } // end function operator<<
```

Fig. 10.18 | HugeInt member-function and friend-function definitions. (Part 2 of 2.)

```
1   // Fig. 10.19: fig10_19.cpp
2   // HugeInt test program.
3   #include <iostream>
4   #include "Hugeint.h"
5   using namespace std;
6
7   int main()
8   {
```

Fig. 10.19 | HugeInt test program. (Part 1 of 2.)

```
9      HugeInt n1( 7654321 );
10     HugeInt n2( 7891234 );
11     HugeInt n3( "99999999999999999999999999999" );
12     HugeInt n4( "1" );
13     HugeInt n5;
14
15     cout << "n1 is " << n1 << "\nn2 is " << n2
16          << "\nn3 is " << n3 << "\nn4 is " << n4
17          << "\nn5 is " << n5 << "\n\n";
18
19     n5 = n1 + n2;
20     cout << n1 << " + " << n2 << " = " << n5 << "\n\n";
21
22     cout << n3 << " + " << n4 << "\n= " << ( n3 + n4 ) << "\n\n";
23
24     n5 = n1 + 9;
25     cout << n1 << " + " << 9 << " = " << n5 << "\n\n";
26
27     n5 = n2 + "10000";
28     cout << n2 << " + " << "10000" << " = " << n5 << endl;
29  } // end main
```

```
n1 is 7654321
n2 is 7891234
n3 is 99999999999999999999999999999
n4 is 1
n5 is 0

7654321 + 7891234 = 15545555

99999999999999999999999999999 + 1
= 100000000000000000000000000000

7654321 + 9 = 7654330

7891234 + 10000 = 7901234
```

Fig. 10.19 | HugeInt test program. (Part 2 of 2.)

10.10 *(RationalNumber Class)* Create a class RationalNumber (fractions) with these capabilities:
  a) Create a constructor that prevents a 0 denominator in a fraction, reduces or simplifies fractions that are not in reduced form and avoids negative denominators.
  b) Overload the addition, subtraction, multiplication and division operators for this class.
  c) Overload the relational and equality operators for this class.

10.11 *(Polynomial Class)* Develop class Polynomial. The internal representation of a Polynomial is an array of terms. Each term contains a coefficient and an exponent, e.g., the term

$$2x^4$$

has the coefficient 2 and the exponent 4. Develop a complete class containing proper constructor and destructor functions as well as *set* and *get* functions. The class should also provide the following overloaded operator capabilities:
  a) Overload the addition operator (+) to add two Polynomials.
  b) Overload the subtraction operator (-) to subtract two Polynomials.
  c) Overload the assignment operator to assign one Polynomial to another.
  d) Overload the multiplication operator (*) to multiply two Polynomials.
  e) Overload the addition assignment operator (+=), subtraction assignment operator (-=), and multiplication assignment operator (*=).

11

Object-Oriented Programming: Inheritance

Say not you know another entirely, till you have divided an inheritance with him.
—Johann Kasper Lavater

This method is to define as the number of a class the class of all classes similar to the given class.
—Bertrand Russell

Save base authority from others' books.
—William Shakespeare

Objectives

In this chapter you'll learn:

- What inheritance is and how it promotes software reuse.

- The notions of base classes and derived classes and the relationships between them.

- The **protected** member access specifier.

- The use of constructors and destructors in inheritance hierarchies.

- The order in which constructors and destructors are called in inheritance hierarchies.

- The differences between **public**, **protected** and **private** inheritance.

- To use inheritance to customize existing software.

11.1 Introduction

This chapter continues our discussion of object-oriented programming (OOP) by introducing **inheritance**—a form of software reuse in which you create a class that absorbs an existing class's capabilities, then *customizes* or enhances them. Software reuse saves time during program development by taking advantage of proven, high-quality software.

When creating a class, instead of writing completely new data members and member functions, you can specify that the new class should **inherit** the members of an existing class. This existing class is called the **base class**, and the new class is called the **derived class**. Other programming languages, such as Java and C#, refer to the base class as the **superclass** and the derived class as the **subclass**. A derived class represents a *more specialized* group of objects.

C++ offers public, protected and private inheritance. In this chapter, we concentrate on public inheritance and briefly explain the other two. *With public inheritance, every object of a derived class is also an object of that derived class's base class.* However, base-class objects are *not* objects of their derived classes. For example, if we have Vehicle as a base class and Car as a derived class, then all Cars are Vehicles, but not all Vehicles are Cars—for example, a Vehicle could also be a Truck or a Boat.

We distinguish between the *is-a* **relationship** and the *has-a* relationship. The *is-a* relationship represents inheritance. In an *is-a* relationship, an object of a derived class also can be treated as an object of its base class—for example, a Car *is a* Vehicle, so any attributes and behaviors of a Vehicle are also attributes and behaviors of a Car. By contrast, the *has-a* relationship represents *composition*, which was discussed in Chapter 9. In a *has-a* relationship, an object *contains* one or more objects of other classes as members. For example, a Car has many components—it *has a* steering wheel, *has a* brake pedal, *has a* transmission, etc.

11.2 Base Classes and Derived Classes

Figure 11.1 lists several simple examples of base classes and derived classes. Base classes tend to be *more general* and derived classes tend to be *more specific*.

Base class	Derived classes
Student	GraduateStudent, UndergraduateStudent
Shape	Circle, Triangle, Rectangle, Sphere, Cube
Loan	CarLoan, HomeImprovementLoan, MortgageLoan
Employee	Faculty, Staff
Account	CheckingAccount, SavingsAccount

Fig. 11.1 | Inheritance examples.

Because every derived-class object *is an* object of its base class, and one base class can have *many* derived classes, the set of objects represented by a base class typically is *larger* than the set of objects represented by any of its derived classes. For example, the base class Vehicle represents all vehicles, including cars, trucks, boats, airplanes, bicycles and so on. By contrast, derived class Car represents a *smaller, more specific* subset of all vehicles.

Inheritance relationships form **class hierarchies**. A base class exists in a hierarchical relationship with its derived classes. Although classes can exist independently, once they're employed in inheritance relationships, they become affiliated with other classes. A class becomes either a base class—supplying members to other classes, a derived class—inheriting its members from other classes, or *both*.

CommunityMember Class Hierarchy

Let's develop a simple inheritance hierarchy with five levels (represented by the UML class diagram in Fig. 11.2). A university community has thousands of CommunityMembers.

These CommunityMembers consist of Employees, Students and alumni (each of class Alumnus). Employees are either Faculty or Staff. Faculty are either Administrators or

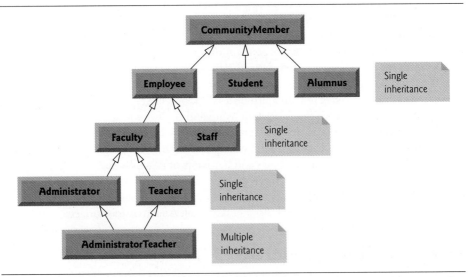

Fig. 11.2 | Inheritance hierarchy for university CommunityMembers.

Teachers. Some Administrators, however, are also Teachers. We've used *multiple inheritance* to form class AdministratorTeacher. With **single** inheritance, a class is derived from *one* base class. With **multiple** inheritance, a derived class inherits simultaneously from *two or more* (possibly unrelated) base classes. We discuss multiple inheritance in Chapter 23, Other Topics, but multiple inheritance is generally discouraged.

Each arrow in the hierarchy (Fig. 11.2) represents an *is-a* relationship. For example, as we follow the arrows in this class hierarchy, we can state "an Employee *is a* CommunityMember" and "a Teacher *is a* Faculty member." CommunityMember is the direct base class of Employee, Student and Alumnus. In addition, CommunityMember is an indirect base class of all the other classes in the diagram. An indirect base class is inherited from two or more levels up the class hierarchy.

Starting from the bottom of the diagram, you can follow the arrows upwards and apply the *is-a* relationship to the topmost base class. For example, an AdministratorTeacher *is an* Administrator, *is a* Faculty member, *is an* Employee and *is a* CommunityMember.

Shape Class Hierarchy

Now consider the Shape inheritance hierarchy in Fig. 11.3. This hierarchy begins with base class Shape. Classes TwoDimensionalShape and ThreeDimensionalShape derive from base class Shape—a Shape *is a* TwoDimensionalShape or *is a* ThreeDimensionalShape. The third level of this hierarchy contains *more specific* types of TwoDimensionalShapes and ThreeDimensionalShapes. As in Fig. 11.2, we can follow the arrows from the bottom of the diagram upwards to the topmost base class in this hierarchy to identify several *is-a* relationships. For instance, a Triangle *is a* TwoDimensionalShape and *is a* Shape, while a Sphere *is a* ThreeDimensionalShape and *is a* Shape.

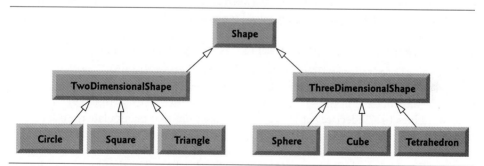

Fig. 11.3 | Inheritance hierarchy for Shapes.

To specify that class TwoDimensionalShape (Fig. 11.3) is derived from (or inherits from) class Shape, class TwoDimensionalShape's definition could begin as follows:

```
class TwoDimensionalShape : public Shape
```

This is an example of **public** inheritance, the most commonly used form. We'll also discuss **private** inheritance and **protected** inheritance (Section 11.5). With all forms of inheritance, private members of a base class are *not* accessible directly from that class's derived classes, but these private base-class members are still inherited (i.e., they're still considered parts of the derived classes). With public inheritance, all other base-class members retain their original member access when they become members of the derived class (e.g., public members of the base class become public members of the derived class, and, as we'll soon see, protected members of the base class become protected members of the derived class). Through inherited base-class member functions, the derived class can manipulate private members of the base class (if these inherited member functions provide such functionality in the base class). Note that friend functions are *not* inherited.

Inheritance is *not* appropriate for every class relationship. In Chapter 9, we discussed the *has-a* relationship, in which classes have members that are objects of other classes. Such relationships create classes by *composition* of existing classes. For example, given the classes Employee, BirthDate and TelephoneNumber, it's improper to say that an Employee *is a* BirthDate or that an Employee *is a* TelephoneNumber. However, it is appropriate to say that an Employee *has a* BirthDate and that an Employee *has a* TelephoneNumber.

It's possible to treat base-class objects and derived-class objects similarly; their commonalities are expressed in the members of the base class. Objects of all classes derived from a common base class can be treated as objects of that base class (i.e., such objects have an *is-a* relationship with the base class). In Chapter 12, we consider many examples that take advantage of this relationship.

11.3 Relationship between Base and Derived Classes

In this section, we use an inheritance hierarchy containing types of employees in a company's payroll application to discuss the relationship between a base class and a derived class. Commission employees (who will be represented as objects of a base class) are paid a percentage of their sales, while base-salaried commission employees (who will be represented as objects of a derived class) receive a base salary plus a percentage of their sales. We divide our discussion of the relationship between commission employees and base-salaried commission employees into a carefully paced series of five examples.

11.3.1 Creating and Using a CommissionEmployee Class

Let's examine CommissionEmployee's class definition (Figs. 11.4–11.5). The CommissionEmployee header (Fig. 11.4) specifies class CommissionEmployee's public services, which include a constructor (lines 11–12) and member functions earnings (line 29) and print (line 30). Lines 14–27 declare public *get* and *set* functions that manipulate the class's data members (declared in lines 32–36) firstName, lastName, socialSecurityNumber, grossSales and commissionRate. Member functions setGrossSales (defined in lines 57–63 of Fig. 11.5) and setCommissionRate (defined in lines 72–78 of Fig. 11.5), for example, validate their arguments before assigning the values to data members grossSales and commissionRate, respectively.

```
1   // Fig. 11.4: CommissionEmployee.h
2   // CommissionEmployee class definition represents a commission employee.
3   #ifndef COMMISSION_H
4   #define COMMISSION_H
5
6   #include <string> // C++ standard string class
7
```

Fig. 11.4 | CommissionEmployee class header. (Part 1 of 2.)

```
8    class CommissionEmployee
9    {
10   public:
11      CommissionEmployee( const std::string &, const std::string &,
12         const std::string &, double = 0.0, double = 0.0 );
13
14      void setFirstName( const std::string & ); // set first name
15      std::string getFirstName() const; // return first name
16
17      void setLastName( const std::string & ); // set last name
18      std::string getLastName() const; // return last name
19
20      void setSocialSecurityNumber( const std::string & ); // set SSN
21      std::string getSocialSecurityNumber() const; // return SSN
22
23      void setGrossSales( double ); // set gross sales amount
24      double getGrossSales() const; // return gross sales amount
25
26      void setCommissionRate( double ); // set commission rate (percentage)
27      double getCommissionRate() const; // return commission rate
28
29      double earnings() const; // calculate earnings
30      void print() const; // print CommissionEmployee object
31   private:
32      std::string firstName;
33      std::string lastName;
34      std::string socialSecurityNumber;
35      double grossSales; // gross weekly sales
36      double commissionRate; // commission percentage
37   }; // end class CommissionEmployee
38
39   #endif
```

Fig. 11.4 | CommissionEmployee class header. (Part 2 of 2.)

```
1    // Fig. 11.5: CommissionEmployee.cpp
2    // Class CommissionEmployee member-function definitions.
3    #include <iostream>
4    #include <stdexcept>
5    #include "CommissionEmployee.h" // CommissionEmployee class definition
6    using namespace std;
7
8    // constructor
9    CommissionEmployee::CommissionEmployee(
10      const string &first, const string &last, const string &ssn,
11      double sales, double rate )
12   {
13      firstName = first; // should validate
14      lastName = last; // should validate
15      socialSecurityNumber = ssn; // should validate
16      setGrossSales( sales ); // validate and store gross sales
```

Fig. 11.5 | Implementation file for CommissionEmployee class that represents an employee who is paid a percentage of gross sales. (Part 1 of 3.)

```
17       setCommissionRate( rate ); // validate and store commission rate
18    } // end CommissionEmployee constructor
19
20    // set first name
21    void CommissionEmployee::setFirstName( const string &first )
22    {
23       firstName = first; // should validate
24    } // end function setFirstName
25
26    // return first name
27    string CommissionEmployee::getFirstName() const
28    {
29       return firstName;
30    } // end function getFirstName
31
32    // set last name
33    void CommissionEmployee::setLastName( const string &last )
34    {
35       lastName = last; // should validate
36    } // end function setLastName
37
38    // return last name
39    string CommissionEmployee::getLastName() const
40    {
41       return lastName;
42    } // end function getLastName
43
44    // set social security number
45    void CommissionEmployee::setSocialSecurityNumber( const string &ssn )
46    {
47       socialSecurityNumber = ssn; // should validate
48    } // end function setSocialSecurityNumber
49
50    // return social security number
51    string CommissionEmployee::getSocialSecurityNumber() const
52    {
53       return socialSecurityNumber;
54    } // end function getSocialSecurityNumber
55
56    // set gross sales amount
57    void CommissionEmployee::setGrossSales( double sales )
58    {
59       if ( sales >= 0.0 )
60          grossSales = sales;
61       else
62          throw invalid_argument( "Gross sales must be >= 0.0" );
63    } // end function setGrossSales
64
65    // return gross sales amount
66    double CommissionEmployee::getGrossSales() const
67    {
```

Fig. 11.5 | Implementation file for CommissionEmployee class that represents an employee who is paid a percentage of gross sales. (Part 2 of 3.)

```
68        return grossSales;
69    } // end function getGrossSales
70
71    // set commission rate
72    void CommissionEmployee::setCommissionRate( double rate )
73    {
74        if ( rate > 0.0 && rate < 1.0 )
75            commissionRate = rate;
76        else
77            throw invalid_argument( "Commission rate must be > 0.0 and < 1.0" );
78    } // end function setCommissionRate
79
80    // return commission rate
81    double CommissionEmployee::getCommissionRate() const
82    {
83        return commissionRate;
84    } // end function getCommissionRate
85
86    // calculate earnings
87    double CommissionEmployee::earnings() const
88    {
89        return commissionRate * grossSales;
90    } // end function earnings
91
92    // print CommissionEmployee object
93    void CommissionEmployee::print() const
94    {
95        cout << "commission employee: " << firstName << ' ' << lastName
96            << "\nsocial security number: " << socialSecurityNumber
97            << "\ngross sales: " << grossSales
98            << "\ncommission rate: " << commissionRate;
99    } // end function print
```

Fig. 11.5 | Implementation file for CommissionEmployee class that represents an employee who is paid a percentage of gross sales. (Part 3 of 3.)

CommissionEmployee *Constructor*

The CommissionEmployee constructor definition *purposely does not use member-initializer syntax* in the first several examples of this section, so that we can demonstrate how private and protected specifiers affect member access in derived classes. As shown in Fig. 11.5, lines 13–15, we assign values to data members firstName, lastName and socialSecurityNumber in the constructor body. Later in this section, we'll return to using member-initializer lists in the constructors.

We do not validate the values of the constructor's arguments first, last and ssn before assigning them to the corresponding data members. We certainly could validate the first and last names—perhaps by ensuring that they're of a reasonable length. Similarly, a social security number could be validated to ensure that it contains nine digits, with or without dashes (e.g., 123-45-6789 or 123456789).

CommissionEmployee *Member Functions* earnings *and* print

Member function earnings (lines 87–90) calculates a CommissionEmployee's earnings. Line 89 multiplies the commissionRate by the grossSales and returns the result. Member function print (lines 93–99) displays the values of a CommissionEmployee object's data members.

Testing Class CommissionEmployee
Figure 11.6 tests class CommissionEmployee. Lines 11–12 instantiate CommissionEmployee object employee and invoke the constructor to initialize the object with "Sue" as the first name, "Jones" as the last name, "222-22-2222" as the social security number, 10000 as the gross sales amount and .06 as the commission rate. Lines 19–24 use employee's *get* functions to display the values of its data members. Lines 26–27 invoke the object's member functions setGrossSales and setCommissionRate to change the values of data members grossSales and commissionRate, respectively. Line 31 then calls employee's print member function to output the updated CommissionEmployee information. Finally, line 34 displays the CommissionEmployee's earnings, calculated by the object's earnings member function using the updated values of data members grossSales and commissionRate.

```cpp
 1  // Fig. 11.6: fig11_06.cpp
 2  // CommissionEmployee class test program.
 3  #include <iostream>
 4  #include <iomanip>
 5  #include "CommissionEmployee.h" // CommissionEmployee class definition
 6  using namespace std;
 7
 8  int main()
 9  {
10     // instantiate a CommissionEmployee object
11     CommissionEmployee employee(
12        "Sue", "Jones", "222-22-2222", 10000, .06 );
13
14     // set floating-point output formatting
15     cout << fixed << setprecision( 2 );
16
17     // get commission employee data
18     cout << "Employee information obtained by get functions: \n"
19        << "\nFirst name is " << employee.getFirstName()
20        << "\nLast name is " << employee.getLastName()
21        << "\nSocial security number is "
22        << employee.getSocialSecurityNumber()
23        << "\nGross sales is " << employee.getGrossSales()
24        << "\nCommission rate is " << employee.getCommissionRate() << endl;
25
26     employee.setGrossSales( 8000 ); // set gross sales
27     employee.setCommissionRate( .1 ); // set commission rate
28
29     cout << "\nUpdated employee information output by print function: \n"
30        << endl;
31     employee.print(); // display the new employee information
32
33     // display the employee's earnings
34     cout << "\n\nEmployee's earnings: $" << employee.earnings() << endl;
35  } // end main
```

Fig. 11.6 | CommissionEmployee class test program. (Part 1 of 2.)

```
Employee information obtained by get functions:

First name is Sue
Last name is Jones
Social security number is 222-22-2222
Gross sales is 10000.00
Commission rate is 0.06

Updated employee information output by print function:

commission employee: Sue Jones
social security number: 222-22-2222
gross sales: 8000.00
commission rate: 0.10

Employee's earnings: $800.00
```

Fig. 11.6 | CommissionEmployee class test program. (Part 2 of 2.)

11.3.2 Creating a BasePlusCommissionEmployee Class Without Using Inheritance

We now discuss the second part of our introduction to inheritance by creating and testing (a completely new and independent) class BasePlusCommissionEmployee (Figs. 11.7–11.8), which contains a first name, last name, social security number, gross sales amount, commission rate *and* base salary.

```cpp
1   // Fig. 11.7: BasePlusCommissionEmployee.h
2   // BasePlusCommissionEmployee class definition represents an employee
3   // that receives a base salary in addition to commission.
4   #ifndef BASEPLUS_H
5   #define BASEPLUS_H
6
7   #include <string> // C++ standard string class
8
9   class BasePlusCommissionEmployee
10  {
11  public:
12     BasePlusCommissionEmployee( const std::string &, const std::string &,
13        const std::string &, double = 0.0, double = 0.0, double = 0.0 );
14
15     void setFirstName( const std::string & ); // set first name
16     std::string getFirstName() const; // return first name
17
18     void setLastName( const std::string & ); // set last name
19     std::string getLastName() const; // return last name
20
21     void setSocialSecurityNumber( const std::string & ); // set SSN
22     std::string getSocialSecurityNumber() const; // return SSN
23
24     void setGrossSales( double ); // set gross sales amount
25     double getGrossSales() const; // return gross sales amount
```

Fig. 11.7 | BasePlusCommissionEmployee class header. (Part 1 of 2.)

```
26
27      void setCommissionRate( double ); // set commission rate
28      double getCommissionRate() const; // return commission rate
29
30      void setBaseSalary( double ); // set base salary
31      double getBaseSalary() const; // return base salary
32
33      double earnings() const; // calculate earnings
34      void print() const; // print BasePlusCommissionEmployee object
35   private:
36      std::string firstName;
37      std::string lastName;
38      std::string socialSecurityNumber;
39      double grossSales; // gross weekly sales
40      double commissionRate; // commission percentage
41      double baseSalary; // base salary
42   }; // end class BasePlusCommissionEmployee
43
44   #endif
```

Fig. 11.7 | BasePlusCommissionEmployee class header. (Part 2 of 2.)

```
1    // Fig. 11.8: BasePlusCommissionEmployee.cpp
2    // Class BasePlusCommissionEmployee member-function definitions.
3    #include <iostream>
4    #include <stdexcept>
5    #include "BasePlusCommissionEmployee.h"
6    using namespace std;
7
8    // constructor
9    BasePlusCommissionEmployee::BasePlusCommissionEmployee(
10      const string &first, const string &last, const string &ssn,
11      double sales, double rate, double salary )
12   {
13      firstName = first; // should validate
14      lastName = last; // should validate
15      socialSecurityNumber = ssn; // should validate
16      setGrossSales( sales ); // validate and store gross sales
17      setCommissionRate( rate ); // validate and store commission rate
18      setBaseSalary( salary ); // validate and store base salary
19   } // end BasePlusCommissionEmployee constructor
20
21   // set first name
22   void BasePlusCommissionEmployee::setFirstName( const string &first )
23   {
24      firstName = first; // should validate
25   } // end function setFirstName
26
27   // return first name
28   string BasePlusCommissionEmployee::getFirstName() const
29   {
```

Fig. 11.8 | BasePlusCommissionEmployee class represents an employee who receives a base salary in addition to a commission. (Part 1 of 3.)

```
30        return firstName;
31    } // end function getFirstName
32
33    // set last name
34    void BasePlusCommissionEmployee::setLastName( const string &last )
35    {
36       lastName = last; // should validate
37    } // end function setLastName
38
39    // return last name
40    string BasePlusCommissionEmployee::getLastName() const
41    {
42       return lastName;
43    } // end function getLastName
44
45    // set social security number
46    void BasePlusCommissionEmployee::setSocialSecurityNumber(
47       const string &ssn )
48    {
49       socialSecurityNumber = ssn; // should validate
50    } // end function setSocialSecurityNumber
51
52    // return social security number
53    string BasePlusCommissionEmployee::getSocialSecurityNumber() const
54    {
55       return socialSecurityNumber;
56    } // end function getSocialSecurityNumber
57
58    // set gross sales amount
59    void BasePlusCommissionEmployee::setGrossSales( double sales )
60    {
61       if ( sales >= 0.0 )
62          grossSales = sales;
63       else
64          throw invalid_argument( "Gross sales must be >= 0.0" );
65    } // end function setGrossSales
66
67    // return gross sales amount
68    double BasePlusCommissionEmployee::getGrossSales() const
69    {
70       return grossSales;
71    } // end function getGrossSales
72
73    // set commission rate
74    void BasePlusCommissionEmployee::setCommissionRate( double rate )
75    {
76       if ( rate > 0.0 && rate < 1.0 )
77          commissionRate = rate;
78       else
79          throw invalid_argument( "Commission rate must be > 0.0 and < 1.0" );
80    } // end function setCommissionRate
81
```

Fig. 11.8 | BasePlusCommissionEmployee class represents an employee who receives a base salary in addition to a commission. (Part 2 of 3.)

```
82   // return commission rate
83   double BasePlusCommissionEmployee::getCommissionRate() const
84   {
85      return commissionRate;
86   } // end function getCommissionRate
87
88   // set base salary
89   void BasePlusCommissionEmployee::setBaseSalary( double salary )
90   {
91      if ( salary >= 0.0 )
92         baseSalary = salary;
93      else
94         throw invalid_argument( "Salary must be >= 0.0" );
95   } // end function setBaseSalary
96
97   // return base salary
98   double BasePlusCommissionEmployee::getBaseSalary() const
99   {
100     return baseSalary;
101  } // end function getBaseSalary
102
103  // calculate earnings
104  double BasePlusCommissionEmployee::earnings() const
105  {
106     return baseSalary + ( commissionRate * grossSales );
107  } // end function earnings
108
109  // print BasePlusCommissionEmployee object
110  void BasePlusCommissionEmployee::print() const
111  {
112     cout << "base-salaried commission employee: " << firstName << ' '
113        << lastName << "\nsocial security number: " << socialSecurityNumber
114        << "\ngross sales: " << grossSales
115        << "\ncommission rate: " << commissionRate
116        << "\nbase salary: " << baseSalary;
117  } // end function print
```

Fig. 11.8 | BasePlusCommissionEmployee class represents an employee who receives a base salary in addition to a commission. (Part 3 of 3.)

Defining Class ***BasePlusCommissionEmployee***

The BasePlusCommissionEmployee header (Fig. 11.7) specifies class BasePlusCommissionEmployee's public services, which include the BasePlusCommissionEmployee constructor (lines 12–13) and member functions earnings (line 33) and print (line 34). Lines 15–31 declare public *get* and *set* functions for the class's private data members (declared in lines 36–41) firstName, lastName, socialSecurityNumber, grossSales, commissionRate *and* baseSalary. These variables and member functions encapsulate all the necessary features of a base-salaried commission employee. Note the similarity between this class and class CommissionEmployee (Figs. 11.4–11.5)—in this example, we do *not* yet exploit that similarity.

Class BasePlusCommissionEmployee's earnings member function (defined in lines 104–107 of Fig. 11.8) computes the earnings of a base-salaried commission employee.

Line 106 returns the result of adding the employee's base salary to the product of the commission rate and the employee's gross sales.

Testing Class *BasePlusCommissionEmployee*

Figure 11.9 tests class BasePlusCommissionEmployee. Lines 11–12 instantiate object employee of class BasePlusCommissionEmployee, passing "Bob", "Lewis", "333-33-3333", 5000, .04 and 300 to the constructor as the first name, last name, social security number, gross sales, commission rate *and* base salary, respectively. Lines 19–25 use BasePlus-CommissionEmployee's *get* functions to retrieve the values of the object's data members for output. Line 27 invokes the object's setBaseSalary member function to change the base salary. Member function setBaseSalary (Fig. 11.8, lines 89–95) ensures that data member baseSalary is not assigned a negative value, because an employee's base salary cannot be negative. Line 31 of Fig. 11.9 invokes the object's print member function to output the updated BasePlusCommissionEmployee's information, and line 34 calls member function earnings to display the BasePlusCommissionEmployee's earnings.

```cpp
1   // Fig. 11.9: fig11_09.cpp
2   // BasePlusCommissionEmployee class test program.
3   #include <iostream>
4   #include <iomanip>
5   #include "BasePlusCommissionEmployee.h"
6   using namespace std;
7
8   int main()
9   {
10     // instantiate BasePlusCommissionEmployee object
11     BasePlusCommissionEmployee
12       employee( "Bob", "Lewis", "333-33-3333", 5000, .04, 300 );
13
14     // set floating-point output formatting
15     cout << fixed << setprecision( 2 );
16
17     // get commission employee data
18     cout << "Employee information obtained by get functions: \n"
19       << "\nFirst name is " << employee.getFirstName()
20       << "\nLast name is " << employee.getLastName()
21       << "\nSocial security number is "
22       << employee.getSocialSecurityNumber()
23       << "\nGross sales is " << employee.getGrossSales()
24       << "\nCommission rate is " << employee.getCommissionRate()
25       << "\nBase salary is " << employee.getBaseSalary() << endl;
26
27     employee.setBaseSalary( 1000 ); // set base salary
28
29     cout << "\nUpdated employee information output by print function: \n"
30       << endl;
31     employee.print(); // display the new employee information
32
33     // display the employee's earnings
34     cout << "\n\nEmployee's earnings: $" << employee.earnings() << endl;
35   } // end main
```

Fig. 11.9 | BasePlusCommissionEmployee class test program. (Part 1 of 2.)

```
Employee information obtained by get functions:

First name is Bob
Last name is Lewis
Social security number is 333-33-3333
Gross sales is 5000.00
Commission rate is 0.04
Base salary is 300.00

Updated employee information output by print function:

base-salaried commission employee: Bob Lewis
social security number: 333-33-3333
gross sales: 5000.00
commission rate: 0.04
base salary: 1000.00

Employee's earnings: $1200.00
```

Fig. 11.9 | BasePlusCommissionEmployee class test program. (Part 2 of 2.)

Exploring the Similarities Between Class *BasePlusCommissionEmployee* and Class *CommissionEmployee*

Most of the code for class BasePlusCommissionEmployee (Figs. 11.7–11.8) is *similar, if not identical*, to the code for class CommissionEmployee (Figs. 11.4–11.5). For example, in class BasePlusCommissionEmployee, private data members firstName and lastName and member functions setFirstName, getFirstName, setLastName and getLastName are identical to those of class CommissionEmployee. Classes CommissionEmployee and BasePlusCommissionEmployee also both contain private data members socialSecurityNumber, commissionRate and grossSales, as well as *get* and *set* functions to manipulate these members. In addition, the BasePlusCommissionEmployee constructor is *almost* identical to that of class CommissionEmployee, except that BasePlusCommissionEmployee's constructor *also* sets the baseSalary. The other additions to class BasePlusCommissionEmployee are private data member baseSalary *and* member functions setBaseSalary and getBaseSalary. Class BasePlusCommissionEmployee's print member function is *nearly identical* to that of class CommissionEmployee, except that BasePlusCommissionEmployee's print *also* outputs the value of data member baseSalary.

We literally *copied* code from class CommissionEmployee and *pasted* it into class BasePlusCommissionEmployee, then modified class BasePlusCommissionEmployee to include a base salary and member functions that manipulate the base salary. This *copy-and-paste approach* is error prone and time consuming.

Software Engineering Observation 11.1

Copying and pasting code *from one class to another can spread many physical* copies of the same code *and can spread* errors *throughout a system, creating a code-maintenance nightmare. To avoid duplicating code (and possibly errors),* use inheritance, *rather than the "copy-and-paste" approach, in situations where you want one class to "absorb" the data members and member functions of another class.*

>
> ## Software Engineering Observation 11.2
> *With inheritance, the common data members and member functions of all the classes in the hierarchy are declared in a base class. When changes are required for these common features, you need to make the changes only in the base class—derived classes then inherit the changes. Without inheritance, changes would need to be made to all the source code files that contain a copy of the code in question.*

11.3.3 Creating a CommissionEmployee-BasePlusCommissionEmployee Inheritance Hierarchy

Now we create and test a new BasePlusCommissionEmployee class (Figs. 11.10–11.11) that *derives from* class CommissionEmployee (Figs. 11.4–11.5). In this example, a Base-PlusCommissionEmployee object *is a* CommissionEmployee (because inheritance passes on the capabilities of class CommissionEmployee), but class BasePlusCommissionEmployee *also* has data member baseSalary (Fig. 11.10, line 22). The *colon (:)* in line 10 of the class definition indicates inheritance. Keyword public indicates the *type of inheritance*. As a derived class (formed with public inheritance), BasePlusCommissionEmployee inherits *all* the members of class CommissionEmployee, *except* for the constructor each class provides its *own* constructors that are specific to the class. (Destructors, too, are not inherited.) Thus, the public services of BasePlusCommissionEmployee include its constructor (lines 13–14) and the public member functions inherited from class CommissionEmployee—*although we cannot see these inherited member functions* in BasePlusCommissionEmployee's source code, they're nevertheless a part of derived class BasePlusCommissionEmployee. The derived class's public services also include member functions setBaseSalary, get-BaseSalary, earnings and print (lines 16–20).

```
1   // Fig. 11.10: BasePlusCommissionEmployee.h
2   // BasePlusCommissionEmployee class derived from class
3   // CommissionEmployee.
4   #ifndef BASEPLUS_H
5   #define BASEPLUS_H
6
7   #include <string> // C++ standard string class
8   #include "CommissionEmployee.h" // CommissionEmployee class declaration
9
10  class BasePlusCommissionEmployee : public CommissionEmployee
11  {
12  public:
13     BasePlusCommissionEmployee( const std::string &, const std::string &,
14        const std::string &, double = 0.0, double = 0.0, double = 0.0 );
15
16     void setBaseSalary( double ); // set base salary
17     double getBaseSalary() const; // return base salary
18
19     double earnings() const; // calculate earnings
20     void print() const; // print BasePlusCommissionEmployee object
```

Fig. 11.10 | BasePlusCommissionEmployee class definition indicating inheritance relationship with class CommissionEmployee. (Part 1 of 2.)

```
21    private:
22       double baseSalary; // base salary
23    }; // end class BasePlusCommissionEmployee
24
25    #endif
```

Fig. 11.10 | BasePlusCommissionEmployee class definition indicating inheritance relationship with class CommissionEmployee. (Part 2 of 2.)

```
 1    // Fig. 11.11: BasePlusCommissionEmployee.cpp
 2    // Class BasePlusCommissionEmployee member-function definitions.
 3    #include <iostream>
 4    #include <stdexcept>
 5    #include "BasePlusCommissionEmployee.h"
 6    using namespace std;
 7
 8    // constructor
 9    BasePlusCommissionEmployee::BasePlusCommissionEmployee(
10       const string &first, const string &last, const string &ssn,
11       double sales, double rate, double salary )
12       // explicitly call base-class constructor
13       : CommissionEmployee( first, last, ssn, sales, rate )
14    {
15       setBaseSalary( salary ); // validate and store base salary
16    } // end BasePlusCommissionEmployee constructor
17
18    // set base salary
19    void BasePlusCommissionEmployee::setBaseSalary( double salary )
20    {
21       if ( salary >= 0.0 )
22          baseSalary = salary;
23       else
24          throw invalid_argument( "Salary must be >= 0.0" );
25    } // end function setBaseSalary
26
27    // return base salary
28    double BasePlusCommissionEmployee::getBaseSalary() const
29    {
30       return baseSalary;
31    } // end function getBaseSalary
32
33    // calculate earnings
34    double BasePlusCommissionEmployee::earnings() const
35    {
36       // derived class cannot access the base class's private data
37       return baseSalary + ( commissionRate * grossSales );
38    } // end function earnings
39
```

Fig. 11.11 | BasePlusCommissionEmployee implementation file: private base-class data cannot be accessed from derived class. (Part 1 of 2.)

```
40    // print BasePlusCommissionEmployee object
41    void BasePlusCommissionEmployee::print() const
42    {
43       // derived class cannot access the base class's private data
44       cout << "base-salaried commission employee: " << firstName << ' '
45          << lastName << "\nsocial security number: " << socialSecurityNumber
46          << "\ngross sales: " << grossSales
47          << "\ncommission rate: " << commissionRate
48          << "\nbase salary: " << baseSalary;
49    } // end function print
```

Compilation Errors from the LLVM Compiler in Xcode 4.5

```
BasePlusCommissionEmployee.cpp:37:26:
   'commissionRate' is a private member of 'CommissionEmployee'
BasePlusCommissionEmployee.cpp:37:43:
   'grossSales' is a private member of 'CommissionEmployee'
BasePlusCommissionEmployee.cpp:44:53:
   'firstName' is a private member of 'CommissionEmployee'
BasePlusCommissionEmployee.cpp:45:10:
   'lastName' is a private member of 'CommissionEmployee'
BasePlusCommissionEmployee.cpp:45:54:
   'socialSecurityNumber' is a private member of 'CommissionEmployee'
BasePlusCommissionEmployee.cpp:46:31:
   'grossSales' is a private member of 'CommissionEmployee'
BasePlusCommissionEmployee.cpp:47:35:
   'commissionRate' is a private member of 'CommissionEmployee'
```

Fig. 11.11 | BasePlusCommissionEmployee implementation file: private base-class data cannot be accessed from derived class. (Part 2 of 2.)

Figure 11.11 shows BasePlusCommissionEmployee's member-function implementations. The constructor (lines 9–16) introduces **base-class initializer syntax** (line 13), which uses a member initializer to pass arguments to the base-class (CommissionEmployee) constructor. C++ requires that a derived-class constructor call its base-class constructor to initialize the base-class data members that are inherited into the derived class. Line 13 does this by *explicitly* invoking the CommissionEmployee constructor by name, passing the constructor's parameters first, last, ssn, sales and rate as arguments to initialize the base-class data members firstName, lastName, socialSecurityNumber, grossSales and commissionRate, respectively. If BasePlusCommissionEmployee's constructor did *not* invoke class CommissionEmployee's constructor *explicitly*, C++ would attempt to invoke class CommissionEmployee's default constructor implicitly—but the class does *not* have such a constructor, so the compiler would issue an *error*. Recall from Chapter 3 that the compiler provides a default constructor with no parameters in any class that does *not* explicitly include a constructor. However, CommissionEmployee *does* explicitly include a constructor, so a default constructor is *not* provided.

Common Programming Error 11.1

When a derived-class constructor calls a base-class constructor, the arguments passed to the base-class constructor must be consistent with the number and types of parameters specified in one of the base-class constructors; otherwise, a compilation error occurs.

Performance Tip 11.1

In a derived-class constructor, invoking base-class constructors and initializing member objects explicitly in the member initializer list prevents duplicate initialization in which a default constructor is called, then data members are modified again in the derived-class constructor's body.

Compilation Errors from Accessing Base-Class *private* Members

The compiler generates errors for line 37 of Fig. 11.11 because base class CommissionEmployee's data members commissionRate and grossSales are private—derived class BasePlusCommissionEmployee's member functions are *not* allowed to access base class CommissionEmployee's private data. The compiler issues additional errors in lines 44–47 of BasePlusCommissionEmployee's print member function for the same reason. As you can see, C++ rigidly enforces restrictions on accessing private data members, so that *even a derived class (which is intimately related to its base class) cannot access the base class's private data.*

Preventing the Errors in *BasePlusCommissionEmployee*

We purposely included the erroneous code in Fig. 11.11 to emphasize that a derived class's member functions *cannot* access its base class's private data. The errors in BasePlusCommissionEmployee could have been prevented by using the *get* member functions inherited from class CommissionEmployee. For example, line 37 could have invoked getCommissionRate and getGrossSales to access CommissionEmployee's private data members commissionRate and grossSales, respectively. Similarly, lines 44–47 could have used appropriate *get* member functions to retrieve the values of the base class's data members. In the next example, we show how using protected data *also* allows us to avoid the errors encountered in this example.

Including the Base-Class Header in the Derived-Class Header with *#include*

Notice that we #include the base class's header in the derived class's header (line 8 of Fig. 11.10). This is necessary for three reasons. First, for the derived class to use the base class's name in line 10, we must tell the compiler that the base class exists—the class definition in CommissionEmployee.h does exactly that.

The second reason is that the compiler uses a class definition to determine the *size* of an object of that class (as we discussed in Section 3.6). A client program that creates an object of a class #includes the class definition to enable the compiler to reserve the proper amount of memory for the object. When using inheritance, a derived-class object's size depends on the data members declared explicitly in its class definition *and* the data members *inherited* from its direct and indirect base classes. Including the base class's definition in line 8 allows the compiler to determine the memory requirements for the base class's data members that become part of a derived-class object and thus contribute to the total size of the derived-class object.

The last reason for line 8 is to allow the compiler to determine whether the derived class uses the base class's inherited members properly. For example, in the program of Figs. 11.10–11.11, the compiler uses the base-class header to determine that the data members being accessed by the derived class are private in the base class. Since these are *inaccessible* to the derived class, the compiler generates errors. The compiler also uses the base class's *function prototypes* to *validate* function calls made by the derived class to the inherited base-class functions.

Linking Process in an Inheritance Hierarchy

In Section 3.7, we discussed the linking process for creating an executable GradeBook application. In that example, you saw that the client's object code was linked with the object code for class GradeBook, as well as the object code for any C++ Standard Library classes used in either the client code or in class GradeBook.

The linking process is similar for a program that uses classes in an inheritance hierarchy. The process requires the object code for all classes used in the program and the object code for the direct and indirect base classes of any derived classes used by the program. Suppose a client wants to create an application that uses class BasePlusCommission-Employee, which is a derived class of CommissionEmployee (we'll see an example of this in Section 11.3.4). When compiling the client application, the client's object code must be linked with the object code for classes BasePlusCommissionEmployee and Commission-Employee, because BasePlusCommissionEmployee inherits member functions from its base class CommissionEmployee. The code is also linked with the object code for any C++ Standard Library classes used in class CommissionEmployee, class BasePlusCommission-Employee or the client code. This provides the program with access to the implementations of all of the functionality that the program may use.

11.3.4 CommissionEmployee–BasePlusCommissionEmployee Inheritance Hierarchy Using protected Data

Chapter 3 introduced access specifiers public and private. A base class's public members are accessible within its body and anywhere that the program has a handle (i.e., a name, reference or pointer) to an object of that class or one of its derived classes. A base class's private members are accessible only within its body and to the friends of that base class. In this section, we introduce the access specifier **protected**.

Using protected access offers an intermediate level of protection between public and private access. To enable class BasePlusCommissionEmployee to *directly access* CommissionEmployee data members firstName, lastName, socialSecurityNumber, grossSales and commissionRate, we can declare those members as protected in the base class. A base class's protected members *can* be accessed within the body of that base class, by members and friends of that base class, and by members and friends of any classes derived from that base class.

*Defining Base Class **CommissionEmployee** with **protected** Data*

Class CommissionEmployee (Fig. 11.12) now declares data members firstName, last-Name, socialSecurityNumber, grossSales and commissionRate as protected (lines 31–36) rather than private. The member-function implementations are identical to those in Fig. 11.5, so CommissionEmployee.cpp is not shown here.

```
1   // Fig. 11.12: CommissionEmployee.h
2   // CommissionEmployee class definition with protected data.
3   #ifndef COMMISSION_H
4   #define COMMISSION_H
5
```

Fig. 11.12 | CommissionEmployee class definition that declares protected data to allow access by derived classes. (Part 1 of 2.)

```
 6   #include <string> // C++ standard string class
 7
 8   class CommissionEmployee
 9   {
10   public:
11      CommissionEmployee( const std::string &, const std::string &,
12         const std::string &, double = 0.0, double = 0.0 );
13
14      void setFirstName( const std::string & ); // set first name
15      std::string getFirstName() const; // return first name
16
17      void setLastName( const std::string & ); // set last name
18      std::string getLastName() const; // return last name
19
20      void setSocialSecurityNumber( const std::string & ); // set SSN
21      std::string getSocialSecurityNumber() const; // return SSN
22
23      void setGrossSales( double ); // set gross sales amount
24      double getGrossSales() const; // return gross sales amount
25
26      void setCommissionRate( double ); // set commission rate
27      double getCommissionRate() const; // return commission rate
28
29      double earnings() const; // calculate earnings
30      void print() const; // print CommissionEmployee object
31   protected:
32      std::string firstName;
33      std::string lastName;
34      std::string socialSecurityNumber;
35      double grossSales; // gross weekly sales
36      double commissionRate; // commission percentage
37   }; // end class CommissionEmployee
38
39   #endif
```

Fig. 11.12 | CommissionEmployee class definition that declares protected data to allow access by derived classes. (Part 2 of 2.)

Class *BasePlusCommissionEmployee*

The definition of class BasePlusCommissionEmployee from Figs. 11.10–11.11 remains *unchanged*, so we do *not* show it again here. Now that BasePlusCommissionEmployee inherits from the updated class CommissionEmployee (Fig. 11.12), BasePlusCommissionEmployee objects *can* access inherited data members that are declared protected in class CommissionEmployee (i.e., data members firstName, lastName, socialSecurityNumber, grossSales and commissionRate). As a result, the compiler does *not* generate errors when compiling the BasePlusCommissionEmployee earnings and print member-function definitions in Fig. 11.11 (lines 34–38 and 41–49, respectively). This shows the special privileges that a derived class is granted to access protected base-class data members. Objects of a derived class also can access protected members in *any* of that derived class's *indirect* base classes.

Class BasePlusCommissionEmployee does *not* inherit class CommissionEmployee's constructor. However, class BasePlusCommissionEmployee's constructor (Fig. 11.11, lines 9–16) calls class CommissionEmployee's constructor explicitly with member initializer syntax (line 13). Recall that BasePlusCommissionEmployee's constructor must *explicitly* call the constructor of class CommissionEmployee, because CommissionEmployee does *not* contain a default constructor that could be invoked implicitly.

Testing the Modified *BasePlusCommissionEmployee* Class

To test the updated class hierarchy, we reused the test program from Fig. 11.9. As shown in Fig. 11.13, the output is identical to that of Fig. 11.9. We created the first class Base-PlusCommissionEmployee *without using inheritance* and created this version of Base-PlusCommissionEmployee *using inheritance*; however, both classes provide the *same* functionality. The code for class BasePlusCommissionEmployee (i.e., the header and implementation files), which is 74 lines, is considerably *shorter* than the code for the noninherited version of the class, which is 161 lines, because the inherited version absorbs part of its functionality from CommissionEmployee, whereas the noninherited version does not absorb any functionality. Also, there is now only *one* copy of the CommissionEmployee functionality declared and defined in class CommissionEmployee. This makes the source code easier to maintain, modify and debug, because the source code related to a CommissionEmployee exists only in the files CommissionEmployee.h and CommissionEmployee.cpp.

```
Employee information obtained by get functions:

First name is Bob
Last name is Lewis
Social security number is 333-33-3333
Gross sales is 5000.00
Commission rate is 0.04
Base salary is 300.00

Updated employee information output by print function:

base-salaried commission employee: Bob Lewis
social security number: 333-33-3333
gross sales: 5000.00
commission rate: 0.04
base salary: 1000.00

Employee's earnings: $1200.00
```

Fig. 11.13 | protected base-class data can be accessed from derived class.

Notes on Using *protected* Data

In this example, we declared base-class data members as protected, so derived classes can modify the data directly. Inheriting protected data members slightly improves performance, because we can directly access the members without incurring the overhead of calls to *set* or *get* member functions.

Software Engineering Observation 11.3

In most cases, it's better to use private *data members to encourage proper software engineering, and leave code optimization issues to the compiler. Your code will be easier to maintain, modify and debug.*

Using protected data members creates two serious problems. First, the derived-class object does *not* have to use a member function to set the value of the base class's protected data member. An *invalid* value can easily be assigned to the protected data member, thus leaving the object in an *inconsistent* state—e.g., with CommissionEmployee's data member grossSales declared as protected, a derived-class object can assign a negative value to grossSales. The second problem with using protected data members is that derived-class member functions are more likely to be written so that they *depend on the base-class implementation*. Derived classes should depend only on the base-class services (i.e., non-private member functions) and *not* on the base-class implementation. With protected data members in the base class, if the base-class implementation changes, we may need to modify *all* derived classes of that base class. For example, if for some reason we were to change the names of data members firstName and lastName to first and last, then we'd have to do so for all occurrences in which a derived class references these base-class data members directly. Such software is said to be **fragile** or **brittle**, because a small change in the base class can "break" derived-class implementation. You should be able to change the base-class implementation while still providing the *same* services to derived classes. Of course, if the base-class services change, we must reimplement our derived classes—good object-oriented design attempts to prevent this.

Software Engineering Observation 11.4

It's appropriate to use the protected access specifier when a base class should provide a service (i.e., a non-private member function) only to its derived classes and friends.

Software Engineering Observation 11.5

Declaring base-class data members private (as opposed to declaring them protected) enables you to change the base-class implementation without having to change derived-class implementations.

11.3.5 CommissionEmployee–BasePlusCommissionEmployee Inheritance Hierarchy Using private Data

We now reexamine our hierarchy once more, this time using the *best software engineering practices*. Class CommissionEmployee now declares data members firstName, lastName, socialSecurityNumber, grossSales and commissionRate as private as shown previously in lines 31–36 of Fig. 11.4.

Changes to Class CommissionEmployee's Member Function Definitions
In the CommissionEmployee constructor implementation (Fig. 11.14, lines 9–16), we use member initializers (line 12) to set the values of the members firstName, lastName and socialSecurityNumber. We show how the derived-class BasePlusCommissionEmployee (Fig. 11.15) can invoke non-private base-class member functions (setFirstName, getFirstName, setLastName, getLastName, setSocialSecurityNumber and getSocialSecurityNumber) to manipulate these data members.

In the body of the constructor and in the bodies of member function's earnings (Fig. 11.14, lines 85–88) and print (lines 91–98), we call the class's *set* and *get* member functions to access the class's private data members. If we decide to change the data member names, the earnings and print definitions will *not* require modification—only the definitions of the *get* and *set* member functions that directly manipulate the data members will need to change. *These changes occur solely within the base class—no changes to the derived class are needed.* Localizing the effects of changes like this is a good software engineering practice.

```cpp
1   // Fig. 11.14: CommissionEmployee.cpp
2   // Class CommissionEmployee member-function definitions.
3   #include <iostream>
4   #include <stdexcept>
5   #include "CommissionEmployee.h" // CommissionEmployee class definition
6   using namespace std;
7
8   // constructor
9   CommissionEmployee::CommissionEmployee(
10     const string &first, const string &last, const string &ssn,
11     double sales, double rate )
12     : firstName( first ), lastName( last ), socialSecurityNumber( ssn )
13  {
14     setGrossSales( sales ); // validate and store gross sales
15     setCommissionRate( rate ); // validate and store commission rate
16  } // end CommissionEmployee constructor
17
18  // set first name
19  void CommissionEmployee::setFirstName( const string &first )
20  {
21     firstName = first; // should validate
22  } // end function setFirstName
23
24  // return first name
25  string CommissionEmployee::getFirstName() const
26  {
27     return firstName;
28  } // end function getFirstName
29
30  // set last name
31  void CommissionEmployee::setLastName( const string &last )
32  {
33     lastName = last; // should validate
34  } // end function setLastName
35
36  // return last name
37  string CommissionEmployee::getLastName() const
38  {
39     return lastName;
40  } // end function getLastName
41
42  // set social security number
43  void CommissionEmployee::setSocialSecurityNumber( const string &ssn )
44  {
45     socialSecurityNumber = ssn; // should validate
46  } // end function setSocialSecurityNumber
47
```

Fig. 11.14 | CommissionEmployee class implementation file: CommissionEmployee class uses member functions to manipulate its private data. (Part 1 of 2.)

```cpp
48   // return social security number
49   string CommissionEmployee::getSocialSecurityNumber() const
50   {
51      return socialSecurityNumber;
52   } // end function getSocialSecurityNumber
53
54   // set gross sales amount
55   void CommissionEmployee::setGrossSales( double sales )
56   {
57      if ( sales >= 0.0 )
58         grossSales = sales;
59      else
60         throw invalid_argument( "Gross sales must be >= 0.0" );
61   } // end function setGrossSales
62
63   // return gross sales amount
64   double CommissionEmployee::getGrossSales() const
65   {
66      return grossSales;
67   } // end function getGrossSales
68
69   // set commission rate
70   void CommissionEmployee::setCommissionRate( double rate )
71   {
72      if ( rate > 0.0 && rate < 1.0 )
73         commissionRate = rate;
74      else
75         throw invalid_argument( "Commission rate must be > 0.0 and < 1.0" );
76   } // end function setCommissionRate
77
78   // return commission rate
79   double CommissionEmployee::getCommissionRate() const
80   {
81      return commissionRate;
82   } // end function getCommissionRate
83
84   // calculate earnings
85   double CommissionEmployee::earnings() const
86   {
87      return getCommissionRate() * getGrossSales();
88   } // end function earnings
89
90   // print CommissionEmployee object
91   void CommissionEmployee::print() const
92   {
93      cout << "commission employee: "
94         << getFirstName() << ' ' << getLastName()
95         << "\nsocial security number: " << getSocialSecurityNumber()
96         << "\ngross sales: " << getGrossSales()
97         << "\ncommission rate: " << getCommissionRate();
98   } // end function print
```

Fig. 11.14 | CommissionEmployee class implementation file: CommissionEmployee class uses member functions to manipulate its private data. (Part 2 of 2.)

Performance Tip 11.2

Using a member function to access a data member's value can be slightly slower than accessing the data directly. However, today's optimizing compilers are carefully designed to perform many optimizations implicitly (such as inlining set and get member-function calls). You should write code that adheres to proper software engineering principles, and leave optimization to the compiler. A good rule is, "Do not second-guess the compiler."

*Changes to Class **BasePlusCommissionEmployee**'s Member Function Definitions*
Class BasePlusCommissionEmployee inherits CommissionEmployee's public member functions and can access the private base-class members via the inherited member functions. The class's header remains unchanged from Fig. 11.10. The class has several changes to its member-function implementations (Fig. 11.15) that distinguish it from the previous version of the class (Figs. 11.10–11.11). Member functions earnings (Fig. 11.15, lines 34–37) and print (lines 40–48) each invoke member function getBaseSalary to obtain the base salary value, rather than accessing baseSalary directly. This insulates earnings and print from potential changes to the implementation of data member baseSalary. For example, if we decide to rename data member baseSalary or change its type, only member functions setBaseSalary and getBaseSalary will need to change.

```
1   // Fig. 11.15: BasePlusCommissionEmployee.cpp
2   // Class BasePlusCommissionEmployee member-function definitions.
3   #include <iostream>
4   #include <stdexcept>
5   #include "BasePlusCommissionEmployee.h"
6   using namespace std;
7
8   // constructor
9   BasePlusCommissionEmployee::BasePlusCommissionEmployee(
10      const string &first, const string &last, const string &ssn,
11      double sales, double rate, double salary )
12      // explicitly call base-class constructor
13      : CommissionEmployee( first, last, ssn, sales, rate )
14   {
15      setBaseSalary( salary ); // validate and store base salary
16   } // end BasePlusCommissionEmployee constructor
17
18   // set base salary
19   void BasePlusCommissionEmployee::setBaseSalary( double salary )
20   {
21      if ( salary >= 0.0 )
22         baseSalary = salary;
23      else
24         throw invalid_argument( "Salary must be >= 0.0" );
25   } // end function setBaseSalary
26
27   // return base salary
28   double BasePlusCommissionEmployee::getBaseSalary() const
29   {
```

Fig. 11.15 | BasePlusCommissionEmployee class that inherits from class CommissionEmployee but cannot directly access the class's private data. (Part 1 of 2.)

```
30        return baseSalary;
31    } // end function getBaseSalary
32
33    // calculate earnings
34    double BasePlusCommissionEmployee::earnings() const
35    {
36        return getBaseSalary() + CommissionEmployee::earnings();
37    } // end function earnings
38
39    // print BasePlusCommissionEmployee object
40    void BasePlusCommissionEmployee::print() const
41    {
42        cout << "base-salaried ";
43
44        // invoke CommissionEmployee's print function
45        CommissionEmployee::print();
46
47        cout << "\nbase salary: " << getBaseSalary();
48    } // end function print
```

Fig. 11.15 | BasePlusCommissionEmployee class that inherits from class
CommissionEmployee but cannot directly access the class's private data. (Part 2 of 2.)

BasePlusCommissionEmployee* Member Function *earnings

Class BasePlusCommissionEmployee's earnings function (Fig. 11.15, lines 34–37) redefines class CommissionEmployee's earnings member function (Fig. 11.14, lines 85–88) to
calculate the earnings of a base-salaried commission employee. Class BasePlusCommissionEmployee's version of earnings obtains the portion of the employee's earnings based
on commission alone by calling base-class CommissionEmployee's earnings function with
the expression CommissionEmployee::earnings() (Fig. 11.15, line 36). BasePlus-
CommissionEmployee's earnings function then adds the base salary to this value to calculate the total earnings of the employee. Note the syntax used to invoke a redefined base-
class member function from a derived class—place the base-class name and the scope resolution operator (::) before the base-class member-function name. This member-function
invocation is a good software engineering practice: Recall from Chapter 9 that, if an object's
member function performs the actions needed by another object, we should call that member function rather than duplicating its code body. By having BasePlusCommissionEmployee's earnings function invoke CommissionEmployee's earnings function to calculate
part of a BasePlusCommissionEmployee object's earnings, we avoid duplicating the code
and reduce code-maintenance problems.

Common Programming Error 11.2

*When a base-class member function is redefined in a derived class, the derived-class version
often calls the base-class version to do additional work. Failure to use the :: operator prefixed
with the name of the base class when referencing the base class's member function causes infinite recursion, because the derived-class member function would then call itself.*

BasePlusCommissionEmployee* Member Function *print

Similarly, BasePlusCommissionEmployee's print function (Fig. 11.15, lines 40–48) redefines class CommissionEmployee's print function (Fig. 11.14, lines 91–98) to output the ap-

propriate base-salaried commission employee information. The new version displays part of a BasePlusCommissionEmployee object's information (i.e., the string "commission employee" and the values of class CommissionEmployee's private data members) by calling CommissionEmployee's print member function with the qualified name CommissionEmployee::print() (Fig. 11.15, line 45). BasePlusCommissionEmployee's print function then outputs the remainder of a BasePlusCommissionEmployee object's information (i.e., the value of class BasePlusCommissionEmployee's base salary).

Testing the Modified Class Hierarchy
Once again, this example uses the BasePlusCommissionEmployee test program from Fig. 11.9 and produces the same output. Although each "base-salaried commission employee" class behaves identically, the version in this example is the best engineered. *By using inheritance and by calling member functions that hide the data and ensure consistency, we've efficiently and effectively constructed a well-engineered class.*

Summary of the *CommissionEmployee–BasePlusCommissionEmployee* Examples
In this section, you saw an evolutionary set of examples that was carefully designed to teach key capabilities for good software engineering with inheritance. You learned how to create a derived class using inheritance, how to use protected base-class members to enable a derived class to access inherited base-class data members and how to redefine base-class functions to provide versions that are more appropriate for derived-class objects. In addition, you learned how to apply software engineering techniques from Chapter 9 and this chapter to create classes that are easy to maintain, modify and debug.

11.4 Constructors and Destructors in Derived Classes

As we explained in the preceding section, instantiating a derived-class object begins a *chain* of constructor calls in which the derived-class constructor, before performing its own tasks, invokes its direct base class's constructor either explicitly (via a base-class member initializer) or implicitly (calling the base class's default constructor). Similarly, if the base class is derived from another class, the base-class constructor is required to invoke the constructor of the next class up in the hierarchy, and so on. The last constructor called in this chain is the one of the class at the base of the hierarchy, whose body actually finishes executing *first*. The most derived-class constructor's body finishes executing *last*. Each base-class constructor initializes the base-class data members that the derived-class object inherits. In the CommissionEmployee/BasePlusCommissionEmployee hierarchy that we've been studying, when a program creates a BasePlusCommissionEmployee object, the CommissionEmployee constructor is called. Since class CommissionEmployee is at the base of the hierarchy, its constructor executes, initializing the private CommissionEmployee data members that are part of the BasePlusCommissionEmployee object. When CommissionEmployee's constructor completes execution, it returns control to BasePlusCommissionEmployee's constructor, which initializes the BasePlusCommissionEmployee object's baseSalary.

Software Engineering Observation 11.6
When a program creates a derived-class object, the derived-class constructor immediately calls the base-class constructor, the base-class constructor's body executes, then the derived class's member initializers execute and finally the derived-class constructor's body executes. This process cascades up the hierarchy if it contains more than two levels.

When a derived-class object is destroyed, the program calls that object's destructor. This begins a chain (or cascade) of destructor calls in which the derived-class destructor and the destructors of the direct and indirect base classes and the classes' members execute in *reverse* of the order in which the constructors executed. When a derived-class object's destructor is called, the destructor performs its task, then invokes the destructor of the next base class up the hierarchy. This process repeats until the destructor of the final base class at the top of the hierarchy is called. Then the object is removed from memory.

Software Engineering Observation 11.7

Suppose that we create an object of a derived class where both the base class and the derived class contain (via composition) objects of other classes. When an object of that derived class is created, first the constructors for the base class's member objects execute, then the base-class constructor body executes, then the constructors for the derived class's member objects execute, then the derived class's constructor body executes. Destructors for derived-class objects are called in the reverse of the order in which their corresponding constructors are called.

Base-class constructors, destructors and overloaded assignment operators (Chapter 10) are *not* inherited by derived classes. Derived-class constructors, destructors and overloaded assignment operators, however, can call base-class versions.

C++11: Inheriting Base Class Constructors

Sometimes a derived class's constructors simply mimic the base class's constructors. A frequently requested convenience feature for C++11 was the ability to *inherit* a base class's constructors. You can now do this by *explicitly* including a using declaration of the form

```
using BaseClass::BaseClass;
```

anywhere in the derived-class definition. In the preceding declaration, *BaseClass* is the base class's name. With a few exceptions (listed below), for each constructor in the base class, the compiler generates a derived-class constructor that calls the corresponding base-class constructor. The generated constructors perform only *default initialization* for the derived class's additional data members. When you inherit constructors:

- By default, each inherited constructor has the *same* access level (public, protected or private) as its corresponding base-class constructor.
- The default, copy and move constructors are *not* inherited.
- If a constructor is *deleted* in the base class by placing = delete in its prototype, the corresponding constructor in the derived class is *also* deleted.
- If the derived class does not *explicitly* define constructors, the compiler generates a default constructor in the derived class—*even* if it inherits other constructors from its base class.
- If a constructor that you *explicitly* define in a derived class has the *same* parameter list as a base-class constructor, then the base-class constructor is *not* inherited.
- A base-class constructor's default arguments are *not* inherited. Instead, the compiler generates *overloaded constructors* in the derived class. For example, if the base class declares the constructor

```
BaseClass( int = 0, double = 0.0 );
```

the compiler generates the following *two* derived-class constructors *without* default arguments

```
DerivedClass( int );
DerivedClass( int, double );
```

These each call the *BaseClass* constructor that specifies the default arguments.

11.5 public, protected and private Inheritance

When deriving a class from a base class, the base class may be inherited through `public`, `protected` or `private` inheritance. We normally use `public` inheritance in this book. Use of `protected` inheritance is rare. Chapter 19 demonstrates `private` inheritance as an alternative to composition. Figure 11.16 summarizes for each type of inheritance the accessibility of base-class members in a derived class. The first column contains the base-class access specifiers.

Base-class member-access specifier	Type of inheritance		
	public inheritance	**protected** inheritance	**private** inheritance
public	**public** in derived class. Can be accessed directly by member functions, **friend** functions and nonmember functions.	**protected** in derived class. Can be accessed directly by member functions and **friend** functions.	**private** in derived class. Can be accessed directly by member functions and **friend** functions.
protected	**protected** in derived class. Can be accessed directly by member functions and **friend** functions.	**protected** in derived class. Can be accessed directly by member functions and **friend** functions.	**private** in derived class. Can be accessed directly by member functions and **friend** functions.
private	Hidden in derived class. Can be accessed by member functions and **friend** functions through **public** or **protected** member functions of the base class.	Hidden in derived class. Can be accessed by member functions and **friend** functions through **public** or **protected** member functions of the base class.	Hidden in derived class. Can be accessed by member functions and **friend** functions through **public** or **protected** member functions of the base class.

Fig. 11.16 | Summary of base-class member accessibility in a derived class.

When deriving a class with `public` inheritance, `public` members of the base class become `public` members of the derived class, and `protected` members of the base class become `protected` members of the derived class. A base class's `private` members are *never* accessible directly from a derived class, but can be accessed through calls to the `public` and `protected` members of the base class.

When deriving a class with protected inheritance, public and protected members of the base class become protected members of the derived class. When deriving a class with private inheritance, public and protected members of the base class become private members (e.g., the functions become utility functions) of the derived class. Private and protected inheritance are not *is-a* relationships.

11.6 Software Engineering with Inheritance

Sometimes it's difficult for students to appreciate the scope of problems faced by designers who work on large-scale software projects in industry. People experienced with such projects say that effective software reuse improves the software development process. Object-oriented programming facilitates software reuse, thus shortening development times and enhancing software quality.

When we use inheritance to create a new class from an existing one, the new class inherits the data members and member functions of the existing class, as described in Fig. 11.16. We can customize the new class to meet our needs by redefining base-class members and by including additional members. The derived-class programmer does this in C++ *without* accessing the base class's source code (the derived class must be able to *link* to the base class's object code). This powerful capability is attractive to software developers. They can develop proprietary classes for sale or license and make these classes available to users in object-code format. Users then can derive new classes from these library classes rapidly and without accessing the proprietary source code. The software developers need to supply the headers along with the object code

The availability of substantial and useful class libraries delivers the maximum benefits of software reuse through inheritance. The standard C++ libraries tend to be general purpose and limited in scope. There is a worldwide commitment to the development of class libraries for a huge variety of application arenas.

Software Engineering Observation 11.8

At the design stage in an object-oriented system, the designer often determines that certain classes are closely related. The designer should "factor out" common attributes and behaviors and place these in a base class, then use inheritance to form derived classes.

Software Engineering Observation 11.9

Creating a derived class does not affect its base class's source code. Inheritance preserves the integrity of the base class.

11.7 Wrap-Up

This chapter introduced inheritance—the ability to create a class by absorbing an existing class's data members and member functions and embellishing them with new capabilities. Through a series of examples using an employee inheritance hierarchy, you learned the notions of base classes and derived classes and used public inheritance to create a derived class that inherits members from a base class. The chapter introduced the access specifier protected—derived-class member functions can access protected base-class members. You learned how to access redefined base-class members by qualifying their names with the base-class name and scope resolution operator (::). You also saw the order in which constructors and destructors are called for objects of classes that are part of an inheritance hierarchy. Finally, we explained the three types of inheritance—`public`, `protected` and `private`—and the accessibility of base-class members in a derived class when using each type.

In Chapter 12, Object-Oriented Programming: Polymorphism, we build on our discussion of inheritance by introducing polymorphism—an object-oriented concept that enables us to write programs that handle, in a more general manner, objects of a wide variety of classes related by inheritance. After studying Chapter 12, you'll be familiar with classes, objects, encapsulation, inheritance and polymorphism—the essential concepts of object-oriented programming.

Summary

Section 11.1 Introduction
- Software reuse reduces program development time and cost.
- Inheritance (p. 517) is a form of software reuse in which you create a class that absorbs an existing class's capabilities, then customizes or enhances them. The existing class is called the base class (p. 517), and the new class is referred to as the derived class (p. 517).
- Every object of a derived class is also an object of that class's base class. However, a base-class object is not an object of that class's derived classes.
- The *is-a* relationship (p. 517) represents inheritance. In an *is-a* relationship, an object of a derived class also can be treated as an object of its base class.
- The *has-a* relationship (p. 517) represents composition—an object contains one or more objects of other classes as members, but does not disclose their behavior directly in its interface.

Section 11.2 Base Classes and Derived Classes
- A direct base class (p. 519) is the one from which a derived class explicitly inherits. An indirect base class (p. 519) is inherited from two or more levels up the class hierarchy (p. 518).
- With single inheritance (p. 519), a class is derived from one base class. With multiple inheritance (p. 519), a class inherits from multiple (possibly unrelated) base classes.
- A derived class represents a more specialized group of objects.
- Inheritance relationships form class hierarchies.
- It's possible to treat base-class objects and derived-class objects similarly; the commonality shared between the object types is expressed in the base class's data members and member functions.

Section 11.4 Constructors and Destructors in Derived Classes
- When an object of a derived class is instantiated, the base class's constructor is called immediately to initialize the base-class data members in the derived-class object, then the derived-class constructor initializes the additional derived-class data members.
- When a derived-class object is destroyed, the destructors are called in the reverse order of the constructors—first the derived-class destructor is called, then the base-class destructor is called.
- A base class's `public` members are accessible anywhere that the program has a handle to an object of that base class or to an object of one of that base class's derived classes—or, when using the scope resolution operator, whenever the class's name is in scope.
- A base class's `private` members are accessible only within the base class or from its friends.
- A base class's `protected` members can be accessed by members and `friend`s of that base class and by members and `friend`s of any classes derived from that base class.

- In C++11, a derived class can inherit constructors from its base class by including anywhere in the derived-class definition a `using` declaration of the form

  using *BaseClass*::*BaseClass*;

Section 11.5 `public`, `protected` *and* `private` *Inheritance*

- Declaring data members `private`, while providing non-`private` member functions to manipulate and perform validity checking on this data, enforces good software engineering.

- When deriving a class, the base class may be declared as either `public`, `protected` or `private`.

- When deriving a class with `public` inheritance (p. 519), `public` members of the base class become `public` members of the derived class, and `protected` members of the base class become `protected` members of the derived class.

- When deriving a class with `protected` inheritance (p. 519), `public` and `protected` members of the base class become `protected` members of the derived class.

- When deriving a class with `private` inheritance (p. 519), `public` and `protected` members of the base class become `private` members of the derived class.

Self-Review Exercises

11.1 Fill in the blanks in each of the following statements:
- a) _____ is a form of software reuse in which new classes absorb the data and behaviors of existing classes and embellish these classes with new capabilities.
- b) A base class's _____ members can be accessed in the base-class definition, in derived-class definitions and in `friends` of the base class its derived classes.
- c) In a(n) _____ relationship, an object of a derived class also can be treated as an object of its base class.
- d) In a(n) _____ relationship, a class object has one or more objects of other classes as members.
- e) In single inheritance, a class exists in a(n) _____ relationship with its derived classes.
- f) A base class's _____ members are accessible within that base class and anywhere that the program has a handle to an object of that class or one of its derived classes.
- g) A base class's `protected` access members have a level of protection between those of `public` and _____ access.
- h) C++ provides for _____, which allows a derived class to inherit from many base classes, even if the base classes are unrelated.
- i) When an object of a derived class is instantiated, the base class's _____ is called implicitly or explicitly to do any necessary initialization of the base-class data members in the derived-class object.
- j) When deriving a class with `public` inheritance, `public` members of the base class become _____ members of the derived class, and `protected` members of the base class become _____ members of the derived class.
- k) When deriving a class from with `protected` inheritance, `public` members of the base class become _____ members of the derived class, and `protected` members of the base class become _____ members of the derived class.

11.2 State whether each of the following is *true* or *false*. If *false*, explain why.
- a) Software reuse reduces program development time and cost.
- b) A direct base class is the one from which a derived class explicitly inherits.
- c) A base class's `public` members are accessible only within the base class or from its friends.
- d) When deriving a class, the base class may be declared as either `public`, `protected` or `private`.
- e) With multi inheritance, a class is derived from one base class.

Answers to Self-Review Exercises

11.1 a) Inheritance. b) protected. c) *is-a* or inheritance (for public inheritance). d) *has-a* or composition or aggregation. e) hierarchical. f) public. g) private. h) multiple inheritance. i) constructor. j) public, protected. k) protected, protected.

11.2 a) True. b) True. c) False. A base class's private members are accessible only within the base class or from its friends. d) True. e) False. With single inheritance, a class is derived from one base class.

Exercises

11.3 *(Composition as an Alternative to Inheritance)* Many programs written with inheritance could be written with composition instead, and vice versa. Rewrite class BasePlusCommissionEmployee of the CommissionEmployee–BasePlusCommissionEmployee hierarchy to use composition rather than inheritance. After you do this, assess the relative merits of the two approaches for designing classes CommissionEmployee and BasePlusCommissionEmployee, as well as for object-oriented programs in general. Which approach is more natural? Why?

11.4 *(Inheritance Advantage)* Discuss the ways in which inheritance promotes software reuse, saves time during program development and helps prevent errors.

11.5 *(Protected vs. Private Base Classes)* Some programmers prefer not to use protected access because they believe it breaks the encapsulation of the base class. Discuss the relative merits of using protected access vs. using private access in base classes.

11.6 *(Student Inheritance Hierarchy)* Draw an inheritance hierarchy for students at a university similar to the hierarchy shown in Fig. 11.2. Use Student as the base class of the hierarchy, then include classes UndergraduateStudent and GraduateStudent that derive from Student. Continue to extend the hierarchy as deep (i.e., as many levels) as possible. For example, Freshman, Sophomore, Junior and Senior might derive from UndergraduateStudent, and DoctoralStudent and MastersStudent might derive from GraduateStudent. After drawing the hierarchy, discuss the relationships that exist between the classes. [*Note:* You do not need to write any code for this exercise.]

11.7 *(Richer Shape Hierarchy)* The world of shapes is much richer than the shapes included in the inheritance hierarchy of Fig. 11.3. Write down all the shapes you can think of—both two-dimensional and three-dimensional—and form them into a more complete Shape hierarchy with as many levels as possible. Your hierarchy should have the base class Shape from which class TwoDimensionalShape and class ThreeDimensionalShape are derived. [*Note:* You do not need to write any code for this exercise.] We'll use this hierarchy in the exercises of Chapter 12 to process a set of distinct shapes as objects of base-class Shape. (This technique, called polymorphism, is the subject of Chapter 12.)

11.8 *(Quadrilateral Inheritance Hierarchy)* Draw an inheritance hierarchy for classes Quadrilateral, Trapezoid, Parallelogram, Rectangle and Square. Use Quadrilateral as the base class of the hierarchy. Make the hierarchy as deep as possible.

11.9 *(Package Inheritance Hierarchy)* Package-delivery services, such as FedEx®, DHL® and UPS®, offer a number of different shipping options, each with specific costs associated. Create an inheritance hierarchy to represent various types of packages. Use class Package as the base class of the hierarchy, then include classes TwoDayPackage and OvernightPackage that derive from Package. Base class Package should include data members representing the name, address, city, state and ZIP code for both the sender and the recipient of the package, in addition to data members that store the weight (in ounces) and cost per ounce to ship the package. Package's constructor should initialize these data members. Ensure that the weight and cost per ounce contain positive values. Package should provide a public member function calculateCost that returns a double indicating the cost associated with shipping the package. Package's calculateCost function should determine the cost by multiplying the weight by the cost per ounce. Derived class TwoDayPackage should inherit the functionality of base class Package, but also include a data member that represents a flat fee that the shipping company charges for two-day-delivery service. TwoDayPackage's constructor should receive a value to initialize this data member. TwoDayPackage should redefine member function calculate-Cost so that it computes the shipping cost by adding the flat fee to the weight-based cost calculated by base class Package's calculateCost function. Class OvernightPackage should inherit directly from class Package and contain an additional data member representing an additional fee per ounce charged for overnight-delivery service. OvernightPackage should redefine member function calculateCost so that it adds the additional fee per ounce to the standard cost per ounce before calculating the shipping cost. Write a test program that creates objects of each type of Package and tests member function calculateCost.

11.10 *(Account Inheritance Hierarchy)* Create an inheritance hierarchy that a bank might use to represent customers' bank accounts. All customers at this bank can deposit (i.e., credit) money into their accounts and withdraw (i.e., debit) money from their accounts. More specific types of accounts also exist. Savings accounts, for instance, earn interest on the money they hold. Checking accounts, on the other hand, charge a fee per transaction (i.e., credit or debit).

Create an inheritance hierarchy containing base class Account and derived classes Savings-Account and CheckingAccount that inherit from class Account. Base class Account should include one data member of type double to represent the account balance. The class should provide a constructor that receives an initial balance and uses it to initialize the data member. The constructor should validate the initial balance to ensure that it's greater than or equal to 0.0. If not, the balance should be set to 0.0 and the constructor should display an error message, indicating that the initial balance was invalid. The class should provide three member functions. Member function credit should add an amount to the current balance. Member function debit should withdraw money from the Account and ensure that the debit amount does not exceed the Account's balance. If it does, the balance should be left unchanged and the function should print the message "Debit amount exceeded account balance." Member function getBalance should return the current balance.

Derived class SavingsAccount should inherit the functionality of an Account, but also include a data member of type double indicating the interest rate (percentage) assigned to the Account. SavingsAccount's constructor should receive the initial balance, as well as an initial value for the SavingsAccount's interest rate. SavingsAccount should provide a public member function calculateInterest that returns a double indicating the amount of interest earned by an account. Member function calculateInterest should determine this amount by multiplying the interest rate by the account balance. [*Note:* SavingsAccount should inherit member functions credit and debit as is without redefining them.]

Derived class CheckingAccount should inherit from base class Account and include an additional data member of type double that represents the fee charged per transaction. Checking-Account's constructor should receive the initial balance, as well as a parameter indicating a fee amount. Class CheckingAccount should redefine member functions credit and debit so that they subtract the fee from the account balance whenever either transaction is performed successfully. CheckingAccount's versions of these functions should invoke the base-class Account version to perform the updates to an account balance. CheckingAccount's debit function should charge a fee only if money is actually withdrawn (i.e., the debit amount does not exceed the account balance). [*Hint:* Define Account's debit function so that it returns a bool indicating whether money was withdrawn. Then use the return value to determine whether a fee should be charged.]

After defining the classes in this hierarchy, write a program that creates objects of each class and tests their member functions. Add interest to the SavingsAccount object by first invoking its calculateInterest function, then passing the returned interest amount to the object's credit function.

Object-Oriented Programming: Polymorphism

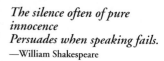

The silence often of pure innocence
Persuades when speaking fails.
—William Shakespeare

General propositions do not decide concrete cases.
—Oliver Wendell Holmes

A philosopher of imposing stature doesn't think in a vacuum. Even his most abstract ideas are, to some extent, conditioned by what is or is not known in the time when he lives.
—Alfred North Whitehead

Objectives

In this chapter you'll learn:

- How polymorphism makes programming more convenient and systems more extensible.

- The distinction between abstract and concrete classes and how to create abstract classes.

- To use runtime type information (RTTI).

- How C++ implements **virtual** functions and dynamic binding.

- How **virtual** destructors ensure that all appropriate destructors run on an object.

12.1 Introduction

We now continue our study of OOP by explaining and demonstrating **polymorphism** with inheritance hierarchies. Polymorphism enables you to "program in the *general*" rather than "program in the *specific*." In particular, polymorphism enables you to write programs that process objects of classes that are part of the *same* class hierarchy as if they were all objects of the hierarchy's base class. As we'll soon see, polymorphism works off base-class *pointer handles* and base-class *reference handles*, but *not* off name handles.

Implementing for Extensibility

With polymorphism, you can design and implement systems that are easily *extensible*—new classes can be added with little or no modification to the general portions of the program, as long as the new classes are part of the inheritance hierarchy that the program processes generally. The only parts of a program that must be altered to accommodate new classes are those that require direct knowledge of the new classes that you add to the hierarchy. For example, if we create class `Tortoise` that inherits from class `Animal` (which might respond to a move message by crawling one inch), we need to write only the `Tortoise` class and the part of the simulation that instantiates a `Tortoise` object. The portions of the simulation that process each `Animal` generally can remain the same.

Optional Discussion of Polymorphism "Under the Hood"

A key feature of this chapter is its (optional) detailed discussion of polymorphism, `virtual` functions and dynamic binding "under the hood," which uses a detailed diagram to explain how polymorphism can be implemented in C++.

12.2 Introduction to Polymorphism: Polymorphic Video Game

Suppose that we design a video game that manipulates objects of many *different* types, including objects of classes Martian, Venutian, Plutonian, SpaceShip and LaserBeam. Imagine that each of these classes inherits from the common base class SpaceObject, which contains the member function draw. Each derived class implements this function in a manner appropriate for that class. A screen-manager program maintains a container (e.g., a vector) that holds SpaceObject *pointers* to objects of the various classes. To refresh the screen, the screen manager periodically sends each object the *same* message—namely, draw. Each type of object responds in a unique way. For example, a Martian object might draw itself in red with the appropriate number of antennae, a SpaceShip object might draw itself as a silver flying saucer, and a LaserBeam object might draw itself as a bright red beam across the screen. The *same* message (in this case, draw) sent to a *variety* of objects has *many forms* of results—hence the term polymorphism.

A polymorphic screen manager facilitates adding new classes to a system with minimal modifications to its code. Suppose that we want to add objects of class Mercurian to our video game. To do so, we must build a class Mercurian that inherits from SpaceObject, but provides its own definition of member function draw. Then, when *pointers* to objects of class Mercurian appear in the container, you do not need to modify the code for the screen manager. The screen manager invokes member function draw on *every* object in the container, *regardless* of the object's type, so the new Mercurian objects simply "plug right in." Thus, without modifying the system (other than to build and include the classes themselves), you can use polymorphism to accommodate additional classes, including ones that were *not even envisioned* when the system was created.

Software Engineering Observation 12.1
Polymorphism enables you to deal in generalities *and let the execution-time environment concern itself with the* specifics. *You can direct a variety of objects to behave in manners appropriate to those objects* without even knowing their types—*as long as those objects belong to the same inheritance hierarchy and are being accessed off a common base-class pointer or a common base-class reference.*

Software Engineering Observation 12.2
Polymorphism promotes extensibility: *Software written to invoke polymorphic behavior is written* independently *of the specific types of the objects to which messages are sent. Thus,* new *types of objects that can respond to* existing *messages can be incorporated into such a system without modifying the base system. Only client code that instantiates new objects must be modified to accommodate new types.*

12.3 Relationships Among Objects in an Inheritance Hierarchy

Section 11.3 created an employee class hierarchy, in which class BasePlusCommission-Employee inherited from class CommissionEmployee. The Chapter 11 examples manipulated CommissionEmployee and BasePlusCommissionEmployee objects by using the objects' names to invoke their member functions. We now examine the relationships among classes in a hierarchy more closely. The next several sections present a series of examples that demonstrate how base-class and derived-class *pointers* can be aimed at base-class and derived-class objects, and how those pointers can be used to invoke member functions that manipulate those objects.

- In Section 12.3.1, we assign the address of a derived-class object to a base-class pointer, then show that invoking a function via the base-class pointer invokes the *base-class functionality* in the derived-class object—i.e., the *type of the handle determines which function is called.*

- In Section 12.3.2, we assign the address of a base-class object to a derived-class pointer, which results in a compilation error. We discuss the error message and investigate why the compiler does *not* allow such an assignment.

- In Section 12.3.3, we assign the address of a derived-class object to a base-class pointer, then examine how the base-class pointer can be used to invoke only the base-class functionality—*when we attempt to invoke derived-class member functions through the base-class pointer, compilation errors occur.*

- Finally, in Section 12.3.4, we demonstrate how to get polymorphic behavior from base-class pointers aimed at derived-class objects. We introduce virtual functions and polymorphism by declaring a base-class function as virtual. We then assign the address of a derived-class object to the base-class pointer and use that pointer to invoke derived-class functionality—*precisely the capability we need to achieve polymorphic behavior.*

A key concept in these examples is to demonstrate that with public inheritance *an object of a derived class can be treated as an object of its base class.* This enables various interesting manipulations. For example, a program can create an array of base-class pointers that point to objects of many derived-class types. Despite the fact that the derived-class objects are of *different types*, the compiler allows this because each derived-class object *is an* object of its base class. However, *we cannot treat a base-class object as an object of any of its derived classes.* For example, a CommissionEmployee is not a BasePlusCommissionEmployee in the hierarchy defined in Chapter 11—a CommissionEmployee does *not* have a baseSalary data member and does *not* have member functions setBaseSalary and getBaseSalary. The *is-a* relationship applies only from a *derived class* to its *direct and indirect base classes.*

12.3.1 Invoking Base-Class Functions from Derived-Class Objects

The example in Fig. 12.1 reuses the final versions of classes CommissionEmployee and BasePlusCommissionEmployee from Section 11.3.5. The example demonstrates three ways to aim base- and derived-class pointers at base- and derived-class objects. The first two are natural and straightforward—we aim a base-class pointer at a base-class object and invoke base-class functionality, and we aim a derived-class pointer at a derived-class object and invoke derived-class functionality. Then, we demonstrate the relationship between derived classes and base classes (i.e., the *is-a* relationship of inheritance) by aiming a base-class pointer at a derived-class object and showing that the base-class functionality is indeed available in the derived-class object.

```cpp
 1  // Fig. 12.1: fig12_01.cpp
 2  // Aiming base-class and derived-class pointers at base-class
 3  // and derived-class objects, respectively.
 4  #include <iostream>
 5  #include <iomanip>
 6  #include "CommissionEmployee.h"
 7  #include "BasePlusCommissionEmployee.h"
 8  using namespace std;
 9
10  int main()
11  {
12     // create base-class object
13     CommissionEmployee commissionEmployee(
14        "Sue", "Jones", "222-22-2222", 10000, .06 );
15
16     // create base-class pointer
17     CommissionEmployee *commissionEmployeePtr = nullptr;
18
19     // create derived-class object
20     BasePlusCommissionEmployee basePlusCommissionEmployee(
21        "Bob", "Lewis", "333-33-3333", 5000, .04, 300 );
22
23     // create derived-class pointer
24     BasePlusCommissionEmployee *basePlusCommissionEmployeePtr = nullptr;
25
26     // set floating-point output formatting
27     cout << fixed << setprecision( 2 );
28
29     // output objects commissionEmployee and basePlusCommissionEmployee
30     cout << "Print base-class and derived-class objects:\n\n";
31     commissionEmployee.print(); // invokes base-class print
32     cout << "\n\n";
33     basePlusCommissionEmployee.print(); // invokes derived-class print
34
35     // aim base-class pointer at base-class object and print
36     commissionEmployeePtr = &commissionEmployee; // perfectly natural
37     cout << "\n\n\nCalling print with base-class pointer to "
38        << "\nbase-class object invokes base-class print function:\n\n";
39     commissionEmployeePtr->print(); // invokes base-class print
40
41     // aim derived-class pointer at derived-class object and print
42     basePlusCommissionEmployeePtr = &basePlusCommissionEmployee; // natural
43     cout << "\n\n\nCalling print with derived-class pointer to "
44        << "\nderived-class object invokes derived-class "
45        << "print function:\n\n";
46     basePlusCommissionEmployeePtr->print(); // invokes derived-class print
47
48     // aim base-class pointer at derived-class object and print
49     commissionEmployeePtr = &basePlusCommissionEmployee;
50     cout << "\n\n\nCalling print with base-class pointer to "
51        << "derived-class object\ninvokes base-class print "
```

Fig. 12.1 | Assigning addresses of base-class and derived-class objects to base-class and derived-class pointers. (Part 1 of 2.)

```
52          << "function on that derived-class object:\n\n";
53      commissionEmployeePtr->print(); // invokes base-class print
54      cout << endl;
55  } // end main
```

```
Print base-class and derived-class objects:

commission employee: Sue Jones
social security number: 222-22-2222
gross sales: 10000.00
commission rate: 0.06

base-salaried commission employee: Bob Lewis
social security number: 333-33-3333
gross sales: 5000.00
commission rate: 0.04
base salary: 300.00


Calling print with base-class pointer to
base-class object invokes base-class print function:

commission employee: Sue Jones
social security number: 222-22-2222
gross sales: 10000.00
commission rate: 0.06


Calling print with derived-class pointer to
derived-class object invokes derived-class print function:

base-salaried commission employee: Bob Lewis
social security number: 333-33-3333
gross sales: 5000.00
commission rate: 0.04
base salary: 300.00


Calling print with base-class pointer to derived-class object
invokes base-class print function on that derived-class object:

commission employee: Bob Lewis
social security number: 333-33-3333
gross sales: 5000.00
commission rate: 0.04        ──── Notice that the base salary is *not* displayed
```

Fig. 12.1 | Assigning addresses of base-class and derived-class objects to base-class and derived-class pointers. (Part 2 of 2.)

Recall that each BasePlusCommissionEmployee object *is a* CommissionEmployee that *also* has a base salary. Class BasePlusCommissionEmployee's earnings member function (lines 34–37 of Fig. 11.15) redefines class CommissionEmployee's earnings member function (lines 85–88 of Fig. 11.14) to include the object's base salary. Class BasePlusCommissionEmployee's print member function (lines 40–48 of Fig. 11.15) redefines class CommissionEmployee's version (lines 91–98 of Fig. 11.14) to display the same information *plus* the employee's base salary.

Creating Objects and Displaying Their Contents
In Fig. 12.1, lines 13–14 create a CommissionEmployee object and line 17 creates a pointer to a CommissionEmployee object; lines 20–21 create a BasePlusCommissionEmployee object and line 24 creates a pointer to a BasePlusCommissionEmployee object. Lines 31 and 33 use each object's name to invoke its print member function.

Aiming a Base-Class Pointer at a Base-Class Object
Line 36 assigns the address of base-class object commissionEmployee to base-class pointer commissionEmployeePtr, which line 39 uses to invoke member function print on that CommissionEmployee object. This invokes the version of print defined in base class CommissionEmployee.

Aiming a Derived-Class Pointer at a Derived-Class Object
Similarly, line 42 assigns the address of derived-class object basePlusCommissionEmployee to derived-class pointer basePlusCommissionEmployeePtr, which line 46 uses to invoke member function print on that BasePlusCommissionEmployee object. This invokes the version of print defined in derived class BasePlusCommissionEmployee.

Aiming a Base-Class Pointer at a Derived-Class Object
Line 49 then assigns the address of derived-class object basePlusCommissionEmployee to base-class pointer commissionEmployeePtr, which line 53 uses to invoke member function print. This "crossover" is allowed because an object of a derived class *is an* object of its base class. Despite the fact that the base class CommissionEmployee pointer points to a *derived class* BasePlusCommissionEmployee object, the *base class* CommissionEmployee's print member function is invoked (rather than BasePlusCommissionEmployee's print function). The output of each print member-function invocation in this program reveals that *the invoked functionality depends on the type of the pointer (or reference) used to invoke the function, not the type of the object for which the member function is called*. In Section 12.3.4, when we introduce virtual functions, we demonstrate that it's possible to invoke the object type's functionality, *rather than* invoke the handle type's functionality. We'll see that this is crucial to implementing polymorphic behavior—the key topic of this chapter.

12.3.2 Aiming Derived-Class Pointers at Base-Class Objects

In Section 12.3.1, we assigned the address of a derived-class object to a base-class pointer and explained that the C++ compiler allows this assignment, because a derived-class object *is a* base-class object. We take the opposite approach in Fig. 12.2, as we aim a derived-class pointer at a base-class object. [*Note:* This program reuses the final versions of classes CommissionEmployee and BasePlusCommissionEmployee from Section 11.3.5.] Lines 8–9 of Fig. 12.2 create a CommissionEmployee object, and line 10 creates a BasePlusCommissionEmployee pointer. Line 14 attempts to assign the address of base-class object commissionEmployee to derived-class pointer basePlusCommissionEmployeePtr, but the compiler generates an error. The compiler prevents this assignment, because a CommissionEmployee is *not* a BasePlusCommissionEmployee.

Consider the consequences if the compiler were to allow this assignment. Through a BasePlusCommissionEmployee pointer, we can invoke *every* BasePlusCommissionEmployee member function, including setBaseSalary, for the object to which the pointer points (i.e., the base-class object commissionEmployee). However, the CommissionEmployee object does *not* provide a setBaseSalary member function, *nor* does it provide a baseSalary data member to set. This could lead to problems, because member function setBaseSalary would assume that there is a baseSalary data member to set at its "usual location" in a BasePlusCommissionEmployee object. This memory does not belong to the CommissionEmployee object, so member function setBaseSalary might overwrite other important data in memory, possibly data that belongs to a different object.

```
 1   // Fig. 12.2: fig12_02.cpp
 2   // Aiming a derived-class pointer at a base-class object.
 3   #include "CommissionEmployee.h"
 4   #include "BasePlusCommissionEmployee.h"
 5
 6   int main()
 7   {
 8      CommissionEmployee commissionEmployee(
 9         "Sue", "Jones", "222-22-2222", 10000, .06 );
10      BasePlusCommissionEmployee *basePlusCommissionEmployeePtr = nullptr;
11
12      // aim derived-class pointer at base-class object
13      // Error: a CommissionEmployee is not a BasePlusCommissionEmployee
14      basePlusCommissionEmployeePtr = &commissionEmployee;
15   } // end main
```

Microsoft Visual C++ compiler error message:

```
C:\cpphtp8_examples\ch12\Fig12_02\fig12_02.cpp(14): error C2440: '=' :
    cannot convert from 'CommissionEmployee *' to 'BasePlusCommissionEmployee *'
        Cast from base to derived requires dynamic_cast or static_cast
```

Fig. 12.2 | Aiming a derived-class pointer at a base-class object.

12.3.3 Derived-Class Member-Function Calls via Base-Class Pointers

Off a base-class pointer, the compiler allows us to invoke *only* base-class member functions. Thus, if a base-class pointer is aimed at a derived-class object, and an attempt is made to access a *derived-class-only member function*, a compilation error will occur.

Figure 12.3 shows the consequences of attempting to invoke a derived-class member function off a base-class pointer. [*Note:* We're again reusing the versions of classes CommissionEmployee and BasePlusCommissionEmployee from Section 11.3.5.] Line 11 creates commissionEmployeePtr—a pointer to a CommissionEmployee object—and lines 12–13 create a BasePlusCommissionEmployee object. Line 16 aims the base-class commissionEmployeePtr at derived-class object basePlusCommissionEmployee. Recall from Section 12.3.1 that this is allowed, because a BasePlusCommissionEmployee *is a* CommissionEmployee (in the sense that a BasePlusCommissionEmployee object contains all the functionality of a CommissionEmployee object). Lines 20–24 invoke base-class member functions getFirstName, getLastName, getSocialSecurityNumber, getGrossSales and getCommissionRate off the base-class pointer. All of these calls are allowed, because BasePlusCommissionEmployee *inherits* these member functions from CommissionEmployee. We know that commissionEmployeePtr is aimed at a BasePlusCommissionEmployee object, so in lines 28–29 we attempt to invoke BasePlusCommissionEmployee member functions getBaseSalary and setBaseSalary. The compiler generates errors on both of these calls, because they're *not* made to member functions of base-class CommissionEmployee. The handle can be used to invoke *only* those functions that are members of that handle's associated class type. (In this case, off a CommissionEmployee *, we can invoke only CommissionEmployee member functions setFirstName, getFirstName, setLastName, getLastName, setSocialSecurityNumber, getSocialSecurityNumber, setGrossSales, getGrossSales, setCommissionRate, getCommissionRate, earnings and print.)

```cpp
 1   // Fig. 12.3: fig12_03.cpp
 2   // Attempting to invoke derived-class-only member functions
 3   // via a base-class pointer.
 4   #include <string>
 5   #include "CommissionEmployee.h"
 6   #include "BasePlusCommissionEmployee.h"
 7   using namespace std;
 8
 9   int main()
10   {
11      CommissionEmployee *commissionEmployeePtr = nullptr; // base class ptr
12      BasePlusCommissionEmployee basePlusCommissionEmployee(
13         "Bob", "Lewis", "333-33-3333", 5000, .04, 300 ); // derived class
14
15      // aim base-class pointer at derived-class object (allowed)
16      commissionEmployeePtr = &basePlusCommissionEmployee;
17
18      // invoke base-class member functions on derived-class
19      // object through base-class pointer (allowed)
20      string firstName = commissionEmployeePtr->getFirstName();
21      string lastName = commissionEmployeePtr->getLastName();
22      string ssn = commissionEmployeePtr->getSocialSecurityNumber();
23      double grossSales = commissionEmployeePtr->getGrossSales();
24      double commissionRate = commissionEmployeePtr->getCommissionRate();
25
26      // attempt to invoke derived-class-only member functions
27      // on derived-class object through base-class pointer (disallowed)
28      double baseSalary = commissionEmployeePtr->getBaseSalary();
29      commissionEmployeePtr->setBaseSalary( 500 );
30   } // end main
```

GNU C++ compiler error messages:

```
fig12_03.cpp:28:47: error: 'class CommissionEmployee' has no member named
   'getBaseSalary'
fig12_03.cpp:29:27: error: 'class CommissionEmployee' has no member named
   'setBaseSalary'
```

Fig. 12.3 | Attempting to invoke derived-class-only functions via a base-class pointer.

Downcasting

The compiler will allow access to derived-class-only members from a base-class pointer that's aimed at a derived-class object *if* we explicitly cast the base-class pointer to a derived-class pointer—this is known as **downcasting**. As you know, it's possible to aim a base-class pointer at a derived-class object. However, as we demonstrated in Fig. 12.3, a base-class pointer can be used to invoke *only* the functions declared in the base class. Downcasting allows a derived-class-specific operation on a derived-class object pointed to by a base-class pointer. After a downcast, the program *can* invoke derived-class functions that are not in the base class. Downcasting is a potentially dangerous operation. Section 12.8 demonstrates how to *safely* use downcasting.

Software Engineering Observation 12.3

If the address of a derived-class object has been assigned to a pointer of one of its direct or indirect base classes, it's acceptable to cast that base-class pointer back to a pointer of the derived-class type. In fact, this must *be done to call derived-class member functions that do not appear in the base class.*

12.3.4 Virtual Functions and Virtual Destructors

In Section 12.3.1, we aimed a base-class `CommissionEmployee` pointer at a derived-class `BasePlusCommissionEmployee` object, then invoked member function `print` through that pointer. Recall that the *type of the handle* determined which class's functionality to invoke. In that case, the `CommissionEmployee` pointer invoked the `CommissionEmployee` member function `print` on the `BasePlusCommissionEmployee` object, even though the pointer was aimed at a `BasePlusCommissionEmployee` object that has its own custom `print` function.

Software Engineering Observation 12.4

With `virtual` *functions, the type of the object, not the type of the handle used to invoke the member function, determines which version of a* `virtual` *function to invoke.*

Why `virtual` Functions Are Useful

First, we consider why `virtual` functions are useful. Suppose that shape classes such as `Circle`, `Triangle`, `Rectangle` and `Square` are all derived from base class `Shape`. Each of these classes might be endowed with the ability to *draw itself* via a member function `draw`, but the function for each shape is quite different. In a program that draws a set of shapes, it would be useful to be able to treat all the shapes generally as objects of the base class `Shape`. Then, to draw any shape, we could simply use a base-class `Shape` pointer to invoke function `draw` and let the program determine *dynamically* (i.e., at runtime) which derived-class `draw` function to use, based on the type of the object to which the base-class `Shape` pointer points at any given time. This is *polymorphic behavior*.

Declaring `virtual` Functions

To enable this behavior, we declare `draw` in the base class as a **`virtual` function**, and we override `draw` in *each* of the derived classes to draw the appropriate shape. From an implementation perspective, *overriding* a function is no different than *redefining* one (which is the approach we've been using until now). An overridden function in a derived class has the *same signature and return type* (i.e., *prototype*) as the function it overrides in its base class. If we do not declare the base-class function as `virtual`, we can *redefine* that function. By contrast, if we declare the base-class function as `virtual`, we can *override* that function to enable *polymorphic behavior*. We declare a `virtual` function by preceding the function's prototype with the keyword `virtual` in the base class. For example,

```
virtual void draw() const;
```

would appear in base class Shape. The preceding prototype declares that function draw is a virtual function that takes no arguments and returns nothing. This function is declared const because a draw function typically would not make changes to the Shape object on which it's invoked—virtual functions do *not* have to be const functions.

Software Engineering Observation 12.5
Once a function is declared virtual, it remains virtual all the way down the inheritance hierarchy from that point, even if that function is not explicitly declared virtual when a derived class overrides it.

Good Programming Practice 12.1
Even though certain functions are implicitly virtual because of a declaration made higher in the class hierarchy, explicitly declare these functions virtual at every level of the class hierarchy to promote program clarity.

Software Engineering Observation 12.6
When a derived class chooses not *to override a virtual function from its base class, the derived class simply inherits its base class's virtual function implementation.*

Invoking a virtual Function Through a Base-Class Pointer or Reference
If a program invokes a virtual function through a base-class pointer to a derived-class object (e.g., shapePtr->draw()) or a base-class reference to a derived-class object (e.g., shapeRef.draw()), the program will choose the correct derived-class draw function *dynamically* (i.e., at execution time) *based on the object type—not the pointer or reference type*. Choosing the appropriate function to call at execution time (rather than at compile time) is known as **dynamic binding** or **late binding**.

Invoking a virtual Function Through an Object's Name
When a virtual function is called by referencing a specific object by *name* and using the dot member-selection operator (e.g., squareObject.draw()), the function invocation is *resolved at compile time* (this is called **static binding**) and the virtual function that's called is the one defined for (or inherited by) the class of that particular object—this is *not* polymorphic behavior. Thus, dynamic binding with virtual functions occurs only off pointers (and, as we'll soon see, references).

virtual Functions in the CommissionEmployee Hierarchy
Now let's see how virtual functions can enable polymorphic behavior in our employee hierarchy. Figures 12.4–12.5 are the headers for classes CommissionEmployee and BasePlusCommissionEmployee, respectively. We modified these to declare each class's earnings and print member functions as virtual (lines 29–30 of Fig. 12.4 and lines 19–20 of Fig. 12.5). Because functions earnings and print are virtual in class CommissionEmployee, class BasePlusCommissionEmployee's earnings and print functions *override* class CommissionEmployee's. In addition, class BasePlusCommissionEmployee's earnings and print functions are declared **override**.

> ### Error-Prevention Tip 12.1
>
> *Apply C++11's* override *keyword to every overridden function in a derived-class. This forces the compiler to check whether the base class has a member function with the same name and parameter list (i.e., the same signature). If not, the compiler generates an error.*

Now, if we aim a base-class `CommissionEmployee` pointer at a derived-class `BasePlusCommissionEmployee` object, and the program uses that pointer to call either function `earnings` or `print`, the `BasePlusCommissionEmployee` object's corresponding function will be invoked. There were *no* changes to the member-function implementations of classes `CommissionEmployee` and `BasePlusCommissionEmployee`, so we reuse the versions of Figs. 11.14 and 11.15.

```
 1   // Fig. 12.4: CommissionEmployee.h
 2   // CommissionEmployee class header declares earnings and print as virtual.
 3   #ifndef COMMISSION_H
 4   #define COMMISSION_H
 5
 6   #include <string> // C++ standard string class
 7
 8   class CommissionEmployee
 9   {
10   public:
11      CommissionEmployee( const std::string &, const std::string &,
12         const std::string &, double = 0.0, double = 0.0 );
13
14      void setFirstName( const std::string & ); // set first name
15      std::string getFirstName() const; // return first name
16
17      void setLastName( const std::string & ); // set last name
18      std::string getLastName() const; // return last name
19
20      void setSocialSecurityNumber( const std::string & ); // set SSN
21      std::string getSocialSecurityNumber() const; // return SSN
22
23      void setGrossSales( double ); // set gross sales amount
24      double getGrossSales() const; // return gross sales amount
25
26      void setCommissionRate( double ); // set commission rate
27      double getCommissionRate() const; // return commission rate
28
29      virtual double earnings() const; // calculate earnings
30      virtual void print() const; // print object
31   private:
32      std::string firstName;
33      std::string lastName;
34      std::string socialSecurityNumber;
35      double grossSales; // gross weekly sales
36      double commissionRate; // commission percentage
37   }; // end class CommissionEmployee
38
39   #endif
```

Fig. 12.4 | `CommissionEmployee` class header declares `earnings` and `print` as `virtual`.

```
 1   // Fig. 12.5: BasePlusCommissionEmployee.h
 2   // BasePlusCommissionEmployee class derived from class
 3   // CommissionEmployee.
 4   #ifndef BASEPLUS_H
 5   #define BASEPLUS_H
 6
 7   #include <string> // C++ standard string class
 8   #include "CommissionEmployee.h" // CommissionEmployee class declaration
 9
10   class BasePlusCommissionEmployee : public CommissionEmployee
11   {
12   public:
13      BasePlusCommissionEmployee( const std::string &, const std::string &,
14         const std::string &, double = 0.0, double = 0.0, double = 0.0 );
15
16      void setBaseSalary( double ); // set base salary
17      double getBaseSalary() const; // return base salary
18
19      virtual double earnings() const override; // calculate earnings
20      virtual void print() const override; // print object
21   private:
22      double baseSalary; // base salary
23   }; // end class BasePlusCommissionEmployee
24
25   #endif
```

Fig. 12.5 | BasePlusCommissionEmployee class header declares earnings and print functions as virtual and override.

We modified Fig. 12.1 to create the program of Fig. 12.6. Lines 40–51 of Fig. 12.6 demonstrate again that a CommissionEmployee pointer aimed at a CommissionEmployee object can be used to invoke CommissionEmployee functionality, and a BasePlusCommissionEmployee pointer aimed at a BasePlusCommissionEmployee object can be used to invoke BasePlusCommissionEmployee functionality. Line 54 aims the base-class pointer commissionEmployeePtr at derived-class object basePlusCommissionEmployee. Note that when line 61 invokes member function print off the base-class pointer, the derived-class BasePlusCommissionEmployee's print member function is invoked, so line 61 outputs different text than line 53 does in Fig. 12.1 (when member function print was *not* declared virtual). We see that declaring a member function virtual causes the program to dynamically determine which function to invoke *based on the type of object to which the handle points, rather than on the type of the handle*. Note again that when commissionEmployeePtr points to a CommissionEmployee object, class CommissionEmployee's print function is invoked (Fig. 12.6, line 40), and when CommissionEmployeePtr points to a BasePlusCommissionEmployee object, class BasePlusCommissionEmployee's print function is invoked (line 61). Thus, the same message—print, in this case—sent (off a base-class pointer) to a variety of objects related by inheritance to that base class, takes on many forms—this is polymorphic behavior.

```
 1   // Fig. 12.6: fig12_06.cpp
 2   // Introducing polymorphism, virtual functions and dynamic binding.
 3   #include <iostream>
 4   #include <iomanip>
 5   #include "CommissionEmployee.h"
 6   #include "BasePlusCommissionEmployee.h"
 7   using namespace std;
 8
 9   int main()
10   {
11      // create base-class object
12      CommissionEmployee commissionEmployee(
13         "Sue", "Jones", "222-22-2222", 10000, .06 );
14
15      // create base-class pointer
16      CommissionEmployee *commissionEmployeePtr = nullptr;
17
18      // create derived-class object
19      BasePlusCommissionEmployee basePlusCommissionEmployee(
20         "Bob", "Lewis", "333-33-3333", 5000, .04, 300 );
21
22      // create derived-class pointer
23      BasePlusCommissionEmployee *basePlusCommissionEmployeePtr = nullptr;
24
25      // set floating-point output formatting
26      cout << fixed << setprecision( 2 );
27
28      // output objects using static binding
29      cout << "Invoking print function on base-class and derived-class "
30         << "\nobjects with static binding\n\n";
31      commissionEmployee.print(); // static binding
32      cout << "\n\n";
33      basePlusCommissionEmployee.print(); // static binding
34
35      // output objects using dynamic binding
36      cout << "\n\n\nInvoking print function on base-class and "
37         << "derived-class \nobjects with dynamic binding";
38
39      // aim base-class pointer at base-class object and print
40      commissionEmployeePtr = &commissionEmployee;
41      cout << "\n\nCalling virtual function print with base-class pointer"
42         << "\nto base-class object invokes base-class "
43         << "print function:\n\n";
44      commissionEmployeePtr->print(); // invokes base-class print
45
46      // aim derived-class pointer at derived-class object and print
47      basePlusCommissionEmployeePtr = &basePlusCommissionEmployee;
48      cout << "\n\nCalling virtual function print with derived-class "
49         << "pointer\nto derived-class object invokes derived-class "
50         << "print function:\n\n";
51      basePlusCommissionEmployeePtr->print(); // invokes derived-class print
```

Fig. 12.6 | Demonstrating polymorphism by invoking a derived-class `virtual` function via a base-class pointer to a derived-class object. (Part 1 of 2.)

```
52
53       // aim base-class pointer at derived-class object and print
54       commissionEmployeePtr = &basePlusCommissionEmployee;
55       cout << "\n\nCalling virtual function print with base-class pointer"
56          << "\nto derived-class object invokes derived-class "
57          << "print function:\n\n";
58
59       // polymorphism; invokes BasePlusCommissionEmployee's print;
60       // base-class pointer to derived-class object
61       commissionEmployeePtr->print();
62       cout << endl;
63    } // end main
```

```
Invoking print function on base-class and derived-class
objects with static binding

commission employee: Sue Jones
social security number: 222-22-2222
gross sales: 10000.00
commission rate: 0.06

base-salaried commission employee: Bob Lewis
social security number: 333-33-3333
gross sales: 5000.00
commission rate: 0.04
base salary: 300.00


Invoking print function on base-class and derived-class
objects with dynamic binding

Calling virtual function print with base-class pointer
to base-class object invokes base-class print function:

commission employee: Sue Jones
social security number: 222-22-2222
gross sales: 10000.00
commission rate: 0.06

Calling virtual function print with derived-class pointer
to derived-class object invokes derived-class print function:

base-salaried commission employee: Bob Lewis
social security number: 333-33-3333
gross sales: 5000.00
commission rate: 0.04
base salary: 300.00

Calling virtual function print with base-class pointer
to derived-class object invokes derived-class print function:

base-salaried commission employee: Bob Lewis
social security number: 333-33-3333
gross sales: 5000.00
commission rate: 0.04
base salary: 300.00——— Notice that the base salary is now displayed
```

Fig. 12.6 | Demonstrating polymorphism by invoking a derived-class virtual function via a base-class pointer to a derived-class object. (Part 2 of 2.)

virtual Destructors

A problem can occur when using polymorphism to process dynamically allocated objects of a class hierarchy. So far you've seen destructors that are not declared with keyword virtual. If a derived-class object with a non-virtual destructor is destroyed by applying the delete operator to a *base-class pointer* to the object, the C++ standard specifies that the behavior is *undefined*.

The simple solution to this problem is to create a public **virtual destructor** in the base class. If a base class destructor is declared virtual, the destructors of any derived classes are *also* virtual and they *override* the base class destructor. For example, in class CommissionEmployee's definition, we can define the virtual destructor as follows:

```
virtual ~CommissionEmployee() { }
```

Now, if an object in the hierarchy is destroyed explicitly by applying the delete operator to a *base-class pointer*, the destructor for the *appropriate class* is called based on the object to which the base-class pointer points. Remember, when a derived-class object is destroyed, the base-class part of the derived-class object is also destroyed, so it's important for the destructors of *both* the derived and base classes to execute. The base-class destructor automatically executes after the derived-class destructor. From this point forward, we'll include a virtual destructor in *every* class that contains virtual functions.

Error-Prevention Tip 12.2

If a class has virtual functions, always provide a virtual destructor, even if one is not required for the class. This ensures that a custom derived-class destructor (if there is one) will be invoked when a derived-class object is deleted via a base class pointer.

Common Programming Error 12.1

Constructors cannot be virtual. Declaring a constructor virtual is a compilation error.

C++11: final Member Functions and Classes

Prior to C++11, a derived class could override *any* of its base class's virtual functions. In C++11, a base-class virtual function that's declared **final** in its prototype, as in

```
virtual someFunction( parameters ) final;
```

cannot be overridden in any derived class—this guarantees that the base class's final member function definition will be used by all base-class objects and by all objects of the base class's direct *and* indirect derived classes. Similarly, prior to C++11, *any* existing class could be used as a base class in a hierarchy. As of C++11, you can declare a class as final to prevent it from being used as a base class, as in

```
class MyClass final // this class cannot be a base class
{
    // class body
};
```

Attempting to override a final member function or inherit from a final base class results in a compilation error.

12.4 Type Fields and switch Statements

One way to determine the type of an object is to use a switch statement to check the value of a field in the object. This allows us to distinguish among object types, then invoke an appropriate action for a particular object. For example, in a hierarchy of shapes in which each shape object has a shapeType attribute, a switch statement could check the object's shapeType to determine which print function to call.

Using switch logic exposes programs to a variety of potential problems. For example, you might forget to include a type test when one is warranted, or might forget to test all possible cases in a switch statement. When modifying a switch-based system by adding new types, you might forget to insert the new cases in *all* relevant switch statements. Every addition or deletion of a class requires the modification of every switch statement in the system; tracking these statements down can be time consuming and error prone.

Software Engineering Observation 12.7
Polymorphic programming can eliminate the need for switch logic. By using the polymorphism mechanism to perform the equivalent logic, you can avoid the kinds of errors typically associated with switch logic.

Software Engineering Observation 12.8
An interesting consequence of using polymorphism is that programs take on a simplified appearance. They contain less branching logic and simpler sequential code.

12.5 Abstract Classes and Pure virtual Functions

When we think of a class as a type, we assume that programs will create objects of that type. However, there are cases in which it's useful to define *classes from which you never intend to instantiate any objects*. Such classes are called abstract classes. Because these classes normally are used as base classes in inheritance hierarchies, we refer to them as abstract base classes. These classes cannot be used to instantiate objects, because, as we'll soon see, abstract classes are *incomplete*—derived classes must define the "missing pieces" before objects of these classes can be instantiated. We build programs with abstract classes in Section 12.6.

An abstract class is a base class from which other classes can inherit. Classes that can be used to instantiate objects are called concrete classes. Such classes define or inherit implementations for *every* member function they declare. We could have an *abstract* base class TwoDimensionalShape and derive such *concrete* classes as Square, Circle and Triangle. We could also have an *abstract* base class ThreeDimensionalShape and derive such *concrete* classes as Cube, Sphere and Cylinder. Abstract base classes are *too generic* to define real objects; we need to be *more specific* before we can think of instantiating objects. For example, if someone tells you to "draw the two-dimensional shape," what shape would you draw? Concrete classes provide the *specifics* that make it possible to instantiate objects.

An inheritance hierarchy does *not* need to contain any abstract classes, but many object-oriented systems have class hierarchies headed by abstract base classes. In some cases, abstract classes constitute the top few levels of the hierarchy. A good example of this is the shape hierarchy in Fig. 11.3, which begins with abstract base class Shape. On the next level of the hierarchy we have two more abstract base classes—TwoDimensionalShape and `ThreeDimensionalShape`. The next level of the hierarchy defines *concrete* classes for two-dimensional shapes (namely, `Circle`, `Square` and `Triangle`) and for three-dimensional shapes (namely, `Sphere`, `Cube` and `Tetrahedron`).

Pure Virtual Functions

A class is made abstract by declaring one or more of its `virtual` functions to be "pure." A pure `virtual` function is specified by placing "= 0" in its declaration, as in

```
virtual void draw() const = 0; // pure virtual function
```

The "= 0" is a **pure specifier**. Pure `virtual` functions typically do *not* provide implementations, though they can. Each *concrete* derived class *must override all* base-class pure `virtual` functions with concrete implementations of those functions; otherwise, the derived class is also abstract. The difference between a `virtual` function and a pure `virtual` function is that a `virtual` function *has* an implementation and gives the derived class the *option* of overriding the function; by contrast, a pure `virtual` function does *not* have an implementation and *requires* the derived class to override the function for that derived class to be concrete; otherwise the derived class remains *abstract*.

Pure `virtual` functions are used when it does *not* make sense for the base class to have an implementation of a function, but you want all concrete derived classes to implement the function. Returning to our earlier example of space objects, it does not make sense for the base class `SpaceObject` to have an implementation for function `draw` (as there is no way to draw a generic space object without having more information about what type of space object is being drawn). An example of a function that would be defined as `virtual` (and not pure `virtual`) would be one that returns a name for the object. We can name a generic `SpaceObject` (for instance, as `"space object"`), so a default implementation for this function can be provided, and the function does not need to be *pure* `virtual`. The function is still declared `virtual`, however, because it's expected that derived classes will override this function to provide *more specific* names for the derived-class objects.

Software Engineering Observation 12.9

An abstract class defines a common public interface for the various classes in a class hierarchy. An abstract class contains one or more pure `virtual` functions that concrete derived classes must override.

Common Programming Error 12.2

Failure to override a pure `virtual` function in a derived class makes that class abstract. Attempting to instantiate an object of an abstract class causes a compilation error.

Software Engineering Observation 12.10

An abstract class has at least one pure `virtual` function. An abstract class also can have data members and concrete functions (including constructors and destructors), which are subject to the normal rules of inheritance by derived classes.

Although we *cannot* instantiate objects of an abstract base class, we *can* use the abstract base class to declare *pointers* and *references* that can refer to objects of any *concrete* classes derived from the abstract class. Programs typically use such pointers and references to manipulate derived-class objects polymorphically.

Device Drivers and Polymorphism

Polymorphism is particularly effective for implementing *layered software systems*. In operating systems, for example, each type of physical device could operate quite differently from the others. Even so, commands to *read* or *write* data from and to devices may have a certain uniformity. The *write* message sent to a *device-driver* object needs to be interpreted specifically in the context of that device driver and how that device driver manipulates devices of a specific type. However, the *write* call itself really is no different from the *write* to any other device in the system—place some number of *bytes* from memory onto that device. An object-oriented operating system could use an abstract base class to provide an interface appropriate for all device drivers. Then, through inheritance from that abstract base class, derived classes are formed that all operate similarly. The capabilities (i.e., the public functions) offered by the device drivers are provided as pure virtual functions in the abstract base class. The implementations of these pure virtual functions are provided in the derived classes that correspond to the specific types of device drivers. This architecture also allows new devices to be *added* to a system easily. The user can just plug in the device and install its new device driver. The operating system "talks" to this new device through its device driver, which has the same public member functions as all other device drivers—those defined in the device driver abstract base class.

12.6 Case Study: Payroll System Using Polymorphism

This section reexamines the CommissionEmployee–BasePlusCommissionEmployee hierarchy that we explored throughout Section 11.3. In this example, we use an abstract class and polymorphism to perform payroll calculations based on the type of employee. We create an enhanced employee hierarchy to solve the following problem:

> *A company pays its employees weekly. The employees are of three types:* Salaried employees *are paid a fixed weekly salary regardless of the number of hours worked,* commission employees *are paid a percentage of their sales and* base-salary-plus-commission employees *receive a base salary plus a percentage of their sales. For the current pay period, the company has decided to reward base-salary-plus-commission employees by adding 10 percent to their base salaries. The company wants to implement a C++ program that performs its payroll calculations polymorphically.*

We use abstract class Employee to represent the general concept of an employee. The classes that derive directly from Employee are SalariedEmployee and CommissionEmployee. Class BasePlusCommissionEmployee—derived from CommissionEmployee—represents the last employee type. The UML class diagram in Fig. 12.7 shows the inheritance hierarchy for our polymorphic employee payroll application. The abstract class name Employee is *italicized*, as per the convention of the UML.

Abstract base class Employee declares the "interface" to the hierarchy—that is, the set of member functions that a program can invoke on all Employee objects. Each employee, regardless of the way his or her earnings are calculated, has a first name, a last name and a social security number, so private data members firstName, lastName and socialSecurityNumber appear in abstract base class Employee.

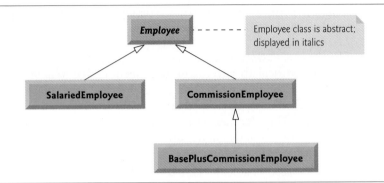

Fig. 12.7 | Employee hierarchy UML class diagram.

 Software Engineering Observation 12.11

A derived class can inherit interface and/or implementation from a base class. Hierarchies designed for implementation inheritance tend to have their functionality high in the hierarchy—each new derived class inherits one or more member functions that were defined in a base class, and the derived class uses the base-class definitions. Hierarchies designed for interface inheritance tend to have their functionality lower in the hierarchy—a base class specifies one or more functions that should be defined for each class in the hierarchy (i.e., they have the same prototype), but the individual derived classes provide their own implementations of the function(s).

The following sections implement the Employee class hierarchy. The first five each implement one of the abstract or concrete classes. The last section implements a test program that builds objects of all these classes and processes the objects polymorphically.

12.6.1 Creating Abstract Base Class Employee

Class Employee (Figs. 12.9–12.10, discussed in further detail shortly) provides functions earnings and print, in addition to various *get* and *set* functions that manipulate Employee's data members. An earnings function certainly applies generally to all employees, but each earnings calculation depends on the employee's class. So we declare earnings as pure virtual in base class Employee because *a default implementation does not make sense* for that function—there is not enough information to determine what amount earnings should return. Each derived class *overrides* earnings with an appropriate implementation. To calculate an employee's earnings, the program assigns the address of an employee's object to a base class Employee *pointer*, then invokes the earnings function on that object. We maintain a vector of Employee pointers, each of which points to an Employee object. *Of course, there cannot be Employee objects, because Employee is an abstract class—because of inheritance, however, all objects of all concrete derived classes of Employee may nevertheless be thought of as Employee objects.* The program iterates through the vector and calls function earnings for each Employee object. C++ processes these function calls *polymorphically.* Including earnings as a pure virtual function in Employee *forces* every direct derived class of Employee that wishes to be a *concrete* class to *override* earnings.

Function print in class Employee displays the first name, last name and social security number of the employee. As we'll see, each derived class of Employee overrides function print to output the employee's type (e.g., `"salaried employee:"`) followed by the rest of the employee's information. Function `print` in the derived classes could also call `earnings`, even though `earnings` is a pure-`virtual` function in base class `Employee`.

The diagram in Fig. 12.8 shows each of the four classes in the hierarchy down the left side and functions `earnings` and `print` across the top. For each class, the diagram shows the desired results of each function. Italic text represents where the values from a particular object are used in the `earnings` and `print` functions. Class `Employee` specifies "= 0" for function `earnings` to indicate that this is a pure `virtual` function and hence has *no* implementation. Each derived class overrides this function to provide an appropriate implementation. We do *not* list base class `Employee`'s *get* and *set* functions because they're *not* overridden in any of the derived classes—each of these functions is inherited and used "as is" by each of the derived classes.

	earnings	print
Employee	= 0	*firstName lastName* `social security number:` *SSN*
Salaried-Employee	*weeklySalary*	`salaried employee:` *firstName lastName* `social security number:` *SSN* `weekly salary:` *weeklySalary*
Commission-Employee	*commissionRate * grossSales*	`commission employee:` *firstName lastName* `social security number:` *SSN* `gross sales:` *grossSales*; `commission rate:` *commissionRate*
BasePlus-Commission-Employee	*(commissionRate *** *grossSales) + baseSalary*	`base-salaried commission employee:` *firstName lastName* `social security number:` *SSN* `gross sales:` *grossSales*; `commission rate:` *commissionRate*; `base salary:` *baseSalary*

Fig. 12.8 | Polymorphic interface for the `Employee` hierarchy classes.

Employee Class Header

Let's consider class `Employee`'s header (Fig. 12.9). The `public` member functions include a constructor that takes the first name, last name and social security number as arguments (lines 11–12); a virtual destructor (line 13); *set* functions that set the first name, last name and social security number (lines 15, 18 and 21, respectively); *get* functions that return the first name, last name and social security number (lines 16, 19 and 22, respectively); pure `virtual` function `earnings` (line 25) and `virtual` function `print` (line 26).

```
1   // Fig. 12.9: Employee.h
2   // Employee abstract base class.
3   #ifndef EMPLOYEE_H
```

Fig. 12.9 | Employee abstract base class. (Part 1 of 2.)

```
4   #define EMPLOYEE_H
5
6   #include <string> // C++ standard string class
7
8   class Employee
9   {
10  public:
11      Employee( const std::string &, const std::string &,
12          const std::string & );
13      virtual ~Employee() { } // virtual destructor
14
15      void setFirstName( const std::string & ); // set first name
16      std::string getFirstName() const; // return first name
17
18      void setLastName( const std::string & ); // set last name
19      std::string getLastName() const; // return last name
20
21      void setSocialSecurityNumber( const std::string & ); // set SSN
22      std::string getSocialSecurityNumber() const; // return SSN
23
24      // pure virtual function makes Employee an abstract base class
25      virtual double earnings() const = 0; // pure virtual
26      virtual void print() const; // virtual
27  private:
28      std::string firstName;
29      std::string lastName;
30      std::string socialSecurityNumber;
31  }; // end class Employee
32
33  #endif // EMPLOYEE_H
```

Fig. 12.9 | Employee abstract base class. (Part 2 of 2.)

Recall that we declared earnings as a pure virtual function because first we must know the *specific* Employee type to determine the appropriate earnings calculations. Declaring this function as pure virtual indicates that each concrete derived class *must* provide an earnings implementation and that a program can use base-class Employee pointers to invoke function earnings *polymorphically* for *any* type of Employee.

Employee Class Member-Function Definitions

Figure 12.10 contains the member-function definitions for class Employee. No implementation is provided for virtual function earnings. The Employee constructor (lines 9–14) does not validate the social security number. Normally, such validation should be provided.

```
1   // Fig. 12.10: Employee.cpp
2   // Abstract-base-class Employee member-function definitions.
3   // Note: No definitions are given for pure virtual functions.
4   #include <iostream>
5   #include "Employee.h" // Employee class definition
6   using namespace std;
```

Fig. 12.10 | Employee class implementation file. (Part 1 of 2.)

```cpp
7
8   // constructor
9   Employee::Employee( const string &first, const string &last,
10     const string &ssn )
11     : firstName( first ), lastName( last ), socialSecurityNumber( ssn )
12  {
13     // empty body
14  } // end Employee constructor
15
16  // set first name
17  void Employee::setFirstName( const string &first )
18  {
19     firstName = first;
20  } // end function setFirstName
21
22  // return first name
23  string Employee::getFirstName() const
24  {
25     return firstName;
26  } // end function getFirstName
27
28  // set last name
29  void Employee::setLastName( const string &last )
30  {
31     lastName = last;
32  } // end function setLastName
33
34  // return last name
35  string Employee::getLastName() const
36  {
37     return lastName;
38  } // end function getLastName
39
40  // set social security number
41  void Employee::setSocialSecurityNumber( const string &ssn )
42  {
43     socialSecurityNumber = ssn; // should validate
44  } // end function setSocialSecurityNumber
45
46  // return social security number
47  string Employee::getSocialSecurityNumber() const
48  {
49     return socialSecurityNumber;
50  } // end function getSocialSecurityNumber
51
52  // print Employee's information (virtual, but not pure virtual)
53  void Employee::print() const
54  {
55     cout << getFirstName() << ' ' << getLastName()
56        << "\nsocial security number: " << getSocialSecurityNumber();
57  } // end function print
```

Fig. 12.10 | Employee class implementation file. (Part 2 of 2.)

The `virtual` function `print` (lines 53–57) provides an *implementation* that will be *overridden* in *each* of the derived classes. Each of these functions will, however, use the abstract class's version of `print` to print information *common to all classes* in the `Employee` hierarchy.

12.6.2 Creating Concrete Derived Class `SalariedEmployee`

Class `SalariedEmployee` (Figs. 12.11–12.12) derives from class `Employee` (line 9 of Fig. 12.11). The `public` member functions include a constructor that takes a first name, a last name, a social security number and a weekly salary as arguments (lines 12–13); a `virtual` destructor (line 14); a *set* function to assign a new nonnegative value to data member `weeklySalary` (line 16); a *get* function to return `weeklySalary`'s value (line 17); a `virtual` function `earnings` that calculates a `SalariedEmployee`'s earnings (line 20) and a `virtual` function `print` (line 21) that outputs the employee's type, namely, `"salaried employee: "` followed by employee-specific information produced by base class `Employee`'s `print` function and `SalariedEmployee`'s `getWeeklySalary` function.

```
1   // Fig. 12.11: SalariedEmployee.h
2   // SalariedEmployee class derived from Employee.
3   #ifndef SALARIED_H
4   #define SALARIED_H
5
6   #include <string> // C++ standard string class
7   #include "Employee.h" // Employee class definition
8
9   class SalariedEmployee : public Employee
10  {
11  public:
12     SalariedEmployee( const std::string &, const std::string &,
13        const std::string &, double = 0.0 );
14     virtual ~SalariedEmployee() { } // virtual destructor
15
16     void setWeeklySalary( double ); // set weekly salary
17     double getWeeklySalary() const; // return weekly salary
18
19     // keyword virtual signals intent to override
20     virtual double earnings() const override; // calculate earnings
21     virtual void print() const override; // print object
22  private:
23     double weeklySalary; // salary per week
24  }; // end class SalariedEmployee
25
26  #endif // SALARIED_H
```

Fig. 12.11 | `SalariedEmployee` class header.

SalariedEmployee Class Member-Function Definitions
Figure 12.12 contains the member-function definitions for `SalariedEmployee`. The class's constructor passes the first name, last name and social security number to the Employee constructor (line 11) to initialize the `private` data members that are inherited from the base class, but not directly accessible in the derived class. Function `earnings`

(lines 33–36) overrides pure virtual function earnings in Employee to provide a *concrete* implementation that returns the SalariedEmployee's weekly salary. If we did not define earnings, class SalariedEmployee would be an *abstract* class, and any attempt to instantiate a SalariedEmployee object would cause a compilation error. In class SalariedEmployee's header, we declared member functions earnings and print as virtual (lines 20–21 of Fig. 12.11)—actually, placing the virtual keyword before these member functions is *redundant*. We defined them as virtual in base class Employee, so they remain virtual functions throughout the class hierarchy. Explicitly declaring such functions virtual at every level of the hierarchy promotes program clarity. Not declaring earnings as pure virtual signals our intent to provide an implementation in this concrete class.

```cpp
1   // Fig. 12.12: SalariedEmployee.cpp
2   // SalariedEmployee class member-function definitions.
3   #include <iostream>
4   #include <stdexcept>
5   #include "SalariedEmployee.h" // SalariedEmployee class definition
6   using namespace std;
7
8   // constructor
9   SalariedEmployee::SalariedEmployee( const string &first,
10     const string &last, const string &ssn, double salary )
11     : Employee( first, last, ssn )
12  {
13     setWeeklySalary( salary );
14  } // end SalariedEmployee constructor
15
16  // set salary
17  void SalariedEmployee::setWeeklySalary( double salary )
18  {
19     if ( salary >= 0.0 )
20        weeklySalary = salary;
21     else
22        throw invalid_argument( "Weekly salary must be >= 0.0" );
23  } // end function setWeeklySalary
24
25  // return salary
26  double SalariedEmployee::getWeeklySalary() const
27  {
28     return weeklySalary;
29  } // end function getWeeklySalary
30
31  // calculate earnings;
32  // override pure virtual function earnings in Employee
33  double SalariedEmployee::earnings() const
34  {
35     return getWeeklySalary();
36  } // end function earnings
37
38  // print SalariedEmployee's information
39  void SalariedEmployee::print() const
40  {
```

Fig. 12.12 | SalariedEmployee class implementation file. (Part 1 of 2.)

```
41        cout << "salaried employee: ";
42        Employee::print(); // reuse abstract base-class print function
43        cout << "\nweekly salary: " << getWeeklySalary();
44    } // end function print
```

Fig. 12.12 | SalariedEmployee class implementation file. (Part 2 of 2.)

Function print of class SalariedEmployee (lines 39–44 of Fig. 12.12) overrides Employee function print. If class SalariedEmployee did not override print, Salaried-Employee would inherit the Employee version of print. In that case, SalariedEmployee's print function would simply return the employee's full name and social security number, which does not adequately represent a SalariedEmployee. To print a SalariedEmployee's complete information, the derived class's print function outputs "salaried employee: " followed by the base-class Employee-specific information (i.e., first name, last name and social security number) printed by *invoking the base class's print function* using the scope resolution operator (line 42)—this is a nice example of code reuse. Without the scope resolution operator, the print call would cause *infinite recursion*. The output produced by SalariedEmployee's print function also contains the employee's weekly salary obtained by invoking the class's getWeeklySalary function.

12.6.3 Creating Concrete Derived Class CommissionEmployee

Class CommissionEmployee (Figs. 12.13–12.14) derives from Employee (Fig. 12.13, line 9). The member-function implementations (Fig. 12.14) include a constructor (lines 9–15) that takes a first name, last name, social security number, sales amount and commission rate; *set* functions (lines 18–24 and 33–39) to assign new values to data members commissionRate and grossSales, respectively; *get* functions (lines 27–30 and 42–45) that retrieve their values; function earnings (lines 48–51) to calculate a CommissionEmployee's earnings; and function print (lines 54–60) to output the employee's type, namely, "commission employee: " and employee-specific information. The constructor passes the first name, last name and social security number to the Employee constructor (line 11) to initialize Employee's private data members. Function print calls base-class function print (line 57) to display the Employee-specific information.

```
 1    // Fig. 12.13: CommissionEmployee.h
 2    // CommissionEmployee class derived from Employee.
 3    #ifndef COMMISSION_H
 4    #define COMMISSION_H
 5
 6    #include <string> // C++ standard string class
 7    #include "Employee.h" // Employee class definition
 8
 9    class CommissionEmployee : public Employee
10    {
11    public:
12       CommissionEmployee( const std::string &, const std::string &,
13          const std::string &, double = 0.0, double = 0.0 );
```

Fig. 12.13 | CommissionEmployee class header. (Part 1 of 2.)

```
14       virtual ~CommissionEmployee() { } // virtual destructor
15
16       void setCommissionRate( double ); // set commission rate
17       double getCommissionRate() const; // return commission rate
18
19       void setGrossSales( double ); // set gross sales amount
20       double getGrossSales() const; // return gross sales amount
21
22       // keyword virtual signals intent to override
23       virtual double earnings() const override; // calculate earnings
24       virtual void print() const override; // print object
25    private:
26       double grossSales; // gross weekly sales
27       double commissionRate; // commission percentage
28    }; // end class CommissionEmployee
29
30    #endif // COMMISSION_H
```

Fig. 12.13 | CommissionEmployee class header. (Part 2 of 2.)

```
1    // Fig. 12.14: CommissionEmployee.cpp
2    // CommissionEmployee class member-function definitions.
3    #include <iostream>
4    #include <stdexcept>
5    #include "CommissionEmployee.h" // CommissionEmployee class definition
6    using namespace std;
7
8    // constructor
9    CommissionEmployee::CommissionEmployee( const string &first,
10      const string &last, const string &ssn, double sales, double rate )
11      : Employee( first, last, ssn )
12   {
13      setGrossSales( sales );
14      setCommissionRate( rate );
15   } // end CommissionEmployee constructor
16
17   // set gross sales amount
18   void CommissionEmployee::setGrossSales( double sales )
19   {
20      if ( sales >= 0.0 )
21         grossSales = sales;
22      else
23         throw invalid_argument( "Gross sales must be >= 0.0" );
24   } // end function setGrossSales
25
26   // return gross sales amount
27   double CommissionEmployee::getGrossSales() const
28   {
29      return grossSales;
30   } // end function getGrossSales
31
```

Fig. 12.14 | CommissionEmployee class implementation file. (Part 1 of 2.)

```
32   // set commission rate
33   void CommissionEmployee::setCommissionRate( double rate )
34   {
35      if ( rate > 0.0 && rate < 1.0 )
36         commissionRate = rate;
37      else
38         throw invalid_argument( "Commission rate must be > 0.0 and < 1.0" );
39   } // end function setCommissionRate
40
41   // return commission rate
42   double CommissionEmployee::getCommissionRate() const
43   {
44      return commissionRate;
45   } // end function getCommissionRate
46
47   // calculate earnings; override pure virtual function earnings in Employee
48   double CommissionEmployee::earnings() const
49   {
50      return getCommissionRate() * getGrossSales();
51   } // end function earnings
52
53   // print CommissionEmployee's information
54   void CommissionEmployee::print() const
55   {
56      cout << "commission employee: ";
57      Employee::print(); // code reuse
58      cout << "\ngross sales: " << getGrossSales()
59         << "; commission rate: " << getCommissionRate();
60   } // end function print
```

Fig. 12.14 | CommissionEmployee class implementation file. (Part 2 of 2.)

12.6.4 Creating Indirect Concrete Derived Class BasePlusCommissionEmployee

Class BasePlusCommissionEmployee (Figs. 12.15–12.16) directly inherits from class CommissionEmployee (line 9 of Fig. 12.15) and therefore is an *indirect* derived class of class Employee. Class BasePlusCommissionEmployee's member-function implementations include a constructor (lines 9–15 of Fig. 12.16) that takes as arguments a first name, a last name, a social security number, a sales amount, a commission rate *and* a base salary. It then passes the first name, last name, social security number, sales amount and commission rate to the CommissionEmployee constructor (line 12) to initialize the inherited members. BasePlusCommissionEmployee also contains a *set* function (lines 18–24) to assign a new value to data member baseSalary and a *get* function (lines 27–30) to return baseSalary's value. Function earnings (lines 34–37) calculates a BasePlusCommissionEmployee's earnings. Line 36 in function earnings calls base-class CommissionEmployee's earnings function to calculate the commission-based portion of the employee's earnings. This is another nice example of code reuse. BasePlusCommissionEmployee's print function (lines 40–45) outputs "base-salaried", followed by the output of base-class CommissionEmployee's print function (another example of code reuse), then the base salary. The resulting output begins with "base-salaried commission employee: " followed by the rest of the Base-

PlusCommissionEmployee's information. Recall that CommissionEmployee's print displays the employee's first name, last name and social security number by invoking the print function of its base class (i.e., Employee)—yet another example of code reuse. BasePlusCommissionEmployee's print initiates a chain of functions calls that spans *all three levels* of the Employee hierarchy.

```
1   // Fig. 12.15: BasePlusCommissionEmployee.h
2   // BasePlusCommissionEmployee class derived from CommissionEmployee.
3   #ifndef BASEPLUS_H
4   #define BASEPLUS_H
5
6   #include <string> // C++ standard string class
7   #include "CommissionEmployee.h" // CommissionEmployee class definition
8
9   class BasePlusCommissionEmployee : public CommissionEmployee
10  {
11  public:
12     BasePlusCommissionEmployee( const std::string &, const std::string &,
13        const std::string &, double = 0.0, double = 0.0, double = 0.0 );
14     virtual ~CommissionEmployee() { } // virtual destructor
15
16     void setBaseSalary( double ); // set base salary
17     double getBaseSalary() const; // return base salary
18
19     // keyword virtual signals intent to override
20     virtual double earnings() const override; // calculate earnings
21     virtual void print() const override; // print object
22  private:
23     double baseSalary; // base salary per week
24  }; // end class BasePlusCommissionEmployee
25
26  #endif // BASEPLUS_H
```

Fig. 12.15 | BasePlusCommissionEmployee class header.

```
1   // Fig. 12.16: BasePlusCommissionEmployee.cpp
2   // BasePlusCommissionEmployee member-function definitions.
3   #include <iostream>
4   #include <stdexcept>
5   #include "BasePlusCommissionEmployee.h"
6   using namespace std;
7
8   // constructor
9   BasePlusCommissionEmployee::BasePlusCommissionEmployee(
10     const string &first, const string &last, const string &ssn,
11     double sales, double rate, double salary )
12     : CommissionEmployee( first, last, ssn, sales, rate )
13  {
14     setBaseSalary( salary ); // validate and store base salary
15  } // end BasePlusCommissionEmployee constructor
16
```

Fig. 12.16 | BasePlusCommissionEmployee class implementation file. (Part 1 of 2.)

```
17   // set base salary
18   void BasePlusCommissionEmployee::setBaseSalary( double salary )
19   {
20      if ( salary >= 0.0 )
21         baseSalary = salary;
22      else
23         throw invalid_argument( "Salary must be >= 0.0" );
24   } // end function setBaseSalary
25
26   // return base salary
27   double BasePlusCommissionEmployee::getBaseSalary() const
28   {
29      return baseSalary;
30   } // end function getBaseSalary
31
32   // calculate earnings;
33   // override virtual function earnings in CommissionEmployee
34   double BasePlusCommissionEmployee::earnings() const
35   {
36      return getBaseSalary() + CommissionEmployee::earnings();
37   } // end function earnings
38
39   // print BasePlusCommissionEmployee's information
40   void BasePlusCommissionEmployee::print() const
41   {
42      cout << "base-salaried ";
43      CommissionEmployee::print(); // code reuse
44      cout << "; base salary: " << getBaseSalary();
45   } // end function print
```

Fig. 12.16 | BasePlusCommissionEmployee class implementation file. (Part 2 of 2.)

12.6.5 Demonstrating Polymorphic Processing

To test our Employee hierarchy, the program in Fig. 12.17 creates an object of each of the three concrete classes SalariedEmployee, CommissionEmployee and BasePlusCommissionEmployee. The program manipulates these objects, first with *static binding*, then *polymorphically*, using a vector of Employee pointers. Lines 22–27 create objects of each of the three concrete Employee derived classes. Lines 32–38 output each Employee's information and earnings. Each member-function invocation in lines 32–37 is an example of *static binding*—at *compile time*, because we are using *name handles* (not *pointers* or *references* that could be set at *execution time*), the *compiler* can identify each object's type to determine which print and earnings functions are called.

```
1   // Fig. 12.17: fig12_17.cpp
2   // Processing Employee derived-class objects individually
3   // and polymorphically using dynamic binding.
4   #include <iostream>
5   #include <iomanip>
6   #include <vector>
```

Fig. 12.17 | Employee class hierarchy driver program. (Part 1 of 4.)

```
7   #include "Employee.h"
8   #include "SalariedEmployee.h"
9   #include "CommissionEmployee.h"
10  #include "BasePlusCommissionEmployee.h"
11  using namespace std;
12
13  void virtualViaPointer( const Employee * const ); // prototype
14  void virtualViaReference( const Employee & ); // prototype
15
16  int main()
17  {
18     // set floating-point output formatting
19     cout << fixed << setprecision( 2 );
20
21     // create derived-class objects
22     SalariedEmployee salariedEmployee(
23        "John", "Smith", "111-11-1111", 800 );
24     CommissionEmployee commissionEmployee(
25        "Sue", "Jones", "333-33-3333", 10000, .06 );
26     BasePlusCommissionEmployee basePlusCommissionEmployee(
27        "Bob", "Lewis", "444-44-4444", 5000, .04, 300 );
28
29     cout << "Employees processed individually using static binding:\n\n";
30
31     // output each Employee's information and earnings using static binding
32     salariedEmployee.print();
33     cout << "\nearned $" << salariedEmployee.earnings() << "\n\n";
34     commissionEmployee.print();
35     cout << "\nearned $" << commissionEmployee.earnings() << "\n\n";
36     basePlusCommissionEmployee.print();
37     cout << "\nearned $" << basePlusCommissionEmployee.earnings()
38        << "\n\n";
39
40     // create vector of three base-class pointers
41     vector< Employee * > employees( 3 );
42
43     // initialize vector with pointers to Employees
44     employees[ 0 ] = &salariedEmployee;
45     employees[ 1 ] = &commissionEmployee;
46     employees[ 2 ] = &basePlusCommissionEmployee;
47
48     cout << "Employees processed polymorphically via dynamic binding:\n\n";
49
50     // call virtualViaPointer to print each Employee's information
51     // and earnings using dynamic binding
52     cout << "Virtual function calls made off base-class pointers:\n\n";
53
54     for ( const Employee *employeePtr : employees )
55        virtualViaPointer( employeePtr );
56
57     // call virtualViaReference to print each Employee's information
58     // and earnings using dynamic binding
59     cout << "Virtual function calls made off base-class references:\n\n";
```

Fig. 12.17 | Employee class hierarchy driver program. (Part 2 of 4.)

```
60
61     for ( const Employee *employeePtr : employees )
62        virtualViaReference( *employeePtr ); // note dereferencing
63  } // end main
64
65  // call Employee virtual functions print and earnings off a
66  // base-class pointer using dynamic binding
67  void virtualViaPointer( const Employee * const baseClassPtr )
68  {
69     baseClassPtr->print();
70     cout << "\nearned $" << baseClassPtr->earnings() << "\n\n";
71  } // end function virtualViaPointer
72
73  // call Employee virtual functions print and earnings off a
74  // base-class reference using dynamic binding
75  void virtualViaReference( const Employee &baseClassRef )
76  {
77     baseClassRef.print();
78     cout << "\nearned $" << baseClassRef.earnings() << "\n\n";
79  } // end function virtualViaReference
```

```
Employees processed individually using static binding:

salaried employee: John Smith
social security number: 111-11-1111
weekly salary: 800.00
earned $800.00

commission employee: Sue Jones
social security number: 333-33-3333
gross sales: 10000.00; commission rate: 0.06
earned $600.00

base-salaried commission employee: Bob Lewis
social security number: 444-44-4444
gross sales: 5000.00; commission rate: 0.04; base salary: 300.00
earned $500.00

Employees processed polymorphically using dynamic binding:

Virtual function calls made off base-class pointers:

salaried employee: John Smith
social security number: 111-11-1111
weekly salary: 800.00
earned $800.00

commission employee: Sue Jones
social security number: 333-33-3333
gross sales: 10000.00; commission rate: 0.06
earned $600.00

base-salaried commission employee: Bob Lewis
social security number: 444-44-4444
gross sales: 5000.00; commission rate: 0.04; base salary: 300.00
earned $500.00
```

Fig. 12.17 | Employee class hierarchy driver program. (Part 3 of 4.)

```
Virtual function calls made off base-class references:

salaried employee: John Smith
social security number: 111-11-1111
weekly salary: 800.00
earned $800.00

commission employee: Sue Jones
social security number: 333-33-3333
gross sales: 10000.00; commission rate: 0.06
earned $600.00

base-salaried commission employee: Bob Lewis
social security number: 444-44-4444
gross sales: 5000.00; commission rate: 0.04; base salary: 300.00
earned $500.00
```

Fig. 12.17 | Employee class hierarchy driver program. (Part 4 of 4.)

Line 41 creates the vector employees, which contains three Employee pointers. Line 44 aims employees[0] at object salariedEmployee. Line 45 aims employees[1] at object commissionEmployee. Line 46 aims employee[2] at object basePlusCommissionEmployee. The compiler allows these assignments, because a SalariedEmployee *is an* Employee, a CommissionEmployee *is an* Employee and a BasePlusCommissionEmployee *is an* Employee. Therefore, we can assign the addresses of SalariedEmployee, CommissionEmployee and BasePlusCommissionEmployee objects to base-class Employee pointers, even though Employee is an *abstract* class.

Lines 54–55 traverse vector employees and invoke function virtualViaPointer (lines 67–71) for each element in employees. Function virtualViaPointer receives in parameter baseClassPtr the address stored in an employees element. Each call to virtualViaPointer uses baseClassPtr to invoke virtual functions print (line 69) and earnings (line 70). Function virtualViaPointer does *not* contain *any* SalariedEmployee, CommissionEmployee or BasePlusCommissionEmployee type information. The function knows *only* about base-class type Employee. Therefore, the compiler *cannot know* which concrete class's functions to call through baseClassPtr. Yet at execution time, each virtual-function invocation *correctly* calls the function on the object to which baseClassPtr currently points. The output illustrates that *the appropriate functions for each class are indeed invoked* and that each object's proper information is displayed. For instance, the weekly salary is displayed for the SalariedEmployee, and the gross sales are displayed for the CommissionEmployee and BasePlusCommissionEmployee. Also, obtaining the earnings of each Employee polymorphically in line 70 produces the same results as obtaining these employees' earnings via *static binding* in lines 33, 35 and 37. All virtual function calls to print and earnings are resolved at *runtime* with *dynamic binding*.

Finally, lines 61–62 traverse employees and invoke function virtualViaReference (lines 75–79) for each vector element. Function virtualViaReference receives in its parameter baseClassRef (of type const Employee &) a *reference* to the object obtained by *dereferencing the pointer* stored in each employees element (line 62). Each call to virtualViaReference invokes virtual functions print (line 77) and earnings (line 78) via baseClassRef to demonstrate that *polymorphic processing occurs with base-class references as well.*

Each virtual-function invocation calls the function on the object to which baseClassRef refers at runtime. This is another example of *dynamic binding*. The output produced using base-class references is identical to the output produced using base-class pointers.

12.7 (Optional) Polymorphism, Virtual Functions and Dynamic Binding "Under the Hood"

C++ makes polymorphism easy to program. It's certainly possible to program for polymorphism in non-object-oriented languages such as C, but doing so requires complex and potentially dangerous pointer manipulations. This section discusses how C++ can implement polymorphism, virtual functions and dynamic binding internally. This will give you a solid understanding of how these capabilities really work. More importantly, it will help you appreciate the *overhead* of polymorphism—in terms of additional *memory consumption* and *processor time*. This can help you determine when to use polymorphism and when to avoid it. C++ Standard Library classes like array and vector are implemented *without* polymorphism and virtual functions to avoid the associated execution-time overhead and achieve optimal performance.

First, we'll explain the data structures that the compiler builds at *compile time* to support polymorphism at execution time. You'll see that polymorphism is accomplished through three levels of pointers, i.e., *triple indirection*. Then we'll show how an executing program uses these data structures to execute virtual functions and achieve the *dynamic binding* associated with polymorphism. Our discussion explains one *possible* implementation; this is not a language requirement.

When C++ compiles a class that has one or more virtual functions, it builds a **virtual function table** (*vtable*) for that class. The *vtable* contains pointers to the class's virtual functions. Just as the name of a built-in array contains the address in memory of the array's first element, a **pointer to a function** contains the starting address in memory of the code that performs the function's task. An executing program uses the *vtable* to select the proper function implementation each time a virtual function of that class is called. The leftmost column of Fig. 12.18 illustrates the *vtables* for the classes Employee, SalariedEmployee, CommissionEmployee and BasePlusCommissionEmployee.

Employee *Class* vtable

In the Employee class *vtable*, the first function pointer is set to 0 (i.e., nullptr), because function earnings is a *pure* virtual function and therefore *lacks an implementation*. The second function pointer points to function print, which displays the employee's full name and social security number. [*Note:* We've abbreviated the output of each print function in this figure to conserve space.] Any class that has one or more null pointers in its *vtable* is an *abstract* class. Classes without any null *vtable* pointers (such as SalariedEmployee, CommissionEmployee and BasePlusCommissionEmployee) are *concrete* classes.

SalariedEmployee *Class* vtable

Class SalariedEmployee overrides function earnings to return the employee's weekly salary, so the function pointer points to the earnings function of class SalariedEmployee. SalariedEmployee also overrides print, so the corresponding function pointer points to the SalariedEmployee member function that prints "salaried employee: " followed by the employee's name, social security number and weekly salary.

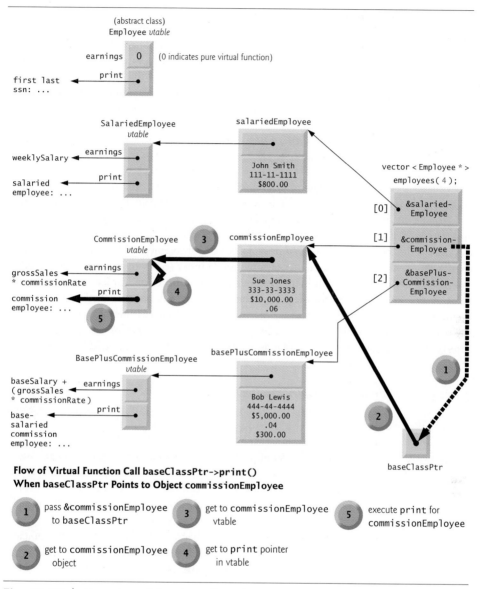

**Flow of Virtual Function Call baseClassPtr->print()
When baseClassPtr Points to Object commissionEmployee**

1 pass &commissionEmployee to baseClassPtr

2 get to commissionEmployee object

3 get to commissionEmployee vtable

4 get to print pointer in vtable

5 execute print for commissionEmployee

Fig. 12.18 | How virtual function calls work.

CommissionEmployee *Class* vtable

The earnings function pointer in the *vtable* for class CommissionEmployee points to CommissionEmployee's earnings function that returns the employee's gross sales multiplied by the commission rate. The print function pointer points to the CommissionEmployee version of the function, which prints the employee's type, name, social security number, commission rate and gross sales. As in class HourlyEmployee, both functions override the functions in class Employee.

BasePlusCommissionEmployee Class vtable

The earnings function pointer in the *vtable* for class BasePlusCommissionEmployee points to the BasePlusCommissionEmployee's earnings function, which returns the employee's base salary plus gross sales multiplied by commission rate. The print function pointer points to the BasePlusCommissionEmployee version of the function, which prints the employee's base salary plus the type, name, social security number, commission rate and gross sales. Both functions override the functions in class CommissionEmployee.

Inheriting Concrete virtual Functions

In our Employee case study, each *concrete* class provides its own implementation for virtual functions earnings and print. You've learned that each class which inherits *directly* from abstract base class Employee *must implement earnings* in order to be a *concrete* class, because earnings is a pure virtual function. These classes do *not* need to implement function print, however, to be considered concrete—print is *not a pure* virtual function and derived classes can inherit class Employee's implementation of print. Furthermore, class BasePlusCommissionEmployee does *not* have to implement either function print or earnings—both function implementations can be inherited from concrete class CommissionEmployee. If a class in our hierarchy were to inherit function implementations in this manner, the *vtable* pointers for these functions would simply point to the function implementation that was being inherited. For example, if BasePlusCommissionEmployee did not override earnings, the earnings function pointer in the *vtable* for class BasePlusCommissionEmployee would point to the same earnings function as the *vtable* for class CommissionEmployee points to.

Three Levels of Pointers to Implement Polymorphism

Polymorphism is accomplished through an elegant data structure involving *three levels of pointers*. We've discussed one level—the function pointers in the *vtable*. These point to the actual functions that execute when a virtual function is invoked.

Now we consider the second level of pointers. *Whenever an object of a class with one or more virtual functions is instantiated, the compiler attaches to the object a pointer to the* vtable *for that class.* This pointer is normally at the front of the object, but it isn't required to be implemented that way. In Fig. 12.18, these pointers are associated with the objects created in Fig. 12.17 (one object for each of the types SalariedEmployee, CommissionEmployee and BasePlusCommissionEmployee). The diagram displays each of the object's data member values. For example, the salariedEmployee object contains a pointer to the SalariedEmployee *vtable*; the object also contains the values John Smith, 111-11-1111 and $800.00.

The third level of pointers simply contains the handles to the objects that receive the virtual function calls. The handles in this level may also be *references*. Fig. 12.18 depicts the vector employees that contains Employee *pointers*.

Now let's see how a typical virtual function call executes. Consider the call baseClassPtr->print() in function virtualViaPointer (line 69 of Fig. 12.17). Assume that baseClassPtr contains employees[1] (i.e., the address of object commissionEmployee in employees). When the compiler compiles this statement, it determines that the call is indeed being made via a *base-class pointer* and that print is a virtual function.

The compiler determines that print is the *second* entry in each of the *vtables*. To locate this entry, the compiler notes that it will need to skip the first entry. Thus, the compiler compiles an **offset** or **displacement** into the table of machine-language object-code pointers to find the code that will execute the virtual function call. The size in bytes of the offset depends on the number of bytes used to represent a function pointer on an individual platform. For example, on a 32-bit platform, a pointer is typically stored in four bytes, whereas on a 64-bit platform, a pointer is typically stored in eight bytes. We assume four bytes for this discussion.

The compiler generates code that performs the following operations [*Note:* The numbers in the list correspond to the circled numbers in Fig. 12.18]:

1. Select the ith entry of employees (in this case, the address of object commission-Employee), and pass it as an argument to function virtualViaPointer. This sets parameter baseClassPtr to point to commissionEmployee.

2. *Dereference* that pointer to get to the commissionEmployee object—which, as you recall, begins with a pointer to the CommissionEmployee *vtable*.

3. *Dereference* commissionEmployee's *vtable* pointer to get to the CommissionEmployee *vtable*.

4. Skip the offset of four bytes to select the print function pointer.

5. *Dereference* the print function pointer to form the "name" of the actual function to execute, and use the function call operator () to execute the appropriate print function, which in this case prints the employee's type, name, social security number, gross sales and commission rate.

Fig. 12.18's data structures may appear to be complex, but this complexity is managed by the compiler and *hidden* from you, making polymorphic programming straightforward. The pointer dereferencing operations and memory accesses that occur on every virtual function call require some additional execution time. The *vtables* and the *vtable* pointers added to the objects require some additional memory.

Performance Tip 12.1
Polymorphism, as typically implemented with virtual functions and dynamic binding in C++, is efficient. You can use these capabilities with nominal impact on performance.

Performance Tip 12.2
Virtual functions and dynamic binding enable polymorphic programming as an alternative to switch logic programming. Optimizing compilers normally generate polymorphic code that's nearly as efficient as hand-coded switch-based logic. Polymorphism's overhead is acceptable for most applications. In some situations—such as real-time applications with stringent performance requirements—polymorphism's overhead may be too high.

12.8 Case Study: Payroll System Using Polymorphism and Runtime Type Information with Downcasting, dynamic_cast, typeid and type_info

Recall from the problem statement at the beginning of Section 12.6 that, for the current pay period, our fictitious company has decided to reward BasePlusCommissionEmployees by adding 10 percent to their base salaries. When processing Employee objects polymorphically in Section 12.6.5, we did not need to worry about the "specifics." Now, however, to adjust the base salaries of BasePlusCommissionEmployees, we have to determine the *specific type* of each Employee object *at execution time*, then act appropriately. This section demonstrates the powerful capabilities of **runtime type information (RTTI)** and **dynamic casting**, which enable a program to determine an object's type at execution time and act on that object accordingly.[1]

Figure 12.19 uses the Employee hierarchy developed in Section 12.6 and increases by 10 percent the base salary of each BasePlusCommissionEmployee. Line 21 declares three-element vector employees that stores pointers to Employee objects. Lines 24–29 populate the vector with the *addresses* of *dynamically allocated* objects of classes SalariedEmployee (Figs. 12.11–12.12), CommissionEmployee (Figs. 12.13–12.14) and BasePlusCommissionEmployee (Figs. 12.15–12.16). Lines 32–52 iterate through the employees vector and display each Employee's information by invoking member function print (line 34). Recall that because print is declared virtual in *base class* Employee, the system invokes the appropriate *derived-class* object's print function.

```
1   // Fig. 12.19: fig12_19.cpp
2   // Demonstrating downcasting and runtime type information.
3   // NOTE: You may need to enable RTTI on your compiler
4   // before you can compile this application.
5   #include <iostream>
6   #include <iomanip>
7   #include <vector>
8   #include <typeinfo>
9   #include "Employee.h"
10  #include "SalariedEmployee.h"
11  #include "CommissionEmployee.h"
12  #include "BasePlusCommissionEmployee.h"
13  using namespace std;
14
15  int main()
16  {
17     // set floating-point output formatting
18     cout << fixed << setprecision( 2 );
19
20     // create vector of three base-class pointers
21     vector < Employee * > employees( 3 );
22
23     // initialize vector with various kinds of Employees
24     employees[ 0 ] = new SalariedEmployee(
25        "John", "Smith", "111-11-1111", 800 );
26     employees[ 1 ] = new CommissionEmployee(
27        "Sue", "Jones", "333-33-3333", 10000, .06 );
28     employees[ 2 ] = new BasePlusCommissionEmployee(
29        "Bob", "Lewis", "444-44-4444", 5000, .04, 300 );
30
```

Fig. 12.19 | Demonstrating downcasting and runtime type information. (Part 1 of 2.)

---

1. Some compilers require that RTTI be enabled before it can be used in a program. The compilers we used for testing this book's examples—GNU C++ 4.7, Visual C++ 2012 and Xcode 4.5 LLVM—each enable RTTI by default.

```
31      // polymorphically process each element in vector employees
32      for ( Employee *employeePtr : employees )
33      {
34         employeePtr->print(); // output employee information
35         cout << endl;
36
37         // attempt to downcast pointer
38         BasePlusCommissionEmployee *derivedPtr =
39            dynamic_cast < BasePlusCommissionEmployee * >( employeePtr );
40
41         // determine whether element points to a BasePlusCommissionEmployee
42         if ( derivedPtr != nullptr ) // true for "is a" relationship
43         {
44            double oldBaseSalary = derivedPtr->getBaseSalary();
45            cout << "old base salary: $" << oldBaseSalary << endl;
46            derivedPtr->setBaseSalary( 1.10 * oldBaseSalary );
47            cout << "new base salary with 10% increase is: $"
48               << derivedPtr->getBaseSalary() << endl;
49         } // end if
50
51         cout << "earned $" << employeePtr->earnings() << "\n\n";
52      } // end for
53
54      // release objects pointed to by vector's elements
55      for ( const Employee *employeePtr : employees )
56      {
57         // output class name
58         cout << "deleting object of "
59            << typeid( *employeePtr ).name() << endl;
60
61         delete employeePtr;
62      } // end for
63   } // end main
```

```
salaried employee: John Smith
social security number: 111-11-1111
weekly salary: 800.00
earned $800.00

commission employee: Sue Jones
social security number: 333-33-3333
gross sales: 10000.00; commission rate: 0.06
earned $600.00

base-salaried commission employee: Bob Lewis
social security number: 444-44-4444
gross sales: 5000.00; commission rate: 0.04; base salary: 300.00
old base salary: $300.00
new base salary with 10% increase is: $330.00
earned $530.00

deleting object of class SalariedEmployee
deleting object of class CommissionEmployee
deleting object of class BasePlusCommissionEmployee
```

Fig. 12.19 | Demonstrating downcasting and runtime type information. (Part 2 of 2.)

Determining an Object's Type with dynamic_cast

In this example, as we encounter a BasePlusCommissionEmployee object, we wish to increase its base salary by 10 percent. Since we process the Employees polymorphically, we cannot (with the techniques you've learned so far) be certain as to which type of Employee is being manipulated at any given time. This creates a problem, because BasePlusCommission-Employee employees *must* be identified when we encounter them so they can receive the 10 percent salary increase. To accomplish this, we use operator **dynamic_cast** (line 39) to determine whether the current Employee's type is BasePlusCommissionEmployee. This is the *downcast* operation we referred to in Section 12.3.3. Lines 38–39 *dynamically downcast* employeePtr from type Employee * to type BasePlusCommissionEmployee *. If employeePtr points to an object that *is a* BasePlusCommissionEmployee object, then that object's *address* is assigned to derived-class pointer derivedPtr; otherwise, nullptr is assigned to derivedPtr. Note that dynamic_cast rather than static_cast is *required* here to perform type checking on the underlying object—a static_cast would simply cast the Employee * to a BasePlusCommissionEmployee * regardless of the underlying object's type. With a static_cast, the program would attempt to increase *every* Employee's base salary, resulting in undefined behavior for each object that is not a BasePlusCommissionEmployee.

If the value returned by the dynamic_cast operator in lines 38–39 *is not* nullptr, the object *is* the correct type, and the if statement (lines 42–49) performs the special processing required for the BasePlusCommissionEmployee object. Lines 44, 46 and 48 invoke BasePlusCommissionEmployee functions getBaseSalary and setBaseSalary to retrieve and update the employee's salary.

*Calculating the Current **Employee**'s Earnings*

Line 51 invokes member function earnings on the object to which employeePtr points. Recall that earnings is declared virtual in the base class, so the program invokes the derived-class object's earnings function—another example of *dynamic binding*.

*Displaying an **Employee**'s Type*

Lines 55–62 display each employee's *object type* and uses the delete operator to deallocate the dynamic memory to which each vector element points. Operator **typeid** (line 59) returns a *reference* to an object of class **type_info** that contains the information about the type of its operand, including the name of that type. When invoked, type_info member function **name** (line 59) returns a pointer-based string containing the typeid argument's *type name* (e.g., "class BasePlusCommissionEmployee"). To use typeid, the program must include header **<typeinfo>** (line 8).

Portability Tip 12.1

The string returned by type_info member function name may vary by compiler.

*Compilation Errors That We Avoided By Using **dynamic_cast***

We avoid several compilation errors in this example by *downcasting* an Employee pointer to a BasePlusCommissionEmployee pointer (lines 38–39). If we remove the dynamic_cast from line 39 and attempt to assign the current Employee pointer directly to BasePlusCommissionEmployee pointer derivedPtr, we'll receive a compilation error. C++ does *not* allow a program to assign a base-class pointer to a derived-class pointer because the *is-a* relationship does *not* apply—a CommissionEmployee is *not* a BasePlusCommissionEmployee. The *is-a* relationship applies only between the derived class and its base classes, not vice versa.

Similarly, if lines 44, 46 and 48 used the current base-class pointer from employees, rather than derived-class pointer derivedPtr, to invoke derived-class-only functions get-BaseSalary and setBaseSalary, we would receive a compilation error at each of these lines. As you learned in Section 12.3.3, attempting to invoke *derived-class-only functions* through a *base-class pointer* is *not* allowed. Although lines 44, 46 and 48 execute only if commissionPtr is not nullptr (i.e., if the cast *can* be performed), we *cannot* attempt to invoke derived-class BasePlusCommissionEmployee functions getBaseSalary and setBaseSalary on the base-class Employee pointer. Recall that, using a base class Employee pointer, we can invoke only functions found in base class Employee—earnings, print and Employee's *get* and *set* functions.

12.9 Wrap-Up

In this chapter we discussed polymorphism, which enables us to "program in the general" rather than "program in the specific," and we showed how this makes programs more extensible. We began with an example of how polymorphism would allow a screen manager to display several "space" objects. We then demonstrated how base-class and derived-class pointers can be aimed at base-class and derived-class objects. We said that aiming base-class pointers at base-class objects is natural, as is aiming derived-class pointers at derived-class objects. Aiming base-class pointers at derived-class objects is also natural because a derived-class object *is an* object of its base class. You learned why aiming derived-class pointers at base-class objects is dangerous and why the compiler disallows such assignments. We introduced virtual functions, which enable the proper functions to be called when objects at various levels of an inheritance hierarchy are referenced (at execution time) via base-class pointers or references. This is known as dynamic binding or late binding. We discussed virtual destructors, and how they ensure that all appropriate destructors in an inheritance hierarchy run on a derived-class object when that object is deleted via a base-class pointer or reference. We then discussed pure virtual functions and abstract classes (classes with one or more pure virtual functions). You learned that abstract classes cannot be used to instantiate objects, while concrete classes can. We then demonstrated using abstract classes in an inheritance hierarchy. You learned how polymorphism works "under the hood" with *vtables* that are created by the compiler. We used runtime type information (RTTI) and dynamic casting to determine the type of an object at execution time and act on that object accordingly. We also used the typeid operator to get a type_info object containing a given object's type information.

In the next chapter, we discuss many of C++'s I/O capabilities and demonstrate several stream manipulators that perform various formatting tasks.

Summary

Section 12.1 Introduction
- Polymorphism (p. 552) enables us to "program in the general" rather than "program in the specific."
- Polymorphism enables us to write programs that process objects of classes that are part of the same class hierarchy as if they were all objects of the hierarchy's base class.

- With polymorphism, we can design and implement systems that are easily extensible—new classes can be added with little or no modification to the general portions of the program. The only parts of a program that must be altered to accommodate new classes are those that require direct knowledge of the new classes that you add to the hierarchy.

Section 12.2 Introduction to Polymorphism: Polymorphic Video Game
- With polymorphism, one function call can cause different actions to occur, depending on the type of the object on which the function is invoked.
- This makes it possible to design and implement more extensible systems. Programs can be written to process objects of types that may not exist when the program is under development.

Section 12.3 Relationships Among Objects in an Inheritance Hierarchy
- C++ enables polymorphism—the ability for objects of different classes related by inheritance to respond differently to the same member-function call.
- Polymorphism is implemented via virtual functions (p. 560) and dynamic binding (p. 561).
- When a base-class pointer or reference is used to call a virtual function, C++ chooses the correct overridden function in the appropriate derived class associated with the object.
- If a virtual function is called by referencing a specific object by name and using the dot member-selection operator, the reference is resolved at compile time (this is called static binding; p. 561); the virtual function that is called is the one defined for the class of that particular object.
- Derived classes can override a base-class virtual function if necessary, but if they do not, the base class's implementation is used.
- Declare the base-class destructor virtual (p. 566) if the class contains virtual functions. This makes all derived-class destructors virtual, even though they do not have the same name as the base-class destructor. If an object in the hierarchy is destroyed explicitly by applying the delete operator to a base-class pointer to a derived-class object, the destructor for the appropriate class is called. After a derived-class destructor runs, the destructors for all of that class's base classes run all the way up the hierarchy.

Section 12.4 Type Fields and switch Statements
- Polymorphic programming with virtual functions can eliminate the need for switch logic. You can use the virtual function mechanism to perform the equivalent logic automatically, thus avoiding the kinds of errors typically associated with switch logic.

Section 12.5 Abstract Classes and Pure virtual Functions
- Abstract classes (p. 567) are typically used as base classes, so we refer to them as abstract base classes (p. 567). No objects of an abstract class may be instantiated.
- Classes from which objects can be instantiated are concrete classes (p. 567).
- You create an abstract class by declaring one or more pure virtual functions (p. 568) with pure specifiers (= 0) in their declarations.
- If a class is derived from a class with a pure virtual function and that derived class does not supply a definition for that pure virtual function, then that virtual function remains pure in the derived class. Consequently, the derived class is also an abstract class.
- Although we cannot instantiate objects of abstract base classes, we can declare pointers and references to objects of abstract base classes. Such pointers and references can be used to enable polymorphic manipulations of derived-class objects instantiated from concrete derived classes.

Section 12.7 (Optional) Polymorphism, Virtual Functions and Dynamic Binding "Under the Hood"

- Dynamic binding requires that at runtime, the call to a virtual member function be routed to the virtual function version appropriate for the class. A virtual function table called the *vtable* (p. 584) is implemented as an array containing function pointers. Each class with virtual functions has a *vtable*. For each virtual function in the class, the *vtable* has an entry containing a function pointer to the version of the virtual function to use for an object of that class. The virtual function to use for a particular class could be the function defined in that class, or it could be a function inherited either directly or indirectly from a base class higher in the hierarchy.

- When a base class provides a virtual member function, derived classes can override the virtual function, but they do not have to override it.

- Each object of a class with virtual functions contains a pointer to the *vtable* for that class. When a function call is made from a base-class pointer to a derived-class object, the appropriate function pointer in the *vtable* is obtained and dereferenced to complete the call at execution time.

- Any class that has one or more nullptr pointers in its *vtable* is an abstract class. Classes without any nullptr *vtable* pointers are concrete classes.

- New kinds of classes are regularly added to systems and accommodated by dynamic binding.

Section 12.8 Case Study: Payroll System Using Polymorphism and Runtime Type Information with Downcasting, **dynamic_cast**, **typeid** and **type_info**

- Operator dynamic_cast (p. 588) checks the type of the object to which a pointer points, then determines whether the type has an *is-a* relationship with the type to which the pointer is being converted. If so, dynamic_cast returns the object's address. If not, dynamic_cast returns nullptr.

- Operator typeid (p. 590) returns a reference to a type_info object (p. 590) that contains information about the operand's type, including the type name. To use typeid, the program must include header <typeinfo> (p. 590).

- When invoked, type_info member function name (p. 590) returns a pointer-based string that contains the name of the type that the type_info object represents.

- Operators dynamic_cast and typeid are part of C++'s runtime type information (RTTI; p. 588) feature, which allows a program to determine an object's type at runtime.

Self-Review Exercises

12.1 Fill in the blanks in each of the following statements:
   a) Treating a base-class object as a(n) _____ can cause errors.
   b) Polymorphism helps eliminate _____ logic.
   c) If a class contains at least one pure virtual function, it's a(n) _____ class.
   d) Classes from which objects can be instantiated are called _____ classes.
   e) Operator _____ can be used to downcast base-class pointers safely.
   f) Operator typeid returns a reference to a(n) _____ object.
   g) _____ involves using a base-class pointer or reference to invoke virtual functions on base-class and derived-class objects.
   h) Overridable functions are declared using keyword _____.
   i) Casting a base-class pointer to a derived-class pointer is called _____.

12.2 State whether each of the following is *true* or *false*. If *false*, explain why.
   a) Polymorphism enables "programming in the specific."
   b) With polymorphism, one function call can cause different actions to occur.
   c) Polymorphism is implemented only via dynamic binding.

  d) After the derived-class destructor runs, the destructors for all of that class's base classes
     run all the way up the hierarchy.
  e) Objects of an abstract class may be instantiated.

Answers to Self-Review Exercises

12.1   a) derived-class object. b) `switch`. c) abstract. d) concrete. e) `dynamic_cast`. f) `type_info`.
g) Polymorphism. h) `virtual`. i) downcasting.

12.2   a) False. Polymorphism enables "programming in the general". b) True. c) False. Polymorphism is implemented via virtual functions and dynamic binding. d) True. e) False. Objects of an abstract class may be instantiated.

Exercises

12.3   *(Extensibility using Polymorphism)* How is it that polymorphism enables us to design and implement systems that are easily extensible?

12.4   *(Derive Class Member call via Base Class Pointer)* Discuss the problems of accessing a derived-class-only member function using a base class pointer.

12.5   *(Abstract vs. Concrete Class)* Distinguish between abstract class and concrete class. Which are the situations were abstract class is used?

12.6   *(Abstraction and Derive Class)* Under what circumstances is a derived class is also an abstract class?

12.7   *(`dynamic_cast` vs. `static_cast`)* Distinguish between `dynamic_cast` and `static_cast`. What is the significance if `dynamic_cast` returns `nullptr`?

12.8   *(Overriding vs. Overloading)* Distinguish between overriding and overloading.

12.9   *(Abstract Base Classes)* Suggest one or more levels of abstract base classes for the `Shape` hierarchy discussed in this chapter and shown in Fig. 11.3. (The first level is `Shape`, and the second level consists of the classes `TwoDimensionalShape` and `ThreeDimensionalShape`.)

12.10   *(Runtime type information)* How does runtime type information help to determine an object's type?

12.11   *(Polymorphic Application)* You've been asked to develop a flight simulator that will have elaborate graphical outputs. Explain why polymorphic programming could be especially effective for a problem of this nature.

12.12   *(Payroll System Modification)* Modify the payroll system of Figs. 12.9–12.17 to include `private` data member `birthDate` in class `Employee`. Use class `Date` from Figs. 10.6–10.7 to represent an employee's birthday. Assume that payroll is processed once per month. Create a `vector` of `Employee` references to store the various employee objects. In a loop, calculate the payroll for each `Employee` (polymorphically), and add a $100.00 bonus to the person's payroll amount if the current month is the month in which the `Employee`'s birthday occurs.

12.13   *(Package Inheritance Hierarchy)* Use the `Package` inheritance hierarchy created in Exercise 11.9 to create a program that displays the address information and calculates the shipping costs for several `Packages`. The program should contain a `vector` of `Package` pointers to objects of classes `TwoDayPackage` and `OvernightPackage`. Loop through the `vector` to process the `Packages` polymorphically. For each `Package`, invoke *get* functions to obtain the address information of the sender and the recipient, then print the two addresses as they would appear on mailing labels. Also, call each `Package`'s `calculateCost` member function and print the result. Keep track of the total shipping cost for all `Packages` in the `vector`, and display this total when the loop terminates.

12.14 *(Polymorphic Banking Program Using Account Hierarchy)* Develop a polymorphic banking program using the Account hierarchy created in Exercise 11.10. Create a vector of Account pointers to SavingsAccount and CheckingAccount objects. For each Account in the vector, allow the user to specify an amount of money to withdraw from the Account using member function debit and an amount of money to deposit into the Account using member function credit. As you process each Account, determine its type. If an Account is a SavingsAccount, calculate the amount of interest owed to the Account using member function calculateInterest, then add the interest to the account balance using member function credit. After processing an Account, print the updated account balance obtained by invoking base-class member function getBalance.

12.15 *(Payroll System Modification)* Modify the payroll system of Figs. 12.9–12.17 to include additional Employee subclasses PieceWorker and HourlyWorker. A PieceWorker represents an employee whose pay is based on the number of pieces of merchandise produced. An HourlyWorker represents an employee whose pay is based on an hourly wage and the number of hours worked. Hourly workers receive overtime pay (1.5 times the hourly wage) for all hours worked in excess of 40 hours.

Class PieceWorker should contain private instance variables wage (to store the employee's wage per piece) and pieces (to store the number of pieces produced). Class HourlyWorker should contain private instance variables wage (to store the employee's wage per hour) and hours (to store the hours worked). In class PieceWorker, provide a concrete implementation of method earnings that calculates the employee's earnings by multiplying the number of pieces produced by the wage per piece. In class HourlyWorker, provide a concrete implementation of method earnings that calculates the employee's earnings by multiplying the number of hours worked by the wage per hour. If the number of hours worked is over 40, be sure to pay the HourlyWorker for the overtime hours. Add a pointer to an object of each new class into the vector of Employee pointers in main. For each Employee, display its string representation and earnings.

Making a Difference

12.16 *(CarbonFootprint Abstract Class: Polymorphism)* Using an abstract class with only pure virtual functions, you can specify similar behaviors for possibly disparate classes. Governments and companies worldwide are becoming increasingly concerned with carbon footprints (annual releases of carbon dioxide into the atmosphere) from buildings burning various types of fuels for heat, vehicles burning fuels for power, and the like. Many scientists blame these greenhouse gases for the phenomenon called global warming. Create three small classes unrelated by inheritance—classes Building, Car and Bicycle. Give each class some unique appropriate attributes and behaviors that it does not have in common with other classes. Write an abstract class CarbonFootprint with only a pure virtual getCarbonFootprint method. Have each of your classes inherit from that abstract class and implement the getCarbonFootprint method to calculate an appropriate carbon footprint for that class (check out a few websites that explain how to calculate carbon footprints). Write an application that creates objects of each of the three classes, places pointers to those objects in a vector of CarbonFootprint pointers, then iterates through the vector, polymorphically invoking each object's getCarbonFootprint method. For each object, print some identifying information and the object's carbon footprint.

13

Stream Input/Output:
A Deeper Look

Consciousness ... does not appear to itself chopped up in bits ... A "river" or a "stream" are the metaphors by which it is most naturally described.
—William James

Objectives

In this chapter you'll learn:

- To use C++ object-oriented stream input/output.

- To format input and output.

- The stream-I/O class hierarchy.

- To use stream manipulators.

- To control justification and padding.

- To determine the success or failure of input/output operations.

- To tie output streams to input streams.

13.1 Introduction

This chapter discusses a range of capabilities sufficient for performing most common I/O operations and overviews the remaining capabilities. We discussed some of these features earlier in the text; now we provide a more complete treatment. Many of the I/O features that we'll discuss are object oriented. This style of I/O makes use of other C++ features, such as references, function overloading and operator overloading.

C++ uses *type-safe I/O*. Each I/O operation is executed in a manner sensitive to the data type. If an I/O function has been defined to handle a particular data type, then that member function is called to handle that data type. If there is no match between the type of the actual data and a function for handling that data type, the compiler generates an error. Thus, improper data cannot "sneak" through the system (as can occur in C, allowing for some subtle and bizarre errors).

Users can specify how to perform I/O for objects of user-defined types by overloading the stream insertion operator (<<) and the stream extraction operator (>>). This extensibility is one of C++'s most valuable features.

Software Engineering Observation 13.1

Use the C++-style I/O exclusively in C++ programs, even though C-style I/O is available to C++ programmers.

Error-Prevention Tip 13.1

C++ I/O is type safe.

Software Engineering Observation 13.2

C++ enables a common treatment of I/O for predefined types and user-defined types. This commonality facilitates software development and reuse.

13.2 Streams

C++ I/O occurs in **streams**, which are sequences of bytes. In input operations, the bytes flow from a device (e.g., a keyboard, a disk drive, a network connection, etc.) to main memory. In output operations, bytes flow from main memory to a device (e.g., a display screen, a printer, a disk drive, a network connection, etc.).

An application associates meaning with bytes. The bytes could represent characters, raw data, graphics images, digital speech, digital video or any other information an application may require. The system I/O mechanisms should transfer bytes from devices to memory (and vice versa) consistently and reliably. Such transfers often involve some mechanical motion, such as the rotation of a disk or a tape, or the typing of keystrokes at a keyboard. The time these transfers take typically is far greater than the time the processor requires to manipulate data internally. Thus, I/O operations require careful planning and tuning to ensure optimal performance.

C++ provides both "low-level" and "high-level" I/O capabilities. Low-level I/O capabilities (i.e., **unformatted I/O**) specify that some number of bytes should be transferred device-to-memory or memory-to-device. In such transfers, the individual byte is the item of interest. Such low-level capabilities provide high-speed, high-volume transfers but are not particularly convenient.

Programmers generally prefer a higher-level view of I/O (i.e., **formatted I/O**), in which bytes are grouped into meaningful units, such as integers, floating-point numbers, characters, strings and user-defined types. These type-oriented capabilities are satisfactory for most I/O other than high-volume file processing.

Performance Tip 13.1

Use unformatted I/O for the best performance in high-volume file processing.

Portability Tip 13.1

Unformatted I/O is not portable across all platforms.

13.2.1 Classic Streams vs. Standard Streams

In the past, the C++ **classic stream** libraries enabled input and output of chars. Because a char normally occupies *one* byte, it can represent only a limited set of characters (such as those in the ASCII character set used by most readers of this book, or other popular character sets). However, many languages use alphabets that contain more characters than a single-byte char can represent. The ASCII character set does not provide these characters; the Unicode® character set does. Unicode is an extensive international character set that represents the majority of the world's "commercially viable" languages, mathematical symbols and much more. For more information on Unicode, visit `www.unicode.org`.

C++ includes the standard stream libraries, which enable developers to build systems capable of performing I/O operations with Unicode characters. For this purpose, C++ includes the type `wchar_t`, which among other uses can store Unicode characters. The C++ standard also redesigned the classic C++ stream classes, which processed only `char`s, as class templates with specializations for processing characters of types `char` and `wchar_t`, respectively. We use the `char` specializations. The size of type `wchar_t` is not specified by the standard. C++11's new `char16_t` and `char32_t` types for representing Unicode characters were added to provide character types with explicitly specified sizes.

13.2.2 `iostream` Library Headers

The C++ `iostream` library provides hundreds of I/O capabilities. Several headers contain portions of the library interface.

Most C++ programs include the `<iostream>` header, which declares basic services required for all stream-I/O operations. The `<iostream>` header defines the `cin`, `cout`, `cerr` and `clog` objects, which correspond to the standard input stream, the standard output stream, the unbuffered standard error stream and the buffered standard error stream, respectively. (`cerr` and `clog` are discussed in Section 13.2.3.) Both unformatted- and formatted-I/O services are provided.

The `<iomanip>` header declares services useful for performing formatted I/O with so-called parameterized stream manipulators, such as `setw` and `setprecision`.

The `<fstream>` header declares services for file processing. We use this header in the file-processing programs of Chapter 14.

13.2.3 Stream Input/Output Classes and Objects

The `iostream` library provides many templates for handling common I/O operations. For example, class template **basic_istream** supports stream-input operations, class template **basic_ostream** supports stream-output operations, and class template **basic_iostream** supports both stream-input and stream-output operations. Each template has a predefined template specialization that enables `char` I/O. In addition, the `iostream` library provides a set of `typedef`s that provide aliases for these template specializations. The **typedef** specifier declares synonyms (aliases) for data types. You'll sometimes use `typedef` to create shorter or more readable type names. For example, the statement

```
typedef Card *CardPtr;
```

defines an additional type name, CardPtr, as a *synonym* for type Card *. Creating a name using `typedef` does *not* create a data type; it creates only a new type name. Section 22.3 discusses `typedef` in detail. The typedef **istream** represents a basic_istream<char> that enables `char` input. Similarly, the typedef **ostream** represents a basic_ostream<char> that enables `char` output. Also, the typedef **iostream** represents a basic_iostream<char> that enables both `char` input and output. We use these `typedef`s throughout this chapter.

Stream-I/O Template Hierarchy and Operator Overloading
Templates basic_istream and basic_ostream both derive through single inheritance from base template **basic_ios**.[1] Template basic_iostream derives through *multiple in-*

heritance[2] from templates `basic_istream` and `basic_ostream`. The UML class diagram of Fig. 13.1 summarizes these inheritance relationships.

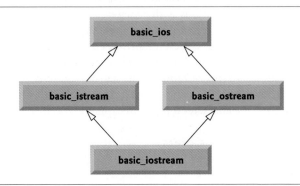

Fig. 13.1 | Stream-I/O template hierarchy portion.

Operator overloading provides a convenient notation for performing input/output. The *left-shift operator (<<)* is overloaded to designate stream output and is referred to as the *stream insertion operator*. The *right-shift operator (>>)* is overloaded to designate stream input and is referred to as the *stream extraction operator*. These operators are used with the standard stream objects `cin`, `cout`, `cerr` and `clog` and, commonly, with stream objects you create in your own code.

Standard Stream Objects *cin, cout, cerr and clog*

Predefined object `cin` is an `istream` instance and is said to be "connected to" (or attached to) the *standard input device*, which usually is the keyboard. The stream extraction operator (>>) as used in the following statement causes a value for integer variable `grade` (assuming that `grade` has been declared as an `int` variable) to be input from `cin` to memory:

```
cin >> grade; // data "flows" in the direction of the arrows
```

The compiler determines the data type of `grade` and selects the appropriate overloaded stream extraction operator. Assuming that `grade` has been declared properly, the stream extraction operator does not require additional type information (as is the case, for example, in C-style I/O). The >> operator is overloaded to input data items of fundamental types, strings and pointer values.

The predefined object `cout` is an `ostream` instance and is said to be "connected to" the *standard output device*, which usually is the display screen. The stream insertion operator (<<), as used in the following statement, causes the value of variable `grade` to be output from memory to the standard output device:

```
cout << grade; // data "flows" in the direction of the arrows
```

The compiler determines the data type of `grade` (assuming `grade` has been declared properly) and selects the appropriate stream insertion operator. The << operator is overloaded to output data items of fundamental types, strings and pointer values.

---

1. This chapter discusses templates only in the context of the template specializations for char I/O.
2. Multiple inheritance is discussed in Chapter 23, Other Topics.

The predefined object cerr is an ostream instance and is said to be "connected to" the *standard error device*, normally the screen. Outputs to object cerr are unbuffered, implying that each stream insertion to cerr causes its output to appear *immediately*—this is appropriate for notifying a user promptly about errors.

The predefined object clog is an instance of the ostream class and is said to be "connected to" the *standard error device*. Outputs to clog are buffered. This means that each insertion to clog could cause its output to be held in a buffer (that is, an area in memory) until the buffer is filled or until the buffer is flushed. Buffering is an I/O performance-enhancement technique discussed in operating-systems courses.

File-Processing Templates

C++ file processing uses class templates basic_ifstream (for file input), basic_ofstream (for file output) and basic_fstream (for file input and output). As with the standard streams, C++ provides typedefs for working with these class templates. For example, the typedef ifstream represents a basic_ifstream<char> that enables char input from a file. Similarly, typedef ofstream represents a basic_ofstream<char> that enables char output to a file. Also, typedef fstream represents a basic_fstream<char> that enables char input from, and output to, a file. Template basic_ifstream inherits from basic_istream, basic_ofstream inherits from basic_ostream and basic_fstream inherits from basic_iostream. The UML class diagram of Fig. 13.2 summarizes the various inheritance relationships of the I/O-related classes. The full stream-I/O class hierarchy provides most of the capabilities that you need. Consult the class-library reference for your C++ system for additional file-processing information.

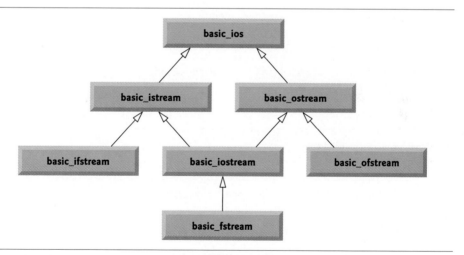

Fig. 13.2 | Stream-I/O template hierarchy portion showing the main file-processing templates.

13.3 Stream Output

Formatted and unformatted output capabilities are provided by ostream. Capabilities include output of standard data types with the stream insertion operator (<<); output of characters via the put member function; unformatted output via the write member function; output of integers in decimal, octal and hexadecimal formats; output of floating-point values with various precision, with forced decimal points, in scientific notation and in fixed notation; output of data justified in fields of designated widths; output of data in fields padded with specified characters; and output of uppercase letters in scientific notation and hexadecimal notation.

13.3.1 Output of char * Variables

C++ determines data types automatically—an improvement over C, but this feature sometimes "gets in the way." For example, suppose we want to print the address stored in a char * pointer. The << operator has been overloaded to output a char * as a *null-terminated C-style string*. To output the *address*, you can cast the char * to a void * (this can be done to any pointer variable). Figure 13.3 demonstrates printing a char * variable in both string and address formats. The address prints here as a hexadecimal (base-16) number—in general, the way addresses print is *implementation dependent*. To learn more about hexadecimal numbers, see Appendix D. We say more about controlling the bases of numbers in Section 13.6.1 and Section 13.7.4.

```cpp
1   // Fig. 13.3: fig13_03.cpp
2   // Printing the address stored in a char * variable.
3   #include <iostream>
4   using namespace std;
5
6   int main()
7   {
8      const char *const word = "again";
9
10     // display value of char *, then display value of char *
11     // after a static_cast to void *
12     cout << "Value of word is: " << word << endl
13        << "Value of static_cast< const void * >( word ) is: "
14        << static_cast< const void * >( word ) << endl;
15  } // end main
```

```
Value of word is: again
Value of static_cast< const void * >( word ) is: 0135CC70
```

Fig. 13.3 | Printing the address stored in a char * variable.

13.3.2 Character Output Using Member Function put

We can use the put member function to output characters. For example, the statement

```cpp
cout.put( 'A' );
```

displays a single character A. Calls to put may be *cascaded*, as in the statement

```cpp
cout.put( 'A' ).put( '\n' );
```

which outputs the letter A followed by a newline character. As with <<, the preceding statement executes in this manner, because the dot operator (.) associates from left to right, and the put member function returns a reference to the ostream object (cout) that received the put call. The put function also may be called with a numeric expression that represents an ASCII value, as in the following statement, which also outputs A:

```
cout.put( 65 );
```

13.4 Stream Input

Now let's consider stream input. Formatted and unformatted input capabilities are provided by istream. The stream extraction operator (>>) normally skips white-space characters (such as blanks, tabs and newlines) in the input stream; later we'll see how to change this behavior. After each input, the stream extraction operator returns a *reference* to the stream object that received the extraction message (e.g., cin in the expression cin >> grade). If that reference is used as a condition (e.g., in a while statement's loop-continuation condition), the stream's overloaded void * cast operator function is implicitly invoked to convert the reference into a non-null pointer value or the null pointer based on the success or failure, respectively, of the last input operation. A non-null pointer converts to the bool value true to indicate success and the null pointer converts to the bool value false to indicate failure. When an attempt is made to read past the end of a stream, the stream's overloaded void * cast operator returns the *null pointer* to indicate *end-of-file*.

Each stream object contains a set of **state bits** used to control the stream's state (i.e., formatting, setting error states, etc.). These bits are used by the stream's overloaded void * cast operator to determine whether to return a non-null pointer or the null pointer. Stream extraction causes the stream's **failbit** to be set if data of the wrong type is input and causes the stream's **badbit** to be set if the operation fails. Section 13.7 and Section 13.8 discuss stream state bits in detail, then show how to test these bits after an I/O operation.

13.4.1 get and getline Member Functions

The **get** member function with *no arguments* inputs *one* character from the designated stream (including white-space characters and other nongraphic characters, such as the key sequence that represents end-of-file) and returns it as the value of the function call. This version of get returns EOF when *end-of-file* is encountered on the stream.

Using Member Functions eof, get and put

Figure 13.4 demonstrates the use of member functions eof and get on input stream cin and member function put on output stream cout. Recall from Chapter 5 that EOF is represented as an int. This program reads characters into the int variable character, so that we can test each character entered to see if it's EOF. The program first prints the value of cin.eof()—i.e., false (0 on the output)—to show that *end-of-file* has *not* occurred on cin. The user enters a line of text and presses *Enter* followed by end-of-file (*<Ctrl> z* on Microsoft Windows systems, *<Ctrl> d* on Linux and Mac systems). Line 15 reads each character, which line 16 outputs to cout using member function put. When end-of-file is encountered, the while statement ends, and line 20 displays the value of cin.eof(), which is now true (1 on the output), to show that end-of-file has been set on cin. This program uses the version of istream member function get that takes no arguments and returns the character being input (line 15). Function eof returns true only after the program attempts to read past the last character in the stream.

```
 1    // Fig. 13.4: fig13_04.cpp
 2    // get, put and eof member functions.
 3    #include <iostream>
 4    using namespace std;
 5
 6    int main()
 7    {
 8       int character; // use int, because char cannot represent EOF
 9
10       // prompt user to enter line of text
11       cout << "Before input, cin.eof() is " << cin.eof() << endl
12          << "Enter a sentence followed by end-of-file:" << endl;
13
14       // use get to read each character; use put to display it
15       while ( ( character = cin.get() ) != EOF )
16          cout.put( character );
17
18       // display end-of-file character
19       cout << "\nEOF in this system is: " << character << endl;
20       cout << "After input of EOF, cin.eof() is " << cin.eof() << endl;
21    } // end main
```

```
Before input, cin.eof() is 0
Enter a sentence followed by end-of-file:
Testing the get and put member functions
Testing the get and put member functions
^Z

EOF in this system is: -1
After input of EOF, cin.eof() is 1
```

Fig. 13.4 | get, put and eof member functions.

The get member function with a character-reference argument inputs the next character from the input stream (even if this is a *white-space character*) and stores it in the character argument. This version of get returns a reference to the istream object for which the get member function is being invoked.

A third version of get takes three arguments—a built-in array of chars, a size limit and a delimiter (with default value '\n'). This version reads characters from the input stream. It either reads *one fewer* than the specified maximum number of characters and terminates or terminates as soon as the *delimiter* is read. A null character is inserted to terminate the input string in the character array used as a buffer by the program. The delimiter is not placed in the character array but *does remain in the input stream* (the delimiter will be the next character read). Thus, the result of a second consecutive get is an empty line, unless the delimiter character is removed from the input stream (possibly with cin.ignore()).

Comparing cin and cin.get

Figure 13.5 compares input using stream extraction with cin (which reads characters until a white-space character is encountered) and input using cin.get. The call to cin.get (line 22) does *not* specify a delimiter, so the *default* '\n' character is used.

```cpp
 1   // Fig. 13.5: fig13_05.cpp
 2   // Contrasting input of a string via cin and cin.get.
 3   #include <iostream>
 4   using namespace std;
 5
 6   int main()
 7   {
 8      // create two char arrays, each with 80 elements
 9      const int SIZE = 80;
10      char buffer1[ SIZE ];
11      char buffer2[ SIZE ];
12
13      // use cin to input characters into buffer1
14      cout << "Enter a sentence:" << endl;
15      cin >> buffer1;
16
17      // display buffer1 contents
18      cout << "\nThe string read with cin was:" << endl
19         << buffer1 << endl << endl;
20
21      // use cin.get to input characters into buffer2
22      cin.get( buffer2, SIZE );
23
24      // display buffer2 contents
25      cout << "The string read with cin.get was:" << endl
26         << buffer2 << endl;
27   } // end main
```

```
Enter a sentence:
Contrasting string input with cin and cin.get

The string read with cin was:
Contrasting

The string read with cin.get was:
 string input with cin and cin.get
```

Fig. 13.5 | Contrasting input of a string via cin and cin.get.

Using Member Function getline
Member function **getline** operates similarly to the third version of the get member function and *inserts a null character* after the line in the built-in array of chars. The getline function removes the delimiter from the stream (i.e., reads the character and discards it), but does *not* store it in the character array. The program of Fig. 13.6 demonstrates the use of the getline member function to input a line of text (line 13).

```cpp
 1   // Fig. 13.6: fig13_06.cpp
 2   // Inputting characters using cin member function getline.
 3   #include <iostream>
 4   using namespace std;
```

Fig. 13.6 | Inputting characters using cin member function getline. (Part 1 of 2.)

```
 5
 6   int main()
 7   {
 8      const int SIZE = 80;
 9      char buffer[ SIZE ]; // create array of 80 characters
10
11      // input characters in buffer via cin function getline
12      cout << "Enter a sentence:" << endl;
13      cin.getline( buffer, SIZE );
14
15      // display buffer contents
16      cout << "\nThe sentence entered is:" << endl << buffer << endl;
17   } // end main
```

```
Enter a sentence:
Using the getline member function

The sentence entered is:
Using the getline member function
```

Fig. 13.6 | Inputting characters using `cin` member function `getline`. (Part 2 of 2.)

13.4.2 `istream` Member Functions peek, putback and ignore

The **ignore** member function of `istream` reads and discards a designated number of characters (the default is *one*) or terminates upon encountering a designated delimiter (the default is EOF, which causes `ignore` to skip to the end of the file when reading from a file).

The **putback** member function places the previous character obtained by a `get` from an input stream back into that stream. This function is useful for applications that scan an input stream looking for a field beginning with a specific character. When that character is input, the application returns the character to the stream, so the character can be included in the input data.

The **peek** member function returns the next character from an input stream but does not remove the character from the stream.

13.4.3 Type-Safe I/O

C++ offers type-safe I/O. The << and >> operators are overloaded to accept data items of *specific* types. If unexpected data is processed, various error bits are set, which the user may test to determine whether an I/O operation succeeded or failed. If operators << and >> have not been overloaded for a user-defined type and you attempt to input into or output the contents of an object of that user-defined type, the compiler reports an error. This enables the program to "stay in control." We discuss these error states in Section 13.8.

13.5 Unformatted I/O Using read, write and gcount

Unformatted input/output is performed using the **read** and **write** member functions of `istream` and `ostream`, respectively. Member function read inputs *bytes* to a built-in array of chars in memory; member function write outputs bytes from a built-in array of chars. These bytes are *not formatted* in any way. They're input or output as raw bytes. For example, the call

```
char buffer[] = "HAPPY BIRTHDAY";
cout.write( buffer, 10 );
```

outputs the first 10 bytes of buffer (including null characters, if any, that would cause output with cout and << to terminate). The call

```
cout.write( "ABCDEFGHIJKLMNOPQRSTUVWXYZ", 10 );
```

displays the first 10 characters of the alphabet.

The read member function inputs a designated number of characters into a built-in array of chars. If *fewer* than the designated number of characters are read, failbit is set. Section 13.8 shows how to determine whether failbit has been set. Member function **gcount** reports the number of characters read by the last input operation.

Figure 13.7 demonstrates istream member functions read and gcount, and ostream member function write. The program inputs 20 characters (from a longer input sequence) into the array buffer with read (line 13), determines the number of characters input with gcount (line 17) and outputs the characters in buffer with write (line 17).

```cpp
1   // Fig. 13.7: fig13_07.cpp
2   // Unformatted I/O using read, gcount and write.
3   #include <iostream>
4   using namespace std;
5
6   int main()
7   {
8      const int SIZE = 80;
9      char buffer[ SIZE ]; // create array of 80 characters
10
11     // use function read to input characters into buffer
12     cout << "Enter a sentence:" << endl;
13     cin.read( buffer, 20 );
14
15     // use functions write and gcount to display buffer characters
16     cout << endl << "The sentence entered was:" << endl;
17     cout.write( buffer, cin.gcount() );
18     cout << endl;
19  } // end main
```

```
Enter a sentence:
Using the read, write, and gcount member functions
The sentence entered was:
Using the read, writ
```

Fig. 13.7 | Unformatted I/O using read, gcount and write.

13.6 Introduction to Stream Manipulators

C++ provides various **stream manipulators** that perform formatting tasks. The stream manipulators provide capabilities such as setting field widths, setting precision, setting and unsetting format state, setting the fill character in fields, flushing streams, inserting a newline into the output stream (and flushing the stream), inserting a null character into the output stream and skipping white space in the input stream. These features are described in the following sections.

13.6.1 Integral Stream Base: dec, oct, hex and setbase

Integers are interpreted normally as decimal (base-10) values. To change the base in which integers are interpreted on a stream, insert the **hex** manipulator to set the base to hexadecimal (base 16) or insert the **oct** manipulator to set the base to octal (base 8). Insert the **dec** manipulator to reset the stream base to decimal. These are all *sticky* manipulators.

A stream's base also may be changed by the **setbase** stream manipulator, which takes an int argument of 10, 8, or 16 to set the base to decimal, octal or hexadecimal, respectively. Because setbase takes an argument, it's called a *parameterized stream manipulator*. Parameterized stream manipulators like setbase require the header <iomanip>. The stream base value remains the same until changed explicitly; setbase settings are sticky. Figure 13.8 demonstrates stream manipulators hex, oct, dec and setbase. For more information on decimal, octal and hexadecimal numbers, see Appendix D.

```cpp
1   // Fig. 13.8: fig13_08.cpp
2   // Using stream manipulators hex, oct, dec and setbase.
3   #include <iostream>
4   #include <iomanip>
5   using namespace std;
6
7   int main()
8   {
9      int number;
10
11     cout << "Enter a decimal number: ";
12     cin >> number; // input number
13
14     // use hex stream manipulator to show hexadecimal number
15     cout << number << " in hexadecimal is: " << hex
16        << number << endl;
17
18     // use oct stream manipulator to show octal number
19     cout << dec << number << " in octal is: "
20        << oct << number << endl;
21
22     // use setbase stream manipulator to show decimal number
23     cout << setbase( 10 ) << number << " in decimal is: "
24        << number << endl;
25   } // end main
```

```
Enter a decimal number: 20
20 in hexadecimal is: 14
20 in octal is: 24
20 in decimal is: 20
```

Fig. 13.8 | Using stream manipulators hex, oct, dec and setbase.

13.6.2 Floating-Point Precision (precision, setprecision)

We can control the precision of floating-point numbers (i.e., the number of digits to the right of the decimal point) by using either the setprecision stream manipulator or the precision member function of ios_base. A call to either of these sets the precision for all subsequent output operations until the next precision-setting call. A call to member function precision with no argument returns the current precision setting (this is what you need to use so that you can *restore the original precision* eventually after a sticky setting is no longer needed). The program of Fig. 13.9 uses both member function precision (line 22) and the setprecision manipulator (line 31) to print a table that shows the square root of 2, with precision varying from 0 to 9.

```cpp
1   // Fig. 13.9: fig13_09.cpp
2   // Controlling precision of floating-point values.
3   #include <iostream>
4   #include <iomanip>
5   #include <cmath>
6   using namespace std;
7
8   int main()
9   {
10      double root2 = sqrt( 2.0 ); // calculate square root of 2
11      int places; // precision, vary from 0-9
12
13      cout << "Square root of 2 with precisions 0-9." << endl
14         << "Precision set by ios_base member function "
15         << "precision:" << endl;
16
17      cout << fixed; // use fixed-point notation
18
19      // display square root using ios_base function precision
20      for ( places = 0; places <= 9; ++places )
21      {
22         cout.precision( places );
23         cout << root2 << endl;
24      } // end for
25
26      cout << "\nPrecision set by stream manipulator "
27         << "setprecision:" << endl;
28
29      // set precision for each digit, then display square root
30      for ( places = 0; places <= 9; ++places )
31         cout << setprecision( places ) << root2 << endl;
32   } // end main
```

```
Square root of 2 with precisions 0-9.
Precision set by ios_base member function precision:
1
1.4
1.41
1.414
1.4142
1.41421
1.414214
1.4142136
1.41421356
1.414213562
```

Fig. 13.9 | Controlling precision of floating-point values. (Part 1 of 2.)

```
Precision set by stream manipulator setprecision:
1
1.4
1.41
1.414
1.4142
1.41421
1.414214
1.4142136
1.41421356
1.414213562
```

Fig. 13.9 | Controlling precision of floating-point values. (Part 2 of 2.)

13.6.3 Field Width (width, setw)

The width member function (of base class ios_base) sets the *field width* (i.e., the number of character positions in which a value should be output or the maximum number of characters that should be input) and *returns the previous width*. If values output are narrower than the field width, **fill characters** are inserted as **padding**. A value wider than the designated width will *not* be truncated—the *full number* will be printed. The width function with no argument returns the current setting.

Common Programming Error 13.1

The width setting applies only for the next insertion or extraction (i.e., the width setting is not sticky); afterward, the width is set implicitly to 0 (that is, input and output will be performed with default settings). Assuming that the width setting applies to all subsequent outputs is a logic error.

Common Programming Error 13.2

When a field is not sufficiently wide to handle outputs, the outputs print as wide as necessary, which can yield confusing outputs.

Figure 13.10 demonstrates the use of the width member function on both input and output. On input into a char array, *a maximum of one fewer characters than the width will be read*, because provision is made for the null character to be placed in the input string. Remember that stream extraction *terminates* when *nonleading white space* is encountered. The setw stream manipulator also may be used to set the field width. [*Note:* When prompted for input in Fig. 13.10, the user should enter a line of text and press *Enter* followed by end-of-file (*<Ctrl> z* on Microsoft Windows systems and *<Ctrl> d* on Linux and OS X systems).]

```
 1   // Fig. 13.10: fig13_10.cpp
 2   // width member function of class ios_base.
 3   #include <iostream>
 4   using namespace std;
 5
```

Fig. 13.10 | width member function of class ios_base. (Part 1 of 2.)

```
6   int main()
7   {
8       int widthValue = 4;
9       char sentence[ 10 ];
10
11      cout << "Enter a sentence:" << endl;
12      cin.width( 5 ); // input only 5 characters from sentence
13
14      // set field width, then display characters based on that width
15      while ( cin >> sentence )
16      {
17          cout.width( widthValue++ );
18          cout << sentence << endl;
19          cin.width( 5 ); // input 5 more characters from sentence
20      } // end while
21  } // end main
```

```
Enter a sentence:
This is a test of the width member function
This
   is
     a
  test
     of
    the
    widt
        h
      memb
        er
      func
       tion
```

Fig. 13.10 | `width` member function of class `ios_base`. (Part 2 of 2.)

13.6.4 User-Defined Output Stream Manipulators

You can create your own stream manipulators. Figure 13.11 shows how to create and use *new* nonparameterized stream manipulators `bell` (lines 8–11), `carriageReturn` (lines 14–17), `tab` (lines 20–23) and `endLine` (lines 27–30). For output stream manipulators, the return type and parameter must be of type `ostream &`. When line 35 inserts the `endLine` manipulator in the output stream, function `endLine` is called and line 29 outputs the escape sequence \n and the `flush` manipulator (which flushes the output buffer) to the standard output stream `cout`. Similarly, when lines 35–44 insert the manipulators `tab`, `bell` and `carriageReturn` in the output stream, their corresponding functions—`tab` (line 20), `bell` (line 8) and `carriageReturn` (line 14) are called, which in turn output various escape sequences.

```
1   // Fig. 13.11: fig13_11.cpp
2   // Creating and testing user-defined, nonparameterized
3   // stream manipulators.
4   #include <iostream>
5   using namespace std;
```

Fig. 13.11 | User-defined, nonparameterized stream manipulators. (Part 1 of 2.)

```
6
7    // bell manipulator (using escape sequence \a)
8    ostream& bell( ostream& output )
9    {
10      return output << '\a'; // issue system beep
11   } // end bell manipulator
12
13   // carriageReturn manipulator (using escape sequence \r)
14   ostream& carriageReturn( ostream& output )
15   {
16      return output << '\r'; // issue carriage return
17   } // end carriageReturn manipulator
18
19   // tab manipulator (using escape sequence \t)
20   ostream& tab( ostream& output )
21   {
22      return output << '\t'; // issue tab
23   } // end tab manipulator
24
25   // endLine manipulator (using escape sequence \n and flush stream
26   // manipulator to simulate endl)
27   ostream& endLine( ostream& output )
28   {
29      return output << '\n' << flush; // issue endl-like end of line
30   } // end endLine manipulator
31
32   int main()
33   {
34      // use tab and endLine manipulators
35      cout << "Testing the tab manipulator:" << endLine
36         << 'a' << tab << 'b' << tab << 'c' << endLine;
37
38      cout << "Testing the carriageReturn and bell manipulators:"
39         << endLine << ".........";
40
41      cout << bell; // use bell manipulator
42
43      // use carriageReturn and endLine manipulators
44      cout << carriageReturn << "-----" << endLine;
45   } // end main
```

```
Testing the tab manipulator:
a       b       c
Testing the carriageReturn and bell manipulators:
-----.....
```

Fig. 13.11 | User-defined, nonparameterized stream manipulators. (Part 2 of 2.)

13.7 Stream Format States and Stream Manipulators

Various stream manipulators can be used to specify the kinds of formatting to be performed during stream-I/O operations. Stream manipulators control the output's format settings. Figure 13.12 lists each stream manipulator that controls a given stream's format state. All these manipulators belong to class `ios_base`. We show examples of most of these stream manipulators in the next several sections.

Manipulator	Description
skipws	*Skip white-space characters* on an input stream. This setting is reset with stream manipulator `noskipws`.
left	*Left justify* output in a field. *Padding* characters appear to the *right* if necessary.
right	*Right justify* output in a field. Padding characters appear to the *left* if necessary.
internal	Indicate that a number's *sign* should be *left justified* in a field and a number's *magnitude* should be *right justified* in that same field (i.e., *padding* characters appear *between* the sign and the number).
boolalpha	Specify that `bool` *values* should be displayed as the word `true` or `false`. The manipulator `noboolalpha` sets the stream back to displaying bool values as 1 (true) and 0 (false).
dec	Specify that integers should be treated as *decimal* (base 10) values.
oct	Specify that integers should be treated as *octal* (base 8) values.
hex	Specify that integers should be treated as *hexadecimal* (base 16) values.
showbase	Specify that the *base* of a number is to be output *ahead* of the number (a leading 0 for octals; a leading 0x or 0X for hexadecimals). This setting is reset with stream manipulator `noshowbase`.
showpoint	Specify that floating-point numbers should be output with a *decimal point*. This is used normally with `fixed` to *guarantee* a certain number of digits to the *right* of the decimal point, even if they're zeros. This setting is reset with stream manipulator `noshowpoint`.
uppercase	Specify that *uppercase letters* (i.e., X and A through F) should be used in a *hexadecimal* integer and that *uppercase* E should be used when representing a floating-point value in *scientific notation*. This setting is reset with stream manipulator `nouppercase`.
showpos	Specify that *positive* numbers should be preceded by a plus sign (+). This setting is reset with stream manipulator `noshowpos`.
scientific	Specify output of a floating-point value in *scientific notation*.
fixed	Specify output of a floating-point value in *fixed-point notation* with a specific number of digits to the *right* of the decimal point.

Fig. 13.12 | Format state stream manipulators from `<iostream>`.

13.7.1 Trailing Zeros and Decimal Points (`showpoint`)

Stream manipulator `showpoint` is a sticky setting that forces a floating-point number to be output with its *decimal point* and *trailing zeros*. For example, the floating-point value 79.0 prints as 79 without using `showpoint` and prints as 79.000000 (or as many trailing zeros as are specified by the current *precision*) using `showpoint`. To reset the `showpoint` setting, output the stream manipulator `noshowpoint`. The program in Fig. 13.13 shows how to use stream manipulator `showpoint` to control the printing of *trailing zeros* and *decimal points* for floating-point values. Recall that the *default precision* of a floating-point number is 6. When neither the `fixed` nor the `scientific` stream manipulator is used, the precision represents the number of significant digits to display (i.e., the total number of digits to display), *not* the number of digits to display after decimal point.

```cpp
1   // Fig. 13.13: fig13_13.cpp
2   // Controlling the printing of trailing zeros and
3   // decimal points in floating-point values.
4   #include <iostream>
5   using namespace std;
6
7   int main()
8   {
9      // display double values with default stream format
10     cout << "Before using showpoint" << endl
11        << "9.9900 prints as: " << 9.9900 << endl
12        << "9.9000 prints as: " << 9.9000 << endl
13        << "9.0000 prints as: " << 9.0000 << endl << endl;
14
15     // display double value after showpoint
16     cout << showpoint
17        << "After using showpoint" << endl
18        << "9.9900 prints as: " << 9.9900 << endl
19        << "9.9000 prints as: " << 9.9000 << endl
20        << "9.0000 prints as: " << 9.0000 << endl;
21  } // end main
```

```
Before using showpoint
9.9900 prints as: 9.99
9.9000 prints as: 9.9
9.0000 prints as: 9

After using showpoint
9.9900 prints as: 9.99000
9.9000 prints as: 9.90000
9.0000 prints as: 9.00000
```

Fig. 13.13 | Controlling the printing of trailing zeros and decimal points in floating-point values.

13.7.2 Justification (`left`, `right` and `internal`)

Stream manipulators `left` and `right` enable fields to be *left justified* with *padding* characters to the *right* or *right justified* with *padding* characters to the *left*, respectively. The padding character is specified by the `fill` member function or the `setfill` parameterized stream manipulator (which we discuss in Section 13.7.3). Figure 13.14 uses the `setw`, `left` and `right` manipulators to left justify and right justify integer data in a field.

```cpp
1   // Fig. 13.14: fig13_14.cpp
2   // Left and right justification with stream manipulators left and right.
3   #include <iostream>
```

Fig. 13.14 | Left and right justification with stream manipulators `left` and `right`. (Part 1 of 2.)

```
4    #include <iomanip>
5    using namespace std;
6
7    int main()
8    {
9       int x = 12345;
10
11      // display x right justified (default)
12      cout << "Default is right justified:" << endl
13         << setw( 10 ) << x;
14
15      // use left manipulator to display x left justified
16      cout << "\n\nUse std::left to left justify x:\n"
17         << left << setw( 10 ) << x;
18
19      // use right manipulator to display x right justified
20      cout << "\n\nUse std::right to right justify x:\n"
21         << right << setw( 10 ) << x << endl;
22   } // end main
```

```
Default is right justified:
    12345

Use std::left to left justify x:
12345

Use std::right to right justify x:
    12345
```

Fig. 13.14 | Left and right justification with stream manipulators `left` and `right`. (Part 2 of 2.)

Stream manipulator **internal** indicates that a number's *sign* (or *base* when using stream manipulator showbase) should be *left justified* within a field, that the number's *magnitude* should be *right justified* and that *intervening spaces* should be *padded* with the *fill character*. Figure 13.15 shows the internal stream manipulator specifying internal spacing (line 10). Note that **showpos** forces the plus sign to print (line 10). To reset the showpos setting, output the stream manipulator **noshowpos**.

```
1    // Fig. 13.15: fig13_15.cpp
2    // Printing an integer with internal spacing and plus sign.
3    #include <iostream>
4    #include <iomanip>
5    using namespace std;
6
7    int main()
8    {
9       // display value with internal spacing and plus sign
10      cout << internal << showpos << setw( 10 ) << 123 << endl;
11   } // end main
```

Fig. 13.15 | Printing an integer with internal spacing and plus sign. (Part 1 of 2.)

+	123

Fig. 13.15 | Printing an integer with internal spacing and plus sign. (Part 2 of 2.)

13.7.3 Padding (`fill`, `setfill`)

The `fill` member function specifies the *fill character* to be used with justified fields; *spaces* are used for padding by *default*. The function returns the prior padding character. The `setfill` manipulator also sets the *padding character*. Figure 13.16 demonstrates function `fill` (line 30) and stream manipulator `setfill` (lines 34 and 37) to set the fill character.

```cpp
// Fig. 13.16: fig13_16.cpp
// Using member function fill and stream manipulator setfill to change
// the padding character for fields larger than the printed value.
#include <iostream>
#include <iomanip>
using namespace std;

int main()
{
   int x = 10000;

   // display x
   cout << x << " printed as int right and left justified\n"
      << "and as hex with internal justification.\n"
      << "Using the default pad character (space):" << endl;

   // display x with base
   cout << showbase << setw( 10 ) << x << endl;

   // display x with left justification
   cout << left << setw( 10 ) << x << endl;

   // display x as hex with internal justification
   cout << internal << setw( 10 ) << hex << x << endl << endl;

   cout << "Using various padding characters:" << endl;

   // display x using padded characters (right justification)
   cout << right;
   cout.fill( '*' );
   cout << setw( 10 ) << dec << x << endl;

   // display x using padded characters (left justification)
   cout << left << setw( 10 ) << setfill( '%' ) << x << endl;

   // display x using padded characters (internal justification)
   cout << internal << setw( 10 ) << setfill( '^' ) << hex
      << x << endl;
} // end main
```

Fig. 13.16 | Using member function `fill` and stream manipulator `setfill` to change the padding character for fields larger than the printed values. (Part 1 of 2.)

```
10000 printed as int right and left justified
and as hex with internal justification.
Using the default pad character (space):
     10000
10000
0x    2710

Using various padding characters:
*****10000
10000%%%%%
0x^^^^2710
```

Fig. 13.16 | Using member function `fill` and stream manipulator `setfill` to change the padding character for fields larger than the printed values. (Part 2 of 2.)

13.7.4 Integral Stream Base (dec, oct, hex, showbase)

C++ provides stream manipulators **dec**, **hex** and **oct** to specify that integers are to be displayed as decimal, hexadecimal and octal values, respectively. Stream insertions *default* to *decimal* if none of these manipulators is used. With stream extraction, integers prefixed with 0 (zero) are treated as *octal* values, integers prefixed with 0x or 0X are treated as *hexadecimal* values, and all other integers are treated as *decimal* values. Once a particular base is specified for a stream, all integers on that stream are processed using that base until a different base is specified or until the program terminates.

Stream manipulator **showbase** forces the *base* of an integral value to be output. Decimal numbers are output by default, octal numbers are output with a leading 0, and hexadecimal numbers are output with either a leading 0x or a leading 0X (as we discuss in Section 13.7.6, stream manipulator **uppercase** determines which option is chosen). Figure 13.17 demonstrates the use of stream manipulator **showbase** to force an integer to print in decimal, octal and hexadecimal formats. To reset the showbase setting, output the stream manipulator **noshowbase**.

```cpp
 1   // Fig. 13.17: fig13_17.cpp
 2   // Stream manipulator showbase.
 3   #include <iostream>
 4   using namespace std;
 5
 6   int main()
 7   {
 8      int x = 100;
 9
10      // use showbase to show number base
11      cout << "Printing integers preceded by their base:" << endl
12         << showbase;
13
14      cout << x << endl; // print decimal value
15      cout << oct << x << endl; // print octal value
16      cout << hex << x << endl; // print hexadecimal value
17   } // end main
```

Fig. 13.17 | Stream manipulator `showbase`. (Part 1 of 2.)

```
Printing integers preceded by their base:
100
0144
0x64
```

Fig. 13.17 | Stream manipulator showbase. (Part 2 of 2.)

13.7.5 Floating-Point Numbers; Scientific and Fixed Notation (scientific, fixed)

The sticky stream manipulators scientific and fixed control the output format of floating-point numbers. Stream manipulator **scientific** forces the output of a floating-point number to display in scientific format. Stream manipulator **fixed** forces a floating-point number to display a specific number of digits (as specified by member function precision or stream manipulator setprecision) to the right of the decimal point. Without using another manipulator, the floating-point-number value determines the output format.

Figure 13.18 demonstrates displaying floating-point numbers in fixed and scientific formats using stream manipulators scientific (line 18) and fixed (line 22). The exponent format in scientific notation might differ across different compilers.

```cpp
1   // Fig. 13.18: fig13_18.cpp
2   // Floating-point values displayed in system default,
3   // scientific and fixed formats.
4   #include <iostream>
5   using namespace std;
6
7   int main()
8   {
9      double x = 0.001234567;
10     double y = 1.946e9;
11
12     // display x and y in default format
13     cout << "Displayed in default format:" << endl
14        << x << '\t' << y << endl;
15
16     // display x and y in scientific format
17     cout << "\nDisplayed in scientific format:" << endl
18        << scientific << x << '\t' << y << endl;
19
20     // display x and y in fixed format
21     cout << "\nDisplayed in fixed format:" << endl
22        << fixed << x << '\t' << y << endl;
23   } // end main
```

```
Displayed in default format:
0.00123457      1.946e+009

Displayed in scientific format:
1.234567e-003   1.946000e+009
```

Fig. 13.18 | Floating-point values displayed in default, scientific and fixed formats. (Part 1 of 2.)

```
Displayed in fixed format:
0.001235         1946000000.000000
```

Fig. 13.18 | Floating-point values displayed in default, scientific and fixed formats. (Part 2 of 2.)

13.7.6 Uppercase/Lowercase Control (uppercase)

Stream manipulator **uppercase** outputs an uppercase X or E with hexadecimal-integer values or with scientific notation floating-point values, respectively (Fig. 13.19). Using stream manipulator uppercase also causes all letters in a hexadecimal value to be uppercase. By *default*, the letters for hexadecimal values and the exponents in scientific notation floating-point values appear in *lowercase*. To reset the uppercase setting, output the stream manipulator **nouppercase**.

```
1   // Fig. 13.19: fig13_19.cpp
2   // Stream manipulator uppercase.
3   #include <iostream>
4   using namespace std;
5
6   int main()
7   {
8      cout << "Printing uppercase letters in scientific" << endl
9         << "notation exponents and hexadecimal values:" << endl;
10
11     // use std:uppercase to display uppercase letters; use std::hex and
12     // std::showbase to display hexadecimal value and its base
13     cout << uppercase << 4.345e10 << endl
14        << hex << showbase << 123456789 << endl;
15  } // end main
```

```
Printing uppercase letters in scientific
notation exponents and hexadecimal values:
4.345E+010
0X75BCD15
```

Fig. 13.19 | Stream manipulator uppercase.

13.7.7 Specifying Boolean Format (boolalpha)

C++ provides data type bool, whose values may be false or true, as a preferred alternative to the old style of using 0 to indicate false and nonzero to indicate true. A bool variable outputs as 0 or 1 by *default*. However, we can use stream manipulator **boolalpha** to set the output stream to display bool values as the strings "true" and "false". Use stream manipulator **noboolalpha** to set the output stream to display bool values as integers (i.e., the default setting). The program of Fig. 13.20 demonstrates these stream manipulators. Line 11 displays the bool value, which line 8 sets to true, as an integer. Line 15 uses manipulator boolalpha to display the bool value as a string. Lines 18–19 then change the bool's value and use manipulator noboolalpha, so line 22 can display the bool value as an integer. Line 26 uses manipulator boolalpha to display the bool value as a string. Both boolalpha and noboolalpha are sticky settings.

Good Programming Practice 13.1

Displaying bool *values as* true *or* false, *rather than nonzero or 0, respectively, makes program outputs clearer.*

```
 1   // Fig. 13.20: fig13_20.cpp
 2   // Stream manipulators boolalpha and noboolalpha.
 3   #include <iostream>
 4   using namespace std;
 5
 6   int main()
 7   {
 8      bool booleanValue = true;
 9
10      // display default true booleanValue
11      cout << "booleanValue is " << booleanValue << endl;
12
13      // display booleanValue after using boolalpha
14      cout << "booleanValue (after using boolalpha) is "
15         << boolalpha << booleanValue << endl << endl;
16
17      cout << "switch booleanValue and use noboolalpha" << endl;
18      booleanValue = false; // change booleanValue
19      cout << noboolalpha << endl; // use noboolalpha
20
21      // display default false booleanValue after using noboolalpha
22      cout << "booleanValue is " << booleanValue << endl;
23
24      // display booleanValue after using boolalpha again
25      cout << "booleanValue (after using boolalpha) is "
26         << boolalpha << booleanValue << endl;
27   } // end main
```

```
booleanValue is 1
booleanValue (after using boolalpha) is true

switch booleanValue and use noboolalpha

booleanValue is 0
booleanValue (after using boolalpha) is false
```

Fig. 13.20 | Stream manipulators boolalpha and noboolalpha.

13.7.8 Setting and Resetting the Format State via Member Function flags

Throughout Section 13.7, we've been using stream manipulators to change output format characteristics. We now discuss how to return an output stream's format to its default state after having applied several manipulations. Member function flags without an argument returns the current format settings as an fmtflags data type (of class ios_base), which represents the format state. Member function flags with an fmtflags argument sets the format state as specified by the argument and returns the prior state settings. The initial settings of the value that flags returns might differ across several systems. The program of Fig. 13.21 uses member function `flags` to save the stream's original format state (line 17), then restore the original format settings (line 25).

```cpp
 1   // Fig. 13.21: fig13_21.cpp
 2   // flags member function.
 3   #include <iostream>
 4   using namespace std;
 5
 6   int main()
 7   {
 8      int integerValue = 1000;
 9      double doubleValue = 0.0947628;
10
11      // display flags value, int and double values (original format)
12      cout << "The value of the flags variable is: " << cout.flags()
13         << "\nPrint int and double in original format:\n"
14         << integerValue << '\t' << doubleValue << endl << endl;
15
16      // use cout flags function to save original format
17      ios_base::fmtflags originalFormat = cout.flags();
18      cout << showbase << oct << scientific; // change format
19
20      // display flags value, int and double values (new format)
21      cout << "The value of the flags variable is: " << cout.flags()
22         << "\nPrint int and double in a new format:\n"
23         << integerValue << '\t' << doubleValue << endl << endl;
24
25      cout.flags( originalFormat ); // restore format
26
27      // display flags value, int and double values (original format)
28      cout << "The restored value of the flags variable is: "
29         << cout.flags()
30         << "\nPrint values in original format again:\n"
31         << integerValue << '\t' << doubleValue << endl;
32   } // end main
```

```
The value of the flags variable is: 513
Print int and double in original format:
1000    0.0947628

The value of the flags variable is: 012011
Print int and double in a new format:
01750    9.476280e-002

The restored value of the flags variable is: 513
Print values in original format again:
1000    0.0947628
```

Fig. 13.21 | `flags` member function.

13.8 Stream Error States

The state of a stream may be tested through bits in class `ios_base`. Earlier in the book, we indicated that you can test, for example, whether an input was successful. Figure 13.22

shows how to test these state bits. In industrial-strength code, you'll want to perform similar tests on your I/O operations.

```cpp
1   // Fig. 13.22: fig13_22.cpp
2   // Testing error states.
3   #include <iostream>
4   using namespace std;
5
6   int main()
7   {
8       int integerValue;
9
10      // display results of cin functions
11      cout << "Before a bad input operation:"
12          << "\ncin.rdstate(): " << cin.rdstate()
13          << "\n     cin.eof(): " << cin.eof()
14          << "\n    cin.fail(): " << cin.fail()
15          << "\n     cin.bad(): " << cin.bad()
16          << "\n    cin.good(): " << cin.good()
17          << "\n\nExpects an integer, but enter a character: ";
18
19      cin >> integerValue; // enter character value
20      cout << endl;
21
22      // display results of cin functions after bad input
23      cout << "After a bad input operation:"
24          << "\ncin.rdstate(): " << cin.rdstate()
25          << "\n     cin.eof(): " << cin.eof()
26          << "\n    cin.fail(): " << cin.fail()
27          << "\n     cin.bad(): " << cin.bad()
28          << "\n    cin.good(): " << cin.good() << endl << endl;
29
30      cin.clear(); // clear stream
31
32      // display results of cin functions after clearing cin
33      cout << "After cin.clear()" << "\ncin.fail(): " << cin.fail()
34          << "\ncin.good(): " << cin.good() << endl;
35  } // end main
```

```
Before a bad input operation:
cin.rdstate(): 0
    cin.eof(): 0
   cin.fail(): 0
    cin.bad(): 0
   cin.good(): 1

Expects an integer, but enter a character: A

After a bad input operation:
cin.rdstate(): 2
    cin.eof(): 0
   cin.fail(): 1
```

Fig. 13.22 | Testing error states. (Part 1 of 2.)

```
      cin.bad(): 0
      cin.good(): 0

After cin.clear()
cin.fail(): 0
cin.good(): 1
```

Fig. 13.22 | Testing error states. (Part 2 of 2.)

The **eofbit** is set for an input stream after *end-of-file* is encountered. A program can use member function **eof** to determine whether end-of-file has been encountered on a stream after an attempt to extract data *beyond* the end of the stream. The call

```
    cin.eof()
```

returns true if end-of-file has been encountered on cin and false otherwise.

The **failbit** is set for a stream when a *format error* occurs on the stream and no characters are input (e.g., when you attempt to read a *number* and the user enters a *string*). When such an error occurs, the characters are *not* lost. The **fail** member function reports whether a stream operation has failed. Usually, recovering from such errors is possible.

The **badbit** is set for a stream when an error occurs that results in the *loss of data*. The **bad** member function reports whether a stream operation *failed*. Generally, such serious failures are nonrecoverable.

The **goodbit** is set for a stream if *none* of the bits eofbit, failbit or badbit is set for the stream.

The **good** member function returns true if the bad, fail and eof functions would *all* return false. I/O operations should be performed only on "good" streams.

The **rdstate** member function returns the stream's *error state*. Calling cout.rdstate, for example, would return the stream's state, which then could be tested by a switch statement that examines eofbit, badbit, failbit and goodbit. The *preferred* means of testing the state of a stream is to use member functions eof, bad, fail and good—using these functions does not require you to be familiar with particular status bits.

The **clear** member function is used to *restore* a stream's state to "good," so that I/O may proceed on that stream. The default argument for clear is goodbit, so the statement

```
    cin.clear();
```

clears cin and sets goodbit for the stream. The statement

```
    cin.clear( ios::failbit )
```

sets the failbit. You might want to do this when performing input on cin with a user-defined type and encountering a problem. The name clear might seem inappropriate in this context, but it's correct.

The program of Fig. 13.22 demonstrates member functions rdstate, eof, fail, bad, good and clear. The actual values output may differ across different compilers.

The **operator!** member function of basic_ios returns true if the badbit is set, the failbit is set or *both* are set. The operator void * member function returns false (0) if the badbit is set, the failbit is set or both are set. These functions are useful in file processing when a true/false condition is being tested under the control of a selection statement or repetition statement.

13.9 Tying an Output Stream to an Input Stream

Interactive applications generally involve an `istream` for input *and* an `ostream` for output. When a prompting message appears on the screen, the user responds by entering the appropriate data. Obviously, the prompt needs to appear *before* the input operation proceeds. With output buffering, outputs appear only when the buffer *fills*, when outputs are *flushed* explicitly by the program or automatically at the end of the program. C++ provides member function `tie` to synchronize (i.e., "tie together") the operation of an `istream` and an `ostream` to ensure that outputs appear *before* their subsequent inputs. The call

```
cin.tie( &cout );
```

ties `cout` (an `ostream`) to `cin` (an `istream`). Actually, this particular call is redundant, because C++ performs this operation automatically to create a user's standard input/output environment. However, the user would tie other `istream`/`ostream` pairs explicitly. To untie an input stream, `inputStream`, from an output stream, use the call

```
inputStream.tie( 0 );
```

13.10 Wrap-Up

This chapter summarized how C++ performs input/output using streams. You learned about the stream-I/O classes and objects, as well as the stream I/O template class hierarchy. We discussed `ostream`'s formatted and unformatted output capabilities performed by the `put` and `write` functions. You learned about `istream`'s formatted and unformatted input capabilities performed by the `eof`, `get`, `getline`, `peek`, `putback`, `ignore` and `read` functions. We discussed stream manipulators and member functions that perform formatting tasks—`dec`, `oct`, `hex` and `setbase` for displaying integers; `precision` and `setprecision` for controlling floating-point precision; and `width` and `setw` for setting field width. You also learned additional formatting `iostream` manipulators and member functions—`showpoint` for displaying decimal point and trailing zeros; `left`, `right` and `internal` for justification; `fill` and `setfill` for padding; `scientific` and `fixed` for displaying floating-point numbers in scientific and fixed notation; `uppercase` for uppercase/lowercase control; `boolalpha` for specifying boolean format; and `flags` and `fmtflags` for resetting the format state.

In the next chapter, you'll learn about file processing, including how persistent data is stored and how to manipulate it.

Summary

Section 13.1 Introduction
- I/O operations are performed in a manner sensitive to the type of the data.

Section 13.2 Streams
- C++ I/O occurs in streams (p. 598). A stream is a sequence of bytes.
- Low-level I/O-capabilities specify that bytes should be transferred device-to-memory or memory-to-device. High-level I/O is performed with bytes grouped into meaningful units such as integers, strings and user-defined types.

- C++ provides both unformatted-I/O and formatted-I/O operations. Unformatted-I/O (p. 598) transfers are fast, but process raw data that is difficult for people to use. Formatted I/O processes data in meaningful units, but requires extra processing time that can degrade the performance.
- The `<iostream>` header declares all stream-I/O operations (p. 599).
- The `<iomanip>` header declares the parameterized stream manipulators (p. 599).
- The `<fstream>` header declares file-processing operations (p. 601).
- The `basic_istream` template (p. 599) supports stream-input operations.
- The `basic_ostream` template (p. 599) supports stream-output operations.
- The `basic_iostream` template supports both stream-input and stream-output operations.
- Templates `basic_istream` and the `basic_ostream` each derive from the `basic_ios` (p. 599) template.
- Template `basic_iostream` derives from both the `basic_istream` and `basic_ostream` templates.
- The `istream` object `cin` is tied to the standard input device, normally the keyboard.
- The `ostream` object `cout` is tied to the standard output device, normally the screen.
- The `ostream` object `cerr` is tied to the standard error device, normally the screen. Outputs to `cerr` are unbuffered (p. 601)—each insertion to `cerr` appears immediately.
- The `ostream` object `clog` is tied to the standard error device, normally the screen. Outputs to `clog` are buffered (p. 601).
- The C++ compiler determines data types automatically for input and output.

Section 13.3 Stream Output
- Addresses are displayed in hexadecimal format by default.
- To print the address in a pointer variable, cast the pointer to `void *`.
- Member function `put` outputs one character. Calls to `put` may be cascaded.

Section 13.4 Stream Input
- Stream input is performed with the stream extraction operator `>>`, which automatically skips whitespace characters (p. 603) in the input stream and returns `false` after end-of-file is encountered.
- Stream extraction causes `failbit` (p. 603) to be set for improper input and `badbit` (p. 603) to be set if the operation fails.
- A series of values can be input using the stream extraction operation in a `while` loop header. The extraction returns 0 when end-of-file is encountered or an error occurs.
- The `get` member function (p. 603) with no arguments inputs one character and returns the character; `EOF` is returned if end-of-file is encountered on the stream.
- Member function `get` with a character-reference argument inputs the next character from the input stream and stores it in the character argument. This version of `get` returns a reference to the `istream` object (p. 599) for which the `get` member function is being invoked.
- Member function `get` with three arguments—a character array, a size limit and a delimiter (with default value newline)—reads characters from the input stream up to a maximum of limit – 1 characters, or until the delimiter is read. The input string is terminated with a null character. The delimiter is not placed in the character array but remains in the input stream.
- Member function `getline` (p. 605) operates like the three-argument `get` member function. The `getline` function removes the delimiter from the input stream but does not store it in the string.
- Member function `ignore` (p. 606) skips the specified number of characters (the default is 1) in the input stream; it terminates if the specified delimiter is encountered (the default delimiter is `EOF`).

- The putback member function (p. 606) places the previous character obtained by a get on a stream back into that stream.

- The peek member function (p. 606) returns the next character from an input stream but does not extract (remove) the character from the stream.

- C++ offers type-safe I/O (p. 606). If unexpected data is processed by the << and >> operators, various error bits are set, which can be tested to determine whether an I/O operation succeeded or failed. If operator << has not been overloaded for a user-defined type, a compiler error is reported.

Section 13.5 Unformatted I/O Using **read, write** and **gcount**

- Unformatted I/O is performed with member functions read and write (p. 606). These input or output bytes to or from memory, beginning at a designated memory address.

- The gcount member function (p. 607) returns the number of characters input by the previous read operation on that stream.

- Member function read inputs a specified number of characters into a character array. failbit is set if fewer than the specified number of characters are read.

Section 13.6 Introduction to Stream Manipulators

- To change the base in which integers output, use the manipulator hex (p. 608) to set the base to hexadecimal (base 16) or oct (p. 608) to set the base to octal (base 8). Use manipulator dec (p. 608) to reset the base to decimal. The base remains the same until changed explicitly.

- The parameterized stream manipulator setbase (p. 608) also sets the base for integer output. setbase takes one integer argument of 10, 8 or 16 to set the base.

- Floating-point precision can be controlled with the setprecision stream manipulator or the precision member function (p. 608). Both set the precision for all subsequent output operations until the next precision-setting call. The precision member function with no argument returns the current precision value.

- Parameterized manipulators require the inclusion of the <iomanip> header.

- Member function width (p. 610) sets the field width and returns the previous width. Values narrower than the field are padded with fill characters (p. 610). The field-width setting applies only for the next insertion or extraction, then input is performed using the default settings. Values wider than a field are printed in their entirety. Function width with no argument returns the current width setting. Manipulator setw also sets the width.

- For input, the setw stream manipulator establishes a maximum string size; if a larger string is entered, the larger line is broken into pieces no larger than the designated size.

- You can create your own stream manipulators.

Section 13.7 Stream Format States and Stream Manipulators

- Stream manipulator showpoint (p. 613) forces a floating-point number to be output with a decimal point and with the number of significant digits specified by the precision.

- Stream manipulators left and right (p. 614) cause fields to be left justified with padding characters to the right or right justified with padding characters to the left.

- Stream manipulator internal (p. 615) indicates that a number's sign (or base when using stream manipulator showbase; p. 617) should be left justified within a field, its magnitude should be right justified and intervening spaces should be padded with the fill character.

- Member function fill (p. 616) specifies the fill character to be used with stream manipulators left, right and internal (space is the default); the prior padding character is returned. Stream manipulator setfill (p. 616) also sets the fill character.

- Stream manipulators oct, hex and dec specify that integers are to be treated as octal, hexadecimal or decimal values, respectively. Integer output defaults to decimal if none of these is set; stream extractions process the data in the form the data is supplied.

- Stream manipulator showbase forces the base of an integral value to be output.

- Stream manipulator scientific (p. 618) is used to output a floating-point number in scientific format. Stream manipulator fixed (p. 618) is used to output a floating-point number with the precision specified by the precision member function.

- Stream manipulator uppercase (p. 613) outputs an uppercase X or E for hexadecimal integers and scientific notation floating-point values, respectively. Hexadecimal values appear in all uppercase.

- Member function flags (p. 620) with no argument returns the current format state (p. 620) as a long value. Function flags with a long argument sets the format state specified by the argument.

Section 13.8 Stream Error States

- The state of a stream may be tested through bits in class ios_base.

- The eofbit (p. 623) is set for an input stream after end-of-file is encountered during an input operation. The eof member function (p. 623) reports whether the eofbit has been set.

- A stream's failbit is set when a format error occurs. The fail member function (p. 623) reports whether a stream operation has failed; it's normally possible to recover from such errors.

- A stream's badbit is set when an error occurs that results in data loss. Member function bad reports whether a stream operation failed. Such serious failures are normally nonrecoverable.

- The good member function (p. 623) returns true if the bad, fail and eof functions would all return false. I/O operations should be performed only on "good" streams.

- The rdstate member function (p. 623) returns the error state of the stream.

- Member function clear (p. 623) restores a stream's state to "good," so that I/O may proceed.

Section 13.9 Tying an Output Stream to an Input Stream

- C++ provides the tie member function (p. 624) to synchronize istream and ostream operations to ensure that outputs appear before subsequent inputs.

Self-Review Exercises

13.1   *(Fill in the Blanks)* Answer each of the following:
  a) Input/output in C++ occurs as _____ of bytes.
  b) The stream manipulators for justification are _____, _____ and _____.
  c) Member function _____ can be used to set and reset format state.
  d) Most C++ programs that do I/O should include the _____ header that contains the declarations required for all stream-I/O operations.
  e) When using parameterized manipulators, the header _____ must be included.
  f) Header _____ contains the declarations required for file processing.
  g) The ostream member function _____ is used to perform unformatted output.
  h) Input operations are supported by class _____.
  i) Standard error stream outputs are directed to the stream objects _____ or _____.
  j) Output operations are supported by class _____.
  k) The symbol for the stream insertion operator is _____.
  l) The four objects that correspond to the standard devices on the system include _____, _____, _____ and _____.
  m) The symbol for the stream extraction operator is _____.

n) The stream manipulators _____, _____ and _____ specify that integers should be displayed in octal, hexadecimal and decimal formats, respectively.

o) The _____ stream manipulator causes positive numbers to display with a plus sign.

13.2 *(True or False)* State whether the following are *true* or *false*. If the answer is *false*, explain why.

a) The stream member function flags with a long argument sets the flags state variable to its argument and returns its previous value.

b) The stream insertion operator << and the stream extraction operator >> are overloaded to handle all standard data types—including strings and memory addresses (stream insertion only)—and all user-defined data types.

c) The stream member function flags with no arguments resets the stream's format state.

d) The stream extraction operator >> can be overloaded with an operator function that takes an istream reference and a reference to a user-defined type as arguments and returns an istream reference.

e) The stream insertion operator << can be overloaded with an operator function that takes an istream reference and a reference to a user-defined type as arguments and returns an istream reference.

f) Input with the stream extraction operator >> always skips leading white-space characters in the input stream, by default.

g) The stream member function rdstate returns the current state of the stream.

h) The cout stream normally is connected to the display screen.

i) The stream member function good returns true if the bad, fail and eof member functions all return false.

j) The cin stream normally is connected to the display screen.

k) If a nonrecoverable error occurs during a stream operation, the bad member function will return true.

l) Output to cerr is unbuffered and output to clog is buffered.

m) Stream manipulator showpoint forces floating-point values to print with the default six digits of precision unless the precision value has been changed, in which case floating-point values print with the specified precision.

n) The ostream member function put outputs the specified number of characters.

o) The stream manipulators dec, oct and hex affect only the next integer output operation.

13.3 *(Write a C++ Statement)* For each of the following, write a single statement that performs the indicated task.

a) Output the string "Enter your name: ".

b) Use a stream manipulator that causes the exponent in scientific notation and the letters in hexadecimal values to print in capital letters.

c) Output the address of the variable myString of type char *.

d) Use a stream manipulator to ensure that floating-point values print in scientific notation.

e) Output the address in variable integerPtr of type int *.

f) Use a stream manipulator such that, when integer values are output, the integer base for octal and hexadecimal values is displayed.

g) Output the value pointed to by floatPtr of type float *.

h) Use a stream member function to set the fill character to '*' for printing in field widths larger than the values being output. Repeat this statement with a stream manipulator.

i) Output the characters '0' and 'K' in one statement with ostream function put.

j) Get the value of the next character to input without extracting it from the stream.

k) Input a single character into variable charValue of type char, using the istream member function get in two different ways.

l) Input and discard the next six characters in the input stream.

m) Use istream member function read to input 50 characters into char array line.
n) Read 10 characters into character array name. Stop reading characters if the '.' delimiter is encountered. Do not remove the delimiter from the input stream. Write another statement that performs this task and removes the delimiter from the input.
o) Use the istream member function gcount to determine the number of characters input into character array line by the last call to istream member function read, and output that number of characters, using ostream member function write.
p) Output 124, 18.376, 'Z', 1000000 and "String", separated by spaces.
q) Display cout's current precision setting.
r) Input an integer value into int variable months and a floating-point value into float variable percentageRate.
s) Print 1.92, 1.925 and 1.9258 separated by tabs and with 3 digits of precision, using a stream manipulator.
t) Print integer 100 in octal, hexadecimal and decimal, using stream manipulators and separated by tabs.
u) Print integer 100 in decimal, octal and hexadecimal separated by tabs, using a stream manipulator to change the base.
v) Print 1234 right justified in a 10-digit field.
w) Read characters into character array line until the character 'z' is encountered, up to a limit of 20 characters (including a terminating null character). Do not extract the delimiter character from the stream.
x) Use integer variables x and y to specify the field width and precision used to display the double value 87.4573, and display the value.

13.4 *(Find and Correct Code Errors)* Identify the error in each of the following statements and explain how to correct it.
a) `cout << "Value of x < y is: " << x < y;`
b) The following statement should print the integer value of 'A'.
`cout << 'A';`
c) `cout << 'A string in quotes';`

13.5 *(Show Outputs)* For each of the following, show the output.
a)
```
cout << "123456789" << endl;
cout.width( 5 );
cout.fill( '$' );
cout << 12 << endl << 12;
```
b) `cout << setw( 8 ) << setfill( '*' ) << 1000;`
c) `cout << setw( 9 ) << setprecision( 3 ) << 1024.987344;`
d) `cout << showbase << oct << 100 << endl << hex << 100;`
e) `cout << 10000 << endl << showpos << 10000;`
f) `cout << setw( 10 ) << setprecision( 2 ) << scientific << 244.93739;`

Answers to Self-Review Exercises

13.1 a) streams. b) left, right and internal. c) flags. d) <iostream>. e) <iomanip>. f) <fstream>. g) write. h) istream. i) cerr or clog. j) ostream. k) <<. l) cin, cout, cerr and clog. m) >>. n) oct, hex and dec. o) showpos.

13.2 a) False. The stream member function flags with a fmtflags argument sets the flags state variable to its argument and returns the prior state settings. b) False. The stream insertion and stream extraction operators are not overloaded for all user-defined types. You must specifically provide the overloaded operator functions to overload the stream operators for use with each user-defined type you create. c) False. The stream member function flags with no arguments returns the

current format settings as a fmtflags data type, which represents the format state. d) True. e) False.
To overload the stream insertion operator <<, the overloaded operator function must take an
ostream reference and a reference to a user-defined type as arguments and return an ostream reference. f) True. g) True. h) True. i) True. j) False. The cin stream is connected to the standard input
of the computer, which normally is the keyboard. k) True. l) True. m) True. n) False. The ostream
member function put outputs its single-character argument. o) False. The stream manipulators dec,
oct and hex set the output format state for integers to the specified base until the base is changed
again or the program terminates.

13.3 a) `cout << "Enter your name: ";`
   b) `cout << uppercase;`
   c) `cout << static_cast< void * >( myString );`
   d) `cout << scientific;`
   e) `cout << integerPtr;`
   f) `cout << showbase;`
   g) `cout << *floatPtr;`
   h) `cout.fill( '*' );`
       `cout << setfill( '*' );`
   i) `cout.put( 'O' ).put( 'K' );`
   j) `cin.peek();`
   k) `charValue = cin.get();`
       `cin.get( charValue );`
   l) `cin.ignore( 6 );`
   m) `cin.read( line, 50 );`
   n) `cin.get( name, 10, '.' );`
       `cin.getline( name, 10, '.' );`
   o) `cout.write( line, cin.gcount() );`
   p) `cout << 124 << ' ' << 18.376 << ' ' << "Z " << 1000000 << " String";`
   q) `cout << cout.precision();`
   r) `cin >> months >> percentageRate;`
   s) `cout << setprecision( 3 ) << 1.92 << '\t' << 1.925 << '\t' << 1.9258;`
   t) `cout << oct << 100 << '\t' << hex << 100 << '\t' << dec << 100;`
   u) `cout << 100 << '\t' << setbase( 8 ) << 100 << '\t' << setbase( 16 ) << 100;`
   v) `cout << setw( 10 ) << 1234;`
   w) `cin.get( line, 20, 'z' );`
   x) `cout << setw( x ) << setprecision( y ) << 87.4573;`

13.4 a) *Error:* The precedence of the << operator is higher than that of <, which causes the
statement to be evaluated improperly and also causes a compiler error.
   Correction: Place parentheses around the expression x < y.
   b) *Error:* In C++, characters are not treated as small integers, as they are in C.
   Correction: To print the numerical value for a character in the computer's character set,
   the character must be cast to an integer value, as in the following:
       `cout << static_cast< int >( 'A' );`
   c) *Error:* Quote characters cannot be printed in a string unless an escape sequence is used.
   Correction: Print the string:
       `cout << "\'A string in quotes\'";`

13.5 a) 123456789
       $$$12
       12
   b) ****1000
   c) 1024.9873

d) 0144
    0x64
e) 10000
    +10000
f) 2.45e+002

Exercises

13.6   *(Write C++ Statements)* Write a statement for each of the following:
  a) Print integer 40000 left justified in a 15-digit field.
  b) Read a string into character array variable `state`.
  c) Print 200 with and without a sign.
  d) Print the decimal value 100 in hexadecimal form preceded by 0x.
  e) Read characters into array `charArray` until the character `'p'` is encountered, up to a limit of 10 characters (including the terminating null character). Extract the delimiter from the input stream, and discard it.
  f) Print 1.234 in a 9-digit field with preceding zeros.

13.7   *(Inputting Decimal, Octal and Hexadecimal Values)* Write a program to test the inputting of integer values in decimal, octal and hexadecimal formats. Output each integer read by the program in all three formats. Test the program with the following input data: 10, 010, 0x10.

13.8   *(Printing Pointer Values as Integers)* Write a program that prints pointer values, using casts to all the integer data types. Which ones print strange values? Which ones cause errors?

13.9   *(Printing with Field Widths)* Write a program to test the results of printing the integer value 12345 and the floating-point value 1.2345 in various-sized fields. What happens when the values are printed in fields containing fewer digits than the values?

13.10   *(Rounding)* Write a program that prints the value 100.453627 rounded to the nearest digit, tenth, hundredth, thousandth and ten-thousandth.

13.11   *(Length of a String)* Write a program that inputs a string from the keyboard and determines the length of the string. Print the string in a field width that is twice the length of the string.

13.12   *(Converting Fahrenheit to Celsius)* Write a program that converts integer Fahrenheit temperatures from 0 to 212 degrees to floating-point Celsius temperatures with 3 digits of precision. Use the formula

```
celsius = 5.0 / 9.0 * ( fahrenheit - 32 );
```

to perform the calculation. The output should be printed in two right-justified columns and the Celsius temperatures should be preceded by a sign for both positive and negative values.

13.13   In some programming languages, strings are entered surrounded by either single or double quotation marks. Write a program that reads the three strings suzy, "suzy" and 'suzy'. Are the single and double quotes ignored or read as part of the string?

13.14   *(Reading Phone Numbers with and Overloaded Stream Extraction Operator)* In Fig. 10.5, the stream extraction and stream insertion operators were overloaded for input and output of objects of the PhoneNumber class. Rewrite the stream extraction operator to perform the following error checking on input. The operator>> function will need to be reimplemented.
  a) Input the entire phone number into an array. Test that the proper number of characters has been entered. There should be a total of 14 characters read for a phone number of the form (800) 555-1212. Use ios_base-member-function `clear` to set `failbit` for improper input.

b) The area code and exchange do not begin with 0 or 1. Test the first digit of the area-code and exchange portions of the phone number to be sure that neither begins with 0 or 1. Use ios_base-member-function clear to set failbit for improper input.

c) The middle digit of an area code used to be limited to 0 or 1 (though this has changed). Test the middle digit for a value of 0 or 1. Use the ios_base-member-function clear to set failbit for improper input. If none of the above operations results in failbit being set for improper input, copy the parts of the telephone number into the PhoneNumber object's areaCode, exchange and line members. If failbit has been set on the input, have the program print an error message and end, rather than print the phone number.

13.15 *(Point Class)* Write a program that accomplishes each of the following:

a) Create a user-defined class Point that contains the private integer data members xCoordinate and yCoordinate and declares stream insertion and stream extraction over-loaded operator functions as friends of the class.

b) Define the stream insertion and stream extraction operator functions. The stream extraction operator function should determine whether the data entered is valid, and, if not, it should set the failbit to indicate improper input. The stream insertion operator should not be able to display the point after an input error occurred.

c) Write a main function that tests input and output of user-defined class Point, using the overloaded stream extraction and stream insertion operators.

13.16 *(Complex Class)* Write a program that accomplishes each of the following:

a) Create a user-defined class Complex that contains the private integer data members real and imaginary and declares stream insertion and stream extraction overloaded operator functions as friends of the class.

b) Define the stream insertion and stream extraction operator functions. The stream extraction operator function should determine whether the data entered is valid, and, if not, it should set failbit to indicate improper input. The input should be of the form

   3 + 8i

c) The values can be negative or positive, and it's possible that one of the two values is not provided, in which case the appropriate data member should be set to 0. The stream insertion operator should not be able to display the point if an input error occurred. For negative imaginary values, a minus sign should be printed rather than a plus sign.

d) Write a main function that tests input and output of user-defined class Complex, using the overloaded stream extraction and stream insertion operators.

13.17 *(Printing a Table of ASCII Values)* Write a program that uses a for statement to print a table of ASCII values for the characters in the ASCII character set from 33 to 126. The program should print the decimal value, octal value, hexadecimal value and character value for each character. Use the stream manipulators dec, oct and hex to print the integer values.

13.18 *(String-Terminating Null Character)* Write a program to show that the getline and three-argument get istream member functions both end the input string with a string-terminating null character. Also, show that get leaves the delimiter character on the input stream, whereas getline extracts the delimiter character and discards it. What happens to the unread characters in the stream?

File Processing

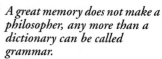

A great memory does not make a philosopher, any more than a dictionary can be called grammar.
—John Henry, Cardinal Newman

I can only assume that a "Do Not File" document is filed in a "Do Not File" file.
—Senator Frank Church
Senate Intelligence Subcommittee
Hearing, 1975

Objectives

In this chapter you'll learn:

- To create, read, write and update files.

- Sequential file processing.

- Random-access file processing.

- To use high-performance unformatted I/O operations.

- The differences between formatted-data and raw-data file processing.

- To build a transaction-processing program using random-access file processing.

- To understand the concept of object serialization.

14.1 Introduction

Storage of data in memory is *temporary*. **Files** are used for **data persistence**—*permanent* retention of data. Computers store files on **secondary storage devices**, such as hard disks, CDs, DVDs, flash drives and tapes. In this chapter, we explain how to build C++ programs that create, update and process data files. We consider both *sequential files* and *random-access files*. We compare *formatted-data* file processing and *raw-data* file processing. We examine techniques for input of data from, and output of data to, `string` streams rather than files in Chapter 21.

14.2 Files and Streams

C++ views each file simply as *a sequence of bytes* (Fig. 14.1). Each file ends either with an **end-of-file marker** or at a specific byte number recorded in an operating-system-maintained, administrative data structure. When a file is *opened*, an object is created, and a stream is associated with the object. In Chapter 13, we saw that objects `cin`, `cout`, `cerr` and `clog` are created when `<iostream>` is included. The streams associated with these objects provide communication channels between a program and a particular file or device. For example, the `cin` object (standard input stream object) enables a program to input data from the keyboard or from other devices, the `cout` object (standard output stream object) enables a program to output data to the screen or other devices, and the `cerr` and `clog` objects (standard error stream objects) enable a program to output error messages to the screen or other devices.

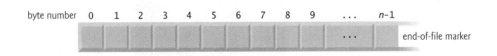

byte number   0   1   2   3   4   5   6   7   8   9   ...   *n*-1

... end-of-file marker

Fig. 14.1 | C++'s simple view of a file of *n* bytes.

File-Processing Class Templates

To perform file processing in C++, headers `<iostream>` and `<fstream>` must be included. Header `<fstream>` includes the definitions for the stream class templates `basic_ifstream` (for file input), `basic_ofstream` (for file output) and `basic_fstream` (for file input *and* output). Each class template has a predefined template specialization that enables char I/O. In addition, the `<fstream>` library provides `typedef` aliases for these template specializations. For example, the `typedef ifstream` represents a specialization of `basic_ifstream` that enables char input from a file. Similarly, `typedef ofstream` represents a specialization of `basic_ofstream` that enables char output to files. Also, `typedef fstream` represents a specialization of `basic_fstream` that enables char input from, *and* output to, files.

These templates derive from the class templates `basic_istream`, `basic_ostream` and `basic_iostream`, respectively. Thus, all member functions, operators and manipulators that belong to these templates (which we described in Chapter 13) also can be applied to file streams. Figure 14.2 summarizes the inheritance relationships of the I/O classes that we've discussed to this point.

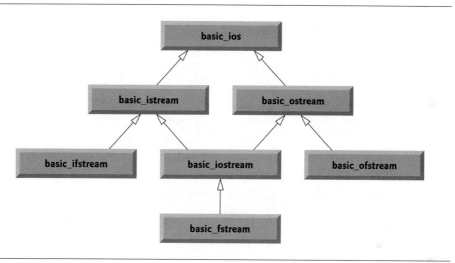

Fig. 14.2 | Portion of stream I/O template hierarchy.

14.3 Creating a Sequential File

C++ imposes no structure on a file. Thus, a concept like that of a "record" does not exist in a C++ file. You must structure files to meet the application's requirements. The following example shows how you can impose a simple record structure on a file.

Figure 14.3 creates a sequential file that might be used in an accounts-receivable system to help manage the money owed to a company by its credit clients. For each client, the program obtains the client's account number, name and balance (i.e., the amount the client owes the company for goods and services received in the past). The data obtained for each client constitutes a *record* for that client. The account number serves as the *record key*; that is, the program creates and maintains the records of the file in account number order. This program assumes the user enters the records in account number order. In a comprehensive accounts receivable system, a sorting capability would be provided for the user to enter records *in any* order—the records then would be *sorted* and written to the file.

```
 1   // Fig. 14.3: Fig14_03.cpp
 2   // Create a sequential file.
 3   #include <iostream>
 4   #include <string>
 5   #include <fstream> // contains file stream processing types
 6   #include <cstdlib> // exit function prototype
 7   using namespace std;
 8
 9   int main()
10   {
11      // ofstream constructor opens file
12      ofstream outClientFile( "clients.txt", ios::out );
13
14      // exit program if unable to create file
15      if ( !outClientFile ) // overloaded ! operator
16      {
17         cerr << "File could not be opened" << endl;
18         exit( EXIT_FAILURE );
19      } // end if
20
21      cout << "Enter the account, name, and balance." << endl
22           << "Enter end-of-file to end input.\n? ";
23
24      int account; // the account number
25      string name; // the account owner's name
26      double balance; // the account balance
27
28      // read account, name and balance from cin, then place in file
29      while ( cin >> account >> name >> balance )
30      {
31         outClientFile << account << ' ' << name << ' ' << balance << endl;
32         cout << "? ";
33      } // end while
34   } // end main
```

```
Enter the account, name, and balance.
Enter end-of-file to end input.
? 100 Jones 24.98
? 200 Doe 345.67
? 300 White 0.00
? 400 Stone -42.16
? 500 Rich 224.62
? ^Z
```

Fig. 14.3 | Create a sequential file.

Opening a File

Figure 14.3 writes data to a file, so we open the file for output by creating an ofstream object. Two arguments are passed to the object's constructor—the filename and the file-open mode (line 12). For an ofstream object, the file-open mode can be either ios::out (the default) to *output* data to a file or ios::app to *append* data to the end of a file (without modifying any data already in the file). Since ios::out is the default, the second constructor argument in line 12 is not required. Existing files opened with mode ios::out are truncated—all data in the file is *discarded*. If the specified file does *not* yet exist, then the ofstream object *creates* the file, using that filename. Prior to C++11, the filename was specified as a pointer-based string—as of C++11, it can also be specified as a string object.

> **Error-Prevention Tip 14.1**
> *Use caution when opening an existing file for output (ios::out), especially when you want to preserve the file's contents, which will be discarded without warning.*

Line 12 creates an ofstream object named outClientFile associated with the file clients.txt that's opened for output. The arguments "clients.txt" and ios::out are passed to the ofstream constructor, which opens the file—this establishes a "line of communication" with the file. By *default*, ofstream objects are opened for *output*, so line 12 could have used the alternate statement

```
ofstream outClientFile( "clients.txt" );
```

to open clients.txt for output. Figure 14.4 lists the file-open modes. These modes can also be combined, as we discuss in Section 14.8.

Mode	Description
ios::app	*Append* all output to the end of the file.
ios::ate	Open a file for output and move to the end of the file (normally used to append data to a file). Data can be written *anywhere* in the file.
ios::in	Open a file for *input*.
ios::out	Open a file for *output*.
ios::trunc	*Discard* the file's contents (this also is the default action for ios::out).
ios::binary	Open a file for binary, i.e., *nontext*, input or output.

Fig. 14.4 | File open modes.

Opening a File via the open Member Function
You can create an ofstream object *without* opening a specific file—in this case, a file can be attached to the object later. For example, the statement

```
ofstream outClientFile;
```

creates an ofstream object that's not yet associated with a file. The ofstream member function **open** opens a file and attaches it to an *existing* ofstream object as follows:

```
outClientFile.open( "clients.txt", ios::out );
```

> **Error-Prevention Tip 14.2**
> *Some operating systems allow you to open the same file multiple times simultaneously. Avoid doing this because it can lead to subtle problems.*

Testing Whether a File Was Opened Successfully
After creating an ofstream object and *attempting* to open it, the program tests whether the open operation was *successful*. The if statement in lines 15–19 uses the *overloaded* ios mem-

ber function `operator!` to determine whether the open operation succeeded. The condition returns a `true` value if either the `failbit` or the `badbit` (see Chapter 13) is set for the stream on the open operation. Some possible errors are attempting to open a *nonexistent* file for reading, attempting to open a file for reading or writing from a directory that you don't have permission to access, and opening a file for writing when no disk space is available.

If the condition indicates an unsuccessful attempt to open the file, line 17 outputs the error message `"File could not be opened"`, and line 18 invokes function `exit` to terminate the program. The argument to `exit` is returned to the environment from which the program was invoked. Passing `EXIT_SUCCESS` (also defined in `<cstdlib>`) to `exit` indicates that the program terminated *normally*; passing any other value (in this case `EXIT_FAILURE`) indicates that the program terminated due to an *error*.

The Overloaded **void** * Operator

Another *overloaded* `ios` member function—`operator void *`—converts the stream to a pointer, so it can be tested as 0 (i.e., the null pointer) or nonzero (i.e., any other pointer value). When a pointer value is used as a condition, C++ interprets a null pointer in a condition as the `bool` value `false` and interprets a non-null pointer as the `bool` value `true`. If the `failbit` or `badbit` has been set for the stream, 0 (`false`) is returned. The condition in the `while` statement of lines 29–33 invokes the `operator void *` member function on `cin` *implicitly*. The condition remains `true` as long as neither the `failbit` nor the `badbit` has been set for `cin`. Entering the *end-of-file* indicator sets the `failbit` for `cin`. The `operator void *` function can be used to test an input object for end-of-file, but you can also call member function `eof` on the input object.

Processing Data

If line 12 opens the file successfully, the program begins processing data. Lines 21–22 prompt the user to enter either the various fields for each record or the end-of-file indicator when data entry is complete. Figure 14.5 lists the keyboard combinations for entering end-of-file for various computer systems.

Computer system	Keyboard combination
UNIX/Linux/Mac OS X	*<Ctrl-d>* (on a line by itself)
Microsoft Windows	*<Ctrl-z>* (sometimes followed by pressing *Enter*)

Fig. 14.5 | End-of-file key combinations.

Line 29 extracts each set of data and determines whether end-of-file has been entered. When end-of-file is encountered or bad data is entered, `operator void *` returns the null pointer (which converts to the `bool` value `false`) and the `while` statement terminates. The user enters end-of-file to inform the program to process no additional data. The end-of-file indicator is set when the user enters the end-of-file key combination. The `while` statement loops until the end-of-file indicator is set (or bad data is entered).

Line 31 writes a set of data to the file `clients.txt`, using the stream insertion operator `<<` and the `outClientFile` object associated with the file at the beginning of the program. The data may be retrieved by a program designed to read the file (see Section 14.4). The file created in Fig. 14.3 is simply a *text file*, so it can be viewed by any text editor.

Closing a File
Once the user enters the end-of-file indicator, `main` terminates. This implicitly invokes `outClientFile`'s destructor, which *closes* the `clients.txt` file. You also can close the `ofstream` object *explicitly*, using member function `close` as follows:

```
outClientFile.close();
```

Error-Prevention Tip 14.3

Always close a file as soon as it's no longer needed in a program

The Sample Execution
In the sample execution for the program of Fig. 14.3, the user enters information for five accounts, then signals that data entry is complete by entering end-of-file (^Z is displayed for Microsoft Windows). This dialog window does *not* show how the data records appear in the file. To verify that the program created the file successfully, the next section shows how to create a program that reads this file and prints its contents.

14.4 Reading Data from a Sequential File

Files store data so it may be *retrieved* for processing when needed. The previous section demonstrated how to create a file for sequential access. We now discuss how to *read* data sequentially from a file. Figure 14.6 reads and displays the records from the `clients.txt` file that we created using the program of Fig. 14.3. Creating an `ifstream` object opens a file for *input*. The `ifstream` constructor can receive the filename and the file open mode as arguments. Line 15 creates an `ifstream` object called `inClientFile` and associates it with the `clients.txt` file. The arguments in parentheses are passed to the `ifstream` constructor, which opens the file and establishes a "line of communication" with the file.

Good Programming Practice 14.1

If a file's contents should not be modified, use `ios::in` to open it only for input. This prevents unintentional modification of the file's contents and is another example of the principle of least privilege.

```
 1   // Fig. 14.6: Fig14_06.cpp
 2   // Reading and printing a sequential file.
 3   #include <iostream>
 4   #include <fstream> // file stream
 5   #include <iomanip>
 6   #include <string>
 7   #include <cstdlib>
 8   using namespace std;
 9
10   void outputLine( int, const string &, double ); // prototype
```

Fig. 14.6 | Reading and printing a sequential file. (Part 1 of 2.)

```
11
12   int main()
13   {
14      // ifstream constructor opens the file
15      ifstream inClientFile( "clients.txt", ios::in );
16
17      // exit program if ifstream could not open file
18      if ( !inClientFile )
19      {
20         cerr << "File could not be opened" << endl;
21         exit( EXIT_FAILURE );
22      } // end if
23
24      int account; // the account number
25      string name; // the account owner's name
26      double balance; // the account balance
27
28      cout << left << setw( 10 ) << "Account" << setw( 13 )
29         << "Name" << "Balance" << endl << fixed << showpoint;
30
31      // display each record in file
32      while ( inClientFile >> account >> name >> balance )
33         outputLine( account, name, balance );
34   } // end main
35
36   // display single record from file
37   void outputLine( int account, const string &name, double balance )
38   {
39      cout << left << setw( 10 ) << account << setw( 13 ) << name
40         << setw( 7 ) << setprecision( 2 ) << right << balance << endl;
41   } // end function outputLine
```

```
Account   Name        Balance
100       Jones         24.98
200       Doe          345.67
300       White          0.00
400       Stone        -42.16
500       Rich         224.62
```

Fig. 14.6 | Reading and printing a sequential file. (Part 2 of 2.)

Opening a File for Input

Objects of class ifstream are opened for *input* by default, so the statement

```
ifstream inClientFile( "clients.txt" );
```

opens clients.txt for input. Just as with an ofstream object, an ifstream object can be created without opening a specific file, because a file can be attached to it later.

Ensuring That the File Was Opened

Before attempting to retrieve data from the file, the program uses the condition !inClientFile to determine whether the file was opened successfully.

Reading from the File

Line 32 reads a set of data (i.e., a record) from the file. After line 32 executes the first time, account has the value 100, name has the value "Jones" and balance has the value 24.98. Each time line 32 executes, it reads another record from the file into the variables account, name and balance. Line 33 displays the records, using function outputLine (lines 37–41), which uses parameterized stream manipulators to format the data for display. When the end of file has been reached, the *implicit call to operator void * in the while condition* returns the null pointer (which converts to the bool value false), the ifstream destructor closes the file and the program terminates.

File Position Pointers

To retrieve data sequentially from a file, programs normally start reading from the beginning of the file and read all the data consecutively until the desired data is found. It might be necessary to process the file sequentially several times (from the beginning of the file) during the execution of a program. Both istream and ostream provide member functions for *repositioning the file-position pointer* (the byte number of the next byte in the file to be read or written). These member functions are **seekg** ("seek get") for istream and **seekp** ("seek put") for ostream. Each istream object has a *get pointer*, which indicates the byte number in the file from which the next *input* is to occur, and each ostream object has a *put pointer*, which indicates the byte number in the file at which the next *output* should be placed. The statement

```
inClientFile.seekg( 0 );
```

repositions the file-position pointer to the *beginning* of the file (location 0) attached to inClientFile. The argument to seekg is a long integer. A second argument can be specified to indicate the seek direction, which can be **ios::beg** (the default) for positioning relative to the *beginning* of a stream, **ios::cur** for positioning relative to the *current position* in a stream or **ios::end** for positioning relative to the *end* of a stream. The file-position pointer is an integer value that specifies the location in the file as a number of bytes from the file's starting location (this is also referred to as the offset from the beginning of the file). Some examples of positioning the *get* file-position pointer are

```
// position to the nth byte of fileObject (assumes ios::beg)
fileObject.seekg( n );

// position n bytes forward in fileObject
fileObject.seekg( n, ios::cur );

// position n bytes back from end of fileObject
fileObject.seekg( n, ios::end );

// position at end of fileObject
fileObject.seekg( 0, ios::end );
```

The same operations can be performed using ostream member function seekp. Member functions **tellg** and **tellp** are provided to return the current locations of the *get* and *put* pointers, respectively. The following statement assigns the *get* file-position pointer value to variable location of type long:

```
location = fileObject.tellg();
```

Credit Inquiry Program

Figure 14.7 enables a credit manager to display the account information for those customers with zero balances (i.e., customers who do not owe the company any money), credit (negative) balances (i.e., customers to whom the company owes money), and debit (positive) balances (i.e., customers who owe the company money for goods and services received in the past). The program displays a menu and allows the credit manager to enter one of three options to obtain credit information. Option 1 produces a list of accounts with zero balances. Option 2 produces a list of accounts with credit balances. Option 3 produces a list of accounts with debit balances. Option 4 terminates program execution. Entering an invalid option displays the prompt to enter another choice. Lines 64–65 enable the program to read from the beginning of the file after end-of-file has been read.

```cpp
1   // Fig. 14.7: Fig14_07.cpp
2   // Credit inquiry program.
3   #include <iostream>
4   #include <fstream>
5   #include <iomanip>
6   #include <string>
7   #include <cstdlib>
8   using namespace std;
9
10  enum RequestType { ZERO_BALANCE = 1, CREDIT_BALANCE, DEBIT_BALANCE, END };
11  int getRequest();
12  bool shouldDisplay( int, double );
13  void outputLine( int, const string &, double );
14
15  int main()
16  {
17     // ifstream constructor opens the file
18     ifstream inClientFile( "clients.txt", ios::in );
19
20     // exit program if ifstream could not open file
21     if ( !inClientFile )
22     {
23        cerr << "File could not be opened" << endl;
24        exit( EXIT_FAILURE );
25     } // end if
26
27     int account; // the account number
28     string name; // the account owner's name
29     double balance; // the account balance
30
31     // get user's request (e.g., zero, credit or debit balance)
32     int request = getRequest();
33
34     // process user's request
35     while ( request != END )
36     {
37        switch ( request )
38        {
```

Fig. 14.7 | Credit inquiry program. (Part 1 of 4.)

```
39              case ZERO_BALANCE:
40                  cout << "\nAccounts with zero balances:\n";
41                  break;
42              case CREDIT_BALANCE:
43                  cout << "\nAccounts with credit balances:\n";
44                  break;
45              case DEBIT_BALANCE:
46                  cout << "\nAccounts with debit balances:\n";
47                  break;
48          } // end switch
49
50          // read account, name and balance from file
51          inClientFile >> account >> name >> balance;
52
53          // display file contents (until eof)
54          while ( !inClientFile.eof() )
55          {
56              // display record
57              if ( shouldDisplay( request, balance ) )
58                  outputLine( account, name, balance );
59
60              // read account, name and balance from file
61              inClientFile >> account >> name >> balance;
62          } // end inner while
63
64          inClientFile.clear(); // reset eof for next input
65          inClientFile.seekg( 0 ); // reposition to beginning of file
66          request = getRequest(); // get additional request from user
67      } // end outer while
68
69      cout << "End of run." << endl;
70  } // end main
71
72  // obtain request from user
73  int getRequest()
74  {
75      int request; // request from user
76
77      // display request options
78      cout << "\nEnter request" << endl
79          << " 1 - List accounts with zero balances" << endl
80          << " 2 - List accounts with credit balances" << endl
81          << " 3 - List accounts with debit balances" << endl
82          << " 4 - End of run" << fixed << showpoint;
83
84      do // input user request
85      {
86          cout << "\n? ";
87          cin >> request;
88      } while ( request < ZERO_BALANCE && request > END );
89
90      return request;
91  } // end function getRequest
```

Fig. 14.7 | Credit inquiry program. (Part 2 of 4.)

```
92
93   // determine whether to display given record
94   bool shouldDisplay( int type, double balance )
95   {
96      // determine whether to display zero balances
97      if ( type == ZERO_BALANCE && balance == 0 )
98         return true;
99
100     // determine whether to display credit balances
101     if ( type == CREDIT_BALANCE && balance < 0 )
102        return true;
103
104     // determine whether to display debit balances
105     if ( type == DEBIT_BALANCE && balance > 0 )
106        return true;
107
108     return false;
109  } // end function shouldDisplay
110
111  // display single record from file
112  void outputLine( int account, const string &name, double balance )
113  {
114     cout << left << setw( 10 ) << account << setw( 13 ) << name
115        << setw( 7 ) << setprecision( 2 ) << right << balance << endl;
116  } // end function outputLine
```

```
Enter request
 1 - List accounts with zero balances
 2 - List accounts with credit balances
 3 - List accounts with debit balances
 4 - End of run
? 1

Accounts with zero balances:
300      White          0.00

Enter request
 1 - List accounts with zero balances
 2 - List accounts with credit balances
 3 - List accounts with debit balances
 4 - End of run
? 2

Accounts with credit balances:
400      Stone         -42.16

Enter request
 1 - List accounts with zero balances
 2 - List accounts with credit balances
 3 - List accounts with debit balances
 4 - End of run
? 3

Accounts with debit balances:
100      Jones         24.98
200      Doe          345.67
500      Rich         224.62
```

Fig. 14.7 | Credit inquiry program. (Part 3 of 4.)

```
Enter request
 1 - List accounts with zero balances
 2 - List accounts with credit balances
 3 - List accounts with debit balances
 4 - End of run
? 4
End of run.
```

Fig. 14.7 | Credit inquiry program. (Part 4 of 4.)

14.5 Updating Sequential Files

Data that is formatted and written to a sequential file as shown in Section 14.3 cannot be modified without the risk of destroying other data in the file. For example, if the name "White" needs to be changed to "Worthington," the old name cannot be overwritten without corrupting the file. The record for White was written to the file as

```
300 White 0.00
```

If this record were rewritten beginning at the same location in the file using the longer name, the record would be

```
300 Worthington 0.00
```

The new record contains six more characters than the original record. Therefore, the characters beyond the second "o" in "Worthington" would overwrite the beginning of the next sequential record in the file. The problem is that, in the formatted input/output model using the stream insertion operator << and the stream extraction operator >>, fields—and hence records—can vary in size. For example, values 7, 14, –117, 2074, and 27383 are all ints, which store the same number of "raw data" bytes internally (typically four bytes on 32-bit machines and eight bytes on 64-bit machines). However, these integers become different-sized fields, depending on their actual values, when output as formatted text (character sequences). Therefore, the formatted input/output model usually is not used to update records *in place*. Sections 14.6–14.10 show how to perform in-place updates with fixed-length records.

Such updating can be done awkwardly. For example, to make the preceding name change, the records before 300 White 0.00 in a sequential file could be *copied* to a new file, the updated record then written to the new file, and the records after 300 White 0.00 copied to the new file. Then the old file could be deleted and the new file renamed. This requires processing *every* record in the file to update one record. If many records are being updated in one pass of the file, though, this technique can be acceptable.

14.6 Random-Access Files

So far, we've seen how to create sequential files and search them to locate information. Sequential files are inappropriate for instant-access applications, in which a particular record must be located immediately. Common instant-access applications are airline reservation systems, banking systems, point-of-sale systems, automated teller machines and other kinds of transaction-processing systems that require rapid access to specific data. A bank might have hundreds of thousands (or even millions) of other customers, yet, when a customer uses an automated teller machine, the program checks that customer's account in a few seconds or less for sufficient funds. This kind of instant access is made possible with random-access files. Individual records of a random-access file can be accessed directly (and quickly) without having to search other records.

As we've said, C++ does not impose structure on a file. So the application that wants to use random-access files must create them. A variety of techniques can be used. Perhaps the easiest method is to require that all records in a file be of the *same fixed length*. Using same-size, fixed-length records makes it easy for a program to quickly calculate (as a function of the record size and the record key) the exact location of any record relative to the beginning of the file. We'll soon see how this facilitates *immediate access* to specific records, even in large files.

Figure 14.8 illustrates C++'s view of a random-access file composed of fixed-length records (each record, in this case, is 100 bytes long). A random-access file is like a railroad train with many same-size cars—some empty and some with contents.

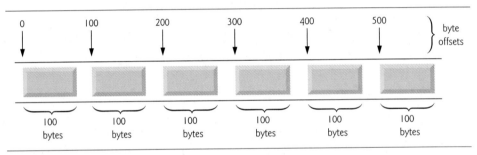

Fig. 14.8 | C++ view of a random-access file.

Data can be inserted into a random-access file without destroying other data in the file. Data stored previously also can be updated or deleted without rewriting the entire file. In the following sections, we explain how to create a random-access file, enter data into the file, read the data both sequentially and randomly, update the data and delete data that is no longer needed.

14.7 Creating a Random-Access File

The `ostream` member function `write` outputs to the specified stream a fixed number of bytes, beginning at a specific location in memory. When the stream is associated with a file, function `write` writes the data *at the location in the file specified by the put file-position pointer*. The `istream` member function **read** inputs a fixed number of bytes from the specified stream to an area in memory beginning at a specified address. If the stream is associated with a file, function `read` inputs bytes at the location in the file specified by the "get" file-position pointer.

Writing Bytes with `ostream` *Member Function* `write`
When writing the integer `number` to a file, instead of using the statement

```
outFile << number;
```

which for a four-byte integer could print as few digits as one or as many as 11 (10 digits plus a sign, each requiring a single byte of storage), we can use the statement

```
outFile.write( reinterpret_cast< const char * >( &number ),
    sizeof( number ) );
```

which always writes the *binary* version of the integer number's *four* bytes (on a machine with four-byte integers). Function `write` treats its first argument as a group of bytes by viewing the object in memory as a `const char *`, which is a pointer to a byte. Starting from that location, function `write` outputs the number of bytes specified by its second argument—an integer of type `size_t`. As we'll see, `istream` function `read` can subsequently be used to read the four bytes back into integer variable `number`.

Converting Between Pointer Types with the `reinterpret_cast` Operator

Unfortunately, most pointers that we pass to function `write` as the first argument are *not* of type `const char *`. To output objects of other types, we must convert the pointers to those objects to type `const char *`; otherwise, the compiler will not compile calls to function `write`. C++ provides the `reinterpret_cast` operator for cases like this in which a pointer of one type must be cast to an *unrelated* pointer type. Without a `reinterpret_cast`, the `write` statement that outputs the integer `number` will not compile because the compiler does *not* allow a pointer of type `int *` (the type returned by the expression `&number`) to be passed to a function that expects an argument of type `const char *`—as far as the compiler is concerned, these types are *inconsistent*.

A `reinterpret_cast` is performed at *compile time* and does *not* change the value of the object to which its operand points. Instead, it requests that the compiler reinterpret the operand as the target type (specified in the angle brackets following the keyword `reinterpret_cast`). In Fig. 14.11, we use `reinterpret_cast` to convert a `ClientData` pointer to a `const char *`, which reinterprets a `ClientData` object as bytes to be output to a file. Random-access file-processing programs rarely write a single field to a file. Typically, they write one object of a class at a time, as we show in the following examples.

Error-Prevention Tip 14.4

It's easy to use `reinterpret_cast` to perform dangerous manipulations that could lead to serious execution-time errors.

Portability Tip 14.1

`reinterpret_cast` is compiler dependent and can cause programs to behave differently on different platforms. Use this operator only if it's absolutely necessary.

Portability Tip 14.2

A program that reads unformatted data (written by `write`) must be compiled and executed on a system compatible with the program that wrote the data, because different systems may represent internal data differently.

Credit Processing Program

Consider the following problem statement:

> Create a credit-processing program capable of storing at most 100 fixed-length records for a company that can have up to 100 customers. Each record should consist of an account number that acts as the record key, a last name, a first name and a balance. The program should be able to update an account, insert a new account, delete an account and insert all the account records into a formatted text file for printing.

The next few sections create this credit-processing program. Figure 14.11 illustrates opening a random-access file, defining the record format using an object of class ClientData (Figs. 14.9–14.10) and writing data to the disk in *binary* format. This program initializes all 100 records of the file credit.dat with *empty* objects, using function write. Each empty object contains the account number 0, emptylast and first name strings and the balance 0.0. Each record is initialized with the space in which the account data will be stored.

```cpp
1   // Fig. 14.9: ClientData.h
2   // Class ClientData definition used in Fig. 14.11-Fig. 14.14.
3   #ifndef CLIENTDATA_H
4   #define CLIENTDATA_H
5
6   #include <string>
7
8   class ClientData
9   {
10  public:
11     // default ClientData constructor
12     ClientData( int = 0, const std::string & = "",
13        const std::string & = "", double = 0.0 );
14
15     // accessor functions for accountNumber
16     void setAccountNumber( int );
17     int getAccountNumber() const;
18
19     // accessor functions for lastName
20     void setLastName( const std::string & );
21     std::string getLastName() const;
22
23     // accessor functions for firstName
24     void setFirstName( const std::string & );
25     std::string getFirstName() const;
26
27     // accessor functions for balance
28     void setBalance( double );
29     double getBalance() const;
30  private:
31     int accountNumber;
32     char lastName[ 15 ];
33     char firstName[ 10 ];
34     double balance;
35  }; // end class ClientData
36
37  #endif
```

Fig. 14.9 | ClientData class header.

```cpp
1   // Fig. 14.10: ClientData.cpp
2   // Class ClientData stores customer's credit information.
3   #include <string>
```

Fig. 14.10 | ClientData class represents a customer's credit information. (Part 1 of 3.)

```
 4   #include "ClientData.h"
 5   using namespace std;
 6
 7   // default ClientData constructor
 8   ClientData::ClientData( int accountNumberValue, const string &lastName,
 9      const string &firstName, double balanceValue )
10      : accountNumber( accountNumberValue ), balance( balanceValue )
11   {
12      setLastName( lastNameValue );
13      setFirstName( firstNameValue );
14   } // end ClientData constructor
15
16   // get account-number value
17   int ClientData::getAccountNumber() const
18   {
19      return accountNumber;
20   } // end function getAccountNumber
21
22   // set account-number value
23   void ClientData::setAccountNumber( int accountNumberValue )
24   {
25      accountNumber = accountNumberValue; // should validate
26   } // end function setAccountNumber
27
28   // get last-name value
29   string ClientData::getLastName() const
30   {
31      return lastName;
32   } // end function getLastName
33
34   // set last-name value
35   void ClientData::setLastName( const string &lastNameString )
36   {
37      // copy at most 15 characters from string to lastName
38      int length = lastNameString.size();
39      length = ( length < 15 ? length : 14 );
40      lastNameString.copy( lastName, length );
41      lastName[ length ] = '\0'; // append null character to lastName
42   } // end function setLastName
43
44   // get first-name value
45   string ClientData::getFirstName() const
46   {
47      return firstName;
48   } // end function getFirstName
49
50   // set first-name value
51   void ClientData::setFirstName( const string &firstNameString )
52   {
53      // copy at most 10 characters from string to firstName
54      int length = firstNameString.size();
```

Fig. 14.10 | ClientData class represents a customer's credit information. (Part 2 of 3.)

```
55      length = ( length < 10 ? length : 9 );
56      firstNameString.copy( firstName, length );
57      firstName[ length ] = '\0'; // append null character to firstName
58   } // end function setFirstName
59
60   // get balance value
61   double ClientData::getBalance() const
62   {
63      return balance;
64   } // end function getBalance
65
66   // set balance value
67   void ClientData::setBalance( double balanceValue )
68   {
69      balance = balanceValue;
70   } // end function setBalance
```

Fig. 14.10 | ClientData class represents a customer's credit information. (Part 3 of 3.)

Objects of class string *do not have uniform size*, rather they use dynamically allocated memory to accommodate strings of various lengths. We must maintain fixed-length records, so class ClientData stores the client's first and last name in fixed-length char arrays (declared in Fig. 14.9, lines 32–33). Member functions setLastName (Fig. 14.10, lines 35–42) and setFirstName (Fig. 14.10, lines 51–58) each copy the characters of a string object into the corresponding char array. Consider function setLastName. Line 38 invokes string member function size to get the length of lastNameString. Line 39 ensures that length is fewer than 15 characters, then line 40 copies length characters from lastNameString into the char array lastName using string member function copy. Member function setFirstName performs the same steps for the first name.

Opening a File for Output in Binary Mode
In Fig. 14.11, line 11 creates an ofstream object for the file credit.dat. The second argument to the constructor—ios::out | ios::binary—indicates that we are opening the file for output in *binary mode*, which is *required* if we are to write *fixed-length records*. Multiple file-open modes are combined by separating each open mode from the next with the | operator, which is known as the *bitwise inclusive OR operator*. (Chapter 22 discusses this operator in detail.) Lines 24–25 cause the blankClient (which was constructed with default arguments at line 20) to be written to the credit.dat file associated with ofstream object outCredit. Remember that operator sizeof returns the size in bytes of the object contained in parentheses (see Chapter 8). The first argument to function write at line 24 must be of type const char *. However, the data type of &blankClient is ClientData *. To convert &blankClient to const char *, line 24 uses the cast operator reinterpret_cast, so the call to write compiles without issuing a compilation error.

```
1   // Fig. 14.11: Fig14_11.cpp
2   // Creating a randomly accessed file.
3   #include <iostream>
```

Fig. 14.11 | Creating a random-access file with 100 blank records sequentially. (Part 1 of 2.)

```
4    #include <fstream>
5    #include <cstdlib>
6    #include "ClientData.h" // ClientData class definition
7    using namespace std;
8
9    int main()
10   {
11      ofstream outCredit( "credit.dat", ios::out | ios::binary );
12
13      // exit program if ofstream could not open file
14      if ( !outCredit )
15      {
16         cerr << "File could not be opened." << endl;
17         exit( EXIT_FAILURE );
18      } // end if
19
20      ClientData blankClient; // constructor zeros out each data member
21
22      // output 100 blank records to file
23      for ( int i = 0; i < 100; ++i )
24         outCredit.write( reinterpret_cast< const char * >( &blankClient ),
25            sizeof( ClientData ) );
26   } // end main
```

Fig. 14.11 | Creating a random-access file with 100 blank records sequentially. (Part 2 of 2.)

14.8 Writing Data Randomly to a Random-Access File

Figure 14.12 writes data to the file credit.dat and uses the combination of fstream functions seekp and write to store data at *exact* locations in the file. Function seekp sets the *put* file-position pointer to a specific position in the file, then function write outputs the data. Line 6 includes the header ClientData.h defined in Fig. 14.9, so the program can use ClientData objects.

```
1    // Fig. 14.12: Fig14_12.cpp
2    // Writing to a random-access file.
3    #include <iostream>
4    #include <fstream>
5    #include <cstdlib>
6    #include "ClientData.h" // ClientData class definition
7    using namespace std;
8
9    int main()
10   {
11      int accountNumber;
12      string lastName;
13      string firstName;
14      double balance;
15
16      fstream outCredit( "credit.dat", ios::in | ios::out | ios::binary );
```

Fig. 14.12 | Writing to a random-access file. (Part 1 of 3.)

```
17
18      // exit program if fstream cannot open file
19      if ( !outCredit )
20      {
21        cerr << "File could not be opened." << endl;
22        exit( EXIT_FAILURE );
23      } // end if
24
25      cout << "Enter account number (1 to 100, 0 to end input)\n? ";
26
27      // require user to specify account number
28      ClientData client;
29      cin >> accountNumber;
30
31      // user enters information, which is copied into file
32      while ( accountNumber > 0 && accountNumber <= 100 )
33      {
34        // user enters last name, first name and balance
35        cout << "Enter lastname, firstname, balance\n? ";
36        cin >> lastName;
37        cin >> firstName;
38        cin >> balance;
39
40        // set record accountNumber, lastName, firstName and balance values
41        client.setAccountNumber( accountNumber );
42        client.setLastName( lastName );
43        client.setFirstName( firstName );
44        client.setBalance( balance );
45
46        // seek position in file of user-specified record
47        outCredit.seekp( ( client.getAccountNumber() - 1 ) *
48          sizeof( ClientData ) );
49
50        // write user-specified information in file
51        outCredit.write( reinterpret_cast< const char * >( &client ),
52          sizeof( ClientData ) );
53
54        // enable user to enter another account
55        cout << "Enter account number\n? ";
56        cin >> accountNumber;
57      } // end while
58    } // end main
```

```
Enter account number (1 to 100, 0 to end input)
? 37
Enter lastname, firstname, balance
? Barker Doug 0.00
Enter account number
? 29
Enter lastname, firstname, balance
? Brown Nancy -24.54
Enter account number
? 96
```

Fig. 14.12 | Writing to a random-access file. (Part 2 of 3.)

```
Enter lastname, firstname, balance
? Stone Sam 34.98
Enter account number
? 88
Enter lastname, firstname, balance
? Smith Dave 258.34
Enter account number
? 33
Enter lastname, firstname, balance
? Dunn Stacey 314.33
Enter account number
? 0
```

Fig. 14.12 | Writing to a random-access file. (Part 3 of 3.)

Opening a File for Input and Output in Binary Mode
Line 16 uses the fstream object outCredit to open the existing credit.dat file. The file is opened for input and output in *binary mode* by combining the file-open modes ios::in, ios::out and ios::binary. Opening the existing credit.dat file in this manner ensures that this program can manipulate the records written to the file by the program of Fig. 14.11, rather than creating the file from scratch.

Positioning the File Position Pointer
Lines 47–48 position the *put* file-position pointer for object outCredit to the byte location calculated by

```
( client.getAccountNumber() - 1 ) * sizeof( ClientData )
```

Because the account number is between 1 and 100, 1 is subtracted from the account number when calculating the byte location of the record. Thus, for record 1, the file-position pointer is set to byte 0 of the file.

14.9 Reading from a Random-Access File Sequentially

In the previous sections, we created a random-access file and wrote data to that file. In this section, we develop a program that reads the file sequentially and prints only those records that contain data. These programs produce an additional benefit. See if you can determine what it is; we'll reveal it at the end of this section.

The istream function read inputs a specified number of bytes from the current position in the specified stream into an object. For example, lines 31–32 from Fig. 14.13 read the number of bytes specified by sizeof(ClientData) from the file associated with ifstream object inCredit and store the data in the client record. Function read requires a first argument of type char *. Since &client is of type ClientData *, &client must be cast to char * using the cast operator reinterpret_cast.

```
1   // Fig. 14.13: Fig14_13.cpp
2   // Reading a random-access file sequentially.
3   #include <iostream>
```

Fig. 14.13 | Reading a random-access file sequentially. (Part 1 of 3.)

```
 4   #include <iomanip>
 5   #include <fstream>
 6   #include <cstdlib>
 7   #include "ClientData.h" // ClientData class definition
 8   using namespace std;
 9
10   void outputLine( ostream&, const ClientData & ); // prototype
11
12   int main()
13   {
14      ifstream inCredit( "credit.dat", ios::in | ios::binary );
15
16      // exit program if ifstream cannot open file
17      if ( !inCredit )
18      {
19         cerr << "File could not be opened." << endl;
20         exit( EXIT_FAILURE );
21      } // end if
22
23      // output column heads
24      cout << left << setw( 10 ) << "Account" << setw( 16 )
25         << "Last Name" << setw( 11 ) << "First Name" << left
26         << setw( 10 ) << right << "Balance" << endl;
27
28      ClientData client; // create record
29
30      // read first record from file
31      inCredit.read( reinterpret_cast< char * >( &client ),
32         sizeof( ClientData ) );
33
34      // read all records from file
35      while ( inCredit && !inCredit.eof() )
36      {
37         // display record
38         if ( client.getAccountNumber() != 0 )
39            outputLine( cout, client );
40
41         // read next from file
42         inCredit.read( reinterpret_cast< char * >( &client ),
43            sizeof( ClientData ) );
44      } // end while
45   } // end main
46
47   // display single record
48   void outputLine( ostream &output, const ClientData &record )
49   {
50      output << left << setw( 10 ) << record.getAccountNumber()
51         << setw( 16 ) << record.getLastName()
52         << setw( 11 ) << record.getFirstName()
53         << setw( 10 ) << setprecision( 2 ) << right << fixed
54         << showpoint << record.getBalance() << endl;
55   } // end function outputLine
```

Fig. 14.13 | Reading a random-access file sequentially. (Part 2 of 3.)

```
Account   Last Name    First Name   Balance
29        Brown        Nancy        -24.54
33        Dunn         Stacey       314.33
37        Barker       Doug           0.00
88        Smith        Dave         258.34
96        Stone        Sam           34.98
```

Fig. 14.13 | Reading a random-access file sequentially. (Part 3 of 3.)

Figure 14.13 reads every record in the credit.dat file sequentially, checks each record to determine whether it contains data, and displays formatted outputs for records containing data. The condition in line 35 uses the ios member function eof to determine when the end of file is reached and causes execution of the while statement to terminate. Also, if an error occurs when reading from the file, the loop terminates, because inCredit evaluates to false. The data input from the file is output by function outputLine (lines 48–55), which takes two arguments—an ostream object and a clientData structure to be output. The ostream parameter type is interesting, because any ostream object (such as cout) or any object of a derived class of ostream (such as an object of type ofstream) can be supplied as the argument. This means that the *same* function can be used, for example, to perform output to the standard-output stream and to a file stream without writing separate functions.

What about that additional benefit we promised? If you examine the output window, you'll notice that the records are listed in *sorted order* (by account number). This is a consequence of how we stored these records in the file, using direct-access techniques. Sorting using direct-access techniques is relatively fast. *The speed is achieved by making the file large enough to hold every possible record that might be created.* This, of course, means that the file could be occupied *sparsely* most of the time, resulting in a waste of storage. This is an example of the *space-time trade-off:* By using *large amounts of space*, we can develop *a much faster sorting algorithm*. Fortunately, the continuous reduction in price of storage units has made this less of an issue.

14.10 Case Study: A Transaction-Processing Program

We now present a substantial transaction-processing program (Fig. 14.14) using a random-access file to achieve instant-access processing. The program maintains a bank's account information. It updates existing accounts, adds new accounts, deletes accounts and stores a formatted listing of all current accounts in a text file. We assume that the program of Fig. 14.11 has been executed to create the file credit.dat and that the program of Fig. 14.12 has been executed to insert the initial data. Line 25 opens the credit.dat file by creating an fstream object for both reading and writing in binary format.

```
1   // Fig. 14.14: Fig14_14.cpp
2   // This program reads a random-access file sequentially, updates
3   // data previously written to the file, creates data to be placed
4   // in the file, and deletes data previously stored in the file.
```

Fig. 14.14 | Bank account program. (Part 1 of 6.)

```
5   #include <iostream>
6   #include <fstream>
7   #include <iomanip>
8   #include <cstdlib>
9   #include "ClientData.h" // ClientData class definition
10  using namespace std;
11
12  int enterChoice();
13  void createTextFile( fstream& );
14  void updateRecord( fstream& );
15  void newRecord( fstream& );
16  void deleteRecord( fstream& );
17  void outputLine( ostream&, const ClientData & );
18  int getAccount( const char * const );
19
20  enum Choices { PRINT = 1, UPDATE, NEW, DELETE, END };
21
22  int main()
23  {
24     // open file for reading and writing
25     fstream inOutCredit( "credit.dat", ios::in | ios::out | ios::binary );
26
27     // exit program if fstream cannot open file
28     if ( !inOutCredit )
29     {
30        cerr << "File could not be opened." << endl;
31        exit ( EXIT_FAILURE );
32     } // end if
33
34     int choice; // store user choice
35
36     // enable user to specify action
37     while ( ( choice = enterChoice() ) != END )
38     {
39        switch ( choice )
40        {
41           case PRINT: // create text file from record file
42              createTextFile( inOutCredit );
43              break;
44           case UPDATE: // update record
45              updateRecord( inOutCredit );
46              break;
47           case NEW: // create record
48              newRecord( inOutCredit );
49              break;
50           case DELETE: // delete existing record
51              deleteRecord( inOutCredit );
52              break;
53           default: // display error if user does not select valid choice
54              cerr << "Incorrect choice" << endl;
55              break;
56        } // end switch
57
```

Fig. 14.14 | Bank account program. (Part 2 of 6.)

```
58          inOutCredit.clear(); // reset end-of-file indicator
59       } // end while
60    } // end main
61
62    // enable user to input menu choice
63    int enterChoice()
64    {
65       // display available options
66       cout << "\nEnter your choice" << endl
67          << "1 - store a formatted text file of accounts" << endl
68          << "    called \"print.txt\" for printing" << endl
69          << "2 - update an account" << endl
70          << "3 - add a new account" << endl
71          << "4 - delete an account" << endl
72          << "5 - end program\n? ";
73
74       int menuChoice;
75       cin >> menuChoice; // input menu selection from user
76       return menuChoice;
77    } // end function enterChoice
78
79    // create formatted text file for printing
80    void createTextFile( fstream &readFromFile )
81    {
82       // create text file
83       ofstream outPrintFile( "print.txt", ios::out );
84
85       // exit program if ofstream cannot create file
86       if ( !outPrintFile )
87       {
88          cerr << "File could not be created." << endl;
89          exit( EXIT_FAILURE );
90       } // end if
91
92       // output column heads
93       outPrintFile << left << setw( 10 ) << "Account" << setw( 16 )
94          << "Last Name" << setw( 11 ) << "First Name" << right
95          << setw( 10 ) << "Balance" << endl;
96
97       // set file-position pointer to beginning of readFromFile
98       readFromFile.seekg( 0 );
99
100      // read first record from record file
101      ClientData client;
102      readFromFile.read( reinterpret_cast< char * >( &client ),
103         sizeof( ClientData ) );
104
105      // copy all records from record file into text file
106      while ( !readFromFile.eof() )
107      {
108         // write single record to text file
109         if ( client.getAccountNumber() != 0 ) // skip empty records
110            outputLine( outPrintFile, client );
```

Fig. 14.14 | Bank account program. (Part 3 of 6.)

```
III
II2        // read next record from record file
II3        readFromFile.read( reinterpret_cast< char * >( &client ),
II4           sizeof( ClientData ) );
II5     } // end while
II6  } // end function createTextFile
II7
II8  // update balance in record
II9  void updateRecord( fstream &updateFile )
I20  {
I2I     // obtain number of account to update
I22     int accountNumber = getAccount( "Enter account to update" );
I23
I24     // move file-position pointer to correct record in file
I25     updateFile.seekg( ( accountNumber - 1 ) * sizeof( ClientData ) );
I26
I27     // read first record from file
I28     ClientData client;
I29     updateFile.read( reinterpret_cast< char * >( &client ),
I30        sizeof( ClientData ) );
I3I
I32     // update record
I33     if ( client.getAccountNumber() != 0 )
I34     {
I35        outputLine( cout, client ); // display the record
I36
I37        // request user to specify transaction
I38        cout << "\nEnter charge (+) or payment (-): ";
I39        double transaction; // charge or payment
I40        cin >> transaction;
I4I
I42        // update record balance
I43        double oldBalance = client.getBalance();
I44        client.setBalance( oldBalance + transaction );
I45        outputLine( cout, client ); // display the record
I46
I47        // move file-position pointer to correct record in file
I48        updateFile.seekp( ( accountNumber - 1 ) * sizeof( ClientData ) );
I49
I50        // write updated record over old record in file
I5I        updateFile.write( reinterpret_cast< const char * >( &client ),
I52           sizeof( ClientData ) );
I53     } // end if
I54     else // display error if account does not exist
I55        cerr << "Account #" << accountNumber
I56           << " has no information." << endl;
I57  } // end function updateRecord
I58
I59  // create and insert record
I60  void newRecord( fstream &insertInFile )
I6I  {
I62     // obtain number of account to create
I63     int accountNumber = getAccount( "Enter new account number" );
```

Fig. 14.14 | Bank account program. (Part 4 of 6.)

```
164
165     // move file-position pointer to correct record in file
166     insertInFile.seekg( ( accountNumber - 1 ) * sizeof( ClientData ) );
167
168     // read record from file
169     ClientData client;
170     insertInFile.read( reinterpret_cast< char * >( &client ),
171        sizeof( ClientData ) );
172
173     // create record, if record does not previously exist
174     if ( client.getAccountNumber() == 0 )
175     {
176        string lastName;
177        string firstName;
178        double balance;
179
180        // user enters last name, first name and balance
181        cout << "Enter lastname, firstname, balance\n? ";
182        cin >> setw( 15 ) >> lastName;
183        cin >> setw( 10 ) >> firstName;
184        cin >> balance;
185
186        // use values to populate account values
187        client.setLastName( lastName );
188        client.setFirstName( firstName );
189        client.setBalance( balance );
190        client.setAccountNumber( accountNumber );
191
192        // move file-position pointer to correct record in file
193        insertInFile.seekp( ( accountNumber - 1 ) * sizeof( ClientData ) );
194
195        // insert record in file
196        insertInFile.write( reinterpret_cast< const char * >( &client ),
197           sizeof( ClientData ) );
198     } // end if
199     else // display error if account already exists
200        cerr << "Account #" << accountNumber
201           << " already contains information." << endl;
202  } // end function newRecord
203
204  // delete an existing record
205  void deleteRecord( fstream &deleteFromFile )
206  {
207     // obtain number of account to delete
208     int accountNumber = getAccount( "Enter account to delete" );
209
210     // move file-position pointer to correct record in file
211     deleteFromFile.seekg( ( accountNumber - 1 ) * sizeof( ClientData ) );
212
213     // read record from file
214     ClientData client;
215     deleteFromFile.read( reinterpret_cast< char * >( &client ),
216        sizeof( ClientData ) );
```

Fig. 14.14 | Bank account program. (Part 5 of 6.)

```
217
218     // delete record, if record exists in file
219     if ( client.getAccountNumber() != 0 )
220     {
221        ClientData blankClient; // create blank record
222
223        // move file-position pointer to correct record in file
224        deleteFromFile.seekp( ( accountNumber - 1 ) *
225           sizeof( ClientData ) );
226
227        // replace existing record with blank record
228        deleteFromFile.write(
229           reinterpret_cast< const char * >( &blankClient ),
230           sizeof( ClientData ) );
231
232        cout << "Account #" << accountNumber << " deleted.\n";
233     } // end if
234     else // display error if record does not exist
235        cerr << "Account #" << accountNumber << " is empty.\n";
236  } // end deleteRecord
237
238  // display single record
239  void outputLine( ostream &output, const ClientData &record )
240  {
241     output << left << setw( 10 ) << record.getAccountNumber()
242        << setw( 16 ) << record.getLastName()
243        << setw( 11 ) << record.getFirstName()
244        << setw( 10 ) << setprecision( 2 ) << right << fixed
245        << showpoint << record.getBalance() << endl;
246  } // end function outputLine
247
248  // obtain account-number value from user
249  int getAccount( const char * const prompt )
250  {
251     int accountNumber;
252
253     // obtain account-number value
254     do
255     {
256        cout << prompt << " (1 - 100): ";
257        cin >> accountNumber;
258     } while ( accountNumber < 1 || accountNumber > 100 );
259
260     return accountNumber;
261  } // end function getAccount
```

Fig. 14.14 | Bank account program. (Part 6 of 6.)

The program has five options (Option 5 is for terminating the program). Option 1 calls function createTextFile to store a formatted list of all the account information in a text file called print.txt that may be printed. Function createTextFile (lines 80–116) takes an fstream object as an argument to be used to input data from the credit.dat file. Function createTextFile invokes istream member function read (lines 102–103) and uses the sequential-file-access techniques of Fig. 14.13 to input data from credit.dat.

Function outputLine, discussed in Section 14.9, outputs the data to file print.txt. Note that function createTextFile uses istream member function seekg (line 98) to ensure that the file-position pointer is at the beginning of the file. After choosing Option 1, the print.txt file contains

```
Account    Last Name      First Name    Balance
29         Brown          Nancy          -24.54
33         Dunn           Stacey         314.33
37         Barker         Doug             0.00
88         Smith          Dave           258.34
96         Stone          Sam             34.98
```

Option 2 calls updateRecord (lines 119–157) to update an account. This function updates only an *existing* record, so the function first determines whether the specified record is *empty*. Lines 129–130 read data into object client, using istream member function read. Then line 133 compares the value returned by getAccountNumber of the client object to zero to determine whether the record contains information. If this value is zero, lines 155–156 print an error message indicating that the record is empty. If the record contains information, line 135 displays the record, using function outputLine, line 140 inputs the transaction amount and lines 143–152 calculate the new balance and rewrite the record to the file. A typical execution for Option 2 is

```
Enter account to update (1 - 100): 37
37          Barker          Doug             0.00

Enter charge (+) or payment (-): +87.99
37          Barker          Doug            87.99
```

Option 3 calls function newRecord (lines 160–202) to add a new account to the file. If the user enters an account number for an *existing* account, newRecord displays an error message indicating that the account exists (lines 200–201). This function adds a new account in the same manner as the program of Fig. 14.12. A typical execution for Option 3 is

```
Enter new account number (1 - 100): 22
Enter lastname, firstname, balance
? Johnston Sarah 247.45
```

Option 4 calls function deleteRecord (lines 205–236) to delete a record from the file. Line 208 prompts the user to enter the account number. Only an *existing* record may be deleted, so, if the specified account is empty, line 235 displays an error message. If the account exists, lines 221–230 reinitialize that account by copying an empty record (blank-Client) to the file. Line 232 displays a message to inform the user that the record has been deleted. A typical execution for Option 4 is

```
Enter account to delete (1 - 100): 29
Account #29 deleted.
```

14.11 Object Serialization

This chapter and Chapter 13 introduced the object-oriented style of input/output. However, our examples concentrated on I/O of fundamental types rather than objects of user-defined types. In Chapter 10, we showed how to input and output objects using operator overloading. We accomplished object input by overloading the stream extraction operator, >>, for the appropriate `istream`. We accomplished object output by overloading the stream insertion operator, <<, for the appropriate `ostream`. In both cases, only an object's data members were input or output, and, in each case, they were in a format meaningful only for objects of that particular type. An object's member functions are *not* input or output with the object's data; rather, *one copy of the class's member functions remains available internally and is shared by all objects of the class.*

When object data members are output to a disk file, we *lose* the object's type information. We store only the values of the object's attributes, not type information, on the disk. If the program that reads this data knows the object type to which the data corresponds, the program can read the data into an object of that type as we did in our random-access file examples.

An interesting problem occurs when we store objects of different types in the same file. How can we distinguish them (or their collections of data members) as we read them into a program? The problem is that objects typically do *not* have type fields (we discussed this issue in Chapter 12).

One approach used by several programming languages is called **object serialization**. A so-called **serialized object** is an object represented as a sequence of bytes that includes the object's *data* as well as information about the object's *type* and the *types of data stored in the object*. After a serialized object has been written to a file, it can be read from the file and **deserialized**—that is, the type information and bytes that represent the object and its data can be used to *recreate* the object in memory. C++ does *not* provide a built-in serialization mechanism; however, there are third party and open source C++ libraries that support object serialization. The open source Boost C++ Libraries (`www.boost.org`) provide support for serializing objects in text, binary and extensible markup language (XML) formats (`www.boost.org/libs/serialization/doc/index.html`).

14.12 Wrap-Up

In this chapter, we presented various file-processing techniques to manipulate persistent data. You were introduced to the differences between character-based and byte-based streams, and to several file-processing class templates in header `<fstream>`. Then, you learned how to use sequential file processing to manipulate records stored in order, by a record-key field. You also learned how to use random-access files to "instantly" retrieve and manipulate fixed-length records. We presented a substantial transaction-processing program using a random-access file to achieve "instant-access" processing. Finally, we discussed the basic concepts of object serialization. We introduced the Standard Library array and `vector` classes in Chapter 7. In the next chapter, you'll learn about the Standard Library's other predefined data structures (known as containers) as well as the basics of iterators, which are used to manipulate container elements.

Summary

Section 14.1 Introduction
- Files are used for data persistence (p. 634)—permanent retention of data.
- Computers store files on secondary storage devices (p. 634), such as hard disks, CDs, DVDs, flash memory and tapes.

Section 14.2 Files and Streams
- C++ views each file simply as a sequence of bytes.
- Each file ends either with an end-of-file marker (p. 634) or at a specific byte number recorded in a system-maintained, administrative data structure.
- When a file is opened, an object is created, and a stream is associated with the object.
- To perform file processing in C++, headers `<iostream>` and `<fstream>` must be included.
- Header `<fstream>` (p. 634) includes the definitions for the stream class templates `basic_ifstream` (for file input), `basic_ofstream` (for file output) and `basic_fstream` (for file input and output).
- Each class template has a predefined template specialization that enables char I/O. The `<fstream>` library provides `typedef` aliases for these template specializations. The `typedef` `ifstream` represents a specialization of `basic_ifstream` that enables char input from a file. The `typedef` `ofstream` represents a specialization of `basic_ofstream` that enables char output to files. The `typedef` `fstream` (p. 634) represents a specialization of `basic_fstream` that enables char input from, and output to, files.
- The file-processing templates derive from class templates `basic_istream`, `basic_ostream` and `basic_iostream`, respectively. Thus, all member functions, operators and manipulators that belong to these templates also can be applied to file streams.

Section 14.3 Creating a Sequential File
- C++ imposes no structure on a file; you must structure files to meet the application's requirements.
- A file can be opened for output when an `ofstream` object is created. Two arguments are passed to the object's constructor—the filename (p. 636) and the file-open mode (p. 636).
- For an `ofstream` (p. 636) object, the file-open mode can be either `ios::out` (p. 636) to output data to a file or `ios::app` (p. 636) to append data to the end of a file. Existing files opened with mode `ios::out` are truncated (p. 637). If the specified file does not exist, the `ofstream` object creates the file using that filename.
- By default, `ofstream` objects are opened for output.
- An `ofstream` object can be created without opening a specific file—a file can be attached to the object later with member function `open` (p. 637).
- The `ios` member function `operator!` determines whether a stream was opened correctly. This operator can be used in a condition that returns a true value if either the `failbit` or the `badbit` is set for the stream on the open operation.
- The `ios` member function `operator void *` converts a stream to a pointer, so it can be compared to 0. When a pointer value is used as a condition, a null pointer represents `false` and a non-null pointer represents `true`. If the `failbit` or `badbit` has been set for a stream, 0 (`false`) is returned.
- Entering the end-of-file indicator sets the `failbit` for `cin`.
- The `operator void *` function can be used to test an input object for end-of-file instead of calling the `eof` member function explicitly on the input object.
- When a stream object's destructor is called, the corresponding stream is closed. You also can close the stream object explicitly, using the stream's `close` member function.

Section 14.4 Reading Data from a Sequential File

- Files store data so it may be retrieved for processing when needed.

- Creating an ifstream object opens a file for input. The ifstream constructor can receive the file-name and the file open mode as arguments.

- Open a file for input only if the file's contents should not be modified.

- Objects of class ifstream are opened for input by default.

- An ifstream object can be created without opening a specific file; a file can be attached to it later.

- To retrieve data sequentially from a file, programs normally start reading from the beginning of the file and read all the data consecutively until the desired data is found.

- The member functions for repositioning the file-position pointer (p. 641) are seekg ("seek get"; p. 641) for istream and seekp ("seek put"; p. 641) for ostream. Each istream has a "get pointer," which indicates the byte number in the file from which the next input is to occur, and each ostream has a "put pointer," which indicates the byte number in the file at which the next output should be placed.

- The argument to seekg (p. 641) is a long integer. A second argument can be specified to indicate the seek direction (p. 641), which can be ios::beg (the default; p. 641) for positioning relative to the beginning of a stream, ios::cur (p. 641) for positioning relative to the current position in a stream or ios::end (p. 641) for positioning relative to the end of a stream.

- The file-position pointer (p. 641) is an integer value that specifies the location in the file as a number of bytes from the file's starting location (i.e., the offset (p. 641) from the beginning of the file).

- Member functions tellg (p. 641) and tellp (p. 641) are provided to return the current locations of the "get" and "put" pointers, respectively.

Section 14.5 Updating Sequential Files

- Data that is formatted and written to a sequential file cannot be modified without the risk of destroying other data in the file. The problem is that records can vary in size.

Section 14.6 Random-Access Files

- Sequential files are inappropriate for instant-access applications (p. 645), in which a particular record must be located immediately.

- Instant access is made possible with random-access files (p. 646). Individual records of a random-access file can be accessed directly (and quickly) without having to search other records.

- The easiest method to format files for random access is to require that all records in a file be of the same fixed length. Using same-size, fixed-length records makes it easy for a program to calculate (as a function of the record size and the record key) the exact location of any record relative to the beginning of the file.

- Data can be inserted into a random-access file without destroying other data in the file.

- Data stored previously can be updated or deleted without rewriting the entire file.

Section 14.7 Creating a Random-Access File

- The ostream member function write outputs a fixed number of bytes, beginning at a specific location in memory, to the specified stream. Function write writes the data at the location in the file specified by the "put" file-position pointer.

- The istream member function read (p. 646) inputs a fixed number of bytes from the specified stream to an area in memory beginning at a specified address. If the stream is associated with a file, function read inputs bytes at the location in the file specified by the "get" file-position pointer.

- Function write treats its first argument as a group of bytes by viewing the object in memory as a const char *, which is a pointer to a byte (remember that a char is one byte). Starting from that location, function write outputs the number of bytes specified by its second argument. The istream function read can subsequently be used to read the bytes back into memory.

- The reinterpret_cast operator (p. 647) converts a pointer of one type to an unrelated pointer type.

- A reinterpret_cast is performed at compile time and does not change the value of the object to which its operand points.

- A program that reads unformatted data must be compiled and executed on a system compatible with the program that wrote the data—different systems may represent internal data differently.

- Objects of class string do not have uniform size, rather they use dynamically allocated memory to accommodate strings of various lengths.

Section 14.8 Writing Data Randomly to a Random-Access File

- Multiple file-open modes are combined by separating each open mode from the next with the bitwise inclusive OR operator (|).

- The string member function size (p. 650) gets the length of a string.

- The file open mode ios::binary (p. 650) indicates that a file should be opened in binary mode.

Section 14.9 Reading from a Random-Access File Sequentially

- The istream function read inputs a specified number of bytes from the current position in the specified stream into an object.

- A function that receives an ostream parameter can receive any ostream object (such as cout) or any object of a derived class of ostream (such as an object of type ofstream) as an argument. This means that the same function can be used, for example, to perform output to the standard-output stream and to a file stream without writing separate functions.

Section 14.11 Object Serialization

- When object data members are output to a disk file, we lose the object's type information. We store only the values of the object's attributes, not type information, on the disk. If the program that reads this data knows the object type to which the data corresponds, the program can read the data into an object of that type.

- A so-called serialized object (p. 662) is an object represented as a sequence of bytes that includes the object's data as well as information about the object's type and the types of data stored in the object. A serialized object can be read from the file and deserialized (p. 662).

- The open source Boost Libraries provide support for serializing objects (p. 662) in text, binary and extensible markup language (XML) formats.

Self-Review Exercises

14.1 *(Fill in the Blanks)* Fill in the blanks in each of the following:
  a) Member function _____ of the file streams fstream, ifstream and ofstream closes a file.
  b) The istream member function _____ reads a character from the specified stream.
  c) Member function _____ of the file streams fstream, ifstream and ofstream opens a file.
  d) The istream member function _____ is normally used when reading data from a file in random-access applications.

e) Member functions _____ and _____ of istream and ostream set the file-position pointer to a specific location in an input or output stream, respectively.

14.2 *(True or False)* State which of the following are *true* and which are *false*. If *false*, explain why.

a) Member function read cannot be used to read data from the input object cin.
b) You must create the cin, cout, cerr and clog objects explicitly.
c) A program must call function close explicitly to close a file associated with an if-stream, ofstream or fstream object.
d) If the file-position pointer points to a location in a sequential file other than the beginning of the file, the file must be closed and reopened to read from the beginning of the file.
e) The ostream member function write can write to standard-output stream cout.
f) Data in sequential files always is updated without overwriting nearby data.
g) Searching all records in a random-access file to find a specific record is unnecessary.
h) Records in random-access files must be of uniform length.
i) Member functions seekp and seekg must seek relative to the beginning of a file.

14.3 Assume that each of the following statements applies to the same program.

a) Write a statement that opens file oldmast.dat for input; use an ifstream object called inOldMaster.
b) Write a statement that opens file trans.dat for input; use an ifstream object called inTransaction.
c) Write a statement that opens file newmast.dat for output (and creation); use ofstream object outNewMaster.
d) Write a statement that reads a record from the file oldmast.dat. The record consists of integer accountNumber, string name and floating-point currentBalance. Use ifstream object inOldMaster.
e) Write a statement that reads a record from the file trans.dat. The record consists of integer accountNum and floating-point dollarAmount. Use ifstream object inTransaction.
f) Write a statement that writes a record to the file newmast.dat. The record consists of integer accountNum, string name, and floating-point currentBalance. Use ofstream object outNewMaster.

14.4 Find the error(s) and show how to correct it (them) in each of the following.

a) File payables.dat referred to by ofstream object outPayable has not been opened.

```
outPayable << account << company << amount << endl;
```

b) The following statement should read a record from the file payables.dat. The ifstream object inPayable refers to this file, and istream object inReceivable refers to the file receivables.dat.

```
inReceivable >> account >> company >> amount;
```

c) The file tools.dat should be opened to add data to the file without discarding the current data.

```
ofstream outTools( "tools.dat", ios::out );
```

Answers to Self-Review Exercises

14.1 a) close. b) get. c) open. d) read. e) seekg, seekp.

14.2 a) False. Function read can read from any input stream object derived from istream.

b) False. These four streams are created automatically for you. The <iostream> header must be included in a file to use them. This header includes declarations for each pre-defined stream object.

c) False. The files will be closed when destructors for ifstream, ofstream or fstream objects execute when the stream objects go out of scope or before program execution terminates, but it's a good programming practice to close all files explicitly with close once they're no longer needed.

d) False. Member function seekg can be used to reposition the "put" or "get" file-position pointer to the beginning of the file.

e) True.

f) False. In most cases, sequential file records are not of uniform length. Therefore, it's possible that updating a record will cause other data to be overwritten.

g) True.

h) False. Records in a random-access file normally are of uniform length.

i) False. It's possible to seek from the beginning of the file, from the end of the file and from the current position in the file.

14.3 a) `ifstream inOldMaster( "oldmast.dat", ios::in );`

     b) `ifstream inTransaction( "trans.dat", ios::in );`

     c) `ofstream outNewMaster( "newmast.dat", ios::out );`

     d) `inOldMaster >> accountNumber >> name >> currentBalance;`

     e) `inTransaction >> accountNum >> dollarAmount;`

     f) `outNewMaster << accountNum << " " << name << " " << currentBalance;`

14.4 a) *Error:* The file payables.dat has not been opened before the attempt is made to output data to the stream.
Correction: Use ostream function open to open payables.dat for output.

     b) *Error:* The incorrect istream object is being used to read a record from the file named payables.dat.
Correction: Use istream object inPayable to refer to payables.dat.

     c) *Error:* The file's contents are discarded because the file is opened for output (ios::out).
Correction: To add data to the file, open the file either for updating (ios::ate) or for appending (ios::app).

Exercises

14.5 *(Fill in the Blanks)* Fill in the blanks in each of the following:

a) Computers store large amounts of data on secondary storage devices as _____.

b) The standard stream objects declared by header <iostream> are _____, _____, _____ and _____.

c) ostream member function _____ outputs a character to the specified stream.

d) ostream member function _____ is generally used to write data to a randomly accessed file.

e) istream member function _____ repositions the file-position pointer in a file.

14.6 *(File Matching)* Exercise 14.3 asked you to write a series of single statements. Actually, these statements form the core of an important type of file-processing program, namely, a file-matching program. In commercial data processing, it's common to have several files in each application system. In an accounts receivable system, for example, there is generally a master file containing detailed information about each customer, such as the customer's name, address, telephone number, outstanding balance, credit limit, discount terms, contract arrangements and, possibly, a condensed history of recent purchases and cash payments.

As transactions occur (e.g., sales are made and cash payments arrive), they're entered into a file. At the end of each business period (a month for some companies, a week for others and a day in some cases), the file of transactions (called trans.dat in Exercise 14.3) is applied to the master file (called oldmast.dat in Exercise 14.3), thus updating each account's record of purchases and payments. During an updating run, the master file is rewritten as a new file (newmast.dat), which is then used at the end of the next business period to begin the updating process again.

File-matching programs must deal with certain problems that do not exist in single-file programs. For example, a match does not always occur. A customer on the master file might not have made any purchases or cash payments in the current business period, and therefore no record for this customer will appear on the transaction file. Similarly, a customer who did make some purchases or cash payments may have just moved to this community, and the company may not have had a chance to create a master record for this customer.

Use the statements from Exercise 14.3 as a basis for writing a complete file-matching accounts receivable program. Use the account number on each file as the record key for matching purposes. Assume that each file is a sequential file with records stored in increasing order by account number.

When a match occurs (i.e., records with the same account number appear on both the master and transaction files), add the dollar amount on the transaction file to the current balance on the master file, and write the newmast.dat record. (Assume purchases are indicated by positive amounts on the transaction file and payments are indicated by negative amounts.) When there is a master record for a particular account but no corresponding transaction record, merely write the master record to newmast.dat. When there is a transaction record but no corresponding master record, print the error message "Unmatched transaction record for account number ..." (fill in the account number from the transaction record).

14.7 *(File Matching Test Data)* After writing the program of Exercise 14.6, write a simple program to create some test data for checking out the program. Use the following sample account data:

Master file Account number	Name	Balance
100	Alan Jones	348.17
300	Mary Smith	27.19
500	Sam Sharp	0.00
700	Suzy Green	–14.22

Transaction file Account number	Transaction amount
100	27.14
300	62.11
400	100.56
900	82.17

14.8 *(File Matching Test)* Run the program of Exercise 14.6, using the files of test data created in Exercise 14.7. Print the new master file. Check that the accounts have been updated correctly.

14.9 *(File Matching Enhancement)* It's common to have several transaction records with the same record key, because a particular customer might make several purchases and cash payments during a business period. Rewrite your accounts receivable file-matching program of Exercise 14.6 to provide for the possibility of handling several transaction records with the same record key. Modify the test data of Exercise 14.7 to include the following additional transaction records:

Account number	Dollar amount
300	83.89
700	80.78
700	1.53

14.10 Write a series of statements that accomplish each of the following. Assume that we've defined class `Person` that contains the `private` data members

```
char lastName[ 15 ];
char firstName[ 10 ];
int age;
int id;
```

and `public` member functions

```
// accessor functions for id
void setId( int );
int getId() const;

// accessor functions for lastName
void setLastName( const string & );
string getLastName() const;

// accessor functions for firstName
void setFirstName( const string & );
string getFirstName() const;

// accessor functions for age
void setAge( int );
int getAge() const;
```

Also assume that any random-access files have been opened properly.

a) Initialize `nameage.dat` with 100 records that store values `lastName ="unassigned"`, `firstName = ""` and `age = 0`.

b) Input 10 last names, first names and ages, and write them to the file.

c) Update a record that already contains information. If the record does not contain information, inform the user `"No info"`.

d) Delete a record that contains information by reinitializing that particular record.

14.11 *(Hardware Inventory)* You are the owner of a hardware store and need to keep an inventory that can tell you what different tools you have, how many of each you have on hand and the cost of each one. Write a program that initializes the random-access file `hardware.dat` to 100 empty records, lets you input the data concerning each tool, enables you to list all your tools, lets you delete a record for a tool that you no longer have and lets you update *any* information in the file. The tool identification number should be the record number. Use the following information to start your file:

Record #	Tool name	Quantity	Cost
3	Electric sander	7	57.98
17	Hammer	76	11.99
24	Jig saw	21	11.00
39	Lawn mower	3	79.50
56	Power saw	18	99.99
68	Screwdriver	106	6.99
77	Sledge hammer	11	21.50
83	Wrench	34	7.50

14.12 (*Telephone Number Word Generator*) Standard telephone keypads contain the digits 0 through 9. The numbers 2 through 9 each have three letters associated with them, as is indicated by the following table:

Digit	Letter	Digit	Letter
2	A B C	6	M N O
3	D E F	7	P Q R S
4	G H I	8	T U V
5	J K L	9	W X Y Z

Many people find it difficult to memorize phone numbers, so they use the correspondence between digits and letters to develop seven-letter words that correspond to their phone numbers. For example, a person whose telephone number is 686-2377 might use the correspondence indicated in the above table to develop the seven-letter word "NUMBERS."

Businesses frequently attempt to get telephone numbers that are easy for their clients to remember. If a business can advertise a simple word for its customers to dial, then no doubt the business will receive a few more calls. Each seven-letter word corresponds to exactly one seven-digit telephone number. The restaurant wishing to increase its take-home business could surely do so with the number 825-3688 (i.e., "TAKEOUT"). Each seven-digit phone number corresponds to many separate seven-letter words. Unfortunately, most of these represent unrecognizable juxtapositions of letters. It's possible, however, that the owner of a barber shop would be pleased to know that the shop's telephone number, 424-7288, corresponds to "HAIRCUT." A veterinarian with the phone number 738-2273 would be happy to know that the number corresponds to "PETCARE."

Write a program that, given a seven-digit number, writes to a file every possible seven-letter word corresponding to that number. There are 2187 (3 to the seventh power) such words. Avoid phone numbers with the digits 0 and 1.

14.13 (*sizeof Operator*) Write a program that uses the sizeof operator to determine the sizes in bytes of the various data types on your computer system. Write the results to the file data-size.dat, so that you may print the results later. The results should be displayed in two-column format with the type name in the left column and the size of the type in right column, as in:

```
char                    1
unsigned char           1
short int               2
unsigned short int      2
int                     4
unsigned int            4
long int                4
unsigned long int       4
float                   4
double                  8
long double            10
```

[*Note:* The sizes of the built-in data types on your computer might differ from those listed here.]

Making a Difference

14.14   *(Phishing Scanner)* Phishing is a form of identity theft in which, in an e-mail, a sender posing as a trustworthy source attempts to acquire private information, such as your user names, passwords, credit-card numbers and social security number. Phishing e-mails claiming to be from popular banks, credit-card companies, auction sites, social networks and online payment services may look quite legitimate. These fraudulent messages often provide links to spoofed (fake) websites where you're asked to enter sensitive information.

Visit Security Extra (www.securityextra.com/), www.snopes.com and other websites to find lists of the top phishing scams. Also check out the Anti-Phishing Working Group

www.antiphishing.org/

and the FBI's Cyber Investigations website

www.fbi.gov/cyberinvest/cyberhome.htm

where you'll find information about the latest scams and how to protect yourself.

Create a list of 30 words, phrases and company names commonly found in phishing messages. Assign a point value to each based on your estimate of its likeliness to be in a phishing message (e.g., one point if it's somewhat likely, two points if moderately likely, or three points if highly likely). Write a program that scans a file of text for these terms and phrases. For each occurrence of a keyword or phrase within the text file, add the assigned point value to the total points for that word or phrase. For each keyword or phrase found, output one line with the word or phrase, the number of occurrences and the point total. Then show the point total for the entire message. Does your program assign a high point total to some actual phishing e-mails you've received? Does it assign a high point total to some legitimate e-mails you've received?

15

Standard Library Containers and Iterators

They are the books,
the arts, the academes,
That show, contain, and
nourish all the world.
—William Shakespeare

Journey over all the
universe in a map.
—Miguel de Cervantes

Objectives

In this chapter you'll:

- Introduce the Standard Library containers, iterators and algorithms.

- Use the **vector**, **list** and **deque** sequence containers.

- Use the **set**, **multiset**, **map** and **multimap** associative containers.

- Use the **stack**, **queue** and **priority_queue** container adapters.

- Use iterators to access container elements.

- Use the **copy** algorithm and **ostream_iterator**s to output a container.

- Use the **bitset** "near container" to implement the Sieve of Eratosthenes for determining prime numbers.

15.1 Introduction

The Standard Library defines powerful, template-based, reusable components that implement many common data structures and algorithms used to process those data structures. We began introducing templates in Chapters 6–7 and use them extensively here and in Chapters 16 and 19. Historically, the features presented in this chapter were often referred to as the *Standard Template Library* or *STL*.[1] We'll occasionally refer to these features as the STL. In the C++ standard document, these features are simply referred to as part of the C++ Standard Library.

Containers, Iterators and Algorithms
This chapter introduces three key components of the Standard Library—**containers** (*templatized* data structures), iterators and algorithms. Containers are data structures capable of storing objects of *almost* any data type (there are some restrictions). We'll see that there are three styles of container classes—*first-class containers, container adapters* and *near containers*.

Common Member Functions Among Containers
Each container has associated member functions—a subset of these is defined in *all* containers. We illustrate most of this common functionality in our examples of `array` (which was introduced in Chapter 7), `vector` (which was introduced in Chapter 7 and we cover in more depth here), `list` (Section 15.5.2) and `deque` (Section 15.5.3).

Iterators
Iterators, which have properties similar to those of *pointers*, are used to manipulate container elements. *Built-in arrays* also can be manipulated by Standard Library algorithms, using pointers as iterators. We'll see that manipulating containers with iterators is convenient and provides tremendous expressive power when combined with Standard Library algorithms—in some cases, reducing many lines of code to a single statement.

---

1. The STL was developed by Alexander Stepanov and Meng Lee at Hewlett-Packard and is based on their generic programming research, with significant contributions from David Musser.

Algorithms
Standard Library **algorithms** are function templates that perform such common data manipulations as *searching*, *sorting* and *comparing elements or entire containers*. The Standard Library provides *many* algorithms. Most of them use iterators to access container elements. Each algorithm has *minimum requirements* for the types of iterators that can be used with it. We'll see that containers support specific iterator types, some more powerful than others. A *container's* supported iterator type determines whether the container can be used with a specific algorithm. Iterators encapsulate the mechanisms used to access container elements. This encapsulation enables many of the algorithms to be applied to various containers *independently* of the underlying container implementation. This also enables you to create new algorithms that can process the elements of *multiple* container types.

Custom Templatized Data Structures
In Chapter 19, we'll build our own *custom* templatized data structures, including linked lists, queues, stacks and trees. We'll carefully weave linked objects together with pointers. Pointer-based code is complex and error-prone—the slightest omissions or oversights can lead to serious *memory-access violations* and *memory-leak* errors with no forewarning from the compiler. If many programmers on a large project implement custom containers and algorithms for different tasks, the code becomes difficult to modify, maintain and debug.

Software Engineering Observation 15.1
Avoid reinventing the wheel; program with the components of the C++ Standard Library.

Error-Prevention Tip 15.1
The prepackaged, templatized Standard Library containers are sufficient for most applications. Using the Standard Library helps you reduce testing and debugging time.

Performance Tip 15.1
The Standard Library was conceived and designed for performance and flexibility.

15.2 Introduction to Containers

The Standard Library container types are shown in Fig. 15.1. The containers are divided into four major categories—sequence containers, ordered associative containers, unordered associative containers and container adapters.

Container class	Description
Sequence containers	
array	Fixed size. Direct access to any element.
deque	Rapid insertions and deletions at front or back. Direct access to any element.
forward_list	Singly linked list, rapid insertion and deletion anywhere. New in C++11.

Fig. 15.1 | Standard Library container classes and container adapters. (Part 1 of 2.)

Container class	Description
list	Doubly linked list, rapid insertion and deletion anywhere.
vector	Rapid insertions and deletions at back. Direct access to any element.
Ordered associative containers—keys are maintained in sorted order	
set	Rapid lookup, no duplicates allowed.
multiset	Rapid lookup, duplicates allowed.
map	One-to-one mapping, no duplicates allowed, rapid key-based lookup.
multimap	One-to-many mapping, duplicates allowed, rapid key-based lookup.
Unordered associative containers	
unordered_set	Rapid lookup, no duplicates allowed.
unordered_multiset	Rapid lookup, duplicates allowed.
unordered_map	One-to-one mapping, no duplicates allowed, rapid key-based lookup.
unordered_multimap	One-to-many mapping, duplicates allowed, rapid key-based lookup.
Container adapters	
stack	Last-in, first-out (LIFO).
queue	First-in, first-out (FIFO).
priority_queue	Highest-priority element is always the first element out.

Fig. 15.1 | Standard Library container classes and container adapters. (Part 2 of 2.)

Containers Overview

The *sequence containers* represent *linear* data structures (i.e., all of their elements are conceptually "lined up in a row"), such as arrays, vectors and linked lists. We'll study linked data structures in Chapter 19, Custom Templatized Data Structures. *Associative containers* are *nonlinear* data structures that typically can locate elements stored in the containers quickly. Such containers can store sets of values or key–value pairs. As of C++11, the keys in associative containers are *immutable* (they cannot be modified). The sequence containers and associative containers are collectively referred to as the **first-class containers**. Stacks and queues are typically constrained versions of sequence containers. For this reason, the Standard Library implements class templates stack, queue and priority_queue as **container adapters** that enable a program to view a sequence container in a constrained manner. Class string supports the same functionality as a *sequence container*, but stores only character data.

Near Containers

There are other container types that are considered **near containers**—built-in arrays, bitsets for maintaining sets of flag values and valarrays for performing high-speed *mathematical vector* (not to be confused with the vector container) operations. These types are considered *near containers* because they exhibit some, but not all, capabilities of the *first-class containers*.

Common Container Functions

Most containers provide similar functionality. Many operations apply to all containers, and other operations apply to subsets of similar containers. Figure 15.2 describes the many functions that are commonly available in most Standard Library containers. Overloaded operators <, <=, >, >=, == and != are *not* provided for priority_queues. Overloaded operators <, <=, > and >= are *not* provided for the *unordered associative containers*. Member functions rbegin, rend, crbegin and crend are *not* available in a forward_list. Before using any container, you should study its capabilities.

Member function	Description
default constructor	A constructor that *initializes an empty container.* Normally, each container has several constructors that provide different ways to initialize the container.
copy constructor	A constructor that initializes the container to be a *copy of an existing container* of the same type.
move constructor	A move constructor (new in C++11 and discussed in Chapter 24) moves the contents of an existing container of the same type into a new container. This avoids the overhead of copying each element of the argument container.
destructor	Destructor function for cleanup after a container is no longer needed.
empty	Returns true if there are *no* elements in the container; otherwise, returns false.
insert	Inserts an item in the container.
size	Returns the number of elements currently in the container.
copy operator=	Copies the elements of one container into another.
move operator=	The move assignment operator (new in C++11 and discussed in Chapter 24) moves the elements of one container into another. This avoids the overhead of copying each element of the argument container.
operator<	Returns true if the contents of the first container are *less than* the second; otherwise, returns false.
operator<=	Returns true if the contents of the first container are *less than or equal to* the second; otherwise, returns false.
operator>	Returns true if the contents of the first container are *greater than* the second; otherwise, returns false.
operator>=	Returns true if the contents of the first container are *greater than or equal to* the second; otherwise, returns false.
operator==	Returns true if the contents of the first container are *equal to* the contents of the second; otherwise, returns false.
operator!=	Returns true if the contents of the first container are *not equal to* the contents of the second; otherwise, returns false.
swap	Swaps the elements of two containers. As of C++11, there is now a non-member function version of swap that swaps the contents of its two arguments (which must be of the same container type) using move operations rather than copy operations.

Fig. 15.2 | Common member functions for most Standard Library containers. (Part 1 of 2.)

Member function	Description
max_size	Returns the *maximum number of elements* for a container.
begin	Overloaded to return either an iterator or a const_iterator that refers to the *first element* of the container.
end	Overloaded to return either an iterator or a const_iterator that refers to the *next position after the end* of the container.
cbegin (C++11)	Returns a const_iterator that refers to the container's *first element*.
cend (C++11)	Returns a const_iterator that refers to the *next position after the end* of the container.
rbegin	The two versions of this function return either a reverse_iterator or a const_reverse_iterator that refers to the *last element* of the container.
rend	The two versions of this function return either a reverse_iterator or a const_reverse_iterator that refers to the *position before the first element* of the container.
crbegin (C++11)	Returns a const_reverse_iterator that refers to the *last element* of the container.
crend (C++11)	Returns a const_reverse_iterator that refers to the *position before the first element* of the container.
erase	Removes *one or more* elements from the container.
clear	Removes *all* elements from the container.

Fig. 15.2 | Common member functions for most Standard Library containers. (Part 2 of 2.)

First-Class Container Common Nested Types

Figure 15.3 shows the common first-class container *nested types* (types defined inside each container class definition). These are used in template-based declarations of variables, parameters to functions and return values from functions (as you'll see in this chapter and Chapter 16). For example, value_type in each container always represents the type of elements stored in the container. The types reverse_iterator and const_reverse_iterator are not provided by class forward_list.

typedef	Description
allocator_type	The type of the object used to allocate the container's memory—not included in class template array.
value_type	The type of element stored in the container.
reference	A reference for the container's element type.
const_reference	A reference for the container's element type that can be used only to *read* elements in the container and to perform const operations.
pointer	A pointer for the container's element type.

Fig. 15.3 | Nested types found in first-class containers. (Part 1 of 2.)

typedef	Description
const_pointer	A pointer for the container's element type that can be used only to *read* elements and to perform const operations.
iterator	An iterator that points to an element of the container's element type.
const_iterator	An iterator that points to an element of the container's element type. Used only only to *read* elements and to perform const operations.
reverse_iterator	A reverse iterator that points to an element of the container's element type. Used to iterate through a container in reverse.
const_reverse_iterator	A reverse iterator that points to an element of the container's element type and can be used only to *read* elements and to perform const operations. Used to iterate through a container in reverse.
difference_type	The type of the result of subtracting two iterators that refer to the same container (operator- is not defined for iterators of lists and associative containers).
size_type	The type used to count items in a container and index through a sequence container (cannot index through a list).

Fig. 15.3 | Nested types found in first-class containers. (Part 2 of 2.)

Requirements for Container Elements

Before using a Standard Library container, it's important to ensure that the type of objects being stored in the container supports a *minimum* set of functionality. When an object is inserted into a container, a *copy* of the object is made. For this reason, the object type should provide a *copy constructor* and *copy assignment operator* (custom or default versions, depending on whether the class uses dynamic memory). Also, the *ordered associative containers* and many algorithms require elements to be *compared*—for this reason, the object type should provide *less-than (<)* and *equality (==)* operators. As of C++11, objects can also be *moved* into container elements, in which case the object type needs a *move constructor* and *move assignment operator*—Chapter 24 discusses *move semantics*.

15.3 Introduction to Iterators

Iterators have many similarities to *pointers* and are used to point to *first-class container* elements and for other purposes. Iterators hold *state* information sensitive to the particular containers on which they operate; thus, iterators are implemented for each type of container. Certain iterator operations are uniform across containers. For example, the *dereferencing operator (*)* dereferences an iterator so that you can use the element to which it points. The ++ *operation on an iterator* moves it to the container's *next element* (much as incrementing a pointer into a built-in array aims the pointer at the next array element).

First-class containers provide member functions begin and end. Function **begin** returns an iterator pointing to the *first* element of the container. Function **end** returns an iterator pointing to the *first element past the end of the container* (one past the end)—a non-existent element that's frequently used to determine when the end of a container is reached. If iterator i points to a particular element, then ++i points to the "next" element and *i refers to the element pointed to by i. The iterator resulting from end is typically used in an equality or inequality comparison to determine whether the "moving iterator" (i in this case) has reached the end of the container.

An object of a container's iterator type refers to a container element that *can* be modified. An object of a container's const_iterator type refers to a container element that *cannot* be modified.

Using istream_iterator for Input and ostream_iterator for Output

We use iterators with sequences (also called ranges). These sequences can be in containers, or they can be input sequences or output sequences. The program of Fig. 15.4 demonstrates input from the standard input (a sequence of data for input into a program), using an istream_iterator, and output to the standard output (a sequence of data for output from a program), using an ostream_iterator. The program inputs two integers from the user at the keyboard and displays the sum of the integers. As you'll see later in this chapter, istream_iterators and ostream_iterators can be used with the Standard Library algorithms to create powerful statements. For example, you can use an ostream_iterator with the copy algorithm to copy a container's *entire* contents to the standard output stream with a single statement.

```
1   // Fig. 15.4: fig15_04.cpp
2   // Demonstrating input and output with iterators.
3   #include <iostream>
4   #include <iterator> // ostream_iterator and istream_iterator
5   using namespace std;
6
7   int main()
8   {
9      cout << "Enter two integers: ";
10
11     // create istream_iterator for reading int values from cin
12     istream_iterator< int > inputInt( cin );
13
14     int number1 = *inputInt; // read int from standard input
15     ++inputInt; // move iterator to next input value
16     int number2 = *inputInt; // read int from standard input
17
18     // create ostream_iterator for writing int values to cout
19     ostream_iterator< int > outputInt( cout );
20
21     cout << "The sum is: ";
22     *outputInt = number1 + number2; // output result to cout
23     cout << endl;
24   } // end main
```

```
Enter two integers: 12 25
The sum is: 37
```

Fig. 15.4 | Demonstrating input and output with iterators.

istream_iterator

Line 12 creates an istream_iterator that's capable of *extracting* (inputting) int values from the standard input object cin. Line 14 *dereferences* iterator inputInt to read the first integer from cin and assigns that integer to number1. The dereferencing operator * applied to iterator inputInt gets the value from the stream associated with inputInt; this is similar to *dereferencing a pointer*. Line 15 positions iterator inputInt to the next value in the input stream. Line 16 inputs the next integer from inputInt and assigns it to number2.

ostream_iterator

Line 19 creates an ostream_iterator that's capable of inserting (outputting) int values in the standard output object cout. Line 22 outputs an integer to cout by assigning to *outputInt the sum of number1 and number2. Notice that we use the dereferenced outputInt iterator as an *lvalue* in the assignment statement. If you want to output another value using outputInt, the iterator must be incremented with ++ first. Either the prefix or postfix increment can be used—we use the prefix form for *performance* reasons because it does not create a temporary object.

> **Error-Prevention Tip 15.2**
>
> *The * (dereferencing) operator when applied to a const iterator returns a reference to const for the container element, disallowing the use of non-const member functions.*

Iterator Categories and Iterator Category Hierarchy

Figure 15.5 shows the iterator categories. Each category provides a specific set of functionality. Figure 15.6 illustrates the hierarchy of iterator categories. As you follow the hierarchy from bottom to top, each iterator category supports all the functionality of the categories *below* it in the figure. Thus the "weakest" iterator types are at the bottom and the most powerful one is at the top. Note that this is *not* an inheritance hierarchy.

Category	Description
random access	Combines the capabilities of a *bidirectional iterator* with the ability to *directly* access *any* element of the container, i.e., to jump forward or backward by an arbitrary number of elements. These can also be compared with relational operators.
bidirectional	Combines the capabilities of a *forward iterator* with the ability to move in the *backward* direction (i.e., from the end of the container toward the beginning). Bidirectional iterators support multipass algorithms.
forward	Combines the capabilities of *input and output iterators* and retains their position in the container (as state information). Such iterators can be used to pass through a sequence more than once (for so-called multipass algorithms).
output	Used to write an element to a container. An output iterator can move only in the *forward* direction one element at a time. Output iterators support *only* one-pass algorithms—the same output iterator *cannot* be used to pass through a sequence twice.
input	Used to read an element from a container. An input iterator can move only in the *forward* direction (i.e., from the beginning of the container to the end) one element at a time. Input iterators support *only* one-pass algorithms—the same input iterator *cannot* be used to pass through a sequence twice.

Fig. 15.5 | Iterator categories.

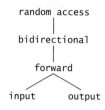

Fig. 15.6 | Iterator category hierarchy.

Container Support for Iterators

The iterator category that each container supports determines whether that container can be used with specific algorithms. *Containers that support random-access iterators can be used with all Standard Library algorithms*—with the exception that if an algorithm requires changes to a container's size, the algorithm can't be used on built-in arrays or `array` objects. Pointers into *built-in* arrays can be used in place of iterators with most algorithms. Figure 15.7 shows the iterator category of each container. The first-class containers, `string`s and built-in arrays are all traversable with iterators.

Container	Iterator type	Container	Iterator type
Sequence containers (first class)		*Unordered associative containers (first class)*	
`vector`	random access	`unordered_set`	bidirectional
`array`	random access	`unordered_multiset`	bidirectional
`deque`	random access	`unordered_map`	bidirectional
`list`	bidirectional	`unordered_multimap`	bidirectional
`forward_list`	forward		
Ordered associative containers (first class)		*Container adapters*	
`set`	bidirectional	`stack`	none
`multiset`	bidirectional	`queue`	none
`map`	bidirectional	`priority_queue`	none
`multimap`	bidirectional		

Fig. 15.7 | Iterator types supported by each container.

Predefined Iterator `typedef`s

Figure 15.8 shows the predefined iterator `typedef`s that are found in the Standard Library container class definitions. Not every `typedef` is defined for every container. We use `const` versions of the iterators for traversing `const` *containers* or non-`const` containers that should not be modified. We use *reverse iterators* to traverse containers in the *reverse* direction.

 Error-Prevention Tip 15.3

Operations performed on a `const_iterator` *return references to* `const` *to prevent modification to elements of the container being manipulated. Using* `const_iterator`s *where appropriate is another example of the principle of least privilege.*

Predefined `typedefs` for iterator types	Direction of ++	Capability
`iterator`	forward	read/write
`const_iterator`	forward	read
`reverse_iterator`	backward	read/write
`const_reverse_iterator`	backward	read

Fig. 15.8 | Iterator `typedefs`.

Iterator Operations
Figure 15.9 shows operations that can be performed on each iterator type. In addition to the operators shown for all iterators, iterators must provide default constructors, copy constructors and copy assignment operators. A *forward* iterator supports ++ and all of the *input* and *output* iterator capabilities. A *bidirectional* iterator supports -- and all the capabilities of *forward* iterators. A *random access* iterator supports all of the operations shown in the table. For input iterators and output iterators, it's not possible to save the iterator then use the saved value later.

Iterator operation	Description
All iterators	
`++p`	Preincrement an iterator.
`p++`	Postincrement an iterator.
`p = p1`	Assign one iterator to another.
Input iterators	
`*p`	Dereference an iterator as an *rvalue*.
`p->m`	Use the iterator to read the element `m`.
`p == p1`	Compare iterators for equality.
`p != p1`	Compare iterators for inequality.
Output iterators	
`*p`	Dereference an iterator as an *lvalue*.
`p = p1`	Assign one iterator to another.
Forward iterators	Forward iterators provide all the functionality of both input iterators and output iterators.
Bidirectional iterators	
`--p`	Predecrement an iterator.
`p--`	Postdecrement an iterator.
Random-access iterators	
`p += i`	Increment the iterator `p` by `i` positions.
`p -= i`	Decrement the iterator `p` by `i` positions.

Fig. 15.9 | Iterator operations for each type of iterator. (Part 1 of 2.)

Iterator operation	Description
p + i *or* i + p	Expression value is an iterator positioned at p incremented by i positions.
p - i	Expression value is an iterator positioned at p decremented by i positions.
p - p1	Expression value is an integer representing the distance between two elements in the same container.
p[i]	Return a reference to the element offset from p by i positions
p < p1	Return true if iterator p is *less than* iterator p1 (i.e., iterator p is *before* iterator p1 in the container); otherwise, return false.
p <= p1	Return true if iterator p is *less than or equal to* iterator p1 (i.e., iterator p is *before* iterator p1 or *at the same location* as iterator p1 in the container); otherwise, return false.
p > p1	Return true if iterator p is *greater than* iterator p1 (i.e., iterator p is *after* iterator p1 in the container); otherwise, return false.
p >= p1	Return true if iterator p is *greater than or equal to* iterator p1 (i.e., iterator p is *after* iterator p1 or *at the same location* as iterator p1 in the container); otherwise, return false.

Fig. 15.9 | Iterator operations for each type of iterator. (Part 2 of 2.)

15.4 Introduction to Algorithms

The Standard Library provides scores of *algorithms* you'll use frequently to manipulate a variety of containers. *Inserting, deleting, searching, sorting* and others are appropriate for some or all of the sequence and associative containers. *The algorithms operate on container elements only indirectly through iterators.* Many algorithms operate on sequences of elements defined by iterators pointing to the *first element* of the sequence and to *one element past the last element.* It's also possible to *create your own new algorithms* that operate in a similar fashion so they can be used with the Standard Library containers and iterators. In this chapter, we'll use the copy algorithm in many examples to copy a container's contents to the standard output. We discuss many Standard Library algorithms in Chapter 16.

15.5 Sequence Containers

The C++ Standard Template Library provides five *sequence containers*—array, vector, deque, list and forward_list. Class templates array, vector and deque are based on built-in arrays. Class templates list and forward_list implement linked-list data structures, which we discuss in Chapter 19. We've already discussed and used class template array extensively, so we do not cover it again here.

Performance and Choosing the Appropriate Container
Figure 15.2 presented the operations common to *most* of the Standard Library containers. Beyond these operations, each container typically provides a variety of other capabilities. Many of these are common to several containers, but they're not always equally efficient for each container.

Software Engineering Observation 15.2

It's usually preferable to reuse Standard Library containers rather than developing customized templatized data structures. For novices, vector is typically satisfactory for most applications.

Performance Tip 15.2

Insertion at the back of a vector is efficient. The vector simply grows, if necessary, to accommodate the new item. It's expensive to insert (or delete) an element in the middle of a vector—the entire portion of the vector after the insertion (or deletion) point must be moved, because vector elements occupy contiguous cells in memory.

Performance Tip 15.3

Applications that require frequent insertions and deletions at both ends of a container normally use a deque rather than a vector. Although we can insert and delete elements at the front and back of both a vector and a deque, class deque is more efficient than vector for doing insertions and deletions at the front.

Performance Tip 15.4

Applications with frequent insertions and deletions in the middle and/or at the extremes of a container normally use a list, due to its efficient implementation of insertion and deletion anywhere in the data structure.

15.5.1 vector Sequence Container

Class template vector, which we introduced in Section 7.10, provides a data structure with *contiguous* memory locations. This enables efficient, direct access to any element of a vector via the subscript operator [], exactly as with a built-in array. Like class template array, template vector is most commonly used when the data in the container must be easily accessible via a subscript or will be sorted, and when the number of elements may need to grow. When a vector's memory is exhausted, the vector *allocates* a larger built-in array, *copies* (or *moves*; Chapter 24)the original elements into the new built-in array and *deallocates* the old built-in array. .

Performance Tip 15.5

Choose the vector container for the best random-access performance in a container that can grow.

Performance Tip 15.6

Objects of class template vector provide rapid indexed access with the overloaded subscript operator [] because they're stored in contiguous memory like a built-in array or an array object.

Using *vectors and Iterators*

Figure 15.10 illustrates several functions of the vector class template. Many of these functions are available in every *first-class container*. You must include header <vector> to use class template vector.

```cpp
 1   // Fig. 15.10: Fig15_10.cpp
 2   // Standard Library vector class template.
 3   #include <iostream>
 4   #include <vector> // vector class-template definition
 5   using namespace std;
 6
 7   // prototype for function template printVector
 8   template < typename T > void printVector( const vector< T > &integers2 );
 9
10   int main()
11   {
12      const size_t SIZE = 6; // define array size
13      int values[ SIZE ] = { 1, 2, 3, 4, 5, 6 }; // initialize values
14      vector< int > integers; // create vector of ints
15
16      cout << "The initial size of integers is: " << integers.size()
17         << "\nThe initial capacity of integers is: " << integers.capacity();
18
19      // function push_back is in vector, deque and list
20      integers.push_back( 2 );
21      integers.push_back( 3 );
22      integers.push_back( 4 );
23
24      cout << "\nThe size of integers is: " << integers.size()
25         << "\nThe capacity of integers is: " << integers.capacity();
26      cout << "\n\nOutput built-in array using pointer notation: ";
27
28      // display array using pointer notation
29      for ( const int *ptr = begin( values ); ptr != end( values ); ++ptr )
30         cout << *ptr << ' ';
31
32      cout << "\nOutput vector using iterator notation: ";
33      printVector( integers );
34      cout << "\nReversed contents of vector integers: ";
35
36      // display vector in reverse order using const_reverse_iterator
37      for ( auto reverseIterator = integers.crbegin();
38         reverseIterator!= integers.crend(); ++reverseIterator )
39         cout << *reverseIterator << ' ';
40
41      cout << endl;
42   } // end main
43
44   // function template for outputting vector elements
45   template < typename T > void printVector( const vector< T > &integers2 )
46   {
47      // display vector elements using const_iterator
48      for ( auto constIterator = integers2.cbegin();
49         constIterator != integers2.cend(); ++constIterator )
50         cout << *constIterator << ' ';
51   } // end function printVector
```

Fig. 15.10 | Standard Library vector class template. (Part 1 of 2.)

```
The initial size of integers is: 0
The initial capacity of integers is: 0
The size of integers is: 3
The capacity of integers is: 4

Output built-in array using pointer notation: 1 2 3 4 5 6
Output vector using iterator notation: 2 3 4
Reversed contents of vector integers: 4 3 2
```

Fig. 15.10 | Standard Library vector class template. (Part 2 of 2.)

Creating a vector

Line 14 defines an instance called integers of class template vector that stores int values. When this object is instantiated, an empty vector is created with size 0 (i.e., the number of elements stored in the vector) and capacity 0 (i.e., the number of elements that can be stored without allocating more memory to the vector).

vector Member Functions size and capacity

Lines 16 and 17 demonstrate the size and capacity functions; each initially returns 0 for vector v in this example. Function size—available in *every* container except forward_list—returns the number of elements currently stored in the container. Function **capacity** (specific to vector and deque) returns the number of elements that can be stored in the vector before the vector needs to *dynamically resize itself* to accommodate more elements.

vector Member Function push_back

Lines 20–22 use function **push_back**—available in *sequence containers* other than array and forward_list—to add an element to the end of the vector. If an element is added to a full vector, the vector increases its size—some implementations have the vector *double* its capacity. Sequence containers other than array and vector also provide a **push_front** function.

Performance Tip 15.7
It can be wasteful to double a vector's size when more space is needed. For example, a full vector of 1,000,000 elements resizes to accommodate 2,000,000 elements when a new element is added. This leaves 999,999 unused elements. You can use resize and reserve to control space usage better.

Updated size and capacity After Modifying a vector

Lines 24 and 25 use size and capacity to illustrate the new size and capacity of the vector after the three push_back operations. Function size returns 3—the number of elements added to the vector. Function capacity returns 4 (though this could vary by compiler), indicating that we can add one more element before the vector needs to add more memory. When we added the first element, the vector allocated space for one element, and the size became 1 to indicate that the vector contained only one element. When we added the second element, the capacity *doubled* to 2 and the size became 2 as well. When we added the third element, the capacity doubled again to 4. So we can actually add another element before the vector needs to allocate more space. When the vector eventually fills its allocated capacity and the program attempts to add one more element to the vector, the vector will double its capacity to eight elements.

vector *Growth*

The manner in which a vector grows to accommodate more elements—a time consuming operation—is *not* specified by the C++ Standard. C++ library implementers use various clever schemes to minimize the overhead of *resizing* a vector. Hence, the output of this program may vary, depending on the version of vector that comes with your compiler. Some library implementers allocate a large initial capacity. If a vector stores a small number of elements, such capacity may be a waste of space. However, it can greatly improve performance if a program adds many elements to a vector and does not have to reallocate memory to accommodate those elements. This is a classic *space–time trade-off*. Library implementors must balance the amount of memory used against the amount of time required to perform various vector operations.

Outputting Built-in Array Contents with Pointers

Lines 29–30 demonstrate how to output the contents of the built-in array values using pointers and pointer arithmetic. Pointers into a built-in array can be used as iterators. Recall from Section 8.5 that C++11 functions begin and end (line 29) from the <iterator> header each take a built-in array as an argument. Function begin returns an iterator pointing to the built-in array's first element and function end returns an iterator representing the position one element *after* the end of the built-in array. Functions begin and end may *also* receive container objects as arguments. Note that we use the != operator in the loop-continuation condition. When iterating using pointers to built-in array elements, it's common for the loop-continuation condition to test whether the pointer has reached the end of the built-in array. This technique is commonly used by the standard library algorithms.

Outputting vector *Contents with Iterators*

Line 33 calls function printVector (defined in lines 45–51) to output the contents of a vector using iterators. The function receives a reference to a const vector. The for statement in lines 48–50 initializes control variable constIterator using vector member function **cbegin** (new in C++11), which returns a const_iterator to the vector's first element. We infer the control variable's type (vector<int>::const_iterator) using the auto keyword. Prior to C++11, you would have used the overloaded begin member function to get the const_iterator—when called on a const container, begin returns a const_iterator. The other version of begin returns an iterator that can be used for non-const containers.

The loop continues as long as constIterator has not reached the end of the vector. This is determined by comparing constIterator to the result of calling the vector's **cend** member function (also new in C++11), which returns a const_iterator indicating the *location past the last element* of the vector. If constIterator is equal to this value, the end of the vector has been reached. Prior to C++11, you would have used the overloaded end member function to get the const_iterator. Functions cbegin, begin, cend and end are available for all first-class containers.

The body of the loop dereferences constIterator to get the current element's value. Remember that the iterator acts like a pointer to the element and that operator * is overloaded to return a reference to the element. The expression ++constIterator (line 49)

positions the iterator to the vector's next element. Note that lines 48–50 could have been replaced with the following range-based for statement:

```
for ( auto const &item : integers2 )
    cout << item << ' ';
```

Common Programming Error 15.1
Attempting to dereference an iterator positioned outside its container is a runtime logic error. In particular, the iterator returned by end should not be dereferenced or incremented.

Displaying the vector's Contents in Reverse with const_reverse_iterators

Lines 37–39 use a for statement (similar to the one in printVector) to iterate through the vector in reverse. C++11 now includes vector member function **crbegin** and **crend** which return const_reverse_iterators that represent the starting and ending points when iterating through a container in reverse. Most first-class containers support this type of iterator. As with functions cbegin and cend, prior to C++11 you would have used the overloaded member functions **rbegin** and **rend** to obtain const_reverse_iterators or reverse_iterators, based on whether the container is const.

C++11: shrink_to_fit

As of C++11, you can ask a vector or deque to return unneeded memory to the system by calling member function **shrink_to_fit**. This *requests* that the container reduce its capacity to the number of elements in the container. According to the C++ standard, implementations can *ignore* this request so that they can perform implementation-specific optimizations.

vector Element-Manipulation Functions

Figure 15.11 illustrates functions for retrieving and manipulating vector elements. Line 16 uses an overloaded vector constructor that takes two iterators as arguments to initialize integers. Line 16 initializes integers with the contents of the array values from beginning of values up to—but not including—values.cend() (which points to the element *after* the end of values). In C++11, you can use list initializers to initialize vectors as in

```
vector< int > integers{ 1, 2, 3, 4, 5, 6 };
```

or

```
vector< int > integers = { 1, 2, 3, 4, 5, 6 };
```

However, these are not fully supported across compilers yet. For this reason, this chapter's examples frequently initialize other containers with array contents as in line 16.

```
1   // Fig. 15.11: fig15_15.cpp
2   // Testing Standard Library vector class template
3   // element-manipulation functions.
4   #include <iostream>
```

Fig. 15.11 | vector class template element-manipulation functions. (Part 1 of 3.)

```cpp
 5    #include <array> // array class-template definition
 6    #include <vector> // vector class-template definition
 7    #include <algorithm> // copy algorithm
 8    #include <iterator> // ostream_iterator iterator
 9    #include <stdexcept> // out_of_range exception
10    using namespace std;
11
12    int main()
13    {
14       const size_t SIZE = 6;
15       array< int, SIZE > values = { 1, 2, 3, 4, 5, 6 };
16       vector< int > integers( values.cbegin(), values.cend() );
17       ostream_iterator< int > output( cout, " " );
18
19       cout << "Vector integers contains: ";
20       copy( integers.cbegin(), integers.cend(), output );
21
22       cout << "\nFirst element of integers: " << integers.front()
23          << "\nLast element of integers: " << integers.back();
24
25       integers[ 0 ] = 7; // set first element to 7
26       integers.at( 2 ) = 10; // set element at position 2 to 10
27
28       // insert 22 as 2nd element
29       integers.insert( integers.cbegin() + 1, 22 );
30
31       cout << "\n\nContents of vector integers after changes: ";
32       copy( integers.cbegin(), integers.cend(), output );
33
34       // access out-of-range element
35       try
36       {
37          integers.at( 100 ) = 777;
38       } // end try
39       catch ( out_of_range &outOfRange ) // out_of_range exception
40       {
41          cout << "\n\nException: " << outOfRange.what();
42       } // end catch
43
44       // erase first element
45       integers.erase( integers.cbegin() );
46       cout << "\n\nVector integers after erasing first element: ";
47       copy( integers.cbegin(), integers.cend(), output );
48
49       // erase remaining elements
50       integers.erase( integers.cbegin(), integers.cend() );
51       cout << "\nAfter erasing all elements, vector integers "
52          << ( integers.empty() ? "is" : "is not" ) << " empty";
53
54       // insert elements from the array values
55       integers.insert( integers.cbegin(), values.cbegin(), values.cend() );
56       cout << "\n\nContents of vector integers before clear: ";
57       copy( integers.cbegin(), integers.cend(), output );
```

Fig. 15.11 | vector class template element-manipulation functions. (Part 2 of 3.)

```
58
59     // empty integers; clear calls erase to empty a collection
60     integers.clear();
61     cout << "\nAfter clear, vector integers "
62        << ( integers.empty() ? "is" : "is not" ) << " empty" << endl;
63  } // end main
```

```
Vector integers contains: 1 2 3 4 5 6
First element of integers: 1
Last element of integers: 6

Contents of vector integers after changes: 7 22 2 10 4 5 6

Exception: invalid vector<T> subscript

Vector integers after erasing first element: 22 2 10 4 5 6
After erasing all elements, vector integers is empty

Contents of vector integers before clear: 1 2 3 4 5 6
After clear, vector integers is empty
```

Fig. 15.11 | vector class template element-manipulation functions. (Part 3 of 3.)

ostream_iterator

Line 17 defines an ostream_iterator called output that can be used to output integers separated by single spaces via cout. An ostream_iterator<int> outputs only values of type int or a compatible type. The first argument to the constructor specifies the output stream, and the second argument is a string specifying the separator for the values output—in this case, the string contains a space character. We use the ostream_iterator (defined in header <iterator>) to output the contents of the vector in this example.

copy Algorithm

Line 20 uses Standard Library algorithm **copy** (from header **<algorithm>**) to output the entire contents of integers to the standard output. The algorithm copies each element in a range from the location specified by the iterator in its first argument and up to, but *not* including, the location specified by the iterator in its second argument. These two arguments must satisfy *input iterator* requirements—they must be iterators through which values can be read from a container, such as const_iterators. They must also represent a range of elements—applying ++ to the first iterator must eventually cause it to reach the second iterator argument in the range. The elements are copied to the location specified by the *output iterator* (i.e., an iterator through which a value can be stored or output) specified as the last argument. In this case, the *output iterator* is an ostream_iterator that's attached to cout, so the elements are copied to the standard output.

vector Member Functions front and back

Lines 22–23 use functions **front** and **back** (available for most *sequence containers*) to determine the vector's first and last elements, respectively. Notice the difference between functions front and begin. Function front returns a reference to the first element in the vector, while function begin returns a *random access iterator* pointing to the first element in the vector. Also notice the difference between functions back and end. Function back returns a reference to the vector's last element, whereas function end returns a *random access iterator* pointing to the location *after* the last element.

Common Programming Error 15.2
The vector must not be empty; otherwise, the results of front *and* back *are undefined.*

Accessing vector Elements

Lines 25–26 illustrate two ways to access vector elements. These can also be used with deque containers. Line 25 uses the subscript operator that's overloaded to return either a reference to the value at the specified location or a reference to that const value, depending on whether the container is const. Function at (line 26) performs the same operation, but with *bounds checking*. Function at first checks the value supplied as an argument and determines whether it's in the vector's bounds. If not, function at throws an out_of_range exception (as demonstrated in lines 35–42). Figure 15.12 shows some of the Standard Library exception types. (The Standard Library exception types are discussed in Chapter 17.)

Exception type	Description
out_of_range	Indicates when subscript is out of range—e.g., when an invalid subscript is specified to vector member function at.
invalid_argument	Indicates an invalid argument was passed to a function.
length_error	Indicates an attempt to create too long a container, string, etc.
bad_alloc	Indicates that an attempt to allocate memory with new (or with an allocator) failed because not enough memory was available.

Fig. 15.12 | Some exception types in header <stdexcept>.

vector Member Function insert

Line 29 uses one of the several overloaded **insert** functions provided by each *sequence container* (except array, which has a fixed size, and forward_list, which has the function insert_after instead). Line 29 inserts the value 22 before the element at the location specified by the iterator in the first argument. In this example, the iterator is pointing to the vector's second element, so 22 is inserted as the second element and the original second element becomes the third element. Other versions of insert allow inserting multiple copies of the same value starting at a particular position, or inserting a range of values from another container, starting at a particular position. As of C++11, this version of member function insert returns an iterator pointing to the item that was inserted.

vector Member Function erase

Lines 45 and 50 use the two **erase** functions that are available in all *first-class containers* (except array, which has a fixed size, and forward_list, which has the function erase_after instead). Line 45 erases the element at the location specified by the iterator argument (in this example, the first element). Line 50 specifies that all elements in the range specified by the two iterator arguments should be erased. In this example, all the elements are erased. Line 52 uses function **empty** (available for all containers and adapters) to confirm that the vector is empty.

Common Programming Error 15.3

Normally erase *destroys the objects that are erased from a container. However, erasing an element that contains a pointer to a dynamically allocated object does* not delete *the dynamically allocated memory—this can lead to a memory leak. If the element is a* unique_ptr, *the* unique_ptr *would be destroyed and the dynamically allocated memory would* be deleted. *If the element is a* shared_ptr, *the reference count to the dynamically allocated object would be decremented and the memory would be deleted only if the reference count reached 0.*

vector Member Function insert *with Three Arguments (Range* insert*)*

Line 55 demonstrates the version of function insert that uses the second and third arguments to specify the starting location and ending location in a sequence of values (in this case, from the array values) that should be inserted into the vector. Remember that the ending location specifies the position in the sequence *after* the last element to be inserted; copying occurs up to, but *not* including, this location. As of C++11, this version of member function insert returns an iterator pointing to the first item that was inserted—if nothing was inserted, the function returns its first argument.

vector Member Function clear

Finally, line 60 uses function clear (found in all *first-class containers* except array) to empty the vector—this does not necessarily return any of the vector's memory to the system. [*Note:* We'll cover many common container member functions in the next few sections. We'll also cover many functions that are specific to each container.]

15.5.2 list Sequence Container

The list *sequence container* (from header <list>) allows insertion and deletion operations at *any* location in the container. If most of the insertions and deletions occur at the *ends* of the container, the deque data structure (Section 15.5.3) provides a more efficient implementation. Class template list is implemented as a *doubly linked list*—every node in the list contains a pointer to the previous node in the list and to the next node in the list. This enables class template list to support *bidirectional iterators* that allow the container to be traversed both forward and backward. Any algorithm that requires *input, output, forward* or *bidirectional iterators* can operate on a list. Many list member functions manipulate the elements of the container as an ordered set of elements.

C++11: forward_list Container

C++11 now includes the new **forward_list** sequence container (header <forward_list>), which is implemented as a *singly linked list*—every node in the list contains a pointer to the next node in the list. This enables class template list to support *forward iterators* that allow the container to be traversed in the forward direction. Any algorithm that requires *input, output* or *forward iterators* can operate on a forward_list.

list Member Functions

In addition to the member functions in Fig. 15.2 and the common member functions of all *sequence containers* discussed in Section 15.5, class template list provides other member functions, including splice, push_front, pop_front, remove, remove_if, unique, merge, reverse and sort. Several of these member functions are list-optimized implementations of the Standard Library algorithms presented in Chapter 16. Both push_front and pop_front are also supported by forward_list and deque. Figure 15.13 demonstrates several features of class list. Remember that many of the functions presented in Figs. 15.10–15.11 can be used with class list, so we focus on the new features in this example's discussion.

```cpp
1   // Fig. 15.13: fig15_13.cpp
2   // Standard library list class template.
3   #include <iostream>
4   #include <array>
5   #include <list> // list class-template definition
6   #include <algorithm> // copy algorithm
7   #include <iterator> // ostream_iterator
8   using namespace std;
9
10  // prototype for function template printList
11  template < typename T > void printList( const list< T > &listRef );
12
13  int main()
14  {
15     const size_t SIZE = 4;
16     array< int, SIZE > ints = { 2, 6, 4, 8 };
17     list< int > values; // create list of ints
18     list< int > otherValues; // create list of ints
19
20     // insert items in values
21     values.push_front( 1 );
22     values.push_front( 2 );
23     values.push_back( 4 );
24     values.push_back( 3 );
25
26     cout << "values contains: ";
27     printList( values );
28
29     values.sort(); // sort values
30     cout << "\nvalues after sorting contains: ";
31     printList( values );
32
33     // insert elements of ints into otherValues
34     otherValues.insert( otherValues.cbegin(), ints.cbegin(), ints.cend() );
35     cout << "\nAfter insert, otherValues contains: ";
36     printList( otherValues );
37
38     // remove otherValues elements and insert at end of values
39     values.splice( values.cend(), otherValues );
40     cout << "\nAfter splice, values contains: ";
41     printList( values );
42
43     values.sort(); // sort values
44     cout << "\nAfter sort, values contains: ";
45     printList( values );
46
```

Fig. 15.13 | Standard Library list class template. (Part 1 of 3.)

```
47       // insert elements of ints into otherValues
48       otherValues.insert( otherValues.cbegin(), ints.cbegin(), ints.cend() );
49       otherValues.sort(); // sort the list
50       cout << "\nAfter insert and sort, otherValues contains: ";
51       printList( otherValues );
52
53       // remove otherValues elements and insert into values in sorted order
54       values.merge( otherValues );
55       cout << "\nAfter merge:\n   values contains: ";
56       printList( values );
57       cout << "\n   otherValues contains: ";
58       printList( otherValues );
59
60       values.pop_front(); // remove element from front
61       values.pop_back(); // remove element from back
62       cout << "\nAfter pop_front and pop_back:\n   values contains: "
63       printList( values );
64
65       values.unique(); // remove duplicate elements
66       cout << "\nAfter unique, values contains: ";
67       printList( values );
68
69       // swap elements of values and otherValues
70       values.swap( otherValues );
71       cout << "\nAfter swap:\n   values contains: ";
72       printList( values );
73       cout << "\n   otherValues contains: ";
74       printList( otherValues );
75
76       // replace contents of values with elements of otherValues
77       values.assign( otherValues.cbegin(), otherValues.cend() );
78       cout << "\nAfter assign, values contains: ";
79       printList( values );
80
81       // remove otherValues elements and insert into values in sorted order
82       values.merge( otherValues );
83       cout << "\nAfter merge, values contains: ";
84       printList( values );
85
86       values.remove( 4 ); // remove all 4s
87       cout << "\nAfter remove( 4 ), values contains: ";
88       printList( values );
89       cout << endl;
90    } // end main
91
92    // printList function template definition; uses
93    // ostream_iterator and copy algorithm to output list elements
94    template < typename T > void printList( const list< T > &listRef )
95    {
96       if ( listRef.empty() ) // list is empty
97          cout << "List is empty";
98       else
99       {
```

Fig. 15.13 | Standard Library list class template. (Part 2 of 3.)

```
100          ostream_iterator< T > output( cout, " " );
101          copy( listRef.cbegin(), listRef.cend(), output );
102      } // end else
103  } // end function printList
```

```
values contains: 2 1 4 3
values after sorting contains: 1 2 3 4
After insert, otherValues contains: 2 6 4 8
After splice, values contains: 1 2 3 4 2 6 4 8
After sort, values contains: 1 2 2 3 4 4 6 8
After insert and sort, otherValues contains: 2 4 6 8
After merge:
   values contains: 1 2 2 2 3 4 4 4 6 6 8 8
   otherValues contains: List is empty
After pop_front and pop_back:
   values contains: 2 2 2 3 4 4 4 6 6 8r
After unique, values contains: 2 3 4 6 8
After swap:
   values contains: List is empty
   otherValues contains: 2 3 4 6 8
After assign, values contains: 2 3 4 6 8
After merge, values contains: 2 2 3 3 4 4 6 6 8 8
After remove( 4 ), values contains: 2 2 3 3 6 6 8 8
```

Fig. 15.13 | Standard Library `list` class template. (Part 3 of 3.)

Creating `list` Objects

Lines 17–18 instantiate two `list` objects capable of storing `int`s. Lines 21–22 use function **push_front** to insert integers at the beginning of `values`. Function `push_front` is specific to classes `forward_list`, `list` and `deque`. Lines 23–24 use function `push_back` to insert integers at the end of `values`. *Function `push_back` is common to all sequence containers*, except `array` and `forward_list`.

`list` Member Function `sort`

Line 29 uses `list` member function **sort** to arrange the elements in the `list` in *ascending order*. [*Note:* This is different from the `sort` in the Standard Library algorithms.] A second version of function `sort` allows you to supply a *binary predicate function* that takes two arguments (values in the list), performs a comparison and returns a `bool` value indicating whether the first argument should come before the second in the sorted contents. This function determines the order in which the elements of the `list` are sorted. This version could be particularly useful for a `list` that stores pointers rather than values. [*Note:* We demonstrate a *unary predicate function* in Fig. 16.3. A unary predicate function takes a single argument, performs a comparison using that argument and returns a `bool` value indicating the result.]

`list` Member Function `splice`

Line 39 uses `list` function **splice** to remove the elements in `otherValues` and insert them into `values` before the iterator position specified as the first argument. There are two other versions of this function. Function `splice` with three arguments allows one element to be removed from the container specified as the second argument from the location specified by the iterator in the third argument. Function `splice` with four arguments uses the last two arguments to specify a range of locations that should be removed from the container in the second argument and placed at the location specified in the first argument. Class template `forward_list` provides a similar member function named `splice_after`.

`list` *Member Function* `merge`

After inserting more elements in `otherValues` and *sorting* both `values` and `otherValues`, line 54 uses `list` member function **merge** to remove all elements of `otherValues` and insert them in sorted order into `values`. Both `list`s *must* be *sorted* in the *same* order before this operation is performed. A second version of `merge` enables you to supply a *binary predicate function* that takes two arguments (values in the list) and returns a `bool` value. The predicate function specifies the sorting order used by `merge`.

`list` *Member Function* `pop_front`

Line 60 uses `list` function **pop_front** to remove the first element in the `list`. Line 60 uses function **pop_back** (available for *sequence containers* other than `array` and `forward_list`) to remove the last element in the `list`.

`list` *Member Function* `unique`

Line 65 uses `list` function **unique** to *remove duplicate elements* in the `list`. The `list` should be in *sorted* order (so that all duplicates are side by side) before this operation is performed, to guarantee that all duplicates are eliminated. A second version of `unique` enables you to supply a *predicate function* that takes two arguments (values in the list) and returns a `bool` value specifying whether two elements are equal.

`list` *Member Function* `swap`

Line 70 uses function **swap** (available to all *first-class containers*) to exchange the contents of `values` with the contents of `otherValues`.

`list` *Member Functions* `assign` *and* `remove`

Line 77 uses `list` function **assign** (available to all *sequence containers*) to replace the contents of `values` with the contents of `otherValues` in the range specified by the two iterator arguments. A second version of `assign` replaces the original contents with copies of the value specified in the second argument. The first argument of the function specifies the number of copies. Line 86 uses `list` function **remove** to delete all copies of the value 4 from the `list`.

15.5.3 deque Sequence Container

Class **deque** provides many of the benefits of a `vector` and a `list` in one container. The term deque is short for "double-ended queue." Class deque is implemented to provide efficient indexed access (using subscripting) for reading and modifying its elements, much like a `vector`. Class deque is also implemented for *efficient insertion and deletion operations at its front and back*, much like a `list` (although a `list` is also capable of efficient insertions and deletions in the *middle* of the `list`). Class deque provides support for random-access iterators, so deques can be used with all Standard Library algorithms. One of the most common uses of a deque is to maintain a *first-in, first-out queue* of elements. In fact, a deque is the default underlying implementation for the queue adaptor (Section 15.7.2).

Additional storage for a deque can be allocated at either end of the deque in blocks of memory that are typically maintained as a built-in array of pointers to those blocks.[2] Due to the *noncontiguous memory layout* of a deque, a deque iterator must be more "intelligent" than the pointers that are used to iterate through vectors, arrays or built-in arrays.

Performance Tip 15.8
In general, deque has higher overhead than vector.

Performance Tip 15.9
Insertions and deletions in the middle of a deque are optimized to minimize the number of elements copied, so it's more efficient than a vector but less efficient than a list for this kind of modification.

Class deque provides the same basic operations as class vector, but like list adds member functions **push_front** and **pop_front** to allow insertion and deletion at the beginning of the deque, respectively.

Figure 15.14 demonstrates features of class deque. Remember that many of the functions presented in Fig. 15.10, Fig. 15.11 and Fig. 15.13 also can be used with class deque. Header **<deque>** must be included to use class deque.

```cpp
1   // Fig. 15.14: fig15_14.cpp
2   // Standard Library deque class template.
3   #include <iostream>
4   #include <deque> // deque class-template definition
5   #include <algorithm> // copy algorithm
6   #include <iterator> // ostream_iterator
7   using namespace std;
8
9   int main()
10  {
11     deque< double > values; // create deque of doubles
12     ostream_iterator< double > output( cout, " " );
13
14     // insert elements in values
15     values.push_front( 2.2 );
16     values.push_front( 3.5 );
17     values.push_back( 1.1 );
18
19     cout << "values contains: ";
20
21     // use subscript operator to obtain elements of values
22     for ( size_t i = 0; i < values.size(); ++i )
23        cout << values[ i ] << ' ';
24
25     values.pop_front(); // remove first element
26     cout << "\nAfter pop_front, values contains: ";
27     copy( values.cbegin(), values.cend(), output );
28
```

Fig. 15.14 | Standard Library deque class template. (Part 1 of 2.)

2. This is an implementation-specific detail, not a requirement of the C++ standard.

```
29      // use subscript operator to modify element at location 1
30      values[ 1 ] = 5.4;
31      cout << "\nAfter values[ 1 ] = 5.4, values contains: ";
32      copy( values.cbegin(), values.cend(), output );
33      cout << endl;
34   } // end main
```

```
values contains: 3.5 2.2 1.1
After pop_front, values contains: 2.2 1.1
After values[ 1 ] = 5.4, values contains: 2.2 5.4
```

Fig. 15.14 | Standard Library deque class template. (Part 2 of 2.)

Line 11 instantiates a deque that can store double values. Lines 15–17 use functions push_front and push_back to insert elements at the beginning and end of the deque.

The for statement in lines 22–23 uses the subscript operator to retrieve the value in each element of the deque for output. The condition uses function size to ensure that we do not attempt to access an element *outside* the bounds of the deque.

Line 25 uses function pop_front to demonstrate removing the first element of the deque. Line 30 uses the subscript operator to obtain an *lvalue*. This enables values to be assigned directly to any element of the deque.

15.6 Associative Containers

The *associative containers* provide *direct access* to store and retrieve elements via keys (often called search keys). The four *ordered associative containers* are multiset, set, multimap and map. Each of these maintains its keys in *sorted order*. There are also four corresponding *unordered associative containers*—unordered_multiset, unordered_set, unordered_multimap and unordered_map—that offer most of the same capabilities as their ordered counterparts. The primary difference between the ordered and unordered associative containers is that the unordered ones do *not* maintain their keys in *sorted* order. In this section, we focus on the *ordered associative containers*.

Performance Tip 15.10

The unordered associative containers might offer better performance for cases in which it's not necessary to maintain keys in sorted order.

Iterating through an *ordered associative container* traverses it in the sort order for that container. Classes **multiset** and **set** provide operations for manipulating sets of values where the values are the keys—there is *not* a separate value associated with each key. The primary difference between a multiset and a set is that a multiset *allows duplicate keys* and a set does not. Classes **multimap** and **map** provide operations for manipulating values associated with keys (these values are sometimes referred to as **mapped values**). The primary difference between a multimap and a map is that a multimap allows *duplicate keys* with associated values to be stored and a map allows only *unique keys* with associated values. In addition to the common container member functions, *ordered associative containers* also support several other member functions that are specific to associative containers. Examples of each of the *ordered associative containers* and their common member functions are presented in the next several subsections.

15.6.1 `multiset` Associative Container

The `multiset` *ordered associative container* (from header `<set>`) provides fast storage and retrieval of keys and allows duplicate keys. The elements' ordering is determined by a so-called comparator function object. For example, in an integer `multiset`, elements can be sorted in *ascending order* by ordering the keys with comparator function object `less<int>`. We discuss function objects in detail in Section 16.4. For this chapter, we'll simply show how to use `less<int>` when declaring ordered associative containers. The data type of the keys in all *ordered associative containers* must support comparison based on the comparator function object—keys sorted with `less<T>` must support comparison with `operator<`. If the keys used in the *ordered associative containers* are of user-defined data types, those types must supply the appropriate comparison operators. A `multiset` supports *bidirectional iterators* (but not *random-access iterators*). In if the order of the keys is not important, you can use `unordered_multiset` (header `<unordered_set>`) instead.

Figure 15.15 demonstrates the `multiset` *ordered associative container* for a `multiset` of `int`s with keys that are sorted in *ascending order*. Containers `multiset` and `set` (Section 15.6.2) provide the same basic functionality.

```cpp
// Fig. 15.15: fig15_15.cpp
// Standard Library multiset class template
#include <array>
#include <iostream>
#include <set> // multiset class-template definition
#include <algorithm> // copy algorithm
#include <iterator> // ostream_iterator
using namespace std;

int main()
{
   const size_t SIZE = 10;
   array< int, SIZE > a = { 7, 22, 9, 1, 18, 30, 100, 22, 85, 13 };
   multiset< int, less< int > > intMultiset; // multiset of ints
   ostream_iterator< int > output( cout, " " );

   cout << "There are currently " << intMultiset.count( 15 )
      << " values of 15 in the multiset\n";

   intMultiset.insert( 15 ); // insert 15 in intMultiset
   intMultiset.insert( 15 ); // insert 15 in intMultiset
   cout << "After inserts, there are " << intMultiset.count( 15 )
      << " values of 15 in the multiset\n\n";

   // find 15 in intMultiset; find returns iterator
   auto result = intMultiset.find( 15 );

   if ( result != intMultiset.end() ) // if iterator not at end
      cout << "Found value 15\n"; // found search value 15
```

Fig. 15.15 | Standard Library `multiset` class template. (Part 1 of 2.)

```
30
31      // find 20 in intMultiset; find returns iterator
32      result = intMultiset.find( 20 );
33
34      if ( result == intMultiset.end() ) // will be true hence
35         cout << "Did not find value 20\n"; // did not find 20
36
37      // insert elements of array a into intMultiset
38      intMultiset.insert( a.cbegin(), a.cend() );
39      cout << "\nAfter insert, intMultiset contains:\n";
40      copy( intMultiset.begin(), intMultiset.end(), output );
41
42      // determine lower and upper bound of 22 in intMultiset
43      cout << "\n\nLower bound of 22: "
44         << *( intMultiset.lower_bound( 22 ) );
45      cout << "\nUpper bound of 22: " << *( intMultiset.upper_bound( 22 ) );
46
47      // use equal_range to determine lower and upper bound
48      // of 22 in intMultiset
49      auto p = intMultiset.equal_range( 22 );
50
51      cout << "\n\nequal_range of 22:" << "\n   Lower bound: "
52         << *( p.first ) << "\n   Upper bound: " << *( p.second );
53      cout << endl;
54   } // end main
```

```
There are currently 0 values of 15 in the multiset
After inserts, there are 2 values of 15 in the multiset

Found value 15
Did not find value 20

After insert, intMultiset contains:
1 7 9 13 15 15 18 22 22 30 85 100

Lower bound of 22: 22
Upper bound of 22: 30

equal_range of 22:
   Lower bound: 22
   Upper bound: 30
```

Fig. 15.15 | Standard Library multiset class template. (Part 2 of 2.)

Creating a multiset

Line 14 creates a multiset of ints ordered in *ascending order*, using the function object less<int>. *Ascending order* is the default for a multiset, so less<int> can be omitted. C++11 fixes a compiler issue with spacing between the closing > of less<int> and the closing > of the multiset type. Before C++11, if you specified this multiset's type as

```
multiset<int, less<int>> intMultiset;
```

the compiler would treat >> at the end of the type as the >> operator and generate a compilation error. For this reason, you were required to put a space between the closing > of less<int> and the closing > of the multiset type (or any other similar template type, such as vector<vector<int>>). As of C++11, the preceding declaration compiles correctly.

multiset *Member Function* count
Line 17 uses function **count** (available to all *associative containers*) to count the number of occurrences of the value 15 currently in the multiset.

multiset *Member Function* insert
Lines 20–21 use one of the several overloaded versions of function insert to add the value 15 to the multiset twice. A second version of insert takes an iterator and a value as arguments and begins the search for the insertion point from the iterator position specified. A third version of insert takes two iterators as arguments that specify a range of values to add to the multiset from another container.

multiset *Member Function* find
Line 26 uses function **find** (available to all *associative containers*) to locate the value 15 in the multiset. Function find returns an iterator or a const_iterator pointing to the location at which the value is found. If the value is *not* found, find returns an iterator or a const_iterator equal to the value returned by calling end on the container. Line 32 demonstrates this case.

Inserting Elements of Another Container into a multiset
Line 38 uses function insert to insert the elements of array a into the multiset. In line 40, the copy algorithm copies the elements of the multiset to the standard output in *ascending order.*

multiset *Member Functions* lower_bound *and* upper_bound
Lines 44 and 45 use functions **lower_bound** and **upper_bound** (available in all *associative containers*) to locate the earliest occurrence of the value 22 in the multiset and the element *after* the last occurrence of the value 22 in the multiset. Both functions return iterators or const_iterators pointing to the appropriate location or the iterator returned by end if the value is not in the multiset.

pair *Objects and* multiset *Member Function* equal_range
Line 49 creates and intializes a pair object called p. Once again, we use C++11's auto keyword to infer the variable's type from its initializer—in this case, the return value of multiset member function equal_range, which is a pair object. Such objects associate pairs of values. The contents of a p will be two const_iterators for our multiset of ints. The multiset function **equal_range** returns a pair containing the results of calling both lower_bound and upper_bound. Type pair contains two public data members called **first** and **second**. Line 49 uses function equal_range to determine the lower_bound and upper_bound of 22 in the multiset. Line 52 uses p.first and p.second to access the lower_bound and upper_bound. We *dereferenced* the iterators to output the values at the locations returned from equal_range. Though we did not do so here, you should always ensure that the iterators returned by lower_bound, upper_bound and equal_range are not equal to the container's *end* iterator before dereferencing the iterators.

C++11: Variadic Class Template tuple

C++ also includes class template tuple, which is similar to pair, but can hold any number of items of various types. As of C++11, class template tuple has been reimplemented using *variadic templates*—templates that can receive a *variable* number of arguments. We discuss tuple and variadic templates in Chapter 24, C++11: Additional Features.

15.6.2 set Associative Container

The *set associative container* (from header <set>) is used for fast storage and retrieval of *unique* keys. The implementation of a set is identical to that of a multiset, except that a set must have unique keys. Therefore, if an attempt is made to insert a *duplicate* key into a set, the duplicate is ignored; because this is the intended mathematical behavior of a set, we do not identify it as a common programming error. A set supports *bidirectional iterators* (but not *random-access iterators*). If the order of the keys is not important, you can use unordered_set (header <unordered_set>) instead. Figure 15.16 demonstrates a set of doubles.

```cpp
1   // Fig. 15.16: fig15_16.cpp
2   // Standard Library set class template.
3   #include <iostream>
4   #include <array>
5   #include <set>
6   #include <algorithm>
7   #include <iterator> // ostream_iterator
8   using namespace std;
9
10  int main()
11  {
12     const size_t SIZE = 5;
13     array< double, SIZE > a = { 2.1, 4.2, 9.5, 2.1, 3.7 };
14     set< double, less< double > > doubleSet( a.begin(), a.end() );
15     ostream_iterator< double > output( cout, " " );
16
17     cout << "doubleSet contains: ";
18     copy( doubleSet.begin(), doubleSet.end(), output );
19
20     // insert 13.8 in doubleSet; insert returns pair in which
21     // p.first represents location of 13.8 in doubleSet and
22     // p.second represents whether 13.8 was inserted
23     auto p = doubleSet.insert( 13.8 ); // value not in set
24     cout << "\n\n" << *( p.first )
25        << ( p.second ? " was" : " was not" ) << " inserted";
26     cout << "\ndoubleSet contains: ";
27     copy( doubleSet.begin(), doubleSet.end(), output );
28
29     // insert 9.5 in doubleSet
30     p = doubleSet.insert( 9.5 ); // value already in set
31     cout << "\n\n" << *( p.first )
32        << ( p.second ? " was" : " was not" ) << " inserted";
33     cout << "\ndoubleSet contains: ";
```

Fig. 15.16 | Standard Library set class template. (Part 1 of 2.)

```
34      copy( doubleSet.begin(), doubleSet.end(), output );
35      cout << endl;
36   } // end main
```

```
doubleSet contains: 2.1 3.7 4.2 9.5

13.8 was inserted
doubleSet contains: 2.1 3.7 4.2 9.5 13.8

9.5 was not inserted
doubleSet contains: 2.1 3.7 4.2 9.5 13.8
```

Fig. 15.16 | Standard Library set class template. (Part 2 of 2.)

Line 14 creates a set of doubles ordered in *ascending order*, using the function object less<double>. The constructor call takes all the elements in array a and inserts them into the set. Line 18 uses algorithm copy to output the contents of the set. Notice that the value 2.1—which appeared twice in array—appears only *once* in doubleSet. This is because container set does *not* allow duplicates.

Line 23 defines and initializes a pair to store the result of a call to set function insert. The pair returned consists of a const_iterator pointing to the item in the set inserted and a bool value indicating whether the item was inserted—true if the item was not in the set; false if it was.

Line 23 uses function insert to place the value 13.8 in the set. The returned pair, p, contains an iterator p.first pointing to the value 13.8 in the set and a bool value that's true because the value was inserted. Line 30 attempts to insert 9.5, which is already in the set. The output shows that 9.5 was not inserted again because sets don't allow duplicate keys. In this case, p.first in the returned pair points to the existing 9.5 in the set.

15.6.3 multimap Associative Container

The *multimap associative container* is used for fast storage and retrieval of keys and associated values (often called key–value pairs). Many of the functions used with multisets and sets are also used with multimaps and maps. The elements of multimaps and maps are pairs of keys and values instead of individual values. When inserting into a multimap or map, a pair object that contains the key and the value is used. The ordering of the keys is determined by a *comparator function object*. For example, in a multimap that uses integers as the key type, keys can be sorted in *ascending order* by ordering them with *comparator function object* less<int>. Duplicate keys are allowed in a multimap, so multiple values can be associated with a single key. This is called a **one-to-many relationship**. For example, in a credit-card transaction-processing system, one credit-card account can have many associated transactions; in a university, one student can take many courses, and one professor can teach many students; in the military, one rank (like "private") has many people. A multimap supports *bidirectional iterators*, but not *random-access iterators*. Figure 15.17 demonstrates the *multimap associative container*. Header **<map>** must be included to use class multimap. If the order of the keys is not important, you can use unordered_multimap (header <unordered_map>) instead.

Performance Tip 15.11

A multimap *is implemented to efficiently locate all values paired with a given key.*

```cpp
1   // Fig. 15.17: fig15_17.cpp
2   // Standard Library multimap class template.
3   #include <iostream>
4   #include <map> // multimap class-template definition
5   using namespace std;
6
7   int main()
8   {
9      multimap< int, double, less< int > > pairs; // create multimap
10
11     cout << "There are currently " << pairs.count( 15 )
12        << " pairs with key 15 in the multimap\n";
13
14     // insert two value_type objects in pairs
15     pairs.insert( make_pair( 15, 2.7 ) );
16     pairs.insert( make_pair( 15, 99.3 ) );
17
18     cout << "After inserts, there are " << pairs.count( 15 )
19        << " pairs with key 15\n\n";
20
21     // insert five value_type objects in pairs
22     pairs.insert( make_pair( 30, 111.11 ) );
23     pairs.insert( make_pair( 10, 22.22 ) );
24     pairs.insert( make_pair( 25, 33.333 ) );
25     pairs.insert( make_pair( 20, 9.345 ) );
26     pairs.insert( make_pair( 5, 77.54 ) );
27
28     cout << "Multimap pairs contains:\nKey\tValue\n";
29
30     // walk through elements of pairs
31     for ( auto mapItem : pairs )
32        cout << mapItem.first << '\t' << mapItem.second << '\n';
33
34     cout << endl;
35  } // end main
```

```
There are currently 0 pairs with key 15 in the multimap
After inserts, there are 2 pairs with key 15

Multimap pairs contains:
Key     Value
5       77.54
10      22.22
15      2.7
15      99.3
20      9.345
25      33.333
30      111.11
```

Fig. 15.17 | Standard Library multimap class template.

Line 9 creates a `multimap` in which the key type is `int`, the type of a key's associated value is `double` and the elements are ordered in *ascending order*. Line 11 uses function `count` to determine the number of key–value pairs with a key of 15 (none yet, since the container is currently empty).

Line 15 uses function `insert` to add a new key–value pair to the `multimap`. The expression `make_pair( 15, 2.7 )` creates a `pair` object in which `first` is the key (15) of type `int` and `second` is the value (2.7) of type `double`. Function `make_pair` automatically uses the types that you specified for the keys and values in the `multimap`'s declaration (line 9). Line 16 inserts another `pair` object with the key 15 and the value 99.3. Then lines 18–19 output the number of pairs with key 15. As of C++11, you can use list initalization for `pair` objects, so line 15 can be simplified as

```
pairs.insert( { 15, 2.7 } );
```

Similarly, C++11 enables you to use list initialization to initialize an object being returned from a function. For example, if a function returns a `pair` containing an `int` and a `double`, you could write:

```
return { 15, 2.7 };
```

Lines 22–26 insert five additional `pairs` into the `multimap`. The range-based `for` statement in lines 31–32 outputs the contents of the `multimap`, including both keys and values. We infer the type of the loop's control variable (a `pair` containing an `int` key and a `double` value) with keyword `auto`. Line 32 accesses the members of the current `pair` in each element of the `multimap`. Notice in the output that the keys appear in *ascending order*.

C++11: List Initializing a Key–Value Pair Container

In this example, we used separate calls to member function insert to place key–value pairs in a `multimap`. If you know the key–value pairs in advance, you can use list initialization when you create the `multimap`. For example, the following statement initializes a `multimap` with three key–value pairs that are represented by the sublists in the main intializer list:

```
multimap< int, double, less< int > > pairs =
   { { 10, 22.22 }, { 20, 9.345 }, { 5, 77.54 } };
```

15.6.4 map Associative Container

The *map associative container* (from header `<map>`) performs fast storage and retrieval of *unique keys* and *associated values*. Duplicate keys are *not* allowed—a single value can be associated with each key. This is called a **one-to-one mapping**. For example, a company that uses unique employee numbers, such as 100, 200 and 300, might have a map that associates employee numbers with their telephone extensions—4321, 4115 and 5217, respectively. With a map you specify the key and get back the associated data quickly. Providing the key in a map's subscript operator [] locates the value associated with that key in the map. Insertions and deletions can be made *anywhere* in a map. If the order of the keys is not important, you can use unordered_map (header `<unordered_map>`) instead.

Figure 15.18 demonstrates a map and uses the same features as Fig. 15.17 to demonstrate the subscript operator. Lines 27–28 use the subscript operator of class map. When the subscript is a key that's already in the map (line 27), the operator returns a reference to the associated value. When the subscript is a key that's *not* in the map (line 18), the operator inserts the key in the map and returns a reference that can be used to associate a value with that key. Line 27 replaces the value for the key 25 (previously 33.333 as specified in line 16) with a new value, 9999.99. Line 28 inserts a new key–value pair in the map (called creating an association).

```cpp
1   // Fig. 15.18: fig15_18.cpp
2   // Standard Library class map class template.
3   #include <iostream>
4   #include <map> // map class-template definition
5   using namespace std;
6
7   int main()
8   {
9      map< int, double, less< int > > pairs;
10
11     // insert eight value_type objects in pairs
12     pairs.insert( make_pair( 15, 2.7 ) );
13     pairs.insert( make_pair( 30, 111.11 ) );
14     pairs.insert( make_pair( 5, 1010.1 ) );
15     pairs.insert( make_pair( 10, 22.22 ) );
16     pairs.insert( make_pair( 25, 33.333 ) );
17     pairs.insert( make_pair( 5, 77.54 ) ); // dup ignored
18     pairs.insert( make_pair( 20, 9.345 ) );
19     pairs.insert( make_pair( 15, 99.3 ) ); // dup ignored
20
21     cout << "pairs contains:\nKey\tValue\n";
22
23     // walk through elements of pairs
24     for ( auto mapItem : pairs )
25        cout << mapItem.first << '\t' << mapItem.second << '\n';
26
27     pairs[ 25 ] = 9999.99; // use subscripting to change value for key 25
28     pairs[ 40 ] = 8765.43; // use subscripting to insert value for key 40
29
30     cout << "\nAfter subscript operations, pairs contains:\nKey\tValue\n";
31
32     // use const_iterator to walk through elements of pairs
33     for ( auto mapItem : pairs )
34        cout << mapItem.first << '\t' << mapItem.second << '\n';
35
36     cout << endl;
37  } // end main
```

```
pairs contains:
Key     Value
5       1010.1
10      22.22
15      2.7
20      9.345
25      33.333
30      111.11
```

Fig. 15.18 | Standard Library map class template. (Part 1 of 2.)

```
After subscript operations, pairs contains:
Key      Value
5        1010.1
10       22.22
15       2.7
20       9.345
25       9999.99
30       111.11
40       8765.43
```

Fig. 15.18 | Standard Library map class template. (Part 2 of 2.)

15.7 Container Adapters

The three **container adapters** are stack, queue and priority_queue. Container adapters are *not first-class containers*, because they do *not* provide the actual data-structure implementation in which elements can be stored and because adapters do *not* support iterators. The benefit of an *adapter class* is that you can choose an appropriate underlying data structure. All three *adapter classes* provide member functions **push** and **pop** that properly insert an element into each adapter data structure and properly remove an element from each adapter data structure. The next several subsections provide examples of the adapter classes.

15.7.1 stack Adapter

Class **stack** (from header <stack>) enables insertions into and deletions from the underlying container at one end called the *top*, so a stack is commonly referred to as a *last-in, first-out* data structure. We introduced stacks in our discussion of the function-call stack in Section 6.12. A stack can be implemented with vector, list or deque. This example creates three integer stacks, using vector, list and deque as the underlying data structure to represent the stack. By default, a stack is implemented with a deque. The stack operations are push to insert an element at the *top* of the stack (implemented by calling function push_back of the underlying container), pop to remove the *top* element of the stack (implemented by calling function pop_back of the underlying container), **top** to get a reference to the top element of the stack (implemented by calling function back of the underlying container), empty to determine whether the stack is empty (implemented by calling function empty of the underlying container) and size to get the number of elements in the stack (implemented by calling function size of the underlying container). In Chapter 19, we'll show you how to develop your own custom stack class template.

Figure 15.19 demonstrates the stack adapter class. Lines 18, 21 and 24 instantiate three integer stacks. Line 18 specifies a stack of integers that uses the default deque container as its underlying data structure. Line 21 specifies a stack of integers that uses a vector of integers as its underlying data structure. Line 24 specifies a stack of integers that uses a list of integers as its underlying data structure.

```
1   // Fig. 15.19: fig15_19.cpp
2   // Standard Library stack adapter class.
3   #include <iostream>
```

Fig. 15.19 | Standard Library stack adapter class. (Part 1 of 3.)

```cpp
 4   #include <stack> // stack adapter definition
 5   #include <vector> // vector class-template definition
 6   #include <list> // list class-template definition
 7   using namespace std;
 8
 9   // pushElements function-template prototype
10   template< typename T > void pushElements( T &stackRef );
11
12   // popElements function-template prototype
13   template< typename T > void popElements( T &stackRef );
14
15   int main()
16   {
17      // stack with default underlying deque
18      stack< int > intDequeStack;
19
20      // stack with underlying vector
21      stack< int, vector< int > > intVectorStack;
22
23      // stack with underlying list
24      stack< int, list< int > > intListStack;
25
26      // push the values 0-9 onto each stack
27      cout << "Pushing onto intDequeStack: ";
28      pushElements( intDequeStack );
29      cout << "\nPushing onto intVectorStack: ";
30      pushElements( intVectorStack );
31      cout << "\nPushing onto intListStack: ";
32      pushElements( intListStack );
33      cout << endl << endl;
34
35      // display and remove elements from each stack
36      cout << "Popping from intDequeStack: ";
37      popElements( intDequeStack );
38      cout << "\nPopping from intVectorStack: ";
39      popElements( intVectorStack );
40      cout << "\nPopping from intListStack: ";
41      popElements( intListStack );
42      cout << endl;
43   } // end main
44
45   // push elements onto stack object to which stackRef refers
46   template< typename T > void pushElements( T &stackRef )
47   {
48      for ( int i = 0; i < 10; ++i )
49      {
50         stackRef.push( i ); // push element onto stack
51         cout << stackRef.top() << ' '; // view (and display) top element
52      } // end for
53   } // end function pushElements
54
```

Fig. 15.19 | Standard Library stack adapter class. (Part 2 of 3.)

```
55    // pop elements from stack object to which stackRef refers
56    template< typename T > void popElements( T &stackRef )
57    {
58       while ( !stackRef.empty() )
59       {
60          cout << stackRef.top() << ' '; // view (and display) top element
61          stackRef.pop(); // remove top element
62       } // end while
63    } // end function popElements
```

```
Pushing onto intDequeStack: 0 1 2 3 4 5 6 7 8 9
Pushing onto intVectorStack: 0 1 2 3 4 5 6 7 8 9
Pushing onto intListStack: 0 1 2 3 4 5 6 7 8 9

Popping from intDequeStack: 9 8 7 6 5 4 3 2 1 0
Popping from intVectorStack: 9 8 7 6 5 4 3 2 1 0
Popping from intListStack: 9 8 7 6 5 4 3 2 1 0
```

Fig. 15.19 | Standard Library stack adapter class. (Part 3 of 3.)

Function pushElements (lines 46–53) pushes the elements onto each stack. Line 50 uses function push (available in each *adapter class*) to place an integer on top of the stack. Line 51 uses stack function top to retrieve the *top* element of the stack for output. *Function top does not remove the top element.*

Function popElements (lines 56–63) pops the elements off each stack. Line 60 uses stack function top to retrieve the top element of the stack for output. Line 61 uses function pop (available in each *adapter class*) to remove the *top* element of the stack. Function pop does *not* return a value.

15.7.2 queue Adapter

A queue is similar to a *waiting line*. The item that has been in the queue the *longest* is the *next* one removed—so a queue is referred to as a **first-in, first-out (FIFO)** data structure. Class **queue** (from header **<queue>**) enables insertions at the *back* of the underlying data structure and deletions from the *front*. A queue can store its elements in objects of the Standard Library's list or deque containers. By default, a queue is implemented with a deque. The common queue operations are push to insert an element at the back of the queue (implemented by calling function push_back of the underlying container), pop to remove the element at the front of the queue (implemented by calling function pop_front of the underlying container), **front** to get a reference to the *first* element in the queue (implemented by calling function front of the underlying container), **back** to get a reference to the *last* element in the queue (implemented by calling function back of the underlying container), empty to determine whether the queue is *empty* (implemented by calling function empty of the underlying container) and size to get the number of elements in the queue (implemented by calling function size of the underlying container). In Chapter 19, we'll show you how to develop your own custom queue class template.

Figure 15.20 demonstrates the queue adapter class. Line 9 instantiates a queue of doubles. Lines 12–14 use function push to add elements to the queue. The while statement in lines 19–23 uses function empty (available in *all* containers) to determine whether the queue is empty (line 19). While there are more elements in the queue, line 21 uses queue function front to read (but not remove) the first element in the queue for output. Line 22 removes the first element in the queue with function pop (available in all *adapter classes*).

```
1   // Fig. 15.20: fig15_20.cpp
2   // Standard Library queue adapter class template.
3   #include <iostream>
4   #include <queue> // queue adapter definition
5   using namespace std;
6
7   int main()
8   {
9      queue< double > values; // queue with doubles
10
11     // push elements onto queue values
12     values.push( 3.2 );
13     values.push( 9.8 );
14     values.push( 5.4 );
15
16     cout << "Popping from values: ";
17
18     // pop elements from queue
19     while ( !values.empty() )
20     {
21        cout << values.front() << ' '; // view front element
22        values.pop(); // remove element
23     } // end while
24
25     cout << endl;
26  } // end main
```

```
Popping from values: 3.2 9.8 5.4
```

Fig. 15.20 | Standard Library queue adapter class templates.

15.7.3 priority_queue Adapter

Class **priority_queue** (from header <queue>) provides functionality that enables *insertions* in *sorted order* into the underlying data structure and deletions from the *front* of the underlying data structure. By default, a priority_queue's elements are stored in a vector. When elements are added to a priority_queue, they're inserted in *priority order*, such that the highest-priority element (i.e., the *largest* value) will be the first element removed from the priority_queue. This is usually accomplished by arranging the elements in a data structure called a **heap** (not to be confused with the heap for dynamically allocated memory) that always maintains the largest value (i.e., highest-priority element) at the front of the data structure. We use the Standard Library's *heap algorithms* in Section 16.3.12. The comparison of elements is performed with *comparator function object* less<T> by default, but you can supply a different comparator.

There are several common priority_queue operations. Function push inserts an element at the appropriate location based on *priority order* of the priority_queue (implemented by calling function push_back of the underlying container, which then reorders the elements in priority order. Function pop removes the *highest-priority* element of the priority_queue (implemented by calling function pop_back of the underlying container after removing the top element of the heap). **top** gets a reference to the *top* element of the priority_queue (implemented by calling function front of the underlying container). empty determines whether the priority_queue is *empty* (implemented by calling function empty of the underlying container). size gets the number of elements in the priority_queue (implemented by calling function size of the underlying container).

Figure 15.21 demonstrates the priority_queue adapter class. Line 9 instantiates a priority_queue that stores double values and uses a vector as the underlying data structure. Lines 12–14 use function push to add elements to the priority_queue. The while statement in lines 19–23 uses function empty (available in *all* containers) to determine whether the priority_queue is empty (line 19). While there are more elements, line 21 uses priority_queue function top to retrieve the *highest-priority* element (i.e., the largest value) in the priority_queue for output. Line 22 removes the *highest-priority* element in the priority_queue with function pop (available in all adapter classes).

```cpp
 1  // Fig. 15.21: fig15_21.cpp
 2  // Standard Library priority_queue adapter class.
 3  #include <iostream>
 4  #include <queue> // priority_queue adapter definition
 5  using namespace std;
 6
 7  int main()
 8  {
 9     priority_queue< double > priorities; // create priority_queue
10
11     // push elements onto priorities
12     priorities.push( 3.2 );
13     priorities.push( 9.8 );
14     priorities.push( 5.4 );
15
16     cout << "Popping from priorities: ";
17
18     // pop element from priority_queue
19     while ( !priorities.empty() )
20     {
21        cout << priorities.top() << ' '; // view top element
22        priorities.pop(); // remove top element
23     } // end while
24
25     cout << endl;
26  } // end main
```

```
Popping from priorities: 9.8 5.4 3.2
```

Fig. 15.21 | Standard Library priority_queue adapter class.

15.8 Class bitset

Class bitset makes it easy to create and manipulate bit sets, which are useful for representing a set of bit flags. bitsets are fixed in size at compile time. Class bitset is an alternate tool for *bit manipulation*, discussed in Chapter 22.

The declaration

```
bitset< size > b;
```

creates `bitset` b, in which every on of the `size` bits is initially 0 ("off").

The statement

```
b.set( bitNumber );
```

sets bit `bitNumber` of `bitset` b "on." The expression `b.set()` sets all bits in b "on."

The statement

```
b.reset( bitNumber );
```

sets bit `bitNumber` of `bitset` b "off." The expression `b.reset()` sets all bits in b "off."

The statement

```
b.flip( bitNumber );
```

"flips" bit `bitNumber` of `bitset` b (e.g., if the bit is "on", `flip` sets it "off"). The expression `b.flip()` flips all bits in b.

The statement

```
b[ bitNumber ];
```

returns a reference to the bit `bitNumber` of `bitset` b. Similarly,

```
b.at( bitNumber );
```

performs range checking on `bitNumber` first. Then, if `bitNumber` is in range, at returns a reference to the bit. Otherwise, at throws an `out_of_range` exception.

The statement

```
b.test( bitNumber );
```

performs *range checking* on `bitNumber` first. If `bitNumber` is in range, `test` returns `true` if the bit is on, `false` it's off. Otherwise, `test` throws an `out_of_range` exception.

The expression

```
b.size()
```

returns the number of bits in `bitset` b.

The expression

```
b.count()
```

returns the number of bits that are set in `bitset` b.

The expression

```
b.any()
```

returns `true` if any bit is set in `bitset` b.

The expression

```
b.all()
```

returns `true` if all of the bits are set in `bitset` b.

The expression

```
b.none()
```

returns true if none of the bits is set in bitset b.

The expressions

```
b == b1
b != b1
```

compare the two bitsets for equality and inequality, respectively.

Each of the bitwise assignment operators &=, |= and ^= (discussed in detail in Section 22.5) can be used to combine bitsets. For example,

```
b &= b1;
```

performs a bit-by-bit logical AND between bitsets b and b1. The result is stored in b. Bitwise logical OR and bitwise logical XOR are performed by

```
b |= b1;
b ^= b2;
```

The expression

```
b >>= n;
```

shifts the bits in bitset b right by n positions.

The expression

```
b <<= n;
```

shifts the bits in bitset b left by n positions.

The expressions

```
b.to_string()
b.to_ulong()
```

convert bitset b to a string and an unsigned long, respectively.

15.9 Wrap-Up

In this chapter, we introduced three key components of the Standard Library—containers, iterators and algorithms. You learned about the linear *sequence containers*, array (Chapter 7), vector, deque, forward_list and list, which all represent linear data structures. We discussed the nonlinear *associative containers*, set, multiset, map and multimap and their unordered versions. You also saw that the *container adapters* stack, queue and priority_queue can be used to restrict the operations of the sequence containers vector, deque and list for the purpose of implementing the specialized data structures represented by the container adapters. You learned the categories of iterators and that each algorithm can be used with any container that supports the minimum iterator functionality that the algorithm requires. You also learned class bitset, which makes it easy to create and manipulate bit sets as a container.

The next chapter continues our discussion of the Standard Library's containers, iterators and algorithms with a detailed treatment of algorithms. You'll also learn about function pointers, function objects and C++11's new lambda expressions.

Summary

Section 15.1 Introduction
- The C++ Standard Library defines powerful, template-based, reusable components for common data structures, and algorithms used to process those data structures.
- There are three container-class categories—first-class containers, container adapters and near containers.
- Iterators, which have properties similar to those of pointers, are used to manipulate container elements.
- Standard Library algorithms are function templates that perform such common data manipulations as searching, sorting and comparing elements or entire containers.

Section 15.2 Introduction to Containers
- Containers are divided into sequence containers, ordered associative containers, unordered associative containers and container adapters (p. 674).
- The sequence containers (p. 674) represent linear data structures.
- Associative containers are nonlinear containers that quickly locate elements stored in them, such as sets of values or key–value pairs (p. 675).
- Sequence containers and associative containers are collectively referred to as first-class containers.
- Class templates `stack`, `queue` and `priority_queue` are container adapters that enable a program to view a sequence container in a constrained manner.
- Near containers (p. 675; built-in arrays, `bitset`s and `valarray`s) exhibit capabilities similar to those of the first-class containers, but do not support all the first-class-container capabilities.
- Most containers provide similar functionality. Many operations apply to all containers, and other operations apply to subsets of similar containers.
- First-class containers define many common nested types that are used in template-based declarations of variables, parameters to functions and return values from functions.

Section 15.3 Introduction to Iterators
- Iterators have many similarities to pointers and are used to point to first-class container elements.
- First-class container function `begin` (p. 678) returns an iterator pointing to the first element of a container. Function `end` (p. 678) returns an iterator pointer after the container's last element (one past the end)—typically used in a loop to indicate when to terminate processing of the container's elements.
- An `istream_iterator` (p. 679) is capable of extracting values in a type-safe manner from an input stream. An `ostream_iterator` (p. 679) is capable of inserting values in an output stream.
- A random-access iterator (p. 681) has the capabilities of a bidirectional iterator and the ability to directly access any element of the container.
- A bidirectional iterator (p. 680) has the capabilities of a forward iterator and can move backwards.
- A forward iterator (p. 680) combines the capabilities of input and output iterators.
- Input and output iterators (p. 680) can move only in the forward direction one element at a time.

Section 15.4 Introduction to Algorithms
- The Standard Library algorithms operate on container elements only indirectly through iterators.
- Many algorithms operate on sequences of elements defined by iterators pointing to the first element of the sequence and to one element past the last element.

Section 15.5 Sequence Containers

- The Standard Library provides sequence containers `array`, `vector`, `forward_list`, `list` and `deque`. Class templates `array`, `vector` and `deque` are based on built-in arrays. Class templates `forward_list` and `list` implements a linked-list data structure.

Section 15.5.1 `vector` Sequence Container

- Function `capacity` (p. 686) returns the number of elements that can be stored in a vector before the vector dynamically resizes itself to accommodate more elements.

- Sequence container function `push_back` (p. 686) adds an element to the end of a container.

- `vector` member function `cbegin` (p. 687; new in C++11) returns a `const_iterator` to the vector's first element.

- `vector` member function `cend` (p. 687; new in C++11) returns a `const_iterator` to the location past the last element of the `vector`.

- `vector` member function `crbegin` (p. 688; new in C++11) returns a `const_reverse_iterator` to the `vector`'s last element.

- `vector` member function `crend` (p. 688; new in C++11) returns a `const_reverse_iterator` to the location before the first element of the `vector`.

- As of C++11, you can ask a `vector` or `deque` to return unneeded memory to the system by calling member function `shrink_to_fit` (p. 688).

- As of C++11, you can use list initializers to initialize the elements of `vector`s and other containers.

- Algorithm `copy` (p. 690; from header `<algorithm>`) copies each element in a range starting with the location specified by its first iterator argument up to, but not including, the one specified by its second iterator argument.

- Function `front` (p. 690) returns a reference to the first element in a sequence container. Function `begin` returns an iterator pointing to the beginning of a sequence container.

- Function `back` (p. 690) returns a reference to the last element in a sequence container (except `forward_list`). Function `end` returns an iterator pointing to the element one past the end of a sequence container.

- Sequence container function `insert` (p. 691) inserts value(s) before the element at a specific location and returns an iterator pointing to the inserted item or the first of the inserted items.

- Function `erase` (p. 691; in all first-class containers except `forward_list`) removes specific element(s) from the container.

- Function `empty` (p. 691; in all containers and adapters) returns `true` if the container is empty.

- Function `clear` (p. 692; in all first-class containers) empties the container.

Section 15.5.2 `list` Sequence Container

- The `list` sequence container (p. 692; from header `<list>`) implements a doubly linked list that provides an efficient implementation for inserting and deleting anywhere in the container.

- The `forward_list` sequence container (p. 692; from header `<forward_list>`) implements a singly linked list that supports only forward iterators.

- `list` member function `push_front` (p. 695) inserts values at the beginning of a list.

- `list` member function `sort` (p. 695) arranges the elements in the list in ascending order.

- `list` member function `splice` (p. 695) removes elements in one `list` and inserts them into another `list` at a specific position.

- `list` member function `unique` (p. 696) removes duplicate elements in a `list`.

- `list` member function `assign` (p. 696) replaces the contents of one `list` with those of another.
- `list` member function `remove` (p. 696) deletes all copies of a specified value from a `list`.

Section 15.5.3 deque *Sequence Container*

- Class template `deque` (p. 697) provides the same operations as `vector`, but adds member functions `push_front` and `pop_front` (p. 696) to allow insertion and deletion at the beginning of a `deque`, respectively. Header `<deque>` must be included to use class template `deque`.

Section 15.6 Associative Containers

- The Standard Library's associative containers provide direct access to store and retrieve elements via keys (p. 698).
- The four ordered associative containers (p. 698) are `multiset`, `set`, `multimap` and `map`.
- The four unordered associative containers (p. 698) are `unordered_multiset`, `unordered_set`, `unordered_multimap` and `unordered_map`. These are nearly identical to their ordered counterparts, but do not maintain keys in sorted order.
- Class templates `multiset` and `set` provide operations for manipulating sets of values where the values are the keys—there is not a separate value associated with each key. Header `<set>` must be included to use class templates `set` and `multiset`.
- A `multiset` allows duplicate keys and a `set` does not.

Section 15.6.1 multiset *Associative Container*

- The `multiset` associative container (p. 698) provides fast storage and retrieval of keys and allows duplicate keys. The key order is determined by a comparator function object. If the order of the keys is not important, you can use `unordered_multiset` (header `<unordered_set>`) instead.
- A `multiset`'s keys can be sorted in ascending order by ordering the keys with comparator function object `less<T>` (p. 699).
- The type of the keys in all associative containers must support comparison properly based on the comparator function object specified.
- A `multiset` supports bidirectional iterators.
- Header `<set>` (p. 699) must be included to use class `multiset`.
- Function `count` (p. 701; available to all associative containers) counts the number of occurrences of the specified value currently in a container.
- Function `find` (p. 701; available to all associative containers) locates a specified value in a container.
- Associative container functions `lower_bound` and `upper_bound` (p. 701) locate the earliest occurrence of the specified value in a container and the element after the value's last occurrence, respectively.
- Associative container function `equal_range` (p. 701) returns a `pair` containing the results of both a `lower_bound` and an `upper_bound` operation.
- C++ also includes class template `tuple`, which is similar to `pair`, but can hold any number of items of various types.

Section 15.6.2 set *Associative Container*

- The `set` associative container is used for fast storage and retrieval of unique keys. If the order of the keys is not important, you can use `unordered_set` (header `<unordered_set>`) instead.
- If an attempt is made to insert a duplicate key into a `set`, the duplicate is ignored.

- A set supports bidirectional iterators.
- Header <set> must be included to use class set.

Section 15.6.3 `multimap` *Associative Container*
- Containers multimap and map provide operations for manipulating key–value pairs. If the order of the keys is not important, you can use unordered_multimap (header <unordered_map>) instead.
- The primary difference between a multimap and a map is that a multimap allows duplicate keys with associated values to be stored and a map allows only unique keys with associated values.
- The multimap associative container is used for fast storage and retrieval of key–value pairs.
- Duplicate keys are allowed in a multimap, so multiple values can be associated with a single key. This is called a one-to-many relationship.
- Header <map> (p. 703) must be included to use class templates map and multimap.
- Function make_pair automatically creates a pair using the types specified in the multimap's declaration.
- In C++11, if you know the key–value pairs in advance, you can use list initialization when you create a multimap.

Section 15.6.4 `map` *Associative Container*
- Duplicate keys are not allowed in a map, so only a single value can be associated with each key. This is called a one-to-one mapping (p. 705). If the order of the keys is not important, you can use unordered_map (header <unordered_map>) instead.

Section 15.7 *Container Adapters*
- The container adapters are stack, queue and priority_queue.
- Adapters are not first-class containers, because they do not provide the actual data structure implementation in which elements can be stored and they do not support iterators.
- All three adapter class templates provide member functions push and pop (p. 707) that properly insert an element into and remove an element from each adapter data structure, respectively.

Section 15.7.1 `stack` *Adapter*
- Class template stack (p. 707) is a last-in, first-out data structure. Header <stack> (p. 707) must be included to use class template stack.
- The stack member function top (p. 707) returns a reference to the top element of the stack (implemented by calling function back of the underlying container).
- The stack member function empty determines whether the stack is empty (implemented by calling function empty of the underlying container).
- The stack member function size returns the number of elements in the stack (implemented by calling function size of the underlying container).

Section 15.7.2 `queue` *Adapter*
- Class template queue (p. 709) implements a FIFO data structure. Header <queue> (p. 709) must be included to use a queue or a priority_queue.
- The queue member function front returns a reference to the first element in the queue.
- The queue member function back (p. 709) returns a reference to the last element in the queue.
- The queue member function empty determines whether the queue is empty.
- The queue member function size returns the number of elements in the queue.

Section 15.7.3 `priority_queue` *Adapter*
- Class template `priority_queue` provides functionality that enables insertions in sorted order into the underlying data structure and deletions from the front of the underlying data structure.
- The common `priority_queue` (p. 710) operations are `push`, `pop`, `top`, `empty` and `size`.

Section 15.8 Class `bitset`
- Class template `bitset` (p. 711) makes it easy to create and manipulate bit sets, which are useful for representing a set of bit flags.

Self-Review Exercises

15.1   State whether each of the following is *true* or *false*. If *false*, explain why.
- a) Pointer-based code is complex and error-prone—the slightest omissions or oversights can lead to serious memory-access violations and memory-leak errors that the compiler will warn you about.
- b) deques offer rapid insertions and deletions at front or back and direct access to any element.
- c) `lists` are singly linked lists and offer rapid insertion and deletion anywhere.
- d) `multimaps` offer one-to-many mapping with duplicates allowed and rapid key-based lookup.
- e) Associative containers are nonlinear data structures that typically can locate elements stored in the containers quickly.
- f) The container member function `cbegin` returns an `iterator` that refers to the container's first element.
- g) The `++` operation on an iterator moves it to the container's next element.
- h) The `*` (dereferencing) operator when applied to a `const` iterator returns a `const` reference to the container element, allowing the use of non-`const` member functions.
- i) Using `iterators` where appropriate is another example of the principle of least privilege.
- j) Many algorithms operate on sequences of elements defined by iterators pointing to the first element of the sequence and to the last element.
- k) Function `capacity` returns the number of elements that can be stored in the `vector` before the `vector` needs to dynamically resize itself to accommodate more elements.
- l) One of the most common uses of a deque is to maintain a first-in, first-out queue of elements. In fact, a deque is the default underlying implementation for the queue adaptor.
- m) `push_front` is available only for class `list`.
- n) Insertions and deletions can be made only at the front and back of a map.
- o) Class queue enables insertions at the front of the underlying data structure and deletions from the back (commonly referred to as a first-in, first-out data structure).

15.2   Fill in the blanks in each of the following statements:
- a) The three key components of the "STL" portion of the Standard Library are _____, _____ and _____.
- b) Built-in arrays can be manipulated by Standard Library algorithms, using _____ as iterators.
- c) The Standard Library container adapter most closely associated with the last-in, first-out (LIFO) insertion-and-removal discipline is the _____.
- d) The sequence containers and _____ containers are collectively referred to as the first-class containers.
- e) A(n) _____ constructor initializes the container to be a copy of an existing container of the same type.

f) The _____ container member function returns true if there are no elements in the container; otherwise, returns false.

g) The _____ container member function (new in C++11) moves the elements of one container into another—this avoids the overhead of copying each element of the argument container.

h) The container member function _____ is overloaded to return either an iterator or a const_iterator that refers to the first element of the container.

i) Operations performed on a const_iterator return _____ to prevent modification to elements of the container being manipulated.

j) The Standard Library sequence containers are array, vector, deque, _____ and _____.

k) Choose the _____ container for the best random-access performance in a container that can grow.

l) Function push_back, which is available in sequence containers other than _____, adds an element to the end of the container.

m) As with cbegin and cend, C++11 now includes vector member function crbegin and crend which return _____ that represent the starting and ending points when iterating through a container in reverse.

n) A unary _____ function takes a single argument, performs a comparison using that argument and returns a bool value indicating the result.

o) The primary difference between the ordered and unordered associative containers is _____.

p) The primary difference between a multimap and a map is _____.

q) C++11 introduces class template tuple, which is similar to pair, but can _____.

r) The map associative container performs fast storage and retrieval of unique keys and associated values. Duplicate keys are not allowed—a single value can be associated with each key. This is called a(n) _____ mapping.

s) Class _____ provides functionality that enables insertions in sorted order into the underlying data structure and deletions from the front of the underlying data structure.

15.3 Write a statement or expression that performs each of the following bitset tasks:

a) Write a declaration that creates bitset flags of size size, in which every bit is initially 0.

b) Write a statement that sets bit bitNumber of bitset flags "off."

c) Write a statement that returns a reference to the bit bitNumber of bitset flags.

d) Write an expression that returns the number of bits that are set in bitset flags.

e) Write an expression that returns true if all of the bits are set in bitset flags.

f) Write an expression that compares bitsets flags and otherFlags for inequality.

g) Write an expression that shifts the bits in bitset flags left by n positions.

Answers to Self-Review Exercises

15.1   a) False. The compiler does not warn about these kinds of execution-time errors. b) True. c) False. They are doubly linked lists. d) True. e) True. f) False. It returns a const_iterator. g) True. h) False. Disallowing the use of non-const member functions. i) False. Using const_iterators where are appropriate is another example of the principle of least privilege. j) False. Many algorithms operate on sequences of elements defined by iterators pointing to the first element of the sequence and to one element past the last element. k) True. l) True. m) False. It's also available for class deque. n) False. Insertions and deletions can be made anywhere in a map. o) False. Insertions may occur only at the back and deletions may occur only at the front.

15.2   a) containers, iterators and algorithms. b) pointers. c) stack. d) associative. e) copy. f) empty. g) move version of operator=. h) begin. i) const references. j) list and forward_list.

k) vector. l) array. m) `const_reverse_iterators`. n) predicate. o) the unordered ones do not maintain their keys in sorted order. p) A `multimap` allows duplicate keys with associated values to be stored and a map allows only unique keys with associated values. q) hold any number of items of various types. r) one-to-one. s) `priority_queue`.

15.3   a) `bitset< size > flags;`
  b) `flags.reset( bitNumber );`
  c) `flags[ bitNumber ];`
  d) `flags.count()`
  e) `flags.all()`
  f) `flags != otherFlags`
  g) `flags <<= n;`

Exercises

15.4   State whether each of the following is *true* or *false*. If *false*, explain why.
  a) Many of the Standard Library algorithms can be applied to various containers independently of the underlying container implementation.
  b) `arrays` are fixed in size and offer direct access to any element.
  c) `forward_lists` are singly linked lists, that offer rapid insertion and deletion only at the front and the back.
  d) `sets` offer rapid lookup and duplicates are allowed.
  e) In a `priority_queue`, the lowest-priority element is always the first element out.
  f) The sequence containers represent non-linear data structures.
  g) As of C++11, there is now a non-member function version of `swap` that swaps the contents of its two arguments (which must be of different container types) using move operations rather than copy operations.
  h) Container member function `erase` removes all elements from the container.
  i) An object of type `iterator` refers to a container element that *can* be modified.
  j) We use const versions of the iterators for traversing read-only containers.
  k) For input iterators and output iterators, it's common to save the iterator then use the saved value later.
  l) Class templates `array`, `vector` and `deque` are based on built-in arrays.
  m) Attempting to dereference an iterator positioned outside its container is a compilation error. In particular, the iterator returned by `end` should not be dereferenced or incremented.
  n) Insertions and deletions in the middle of a `deque` are optimized to minimize the number of elements copied, so it's more efficient than a `vector` but less efficient than a `list` for this kind of modification.
  o) Container `set` does *not* allow duplicates.
  p) Class `stack` (from header `<stack>`) enables insertions into and deletions from the underlying data structure at one end (commonly referred to as a last-in, first-out data structure).
  q) Function `empty` is available in all containers except the deque.

15.5   Fill in the blanks in each of the following statements:
  a) The three styles of container classes are first-class containers, _____ and near containers.
  b) Containers are divided into four major categories—sequence containers, ordered associative containers, _____ and container adapters.
  c) The Standard Library container adapter most closely associated with the first-in, first-out (FIFO) insertion-and-removal discipline is the _____.

d) Built-in arrays, `bitset`s and `valarray`s are all _____ containers.

e) A(n) _____ constructor (new in C++11) moves the contents of an existing container of the same type into a new container, without the overhead of copying each element of the argument container.

f) The _____ container member function returns the number of elements currently in the container.

g) The _____ container member function returns `true` if the contents of the first container are not equal to the contents of the second; otherwise, returns `false`.

h) We use iterators with sequences—these can be input sequences or output sequences, or they can be _____.

i) The Standard Library algorithms operate on container elements only indirectly through _____.

j) Applications with frequent insertions and deletions in the middle and/or at the extremes of a container normally use a(n) _____.

k) Function _____ is available in *every* first-class container (except `forward_list`) and it returns the number of elements currently stored in the container.

l) It can be wasteful to double a `vector`'s size when more space is needed. For example, a full `vector` of 1,000,000 elements resizes to accommodate 2,000,000 elements when a new element is added, leaving 999,999 unused elements. You can use _____ and _____ to control space usage better.

m) As of C++11, you can ask a `vector` or `deque` to return unneeded memory to the system by calling member function _____.

n) The associative containers provide direct access to store and retrieve elements via keys (often called search keys). The ordered associative containers are `multiset`, `set`, _____ and _____.

o) Classes _____ and _____ provide operations for manipulating sets of values where the values are the keys—there is *not* a separate value associated with each key.

p) We use C++11's auto keyword _____.

q) A `multimap` is implemented to efficiently locate all values paired with a given _____.

r) The Standard Library container adapters are `stack`, `queue` and _____.

Discussion Questions

15.6 Why are iterators used? Explain the similarity with pointers.

15.7 What is the use of Standard Library algorithms?

15.8 What are the major categories of Standard Library containers? Which is the newest sequence of containers in C++11?

15.9 What is the use of near containers?

15.10 What is the use of copy constructors and move constructors?

15.11 How does the Standard Library algorithm copy work?

15.12 Describe how a list sequence container works.

15.13 When would you prefer a `list` to an array?

15.14 How does a multimap associative container act as a fast storage?

15.15 Use C++11 list initializers to initialize the `vector` names with the strings `"Cavendis"`, `"Banister"`, `"Crol"` and `"Anderson"`. Show both common syntaxes.

15.16 What are the different types of container adapters? Why are container adapters not first-class containers?

15.17 Describe the use of the class `priority_queue`.

15.18 What is the use of class `bitset`?

15.19 What are the different types of unordered associative containers? Explain each.

15.20 Explain the push, pop and top operations of a stack.

15.21 Explain the container support for iterators.

15.22 What are the requirements for c ontainer elements?

Programming Exercises

15.23 *(Palindromes)* Write a function template `palindrome` that takes a vector parameter and returns true or false according to whether the vector does or does not read the same forward as backward (e.g., a vector containing 1, 2, 3, 2, 1 is a palindrome, but a vector containing 1, 2, 3, 4 is not).

15.24 *(Sieve of Eratosthenes with `bitset`)* This exercises revisits the *Sieve of Eratosthenes* for finding prime numbers that we discussed in Exercise 7.27. Use a `bitset` to implement the algorithm. Your program should display all the prime numbers from 2 to 1023, then allow the user to enter a number to determine whether that number is prime.

15.25 *(Sieve of Eratosthenes)* Modify Exercise 15.24, the Sieve of Eratosthenes, so that, if the number the user inputs into the program is not prime, the program displays the prime factors of the number. Remember that a prime number's factors are only 1 and the prime number itself. Every nonprime number has a unique prime factorization. For example, the factors of 54 are 2, 3, 3 and 3. When these values are multiplied together, the result is 54. For the number 54, the prime factors output should be 2 and 3.

15.26 *(Prime Factors)* Modify Exercise 15.25 so that, if the number the user inputs into the program is not prime, the program displays the prime factors of the number and the number of times each prime factor appears in the unique prime factorization. For example, the output for the number 54 should be

```
The unique prime factorization of 54 is: 2 * 3 * 3 * 3
```

Recommended Reading

Abrahams, D., and A. Gurtovoy. *C++ Template Metaprogramming: Concepts, Tools, and Techniques from Boost and Beyond.* Boston: Addison-Wesley Professional, 2004.

Ammeraal, L. *STL for C++ Programmers.* New York: John Wiley & Sons, 1997.

Austern, M. H. *Generic Programming and the STL: Using and Extending the C++ Standard Template Library.* Boston: Addison-Wesley, 2000.

Becker, P. *The C++ Standard Library Extensions: A Tutorial and Reference.* Boston: Addison-Wesley Professional, 2006.

Glass, G., and B. Schuchert. *The STL <Primer>.* Upper Saddle River, NJ: Prentice Hall PTR, 1995.

Heller, S., and Chrysalis Software Corp., *C++: A Dialog: Programming with the C++ Standard Library.* New York, Prentice Hall PTR, 2002.

Josuttis, N. *The C++ Standard Library: A Tutorial and Reference (2nd edition).* Boston: Addison-Wesley Professional, 2012.

Josuttis, N. *The C++ Standard Library: A Tutorial and Handbook.* Boston: Addison-Wesley, 2000.

Karlsson, B. Beyond *the C++ Standard Library: An Introduction to Boost.* Boston: Addison-Wesley Professional, 2005.

Koenig, A., and B. Moo. *Ruminations on C++.* Boston: Addison-Wesley, 1997.

Lippman, S., J. Lajoie, and B. Moo. *C++ Primer (Fifth Edition).* Boston: Addison-Wesley Professional, 2012.

Meyers, S. *Effective STL: 50 Specific Ways to Improve Your Use of the Standard Template Library.* Boston: Addison-Wesley, 2001.

Musser, D. R., G. Derge and A. Saini. *STL Tutorial and Reference Guide: C++ Programming with the Standard Template Library, Second Edition.* Boston: Addison-Wesley, 2010.

Musser, D. R., and A. A. Stepanov. "Algorithm-Oriented Generic Libraries," *Software Practice and Experience,* Vol. 24, No. 7, July 1994.

Nelson, M. *C++ Programmer's Guide to the Standard Template Library.* Foster City, CA: Programmer's Press, 1995.

Pohl, I. *C++ Distilled: A Concise ANSI/ISO Reference and Style Guide.* Boston: Addison-Wesley, 1997.

Reese, G. *C++ Standard Library Practical Tips.* Hingham, MA: Charles River Media, 2005.

Robson, R. *Using the STL: The C++ Standard Template Library, Second Edition.* New York: Springer, 2000.

Schildt, H. *STL Programming from the Ground Up, Third Edition.* New York: McGraw-Hill Osborne Media, 2003.

Schildt, H. *STL Programming from the Ground Up.* New York: Osborne McGraw-Hill, 1999.

Stepanov, A., and M. Lee. "The Standard Template Library," *Internet Distribution* 31 October 1995 <www.cs.rpi.edu/~musser/doc.ps>.

Stroustrup, B. "C++11—the New ISO C++ Standard" <www.stroustrup.com/C++11FAQ.html>.

Stroustrup, B. "Making a vector Fit for a Standard," *The C++ Report,* October 1994.

Stroustrup, B. *The Design and Evolution of C++.* Boston: Addison-Wesley, 1994.

Stroustrup, B. T*he C++ Programming Language, Fourth Edition.* Boston: Addison-Wesley Professional, 2013.

Stroustrup, B. *The C++ Programming Language, Third Edition.* Boston: Addison-Wesley, 2000.

Vandevoorde, D., and N. Josuttis. *C++ Templates: The Complete Guide.* Boston: Addison-Wesley, 2003.

Vilot, M. J., "An Introduction to the Standard Template Library," *The C++ Report,* Vol. 6, No. 8, October 1994.

Wilson, M. *Extended STL, Volume 1: Collections and Iterators.* Boston: Addison-Wesley, 2007.

Standard Library Algorithms

*The historian is a prophet in
reverse.*
—Friedrich von Schlegel

*Attempt the end, and never
stand to doubt; Nothing's so
hard but search will find it out.*
—Robert Herrick

Objectives

In this chapter you'll:

- Program with many of the
  dozens of Standard Library
  algorithms.

- Use iterators with algorithms
  to access and manipulate the
  elements of Standard Library
  containers.

- Pass function pointers,
  function objects and lambda
  expressions into Standard
  Library algorithms.

16.1 Introduction

This chapter continues our discussion of the Standard Library's containers, iterators and algorithms by focusing on algorithms that perform common data manipulations such as *searching*, *sorting* and *comparing elements or entire containers*. The Standard Library provides over 90 algorithms, many of which are new in C++11. The complete list can be found in Sections 25 and 26.7 of the C++ standard document and there are various online references where you can learn about each algorithm, such as en.cppreference.com/w/cpp/algorithm. Most of them use iterators to access container elements. As you'll see, various algorithms can receive a *function pointer* (a pointer to a function's code) as an argument. Such algorithms use the pointer to call the function—typically with one or two container elements as arguments. We'll introduce function pointers in more detail in this chapter. Later in the chapter we'll present the concept of a *function object*, which is similar to a function pointer but is implemented as an object of a class that has an overloaded function-call operator (`operator()`) so that the object can be used like a function name. Finally, we'll introduce *lambda expressions*—C++11's new shorthand mechanism for creating *anonymous function objects* (that is, function objects that do not have names).

16.2 Minimum Iterator Requirements

With few exceptions, the Standard Library separates algorithms from containers. This makes it much easier to add new algorithms. An important part of every container is the *type of iterator* it supports (Fig. 15.7). This determines which algorithms can be applied to the container. For example, both `vector`s and `array`s support *random-access iterators* that provide *all* of the iterator operations shown in Fig. 15.9. *All* Standard Library algorithms can operate on `vector`s and the ones that do not modify a container's size can also operate on `array`s. Each Standard Library algorithm that takes iterator arguments requires those iterators to provide a minimum level of functionality. If an algorithm requires a *forward iterator*, for example, that algorithm can operate on any container that supports *forward iterators*, *bidirectional iterators* or *random-access iterators*.

Software Engineering Observation 16.1

Standard Library algorithms do not depend on the implementation details of the containers on which they operate. As long as a container's (or built-in array's) iterators satisfy the requirements of an algorithm, the algorithm can work on the container.

Portability Tip 16.1

Because Standard Library algorithms process containers only indirectly through iterators, one algorithm can often be used with many different containers.

Software Engineering Observation 16.2

The Standard Library containers are implemented concisely. The algorithms are separated from the containers and operate on elements of the containers only indirectly through iterators. This separation makes it easier to write generic algorithms applicable to a variety of container classes.

Software Engineering Observation 16.3

Using the "weakest iterator" that yields acceptable performance helps produce maximally reusable components. For example, if an algorithm requires only forward iterators, it can be used with any container that supports forward iterators, bidirectional iterators or random-access iterators. However, an algorithm that requires random-access iterators can be used only with containers that have random-access iterators.

Iterator Invalidation

Iterators simply *point* to container elements, so it's possible for iterators to become *invalid* when certain container modifications occur. For example, if you invoke clear on a vector, *all* of its elements are *removed*. If a program had any iterators that pointed to that vector's elements before clear was called, those iterators would now be *invalid*. Section 23 of the C++ standard discusses all the cases in which iterators (and pointers and references) are invalidated for each Standard Library container. Here we summarize when iterators are invalidated during *insert* and *erase* operations.

When *inserting* into a:

- vector—If the vector is reallocated, all iterators pointing to that vector are invalidated. Otherwise, iterators from the insertion point to the end of the vector are invalidated.

- deque—All iterators are invalidated.

- list or forward_list—All iterators *remain valid*.

- Ordered associative container—All iterators *remain valid*.

- Unordered associative container—All iterators are invalidated if the containers need to be reallocated.

When *erasing* from a container, iterators to the *erased* elements are invalidated. In addition:

- vector—Iterators from the erased element to the end of the vector are invalidated.

- deque—If an element in the middle of the deque is erased, all iterators are invalidated.

16.3 Algorithms

Sections 16.3.1–16.3.13 demonstrate many of the Standard Library algorithms.

16.3.1 `fill`, `fill_n`, `generate` and `generate_n`

Figure 16.1 demonstrates algorithms `fill`, `fill_n`, `generate` and `generate_n`. Algorithms `fill` and `fill_n` set every element in a range of container elements to a specific value. Algorithms **generate** and **generate_n** use a generator function to create values for every element in a *range* of container elements. The *generator function* takes no arguments and returns a value that can be placed in an element of the container.

```cpp
1   // Fig. 16.1: fig16_01.cpp
2   // Algorithms fill, fill_n, generate and generate_n.
3   #include <iostream>
4   #include <algorithm> // algorithm definitions
5   #include <array> // array class-template definition
6   #include <iterator> // ostream_iterator
7   using namespace std;
8
9   char nextLetter(); // prototype of generator function
10
11  int main()
12  {
13     array< char, 10 > chars;
14     ostream_iterator< char > output( cout, " " );
15     fill( chars.begin(), chars.end(), '5' ); // fill chars with 5s
16
17     cout << "chars after filling with 5s:\n";
18     copy( chars.cbegin(), chars.cend(), output );
19
20     // fill first five elements of chars with As
21     fill_n( chars.begin(), 5, 'A' );
22
23     cout << "\n\nchars after filling five elements with As:\n";
24     copy( chars.cbegin(), chars.cend(), output );
25
26     // generate values for all elements of chars with nextLetter
27     generate( chars.begin(), chars.end(), nextLetter );
28
29     cout << "\n\nchars after generating letters A-J:\n";
30     copy( chars.cbegin(), chars.cend(), output );
31
32     // generate values for first five elements of chars with nextLetter
33     generate_n( chars.begin(), 5, nextLetter );
34
35     cout << "\n\nchars after generating K-O for the"
36        << " first five elements:\n";
37     copy( chars.cbegin(), chars.cend(), output );
38     cout << endl;
39  } // end main
40
```

Fig. 16.1 | Algorithms `fill`, `fill_n`, `generate` and `generate_n`. (Part 1 of 2.)

```
41    // generator function returns next letter (starts with A)
42    char nextLetter()
43    {
44        static char letter = 'A';
45        return letter++;
46    } // end function nextLetter
```

```
chars after filling with 5s:
5 5 5 5 5 5 5 5 5 5

chars after filling five elements with As:
A A A A A 5 5 5 5 5

chars after generating letters A-J:
A B C D E F G H I J

chars after generating K-O for the first five elements:
K L M N O F G H I J
```

Fig. 16.1 | Algorithms fill, fill_n, generate and generate_n. (Part 2 of 2.)

fill Algorithm
Line 13 defines a 10-element array of char values. Line 15 uses the fill algorithm to place the character '5' in every element of chars from chars.begin() up to, but *not* including, chars.end(). The iterators supplied as the first and second argument must be at least *forward iterators* (i.e., they can be used for both input from a container and output to a container in the *forward* direction).

fill_n Algorithm
Line 21 uses the fill_n algorithm to place the character 'A' in the first five elements of chars. The iterator supplied as the first argument must be at least an *output iterator* (i.e., it can be used to *write* into a container in the *forward* direction). The second argument specifies the number of elements to fill. The third argument specifies the value to place in each element.

generate Algorithm
Line 27 uses the generate algorithm to place the result of a call to *generator function* nextLetter in every element of chars from chars.begin() up to, but *not* including, chars.end(). The iterators supplied as the first and second arguments must be at least *forward iterators*. Function nextLetter (lines 42–46) begins with the character 'A' maintained in a static local variable. The statement in line 45 postincrements the value of letter and returns the old value of letter each time nextLetter is called.

generate_n Algorithm
Line 33 uses the generate_n algorithm to place the result of a call to *generator function* nextLetter in five elements of chars, starting from chars.begin(). The iterator supplied as the first argument must be at least an *output iterator*.

A Note About Reading Standard Library Algorithm Documentation
When you look at the Standard Library algorithms documentation for algorithms that can receive function pointers as arguments, you'll notice in the documentation that the corre-

sponding parameters do *not* show pointer declarations. Such parameters can actually receive as arguments *function pointers, function objects* (Section 16.4) or *lambda expressions* (Section 16.5). For this reason, the Standard Library declares such parameters using more generic names.

For example, the `generate` algorithm's prototype is listed in the C++ standard document as:

```
template<class ForwardIterator, class Generator>
void generate(ForwardIterator first, ForwardIterator last,
    Generator gen);
```

indicating that `generate` expects as arguments *ForwardIterators* representing the range of elements to process and a *Generator function*. The standard explains that the algorithm calls the `Generator` function to obtain a value for each element in the range specified by the *ForwardIterators*. The standard also specifies that the `Generator` must take no arguments and return a value of the element type.

Similar documentation is provided for each algorithm that can receive a function pointer, function object or lambda expression. In most of this chapter's examples, as we present each algorithm, we specify the requirements for such parameters. We typically do so in the context of functions, and pass function pointers into the algorithms. In Sections 16.4–16.5, we discuss how to create and use function objects and lambda expressions that you can pass to algorithms.

16.3.2 equal, `mismatch` and `lexicographical_compare`

Figure 16.2 demonstrates comparing sequences of values for equality using algorithms `equal`, `mismatch` and `lexicographical_compare`.

```
1   // Fig. 16.2: fig16_02.cpp
2   // Algorithms equal, mismatch and lexicographical_compare.
3   #include <iostream>
4   #include <algorithm> // algorithm definitions
5   #include <array> // array class-template definition
6   #include <iterator> // ostream_iterator
7   using namespace std;
8
9   int main()
10  {
11     const size_t SIZE = 10;
12     array< int, SIZE > a1 = { 1, 2, 3, 4, 5, 6, 7, 8, 9, 10 };
13     array< int, SIZE > a2( a1 ); // initializes a2 with copy of a1
14     array< int, SIZE > a3 = { 1, 2, 3, 4, 1000, 6, 7, 8, 9, 10 };
15     ostream_iterator< int > output( cout, " " );
16
17     cout << "a1 contains: ";
18     copy( a1.cbegin(), a1.cend(), output );
19     cout << "\na2 contains: ";
20     copy( a2.cbegin(), a2.cend(), output );
21     cout << "\na3 contains: ";
22     copy( a3.cbegin(), a3.cend(), output );
```

Fig. 16.2 | Algorithms `equal`, `mismatch` and `lexicographical_compare`. (Part I of 2.)

```
23
24      // compare a1 and a2 for equality
25      bool result = equal( a1.cbegin(), a1.cend(), a2.cbegin() );
26      cout << "\n\a1 " << ( result ? "is" : "is not" )
27         << " equal to a2.\n";
28
29      // compare a1 and a3 for equality
30      result = equal( a1.cbegin(), a1.cend(), a3.cbegin() );
31      cout << "a1 " << ( result ? "is" : "is not" ) << " equal to a3.\n";
32
33      // check for mismatch between a1 and a3
34      auto location = mismatch( a1.cbegin(), a1.cend(), a3.cbegin() );
35      cout << "\nThere is a mismatch between a1 and a3 at location "
36         << ( location.first - a1.begin() ) << "\nwhere a1 contains "
37         << *location.first << " and a3 contains " << *location.second
38         << "\n\n";
39
40      char c1[ SIZE ] = "HELLO";
41      char c2[ SIZE ] = "BYE BYE";
42
43      // perform lexicographical comparison of c1 and c2
44      result = lexicographical_compare(
45         begin( c1 ), end( c1 ), begin( c2 ), end( c2 ) );
46      cout << c1 << ( result ? " is less than " :
47         " is greater than or equal to " )  << c2 << endl;
48   } // end main
```

```
a1 contains: 1 2 3 4 5 6 7 8 9 10
a2 contains: 1 2 3 4 5 6 7 8 9 10
a3 contains: 1 2 3 4 1000 6 7 8 9 10

a1 is equal to a2.
a1 is not equal to a3.

There is a mismatch between a1 and a3 at location 4
where a1 contains 5 and a3 contains 1000

HELLO is greater than or equal to BYE BYE
```

Fig. 16.2 | Algorithms `equal`, `mismatch` and `lexicographical_compare`. (Part 2 of 2.)

equal Algorithm

Line 25 uses the **equal** algorithm to compare two sequences of values for equality. The second sequence must contain at least as many elements as the first—equal returns false if the sequences are *not* of the same length. The == operator (whether built-in or overloaded) performs the element comparisons. In this example, the elements in a1 from a1.cbegin() up to, but *not* including, a1.cend() are compared to the elements in a2 starting from a2.cbegin(). In this example, a1 and a2 are equal. The three iterator arguments must be at least *input iterators* (i.e., they can be used for input from a sequence in the *forward* direction). Line 30 uses function equal to compare a1 and a3, which are *not* equal.

equal Algorithm with Binary Predicate Function

Another version of equal takes a *binary predicate function* as a fourth parameter. The binary predicate function receives the two elements being compared and returns a bool value indicating whether the elements are equal. This can be useful in sequences that store objects or pointers to values rather than actual values, because you can define one or more comparisons. For example, you can compare `Employee` objects for age, social security number, or location rather than comparing entire objects. You can compare what pointers refer to rather than comparing the pointer values (i.e., the addresses stored in the pointers).

mismatch *Algorithm*

Lines 34 calls the `mismatch` algorithm to compare two sequences of values. The algorithm returns a `pair` of iterators indicating the location in each sequence of the *mismatched* elements. If all the elements match, the two iterators in the `pair` are equal to the end iterator for each sequence. The three iterator arguments must be at least *input iterators*. We *infer* the type of the `pair` object `location` with C++11's auto keyword (line 34). Line 36 determines the actual location of the mismatch in the `arrays` with the expression `location.first - a1.begin()`, which evaluates to the number of elements between the iterators (this is analogous to pointer arithmetic; Chapter 8). This corresponds to the element number in this example, because the comparison is performed from the beginning of each `array`. As with `equal`, there is another version of `mismatch` that takes a *binary predicate function* as a fourth parameter.

lexicographical_compare *Algorithm*

Lines 44–45 use the `lexicographical_compare` algorithm to compare the contents of two char built-in arrays. This algorithm's four iterator arguments must be at least *input iterators*. As you know, pointers into built-in arrays are *random-access iterators*. The first two iterator arguments specify the range of locations in the first sequence. The last two specify the range of locations in the second sequence. Once again, we use the C++11 begin and end functions to determine the range of elements for each built-in array. While iterating through the sequences, the `lexicographical_compare` checks if the element in the first sequence is less than the corresponding element in the second sequence. If so, the algorithm returns `true`. If the element in the first sequence is greater than or equal to the element in the second sequence, the algorithm returns `false`. This algorithm can be used to arrange sequences *lexicographically*. Typically, such sequences contain strings.

16.3.3 remove, remove_if, remove_copy and remove_copy_if

Figure 16.3 demonstrates removing values from a sequence with algorithms remove, remove_if, remove_copy and remove_copy_if.

```
1   // Fig. 16.3: fig16_03.cpp
2   // Algorithms remove, remove_if, remove_copy and remove_copy_if.
3   #include <iostream>
4   #include <algorithm> // algorithm definitions
5   #include <array> // array class-template definition
6   #include <iterator> // ostream_iterator
7   using namespace std;
8
9   bool greater9( int ); // prototype
10
```

Fig. 16.3 | Algorithms remove, remove_if, remove_copy and remove_copy_if. (Part 1 of 3.)

```
11   int main()
12   {
13      const size_t SIZE = 10;
14      array< int, SIZE > init = { 10, 2, 10, 4, 16, 6, 14, 8, 12, 10 };
15      ostream_iterator< int > output( cout, " " );
16
17      array< int, SIZE > a1( init ); // initialize with copy of init
18      cout << "a1 before removing all 10s:\n   ";
19      copy( a1.cbegin(), a1.cend(), output );
20
21      // remove all 10s from a1
22      auto newLastElement = remove( a1.begin(), a1.end(), 10 );
23      cout << "\a1 after removing all 10s:\n   ";
24      copy( a1.begin(), newLastElement, output );
25
26      array< int, SIZE > a2( init ); // initialize with copy of init
27      array< int, SIZE > c = { 0 }; // initialize to 0s
28      cout << "\n\a2 before removing all 10s and copying:\n   ";
29      copy( a2.cbegin(), a2.cend(), output );
30
31      // copy from a2 to c, removing 10s in the process
32      remove_copy( a2.cbegin(), a2.cend(), c.begin(), 10 );
33      cout << "\nc after removing all 10s from a2:\n   ";
34      copy( c.cbegin(), c.cend(), output );
35
36      array< int, SIZE > a3( init ); // initialize with copy of init
37      cout << "\n\na3 before removing all elements greater than 9:\n   ";
38      copy( a3.cbegin(), a3.cend(), output );
39
40      // remove elements greater than 9 from a3
41      newLastElement = remove_if( a3.begin(), a3.end(), greater9 );
42      cout << "\na3 after removing all elements greater than 9:\n   ";
43      copy( a3.begin(), newLastElement, output );
44
45      array< int, SIZE > a4( init ); // initialize with copy of init
46      array< int, SIZE > c2 = { 0 }; // initialize to 0s
47      cout << "\n\na4 before removing all elements"
48         << "\ngreater than 9 and copying:\n   ";
49      copy( a4.cbegin(), a4.cend(), output );
50
51      // copy elements from a4 to c2, removing elements greater
52      // than 9 in the process
53      remove_copy_if( a4.cbegin(), a4.cend(), c2.begin(), greater9 );
54      cout << "\nc2 after removing all elements"
55         << "\ngreater than 9 from a4:\n   ";
56      copy( c2.cbegin(), c2.cend(), output );
57      cout << endl;
58   } // end main
59
60   // determine whether argument is greater than 9
61   bool greater9( int x )
62   {
```

Fig. 16.3 | Algorithms remove, remove_if, remove_copy and remove_copy_if. (Part 2 of 3.)

```
63        return x > 9;
64    } // end function greater9
```

```
a1 before removing all 10s:
   10 2 10 4 16 6 14 8 12 10
a1 after removing all 10s:
   2 4 16 6 14 8 12

a2 before removing all 10s and copying:
   10 2 10 4 16 6 14 8 12 10
c after removing all 10s from a2:
   2 4 16 6 14 8 12 0 0 0

a3 before removing all elements greater than 9:
   10 2 10 4 16 6 14 8 12 10
a3 after removing all elements greater than 9:
   2 4 6 8

a4 before removing all elements
greater than 9 and copying:
   10 2 10 4 16 6 14 8 12 10
c2 after removing all elements
greater than 9 from a4:
   2 4 6 8 0 0 0 0 0 0
```

Fig. 16.3 | Algorithms remove, remove_if, remove_copy and remove_copy_if. (Part 3 of 3.)

remove *Algorithm*

Line 22 uses the **remove** algorithm to eliminate from a1 *all* elements with the value 10 in the range from a1.begin() up to, but *not* including, a1.end(). The first two iterator arguments must be *forward iterators*. This algorithm does *not* modify the number of elements in the container or destroy the eliminated elements, but it does move *all* elements that are *not* eliminated toward the *beginning* of the container. The algorithm returns an iterator positioned after the last element that was not removed. Elements from the iterator position to the end of the container have *unspecified* values.

remove_copy *Algorithm*

Line 32 uses the **remove_copy** algorithm to copy *all* elements from a2 that do *not* have the value 10 in the range from a2.cbegin() up to, but *not* including, a2.cend(). The elements are placed in c, starting at position c.begin(). The iterators supplied as the first two arguments must be *input iterators*. The iterator supplied as the third argument must be an *output iterator* so that the element being copied can be *inserted* into the copy location. This algorithm returns an iterator positioned after the last element copied into vector c.

remove_if *Algorithm*

Line 41 uses the **remove_if** algorithm to delete from a3 *all* those elements in the range from a3.begin() up to, but *not* including, a3.end() for which our user-defined unary *predicate function* greater9 returns true. Function greater9 (defined in lines 61–64) returns true if the value passed to it is greater than 9; otherwise, it returns false. The iterators supplied as the first two arguments must be *forward iterators*. This algorithm does *not* modify the number of elements in the container, but it does move to the *beginning* of the container *all* elements that are *not* removed. This algorithm returns an iterator positioned after the last element that was *not* removed. All elements from the iterator position to the end of the container have *undefined* values.

remove_copy_if *Algorithm*

Line 53 uses the `remove_copy_if` algorithm to copy all those elements from a4 in the range from a4.cbegin() up to, but *not* including, a4.cend() for which the *unary predicate function* greater9 returns true. The elements are placed in c2, starting at c2.begin(). The iterators supplied as the first two arguments must be *input iterators*. The iterator supplied as the third argument must be an *output iterator* so that the element being copied can be *assigned* to the copy location. This algorithm returns an iterator positioned after the *last* element copied into c2.

16.3.4 replace, replace_if, replace_copy and replace_copy_if

Figure 16.4 demonstrates replacing values from a sequence using algorithms replace, replace_if, replace_copy and replace_copy_if.

```cpp
 1   // Fig. 16.4: fig16_04.cpp
 2   // Algorithms replace, replace_if, replace_copy and replace_copy_if.
 3   #include <iostream>
 4   #include <algorithm>
 5   #include <array>
 6   #include <iterator> // ostream_iterator
 7   using namespace std;
 8
 9   bool greater9( int ); // predicate function prototype
10
11   int main()
12   {
13      const size_t SIZE = 10;
14      array< int, SIZE > init = = { 10, 2, 10, 4, 16, 6, 14, 8, 12, 10 };
15      ostream_iterator< int > output( cout, " " );
16
17      array< int, SIZE > a1( init ); // initialize with copy of init
18      cout << "a1 before replacing all 10s:\n   ";
19      copy( a1.cbegin(), a1.cend(), output );
20
21      // replace all 10s in a1 with 100
22      replace( a1.begin(), a1.end(), 10, 100 );
23      cout << "\na1 after replacing 10s with 100s:\n   ";
24      copy( a1.cbegin(), a1.cend(), output );
25
26      array< int, SIZE > a2( init ); // initialize with copy of init
27      array< int, SIZE > c1; // instantiate c1
28      cout << "\n\na2 before replacing all 10s and copying:\n   ";
29      copy( a2.cbegin(), a2.cend(), output );
30
31      // copy from a2 to c1, replacing 10s with 100s
32      replace_copy( a2.cbegin(), a2.cend(), c1.begin(), 10, 100 );
```

Fig. 16.4 | Algorithms replace, replace_if, replace_copy and replace_copy_if. (Part 1 of 2.)

```
33          cout << "\nc1 after replacing all 10s in a2:\n    ";
34          copy( c1.cbegin(), c1.cend(), output );
35
36          array< int, SIZE > a3( init ); // initialize with copy of init
37          cout << "\n\na3 before replacing values greater than 9:\n    ";
38          copy( a3.cbegin(), a3.cend(), output );
39
40          // replace values greater than 9 in a3 with 100
41          replace_if( a3.begin(), a3.end(), greater9, 100 );
42          cout << "\na3 after replacing all values greater"
43             << "\nthan 9 with 100s:\n    ";
44          copy( a3.cbegin(), a3.cend(), output );
45
46          array< int, SIZE > a4( init ); // initialize with copy of init
47          array< int, SIZE > c2; // instantiate c2'
48          cout << "\n\na4 before replacing all values greater "
49             << "than 9 and copying:\n    ";
50          copy( a4.cbegin(), a4.cend(), output );
51
52          // copy a4 to c2, replacing elements greater than 9 with 100
53          replace_copy_if( a4.cbegin(), a4.cend(), c2.begin(), greater9, 100 );
54          cout << "\nc2 after replacing all values greater than 9 in v4:\n    ";
55          copy( c2.begin(), c2.end(), output );
56          cout << endl;
57   } // end main
58
59   // determine whether argument is greater than 9
60   bool greater9( int x )
61   {
62       return x > 9;
63   } // end function greater9
```

```
a1 before replacing all 10s:
   10 2 10 4 16 6 14 8 12 10
a1 after replacing 10s with 100s:
   100 2 100 4 16 6 14 8 12 100

a2 before replacing all 10s and copying:
   10 2 10 4 16 6 14 8 12 10
c1 after replacing all 10s in a2:
   100 2 100 4 16 6 14 8 12 100

a3 before replacing values greater than 9:
   10 2 10 4 16 6 14 8 12 10
a3 after replacing all values greater
than 9 with 100s:
   100 2 100 4 100 6 100 8 100 100

a4 before replacing all values greater than 9 and copying:
   10 2 10 4 16 6 14 8 12 10
c2 after replacing all values greater than 9 in a4:
   100 2 100 4 100 6 100 8 100 100
```

Fig. 16.4 | Algorithms replace, replace_if, replace_copy and replace_copy_if. (Part 2 of 2.)

replace Algorithm

Line 22 uses the `replace` algorithm to replace *all* elements with the value 10 in the range a1.begin() up to, but *not* including, a1.end() with the new value 100. The iterators supplied as the first two arguments must be *forward iterators* so that the algorithm can *modify* the elements in the sequence.

replace_copy Algorithm

Line 32 uses the `replace_copy` algorithm to copy *all* elements in the range a2.cbegin() up to, but *not* including, a2.cend(), replacing *all* elements with the value 10 with the new value 100. The elements are copied into c1, starting at position c1.begin(). The iterators supplied as the first two arguments must be *input iterators*. The iterator supplied as the third argument must be an *output iterator* so that the element being copied can be *assigned* to the copy location. This function returns an iterator positioned after the *last* element copied into c1.

replace_if Algorithm

Line 41 uses the `replace_if` algorithm to replace *all* those elements from a3.begin() up to, but *not* including, a3.end() for which the *unary predicate function* greater9 returns true. Function greater9 (defined in lines 60–63) returns true if the value passed to it is greater than 9; otherwise, it returns false. The value 100 replaces each value greater than 9. The iterators supplied as the first two arguments must be *forward iterators*.

replace_copy_if Algorithm

Line 53 uses the `replace_copy_if` algorithm to copy *all* elements from a4.cbegin() up to, but *not* including, a4.cend(). Elements for which the *unary predicate function* greater9 returns true are replaced with the value 100. The elements are placed in c2, starting at position c2.begin(). The iterators supplied as the first two arguments must be *input iterators*. The iterator supplied as the third argument must be an *output iterator* so that the element being copied can be *assigned* to the copy location. This algorithm returns an iterator positioned after the *last* element copied into c2.

16.3.5 Mathematical Algorithms

Figure 16.5 demonstrates several common mathematical algorithms, including `random_shuffle`, `count`, `count_if`, `min_element`, `max_element`, `minmax_element`, `accumulate`, `for_each` and `transform`.

```cpp
 1   // Fig. 16.5: fig16_05.cpp
 2   // Mathematical algorithms of the Standard Library.
 3   #include <iostream>
 4   #include <algorithm> // algorithm definitions
 5   #include <numeric> // accumulate is defined here
 6   #include <array>
 7   #include <iterator>
 8   using namespace std;
 9
10   bool greater9( int ); // predicate function prototype
```

Fig. 16.5 | Mathematical algorithms of the Standard Library. (Part 1 of 3.)

```
11    void outputSquare( int ); // output square of a value
12    int calculateCube( int ); // calculate cube of a value
13
14    int main()
15    {
16       const size_t SIZE = 10;
17       array< int, SIZE > a1 = { 1, 2, 3, 4, 5, 6, 7, 8, 9, 10 };
18       ostream_iterator< int > output( cout, " " );
19
20       cout << "a1 before random_shuffle: ";
21       copy( a1.cbegin(), a1.cend(), output );
22
23       random_shuffle( a1.begin(), a1.end() ); // shuffle elements of a1
24       cout << "\na1 after random_shuffle: ";
25       copy( a1.cbegin(), a1.cend(), output );
26
27       array< int, SIZE > a2 = { 100, 2, 8, 1, 50, 3, 8, 8, 9, 10 };
28       cout << "\n\na2 contains: ";
29       copy( a2.cbegin(), a2.cend(), output );
30
31       // count number of elements in a2 with value 8
32       int result = count( a2.cbegin(), a2.cend(), 8 );
33       cout << "\nNumber of elements matching 8: " << result;
34
35       // count number of elements in a2 that are greater than 9
36       result = count_if( a2.cbegin(), a2.cend(), greater9 );
37       cout << "\nNumber of elements greater than 9: " << result;
38
39       // locate minimum element in a2
40       cout << "\n\nMinimum element in a2 is: "
41          << *( min_element( a2.cbegin(), a2.cend() ) );
42
43       // locate maximum element in a2
44       cout << "\nMaximum element in a2 is: "
45          << *( max_element( a2.cbegin(), a2.cend() ) );
46
47       // locate minimum and maximum elements in a2
48       auto minAndMax = minmax_element( a2.cbegin(), a2.cend() );
49       cout << "\nThe minimum and maximum elements in a2 are "
50          << *minAndMax.first << " and " << *minAndMax.second
51          << ", respectively";
52
53       // calculate sum of elements in a1
54       cout << "\n\nThe total of the elements in a1 is: "
55          << accumulate( a1.cbegin(), a1.cend(), 0 );
56
57       // output square of every element in a1
58       cout << "\n\nThe square of every integer in a1 is:\n";
59       for_each( a1.cbegin(), a1.cend(), outputSquare );
60
61       array< int, SIZE > cubes; // instantiate cubes
62
```

Fig. 16.5 | Mathematical algorithms of the Standard Library. (Part 2 of 3.)

```
63      // calculate cube of each element in a1; place results in cubes
64      transform( a1.cbegin(), a1.cend(), cubes.begin(), calculateCube );
65      cout << "\n\nThe cube of every integer in a1 is:\n";
66      copy( cubes.cbegin(), cubes.cend(), output );
67      cout << endl;
68   } // end main
69
70   // determine whether argument is greater than 9
71   bool greater9( int value )
72   {
73      return value > 9;
74   } // end function greater9
75
76   // output square of argument
77   void outputSquare( int value )
78   {
79      cout << value * value << ' ';
80   } // end function outputSquare
81
82   // return cube of argument
83   int calculateCube( int value )
84   {
85      return value * value * value;
86   } // end function calculateCube
```

```
a1 before random_shuffle: 1 2 3 4 5 6 7 8 9 10
a1 after random_shuffle: 9 2 10 3 1 6 8 4 5 7

a2 contains: 100 2 8 1 50 3 8 8 9 10
Number of elements matching 8: 3
Number of elements greater than 9: 3

Minimum element in a2 is: 1
Maximum element in a2 is: 100
The minimum and maximum elements in a2 are 1 and 100, respectively

The total of the elements in a1 is: 55

The square of every integer in a1 is:
81 4 100 9 1 36 64 16 25 49

The cube of every integer in a1 is:
729 8 1000 27 1 216 512 64 125 343
```

Fig. 16.5 | Mathematical algorithms of the Standard Library. (Part 3 of 3.)

random_shuffle *Algorithm*

Line 23 uses the **random_shuffle** algorithm to reorder randomly the elements in the range a1.begin() up to, but *not* including, a1.end(). This algorithm takes *two random-access iterator* arguments. This version of random_shuffle uses rand for randomization and produces the same results each time you run the program unless you seed the random-number generator with srand. Another version of random_shuffle receives as its third argument a C++11 uniform random-number generator.

count *Algorithm*

Line 32 uses the `count` algorithm to count the elements with the value 8 in the range `a2.cbegin()` up to, but *not* including, `a2.cend()`. This algorithm requires its two iterator arguments to be at least *input iterators.*

count_if *Algorithm*

Line 36 uses the `count_if` algorithm to count elements in the range from `a2.cbegin()` up to, but *not* including, `a2.cend()` for which the *predicate function* `greater9` returns `true`. Algorithm `count_if` requires its two iterator arguments to be at least *input iterators.*

min_element *Algorithm*

Line 41 uses the `min_element` algorithm to locate the *smallest* element in the range from `a2.cbegin()` up to, but *not* including, `a2.cend()`. The algorithm returns a *forward iterator* located at the *first* smallest element, or `a2.end()` if the range is *empty.* The algorithm's two iterator arguments must be at least *forward iterators.* A second version of this algorithm takes as its third argument a binary function that compares two elements in the sequence. This algorithm returns the `bool` value `true` if the first argument is *less than* the second.

> **Error-Prevention Tip 16.1**
> *It's a good practice to check that the range specified in a call to* `min_element` *is not empty and that the return value is not the "past the end" iterator.*

max_element *Algorithm*

Line 45 uses the `max_element` algorithm to locate the *largest* element in the range from `a2.cbegin()` up to, but *not* including, `a2.cend()`. The algorithm returns a *forward iterator* located at the *first* largest element. The algorithm's two iterator arguments must be at least *forward iterators.* A second version of this algorithm takes as its third argument a *binary predicate function* that compares the elements in the sequence. The binary function takes two arguments and returns the `bool` value `true` if the first argument is *less than* the second.

C++11: minmax_element *Algorithm*

Line 48 uses the new C++11 `minmax_element` algorithm to locate both the *smallest* and *largest* elements in the range from `a2.cbegin()` up to, but *not* including, `a2.cend()`. The algorithm returns a pair of *forward iterators* located at the smallest and largest elements, respectively. If there are duplicate smallest or largest elements, the iterators are located at the first smallest and last largest values. The algorithm's two iterator arguments must be at least *forward iterators.* A second version of this algorithm takes as its third argument a *binary predicate function* that compares the elements in the sequence. The binary function takes two arguments and returns the `bool` value `true` if the first argument is *less than* the second.

accumulate *Algorithm*

Line 55 uses the `accumulate` algorithm (the template of which is in header `<numeric>`) to sum the values in the range from `a1.cbegin()` up to, but *not* including, `a1.cend()`. The algorithm's two iterator arguments must be at least *input iterators* and its third argument represents the initial value of the total. A second version of this algorithm takes as its fourth argument a general function that determines how elements are accumulated. The general function must take *two* arguments and return a result. The first argument to this function is the current value of the accumulation. The second argument is the value of the current element in the sequence being accumulated.

for_each Algorithm

Line 59 uses the `for_each` algorithm to apply a general function to every element in the range from a1.cbegin() up to, but *not* including, a1.cend(). The general function takes the current element as an argument and may modify that element (if it's received by reference and is not const). Algorithm for_each requires its two iterator arguments to be at least *input iterators*.

transform Algorithm

Line 63 uses the `transform` algorithm to apply a general function to *every* element in the range from a1.cbegin() up to, but *not* including, a1.cend(). The general function (the fourth argument) should take the current element as an argument, must *not* modify the element and should return the transformed value. Algorithm transform requires its first two iterator arguments to be at least *input iterators* and its third argument to be at least an *output iterator*. The third argument specifies where the transformed values should be placed. Note that the third argument can equal the first. Another version of transform accepts five arguments—the first two arguments are *input iterators* that specify a range of elements from one source container, the third argument is an *input iterator* that specifies the first element in another source container, the fourth argument is an *output iterator* that specifies where the transformed values should be placed and the last argument is a general function that takes two arguments. This version of transform takes one element from each of the two input sources and applies the general function to that pair of elements, then places the transformed value at the location specified by the fourth argument.

16.3.6 Basic Searching and Sorting Algorithms

Figure 16.6 demonstrates some basic searching and sorting Standard Library algorithms, including find, find_if, sort, binary_search, all_of, any_of, none_of and find_if_not.

```
1   // Fig. 16.6: fig16_06.cpp
2   // Standard Library search and sort algorithms.
3   #include <iostream>
4   #include <algorithm> // algorithm definitions
5   #include <array> // array class-template definition
6   #include <iterator>
7   using namespace std;
8
9   bool greater10( int value ); // predicate function prototype
10
11  int main()
12  {
13     const size_t SIZE = 10;
14     array< int, SIZE > a = { 10, 2, 17, 5, 16, 8, 13, 11, 20, 7 };
15     ostream_iterator< int > output( cout, " " );
```

Fig. 16.6 | Standard Library search and sort algorithms. (Part 1 of 3.)

```
16
17        cout << "array a contains: ";
18        copy( a.cbegin(), a.cend(), output ); // display output vector
19
20        // locate first occurrence of 16 in a
21        auto location = find( a.cbegin(), a.cend(), 16 );
22
23        if ( location != a.cend() ) // found 16
24           cout << "\n\nFound 16 at location " << ( location - a.cbegin() );
25        else // 16 not found
26           cout << "\n\n16 not found";
27
28        // locate first occurrence of 100 in a
29        location = find( a.cbegin(), a.cend(), 100 );
30
31        if ( location != a.cend() ) // found 100
32           cout << "\nFound 100 at location " << ( location - a.cbegin() );
33        else // 100 not found
34           cout << "\n100 not found";
35
36        // locate first occurrence of value greater than 10 in a
37        location = find_if( a.cbegin(), a.cend(), greater10 );
38
39        if ( location != a.cend() ) // found value greater than 10
40           cout << "\n\nThe first value greater than 10 is " << *location
41              << "\nfound at location " << ( location - a.cbegin() );
42        else // value greater than 10 not found
43           cout << "\n\nNo values greater than 10 were found";
44
45        // sort elements of a
46        sort( a.begin(), a.end() );
47        cout << "\n\narray a after sort: ";
48        copy( a.cbegin(), a.cend(), output );
49
50        // use binary_search to locate 13 in a
51        if ( binary_search( a.cbegin(), a.cend(), 13 ) )
52           cout << "\n\n13 was found in a";
53        else
54           cout << "\n\n13 was not found in a";
55
56        // use binary_search to locate 100 in a
57        if ( binary_search( a.cbegin(), a.cend(), 100 ) )
58           cout << "\n100 was found in a";
59        else
60           cout << "\n100 was not found in a";
61
62        // determine whether all of the elements of a are greater than 10
63        if ( all_of( a.cbegin(), a.cend(), greater10 ) )
64           cout << "\n\nAll the elements in a are greater than 10";
65        else
66           cout << "\n\nSome elements in a are not greater than 10";
67
```

Fig. 16.6 | Standard Library search and sort algorithms. (Part 2 of 3.)

```
68      // determine whether any of the elements of a are greater than 10
69      if ( any_of( a.cbegin(), a.cend(), greater10 ) )
70         cout << "\n\nSome of the elements in a are greater than 10";
71      else
72         cout << "\n\nNone of the elements in a are greater than 10";
73
74      // determine whether none of the elements of a are greater than 10
75      if ( none_of( a.cbegin(), a.cend(), greater10 ) )
76         cout << "\n\nNone of the elements in a are greater than 10";
77      else
78         cout << "\n\nSome of the elements in a are greater than 10";
79
80      // locate first occurrence of value that's not greater than 10 in a
81      location = find_if_not( a.cbegin(), a.cend(), greater10 );
82
83      if ( location != a.cend() ) // found a value less than or eqaul to 10
84         cout << "\n\nThe first value not greater than 10 is " << *location
85            << "\nfound at location " << ( location - a.cbegin() );
86      else // no values less than or equal to 10 were found
87         cout << "\n\nOnly values greater than 10 were found";
88
89      cout << endl;
90   } // end main
91
92   // determine whether argument is greater than 10
93   bool greater10( int value )
94   {
95      return value > 10;
96   } // end function greater10
```

```
array a contains: 10 2 17 5 16 8 13 11 20 7

Found 16 at location 4
100 not found

The first value greater than 10 is 17
found at location 2

array a after sort: 2 5 7 8 10 11 13 16 17 20

13 was found in a
100 was not found in a

Some elements in a are not greater than 10

Some of the elements in a are greater than 10

Some of the elements in a are greater than 10

The first value not greater than 10 is 2
found at location 0
```

Fig. 16.6 | Standard Library search and sort algorithms. (Part 3 of 3.)

find Algorithm

Line 21 uses the **find** algorithm to locate the value 16 in the range from a.cbegin() up to, but not including, a.cend(). The algorithm requires its two iterator arguments to be at least *input iterators* and returns an *input iterator* that either is positioned at the first element containing the value or indicates the end of the sequence (as is the case in line 29).

find_if *Algorithm*
Line 37 uses the `find_if` algorithm (a linear search) to locate the first value in the range from a.cbegin() up to, but *not* including, a.cend() for which the *unary predicate function* greater10 returns `true`. Function greater10 (defined in lines 93–96) takes an integer and returns a `bool` value indicating whether the integer argument is *greater than* 10. Algorithm `find_if` requires its two iterator arguments to be at least *input iterators*. The algorithm returns an *input iterator* that either is positioned at the first element containing a value for which the predicate function returns `true` or indicates the end of the sequence.

sort *Algorithm*
Line 46 uses **sort** algorithm to arrange the elements in the range from a.begin() up to, but *not* including, a.end() in *ascending order*. The algorithm requires its two iterator arguments to be *random-access iterators*. A second version of this algorithm takes a third argument that's a *binary predicate function* taking two arguments that are values in the sequence and returning a `bool` indicating the *sorting order*—if the return value is `true`, the two elements being compared are in *sorted order*.

binary_search *Algorithm*
Line 51 uses the **binary_search** algorithm to determine whether the value 13 is in the range from a.cbegin() up to, but *not* including, a.cend(). The values must be sorted in *ascending order*. Algorithm binary_search requires its two iterator arguments to be at least *forward iterators*. The algorithm returns a `bool` indicating whether the value was found in the sequence. Line 57 demonstrates a call to binary_search in which the value is *not* found. A second version of this algorithm takes a fourth argument that's a *binary predicate function* taking two arguments that are values in the sequence and returning a `bool`. The predicate function returns `true` if the two elements being compared are in *sorted order*. To obtain the *location* of the search key in the container, use the lower_bound or find algorithms.

C++11: all_of *Algorithm*
Line 63 uses the **all_of** algorithm to determine whether the *unary predicate function* greater10 returns `true` for *all* of the elements in the range from a.cbegin() up to, but *not* including, a.cend(). Algorithm all_of requires its two iterator arguments to be at least *input iterators*.

C++11: any_of *Algorithm*
Line 69 uses the **any_of** algorithm to determine whether the *unary predicate function* greater10 returns `true` for *at least one* of the elements in the range from a.cbegin() up to, but *not* including, a.cend(). Algorithm any_of requires its two iterator arguments to be at least *input iterators*.

C++11: none_of *Algorithm*
Line 75 uses the **none_of** algorithm to determine whether the *unary predicate function* greater10 returns `false` for *all* of the elements in the range from a.cbegin() up to, but *not* including, a.cend(). Algorithm none_of requires its two iterator arguments to be at least *input iterators*.

C++11: find_if_not Algorithm

Line 81 uses the **find_if_not** algorithm to locate the first value in the range from a.cbegin() up to, but *not* including, a.cend() for which the *unary predicate function* greater10 returns false. Algorithm find_if requires its two iterator arguments to be at least *input iterators*. The algorithm returns an *input iterator* that either is positioned at the first element containing a value for which the predicate function returns false or indicates the end of the sequence.

16.3.7 swap, iter_swap and swap_ranges

Figure 16.7 demonstrates algorithms swap, iter_swap and swap_ranges for *swapping* elements.

```
1   // Fig. 16.7: fig16_07.cpp
2   // Algorithms iter_swap, swap and swap_ranges.
3   #include <iostream>
4   #include <array>
5   #include <algorithm> // algorithm definitions
6   #include <iterator>
7   using namespace std;
8
9   int main()
10  {
11     const size_t SIZE = 10;
12     array< int, SIZE > a = { 1, 2, 3, 4, 5, 6, 7, 8, 9, 10 };
13     ostream_iterator< int > output( cout, " " );
14
15     cout << "Array a contains:\n   ";
16     copy( a.cbegin(), a.cend(), output ); // display array a
17
18     swap( a[ 0 ], a[ 1 ] ); // swap elements at locations 0 and 1 of a
19
20     cout << "\nArray a after swapping a[0] and a[1] using swap:\n   ";
21     copy( a.cbegin(), a.cend(), output ); // display array a
22
23     // use iterators to swap elements at locations 0 and 1 of array a
24     iter_swap( a.begin(), a.begin() + 1 ); // swap with iterators
25     cout << "\nArray a after swapping a[0] and a[1] using iter_swap:\n   ";
26     copy( a.cbegin(), a.cend(), output );
27
28     // swap elements in first five elements of array a with
29     // elements in last five elements of array a
30     swap_ranges( a.begin(), a.begin() + 5, a.begin() + 5 );
31
32     cout << "\nArray a after swapping the first five elements\n"
33          << "with the last five elements:\n   ";
34     copy( a.cbegin(), a.cend(), output );
35     cout << endl;
36  } // end main
```

Fig. 16.7 | Algorithms iter_swap, swap and swap_ranges. (Part 1 of 2.)

```
Array a contains:
   1 2 3 4 5 6 7 8 9 10
Array a after swapping a[0] and a[1] using swap:
   2 1 3 4 5 6 7 8 9 10
Array a after swapping a[0] and a[1] using iter_swap:
   1 2 3 4 5 6 7 8 9 10
Array a after swapping the first five elements
with the last five elements:
   6 7 8 9 10 1 2 3 4 5
```

Fig. 16.7 | Algorithms `iter_swap`, swap and `swap_ranges`. (Part 2 of 2.)

swap *Algorithm*

Line 18 uses the **swap** algorithm to exchange two values. In this example, the first and second elements of `array` a are exchanged. The function takes as arguments references to the two values being exchanged.

`iter_swap` *Algorithm*

Line 24 uses function **iter_swap** to exchange the two elements. The function takes two *forward iterator* arguments (in this case, iterators to elements of an `array`) and exchanges the values in the elements to which the iterators refer.

`swap_ranges` *Algorithm*

Line 30 uses function **swap_ranges** to exchange the elements from a.begin() up to, but not including, a.begin() + 5 with the elements beginning at position a.begin() + 5. The function requires three *forward iterator* arguments. The first two arguments specify the range of elements in the first sequence that will be exchanged with the elements in the second sequence starting from the iterator in the third argument. In this example, the two sequences of values are in the same `array`, but the sequences can be from different arrays or containers. The sequences must not overlap. The destination sequence must be large enough to contain all the elements of the ranges being swapped.

16.3.8 copy_backward, merge, unique and reverse

Figure 16.8 demonstrates algorithms copy_backward, merge, unique and reverse.

```cpp
1  // Fig. 16.8: fig16_08.cpp
2  // Algorithms copy_backward, merge, unique and reverse.
3  #include <iostream>
4  #include <algorithm> // algorithm definitions
5  #include <array> // array class-template definition
6  #include <iterator> // ostream_iterator
7  using namespace std;
8
9  int main()
10 {
11    const size_t SIZE = 5;
12    array< int, SIZE > a1 = { 1, 3, 5, 7, 9 };
```

Fig. 16.8 | Algorithms copy_backward, merge, unique and reverse. (Part 1 of 2.)

```
13      array< int, SIZE > a2 = { 2, 4, 5, 7, 9 };
14      ostream_iterator< int > output( cout, " " );
15
16      cout << "array a1 contains: ";
17      copy( a1.cbegin(), a1.cend(), output ); // display a1
18      cout << "\narray a2 contains: ";
19      copy( a2.cbegin(), a2.cend(), output ); // display a2
20
21      array< int, SIZE > results;
22
23      // place elements of a1 into results in reverse order
24      copy_backward( a1.cbegin(), a1.cend(), results.end() );
25      cout << "\n\nAfter copy_backward, results contains: ";
26      copy( results.cbegin(), results.cend(), output );
27
28      array< int, SIZE + SIZE >  results2;
29
30      // merge elements of a1 and a2 into results2 in sorted order
31      merge( a1.cbegin(), a1.cend(), a2.cbegin(), a2.cend(),
32          results2.begin() );
33
34      cout << "\n\nAfter merge of a1 and a2 results2 contains: ";
35      copy( results2.cbegin(), results2.cend(), output );
36
37      // eliminate duplicate values from results2
38      auto endLocation = unique( results2.begin(), results2.end() );
39
40      cout << "\n\nAfter unique results2 contains: ";
41      copy( results2.begin(), endLocation, output );
42
43      cout << "\n\narray a1 after reverse: ";
44      reverse( a1.begin(), a1.end() ); // reverse elements of a1
45      copy( a1.cbegin(), a1.cend(), output );
46      cout << endl;
47   } // end main
```

```
array a1 contains: 1 3 5 7 9
array a2 contains: 2 4 5 7 9

After copy_backward, results contains: 1 3 5 7 9

After merge of a1 and a2 results2 contains: 1 2 3 4 5 5 7 7 9 9

After unique results2 contains: 1 2 3 4 5 7 9

array a1 after reverse: 9 7 5 3 1
```

Fig. 16.8 | Algorithms copy_backward, merge, unique and reverse. (Part 2 of 2.)

copy_backward *Algorithm*

Line 24 uses the **copy_backward** algorithm to copy elements in the range from a1.cbegin() up to, but *not* including, a1.cend(), placing the elements in results by starting from the element before results.end() and working toward the beginning of the array. The algorithm returns an iterator positioned at the *last* element copied into the results (i.e., the beginning of `results`, because of the backward copy). The elements are placed in `results` in the same order as `a1`. This algorithm requires three *bidirectional iterator* arguments (iterators that can be *incremented* and *decremented* to iterate *forward* and *backward* through a sequence, respectively). One difference between `copy_backward` and `copy` is that the iterator returned from `copy` is positioned *after* the last element copied and the one returned from `copy_backward` is positioned *at* the last element copied (i.e., the first element in the sequence). Also, `copy_backward` *can* manipulate *overlapping* ranges of elements in a container as long as the first element to copy is *not* in the destination range of elements.

In addition to the `copy` and `copy_backward` algorithms, C++11 now includes the **move** and **move_backward** algorithms. These use C++11's new move semantics (discussed in Chapter 24, C++11: Additional Features) to move, rather than copy, objects from one container to another.

merge *Algorithm*

Lines 31–32 use the **merge** algorithm to combine two *sorted ascending sequences* of values into a third sorted ascending sequence. The algorithm requires five iterator arguments. The first four must be at least *input iterators* and the last must be at least an *output iterator*. The first two arguments specify the range of elements in the first sorted sequence (`a1`), the second two arguments specify the range of elements in the second sorted sequence (`a2`) and the last argument specifies the starting location in the third sequence (`results2`) where the elements will be merged. A second version of this algorithm takes as its sixth argument a *binary predicate function* that specifies the *sorting order*.

back_inserter, front_inserter *and* inserter *Iterator Adapters*

Line 28 creates the `array results2` with the number of elements in `a1` and `a2`. Using the `merge` algorithm requires that the sequence where the results are stored be at least the size of the sequences being merged. If you do not want to allocate the number of elements for the resulting sequence before the `merge` operation, you can use the following statements:

```
vector< int > results2;
merge( a1.begin(), a1.end(), a2.begin(), a2.end(),
    back_inserter( results2 ) );
```

The argument `back_inserter(results2)` uses function template **back_inserter** (header `<iterator>`) for the `vector results2`. A `back_inserter` calls the container's default `push_back` function to insert an element at the *end* of the container. If an element is inserted into a container that has no more space available, *the container grows in size*—which is why we used a `vector` in the preceding statements, because `arrays` are fixed size. Thus, the number of elements in the container does *not* have to be known in advance. There are two other inserters—**front_inserter** (uses `push_front` to insert an element at the *beginning* of a container specified as its argument) and **inserter** (uses `insert` to insert an element *at* the iterator supplied as its second argument in the container supplied as its first argument).

unique *Algorithm*

Line 38 uses the **unique** algorithm on the *sorted* sequence of elements in the range from `results2.begin()` up to, but *not* including, `results2.end()`. After this algorithm is applied to a sorted sequence with *duplicate* values, only a *single* copy of each value remains in the sequence. The algorithm takes two arguments that must be at least *forward iterators*.

The algorithm returns an iterator positioned *after the last element* in the sequence of unique values. The values of all elements in the container after the last unique value are *undefined*. A second version of this algorithm takes as a third argument a *binary predicate function* specifying how to compare two elements for *equality*.

reverse *Algorithm*

Line 44 uses the **reverse** algorithm to reverse all the elements in the range from a1.begin() up to, but *not* including, a1.end(). The algorithm takes two arguments that must be at least *bidirectional iterators*.

C++11: copy_if *and* copy_n *Algorithms*

C++11 now includes the new copy algorithms copy_if and copy_n. The **copy_if** algorithm copies each element from a range if the *unary predicate function* in its fourth argument returns **true** for that element. The iterators supplied as the first two arguments must be *input iterators*. The iterator supplied as the third argument must be an *output iterator* so that the element being copied can be *assigned* to the copy location. This algorithm returns an iterator positioned after the *last* element copied.

The **copy_n** algorithm copies the number of elements specified by its second argument from the location specified by its first argument (an *input iterator*). The elements are output to the location specified by its third argument (an *output iterator*).

16.3.9 `inplace_merge`, `unique_copy` and `reverse_copy`

Figure 16.9 demonstrates algorithms `inplace_merge`, `unique_copy` and `reverse_copy`.

```cpp
 1   // Fig. 16.9: fig16_09.cpp
 2   // Algorithms inplace_merge, reverse_copy and unique_copy.
 3   #include <iostream>
 4   #include <algorithm> // algorithm definitions
 5   #include <array> // array class-template definition
 6   #include <vector> // vector class-template definition
 7   #include <iterator> // back_inserter definition
 8   using namespace std;
 9
10   int main()
11   {
12      const int SIZE = 10;
13      array< int, SIZE > a1 = { 1, 3, 5, 7, 9, 1, 3, 5, 7, 9 };
14      ostream_iterator< int > output( cout, " " );
15
16      cout << "array a1 contains: ";
17      copy( a1.cbegin(), a1.cend(), output );
18
19      // merge first half of a1 with second half of a1 such that
20      // a1 contains sorted set of elements after merge
21      inplace_merge( a1.begin(), a1.begin() + 5, a1.end() );
22
23      cout << "\nAfter inplace_merge, a1 contains: ";
24      copy( a1.cbegin(), a1.cend(), output );
```

Fig. 16.9 | Algorithms `inplace_merge`, `reverse_copy` and `unique_copy`. (Part I of 2.)

```
25
26      vector< int > results1;
27
28      // copy only unique elements of a1 into results1
29      unique_copy( a1.cbegin(), a1.cend(), back_inserter( results1 ) );
30      cout << "\nAfter unique_copy results1 contains: ";
31      copy( results1.cbegin(), results1.cend(), output );
32
33      vector< int > results2;
34
35      // copy elements of a1 into results2 in reverse order
36      reverse_copy( a1.cbegin(), a1.cend(), back_inserter( results2 ) );
37      cout << "\nAfter reverse_copy, results2 contains: ";
38      copy( results2.cbegin(), results2.cend(), output );
39      cout << endl;
40  } // end main
```

```
array a1 contains: 1 3 5 7 9 1 3 5 7 9
After inplace_merge, a1 contains: 1 1 3 3 5 5 7 7 9 9
After unique_copy results1 contains: 1 3 5 7 9
After reverse_copy, results2 contains: 9 9 7 7 5 5 3 3 1 1
```

Fig. 16.9 | Algorithms `inplace_merge`, `reverse_copy` and `unique_copy`. (Part 2 of 2.)

inplace_merge *Algorithm*

Line 21 uses the **inplace_merge** algorithm to merge two *sorted sequences* of elements in the *same* container. In this example, the elements from a1.begin() up to, but *not* including, a1.begin() + 5 are merged with the elements from a1.begin() + 5 up to, but *not* including, a1.end(). This algorithm requires its three iterator arguments to be at least *bidirectional iterators*. A second version of this algorithm takes as a fourth argument a *binary predicate function* for comparing elements in the two sequences.

unique_copy *Algorithm*

Line 29 uses the **unique_copy** algorithm to make a copy of all the unique elements in the sorted sequence of values from a1.cbegin() up to, but *not* including, a1.cend(). The copied elements are placed into vector results1. The first two arguments must be at least *input iterators* and the last must be at least an *output iterator*. In this example, we did *not* preallocate enough elements in results1 to store *all* the elements copied from a1. Instead, we use function back_inserter (defined in header <iterator>) to add elements to the end of results1. The back_inserter uses vector's push_back member function to insert elements at the end of the vector. Because the back_inserter *inserts* an element *rather than replacing* an existing element's value, the vector is able to grow to accommodate additional elements. A second version of the unique_copy algorithm takes as a fourth argument a *binary predicate function* for comparing elements for *equality*.

reverse_copy *Algorithm*

Line 36 uses the **reverse_copy** algorithm to make a reversed copy of the elements in the range from a1.cbegin() up to, but *not* including, a1.cend(). The copied elements are inserted into results2 using a back_inserter object to ensure that the vector can *grow* to accommodate the appropriate number of elements copied. Algorithm `reverse_copy` requires its first two iterator arguments to be at least *bidirectional iterators* and its third to be at least an *output iterator*.

16.3.10 Set Operations

Figure 16.10 demonstrates algorithms `includes`, `set_difference`, `set_intersection`, `set_symmetric_difference` and `set_union` for manipulating *sets of sorted values*.

```cpp
1   // Fig. 16.10: fig16_10.cpp
2   // Algorithms includes, set_difference, set_intersection,
3   // set_symmetric_difference and set_union.
4   #include <iostream>
5   #include <array>
6   #include <algorithm> // algorithm definitions
7   #include <iterator> // ostream_iterator
8   using namespace std;
9
10  int main()
11  {
12     const size_t SIZE1 = 10, SIZE2 = 5, SIZE3 = 20;
13     array< int, SIZE1 > a1 = { 1, 2, 3, 4, 5, 6, 7, 8, 9, 10 };
14     array< int, SIZE2 > a2 = { 4, 5, 6, 7, 8 };
15     array< int, SIZE2 > a3 = { 4, 5, 6, 11, 15 };
16     ostream_iterator< int > output( cout, " " );
17
18     cout << "a1 contains: ";
19     copy( a1.cbegin(), a1.cend(), output ); // display array a1
20     cout << "\na2 contains: ";
21     copy( a2.cbegin(), a2.cend(), output ); // display array a2
22     cout << "\na3 contains: ";
23     copy( a3.cbegin(), a3.cend(), output ); // display array a3
24
25     // determine whether a2 is completely contained in a1
26     if ( includes( a1.cbegin(), a1.cend(), a2.cbegin(), a2.cend() ) )
27        cout << "\n\na1 includes a2";
28     else
29        cout << "\n\na1 does not include a2";
30
31     // determine whether a3 is completely contained in a1
32     if ( includes( a1.cbegin(), a1.cend(), a3.cbegin(), a3.cend() ) )
33        cout << "\na1 includes a3";
34     else
35        cout << "\na1 does not include a3";
36
37     array< int, SIZE1 > difference;
38
39     // determine elements of a1 not in a2
40     auto result1 = set_difference( a1.cbegin(), a1.cend(),
41        a2.cbegin(), a2.cend(), difference.begin() );
```

Fig. 16.10 | Algorithms `includes`, `set_difference`, `set_intersection`, `set_symmetric_difference` and `set_union`. (Part 1 of 2.)

```
42        cout << "\n\nset_difference of a1 and a2 is: ";
43        copy( difference.begin(), result1, output );
44
45        array< int, SIZE1 > intersection;
46
47        // determine elements in both a1 and a2
48        auto result2 = set_intersection( a1.cbegin(), a1.cend(),
49           a2.cbegin(), a2.cend(), intersection.begin() );
50        cout << "\n\nset_intersection of a1 and a2 is: ";
51        copy( intersection.begin(), result2, output );
52
53        array< int, SIZE1 + SIZE2 > symmetric_difference;
54
55        // determine elements of a1 that are not in a2 and
56        // elements of a2 that are not in a1
57        auto result3 = set_symmetric_difference( a1.cbegin(), a1.cend(),
58           a3.cbegin(), a3.cend(), symmetric_difference.begin() );
59        cout << "\n\nset_symmetric_difference of a1 and a3 is: ";
60        copy( symmetric_difference.begin(), result3, output );
61
62        array< int, SIZE3 > unionSet;
63
64        // determine elements that are in either or both sets
65        auto result4 = set_union( a1.cbegin(), a1.cend(),
66           a3.cbegin(), a3.cend(), unionSet.begin() );
67        cout << "\n\nset_union of a1 and a3 is: ";
68        copy( unionSet.begin(), result4, output );
69        cout << endl;
70     } // end main
```

```
a1 contains: 1 2 3 4 5 6 7 8 9 10
a2 contains: 4 5 6 7 8
a3 contains: 4 5 6 11 15

a1 includes a2
a1 does not include a3

set_difference of a1 and a2 is: 1 2 3 9 10

set_intersection of a1 and a2 is: 4 5 6 7 8

set_symmetric_difference of a1 and a3 is: 1 2 3 7 8 9 10 11 15

set_union of a1 and a3 is: 1 2 3 4 5 6 7 8 9 10 11 15
```

Fig. 16.10 | Algorithms includes, set_difference, set_intersection, set_symmetric_difference and set_union. (Part 2 of 2.)

includes Algorithm

Lines 26 and 32 call the `includes` algorithm, which compares two sets of *sorted* values to determine whether *every* element of the second set is in the first set. If so, `includes` returns `true`; otherwise, it returns `false`. The first two iterator arguments must be at least *input iterators* and must describe the first set of values. In line 26, the first set consists of the elements from a1.cbegin() up to, but *not* including, a1.cend(). The last two iterator arguments must be at least *input iterators* and must describe the second set of values. In this example, the second set consists of the elements from a2.cbegin() up to, but *not* including, a2.cend(). A second version of algorithm includes takes a fifth argument that's a *binary predicate function* indicating the order in which the elements were originally sorted. The two sequences must be sorted using the *same comparison function*.

set_difference *Algorithm*
Lines 40–41 use the set_difference algorithm to find the elements from the first set of sorted values that are *not* in the second set of sorted values (both sets of values must be in *ascending order*). The elements that are *different* are copied into the fifth argument (in this case, the array difference). The first two iterator arguments must be at least *input iterators* for the first set of values. The next two iterator arguments must be at least *input iterators* for the second set of values. The fifth argument must be at least an *output iterator* indicating where to store a copy of the values that are *different*. The algorithm returns an *output iterator* positioned immediately after the *last* value copied into the set to which the fifth argument points. A second version of set_difference takes a sixth argument that's a *binary predicate function* indicating the *order* in which the elements were *originally sorted*. The two sequences must be sorted using the *same comparison function*.

set_intersection *Algorithm*
Lines 48–49 use the set_intersection algorithm to determine the elements from the first set of sorted values that *are* in the second set of sorted values (both sets of values must be in *ascending* order). The elements *common to both sets* are copied into the fifth argument (in this case, array intersection). The first two iterator arguments must be at least *input iterators* for the first set of values. The next two iterator arguments must be at least *input iterators* for the second set of values. The fifth argument must be at least an *output iterator* indicating where to store a copy of the values that are the same. The algorithm returns an *output iterator* positioned immediately after the last value copied into the set to which the fifth argument points. A second version of set_intersection takes a sixth argument that's a *binary predicate function* indicating the order in which the elements were *originally* sorted. The two sequences must be sorted using the *same comparison function*.

set_symmetric_difference *Algorithm*
Lines 57–58 use the set_symmetric_difference algorithm to determine the elements in the first set that are *not* in the second set and the elements in the second set that are *not* in the first set (both sets must be in *ascending order*). The elements that are *different* are copied from both sets into the fifth argument (the array symmetric_difference). The first two iterator arguments must be at least *input iterators* for the first set of values. The next two iterator arguments must be at least *input iterators* for the second set of values. The fifth argument must be at least an *output iterator* indicating where to store a copy of the values that are different. The algorithm returns an *output iterator* positioned immediately after the *last* value copied into the set to which the fifth argument points. A second version of set_symmetric_difference takes a sixth argument that's a *binary predicate function* indicating the order in which the elements were originally sorted. The two sequences must be sorted using the *same comparison function*.

set_union *Algorithm*

Lines 65–66 use the `set_union` algorithm to create a set of all the elements that are in *either or both* of the two sorted sets (both sets of values must be in *ascending order*). The elements are copied from both sets into the fifth argument (in this case the array `unionSet`). Elements that appear in *both* sets are only copied from the first set. The first two iterator arguments must be at least *input iterators* for the first set of values. The next two iterator arguments must be at least *input iterators* for the second set of values. The fifth argument must be at least an *output iterator* indicating where to store the copied elements. The algorithm returns an *output iterator* positioned immediately after the *last* value copied into the set to which the fifth argument points. A second version of `set_union` takes a sixth argument that's a *binary predicate function* indicating the order in which the elements were *originally* sorted. The two sequences must be sorted using the *same comparison function*.

16.3.11 `lower_bound`, `upper_bound` and `equal_range`

Figure 16.11 demonstrates algorithms `lower_bound`, `upper_bound` and `equal_range`.

```
1   // Fig. 16.11: fig16_11.cpp
2   // Algorithms lower_bound, upper_bound and
3   // equal_range for a sorted sequence of values.
4   #include <iostream>
5   #include <algorithm> // algorithm definitions
6   #include <array> // aray class-template definition
7   #include <iterator> // ostream_iterator
8   using namespace std;
9
10  int main()
11  {
12     const size_t SIZE = 10;
13     array< int, SIZE > a = { 2, 2, 4, 4, 4, 6, 6, 6, 6, 8 };
14     ostream_iterator< int > output( cout, " " );
15
16     cout << "array a contains:\n";
17     copy( a.cbegin(), a.cend(), output );
18
19     // determine lower-bound insertion point for 6 in a
20     auto lower = lower_bound( a.cbegin(), a.cend(), 6 );
21     cout << "\n\nLower bound of 6 is element "
22        << ( lower - a.cbegin() ) << " of array a";
23
24     // determine upper-bound insertion point for 6 in a
25     auto upper = upper_bound( a.cbegin(), a.cend(), 6 );
26     cout << "\nUpper bound of 6 is element "
27        << ( upper - a.cbegin() ) << " of array a";
28
29     // use equal_range to determine both the lower- and
30     // upper-bound insertion points for 6
31     auto eq = equal_range( a.cbegin(), a.cend(), 6 );
```

Fig. 16.11 | Algorithms `lower_bound`, `upper_bound` and `equal_range` for a sorted sequence of values. (Part 1 of 2.)

```
32      cout << "\nUsing equal_range:\n   Lower bound of 6 is element "
33         << ( eq.first - a.cbegin() ) << " of array a";
34      cout << "\n   Upper bound of 6 is element "
35         << ( eq.second - a.cbegin() ) << " of array a";
36      cout << "\n\nUse lower_bound to locate the first point\n"
37         << "at which 5 can be inserted in order";
38
39      // determine lower-bound insertion point for 5 in a
40      lower = lower_bound( a.cbegin(), a.cend(), 5 );
41      cout << "\n   Lower bound of 5 is element "
42         << ( lower - a.cbegin() ) << " of array a";
43      cout << "\n\nUse upper_bound to locate the last point\n"
44         << "at which 7 can be inserted in order";
45
46      // determine upper-bound insertion point for 7 in a
47      upper = upper_bound( a.cbegin(), a.cend(), 7 );
48      cout << "\n   Upper bound of 7 is element "
49         << ( upper - a.cbegin() ) << " of array a";
50      cout << "\n\nUse equal_range to locate the first and\n"
51         << "last point at which 5 can be inserted in order";
52
53      // use equal_range to determine both the lower- and
54      // upper-bound insertion points for 5
55      eq = equal_range( a.cbegin(), a.cend(), 5 );
56      cout << "\n   Lower bound of 5 is element "
57         << ( eq.first - a.cbegin() ) << " of array a";
58      cout << "\n   Upper bound of 5 is element "
59         << ( eq.second - a.cbegin() ) << " of array a" << endl;
60   } // end main
```

```
Array a contains:
2 2 4 4 4 6 6 6 6 8

Lower bound of 6 is element 5 of array a
Upper bound of 6 is element 9 of array a
Using equal_range:
   Lower bound of 6 is element 5 of array a
   Upper bound of 6 is element 9 of array a

Use lower_bound to locate the first point
at which 5 can be inserted in order
   Lower bound of 5 is element 5 of array a

Use upper_bound to locate the last point
at which 7 can be inserted in order
   Upper bound of 7 is element 9 of array a

Use equal_range to locate the first and
last point at which 5 can be inserted in order
   Lower bound of 5 is element 5 of array a
   Upper bound of 5 is element 5 of array a
```

Fig. 16.11 | Algorithms lower_bound, upper_bound and equal_range for a sorted sequence of values. (Part 2 of 2.)

`lower_bound` *Algorithm*

Line 20 uses the `lower_bound` algorithm to find the first location in a sorted sequence of values at which the third argument could be inserted in the sequence such that the sequence would still be *sorted in ascending order*. The first two iterator arguments must be at least *forward iterators*. The third argument is the value for which to determine the lower bound. The algorithm returns a *forward iterator* pointing to the position at which the insert can occur. A second version of lower_bound takes as a fourth argument a *binary predicate function* indicating the order in which the elements were *originally* sorted.

`upper_bound` *Algorithm*

Line 25 uses the `upper_bound` algorithm to find the last location in a sorted sequence of values at which the third argument could be inserted in the sequence such that the sequence would still be sorted in *ascending order*. The first two iterator arguments must be at least *forward iterators*. The third argument is the value for which to determine the upper bound. The algorithm returns a *forward iterator* pointing to the position at which the insert can occur. A second version of upper_bound takes as a fourth argument a *binary predicate function* indicating the order in which the elements were *originally* sorted.

`equal_range` *Algorithm*

Line 31 uses the `equal_range` algorithm to return a `pair` of *forward iterators* containing the results of performing both a `lower_bound` and an `upper_bound` operation. The first two arguments must be at least *forward iterators*. The third is the value for which to locate the equal range. The algorithm returns a `pair` of *forward iterators* for the lower bound (`eq.first`) and upper bound (`eq.second`), respectively.

Locating Insertion Points in Sorted Sequences

Algorithms `lower_bound`, `upper_bound` and `equal_range` are often used to locate *insertion points* in sorted sequences. Line 40 uses `lower_bound` to locate the first point at which 5 can be inserted in order in a. Line 47 uses `upper_bound` to locate the last point at which 7 can be inserted in order in a. Line 55 uses `equal_range` to locate the first and last points at which 5 can be inserted in order in a.

16.3.12 Heapsort

Figure 16.12 demonstrates the Standard Library algorithms for performing the heapsort sorting algorithm, in which an array of elements is arranged into a data structure called a *heap*. Heapsort is discussed in detail in computer science courses called "Data Structures" and "Algorithms." For more information and additional resources, see:

```
en.wikipedia.org/wiki/Heapsort
```

```
1   // Fig. 16.12: fig16_12.cpp
2   // Algorithms push_heap, pop_heap, make_heap and sort_heap.
3   #include <iostream>
4   #include <algorithm>
5   #include <array>
```

Fig. 16.12 | Algorithms push_heap, pop_heap, make_heap and sort_heap. (Part 1 of 3.)

```
6   #include <vector>
7   #include <iterator>
8   using namespace std;
9
10  int main()
11  {
12     const size_t SIZE = 10;
13     array< int, SIZE > init = { 3, 100, 52, 77, 22, 31, 1, 98, 13, 40 };
14     array< int, SIZE > a( init ); // copy of init
15     ostream_iterator< int > output( cout, " " );
16
17     cout << "Array a before make_heap:\n";
18     copy( a.cbegin(), a.cend(), output );
19
20     make_heap( a.begin(), a.end() ); // create heap from array a
21     cout << "\Array a after make_heap:\n";
22     copy( a.cbegin(), a.cend(), output );
23
24     sort_heap( a.begin(), a.end() ); // sort elements with sort_heap
25     cout << "\Array a after sort_heap:\n";
26     copy( a.cbegin(), a.cend(), output );
27
28     // perform the heapsort with push_heap and pop_heap
29     cout << "\n\nArray init contains: ";
30     copy( init.cbegin(), init.cend(), output ); // display array init
31     cout << endl;
32
33     vector< int > v;
34
35     // place elements of array init into v and
36     // maintain elements of v in heap
37     for ( size_t i = 0; i < SIZE; ++i )
38     {
39        v.push_back( init[ i ] );
40        push_heap( v.begin(), v.end() );
41        cout << "\nv after push_heap(init[" << i << "]): ";
42        copy( v.cbegin(), v.cend(), output );
43     } // end for
44
45     cout << endl;
46
47     // remove elements from heap in sorted order
48     for ( size_t  j = 0; j < v.size(); ++j )
49     {
50        cout << "\nv after " << v[ 0 ] << " popped from heap\n";
51        pop_heap( v.begin(), v.end() - j );
52        copy( v.cbegin(), v.cend(), output );
53     } // end for
54
55     cout << endl;
56  } // end main
```

Fig. 16.12 | Algorithms push_heap, pop_heap, make_heap and sort_heap. (Part 2 of 3.)

```
Array a before make_heap:
3 100 52 77 22 31 1 98 13 40
Array a after make_heap:
100 98 52 77 40 31 1 3 13 22
Array a after sort_heap:
1 3 13 22 31 40 52 77 98 100

Array init contains: 3 100 52 77 22 31 1 98 13 40

v after push_heap(init[0]): 3
v after push_heap(init[1]): 100 3
v after push_heap(init[2]): 100 3 52
v after push_heap(init[3]): 100 77 52 3
v after push_heap(init[4]): 100 77 52 3 22
v after push_heap(init[5]): 100 77 52 3 22 31
v after push_heap(init[6]): 100 77 52 3 22 31 1
v after push_heap(init[7]): 100 98 52 77 22 31 1 3
v after push_heap(init[8]): 100 98 52 77 22 31 1 3 13
v after push_heap(init[9]): 100 98 52 77 40 31 1 3 13 22

v after 100 popped from heap
98 77 52 22 40 31 1 3 13 100
v after 98 popped from heap
77 40 52 22 13 31 1 3 98 100
v after 77 popped from heap
52 40 31 22 13 3 1 77 98 100
v after 52 popped from heap
40 22 31 1 13 3 52 77 98 100
v after 40 popped from heap
31 22 3 1 13 40 52 77 98 100
v after 31 popped from heap
22 13 3 1 31 40 52 77 98 100
v after 22 popped from heap
13 1 3 22 31 40 52 77 98 100
v after 13 popped from heap
3 1 13 22 31 40 52 77 98 100
v after 3 popped from heap
1 3 13 22 31 40 52 77 98 100
v after 1 popped from heap
1 3 13 22 31 40 52 77 98 100
```

Fig. 16.12 | Algorithms push_heap, pop_heap, make_heap and sort_heap. (Part 3 of 3.)

make_heap Algorithm

Line 20 uses the make_heap algorithm to take a sequence of values in the range from a.begin() up to, but *not* including, a.end() and *create a heap* that can be used to produce a *sorted sequence*. The two iterator arguments must be *random-access iterators*, so this algorithm will work only with arrays, vectors and deques. A second version of this algorithm takes as a third argument a *binary predicate function* for *comparing* values.

sort_heap Algorithm

Line 24 uses the **sort_heap** algorithm to *sort a sequence of values* in the range from a.begin() up to, but *not* including, a.end() that are already arranged in a heap. The two iterator arguments must be *random-access iterators*. A second version of this algorithm takes as a third argument a *binary predicate function* for *comparing* values.

push_heap Algorithm

Line 40 uses the **push_heap** algorithm to *add a new value into a heap*. We take one element of array **init** at a time, *append it* to the *end* of vector **v** and perform the push_heap operation. If the appended element is the *only* element in the vector, the vector is *already* a heap. Otherwise, push_heap rearranges the vector elements into a heap. Each time push_heap is called, it assumes that the *last* element currently in the vector (i.e., the one that's appended before the push_heap call) is the element being added to the heap and that all other elements in the vector are already arranged as a heap. The two iterator arguments to push_heap must be *random-access iterators*. A second version of this algorithm takes as a third argument a *binary predicate function* for *comparing* values.

pop_heap Algorithm

Line 51 uses **pop_heap** to remove the *top* heap element. This algorithm assumes that the elements in the range specified by its two *random-access iterator* arguments are already a heap. Repeatedly removing the *top* heap element results in a sorted sequence of values. Algorithm pop_heap *swaps* the *first* heap element (v.begin()) with the *last* heap element (the element before v.end() - j), then ensures that the elements up to, but *not* including, the last element still form a heap. Notice in the output that, after the pop_heap operations, the vector is *sorted* in *ascending order*. A second version of this algorithm takes as a third argument a *binary predicate function* for comparing values.

C++11: **is_heap** *and* **is_heap_until** *Algorithms*

In addition to the make_heap, sort_heap, push_heap and pop_heap algorithms presented in Fig. 16.12, C++11 now includes the new algorithms is_heap and is_heap_until. The is_heap algorithm returns true if the elements in the specified range represent a heap. A second version of this algorithm takes as a third argument a *binary predicate function* for comparing values.

The is_heap_until algorithm checks the specified range of values and returns an iterator pointing to the last item in the range for which the elements up to, but not including, that iterator represent a heap.

16.3.13 min, max, minmax and minmax_element

Figure 16.13 demonstrates algorithms min, max, minmax and minmax_element.

```
 1   // Fig. 16.13: fig16_13.cpp
 2   // Algorithms min, max, minmax and minmax_element.
 3   #include <iostream>
 4   #include <array>
 5   #include <algorithm>
 6   using namespace std;
 7
 8   int main()
 9   {
10      cout << "The minimum of 12 and 7 is: " << min( 12, 7 );
11      cout << "\nThe maximum of 12 and 7 is: " << max( 12, 7 );
12      cout << "\nThe minimum of 'G' and 'Z' is: " << min( 'G', 'Z' );
```

Fig. 16.13 | Algorithms min, max, minmax and minmax_element. (Part 1 of 2.)

```
13      cout << "\nThe maximum of 'G' and 'Z' is: " << max( 'G', 'Z' );
14
15      // determine which argument is the min and which is the max
16      auto result1 = minmax( 12, 7 );
17      cout << "\n\nThe minimum of 12 and 7 is: " << result1.first
18         << "\nThe maximum of 12 and 7 is: " << result1.second;
19
20      array< int, 10 > items = { 3, 100, 52, 77, 22, 31, 1, 98, 13, 40 };
21      ostream_iterator< int > output( cout, " " );
22
23      cout << "\n\nArray items contains: ";
24      copy( items.cbegin(), items.cend(), output );
25
26      auto result2 = minmax_element( items.cbegin(), items.cend() );
27      cout << "\nThe minimum element in items is: " << *result2.first
28         << "\nThe maximum element in items is: " << *result2.second
29         << endl;
30   } // end main
```

```
The minimum of 12 and 7 is: 7
The maximum of 12 and 7 is: 12
The minimum of 'G' and 'Z' is: G
The maximum of 'G' and 'Z' is: Z

The minimum of 12 and 7 is: 7
The maximum of 12 and 7 is: 12

Array items contains: 3 100 52 77 22 31 1 98 13 40
The minimum element in items is: 1
The maximum element in items is: 100
```

Fig. 16.13 | Algorithms min, max, minmax and minmax_element. (Part 2 of 2.)

Algorithms *min* and *max* with Two Parameters
Algorithms min and max (demonstrated in lines 10–13) determine the minimum and the maximum of two elements, respectively.

C++11: *min* and *max* Algorithms with `initializer_list` Parameters

C++11 now includes overloaded versions of the algorithms min and max that each receive an initializer_list parameter and return the smallest or largest item in the list initializer that's passed as an argument. For example, the following statement returns 7:

```
int minumum = min( { 10, 7, 14, 21, 17 } );
```

Each of these new min and max algorithms is overloaded with a version that takes as a second argument a *binary predicate function* for comparing values.

C++11: *minmax* Algorithm
C++11 now includes the minmax algorithm (line 16) that receives two items and returns a pair in which the smaller item is stored in first and the larger item is stored in second. A second version of this algorithm takes as a third argument a *binary predicate function* for comparing values.

C++11: `minmax_element` *Algorithm*

C++11 now includes the `minmax_element` algorithm (line 26) that receives two *input iterators* representing a range of elements and returns a `pair` of iterators in which `first` points to the smallest element in the range and `second` points to the largest. A second version of this algorithm takes as a third argument a *binary predicate function* for comparing values.

16.4 Function Objects

Many Standard Library algorithms allow you to pass a *function pointer* into the algorithm to help the algorithm perform its task. For example, the `binary_search` algorithm that we discussed in Section 16.3.6 is overloaded with a version that requires as its fourth parameter a *function pointer* that takes two arguments and returns a `bool` value. The algorithm uses this function to compare the search key to an element in the collection. The function returns `true` if the search key and element being compared are equal; otherwise, the function returns `false`. This enables `binary_search` to search a collection of elements for which the element type does *not* provide an overloaded equality < operator.

Any algorithm that can receive a *function pointer* can also receive an object of a class that overloads the function-call operator (parentheses) with a function named `operator()`, provided that the overloaded operator meets the requirements of the algorithm—in the case of `binary_search`, it must receive two arguments and return a `bool`. An object of such a class is known as a **function object** and can be used syntactically and semantically like a function or *function pointer*—the overloaded parentheses operator is invoked by using a function object's name followed by parentheses containing the arguments to the function. Most algorithms can use function objects and functions interchangeably. As you'll learn in Section 16.5, C++11's lambda expressions can also be used where function pointers and function objects are used.

Advantages of Function Objects Over Function Pointers

Function objects provide several advantages over *function pointers*. The compiler can inline a *function object's* overloaded `operator()` to improve performance. Also, since they're objects of classes, *function objects* can have data members that `operator()` can use to perform its task.

Predefined Function Objects of the Standard Template Library

Many predefined *function objects* can be found in the header `<functional>`. Figure 16.14 lists several of the dozens of Standard Library *function objects*, which are all implemented as class templates. Section 20.8 of the C++ standard contains the complete list of function objects. We used the *function object* `less<T>` in the `set`, `multiset` and `priority_queue` examples, to specify the sorting order for elements in a container.

Using the `accumulate` Algorithm

Figure 16.15 uses the `accumulate` numeric algorithm (introduced in Fig. 16.5) to calculate the sum of the squares of the elements in an `array`. The fourth argument to `accumulate` is a **binary function object** (that is, a *function object* for which `operator()` takes two arguments) or a *function pointer* to a **binary function** (that is, a function that takes two arguments). Function `accumulate` is demonstrated twice—once with a *function pointer* and once with a *function object*.

Function object	Type	Function object	Type
divides< T >	arithmetic	logical_or< T >	logical
equal_to< T >	relational	minus< T >	arithmetic
greater< T >	relational	modulus< T >	arithmetic
greater_equal< T >	relational	negate< T >	arithmetic
less< T >	relational	not_equal_to< T >	relational
less_equal< T >	relational	plus< T >	arithmetic
logical_and< T >	logical	multiplies< T >	arithmetic
logical_not< T >	logical		

Fig. 16.14 | Function objects in the Standard Library.

```cpp
1   // Fig. 16.15: fig16_15.cpp
2   // Demonstrating function objects.
3   #include <iostream>
4   #include <array> // array class-template definition
5   #include <algorithm> // copy algorithm
6   #include <numeric> // accumulate algorithm
7   #include <functional> // binary_function definition
8   #include <iterator> // ostream_iterator
9   using namespace std;
10
11  // binary function adds square of its second argument and the
12  // running total in its first argument, then returns the sum
13  int sumSquares( int total, int value )
14  {
15     return total + value * value;
16  } // end function sumSquares
17
18  // Class template SumSquaresClass defines overloaded operator()
19  // that adds the square of its second argument and running
20  // total in its first argument, then returns sum
21  template< typename T >
22  class SumSquaresClass
23  {
24  public:
25     // add square of value to total and return result
26     T operator()( const T &total, const T &value )
27     {
28        return total + value * value;
29     } // end function operator()
30  }; // end class SumSquaresClass
31
32  int main()
33  {
34     const size_t SIZE = 10;
35     array< int, SIZE > integers = { 1, 2, 3, 4, 5, 6, 7, 8, 9, 10 };
```

Fig. 16.15 | Binary function object. (Part 1 of 2.)

```
36        ostream_iterator< int > output( cout, " " );
37
38        cout << "array integers contains:\n";
39        copy( integers.cbegin(), integers.cend(), output );
40
41        // calculate sum of squares of elements of array integers
42        // using binary function sumSquares
43        int result = accumulate( integers.cbegin(), integers.cend(),
44           0, sumSquares );
45
46        cout << "\n\nSum of squares of elements in integers using "
47           << "binary\nfunction sumSquares: " << result;
48
49        // calculate sum of squares of elements of array integers
50        // using binary function object
51        result = accumulate( integers.cbegin(), integers.cend(),
52           0, SumSquaresClass< int >() );
53
54        cout << "\n\nSum of squares of elements in integers using "
55           << "binary\nfunction object of type "
56           << "SumSquaresClass< int >: " << result << endl;
57    } // end main
```

```
array integers contains:
1 2 3 4 5 6 7 8 9 10

Sum of squares of elements in integers using binary
function sumSquares: 385

Sum of squares of elements in integers using binary
function object of type SumSquaresClass< int >: 385
```

Fig. 16.15 | Binary function object. (Part 2 of 2.)

Function sumSquares

Lines 13–16 define a function sumSquares that squares its second argument value, adds that square and its first argument total and returns the sum. Function accumulate will pass each of the elements of the sequence over which it iterates as the second argument to sumSquares in the example. On the first call to sumSquares, the first argument will be the initial value of the total (which is supplied as the third argument to accumulate; 0 in this program). All subsequent calls to sumSquares receive as the first argument the running sum returned by the previous call to sumSquares. When accumulate completes, it returns the sum of the squares of all the elements in the sequence.

Class SumSquaresClass

Lines 21–30 define the class template SumSquaresClass with an overloaded operator() that has two parameters and returns a value—the requirements for a binary function object. On the first call to the *function object*, the first argument will be the initial value of the total (which is supplied as the third argument to accumulate; 0 in this program) and the second argument will be the first element in array integers. All subsequent calls to operator receive as the first argument the result returned by the previous call to the *func-*

tion object, and the second argument will be the next element in the array. When accumulate completes, it returns the sum of the squares of all the elements in the array.

Passing Function Pointers and Function Objects to Algorithm **accumulate**

Lines 43–44 call function accumulate with a *pointer to function* sumSquares as its last argument. Similarly, the statement in lines 51–52 calls accumulate with an object of class SumSquaresClass as the last argument. The expression SumSquaresClass<int>() creates (and calls the default constructor for) an instance of class SumSquaresClass (a *function object*) that's passed to accumulate, which invokes the function operator(). Lines 51–52 could be written as two separate statements, as follows:

```
SumSquaresClass< int > sumSquaresObject;
result = accumulate( integers.cbegin(), integers.cend(),
    0, sumSquaresObject );
```

The first line defines an object of class SumSquaresClass. That object is then passed to accumulate.

16.5 Lambda Expressions

As you've seen in this chapter, many algorithms can receive function pointers or function objects as parameters. Before you can pass a function pointer or function object to an algorithm, the corresponding function or class must have been declared.

C++11's Lambda expressions (or lambda functions) enable you to define anonymous function objects *where they're passed* to a function. They're defined locally inside functions and can "capture" (by value or by reference) the local variables of the enclosing function then manipulate these variables in the lambda's body. Figure 16.16 demonstrates a simple lambda expression example that doubles the value of each element in an int array.

```cpp
 1   // Fig. 16.16: fig16_16.cpp
 2   // Lambda expressions.
 3   #include <iostream>
 4   #include <array>
 5   #include <algorithm>
 6   using namespace std;
 7
 8   int main()
 9   {
10      const size_t SIZE = 4; // size of array values
11      array< int, SIZE > values = { 1, 2, 3, 4 }; // initialize values
12
13      // output each element multiplied by two
14      for_each( values.cbegin(), values.cend(),
15         []( int i ) { cout << i * 2 << endl; } );
16
17      int sum = 0; // initialize sum to zero
18
19      // add each element to sum
20      for_each( values.cbegin(), values.cend(),
21         [ &sum ]( int i ) { sum += i; } );
```

Fig. 16.16 | Lambda expressions. (Part 1 of 2.)

```
22
23      cout << "sum is " << sum << endl; // output sum
24  } // end main
```

```
2
4
6
8
sum is 10
```

Fig. 16.16 | Lambda expressions. (Part 2 of 2.)

Lines 10 and 11 declare and initialize a small array of ints named values. Lines 14–15 call the for_each algorithm on the elements of values. The third argument (line 15) to for_each is a *lambda expression*. Lambdas begin with *lambda introducer* ([]), followed by a parameter list and function body. Return types can be inferred automatically if the body is a single statement of the form return *expression*;—otherwise, the return type is void by default or you can explicitly use a *trailing return type* (introduced in Section 6.19). The compiler converts the lambda expression into a function object. The lambda expression in line 15 receives an int, multiplies it by 2 and displays the result. The for_each algorithm passes each element of the array to the lambda.

The second call to the for_each algorithm (lines 20–21) calculates the sum of the array elements. The lambda introducer [&sum] indicates that this lambda expression *captures* the local variable sum *by reference* (note the use of the ampersand), so that the lambda can modify sum's value. Without the ampersand, sum would be captured by value and the local variable outside the lambda expression would *not* be updated. The for_each algorithm passes each element of values to the lambda, which adds the value to the sum. Line 23 then displays the value of sum.

You can assign lambda expressions to variables, which can then be used to invoke the lambda expression or pass it to other functions. For example, you can assign the lambda expression in line 15 to a variable as follows:

```
auto myLambda = []( int i ) { cout << i * 2 << endl; };
```

You can then use the variable name as a function name to invoke the lambda as in:

```
myLambda( 10 ); // outputs 20
```

16.6 Standard Library Algorithm Summary

The C++ standard specifies over 90 algorithms—many overloaded with two or more versions. The standard separates the algorithms into several categories—*mutating sequence algorithms, nonmodifying sequence algorithms, sorting and related algorithms* and *generalized numeric operations.* To learn about the algorithms that we did not present in this chapter, see your compiler's documentation or visit sites such as

```
en.cppreference.com/w/cpp/algorithm
msdn.microsoft.com/en-us/library/yah1y2x8.aspx
```

Mutating Sequence Algorithms

Figure 16.17 shows many of the mutating-sequence algorithms—i.e., algorithms that modify the containers they operate on. Algorithms new in C++11 are marked with an * in Figs. 16.17–16.20. Algorithms presented in this chapter are shown in **bold**.

Mutating sequence algorithms from header `<algorithm>`			
copy	copy_n*	copy_if*	copy_backward
move*	move_backward*	**swap**	swap_ranges
iter_swap	**transform**	**replace**	**replace_if**
replace_copy	replace_copy_if	**fill**	**fill_n**
generate	generate_n	**remove**	**remove_if**
remove_copy	remove_copy_if	**unique**	**unique_copy**
reverse	**reverse_copy**	rotate	rotate_copy
random_shuffle	shuffle*	is_partitioned*	partition
stable_partition	partition_copy*	partition_point*	

Fig. 16.17 | Mutating-sequence algorithms from header `<algorithm>`.

Nonmodifying Sequence Algorithms

Figure 16.18 shows the nonmodifying sequence algorithms—i.e., algorithms that do *not* modify the containers they operate on.

Nonmodifying sequence algorithms from header `<algorithm>`			
all_of*	**any_of***	**none_of***	for_each
find	**find_if**	**find_if_not***	find_end
find_first_of	adjacent_find	**count**	**count_if**
mismatch	**equal**	is_permutation*	search
search_n			

Fig. 16.18 | Nonmodifying sequence algorithms from header `<algorithm>`.

Sorting and Related Algorithms

Figure 16.19 shows the *sorting and related algorithms*.

Sorting and related algorithms from header `<algorithm>`			
sort	stable_sort	partial_sort	partial_sort_copy
is_sorted*	is_sorted_until*	nth_element	**lower_bound**
upper_bound	**equal_range**	**binary_search**	**merge**

Fig. 16.19 | Sorting and related algorithms from header `<algorithm>`. (Part 1 of 2.)

Sorting and related algorithms from header `<algorithm>`			
inplace_merge	includes	set_union	set_intersection
set_difference	set_symmetric_difference		push_heap
pop_heap	make_heap	sort_heap	is_heap*
is_heap_until*	min	max	minmax*
min_element	max_element	minmax_element*	lexicographical_compare
next_permutation	prev_permutation		

Fig. 16.19 | Sorting and related algorithms from header <algorithm>. (Part 2 of 2.)

Numerical Algorithms
Figure 16.20 shows the numerical algorithms of the header `<numeric>`.

Numerical algorithms from header `<numeric>`		
accumulate	partial_sum	iota*
inner_product	adjacent_difference	

Fig. 16.20 | Numerical algorithms from header <numeric>.

16.7 Wrap-Up

In this chapter, we demonstrated many of the Standard Library algorithms, including mathematical algorithms, basic searching and sorting algorithms and set operations. You learned the types of iterators each algorithm requires and that each algorithm can be used with any container that supports the minimum iterator functionality the algorithm requires. We introduced function objects that work syntactically and semantically like ordinary functions, but offer advantages such as performance and the ability to store data. Finally, you used lambda expressions to create function objects inline then passed them to Standard Library algorithms.

We introduced exception handling earlier in the book in our discussion of arrays. In the next chapter, we take a deeper look at C++'s rich set of exception handling capabilities.

Summary

Section 16.1 Introduction
• Standard Library algorithms are functions that perform such common data manipulations as searching, sorting and comparing elements or entire containers.

Section 16.3.1 *fill, fill_n, generate and generate_n*
• Algorithms fill and fill_n (p. 727) set every element in a range of container elements to a specific value.

- Algorithms `generate` and `generate_n` (p. 727) use a generator function (p. 727) or function object to create values for every element in a range of container elements.

Section 16.3.2 `equal`, `mismatch` and `lexicographical_compare`
- Algorithm `equal` (p. 730) compares two sequences of values for equality.
- Algorithm `mismatch` (p. 731) compares two sequences of values and returns a pair of iterators indicating the location in each sequence of the mismatched elements.
- Algorithm `lexicographical_compare` (p. 731) compares the contents of two sequences.

Section 16.3.3 `remove`, `remove_if`, `remove_copy` and `remove_copy_if`
- Algorithm `remove` (p. 733) eliminates all elements with a specific value in a certain range.
- Algorithm `remove_copy` (p. 733) copies all elements that do not have a specific value in a certain range.
- Algorithm `remove_if` (p. 733) deletes all elements that satisfy the `if` condition in a certain range.
- Algorithm `remove_copy_if` (p. 734) copies all elements that satisfy the `if` condition in a certain range.

Section 16.3.4 `replace`, `replace_if`, `replace_copy` and `replace_copy_if`
- Algorithm `replace` (p. 736) replaces all elements with a specific value in certain range.
- Algorithm `replace_copy` (p. 736) copies all elements in a range, replacing all elements of one value with a different value.
- Algorithm `replace_if` (p. 736) replaces all elements that satisfy the `if` condition in a certain range.
- Algorithm `replace_copy_if` (p. 736) copies all elements in a range, replacing all elements that satisfy the `if` condition in a range.

Section 16.3.5 Mathematical Algorithms
- Algorithm `random_shuffle` (p. 738) reorders randomly the elements in a certain range.
- Algorithm `count` (p. 739) counts the elements with a specific value in a certain range.
- Algorithm `count_if` (p. 739) counts the elements that satisfy the `if` condition in a certain range.
- Algorithm `min_element` (p. 739) locates the smallest element in a certain range.
- Algorithm `max_element` (p. 739) locates the largest element in a certain range.
- Algorithm `minmax_element` (p. 739) locates the smallest and largest elements in a certain range.
- Algorithm `accumulate` (p. 739) sums the values in a certain range.
- Algorithm `for_each` (p. 740) applies a general function or function object to every element in a range.
- Algorithm `transform` (p. 740) applies a general function or function object to every element in a range and replaces each element with the result of the function.

Section 16.3.6 Basic Searching and Sorting Algorithms
- Algorithm `find` (p. 742) locates a specific value in a certain range.
- Algorithm `find_if` (p. 743) locates the first value in a certain range that satisfies the `if` condition.
- Algorithm `sort` (p. 743) arranges the elements in a certain range in ascending order or an order specified by a predicate.
- Algorithm `binary_search` (p. 743) determines whether a specific value is in a sorted range of elements.

- Algorithm all_of (p. 743) determines whether a unary predicate function returns true for all of the elements in the range.

- Algorithm any_of (p. 743) determines whether a unary predicate function returns true for any of the elements in the range.

- Algorithm none_of (p. 743) determines whether a unary predicate function returns false for all of the elements in the range.

- Algorithm find_if_not (p. 744) locates the first value in a certain range that do not satisfy the if condition.

Section 16.3.7 swap, iter_swap and swap_ranges
- Algorithm swap (p. 745) exchanges two values.

- Algorithm iter_swap (p. 745) exchanges the two elements to which the two iterator arguments point.

- Algorithm swap_ranges (p. 745) exchanges the elements in a certain range.

Section 16.3.8 copy_backward, merge, unique and reverse
- Algorithm copy_backward (p. 746) copies elements in a range and places the elements into a container starting from the end and working toward the front.

- Algorithm move (p. 747) moves elements in a range from one container to another.

- Algorithm move_backward (p. 747) moves elements in a range from one container to another starting from the end and working toward the front.

- Algorithm merge (p. 747) combines two sorted ascending sequences of values into a third sorted ascending sequence.

- Algorithm unique (p. 747) removes duplicated elements in a certain range of a sorted sequence.

- Algorithm copy_if (p. 748) copies each element from a range if a unary predicate function returns true for that element.

- Algorithm reverse (p. 748) reverses all the elements in a certain range.

- Algorithm copy_n (p. 748) copies a specified number of elements starting from a specified location and places them into a container starting at the specified location.

Section 16.3.9 inplace_merge, unique_copy and reverse_copy
- Algorithm inplace_merge (p. 749) merges two sorted sequences of elements in the same container.

- Algorithm unique_copy (p. 749) makes a copy of all the unique elements in the sorted sequence of values in a certain range.

- Algorithm reverse_copy (p. 749) makes a reversed copy of the elements in a certain range.

Section 16.3.10 Set Operations
- The set algorithm includes (p. 751) compares two sets of sorted values to determine whether every element of the second set is in the first set.

- The set algorithm set_difference (p. 752) finds the elements from the first set of sorted values that are not in the second set of sorted values (both sets of values must be in ascending order).

- The set algorithm set_intersection (p. 752) determines the elements from the first set of sorted values that are in the second set of sorted values (both sets of values must be in ascending order).

- The set algorithm set_symmetric_difference (p. 752) determines the elements in the first set that are not in the second set and the elements in the second set that are not in the first set (both sets of values must be in ascending order).

- The set algorithm set_union (p. 753) creates a set of all the elements that are in either or both of the two sorted sets (both sets of values must be in ascending order).

Section 16.3.11 *lower_bound, upper_bound and equal_range*

- Algorithm lower_bound (p. 755) finds the first location in a sorted sequence of values at which the third argument could be inserted in the sequence such that the sequence would still be sorted in ascending order.

- Algorithm upper_bound (p. 755) finds the last location in a sorted sequence of values at which the third argument could be inserted in the sequence such that the sequence would still be sorted in ascending order.

- Algorithm equal_range (p. 755) returns the lower bound and upper bound as a pair.

Section 16.3.12 *Heapsort*

- Algorithm make_heap (p. 757) takes a sequence of values in a certain range and creates a heap that can be used to produce a sorted sequence.

- Algorithm sort_heap (p. 757) sorts a sequence of values in a certain range of a heap.

- Algorithm pop_heap (p. 758) removes the top heap element.

- Algorithm is_heap (p. 758) returns true if the elements in the specified range represent a heap.

- Algorithm is_heap_until (p. 758) checks the specified range of values and returns an iterator pointing to the last item in the range for which the elements up to, but not including, that iterator represent a heap.

Section 16.3.13 *min, max, minmax and minmax_element*

- Algorithms min and max (p. 759) determine the minimum of two elements and the maximum of two elements, respectively.

- C++11 now includes overloaded versions of the algorithms min and max that each receive an initializer_list parameter and return the smallest or largest item in the list initializer that's passed as an argument. Each is overloaded with a version that takes as a second argument a *binary predicate function* for comparing values.

- C++11 now includes the minmax algorithm (p. 759) that receives two items and returns a pair in which the smaller item is stored in first and the larger item is stored in second. A second version of this algorithm takes as a third argument a binary predicate function for comparing values.

- C++11 now includes the minmax_element algorithm (p. 739) that receives two input iterators representing a range of elements and returns a pair of iterators in which first points to the smallest element in the range and second points to the largest. A second version of this algorithm takes as a third argument a binary predicate function for comparing values.

Section 16.4 *Function Objects*

- A function object (p. 760) is an instance of a class that overloads operator().

- The Standard Library provides many predefined function objects, which can be found in header <functional> (p. 760).

- Binary function objects (p. 760) take two arguments and return a value.

Section 16.5 *Lambda Expressions*

- Lambda expressions (or lambda functions; p. 763) provide a simplified syntax for defining function objects directly where they are used.

- A lambda function can capture local variables (by value or by reference) and manipulate them inside the lambda's body.
- Lambdas begin with the lambda introducer [], followed by a parameter and function body. Return types can be inferred automatically if the body is a single statement of the form return *expression*;—otherwise, the return type is void by default.
- To capture a local variable, specify it in the lambda introducer. To capture by reference, use an ampersand.

Self-Review Exercises

16.1   State whether each of the following is *true* or *false*. If *false*, explain why.
- a) Standard Library algorithms can operate on C-like pointer-based arrays.
- b) Standard Library algorithms are encapsulated as member functions within each container class.
- c) When using the remove algorithm on a container, the algorithm does not decrease the size of the container from which elements are being removed.
- d) One disadvantage of using Standard Library algorithms is that they depend on the implementation details of the containers on which they operate.
- e) The remove_if algorithm does not modify the number of elements in the container, but it does move to the beginning of the container all elements that are not removed.
- f) The find_if_not algorithm locates all the values in the range for which the specified unary predicate function returns false.
- g) Use the set_union algorithm to create a set of all the elements that are in either or both of the two sorted sets (both sets of values must be in ascending order).

16.2   Fill in the blanks in each of the following statements:
- a) Standard Library algorithms operate on container elements indirectly, using _____.
- b) The sort algorithm requires a(n) _____ iterator.
- c) Algorithms _____ and _____ set every element in a range of container elements to a specific value.
- d) The _____ algorithm compares two sequences of values for equality.
- e) The C++11 _____ algorithm locates both the smallest and largest elements in a range.
- f) A back_inserter calls the container's default _____ function to insert an element at the end of the container. If an element is inserted into a container that has no more space available, the container grows in size.
- g) Any algorithm that can receive a function pointer can also receive an object of a class that overloads the parentheses operator with a function named operator(), provided that the overloaded operator meets the requirements of the algorithm. An object of such a class is known as a(n) _____ and can be used syntactically and semantically like a function or function pointer.

16.3   Write a statement to peform each of the following tasks:
- a) Use the fill algorithm to fill the entire array of strings named items with "hello".
- b) Function nextInt returns the next int value in sequence starting with 0 the first time it's called. Use the generate algorithm and the nextInt function to fill the array of ints named integers.
- c) Use the equal algorithm to compare two lists (strings1 and strings2) for equality. Store the result in bool variable result.
- d) Use the remove_if algorithm to remove from the vector of strings named colors all of the strings that start with "bl". Function startsWithBL returns true if its argument string starts with "bl". Store the iterator that the algorithm returns in newLastElement.

e) Use the `replace_if` algorithm to replace with 0 all elements with values greater than 100 in the array of `int`s named `values`. Function `greaterThan100` returns `true` if its argument is greater than 100.

f) Use the `minmax_element` algorithm to find the smallest and largest values in the array of `double`s named `temperatures`. Store the `pair` of iterators that's returned in `result`.

g) Use the `sort` algorithm to sort the array of `string`s named `colors`.

h) Use the `reverse` algorithm to reverse order of the elements in the array of `string`s named `colors`.

i) Use the `merge` algorithm to merge the contents of the two sorted arrays named `values1` and `values2` into a third array named `results`.

j) Write a lambda expression that returns the square of its `int` argument and assign the lambda expression to variable `squareInt`.

Answers to Self-Review Exercises

16.1 a) True.

b) False. STL algorithms are not member functions. They operate indirectly on containers, through iterators.

c) True.

d) False. Standard Library algorithms do not depend on the implementation details of the containers on which they operate.

e) True.

f) False. It locates only the first value in the range for which the specified unary predicate function returns `false`.

g) True.

16.2 a) Iterators. b) random-access. c) `fill`, `fill_n`. d) `equal`. e) `minmax_element`. f) `push_back`. g) function object.

16.3 a) `fill( items.begin(), items.end(), "hello" );`

b) `generate( integers.begin(), integers.end(), nextInt );`

c) `bool result =`
    `equal( strings1.cbegin(), strings1.cend(), strings2.cbegin() );`

d) `auto newLastElement =`
    `remove_if( colors.begin(), colors.end(), startsWithBL );`

e) `replace_if( values.begin(), values.end(), greaterThan100 );`

f) `auto result =`
    `minmax_element( temperatures.cbegin(), temperatures.cend() );`

g) `sort( colors.begin(), colors.end() );`

h) `reverse( colors.begin(), colors.end() );`

i) `merge( values1.cbegin(), values1.cend(), values2.cbegin(), values2.cend(),`
    `results.begin() );`

j) `auto squareInt = []( int i ) { return i * i; };`

Exercises

16.4 State whether each of the following is *true* or *false*. If *false*, explain why.

a) Because Standard Library algorithms process containers directly, one algorithm can often be used with many different containers.

b) Use the `for_each` algorithm to apply a general function to every element in a range; for_each does not modify the sequence.

c) By default, the `sort` algorithm arranges the elements in a range in ascending order.

    d) Use the merge algorithm to form a new sequence by placing the second sequence after the first.

    e) Use the set_intersection algorithm to find the elements from a first set of sorted values that are not in a second set of sorted values (both sets of values must be in ascending order).

    f) Algorithms lower_bound, upper_bound and equal_range are often used to locate insertion points in sorted sequences.

    g) Lambda expressions can also be used where function pointers and function objects are used in algorithms.

    h) C++11's Lambda expressions are defined locally inside functions and can "capture" (by value or by reference) the local variables of the enclosing function then manipulate these variables in the lambda's body.

16.5 Fill in the blanks in each of the following statements:

    a) As long as a container's (or built-in array's) _____ satisfy the requirements of an algorithm, the algorithm can work on the container.

    b) Algorithms generate and generate_n use a(n) _____ function to create values for every element in a *range* of container elements. That type of function takes no arguments and returns a value that can be placed in an element of the container.

    c) Pointers into built-in arrays are _____ iterators.

    d) Use the _____ algorithm (the template of which is in header <numeric>) to sum the values in a range.

    e) Use the _____ algorithm to apply a general function to every element in a range when you need to modify those elements.

    f) In order to work properly, the binary_search algorithm requires that the sequence of values must be _____.

    g) Use the function iter_swap to exchange the elements that are pointed to by two _____ iterators and exchanges the values in those elements.

    h) C++11 now includes the minmax algorithm that receives two items and returns a(n) _____ in which the smaller item is stored in first and the larger item is stored in second.

    i) _____ algorithms modify the containers they operate on.

16.6 Distinguish between the copy_if and copy_n algorithms.

16.7 What happens when you apply the sort_heap algorithm to a set of elements in a heap?

16.8 *(Duplicate Elimination)* Read 20 integers into an array. Next, use the unique algorithm to reduce the array to the unique values entered by the user. Use the copy algorithm to display the unique values.

16.9 *(Duplicate Elimination)* Modify Exercise 16.8 to use the unique_copy algorithm. The unique values should be inserted into a vector that's initially empty. Use a back_inserter to enabled the vector to grow as new items are added. Use the copy algorithm to display the unique values.

16.10 *(Reading Data from a File)* Use an istream_iterator<int>, the copy algorithm and a back_inserter to read the contents of a text file that contains int values separated by whitespace. Place the int values into a vector of ints. The first argument to the copy algorithm should be the istream_iterator<int> object that's associated with the text file's ifstream object. The second argument should be an istream_iterator<int> object that's initialized using the class template istream_iterator's default constructor—the resulting object can be used as an "end" iterator. After reading the file's contents, display the contents of the resulting vector.

16.11 *(Merging Ordered Lists)* Write a program that uses Standard Library algorithms to merge two ordered `list`s of `string`s into a single ordered `list` of `string`s, then displays the resulting `list`.

16.12 *(Palindrome Tester)* A palindrome is a `string` that is spelled the same way forward and backward. Examples of palindromes include "radar" and "able was i ere i saw elba." Write a function `palindromeTester` that uses the `reverse` algorithm on an a copy of a `string`, then compares the original `string` and the reversed `string` to determine whether the original `string` is a palindrome. Like the Standard Library containers, `string` objects provide functions like `begin` and `end` to obtain iterators that point to characters in a `string`. Assume that the original `string` contains all lowercase letters and does not contain any punctuation. Use function `palindromeTester` in a program.

16.13 *(Enhanced Palindrome Tester)* Enhance Exercise 16.12's `palindromeTester` function to allow strings containing uppercase and lowercase letters and punctuation. Before testing if the original string is a palindrome, function `palindromeTester` should convert the `string` to lowercase letters and eliminate any punctuation. For simplicity, assume the only punctuations characters can be

> `. , ! ; : ( )`

You can use the `copy_if` algorithm and a `back_inserter` to make a copy of the original `string`, eliminate the punctuation characters and place the characters into a new `string` object.

17

Exception Handling: A Deeper Look

*It is common sense to take a
method and try it. If it fails,
admit it frankly and try
another. But above all, try
something.*
—Franklin Delano Roosevelt

*If they're running and they don't
look where they're going
I have to come out from
somewhere and catch them.*
—Jerome David Salinger

Objectives

In this chapter you'll learn:

- To use **try**, `catch` and
  `throw` to detect, handle and
  indicate exceptions,
  respectively.

- To declare new exception
  classes.

- How stack unwinding
  enables exceptions not
  caught in one scope to be
  caught in another.

- To handle **new** failures.

- To use `unique_ptr` to
  prevent memory leaks.

- To understand the standard
  exception hierarchy.

17.1 Introduction

As you know from Section 7.10, an **exception** is an indication of a problem that occurs during a program's execution. **Exception handling** enables you to create applications that can resolve (or handle) exceptions. In many cases, this allows a program to continue executing as if no problem had been encountered. The features presented in this chapter enable you to write **robust** and **fault-tolerant programs** that can deal with problems and continue executing or terminate gracefully.

We begin with a review of exception-handling concepts via an example that demonstrates handling an exception that occurs when a function attempts to divide by zero. We show how to handle exceptions that occur in a constructor or destructor and exceptions that occur if operator new fails to allocate memory for an object. We introduce several C++ Standard Library exception handling classes and show you how to create your own.

Software Engineering Observation 17.1

Exception handling provides a standard mechanism for processing errors. This is especially important when working on a project with a large team of programmers.

Software Engineering Observation 17.2

Incorporate your exception-handling strategy into your system from its inception. Including effective exception handling after a system has been implemented can be difficult.

Error-Prevention Tip 17.1

Without exception handling, it's common for a function to calculate and return a value on success or return an error indicator on failure. A common problem with this achitecture is using the return value in a subsequent calculation without first checking whether the value is the error indicator. Exception handling eliminates this problem.

17.2 Example: Handling an Attempt to Divide by Zero

Let's consider a simple example of exception handling (Figs. 17.1–17.2). We show how to deal with a common arithmetic problem—*division by zero*. Division by zero using integer arithmetic typically causes a program to terminate prematurely. In floating-point arithmetic, many C++ implementations allow division by zero, in which case a result of positive or negative infinity is displayed as INF or -INF, respectively.

In this example, we define a function named quotient that receives two integers input by the user and divides its first int parameter by its second int parameter. Before performing the division, the function casts the first int parameter's value to type double. Then, the second int parameter's value is (implicitly) promoted to type double for the calculation. So function quotient actually performs the division using two double values and returns a double result.

Although division by zero is often allowed in floating-point arithmetic, for the purpose of this example we treat any attempt to divide by zero as an error. Thus, function quotient tests its second parameter to ensure that it isn't zero before allowing the division to proceed. If the second parameter is zero, the function *throws an exception* to indicate to the caller that a problem occurred. The caller (main in this example) can then process the exception and allow the user to type two new values before calling function quotient again. In this way, the program can continue executing even after an improper value is entered, thus making the program more robust.

The example consists of two files. DivideByZeroException.h (Fig. 17.1) defines an *exception class* that represents the type of the problem that might occur in the example, and fig17_02.cpp (Fig. 17.2) defines the quotient function and the main function that calls it. Function main contains the code that demonstrates exception handling.

Defining an Exception Class to Represent the Type of Problem That Might Occur

Figure 17.1 defines class DivideByZeroException as a derived class of Standard Library class runtime_error (from header <stdexcept>). Class runtime_error—a derived class of **exception** (from header <exception>)—is the C++ standard base class for representing runtime errors. Class exception is the standard C++ base class for exception in the C++ Standard Library. (Section 17.10 discusses class exception and its derived classes in detail.) A typical exception class that derives from the runtime_error class defines only a constructor (e.g., lines 11–12) that passes an error-message string to the base-class runtime_error constructor. Every exception class that derives directly or indirectly from exception contains the virtual function **what**, which returns an exception object's error message. You're not required to derive a custom exception class, such as DivideByZeroException, from the standard exception classes provided by C++. However, doing so allows you to use the virtual function what to obtain an appropriate error message. We use an object of this DivideByZeroException class in Fig. 17.2 to indicate when an attempt is made to divide by zero.

```
I   // Fig. 17.1: DivideByZeroException.h
2   // Class DivideByZeroException definition.
3   #include <stdexcept> // stdexcept header contains runtime_error
4
5   // DivideByZeroException objects should be thrown by functions
6   // upon detecting division-by-zero exceptions
7   class DivideByZeroException : public std::runtime_error
8   {
9   public:
10     // constructor specifies default error message
11     DivideByZeroException()
12        : std::runtime_error( "attempted to divide by zero" ) {}
13  }; // end class DivideByZeroException
```

Fig. 17.1 | Class DivideByZeroException definition.

Demonstrating Exception Handling

Figure 17.2 uses exception handling to wrap code that might throw a DivideByZeroException and to handle that exception, should one occur. The user enters two integers, which are passed as arguments to function quotient (lines 10–18). This function divides its first parameter (numerator) by its second parameter (denominator). Assuming that the user does not specify 0 as the denominator for the division, function quotient returns the division result. If the user inputs 0 for the denominator, quotient throws an exception. In the sample output, the first two lines show a successful calculation, and the next two show a failure due to an attempt to divide by zero. When the exception occurs, the program informs the user of the mistake and prompts the user to input two new integers. After we discuss the code, we'll consider the user inputs and flow of program control that yield *these outputs*.

```
1   // Fig. 17.2: fig17_02.cpp
2   // Example that throws exceptions on
3   // attempts to divide by zero.
4   #include <iostream>
5   #include "DivideByZeroException.h" // DivideByZeroException class
6   using namespace std;
7
8   // perform division and throw DivideByZeroException object if
9   // divide-by-zero exception occurs
10  double quotient( int numerator, int denominator )
11  {
12     // throw DivideByZeroException if trying to divide by zero
13     if ( denominator == 0 )
14        throw DivideByZeroException(); // terminate function
15
16     // return division result
17     return static_cast< double >( numerator ) / denominator;
18  } // end function quotient
19
20  int main()
21  {
22     int number1; // user-specified numerator
23     int number2; // user-specified denominator
24
25     cout << "Enter two integers (end-of-file to end): ";
26
27     // enable user to enter two integers to divide
28     while ( cin >> number1 >> number2 )
29     {
30        // try block contains code that might throw exception
31        // and code that will not execute if an exception occurs
32        try
33        {
34           double result = quotient( number1, number2 );
35           cout << "The quotient is: " << result << endl;
36        } // end try
37        catch ( DivideByZeroException &divideByZeroException )
38        {
```

Fig. 17.2 | Example that throws exceptions on attempts to divide by zero. (Part 1 of 2.)

```
39                 cout << "Exception occurred: "
40                     << divideByZeroException.what() << endl;
41         } // end catch
42
43         cout << "\nEnter two integers (end-of-file to end): ";
44     } // end while
45
46     cout << endl;
47 } // end main
```

```
Enter two integers (end-of-file to end): 100 7
The quotient is: 14.2857

Enter two integers (end-of-file to end): 100 0
Exception occurred: attempted to divide by zero

Enter two integers (end-of-file to end): ^Z
```

Fig. 17.2 | Example that throws exceptions on attempts to divide by zero. (Part 2 of 2.)

Enclosing Code in a try Block

The program begins by prompting the user to enter two integers. The integers are input in the condition of the while loop (line 28). Line 34 passes the values to function quotient (lines 10–18), which either divides the integers and returns a result, or throws an exception (i.e., indicates that an error occurred) on an attempt to divide by zero. Exception handling is geared to situations in which the function that detects an error is unable to handle it.

As you learned in Section 7.10, try blocks enable exception handling, enclosing statements that might cause exceptions and statements that should be skipped if an exception occurs. The try block in lines 32–36 encloses the invocation of function quotient and the statement that displays the division result. In this example, because the invocation of function quotient (line 34) can *throw* an exception, we enclose this function invocation in a try block. Enclosing the output statement (line 35) in the try block ensures that the output will occur *only* if function quotient returns a result.

Software Engineering Observation 17.3

Exceptions may surface through explicitly mentioned code in a try block, through calls to other functions and through deeply nested function calls initiated by code in a try block.

Defining a catch Handler to Process a DivideByZeroException

You saw in Section 7.10 that exceptions are processed by catch handlers. At least one catch handler (lines 37–41) *must* immediately follow each try block. An exception parameter should *always* be declared as a *reference* to the type of exception the catch handler can process (DivideByZeroException in this case)—this prevents copying the exception object when it's caught and allows a catch handler to properly catch derived-class exceptions as well. When an exception occurs in a try block, the catch handler that executes is the first one whose type *matches* the type of the exception that occurred (i.e., the type in the catch block matches the thrown exception type exactly or is a *direct or indirect* base class of it). If an exception parameter includes an *optional* parameter name, the catch handler can use that parameter name to interact with the caught exception in the body of the catch handler, which is delimited by braces ({ and }). A catch handler typically reports the error to the user, logs it to a file, terminates the program gracefully or tries an alternate strategy to accomplish the failed task. In this example, the catch handler simply reports that the user attempted to divide by zero. Then the program prompts the user to enter two new integer values.

Common Programming Error 17.1

It's a syntax error to place code between a try block and its corresponding catch handlers or between its catch handlers.

Common Programming Error 17.2

Each catch handler can have only a single parameter—specifying a comma-separated list of exception parameters is a syntax error.

Common Programming Error 17.3

It's a compilation error to catch the same type in multiple catch handlers following a single try block.

Termination Model of Exception Handling

If an exception occurs as the result of a statement in a try block, the try block expires (i.e., terminates immediately). Next, the program searches for the first catch handler that can process the type of exception that occurred. The program locates the matching catch by comparing the thrown exception's type to each catch's exception-parameter type until the program finds a match. A match occurs if the types are *identical* or if the thrown exception's type is a *derived class* of the exception-parameter type. When a match occurs, the code in the matching catch handler executes. When a catch handler finishes processing by reaching its closing right brace (}), the exception is considered handled and the local variables defined within the catch handler (including the catch parameter) go out of scope. Program control does *not* return to the point at which the exception occurred (known as the throw point), because the try block has *expired*. Rather, control resumes with the first statement (line 43) after the last catch handler following the try block. This is known as the termination model of exception handling. Some languages use the resumption model of exception handling, in which, after an exception is handled, control resumes just after the throw point. As with any other block of code, *when a try block terminates, local variables defined in the block go out of scope.*

Common Programming Error 17.4

Logic errors can occur if you assume that after an exception is handled, control will return to the first statement after the throw point.

Error-Prevention Tip 17.2

With exception handling, a program can continue executing (rather than terminating) after dealing with a problem. This helps ensure the kind of robust applications that contribute to what's called mission-critical computing or business-critical computing.

If the try block completes its execution successfully (i.e., no exceptions occur in the try block), then the program ignores the catch handlers and program control continues with the first statement after the last catch following that try block.

If an exception that occurs in a try block has *no* matching catch handler, or if an exception occurs in a statement that is *not* in a try block, the function that contains the statement terminates immediately, and the program attempts to locate an enclosing try block in the calling function. This process is called **stack unwinding** and is discussed in Section 17.4.

Flow of Program Control When the User Enters a Nonzero Denominator

Consider the flow of control when the user inputs the numerator 100 and the denominator 7. In line 13, function quotient determines that the denominator is not zero, so line 17 performs the division and returns the result (14.2857) to line 34 as a double. Program control then continues sequentially from line 34, so line 35 displays the division result—line 36 ends the try block. Because the try block completed successfully and did *not* throw an exception, the program does *not* execute the statements contained in the catch handler (lines 37–41), and control continues to line 43 (the first line of code after the catch handler), which prompts the user to enter two more integers.

Flow of Program Control When the User Enters a Denominator of Zero

Now consider the case in which the user inputs the numerator 100 and the denominator 0. In line 13, quotient determines that the denominator is zero, which indicates an attempt to divide by zero. Line 14 throws an exception, which we represent as an object of class DivideByZeroException (Fig. 17.1).

To throw an exception, line 14 in Fig. 17.2 uses keyword **throw** followed by an operand of the type of exception to throw. Normally, a throw statement specifies *one* operand. (In Section 17.3, we discuss how to use a throw statement with *no* operand.) The operand of a throw can be of *any* type (but it must be copy constructable). If the operand is an object, we call it an **exception object**—in this example, the exception object is of type DivideByZeroException. However, a throw operand also can assume other values, such as the value of an expression that does *not* result in an object of a class (e.g., throw x > 5) or the value of an int (e.g., throw 5). The examples in this chapter focus exclusively on throwing objects of exception classes.

Error-Prevention Tip 17.3
In general, you should throw only objects of exception class types.

As part of throwing an exception, the throw operand is created and used to initialize the parameter in the catch handler, which we discuss momentarily. The throw statement in line 14 creates a DivideByZeroException object. When line 14 throws the exception, function quotient exits immediately. So, line 14 throws the exception *before* function quotient can perform the division in line 17. This is a central characteristic of exception handling: *If your program explicitly throws an exception, it should do so before the error has an opportunity to occur.*

Because we enclosed the call to quotient (line 34) in a try block, program control enters the catch handler (lines 37–41) that immediately follows the try block. This catch handler serves as the exception handler for the divide-by-zero exception. In general, when an exception is thrown within a try block, the exception is caught by a catch handler that specifies the type matching the thrown exception. In this program, the catch handler specifies that it catches DivideByZeroException objects—this type matches the object type thrown in function quotient. Actually, the catch handler catches a *reference* to the

DivideByZeroException object created by function quotient's throw statement (line 14), so that the catch handler does *not* make a copy of the exception object.

The catch's body (lines 39–40) prints the error message returned by function what of base-class runtime_error—i.e., the string that the DivideByZeroException constructor (lines 11–12 in Fig. 17.1) passed to the runtime_error base-class constructor.

Good Programming Practice 17.1

Associating each type of runtime error with an appropriately named exception type improves program clarity.

17.3 Rethrowing an Exception

A function might use a resource—like a file—and might want to release the resource (i.e., close the file) if an exception occurs. An exception handler, upon receiving an exception, can release the resource then notify its caller than an exception occurred by **rethrowing the exception** via the statement

```
throw;
```

Regardless of whether a handler can process an exception, the handler can *rethrow* the exception for further processing outside the handler. The next enclosing try block detects the rethrown exception, which a catch handler listed after that enclosing try block attempts to handle.

Common Programming Error 17.5

Executing an empty throw statement outside a catch handler abandons exception processing and terminates the program immediately.

The program of Fig. 17.3 demonstrates rethrowing an exception. In main's try block (lines 29–34), line 32 calls function throwException (lines 8–24). The throwException function also contains a try block (lines 11–15), from which the throw statement in line 14 throws an instance of standard-library-class exception. Function throwException's catch handler (lines 16–21) catches this exception, prints an error message (lines 18–19) and rethrows the exception (line 20). This terminates function throwException and returns control to line 32 in the try...catch block in main. The try block *terminates* (so line 33 does *not* execute), and the catch handler in main (lines 35–38) catches this exception and prints an error message (line 37). Since we do not use the exception parameters in the catch handlers of this example, we omit the exception parameter names and specify only the type of exception to catch (lines 16 and 35).

```
1    // Fig. 17.3: fig17_03.cpp
2    // Rethrowing an exception.
3    #include <iostream>
4    #include <exception>
5    using namespace std;
6
```

Fig. 17.3 | Rethrowing an exception. (Part 1 of 2.)

```
 7   // throw, catch and rethrow exception
 8   void throwException()
 9   {
10      // throw exception and catch it immediately
11      try
12      {
13         cout << "  Function throwException throws an exception\n";
14         throw exception(); // generate exception
15      } // end try
16      catch ( exception & ) // handle exception
17      {
18         cout << "  Exception handled in function throwException"
19            << "\n  Function throwException rethrows exception";
20         throw; // rethrow exception for further processing
21      } // end catch
22
23      cout << "This also should not print\n";
24   } // end function throwException
25
26   int main()
27   {
28      // throw exception
29      try
30      {
31         cout << "\nmain invokes function throwException\n";
32         throwException();
33         cout << "This should not print\n";
34      } // end try
35      catch ( exception & ) // handle exception
36      {
37         cout << "\n\nException handled in main\n";
38      } // end catch
39
40      cout << "Program control continues after catch in main\n";
41   } // end main
```

```
main invokes function throwException
  Function throwException throws an exception
  Exception handled in function throwException
  Function throwException rethrows exception

Exception handled in main
Program control continues after catch in main
```

Fig. 17.3 | Rethrowing an exception. (Part 2 of 2.)

17.4 Stack Unwinding

When an exception is thrown but not caught in a particular scope, the function call stack is "unwound," and an attempt is made to catch the exception in the next outer try...catch block. Unwinding the function call stack means that the function in which the exception was not caught terminates, all local variables that have completed intitialization in that function are destroyed and control returns to the statement that originally invoked that function. If a try block encloses that statement, an attempt is made to catch the exception. If a try block does *not* enclose that statement, stack unwinding occurs again. If no catch handler ever catches this exception, the program terminates. The program of Fig. 17.4 demonstrates stack unwinding.

```cpp
1   // Fig. 17.4: fig17_04.cpp
2   // Demonstrating stack unwinding.
3   #include <iostream>
4   #include <stdexcept>
5   using namespace std;
6
7   // function3 throws runtime error
8   void function3()
9   {
10     cout << "In function 3" << endl;
11
12     // no try block, stack unwinding occurs, return control to function2
13     throw runtime_error( "runtime_error in function3" ); // no print
14  } // end function3
15
16  // function2 invokes function3
17  void function2()
18  {
19     cout << "function3 is called inside function2" << endl;
20     function3(); // stack unwinding occurs, return control to function1
21  } // end function2
22
23  // function1 invokes function2
24  void function1()
25  {
26     cout << "function2 is called inside function1" << endl;
27     function2(); // stack unwinding occurs, return control to main
28  } // end function1
29
30  // demonstrate stack unwinding
31  int main()
32  {
33     // invoke function1
34     try
35     {
36        cout << "function1 is called inside main" << endl;
37        function1(); // call function1 which throws runtime_error
38     } // end try
39     catch ( runtime_error &error ) // handle runtime error
40     {
41        cout << "Exception occurred: " << error.what() << endl;
42        cout << "Exception handled in main" << endl;
43     } // end catch
44  } // end main
```

Fig. 17.4 | Stack unwinding. (Part 1 of 2.)

```
function1 is called inside main
function2 is called inside function1
function3 is called inside function2
In function 3
Exception occurred: runtime_error in function3
Exception handled in main
```

Fig. 17.4 | Stack unwinding. (Part 2 of 2.)

In main, the try block (lines 34–38) calls function1 (lines 24–28). Next, function1 calls function2 (lines 17–21), which in turn calls function3 (lines 8–14). Line 13 of function3 throws a runtime_error object. However, because no try block encloses the throw statement in line 13, stack unwinding occurs—function3 terminates at line 13, then returns control to the statement in function2 that invoked function3 (i.e., line 20). Because no try block encloses line 20, stack unwinding occurs again—function2 terminates at line 20 and returns control to the statement in function1 that invoked function2 (i.e., line 27). Because no try block encloses line 27, stack unwinding occurs one more time—function1 terminates at line 27 and returns control to the statement in main that invoked function1 (i.e., line 37). The try block of lines 34–38 encloses this statement, so the first matching catch handler located after this try block (line 39–43) catches and processes the exception. Line 41 uses function what to display the exception message.

17.5 When to Use Exception Handling

Exception handling is designed to process **synchronous errors**, which occur when a statement executes, such as *out-of-range array subscripts*, *arithmetic overflow* (i.e., a value outside the representable range of values), *division by zero*, *invalid function parameters* and *unsuccessful memory allocation* (due to lack of memory). Exception handling is not designed to process errors associated with **asynchronous events** (e.g., disk I/O completions, network message arrivals, mouse clicks and keystrokes), which occur in parallel with, and independent of, the program's flow of control.

Software Engineering Observation 17.4

Exception handling provides a single, uniform technique for processing problems. This helps programmers on large projects understand each other's error-processing code.

Software Engineering Observation 17.5

Exception handling enables predefined software components to communicate problems to application-specific components, which can then process the problems in an application-specific manner.

Exception handling also is useful for processing problems that occur when a program interacts with software elements, such as member functions, constructors, destructors and classes. Such software elements often use exceptions to notify programs when problems occur. This enables you to implement *customized error handling* for each application.

Software Engineering Observation 17.6

Functions with common error conditions should return nullptr, 0 *or other appropriate values, such as* bools, *rather than throw exceptions. A program calling such a function can check the return value to determine success or failure of the function call.*

Complex applications normally consist of predefined software components and application-specific components that use the predefined components. When a predefined component encounters a problem, that component needs a mechanism to communicate the problem to the application-specific component—*the predefined component cannot know in advance how each application processes a problem that occurs.*

C++11: Declaring Functions That Do Not Throw Exceptions

As of C++11, if a function does not throw any exceptions *and* does not call any functions that throw exceptions, you should explicitly state that a function *does not* throw exceptions. This indicates to client-code programmers that there's no need to place calls to the function in a try block. Simply add **noexcept** to the right of the function's parameter list in both the prototype and the definition. For a const member function, place noexcept after const. If a function that's declared noexcept calls another function that throws an exception or executes a throw statement, the program terminates. We'll say more about noexcept in Chapter 24.

17.6 Constructors, Destructors and Exception Handling

First, let's discuss an issue that we've mentioned but not yet resolved satisfactorily: What happens when an error is detected in a *constructor*? For example, how should an object's constructor respond when it receives invalid data? Because the constructor *cannot return a value* to indicate an error, we must choose an alternative means of indicating that the object has not been constructed properly. One scheme is to return the improperly constructed object and hope that anyone using it would make appropriate tests to determine that it's in an inconsistent state. Another scheme is to set some variable outside the constructor. The preferred alternative is to require the constructor to throw an exception that contains the error information, thus offering an opportunity for the program to handle the failure.

Before an exception is thrown by a constructor, destructors are called for any member objects whose constructors have run to completion as part of the object being constructed. Destructors are called for every automatic object constructed in a try block before the exception is caught. Stack unwinding is guaranteed to have been completed at the point that an exception handler begins executing. If a destructor invoked as a result of stack unwinding throws an exception, the program terminates. This has been linked to various security attacks.

Error-Prevention Tip 17.4

Destructors should catch exceptions to prevent program termination.

Error-Prevention Tip 17.5

Do not throw exceptions from the constructor of an object with static storage duration. Such exceptions cannot be caught.

If an object has member objects, and if an exception is thrown before the outer object is fully constructed, then destructors will be executed for the member objects that have been constructed prior to the occurrence of the exception. If an array of objects has been partially constructed when an exception occurs, only the destructors for the constructed objects in the array will be called.

Error-Prevention Tip 17.6

When an exception is thrown from the constructor for an object that's created in a new *expression, the dynamically allocated memory for that object is released.*

Error-Prevention Tip 17.7

A constructor should throw an exception if a problem occurs while initializing an object. Before doing so, the constructor should release any memory that it dynamically allocated.

Initializing Local Objects to Acquire Resources

An exception could preclude the operation of code that would normally *release a resource* (such as memory or a file), thus causing a **resource leak** that prevents other programs from acquiring the resource. One technique to resolve this problem is to initialize a local object to acquire the resource. When an exception occurs, the destructor for that object will be invoked and can free the resource.

17.7 Exceptions and Inheritance

Various exception classes can be derived from a common base class, as we discussed in Section 17.2, when we created class `DivideByZeroException` as a derived class of class `exception`. If a `catch` handler catches a reference to an exception object of a base-class type, it also can `catch` a reference to all objects of classes publicly derived from that base class—this allows for polymorphic processing of related exceptions.

Error-Prevention Tip 17.8

Using inheritance with exceptions enables an exception handler to catch *related errors with concise notation. One approach is to* catch *each type of reference to a derived-class exception object individually, but a more concise approach is to* catch *pointers or references to base-class exception objects instead. Also, catching pointers or references to derived-class exception objects individually is error prone, especially if you forget to test explicitly for one or more of the derived-class reference types.*

17.8 Processing new Failures

When operator new fails, it throws a **bad_alloc** exception (defined in header <new>).In this section, we present two examples of new failing. The first uses the version of new that throws a bad_alloc exception when new fails. The second uses function **set_new_handler** to handle new failures. [*Note:* The examples in Figs. 17.5–17.6 allocate large amounts of dynamic memory, which could cause your computer to become sluggish.]

new Throwing **bad_alloc** *on Failure*

Figure 17.5 demonstrates new *implicitly* throwing bad_alloc on failure to allocate the requested memory. The `for` statement (lines 16–20) inside the `try` block should loop 50 times and, on each pass, allocate an array of 50,000,000 double values. If new fails and throws a bad_alloc exception, the loop terminates, and the program continues in line 22, where the catch handler catches and processes the exception. Lines 24–25 print the message "Exception occurred:" followed by the message returned from the base-class-exception version of function what (i.e., an implementation-defined exception-specific message, such as "bad allocation" in Microsoft Visual C++). The output shows that the program performed only four iterations of the loop before new failed and threw the bad_alloc exception. Your output might differ based on the physical memory, disk space available for virtual memory on your system and the compiler you're using.

```cpp
1   // Fig. 17.5: fig17_05.cpp
2   // Demonstrating standard new throwing bad_alloc when memory
3   // cannot be allocated.
4   #include <iostream>
5   #include <new> // bad_alloc class is defined here
6   using namespace std;
7
8   int main()
9   {
10     double *ptr[ 50 ];
11
12     // aim each ptr[i] at a big block of memory
13     try
14     {
15       // allocate memory for ptr[ i ]; new throws bad_alloc on failure
16       for ( size_t i = 0; i < 50; ++i )
17       {
18         ptr[ i ] = new double[ 50000000 ]; // may throw exception
19         cout << "ptr[" << i << "] points to 50,000,000 new doubles\n";
20       } // end for
21     } // end try
22     catch ( bad_alloc &memoryAllocationException )
23     {
24       cerr << "Exception occurred: "
25         << memoryAllocationException.what() << endl;
26     } // end catch
27   } // end main
```

```
ptr[0] points to 50,000,000 new doubles
ptr[1] points to 50,000,000 new doubles
ptr[2] points to 50,000,000 new doubles
ptr[3] points to 50,000,000 new doubles
Exception occurred: bad allocation
```

Fig. 17.5 | new throwing bad_alloc on failure.

new Returning nullptr *on Failure*
The C++ standard specifies that programmers can use an older version of new that returns nullptr upon failure. For this purpose, header <new> defines object **nothrow** (of type nothrow_t), which is used as follows:

```cpp
double *ptr = new( nothrow ) double[ 50000000 ];
```

The preceding statement uses the version of new that does *not* throw bad_alloc exceptions (i.e., nothrow) to allocate an array of 50,000,000 doubles.

> **Software Engineering Observation 17.7**
> *To make programs more robust, use the version of new that throws bad_alloc exceptions on failure.*

Handling *new* Failures Using Function *set_new_handler*

An additional feature for handling new failures is function set_new_handler (prototyped in standard header <new>). This function takes as its argument a pointer to a function that takes no arguments and returns void. This pointer points to the function that will be called if new fails. This provides you with a uniform approach to handling all new failures, regardless of where a failure occurs in the program. Once set_new_handler registers a **new handler** in the program, operator new does *not* throw bad_alloc on failure; rather, it defers the error handling to the new-handler function.

If new allocates memory successfully, it returns a pointer to that memory. If new fails to allocate memory and set_new_handler did not register a new-handler function, new throws a bad_alloc exception. If new fails to allocate memory and a new-handler function has been registered, the new-handler function is called. The new-handler function should perform one of the following tasks:

1. Make more memory available by deleting other dynamically allocated memory (or telling the user to close other applications) and return to operator new to attempt to allocate memory again.

2. Throw an exception of type bad_alloc.

3. Call function abort or exit (both found in header <cstdlib>) to terminate the program. These were introduced in Section 9.7.

Figure 17.6 demonstrates set_new_handler. Function customNewHandler (lines 9–13) prints an error message (line 11), then calls abort (line 12) to terminate the program. The output shows that the loop iterated four times before new failed and invoked function customNewHandler. Your output might differ based on the physical memory, disk space available for virtual memory on your system and your compiler.

```
1   // Fig. 17.6: fig17_06.cpp
2   // Demonstrating set_new_handler.
3   #include <iostream>
4   #include <new> // set_new_handler function prototype
5   #include <cstdlib> // abort function prototype
6   using namespace std;
7
8   // handle memory allocation failure
9   void customNewHandler()
10  {
11     cerr << "customNewHandler was called";
12     abort();
13  } // end function customNewHandler
```

Fig. 17.6 | set_new_handler specifying the function to call when new fails. (Part 1 of 2.)

```
14
15   // using set_new_handler to handle failed memory allocation
16   int main()
17   {
18      double *ptr[ 50 ];
19
20      // specify that customNewHandler should be called on
21      // memory allocation failure
22      set_new_handler( customNewHandler );
23
24      // aim each ptr[i] at a big block of memory; customNewHandler will be
25      // called on failed memory allocation
26      for ( size_t i = 0; i < 50; ++i )
27      {
28         ptr[ i ] = new double[ 50000000 ]; // may throw exception
29         cout << "ptr[" << i << "] points to 50,000,000 new doubles\n";
30      } // end for
31   } // end main
```

```
ptr[0] points to 50,000,000 new doubles
ptr[1] points to 50,000,000 new doubles
ptr[2] points to 50,000,000 new doubles
ptr[3] points to 50,000,000 new doubles
customNewHandler was called
```

Fig. 17.6 | `set_new_handler` specifying the function to call when new fails. (Part 2 of 2.)

17.9 Class `unique_ptr` and Dynamic Memory Allocation

A common programming practice is to *allocate* dynamic memory, assign the address of that memory to a pointer, use the pointer to manipulate the memory and *deallocate* the memory with `delete` when the memory is no longer needed. If an exception occurs after successful memory allocation but *before* the `delete` statement executes, a *memory leak* could occur. C++11 provides class template **`unique_ptr`** in header **`<memory>`** to deal with this situation.

An object of class `unique_ptr` maintains a pointer to dynamically allocated memory. When a `unique_ptr` object destructor is called (for example, when a `unique_ptr` object goes out of scope), it performs a `delete` operation on its pointer data member. Class template `unique_ptr` provides overloaded operators * and -> so that a `unique_ptr` object can be used just as a regular pointer variable is. Figure 17.9 demonstrates a `unique_ptr` object that points to a dynamically allocated object of class `Integer` (Figs. 17.7–17.8).

```
1   // Fig. 17.7: Integer.h
2   // Integer class definition.
3
4   class Integer
5   {
```

Fig. 17.7 | `Integer` class definition. (Part 1 of 2.)

```
 6   public:
 7      Integer( int i = 0 ); // Integer default constructor
 8      ~Integer(); // Integer destructor
 9      void setInteger( int i ); // set Integer value
10      int getInteger() const; // return Integer value
11   private:
12      int value;
13   }; // end class Integer
```

Fig. 17.7 | Integer class definition. (Part 2 of 2.)

```
 1   // Fig. 17.8: Integer.cpp
 2   // Integer member function definitions.
 3   #include <iostream>
 4   #include "Integer.h"
 5   using namespace std;
 6
 7   // Integer default constructor
 8   Integer::Integer( int i )
 9      : value( i )
10   {
11      cout << "Constructor for Integer " << value << endl;
12   } // end Integer constructor
13
14   // Integer destructor
15   Integer::~Integer()
16   {
17      cout << "Destructor for Integer " << value << endl;
18   } // end Integer destructor
19
20   // set Integer value
21   void Integer::setInteger( int i )
22   {
23      value = i;
24   } // end function setInteger
25
26   // return Integer value
27   int Integer::getInteger() const
28   {
29      return value;
30   } // end function getInteger
```

Fig. 17.8 | Member function definitions of class Integer.

Line 15 of Fig. 17.9 creates unique_ptr object ptrToInteger and initializes it with a pointer to a dynamically allocated Integer object that contains the value 7. Line 18 uses the unique_ptr overloaded -> operator to invoke function setInteger on the Integer object that ptrToInteger manages. Line 21 uses the unique_ptr overloaded * operator to dereference ptrToInteger, then uses the dot (.) operator to invoke function getInteger on the Integer object. Like a regular pointer, a unique_ptr's -> and * overloaded operators can be used to access the object to which the unique_ptr points.

```
 1   // Fig. 17.9: fig17_09.cpp
 2   // Demonstrating unique_ptr.
 3   #include <iostream>
 4   #include <memory>
 5   using namespace std;
 6
 7   #include "Integer.h"
 8
 9   // use unique_ptr to manipulate Integer object
10   int main()
11   {
12      cout << "Creating a unique_ptr object that points to an Integer\n";
13
14      // "aim" unique_ptr at Integer object
15      unique_ptr< Integer > ptrToInteger( new Integer( 7 ) );
16
17      cout << "\nUsing the unique_ptr to manipulate the Integer\n";
18      ptrToInteger->setInteger( 99 ); // use unique_ptr to set Integer value
19
20      // use unique_ptr to get Integer value
21      cout << "Integer after setInteger: " << ( *ptrToInteger ).getInteger()
22         << "\n\nTerminating program" << endl;
23   } // end main
```

```
Creating a unique_ptr object that points to an Integer
Constructor for Integer 7

Using the unique_ptr to manipulate the Integer
Integer after setInteger: 99

Terminating program
Destructor for Integer 99
```

Fig. 17.9 | `unique_ptr` object manages dynamically allocated memory.

Because `ptrToInteger` is a local automatic variable in `main`, `ptrToInteger` is destroyed when `main` terminates. The `unique_ptr` destructor forces a `delete` of the `Integer` object pointed to by `ptrToInteger`, which in turn calls the `Integer` class destructor. The memory that `Integer` occupies is released, regardless of how control leaves the block (e.g., by a `return` statement or by an exception). Most importantly, using this technique can *prevent memory leaks*. For example, suppose a function returns a pointer aimed at some object. Unfortunately, the function caller that receives this pointer might not `delete` the object, thus resulting in *a memory leak*. However, if the function returns a `unique_ptr` to the object, the object will be deleted automatically when the `unique_ptr` object's destructor gets called.

unique_ptr Notes
The class is called `unique_ptr` because only *one* `unique_ptr` at a time can own a dynamically allocated object. By using its overloaded assignment operator or copy constructor, a `unique_ptr` can *transfer ownership* of the dynamic memory it manages. The *last* `unique_ptr` object that maintains the pointer to the dynamic memory will delete the

memory. This makes `unique_ptr` an ideal mechanism for returning dynamically allocated memory to client code. When the `unique_ptr` goes out of scope in the *client* code, the `unique_ptr`'s destructor destroys the dynamically allocated object and deletes its memory.

unique_ptr to a Built-In Array

You can also use a `unique_ptr` to manage a dynamically allocated built-in array. For example, consider the statement

```
unique_ptr< string[] > ptr( new string[ 10 ] );
```

which dynamically allocates an array of 10 `strings` managed by `ptr`. The type `string[]` indicates that the managed memory is a built-in array containing `strings`. When a `unique_ptr` that manages an array goes out of scope it deletes the memory with `delete []` so that every element of the array receives a destructor call.

A `unique_ptr` that manages an array provides an overloaded `[]` operator for accessing the array's elements. For example, the statement

```
ptr[ 2 ] = "hello";
```

assigns `"hello"` to the `string` at `ptr[2]` and the statement

```
cout << ptr[ 2 ] << endl;
```

displays that `string`.

17.10 Standard Library Exception Hierarchy

Experience has shown that exceptions fall nicely into a number of categories. The C++ Standard Library includes a hierarchy of exception classes, some of which are shown in Fig. 17.10. As we first discussed in Section 17.2, this hierarchy is headed by base-class exception (defined in header `<exception>`), which contains `virtual` function `what` that derived classes can override to issue appropriate error messages.

Immediate derived classes of base-class exception include `runtime_error` and `logic_error` (both defined in header `<stdexcept>`), each of which has several derived classes. Also derived from exception are the exceptions thrown by C++ operators—for example, `bad_alloc` is thrown by `new` (Section 17.8), `bad_cast` is thrown by `dynamic_cast` (Chapter 12) and `bad_typeid` is thrown by `typeid` (Chapter 12).

Common Programming Error 17.6

Placing a catch handler that catches a base-class object before a catch that catches an object of a class derived from that base class is a logic error. The base-class catch catches all objects of classes derived from that base class, so the derived-class catch will never execute.

Class `logic_error` is the base class of several standard exception classes that indicate errors in program logic. For example, class `invalid_argument` indicates that a function received an invalid argument. (Proper coding can, of course, prevent invalid arguments from reaching a function.) Class `length_error` indicates that a length larger than the maximum size allowed for the object being manipulated was used for that object. Class `out_of_range` indicates that a value, such as a subscript into an array, exceeded its allowed range of values.

Class `runtime_error`, which we used briefly in Section 17.4, is the base class of several other standard exception classes that indicate execution-time errors. For example, class

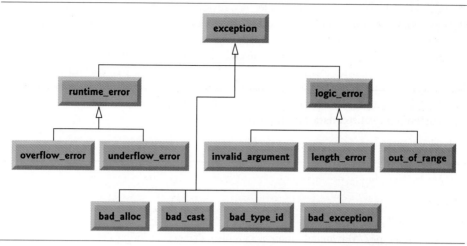

Fig. 17.10 | Some of the Standard Library exception classes.

`overflow_error` describes an arithmetic overflow error (i.e., the result of an arithmetic operation is larger than the largest number that can be stored in the computer) and class `underflow_error` describes an arithmetic underflow error (i.e., the result of an arithmetic operation is smaller than the smallest number that can be stored in the computer).

Common Programming Error 17.7
Exception classes need not be derived from class exception, so catching type exception is not guaranteed to catch all exceptions a program could encounter.

Error-Prevention Tip 17.9
To catch all exceptions potentially thrown in a try block, use catch(...). One weakness with catching exceptions in this way is that the type of the caught exception is unknown. Another weakness is that, without a named parameter, there's no way to refer to the exception object inside the exception handler.

Software Engineering Observation 17.8
The standard exception hierarchy is a good starting point for creating exceptions. You can build programs that can throw standard exceptions, throw exceptions derived from the standard exceptions or throw your own exceptions not derived from the standard exceptions.

Software Engineering Observation 17.9
Use catch(...) to perform recovery that does not depend on the exception type (e.g., releasing common resources). The exception can be rethrown to alert more specific enclosing catch handlers.

17.11 Wrap-Up

In this chapter, you learned how to use exception handling to deal with errors in a program. You learned that exception handling enables you to remove error-handling code from the "main line" of the program's execution. We demonstrated exception handling in the context of a divide-by-zero example. We reviewed how to use try blocks to enclose code that may throw an exception, and how to use catch handlers to deal with exceptions that may arise. You learned how to throw and rethrow exceptions, and how to handle the exceptions that occur in constructors. The chapter continued with discussions of processing new failures, dynamic memory allocation with class unique_ptr and the standard library exception hierarchy. In the next chapter, you'll learn how to build your own custom class templates. In particular, we'll demonstrate the features that you'll need to build your own custom templatized data structures in Chapter 19.

Summary

Section 17.1 Introduction

- An exception (p. 775) is an indication of a problem that occurs during a program's execution.
- Exception handling (p. 775) enables you to create programs that can resolve problems that occur at execution time—often allowing programs to continue executing as if no problems had been encountered. More severe problems may require a program to notify the user of the problem before terminating in a controlled manner.

Section 17.2 Example: Handling an Attempt to Divide by Zero

- Class exception is the standard base class for exceptions classes (p. 776). It provides virtual function what (p. 776) that returns an appropriate error message and can be overridden in derived classes.
- Class runtime_error (p. 776), which is defined in header <stdexcept> (p. 776), is the C++ standard base class for representing runtime errors.
- C++ uses the termination model (p. 779) of exception handling.
- A try block consists of keyword try followed by braces ({}) that define a block of code in which exceptions might occur. The try block encloses statements that might cause exceptions and statements that should not execute if exceptions occur.
- At least one catch handler must immediately follow a try block. Each catch handler specifies an exception parameter that represents the type of exception the catch handler can process.
- If an exception parameter includes an optional parameter name, the catch handler can use that parameter name to interact with a caught exception object (p. 780).
- The point in the program at which an exception occurs is called the throw point (p. 779).
- If an exception occurs in a try block, the try block expires and program control transfers to the first catch in which the exception parameter's type matches that of the thrown exception.
- When a try block terminates, local variables defined in the block go out of scope.
- When a try block terminates due to an exception, the program searches for the first catch handler that matches the type of exception that occurred. A match occurs if the types are identical or if the thrown exception's type is a derived class of the exception-parameter type. When a match occurs, the code contained within the matching catch handler executes.
- When a catch handler finishes processing, the catch parameter and local variables defined within the catch handler go out of scope. Any remaining catch handlers that correspond to the try block are ignored, and execution resumes at the first line of code after the try...catch sequence.
- If no exceptions occur in a try block, the program ignores the catch handler(s) for that block. Program execution resumes with the next statement after the try...catch sequence.

- If an exception that occurs in a try block has no matching catch handler, or if an exception occurs in a statement that is not in a try block, the function that contains the statement terminates immediately, and the program attempts to locate an enclosing try block in the calling function. This process is called stack unwinding (p. 780).

- To throw an exception, use keyword throw followed by an operand that represents the type of exception to throw. The operand of a throw can be of any type.

Section 17.3 Rethrowing an Exception
- The exception handler can defer the exception handling (or perhaps a portion of it) to another exception handler. In either case, the handler achieves this by rethrowing the exception (p. 781).

- Common examples of exceptions are out-of-range array subscripts, arithmetic overflow, division by zero, invalid function parameters and unsuccessful memory allocations.

Section 17.4 Stack Unwinding
- Unwinding the function call stack means that the function in which the exception was not caught terminates, all local variables in that function are destroyed and control returns to the statement that originally invoked that function.

Section 17.5 When to Use Exception Handling
- Exception handling is for synchronous errors (p. 784), which occur when a statement executes.

- Exception handling is not designed to process errors associated with asynchronous events (p. 784), which occur in parallel with, and independent of, the program's flow of control.

- As of C++11, if a function does not throw any exceptions and does not call any functions that throw exceptions, you should explicitly declare the function noexcept (p. 785).

Section 17.6 Constructors, Destructors and Exception Handling
- Exceptions thrown by a constructor cause destructors to be called for any objects built as part of the object being constructed before the exception is thrown.

- Each automatic object constructed in a try block is destructed before an exception is thrown.

- Stack unwinding completes before an exception handler begins executing.

- If a destructor invoked as a result of stack unwinding throws an exception, the program terminates.

- If an object has member objects, and if an exception is thrown before the outer object is fully constructed, then destructors will be executed for the member objects that have been constructed before the exception occurs.

- If an array of objects has been partially constructed when an exception occurs, only the destructors for the constructed array element objects will be called.

- When an exception is thrown from the constructor for an object that is created in a new expression, the dynamically allocated memory for that object is released.

Section 17.7 Exceptions and Inheritance
- If a catch handler catches a reference to an exception object of a base-class type, it also can catch a reference to all objects of classes derived publicly from that base class—this allows for polymorphic processing of related errors.

Section 17.8 Processing new Failures
- The C++ standard document specifies that, when operator new fails, it throws a bad_alloc exception (p. 786), which is defined in header <new>.

- Function set_new_handler (p. 786) takes as its argument a pointer to a function that takes no arguments and returns void. This pointer points to the function that will be called if new fails.

- Once `set_new_handler` registers a new handler (p. 788) in the program, operator `new` does not throw `bad_alloc` on failure; rather, it defers the error handling to the new-handler function.

- If `new` allocates memory successfully, it returns a pointer to that memory.

Section 17.9 Class `unique_ptr` and Dynamic Memory Allocation

- If an exception occurs after successful memory allocation but before the `delete` statement executes, a memory leak could occur.

- The C++ Standard Library provides class template `unique_ptr` (p. 789) to deal with memory leaks.

- An object of class `unique_ptr` maintains a pointer to dynamically allocated memory. A `unique_ptr`'s destructor performs a `delete` operation on the `unique_ptr`'s pointer data member.

- Class template `unique_ptr` provides overloaded operators `*` and `->` so that a `unique_ptr` object can be used just as a regular pointer variable is. A `unique_ptr` also transfers ownership of the dynamic memory it manages via its copy constructor and overloaded assignment operator.

Section 17.10 Standard Library Exception Hierarchy

- The C++ Standard Library includes a hierarchy of exception classes. This hierarchy is headed by base-class `exception`.

- Immediate derived classes of base class `exception` include `runtime_error` and `logic_error` (both defined in header `<stdexcept>`), each of which has several derived classes.

- Several operators throw standard exceptions—operator `new` throws `bad_alloc`, operator `dynamic_cast` throws `bad_cast` (p. 792) and operator `typeid` throws `bad_typeid` (p. 792).

Self-Review Exercises

17.1　What is a robust and fault-tolerant program?

17.2　Give several reasons why exception-handling techniques should not be used for conventional program control.

17.3　Why are exceptions appropriate for dealing with errors produced by library functions?

17.4　What is a "throw point"?

17.5　If no exceptions are thrown in a `try` block, where does control proceed to after the `try` block completes execution?

17.6　What happens if an exception is thrown outside a `try` block?

17.7　Give a key advantage and a key disadvantage of using `catch(...)`.

17.8　What happens if no `catch` handler matches the type of a thrown object?

17.9　What happens if several handlers match the type of the thrown object?

17.10　Why would you specify a base-class type as the type of a `catch` handler, then `throw` objects of derived-class types?

17.11　Suppose a `catch` handler with a precise match to an exception object type is available. Under what circumstances might a different handler be executed for exception objects of that type?

17.12　What is stack unwinding?

17.13　What is "termination model of exception handling"?

17.14　What is an exception object?

Answers to Self-Review Exercises

17.1 A robust and fault-tolerant program can deal with problems and continue executing or terminate gracefully.

17.2 (a) Exception handling is designed to handle infrequently occurring situations that often result in program termination, so compiler writers are not required to implement exception handling to perform optimally. (b) Flow of control with conventional control structures generally is clearer and more efficient than with exceptions. (c) Problems can occur because the stack is unwound when an exception occurs and resources allocated prior to the exception might not be freed. (d) The "additional" exceptions make it more difficult for you to handle the larger number of exception cases.

17.3 It's unlikely that a library function will perform error processing that will meet the unique needs of all users.

17.4 Program control does not return to the point at which the exception occurred, known as the throw point.

17.5 The exception handlers (in the catch handlers) for that try block are skipped, and the program resumes execution after the last catch handler.

17.6 An exception thrown outside a try block causes a call to terminate.

17.7 The form catch(...) catches any type of exception thrown in a try block. An advantage is that all possible exceptions will be caught. A disadvantage is that the catch has no parameter, so it cannot reference information in the thrown object and cannot know the cause of the exception.

17.8 This causes the search for a match to continue in the next enclosing try block if there is one. As this process continues, it might eventually be determined that there is no handler in the program that matches the type of the thrown object; in this case, the program terminates.

17.9 The first matching exception handler after the try block is executed.

17.10 This is a nice way to catch related types of exceptions.

17.11 A base-class handler would catch objects of all derived-class types.

17.12 When an exception is thrown but not caught in a particular scope, the function call stack is "unwound," and an attempt is made to catch the exception in the next outer try...catch block.

17.13 Sometimes, program control does not return to the point at which the exception occurred (known as the throw point), because the try block has expired. Then, control resumes with the first statement after the last catch handler following the try block. This is known as the termination model of exception handling.

17.14 To throw an exception, we use the keyword throw followed by an operand of the type of exception to throw. Normally, a throw statement specifies one operand. The operand of a throw can be of any type (but it must be copy constructable). If the operand is an object, we call it an exception object.

Exercises

17.15 *(Exceptional Conditions)* List various exceptional conditions that have occurred throughout this text. List as many additional exceptional conditions as you can. For each of these exceptions, describe briefly how a program typically would handle the exception, using the exception-handling techniques discussed in this chapter. Some typical exceptions are division by zero, arithmetic overflow, array subscript out of bounds, exhaustion of the free store, etc.

17.16 *(Catch Parameter)* Under what circumstances would you not provide a parameter name when defining the type of the object that will be caught by a handler?

17.17 *(throw Statement)* A program contains the statement

```
throw;
```

Where would you normally expect to find such a statement? What if that statement appeared in a different part of the program?

17.18 *(Exception Handling vs. Other Schemes)* Compare and contrast exception handling with the various other error-processing schemes discussed in the text.

17.19 *(Exception Handling and Program Control)* Why should exceptions *not* be used as an alternate form of program control?

17.20 *(Handling Related Exceptions)* Describe a technique for handling related exceptions.

17.21 *(Throwing Exceptions from a* **catch***)* Suppose a program throws an exception and the appropriate exception handler begins executing. Now suppose that the exception handler itself throws the same exception. Does this create infinite recursion? Write a program to check your observation.

17.22 *(Catching Derived-Class Exceptions)* Use inheritance to create various derived classes of runtime_error. Then show that a catch handler specifying the base class can catch derived-class exceptions.

17.23 *(Throwing the Result of a Conditional Expression)* Throw the result of a conditional expression that returns either a double or an int. Provide an int catch handler and a double catch handler. Show that only the double catch handler executes, regardless of whether the int or the double is returned.

17.24 *(Local Variable Destructors)* Write a program illustrating that all destructors for objects constructed in a block are called before an exception is thrown from that block.

17.25 *(Member Object Destructors)* Write a program illustrating that member object destructors are called for only those member objects that were constructed before an exception occurred.

17.26 *(Catching All Exceptions)* Write a program that demonstrates several exception types being caught with the catch(...) exception handler.

17.27 *(Order of Exception Handlers)* Write a program illustrating that the order of exception handlers is important. The first matching handler is the one that executes. Attempt to compile and run your program two different ways to show that two different handlers execute with two different effects.

17.28 *(Constructors Throwing Exceptions)* Write a program that shows a constructor passing information about constructor failure to an exception handler after a try block.

17.29 *(Rethrowing Exceptions)* Write a program that illustrates rethrowing an exception.

17.30 *(Uncaught Exceptions)* Write a program that illustrates that a function with its own try block does not have to catch every possible error generated within the try. Some exceptions can slip through to, and be handled in, outer scopes.

17.31 *(Stack Unwinding)* Write a program that throws an exception from a deeply nested function and still has the catch handler following the try block enclosing the initial call in main catch the exception.

Introduction to Custom Templates

Behind that outside
pattern the dim shapes
get clearer every day.
It is always the same shape,
only very numerous.
—Charlotte Perkins Gilman

Every man of genius sees the
world at a different angle from
his fellows.
—Havelock Ellis

...our special individuality, as
distinguished from our generic
humanity.
—Oliver Wendell Holmes, Sr.

Objectives

In this chapter you'll:

- Use class templates to create groups of related classes.

- Distinguish between class templates and class-template specializations.

- Learn about nontype template parameters.

- Learn about default template arguments.

- Learn about overloading function templates.

18.1 Introduction

In Chapters 7, 15 and 16, you used many of the Standard Library's *prepackaged* templatized containers and algorithms. Function templates (which were introduced in Chapter 6) and **class templates** enable you to conveniently specify a variety of related (overloaded) functions—called **function-template specializations**—or a variety of related classes—called **class-template specializations**, respectively. This is called **generic programming**. Function templates and class templates are like *stencils* out of which we trace shapes; function-template specializations and class-template specializations are like the separate tracings that all have the same shape, but could, for example, be drawn in different colors and textures.

In this chapter, we demonstrate how to create a custom class template and a function template that manipulates objects of our class-template specializations. We focus on the template capabilities you'll need to build the custom templatized data structures that we present in Chapter 19.[1]

18.2 Class Templates

It's possible to *understand* the concept of a stack (a data structure into which we insert items *only* at the *top* and retrieve those items *only* from the *top* in *last-in, first-out order*) *independent of the type of the items* being placed in the stack. However, to *instantiate* a stack, a data type must be specified. This creates a nice opportunity for software reusability—as you already saw with the stack container adapter in Section 15.7.1. Here, we define a stack *generically* then use *type-specific* versions of this generic stack class.

> **Software Engineering Observation 18.1**
> *Class templates encourage software reusability by enabling a variety of type-specific class-template specializations to be instantiated from a single class template.*

Class templates are called **parameterized types**, because they require one or more *type parameters* to specify how to customize a generic class template to form a *class-template specialization*. To produce many specializations you write only one class-template definition (as we'll do shortly). When a particular specialization is needed, you use a concise, simple notation, and the compiler writes the specialization source code. One Stack class template, for example, could thus become the basis for creating many Stack class-template

---

1. Building custom templates is an advanced topic with many features that are beyond the scope of this book.

specializations (such as "Stack of doubles," "Stack of ints," "Stack of Employees," "Stack of Bills," etc.) used in a program.

Common Programming Error 18.1

To create a template specialization with a user-defined type, the user-defined type must meet the template's requirements. For example, the template might compare objects of the user-defined type with < to determine sorting order, or the template might call a specific member function on an object of the user-defined type. If the user-defined type does not overload the required operator or provide the required functions, compilation errors occur.

Creating Class Template Stack<T>

The Stack class-template definition in Fig. 18.1 looks like a conventional class definition, with a few key differences. First, it's preceded by line 7

```
template< typename T >
```

All class templates begin with keyword **template** followed by a list of template parameters enclosed in angle brackets (< and >); each template parameter that represents a type *must* be preceded by either of the *interchangeable* keywords **typename** or **class**. The type parameter T acts as a placeholder for the Stack's element type. The names of type parameters must be *unique* inside a template definition. You need not specifically use identifier T—any valid identifier can be used. The element type is mentioned generically throughout the Stack class-template definition as T (lines 12, 18 and 42). The type parameter becomes associated with a specific type when you create an object using the class template—at that point, the compiler generates a copy of the class template in which all occurrences of the type parameter are replaced with the specified type. Another key difference is that we did *not* separate the class template's interface from its implementation.

Software Engineering Observation 18.2

Templates are typically defined in headers, which are then #included in the appropriate client source-code files. For class templates, this means that the member functions are also defined in the header—typically inside the class definition's body, as we do in Fig. 18.1.

```
1   // Fig. 18.1: Stack.h
2   // Stack class template.
3   #ifndef STACK_H
4   #define STACK_H
5   #include <deque>
6
7   template< typename T >
8   class Stack
9   {
10  public:
11     // return the top element of the Stack
12     T& top()
13     {
14        return stack.front();
15     } // end function template top
```

Fig. 18.1 | Stack class template. (Part 1 of 2.)

```
16
17      // push an element onto the Stack
18      void push( const T &pushValue )
19      {
20         stack.push_front( pushValue );
21      } // end function template push
22
23      // pop an element from the stack
24      void pop()
25      {
26         stack.pop_front();
27      } // end function template pop
28
29      // determine whether Stack is empty
30      bool isEmpty() const
31      {
32         return stack.empty();
33      } // end function template isEmpty
34
35      // return size of Stack
36      size_t size() const
37      {
38         return stack.size();
39      } // end function template size
40
41   private:
42      std::deque< T > stack; // internal representation of the Stack
43   }; // end class template Stack
44
45   #endif
```

Fig. 18.1 | Stack class template. (Part 2 of 2.)

Class Template Stack<T>'s Data Representation

Section 15.7.1 showed that the Standard Library's stack adapter class can use various containers to store its elements. Of course, a stack requires insertions and deletions *only* at its *top*. So, for example, a vector or a deque could be used to store the stack's elements. A vector supports fast insertions and deletions at its *back*. A deque supports fast insertions and deletions at its *front* and its *back*. A deque is the default representation for the Standard Library's stack adapter because a deque grows more efficiently than a vector. A vector is maintained as a *contiguous* block of memory—when that block is full and a new element is added, the vector allocates a larger contiguous block of memory and *copies* the old elements into that new block. A deque, on the other hand, is typically implemented as list of fixed-size, built-in arrays—new fixed-size built-in arrays are added as necessary and none of the existing elements are copied when new items are added to the front or back. For these reasons, we use a deque (line 42) as the underlying container for our Stack class.

Class Template Stack<T>'s Member Functions

The member-function definitions of a class template are *function templates*, but are not preceded with the template keyword and template parameters in angle brackets (< and >) when they're defined within the class template's body. As you can see, however, they do use the class template's template parameter T to represent the element type. Our Stack class template does *not* define it's own constructors—the *default constructor* provided by the compiler will invoke the deque's default constructor. We also provide the following member functions in Fig. 18.1:

- top (lines 12–15) returns a reference to the Stack's top element.
- push (lines 18–21) places a new element on the top of the Stack.
- pop (lines 24–27) removes the Stack's top element.
- isEmpty (lines 30–33) returns a bool value—true if the Stack is empty and false otherwise.
- size (lines 36–39) returns the number if elements in the Stack.

Each of these member functions *delegates* its responsibility to the appropriate member function of class template deque.

Declaring a Class Template's Member Functions Outside the Class Template Definition
Though we did *not* do so in our Stack class template, member-function definitions can appear *outside* a class template definition. If you do this, each must begin with the template keyword followed by the *same* set of template parameters as the class template. In addition, the member functions must be qualified with the class name and scope resolution operator. For example, you can define the pop function outside the class-template definition as follows:

```
template< typename T >
inline void Stack<T>::pop()
{
    stack.pop_front();
} // end function template pop
```

Stack<T>:: indicates that pop is in the scope of class Stack<T>. The Standard Library's container classes tend to define all their member functions *inside* their class definitions.

Testing Class Template Stack<T>
Now, let's consider the driver (Fig. 18.2) that exercises the Stack class template. The driver begins by instantiating object doubleStack (line 9). This object is declared as a Stack<double> (pronounced "Stack of double"). The compiler associates type double with type parameter T in the class template to produce the source code for a Stack class with elements of type double that actually stores its elements in a deque<double>.

Lines 16–21 invoke push (line 18) to place the double values 1.1, 2.2, 3.3, 4.4 and 5.5 onto doubleStack. Next, lines 26–30 invoke top and pop in a while loop to remove the five values from the stack. Notice in the output of Fig. 18.2, that the values do pop off in *last-in, first-out order*. When doubleStack is empty, the pop loop terminates.

```
1   // Fig. 18.2: fig18_02.cpp
2   // Stack class template test program.
3   #include <iostream>
4   #include "Stack.h" // Stack class template definition
```

Fig. 18.2 | Stack class template test program. (Part 1 of 3.)

```
5   using namespace std;
6
7   int main()
8   {
9      Stack< double > doubleStack; // create a Stack of double
10     const size_t doubleStackSize = 5; // stack size
11     double doubleValue = 1.1; // first value to push
12
13     cout << "Pushing elements onto doubleStack\n";
14
15     // push 5 doubles onto doubleStack
16     for ( size_t i = 0; i < doubleStackSize; ++i )
17     {
18        doubleStack.push( doubleValue );
19        cout << doubleValue << ' ';
20        doubleValue += 1.1;
21     } // end while
22
23     cout << "\n\nPopping elements from doubleStack\n";
24
25     // pop elements from doubleStack
26     while ( !doubleStack.isEmpty() ) // loop while Stack is not empty
27     {
28        cout << doubleStack.top() << ' '; // display top element
29        doubleStack.pop(); // remove top element
30     } // end while
31
32     cout << "\nStack is empty, cannot pop.\n";
33
34     Stack< int > intStack; // create a Stack of int
35     const size_t intStackSize = 10; // stack size
36     int intValue = 1; // first value to push
37
38     cout << "\nPushing elements onto intStack\n";
39
40     // push 10 integers onto intStack
41     for ( size_t i = 0; i < intStackSize; ++i )
42     {
43        intStack.push( intValue );
44        cout << intValue++ << ' ';
45     } // end while
46
47     cout << "\n\nPopping elements from intStack\n";
48
49     // pop elements from intStack
50     while ( !intStack.isEmpty() ) // loop while Stack is not empty
51     {
52        cout << intStack.top() << ' '; // display top element
53        intStack.pop(); // remove top element
54     } // end while
55
56     cout << "\nStack is empty, cannot pop." << endl;
57  } // end main
```

Fig. 18.2 | Stack class template test program. (Part 2 of 3.)

```
Pushing elements onto doubleStack
1.1 2.2 3.3 4.4 5.5

Popping elements from doubleStack
5.5 4.4 3.3 2.2 1.1
Stack is empty, cannot pop

Pushing elements onto intStack
1 2 3 4 5 6 7 8 9 10

Popping elements from intStack
10 9 8 7 6 5 4 3 2 1
Stack is empty, cannot pop
```

Fig. 18.2 | Stack class template test program. (Part 3 of 3.)

Line 34 instantiates int stack intStack with the declaration

```
Stack< int > intStack;
```

(pronounced "intStack is a Stack of int"). Lines 41–45 repeatedly invoke push (line 43) to place values onto intStack, then lines 50–54 repeatedly invoke top and pop to remove values from intStack until it's empty. Once again, notice in the output that the values pop off in last-in, first-out order.

18.3 Function Template to Manipulate a Class-Template Specialization Object

Notice that the code in function main of Fig. 18.2 is *almost identical* for both the double-Stack manipulations in lines 9–32 and the intStack manipulations in lines 34–56. This presents another opportunity to use a function template. Figure 18.3 defines function template testStack (lines 10–39) to perform the same tasks as main in Fig. 18.2—push a series of values onto a Stack<T> and pop the values off a Stack<T>.

```cpp
1   // Fig. 18.3: fig18_03.cpp
2   // Passing a Stack template object
3   // to a function template.
4   #include <iostream>
5   #include <string>
6   #include "Stack.h" // Stack class template definition
7   using namespace std;
8
9   // function template to manipulate Stack< T >
10  template< typename T >
11  void testStack(
12     Stack< T > &theStack, // reference to Stack< T >
13     const T &value, // initial value to push
14     const T &increment, // increment for subsequent values
15     size_t size, // number of items to push
16     const string &stackName ) // name of the Stack< T > object
17  {
```

Fig. 18.3 | Passing a Stack template object to a function template. (Part 1 of 2.)

```
18         cout << "\nPushing elements onto " << stackName << '\n';
19         T pushValue = value;
20
21         // push element onto Stack
22         for ( size_t i = 0; i < size; ++i )
23         {
24            theStack.push( pushValue ); // push element onto Stack
25            cout << pushValue << ' ';
26            pushValue += increment;
27         } // end while
28
29         cout << "\n\nPopping elements from " << stackName << '\n';
30
31         // pop elements from Stack
32         while ( !theStack.isEmpty() ) // loop while Stack is not empty
33         {
34            cout << theStack.top() << ' ';
35            theStack.pop(); // remove top element
36         } // end while
37
38         cout << "\nStack is empty. Cannot pop." << endl;
39      } // end function template testStack
40
41      int main()
42      {
43         Stack< double > doubleStack;
44         const size_t doubleStackSize = 5;
45         testStack( doubleStack, 1.1, 1.1, doubleStackSize, "doubleStack" );
46
47         Stack< int > intStack;
48         const size_t intStackSize = 10;
49         testStack( intStack, 1, 1, intStackSize, "intStack" );
50      } // end main
```

```
Pushing elements onto doubleStack
1.1 2.2 3.3 4.4 5.5

Popping elements from doubleStack
5.5 4.4 3.3 2.2 1.1
Stack is empty, cannot pop

Pushing elements onto intStack
1 2 3 4 5 6 7 8 9 10

Popping elements from intStack
10 9 8 7 6 5 4 3 2 1
Stack is empty, cannot pop
```

Fig. 18.3 | Passing a Stack template object to a function template. (Part 2 of 2.)

Function template testStack uses T (specified at line 10) to represent the data type stored in the Stack<T>. The function template takes five arguments (lines 12–16):

- the Stack<T> to manipulate

- a value of type T that will be the first value pushed onto the Stack<T>
- a value of type T used to increment the values pushed onto the Stack<T>
- the number of elements to push onto the Stack<T>
- a string that represents the name of the Stack<T> object for output purposes

Function main (lines 41–50) instantiates an object of type Stack<double> called doubleStack (line 43) and an object of type Stack<int> called intStack (line 47) and uses these objects in lines 45 and 49. The compiler infers the type of T for testStack from the type used to instantiate the function's first argument (i.e., the type used to instantiate doubleStack or intStack).

18.4 Nontype Parameters

Class template Stack of Section 18.2 used only a type parameter (Fig. 18.1, line 7) in its template declaration. It's also possible to use **nontype template parameters**, which can have default arguments and are treated as constants. For example, the C++ standard's array class template begins with the template declaration:

```
template < class T, size_t N >
```

(Recall that keywords class and typename are *interchangeable* in template declarations.) So, a declaration such as

```
array< double, 100 > salesFigures;
```

creates a 100-element array of doubles class-template specialization, then uses it to instantiate the object salesFigures. The array class template encapsulates a *built-in array*. When you create an array class-template specialization, the array's built-in array data member has the type and size specified in the declaration—in the preceding example, it would be a built-in array of double values with 100 elements.

18.5 Default Arguments for Template Type Parameters

In addition, a type parameter can specify a **default type argument**. For example, the C++ standard's stack *container adapter* class template begins with:

```
template < class T, class Container = deque< T > >
```

which specifies that a stack uses a deque *by default* to store the stack's elements of type T. The declaration

```
stack< int > values;
```

creates a stack of ints class-template specialization (behind the scenes) and uses it to instantiate the object named values. The stack's elements are stored in a deque<int>.

Default type parameters must be the *rightmost* (trailing) parameters in a template's type-parameter list. When you instantiate a template with two or more default arguments, if an omitted argument is not the rightmost, then all type parameters to the right of it also must be omitted. As of C++11, you can now use default type arguments for template type parameters in function templates.

18.6 Overloading Function Templates

Function templates and overloading are intimately related. In Section 6.19, you learned that when overloaded functions perform *identical* operations on *different* types of data, they can be expressed more compactly and conveniently using function templates. You can then write function calls with different types of arguments and let the compiler generate separate *function-template specializations* to handle each function call appropriately. The function-template specializations generated from a given function template all have the same name, so the compiler uses overload resolution to invoke the proper function.

You may also *overload* function templates. For example, you can provide other function templates that specify the *same* function name but *different* function parameters. A function template also can be overloaded by providing nontemplate functions with the same function name but different function parameters.

Matching Process for Overloaded Functions

The compiler performs a matching process to determine what function to call when a function is invoked. It looks at both existing functions and function templates to locate a function or generate a function-template specialization whose function name and argument types are consistent with those of the function call. If there are no matches, the compiler issues an error message. If there are multiple matches for the function call, the compiler attempts to determine the *best* match. If there's *more than one* best match, the call is *ambiguous* and the compiler issues an error message.[2]

18.7 Wrap-Up

This chapter discussed class templates and class-template specializations. We used a class template to create a group of related class-template specializations that each perform identical processing on different data types. We discussed nontype template parameters. We also discussed how to overload a function template to create a customized version that handles a particular data type's processing in a manner that differs from the other function-template specializations. In the next chapter, we demonstrate how to create your own custom templatized dynamic data structures, including linked lists, stacks, queues and binary trees.

---

2. The compiler's process for resolving function calls is complex. The complete details are discussed in Section 13.3.3 of the C++ standard.

Summary

Section 18.1 Introduction
- Templates enable us to specify a range of related (overloaded) functions—called function-template specializations (p. 800)—or a range of related classes—called class-template specializations (p. 800).

Section 18.2 Class Templates
- Class templates provide the means for describing a class generically and for instantiating classes that are type-specific versions of this generic class.

- Class templates are called parameterized types (p. 800); they require type parameters to specify how to customize a generic class template to form a specific class-template specialization.

- To use class-template specializations you write one class template. When you need a new type-specific class, the compiler writes the source code for the class-template specialization.

- A class-template definition (p. 800) looks like a conventional class definition, but it's preceded by `template<typename T>` (or `template<class T>`) to indicate this is a class-template definition. T is a type parameter that acts as a placeholder for the type of the class to create. The type T is mentioned throughout the class definition and member-function definitions as a generic type name.

- The names of template parameters must be unique inside a template definition.

- Member-function definitions outside a class template each begin with the same `template` declaration as their class. Then, each function definition resembles a conventional function definition, except that the generic data in the class always is listed generically as type parameter T. The binary scope-resolution operator is used with the class-template name to tie each member-function definition to the class template's scope.

Section 18.4 Nontype Parameters
- It's possible to use nontype parameters (p. 807) in a class or function template declaration.

Section 18.5 Default Arguments for Template Type Parameters
- You can specify a default type argument (p. 807) for a type parameter in the type-parameter list.

Section 18.6 Overloading Function Templates
- A function template may be overloaded in several ways. We can provide other function templates that specify the same function name but different function parameters. A function template can also be overloaded by providing other nontemplate functions with the same function name, but different function parameters. If both the template and non-template versions match a call, the non-template version will be used.

Self-Review Exercises

18.1 State which of the following are *true* and which are *false*. If *false*, explain why.
   a) Templates enable us to specify a range of related classes called function-template specializations.
   b) The names of template parameters must be unique inside a template definition.
   c) It is not possible to use nontype parameters in a function template declaration.
   d) If both the template and non-template versions of a function match a call, the non-template version will be used.

18.2 Fill in the blanks in each of the following:
   a) Templates enable us to specify, with a single code segment, an entire range of related functions called _____, or an entire range of related classes called _____.
   b) All template definitions begin with the keyword _____, followed by a list of template parameters enclosed in _____.
   c) The related functions generated from a function template all have the same name, so the compiler uses _____ resolution to invoke the proper function.
   d) Class templates also are called _____ types.
   e) The _____ operator is used with a class-template name to tie each member-function definition to the class template's scope.

Answers to Self-Review Exercises

18.1 a) False. Templates enable us to specify a range of related classes called class-template specializations. b) True. c) False. It is possible to use nontype parameters in a function template declaration. d) True.

18.2 a) function-template specializations, class-template specializations. b) `template`, angle brackets (`<` and `>`). c) overload. d) parameterized. e) scope resolution.

Exercises

18.3 *(Operator Overloads in Templates)* Write a simple function template for predicate function `isEqualTo` that compares its two arguments of the same type with the equality operator (`==`) and returns `true` if they are equal and `false` otherwise. Use this function template in a program that calls `isEqualTo` only with a variety of fundamental types. Now write a separate version of the program that calls `isEqualTo` with a user-defined class type, but does not overload the equality operator. What happens when you attempt to run this program? Now overload the equality operator (with the operator function) `operator==`. Now what happens when you attempt to run this program?

18.4 *(Array Class Template)* Reimplement class `Array` from Figs. 10.10–10.11 as a class template. Demonstrate the new `Array` class template in a program.

18.5 Distinguish between the terms "class template" and "class template specialization".

18.6 Explain the mechanism to manipulate a Class-Template Specialization Object using Function Template.

18.7 What's the matching process for overloaded functions?

18.8 The compiler performs a matching process to determine which function-template specialization to call when a function is invoked. Under what circumstances does an attempt to make a match result in a compile error?

18.9 How can you create your own custom templatized dynamic data structures using templates?

18.10 Explain why a C++ program would use the statement

```
Array< Employee > workerList( 100 );
```

18.11 Review your answer to Exercise 18.10. Explain why a C++ program might use the statement

```
Array< Employee > workerList;
```

18.12 Explain the use of the following notation in a C++ program:

```
template< typename T > Array< T >::Array( int s )
```

18.13 Why might you use a nontype parameter with a class template for a container such as an array or stack?

Custom Templatized Data Structures

'Will you walk a little faster?'
said a whiting to a snail,
'There's a porpoise close behind
us, and he's treading on my tail.'
—Lewis Carroll

There is always room at the top.
—Daniel Webster

Push on—keep moving.
—Thomas Morton

I'll turn over a new leaf.
—Miguel de Cervantes

Objectives
In this chapter you'll:

- Form linked data structures using pointers, self-referential classes and recursion.
- Create and manipulate dynamic data structures such as linked lists, queues, stacks and binary trees.
- Use binary search trees for high-speed searching and sorting.
- Learn important applications of linked data structures.
- Create reusable data structures with class templates, inheritance and composition.

19.1 Introduction

We've studied *fixed-size data structures*—such as one- and two-dimensional template-based arrays (Chapter 7) and built-in arrays (Chapter 8)—and various C++ Standard Library *dynamic data structures* (vectors in Chapter 7 and other template-based containers in Chapter 15) that can grow and shrink during execution.

In this chapter, we demonstrate how you can create your own custom templatized dynamic data structures. We discuss several popular and important data structures and implement programs that create and manipulate them:

- Linked lists are collections of data items logically "lined up in a row"—insertions and removals are made *anywhere* in a linked list.

- *Stacks* are important in compilers and operating systems: Insertions and removals are made *only* at one end of a stack—its *top*.

- *Queues* represent *waiting lines*; insertions are made at the *back* (also referred to as the *tail*) of a queue and removals are made from the *front* (also referred to as the *head*) of a queue.

- Binary trees facilitate searching and sorting data, *duplicate elimination* and *compiling* expressions into machine code.

Each of these data structures has many other interesting applications. We use class templates, inheritance and composition to create and package these data structures for reusability and maintainability. The programs employ extensive pointer manipulation. The exercises include a rich collection of useful applications.

Always Prefer the Standard Library's Containers, Iterators and Algorithms, if Possible
The C++ Standard Library's *containers*, *iterators* for traversing those containers and *algorithms* for processing the containers' elements meet the needs of most C++ programmers. The Standard Library code is carefully written to be correct, portable, efficient and extensible. Understanding how to build custom templatized data structures will also help you use the Standard Library containers, iterators and algorithms, more effectively.

Special Section: Building Your Own Compiler
We encourage you to attempt the optional project described in the Special Section: Building Your Own Compiler (www.deitel.com/books/cpphtp9). You've been using a C++ compiler to translate your programs to machine code so that you can execute these programs on your computer. In this project, you'll actually build your own compiler. It will

read a file of statements written in a simple, yet powerful, high-level language similar to early versions of BASIC. Your compiler will translate these statements into a file of Simpletron Machine Language (SML) instructions—SML is the language you learned in the Chapter 8 Special Section: Building Your Own Computer. Your Simpletron Simulator program will then execute the SML program produced by your compiler! The special section discusses the high-level language and the algorithms you'll need to convert each type of high-level language statement into machine code. We provide compiler-theory exercises and in the special section suggest enhancements to both the compiler and the Simpletron Simulator.

19.2 Self-Referential Classes

A self-referential class contains a member that points to a class object of the same class type. For example, the definition

```
class Node
{
public:
    explicit Node( int ); // constructor
    void setData( int ); // set data member
    int getData() const; // get data member
    void setNextPtr( Node * ); // set pointer to next Node
    Node *getNextPtr() const; // get pointer to next Node
private:
    int data; // data stored in this Node
    Node *nextPtr; // pointer to another object of same type
}; // end class Node
```

defines a type, Node. Type Node has two private data members—integer member data and pointer member nextPtr. Member nextPtr points to an object of type Node—an object of the *same* type as the one being declared here, hence the term *self-referential class*. Member nextPtr is referred to as a link—i.e., nextPtr can "tie" an object of type Node to another object of the *same* type. Type Node also has five member functions—a constructor that receives an integer to initialize member data, a setData function to set the value of member data, a getData function to return the value of member data, a setNextPtr function to set the value of member nextPtr and a getNextPtr function to return the value of member nextPtr.

Self-referential class objects can be linked together to form useful data structures such as lists, queues, stacks and trees. Figure 19.1 illustrates two self-referential class objects linked together to form a list. Note that a slash—representing a null pointer (nullptr)—is placed in the link member of the second self-referential class object to indicate that the link does *not* point to another object. The slash is for illustration purposes only; it does *not* correspond to the backslash character in C++. A null pointer normally indicates the *end of a data structure.*

 Common Programming Error 19.1
Not setting the link in the last node of a linked data structure to nullptr *is a (possibly fatal) logic error.*

Fig. 19.1 | Two self-referential class objects linked together.

The following sections discuss lists, stacks, queues and trees. The data structures presented in this chapter are created and maintained with *dynamic memory allocation* (Section 10.9), *self-referential classes*, *class templates* (Chapter 18) and *function templates* (Section 6.19).

19.3 Linked Lists

A linked list is a *linear* collection of self-referential class objects, called **nodes**, connected by **pointer links**—hence, the term "linked" list. A linked list is accessed via a pointer to the list's first node. Each subsequent node is accessed via the *link-pointer member* stored in the previous node. By *convention*, the link pointer in the last node of a list is set to nullptr to mark the end of the list. Data is stored in a linked list *dynamically*—each node is created and destroyed as necessary. A node can contain data of any type, including objects of other classes. If nodes contain base-class pointers to base-class and derived-class objects related by inheritance, we can have a linked list of such nodes and process them *polymorphically* using virtual function calls. Stacks and queues are also **linear data structures** and, as we'll see, can be viewed as constrained versions of linked lists. Trees are **nonlinear data structures**.

Linked lists provide several advantages over array objects and built-in arrays. A linked list is appropriate when the number of data elements to be represented at one time is *unpredictable*. Linked lists are dynamic, so the length of a list can increase or decrease as necessary. The size of an array object or built-in array, however, cannot be altered, because the array size is fixed at compile time. An array object or built-in array can become full. Linked lists become full only when the system has insufficient memory to satisfy additional dynamic storage allocation requests.

Performance Tip 19.1

An array object or built-in array can be declared to contain more elements than the number of items expected, but this can waste memory. Linked lists can provide better memory utilization in these situations. Linked lists allow the program to adapt at runtime. Class template vector (Section 7.10) implements a dynamically resizable array-based data structure.

Linked lists can be maintained in *sorted order* by inserting each new element at the proper point in the list. Existing list elements do *not* need to be moved. Pointers merely need to be updated to point to the correct node.

Performance Tip 19.2

Insertion and deletion in a sorted array object or built-in array can be time consuming—all the elements following the inserted or deleted element must be shifted appropriately. A linked list allows efficient insertion operations anywhere in the list.

Performance Tip 19.3

The elements of an array object or built-in array are stored contiguously in memory. This allows immediate access to any element, because an element's address can be calculated directly based on its position relative to the beginning of the array object or built-in array. Linked lists do not afford such immediate direct access to their elements, so accessing individual elements can be considerably more expensive. The selection of a data structure is typically based on the performance of specific operations used by a program and the order in which the data items are maintained in the data structure. For example, if you have a pointer to the insertion location, it's typically more efficient to insert an item in a sorted linked list than a sorted array object or built-in array.

Linked-list nodes typically are *not* stored contiguously in memory, but logically they *appear* to be contiguous. Figure 19.2 illustrates a linked list with several nodes.

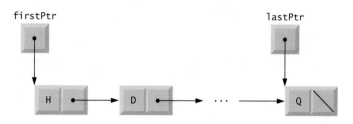

Fig. 19.2 | A graphical representation of a list.

Performance Tip 19.4

Using dynamic memory allocation for data structures that grow and shrink at execution time can save memory.

Testing Our Linked List Implementation
The program of Figs. 19.3–19.5 uses a List *class template* to manipulate a list of integer values and a list of floating-point values. The driver program (Fig. 19.3) has five options:

- insert a value at the beginning of the List
- insert a value at the end of the List
- delete a value from the beginning of the List
- delete a value from the end of the List
- end the List processing

The linked list implementation we present here does not allow insertions and deletions anywhere in the linked list. We ask you to implement these operations in Exercise 19.26. Exercise 19.20 asks you to implement a recursive function that prints a linked list backward, and Exercise 19.21 asks you to implement a recursive function that searches a linked list for a particular data item.

In Fig. 19.3, Lines 69 and 73 create List objects for types int and double, respectively. Lines 70 and 74 invoke the testList function template to manipulate objects.

```
1   // Fig. 19.3: fig19_03.cpp
2   // Manipulating a linked list.
3   #include <iostream>
4   #include <string>
5   #include "List.h" // List class definition
6   using namespace std;
7
8   // display program instructions to user
9   void instructions()
10  {
11     cout << "Enter one of the following:\n"
12        << "  1 to insert at beginning of list\n"
13        << "  2 to insert at end of list\n"
14        << "  3 to delete from beginning of list\n"
15        << "  4 to delete from end of list\n"
16        << "  5 to end list processing\n";
17  } // end function instructions
18
19  // function to test a List
20  template< typename T >
21  void testList( List< T > &listObject, const string &typeName )
22  {
23     cout << "Testing a List of " << typeName << " values\n";
24     instructions(); // display instructions
25
26     int choice; // store user choice
27     T value; // store input value
28
29     do // perform user-selected actions
30     {
31        cout << "? ";
32        cin >> choice;
33
34        switch ( choice )
35        {
36           case 1: // insert at beginning
37              cout << "Enter " << typeName << ": ";
38              cin >> value;
39              listObject.insertAtFront( value );
40              listObject.print();
41              break;
42           case 2: // insert at end
43              cout << "Enter " << typeName << ": ";
44              cin >> value;
45              listObject.insertAtBack( value );
46              listObject.print();
47              break;
48           case 3: // remove from beginning
49              if ( listObject.removeFromFront( value ) )
50                 cout << value << " removed from list\n";
51
52              listObject.print();
53              break;
```

Fig. 19.3 | Manipulating a linked list. (Part 1 of 3.)

```
54                case 4: // remove from end
55                   if ( listObject.removeFromBack( value ) )
56                      cout << value << " removed from list\n";
57
58                   listObject.print();
59                   break;
60            } // end switch
61         } while ( choice < 5 ); // end do...while
62
63         cout << "End list test\n\n";
64      } // end function testList
65
66      int main()
67      {
68         // test List of int values
69         List< int > integerList;
70         testList( integerList, "integer" );
71
72         // test List of double values
73         List< double > doubleList;
74         testList( doubleList, "double" );
75      } // end main
```

```
Testing a List of integer values
Enter one of the following:
  1 to insert at beginning of list
  2 to insert at end of list
  3 to delete from beginning of list
  4 to delete from end of list
  5 to end list processing
? 1
Enter integer: 1
The list is: 1

? 1
Enter integer: 2
The list is: 2 1

? 2
Enter integer: 3
The list is: 2 1 3

? 2
Enter integer: 4
The list is: 2 1 3 4

? 3
2 removed from list
The list is: 1 3 4

? 3
1 removed from list
The list is: 3 4

? 4
4 removed from list
The list is: 3
```

Fig. 19.3 | Manipulating a linked list. (Part 2 of 3.)

```
? 4
3 removed from list
The list is empty

? 5
End list test

Testing a List of double values
Enter one of the following:
   1 to insert at beginning of list
   2 to insert at end of list
   3 to delete from beginning of list
   4 to delete from end of list
   5 to end list processing
? 1
Enter double: 1.1
The list is: 1.1

? 1
Enter double: 2.2
The list is: 2.2 1.1

? 2
Enter double: 3.3
The list is: 2.2 1.1 3.3

? 2
Enter double: 4.4
The list is: 2.2 1.1 3.3 4.4

? 3
2.2 removed from list
The list is: 1.1 3.3 4.4

? 3
1.1 removed from list
The list is: 3.3 4.4

? 4
4.4 removed from list
The list is: 3.3

? 4
3.3 removed from list
The list is empty

? 5
End list test

All nodes destroyed

All nodes destroyed
```

Fig. 19.3 | Manipulating a linked list. (Part 3 of 3.)

Class Template ListNode

Figure 19.3 uses class templates ListNode (Fig. 19.4) and List (Fig. 19.5). Encapsulated in each List object is a linked list of ListNode objects. Class template ListNode (Fig. 19.4) contains private members data and nextPtr (lines 27–28), a constructor (lines 16–20) to initialize these members and function getData (lines 22–25) to return the data in a node. Member data stores a value of type NODETYPE, the type parameter passed to the class template. Member nextPtr stores a pointer to the next ListNode object in the linked list. Line 13 of the ListNode class template definition declares class List<NODETYPE> as a friend. This makes all member functions of a given specialization of class template List friends of the corresponding specialization of class template ListNode, so they can access the private members of ListNode objects of that type. We do this for performance and because these two classes are tightly coupled—only class template List manipulates objects of class template ListNode. Because the ListNode template parameter NODETYPE is used as the template argument for List in the friend declaration, ListNodes specialized with a particular type can be processed only by a List specialized with the *same* type (e.g., a List of int values manages ListNode objects that store int values). To use the type name List<NODETYPE> in line 13, the compiler needs to know that class template List exists. Line 8 is a so-called forward declaration of class template List. A forward declaration tells the compiler that a type exists, even if it has not yet been defined.

Error-Prevention Tip 19.1

Assign nullptr to the link member of a new node. Pointers must be initialized before they're used.

```
1   // Fig. 19.4: ListNode.h
2   // ListNode class-template definition.
3   #ifndef LISTNODE_H
4   #define LISTNODE_H
5
6   // forward declaration of class List required to announce that class
7   // List exists so it can be used in the friend declaration at line 13
8   template< typename NODETYPE > class List;
9
10  template< typename NODETYPE >
11  class ListNode
12  {
13     friend class List< NODETYPE >; // make List a friend
14
15  public:
16     explicit ListNode( const NODETYPE &info ) // constructor
17        : data( info ), nextPtr( nullptr )
18     {
19        // empty body
20     } // end ListNode constructor
21
22     NODETYPE getData() const; // return data in node
23     {
24        return data;
25     } // end function getData
26  private:
27     NODETYPE data; // data
28     ListNode< NODETYPE > *nextPtr; // next node in list
29  }; // end class ListNode
30
31  #endif
```

Fig. 19.4 | ListNode class-template definition.

*Class Template **List***

Lines 148–149 of the List class template (Fig. 19.5) declare private data members first-Ptr and lastPtr—pointers to the List's first and last ListNodes. The default constructor (lines 14–18) initializes both pointers to nullptr. The destructor (lines 21–40) destroys all of the List's ListNode objects when the List is destroyed. The primary List functions are insertAtFront (lines 43–54), insertAtBack (lines 57–68), removeFromFront (lines 71–88) and removeFromBack (lines 91–117). We discuss each of these after Fig. 19.5.

Function isEmpty (lines 120–123) is called a *predicate function*—it *does not alter* the List; rather, it determines whether the List is *empty*. If so, true is returned; otherwise, false is returned. Function print (lines 126–145) displays the List's contents. Utility function getNewNode (lines 152–155) returns a dynamically allocated ListNode object. This function is called from functions insertAtFront and insertAtBack.

```cpp
1   // Fig. 19.5: List.h
2   // List class-template definition.
3   #ifndef LIST_H
4   #define LIST_H
5
6   #include <iostream>
7   #include "ListNode.h" // ListNode class definition
8
9   template< typename NODETYPE >
10  class List
11  {
12  public:
13     // default constructor
14     List()
15        : firstPtr( nullptr ), lastPtr( nullptr )
16     {
17        // empty body
18     } // end List constructor
19
20     // destructor
21     ~List()
22     {
23        if ( !isEmpty() ) // List is not empty
24        {
25           std::cout << "Destroying nodes ...\n";
26
27           ListNode< NODETYPE > *currentPtr = firstPtr;
28           ListNode< NODETYPE > *tempPtr = nullptr;
29
30           while ( currentPtr != nullptr ) // delete remaining nodes
31           {
32              tempPtr = currentPtr;
33              std::cout << tempPtr->data << '\n';
34              currentPtr = currentPtr->nextPtr;
35              delete tempPtr;
36           } // end while
37        } // end if
```

Fig. 19.5 | List class-template definition. (Part 1 of 4.)

```
38
39          std::cout << "All nodes destroyed\n\n";
40       } // end List destructor
41
42       // insert node at front of list
43       void insertAtFront( const NODETYPE &value )
44       {
45          ListNode< NODETYPE > *newPtr = getNewNode( value ); // new node
46
47          if ( isEmpty() ) // List is empty
48             firstPtr = lastPtr = newPtr; // new list has only one node
49          else // List is not empty
50          {
51             newPtr->nextPtr = firstPtr; // point new node to old 1st node
52             firstPtr = newPtr; // aim firstPtr at new node
53          } // end else
54       } // end function insertAtFront
55
56       // insert node at back of list
57       void insertAtBack( const NODETYPE &value )
58       {
59          ListNode< NODETYPE > *newPtr = getNewNode( value ); // new node
60
61          if ( isEmpty() ) // List is empty
62             firstPtr = lastPtr = newPtr; // new list has only one node
63          else // List is not empty
64          {
65             lastPtr->nextPtr = newPtr; // update previous last node
66             lastPtr = newPtr; // new last node
67          } // end else
68       } // end function insertAtBack
69
70       // delete node from front of list
71       bool removeFromFront( NODETYPE &value )
72       {
73          if ( isEmpty() ) // List is empty
74             return false; // delete unsuccessful
75          else
76          {
77             ListNode< NODETYPE > *tempPtr = firstPtr; // hold item to delete
78
79             if ( firstPtr == lastPtr )
80                firstPtr = lastPtr = nullptr; // no nodes remain after removal
81             else
82                firstPtr = firstPtr->nextPtr; // point to previous 2nd node
83
84             value = tempPtr->data; // return data being removed
85             delete tempPtr; // reclaim previous front node
86             return true; // delete successful
87          } // end else
88       } // end function removeFromFront
89
```

Fig. 19.5 | List class-template definition. (Part 2 of 4.)

```
90      // delete node from back of list
91      bool removeFromBack( NODETYPE &value )
92      {
93         if ( isEmpty() ) // List is empty
94            return false; // delete unsuccessful
95         else
96         {
97            ListNode< NODETYPE > *tempPtr = lastPtr; // hold item to delete
98
99            if ( firstPtr == lastPtr ) // List has one element
100              firstPtr = lastPtr = nullptr; // no nodes remain after removal
101           else
102           {
103              ListNode< NODETYPE > *currentPtr = firstPtr;
104
105              // locate second-to-last element
106              while ( currentPtr->nextPtr != lastPtr )
107                 currentPtr = currentPtr->nextPtr; // move to next node
108
109              lastPtr = currentPtr; // remove last node
110              currentPtr->nextPtr = nullptr; // this is now the last node
111           } // end else
112
113           value = tempPtr->data; // return value from old last node
114           delete tempPtr; // reclaim former last node
115           return true; // delete successful
116        } // end else
117     } // end function removeFromBack
118
119     // is List empty?
120     bool isEmpty() const
121     {
122        return firstPtr == nullptr;
123     } // end function isEmpty
124
125     // display contents of List
126     void print() const
127     {
128        if ( isEmpty() ) // List is empty
129        {
130           std::cout << "The list is empty\n\n";
131           return;
132        } // end if
133
134        ListNode< NODETYPE > *currentPtr = firstPtr;
135
136        std::cout << "The list is: ";
137
138        while ( currentPtr != nullptr ) // get element data
139        {
140           std::cout << currentPtr->data << ' ';
141           currentPtr = currentPtr->nextPtr;
142        } // end while
```

Fig. 19.5 | List class-template definition. (Part 3 of 4.)

```
143
144         std::cout << "\n\n";
145     } // end function print
146
147 private:
148     ListNode< NODETYPE > *firstPtr; // pointer to first node
149     ListNode< NODETYPE > *lastPtr; // pointer to last node
150
151     // utility function to allocate new node
152     ListNode< NODETYPE > *getNewNode( const NODETYPE &value )
153     {
154         return new ListNode< NODETYPE >( value );
155     } // end function getNewNode
156 }; // end class List
157
158 #endif
```

Fig. 19.5 | List class-template definition. (Part 4 of 4.)

Member Function *insertAtFront*

Over the next several pages, we discuss each of the member functions of class List in detail. Function insertAtFront (Fig. 19.5, lines 43–54) places a new node at the front of the list. The function consists of several steps:

1. Call function getNewNode (line 45), passing it value, which is a constant reference to the node value to be inserted.

2. Function getNewNode (lines 152–155) uses operator new to create a new list node and return a pointer to this newly allocated node, which is assigned to newPtr in insertAtFront (line 45).

3. If the list is *empty* (line 47), firstPtr and lastPtr are set to newPtr (line 48)—i.e., the first and last node are the same node.

4. If the list is *not empty* (line 49), then the node pointed to by newPtr is threaded into the list by copying firstPtr to newPtr->nextPtr (line 51), so that the new node points to what used to be the first node of the list, and copying newPtr to firstPtr (line 52), so that firstPtr now points to the new first node of the list.

Figure 19.6 illustrates function insertAtFront. Part (a) shows the list and the new node before calling insertAtFront. The dashed arrows in part (b) illustrate *Step 4* of the insertAtFront operation that enables the node containing 12 to become the new list front.

Member Function *insertAtBack*

Function insertAtBack (Fig. 19.5, lines 57–68) places a new node at the back of the list. The function consists of several steps:

1. Call function getNewNode (line 59), passing it value, which is a constant reference to the node value to be inserted.

2. Function getNewNode (lines 152–155) uses operator new to create a new list node and return a pointer to this newly allocated node, which is assigned to newPtr in insertAtBack (line 59).

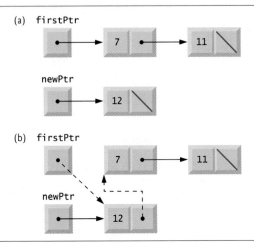

Fig. 19.6 | Operation insertAtFront represented graphically.

3. If the list is *empty* (line 61), then both firstPtr and lastPtr are set to newPtr (line 62).

4. If the list is *not empty* (line 63), then the node pointed to by newPtr is threaded into the list by copying newPtr into lastPtr->nextPtr (line 65), so that the new node is pointed to by what used to be the last node of the list, and copying newPtr to lastPtr (line 66), so that lastPtr now points to the new last node of the list.

Figure 19.7 illustrates an insertAtBack operation. Part (a) of the figure shows the list and the new node before the operation. The dashed arrows in part (b) illustrate *Step 4* of function insertAtBack that enables a new node to be added to the end of a list that's not empty.

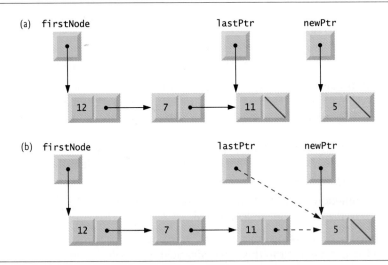

Fig. 19.7 | Operation insertAtBack represented graphically.

Member Function **removeFromFront**

Function removeFromFront (Fig. 19.5, lines 71–88) removes the front node of the list and copies the node value to the reference parameter. The function returns false if an attempt is made to remove a node from an empty list (lines 73–74) and returns true if the removal is successful. The function consists of several steps:

1. Assign tempPtr the address to which firstPtr points (line 77). Eventually, tempPtr will be used to delete the node being removed.

2. If firstPtr is equal to lastPtr (line 79), i.e., if the list has only one element prior to the removal attempt, then set firstPtr and lastPtr to nullptr (line 80) to dethread that node from the list (leaving the list empty).

3. If the list has more than one node prior to removal, then leave lastPtr as is and set firstPtr to firstPtr->nextPtr (line 82); i.e., modify firstPtr to point to what was the second node prior to removal (and is now the new first node).

4. After all these pointer manipulations are complete, copy to reference parameter value the data member of the node being removed (line 84).

5. Now delete the node pointed to by tempPtr (line 85).

6. Return true, indicating successful removal (line 86).

Figure 19.8 illustrates function removeFromFront. Part (a) illustrates the list before the removal operation. Part (b) shows the actual pointer manipulations for removing the front node from a nonempty list.

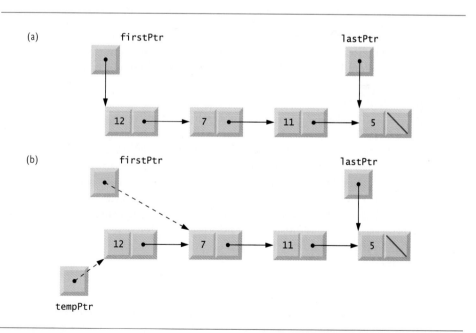

Fig. 19.8 | Operation removeFromFront represented graphically.

*Member Function **removeFromBack***

Function removeFromBack (Fig. 19.5, lines 91–117) removes the back node of the list and copies the node value to the reference parameter. The function returns false if an attempt is made to remove a node from an empty list (lines 93–94) and returns true if the removal is successful. The function consists of several steps:

1. Assign to tempPtr the address to which lastPtr points (line 97). Eventually, tempPtr will be used to delete the node being removed.

2. If firstPtr is equal to lastPtr (line 99), i.e., if the list has only one element prior to the removal attempt, then set firstPtr and lastPtr to nullptr (line 100) to dethread that node from the list (leaving the list empty).

3. If the list has more than one node prior to removal, then assign currentPtr the address to which firstPtr points (line 103) to prepare to "walk the list."

4. Now "walk the list" with currentPtr until it points to the node before the last node. This node will become the last node after the remove operation completes. This is done with a while loop (lines 106–107) that keeps replacing currentPtr by currentPtr->nextPtr, while currentPtr->nextPtr is not lastPtr.

5. Assign lastPtr to the address to which currentPtr points (line 109) to dethread the back node from the list.

6. Set currentPtr->nextPtr to nullptr (line 110) in the new last node of the list.

7. After all the pointer manipulations are complete, copy to reference parameter value the data member of the node being removed (line 113).

8. Now delete the node pointed to by tempPtr (line 114).

9. Return true (line 115), indicating successful removal.

Figure 19.9 illustrates removeFromBack. Part (a) of the figure illustrates the list before the removal operation. Part (b) of the figure shows the actual pointer manipulations.

*Member Function **print***

Function print (lines 126–145) first determines whether the list is *empty* (line 128). If so, it prints "The list is empty" and returns (lines 130–131). Otherwise, it iterates through the list and outputs the value in each node. The function initializes currentPtr as a copy of firstPtr (line 134), then prints the string "The list is: " (line 136). While current-Ptr is not nullptr (line 138), currentPtr->data is printed (line 140) and currentPtr is assigned the value of currentPtr->nextPtr (line 141). Note that if the link in the last node of the list does not have the value nullptr, the printing algorithm will erroneously attempt to print past the end of the list. Our printing algorithm here is identical for linked lists, stacks and queues (because we base each of these data structures on the same linked list infrastructure).

Circular Linked Lists and Double Linked Lists

The kind of linked list we've been discussing is a **singly linked list**—the list begins with a pointer to the first node, and each node contains a pointer to the next node "in sequence." This list terminates with a node whose pointer member has the value nullptr. A singly linked list may be traversed in only *one* direction.

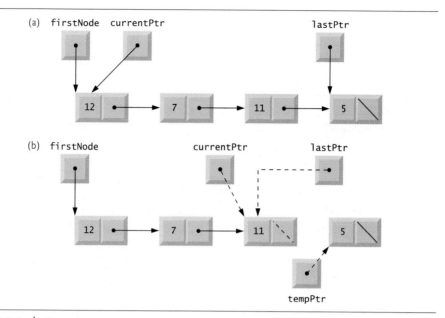

Fig. 19.9 | Operation removeFromBack represented graphically.

A circular, singly linked list (Fig. 19.10) begins with a pointer to the first node, and each node contains a pointer to the next node. The "last node" does not contain nullptr; rather, the pointer in the last node points back to the first node, thus closing the "circle."

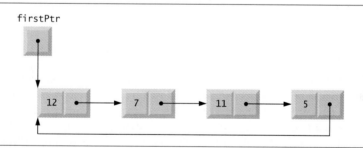

Fig. 19.10 | Circular, singly linked list.

A doubly linked list (Fig. 19.11)—such as the Standard Library list class template—allows traversals *both forward and backward*. Such a list is often implemented with two "start pointers"—one that points to the first element of the list to allow *front-to-back traversal* of the list and one that points to the last element to allow *back-to-front traversal*. Each node has *both* a *forward pointer* to the next node in the list in the forward direction *and* a *backward pointer* to the next node in the list in the backward direction. If your list contains an alphabetized telephone directory, for example, a search for someone whose name begins with a letter near the front of the alphabet might best begin from the front of the list. Searching for someone whose name begins with a letter near the end of the alphabet might best begin from the back of the list.

firstPtr

lastPtr

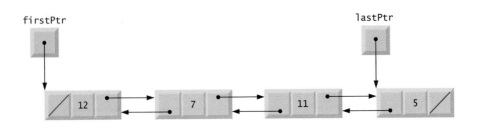

Fig. 19.11 | Doubly linked list.

In a circular, doubly linked list (Fig. 19.12), the *forward pointer* of the last node points to the first node, and the *backward pointer* of the first node points to the last node, thus closing the "circle."

firstPtr

lastPtr

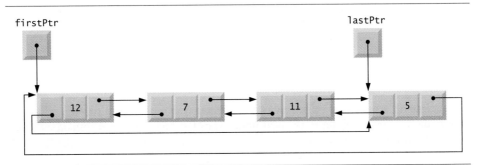

Fig. 19.12 | Circular, doubly linked list.

19.4 Stacks

You learned the notion of a stack in Section 6.12, Section 15.7.1, stack Adapter and Section 18.2. Recall that a nodes can be added to a stack and removed from a stack only at its *top*, so a stack is referred to as a *last-in, first-out (LIFO)* data structure. One way to implement a stack is as a *constrained version* of a linked list. In such an implementation, the link member in the last node of the stack is set to nullptr to indicate the *bottom* of the stack.

The primary member functions used to manipulate a stack are push and pop. Function push *inserts* a new node at the top of the stack. Function pop *removes* a node from the top of the stack, stores the popped value in a reference variable that's passed to the calling function and returns true if the pop operation was successful (false otherwise).

Applications of Stacks
Stacks have many interesting applications:

- In Section 6.12, you learned that when a function call is made, the called function must know how to return to its caller, so the return address is pushed onto a stack. If a series of function calls occurs, the successive return values are pushed onto the stack in last-in, first-out order, so that each function can return to its caller. Stacks support recursive function calls in the same manner as conventional nonrecursive calls.

- Stacks provide the memory for, and store the values of, automatic variables on each invocation of a function. When the function returns to its caller or throws an exception, the destructor (if any) for each local object is called, the space for that function's automatic variables is popped off the stack and those variables are no longer known to the program.

- Stacks are used by compilers in the process of evaluating expressions and generating machine-language code. The exercises explore several applications of stacks, including using them to develop your own complete working compiler.

Taking Advantage of the Relationship Between *Stack* and *List*

We'll take advantage of the close relationship between lists and stacks to implement a stack class primarily by *reusing* our List class template. First, we'll implement the Stack class template via *private inheritance* from our List class template. Then we'll implement an identically performing Stack class template through *composition* by including a List object as a private member of a Stack class template.

Implementing a Class Template *Stack* Class Based By Inheriting from *List*

The program of Figs. 19.13–19.14 creates a Stack class template (Fig. 19.13) primarily through *private inheritance* (line 9) of the List class template of Fig. 19.5. We want the Stack to have member functions push (lines 13–16), pop (lines 19–22), isStackEmpty (lines 25–28) and printStack (lines 31–34). Note that these are essentially the insertAtFront, removeFromFront, isEmpty and print functions of the List class template. Of course, the List class template contains other member functions (i.e., insertAtBack and removeFromBack) that we would not want to make accessible through the public interface to the Stack class. So when we indicate that the Stack class template is to inherit from the List class template, we specify *private inheritance*. This makes all the List class template's member functions private in the Stack class template. When we implement the Stack's member functions, we then have each of these call the appropriate member function of the List class—push calls insertAtFront (line 15), pop calls removeFromFront (line 21), isStackEmpty calls isEmpty (line 27) and printStack calls print (line 33)—this is referred to as delegation.

```
1   // Fig. 19.13: Stack.h
2   // Stack class-template definition.
3   #ifndef STACK_H
4   #define STACK_H
5
6   #include "List.h" // List class definition
7
8   template< typename STACKTYPE >
9   class Stack : private List< STACKTYPE >
10  {
```

Fig. 19.13 | Stack class-template definition. (Part 1 of 2.)

```
11   public:
12      // push calls the List function insertAtFront
13      void push( const STACKTYPE &data )
14      {
15         insertAtFront( data );
16      } // end function push
17
18      // pop calls the List function removeFromFront
19      bool pop( STACKTYPE &data )
20      {
21         return removeFromFront( data );
22      } // end function pop
23
24      // isStackEmpty calls the List function isEmpty
25      bool isStackEmpty() const
26      {
27         return this->isEmpty();
28      } // end function isStackEmpty
29
30      // printStack calls the List function print
31      void printStack() const
32      {
33         this->print();
34      } // end function print
35   }; // end class Stack
36
37   #endif
```

Fig. 19.13 │ Stack class-template definition. (Part 2 of 2.)

Dependent Names in Class Templates

The *explicit use of* this on lines 27 and 33 is required so the compiler can properly resolve identifiers in template definitions. A **dependent name** is an identifier that depends on a template parameter. For example, the call to removeFromFront (line 21) depends on the argument data which has a type that's dependent on the template parameter STACKTYPE. Resolution of *dependent names* occurs when the template is instantiated. In contrast, the identifier for a function that takes no arguments like isEmpty or print in the List superclass is a *non-dependent name*. Such identifiers are normally resolved at the point where the template is defined. If the template has not yet been instantiated, then the code for the function with the *non-dependent name* does not yet exist and some compilers will generate compilation errors. Adding the explicit use of this-> in lines 27 and 33 makes the calls to the base class's member functions dependent on the template parameter and ensures that the code will compile properly.

Testing the Stack Class Template

The stack class template is used in main (Fig. 19.14) to instantiate integer stack intStack of type Stack< int > (line 9). Integers 0 through 2 are pushed onto intStack (lines 14–18), then popped off intStack (lines 23–28). The program uses the Stack class template to create doubleStack of type Stack< double > (line 30). Values 1.1, 2.2 and 3.3 are pushed onto doubleStack (lines 36–41), then popped off doubleStack (lines 46–51).

```cpp
 1   // Fig. 19.14: fig19_14.cpp
 2   // A simple stack program.
 3   #include <iostream>
 4   #include "Stack.h" // Stack class definition
 5   using namespace std;
 6
 7   int main()
 8   {
 9      Stack< int > intStack; // create Stack of ints
10
11      cout << "processing an integer Stack" << endl;
12
13      // push integers onto intStack
14      for ( int i = 0; i < 3; ++i )
15      {
16         intStack.push( i );
17         intStack.printStack();
18      } // end for
19
20      int popInteger; // store int popped from stack
21
22      // pop integers from intStack
23      while ( !intStack.isStackEmpty() )
24      {
25         intStack.pop( popInteger );
26         cout << popInteger << " popped from stack" << endl;
27         intStack.printStack();
28      } // end while
29
30      Stack< double > doubleStack; // create Stack of doubles
31      double value = 1.1;
32
33      cout << "processing a double Stack" << endl;
34
35      // push floating-point values onto doubleStack
36      for ( int j = 0; j < 3; ++j )
37      {
38         doubleStack.push( value );
39         doubleStack.printStack();
40         value += 1.1;
41      } // end for
42
43      double popDouble; // store double popped from stack
44
45      // pop floating-point values from doubleStack
46      while ( !doubleStack.isStackEmpty() )
47      {
48         doubleStack.pop( popDouble );
49         cout << popDouble << " popped from stack" << endl;
50         doubleStack.printStack();
51      } // end while
52   } // end main
```

Fig. 19.14 | A simple stack program. (Part 1 of 2.)

```
processing an integer Stack
The list is: 0

The list is: 1 0

The list is: 2 1 0

2 popped from stack
The list is: 1 0

1 popped from stack
The list is: 0

0 popped from stack
The list is empty

processing a double Stack
The list is: 1.1

The list is: 2.2 1.1

The list is: 3.3 2.2 1.1

3.3 popped from stack
The list is: 2.2 1.1

2.2 popped from stack
The list is: 1.1

1.1 popped from stack
The list is empty

All nodes destroyed

All nodes destroyed
```

Fig. 19.14 | A simple stack program. (Part 2 of 2.)

Implementing a Class Template *Stack Class With Composition of a List Object*

Another way to implement a Stack class template is by reusing the List class template through *composition*. Figure 19.15 is a new implementation of the Stack class template that contains a List< STACKTYPE > object called stackList (line 38). This version of the Stack class template uses class List from Fig. 19.5. To test this class, use the driver program in Fig. 19.14, but include the new header—Stackcomposition.h in line 4 of that file. The output of the program is identical for both versions of class Stack.

```
1   // Fig. 19.15: Stackcomposition.h
2   // Stack class template with a composed List object.
3   #ifndef STACKCOMPOSITION_H
4   #define STACKCOMPOSITION_H
5
```

Fig. 19.15 | Stack class template with a composed List object. (Part 1 of 2.)

```
 6   #include "List.h" // List class definition
 7
 8   template< typename STACKTYPE >
 9   class Stack
10   {
11   public:
12      // no constructor; List constructor does initialization
13
14      // push calls stackList object's insertAtFront member function
15      void push( const STACKTYPE &data )
16      {
17         stackList.insertAtFront( data );
18      } // end function push
19
20      // pop calls stackList object's removeFromFront member function
21      bool pop( STACKTYPE &data )
22      {
23         return stackList.removeFromFront( data );
24      } // end function pop
25
26      // isStackEmpty calls stackList object's isEmpty member function
27      bool isStackEmpty() const
28      {
29         return stackList.isEmpty();
30      } // end function isStackEmpty
31
32      // printStack calls stackList object's print member function
33      void printStack() const
34      {
35         stackList.print();
36      } // end function printStack
37   private:
38      List< STACKTYPE > stackList; // composed List object
39   }; // end class Stack
40
41   #endif
```

Fig. 19.15 | Stack class template with a composed List object. (Part 2 of 2.)

19.5 Queues

Recall that queue nodes are removed only from the *head* of the queue and are inserted only at the *tail* of the queue. For this reason, a queue is referred to as a first-in, *first-out (FIFO)* data structure. The insert and remove operations are known as **enqueue** and **dequeue**.

Applications of Queues
Queues have many applications in computer systems.

- Computers that have a *single* processor can service only one user at a time. Entries for the other users are placed in a queue. Each entry gradually advances to the front of the queue as users receive service. The entry at the front of the queue is the next to receive service.

- Queues are also used to support **print spooling**. For example, a single printer might be shared by all users of a network. Many users can send print jobs to the printer, even when the printer is already busy. These print jobs are placed in a queue until the printer becomes available. A program called a **spooler** manages the queue to ensure that, as each print job completes, the next print job is sent to the printer.

- Information packets also wait in queues in computer networks. Each time a packet arrives at a network node, it must be routed to the next node on the network along the path to the packet's final destination. The routing node routes one packet at a time, so additional packets are enqueued until the router can route them.

- A file server in a computer network handles file access requests from many clients throughout the network. Servers have a limited capacity to service requests from clients. When that capacity is exceeded, client requests wait in queues.

Implementing a Class Template Queue Class Based By Inheriting from List

The program of Figs. 19.16–19.17 creates a Queue class template (Fig. 19.16) through *private inheritance* (line 9) of the List class template from Fig. 19.5. The Queue has member functions enqueue (Fig. 19.16, lines 13–16), dequeue (lines 19–22), isQueueEmpty (lines 25–28) and printQueue (lines 31–34). These are essentially the insertAtBack, removeFromFront, isEmpty and print functions of the List class template. Of course, the List class template contains other member functions that we do *not* want to make accessible through the public interface to the Queue class. So when we indicate that the Queue class template is to inherit the List class template, we specify *private inheritance*. This makes all the List class template's member functions private in the Queue class template. When we implement the Queue's member functions, we have each of these call the appropriate member function of the list class—enqueue calls insertAtBack (line 15), dequeue calls removeFromFront (line 21), isQueueEmpty calls isEmpty (line 27) and printQueue calls print (line 33). As with the Stack example in Fig. 19.13, this *delegation* requires *explicit use of the this pointer* in isQueueEmpty and printQueue to avoid compilation errors.

```
1  // Fig. 19.16: Queue.h
2  // Queue class-template definition.
3  #ifndef QUEUE_H
4  #define QUEUE_H
5
6  #include "List.h" // List class definition
7
8  template< typename QUEUETYPE >
9  class Queue : private List< QUEUETYPE >
10 {
11 public:
12    // enqueue calls List member function insertAtBack
13    void enqueue( const QUEUETYPE &data )
14    {
15       insertAtBack( data );
16    } // end function enqueue
17
```

Fig. 19.16 | Queue class-template definition. (Part 1 of 2.)

```
18    // dequeue calls List member function removeFromFront
19    bool dequeue( QUEUETYPE &data )
20    {
21       return removeFromFront( data );
22    } // end function dequeue
23
24    // isQueueEmpty calls List member function isEmpty
25    bool isQueueEmpty() const
26    {
27       return this->isEmpty();
28    } // end function isQueueEmpty
29
30    // printQueue calls List member function print
31    void printQueue() const
32    {
33       this->print();
34    } // end function printQueue
35  }; // end class Queue
36
37  #endif
```

Fig. 19.16 | Queue class-template definition. (Part 2 of 2.)

Testing the Queue Class Template

Figure 19.17 uses the Queue class template to instantiate integer queue intQueue of type Queue<int> (line 9). Integers 0 through 2 are *enqueued* to intQueue (lines 14–18), then *dequeued* from intQueue in first-in, first-out order (lines 23–28). Next, the program instantiates queue doubleQueue of type Queue< double > (line 30). Values 1.1, 2.2 and 3.3 are *enqueued* to doubleQueue (lines 36–41), then *dequeued* from doubleQueue in first-in, first-out order (lines 46–51).

```
1   // Fig. 19.17: fig19_17.cpp
2   // Queue-processing program.
3   #include <iostream>
4   #include "Queue.h" // Queue class definition
5   using namespace std;
6
7   int main()
8   {
9      Queue< int > intQueue; // create Queue of integers
10
11     cout << "processing an integer Queue" << endl;
12
13     // enqueue integers onto intQueue
14     for ( int i = 0; i < 3; ++i )
15     {
16        intQueue.enqueue( i );
17        intQueue.printQueue();
18     } // end for
19
```

Fig. 19.17 | Queue-processing program. (Part 1 of 3.)

```
20        int dequeueInteger; // store dequeued integer
21
22        // dequeue integers from intQueue
23        while ( !intQueue.isQueueEmpty() )
24        {
25           intQueue.dequeue( dequeueInteger );
26           cout << dequeueInteger << " dequeued" << endl;
27           intQueue.printQueue();
28        } // end while
29
30        Queue< double > doubleQueue; // create Queue of doubles
31        double value = 1.1;
32
33        cout << "processing a double Queue" << endl;
34
35        // enqueue floating-point values onto doubleQueue
36        for ( int j = 0; j < 3; ++j )
37        {
38           doubleQueue.enqueue( value );
39           doubleQueue.printQueue();
40           value += 1.1;
41        } // end for
42
43        double dequeueDouble; // store dequeued double
44
45        // dequeue floating-point values from doubleQueue
46        while ( !doubleQueue.isQueueEmpty() )
47        {
48           doubleQueue.dequeue( dequeueDouble );
49           cout << dequeueDouble << " dequeued" << endl;
50           doubleQueue.printQueue();
51        } // end while
52     } // end main
```

```
processing an integer Queue
The list is: 0

The list is: 0 1

The list is: 0 1 2

0 dequeued
The list is: 1 2

1 dequeued
The list is: 2

2 dequeued
The list is empty

processing a double Queue
The list is: 1.1

The list is: 1.1 2.2

The list is: 1.1 2.2 3.3
```

Fig. 19.17 | Queue-processing program. (Part 2 of 3.)

```
1.1 dequeued
The list is: 2.2 3.3

2.2 dequeued
The list is: 3.3

3.3 dequeued
The list is empty

All nodes destroyed

All nodes destroyed
```

Fig. 19.17 | Queue-processing program. (Part 3 of 3.)

19.6 Trees

Linked lists, stacks and queues are linear data structures. *A tree is a nonlinear, two-dimensional data structure.* Tree nodes contain two or more links. This section discusses **binary trees** (Fig. 19.18)—trees whose nodes all contain two links (none, one or both of which may have the value nullptr).

Basic Terminology

For this discussion, refer to nodes A, B, C and D in Fig. 19.18. The **root node** (node B) is the first node in a tree. Each link in the root node refers to a **child** (nodes A and D). The **left child** (node A) is the root node of the **left subtree** (which contains only node A), and the **right child** (node D) is the root node of the **right subtree** (which contains nodes D and C). The children of a given node are called **siblings** (e.g., nodes A and D are siblings). A node with no children is a **leaf node** (e.g., nodes A and C are leaf nodes). Computer scientists normally draw trees from the root node down—the opposite of how trees grow in nature.

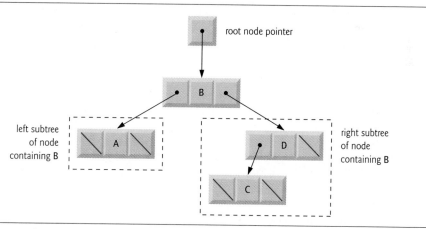

Fig. 19.18 | A graphical representation of a binary tree.

Binary Search Trees

A **binary search tree** (with *no duplicate node values*) has the characteristic that the values in any left subtree are *less than* the value in its **parent node**, and the values in any right subtree are *greater than* the value in its parent node. Figure 19.19 illustrates a binary search tree with 9 values. Note that the shape of the binary search tree that corresponds to a set of data can vary, depending on the *order* in which the values are inserted into the tree.

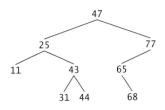

Fig. 19.19 | A binary search tree.

Implementing the Binary Search Tree Program

The program of Figs. 19.20–19.22 creates a binary search tree and traverses it (i.e., walks through all its nodes) three ways—using *recursive* **inorder**, **preorder** and **postorder** traversals. We explain these traversal algorithms shortly.

Testing the Tree Class Template

We begin our discussion with the *driver program* (Fig. 19.20), then continue with the implementations of classes TreeNode (Fig. 19.21) and Tree (Fig. 19.22). Function main (Fig. 19.20) begins by instantiating integer tree intTree of type Tree< int > (line 10). The program prompts for 10 integers, each of which is inserted in the binary tree by calling insertNode (line 19). The program then performs *preorder, inorder* and *postorder traversals* (these are explained shortly) of intTree (lines 23, 26 and 29, respectively). The program then instantiates floating-point tree doubleTree of type Tree< double > (line 31). The program prompts for 10 double values, each of which is inserted in the binary tree by calling insertNode (line 41). The program then performs preorder, inorder and postorder traversals of doubleTree (lines 45, 48 and 51, respectively).

```
 1   // Fig. 19.20: fig19_20.cpp
 2   // Creating and traversing a binary tree.
 3   #include <iostream>
 4   #include <iomanip>
 5   #include "Tree.h" // Tree class definition
 6   using namespace std;
 7
 8   int main()
 9   {
10      Tree< int > intTree; // create Tree of int values
11
12      cout << "Enter 10 integer values:\n";
13
```

Fig. 19.20 | Creating and traversing a binary tree. (Part 1 of 3.)

```
14      // insert 10 integers to intTree
15      for ( int i = 0; i < 10; ++i )
16      {
17         int intValue = 0;
18         cin >> intValue;
19         intTree.insertNode( intValue );
20      } // end for
21
22      cout << "\nPreorder traversal\n";
23      intTree.preOrderTraversal();
24
25      cout << "\nInorder traversal\n";
26      intTree.inOrderTraversal();
27
28      cout << "\nPostorder traversal\n";
29      intTree.postOrderTraversal();
30
31      Tree< double > doubleTree; // create Tree of double values
32
33      cout << fixed << setprecision( 1 )
34         << "\n\n\nEnter 10 double values:\n";
35
36      // insert 10 doubles to doubleTree
37      for ( int j = 0; j < 10; ++j )
38      {
39         double doubleValue = 0.0;
40         cin >> doubleValue;
41         doubleTree.insertNode( doubleValue );
42      } // end for
43
44      cout << "\nPreorder traversal\n";
45      doubleTree.preOrderTraversal();
46
47      cout << "\nInorder traversal\n";
48      doubleTree.inOrderTraversal();
49
50      cout << "\nPostorder traversal\n";
51      doubleTree.postOrderTraversal();
52      cout << endl;
53   } // end main
```

```
Enter 10 integer values:
50 25 75 12 33 67 88 6 13 68

Preorder traversal
50 25 12 6 13 33 75 67 68 88
Inorder traversal
6 12 13 25 33 50 67 68 75 88
Postorder traversal
6 13 12 33 25 68 67 88 75 50

Enter 10 double values:
39.2 16.5 82.7 3.3 65.2 90.8 1.1 4.4 89.5 92.5
```

Fig. 19.20 | Creating and traversing a binary tree. (Part 2 of 3.)

```
Preorder traversal
39.2 16.5 3.3 1.1 4.4 82.7 65.2 90.8 89.5 92.5
Inorder traversal
1.1 3.3 4.4 16.5 39.2 65.2 82.7 89.5 90.8 92.5
Postorder traversal
1.1 4.4 3.3 16.5 65.2 89.5 92.5 90.8 82.7 39.2
```

Fig. 19.20 | Creating and traversing a binary tree. (Part 3 of 3.)

Class Template *TreeNode*

The `TreeNode` class template (Fig. 19.21) definition declares `Tree<NODETYPE>` as its friend (line 13). This makes all member functions of a given specialization of class template `Tree` (Fig. 19.22) friends of the corresponding specialization of class template `TreeNode`, so they can access the `private` members of `TreeNode` objects of that type. Because the `TreeNode` template parameter `NODETYPE` is used as the template argument for `Tree` in the friend declaration, `TreeNode`s specialized with a particular type can be processed only by a `Tree` specialized with the same type (e.g., a `Tree` of `int` values manages `TreeNode` objects that store `int` values).

Lines 30–32 declare a `TreeNode`'s `private` data—the node's `data` value, and pointers `leftPtr` (to the node's *left subtree*) and `rightPtr` (to the node's *right subtree*). The constructor (lines 16–22) sets `data` to the value supplied as a constructor argument and sets pointers `leftPtr` and `rightPtr` to `nullptr` (thus initializing this node to be a *leaf node*). Member function `getData` (lines 25–28) returns the `data` value.

```
1   // Fig. 19.21: TreeNode.h
2   // TreeNode class-template definition.
3   #ifndef TREENODE_H
4   #define TREENODE_H
5
6   // forward declaration of class Tree
7   template< typename NODETYPE > class Tree;
8
9   // TreeNode class-template definition
10  template< typename NODETYPE >
11  class TreeNode
12  {
13     friend class Tree< NODETYPE >;
14  public:
15     // constructor
16     TreeNode( const NODETYPE &d )
17        : leftPtr( nullptr ), // pointer to left subtree
18          data( d ), // tree node data
19          rightPtr( nullptr ) // pointer to right substree
20     {
21        // empty body
22     } // end TreeNode constructor
23
```

Fig. 19.21 | TreeNode class-template definition. (Part 1 of 2.)

```
24       // return copy of node's data
25       NODETYPE getData() const
26       {
27          return data;
28       } // end getData function
29    private:
30       TreeNode< NODETYPE > *leftPtr; // pointer to left subtree
31       NODETYPE data;
32       TreeNode< NODETYPE > *rightPtr; // pointer to right subtree
33    }; // end class TreeNode
34
35    #endif
```

Fig. 19.21 | TreeNode class-template definition. (Part 2 of 2.)

Class Template *Tree*

Class template Tree (Fig. 19.22) has as private data rootPtr (line 42), a pointer to the tree's root node. The Tree constructor (lines 14–15) initializes rootPtr to nullptr to indicate that the tree is initially empty. The class's public member functions are insertNode (lines 18–21) that inserts a new node in the tree and preOrderTraversal (lines 24–27), inOrderTraversal (lines 30–33) and postOrderTraversal (lines 36–39), each of which walks the tree in the designated manner. Each of these member functions calls its own recursive utility function to perform the appropriate operations on the internal representation of the tree, so the program is *not* required to access the underlying private data to perform these functions. Remember that the recursion requires us to pass in a pointer that represents the next subtree to process.

```
1    // Fig. 19.22: Tree.h
2    // Tree class-template definition.
3    #ifndef TREE_H
4    #define TREE_H
5
6    #include <iostream>
7    #include "TreeNode.h"
8
9    // Tree class-template definition
10   template< typename NODETYPE > class Tree
11   {
12   public:
13      // constructor
14      Tree()
15         : rootPtr( nullptr ) { /* empty body */ }
16
17      // insert node in Tree
18      void insertNode( const NODETYPE &value )
19      {
20         insertNodeHelper( &rootPtr, value );
21      } // end function insertNode
22
```

Fig. 19.22 | Tree class-template definition. (Part 1 of 3.)

```
23     // begin preorder traversal of Tree
24     void preOrderTraversal() const
25     {
26        preOrderHelper( rootPtr );
27     } // end function preOrderTraversal
28
29     // begin inorder traversal of Tree
30     void inOrderTraversal() const
31     {
32        inOrderHelper( rootPtr );
33     } // end function inOrderTraversal
34
35     // begin postorder traversal of Tree
36     void postOrderTraversal() const
37     {
38        postOrderHelper( rootPtr );
39     } // end function postOrderTraversal
40
41  private:
42     TreeNode< NODETYPE > *rootPtr;
43
44     // utility function called by insertNode; receives a pointer
45     // to a pointer so that the function can modify pointer's value
46     void insertNodeHelper(
47        TreeNode< NODETYPE > **ptr, const NODETYPE &value )
48     {
49        // subtree is empty; create new TreeNode containing value
50        if ( *ptr == nullptr )
51           *ptr = new TreeNode< NODETYPE >( value );
52        else // subtree is not empty
53        {
54           // data to insert is less than data in current node
55           if ( value < ( *ptr )->data )
56              insertNodeHelper( &( ( *ptr )->leftPtr ), value );
57           else
58           {
59              // data to insert is greater than data in current node
60              if ( value > ( *ptr )->data )
61                 insertNodeHelper( &( ( *ptr )->rightPtr ), value );
62              else // duplicate data value ignored
63                 cout << value << " dup" << endl;
64           } // end else
65        } // end else
66     } // end function insertNodeHelper
67
68     // utility function to perform preorder traversal of Tree
69     void preOrderHelper( TreeNode< NODETYPE > *ptr ) const
70     {
71        if ( ptr != nullptr )
72        {
73           cout << ptr->data << ' '; // process node
74           preOrderHelper( ptr->leftPtr ); // traverse left subtree
```

Fig. 19.22 | Tree class-template definition. (Part 2 of 3.)

```
75              preOrderHelper( ptr->rightPtr ); // traverse right subtree
76          } // end if
77      } // end function preOrderHelper
78
79      // utility function to perform inorder traversal of Tree
80      void inOrderHelper( TreeNode< NODETYPE > *ptr ) const
81      {
82          if ( ptr != nullptr )
83          {
84              inOrderHelper( ptr->leftPtr ); // traverse left subtree
85              cout << ptr->data << ' '; // process node
86              inOrderHelper( ptr->rightPtr ); // traverse right subtree
87          } // end if
88      } // end function inOrderHelper
89
90      // utility function to perform postorder traversal of Tree
91      void postOrderHelper( TreeNode< NODETYPE > *ptr ) const
92      {
93          if ( ptr != nullptr )
94          {
95              postOrderHelper( ptr->leftPtr ); // traverse left subtree
96              postOrderHelper( ptr->rightPtr ); // traverse right subtree
97              cout << ptr->data << ' '; // process node
98          } // end if
99      } // end function postOrderHelper
100 }; // end class Tree
101
102 #endif
```

Fig. 19.22 | Tree class-template definition. (Part 3 of 3.)

Tree Member Function insertNodeHelper

The Tree class's utility function insertNodeHelper (lines 46–66) is called by insertNode (lines 18–21) to recursively insert a node into the tree. *A node can only be inserted as a leaf node in a binary search tree.* If the tree is *empty*, a new TreeNode is created, initialized and inserted in the tree (lines 50–51).

If the tree is *not empty*, the program compares the value to be inserted with the data value in the *root node*. If the insert value is smaller (line 55), the program recursively calls insertNodeHelper (line 56) to insert the value in the *left subtree*. If the insert value is larger (line 60), the program recursively calls insertNodeHelper (line 61) to insert the value in the *right subtree*. If the value to be inserted is identical to the data value in the *root node*, the program prints the message " dup" (line 63) and returns *without inserting the duplicate value into the tree*. Note that insertNode passes the address of rootPtr to insertNode-Helper (line 20) so it can modify the value stored in rootPtr (i.e., the address of the *root node*). To receive a pointer to rootPtr (which is also a pointer), insertNodeHelper's first argument is declared as a *pointer to a pointer* to a TreeNode.

Tree Traversal Functions

Member functions preOrderTraversal (lines 24–27), inOrderTraversal (lines 30–33) and postOrderTraversal (lines 36–39) traverse the tree and print the node values. For the purpose of the following discussion, we use the binary search tree in Fig. 19.23.

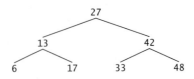

Fig. 19.23 | A binary search tree.

Inorder Traversal Algorithm
Function inOrderTraversal invokes utility function inOrderHelper (lines 80–88) to perform the inorder traversal of the binary tree. The steps for an inorder traversal are:

1. Traverse the *left subtree* with an inorder traversal. (This is performed by the call to inOrderHelper at line 84.)

2. Process the value in the node—i.e., print the node value (line 85).

3. Traverse the *right subtree* with an inorder traversal. (This is performed by the call to inOrderHelper at line 86.)

The value in a node is not processed until the values in its left subtree are processed, because each call to inOrderHelper immediately calls inOrderHelper again with the pointer to the *left subtree*. The inorder traversal of the tree in Fig. 19.23 is

```
6 13 17 27 33 42 48
```

The inorder traversal of a binary search tree prints the node values in *ascending* order. The process of creating a binary search tree actually *sorts* the data—thus, this process is called the **binary tree sort**.

Preorder Traversal Algorithm
Function preOrderTraversal invokes utility function preOrderHelper (lines 69–77) to perform the preorder traversal of the binary tree. The steps for a preorder traversal are:

1. Process the value in the node (line 73).

2. Traverse the *left subtree* with a preorder traversal. (This is performed by the call to preOrderHelper at line 74.)

3. Traverse the *right subtree* with a preorder traversal. (This is performed by the call to preOrderHelper at line 75.)

The value in each node is processed as the node is visited. After the value in a given node is processed, the values in the *left subtree* are processed. Then the values in the *right subtree* are processed. The preorder traversal of the tree in Fig. 19.23 is

```
27 13 6 17 42 33 48
```

Postorder Traversal Algorithm
Function postOrderTraversal invokes utility function postOrderHelper (lines 91–99) to perform the postorder traversal of the binary tree. The steps for a postorder traversal are:

1. Traverse the *left subtree* with a postorder traversal. (This is performed by the call to postOrderHelper at line 95.)

2. Traverse the *right subtree* with a postorder traversal. (This is performed by the call to postOrderHelper at line 96.)

3. Process the value in the node (line 97).

The value in each node is not printed until the values of its children are printed. The post-OrderTraversal of the tree in Fig. 19.23 is

```
    6 17 13 33 48 42 27
```

Duplicate Elimination
The binary search tree facilitates duplicate elimination. As the tree is being created, an attempt to insert a duplicate value will be recognized, because a duplicate will follow the same "go left" or "go right" decisions on each comparison as the original value did when it was inserted in the tree. Thus, the duplicate will eventually be compared with a node containing the same value. The duplicate value may be *discarded* at this point.

Searching a binary tree for a value that matches a key value is also fast. If the tree is balanced, then each branch contains about *half* the number of nodes in the tree. Each comparison of a node to the search key *eliminates half the nodes*. This is called an $O(\log n)$ algorithm (Big O notation is discussed in Chapter 20). So a binary search tree with n elements would require a maximum of $\log_2 n$ comparisons either to find a match or to determine that no match exists. This means, for example, that when searching a (balanced) 1000-element binary search tree, no more than 10 comparisons need to be made, because $2^{10} > 1000$. When searching a (balanced) 1,000,000-element binary search tree, no more than 20 comparisons need to be made, because $2^{20} > 1,000,000$.

Overview of the Binary Tree Exercises
In the exercises, algorithms are presented for several other binary tree operations such as deleting an item from a binary tree, printing a binary tree in a two-dimensional tree format and performing a level-order traversal of a binary tree. The level-order traversal of a binary tree visits the nodes of the tree row by row, starting at the root node level. On each level of the tree, the nodes are visited from left to right. Other binary tree exercises include allowing a binary search tree to contain duplicate values, inserting string values in a binary tree and determining how many levels are contained in a binary tree.

19.7 Wrap-Up

In this chapter, you learned that linked lists are collections of data items that are "linked up in a chain." You also learned that a program can perform insertions and deletions anywhere in a linked list (though our implementation performed insertions and deletions only at the ends of the list). We demonstrated that the stack and queue data structures are constrained versions of lists. For stacks, you saw that insertions and deletions are made only at the top. For queues, you saw that insertions are made at the tail and deletions are made from the head. We also presented the binary tree data structure. You saw a binary search tree that facilitated high-speed searching and sorting of data and efficient duplicate elimination. You learned how to create these data structures for reusability (as templates) and maintainability. In the next chapter, we study various searching and sorting techniques and implement them as function templates.

Summary

Section 19.1 Introduction
- Dynamic data structures (p. 812) grow and shrink during execution.
- Linked lists (p. 812) are collections of data items "lined up in a row"—insertions and removals are made anywhere in a linked list.
- Stacks (p. 812) are important in compilers and operating systems: Insertions and removals are made only at one end of a stack—its top (p. 812).
- Queues (p. 812) represent waiting lines; insertions are made at the back (also referred to as the tail; p. 812) of a queue and removals are made from the front (also referred to as the head; p. 812).
- Binary trees (p. 812) facilitate high-speed searching and sorting of data, efficient duplicate elimination, representation of file-system directories and compilation of expressions into machine code.

Section 19.2 Self-Referential Classes
- A self-referential class (p. 813) contains a pointer that points to an object of the same class type.
- Self-referential class objects can be linked together to form useful data structures such as lists, queues, stacks and trees.

Section 19.3 Linked Lists
- A linked list is a linear collection of self-referential class objects, called nodes, connected by pointer links (p. 814)—hence, the term "linked" list.
- A linked list is accessed via a pointer to the first node of the list. Each subsequent node is accessed via the link-pointer member stored in the previous node and the last node contains a null pointer.
- Linked lists, stacks and queues are linear data structures (p. 814). Trees are nonlinear data structures (p. 814).
- A linked list is appropriate when the number of data elements to be represented is unpredictable.
- Linked lists are dynamic, so the length of a list can increase or decrease as necessary.
- A singly linked list begins with a pointer to the first node, and each node contains a pointer to the next node "in sequence."
- A circular, singly linked list (p. 827) begins with a pointer to the first node, and each node contains a pointer to the next node. The "last node" does not contain a null pointer; rather, the pointer in the last node points back to the first node, thus closing the "circle."
- A doubly linked list (p. 827) allows traversals both forward and backward.
- A doubly linked list is often implemented with two "start pointers"—one that points to the first element to allow front-to-back traversal of the list and one that points to the last element to allow back-to-front traversal. Each node has a pointer to both the next and previous nodes.
- In a circular, doubly linked list (p. 828), the forward pointer of the last node points to the first node, and the backward pointer of the first node points to the last node, thus closing the "circle."

Section 19.4 Stacks
- A stack data structure allows nodes to be added to and removed from the stack only at the top.
- A stack is referred to as a last-in, first-out (LIFO) data structure.
- Function push inserts a new node at the top of the stack. Function pop removes a node from the top of the stack.

- A dependent name (p. 830) is an identifier that depends on the value of a template parameter. Resolution of dependent names occurs when the template is instantiated.

- Non-dependent names (p. 830) are resolved at the point where the template is defined.

Section 19.5 Queues

- A queue is similar to a supermarket checkout line—the first person in line is serviced first, and other customers enter the line at the end and wait to be serviced.

- Queue nodes are removed only from a queue's head and are inserted only at its tail.

- A queue is referred to as a first-in, first-out (FIFO) data structure. The insert and remove operations are known as enqueue and dequeue (p. 833).

Section 19.6 Trees

- Binary trees (p. 837) are trees whose nodes all contain two links (none, one or both of which may have the value nullptr).

- The root node (p. 837) is the first node in a tree.

- Each link in the root node refers to a child. The left child is the root node of the left subtree (p. 837), and the right child is the root node of the right subtree (p. 837).

- The children of a single node are called siblings (p. 837). A node with no children is called a leaf node (p. 837).

- A binary search tree (p. 837) (with no duplicate node values) has the characteristic that the values in any left subtree are less than the value in its parent node (p. 837), and the values in any right subtree are greater than the value in its parent node.

- A node can only be inserted as a leaf node in a binary search tree.

- An inorder traversal (p. 838) of a binary tree traverses the left subtree, processes the value in the root node then traverses the right subtree. The value in a node is not processed until the values in its left subtree are processed. An inorder traversal of a binary search tree processes the nodes in sorted order.

- A preorder traversal (p. 838) processes the value in the root node, traverses the left subtree, then traverses the right subtree. The value in each node is processed as the node is encountered.

- A postorder traversal (p. 838) traverses the left subtree, traverses the right subtree, then processes the root node's value. The value in each node is not processed until the values in both subtrees are processed.

- The binary search tree helps eliminate duplicate data (p. 845). As the tree is being created, an attempt to insert a duplicate value will be recognized and the duplicate value may be discarded.

- The level-order traversal (p. 845) of a binary tree visits the nodes of the tree row by row, starting at the root node level. On each level of the tree, the nodes are visited from left to right.

Self-Review Exercises

19.1 Fill in the blanks in each of the following:

a) A self-_____ class is used to form dynamic data structures that can grow and shrink at execution time

b) The _____ operator is used to dynamically allocate memory and construct an object; this operator returns a pointer to the object.

c) A(n) _____ is a constrained version of a linked list in which nodes can be inserted and deleted only from the start of the list and node values are returned in last-in, first-out order.

d) A function that does not alter a linked list, but looks at the list to determine whether it's empty, is an example of a(n) _____ function.

e) A queue is referred to as a(n) _____ data structure, because the first nodes inserted are the first nodes removed.

f) The pointer to the next node in a linked list is referred to as a(n) _____.

g) The _____ operator is used to destroy an object and release dynamically allocated memory.

h) A(n) _____ is a constrained version of a linked list in which nodes can be inserted only at the end of the list and deleted only from the start of the list.

i) A(n) _____ is a nonlinear, two-dimensional data structure that contains nodes with two or more links.

j) A stack is referred to as a(n) _____ data structure, because the last node inserted is the first node removed.

k) The nodes of a(n) _____ tree contain two link members.

l) The first node of a tree is the _____ node.

m) Each link in a tree node points to a(n) _____ or _____ of that node.

n) A tree node that has no children is called a(n) _____ node.

o) The four traversal algorithms we mentioned in the text for binary search trees are _____, _____, _____ and _____.

19.2 What are the differences between a linked list and a queue?

19.3 What are the differences between a stack and a tree?

19.4 Perhaps a more appropriate title for this chapter would have been "Reusable Data Structures." Comment on how each of the following entities or concepts contributes to the reusability of data structures:

a) classes

b) class templates

c) inheritance

d) `private` inheritance

e) composition

19.5 Provide the inorder, preorder and postorder traversals of the binary search tree of Fig. 19.24.

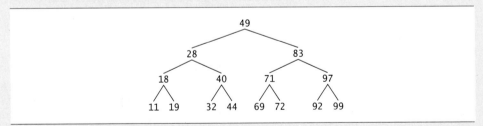

Fig. 19.24 | A 15-node binary search tree.

Answers to Self-Review Exercises

19.1 a) referential. b) `new`. c) stack. d) predicate. e) first-in, first-out (FIFO). f) link. g) `delete`. h) queue. i) tree. j.) last-in, first-out (LIFO). k) binary. l) root. m) child or subtree. n) leaf. o) inorder, preorder, postorder and level order.

19.2 Linked lists are collections of data items logically "lined up in a row"-insertions and removals are made anywhere in a linked list. Queues represent waiting lines; insertions are made at the back (also referred to as the tail) of a queue and removals are made from the front (also referred to as the head) of a queue.

19.3   Stacks are important in compilers and operating systems: Insertions and removals are made only at one end of a stack-it's top. Binary trees facilitate searching and sorting data, duplicate elimination, and compiling expressions into machine code.

19.4   a)   Classes allow us to instantiate as many data structure objects of a certain type (i.e., class) as we wish.

    b)   Class templates enable us to instantiate related classes, each based on different type parameters—we can then generate as many objects of each template class as we like.

    c)   Inheritance enables us to reuse code from a base class in a derived class, so that the derived-class data structure is also a base-class data structure (with `public` inheritance, that is).

    d)   Private inheritance enables us to reuse portions of the code from a base class to form a derived-class data structure; because the inheritance is `private`, all `public` base-class member functions become `private` in the derived class. This enables us to prevent clients of the derived-class data structure from accessing base-class member functions that do not apply to the derived class.

    e)   Composition enables us to reuse code by making a class object data structure a member of a composed class; if we make the class object a `private` member of the composed class, then the class object's `public` member functions are not available through the composed object's interface.

19.5   The inorder traversal is

    11 18 19 28 32 40 44 49 69 71 72 83 92 97 99

The preorder traversal is

    49 28 18 11 19 40 32 44 83 71 69 72 97 92 99

The postorder traversal is

    11 19 18 32 44 40 28 69 72 71 92 99 97 83 49

Exercises

19.6   *(Concatenating Lists)* Write a program that concatenates two linked list objects of characters. The program should include function `concatenate`, which takes references to both list objects as arguments and concatenates the second list to the first list.

19.7   *(Merging Ordered Lists)* Write a program that merges two ordered list objects of integers into a single ordered list object of integers. Function `merge` should receive references to each of the list objects to be merged and a reference to a list object into which the merged elements will be placed.

19.8   *(Summing and Averaging Elements in a List)* Write a program that inserts 25 random integers from 0 to 100 in order in a linked list object. The program should calculate the sum of the elements and the floating-point average of the elements.

19.9   *(Copying a List in Reverse Order)* Write a program that creates a linked list object of 10 characters and creates a second list object containing a copy of the first list, but in reverse order.

19.10   *(Printing a Sentence in Reverse Order with a Stack)* Write a program that inputs a line of text and uses a stack object to print the line reversed.

19.11   *(Palindrome Testing with Stacks)* Write a program that uses a stack object to determine if a string is a palindrome (i.e., the string is spelled identically backward and forward). The program should ignore spaces and punctuation.

19.12 *(Infix-to-Postfix Conversion)* Stacks are used by compilers to help in the process of evaluating expressions and generating machine language code. In this and the next exercise, we investigate how compilers evaluate arithmetic expressions consisting only of constants, operators and parentheses.

Humans generally write expressions like 3 + 4 and 7 / 9 in which the operator (+ or / here) is written between its operands—this is called infix notation. Computers "prefer" postfix notation in which the operator is written to the right of its two operands. The preceding infix expressions would appear in postfix notation as 3 4 + and 7 9 /, respectively.

To evaluate a complex infix expression, a compiler would first convert the expression to postfix notation and evaluate the postfix version of the expression. Each of these algorithms requires only a single left-to-right pass of the expression. Each algorithm uses a stack object in support of its operation, and in each algorithm the stack is used for a different purpose.

In this exercise, you'll write a C++ version of the infix-to-postfix conversion algorithm. In the next exercise, you'll write a C++ version of the postfix expression evaluation algorithm. Later in the chapter, you'll discover that code you write in this exercise can help you implement a complete working compiler.

Write a program that converts an ordinary infix arithmetic expression (assume a valid expression is entered) with single-digit integers such as

```
(6 + 2) * 5 - 8 / 4
```

to a postfix expression. The postfix version of the preceding infix expression is

```
6 2 + 5 * 8 4 / -
```

The program should read the expression into string infix and use modified versions of the stack functions implemented in this chapter to help create the postfix expression in string postfix. The algorithm for creating a postfix expression is as follows:
1) Push a left parenthesis '(' onto the stack.
2) Append a right parenthesis ')' to the end of infix.
3) While the stack is not empty, read infix from left to right and do the following:
>   If the current character in infix is a digit, copy it to the next element of postfix.
>   If the current character in infix is a left parenthesis, push it onto the stack.
>   If the current character in infix is an operator,
>> Pop operators (if there are any) at the top of the stack while they have equal or higher precedence than the current operator, and insert the popped operators in postfix.
>> Push the current character in infix onto the stack.
>   If the current character in infix is a right parenthesis
>> Pop operators from the top of the stack and insert them in postfix until a left parenthesis is at the top of the stack.
>> Pop (and discard) the left parenthesis from the stack.

The following arithmetic operations are allowed in an expression:
+   addition
-   subtraction
*   multiplication
/   division
^   exponentiation
%   modulus

[*Note:* We assume left-to-right associativity for all operators for the purpose of this exercise.] The stack should be maintained with stack nodes, each containing a data member and a pointer to the next stack node.

Some of the functional capabilities you may want to provide are:
a) function convertToPostfix that converts the infix expression to postfix notation

b) function isOperator that determines whether c is an operator

c) function precedence that determines whether the precedence of operator1 is greater than or equal to the precedence of operator2, and, if so, returns true.

d) function push that pushes a value onto the stack

e) function pop that pops a value off the stack

f) function stackTop that returns the top value of the stack without popping the stack

g) function isEmpty that determines if the stack is empty

h) function printStack that prints the stack

19.13 *(Postfix Evaluation)* Write a program that evaluates a postfix expression (assume it's valid) such as

    6 2 + 5 * 8 4 / -

The program should read a postfix expression consisting of digits and operators into a string. Using modified versions of the stack functions implemented earlier in this chapter, the program should scan the expression and evaluate it. The algorithm is as follows:

1) While you have not reached the end of the string, read the expression from left to right.

   If the current character is a digit,

   Push its integer value onto the stack (the integer value of a digit character is its value in the computer's character set minus the value of '0' in the computer's character set).

   Otherwise, if the current character is an *operator*,

   Pop the two top elements of the stack into variables x and y.

   Calculate y *operator* x.

   Push the result of the calculation onto the stack.

2) When you reach the end of the string, pop the top value of the stack. This is the result of the postfix expression.

[Note: In *Step 2* above, if the operator is '/', the top of the stack is 2 and the next element in the stack is 8, then pop 2 into x, pop 8 into y, evaluate 8 / 2 and push the result, 4, back onto the stack. This note also applies to operator '-'.] The arithmetic operations allowed in an expression are

+   addition

–   subtraction

*   multiplication

/   division

^   exponentiation

%   modulus

[Note: We assume left-to-right associativity for all operators for the purpose of this exercise.] The stack should be maintained with stack nodes that contain an int data member and a pointer to the next stack node. You may want to provide the following functional capabilities:

a) function evaluatePostfixExpression that evaluates the postfix expression

b) function calculate that evaluates the expression op1 operator op2

c) function push that pushes a value onto the stack

d) function pop that pops a value off the stack

e) function isEmpty that determines if the stack is empty

f) function printStack that prints the stack

19.14 *(Postfix Evaluation Enhanced)* Modify the postfix evaluator program of Exercise 19.13 so that it can process integer operands larger than 9.

19.15 *(Supermarket Simulation)* Write a program that simulates a checkout line at a supermarket. The line is a queue object. Customers (i.e., customer objects) arrive in random integer intervals of 1–4 minutes. Also, each customer is served in random integer intervals of 1–4 minutes. Obviously, the rates need to be balanced. If the average arrival rate is larger than the average service rate, the queue will grow infinitely. Even with "balanced" rates, randomness can still cause long lines. Run the supermarket simulation for a 12-hour day (720 minutes) using the following algorithm:

1) Choose a random integer from 1 to 4 to determine the minute at which the first customer arrives.

2) At the first customer's arrival time:
   Determine customer's service time (random integer from 1 to 4);
   Begin servicing the customer;
   Schedule arrival time of next customer (random integer 1 to 4 added to the current time).

3) For each minute of the day:
   If the next customer arrives,
      Say so, enqueue the customer, and schedule the arrival time of the next customer;
   If service was completed for the last customer;
      Say so, dequeue next customer to be serviced and determine customer's service completion time (random integer from 1 to 4 added to the current time).

Now run your simulation for 720 minutes, and answer each of the following:

a) What's the maximum number of customers in the queue at any time?

b) What's the longest wait any one customer experiences?

c) What happens if the arrival interval is changed from 1–4 minutes to 1–3 minutes?

19.16 *(Allowing Duplicates in Binary Trees)* Modify the program of Figs. 19.20–19.22 to allow the binary tree object to contain duplicates.

19.17 *(Binary Tree of Strings)* Write a program based on Figs. 19.20–19.22 that inputs a line of text, tokenizes the sentence into separate words (you may want to use the `istringstream` library class), inserts the words in a binary search tree and prints the inorder, preorder and postorder traversals of the tree. Use an OOP approach.

19.18 *(Duplicate Elimination)* In this chapter, we saw that duplicate elimination is straightforward when creating a binary search tree. Describe how you'd perform duplicate elimination using only a one-dimensional array. Compare the performance of array-based duplicate elimination with the performance of binary-search-tree-based duplicate elimination.

19.19 *(Depth of a Binary Tree)* Write a function `depth` that receives a binary tree and determines how many levels it has.

19.20 *(Recursively Print a List Backward)* Write a member function `printListBackward` that recursively outputs the items in a linked list object in reverse order. Write a test program that creates a sorted list of integers and prints the list in reverse order.

19.21 *(Recursively Search a List)* Write a member function `searchList` that recursively searches a linked list object for a specified value. The function should return a pointer to the value if it's found; otherwise, `nullptr` should be returned. Use your function in a test program that creates a list of integers. The program should prompt the user for a value to locate in the list.

19.22 *(Binary Tree Delete)* Deleting items from binary search trees is not as straightforward as the insertion algorithm. There are three cases that are encountered when deleting an item—the item is contained in a leaf node (i.e., it has no children), the item is contained in a node that has one child or the item is contained in a node that has two children.

If the item to be deleted is contained in a leaf node, the node is deleted and the pointer in the parent node is set to `nullptr`.

If the item to be deleted is contained in a node with one child, the pointer in the parent node is set to point to the child node and the node containing the data item is deleted. This causes the child node to take the place of the deleted node in the tree.

The last case is the most difficult. When a node with two children is deleted, another node in the tree must take its place. However, the pointer in the parent node cannot be assigned to point to one of the children of the node to be deleted. In most cases, the resulting binary search tree would not adhere to the following characteristic of binary search trees (with no duplicate values): *The values in any left subtree are less than the value in the parent node, and the values in any right subtree are greater than the value in the parent node.*

Which node is used as a *replacement node* to maintain this characteristic? Either the node containing the largest value in the tree less than the value in the node being deleted, or the node containing the smallest value in the tree greater than the value in the node being deleted. Let's consider the node with the smaller value. In a binary search tree, the largest value less than a parent's value is located in the left subtree of the parent node and is guaranteed to be contained in the rightmost node of the subtree. This node is located by walking down the left subtree to the right until the pointer to the right child of the current node is `nullptr`. We are now pointing to the replacement node, which is either a leaf node or a node with one child to its left. If the replacement node is a leaf node, the steps to perform the deletion are as follows:

1) Store the pointer to the node to be deleted in a temporary pointer variable (this pointer is used to delete the dynamically allocated memory).
2) Set the pointer in the parent of the node being deleted to point to the replacement node.
3) Set the pointer in the parent of the replacement node to `nullptr`.
4) Set the pointer to the right subtree in the replacement node to point to the right subtree of the node to be deleted.
5) Delete the node to which the temporary pointer variable points.

The deletion steps for a replacement node with a left child are similar to those for a replacement node with no children, but the algorithm also must move the child into the replacement node's position in the tree. If the replacement node is a node with a left child, the steps to perform the deletion are as follows:

1) Store the pointer to the node to be deleted in a temporary pointer variable.
2) Set the pointer in the parent of the node being deleted to point to the replacement node.
3) Set the pointer in the parent of the replacement node to point to the left child of the replacement node.
4) Set the pointer to the right subtree in the replacement node to point to the right subtree of the node to be deleted.
5) Delete the node to which the temporary pointer variable points.

Write member function `deleteNode`, which takes as its arguments a pointer to the root node of the tree object and the value to be deleted. The function should locate in the tree the node containing the value to be deleted and use the algorithms discussed here to delete the node. The function should print a message that indicates whether the value is deleted. Modify the program of Figs. 19.20–19.22 to use this function. After deleting an item, call the `inOrder`, `preOrder` and `postOrder` traversal functions to confirm that the delete operation was performed correctly.

19.23 (*Binary Tree Search*) Write member function `binaryTreeSearch`, which attempts to locate a specified value in a binary search tree object. The function should take as arguments a pointer to the binary tree's root node and a search key to locate. If the node containing the search key is found, the function should return a pointer to that node; otherwise, the function should return a `nullptr` pointer.

19.24 (*Level-Order Binary Tree Traversal*) The program of Figs. 19.20–19.22 illustrated three recursive methods of traversing a binary tree—inorder, preorder and postorder traversals. This exercise presents the *level-order traversal* of a binary tree, in which the node values are printed level by level, starting at the root node level. The nodes on each level are printed from left to right. The level-order traversal is not a recursive algorithm. It uses a queue object to control the output of the nodes. The algorithm is as follows:

1) Insert the root node in the queue
2) While there are nodes left in the queue,
    Get the next node in the queue
    Print the node's value
    If the pointer to the left child of the node is not nullptr
        Insert the left child node in the queue
    If the pointer to the right child of the node is not nullptr
        Insert the right child node in the queue.

Write member function levelOrder to perform a level-order traversal of a binary tree object. Modify the program of Figs. 19.20–19.22 to use this function. [*Note:* You'll also need to modify and incorporate the queue-processing functions of Fig. 19.16 in this program.]

19.25 (*Printing Trees*) Write a recursive member function outputTree to display a binary tree object on the screen. The function should output the tree row by row, with the top of the tree at the left of the screen and the bottom of the tree toward the right of the screen. Each row is output vertically. For example, the binary tree illustrated in Fig. 19.24 is output as shown in Fig. 19.25. Note that the rightmost leaf node appears at the top of the output in the rightmost column and the root node appears at the left of the output. Each column of output starts five spaces to the right of the previous column. Function outputTree should receive an argument totalSpaces representing the number of spaces preceding the value to be output (this variable should start at zero, so the root node is output at the left of the screen). The function uses a modified inorder traversal to output the tree—it starts at the rightmost node in the tree and works back to the left. The algorithm is as follows:

While the pointer to the current node is not nullptr
    Recursively call outputTree with the current node's right subtree and totalSpaces + 5
    Use a for structure to count from 1 to totalSpaces and output spaces
    Output the value in the current node
    Set the pointer to the current node to point to the left subtree of the current node
    Increment totalSpaces by 5.

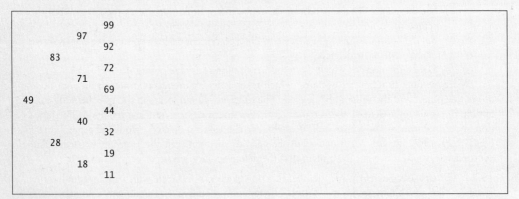

Fig. 19.25 | Outputting the binary tree illustrated in Fig. 19.24.

19.26 (*Insert/Delete Anywhere in a Linked List*) Our linked list class template allowed insertions and deletions at only the front and the back of the linked list. These capabilities were convenient for us when we used private inheritance and composition to produce a stack class template and a queue class template with a minimal amount of code by reusing the list class template. Actually, linked lists are more general than those we provided. Modify the linked list class template we developed in this chapter to handle insertions and deletions anywhere in the list.

19.27 *(List and Queues without Tail Pointers)* Our implementation of a linked list (Figs. 19.4–19.5) used both a firstPtr and a lastPtr. The lastPtr was useful for the insertAtBack and removeFromBack member functions of the List class. The insertAtBack function corresponds to the enqueue member function of the Queue class. Rewrite the List class so that it does not use a lastPtr. Thus, any operations on the tail of a list must begin searching the list from the front. Does this affect our implementation of the Queue class (Fig. 19.16)?

19.28 *(Performance of Binary Tree Sorting and Searching)* One problem with the binary tree sort is that the order in which the data is inserted affects the shape of the tree—for the same collection of data, different orderings can yield binary trees of dramatically different shapes. The performance of the binary tree sorting and searching algorithms is sensitive to the shape of the binary tree. What shape would a binary tree have if its data were inserted in increasing order? in decreasing order? What shape should the tree have to achieve maximal searching performance?

19.29 *(Indexed Lists)* As presented in the text, linked lists must be searched sequentially. For large lists, this can result in poor performance. A common technique for improving list searching performance is to create and maintain an index to the list. An index is a set of pointers to various key places in the list. For example, an application that searches a large list of names could improve performance by creating an index with 26 entries—one for each letter of the alphabet. A search operation for a last name beginning with "Y" would first search the index to determine where the "Y" entries begin and "jump into" the list at that point and search linearly until the desired name was found. This would be much faster than searching the linked list from the beginning. Use the List class of Figs. 19.4–19.5 as the basis of an IndexedList class. Write a program that demonstrates the operation of indexed lists. Be sure to include member functions insertInIndexedList, searchInIndexedList and deleteFromIndexedList.

Special Section: Building Your Own Compiler

In Exercises 8.15–8.17, we introduced Simpletron Machine Language (SML), and you implemented a Simpletron computer simulator to execute SML programs. In Exercises 19.30–19.34, we build a compiler that converts programs written in a high-level programming language to SML. This section "ties" together the entire programming process. You'll write programs in this new high-level language, compile them on the compiler you build and run them on the simulator you built in Exercise 8.16. You should make every effort to implement your compiler in an object-oriented manner. [*Note:* Due to the size of the descriptions for Exercises 19.30–19.34, we've posted them in a PDF document located at www.deitel.com/books/cpphtp9/.]

20

Searching and Sorting

*With sobs and tears
he sorted out
Those of the largest size ...*
—Lewis Carroll

*Attempt the end, and never
stand to doubt;
Nothing's so hard, but search
will find it out.*
—Robert Herrick

*'Tis in my memory lock'd,
And you yourself shall keep the
key of it.*
—William Shakespeare

Objectives

In this chapter you'll:

- Search for a given value in an `array` using linear search and binary search.

- Use Big O notation to express the efficiency of searching and sorting algorithms and to compare their performance.

- Sort an `array` using insertion sort, selection sort and the recursive merge sort algorithms.

- Understand the nature of algorithms of constant, linear and quadratic runtime.

20.1 Introduction

Searching data involves determining whether a value (referred to as the search key) is present in the data and, if so, finding the value's location. Two popular search algorithms are the simple *linear search* (Section 20.2.1) and the faster but more complex *binary search* (Section 20.2.2).

Sorting places data in ascending or descending order, based on one or more sort keys. A list of names could be sorted alphabetically, bank accounts could be sorted by account number, employee payroll records could be sorted by social security number, and so on. You'll learn about *insertion sort* (Section 20.3.1), *selection sort* (Section 20.3.2) and the more efficient, but more complex *merge sort* (Section 20.3.3). Figure 20.1 summarizes the searching and sorting algorithms discussed in the book's examples and exercises. This chapter also introduces **Big O notation**, which is used to characterize an algorithm's worst-case runtime—that is, how hard an algorithm may have to work to solve a problem.

Algorithm	Location	Algorithm	Location
Searching Algorithms		*Sorting Algorithms*	
Linear search	Section 20.2.1	Insertion sort	Section 20.3.1
Binary search	Section 20.2.2	Selection sort	Section 20.3.2
Recursive linear search	Exercise 20.8	Recursive merge sort	Section 20.3.3
Recursive binary search	Exercise 20.9	Bubble sort	Exercises 20.5–20.6
Binary tree search	Section 19.6	Bucket sort	Exercise 20.7
Linear search (linked list)	Exercise 19.21	Recursive quicksort	Exercise 20.10
binary_search standard library function	Section 16.3.6	Binary tree sort	Section 19.6
		sort standard library function	Section 16.3.6
		Heap sort	Section 16.3.12

Fig. 20.1 | Searching and sorting algorithms in this text.

A Note About This Chapter's Examples
The searching and sorting algorithms in this chapter are implemented as function templates that manipulate objects of the array class template. To help you visualize how certain algorithms work, some of the examples display array-element values throughout the searching or sorting process. These output statements slow an algorithm's performance and would *not* be included in industrial-strength code.

20.2 Searching Algorithms

Looking up a phone number, accessing a website and checking a word's definition in a dictionary all involve searching through large amounts of data. A searching algorithm finds an element that matches a given search key, if such an element does, in fact, exist. There are, however, a number of things that differentiate search algorithms from one another. The major difference is the amount of *effort* they require to complete the search. One way to describe this *effort* is with Big O notation. For searching and sorting algorithms, this is particularly dependent on the number of data elements.

In Section 20.2.1, we present the linear search algorithm then discuss the algorithm's *efficiency* as measured by Big O notation. In Section 20.2.2, we introduce the binary search algorithm, which is much more efficient but more complex to implement.

20.2.1 Linear Search

In this section, we discuss the simple linear search for determining whether an *unsorted* array (i.e., an array with element values that are in no particular order) contains a specified search key. Exercise 20.8 at the end of this chapter asks you to implement a recursive version of the linear search.

Function Template `linearSearch`

Function template `linearSearch` (Fig. 20.2, lines 10–18) compares each element of an array with a *search key* (line 14). Because the array is not in any particular order, it's just as likely that the search key will be found in the first element as the last. On average, therefore, the program must compare the search key with *half* of the array's elements. To determine that a value is *not* in the array, the program must compare the search key to *every* array element. Linear search works well for *small* or *unsorted* arrays. However, for large arrays, linear searching is inefficient. If the array is *sorted* (e.g., its elements are in ascending order), you can use the high-speed binary search technique (Section 20.2.2).

```
1   // Fig. 20.2: LinearSearch.cpp
2   // Linear search of an array.
3   #include <iostream>
4   #include <array>
5   using namespace std;
6
7   // compare key to every element of array until location is
8   // found or until end of array is reached; return location of
9   // element if key is found or -1 if key is not found
10  template < typename T, size_t size >
11  int linearSearch( const array< T, size > &items, const T& key )
12  {
13     for ( size_t i = 0; i < items.size(); ++i )
14        if ( key == items[ i ] ) // if found,
15           return i; // return location of key
16
17     return -1; // key not found
18  } // end function linearSearch
```

Fig. 20.2 | Linear search of an array. (Part 1 of 2.)

```
19
20   int main()
21   {
22      const size_t arraySize = 100; // size of array
23      array< int, arraySize > arrayToSearch; // create array
24
25      for ( size_t i = 0; i < arrayToSearch.size(); ++i )
26         arrayToSearch[ i ] = 2 * i; // create some data
27
28      cout << "Enter integer search key: ";
29      int searchKey; // value to locate
30      cin >> searchKey;
31
32      // attempt to locate searchKey in arrayToSearch
33      int element = linearSearch( arrayToSearch, searchKey );
34
35      // display results
36      if ( element != -1 )
37         cout << "Found value in element " << element << endl;
38      else
39         cout << "Value not found" << endl;
40   } // end main
```

```
Enter integer search key: 36
Found value in element 18
```

```
Enter integer search key: 37
Value not found
```

Fig. 20.2 | Linear search of an array. (Part 2 of 2.)

Big O: Constant Runtime

Suppose an algorithm simply tests whether the first element of an array is equal to the second element. If the array has 10 elements, this algorithm requires only *one* comparison. If the array has 1000 elements, the algorithm still requires only *one* comparison. In fact, the algorithm is *independent* of the number of array elements. This algorithm is said to have a **constant runtime**, which is represented in Big O notation as $O(1)$. An algorithm that's $O(1)$ does not necessarily require only one comparison. $O(1)$ just means that the number of comparisons is *constant*—it does *not* grow as the size of the array increases. An algorithm that tests whether the first element of an array is equal to any of the next three elements will always require three comparisons, but in Big O notation it's still considered $O(1)$. $O(1)$ is often pronounced "on the order of 1" or more simply "**order 1**."

Big O: Linear Runtime

An algorithm that tests whether the first element of an array is equal to *any* of the other elements of the array requires at most $n - 1$ comparisons, where n is the number of elements in the array. If the array has 10 elements, the algorithm requires up to nine comparisons. If the array has 1000 elements, the algorithm requires up to 999 comparisons. As n grows larger, the n part of the expression $n - 1$ "dominates," and subtracting one becomes inconsequential. Big O is designed to highlight these dominant terms and ignore terms that become unimportant as n grows. For this reason, an algorithm that requires a total of $n - 1$ comparisons (such as the one we described in this paragraph) is said to be $O(n)$ and is referred to as having a **linear runtime**. $O(n)$ is often pronounced "on the order of n" or more simply "order n."

Big O: Quadratic Runtime

Now suppose you have an algorithm that tests whether *any* element of an array is duplicated elsewhere in the array. The first element must be compared with *all the other elements*. The second element must be compared with all the other elements except the first (it was already compared to the first). The third element then must be compared with all the other elements except the first two. In the end, this algorithm will end up making $(n - 1) + (n - 2) + \ldots + 2 + 1$ or $n^2/2 - n/2$ comparisons. As n increases, the n^2 term *dominates* and the n term becomes inconsequential. Again, Big O notation highlights the n^2 term, leaving $n^2/2$. As we'll soon see, even *constant factors*, such as the 1/2 here, are omitted in Big O notation.

Big O is concerned with how an algorithm's runtime grows in relation to the *number of items processed*. Suppose an algorithm requires n^2 comparisons. With four elements, the algorithm will require 16 comparisons; with eight elements, 64 comparisons. With this algorithm, *doubling* the number of elements *quadruples* the number of comparisons. Consider a similar algorithm requiring $n^2/2$ comparisons. With four elements, the algorithm will require eight comparisons; with eight elements, 32 comparisons. Again, doubling the number of elements quadruples the number of comparisons. Both of these algorithms *grow as the square of n*, so Big O ignores the constant, and both algorithms are considered to be $O(n^2)$, which is referred to as **quadratic runtime** and pronounced "on the order of n-squared" or more simply "order n-squared."

O(n²) Performance

When n is small, $O(n^2)$ algorithms (running on today's billions-of-operations-per-second personal computers) will not noticeably affect performance. But as n grows, you'll start to notice the performance degradation. An $O(n^2)$ algorithm running on a million-element array would require a trillion "operations" (where each could actually require several machine instructions to execute). This could require hours to execute. A billion-element array would require a quintillion operations, a number so large that the algorithm could take decades! Unfortunately, $O(n^2)$ algorithms tend to be easy to write. In this chapter, you'll see algorithms with more favorable Big O measures. Such efficient algorithms often take a bit more cleverness and effort to create, but their superior performance can be worth the extra effort, especially as n gets large.

Linear Search's Runtime

The *linear search* algorithm runs in $O(n)$ time. The worst case in this algorithm is that *every* element must be checked to determine whether the search key is in the array. If the array's size *doubles*, the number of comparisons that the algorithm must perform also *doubles*. Linear search can provide outstanding performance if the element matching the search key happens to be at or near the front of the array. But we seek algorithms that perform well, on average, across *all* searches, including those where the element matching the search key is near the end of the array. If a program needs to perform many searches on large arrays, it may be better to implement a different, more efficient algorithm, such as the *binary search* which we consider in the next section.

Performance Tip 20.1

Sometimes the simplest algorithms perform poorly. Their virtue is that they're easy to program, test and debug. Sometimes more complex algorithms are required to maximize performance.

20.2.2 Binary Search

The **binary search algorithm** is more efficient than the linear search algorithm, but it requires that the array first be *sorted*. This is only worthwhile when the array, once sorted, will be searched a great many times—or when the searching application has *stringent* performance requirements. The first iteration of this algorithm tests the *middle* array element. If this matches the search key, the algorithm ends. Assuming the array is sorted in *ascending* order, then if the search key is *less* than the middle element, the search key cannot match any element in the array's second half so the algorithm continues with only the first *half* (i.e., the first element up to, but *not* including, the middle element). If the search key is *greater* than the middle element, the search key cannot match any element in the array's first half so the algorithm continues with only the second *half* (i.e., the element *after* the middle element through the last element). Each iteration tests the *middle value* of the array's remaining elements. If the element does not match the search key, the algorithm eliminates half of the remaining elements. The algorithm ends either by finding an element that matches the search key or by reducing the sub-array to zero size.

Binary Search of 15 Integer Values
As an example, consider the sorted 15-element array

2	3	5	10	27	30	34	51	56	65	77	81	82	93	99

and the search key 65. A binary search first checks whether the *middle* element (51) is the search key. The search key (65) is larger than 51, so 51 is eliminated from consideration along with the first half of the array (all elements smaller than 51.) Next, the algorithm checks whether 81 (the middle element of the remaining elements) matches the search key. The search key (65) is smaller than 81, so 81 is eliminated from consideration along with the elements larger than 81. After just two tests, the algorithm has narrowed the number of elements to check to three (56, 65 and 77). The algorithm then checks 65 (which matches the search key), and returns the element's index (9). In this case, the algorithm required just *three* comparisons to determine whether the array contained the search key. Using a *linear search* algorithm would have required 10 comparisons. [*Note:* In this example, we've chosen to use an array with 15 elements, so that there will always be an obvious middle element in the array. With an even number of elements, the middle of the array lies between two elements. We implement the algorithm to choose the element with the higher index number.]

Binary Search Example
Figure 20.3 implements and demonstrates the binary-search algorithm. Throughout the program's execution, we use function template displayElements (lines 11–22) to display the portion of the array that's currently being searched.

```
1   // Fig 20.3: BinarySearch.cpp
2   // Binary search of an array.
3   #include <algorithm>
4   #include <array>
5   #include <ctime>
6   #include <iostream>
7   #include <random>
8   using namespace std;
9
10  // display array elements from index low through index high
11  template < typename T, size_t size >
12  void displayElements( const array< T, size > &items,
13     size_t low, size_t high )
14  {
15     for ( size_t i = 0; i < items.size() && i < low; ++i )
16        cout << "   "; // display spaces for alignment
17
18     for ( size_t i = low; i < items.size() && i <= high; ++i )
19        cout << items[ i ] << " "; // display element
20
21     cout << endl;
22  } // end function displayElements
23
24  // perform a binary search on the data
25  template < typename T, size_t size >
26  int binarySearch( const array< T, size > &items, const T& key)
27  {
28     int low = 0; // low index of elements to search
29     int high = items.size() - 1; // high index of elements to search
30     int middle = ( low + high + 1 ) / 2; // middle element
31     int location = -1; // key's index; -1 if not found
32
33     do // loop to search for element
34     {
35        // display remaining elements of array to be searched
36        displayElements( items, low, high );
37
38        // output spaces for alignment
39        for ( int i = 0; i < middle; ++i )
40           cout << "   ";
41
42        cout << " * " << endl; // indicate current middle
43
44        // if the element is found at the middle
45        if ( key == items[ middle ] )
46           location = middle; // location is the current middle
47        else if ( key < items[ middle ] ) // middle is too high
48           high = middle - 1; // eliminate the higher half
49        else // middle element is too low
50           low = middle + 1; // eliminate the lower half
51
52        middle = ( low + high + 1 ) / 2; // recalculate the middle
53     } while ( ( low <= high ) && ( location == -1 ) );
```

Fig. 20.3 | Binary search of an array. (Part 1 of 3.)

```
54
55        return location; // return location of key
56    } // end function binarySearch
57
58    int main()
59    {
60       // use the default random-number generation engine to produce
61       // uniformly distributed pseudorandom int values from 10 to 99
62       default_random_engine engine(
63          static_cast<unsigned int>( time( nullptr ) ) );
64       uniform_int_distribution<unsigned int> randomInt( 10, 99 );
65
66       const size_t arraySize = 15; // size of array
67       array< int, arraySize > arrayToSearch; // create array
68
69       // fill arrayToSearch with random values
70       for ( int &item : arrayToSearch )
71          item = randomInt( engine );
72
73       sort( arrayToSearch.begin(), arrayToSearch.end() ); // sort the array
74
75       // display arrayToSearch's values
76       displayElements( arrayToSearch, 0, arrayToSearch.size() - 1 );
77
78       // get input from user
79       cout << "\nPlease enter an integer value (-1 to quit): ";
80       int searchKey; // value to locate
81       cin >> searchKey; // read an int from user
82       cout << endl;
83
84       // repeatedly input an integer; -1 terminates the program
85       while ( searchKey != -1 )
86       {
87          // use binary search to try to find integer
88          int position = binarySearch( arrayToSearch, searchKey );
89
90          // return value of -1 indicates integer was not found
91          if ( position == -1 )
92             cout << "The integer " << searchKey << " was not found.\n";
93          else
94             cout << "The integer " << searchKey
95                << " was found in position " << position << ".\n";
96
97          // get input from user
98          cout << "\n\nPlease enter an integer value (-1 to quit): ";
99          cin >> searchKey; // read an int from user
100         cout << endl;
101      } // end while
102   } // end main
```

Fig. 20.3 | Binary search of an array. (Part 2 of 3.)

```
10 23 27 48 52 55 58 60 62 63 68 72 75 92 97

Please enter an integer value (-1 to quit): 48

10 23 27 48 52 55 58 60 62 63 68 72 75 92 97
                *
10 23 27 48 52 55 58
             *
The integer 48 was found in position 3.


Please enter an integer value (-1 to quit): 92

10 23 27 48 52 55 58 60 62 63 68 72 75 92 97
                            *
                  62 63 68 72 75 92 97
                            *
                           75 92 97
                              *
The integer 92 was found in position 13.


Please enter an integer value (-1 to quit): 22

10 23 27 48 52 55 58 60 62 63 68 72 75 92 97
                *
10 23 27 48 52 55 58
             *
10 23 27
     *
10
*
The integer 22 was not found.


Please enter an integer value (-1 to quit): -1
```

Fig. 20.3 | Binary search of an array. (Part 3 of 3.)

Function Template binarySearch

Lines 25–56 define function template binarySearch, which has two parameters—a reference to the array to search and a reference to the search key. Lines 28–30 calculate the low end index, high end index and middle index of the portion of the array that the algorithm is currently searching. When binarySearch is first called, low is 0, high is the array's size minus 1 and middle is the average of these two values. Line 31 initializes location to -1—the value that binarySearch returns if the search key is *not* found. Lines 33–53 loop until low is greater than high (indicating that the element was not found) or location does not equal -1 (indicating that the search key was found). Line 45 tests whether the value in the middle element is equal to key. If so, line 46 assigns the middle index to location. Then the loop terminates and location is returned to the caller. Each iteration of the loop that does not find the search key tests a single value (line 45) and eliminates half of the remaining values in the array (line 48 or 50).

Function `main`

Lines 62–64 set up a random-number generator for `int` values from 10–99. Lines 66–71 create an `array` and fill it with random `int`s. Recall that the binary search algorithm requires a *sorted* `array`, so line 73 calls the Standard Library function `sort` to sort `arrayToSearch`'s elements into ascending order. Line 76 displays `arrayToSearch`'s sorted contents.

Lines 85–101 loop until the user enters the value -1. For each search key the user enters, the program performs a binary search of `arrayToSearch` to determine whether it contains the search key. The first line of output from this program shows `arrayToSearch`'s contents in ascending order. When the user instructs the program to search for 48, the program first tests the middle element, which is 60 (as indicated by *). The search key is less than 60, so the program eliminates the second half of the `array` and tests the middle element from the first half of the `array`. The search key equals 48, so the program returns the index 3 after performing just *two* comparisons. The output also shows the results of searching for the values 92 and 22.

Efficiency of Binary Search

In the worst-case scenario, searching a sorted `array` of 1023 elements will take only 10 comparisons when using a binary search. Repeatedly dividing 1023 by 2 (because, after each comparison, we can eliminate from consideration *half* of the remaining elements) and rounding down (because we also remove the middle element) yields the values 511, 255, 127, 63, 31, 15, 7, 3, 1 and 0. The number 1023 ($2^{10} - 1$) is divided by 2 only 10 times to get the value 0, which indicates that there are no more elements to test. Dividing by 2 is equivalent to one comparison in the binary search algorithm. Thus, an `array` of 1,048,575 ($2^{20} - 1$) elements takes a maximum of 20 comparisons to find the key, and an `array` of approximately one billion elements takes a maximum of 30 comparisons to find the key. This is a *tremendous* performance improvement over the linear search. For a one-billion-element `array`, this is a difference between an average of 500 million comparisons for the linear search and a maximum of only 30 comparisons for the binary search! The maximum number of comparisons needed for the binary search of any sorted `array` is the exponent of the first power of 2 greater than the number of elements in the `array`, which is represented as $\log_2 n$. *All logarithms grow at roughly the same rate*, so in Big O notation the base can be omitted. This results in a Big O of $O(\log n)$ for a binary search, which is also known as **logarithmic runtime** and pronounced "on the order of log *n*" or more simply "order log *n*."

20.3 Sorting Algorithms

Sorting data (i.e., placing the data into some particular order, such as *ascending* or *descending*) is one of the most important computing applications. A bank sorts all of its checks by account number so that it can prepare individual bank statements at the end of each month. Telephone companies sort their lists of accounts by last name and, further, by first name to make it easy to find phone numbers. Virtually every organization must sort some data, and often, massive amounts of it. Sorting data is an intriguing, computer-intensive problem that has attracted intense research efforts.

An important point to understand about sorting is that the end result—the sorted `array`*—will be the same no matter which algorithm you use to sort the* `array`*. Your algorithm choice* *affects only the algorithm's runtime and memory use.* The next two sections, introduce the *selection sort* and *insertion sort*—simple algorithms to implement, but inefficient. In each case, we examine the efficiency of the algorithms using Big O notation. We then present the merge sort algorithm, which is much faster but is more difficult to implement.

20.3.1 Insertion Sort

Figure 20.4 uses insertion sort—a simple, but inefficient, sorting algorithm—to sort a 10-element array's values into ascending order. Function template insertionSort (lines 9–28) implements the algorithm.

```cpp
1   // Fig. 20.4: InsertionSort.cpp
2   // Sorting an array into ascending order with insertion sort.
3   #include <array>
4   #include <iomanip>
5   #include <iostream>
6   using namespace std;
7
8   // sort an array into ascending order
9   template < typename T, size_t size >
10  void insertionSort( array< T, size > &items )
11  {
12     // loop over the elements of the array
13     for ( size_t next = 1; next < items.size(); ++next )
14     {
15        T insert = items[ next ]; // save value of next item to insert
16        size_t moveIndex = next; // initialize location to place element
17
18        // search for the location in which to put the current element
19        while ( ( moveIndex > 0 ) && ( items[ moveIndex - 1 ] > insert ) )
20        {
21           // shift element one slot to the right
22           items[ moveIndex ] = items[ moveIndex - 1 ];
23           --moveIndex;
24        } // end while
25
26        items[ moveIndex ] = insert; // place insert item back into array
27     } // end for
28  } // end function insertionSort
29
30  int main()
31  {
32     const size_t arraySize = 10; // size of array
33     array < int, arraySize > data =
34        { 34, 56, 4, 10, 77, 51, 93, 30, 5, 52 };
35
36     cout << "Unsorted array:\n";
37
38     // output original array
39     for ( size_t i = 0; i < arraySize; ++i )
40        cout << setw( 4 ) << data[ i ];
```

Fig. 20.4 | Sorting an array into ascending order with insertion sort. (Part 1 of 2.)

```
41
42        insertionSort( data ); // sort the array
43
44        cout << "\nSorted array:\n";
45
46        // output sorted array
47        for ( size_t i = 0; i < arraySize; ++i )
48           cout << setw( 4 ) << data[ i ];
49
50        cout << endl;
51     } // end main
```

```
Unsorted array:
  34  56   4  10  77  51  93  30   5  52
Sorted array:
   4   5  10  30  34  51  52  56  77  93
```

Fig. 20.4 | Sorting an array into ascending order with insertion sort. (Part 2 of 2.)

Insertion Sort Algorithm

The algorithm's first iteration takes the array's second element and, if it's less than the first element, swaps it with the first element (i.e., the algorithm *inserts* the second element in front of the first element). The second iteration looks at the third element and inserts it into the correct position with respect to the first two elements, so all three elements are in order. At the ith iteration of this algorithm, the first i elements in the original array will be sorted.

First Iteration

Lines 33–34 declare and initialize the array named data with the following values:

```
  34  56   4  10  77  51  93  30   5  52
```

Line 42 passes the array to the insertionSort function, which receives the array in parameter items. The function first looks at items[0] and items[1], whose values are 34 and 56, respectively. These two elements are already in order, so the algorithm continues—if they were out of order, the algorithm would swap them.

Second Iteration

In the second iteration, the algorithm looks at the value of items[2] (that is, 4). This value is less than 56, so the algorithm stores 4 in a temporary variable and moves 56 one element to the right. The algorithm then determines that 4 is less than 34, so it moves 34 one element to the right. At this point, the algorithm has reached the beginning of the array, so it places 4 in items[0]. The array now is

```
   4  34  56  10  77  51  93  30   5  52
```

Third Iteration and Beyond

In the third iteration, the algorithm places the value of items[3] (that is, 10) in the correct location with respect to the first four array elements. The algorithm compares 10 to 56 and moves 56 one element to the right because it's larger than 10. Next, the algorithm compares 10 to 34, moving 34 right one element. When the algorithm compares 10 to 4, it observes that 10 is larger than 4 and places 10 in items[1]. The array now is

| 4 | 10 | 34 | 56 | 77 | 51 | 93 | 30 | 5 | 52 |

Using this algorithm, after the ith iteration, the first $i + 1$ array elements are sorted. They may not be in their *final* locations, however, because the algorithm might encounter smaller values later in the array.

Function Template `insertionSort`

Function template `insertionSort` performs the sorting in lines 13–27, which iterates over the array's elements. In each iteration, line 15 temporarily stores in variable `insert` the value of the element that will be inserted into the array's sorted portion. Line 16 declares and initializes the variable `moveIndex`, which keeps track of where to insert the element. Lines 19–24 loop to locate the correct position where the element should be inserted. The loop terminates either when the program reaches the array's first element or when it reaches an element that's less than the value to insert. Line 22 moves an element to the right, and line 23 decrements the position at which to insert the next element. After the `while` loop ends, line 26 inserts the element into place. When the `for` statement in lines 13–27 terminates, the array's elements are sorted.

Big O: Efficiency of Insertion Sort

Insertion sort is *simple*, but *inefficient*, sorting algorithm. This becomes apparent when sorting *large* arrays. Insertion sort iterates $n - 1$ times, inserting an element into the appropriate position in the elements sorted so far. For each iteration, determining where to insert the element can require comparing the element to each of the preceding elements—$n - 1$ comparisons in the worst case. Each individual repetition statement runs in $O(n)$ time. To determine Big O notation, *nested* statements mean that you must *multiply* the number of comparisons. For each iteration of an outer loop, there will be a certain number of iterations of the inner loop. In this algorithm, for each $O(n)$ iteration of the outer loop, there will be $O(n)$ iterations of the inner loop, resulting in a Big O of $O(n * n)$ or $O(n^2)$.

20.3.2 Selection Sort

Figure 20.5 uses the selection sort algorithm—another easy-to-implement, but inefficient, sorting algorithm—to sort a 10-element array's values into ascending order. Function template `selectionSort` (lines 9–27) implements the algorithm.

```
1   // Fig. 20.5: fig08_13.cpp
2   // Sorting an array into ascending order with selection sort.
3   #include <array>
4   #include <iomanip>
5   #include <iostream>
6   using namespace std;
7
8   // sort an array into ascending order
9   template < typename T, size_t size >
10  void selectionSort( array< T, size > &items )
11  {
```

Fig. 20.5 | Sorting an array into ascending order with selection sort. (Part 1 of 2.)

```
12        // loop over size - 1 elements
13        for ( size_t i = 0; i < items.size() - 1; ++i )
14        {
15           size_t indexOfSmallest = i; // will hold index of smallest element
16
17           // loop to find index of smallest element
18           for ( size_t index = i + 1; index < items.size(); ++index )
19              if ( items[ index ] < items[ indexOfSmallest ] )
20                 indexOfSmallest = index;
21
22           // swap the elements at positions i and indexOfSmallest
23           T hold = items[ i ];
24           items[ i ] = items[ indexOfSmallest ];
25           items[ indexOfSmallest ] = hold;
26        } // end for
27     } // end function insertionSort
28
29     int main()
30     {
31        const size_t arraySize = 10;
32        array < int, arraySize > data =
33           { 34, 56, 4, 10, 77, 51, 93, 30, 5, 52 };
34
35        cout << "Unsorted array:\n";
36
37        // output original array
38        for ( size_t i = 0; i < arraySize; ++i )
39           cout << setw( 4 ) << data[ i ];
40
41        selectionSort( data ); // sort the array
42
43        cout << "\nSorted array:\n";
44
45        // output sorted array
46        for ( size_t i = 0; i < arraySize; ++i )
47           cout << setw( 4 ) << data[ i ];
48
49        cout << endl;
50     } // end main
```

```
Unsorted array:
 34  56   4  10  77  51  93  30   5  52
Sorted array:
  4   5  10  30  34  51  52  56  77  93
```

Fig. 20.5 | Sorting an array into ascending order with selection sort. (Part 2 of 2.)

Selection Sort Algorithm

The algorithm's first iteration selects the smallest element value and swaps it with the first element's value. The second iteration selects the second-smallest element value (which is the smallest of the remaining elements) and swaps it with the second element's value. The algorithm continues until the last iteration selects the second-largest element and swaps it with the second-to-last element's value, leaving the largest value in the last element. After the ith iteration, the smallest i values will be sorted into increasing order in the first i array elements.

First Iteration

Lines 32–33 declare and initialize the array named data with the following values:

| 34 | 56 | 4 | 10 | 77 | 51 | 93 | 30 | 5 | 52 |

The selection sort first determines the smallest value (4) in the array, which is in element 2. The algorithm swaps 4 with the value in element 0 (34), resulting in

| 4 | 56 | 34 | 10 | 77 | 51 | 93 | 30 | 5 | 52 |

Second Iteration

The algorithm then determines the smallest value of the remaining elements (all elements except 4), which is 5, contained in element 8. The program swaps the 5 with the 56 in element 1, resulting in

| 4 | 5 | 34 | 10 | 77 | 51 | 93 | 30 | 56 | 52 |

Third Iteration

On the third iteration, the program determines the next smallest value, 10, and swaps it with the value in element 2 (34).

| 4 | 5 | 10 | 34 | 77 | 51 | 93 | 30 | 56 | 52 |

The process continues until the array is fully sorted.

| 4 | 5 | 10 | 30 | 34 | 51 | 52 | 56 | 77 | 93 |

After the first iteration, the *smallest* element is in the *first* position; after the second iteration, the *two smallest* elements are *in order* in the *first two* positions and so on.

Function Template `selectionSort`

Function template `selectionSort` performs the sorting in lines 13–26. The loop iterates `size - 1` times. Line 15 declares and initializes the variable `indexOfSmallest`, which stores the index of the smallest element in the unsorted portion of the array. Lines 18–20 iterate over the remaining array elements. For each element, line 19 compares the current element's value to the value at `indexOfSmallest`. If the current element is smaller, line 20 assigns the current element's index to `indexOfSmallest`. When this loop finishes, `indexOfSmallest` contains the index of the smallest element remaining in the array. Lines 23–25 then swap the elements at positions `i` and `indexOfSmallest`, using the temporary variable `hold` to store `items[i]`'s value while that element is assigned `items[indexOfSmallest]`.

Efficiency of Selection Sort

The selection sort algorithm iterates $n - 1$ times, each time swapping the smallest remaining element into its sorted position. Locating the smallest remaining element requires $n - 1$ comparisons during the first iteration, $n - 2$ during the second iteration, then $n - 3$, ... , 3, 2, 1. This results in a total of $n(n - 1)/2$ or $(n^2 - n)/2$ comparisons. In Big O notation, smaller terms drop out and constants are ignored, leaving a Big O of $O(n^2)$. Can we develop sorting algorithms that perform *better* than $O(n^2)$?

20.3.3 Merge Sort (A Recursive Implementation)

Merge sort is an *efficient* sorting algorithm but is conceptually *more complex* than insertion sort and selection sort. The merge sort algorithm sorts an array by splitting it into two equal-sized sub-arrays, sorting each sub-array then *merging* them into one larger array. With an odd number of elements, the algorithm creates the two sub-arrays such that one has one more element than the other.

Merge sort performs the merge by looking at each sub-array's first element, which is also the smallest element in that sub-array. Merge sort takes the smallest of these and places it in the first element of merged sorted array. If there are still elements in the sub-array, merge sort looks at the second element in that sub-array (which is now the smallest element remaining) and compares it to the first element in the other sub-array. Merge sort continues this process until the merged array is filled. Once a sub-array has no more elements, the merge copies the other array's remaining elements into the merged array.

Sample Merge

Suppose the algorithm has already merged smaller arrays to create sorted arrays A:

4	10	34	56	77

and B:

5	30	51	52	93

Merge sort merges these arrays into a sorted array. The smallest value in A is 4 (located in the zeroth element of A). The smallest value in B is 5 (located in the zeroth element of B). In order to determine the smallest element in the larger array, the algorithm compares 4 and 5. The value from A is smaller, so 4 becomes the value of the first element in the merged array. The algorithm continues by comparing 10 (the value of the second element in A) to 5 (the value of the first element in B). The value from B is smaller, so 5 becomes the value of the second element in the larger array. The algorithm continues by comparing 10 to 30, with 10 becoming the value of the third element in the array, and so on.

Recursive Implementation

Our merge sort implementation is *recursive*. The *base case* is an array with one element. Such an array is, of course, sorted, so merge sort immediately returns when it's called with a one-element array. The *recursion step* splits an array of two or more elements into two equal-sized sub-arrays, recursively sorts each sub-array, then merges them into one larger, sorted array. [Again, if there is an odd number of elements, one sub-array is one element larger than the other.]

Demonstrating Merge Sort

Figure 20.6 implements and demonstrates the merge sort algorithm. Throughout the program's execution, we use function template displayElements (lines 10–21) to display the portions of the array that are currently being split and merged. Function templates mergeSort (lines 24–49) and merge (lines 52–98) implement the merge sort algorithm. Function main (lines 100–125) creates an array, populates it with random integers, executes the algorithm (line 120) and displays the sorted array. The output from this program displays the splits and merges performed by merge sort, showing the progress of the sort at each step of the algorithm.

```
1    // Fig 20.6: Fig20_06.cpp
2    // Sorting an array into ascending order with merge sort.
3    #include <array>
4    #include <ctime>
5    #include <iostream>
6    #include <random>
7    using namespace std;
8
9    // display array elements from index low through index high
10   template < typename T, size_t size >
11   void displayElements( const array< T, size > &items,
12      size_t low, size_t high )
13   {
14      for ( size_t i = 0; i < items.size() && i < low; ++i )
15         cout << "   "; // display spaces for alignment
16
17      for ( size_t i = low; i < items.size() && i <= high; ++i )
18         cout << items[ i ] << " "; // display element
19
20      cout << endl;
21   } // end function displayElements
22
23   // split array, sort subarrays and merge subarrays into sorted array
24   template < typename T, size_t size >
25   void mergeSort( array< T, size > &items, size_t low, size_t high )
26   {
27      // test base case; size of array equals 1
28      if ( ( high - low ) >= 1 ) // if not base case
29      {
30         int middle1 = ( low + high ) / 2; // calculate middle of array
31         int middle2 = middle1 + 1; // calculate next element over
32
33         // output split step
34         cout << "split:   ";
35         displayElements( items, low, high );
36         cout << "        ";
37         displayElements( items, low, middle1 );
38         cout << "        ";
39         displayElements( items, middle2, high );
40         cout << endl;
41
42         // split array in half; sort each half (recursive calls)
43         mergeSort( items, low, middle1 ); // first half of array
44         mergeSort( items, middle2, high ); // second half of array
45
46         // merge two sorted arrays after split calls return
47         merge( items, low, middle1, middle2, high );
48      } // end if
49   } // end function mergeSort
50
```

Fig. 20.6 | Sorting an array into ascending order with merge sort. (Part 1 of 4.)

```
51   // merge two sorted subarrays into one sorted subarray
52   template < typename T, size_t size >
53   void merge( array< T, size > &items,
54      size_t left, size_t middle1, size_t middle2, size_t right )
55   {
56      size_t leftIndex = left; // index into left subarray
57      size_t rightIndex = middle2; // index into right subarray
58      size_t combinedIndex = left; // index into temporary working array
59      array< T, size > combined; // working array
60
61      // output two subarrays before merging
62      cout << "merge:   ";
63      displayElements( items, left, middle1 );
64      cout << "         ";
65      displayElements( items, middle2, right );
66      cout << endl;
67
68      // merge arrays until reaching end of either
69      while ( leftIndex <= middle1 && rightIndex <= right )
70      {
71         // place smaller of two current elements into result
72         // and move to next space in array
73         if ( items[ leftIndex ] <= items[ rightIndex ] )
74            combined[ combinedIndex++ ] = items[ leftIndex++ ];
75         else
76            combined[ combinedIndex++ ] = items[ rightIndex++ ];
77      } // end while
78
79      if ( leftIndex == middle2 ) // if at end of left array
80      {
81         while ( rightIndex <= right ) // copy in rest of right array
82            combined[ combinedIndex++ ] = items[ rightIndex++ ];
83      } // end if
84      else // at end of right array
85      {
86         while ( leftIndex <= middle1 ) // copy in rest of left array
87            combined[ combinedIndex++ ] = items[ leftIndex++ ];
88      } // end else
89
90      // copy values back into original array
91      for ( size_t i = left; i <= right; ++i )
92         items[ i ] = combined[ i ];
93
94      // output merged array
95      cout << "         ";
96      displayElements( items, left, right );
97      cout << endl;
98   } // end function merge
99
100  int main()
101  {
102     // use the default random-number generation engine to produce
103     // uniformly distributed pseudorandom int values from 10 to 99
```

Fig. 20.6 | Sorting an array into ascending order with merge sort. (Part 2 of 4.)

```
104      default_random_engine engine(
105         static_cast<unsigned int>( time( nullptr ) ) );
106      uniform_int_distribution<unsigned int> randomInt( 10, 99 );
107
108      const size_t arraySize = 10; // size of array
109      array< int, arraySize > data; // create array
110
111      // fill data with random values
112      for ( int &item : data )
113         item = randomInt( engine );
114
115      // display data's values before mergeSort
116      cout << "Unsorted array:" << endl;
117      displayElements( data, 0, data.size() - 1 );
118      cout << endl;
119
120      mergeSort( data, 0, data.size() - 1 ); // sort the array data
121
122      // display data's values after mergeSort
123      cout << "Sorted array:" << endl;
124      displayElements( data, 0, data.size() - 1 );
125   } // end main
```

```
Unsorted array:
 30 47 22 67 79 18 60 78 26 54

split:     30 47 22 67 79 18 60 78 26 54
           30 47 22 67 79
                         18 60 78 26 54

split:     30 47 22 67 79
           30 47 22
                   67 79

split:     30 47 22
           30 47
                 22

split:     30 47
           30
              47

merge:     30
              47
           30 47

merge:     30 47
                 22
           22 30 47

split:             67 79
                   67
                      79
```

Fig. 20.6 | Sorting an array into ascending order with merge sort. (Part 3 of 4.)

```
merge:                67
                          79
                      67 79

merge:     22 30 47
                      67 79
           22 30 47 67 79

split:                    18 60 78 26 54
                          18 60 78
                                   26 54

split:                    18 60 78
                          18 60
                                78

split:                    18 60
                          18
                             60

merge:                    18
                             60
                          18 60

merge:                    18 60
                                78
                          18 60 78

split:                             26 54
                                   26
                                      54

merge:                             26
                                      54
                                   26 54

merge:                    18 60 78
                                   26 54
                          18 26 54 60 78

merge:     22 30 47 67 79
                          18 26 54 60 78
           18 22 26 30 47 54 60 67 78 79

Sorted array:
 18 22 26 30 47 54 60 67 78 79
```

Fig. 20.6 | Sorting an array into ascending order with merge sort. (Part 4 of 4.)

Function *mergeSort*

Recursive function mergeSort (lines 24–49) receives as parameters the array to sort and the low and high indices of the range of elements to sort. Line 28 tests the base case. If the high index minus the low index is 0 (i.e., a one-element sub-array), the function simply returns. If the difference between the indices is greater than or equal to 1, the function splits the array in two—lines 30–31 determine the split point. Next, line 43 recursively calls function mergeSort on the array's first half, and line 44 recursively calls function mergeSort on the array's second half. When these two function calls return, each half is sorted. Line 47 calls function merge (lines 52–98) on the two halves to combine the two sorted arrays into one larger sorted array.

Function merge

Lines 69–77 in function merge loop until the program reaches the end of either sub-array. Line 73 tests which element at the beginning of the two sub-arrays is smaller. If the element in the left sub-array is smaller or both are equal, line 74 places it in position in the combined array. If the element in the right sub-array is smaller, line 76 places it in position in the combined array. When the while loop completes, one entire sub-array is in the combined array, but the other sub-array still contains data. Line 79 tests whether the left sub-array has reached the end. If so, lines 81–82 fill the combined array with the elements of the right sub-array. If the left sub-array has not reached the end, then the right sub-array must have reached the end, and lines 86–87 fill the combined array with the elements of the left sub-array. Finally, lines 91–92 copy the combined array into the original array.

Efficiency of Merge Sort

Merge sort is a far more efficient algorithm than either insertion sort or selection sort—although that may be difficult to believe when looking at the busy output in Fig. 20.6. Consider the first (nonrecursive) call to function mergeSort (line 120). This results in two recursive calls to function mergeSort with sub-arrays that are each approximately half the original array's size, and a single call to function merge. The call to merge requires, at worst, $n - 1$ comparisons to fill the original array, which is $O(n)$. (Recall that each array element is chosen by comparing one element from each of the sub-arrays.) The two calls to function mergeSort result in four more recursive calls to function mergeSort—each with a sub-array approximately one-quarter the size of the original array—and two calls to function merge. These two calls to function merge each require, at worst, $n/2 - 1$ comparisons, for a total number of comparisons of $O(n)$. This process continues, each call to mergeSort generating two additional calls to mergeSort and a call to merge, until the algorithm has split the array into one-element sub-arrays. At each level, $O(n)$ comparisons are required to merge the sub-arrays. Each level splits the size of the arrays in half, so doubling the size of the array requires one more level. Quadrupling the size of the array requires two more levels. This pattern is logarithmic and results in $\log_2 n$ levels. This results in a total efficiency of $O(n \log n)$.

Summary of Searching and Sorting Algorithm Efficiencies

Figure 20.7 summarizes the searching and sorting algorithms we cover in this chapter and lists the Big O for each. Figure 20.8 lists the Big O categories we've covered in this chapter along with a number of values for n to highlight the differences in the growth rates.

Algorithm	Location	Big O
Searching Algorithms		
Linear search	Section 20.2.1	$O(n)$
Binary search	Section 20.2.2	$O(\log n)$

Fig. 20.7 | Searching and sorting algorithms with Big O values. (Part 1 of 2.)

Algorithm	Location	Big O
Recursive linear search	Exercise 20.8	$O(n)$
Recursive binary search	Exercise 20.9	$O(\log n)$
Sorting Algorithms		
Insertion sort	Section 20.3.1	$O(n^2)$
Selection sort	Section 20.3.2	$O(n^2)$
Merge sort	Section 20.3.3	$O(n \log n)$
Bubble sort	Exercises 20.5–20.6	$O(n^2)$
Quicksort	Exercise 20.10	Worst case: $O(n^2)$
		Average case: $O(n \log n)$

Fig. 20.7 | Searching and sorting algorithms with Big O values. (Part 2 of 2.)

n	Approximate decimal value	$O(\log n)$	$O(n)$	$O(n \log n)$	$O(n^2)$
2^{10}	1000	10	2^{10}	$2^{10} \cdot 10$	2^{20}
2^{20}	1,000,000	20	2^{20}	$2^{20} \cdot 20$	2^{40}
2^{30}	1,000,000,000	30	2^{30}	$2^{30} \cdot 30$	2^{60}

Fig. 20.8 | Approximate number of comparisons for common Big O notations.

20.4 Wrap-Up

This chapter discussed searching and sorting data. We began by discussing searching. We first presented the simple, but inefficient linear search algorithm. Then, we presented the binary search algorithm, which is faster but more complex than linear search. Next, we discussed sorting data. You learned two simple, but inefficient sorting techniques—insertion sort and selection sort. Then, we presented the merge sort algorithm, which is more efficient than either the insertion sort or the selection sort. Throughout the chapter we also introduced Big O notation, which helps you express the efficiency of an algorithm by measuring the worst-case runtime of an algorithm. Big O is useful for comparing algorithms so that you can choose the most efficient one. In the next chapter, we discuss typical string-manipulation operations provided by class template `basic_string`. We also introduce string stream-processing capabilities that allow strings to be input from and output to memory.

Summary

Section 20.1 Introduction
- Searching data involves determining whether a search key (p. 857) is present in the data and, if so, returning its location.
- Sorting (p. 857) involves arranging data into order.

- One way to describe the efficiency of an algorithm is with Big O notation (p. 857), which indicates how much work an algorithm must do to solve a problem.

Section 20.2 Searching Algorithms
- A key difference among searching algorithms is the amount of effort they require to return a result.

Section 20.2.1 Linear Search
- The linear search (p. 858) compares each array element with a search key. Because the array is not in any particular order, it's just as likely that the value will be found in the first element as the last. On average, the algorithm must compare the search key with half the array elements. To determine that a value is not in the array, the algorithm must compare the search key to every element in the array.
- Big O describes how an algorithm's effort varies depending on the number of elements in the data.
- An algorithm that's $O(1)$ has a constant runtime (p. 859)—the number of comparisons does not grow as the size of the array increases.
- An $O(n)$ algorithm is referred to as having a linear runtime (p. 860).
- Big O highlights dominant factors and ignores terms that are unimportant with high values of n.
- Big O notation represents the growth rate of algorithm runtimes, so constants are ignored.
- The linear search algorithm runs in $O(n)$ time.
- In the worst case for linear search every element must be checked to determine whether the search element exists. This occurs if the search key is the last element in the array or is not present.

Section 20.2.2 Binary Search
- Binary search (p. 861) is more efficient than linear search, but it requires that the array first be sorted. This is worthwhile only when the array, once sorted, will be searched many times.
- The first iteration of binary search tests the middle element. If this is the search key, the algorithm returns its location. If the search key is less than the middle element, binary search continues with the first half of the array. If the search key is greater than the middle element, binary search continues with the second half. Each iteration tests the middle value of the remaining array and, if the element is not found, eliminates from consideration half of the remaining elements.
- Binary search is more efficient than linear search, because with each comparison it eliminates from consideration half of the elements in the array.
- Binary search runs in $O(\log n)$ (p. 865) time.
- If the size of the array is doubled, binary search requires only one extra comparison to complete.

Section 20.3.1 Insertion Sort
- The first iteration of an insertion sort (p. 866) takes the second element and, if it's less than the first element, swaps it with the first element (i.e., the algorithm *inserts* the second element in front of the first element). The second iteration looks at the third element and inserts it into the correct position with respect to the first two elements, so all three elements are in order. At the ith iteration of this algorithm, the first i elements in the original array will be sorted. For small arrays, the insertion sort is acceptable, but for larger arrays it's inefficient compared to other more sophisticated sorting algorithms.
- The insertion sort algorithm runs in $O(n^2)$ time.

Section 20.3.2 Selection Sort
- The first iteration of selection sort (p. 868) selects the smallest element and swaps it with the first element. The second iteration selects the second-smallest element (which is the smallest remain-

ing element) and swaps it with the second element. This continues until the last iteration selects the second-largest element and swaps it with the second-to-last index, leaving the largest element in the last index. At the ith iteration, the smallest i elements are sorted into the first i elements.

- The selection sort algorithm runs in $O(n^2)$ time (p. 860).

Section 20.3.3 Merge Sort (A Recursive Implementation)
- Merge sort (p. 871) is faster, but more complex to implement, than insertion sort and selection sort.

- The merge sort algorithm sorts an array by splitting the array into two equal-sized sub-arrays, sorting each sub-array and merging the sub-arrays into one larger array.

- Merge sort's base case is an array with one element, which is already sorted. The merge part of merge sort takes two sorted arrays (these could be one-element arrays) and combines them into one larger sorted array.

- Merge sort performs the merge by looking at the first element in each array, which is also the smallest element in each. Merge sort takes the smallest of these and places it in the first element of the larger, sorted array. If there are still elements in the sub-array, merge sort looks at the second element in that sub-array (which is now the smallest element remaining) and compares it to the first element in the other sub-array. Merge sort continues this process until the larger array is filled.

- In the worst case, the first call to merge sort has to make $O(n)$ comparisons to fill the n slots in the final array.

- The merging portion of the merge sort algorithm is performed on two sub-arrays, each of approximately size $n/2$. Creating each of these sub-arrays requires $n/2 - 1$ comparisons for each sub-array, or $O(n)$ comparisons total. This pattern continues, as each level works on twice as many arrays, but each is half the size of the previous array.

- Similar to binary search, this halving results in log n levels, each level requiring $O(n)$ comparisons, for a total efficiency of $O(n \log n)$ (p. 876).

Self-Review Exercises

20.1 Fill in the blanks in each of the following statements:
  a) A selection sort application would take approximately _____ times as long to run on a 128-element array as on a 32-element array.
  b) The efficiency of merge sort is _____.

20.2 What key aspect of both the binary search and the merge sort accounts for the logarithmic portion of their respective Big Os?

20.3 In what sense is the insertion sort superior to the merge sort? In what sense is the merge sort superior to the insertion sort?

20.4 In the text, we say that after the merge sort splits the array into two sub-arrays, it then sorts these two sub-arrays and merges them. Why might someone be puzzled by our statement that "it then sorts these two sub-arrays"?

Answers to Self-Review Exercises

20.1 a) 16, because an $O(n^2)$ algorithm takes 16 times as long to sort four times as much information. b) $O(n \log n)$.

20.2 Both of these algorithms incorporate "halving"—somehow reducing something by half. The binary search eliminates from consideration half of the array after each comparison. The merge sort splits the array in half each time it's called.

20.3   The insertion sort is easier to understand and to implement than the merge sort. The merge sort is far more efficient ($O(n \log n)$) than the insertion sort ($O(n^2)$).

20.4   In a sense, it does not really sort these two sub-arrays. It simply keeps splitting the original array in half until it provides a one-element sub-array, which is, of course, sorted. It then builds up the original two sub-arrays by merging these one-element arrays to form larger sub-arrays, which are then merged, and so on.

Exercises

20.5   *(Bubble Sort)* Implement the bubble sort algorithm—another simple yet inefficient sorting technique. It's called bubble sort or sinking sort because smaller values gradually "bubble" their way to the top of the array (i.e., toward the first element) like air bubbles rising in water, while the larger values sink to the bottom (end) of the array. The technique uses nested loops to make several passes through the array. Each pass compares successive pairs of elements. If a pair is in increasing order (or the values are equal), the bubble sort leaves the values as they are. If a pair is in decreasing order, the bubble sort swaps their values in the array.

The first pass compares the first two element values of the array and swaps them if necessary. It then compares the second and third element values in the array. The end of this pass compares the last two element values in the array and swaps them if necessary. After one pass, the largest value will be in the last element. After two passes, the largest two values will be in the last two elements. Explain why bubble sort is an $O(n^2)$ algorithm.

20.6   *(Enhanced Bubble Sort)* Make the following simple modifications to improve the performance of the bubble sort you developed in Exercise 20.5:

a)   After the first pass, the largest value is guaranteed to be in the highest-numbered element of the array; after the second pass, the two highest values are "in place"; and so on. Instead of making nine comparisons (for a 10-element array) on every pass, modify the bubble sort to make only the eight necessary comparisons on the second pass, seven on the third pass, and so on.

b)   The data in the array may already be in the proper order or near-proper order, so why make nine passes (of a 10-element array) if fewer will suffice? Modify the sort to check at the end of each pass whether any swaps have been made. If none have been made, the data must already be in the proper order, so the program should terminate. If swaps have been made, at least one more pass is needed.

20.7   *(Bucket Sort)* A bucket sort begins with a one-dimensional array of positive integers to be sorted and a two-dimensional array of integers with rows indexed from 0 to 9 and columns indexed from 0 to $n - 1$, where n is the number of values to be sorted. Each row of the two-dimensional array is referred to as a *bucket*. Write a class named BucketSort containing a function called sort that operates as follows:

a)   Place each value of the one-dimensional array into a row of the bucket array, based on the value's "ones" (rightmost) digit. For example, 97 is placed in row 7, 3 is placed in row 3 and 100 is placed in row 0. This procedure is called a *distribution pass*.

b)   Loop through the bucket array row by row, and copy the values back to the original array. This procedure is called a *gathering pass*. The new order of the preceding values in the one-dimensional array is 100, 3 and 97.

c)   Repeat this process for each subsequent digit position (tens, hundreds, thousands, etc.).

On the second (tens digit) pass, 100 is placed in row 0, 3 is placed in row 0 (because 3 has no tens digit) and 97 is placed in row 9. After the gathering pass, the order of the values in the one-dimensional array is 100, 3 and 97. On the third (hundreds digit) pass, 100 is placed in row 1, 3 is placed in row 0 and 97 is placed in row 0 (after the 3). After this last gathering pass, the original array is in sorted order.

Note that the two-dimensional array of buckets is 10 times the length of the integer array being sorted. This sorting technique provides better performance than a bubble sort, but requires much more memory—the bubble sort requires space for only one additional element of data. This comparison is an example of the space–time trade-off: The bucket sort uses more memory than the bubble sort, but performs better. This version of the bucket sort requires copying all the data back to the original array on each pass. Another possibility is to create a second two-dimensional bucket array and repeatedly swap the data between the two bucket arrays.

20.8 (*Recursive Linear Search*) Modify Fig. 20.2 to use recursive function recursiveLinearSearch to perform a linear search of the array. The function should receive the array, the search key and starting index as arguments. If the search key is found, return its index in the array; otherwise, return –1. Each call to the recursive function should check one element value in the array.

20.9 (*Recursive Binary Search*) Modify Fig. 20.3 to use recursive function recursiveBinarySearch to perform a binary search of the array. The function should receive the array, the search key, starting index and ending index as arguments. If the search key is found, return its index in the array. If the search key is not found, return –1.

20.10 (*Quicksort*) The recursive sorting technique called quicksort uses the following basic algorithm for a one-dimensional array of values:

a) *Partitioning Step*: Take the first element of the unsorted array and determine its final location in the sorted array (i.e., all values to the left of the element in the array are less than the element's value, and all values to the right of the element in the array are greater than the element's value—we show how to do this below). We now have one value in its proper location and two unsorted sub-arrays.

b) *Recursion Step*: Perform the *Partitioning Step* on each unsorted sub-array.

Each time *Step 1* is performed on a sub-array, another element is placed in its final location of the sorted array, and two unsorted sub-arrays are created. When a sub-array consists of one element, that sub-array must be sorted; therefore, that element is in its final location.

The basic algorithm seems simple enough, but how do we determine the final position of the first element of each sub-array? As an example, consider the following set of values (the element in bold is the partitioning element—it will be placed in its final location in the sorted array):

37 2 6 4 89 8 10 12 68 45

Starting from the rightmost element of the array, compare each element with **37** until an element less than **37** is found. Then swap **37** and that element. The first element less than **37** is 12, so **37** and 12 are swapped. The values now reside in the array as follows:

12 2 6 4 89 8 10 **37** 68 45

Element 12 is in italics to indicate that it was just swapped with **37**.

Starting from the left of the array, but beginning with the element after 12, compare each element with **37** until an element greater than **37** is found. Then swap **37** and that element. The first element greater than **37** is 89, so **37** and 89 are swapped. The values now reside in the array as follows:

12 2 6 4 **37** 8 10 *89* 68 45

Starting from the right, but beginning with the element before 89, compare each element with **37** until an element less than **37** is found. Then swap **37** and that element. The first element less than **37** is 10, so **37** and 10 are swapped. The values now reside in the array as follows:

12 2 6 4 *10* 8 **37** 89 68 45

Starting from the left, but beginning with the element after 10, compare each element with **37** until an element greater than **37** is found. Then swap **37** and that element. There are no more elements greater than **37**, so when we compare **37** with itself, we know that **37** has been placed in its final location of the sorted array.

Once the partition has been applied to the array, there are two unsorted sub-arrays. The sub-array with values less than 37 contains 12, 2, 6, 4, 10 and 8. The sub-array with values greater than 37 contains 89, 68 and 45. The sort continues with both sub-arrays being partitioned in the same manner as the original array.

Based on the preceding discussion, write recursive function `quickSort` to sort a single-subscripted integer array. The function should receive as arguments an integer array, a starting subscript and an ending subscript. Function `partition` should be called by `quickSort` to perform the partitioning step.

Class **string** and String Stream Processing: A Deeper Look

Suit the action to the word, the word to the action; with this special observance, that you o'erstep not the modesty of nature.
—William Shakespeare

The difference between the almost-right word and the right word is really a large matter — it's the difference between the lightning bug and the lightning.
—Mark Twain

Mum's the word.
—Miguel de Cervantes

I have made this letter longer than usual, because I lack the time to make it short.
—Blaise Pascal

Objectives

In this chapter you'll:

- Manipulate **string** objects.

- Determine **string** characteristics.

- Find, replace and insert characters in **string**s.

- Convert **string** objects to pointer-based strings and vice versa.

- Use **string** iterators.

- Perform input from and output to **string**s in memory.

- Use C++11 numeric conversion functions.

21.1 Introduction

The class template **basic_string** provides typical string-manipulation operations such as copying, searching, etc. The template definition and all support facilities are defined in namespace `std`; these include the `typedef` statement

```
typedef basic_string< char > string;
```

that creates the alias type `string` for `basic_string<char>`. A `typedef` is also provided for the `wchar_t` type (`wstring`). Type `wchar_t`[1] stores characters (e.g., two-byte characters, four-byte characters, etc.) for supporting other character sets. We use `string` exclusively throughout this chapter. To use `strings`, include header `<string>`.

*Initializing a **string** Object*
A `string` object can be initialized with a constructor argument as in

```
string text( "Hello" ); // creates a string from a const char *
```

which creates a `string` containing the characters in `"Hello"`, or with two constructor arguments as in

```
string name( 8, 'x' ); // string of 8 'x' characters
```

which creates a `string` containing eight `'x'` characters. Class `string` also provides a *default constructor* (which creates an *empty* string) and a *copy constructor*. A `string` also can be initialized in its definition as in

```
string month = "March"; // same as: string month( "March" );
```

Remember that = in the preceding declaration is *not* an assignment; rather it's an *implicit call to the string class constructor*, which does the conversion.

---

1. Type wchar_t commonly is used to represent Unicode®, but wchar_t's size is not specified by the standard. C++11 also has types char16_t and char32_t for Unicode support. The Unicode Standard outlines a specification to produce consistent encoding of the world's characters and *symbols*. To learn more about the Unicode Standard, visit www.unicode.org.

strings Are Not Necessarily Null Terminated
Unlike pointer-based char * strings, string objects are not necessarily null terminated. [*Note:* The C++ standard document provides only a description of the capabilities of class string—implementation is platform dependent.]

Length of a string
The length of a string can be retrieved with member function size and with member function length . The subscript operator, [] (which does not perform bounds checking), can be used with strings to access and modify individual characters. A string object has a first subscript of 0 and a last subscript of size() - 1.

Processing strings
Most string member functions take as arguments a *starting subscript location* and the number of characters on which to operate.

string I/O
The stream extraction operator (>>) is overloaded to support strings. The statements

```
string stringObject;
cin >> stringObject;
```

declare a string object and read a string from cin. Input is delimited by whitespace characters. When a delimiter is encountered, the input operation is terminated. Function get-line also is overloaded for strings. Assuming string1 is a string, the statement

```
getline( cin, string1 );
```

reads a string from the keyboard into string1. Input is delimited by a newline ('\n'), so getLine can read a line of text into a string object. You can specify an *alternate delimiter* as the optional third argument to getline.

Validating Input
In earlier chapters, we mentioned the importance of validating user input in industrial-strength code. The capabilities presented in this chapter—and the regular-expression capabilities shown in Section 24.5—are frequently used to perform validation.

21.2 string Assignment and Concatenation

Figure 21.1 demonstrates *string assignment* and *concatenation*. Line 4 includes header <string> for class string. The strings string1, string2 and string3 are created in lines 9–11. Line 13 assigns the value of string1 to string2. After the assignment takes place, string2 is a copy of string1. Line 14 uses member function assign to copy string1 into string3. A separate copy is made (i.e., string1 and string3 are independent objects). Class string also provides an overloaded version of member function assign that copies a specified number of characters, as in

```
targetString.assign( sourceString, start, numberOfCharacters );
```

where sourceString is the string to be copied, start is the starting subscript and num-berOfCharacters is the number of characters to copy.

Line 19 uses the subscript operator to assign 'r' to string3[2] (forming "car") and to assign 'r' to string2[0] (forming "rat"). The strings are then output.

```cpp
1   // Fig. 21.1: Fig21_01.cpp
2   // Demonstrating string assignment and concatenation.
3   #include <iostream>
4   #include <string>
5   using namespace std;
6
7   int main()
8   {
9      string string1( "cat" );
10     string string2; // initialized to the empty string
11     string string3; // initialized to the empty string
12
13     string2 = string1; // assign string1 to string2
14     string3.assign( string1 ); // assign string1 to string3
15     cout << "string1: " << string1 << "\nstring2: " << string2
16        << "\nstring3: " << string3 << "\n\n";
17
18     // modify string2 and string3
19     string2[ 0 ] = string3[ 2 ] = 'r';
20
21     cout << "After modification of string2 and string3:\n" << "string1: "
22        << string1 << "\nstring2: " << string2 << "\nstring3: ";
23
24     // demonstrating member function at
25     for ( size_t i = 0; i < string3.size(); ++i )
26        cout << string3.at( i ); // can throw out_of_range exception
27
28     // declare string4 and string5
29     string string4( string1 + "apult" ); // concatenation
30     string string5; // initialized to the empty string
31
32     // overloaded +=
33     string3 += "pet"; // create "carpet"
34     string1.append( "acomb" ); // create "catacomb"
35
36     // append subscript locations 4 through end of string1 to
37     // create string "comb" (string5 was initially empty)
38     string5.append( string1, 4, string1.size() - 4 );
39
40     cout << "\n\nAfter concatenation:\nstring1: " << string1
41        << "\nstring2: " << string2 << "\nstring3: " << string3
42        << "\nstring4: " << string4 << "\nstring5: " << string5 << endl;
43   } // end main
```

```
string1: cat
string2: cat
string3: cat

After modification of string2 and string3:
string1: cat
string2: rat
string3: car
```

Fig. 21.1 | Demonstrating `string` assignment and concatenation. (Part 1 of 2.)

```
After concatenation:
string1: catacomb
string2: rat
string3: carpet
string4: catapult
string5: comb
```

Fig. 21.1 | Demonstrating string assignment and concatenation. (Part 2 of 2.)

Lines 25–26 output the contents of string3 one character at a time using member function **at**. Member function at provides **checked access** (or **range checking**); i.e., going past the end of the string throws an out_of_range exception. *The subscript operator, [], does not provide checked access.* This is consistent with its use on arrays. Note that you can also iterate through the characters in a string using C++11's range-based for as in

```
for ( char c : string3 )
    cout << c;
```

which ensures that you do not access any elements outside the string's bounds.

Common Programming Error 21.1
Accessing an element beyond the size of the string using the subscript operator is an unreported logic error.

String string4 is declared (line 29) and initialized to the result of concatenating string1 and "apult" using the *overloaded + operator,* which for class string denotes *concatenation.* Line 33 uses the *overloaded addition assignment operator, +=,* to concatenate string3 and "pet". Line 34 uses member function **append** to concatenate string1 and "acomb".

Line 38 appends the string "comb" to empty string string5. This member function is passed the string (string1) to retrieve characters from, the starting subscript in the string (4) and the number of characters to append (the value returned by string1.size() - 4).

21.3 Comparing strings

Class string provides member functions for comparing strings. Figure 21.2 demonstrates class string's comparison capabilities.

```
1   // Fig. 21.2: Fig21_02.cpp
2   // Comparing strings.
3   #include <iostream>
4   #include <string>
5   using namespace std;
6
7   int main()
8   {
9      string string1( "Testing the comparison functions." );
```

Fig. 21.2 | Comparing strings. (Part 1 of 3.)

```
10     string string2( "Hello" );
11     string string3( "stinger" );
12     string string4( string2 ); // "Hello"
13
14     cout << "string1: " << string1 << "\nstring2: " << string2
15        << "\nstring3: " << string3 << "\nstring4: " << string4 << "\n\n";
16
17     // comparing string1 and string4
18     if ( string1 == string4 )
19        cout << "string1 == string4\n";
20     else if ( string1 > string4 )
21          cout << "string1 > string4\n";
22     else // string1 < string4
23        cout << "string1 < string4\n";
24
25     // comparing string1 and string2
26     int result = string1.compare( string2 );
27
28     if ( result == 0 )
29        cout << "string1.compare( string2 ) == 0\n";
30     else if ( result > 0 )
31        cout << "string1.compare( string2 ) > 0\n";
32     else // result < 0
33        cout << "string1.compare( string2 ) < 0\n";
34
35     // comparing string1 (elements 2-5) and string3 (elements 0-5)
36     result = string1.compare( 2, 5, string3, 0, 5 );
37
38     if ( result == 0 )
39        cout << "string1.compare( 2, 5, string3, 0, 5 ) == 0\n";
40     else if ( result > 0 )
41        cout << "string1.compare( 2, 5, string3, 0, 5 ) > 0\n";
42     else // result < 0
43        cout << "string1.compare( 2, 5, string3, 0, 5 ) < 0\n";
44
45     // comparing string2 and string4
46     result = string4.compare( 0, string2.size(), string2 );
47
48     if ( result == 0 )
49        cout << "string4.compare( 0, string2.size(), "
50           << "string2 ) == 0" << endl;
51     else if ( result > 0 )
52        cout << "string4.compare( 0, string2.size(), "
53           << "string2 ) > 0" << endl;
54     else // result < 0
55        cout << "string4.compare( 0, string2.size(), "
56              << "string2 ) < 0" << endl;
57
58     // comparing string2 and string4
59     result = string2.compare( 0, 3, string4 );
60
61     if ( result == 0 )
62        cout << "string2.compare( 0, 3, string4 ) == 0" << endl;
```

Fig. 21.2 | Comparing strings. (Part 2 of 3.)

```
63          else if ( result > 0 )
64              cout << "string2.compare( 0, 3, string4 ) > 0" << endl;
65          else // result < 0
66              cout << "string2.compare( 0, 3, string4 ) < 0" << endl;
67      } // end main
```

```
string1: Testing the comparison functions.
string2: Hello
string3: stinger
string4: Hello

string1 > string4
string1.compare( string2 ) > 0
string1.compare( 2, 5, string3, 0, 5 ) == 0
string4.compare( 0, string2.size(), string2 ) == 0
string2.compare( 0, 3, string4 ) < 0
```

Fig. 21.2 | Comparing strings. (Part 3 of 3.)

The program declares four strings (lines 9–12) and outputs each (lines 14–15). Line 18 tests string1 against string4 for equality using the *overloaded equality operator*. If the condition is true, "string1 == string4" is output. If the condition is false, the condition in line 20 is tested. All the string class overloaded relational and equality operator functions return bool values.

Line 26 uses string member function **compare** to compare string1 to string2. Variable result is assigned 0 if the strings are equivalent, a *positive number* if string1 is lexicographically greater than string2 or a *negative number* if string1 is *lexicographically* less than string2. When we say that a string is *lexicographically* less than another, we mean that the compare method uses the numerical values of the characters (see Appendix B, ASCII Character Set) in each string to determine that the first string is less than the second. Because a string starting with 'T' is considered lexicographically greater than a string starting with 'H', result is assigned a value greater than 0, as confirmed by the output. A lexicon is a dictionary.

Line 36 compares portions of string1 and string3 using an *overloaded* version of member function compare. The first two arguments (2 and 5) specify the *starting subscript* and *length* of the portion of string1 ("sting") to compare with string3. The third argument is the comparison string. The last two arguments (0 and 5) are the *starting subscript* and *length* of the portion of the comparison string being compared (also "sting"). The value assigned to result is 0 for equality, a positive number if string1 is *lexicographically* greater than string3 or a negative number if string1 is *lexicographically* less than string3. The two pieces being compared here are identical, so result is assigned 0.

Line 46 uses another *overloaded* version of function compare to compare string4 and string2. The first two arguments are the same—the *starting subscript* and *length*. The last argument is the comparison string. The value returned is also the same—0 for equality, a positive number if string4 is *lexicographically* greater than string2 or a negative number if string4 is *lexicographically* less than string2. Because the two pieces of strings being compared here are identical, result is assigned 0.

Line 59 calls member function compare to compare the first 3 characters in string2 to string4. Because "Hel" is less than "Hello", a value less than zero is returned.

21.4 Substrings

Class `string` provides member function **substr** for retrieving a substring from a `string`. The result is a new `string` object that's copied from the source `string`. Figure 21.3 demonstrates `substr`. The program declares and initializes a `string` at line 9. Line 13 uses member function `substr` to retrieve a substring from `string1`. The first argument specifies the *beginning subscript* of the desired substring; the second argument specifies the substring's *length*.

```cpp
1   // Fig. 21.3: Fig21_03.cpp
2   // Demonstrating string member function substr.
3   #include <iostream>
4   #include <string>
5   using namespace std;
6
7   int main()
8   {
9      string string1( "The airplane landed on time." );
10
11     // retrieve substring "plane" which
12     // begins at subscript 7 and consists of 5 characters
13     cout << string1.substr( 7, 5 ) << endl;
14  } // end main
```

```
plane
```

Fig. 21.3 | Demonstrating `string` member function `substr`.

21.5 Swapping strings

Class `string` provides member function **swap** for swapping strings. Figure 21.4 swaps two strings. Lines 9–10 declare and initialize `strings first` and `second`. Each `string` is then output. Line 15 uses `string` member function swap to swap the values of `first` and `second`. The two `strings` are printed again to confirm that they were indeed swapped. The `string` member function swap is useful for implementing programs that sort strings.

```cpp
1   // Fig. 21.4: Fig21_04.cpp
2   // Using the swap function to swap two strings.
3   #include <iostream>
4   #include <string>
5   using namespace std;
6
7   int main()
8   {
9      string first( "one" );
10     string second( "two" );
11
12     // output strings
13     cout << "Before swap:\n first: " << first << "\nsecond: " << second;
```

Fig. 21.4 | Using the swap function to swap two `strings`. (Part 1 of 2.)

```
14
15        first.swap( second ); // swap strings
16
17        cout << "\n\nAfter swap:\n first: " << first
18            << "\nsecond: " << second << endl;
19    } // end main
```

```
Before swap:
 first: one
second: two

After swap:
 first: two
second: one
```

Fig. 21.4 | Using the swap function to swap two strings. (Part 2 of 2.)

21.6 string Characteristics

Class string provides member functions for gathering information about a string's *size*, *length, capacity, maximum length* and other characteristics. A string's *size* or *length* is the number of characters currently stored in the string. A string's capacity is the number of characters that can be stored in the string without allocating more memory. The capacity of a string must be at least equal to the current size of the string, though it can be greater. The exact capacity of a string depends on the implementation. The **maximum size** is the largest possible size a string can have. If this value is exceeded, a length_error exception is thrown. Figure 21.5 demonstrates string class member functions for determining various characteristics of strings.

```
1   // Fig. 21.5: Fig21_05.cpp
2   // Printing string characteristics.
3   #include <iostream>
4   #include <string>
5   using namespace std;
6
7   void printStatistics( const string & );
8
9   int main()
10  {
11      string string1; // empty string
12
13      cout << "Statistics before input:\n" << boolalpha;
14      printStatistics( string1 );
15
16      // read in only "tomato" from "tomato soup"
17      cout << "\n\nEnter a string: ";
18      cin >> string1; // delimited by whitespace
19      cout << "The string entered was: " << string1;
20
```

Fig. 21.5 | Printing string characteristics. (Part 1 of 3.)

```
21        cout << "\nStatistics after input:\n";
22        printStatistics( string1 );
23
24        // read in "soup"
25        cin >> string1; // delimited by whitespace
26        cout << "\n\nThe remaining string is: " << string1 << endl;
27        printStatistics( string1 );
28
29        // append 46 characters to string1
30        string1 += "1234567890abcdefghijklmnopqrstuvwxyz1234567890";
31        cout << "\n\nstring1 is now: " << string1 << endl;
32        printStatistics( string1 );
33
34        // add 10 elements to string1
35        string1.resize( string1.size() + 10 );
36        cout << "\n\nStats after resizing by (length + 10):\n";
37        printStatistics( string1 );
38        cout << endl;
39    } // end main
40
41    // display string statistics
42    void printStatistics( const string &stringRef )
43    {
44        cout << "capacity: " << stringRef.capacity() << "\nmax size: "
45            << stringRef.max_size() << "\nsize: " << stringRef.size()
46            << "\nlength: " << stringRef.size()
47            << "\nempty: " << stringRef.empty();
48    } // end printStatistics
```

```
Statistics before input:
capacity: 15
max size: 4294967294
size: 0
length: 0
empty: true

Enter a string: tomato soup
The string entered was: tomato
Statistics after input:
capacity: 15
max size: 4294967294
size: 6
length: 6
empty: false

The remaining string is: soup
capacity: 15
max size: 4294967294
size: 4
length: 4
empty: false

string1 is now: soup1234567890abcdefghijklmnopqrstuvwxyz1234567890
capacity: 63
max size: 4294967294
```

Fig. 21.5 | Printing `string` characteristics. (Part 2 of 3.)

```
size: 50
length: 50
empty: false

Stats after resizing by (length + 10):
capacity: 63
max size: 4294967294
size: 60
length: 60
empty: false
```

Fig. 21.5 | Printing string characteristics. (Part 3 of 3.)

The program declares empty string string1 (line 11) and passes it to function printStatistics (line 14). Function printStatistics (lines 42–48) takes a reference to a const string as an argument and outputs the capacity (using member function capacity), maximum size (using member function max_size), size (using member function size), length (using member function size) and whether the string is empty (using member function empty). The initial call to printStatistics indicates that the initial values for the size and length of string1 are 0.

The size and length of 0 indicate that there are no characters stored in string. Recall that the *size* and *length* are always identical. In this implementation, the maximum size is 4,294,967,294. Object string1 is an empty string, so function empty returns true.

Line 18 inputs a string. In this example, "tomato soup" is input. Because a space character is a delimiter, only "tomato" is stored in string1; however, "soup" remains in the input buffer. Line 22 calls function printStatistics to output statistics for string1. Notice in the output that the length is 6 and the capacity is 15.

Line 25 reads "soup" from the input buffer and stores it in string1, thereby replacing "tomato". Line 27 passes string1 to printStatistics.

Line 30 uses the *overloaded* += operator to concatenate a 46-character-long string to string1. Line 32 passes string1 to printStatistics. The capacity has increased to 63 elements and the length is now 50.

Line 35 uses member function **resize** to increase the length of string1 by 10 characters. The additional elements are set to null characters. The output shows that the capacity has *not* changed and the length is now 60.

21.7 Finding Substrings and Characters in a string

Class string provides const member functions for finding substrings and characters in a string. Figure 21.6 demonstrates the find functions.

```
1   // Fig. 21.6: Fig21_06.cpp
2   // Demonstrating the string find member functions.
3   #include <iostream>
4   #include <string>
```

Fig. 21.6 | Demonstrating the string find member functions. (Part 1 of 2.)

```
 5   using namespace std;
 6
 7   int main()
 8   {
 9      string string1( "noon is 12 pm; midnight is not." );
10      int location;
11
12      // find "is" at location 5 and 24
13      cout << "Original string:\n" << string1
14         << "\n\n(find) \"is\" was found at: " << string1.find( "is" )
15         << "\n(rfind) \"is\" was found at: " << string1.rfind( "is" );
16
17      // find 'o' at location 1
18      location = string1.find_first_of( "misop" );
19      cout << "\n\n(find_first_of) found '" << string1[ location ]
20         << "' from the group \"misop\" at: " << location;
21
22      // find 'o' at location 28
23      location = string1.find_last_of( "misop" );
24      cout << "\n\n(find_last_of) found '" << string1[ location ]
25         << "' from the group \"misop\" at: " << location;
26
27      // find '1' at location 8
28      location = string1.find_first_not_of( "noi spm" );
29      cout << "\n\n(find_first_not_of) '" << string1[ location ]
30         << "' is not contained in \"noi spm\" and was found at: "
31         << location;
32
33      // find '.' at location 13
34      location = string1.find_first_not_of( "12noi spm" );
35      cout << "\n\n(find_first_not_of) '" << string1[ location ]
36         << "' is not contained in \"12noi spm\" and was "
37         << "found at: " << location << endl;
38
39      // search for characters not in string1
40      location = string1.find_first_not_of(
41         "noon is 12 pm; midnight is not." );
42      cout << "\nfind_first_not_of(\"noon is 12 pm; midnight is not.\")"
43         << " returned: " << location << endl;
44   } // end main
```

```
Original string:
noon is 12 pm; midnight is not.
(find) "is" was found at: 5
(rfind) "is" was found at: 24
(find_first_of) found 'o' from the group "misop" at: 1
(find_last_of) found 'o' from the group "misop" at: 28
(find_first_not_of) '1' is not contained in "noi spm" and was found at: 8
(find_first_not_of) '.' is not contained in "12noi spm" and was found at: 13
find_first_not_of("noon is 12 pm; midnight is not.") returned: -1
```

Fig. 21.6 | Demonstrating the `string` find member functions. (Part 2 of 2.)

String string1 is declared and initialized in line 9. Line 14 attempts to find "is" in string1 using function **find**. If "is" is found, the subscript of the starting location of that string is returned. If the string is not found, the value **string::npos** (a public static constant defined in class string) is returned. This value is returned by the string find-related functions to indicate that a substring or character was not found in the string.

Line 15 uses member function **rfind** to search string1 *backward* (i.e., *right-to-left*). If "is" is found, the subscript location is returned. If the string is not found, string::npos is returned. [*Note:* The rest of the find functions presented in this section return the same type unless otherwise noted.]

Line 18 uses member function **find_first_of** to locate the *first* occurrence in string1 of any character in "misop". The searching is done from the beginning of string1. The character 'o' is found in element 1.

Line 23 uses member function **find_last_of** to find the *last* occurrence in string1 of any character in "misop". The searching is done from the end of string1. The character 'o' is found in element 28.

Line 28 uses member function **find_first_not_of** to find the *first* character in string1 *not* contained in "noi spm". The character '1' is found in element 8. Searching is done from the beginning of string1.

Line 34 uses member function find_first_not_of to find the *first* character *not* contained in "12noi spm". The character '.' is found in element 13. Searching is done from the beginning of string1.

Lines 40–41 use member function find_first_not_of to find the *first* character *not* contained in "noon is 12 pm; midnight is not.". In this case, the string being searched contains every character specified in the string argument. Because a character was not found, string::npos (which has the value –1 in this case) is returned.

21.8 Replacing Characters in a string

Figure 21.7 demonstrates string member functions for *replacing* and *erasing* characters. Lines 10–14 declare and initialize string string1. Line 20 uses string member function **erase** to erase everything from (and including) the character in position 62 to the end of string1. [*Note:* Each newline character occupies one character in the string.]

```
1   // Fig. 21.7: Fig21_07.cpp
2   // Demonstrating string member functions erase and replace.
3   #include <iostream>
4   #include <string>
5   using namespace std;
6
7   int main()
8   {
9      // compiler concatenates all parts into one string
10     string string1( "The values in any left subtree"
11        "\nare less than the value in the"
12        "\nparent node and the values in"
13        "\nany right subtree are greater"
14        "\nthan the value in the parent node" );
```

Fig. 21.7 | Demonstrating string member functions erase and replace. (Part 1 of 2.)

```
15
16      cout << "Original string:\n" << string1 << endl << endl;
17
18      // remove all characters from (and including) location 62
19      // through the end of string1
20      string1.erase( 62 );
21
22      // output new string
23      cout << "Original string after erase:\n" << string1
24         << "\nAfter first replacement:\n";
25
26      size_t position = string1.find( " " ); // find first space
27
28      // replace all spaces with period
29      while ( position != string::npos )
30      {
31         string1.replace( position, 1, "." );
32         position = string1.find( " ", position + 1 );
33      } // end while
34
35      cout << string1 << "\nAfter second replacement:\n";
36
37      position = string1.find( "." ); // find first period
38
39      // replace all periods with two semicolons
40      // NOTE: this will overwrite characters
41      while ( position != string::npos )
42      {
43         string1.replace( position, 2, "xxxxx;;yyy", 5, 2 );
44         position = string1.find( ".", position + 1 );
45      } // end while
46
47      cout << string1 << endl;
48   } // end main
```

```
Original string:
The values in any left subtree
are less than the value in the
parent node and the values in
any right subtree are greater
than the value in the parent node

Original string after erase:
The values in any left subtree
are less than the value in the

After first replacement:
The.values.in.any.left.subtree
are.less.than.the.value.in.the

After second replacement:
The;;alues;;n;;ny;;eft;;ubtree
are;;ess;;han;;he;;alue;;n;;he
```

Fig. 21.7 | Demonstrating `string` member functions `erase` and `replace`. (Part 2 of 2.)

Lines 26–33 use `find` to locate each occurrence of the space character. Each space is then *replaced* with a period by a call to `string` member function **replace**. Function `replace` takes three arguments: the *subscript* of the character in the `string` at which replacement should *begin*, the *number of characters to replace* and the *replacement string*. Member function `find` returns `string::npos` when the search character is *not found*. In line 32, 1 is added to `position` to continue searching at the location of the *next* character.

Lines 37–45 use function `find` to find every period and another overloaded function `replace` to replace every period and its following character with two semicolons. The arguments passed to this version of `replace` are the subscript of the element where the replace operation begins, the number of characters to replace, a replacement character string from which a *substring* is selected to use as replacement characters, the element in the character string where the replacement substring begins and the number of characters in the replacement character string to use.

21.9 Inserting Characters into a `string`

Class `string` provides member functions for *inserting* characters into a `string`. Figure 21.8 demonstrates the `string insert` capabilities.

The program declares, initializes then outputs `strings string1, string2, string3` and `string4`. Line 19 uses `string` member function **insert** to insert `string2`'s content before element 10 of `string1`.

Line 22 uses `insert` to insert `string4` before `string3`'s element 3. The last two arguments specify the *starting* and *last* element of `string4` that should be inserted. Using `string::npos` causes the *entire* `string` to be inserted.

```cpp
1   // Fig. 21.8: Fig21_08.cpp
2   // Demonstrating class string insert member functions.
3   #include <iostream>
4   #include <string>
5   using namespace std;
6
7   int main()
8   {
9      string string1( "beginning end" );
10     string string2( "middle " );
11     string string3( "12345678" );
12     string string4( "xx" );
13
14     cout << "Initial strings:\nstring1: " << string1
15        << "\nstring2: " << string2 << "\nstring3: " << string3
16        << "\nstring4: " << string4 << "\n\n";
17
18     // insert "middle" at location 10 in string1
19     string1.insert( 10, string2 );
20
21     // insert "xx" at location 3 in string3
22     string3.insert( 3, string4, 0, string::npos );
23
```

Fig. 21.8 | Demonstrating class `string insert` member functions. (Part 1 of 2.)

```
24        cout << "Strings after insert:\nstring1: " << string1
25            << "\nstring2: " << string2 << "\nstring3: " << string3
26            << "\nstring4: " << string4 << endl;
27  } // end main
```

```
Initial strings:
string1: beginning end
string2: middle
string3: 12345678
string4: xx

Strings after insert:
string1: beginning middle end
string2: middle
string3: 123xx45678
string4: xx
```

Fig. 21.8 | Demonstrating class `string` insert member functions. (Part 2 of 2.)

21.10 Conversion to Pointer-Based char * Strings

You can convert `string` class objects to pointer-based strings. As mentioned earlier, unlike pointer-based strings, `strings` are *not necessarily null terminated*. These conversion functions are useful when a given function takes a pointer-based string as an argument. Figure 21.9 demonstrates conversion of `strings` to pointer-based strings.

```
1   // Fig. 21.9: Fig21_09.cpp
2   // Converting strings to pointer-based strings and character arrays.
3   #include <iostream>
4   #include <string>
5   using namespace std;
6
7   int main()
8   {
9      string string1( "STRINGS" ); // string constructor with char * arg
10     const char *ptr1 = nullptr; // initialize *ptr1
11     size_t length = string1.size();
12     char *ptr2 = new char[ length + 1 ]; // including null
13
14     // copy characters from string1 into allocated memory
15     string1.copy( ptr2, length, 0 ); // copy string1 to ptr2 char *
16     ptr2[ length ] = '\0'; // add null terminator
17
18     cout << "string string1 is " << string1
19         << "\nstring1 converted to a pointer-based string is "
20         << string1.c_str()   << "\nptr1 is ";
21
22     // Assign to pointer ptr1 the const char * returned by
23     // function data(). NOTE: this is a potentially dangerous
```

Fig. 21.9 | Converting `strings` to pointer-based strings and character arrays. (Part 1 of 2.)

```
24        // assignment. If string1 is modified, pointer ptr1 can
25        // become invalid.
26        ptr1 = string1.data(); // non-null terminated char array
27
28        // output each character using pointer
29        for ( size_t i = 0; i < length; ++i )
30           cout << *( ptr1 + i ); // use pointer arithmetic
31
32        cout << "\nptr2 is " << ptr2 << endl;
33        delete [] ptr2; // reclaim dynamically allocated memory
34   } // end main
```

```
string string1 is STRINGS
string1 converted to a pointer-based string is STRINGS
ptr1 is STRINGS
ptr2 is STRINGS
```

Fig. 21.9 | Converting strings to pointer-based strings and character arrays. (Part 2 of 2.)

The program declares a string, a size_t and two char pointers (lines 9–12). The string string1 is initialized to "STRINGS", ptr1 is initialized to nullptr and length is initialized to the length of string1. Memory of sufficient size to hold a pointer-based string equivalent of string string1 is allocated dynamically and attached to char pointer ptr2.

Line 15 uses string member function **copy** to copy object string1 into the char array pointed to by ptr2. Line 16 places a terminating null character in the array pointed to by ptr2.

Line 20 uses function **c_str** to obtain a const char * that points to a null terminated pointer-based string with the same content as string1. The pointer is passed to the stream insertion operator for output.

Line 26 assigns the const char * ptr1 a pointer returned by class string member function **data**. This member function returns a *non-null-terminated* built-in character array. We do *not* modify string string1 in this example. If string1 were to be modified (e.g., the string's dynamic memory changes its address due to a member function call such as string1.insert(0, "abcd");), ptr1 could become invalid—which could lead to unpredictable results.

Lines 29–30 use pointer arithmetic to output the character array pointed to by ptr1. In lines 32–33, the pointer-based string ptr2 is output and the memory allocated for ptr2 is deleted to avoid a memory leak.

Common Programming Error 21.2
Not terminating the character array returned by data with a null character can lead to execution-time errors.

21.11 Iterators

Class string provides *iterators* (introduced in Chapter 15) for forward and backward *traversal* of strings. Iterators provide access to individual characters with a syntax that's similar to pointer operations. *Iterators are not range checked.* Figure 21.10 demonstrates iterators.

```
1   // Fig. 21.10: Fig21_10.cpp
2   // Using an iterator to output a string.
3   #include <iostream>
4   #include <string>
5   using namespace std;
6
7   int main()
8   {
9      string string1( "Testing iterators" );
10     string::const_iterator iterator1 = string1.begin();
11
12     cout << "string1 = " << string1
13        << "\n(Using iterator iterator1) string1 is: ";
14
15     // iterate through string
16     while ( iterator1 != string1.end() )
17     {
18        cout << *iterator1; // dereference iterator to get char
19        ++iterator1; // advance iterator to next char
20     } // end while
21
22     cout << endl;
23  } // end main
```

```
string1 = Testing iterators
(Using iterator iterator1) string1 is: Testing iterators
```

Fig. 21.10 | Using an iterator to output a `string`.

Lines 9–10 declare `string` `string1` and **`string::const_iterator`** `iterator1`. Recall that a `const_iterator` *cannot* be used to modify the data that you're iterating through—in this case the `string`. Iterator `iterator1` is initialized to the beginning of `string1` with the `string` class member function **`begin`**. Two versions of `begin` exist—one that returns an `iterator` for iterating through a non-const `string` and a const version that returns a `const_iterator` for iterating through a const `string`. Line 12 outputs `string1`.

Lines 16–20 use iterator `iterator1` to "walk through" `string1`. Class `string` member function **`end`** returns an `iterator` (or a `const_iterator`) for the position past the last element of `string1`. Each element is printed by *dereferencing the iterator* much as you'd dereference a pointer, and the iterator is advanced one position using operator `++`. In C++11, lines 10 and 16–20 can be replaced with a range-based `for`, as in

```
for ( char c : string1 )
   cout << c;
```

Class `string` provides member functions **`rend`** and **`rbegin`** for accessing individual `string` characters in reverse from the end of a `string` toward the beginning. Member functions `rend` and `rbegin` return **`reverse_iterators`** or **`const_reverse_iterators`** (based on whether the `string` is non-const or const). Exercise 21.8 asks you to write a program that demonstrates these capabilities.

Good Programming Practice 21.1

When the operations involving the iterator should not modify the data being processed, use a const_iterator. *This is another example of employing the principle of least privilege.*

21.12 String Stream Processing

In addition to standard stream I/O and file stream I/O, C++ stream I/O includes capabilities for inputting from, and outputting to, strings in memory. These capabilities often are referred to as in-memory I/O or string stream processing.

Input from a string is supported by class **istringstream**. Output to a string is supported by class **ostringstream**. The class names istringstream and ostringstream are actually *aliases* defined by the typedefs

```
typedef basic_istringstream< char > istringstream;
typedef basic_ostringstream< char > ostringstream;
```

Class templates basic_istringstream and basic_ostringstream provide the same functionality as classes istream and ostream plus other member functions specific to *in-memory formatting*. Programs that use in-memory formatting must include the **<sstream>** and <iostream> headers.

Error-Prevention Tip 21.1

One application of these techniques is data validation. *A program can read an entire line at a time from the input stream into a* string. *Next, a validation routine can scrutinize the contents of the* string *and correct (or repair) the data, if necessary. Then the program can proceed to input from the* string, *knowing that the input data is in the proper format.*

Error-Prevention Tip 21.2

To assist with data validation, C++11 provides powerful regular-expression *capabilities. For example, if a program requires a user to enter a U.S. format telephone number (e.g., (800) 555-1212), you can use a regular-expression pattern to confirm that the user's input matches the expected format. Many websites provide regular expressions for validating email addresses, URLs, phone numbers, addresses and other popular kinds of data. We introduce regular expressions and provide several examples in Chapter 24.*

Software Engineering Observation 21.1

Outputting to a string is a nice way to take advantage of the powerful output formatting capabilities of C++ streams. Data can be prepared in a string to mimic the edited screen format. That string could be written to a disk file to preserve the screen image.

An ostringstream object uses a string object to store the output data. The str member function of class ostringstream returns a copy of that string.

Demonstrating ostringstream
Figure 21.11 demonstrates an ostringstream object. The program creates ostringstream object outputString (line 10) and uses the stream insertion operator to output a series of strings and numerical values to the object.

```cpp
 1   // Fig. 21.11: Fig21_11.cpp
 2   // Using an ostringstream object.
 3   #include <iostream>
 4   #include <string>
 5   #include <sstream> // header for string stream processing
 6   using namespace std;
 7
 8   int main()
 9   {
10      ostringstream outputString; // create ostringstream instance
11
12      string string1( "Output of several data types " );
13      string string2( "to an ostringstream object:" );
14      string string3( "\n          double: " );
15      string string4( "\n             int: " );
16      string string5( "\naddress of int: " );
17
18      double double1 = 123.4567;
19      int integer = 22;
20
21      // output strings, double and int to ostringstream outputString
22      outputString << string1 << string2 << string3 << double1
23         << string4 << integer << string5 << &integer;
24
25      // call str to obtain string contents of the ostringstream
26      cout << "outputString contains:\n" << outputString.str();
27
28      // add additional characters and call str to output string
29      outputString << "\nmore characters added";
30      cout << "\n\nafter additional stream insertions,\n"
31         << "outputString contains:\n" << outputString.str() << endl;
32   } // end main
```

```
outputString contains:
Output of several data types to an ostringstream object:
        double: 123.457
           int: 22
address of int: 0012F540

after additional stream insertions,
outputString contains:
Output of several data types to an ostringstream object:
        double: 123.457
           int: 22
address of int: 0012F540
more characters added
```

Fig. 21.11 | Using an `ostringstream` object.

Lines 22–23 output `string string1`, `string string2`, `string string3`, `double double1`, `string string4`, `int integer`, `string string5` and the address of `int integer`—all to `outputString` in memory. Line 26 uses the stream insertion operator and the call `outputString.str()` to display a copy of the `string` created in lines 22–23. Line 29 demonstrates that more data can be *appended* to the `string` in memory by simply issuing another stream insertion operation to outputString. Lines 30–31 display string outputString after appending additional characters.

An istringstream object inputs data from a string in memory to program variables. Data is stored in an istringstream object as characters. Input from the istringstream object works identically to input from any file. The end of the string is interpreted by the istringstream object as *end-of-file*.

Demonstrating *istringstream*

Figure 21.12 demonstrates input from an istringstream object. Lines 10–11 create string input containing the data and istringstream object inputString constructed to contain the data in string input. The string input contains the data

```
Input test 123 4.7 A
```

which, when read as input to the program, consist of two strings ("Input" and "test"), an int (123), a double (4.7) and a char ('A'). These characters are extracted to variables string1, string2, integer, double1 and character in line 18.

```cpp
1  // Fig. 21.12: Fig21_12.cpp
2  // Demonstrating input from an istringstream object.
3  #include <iostream>
4  #include <string>
5  #include <sstream>
6  using namespace std;
7
8  int main()
9  {
10    string input( "Input test 123 4.7 A" );
11    istringstream inputString( input );
12    string string1;
13    string string2;
14    int integer;
15    double double1;
16    char character;
17
18    inputString >> string1 >> string2 >> integer >> double1 >> character;
19
20    cout << "The following items were extracted\n"
21       << "from the istringstream object:" << "\nstring: " << string1
22       << "\nstring: " << string2 << "\n   int: " << integer
23       << "\ndouble: " << double1 << "\n  char: " << character;
24
25    // attempt to read from empty stream
26    long value;
27    inputString >> value;
28
29    // test stream results
30    if ( inputString.good() )
31       cout << "\n\nlong value is: " << value << endl;
32    else
33       cout << "\n\ninputString is empty" << endl;
34  } // end main
```

Fig. 21.12 | Demonstrating input from an istringstream object. (Part 1 of 2.)

```
The following items were extracted
from the istringstream object:
string: Input
string: test
   int: 123
double: 4.7
  char: A

inputString is empty
```

Fig. 21.12 | Demonstrating input from an `istringstream` object. (Part 2 of 2.)

The data is then output in lines 20–23. The program attempts to read from input-
String again in line 27. The `if` condition in line 30 uses function good (Section 13.8) to
test if any data remains. Because no data remains, the function returns `false` and the `else`
part of the `if...else` statement is executed.

21.13 C++11 Numeric Conversion Functions

C++11 now contains functions for converting from numeric values to `strings` and from
`strings` to numeric values. Though you could previously perform such conversions using
other techniques, the functions presented in this section were added for convenience.

Converting Numeric Values to *string* Objects
C++11's **to_string** function (from the `<string>` header) returns the `string` representation of its numeric argument. The function is overloaded for types `int`, `unsigned int`,
`long`, `unsigned long`, `long long`, `unsigned long long`, `float`, `double` and `long double`.

Converting *string* Objects to Numeric Values
C++11 provides eight functions (Fig. 21.13; from the `<string>` header) for converting
`string` objects to numeric values. Each function attempts to convert the *beginning* of its
`string` argument to a numeric value. If no conversion can be performed, each function
throws an `invalid_argument` exception. If the result of the conversion is out of range for
the function's return type, each function throws an `out_of_range` exception.

Function	Return type	Function	Return type
Functions that convert to integral types		*Functions that convert to floating-point types*	
stoi	int	stof	float
stol	long	stod	double
stoul	unsigned long	stold	long double
stoll	long long		
stoull	unsigned long long		

Fig. 21.13 | C++11 functions that convert from `strings` to numeric types.

*Functions That Convert **strings** to Integral Types*

Consider an example of converting a `string` to an integral value. Assuming the `string`:

```
string s( "100hello" );
```

the following statement converts the beginning of the string to the `int` value 100 and stores that value in `convertedInt`:

```
int convertedInt = stoi( s );
```

Each function that converts a `string` to an integral type actually receives *three* parameters—the last two have default arguments. The parameters are:

- A `string` containing the characters to convert.

- A pointer to a `size_t` variable. The function uses this pointer to store the index of the first character that was *not* converted. The default argument is a null pointer, in which case the function does *not* store the index.

- An `int` from 2 to 36 representing the number's base—the default is base 10.

So, the preceding statement is equivalent to

```
int convertedInt = stoi( s, nullptr, 10 );
```

Given a `size_t` variable named `index`, the statement:

```
int convertedInt = stoi( s, &index, 2 );
```

converts the binary number "100" (base 2) to an `int` (100 in binary is the `int` value 4) and stores in `index` the location of the string's letter "h" (the first character that was not converted).

*Functions That Convert **strings** to Floating-Point Types*

The functions that convert `strings` to floating-point types each receive two parameters:

- A `string` containing the characters to convert.

- A pointer to a `size_t` variable where the function stores the index of the first character that was *not* converted. The default argument is a null pointer, in which case the function does *not* store the index.

Consider an example of converting a `string` to an floating-point value. Assuming the string:

```
string s( "123.45hello" );
```

the following statement converts the beginning of the `string` to the `double` value 123.45 and stores that value in `convertedDouble`:

```
double convertedDouble = stod( s );
```

Again, the second argument is a null pointer by default.

21.14 Wrap-Up

This chapter discussed the details of C++ Standard Library class `string`. We discussed assigning, concatenating, comparing, searching and swapping strings. We also introduced a number of methods to determine string characteristics, to find, replace and insert characters in a string, and to convert `string`s to pointer-based strings and vice versa. You learned about string iterators and performing input from and output to strings in memory. Finally, we introduced C++11's new functions for converting numeric values to `string`s and for converting `string`s to numeric values. In the next chapter, we introduce `struct`s, which are similar to classes, and discuss the manipulation of bits, characters and C strings.

Summary

Section 21.1 Introduction
- Class template `basic_string` provides typical string-manipulation operations.
- The `typedef` statement

      typedef basic_string< char > string;

  creates the alias type `string` for `basic_string<char>` (p. 884). A `typedef` also is provided for the `wchar_t` type (`wstring`).
- To use `string`s, include C++ Standard Library header `<string>`.
- Assigning a single character to a `string` object is permitted in an assignment statement.
- `string`s are not necessarily null terminated.
- Most `string` member functions take as arguments a starting subscript location and the number of characters on which to operate.

Section 21.2 `string` Assignment and Concatenation
- Class `string` provides overloaded `operator=` and member function `assign` (p. 885) for assignments.
- The subscript operator, `[]`, provides read/write access to any element of a `string`.
- `string` member function `at` (p. 887) provides checked access (p. 887)—going past either end of the string throws an `out_of_range` exception. The subscript operator, `[]`, does not provide checked access.
- The overloaded `+` and `+=` operators and member function `append` (p. 887) perform `string` concatenation.

Section 21.3 Comparing `string`s
- Class `string` provides overloaded `==`, `!=`, `<`, `>`, `<=` and `>=` operators for `string` comparisons.
- `string` member function `compare` (p. 889) compares two `string`s (or substrings) and returns 0 if the `string`s are equal, a positive number if the first `string` is lexicographically (p. 889) greater than the second or a negative number if the first string is lexicographically less than the second.

Section 21.4 Substrings
- `string` member function `substr` (p. 890) retrieves a substring from a `string`.

Section 21.5 Swapping `string`s
- `string` member function `swap` (p. 890) swaps the contents of two `string`s.

Section 21.6 `string` Characteristics

- `string` member functions `size` and `length` (p. 885) return the number of characters currently stored in a `string`.
- `string` member function `capacity` (p. 891) returns the total number of characters that can be stored in a `string` without increasing the amount of memory allocated to the `string`.
- `string` member function `max_size` (p. 893) returns the maximum size a `string` can have.
- `string` member function `resize` (p. 893) changes the length of a `string`.
- `string` member function `empty` returns `true` if a `string` is empty.

Section 21.7 Finding Substrings and Characters in a `string`

- Class `string` find functions (p. 895) `find`, `rfind`, `find_first_of`, `find_last_of` and `find_first_not_of` locate substrings or characters in a `string`.

Section 21.8 Replacing Characters in a `string`

- `string` member function `erase` (p. 895) deletes elements of a `string`.
- `string` member function `replace` (p. 897) replaces characters in a `string`.

Section 21.9 Inserting Characters into a `string`

- `string` member function `insert` (p. 897) inserts characters in a `string`.

Section 21.10 Conversion to Pointer-Based `char *` Strings

- `string` member function `c_str` (p. 899) returns a `const char *` pointing to a null-terminated pointer-based string that contains all the characters in a `string`.
- `string` member function `data` (p. 899) returns a `const char *` pointing to a non-null-terminated built-in character array that contains all the characters in a `string`.

Section 21.11 Iterators

- Class `string` provides member functions `begin` and `end` (p. 900) to iterate through individual elements.
- Class `string` provides member functions `rend` and `rbegin` (p. 900) for accessing individual `string` characters in reverse from the end of a `string` toward the beginning.

Section 21.12 String Stream Processing

- Input from a `string` is supported by type `istringstream` (p. 901). Output to a `string` is supported by type `ostringstream` (p. 901).
- `ostringstream` member function `str` (p. 901) returns the `string` from the stream.

Section 21.13 C++11 Numeric Conversion Functions

- C++11's `<string>` header now contains functions for converting from numeric values to string objects and from string objects to numeric values.
- The `to_string` function (p. 904) returns the string representation of its numeric argument and is overloaded for types `int`, `unsigned int`, `long`, `unsigned long`, `long long`, `unsigned long long`, `float`, `double` and `long double`.
- C++11 provides eight functions for converting string objects to numeric values. Each function attempts to convert the beginning of its string argument to a numeric value. If no conversion can be performed, an `invalid_argument` exception occurs. If the result of the convertion is out of range for the function's return type, an `out_of_range` exception occurs.
- Each function that converts a `string` to an integral type receives three parameters—a `string` containing the characters to convert, a pointer to a `size_t` variable where the function stores the

index of the first character that was not converted (a null pointer, by default) and an `int` from 2 to 36 representing the number's base (base 10, by default).

• The functions that convert strings to floating-point types each receive two parameters—a `string` containing the characters to convert and a pointer to a `size_t` variable where the function stores the index of the first character that was not converted (a null pointer, by default).

Self-Review Exercises

21.1 Fill in the blanks in each of the following:
  a) To use `strings`, include C++ Standard Library header _____.
  b) The `string` member function _____ changes the length of a `string`.
  c) _____ member function `str` returns the `string` from the stream.
  d) C++11 provides _____ functions for converting string objects to numeric values.

21.2 State which of the following statements are *true* and which are *false*. If a statement is *false*, explain why.
  a) Assigning a single character to a `string` object is permitted in an assignment statement.
  b) `strings` are necessarily null terminated.
  c) The `string` member function `swapstring` swaps the contents of two `strings`.
  d) The `string` member function `max_size` returns the maximum size a `string` can have.

21.3 Find the error(s) in each of the following, and explain how to correct it (them):
  a) `cout << string1.substr( 7 ) << endl;`
  b) `// resizing a string`
      `string1.resize( string1.size(); + 10 );`

Answers to Self-Review Exercises

21.1 a) `<string>`. b) `resize`. c) `ostringstream`. d) `eight`.

21.2 a) True. b) False. `strings` are not necessarily null terminated. c) False. The `string` member function `swap` swaps the contents of two `strings`. d) True.

21.3 a) *Error*: The `substr` function has one integer argument.
      Correction: The `substr` function requires two integer arguments.
  b) *Error*: A semicolon is given after the `size()` function.
      Correction: Remove the semicolon after the `size()` function.

Exercises

21.4 *(Fill in the Blanks)* Fill in the blanks in each of the following:
  a) The _____ provides read/write access to any element of a `string`.
  b) The `string` member function _____ returns true if a `string` is empty.
  c) The `string` member function _____ inserts characters in a `string`.
  d) Class `string` provides member functions `rend` and _____ for accessing individual `string` characters in reverse from the end of a `string` toward the beginning.

21.5 *(True or False)* State which of the following statements are *true* and which are *false*. If a statement is *false*, explain why.
   a) For converting string objects to numeric values, if no conversion can be performed, an `invalid_argument` exception occurs.
   b) Class `string` provides member functions `begin` and `end` to iterate through individual elements.
   c) The `string` member function `data` returns a `const char *` pointing to a non-null-terminated built-in character array that contains all the characters in a `string`.
   d) Output to a `string` is supported by type `ostringstream`.

21.6 *(Find Code Errors)* Find any errors in the following and explain how to correct them:
   a) `result = string2.compare(3, string4 );`
   b) `stringRef.max_size("hello");`
   c) `size_t position = string1.find(5);`

21.7 *(Simple Encryption)* Some information on the Internet may be encrypted with a simple algorithm known as "rot13," which rotates each character by 13 positions in the alphabet. Thus, `'a'` corresponds to `'n'`, and `'x'` corresponds to `'k'`. rot13 is an example of **symmetric key encryption**. With symmetric key encryption, both the encrypter and decrypter use the same key.
   a) Write a program that encrypts a message using rot13.
   b) Write a program that decrypts the scrambled message using 13 as the key.
   c) After writing the programs of part (a) and part (b), briefly answer the following question: If you did not know the key for part (b), how difficult do you think it would be to break the code? What if you had access to substantial computing power (e.g., supercomputers)? In Exercise 21.24 we ask you to write a program to accomplish this.

21.8 *(Using string Iterators)* Write a program using iterators that demonstrates the use of functions `rbegin` and `rend`.

21.9 *(Words Ending in "r" or "ay")* Write a program that reads in several `strings` and prints only those ending in "r" or "ay". Only lowercase letters should be considered.

21.10 *(string Concatenation)* Write a program that separately inputs a first name and a last name and concatenates the two into a new `string`. Show two techniques for accomplishing this task.

21.11 *(Hangman Game)* Write a program that plays the game of Hangman. The program should pick a word (which is either coded directly into the program or read from a text file) and display the following:

```
Guess the word:    XXXXXX
```

Each X represents a letter. The user tries to guess the letters in the word. The appropriate response yes or no should be displayed after each guess. After each incorrect guess, display the diagram with another body part filled. After seven incorrect guesses, the user should be hanged. The display should look as follows:

```
        O
       /|\
        |
       / \
```

After each guess, display all user guesses. If the user guesses the word correctly, display

```
Congratulations!!! You guessed my word. Play again? yes/no
```

21.12 *(Printing a string Backward)* Write a program that inputs a `string` and prints the `string` backward. Convert all uppercase characters to lowercase and all lowercase characters to uppercase.

21.13 *(Alphabetizing Animal Names)* Write a program that uses the comparison capabilities introduced in this chapter to alphabetize a series of animal names. Only uppercase letters should be used for the comparisons.

21.14 *(Cryptograms)* Write a program that creates a cryptogram out of a `string`. A cryptogram is a message or word in which each letter is replaced with another letter. For example the `string`

```
The bird was named squawk
```

might be scrambled to form

```
cin vrjs otz ethns zxqtop
```

Spaces are not scrambled. In this particular case, `'T'` was replaced with `'x'`, each `'a'` was replaced with `'h'`, etc. Uppercase letters become lowercase letters in the cryptogram. Use techniques similar to those in Exercise 21.7.

21.15 *(Solving Cryptograms)* Modify Exercise 21.14 to allow the user to solve the cryptogram. The user should input two characters at a time: The first character specifies a letter in the cryptogram, and the second letter specifies the replacement letter. If the replacement letter is correct, replace the letter in the cryptogram with the replacement letter in uppercase.

21.16 *(Counting Palindromes)* Write a program that inputs a sentence and counts the number of palindromes in it. A palindrome is a word that reads the same backward and forward. For example, `"tree"` is not a palindrome, but `"noon"` is.

21.17 *(Counting Vowels)* Write a program that counts the total number of vowels in a sentence. Output the frequency of each vowel.

21.18 *(String Insertion)* Write a program that inserts the characters `"******"` in the exact middle of a `string`.

21.19 *(Erasing Characters from a `string`)* Write a program that erases the sequences `"by"` and `"BY"` from a `string`.

21.20 *(Reversing a `string` with Iterators)* Write a program that inputs a line of text and prints the text backward. Use iterators in your solution.

21.21 *(Reversing a `string` with Iterators using Recursion)* Write a recursive version of Exercise 21.20.

21.22 *(Using the `erase` Functions with Iterator Arguments)* Write a program that demonstrates the use of the erase functions that take `iterator` arguments.

21.23 *(Letter Pyramid)* Write a program that generates the following from the `string` `"abcdef-ghijklmnopqrstuvwxyz"`:

```
            a
           bcb
          cdedc
         defgfed
        efghihgfe
       fghijkjihgf
      ghijklmlkjihg
     hijklmnonmlkjih
    ijklmnopqponmlkji
   jklmnopqrsrqponmlkj
  klmnopqrstutsrqponmlk
 lmnopqrstuvwvutsrqponml
mnopqrstuvwxyxwvutsrqponm
nopqrstuvwxyz{zyxwvutsrqpon
```

21.24 *(Simple Decryption)* In Exercise 21.7, we asked you to write a simple encryption algorithm. Write a program that will attempt to decrypt a "rot13" message using simple frequency substitution. (Assume that you do not know the key.) The most frequent letters in the encrypted phrase should be replaced with the most commonly used English letters (a, e, i, o, u, s, t, r, etc.). Write the possibilities to a file. What made the code breaking easy? How can the encryption mechanism be improved?

21.25 *(Enhanced `Employee` Class)* Modify class `Employee` in Figs. 12.9–12.10 by adding a `private` utility function called `isValidSocialSecurityNumber`. This member function should validate the format of a social security number (e.g., `###-##-####`, where # is a digit). If the format is valid, return `true`; otherwise return `false`.

Making a Difference

21.26 *(Cooking with Healthier Ingredients)* Obesity in the United States is increasing at an alarming rate. Check the map from the Centers for Disease Control and Prevention (CDC) at www.cdc.gov/nccdphp/dnpa/Obesity/trend/maps/index.htm, which shows obesity trends in the United States over the last 20 years. As obesity increases, so do occurrences of related problems (e.g., heart disease, high blood pressure, high cholesterol, type 2 diabetes). Write a program that helps users choose healthier ingredients when cooking, and helps those allergic to certain foods (e.g., nuts, gluten) find substitutes. The program should read a recipe from the user and suggest healthier replacements for some of the ingredients. For simplicity, your program should assume the recipe has no abbreviations for measures such as teaspoons, cups, and tablespoons, and uses numerical digits for quantities (e.g., 1 egg, 2 cups) rather than spelling them out (one egg, two cups). Some common substitutions are shown in Fig. 21.14. Your program should display a warning such as, "Always consult your physician before making significant changes to your diet."

Ingredient	Substitution
1 cup sour cream	1 cup yogurt
1 cup milk	1/2 cup evaporated milk and 1/2 cup water
1 teaspoon lemon juice	1/2 teaspoon vinegar
1 cup sugar	1/2 cup honey, 1 cup molasses or 1/4 cup agave nectar
1 cup butter	1 cup yogurt
1 cup flour	1 cup rye or rice flour
1 cup mayonnaise	1 cup cottage cheese or 1/8 cup mayonnaise and 7/8 cup yogurt
1 egg	2 tablespoons cornstarch, arrowroot flour or potato starch or 2 egg whites or 1/2 of a large banana (mashed)
1 cup milk	1 cup soy milk
1/4 cup oil	1/4 cup applesauce
white bread	whole-grain bread

Fig. 21.14 | Common ingredient substitutions.

Your program should take into consideration that replacements are not always one-for-one. For example, if a cake recipe calls for three eggs, it might reasonably use six egg whites instead. Conversion data for measurements and substitutes can be obtained at websites such as:

```
chinesefood.about.com/od/recipeconversionfaqs/f/usmetricrecipes.htm
www.pioneerthinking.com/eggsub.html
www.gourmetsleuth.com/conversions.htm
```

Your program should consider the user's health concerns, such as high cholesterol, high blood pressure, weight loss, gluten allergy, and so on. For high cholesterol, the program should suggest substitutes for eggs and dairy products; if the user wishes to lose weight, low-calorie substitutes for ingredients such as sugar should be suggested.

21.27   *(Spam Scanner)* Spam (or junk e-mail) costs U.S. organizations billions of dollars a year in spam-prevention software, equipment, network resources, bandwidth, and lost productivity. Research online some of the most common spam e-mail messages and words, and check your own junk e-mail folder. Create a list of 30 words and phrases commonly found in spam messages. Write an application in which the user enters an e-mail message. Then, scan the message for each of the 30 keywords or phrases. For each occurrence of one of these within the message, add a point to the message's "spam score." Next, rate the likelihood that the message is spam, based on the number of points it received.

21.28   *(SMS Language)* Short Message Service (SMS) is a communications service that allows sending text messages of 160 or fewer characters between mobile phones. With the proliferation of mobile phone use worldwide, SMS is being used in many developing nations for political purposes (e.g., voicing opinions and opposition), reporting news about natural disasters, and so on. For example, check out comunica.org/radio2.0/archives/87. Since the length of SMS messages is limited, SMS Language—abbreviations of common words and phrases in mobile text messages, e-mails, instant messages, etc.—is often used. For example, "in my opinion" is "IMO" in SMS Language. Research SMS Language online. Write a program in which the user can enter a message using SMS Language; the program should translate it into English (or your own language). Also provide a mechanism to translate text written in English (or your own language) into SMS Language. One potential problem is that one SMS abbreviation could expand into a variety of phrases. For example, IMO (as used above) could also stand for "International Maritime Organization," "in memory of," etc.

Bits, Characters, C Strings and **struct**s

*The same old charitable lie
Repeated as the years scoot by
Perpetually makes a hit—
"You really haven't changed a
bit!"*
—Margaret Fishback

*The chief defect of Henry King
Was chewing little bits of string.*
—Hilaire Belloc

*Vigorous writing is concise. A
sentence should contain no
unnecessary words, a paragraph
no unnecessary sentences.*
—William Strunk, Jr.

Objectives

In this chapter you'll learn:

- To create and use **struct**s and to understand their near equivalence with classes.

- To use **typedef** to create aliases for data types.

- To manipulate data with the bitwise operators and to create bit fields for storing data compactly.

- To use the functions of the character-handling library **<cctype>**.

- To use the string-conversion functions of the general-utilities library **<cstdlib>**.

- To use the string-processing functions of the string-handling library **<cstring>**.

22.1 Introduction

We now discuss structures, their near equivalence with classes, and the manipulation of bits, characters and C strings. Many of the techniques we present here are included for the benefit of those who will work with legacy C and C++ code.

Like classes, C++ structures may contain access specifiers, member functions, constructors and destructors. In fact, *the only differences between structures and classes in C++ is that structure members default to `public` access and class members default to `private` access when no access specifiers are used, and that structures default to `public` inheritance, whereas classes default to `private` inheritance.* Our presentation of structures here is typical of the legacy C code and early C++ code you'll see in industry.

We present a high-performance card shuffling and dealing simulation in which we use structure objects containing C++ `string` objects to represent the cards. We discuss the *bitwise operators* that allow you to access and manipulate the *individual bits* in bytes of data. We also present *bitfields*—special structures that can be used to specify the exact number of bits a variable occupies in memory. These bit-manipulation techniques are common in programs that interact directly with hardware devices that have limited memory. The chapter finishes with examples of many character and C string-manipulation functions—some of which are designed to process blocks of memory as arrays of bytes. The detailed C string treatment in this chapter is mostly for reasons of legacy code support and because there are still remnants of C string use in C++, such as command-line arguments (Appendix F). *New development should use C++ `string` objects rather than C strings.*

22.2 Structure Definitions

Consider the following structure definition:

```
struct Card
{
    string face;
    string suit;
}; // end struct Card
```

Keyword `struct` introduces the definition for structure `Card`. The identifier `Card` is the structure name and is used in C++ to declare variables of the structure type (in C, the type name of the preceding structure is `struct Card`). `Card`'s definition contains two `string` members—`face` and `suit`.

The following declarations

```
Card oneCard;
Card deck[ 52 ];
Card *cardPtr;
```

declare `oneCard` to be a structure variable of type `Card`, `deck` to be an array with 52 elements of type `Card` and `cardPtr` to be a pointer to a `Card` structure. Variables of a given structure type can also be declared by placing a comma-separated list of the variable names between the closing brace of the structure definition and the semicolon that ends the structure definition. For example, the preceding declarations could have been incorporated into the `Card` structure definition as follows:

```
struct Card
{
    string face;
    string suit;
} oneCard, deck[ 52 ], *cardPtr;
```

As with classes, structure members are *not* necessarily stored in *consecutive* bytes of memory. Sometimes there are "holes" in a structure, because some computers store specific data types only on certain memory boundaries for performance reasons, such as half-word, word or double-word boundaries. A word is a standard memory unit used to store data in a computer—usually two, four or eight bytes and typically eight bytes on today's popular 64-bit systems. Consider the following structure definition in which structure objects `sample1` and `sample2` of type `Example` are declared:

```
struct Example
{
    char c;
    int i;
} sample1, sample2;
```

A computer with two-byte words might require that each of the members of `Example` be aligned on a word boundary (i.e., at the beginning of a word—this is *machine dependent*). Figure 22.1 shows a sample storage alignment for an object of type `Example` that's been assigned the character `'a'` and the integer `97` (the bit representations of the values are shown). If the members are stored beginning at word boundaries, there is a one-byte hole (byte 1 in the figure) in the storage for objects of type `Example`. The value in the one-byte hole is *undefined*. If the values in `sample1` and `sample2` are in fact equal, the structure objects might *not* be equal, because the *undefined* one-byte holes are not likely to contain identical values.

Common Programming Error 22.1

Comparing variables of structure types is a compilation error.

Portability Tip 22.1

Because the size of data items of a particular type is machine dependent, and because storage alignment considerations are machine dependent, so too is the representation of a structure.

Fig. 22.1 | Possible storage alignment for an `Example` object, showing an undefined byte.

22.3 typedef

Keyword `typedef` provides a mechanism for creating *synonyms* (or *aliases*) for previously defined data types. Names for structure types are often defined with `typedef` to more readable type names. For example, the statement

```
typedef Card *CardPtr;
```

defines the new type name `CardPtr` as a synonym for type `Card *`.

Creating a new name with `typedef` does *not* create a new type; `typedef` simply creates a *new type name* that can then be used in the program as an alias for an existing type name.

22.4 Example: Card Shuffling and Dealing Simulation

The card shuffling and dealing program in Figs. 22.2–22.4 is similar to the one described in Exercise 9.23. This program represents the deck of cards as an `array` of structures.

```cpp
1  // Fig. 22.2: DeckOfCards.h
2  // Definition of class DeckOfCards that
3  // represents a deck of playing cards.
4  #include <string>
5  #include <array>
6
7  // Card structure definition
8  struct Card
9  {
10    std::string face;
11    std::string suit;
12  }; // end structure Card
13
14  // DeckOfCards class definition
15  class DeckOfCards
16  {
17  public:
18    static const int numberOfCards = 52;
19    static const int faces = 13;
20    static const int suits = 4;
21
22    DeckOfCards(); // constructor initializes deck
23    void shuffle(); // shuffles cards in deck
24    void deal() const; // deals cards in deck
25
```

Fig. 22.2 | Definition of class `DeckOfCards` that represents a deck of playing cards. (Part I of 2.)

```
26   private:
27      std::array< Card, numberOfCards > deck; // represents deck of cards
28   }; // end class DeckOfCards
```

Fig. 22.2 | Definition of class DeckOfCards that represents a deck of playing cards. (Part 2 of 2.)

The constructor (lines 12–31 of Fig. 22.3) initializes the array in order with character strings representing Ace through King of each suit. Function shuffle implements the shuffling algorithm. The function loops through all 52 cards (subscripts 0 to 51). For each card, a number between 0 and 51 is picked randomly. Next, the current Card and the randomly selected Card are swapped in the array. A total of 52 swaps are made in a single pass of the entire array, and the array is shuffled. Because the Card structures were swapped in place in the array, the dealing algorithm implemented in function deal requires only one pass of the array to deal the shuffled cards.

```
 1   // Fig. 22.3: DeckOfCards.cpp
 2   // Member-function definitions for class DeckOfCards that simulates
 3   // the shuffling and dealing of a deck of playing cards.
 4   #include <iostream>
 5   #include <iomanip>
 6   #include <cstdlib> // prototypes for rand and srand
 7   #include <ctime> // prototype for time
 8   #include "DeckOfCards.h" // DeckOfCards class definition
 9   using namespace std;
10
11   // no-argument DeckOfCards constructor intializes deck
12   DeckOfCards::DeckOfCards()
13   {
14      // initialize suit array
15      static string suit[ suits ] =
16         { "Hearts", "Diamonds", "Clubs", "Spades" };
17
18      // initialize face array
19      static string face[ faces ] =
20         { "Ace", "Deuce", "Three", "Four", "Five", "Six", "Seven",
21         "Eight", "Nine", "Ten", "Jack", "Queen", "King" };
22
23      // set values for deck of 52 Cards
24      for ( size_t i = 0; i < deck.size(); ++i )
25      {
26         deck[ i ].face = face[ i % faces ];
27         deck[ i ].suit = suit[ i / faces ];
28      } // end for
29
30      srand( static_cast< size_t >( time( nullptr ) ) ); // seed
31   } // end no-argument DeckOfCards constructor
32
33   // shuffle cards in deck
34   void DeckOfCards::shuffle()
35   {
```

Fig. 22.3 | Member-function definitions for class DeckOfCards. (Part 1 of 2.)

```
36       // shuffle cards randomly
37       for ( size_t i = 0; i < deck.size(); ++i )
38       {
39          int j = rand() % numberOfCards;
40          Card temp = deck[ i ];
41          deck[ i ] = deck[ j ];
42          deck[ j ] = temp;
43       } // end for
44    } // end function shuffle
45
46    // deal cards in deck
47    void DeckOfCards::deal() const
48    {
49       // display each card's face and suit
50       for ( size_t i = 0; i < deck.size(); ++i )
51          cout << right << setw( 5 ) << deck[ i ].face << " of "
52             << left << setw( 8 ) << deck[ i ].suit
53             << ( ( i + 1 ) % 2 ? '\t' : '\n' );
54    } // end function deal
```

Fig. 22.3 | Member-function definitions for class `DeckOfCards`. (Part 2 of 2.)

```
 1    // Fig. 22.4: fig22_04.cpp
 2    // Card shuffling and dealing program.
 3    #include "DeckOfCards.h" // DeckOfCards class definition
 4
 5    int main()
 6    {
 7       DeckOfCards deckOfCards; // create DeckOfCards object
 8       deckOfCards.shuffle(); // shuffle the cards in the deck
 9       deckOfCards.deal(); // deal the cards in the deck
10    } // end main
```

```
King of Clubs          Ten of Diamonds
Five of Diamonds       Jack of Clubs
Seven of Spades        Five of Clubs
Three of Spades        King of Hearts
Ten of Clubs           Eight of Spades
Eight of Hearts        Six of Hearts
Nine of Diamonds       Nine of Clubs
Three of Diamonds      Queen of Hearts
Six of Clubs           Seven of Hearts
Seven of Diamonds      Jack of Diamonds
Jack of Spades         King of Diamonds
Deuce of Diamonds      Four of Clubs
Three of Clubs         Five of Hearts
Eight of Clubs         Ace of Hearts
Deuce of Spades        Ace of Clubs
Ten of Spades          Eight of Diamonds
Ten of Hearts          Six of Spades
Queen of Diamonds      Nine of Hearts
Seven of Clubs         Queen of Clubs
```

Fig. 22.4 | Card shuffling and dealing program. (Part 1 of 2.)

```
Deuce of Clubs          Queen of Spades
Three of Hearts          Five of Spades
Deuce of Hearts          Jack of Hearts
 Four of Hearts           Ace of Diamonds
 Nine of Spades          Four of Diamonds
  Ace of Spades           Six of Diamonds
 Four of Spades          King of Spades
```

Fig. 22.4 | Card shuffling and dealing program. (Part 2 of 2.)

22.5 Bitwise Operators

C++ provides extensive *bit-manipulation* capabilities for getting down to the so-called "bits-and-bytes" level. Operating systems, test-equipment software, networking software and many other kinds of software require that you communicate "directly with the hardware." We introduce each of the *bitwise operators*, and we discuss how to save memory by using *bit fields*.

All data is represented internally by computers as sequences of bits. Each bit can assume the value 0 or the value 1. On most systems, a sequence of eight bits, each of which forms a byte—the standard storage unit for a variable of type char. Other data types are stored in larger numbers of bytes. Bitwise operators are used to manipulate the bits of integral operands (char, short, int and long; both signed and unsigned). Normally the bitwise operators are used with unsigned integers.

Portability Tip 22.2
Bitwise data manipulations are machine dependent.

The bitwise operator discussions in this section show the binary representations of the integer operands. For a detailed explanation of the binary (also called base-2) number system, see Appendix D. Because of the machine-dependent nature of bitwise manipulations, some of these programs might not work on your system without modification.

The bitwise operators are: bitwise AND (&), bitwise inclusive OR (|), bitwise exclusive OR (^), left shift (<<), right shift (>>) and bitwise complement (~)—also known as the one's complement. We've been using &, << and >> for other purposes—this is a classic example of *operator overloading*. The *bitwise AND, bitwise inclusive OR* and *bitwise exclusive OR* operators compare their two operands bit by bit. The *bitwise AND* operator sets each bit in the result to 1 if the corresponding bit in *both* operands is 1. The *bitwise inclusive OR* operator sets each bit in the result to 1 if the corresponding bit in *either (or both)* operand(s) is 1. The *bitwise exclusive OR* operator sets each bit in the result to 1 if the corresponding bit in *either* operand—*but not both*—is 1. The *left-shift* operator shifts the bits of its left operand to the left by the number of bits specified in its right operand. The *right-shift* operator shifts the bits in its left operand to the right by the number of bits specified in its right operand. The *bitwise complement* operator sets all 0 bits in its operand to 1 in the result and sets all 1 bits in its operand to 0 in the result. Detailed discussions of each bitwise operator appear in the following examples. The bitwise operators are summarized in Fig. 22.5.

Operator	Name	Description
&	bitwise AND	The bits in the result are set to 1 if the corresponding bits in the two operands are *both* 1.
|	bitwise inclusive OR	The bits in the result are set to 1 if *one or both* of the corresponding bits in the two operands is 1.
^	bitwise exclusive OR	The bits in the result are set to 1 if *exactly one* of the corresponding bits in the two operands is 1.
<<	left shift	Shifts the bits of the first operand left by the number of bits specified by the second operand; fill from right with 0 bits.
>>	right shift with sign extension	Shifts the bits of the first operand right by the number of bits specified by the second operand; the method of filling from the left is *machine dependent*.
~	bitwise complement	All 0 bits are set to 1 and all 1 bits are set to 0.

Fig. 22.5 | Bitwise operators.

Printing a Binary Representation of an Integral Value

When using the bitwise operators, it's useful to illustrate their precise effects by printing values in their binary representation. The program of Fig. 22.6 prints an `unsigned` integer in its binary representation in groups of eight bits each.

```cpp
// Fig. 22.6: fig22_06.cpp
// Printing an unsigned integer in bits.
#include <iostream>
#include <iomanip>
using namespace std;

void displayBits( unsigned ); // prototype

int main()
{
   unsigned inputValue = 0; // integral value to print in binary

   cout << "Enter an unsigned integer: ";
   cin >> inputValue;
   displayBits( inputValue );
} // end main

// display bits of an unsigned integer value
void displayBits( unsigned value )
{
   const int SHIFT = 8 * sizeof( unsigned ) - 1;
   const unsigned MASK = 1 << SHIFT;

   cout << setw( 10 ) << value << " = ";
```

Fig. 22.6 | Printing an unsigned integer in bits. (Part 1 of 2.)

```
25
26      // display bits
27      for ( unsigned i = 1; i <= SHIFT + 1; ++i )
28      {
29         cout << ( value & MASK ? '1' : '0' );
30         value <<= 1; // shift value left by 1
31
32         if ( i % 8 == 0 ) // output a space after 8 bits
33            cout << ' ';
34      } // end for
35
36      cout << endl;
37   } // end function displayBits
```

```
Enter an unsigned integer: 65000
   65000 = 00000000 00000000 11111101 11101000
```

```
Enter an unsigned integer: 29
   29 = 00000000 00000000 00000000 00011101
```

Fig. 22.6 | Printing an unsigned integer in bits. (Part 2 of 2.)

Function displayBits (lines 19–37) uses the *bitwise AND* operator to combine variable value with constant MASK. Often, the *bitwise AND* operator is used with an operand called a mask—an integer value with specific bits set to 1. Masks are used to *hide* some bits in a value while *selecting* other bits. In displayBits, line 22 assigns constant MASK the value 1 << SHIFT. The value of constant SHIFT was calculated in line 21 with the expression

```
8 * sizeof( unsigned ) - 1
```

which multiplies the number of bytes an unsigned object requires in memory by 8 (the number of bits in a byte) to get the total number of bits required to store an unsigned object, then subtracts 1. The bit representation of 1 << SHIFT on a computer that represents unsigned objects in four bytes of memory is

```
10000000 00000000 00000000 00000000
```

The *left-shift operator* shifts the value 1 from the low-order (rightmost) bit to the high-order (leftmost) bit in MASK, and fills in 0 bits from the right. Line 29 prints a 1 or a 0 for the current leftmost bit of variable value. Assume that variable value contains 65000 (00000000 00000000 11111101 11101000). When value and MASK are combined using &, all the bits except the high-order bit in variable value are "masked off" (hidden), because any bit "ANDed" with 0 yields 0. If the leftmost bit is 1, value & MASK evaluates to

```
00000000 00000000 11111101 11101000    (value)
10000000 00000000 00000000 00000000    (MASK)
-----------------------------------
00000000 00000000 00000000 00000000    (value & MASK)
```

which is interpreted as false, and 0 is printed. Then line 30 shifts variable value left by one bit with the expression value <<= 1 (i.e., value = value << 1). These steps are repeated for each bit variable `value`. Eventually, a bit with a value of 1 is shifted into the leftmost bit position, and the bit manipulation is as follows:

```
11111101 11101000 00000000 00000000   (value)
10000000 00000000 00000000 00000000   (MASK)
---------------------------------
10000000 00000000 00000000 00000000   (value & MASK)
```

Because both left bits are 1s, the expression's result is nonzero (true) and 1 is printed. Figure 22.7 summarizes the results of combining two bits with the bitwise AND operator.

Bit 1	Bit 2	Bit 1 & Bit 2
0	0	0
1	0	0
0	1	0
1	1	1

Fig. 22.7 | Results of combining two bits with the bitwise AND operator (&).

Common Programming Error 22.2
Using the logical AND operator (&&) for the bitwise AND operator (&) and vice versa is a logic error.

The program of Fig. 22.8 demonstrates the *bitwise AND operator*, the *bitwise inclusive OR* operator, the *bitwise exclusive OR* operator and the *bitwise complement operator*. Function `displayBits` (lines 48–66) prints the `unsigned` integer values.

```cpp
1   // Fig. 22.8: fig22_08.cpp
2   // Bitwise AND, inclusive OR,
3   // exclusive OR and complement operators.
4   #include <iostream>
5   #include <iomanip>
6   using namespace std;
7
8   void displayBits( unsigned ); // prototype
9
10  int main()
11  {
12     // demonstrate bitwise &
13     unsigned number1 = 2179876355;
14     unsigned mask = 1;
15     cout << "The result of combining the following\n";
16     displayBits( number1 );
17     displayBits( mask );
18     cout << "using the bitwise AND operator & is\n";
19     displayBits( number1 & mask );
```

Fig. 22.8 | Bitwise AND, inclusive OR, exclusive OR and complement operators. (Part 1 of 3.)

```
20
21        // demonstrate bitwise |
22        number1 = 15;
23        unsigned setBits = 241;
24        cout << "\nThe result of combining the following\n";
25        displayBits( number1 );
26        displayBits( setBits );
27        cout << "using the bitwise inclusive OR operator | is\n";
28        displayBits( number1 | setBits );
29
30        // demonstrate bitwise exclusive OR
31        number1 = 139;
32        unsigned number2 = 199;
33        cout << "\nThe result of combining the following\n";
34        displayBits( number1 );
35        displayBits( number2 );
36        cout << "using the bitwise exclusive OR operator ^ is\n";
37        displayBits( number1 ^ number2 );
38
39        // demonstrate bitwise complement
40        number1 = 21845;
41        cout << "\nThe one's complement of\n";
42        displayBits( number1 );
43        cout << "is" << endl;
44        displayBits( ~number1 );
45    } // end main
46
47    // display bits of an unsigned integer value
48    void displayBits( unsigned value )
49    {
50        const int SHIFT = 8 * sizeof( unsigned ) - 1;
51        const unsigned MASK = 1 << SHIFT;
52
53        cout << setw( 10 ) << value << " = ";
54
55        // display bits
56        for ( unsigned i = 1; i <= SHIFT + 1; ++i )
57        {
58            cout << ( value & MASK ? '1' : '0' );
59            value <<= 1; // shift value left by 1
60
61            if ( i % 8 == 0 ) // output a space after 8 bits
62                cout << ' ';
63        } // end for
64
65        cout << endl;
66    } // end function displayBits
```

```
The result of combining the following
2179876355 = 10000001 11101110 01000110 00000011
         1 = 00000000 00000000 00000000 00000001
using the bitwise AND operator & is
         1 = 00000000 00000000 00000000 00000001
```

Fig. 22.8 | Bitwise AND, inclusive OR, exclusive OR and complement operators. (Part 2 of 3.)

```
The result of combining the following
        15 = 00000000 00000000 00000000 00001111
       241 = 00000000 00000000 00000000 11110001
using the bitwise inclusive OR operator | is
       255 = 00000000 00000000 00000000 11111111

The result of combining the following
       139 = 00000000 00000000 00000000 10001011
       199 = 00000000 00000000 00000000 11000111
using the bitwise exclusive OR operator ^ is
        76 = 00000000 00000000 00000000 01001100

The one's complement of
     21845 = 00000000 00000000 01010101 01010101
is
4294945450 = 11111111 11111111 10101010 10101010
```

Fig. 22.8 | Bitwise AND, inclusive OR, exclusive OR and complement operators. (Part 3 of 3.)

Bitwise AND Operator (&)

In Fig. 22.8, line 13 assigns 2179876355 (10000001 11101110 01000110 00000011) to variable number1, and line 14 assigns 1 (00000000 00000000 00000000 00000001) to variable mask. When mask and number1 are combined using the *bitwise AND operator (&)* in the expression number1 & mask (line 19), the result is 00000000 00000000 00000000 00000001. All the bits except the low-order bit in variable number1 are "masked off" (hidden) by "ANDing" with constant MASK.

Bitwise Inclusive OR Operator (|)

The *bitwise inclusive OR operator* is used to set specific bits to 1 in an operand. In Fig. 22.8, line 22 assigns 15 (00000000 00000000 00000000 00001111) to variable number1, and line 23 assigns 241 (00000000 00000000 00000000 11110001) to variable setBits. When number1 and setBits are combined using the *bitwise inclusive OR operator* in the expression number1 | setBits (line 28), the result is 255 (00000000 00000000 00000000 11111111). Figure 22.9 summarizes the results of combining two bits with the *bitwise inclusive-OR operator*.

Common Programming Error 22.3
Using the logical OR operator (| |) for the bitwise OR operator (|) and vice versa is a logic error.

Bit 1	Bit 2	Bit 1	Bit 2
0	0	0
1	0	1
0	1	1
1	1	1

Fig. 22.9 | Combining two bits with the bitwise inclusive-OR operator (|).

Bitwise Exclusive OR (^)

The *bitwise exclusive OR operator (^)* sets each bit in the result to 1 if *exactly* one of the corresponding bits in its two operands is 1. In Fig. 22.8, lines 31–32 assign variables number1 and number2 the values 139 (00000000 00000000 00000000 10001011) and 199 (00000000 00000000 00000000 11000111), respectively. When these variables are combined with the *bitwise exclusive OR operator* in the expression number1 ^ number2 (line 37), the result is 00000000 00000000 00000000 01001100. Figure 22.10 summarizes the results of combining two bits with the *bitwise exclusive OR operator*.

Bit I	Bit 2	Bit I ^ Bit 2
0	0	0
1	0	1
0	1	1
1	1	0

Fig. 22.10 | Combining two bits with the bitwise exclusive OR operator (^).

Bitwise Complement (~)

The *bitwise complement operator (~)* sets all 1 bits in its operand to 0 in the result and sets all 0 bits to 1 in the result—otherwise referred to as "taking the *one's complement* of the value." In Fig. 22.8, line 40 assigns variable number1 the value 21845 (00000000 00000000 01010101 01010101). When the expression ~number1 evaluates, the result is (11111111 11111111 10101010 10101010).

Bitwise Shift Operators

Figure 22.11 demonstrates the *left-shift operator (<<)* and the *right-shift operator (>>)*. Function displayBits (lines 27–45) prints the unsigned integer values.

```
1   // Fig. 22.11: fig22_11.cpp
2   // Using the bitwise shift operators.
3   #include <iostream>
4   #include <iomanip>
5   using namespace std;
6
7   void displayBits( unsigned ); // prototype
8
9   int main()
10  {
11      unsigned number1 = 960;
12
13      // demonstrate bitwise left shift
14      cout << "The result of left shifting\n";
15      displayBits( number1 );
16      cout << "8 bit positions using the left-shift operator is\n";
```

Fig. 22.11 | Bitwise shift operators. (Part 1 of 2.)

```
17      displayBits( number1 << 8 );
18
19      // demonstrate bitwise right shift
20      cout << "\nThe result of right shifting\n";
21      displayBits( number1 );
22      cout << "8 bit positions using the right-shift operator is\n";
23      displayBits( number1 >> 8 );
24   } // end main
25
26   // display bits of an unsigned integer value
27   void displayBits( unsigned value )
28   {
29      const int SHIFT = 8 * sizeof( unsigned ) - 1;
30      const unsigned MASK = 1 << SHIFT;
31
32      cout << setw( 10 ) << value << " = ";
33
34      // display bits
35      for ( unsigned i = 1; i <= SHIFT + 1; ++i )
36      {
37         cout << ( value & MASK ? '1' : '0' );
38         value <<= 1; // shift value left by 1
39
40         if ( i % 8 == 0 ) // output a space after 8 bits
41            cout << ' ';
42      } // end for
43
44      cout << endl;
45   } // end function displayBits
```

```
The result of left shifting
      960 = 00000000 00000000 00000011 11000000
8 bit positions using the left-shift operator is
   245760 = 00000000 00000011 11000000 00000000

The result of right shifting
      960 = 00000000 00000000 00000011 11000000
8 bit positions using the right-shift operator is
        3 = 00000000 00000000 00000000 00000011
```

Fig. 22.11 | Bitwise shift operators. (Part 2 of 2.)

Left-Shift Operator

The *left-shift operator* (<<) shifts the bits of its left operand to the left by the number of bits specified in its right operand. Bits vacated to the right are replaced with 0s; bits shifted off the left are lost. In Fig. 22.11, line 11 assigns variable number1 the value 960 (00000000 00000000 00000011 11000000). The result of left-shifting variable number1 eight bits in the expression number1 << 8 (line 17) is 245760 (00000000 00000011 11000000 00000000).

Right-Shift Operator

The *right-shift operator* (>>) shifts the bits of its left operand to the right by the number of bits specified in its right operand. Performing a right shift on an unsigned integer causes the vacated bits at the left to be replaced by 0s; bits shifted off the right are lost. In the program of Fig. 22.11, the result of right-shifting number1 in the expression number1 >> 8 (line 23) is 3 (00000000 00000000 00000000 00000011).

Common Programming Error 22.4

The result of shifting a value is undefined if the right operand is negative or if the right operand is greater than or equal to the number of bits in which the left operand is stored.

Portability Tip 22.3

The result of right-shifting a signed value is machine dependent. Some machines fill with zeros and others use the sign bit.

Bitwise Assignment Operators

Each bitwise operator (except the bitwise complement operator) has a corresponding assignment operator. These **bitwise assignment operators** are shown in Fig. 22.12; they're used in a similar manner to the arithmetic assignment operators introduced in Chapter 4.

Bitwise assignment operators	
&=	Bitwise AND assignment operator.
|=	Bitwise inclusive OR assignment operator.
^=	Bitwise exclusive OR assignment operator.
<<=	Left-shift assignment operator.
>>=	Right-shift with sign extension assignment operator.

Fig. 22.12 | Bitwise assignment operators.

Figure 22.13 shows the precedence and associativity of the operators introduced up to this point in the text. They're shown top to bottom in decreasing order of precedence.

Operators	Associativity	Type
:: (unary; right to left) :: (binary; left to right) () (grouping parentheses)	left to right *[See caution in Fig. 2.10 regarding grouping parentheses.]*	primary
() [] . -> ++ -- static_cast<*type*>()	left to right	postfix
++ -- + - ! delete sizeof * ~ & new	right to left	prefix
* / %	left to right	multiplicative
+ -	left to right	additive
<< >>	left to right	shifting
< <= > >=	left to right	relational
== !=	left to right	equality

Fig. 22.13 | Operator precedence and associativity. (Part 1 of 2.)

Operators	Associativity	Type
&	left to right	bitwise AND
^	left to right	bitwise XOR
|	left to right	bitwise OR
&&	left to right	logical AND
||	left to right	logical OR
?:	right to left	conditional
= += -= *= /= %= &= |= ^= <<= >>=	right to left	assignment
,	left to right	comma

Fig. 22.13 | Operator precedence and associativity. (Part 2 of 2.)

22.6 Bit Fields

C++ provides the ability to specify the number of bits in which an integral type or enum type member of a class or a structure is stored. Such a member is referred to as a bit field. Bit fields enable *better memory utilization* by storing data in the minimum number of bits required. Bit field members *must* be declared as an integral or enum type.

Performance Tip 22.1
Bit fields help conserve storage.

Consider the following structure definition:

```
struct BitCard
{
    unsigned face : 4;
    unsigned suit : 2;
    unsigned color : 1;
}; // end struct BitCard
```

The definition contains three unsigned bit fields—face, suit and color—used to represent a card from a deck of 52 cards. A bit field is declared by following an integral type or enum type member with a colon (:) and an integer constant representing the width of the bit field (i.e., the number of bits in which the member is stored). The width must be an integer constant.

The preceding structure definition indicates that member face is stored in four bits, member suit in 2 bits and member color in one bit. The number of bits is based on the desired range of values for each structure member. Member face stores values between 0 (Ace) and 12 (King)—four bits can store a value between 0 and 15. Member suit stores values between 0 and 3 (0 = Diamonds, 1 = Hearts, 2 = Clubs, 3 = Spades)—two bits can store a value between 0 and 3. Finally, member color stores either 0 (Red) or 1 (Black)—one bit can store either 0 or 1.

The program in Figs. 22.14–22.16 creates array deck containing BitCard structures (line 25 of Fig. 22.14). The constructor inserts the 52 cards in the deck array, and function deal prints the 52 cards. Notice that bit fields are accessed exactly as any other structure member is (lines 14–16 and 25–30 of Fig. 22.15). The member color is included as a means of indicating the card color.

```
1   // Fig. 22.14: DeckOfCards.h
2   // Definition of class DeckOfCards that
3   // represents a deck of playing cards.
4   #include <array>
5
6   // BitCard structure definition with bit fields
7   struct BitCard
8   {
9      unsigned face : 4; // 4 bits; 0-15
10     unsigned suit : 2; // 2 bits; 0-3
11     unsigned color : 1; // 1 bit; 0-1
12  }; // end struct BitCard
13
14  // DeckOfCards class definition
15  class DeckOfCards
16  {
17  public:
18     static const int faces = 13;
19     static const int colors = 2; // black and red
20     static const int numberOfCards = 52;
21
22     DeckOfCards(); // constructor initializes deck
23     void deal() const; // deals cards in deck
24  private:
25     std::array< BitCard, numberOfCards > deck; // represents deck of cards
26  }; // end class DeckOfCards
```

Fig. 22.14 | Definition of class DeckOfCards that represents a deck of playing cards.

```
1   // Fig. 22.15: DeckOfCards.cpp
2   // Member-function definitions for class DeckOfCards that simulates
3   // the shuffling and dealing of a deck of playing cards.
4   #include <iostream>
5   #include <iomanip>
6   #include "DeckOfCards.h" // DeckOfCards class definition
7   using namespace std;
8
9   // no-argument DeckOfCards constructor intializes deck
10  DeckOfCards::DeckOfCards()
11  {
12     for ( size_t i = 0; i < deck.size(); ++i )
13     {
14        deck[ i ].face = i % faces; // faces in order
15        deck[ i ].suit = i / faces; // suits in order
16        deck[ i ].color = i / ( faces * colors ); // colors in order
17     } // end for
18  } // end no-argument DeckOfCards constructor
```

Fig. 22.15 | Member-function definitions for class DeckOfCards. (Part 1 of 2.)

```
19
20   // deal cards in deck
21   void DeckOfCards::deal() const
22   {
23      for ( size_t k1 = 0, k2 = k1 + deck.size() / 2;
24         k1 < deck.size() / 2 - 1; ++k1, ++k2 )
25         cout << "Card:" << setw( 3 ) << deck[ k1 ].face
26            << "  Suit:" << setw( 2 ) << deck[ k1 ].suit
27            << "  Color:" << setw( 2 ) << deck[ k1 ].color
28            << "   " << "Card:" << setw( 3 ) << deck[ k2 ].face
29            << "  Suit:" << setw( 2 ) << deck[ k2 ].suit
30            << "  Color:" << setw( 2 ) << deck[ k2 ].color << endl;
31   } // end function deal
```

Fig. 22.15 | Member-function definitions for class `DeckOfCards`. (Part 2 of 2.)

```
1    // Fig. 22.16: fig22_16.cpp
2    // Card shuffling and dealing program.
3    #include "DeckOfCards.h" // DeckOfCards class definition
4
5    int main()
6    {
7       DeckOfCards deckOfCards; // create DeckOfCards object
8       deckOfCards.deal(); // deal the cards in the deck
9    } // end main
```

```
Card:  0  Suit: 0  Color: 0    Card:  0  Suit: 2  Color: 1
Card:  1  Suit: 0  Color: 0    Card:  1  Suit: 2  Color: 1
Card:  2  Suit: 0  Color: 0    Card:  2  Suit: 2  Color: 1
Card:  3  Suit: 0  Color: 0    Card:  3  Suit: 2  Color: 1
Card:  4  Suit: 0  Color: 0    Card:  4  Suit: 2  Color: 1
Card:  5  Suit: 0  Color: 0    Card:  5  Suit: 2  Color: 1
Card:  6  Suit: 0  Color: 0    Card:  6  Suit: 2  Color: 1
Card:  7  Suit: 0  Color: 0    Card:  7  Suit: 2  Color: 1
Card:  8  Suit: 0  Color: 0    Card:  8  Suit: 2  Color: 1
Card:  9  Suit: 0  Color: 0    Card:  9  Suit: 2  Color: 1
Card: 10  Suit: 0  Color: 0    Card: 10  Suit: 2  Color: 1
Card: 11  Suit: 0  Color: 0    Card: 11  Suit: 2  Color: 1
Card: 12  Suit: 0  Color: 0    Card: 12  Suit: 2  Color: 1
Card:  0  Suit: 1  Color: 0    Card:  0  Suit: 3  Color: 1
Card:  1  Suit: 1  Color: 0    Card:  1  Suit: 3  Color: 1
Card:  2  Suit: 1  Color: 0    Card:  2  Suit: 3  Color: 1
Card:  3  Suit: 1  Color: 0    Card:  3  Suit: 3  Color: 1
Card:  4  Suit: 1  Color: 0    Card:  4  Suit: 3  Color: 1
Card:  5  Suit: 1  Color: 0    Card:  5  Suit: 3  Color: 1
Card:  6  Suit: 1  Color: 0    Card:  6  Suit: 3  Color: 1
Card:  7  Suit: 1  Color: 0    Card:  7  Suit: 3  Color: 1
Card:  8  Suit: 1  Color: 0    Card:  8  Suit: 3  Color: 1
Card:  9  Suit: 1  Color: 0    Card:  9  Suit: 3  Color: 1
Card: 10  Suit: 1  Color: 0    Card: 10  Suit: 3  Color: 1
Card: 11  Suit: 1  Color: 0    Card: 11  Suit: 3  Color: 1
Card: 12  Suit: 1  Color: 0    Card: 12  Suit: 3  Color: 1
```

Fig. 22.16 | Bit fields used to store a deck of cards.

It's possible to specify an unnamed bit field, in which case the field is used as padding in the structure. For example, the structure definition uses an unnamed three-bit field as padding—nothing can be stored in those three bits. Member b is stored in another storage unit.

```
struct Example
{
    unsigned a : 13;
    unsigned   : 3; // align to next storage-unit boundary
    unsigned b : 4;
}; // end struct Example
```

An unnamed bit field with a zero width is used to align the next bit field on a new storage-unit boundary. For example, the structure definition

```
struct Example
{
    unsigned a : 13;
    unsigned   : 0; // align to next storage-unit boundary
    unsigned b : 4;
}; // end struct Example
```

uses an unnamed 0-bit field to *skip* the remaining bits (as many as there are) of the storage unit in which a is stored and align b on the *next storage-unit boundary*.

Portability Tip 22.4
Bit-field manipulations are machine dependent. For example, some computers allow bit fields to cross word boundaries, whereas others do not.

Common Programming Error 22.5
Attempting to access individual bits of a bit field with subscripting as if they were elements of an array is a compilation error. Bit fields are not "arrays of bits."

Common Programming Error 22.6
Attempting to take the address of a bit field (the & operator may not be used with bit fields because a pointer can designate only a particular byte in memory and bit fields can start in the middle of a byte) is a compilation error.

Performance Tip 22.2
Although bit fields save space, using them can cause the compiler to generate slower-executing machine-language code. This occurs because it takes extra machine-language operations to access only portions of an addressable storage unit. This is one of many examples of the space–time trade-offs that occur in computer science.

22.7 Character-Handling Library

Most data is entered into computers as *characters*—including letters, digits and various special symbols. In this section, we discuss C++'s capabilities for examining and manipulating individual characters. In the remainder of the chapter, we continue the discussion of *character-string manipulation* that we began in Chapter 8.

The character-handling library includes several functions that perform useful tests and manipulations of character data. Each function receives a character—represented as an `int`—or EOF as an argument. *Characters are often manipulated as integers.* Remember that EOF normally has the value –1 and that some hardware architectures do not allow negative values to be stored in `char` variables. Therefore, the character-handling functions manipulate characters as integers. Figure 22.17 summarizes the functions of the character-handling library. When using functions from the character-handling library, include the `<cctype>` header.

Prototype	Description
`int isdigit( int c )`	Returns 1 if c is a *digit* and 0 otherwise.
`int isalpha( int c )`	Returns 1 if c is a *letter* and 0 otherwise.
`int isalnum( int c )`	Returns 1 if c is a *digit or a letter* and 0 otherwise.
`int isxdigit( int c )`	Returns 1 if c is a *hexadecimal digit* character and 0 otherwise. (See Appendix D for a detailed explanation of binary, octal, decimal and hexadecimal numbers.)
`int islower( int c )`	Returns 1 if c is a *lowercase letter* and 0 otherwise.
`int isupper( int c )`	Returns 1 if c is an *uppercase letter*; 0 otherwise.
`int tolower( int c )`	If c is an *uppercase letter*, `tolower` returns c as a *lowercase letter*. Otherwise, `tolower` returns the argument *unchanged*.
`int toupper( int c )`	If c is a *lowercase letter*, `toupper` returns c as an *uppercase letter*. Otherwise, `toupper` returns the argument *unchanged*.
`int isspace( int c )`	Returns 1 if c is a *whitespace character*—newline (`'\n'`), space (`' '`), form feed (`'\f'`), carriage return (`'\r'`), horizontal tab (`'\t'`), or vertical tab (`'\v'`)—and 0 otherwise.
`int iscntrl( int c )`	Returns 1 if c is a *control character*, such as newline (`'\n'`), form feed (`'\f'`), carriage return (`'\r'`), horizontal tab (`'\t'`), vertical tab (`'\v'`), alert (`'\a'`), or backspace (`'\b'`)—and 0 otherwise.
`int ispunct( int c )`	Returns 1 if c is a *printing character other than a space*, a *digit*, or a *letter* and 0 otherwise.
`int isprint( int c )`	Returns 1 if c is a *printing character including space* (`' '`) and 0 otherwise.
`int isgraph( int c )`	Returns 1 if c is a *printing character other than space* (`' '`) and 0 otherwise.

Fig. 22.17 | Character-handling library functions.

Figure 22.18 demonstrates functions `isdigit`, `isalpha`, `isalnum` and `isxdigit`. Function `isdigit` determines whether its argument is a *digit* (0–9). Function `isalpha` determines whether its argument is an *uppercase letter* (A–Z) or a *lowercase letter* (a–z). Function `isalnum` determines whether its argument is an *uppercase letter, a lowercase letter or a digit*. Function `isxdigit` determines whether its argument is a *hexadecimal digit* (A–F, a–f, 0–9).

```cpp
1   // Fig. 22.18: fig22_18.cpp
2   // Character-handling functions isdigit, isalpha, isalnum and isxdigit.
3   #include <iostream>
4   #include <cctype> // character-handling function prototypes
5   using namespace std;
6
7   int main()
8   {
9      cout << "According to isdigit:\n"
10        << ( isdigit( '8' ) ? "8 is a" : "8 is not a" ) << " digit\n"
11        << ( isdigit( '#' ) ? "# is a" : "# is not a" ) << " digit\n";
12
13     cout << "\nAccording to isalpha:\n"
14        << ( isalpha( 'A' ) ? "A is a" : "A is not a" ) << " letter\n"
15        << ( isalpha( 'b' ) ? "b is a" : "b is not a" ) << " letter\n"
16        << ( isalpha( '&' ) ? "& is a" : "& is not a" ) << " letter\n"
17        << ( isalpha( '4' ) ? "4 is a" : "4 is not a" ) << " letter\n";
18
19     cout << "\nAccording to isalnum:\n"
20        << ( isalnum( 'A' ) ? "A is a" : "A is not a" )
21        << " digit or a letter\n"
22        << ( isalnum( '8' ) ? "8 is a" : "8 is not a" )
23        << " digit or a letter\n"
24        << ( isalnum( '#' ) ? "# is a" : "# is not a" )
25        << " digit or a letter\n";
26
27     cout << "\nAccording to isxdigit:\n"
28        << ( isxdigit( 'F' ) ? "F is a" : "F is not a" )
29        << " hexadecimal digit\n"
30        << ( isxdigit( 'J' ) ? "J is a" : "J is not a" )
31        << " hexadecimal digit\n"
32        << ( isxdigit( '7' ) ? "7 is a" : "7 is not a" )
33        << " hexadecimal digit\n"
34        << ( isxdigit( '$' ) ? "$ is a" : "$ is not a" )
35        << " hexadecimal digit\n"
36        << ( isxdigit( 'f' ) ? "f is a" : "f is not a" )
37        << " hexadecimal digit" << endl;
38  } // end main
```

```
According to isdigit:
8 is a digit
# is not a digi

According to isalpha:
A is a letter
b is a letter
& is not a letter
4 is not a letter

According to isalnum:
A is a digit or a letter
8 is a digit or a letter
# is not a digit or a letter
```

Fig. 22.18 | Character-handling functions isdigit, isalpha, isalnum and isxdigit. (Part 1 of 2.)

```
According to isxdigit:
F is a hexadecimal digit
J is not a hexadecimal digit
7 is a hexadecimal digit
$ is not a hexadecimal digit
f is a hexadecimal digit
```

Fig. 22.18 | Character-handling functions `isdigit`, `isalpha`, `isalnum` and `isxdigit`. (Part 2 of 2.)

Figure 22.18 uses the *conditional operator (?:)* with each function to determine whether the string " is a " or the string " is not a " should be printed in the output for each character tested. For example, line 10 indicates that if '8' is a digit—i.e., if `isdigit` returns a true (nonzero) value—the string "8 is a " is printed. If '8' is not a digit (i.e., if `isdigit` returns 0), the string "8 is not a " is printed.

Figure 22.19 demonstrates functions `islower`, `isupper`, `tolower` and `toupper`. Function `islower` determines whether its argument is a *lowercase letter* (a–z). Function `isupper` determines whether its argument is an *uppercase letter* (A–Z). Function `tolower` converts an uppercase letter to lowercase and returns the lowercase letter—if the argument is not an uppercase letter, `tolower` returns the argument value unchanged. Function `toupper` converts a lowercase letter to uppercase and returns the uppercase letter—if the argument is *not* a lowercase letter, `toupper` returns the argument value *unchanged*.

```cpp
1  // Fig. 22.19: fig22_19.cpp
2  // Character-handling functions islower, isupper, tolower and toupper.
3  #include <iostream>
4  #include <cctype> // character-handling function prototypes
5  using namespace std;
6
7  int main()
8  {
9     cout << "According to islower:\n"
10        << ( islower( 'p' ) ? "p is a" : "p is not a" )
11        << " lowercase letter\n"
12        << ( islower( 'P' ) ? "P is a" : "P is not a" )
13        << " lowercase letter\n"
14        << ( islower( '5' ) ? "5 is a" : "5 is not a" )
15        << " lowercase letter\n"
16        << ( islower( '!' ) ? "! is a" : "! is not a" )
17        << " lowercase letter\n";
18
19     cout << "\nAccording to isupper:\n"
20        << ( isupper( 'D' ) ? "D is an" : "D is not an" )
21        << " uppercase letter\n"
22        << ( isupper( 'd' ) ? "d is an" : "d is not an" )
23        << " uppercase letter\n"
24        << ( isupper( '8' ) ? "8 is an" : "8 is not an" )
```

Fig. 22.19 | Character-handling functions `islower`, `isupper`, `tolower` and `toupper`. (Part 1 of 2.)

```
25            << " uppercase letter\n"
26            << ( isupper( '$' ) ? "$ is an" : "$ is not an" )
27            << " uppercase letter\n";
28
29     cout << "\nu converted to uppercase is "
30            << static_cast< char >( toupper( 'u' ) )
31            << "\n7 converted to uppercase is "
32            << static_cast< char >( toupper( '7' ) )
33            << "\n$ converted to uppercase is "
34            << static_cast< char >( toupper( '$' ) )
35            << "\nL converted to lowercase is "
36            << static_cast< char >( tolower( 'L' ) ) << endl;
37  } // end main
```

```
According to islower:
p is a lowercase letter
P is not a lowercase letter
5 is not a lowercase letter
! is not a lowercase letter

According to isupper:
D is an uppercase letter
d is not an uppercase letter
8 is not an uppercase letter
$ is not an uppercase letter

u converted to uppercase is U
7 converted to uppercase is 7
$ converted to uppercase is $
L converted to lowercase is l
```

Fig. 22.19 | Character-handling functions islower, isupper, tolower and toupper. (Part 2 of 2.)

Figure 22.20 demonstrates functions isspace, iscntrl, ispunct, isprint and isgraph. Function isspace determines whether its argument is a *whitespace character*, such as space (' '), form feed ('\f'), newline ('\n'), carriage return ('\r'), horizontal tab ('\t') or vertical tab ('\v'). Function iscntrl determines whether its argument is a *control character* such as horizontal tab ('\t'), vertical tab ('\v'), form feed ('\f'), alert ('\a'), backspace ('\b'), carriage return ('\r') or newline ('\n'). Function ispunct determines whether its argument is a *printing character other than a space, digit or letter*, such as $, #, (,), [,], {, }, ;, : or %. Function isprint determines whether its argument is a character that can be *displayed on the screen* (including the space character). Function isgraph tests for the same characters as isprint, but the space character is *not* included.

```
1  // Fig. 22.20: fig22_20.cpp
2  // Using functions isspace, iscntrl, ispunct, isprint and isgraph.
3  #include <iostream>
```

Fig. 22.20 | Character-handling functions isspace, iscntrl, ispunct, isprint and isgraph. (Part 1 of 3.)

```
4    #include <cctype> // character-handling function prototypes
5    using namespace std;
6
7    int main()
8    {
9       cout << "According to isspace:\nNewline "
10          << ( isspace( '\n' ) ? "is a" : "is not a" )
11          << " whitespace character\nHorizontal tab "
12          << ( isspace( '\t' ) ? "is a" : "is not a" )
13          << " whitespace character\n"
14          << ( isspace( '%' ) ? "% is a" : "% is not a" )
15          << " whitespace character\n";
16
17       cout << "\nAccording to iscntrl:\nNewline "
18          << ( iscntrl( '\n' ) ? "is a" : "is not a" )
19          << " control character\n"
20          << ( iscntrl( '$' ) ? "$ is a" : "$ is not a" )
21          << " control character\n";
22
23       cout << "\nAccording to ispunct:\n"
24          << ( ispunct( ';' ) ? "; is a" : "; is not a" )
25          << " punctuation character\n"
26          << ( ispunct( 'Y' ) ? "Y is a" : "Y is not a" )
27          << " punctuation character\n"
28          << ( ispunct( '#' ) ? "# is a" : "# is not a" )
29          << " punctuation character\n";
30
31       cout << "\nAccording to isprint:\n"
32          << ( isprint( '$' ) ? "$ is a" : "$ is not a" )
33          << " printing character\nAlert "
34          << ( isprint( '\a' ) ? "is a" : "is not a" )
35          << " printing character\nSpace "
36          << ( isprint( ' ' ) ? "is a" : "is not a" )
37          << " printing character\n";
38
39       cout << "\nAccording to isgraph:\n"
40          << ( isgraph( 'Q' ) ? "Q is a" : "Q is not a" )
41          << " printing character other than a space\nSpace "
42          << ( isgraph( ' ' ) ? "is a" : "is not a" )
43          << " printing character other than a space" << endl;
44    } // end main
```

```
According to isspace:
Newline is a whitespace character
Horizontal tab is a whitespace character
% is not a whitespace character

According to iscntrl:
Newline is a control character
$ is not a control character
```

Fig. 22.20 | Character-handling functions `isspace`, `iscntrl`, `ispunct`, `isprint` and `isgraph`. (Part 2 of 3.)

```
According to ispunct:
; is a punctuation character
Y is not a punctuation character
# is a punctuation character

According to isprint:
$ is a printing character
Alert is not a printing character
Space is a printing character

According to isgraph:
Q is a printing character other than a space
Space is not a printing character other than a space
```

Fig. 22.20 | Character-handling functions isspace, iscntrl, ispunct, isprint and isgraph. (Part 3 of 3.)

22.8 C String-Manipulation Functions

The string-handling library provides any useful functions for manipulating string data, *comparing* strings, *searching* strings for characters and other strings, *tokenizing* strings (separating strings into logical pieces such as the separate words in a sentence) and determining the *length* of strings. This section presents some common string-manipulation functions of the string-handling library (from the *C++ standard library*). The functions are summarized in Fig. 22.21; then each is used in a live-code example. The prototypes for these functions are located in header <cstring>.

Function prototype	Function description
`char *strcpy( char *s1, const char *s2 );`	
	Copies the string s2 into the character array s1. The value of s1 is returned.
`char *strncpy( char *s1, const char *s2, size_t n );`	
	Copies at most n characters of the string s2 into the character array s1. The value of s1 is returned.
`char *strcat( char *s1, const char *s2 );`	
	Appends the string s2 to s1. The first character of s2 overwrites the terminating null character of s1. The value of s1 is returned.
`char *strncat( char *s1, const char *s2, size_t n );`	
	Appends at most n characters of string s2 to string s1. The first character of s2 overwrites the terminating null character of s1. The value of s1 is returned.
`int strcmp( const char *s1, const char *s2 );`	
	Compares the string s1 with the string s2. The function returns a value of zero, less than zero or greater than zero if s1 is equal to, less than or greater than s2, respectively.

Fig. 22.21 | String-manipulation functions of the string-handling library. (Part 1 of 2.)

Function prototype	Function description

`int strncmp( const char *s1, const char *s2, size_t n );`

Compares up to n characters of the string s1 with the string s2. The function returns zero, less than zero or greater than zero if the n-character portion of s1 is equal to, less than or greater than the corresponding n-character portion of s2, respectively.

`char *strtok( char *s1, const char *s2 );`

A sequence of calls to strtok breaks string s1 into *tokens*—logical pieces such as words in a line of text. The string is broken up based on the characters contained in string s2. For instance, if we were to break the string "this:is:a:string" into tokens based on the character ':', the resulting tokens would be "this", "is", "a" and "string". Function strtok returns only one token at a time—the first call contains s1 as the first argument, and subsequent calls to continue tokenizing the same string contain NULL as the first argument. A pointer to the current token is returned by each call. If there are no more tokens when the function is called, NULL is returned.

`size_t strlen( const char *s );`

Determines the length of string s. The number of characters preceding the terminating null character is returned.

Fig. 22.21 | String-manipulation functions of the string-handling library. (Part 2 of 2.)

Several functions in Fig. 22.21 contain parameters with data type `size_t`. This type is defined in the header `<cstring>` to be an unsigned integral type such as `unsigned int` or `unsigned long`.

Common Programming Error 22.7
Forgetting to include the `<cstring>` header when using functions from the string-handling library causes compilation errors.

Copying Strings with **`strcpy` *and* `strncpy`**

Function `strcpy` copies its second argument—a string—into its first argument—a character array that must be large enough to store the string *and its terminating null character*, (which is also copied). Function `strncpy` is much like `strcpy`, except that `strncpy` specifies the number of characters to be copied from the string into the array. Function `strncpy` does *not* necessarily copy the terminating null character of its second argument—a terminating null character is written only if the number of characters to be copied is at least one more than the length of the string. For example, if "test" is the second argument, a terminating null character is written *only* if the third argument to `strncpy` is at least 5 (four characters in "test" plus one terminating null character). If the third argument is larger than 5, null characters are appended to the array until the total number of characters specified by the third argument is written.

Common Programming Error 22.8

When using strncpy, *the terminating null character of the second argument (a char * string) will not be copied if the number of characters specified by* strncpy's *third argument is not greater than the second argument's length. In that case, a fatal error may occur if you do not manually terminate the resulting char * string with a null character.*

Figure 22.22 uses strcpy (line 13) to copy the entire string in array x into array y and uses strncpy (line 19) to copy the first 14 characters of array x into array z. Line 20 appends a null character ('\0') to array z, because the call to strncpy in the program does not write a terminating null character. (The third argument is less than the string length of the second argument plus one.)

```cpp
1   // Fig. 22.22: fig22_22.cpp
2   // Using strcpy and strncpy.
3   #include <iostream>
4   #include <cstring> // prototypes for strcpy and strncpy
5   using namespace std;
6
7   int main()
8   {
9      char x[] = "Happy Birthday to You"; // string length 21
10     char y[ 25 ];
11     char z[ 15 ];
12
13     strcpy( y, x ); // copy contents of x into y
14
15     cout << "The string in array x is: " << x
16        << "\nThe string in array y is: " << y << '\n';
17
18     // copy first 14 characters of x into z
19     strncpy( z, x, 14 ); // does not copy null character
20     z[ 14 ] = '\0'; // append '\0' to z's contents
21
22     cout << "The string in array z is: " << z << endl;
23  } // end main
```

```
The string in array x is: Happy Birthday to You
The string in array y is: Happy Birthday to You
The string in array z is: Happy Birthday
```

Fig. 22.22 | strcpy and strncpy.

Concatenating Strings with strcat and strncat

Function strcat appends its second argument (a string) to its first argument (a character array containing a string). The first character of the second argument replaces the null character ('\0') that terminates the string in the first argument. You must ensure that the array used to store the first string is *large enough* to store the combination of the first string, the second string and the terminating null character (copied from the second string). Function strncat appends a specified number of characters from the second string to the first string and appends a terminating null character to the result. The program of Fig. 22.23 demonstrates function strcat (lines 15 and 25) and function strncat (line 20).

```
 1   // Fig. 22.23: fig23_23.cpp
 2   // Using strcat and strncat.
 3   #include <iostream>
 4   #include <cstring> // prototypes for strcat and strncat
 5   using namespace std;
 6
 7   int main()
 8   {
 9      char s1[ 20 ] = "Happy "; // length 6
10      char s2[] = "New Year "; // length 9
11      char s3[ 40 ] = "";
12
13      cout << "s1 = " << s1 << "\ns2 = " << s2;
14
15      strcat( s1, s2 ); // concatenate s2 to s1 (length 15)
16
17      cout << "\n\nAfter strcat(s1, s2):\ns1 = " << s1 << "\ns2 = " << s2;
18
19      // concatenate first 6 characters of s1 to s3
20      strncat( s3, s1, 6 ); // places '\0' after last character
21
22      cout << "\n\nAfter strncat(s3, s1, 6):\ns1 = " << s1
23         << "\ns3 = " << s3;
24
25      strcat( s3, s1 ); // concatenate s1 to s3
26      cout << "\n\nAfter strcat(s3, s1):\ns1 = " << s1
27         << "\ns3 = " << s3 << endl;
28   } // end main
```

```
s1 = Happy
s2 = New Year

After strcat(s1, s2):
s1 = Happy New Year
s2 = New Year

After strncat(s3, s1, 6):
s1 = Happy New Year
s3 = Happy

After strcat(s3, s1):
s1 = Happy New Year
s3 = Happy Happy New Year
```

Fig. 22.23 | `strcat` and `strncat`.

Comparing Strings with `strcmp` and `strncmp`

Figure 22.24 compares three strings using `strcmp` (lines 15–17) and `strncmp` (lines 20–22). Function `strcmp` compares its first string argument with its second string argument character by character. The function returns zero if the strings are equal, a negative value if the first string is less than the second string and a positive value if the first string is greater than the second string. Function `strncmp` is equivalent to `strcmp`, except that `strncmp` compares up to a specified number of characters. Function `strncmp` stops comparing characters if it reaches the null character in one of its string arguments. The program prints the integer value returned by each function call.

Common Programming Error 22.9

Assuming that strcmp *and* strncmp *return one (a true value) when their arguments are equal is a logic error. Both functions return zero (C++'s false value) for equality. Therefore, when testing two strings for equality, the result of the* strcmp *or* strncmp *function should be compared with zero to determine whether the strings are equal.*

```cpp
1   // Fig. 22.24: fig22_24.cpp
2   // Using strcmp and strncmp.
3   #include <iostream>
4   #include <iomanip>
5   #include <cstring> // prototypes for strcmp and strncmp
6   using namespace std;
7
8   int main()
9   {
10      const char *s1 = "Happy New Year";
11      const char *s2 = "Happy New Year";
12      const char *s3 = "Happy Holidays";
13
14      cout << "s1 = " << s1 << "\ns2 = " << s2 << "\ns3 = " << s3
15         << "\n\nstrcmp(s1, s2) = " << setw( 2 ) << strcmp( s1, s2 )
16         << "\nstrcmp(s1, s3) = " << setw( 2 ) << strcmp( s1, s3 )
17         << "\nstrcmp(s3, s1) = " << setw( 2 ) << strcmp( s3, s1 );
18
19      cout << "\n\nstrncmp(s1, s3, 6) = " << setw( 2 )
20         << strncmp( s1, s3, 6 ) << "\nstrncmp(s1, s3, 7) = " << setw( 2 )
21         << strncmp( s1, s3, 7 ) << "\nstrncmp(s3, s1, 7) = " << setw( 2 )
22         << strncmp( s3, s1, 7 ) << endl;
23   } // end main
```

```
s1 = Happy New Year
s2 = Happy New Year
s3 = Happy Holidays

strcmp(s1, s2) =  0
strcmp(s1, s3) =  1
strcmp(s3, s1) = -1

strncmp(s1, s3, 6) =  0
strncmp(s1, s3, 7) =  1
strncmp(s3, s1, 7) = -1
```

Fig. 22.24 | strcmp and strncmp.

To understand what it means for one string to be "greater than" or "less than" another, consider the process of alphabetizing last names. You'd, no doubt, place "Jones" before "Smith," because the first letter of "Jones" comes before the first letter of "Smith" in the alphabet. But the alphabet is more than just a list of 26 letters—it's an *ordered* list of characters. Each letter occurs in a specific position within the list. "Z" is more than just a letter of the alphabet; "Z" is specifically the 26th letter of the alphabet.

How does the computer know that one letter "comes before" another? All characters are represented inside the computer as numeric codes; when the computer compares two strings, it actually compares the numeric codes of the characters in the strings.

[*Note:* With some compilers, functions `strcmp` and `strncmp` always return -1, 0 or 1, as in the sample output of Fig. 22.24. With other compilers, these functions return 0 or the difference between the numeric codes of the first characters that differ in the strings being compared. For example, when `s1` and `s3` are compared, the first characters that differ between them are the first character of the second word in each string—N (numeric code 78) in `s1` and H (numeric code 72) in `s3`, respectively. In this case, the return value will be 6 (or -6 if `s3` is compared to `s1`).]

Tokenizing a String with `strtok`

Function `strtok` breaks a string into a series of *tokens*. A token is a sequence of characters separated by *delimiting characters* (usually spaces or punctuation marks). For example, in a line of text, each word can be considered a token, and the spaces separating the words can be considered delimiters. Multiple calls to `strtok` are required to break a string into tokens (assuming that the string contains more than one token). The first call to `strtok` contains two arguments, a string to be tokenized and a string containing characters that separate the tokens (i.e., delimiters). Line 15 in Fig. 22.25 assigns to `tokenPtr` a pointer to the first token in `sentence`. The second argument, " ", indicates that tokens in `sentence` are separated by spaces. Function `strtok` searches for the first character in `sentence` that's not a delimiting character (space). This begins the first token. The function then finds the next delimiting character in the string and replaces it with a null ('\0') character. This terminates the current token. Function `strtok` saves (in a `static` variable) a pointer to the next character following the token in `sentence` and returns a pointer to the current token.

```
1   // Fig. 22.25: fig22_25.cpp
2   // Using strtok to tokenize a string.
3   #include <iostream>
4   #include <cstring> // prototype for strtok
5   using namespace std;
6
7   int main()
8   {
9      char sentence[] = "This is a sentence with 7 tokens";
10
11     cout << "The string to be tokenized is:\n" << sentence
12        << "\n\nThe tokens are:\n\n";
13
14     // begin tokenization of sentence
15     char *tokenPtr = strtok( sentence, " " );
16
17     // continue tokenizing sentence until tokenPtr becomes NULL
18     while ( tokenPtr != NULL )
19     {
20        cout << tokenPtr << '\n';
21        tokenPtr = strtok( NULL, " " ); // get next token
22     } // end while
```

Fig. 22.25 | Using `strtok` to tokenize a string. (Part 1 of 2.)

```
23
24      cout << "\nAfter strtok, sentence = " << sentence << endl;
25   } // end main
```

```
The string to be tokenized is:
This is a sentence with 7 tokens

The tokens are:

This
is
a
sentence
with
7
tokens

After strtok, sentence = This
```

Fig. 22.25 | Using strtok to tokenize a string. (Part 2 of 2.)

Subsequent calls to strtok to continue tokenizing sentence contain NULL as the first argument (line 21). The NULL argument indicates that the call to strtok should continue tokenizing from the location in sentence saved by the last call to strtok. Function strtok maintains this saved information in a manner that's not visible to you. If no tokens remain when strtok is called, strtok returns NULL. The program of Fig. 22.25 uses strtok to tokenize the string "This is a sentence with 7 tokens". The program prints each token on a separate line. Line 24 outputs sentence after tokenization. Note that *strtok modifies the input string*; therefore, a copy of the string should be made if the program requires the original after the calls to strtok. When sentence is output after tokenization, only the word "This" prints, because strtok replaced each blank in sentence with a null character ('\0') during the tokenization process.

Common Programming Error 22.10

Not realizing that strtok modifies the string being tokenized, then attempting to use that string as if it were the original unmodified string is a logic error.

Determining String Lengths

Function strlen takes a string as an argument and returns the number of characters in the string—the terminating null character is not included in the length. The length is also the index of the null character. The program of Fig. 22.26 demonstrates function strlen.

```
1   // Fig. 22.26: fig22_26.cpp
2   // Using strlen.
3   #include <iostream>
4   #include <cstring> // prototype for strlen
5   using namespace std;
6
```

Fig. 22.26 | strlen returns the length of a char * string. (Part 1 of 2.)

```
 7   int main()
 8   {
 9      const char *string1 = "abcdefghijklmnopqrstuvwxyz";
10      const char *string2 = "four";
11      const char *string3 = "Boston";
12
13      cout << "The length of \"" << string1 << "\" is " << strlen( string1 )
14          << "\nThe length of \"" << string2 << "\" is " << strlen( string2 )
15          << "\nThe length of \"" << string3 << "\" is " << strlen( string3 )
16          << endl;
17   } // end main
```

```
The length of "abcdefghijklmnopqrstuvwxyz" is 26
The length of "four" is 4
The length of "Boston" is 6
```

Fig. 22.26 | `strlen` returns the length of a `char *` string. (Part 2 of 2.)

22.9 C String-Conversion Functions

In Section 22.8, we discussed several of C++'s most popular C string-manipulation functions. In the next several sections, we cover the remaining functions, including functions for converting strings to numeric values, functions for searching strings and functions for manipulating, comparing and searching blocks of memory.

This section presents the C string-conversion functions from the general-utilities library `<cstdlib>`. These functions convert C strings to integer and floating-point values. In new code, C++ programmers typically use the string stream processing capabilities (Chapter 21) to perform such conversions. Figure 22.27 summarizes the C string-conversion functions. When using functions from the general-utilities library, include the `<cstdlib>` header.

Prototype	Description
`double atof( const char *nPtr )`	Converts the string `nPtr` to `double`. If the string cannot be converted, 0 is returned.
`int atoi( const char *nPtr )`	Converts the string `nPtr` to `int`. If the string cannot be converted, 0 is returned.
`long atol( const char *nPtr )`	Converts the string `nPtr` to `long int`. If the string cannot be converted, 0 is returned.
`double strtod( const char *nPtr, char **endPtr )`	
	Converts the string `nPtr` to `double`. `endPtr` is the address of a pointer to the rest of the string after the `double`. If the string cannot be converted, 0 is returned.

Fig. 22.27 | C string-conversion functions of the general-utilities library. (Part 1 of 2.)

Prototype	Description
`long strtol( const char *nPtr, char **endPtr, int base )`	
	Converts the string nPtr to long. endPtr is the address of a pointer to the rest of the string after the long. If the string cannot be converted, 0 is returned. The base parameter indicates the base of the number to convert (e.g., 8 for octal, 10 for decimal or 16 for hexadecimal). The default is decimal.
`unsigned long strtoul( const char *nPtr, char **endPtr, int base )`	
	Converts the string nPtr to unsigned long. endPtr is the address of a pointer to the rest of the string after the unsigned long. If the string cannot be converted, 0 is returned. The base parameter indicates the base of the number to convert (e.g., 8 for octal, 10 for decimal or 16 for hexadecimal). The default is decimal.

Fig. 22.27 | C string-conversion functions of the general-utilities library. (Part 2 of 2.)

Function `atof` (Fig. 22.28, line 9) converts its argument—a string that represents a floating-point number—to a `double` value. The function returns the `double` value. If the string cannot be converted—for example, if the first character of the string is not a digit—function `atof` returns zero.

```
1   // Fig. 22.28: fig22_28.cpp
2   // Using atof.
3   #include <iostream>
4   #include <cstdlib> // atof prototype
5   using namespace std;
6
7   int main()
8   {
9      double d = atof( "99.0" ); // convert string to double
10
11     cout << "The string \"99.0\" converted to double is " << d
12        << "\nThe converted value divided by 2 is " << d / 2.0 << endl;
13  } // end main
```

```
The string "99.0" converted to double is 99
The converted value divided by 2 is 49.5
```

Fig. 22.28 | String-conversion function atof.

Function `atoi` (Fig. 22.29, line 9) converts its argument—a string of digits that represents an integer—to an `int` value. The function returns the `int` value. If the string cannot be converted, function `atoi` returns zero.

```
1   // Fig. 22.29: fig22_29.cpp
2   // Using atoi.
3   #include <iostream>
4   #include <cstdlib> // atoi prototype
5   using namespace std;
6
7   int main()
8   {
9      int i = atoi( "2593" ); // convert string to int
10
11     cout << "The string \"2593\" converted to int is " << i
12        << "\nThe converted value minus 593 is " << i - 593 << endl;
13  } // end main
```

```
The string "2593" converted to int is 2593
The converted value minus 593 is 2000
```

Fig. 22.29 | String-conversion function `atoi`.

Function **atol** (Fig. 22.30, line 9) converts its argument—a string of digits representing a long integer—to a `long` value. The function returns the `long` value. If the string cannot be converted, function `atol` returns zero. If `int` and `long` are both stored in four bytes, function `atoi` and function `atol` work identically.

```
1   // Fig. 22.30: fig22_30.cpp
2   // Using atol.
3   #include <iostream>
4   #include <cstdlib> // atol prototype
5   using namespace std;
6
7   int main()
8   {
9      long x = atol( "1000000" ); // convert string to long
10
11     cout << "The string \"1000000\" converted to long is " << x
12        << "\nThe converted value divided by 2 is " << x / 2 << endl;
13  } // end main
```

```
The string "1000000" converted to long int is 1000000
The converted value divided by 2 is 500000
```

Fig. 22.30 | String-conversion function `atol`.

Function **strtod** (Fig. 22.31) converts a sequence of characters representing a floating-point value to `double`. Function `strtod` receives two arguments—a string (char *) and the address of a char * pointer (i.e., a char **). The string contains the character sequence to be converted to `double`. The second argument enables `strtod` to modify a char * pointer in the calling function, such that the pointer points to the location of the first character after the converted portion of the string. Line 12 indicates that d is assigned the `double` value converted from `string` and that `stringPtr` is assigned the location of the first character after the converted value (51.2) in `string`.

```
1   // Fig. 22.31: fig22_31.cpp
2   // Using strtod.
3   #include <iostream>
4   #include <cstdlib> // strtod prototype
5   using namespace std;
6
7   int main()
8   {
9      const char *string1 = "51.2% are admitted";
10     char *stringPtr = nullptr;
11
12     double d = strtod( string1, &stringPtr ); // convert to double
13
14     cout << "The string \"" << string1
15        << "\" is converted to the\ndouble value " << d
16        << " and the string \"" << stringPtr << "\"" << endl;
17  } // end main
```

```
The string "51.2% are admitted" is converted to the
double value 51.2 and the string "% are admitted"
```

Fig. 22.31 | String-conversion function `strtod`.

Function `strtol` (Fig. 22.32) converts to `long` a sequence of characters representing an integer. The function receives a string (`char *`), the address of a `char *` pointer and an integer. The string contains the character sequence to convert. The second argument is assigned the location of the first character after the converted portion of the string. The integer specifies the *base* of the value being converted. Line 12 indicates that x is assigned the `long` value converted from `string` and that `remainderPtr` is assigned the location of the first character after the converted value (-1234567) in `string1`. Using a null pointer for the second argument causes the remainder of the string to be ignored. The third argument, 0, indicates that the value to be converted can be in octal (base 8), decimal (base 10) or hexadecimal (base 16). This is determined by the initial characters in the string—0 indicates an octal number, 0x indicates hexadecimal and a number from 1 to 9 indicates decimal.

```
1   // Fig. 22.32: fig22_32.cpp
2   // Using strtol.
3   #include <iostream>
4   #include <cstdlib> // strtol prototype
5   using namespace std;
6
7   int main()
8   {
9      const char *string1 = "-1234567abc";
10     char *remainderPtr = nullptr;
```

Fig. 22.32 | String-conversion function `strtol`. (Part 1 of 2.)

```
11
12    long x = strtol( string1, &remainderPtr, 0 ); // convert to long
13
14    cout << "The original string is \""  << string1
15       << "\"\nThe converted value is "  << x
16       << "\"\nThe remainder of the original string is \"" << remainderPtr
17       << "\"\nThe converted value plus 567 is " << x + 567 << endl;
18  } // end main
```

```
The original string is "-1234567abc"
The converted value is -1234567
The remainder of the original string is "abc"
The converted value plus 567 is -1234000
```

Fig. 22.32 | String-conversion function `strtol`. (Part 2 of 2.)

In a call to function `strtol`, the base can be specified as zero or as any value between 2 and 36. (See Appendix D for a detailed explanation of the octal, decimal, hexadecimal and binary number systems.) Numeric representations of integers from base 11 to base 36 use the characters A–Z to represent the values 10 to 35. For example, hexadecimal values can consist of the digits 0–9 and the characters A–F. A base-11 integer can consist of the digits 0–9 and the character A. A base-24 integer can consist of the digits 0–9 and the characters A–N. A base-36 integer can consist of the digits 0–9 and the characters A–Z. [*Note: The case of the letter used is ignored.*]

Function `strtoul` (Fig. 22.33) converts to `unsigned long` a sequence of characters representing an `unsigned long` integer. The function works identically to `strtol`. Line 13 indicates that x is assigned the `unsigned long` value converted from `string` and that `remainderPtr` is assigned the location of the first character after the converted value (1234567) in `string1`. The third argument, 0, indicates that the value to be converted can be in octal, decimal or hexadecimal format, depending on the initial characters.

```
1   // Fig. 22.33: fig22_33.cpp
2   // Using strtoul.
3   #include <iostream>
4   #include <cstdlib> // strtoul prototype
5   using namespace std;
6
7   int main()
8   {
9      const char *string1 = "1234567abc";
10     char *remainderPtr = nullptr;
11
12     // convert a sequence of characters to unsigned long
13     unsigned long x = strtoul( string1, &remainderPtr, 0 );
14
15     cout << "The original string is \"" << string1
16        << "\"\nThe converted value is " << x
17        << "\"\nThe remainder of the original string is \"" << remainderPtr
```

Fig. 22.33 | String-conversion function `strtoul`. (Part 1 of 2.)

```
18          << "\"\nThe converted value minus 567 is " << x - 567 << endl;
19    } // end main
```

```
The original string is "1234567abc"
The converted value is 1234567
The remainder of the original string is "abc"
The converted value minus 567 is 1234000
```

Fig. 22.33 | String-conversion function `strtoul`. (Part 2 of 2.)

22.10 Search Functions of the C String-Handling Library

This section presents the functions of the string-handling library used to search strings for characters and other strings. The functions are summarized in Fig. 22.34. Functions `strcspn` and `strspn` specify return type `size_t`. Type `size_t` is a type defined by the standard as the integral type of the value returned by operator `sizeof`.

Function `strchr` searches for the first occurrence of a character in a string. If the character is found, `strchr` returns a pointer to the character in the string; otherwise, `strchr` returns a null pointer. The program of Fig. 22.35 uses `strchr` (lines 14 and 22) to search for the first occurrences of `'a'` and `'z'` in the string `"This is a test"`.

Prototype	Description
`char *strchr( const char *s, int c )`	Locates the first occurrence of character c in string s. If c is found, a pointer to c in s is returned. Otherwise, a null pointer is returned.
`char *strrchr( const char *s, int c )`	Searches from the end of string s and locates the last occurrence of character c in string s. If c is found, a pointer to c in string s is returned. Otherwise, a null pointer is returned.
`size_t strspn( const char *s1, const char *s2 )`	Determines and returns the length of the initial segment of string s1 consisting only of characters contained in string s2.
`char *strpbrk( const char *s1, const char *s2 )`	Locates the first occurrence in string s1 of any character in string s2. If a character from string s2 is found, a pointer to the character in string s1 is returned. Otherwise, a null pointer is returned.
`size_t strcspn( const char *s1, const char *s2 )`	Determines and returns the length of the initial segment of string s1 consisting of characters not contained in string s2.
`char *strstr( const char *s1, const char *s2 )`	Locates the first occurrence in string s1 of string s2. If the string is found, a pointer to the string in s1 is returned. Otherwise, a null pointer is returned.

Fig. 22.34 | Search functions of the C string-handling library.

```
 1   // Fig. 22.35: fig22_35.cpp
 2   // Using strchr.
 3   #include <iostream>
 4   #include <cstring> // strchr prototype
 5   using namespace std;
 6
 7   int main()
 8   {
 9      const char *string1 = "This is a test";
10      char character1 = 'a';
11      char character2 = 'z';
12
13      // search for character1 in string1
14      if ( strchr( string1, character1 ) != NULL )
15         cout << '\'' << character1 << "' was found in \""
16            << string1 << "\".\n";
17      else
18         cout << '\'' << character1 << "' was not found in \""
19            << string1 << "\".\n";
20
21      // search for character2 in string1
22      if ( strchr( string1, character2 ) != NULL )
23         cout << '\'' << character2 << "' was found in \""
24            << string1 << "\".\n";
25      else
26         cout << '\'' << character2 << "' was not found in \""
27            << string1 << "\"." << endl;
28   } // end main
```

```
'a' was found in "This is a test".
'z' was not found in "This is a test".
```

Fig. 22.35 | String-search function `strchr`.

Function `strcspn` (Fig. 22.36, line 15) determines the length of the initial part of the string in its first argument that does not contain any characters from the string in its second argument. The function returns the length of the segment.

```
 1   // Fig. 22.36: fig22_36.cpp
 2   // Using strcspn.
 3   #include <iostream>
 4   #include <cstring> // strcspn prototype
 5   using namespace std;
 6
 7   int main()
 8   {
 9      const char *string1 = "The value is 3.14159";
10      const char *string2 = "1234567890";
11
12      cout << "string1 = " << string1 << "\nstring2 = " << string2
13         << "\n\nThe length of the initial segment of string1"
```

Fig. 22.36 | String-search function `strcspn`. (Part 1 of 2.)

```
14              << "\ncontaining no characters from string2 = "
15              << strcspn( string1, string2 ) << endl;
16      } // end main
```

```
string1 = The value is 3.14159
string2 = 1234567890

The length of the initial segment of string1
containing no characters from string2 = 13
```

Fig. 22.36 | String-search function strcspn. (Part 2 of 2.)

Function **strpbrk** searches for the first occurrence in its first string argument of any character in its second string argument. If a character from the second argument is found, strpbrk returns a pointer to the character in the first argument; otherwise, strpbrk returns a null pointer. Line 13 of Fig. 22.37 locates the first occurrence in string1 of any character from string2.

```
 1    // Fig. 22.37: fig22_37.cpp
 2    // Using strpbrk.
 3    #include <iostream>
 4    #include <cstring> // strpbrk prototype
 5    using namespace std;
 6
 7    int main()
 8    {
 9       const char *string1 = "This is a test";
10       const char *string2 = "beware";
11
12       cout << "Of the characters in \"" << string2 << "\"\n'"
13            << *strpbrk( string1, string2 ) << "\' is the first character "
14            << "to appear in\n\"" << string1 << '\"' << endl;
15    } // end main
```

```
Of the characters in "beware"
'a' is the first character to appear in
"This is a test"
```

Fig. 22.37 | String-search function strpbrk.

Function **strrchr** searches for the last occurrence of the specified character in a string. If the character is found, strrchr returns a pointer to the character in the string; otherwise, strrchr returns 0. Line 15 of Fig. 22.38 searches for the last occurrence of the character 'z' in the string "A zoo has many animals including zebras".

```
 1    // Fig. 22.38: fig22_38.cpp
 2    // Using strrchr.
 3    #include <iostream>
 4    #include <cstring> // strrchr prototype
```

Fig. 22.38 | String-search function strrchr. (Part 1 of 2.)

```
5   using namespace std;
6
7   int main()
8   {
9      const char *string1 = "A zoo has many animals including zebras";
10     char c = 'z';
11
12     cout << "string1 = " << string1 << "\n" << endl;
13     cout << "The remainder of string1 beginning with the\n"
14         << "last occurrence of character '"
15         << c << "' is: \"" << strrchr( string1, c ) << '\"' << endl;
16  } // end main
```

```
string1 = A zoo has many animals including zebras

The remainder of string1 beginning with the
last occurrence of character 'z' is: "zebras"
```

Fig. 22.38 | String-search function `strrchr`. (Part 2 of 2.)

Function **strspn** (Fig. 22.39, line 15) determines the length of the initial part of the string in its first argument that contains only characters from the string in its second argument. The function returns the length of the segment.

```
1   // Fig. 22.39: fig22_39.cpp
2   // Using strspn.
3   #include <iostream>
4   #include <cstring> // strspn prototype
5   using namespace std;
6
7   int main()
8   {
9      const char *string1 = "The value is 3.14159";
10     const char *string2 = "aehils Tuv";
11
12     cout << "string1 = " << string1 << "\nstring2 = " << string2
13         << "\n\nThe length of the initial segment of string1\n"
14         << "containing only characters from string2 = "
15         << strspn( string1, string2 ) << endl;
16  } // end main
```

```
string1 = The value is 3.14159
string2 = aehils Tuv

The length of the initial segment of string1
containing only characters from string2 = 13
```

Fig. 22.39 | String-search function `strspn`.

Function **strstr** searches for the first occurrence of its second string argument in its first string argument. If the second string is found in the first string, a pointer to the location of the string in the first argument is returned; otherwise, it returns 0. Line 15 of Fig. 22.40 uses `strstr` to find the string "def" in the string "abcdefabcdef".

```cpp
1   // Fig. 22.40: fig22_40.cpp
2   // Using strstr.
3   #include <iostream>
4   #include <cstring> // strstr prototype
5   using namespace std;
6
7   int main()
8   {
9      const char *string1 = "abcdefabcdef";
10     const char *string2 = "def";
11
12     cout << "string1 = " << string1 << "\nstring2 = " << string2
13        << "\n\nThe remainder of string1 beginning with the\n"
14        << "first occurrence of string2 is: "
15        << strstr( string1, string2 ) << endl;
16  } // end main
```

```
string1 = abcdefabcdef
string2 = def

The remainder of string1 beginning with the
first occurrence of string2 is: defabcdef
```

Fig. 22.40 | String-search function `strstr`.

22.11 Memory Functions of the C String-Handling Library

The string-handling library functions presented in this section facilitate manipulating, comparing and searching blocks of memory. The functions treat blocks of memory as arrays of bytes. These functions can manipulate any block of data. Figure 22.41 summarizes the memory functions of the string-handling library. In the function discussions, "object" refers to a block of data. [*Note:* The string-processing functions in prior sections operate on null-terminated strings. The functions in this section operate on arrays of bytes. The null-character value (i.e., a byte containing 0) has *no* significance with the functions in this section.]

Prototype	Description
`void *memcpy( void *s1, const void *s2, size_t n )`	
	Copies n characters from the object pointed to by s2 into the object pointed to by s1. A pointer to the resulting object is returned. The area from which characters are copied is not allowed to overlap the area to which characters are copied.

Fig. 22.41 | Memory functions of the string-handling library. (Part 1 of 2.)

Prototype	Description

`void *memmove( void *s1, const void *s2, size_t n )`

Copies n characters from the object pointed to by s2 into the object pointed to by s1. The copy is performed as if the characters were first copied from the object pointed to by s2 into a temporary array, then copied from the temporary array into the object pointed to by s1. A pointer to the resulting object is returned. The area from which characters are copied is allowed to overlap the area to which characters are copied.

`int memcmp( const void *s1, const void *s2, size_t n )`

Compares the first n characters of the objects pointed to by s1 and s2. The function returns 0, less than 0, or greater than 0 if s1 is equal to, less than or greater than s2, respectively.

`void *memchr( const void *s, int c, size_t n )`

Locates the first occurrence of c (converted to `unsigned char`) in the first n characters of the object pointed to by s. If c is found, a pointer to c in the object is returned. Otherwise, 0 is returned.

`void *memset( void *s, int c, size_t n )`

Copies c (converted to `unsigned char`) into the first n characters of the object pointed to by s. A pointer to the result is returned.

Fig. 22.41 | Memory functions of the string-handling library. (Part 2 of 2.)

The pointer parameters to these functions are declared void *. In Chapter 8, we saw that *a pointer to any data type can be assigned directly to a pointer of type void *.* For this reason, these functions can receive pointers to any data type. Remember that *a pointer of type void * cannot be assigned directly to a pointer of any other data type.* Because a void * pointer cannot be dereferenced, each function receives a size argument that specifies the number of characters (bytes) the function will process. For simplicity, the examples in this section manipulate character arrays (blocks of characters).

Function `memcpy` copies a specified number of characters (bytes) from the object pointed to by its second argument into the object pointed to by its first argument. The function can receive a pointer to any type of object. The result of this function is undefined if the two objects overlap in memory (i.e., are parts of the same object). The program of Fig. 22.42 uses memcpy (line 14) to copy the string in array s2 to array s1.

```
1   // Fig. 22.42: fig22_42.cpp
2   // Using memcpy.
3   #include <iostream>
4   #include <cstring> // memcpy prototype
5   using namespace std;
6
7   int main()
8   {
9      char s1[ 17 ] = {};
```

Fig. 22.42 | Memory-handling function `memcpy`. (Part 1 of 2.)

```
10
11      // 17 total characters (includes terminating null)
12      char s2[] = "Copy this string";
13
14      memcpy( s1, s2, 17 ); // copy 17 characters from s2 to s1
15
16      cout << "After s2 is copied into s1 with memcpy,\n"
17          << "s1 contains \"" << s1 << '\"' << endl;
18   } // end main
```

```
After s2 is copied into s1 with memcpy,
s1 contains "Copy this string"
```

Fig. 22.42 | Memory-handling function memcpy. (Part 2 of 2.)

Function memmove, like memcpy, copies a specified number of bytes from the object pointed to by its second argument into the object pointed to by its first argument. Copying is performed as if the bytes were copied from the second argument to a temporary array of characters, then copied from the temporary array to the first argument. This allows characters from one part of a string to be copied into another part of the same string.

Common Programming Error 22.11
String-manipulation functions other than memmove that copy characters have undefined results when copying takes place between parts of the same string.

The program in Fig. 22.43 uses memmove (line 13) to copy the last 10 bytes of array x into the first 10 bytes of array x.

```
1   // Fig. 22.43: fig22_43.cpp
2   // Using memmove.
3   #include <iostream>
4   #include <cstring> // memmove prototype
5   using namespace std;
6
7   int main()
8   {
9       char x[] = "Home Sweet Home";
10
11      cout << "The string in array x before memmove is: " << x;
12      cout << "\nThe string in array x after memmove is:  "
13          << static_cast< char * >( memmove( x, &x[ 5 ], 10 ) ) << endl;
14   } // end main
```

```
The string in array x before memmove is: Home Sweet Home
The string in array x after memmove is:  Sweet Home Home
```

Fig. 22.43 | Memory-handling function memmove.

Function memcmp (Fig. 22.44, lines 14–16) compares the specified number of characters of its first argument with the corresponding characters of its second argument. The function returns a value greater than zero if the first argument is greater than the second argument, zero if the arguments are equal, and a value less than zero if the first argument is less than the second argument. [*Note:* With some compilers, function memcmp returns -1, 0 or 1, as in the sample output of Fig. 22.44. With other compilers, this function returns 0 or the difference between the numeric codes of the first characters that differ in the strings being compared. For example, when s1 and s2 are compared, the first character that differs between them is the fifth character of each string—E (numeric code 69) for s1 and X (numeric code 72) for s2. In this case, the return value will be 19 (or -19 when s2 is compared to s1).]

```
1   // Fig. 22.44: fig22_44.cpp
2   // Using memcmp.
3   #include <iostream>
4   #include <iomanip>
5   #include <cstring> // memcmp prototype
6   using namespace std;
7
8   int main()
9   {
10     char s1[] = "ABCDEFG";
11     char s2[] = "ABCDXYZ";
12
13     cout << "s1 = " << s1 << "\ns2 = " << s2 << endl
14       << "\nmemcmp(s1, s2, 4) = " << setw( 3 ) << memcmp( s1, s2, 4 )
15       << "\nmemcmp(s1, s2, 7) = " << setw( 3 ) << memcmp( s1, s2, 7 )
16       << "\nmemcmp(s2, s1, 7) = " << setw( 3 ) << memcmp( s2, s1, 7 )
17       << endl;
18   } // end main
```

```
s1 = ABCDEFG
s2 = ABCDXYZ

memcmp(s1, s2, 4) =   0
memcmp(s1, s2, 7) =  -1
memcmp(s2, s1, 7) =   1
```

Fig. 22.44 | Memory-handling function memcmp.

Function `memchr` searches for the first occurrence of a byte, represented as `unsigned char`, in the specified number of bytes of an object. If the byte is found in the object, a pointer to it is returned; otherwise, the function returns a null pointer. Line 13 of Fig. 22.45 searches for the character (byte) 'r' in the string "This is a string".

```
1   // Fig. 22.45: fig22_45.cpp
2   // Using memchr.
3   #include <iostream>
4   #include <cstring> // memchr prototype
5   using namespace std;
```

Fig. 22.45 | Memory-handling function memchr. (Part 1 of 2.)

```
 6
 7    int main()
 8    {
 9       char s[] = "This is a string";
10
11       cout << "s = " << s << "\n" << endl;
12       cout << "The remainder of s after character 'r' is found is \""
13          << static_cast< char * >( memchr( s, 'r', 16 ) ) << '\"' << endl;
14    } // end main
```

```
s = This is a string

The remainder of s after character 'r' is found is "ring"
```

Fig. 22.45 | Memory-handling function `memchr`. (Part 2 of 2.)

Function **memset** copies the value of the byte in its second argument into a specified number of bytes of the object pointed to by its first argument. Line 13 in Fig. 22.46 uses memset to copy 'b' into the first 7 bytes of string1.

```
 1    // Fig. 22.46: fig22_46.cpp
 2    // Using memset.
 3    #include <iostream>
 4    #include <cstring> // memset prototype
 5    using namespace std;
 6
 7    int main()
 8    {
 9       char string1[ 15 ] = "BBBBBBBBBBBBBB";
10
11       cout << "string1 = " << string1 << endl;
12       cout << "string1 after memset = "
13          << static_cast< char * >( memset( string1, 'b', 7 ) ) << endl;
14    } // end main
```

```
string1 = BBBBBBBBBBBBBB
string1 after memset = bbbbbbbBBBBBBB
```

Fig. 22.46 | Memory-handling function `memset`.

22.12 Wrap-Up

This chapter introduced `struct` definitions, initializing `struct`s and using them with functions. We discussed `typedef`, using it to create aliases to help promote portability. We also introduced bitwise operators to manipulate data and bit fields for storing data compactly. You learned about the string-conversion functions in `<cstlib>` and the string-processing functions in `<cstring>`. In the next chapter, we discuss additional C++ topics.

Summary

Section 22.2 Structure Definitions

- Keyword `struct` (p. 914) begins every structure definition. Between the braces of the structure definition are the structure member declarations.

- A structure definition creates a new data type (p. 914) that can be used to declare variables.

Section 22.3 `typedef`

- Creating a new type name with `typedef` (p. 916) does not create a new type; it creates a name that's synonymous with a type defined previously.

Section 22.5 Bitwise Operators

- The bitwise AND operator (`&`; p. 919) takes two integral operands. A bit in the result is set to one if the corresponding bits in each of the operands are one.

- Masks (p. 921) are used with bitwise AND to hide some bits while preserving others.

- The bitwise inclusive OR operator (`|`; p. 919) takes two operands. A bit in the result is set to one if the corresponding bit in either operand is set to one.

- Each of the bitwise operators (except complement) has a corresponding assignment operator.

- The bitwise exclusive OR operator (`^`; p. 919) takes two operands. A bit in the result is set to one if exactly one of the corresponding bits in the two operands is set to one.

- The left-shift operator (`<<`; p. 919) shifts the bits of its left operand left by the number of bits specified by its right operand. Bits vacated to the right are replaced with zeros.

- The right-shift operator (`>>`; p. 919) shifts the bits of its left operand right by the number of bits specified in its right operand. Right shifting an unsigned integer causes bits vacated at the left to be replaced by zeros. Vacated bits in signed integers can be replaced with zeros or ones.

- The bitwise complement operator (`~`; p. 919) takes one operand and inverts its bits—this produces the one's complement of the operand.

Section 22.6 Bit Fields

- Bit fields (p. 928) reduce storage use by storing data in the minimum number of bits required. Bit-field members must be declared as `int` or `unsigned`.

- A bit field is declared by following an `unsigned` or `int` member name with a colon and the width of the bit field.

- The bit-field width must be an integer constant.

- If a bit field is specified without a name, the field is used as padding (p. 931) in the structure.

- An unnamed bit field with width `0` (p. 931) aligns the next bit field on a new machine-word boundary.

Section 22.7 Character-Handling Library

- Function `islower` (p. 934) determines if its argument is a lowercase letter (a–z). Function `isupper` (p. 934) determines whether its argument is an uppercase letter (A–Z).

- Function `isdigit` (p. 932) determines if its argument is a digit (0–9).

- Function `isalpha` (p. 932) determines if its argument is an uppercase (A–Z) or lowercase letter (a–z).

- Function `isalnum` (p. 932) determines if its argument is an uppercase letter (A–Z), a lowercase letter (a–z), or a digit (0–9).

- Function `isxdigit` (p. 932) determines if its argument is a hexadecimal digit (A–F, a–f, 0–9).

- Function `toupper` (p. 934) converts a lowercase letter to an uppercase letter. Function `tolower` (p. 934) converts an uppercase letter to a lowercase letter.
- Function `isspace` (p. 935) determines if its argument is one of the following whitespace characters: `' '` (space), `'\f'`, `'\n'`, `'\r'`, `'\t'` or `'\v'`.
- Function `iscntrl` (p. 935) determines if its argument is a control character, such as `'\t'`, `'\v'`, `'\f'`, `'\a'`, `'\b'`, `'\r'` or `'\n'`.
- Function `ispunct` (p. 935) determines if its argument is a printing character other than a space, a digit or a letter.
- Function `isprint` (p. 935) determines if its argument is any printing character, including space.
- Function `isgraph` (p. 935) determines if its argument is a printing character other than space.

Section 22.8 C String-Manipulation Functions

- Function `strcpy` (p. 938) copies its second argument into its first argument. You must ensure that the target array is large enough to store the string and its terminating null character.
- Function `strncpy` (p. 938) is equivalent to `strcpy`, but it specifies the number of characters to be copied from the string into the array. The terminating null character will be copied only if the number of characters to be copied is at least one more than the length of the string.
- Function `strcat` (p. 939) appends its second string argument—including the terminating null character—to its first string argument. The first character of the second string replaces the null (`'\0'`) character of the first string. You must ensure that the target array used to store the first string is large enough to store both the first string and the second string.
- Function `strncat` (p. 939) is equivalent to `strcat`, but it appends a specified number of characters from the second string to the first string. A terminating null character is appended to the result.
- Function `strcmp` compares its first string argument with its second string argument character by character. The function returns zero if the strings are equal, a negative value if the first string is less than the second string and a positive value if the first string is greater than the second string.
- Function `strncmp` is equivalent to `strcmp`, but it compares a specified number of characters. If the number of characters in one of the strings is less than the number of characters specified, `strncmp` compares characters until the null character in the shorter string is encountered.
- A sequence of calls to `strtok` (p. 942) breaks a string into tokens that are separated by characters contained in a second string argument. The first call specifies the string to be tokenized as the first argument, and subsequent calls to continue tokenizing the same string specify `NULL` as the first argument. The function returns a pointer to the current token from each call. If there are no more tokens when `strtok` is called, `NULL` is returned.
- Function `strlen` (p. 943) takes a string as an argument and returns the number of characters in the string—the terminating null character is not included in the length of the string.

Section 22.9 C String-Conversion Functions

- Function `atof` (p. 945) converts its argument—a string beginning with a series of digits that represents a floating-point number—to a `double` value.
- Function `atoi` (p. 945) converts its argument—a string beginning with a series of digits that represents an integer—to an `int` value.
- Function `atol` (p. 946) converts its argument—a string beginning with a series of digits that represents a long integer—to a `long` value.
- Function `strtod` (p. 946) converts a sequence of characters representing a floating-point value to `double`. The function receives two arguments—a string (`char *`) and the address of a `char *`

pointer. The string contains the character sequence to be converted, and the pointer to char * is assigned the remainder of the string after the conversion.

- Function `strtol` (p. 947) converts a sequence of characters representing an integer to `long`. It receives a string (char *), the address of a char * pointer and an integer. The string contains the character sequence to be converted, the pointer to char * is assigned the location of the first character after the converted value and the integer specifies the base of the value being converted.

- Function `strtoul` (p. 948) converts a sequence of characters representing an integer to `unsigned long`. It receives a string (char *), the address of a char * pointer and an integer. The string contains the character sequence to be converted, the pointer to char * is assigned the location of the first character after the converted value and the integer specifies the base of the value being converted.

Section 22.10 Search Functions of the C String-Handling Library

- Function `strchr` (p. 949) searches for the first occurrence of a character in a string. If found, `strchr` returns a pointer to the character in the string; otherwise, `strchr` returns a null pointer.

- Function `strcspn` (p. 950) determines the length of the initial part of the string in its first argument that does not contain any characters from the string in its second argument. The function returns the length of the segment.

- Function `strpbrk` (p. 951) searches for the first occurrence in its first argument of any character that appears in its second argument. If a character from the second argument is found, `strpbrk` returns a pointer to the character; otherwise, `strpbrk` returns a null pointer.

- Function `strrchr` (p. 951) searches for the last occurrence of a character in a string. If the character is found, `strrchr` returns a pointer to the character in the string; otherwise, it returns a null pointer.

- Function `strspn` (p. 952) determines the length of the initial part of its first argument that contains only characters from the string in its second argument and returns the length of the segment.

- Function `strstr` (p. 952) searches for the first occurrence of its second string argument in its first string argument. If the second string is found in the first string, a pointer to the location of the string in the first argument is returned; otherwise it returns 0.

Section 22.11 Memory Functions of the C String-Handling Library

- Function `memcpy` (p. 954) copies a specified number of characters from the object to which its second argument points into the object to which its first argument points. The function can receive a pointer to any object. The pointers are received as `void` pointers and converted to `char` pointers for use in the function. Function `memcpy` manipulates the bytes of its argument as characters.

- Function `memmove` (p. 955) copies a specified number of bytes from the object pointed to by its second argument to the object pointed to by its first argument. Copying is accomplished as if the bytes were copied from the second argument to a temporary character array, then copied from the temporary array to the first argument.

- Function `memcmp` (p. 955) compares the specified number of characters of its first and second arguments.

- Function `memchr` (p. 956) searches for the first occurrence of a byte, represented as `unsigned char`, in the specified number of bytes of an object. If the byte is found, a pointer to it is returned; otherwise, a null pointer is returned.

- Function `memset` (p. 957) copies its second argument, treated as an `unsigned char`, to a specified number of bytes of the object pointed to by the first argument.

Self-Review Exercises

22.1   Fill in the blanks in each of the following:

a)   The bits in the result of an expression using the _____ operator are set to one if the corresponding bits in each operand are set to one. Otherwise, the bits are set to zero.

b)   The bits in the result of an expression using the _____ operator are set to one if at least one of the corresponding bits in either operand is set to one. Otherwise, the bits are set to zero.

c)   Keyword _____ introduces a structure declaration.

d)   Keyword _____ is used to create a synonym for a previously defined data type.

e)   Each bit in the result of an expression using the _____ operator is set to one if exactly one of the corresponding bits in either operand is set to one.

f)   The bitwise AND operator & is often used to _____ bits (i.e., to select certain bits from a bit string while zeroing others).

g)   The _____ and _____ operators are used to shift the bits of a value to the left or to the right, respectively.

22.2   Write a single statement or a set of statements to accomplish each of the following:

a)   Define a structure called Part containing int variable partNumber and char array part-Name, whose values may be as long as 25 characters.

b)   Define PartPtr to be a synonym for the type Part *.

c)   Use separate statements to declare variable a to be of type Part, array b[10] to be of type Part and variable ptr to be of type pointer to Part.

d)   Read a part number and a part name from the keyboard into the members of variable a.

e)   Assign the member values of variable a to element three of array b.

f)   Assign the address of array b to the pointer variable ptr.

g)   Print the member values of element three of array b, using the variable ptr and the structure pointer operator to refer to the members.

22.3   Write a single statement to accomplish each of the following. Assume that variables c (which stores a character), x, y and z are of type int; variables d, e and f are of type double; variable ptr is of type char * and arrays s1[100] and s2[100] are of type char.

a)   Convert the character stored in c to an uppercase letter. Assign the result to variable c.

b)   Determine if the value of variable c is a digit. Use the conditional operator as shown in Figs. 22.18–22.20 to print " is a " or " is not a " when the result is displayed.

c)   Convert the string "1234567" to long, and print the value.

d)   Determine whether the value of variable c is a control character. Use the conditional operator to print " is a " or " is not a " when the result is displayed.

e)   Assign to ptr the location of the last occurrence of c in s1.

f)   Convert the string "8.63582" to double, and print the value.

g)   Determine whether the value of c is a letter. Use the conditional operator to print " is a " or " is not a " when the result is displayed.

h)   Assign to ptr the location of the first occurrence of s2 in s1.

i)   Determine whether the value of variable c is a printing character. Use the conditional operator to print " is a " or " is not a " when the result is displayed.

j)   Assign to ptr the location of the first occurrence in s1 of any character from s2.

k)   Assign to ptr the location of the first occurrence of c in s1.

l)   Convert the string "-21" to int, and print the value.

Answers to Self-Review Exercises

22.1   a) bitwise AND (&). b) bitwise inclusive OR (|). c) struct. d) typedef. e) bitwise exclusive OR (^). f) mask. g) left-shift operator (<<), right-shift operator (>>).

22.2 a) `struct Part`
```
      {
          int partNumber;
          char partName[ 26 ];
      };
```
  b) `typedef Part * PartPtr;`
  c) `Part a;`
  `Part b[ 10 ];`
  `Part *ptr;`
  d) `cin >> a.partNumber >> a.partName;`
  e) `b[ 3 ] = a;`
  f) `ptr = b;`
  g) `cout << ( ptr + 3 )->partNumber << ' '`
  `     << ( ptr + 3 )->partName << endl;`

22.3 a) `c = toupper( c );`
  b) `cout << '\'' << c << "\' "`
  `       << ( isdigit( c ) ? "is a" : "is not a" )`
  `       << " digit" << endl;`
  c) `cout << atol( "1234567" ) << endl;`
  d) `cout << '\'' << c << "\' "`
  `       << ( iscntrl( c ) ? "is a" : "is not a" )`
  `       << " control character" << endl;`
  e) `ptr = strrchr( s1, c );`
  f) `out << atof( "8.63582" ) << endl;`
  g) `cout << '\'' << c << "\' "`
  `       << ( isalpha( c ) ? "is a" : "is not a" )`
  `       << " letter" << endl;`
  h) `ptr = strstr( s1, s2 );`
  i) `cout << '\'' << c << "\' "`
  `       << ( isprint( c ) ? "is a" : "is not a" )`
  `       << " printing character" << endl;`
  j) `ptr = strpbrk( s1, s2 );`
  k) `ptr = strchr( s1, c );`
  l) `cout << atoi( "-21" ) << endl;`

Exercises

22.4 *(Defining Structures)* Provide the definition for each of the following structures:
  a) Structure Inventory, containing character array `partName[ 30 ]`, integer `partNumber`, floating-point `price`, integer `stock` and integer `reorder`.
  b) A structure called `Address` that contains character arrays `streetAddress[25]`, `city[20]`, `state[3]` and `zipCode[6]`.
  c) Structure Student, containing arrays `firstName[ 15 ]` and `lastName[ 15 ]` and variable `homeAddress` of type `struct Address` from part (b).
  d) Structure Test, containing 16 bit fields with widths of 1 bit. The names of the bit fields are the letters a to p.

22.5 *(Card Shuffling and Dealing)* Modify Fig. 22.14 to shuffle the cards using the shuffle algorithm in Fig. 22.3. Print the resulting deck in two-column format. Precede each card with its color.

22.6   *(Shifting and Printing an Integer)* Write a program that right-shifts an integer variable four bits. The program should print the integer in bits before and after the shift operation. Does your system place zeros or ones in the vacated bits?

22.7   *(Multiplication Via Bit Shifting)* Left-shifting an unsigned integer by one bit is equivalent to multiplying the value by 2. Write function power2 that takes two integer arguments, number and pow, and calculates

> number * 2^{pow}

Use a shift operator to calculate the result. The program should print the values as integers and as bits.

22.8   *(Packing Characters into Unsigned Integers)* The left-shift operator can be used to pack four character values into a four-byte unsigned integer variable. Write a program that inputs four characters from the keyboard and passes them to function packCharacters. To pack four characters into an unsigned integer variable, assign the first character to the unsigned variable, shift the unsigned variable left by eight bit positions and combine the unsigned variable with the second character using the bitwise inclusive-OR operator, etc. The program should output the characters in their bit format before and after they're packed into the unsigned integer to prove that they're in fact packed correctly in the unsigned variable.

22.9   *(Unpacking Characters from Unsigned Integers)* Using the right-shift operator, the bitwise AND operator and a mask, write function unpackCharacters that takes the unsigned integer from Exercise 22.8 and unpacks it into four characters. To unpack characters from an unsigned four-byte integer, combine the unsigned integer with a mask and right-shift the result. To create the masks t you'll need to unpack the four characters, left-shift the value 255 in the mask variable by eight bits 0, 1, 2 or 3 times (depending on the byte you are unpacking). Then take the combined result each time and right shift it by eight bits the same number of times. Assign each resulting value to a char variable. The program should print the unsigned integer in bits before it's unpacked, then print the characters in bits to confirm that they were unpacked correctly.

22.10   *(Reversing Bits)* Write a program that reverses the order of the bits in an unsigned integer value. The program should input the value from the user and call function reverseBits to print the bits in reverse order. Print the value in bits both before and after the bits are reversed to confirm that the bits are reversed properly.

22.11   *(Testing Characters with the <cctype> Functions)* Write a program that inputs a character from the keyboard and tests the character with each function in the character-handling library. Print the value returned by each function.

22.12   *(Determine the Value)* The following program uses function multiple to determine whether the integer entered from the keyboard is a multiple of some integer X. Examine function multiple, then determine the value of X.

```cpp
// Exercise 22.12: ex22_12.cpp
// This program determines if a value is a multiple of X.
#include <iostream>
using namespace std;

bool multiple( int );

int main()
{
   int y = 0;

   cout << "Enter an integer between 1 and 32000: ";
   cin >> y;
```

```
14
15      if ( multiple( y ) )
16         cout << y << " is a multiple of X" << endl;
17      else
18         cout << y << " is not a multiple of X" << endl;
19   } // end main
20
21   // determine if num is a multiple of X
22   bool multiple( int num )
23   {
24      bool mult = true;
25
26      for ( int i = 0, mask = 1; i < 10; ++i, mask <<= 1 )
27         if ( ( num & mask ) != 0 )
28         {
29            mult = false;
30            break;
31         } // end if
32
33      return mult;
34   } // end function multiple
```

22.13 What does the following program do?

```
1    // Exercise 22.13: ex22_13.cpp
2    #include <iostream>
3    using namespace std;
4
5    bool mystery( unsigned );
6
7    int main()
8    {
9       unsigned x;
10
11      cout << "Enter an integer: ";
12      cin >> x;
13      cout << boolalpha
14           << "The result is " << mystery( x ) << endl;
15   } // end main
16
17   // What does this function do?
18   bool mystery( unsigned bits )
19   {
20      const int SHIFT = 8 * sizeof( unsigned ) - 1;
21      const unsigned MASK = 1 << SHIFT;
22      unsigned total = 0;
23
24      for ( int i = 0; i < SHIFT + 1; ++i, bits <<= 1 )
25         if ( ( bits & MASK ) == MASK )
26            ++total;
27
28      return !( total % 2 );
29   } // end function mystery
```

22.14 Write a program that inputs a line of text with `istream` member function `getline` (as in Chapter 13) into character array `s[100]`. Output the line in uppercase letters and lowercase letters.

22.15 *(Converting Strings to Integers)* Write a program that inputs four strings that represent integers, converts the strings to integers, sums the values and prints the total of the four values. Use only the C string-processing techniques shown in this chapter.

22.16 *(Converting Strings to Floating-Point Numbers)* Write a program that inputs four strings that represent floating-point values, converts the strings to double values, sums the values and prints the total of the four values. Use only the C string-processing techniques shown in this chapter.

22.17 *(Searching for Substrings)* Write a program that inputs a line of text and a search string from the keyboard. Using function `strstr`, locate the first occurrence of the search string in the line of text, and assign the location to variable `searchPtr` of type `char *`. If the search string is found, print the remainder of the line of text beginning with the search string. Then use `strstr` again to locate the next occurrence of the search string in the line of text. If a second occurrence is found, print the remainder of the line of text beginning with the second occurrence. [*Hint:* The second call to `strstr` should contain the expression `searchPtr + 1` as its first argument.]

22.18 *(Searching for Substrings)* Write a program based on the program of Exercise 22.17 that inputs several lines of text and a search string, then uses function `strstr` to determine the total number of occurrences of the string in the lines of text. Print the result.

22.19 *(Searching for Characters)* Write a program that inputs several lines of text and a search character and uses function `strchr` to determine the total number of occurrences of the character in the lines of text.

22.20 *(Searching for Characters)* Write a program based on the program of Exercise 22.19 that inputs several lines of text and uses function `strchr` to determine the total number of occurrences of each letter of the alphabet in the text. Uppercase and lowercase letters should be counted together. Store the totals for each letter in an array, and print the values in tabular format after the totals have been determined.

22.21 *(ASCII Character Set)* The chart in Appendix B shows the numeric code representations for the characters in the ASCII character set. Study this chart, then state whether each of the following is *true* or *false*:
    a) The letter "A" comes before the letter "B."
    b) The digit "9" comes before the digit "0."
    c) The commonly used symbols for addition, subtraction, multiplication and division all come before any of the digits.
    d) The digits come before the letters.
    e) If a sort program sorts strings into ascending sequence, then the program will place the symbol for a right parenthesis before the symbol for a left parenthesis.

22.22 *(Strings Beginning with b)* Write a program that reads a series of strings and prints only those strings beginning with the letter "b."

22.23 *(Strings Ending with ED)* Write a program that reads a series of strings and prints only those strings that end with the letters "ED."

22.24 *(Displaying Characters for Given ASCII Codes)* Write a program that inputs an ASCII code and prints the corresponding character. Modify this program so that it generates all possible three-digit codes in the range 000–255 and attempts to print the corresponding characters. What happens when this program is run?

22.25 *(Write Your Own Character Handling Functions)* Using the ASCII character chart in Appendix B as a guide, write your own versions of the character-handling functions in Fig. 22.17.

22.26 *(Write Your Own String Conversion Functions)* Write your own versions of the functions in Fig. 22.27 for converting strings to numbers.

22.27   *(Write Your Own String Searching Functions)* Write your own versions of the functions in
Fig. 22.34 for searching strings.

22.28   *(Write Your Own Memory Handling Functions)* Write your own versions of the functions
in Fig. 22.41 for manipulating blocks of memory.

22.29   *(What Does the Program Do?)* What does this program do?

```cpp
// Ex. 22.29: ex22_29.cpp
// What does this program do?
#include <iostream>
using namespace std;

bool mystery3( const char *, const char * ); // prototype

int main()
{
   char string1[ 80 ], string2[ 80 ];

   cout << "Enter two strings: ";
   cin >> string1 >> string2;
   cout << "The result is " << mystery3( string1, string2 ) << endl;
} // end main

// What does this function do?
bool mystery3( const char *s1, const char *s2 )
{
   for ( ; *s1 != '\0' && *s2 != '\0'; ++s1, ++s2 )

      if ( *s1 != *s2 )
         return false;

   return true;
} // end function mystery3
```

22.30   *(Comparing Strings)* Write a program that uses function `strcmp` to compare two strings input by the user. The program should state whether the first string is less than, equal to or greater
than the second string.

22.31   *(Comparing Strings)* Write a program that uses function `strncmp` to compare two strings
input by the user. The program should input the number of characters to compare. The program
should state whether the first string is less than, equal to or greater than the second string.

22.32   *(Randomly Creating Sentences)* Write a program that uses random number generation to
create sentences. The program should use four arrays of pointers to char called `article`, `noun`, `verb`
and `preposition`. The program should create a sentence by selecting a word at random from each
array in the following order: `article`, `noun`, `verb`, `preposition`, `article` and `noun`. As each word is
picked, it should be concatenated to the previous words in a character array that's large enough to
hold the entire sentence. The words should be separated by spaces. When the final sentence is output, it should start with a capital letter and end with a period. The program should generate 20 such
sentences.

   The arrays should be filled as follows: The `article` array should contain the articles "the",
"a", "one", "some" and "any"; the noun array should contain the nouns "boy", "girl", "dog",
"town" and "car"; the verb array should contain the verbs "drove", "jumped", "ran", "walked"
and "skipped"; the preposition array should contain the prepositions "to", "from", "over",
"under" and "on".

After completing the program, modify it to produce a short story consisting of several of these sentences. (How about a random term-paper writer!)

22.33 *(Limericks)* A limerick is a humorous five-line verse in which the first and second lines rhyme with the fifth, and the third line rhymes with the fourth. Using techniques similar to those developed in Exercise 22.32, write a C++ program that produces random limericks. Polishing this program to produce good limericks is a challenging problem, but the result will be worth the effort!

22.34 *(Pig Latin)* Write a program that encodes English language phrases into pig Latin. Pig Latin is a form of coded language often used for amusement. Many variations exist in the methods used to form pig Latin phrases. For simplicity, use the following algorithm: To form a pig-Latin phrase from an English-language phrase, tokenize the phrase into words with function `strtok`. To translate each English word into a pig-Latin word, place the first letter of the English word at the end of the English word and add the letters "ay." Thus, the word "jump" becomes "umpjay," the word "the" becomes "hetay" and the word "computer" becomes "omputercay." Blanks between words remain as blanks. Assume that the English phrase consists of words separated by blanks, there are no punctuation marks and all words have two or more letters. Function `printLatinWord` should display each word. [*Hint:* Each time a token is found in a call to `strtok`, pass the token pointer to function `printLatinWord` and print the pig-Latin word.]

22.35 *(Tokenizing Phone Numbers)* Write a program that inputs a telephone number as a string in the form (555) 555-5555. The program should use function `strtok` to extract the area code as a token, the first three digits of the phone number as a token, and the last four digits of the phone number as a token. The seven digits of the phone number should be concatenated into one string. Both the area code and the phone number should be printed.

22.36 *(Tokenizing and Reversing a Sentence)* Write a program that inputs a line of text, tokenizes the line with function `strtok` and outputs the tokens in reverse order.

22.37 *(Alphabetizing Strings)* Use the string-comparison functions discussed in Section 22.8 and the techniques for sorting `arrays` developed in Chapter 7 to write a program that alphabetizes a list of strings. Use the names of 10 towns in your area as data for your program.

22.38 *(Write Your Own String Copy and Concatenation Functions)* Write two versions of each string-copy and string-concatenation function in Fig. 22.21. The first version should use array subscripting, and the second should use pointers and pointer arithmetic.

22.39 *(Write Your Own String Comparison Functions)* Write two versions of each string-comparison function in Fig. 22.21. The first version should use array subscripting, and the second should use pointers and pointer arithmetic.

22.40 *(Write Your Own String Length Function)* Write two versions of function `strlen` in Fig. 22.21. The first version should use array subscripting, and the second should use pointers and pointer arithmetic.

Special Section: Advanced String-Manipulation Exercises

The preceding exercises are keyed to the text and designed to test your understanding of fundamental string-manipulation concepts. This section includes a collection of intermediate and advanced string-manipulation exercises. You should find these problems challenging, yet enjoyable. The problems vary considerably in difficulty. Some require an hour or two of program writing and implementation. Others are useful for lab assignments that might require two or three weeks of study and implementation. Some are challenging term projects.

22.41 *(Text Analysis)* The availability of computers with string-manipulation capabilities has resulted in some rather interesting approaches to analyzing the writings of great authors. Much attention has been focused on whether William Shakespeare ever lived. Some scholars believe there is substantial evidence that Francis Bacon, Christopher Marlowe or other authors actually penned the masterpieces attributed to Shakespeare. Researchers have used computers to find similarities in the writings of these authors. This exercise examines three methods for analyzing texts with a computer. Thousands of texts, including Shakespeare, are available online at www.gutenberg.org.

a) Write a program that reads several lines of text from the keyboard and prints a table indicating the number of occurrences of each letter of the alphabet in the text. For example, the phrase

```
To be, or not to be: that is the question:
```

contains one "a," two "b's," no "c's," etc.

b) Write a program that reads several lines of text and prints a table indicating the number of one-letter words, two-letter words, three-letter words, etc., appearing in the text. For example, the phrase

```
Whether 'tis nobler in the mind to suffer
```

contains the following word lengths and occurrences:

Word length	Occurrences
1	0
2	2
3	1
4	2 (including 'tis)
5	0
6	2
7	1

c) Write a program that reads several lines of text and prints a table indicating the number of occurrences of each different word in the text. The first version of your program should include the words in the table in the same order in which they appear in the text. For example, the lines

```
To be, or not to be: that is the question:
Whether 'tis nobler in the mind to suffer
```

contain the word "to" three times, the word "be" two times, the word "or" once, etc. A more interesting (and useful) printout should then be attempted in which the words are sorted alphabetically.

22.42 *(Word Processing)* One important function in word-processing systems is *type justification*—the alignment of words to both the left and right margins of a page. This generates a professional-looking document that gives the appearance of being set in type rather than prepared on a typewriter. Type justification can be accomplished on computer systems by inserting blank characters between the words in a line so that the rightmost word aligns with the right margin.

Write a program that reads several lines of text and prints this text in type-justified format. Assume that the text is to be printed on paper 8-1/2 inches wide and that one-inch margins are to be allowed on both the left and right sides. Assume that the computer prints 10 characters to the horizontal inch. Therefore, your program should print 6-1/2 inches of text, or 65 characters per line.

22.43 *(Printing Dates in Various Formats)* Dates are commonly printed in several different formats in business correspondence. Two of the more common formats are

```
07/21/1955
July 21, 1955
```

Write a program that reads a date in the first format and prints that date in the second format.

22.44 *(Check Protection)* Computers are frequently employed in check-writing systems such as payroll and accounts-payable applications. Many strange stories circulate regarding weekly paychecks being printed (by mistake) for amounts in excess of $1 million. Weird amounts are printed by computerized check-writing systems, because of human error or machine failure. Systems designers build controls into their systems to prevent such erroneous checks from being issued.

Another serious problem is the intentional alteration of a check amount by someone who intends to cash a check fraudulently. To prevent a dollar amount from being altered, most computerized check-writing systems employ a technique called *check protection*.

Checks designed for imprinting by computer contain a fixed number of spaces in which the computer may print an amount. Suppose that a paycheck contains eight blank spaces in which the computer is supposed to print the amount of a weekly paycheck. If the amount is large, then all eight of those spaces will be filled, for example,

```
1,230.60  (check amount)
--------
12345678  (position numbers)
```

On the other hand, if the amount is less than $1000, then several of the spaces would ordinarily be left blank. For example,

```
   99.87
--------
12345678
```

contains three blank spaces. If a check is printed with blank spaces, it's easier for someone to alter the amount of the check. To prevent a check from being altered, many check-writing systems insert *leading asterisks* to protect the amount as follows:

```
***99.87
--------
12345678
```

Write a program that inputs a dollar amount to be printed on a check then prints the amount in check-protected format with leading asterisks if necessary. Assume that nine spaces are available for printing an amount.

22.45 *(Writing the Word Equivalent of a Check Amount)* Continuing the discussion of the previous example, we reiterate the importance of designing check-writing systems to prevent alteration of check amounts. One common security method requires that the check amount be both written in numbers and "spelled out" in words. Even if someone is able to alter the numerical amount of the check, it's extremely difficult to change the amount in words.

Write a program that inputs a numeric check amount and writes the word equivalent of the amount. Your program should be able to handle check amounts as large as $99.99. For example, the amount 112.43 should be written as

```
ONE HUNDRED TWELVE and 43/100
```

22.46 *(Morse Code)* Perhaps the most famous of all coding schemes is the Morse code, developed by Samuel Morse in 1832 for use with the telegraph system. The Morse code assigns a series of dots and dashes to each letter of the alphabet, each digit and a few special characters (such as period, comma, colon and semicolon). In sound-oriented systems, the dot represents a short sound, and the dash represents a long sound. Other representations of dots and dashes are used with light-oriented systems and signal-flag systems.

Separation between words is indicated by a space, or, quite simply, the absence of a dot or dash. In a sound-oriented system, a space is indicated by a short period of time during which no sound is transmitted. The international version of the Morse code appears in Fig. 22.47.

Write a program that reads an English-language phrase and encodes it in Morse code. Also write a program that reads a phrase in Morse code and converts it into the English-language equivalent. Use one blank between each Morse-coded letter and three blanks between each Morse-coded word.

Character	Code	Character	Code	Character	Code
A	.-	N	-.	*Digits*	
B	-...	O	---	1	.----
C	-.-.	P	.--.	2	..---
D	-..	Q	--.-	3	...--
E	.	R	.-.	4	....-
F	..-.	S	...	5	.....
G	--.	T	-	6	-....
H	....	U	..-	7	--...
I	..	V	...-	8	---..
J	.---	W	.--	9	----.
K	-.-	X	-..-	0	-----
L	.-..	Y	-.--		
M	--	Z	--..		

Fig. 22.47 | Letters and digits as expressed in international Morse code.

22.47 *(Metric Conversion Program)* Write a program that will assist the user with metric conversions. Your program should allow the user to specify the names of the units as strings (i.e., centimeters, liters, grams, etc., for the metric system and inches, quarts, pounds, etc., for the English system) and should respond to simple questions such as

```
"How many inches are in 2 meters?"
"How many liters are in 10 quarts?"
```

Your program should recognize invalid conversions. For example, the question

```
"How many feet are in 5 kilograms?"
```

is not meaningful, because `"feet"` are units of length, while `"kilograms"` are units of weight.

Challenging String-Manipulation Projects

22.48 *(Crossword Puzzle Generator)* Most people have worked a crossword puzzle, but few have ever attempted to generate one. Generating a crossword puzzle is a difficult problem. It's suggested here as a string-manipulation project requiring substantial sophistication and effort. There are many issues that you must resolve to get even the simplest crossword puzzle generator program working. For example, how does one represent the grid of a crossword puzzle inside the computer? Should one use a series of strings, or should two-dimensional arrays be used? You need a source of words (i.e., a computerized dictionary) that can be directly referenced by the program. In what form should these words be stored to facilitate the complex manipulations required by the program? The really ambitious reader will want to generate the "clues" portion of the puzzle, in which the brief hints for each "across" word and each "down" word are printed for the puzzle worker. Merely printing a version of the blank puzzle itself is not a simple problem.

22.49 *(Spelling Checker)* Many popular word-processing software packages have built-in spell checkers. We used spell-checking capabilities in preparing this book and discovered that, no matter how careful we thought we were in writing a chapter, the software was always able to find a few more spelling errors than we were able to catch manually.

In this project, you are asked to develop your own spell-checker utility. We make suggestions to help get you started. You should then consider adding more capabilities. You might find it helpful to use a computerized dictionary as a source of words.

Why do we type so many words with incorrect spellings? In some cases, it's because we simply do not know the correct spelling, so we make a "best guess." In some cases, it's because we transpose two letters (e.g., "defualt" instead of "default"). Sometimes we double-type a letter accidentally (e.g., "hanndy" instead of "handy"). Sometimes we type a nearby key instead of the one we intended (e.g., "biryhday" instead of "birthday"). And so on.

Design and implement a spell-checker program. Your program maintains an array wordList of character strings. You can either enter these strings or obtain them from a computerized dictionary.

Your program asks a user to enter a word. The program then looks up that word in the wordList array. If the word is present in the array, your program should print "Word is spelled correctly."

If the word is not present in the array, your program should print "Word is not spelled correctly." Then your program should try to locate other words in wordList that might be the word the user intended to type. For example, you can try all possible single transpositions of adjacent letters to discover that the word "default" is a direct match to a word in wordList. Of course, this implies that your program will check all other single transpositions, such as "edfault," "dfeault," "deafult," "defalut" and "defautl." When you find a new word that matches one in wordList, print that word in a message such as "Did you mean "default?"."

Implement other tests, such as the replacing of each double letter with a single letter and any other tests you can develop to improve the value of your spell checker.

23

Other Topics

*What's in a name? that which
we call a rose
By any other name would smell
as sweet.*
—William Shakespeare

*O Diamond! Diamond! thou
little knowest the mischief done!*
—Sir Isaac Newton

Objectives

In this chapter you'll learn:

- To use `const_cast` to temporarily treat a `const` object as a non-`const` object.

- To use `namespace`s.

- To use operator keywords.

- To use `mutable` members in `const` objects.

- To use class-member pointer operators `.*` and `->*`.

- To use multiple inheritance.

- The role of `virtual` base classes in multiple inheritance.

23.1 Introduction

We now consider additional C++ features. First, we discuss the `const_cast` operator, which allows you to add or remove the `const` qualification of a variable. Next, we discuss `namespaces`, which can be used to ensure that every identifier in a program has a *unique* name and can help resolve naming conflicts caused by using libraries that have the same variable, function or class names. We then present several *operator keywords* that are useful for programmers who have keyboards that do not support certain characters used in operator symbols, such as !, &, ^, ~ and |. We continue our discussion with the `mutable` storage-class specifier, which enables you to indicate that a data member should *always be modifiable*, even when it appears in an object that's currently being treated as a `const` object by the program. Next we introduce two special operators that you can use with pointers to class members to access a data member or member function *without knowing its name* in advance. Finally, we introduce *multiple inheritance*, which enables a derived class to inherit the members of *several* base classes. As part of this introduction, we discuss potential problems with multiple inheritance and how *virtual inheritance* can be used to solve them.

23.2 const_cast Operator

C++ provides the **`const_cast`** operator for casting away `const` or `volatile` qualification. You declare a variable with the **`volatile`** qualifier when you expect the variable to be modified by hardware or other programs not known to the compiler. Declaring a variable volatile indicates that the compiler should *not optimize* the use of that variable because doing so could affect the ability of those other programs to access and modify the volatile variable.

In general, it's dangerous to use the `const_cast` operator, because it allows a program to modify a variable that was declared `const`. There are cases in which it's desirable, or even necessary, to cast away const-ness. For example, older C and C++ libraries might provide functions that have non-const parameters and that do not modify their parameters—if you wish to pass `const` data to such a function, you'd need to cast away the data's const-ness; otherwise, the compiler would report error messages.

Similarly, you could pass non-const data to a function that treats the data as if it were constant, then returns that data as a constant. In such cases, you might need to cast away the const-ness of the returned data, as we demonstrate in Fig. 23.1.

```
 1   // Fig. 23.1: fig23_01.cpp
 2   // Demonstrating const_cast.
 3   #include <iostream>
 4   #include <cstring> // contains prototypes for functions strcmp and strlen
 5   #include <cctype> // contains prototype for function toupper
 6   using namespace std;
 7
 8   // returns the larger of two C strings
 9   const char *maximum( const char *first, const char *second )
10   {
11      return ( strcmp( first, second ) >= 0 ? first : second );
12   } // end function maximum
13
14   int main()
15   {
16      char s1[] = "hello"; // modifiable array of characters
17      char s2[] = "goodbye"; // modifiable array of characters
18
19      // const_cast required to allow the const char * returned by maximum
20      // to be assigned to the char * variable maxPtr
21      char *maxPtr = const_cast< char * >( maximum( s1, s2 ) );
22
23      cout << "The larger string is: " << maxPtr << endl;
24
25      for ( size_t i = 0; i < strlen( maxPtr ); ++i )
26         maxPtr[ i ] = toupper( maxPtr[ i ] );
27
28      cout << "The larger string capitalized is: " << maxPtr << endl;
29   } // end main
```

```
The larger string is: hello
The larger string capitalized is: HELLO
```

Fig. 23.1 | Demonstrating operator const_cast.

In this program, function maximum (lines 9–12) receives two C strings as const char * parameters and returns a const char * that points to the larger of the two strings. Function main declares the two C strings as non-const char arrays (lines 16–17); thus, these arrays are modifiable. In main, we wish to output the larger of the two C strings, then modify that C string by converting it to uppercase letters.

Function maximum's two parameters are of type const char *, so the function's return type also must be declared as const char *. If the return type is specified as only char *, the compiler issues an error message indicating that the value being returned *cannot* be converted from const char * to char *—a dangerous conversion, because it attempts to treat data that the function believes to be const as if it were non-const data.

Even though function maximum *believes* the data to be constant, we know that the original arrays in main do *not* contain constant data. Therefore, main *should* be able to modify the contents of those arrays as necessary. Since we know these arrays *are* modifiable, we use const_cast (line 21) to *cast away the const-ness* of the pointer returned by maximum, so we can then modify the data in the array representing the larger of the two C strings. We can then use the pointer as the name of a character array in the for statement (lines 25–26) to convert the contents of the larger string to uppercase letters. Without the const_cast in line 21, this program will *not* compile, because you are *not* allowed to assign a pointer of type const char * to a pointer of type char *.

Error-Prevention Tip 23.1

In general, a const_cast should be used only when it is known in advance that the original data is not constant. Otherwise, unexpected results may occur.

23.3 mutable Class Members

In Section 23.2, we introduced the const_cast operator, which allowed us to remove the "const-ness" of a type. A const_cast operation can also be applied to a data member of a const object from the body of a const member function of that object's class. This enables the const member function to modify the data member, even though the object is considered to be const in the body of that function. Such an operation might be performed when most of an object's data members should be considered const, but a particular data member still needs to be modified.

As an example, consider a linked list that maintains its contents in sorted order. Searching through the linked list does not require modifications to the data of the linked list, so the search function could be a const member function of the linked-list class. However, it's conceivable that a linked-list object, in an effort to make future searches more efficient, might keep track of the location of the last successful match. If the next search operation attempts to locate an item that appears later in the list, the search could begin from the location of the last successful match, rather than from the beginning of the list. To do this, the const member function that performs the search must be able to modify the data member that keeps track of the last successful search.

If a data member such as the one described above should *always* be modifiable, C++ provides the storage-class specifier **mutable** as an alternative to const_cast. A mutable data member is always modifiable, even in a const member function or const object.

Portability Tip 23.1

The effect of attempting to modify an object that was defined as constant, regardless of whether that modification was made possible by a const_cast or C-style cast, varies among compilers.

mutable and const_cast are used in different contexts. For a const object with no mutable data members, operator const_cast *must* be used every time a member is to be modified. This greatly reduces the chance of a member being accidentally modified because the member is not permanently modifiable. Operations involving const_cast are typically *hidden* in a member function's implementation. The user of a class might not be aware that a member is being modified.

Software Engineering Observation 23.1

mutable members are useful in classes that have "secret" implementation details that do not contribute to a client's use of an object of the class.

*Mechanical Demonstration of a **mutable** Data Member*
Figure 23.2 demonstrates using a mutable member. The program defines class Test-Mutable (lines 7–21), which contains a constructor, function getValue and a private data member value that's declared mutable. Lines 15–18 define function getValue as a const member function that returns a copy of value. Notice that the function increments mutable data member value in the return statement. Normally, a const member function *cannot* modify data members unless the object on which the function operates—i.e., the one to which this points—is *cast* (using const_cast) to a non-const type. Because value is mutable, this const function *can* modify the data.

```
 1   // Fig. 23.2: fig23_02.cpp
 2   // Demonstrating storage-class specifier mutable.
 3   #include <iostream>
 4   using namespace std;
 5
 6   // class TestMutable definition
 7   class TestMutable
 8   {
 9   public:
10      TestMutable( int v = 0 )
11      {
12         value = v;
13      } // end TestMutable constructor
14
15      int getValue() const
16      {
17         return ++value; // increments value
18      } // end function getValue
19   private:
20      mutable int value; // mutable member
21   }; // end class TestMutable
22
23   int main()
24   {
25      const TestMutable test( 99 );
26
27      cout << "Initial value: " << test.getValue();
28      cout << "\nModified value: " << test.getValue() << endl;
29   } // end main
```

```
Initial value: 99
Modified value: 100
```

Fig. 23.2 | Demonstrating a mutable data member.

Line 25 declares const TestMutable object test and initializes it to 99. Line 27 calls the const member function getValue, which adds one to value and returns its previous contents. Notice that the compiler *allows* the call to member function getValue on the object test because it's a const object and getValue is a const member function. However, getValue *modifies* variable value. Thus, when line 28 invokes getValue again, the new value (100) is output to prove that the mutable data member was indeed *modified*.

23.4 namespaces

A program may include many identifiers defined in different scopes. Sometimes a variable of one scope will "overlap" (i.e., collide) with a variable of the *same* name in a *different* scope, possibly creating a *naming conflict*. Such overlapping can occur at many levels. Identifier overlapping occurs frequently in third-party libraries that happen to use the same names for global identifiers (such as functions). This can cause compilation errors.

C++ solves this problem with **namespaces**. Each **namespace** defines a scope in which identifiers and variables are placed. To use a **namespace** member, either the member's name must be qualified with the **namespace** name and the *scope resolution operator (::),* as in

> *MyNameSpace*::*member*

or a using directive must appear *before* the name is used in the program. Typically, such using statements are placed at the beginning of the file in which members of the namespace are used. For example, placing the following using directive at the beginning of a source-code file

> **using namespace** *MyNameSpace*;

specifies that members of namespace *MyNameSpace* can be used in the file without preceding each member with *MyNameSpace* and the scope resolution operator (::).

A using directive of the form

> **using std::cout;**

brings *one* name into the scope where the directive appears. A using directive of the form

> **using namespace std;**

brings *all* the names from the specified namespace (std) into the scope where the directive appears.

Error-Prevention Tip 23.2

Precede a member with its namespace *name and the scope resolution operator (::) if the possibility exists of a naming conflict.*

Not all namespaces are guaranteed to be unique. Two third-party vendors might inadvertently use the same identifiers for their namespace names. Figure 23.3 demonstrates the use of namespaces.

```
 1   // Fig. 23.3: fig23_03.cpp
 2   // Demonstrating namespaces.
 3   #include <iostream>
 4   using namespace std;
 5
 6   int integer1 = 98; // global variable
 7
 8   // create namespace Example
 9   namespace Example
10   {
```

Fig. 23.3 | Demonstrating the use of namespaces. (Part 1 of 3.)

```
11      // declare two constants and one variable
12      const double PI = 3.14159;
13      const double E = 2.71828;
14      int integer1 = 8;
15
16      void printValues(); // prototype
17
18      // nested namespace
19      namespace Inner
20      {
21         // define enumeration
22         enum Years { FISCAL1 = 1990, FISCAL2, FISCAL3 };
23      } // end Inner namespace
24   } // end Example namespace
25
26   // create unnamed namespace
27   namespace
28   {
29      double doubleInUnnamed = 88.22; // declare variable
30   } // end unnamed namespace
31
32   int main()
33   {
34      // output value doubleInUnnamed of unnamed namespace
35      cout << "doubleInUnnamed = " << doubleInUnnamed;
36
37      // output global variable
38      cout << "\n(global) integer1 = " << integer1;
39
40      // output values of Example namespace
41      cout << "\nPI = " << Example::PI << "\nE = " << Example::E
42         << "\ninteger1 = " << Example::integer1 << "\nFISCAL3 = "
43         << Example::Inner::FISCAL3 << endl;
44
45      Example::printValues(); // invoke printValues function
46   } // end main
47
48   // display variable and constant values
49   void Example::printValues()
50   {
51      cout << "\nIn printValues:\ninteger1 = " << integer1 << "\nPI = "
52         << PI << "\nE = " << E << "\ndoubleInUnnamed = "
53         << doubleInUnnamed << "\n(global) integer1 = " << ::integer1
54         << "\nFISCAL3 = " << Inner::FISCAL3 << endl;
55   } // end printValues
```

```
doubleInUnnamed = 88.22
(global) integer1 = 98
PI = 3.14159
E = 2.71828
integer1 = 8
FISCAL3 = 1992
```

Fig. 23.3 | Demonstrating the use of namespaces. (Part 2 of 3.)

```
In printValues:
integer1 = 8
PI = 3.14159
E = 2.71828
doubleInUnnamed = 88.22
(global) integer1 = 98
FISCAL3 = 1992
```

Fig. 23.3 | Demonstrating the use of namespaces. (Part 3 of 3.)

Defining namespaces

Lines 9–24 use the keyword namespace to define namespace Example. The body of a namespace is delimited by braces ({}). The namespace Example's members consist of two constants (PI and E in lines 12–13), an int (integer1 in line 14), a function (printValues in line 16) and a **nested namespace** (Inner in lines 19–23). Notice that member integer1 has the same name as global variable integer1 (line 6). *Variables that have the same name must have different scopes*—otherwise compilation errors occur. A namespace can contain constants, data, classes, nested namespaces, functions, etc. Definitions of namespaces must occupy the *global scope* or be *nested* within other namespaces. Unlike classes, different namespace members can be defined in separate namespace blocks—each standard library header has a namespace block placing its contents in namespace std.

Lines 27–30 create an **unnamed namespace** containing the member doubleInUnnamed. Variables, classes and functions in an *unnamed namespace* are accessible only in the current **translation unit** (a .cpp file and the files it includes). However, unlike variables, classes or functions with static linkage, those in the *unnamed namespace* may be used as template arguments. The unnamed namespace has an implicit using directive, so its members appear to occupy the **global namespace**, are accessible directly and *do not have to be qualified with a namespace name*. Global variables are also part of the global namespace and are accessible in all scopes following the declaration in the file.

Software Engineering Observation 23.2

Each separate compilation unit has its own unique unnamed namespace; i.e., the unnamed namespace replaces the static linkage specifier.

Accessing namespace Members with Qualified Names

Line 35 outputs the value of variable doubleInUnnamed, which is directly accessible as part of the *unnamed namespace*. Line 38 outputs the value of global variable integer1. For both of these variables, the compiler first attempts to locate a *local* declaration of the variables in main. Since there are no local declarations, the compiler assumes those variables are in the global namespace.

Lines 41–43 output the values of PI, E, integer1 and FISCAL3 from namespace Example. Notice that each must be *qualified* with Example:: because the program does not provide any using directive or declarations indicating that it will use members of namespace Example. In addition, member integer1 must be qualified, because a global variable has the same name. Otherwise, the global variable's value is output. FISCAL3 is a member of nested namespace Inner, so it must be *qualified* with Example::Inner::.

Function `printValues` (defined in lines 49–55) is a member of `Example`, so it can access other members of the `Example` namespace directly *without using a namespace qualifier*. The output statement in lines 51–54 outputs `integer1`, `PI`, `E`, `doubleInUnnamed`, global variable `integer1` and `FISCAL3`. Notice that `PI` and `E` are *not qualified* with `Example`. Variable `doubleInUnnamed` is still *accessible*, because it's in the *unnamed namespace* and the variable name does *not conflict* with any other members of namespace `Example`. The global version of `integer1` must be *qualified* with the scope resolution operator (`::`), because its name *conflicts* with a member of namespace `Example`. Also, `FISCAL3` must be *qualified* with `Inner::`. When accessing members of a *nested* namespace, the members must be qualified with the namespace name (unless the member is being used inside the nested `namespace`).

> **Common Programming Error 23.1**
> *Placing* `main` *in a namespace is a compilation error.*

*us*ing *Directives Should* Not *Be Placed in Headers*

`namespace`s are particularly useful in large-scale applications that use many class libraries. In such cases, there's a higher likelihood of naming conflicts. When working on such projects, there should *never* be a `using` directive in a header. Having one brings the corresponding names into any file that includes the header. This could result in name collisions and subtle, hard-to-find errors. Instead, use only fully qualified names in headers (for example, `std::cout` or `std::string`).

Aliases for **namespace** *Names*

`namespace`s can be *aliased*. For example the statement

```
namespace CPPHTP = CPlusPlusHowToProgram;
```

creates the namespace alias `CPPHTP` for `CPlusPlusHowToProgram`.

23.5 Operator Keywords

The C++ standard provides **operator keywords** (Fig. 23.4) that can be used in place of several C++ operators. You can use operator keywords if you have keyboards that do not support certain characters such as !, &, ^, ~, |, etc.

Operator	Operator keyword	Description
Logical operator keywords		
&&	and	logical AND
||	or	logical OR
!	not	logical NOT
Inequality operator keyword		
!=	not_eq	inequality

Fig. 23.4 | Operator keyword alternatives to operator symbols. (Part 1 of 2.)

Operator	Operator keyword	Description
Bitwise operator keywords		
&	`bitand`	bitwise AND
|	`bitor`	bitwise inclusive OR
^	`xor`	bitwise exclusive OR
~	`compl`	bitwise complement
Bitwise assignment operator keywords		
&=	`and_eq`	bitwise AND assignment
|=	`or_eq`	bitwise inclusive OR assignment
^=	`xor_eq`	bitwise exclusive OR assignment

Fig. 23.4 | Operator keyword alternatives to operator symbols. (Part 2 of 2.)

Figure 23.5 demonstrates the operator keywords. Microsoft Visual C++ 2010 requires the header <ciso646> (line 4) to use the operator keywords. In GNU C++ and LLVM, the operator keywords are always defined and this header is not required.

```
 1   // Fig. 23.5: fig23_05.cpp
 2   // Demonstrating operator keywords.
 3   #include <iostream>
 4   #include <ciso646> // enables operator keywords in Microsoft Visual C++
 5   using namespace std;
 6
 7   int main()
 8   {
 9      bool a = true;
10      bool b = false;
11      int c = 2;
12      int d = 3;
13
14      // sticky setting that causes bool values to display as true or false
15      cout << boolalpha;
16
17      cout << "a = " << a << "; b = " << b
18         << "; c = " << c << "; d = " << d;
19
20      cout << "\n\nLogical operator keywords:";
21      cout << "\n   a and a: " << ( a and a );
22      cout << "\n   a and b: " << ( a and b );
23      cout << "\n    a or a: " << ( a or a );
24      cout << "\n    a or b: " << ( a or b );
25      cout << "\n     not a: " << ( not a );
26      cout << "\n     not b: " << ( not b );
27      cout << "\na not_eq b: " << ( a not_eq b );
28
```

Fig. 23.5 | Demonstrating operator keywords. (Part I of 2.)

```
29        cout << "\n\nBitwise operator keywords:";
30        cout << "\nc bitand d: " << ( c bitand d );
31        cout << "\n c bitor d: " << ( c bitor d );
32        cout << "\n   c xor d: " << ( c xor d );
33        cout << "\n    compl c: " << ( compl c );
34        cout << "\nc and_eq d: " << ( c and_eq d );
35        cout << "\n c or_eq d: " << ( c or_eq d );
36        cout << "\nc xor_eq d: " << ( c xor_eq d ) << endl;
37    } // end main
```

```
a = true; b = false; c = 2; d = 3

Logical operator keywords:
   a and a: true
   a and b: false
    a or a: true
    a or b: true
      not a: false
      not b: true
a not_eq b: true

Bitwise operator keywords:
c bitand d: 2
 c bitor d: 3
   c xor d: 1
    compl c: -3
c and_eq d: 2
 c or_eq d: 3
 c xor_eq d: 0
```

Fig. 23.5 | Demonstrating operator keywords. (Part 2 of 2.)

The program declares and initializes two bool variables and two integer variables (lines 9–12). Logical operations (lines 21–27) are performed with bool variables a and b using the various logical operator keywords. Bitwise operations (lines 30–36) are performed with the int variables c and d using the various bitwise operator keywords. The result of each operation is output.

23.6 Pointers to Class Members (.* and ->*)

C++ provides the .* and ->* operators for accessing class members via pointers. This is a rarely used capability, primarily for advanced C++ programmers. We provide only a mechanical example of using pointers to class members here. Figure 23.6 demonstrates the pointer-to-class-member operators.

```
1    // Fig. 23.6: fig23_06.cpp
2    // Demonstrating operators .* and ->*.
3    #include <iostream>
4    using namespace std;
5
```

Fig. 23.6 | Demonstrating operatprs .* and ->*. (Part I of 2.)

```
 6    // class Test definition
 7    class Test
 8    {
 9    public:
10       void func()
11       {
12          cout << "In func\n";
13       } // end function func
14
15       int value; // public data member
16    }; // end class Test
17
18    void arrowStar( Test * ); // prototype
19    void dotStar( Test * ); // prototype
20
21    int main()
22    {
23       Test test;
24       test.value = 8; // assign value 8
25       arrowStar( &test ); // pass address to arrowStar
26       dotStar( &test ); // pass address to dotStar
27    } // end main
28
29    // access member function of Test object using ->*
30    void arrowStar( Test *testPtr )
31    {
32       void ( Test::*memberPtr )() = &Test::func; // declare function pointer
33       ( testPtr->*memberPtr )(); // invoke function indirectly
34    } // end arrowStar
35
36    // access members of Test object data member using .*
37    void dotStar( Test *testPtr2 )
38    {
39       int Test::*vPtr = &Test::value; // declare pointer
40       cout << ( *testPtr2 ).*vPtr << endl; // access value
41    } // end dotStar
```

```
In test function
8
```

Fig. 23.6 | Demonstrating operatprs .* and ->*. (Part 2 of 2.)

The program declares class Test (lines 7–16), which provides public member function test and public data member value. Lines 18–19 provide prototypes for the functions arrowStar (defined in lines 30–34) and dotStar (defined in lines 37–41), which demonstrate the ->* and .* operators, respectively. Line 23 creates object test, and line 24 assigns 8 to its data member value. Lines 25–26 call functions arrowStar and dotStar with the address of the object test.

Line 32 in function arrowStar declares and initializes variable memPtr as a *pointer to a member function*. In this declaration, Test::* indicates that the variable memPtr is a *pointer to a member* of class Test. To declare a *pointer to a function*, enclose the pointer name preceded by * in parentheses, as in (Test::*memPtr). A *pointer to a function* must specify, as part of its type, both the *return type* of the *function it points to* and the *parameter list* of that function. The function's *return type* appears to the left of the left parenthesis and the *parameter list* appears in a separate set of parentheses to the right of the pointer declaration. In this case, the function has a `void` return type and no parameters. The pointer `memPtr` is initialized with the address of class `Test`'s member function named `test`. The header of the function must match the *function pointer's declaration*—i.e., function `test` must have a `void` return type and no parameters. Notice that the right side of the assignment uses the *address operator (&)* to get the address of the member function `test`. Also, notice that *neither the left side nor the right side of the assignment in line 32 refers to a specific object of class* `Test`. Only the class name is used with the scope resolution operator (`::`). Line 33 invokes the member function stored in `memPtr` (i.e., `test`), using the `->*` operator. Because `memPtr` is a pointer to a member of a class, the `->*` operator must be used rather than the `->` operator to invoke the function.

Line 39 declares and initializes `vPtr` as a pointer to an `int` data member of class `Test`. The right side of the assignment specifies the address of the data member `value`. Line 40 dereferences the pointer `testPtr2`, then uses the `.*` operator to access the member to which `vPtr` points. *The client code can create pointers to class members for only those class members that are accessible to the client code.* In this example, both member function `test` and data member `value` are publicly accessible.

Common Programming Error 23.2

Declaring a member-function pointer without enclosing the pointer name in parentheses is a syntax error.

Common Programming Error 23.3

Declaring a member-function pointer without preceding the pointer name with a class name followed by the scope resolution operator (::) is a syntax error.

Common Programming Error 23.4

*Attempting to use the -> or * operator with a pointer to a class member generates syntax errors.*

23.7 Multiple Inheritance

In Chapters 11 and 12, we discussed *single inheritance, in which each class is derived from exactly one base class.* In C++, a class may be derived from *more than one* base class—a technique known as multiple inheritance in which a derived class inherits the members of two or more base classes. This powerful capability encourages interesting forms of software reuse but can cause a variety of ambiguity problems. *Multiple inheritance is a difficult concept that should be used only by experienced programmers.* In fact, some of the problems associated with multiple inheritance are so subtle that newer programming languages, such as Java and C#, do not enable a class to derive from more than one base class.

Software Engineering Observation 23.3

Great care is required in the design of a system to use multiple inheritance properly; it should not be used when single inheritance and/or composition will do the job.

A common problem with multiple inheritance is that each of the base classes might contain data members or member functions that have the *same name*. This can lead to ambiguity problems when you attempt to compile. Consider the multiple-inheritance example (Figs. 23.7–23.11). Class `Base1` (Fig. 23.7) contains one `protected int` data member—value (line 20), a constructor (lines 10–13) that sets value and `public` member function `getData` (lines 15–18) that returns `value`.

```cpp
1   // Fig. 23.7: Base1.h
2   // Definition of class Base1
3   #ifndef BASE1_H
4   #define BASE1_H
5
6   // class Base1 definition
7   class Base1
8   {
9   public:
10     Base1( int parameterValue )
11        : value( parameterValue )
12     {
13     } // end Base1 constructor
14
15     int getData() const
16     {
17        return value;
18     } // end function getData
19  protected: // accessible to derived classes
20     int value; // inherited by derived class
21  }; // end class Base1
22
23  #endif // BASE1_H
```

Fig. 23.7 | Demonstrating multiple inheritance—`Base1.h`.

Class `Base2` (Fig. 23.8) is similar to class `Base1`, except that its `protected` data is a char named `letter` (line 20). Like class `Base1`, `Base2` has a `public` member function `get-Data`, but this function returns the value of char data member `letter`.

```cpp
1   // Fig. 23.8: Base2.h
2   // Definition of class Base2
3   #ifndef BASE2_H
4   #define BASE2_H
5
6   // class Base2 definition
7   class Base2
8   {
9   public:
10     Base2( char characterData )
11        : letter( characterData )
12     {
13     } // end Base2 constructor
```

Fig. 23.8 | Demonstrating multiple inheritance—`Base2.h`. (Part I of 2.)

```
14
15     char getData() const
16     {
17        return letter;
18     } // end function getData
19  protected: // accessible to derived classes
20     char letter; // inherited by derived class
21  }; // end class Base2
22
23  #endif // BASE2_H
```

Fig. 23.8 | Demonstrating multiple inheritance—`Base2.h`. (Part 2 of 2.)

Class `Derived` (Figs. 23.9–23.10) inherits from both class `Base1` and class `Base2` through *multiple inheritance*. Class `Derived` has a `private` data member of type `double` named `real` (Fig. 23.9, line 20), a constructor to initialize all the data of class `Derived` and a `public` member function `getReal` that returns the value of `double` variable `real`.

```
1   // Fig. 23.9: Derived.h
2   // Definition of class Derived which inherits
3   // multiple base classes (Base1 and Base2).
4   #ifndef DERIVED_H
5   #define DERIVED_H
6
7   #include <iostream>
8   #include "Base1.h"
9   #include "Base2.h"
10  using namespace std;
11
12  // class Derived definition
13  class Derived : public Base1, public Base2
14  {
15     friend ostream &operator<<( ostream &, const Derived & );
16  public:
17     Derived( int, char, double );
18     double getReal() const;
19  private:
20     double real; // derived class's private data
21  }; // end class Derived
22
23  #endif // DERIVED_H
```

Fig. 23.9 | Demonstrating multiple inheritance—`Derived.h`.

```
1   // Fig. 23.10: Derived.cpp
2   // Member-function definitions for class Derived
3   #include "Derived.h"
4
5   // constructor for Derived calls constructors for
6   // class Base1 and class Base2.
```

Fig. 23.10 | Demonstrating multiple inheritance—`Derived.cpp`. (Part 1 of 2.)

```
7   // use member initializers to call base-class constructors
8   Derived::Derived( int integer, char character, double double1 )
9      : Base1( integer ), Base2( character ), real( double1 ) { }
10
11  // return real
12  double Derived::getReal() const
13  {
14     return real;
15  } // end function getReal
16
17  // display all data members of Derived
18  ostream &operator<<( ostream &output, const Derived &derived )
19  {
20     output << "   Integer: " << derived.value << "\n  Character: "
21        << derived.letter << "\nReal number: " << derived.real;
22     return output; // enables cascaded calls
23  } // end operator<<
```

Fig. 23.10 | Demonstrating multiple inheritance—Derived.cpp. (Part 2 of 2.)

To indicate *multiple inheritance* (in Fig. 23.9) we follow the colon (:) after class Derived with a comma-separated list of base classes (line 13). In Fig. 23.10, notice that constructor Derived explicitly calls base-class constructors for each of its base classes—Base1 and Base2—using the member-initializer syntax (line 9). The *base-class constructors are called in the order that the inheritance is specified, not in the order in which their constructors are mentioned. Also, if the base-class constructors are not explicitly called in the member-initializer list, their default constructors will be called implicitly.*

The overloaded stream insertion operator (Fig. 23.10, lines 18–23) uses its second parameter—a reference to a Derived object—to display a Derived object's data. This operator function is a friend of Derived, so operator<< can directly access *all* of class Derived's protected and private members, including the protected data member value (inherited from class Base1), protected data member letter (inherited from class Base2) and private data member real (declared in class Derived).

Now let's examine the main function (Fig. 23.11) that tests the classes in Figs. 23.7–23.10. Line 11 creates Base1 object base1 and initializes it to the int value 10. Line 12 creates Base2 object base2 and initializes it to the char value 'Z'. Line 13 creates Derived object derived and initializes it to contain the int value 7, the char value 'A' and the double value 3.5.

```
1   // Fig. 23.11: fig23_11.cpp
2   // Driver for multiple-inheritance example.
3   #include <iostream>
4   #include "Base1.h"
5   #include "Base2.h"
6   #include "Derived.h"
7   using namespace std;
```

Fig. 23.11 | Demonstrating multiple inheritance. (Part 1 of 2.)

```
8
9    int main()
10   {
11       Base1 base1( 10 ); // create Base1 object
12       Base2 base2( 'Z' ); // create Base2 object
13       Derived derived( 7, 'A', 3.5 ); // create Derived object
14
15       // print data members of base-class objects
16       cout << "Object base1 contains integer " << base1.getData()
17           << "\nObject base2 contains character " << base2.getData()
18           << "\nObject derived contains:\n" << derived << "\n\n";
19
20       // print data members of derived-class object
21       // scope resolution operator resolves getData ambiguity
22       cout << "Data members of Derived can be accessed individually:"
23           << "\n   Integer: " << derived.Base1::getData()
24           << "\n  Character: " << derived.Base2::getData()
25           << "\nReal number: " << derived.getReal() << "\n\n";
26       cout << "Derived can be treated as an object of either base class:\n";
27
28       // treat Derived as a Base1 object
29       Base1 *base1Ptr = &derived;
30       cout << "base1Ptr->getData() yields " << base1Ptr->getData() << '\n';
31
32       // treat Derived as a Base2 object
33       Base2 *base2Ptr = &derived;
34       cout << "base2Ptr->getData() yields " << base2Ptr->getData() << endl;
35   } // end main
```

```
Object base1 contains integer 10
Object base2 contains character Z
Object derived contains:
    Integer: 7
  Character: A
Real number: 3.5

Data members of Derived can be accessed individually:
    Integer: 7
  Character: A
Real number: 3.5

Derived can be treated as an object of either base class:
base1Ptr->getData() yields 7
base2Ptr->getData() yields A
```

Fig. 23.11 | Demonstrating multiple inheritance. (Part 2 of 2.)

Lines 16–18 display each object's data values. For objects base1 and base2, we invoke each object's getData member function. Even though there are *two* getData functions in this example, the calls are *not ambiguous*. In line 16, the compiler knows that base1 is an object of class Base1, so class Base1's getData is called. In line 17, the compiler knows that base2 is an object of class Base2, so class Base2's getData is called. Line 18 displays the contents of object derived using the overloaded stream insertion operator.

Resolving Ambiguity Issues That Arise When a Derived Class Inherits Member Functions of the Same Name from Multiple Base Classes

Lines 22–25 output the contents of object derived again by using the *get* member functions of class Derived. However, there is an *ambiguity* problem, because this object contains two getData functions, one inherited from class Base1 and one inherited from class Base2. This problem is easy to solve by using the scope resolution operator. The expression derived.Base1::getData() gets the value of the variable inherited from class Base1 (i.e., the int variable named value) and derived.Base2::getData() gets the value of the variable inherited from class Base2 (i.e., the char variable named letter). The double value in real is printed *without ambiguity* with the call derived.getReal()—there are no other member functions with that name in the hierarchy.

Demonstrating the Is-A *Relationships in Multiple Inheritance*

The *is-a* relationships of *single inheritance* also apply in *multiple-inheritance* relationships. To demonstrate this, line 29 assigns the address of object derived to the Base1 pointer base1Ptr. This is allowed because an object of class Derived *is an* object of class Base1. Line 30 invokes Base1 member function getData via base1Ptr to obtain the value of only the Base1 part of the object derived. Line 33 assigns the address of object derived to the Base2 pointer base2Ptr. This is allowed because an object of class Derived *is an* object of class Base2. Line 34 invokes Base2 member function getData via base2Ptr to obtain the value of only the Base2 part of the object derived.

23.8 Multiple Inheritance and virtual Base Classes

In Section 23.7, we discussed *multiple inheritance*, the process by which one class inherits from *two or more* classes. Multiple inheritance is used, for example, in the C++ standard library to form class basic_iostream (Fig. 23.12).

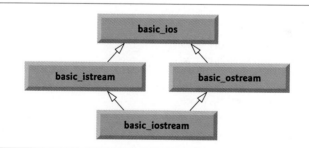

Fig. 23.12 | Multiple inheritance to form class basic_iostream.

Class basic_ios is the base class for both basic_istream and basic_ostream, each of which is formed with *single inheritance*. Class basic_iostream inherits from both basic_istream and basic_ostream. This enables class basic_iostream objects to provide the functionality of basic_istreams and basic_ostreams. In multiple-inheritance hierarchies, the inheritance described in Fig. 23.12 is referred to as **diamond inheritance**

Because classes basic_istream and basic_ostream each inherit from basic_ios, a potential problem exists for basic_iostream. Class basic_iostream could contain *two* copies of the members of class basic_ios—one inherited via class basic_istream and one inherited via class basic_ostream). Such a situation would be *ambiguous* and would result in a compilation error, because the compiler would not know which version of the members from class basic_ios to use. In this section, you'll see how using virtual base classes solves the problem of inheriting duplicate copies of an indirect base class.

Compilation Errors Produced When Ambiguity Arises in Diamond Inheritance
Figure 23.13 demonstrates the *ambiguity* that can occur in *diamond inheritance*. Class Base (lines 8–12) contains pure virtual function print (line 11). Classes DerivedOne (lines 15–23) and DerivedTwo (lines 26–34) each publicly inherit from Base and override function print. Class DerivedOne and class DerivedTwo each contain a base-class subobject—i.e., the members of class Base in this example.

```
 1   // Fig. 23.13: fig23_13.cpp
 2   // Attempting to polymorphically call a function that is
 3   // multiply inherited from two base classes.
 4   #include <iostream>
 5   using namespace std;
 6
 7   // class Base definition
 8   class Base
 9   {
10   public:
11      virtual void print() const = 0; // pure virtual
12   }; // end class Base
13
14   // class DerivedOne definition
15   class DerivedOne : public Base
16   {
17   public:
18      // override print function
19      void print() const
20      {
21         cout << "DerivedOne\n";
22      } // end function print
23   }; // end class DerivedOne
24
25   // class DerivedTwo definition
26   class DerivedTwo : public Base
27   {
28   public:
29      // override print function
30      void print() const
31      {
32         cout << "DerivedTwo\n";
33      } // end function print
34   }; // end class DerivedTwo
35
36   // class Multiple definition
37   class Multiple : public DerivedOne, public DerivedTwo
38   {
```

Fig. 23.13 | Attempting to call a multiply inherited function polymorphically. (Part 1 of 2.)

```
39   public:
40       // qualify which version of function print
41       void print() const
42       {
43          DerivedTwo::print();
44       } // end function print
45   }; // end class Multiple
46
47   int main()
48   {
49       Multiple both; // instantiate Multiple object
50       DerivedOne one; // instantiate DerivedOne object
51       DerivedTwo two; // instantiate DerivedTwo object
52       Base *array[ 3 ]; // create array of base-class pointers
53
54       array[ 0 ] = &both; // ERROR--ambiguous
55       array[ 1 ] = &one;
56       array[ 2 ] = &two;
57
58       // polymorphically invoke print
59       for ( int i = 0; i < 3; ++i )
60          array[ i ] -> print();
61   } // end main
```

Microsoft Visual C++ compiler error message:

```
c:\cpphtp9_examples\ch23\fig23_13\fig23_13.cpp(54) : error C2594: '=' :
   ambiguous conversions from 'Multiple *' to 'Base *'
```

Fig. 23.13 | Attempting to call a multiply inherited function polymorphically. (Part 2 of 2.)

Class `Multiple` (lines 37–45) inherits from *both* class `DerivedOne` and class `DerivedTwo`. In class `Multiple`, function `print` is overridden to call `DerivedTwo`'s `print` (line 43). Notice that we must *qualify* the `print` call with the class name `DerivedTwo` to specify which version of `print` to call.

Function `main` (lines 47–61) declares objects of classes `Multiple` (line 49), `DerivedOne` (line 50) and `DerivedTwo` (line 51). Line 52 declares an array of `Base *` pointers. Each array element is initialized with the address of an object (lines 54–56). An error occurs when the address of `both`—an object of class `Multiple`—is assigned to `array[ 0 ]`. The object `both` actually contains two subobjects of type `Base`, so the compiler does not know which subobject the pointer `array[ 0 ]` should point to, and it generates a compilation error indicating an *ambiguous conversion*.

Eliminating Duplicate Subobjects with `virtual` Base-Class Inheritance
The problem of *duplicate subobjects* is resolved with `virtual` inheritance. When a base class is inherited as `virtual`, only *one* subobject will appear in the derived class—a process called **virtual base-class inheritance**. Figure 23.14 revises the program of Fig. 23.13 to use a `virtual` base class.

```cpp
 1   // Fig. 23.14: fig23_14.cpp
 2   // Using virtual base classes.
 3   #include <iostream>
 4   using namespace std;
 5
 6   // class Base definition
 7   class Base
 8   {
 9   public:
10      virtual void print() const = 0; // pure virtual
11   }; // end class Base
12
13   // class DerivedOne definition
14   class DerivedOne : virtual public Base
15   {
16   public:
17      // override print function
18      void print() const
19      {
20         cout << "DerivedOne\n";
21      } // end function print
22   }; // end DerivedOne class
23
24   // class DerivedTwo definition
25   class DerivedTwo : virtual public Base
26   {
27   public:
28      // override print function
29      void print() const
30      {
31         cout << "DerivedTwo\n";
32      } // end function print
33   }; // end DerivedTwo class
34
35   // class Multiple definition
36   class Multiple : public DerivedOne, public DerivedTwo
37   {
38   public:
39      // qualify which version of function print
40      void print() const
41      {
42         DerivedTwo::print();
43      } // end function print
44   }; // end Multiple class
45
46   int main()
47   {
48      Multiple both; // instantiate Multiple object
49      DerivedOne one; // instantiate DerivedOne object
50      DerivedTwo two; // instantiate DerivedTwo object
51
52      // declare array of base-class pointers and initialize
53      // each element to a derived-class type
```

Fig. 23.14 | Using virtual base classes. (Part 1 of 2.)

```
54        Base *array[ 3 ];
55        array[ 0 ] = &both;
56        array[ 1 ] = &one;
57        array[ 2 ] = &two;
58
59        // polymorphically invoke function print
60        for ( int i = 0; i < 3; ++i )
61            array[ i ]->print();
62    } // end main
```

```
DerivedTwo
DerivedOne
DerivedTwo
```

Fig. 23.14 | Using `virtual` base classes. (Part 2 of 2.)

The key change is that classes `DerivedOne` (line 14) and `DerivedTwo` (line 25) each inherit from `Base` by specifying `virtual public Base`. Since both classes inherit from `Base`, they each contain a *Base subobject*. The benefit of *virtual inheritance* is not clear until class `Multiple` inherits from `DerivedOne` and `DerivedTwo` (line 36). Since each of the base classes used *virtual inheritance* to inherit class `Base`'s members, the compiler ensures that only *one* `Base` subobject is inherited into class `Multiple`. This eliminates the ambiguity error generated by the compiler in Fig. 23.13. The compiler now allows the implicit conversion of the derived-class pointer (`&both`) to the base-class pointer `array[ 0 ]` in line 55 in `main`. The `for` statement in lines 60–61 polymorphically calls `print` for each object.

Constructors in Multiple-Inheritance Hierarchies with `virtual` Base Classes
Implementing hierarchies with `virtual` base classes is simpler if *default constructors* are used for the base classes. Figures 23.13 and 23.14 use compiler-generated *default constructors*. If a `virtual` base class provides a constructor that requires arguments, the derived-class implementations become more complicated, because the most derived class must explicitly invoke the `virtual` base class's constructor.

Software Engineering Observation 23.4
Providing a default constructor for `virtual` base classes simplifies hierarchy design.

23.9 Wrap-Up

In this chapter, you learned how to use the `const_cast` operator to remove the `const` qualification of a variable. We showed how to use `namespaces` to ensure that every identifier in a program has a unique name and explained how `namespaces` can help resolve naming conflicts. You saw several operator keywords to use if your keyboards do not support certain characters used in operator symbols, such as !, &, ^, ~ and |. We showed how the `mutable` storage-class specifier enables you to indicate that a data member should always be modifiable, even when it appears in an object that's currently being treated as a `const`. We also showed the mechanics of using pointers to class members and the `->*` and `.*` operators. Finally, we introduced multiple inheritance and discussed problems associated with allowing a derived class to inherit the members of several base classes. As part of this discussion, we demonstrated how virtual inheritance can be used to solve those problems.

Summary

Section 23.2 const_cast *Operator*
- C++ provides the const_cast operator () for casting away const or volatile qualification.
- A program declares a variable with the volatile qualifier (p. 973) when that program expects the variable to be modified by other programs. Declaring a variable volatile indicates that the compiler should not optimize the use of that variable because doing so could affect the ability of those other programs to access and modify the volatile variable.
- In general, it is dangerous to use the const_cast operator, because it allows a program to modify a variable that was declared const, and thus was not supposed to be modifiable.
- There are cases in which it is desirable, or even necessary, to cast away const-ness. For example, older C and C++ libraries might provide functions with non-const parameters and that do not modify their parameters. If you wish to pass const data to such a function, you'd need to cast away the data's const-ness; otherwise, the compiler would report error messages.
- If you pass non-const data to a function that treats the data as if it were constant, then returns that data as a constant, you might need to cast away the const-ness of the returned data to access and modify that data.

Section 23.3 mutable *Class Members*
- If a data member should always be modifiable, C++ provides the storage-class specifier mutable as an alternative to const_cast. A mutable data member (p. 975) is always modifiable, even in a const member function or const object. This reduces the need to cast away "const-ness."
- mutable and const_cast are used in different contexts. For a const object with no mutable data members, operator const_cast must be used every time a member is to be modified. This greatly reduces the chance of a member being accidentally modified because the member is not permanently modifiable.
- Operations involving const_cast are typically hidden in a member function's implementation. The user of a class might not be aware that a member is being modified.

Section 23.4 namespaces
- A program includes many identifiers defined in different scopes. Sometimes a variable of one scope will "overlap" with a variable of the same name in a different scope, possibly creating a naming conflict. The C++ standard solves this problem with namespaces (p. 977).
- Each namespace defines a scope in which identifiers are placed. To use a namespace member (p. 977), either the member's name must be qualified with the namespace name and the scope resolution operator (::) or a using directive or declaration must appear before the name is used in the program.
- Typically, using statements are placed at the beginning of the file in which members of the namespace are used.
- Not all namespaces are guaranteed to be unique. Two third-party vendors might inadvertently use the same identifiers for their namespace names.
- A namespace can contain constants, data, classes, nested namespaces (p. 979), functions, etc. Definitions of namespaces must occupy the global scope or be nested within other namespaces.

- An unnamed namespace (p. 979) has an implicit using directive, so its members appear to occupy the global namespace, are accessible directly and do not have to be qualified with a namespace name. Global variables are also part of the global namespace.

- When accessing members of a nested namespace, the members must be qualified with the namespace name (unless the member is being used inside the nested namespace).

- Namespaces can be aliased (p. 980).

Section 23.5 Operator Keywords

- The C++ standard provides operator keywords (p. 980) that can be used in place of several C++ operators. Operator keywords are useful for programmers who have keyboards that do not support certain characters such as !, &, ^, ~, |, etc.

Section 23.6 Pointers to Class Members (.* and ->*)

- C++ provides the .* and ->* operators (p. 982) for accessing class members via pointers. This is a rarely used capability that's used primarily by advanced C++ programmers.

- Declaring a pointer to a function requires that you enclose the pointer name preceded by an * in parentheses. A pointer to a function must specify, as part of its type, both the return type of the function it points to and the parameter list of that function.

Section 23.7 Multiple Inheritance

- In C++, a class may be derived from more than one base class—a technique known as multiple inheritance (p. 984), in which a derived class inherits the members of two or more base classes.

- A common problem with multiple inheritance is that each of the base classes might contain data members or member functions that have the same name. This can lead to ambiguity problems when you attempt to compile.

- The *is-a* relationships of single inheritance also apply in multiple-inheritance relationships.

- Multiple inheritance is used in the C++ Standard Library to form class basic_iostream. Class basic_ios is the base class for both basic_istream and basic_ostream. Class basic_iostream inherits from both basic_istream and basic_ostream. In multiple-inheritance hierarchies, the situation described here is referred to as diamond inheritance.

Section 23.8 Multiple Inheritance and virtual Base Classes

- The ambiguity in diamond inheritance (p. 989) occurs when a derived-class object inherits two or more base-class subobjects (p. 990). The problem of duplicate subobjects is resolved with virtual inheritance. When a base class is inherited as virtual, only one subobject will appear in the derived class—a process called virtual base-class inheritance (p. 991).

- Implementing hierarchies with virtual base classes is simpler if default constructors are used for the base classes. If a virtual base class provides a constructor that requires arguments, the implementation of the derived classes becomes more complicated, because the most derived class (p. 993) must explicitly invoke the virtual base class's constructor to initialize the members inherited from the virtual base class.

Self-Review Exercises

23.1   Fill in the blanks for each of the following:

a) C++ provides the _____ operator () for casting away const or volatile qualifications.

b) If a _____ base class provides a constructor that requires arguments, the implementation of the derived classes becomes more complicated.

c) Typically, _____ statements are placed at the beginning of the file in which members of the _____ are used.

    d) In multiple-inheritance hierarchies, the situation described here is referred to as _____ inheritance.

    e) Definitions of namespaces must occupy the _____ scope or be nested within other namespaces.

    f) C++ provides the _____ and _____ operators for accessing class members via pointers.

23.2 State which of the following are *true* and which are *false*. If a statement is *false*, explain why.

    a) The *has-a* relationships of single inheritance also apply in multiple-inheritance relationships.

    b) A program declares a variable with the `volatile` qualifier when that program expects the variable to be modified by other programs.

    c) Two third-party vendors might inadvertently use the same identifiers for their namespace names.

    d) Each namespace defines a scope in which identifiers are placed.

    e) All namespaces are guaranteed to be unique.

Answers to Self-Review Exercises

23.1 a) const_cast. b) `virtual`. c) `using`, `namespace`. d) diamond. e) global. f) .*, ->*

23.2 a) False. The *is-a* relationships of single inheritance also apply in multiple-inheritance relationships. b) True. c) True. d) True. e) False. Not all `namespaces` are guaranteed to be unique.

Exercises

23.3 *(Fill in the Blanks)* Fill in the blanks for each of the following:

    a) Keyword _____ specifies that a `namespace` or `namespace` member is being used.

    b) Operator _____ is the operator keyword for logical OR.

    c) Storage specifier _____ allows a member of a `const` object to be modified.

    d) The _____ qualifier specifies that an object can be modified by other programs.

    e) Precede a member with its _____ name and the scope resolution operator if the possibility exists of a scoping conflict.

    f) The body of a namespace is delimited by _____.

    g) For a `const` object with no _____ data members, operator _____ must be used every time a member is to be modified.

23.4 *(Currency namespace)* Write a namespace, `Currency`, that defines constant members ONE, TWO, FIVE, TEN, TWENTY, FIFTY and HUNDRED. Write two short programs that use `Currency`. One program should make all constants available and the other should make only FIVE available.

23.5 *(Namespaces)* Given the namespaces in Fig. 23.15, determine whether each statement is *true* or *false*. Explain any *false* answers.

    a) Variable `kilometers` is visible within namespace Data.

    b) Object `string1` is visible within namespace Data.

    c) Constant POLAND is not visible within namespace Data.

    d) Constant GERMANY is visible within namespace Data.

    e) Function `function` is visible to namespace Data.

    f) Namespace Data is visible to namespace CountryInformation.

    g) Object `map` is visible to namespace CountryInformation.

    h) Object `string1` is visible within namespace RegionalInformation.

```
 I    namespace CountryInformation
 2    {
 3       using namespace std;
 4       enum Countries { POLAND, SWITZERLAND, GERMANY,
 5                        AUSTRIA, CZECH_REPUBLIC };
 6       int kilometers;
 7       string string1;
 8
 9       namespace RegionalInformation
10       {
11          short getPopulation(); // assume definition exists
12          MapData map; // assume definition exists
13       } // end RegionalInformation
14    } // end CountryInformation
15
16    namespace Data
17    {
18       using namespace CountryInformation::RegionalInformation;
19       void *function( void *, int );
20    } // end Data
```

Fig. 23.15 | namespaces for Exercise 23.5.

23.6 *(mutable vs. const_cast)* Compare and contrast mutable and const_cast. Give at least one example of when one might be preferred over the other. [*Note:* This exercise does not require any code to be written.]

23.7 *(Modifying a const Variable)* Write a program that uses const_cast to modify a const variable. [*Hint:* Use a pointer in your solution to point to the const identifier.]

23.8 *(namespace member)* How would you use a namespace member?

23.9 *(virtual Base Classes)* Write a program that uses virtual base classes. The class at the top of the hierarchy should provide a constructor that takes at least one argument (i.e., do not provide a default constructor). What challenges does this present for the inheritance hierarchy?

23.10 *(Find the Code Errors)* Find the error(s) in each of the following. When possible, explain how to correct each error.
a) namespace Name {
        int x;
        int y;
        mutable int z;
    };
b) int integer = const_cast< int >(double);
c) namespace PCM(111, "hello"); // construct namespace

Chapters on the Web

The following chapters are available as PDF documents from this book's Companion Website, which is accessible from www.pearsoninternationaleditions.com/deitel:

- Chapter 24, C++11: Additional Features
- Chapter 25, ATM Case Study, Part 1: Object-Oriented Design with the UML
- Chapter 26, ATM Case Study, Part 2: Implementing an Object-Oriented Design

These files can be viewed in Adobe® Reader® (get.adobe.com/reader).

New copies of this book come with a Companion Website access code that is located on the inside of the front cover. If the access code is already visible, you purchased a used book. If there is no access code inside the front cover, you purchased an edition that does not come with an access code. In either case, you can purchase access directly from the Companion Website.

A

Operator Precedence and Associativity

Operators are shown in decreasing order of precedence from top to bottom (Fig. A.1).

Operator	Type	Associativity
`::`	binary scope resolution	left to right
`::`	unary scope resolution	
`()`	grouping parentheses *[See caution in Fig. 2.10 regarding grouping parentheses.]*	
`()`	function call	left to right
`[]`	array subscript	
`.`	member selection via object	
`->`	member selection via pointer	
`++`	unary postfix increment	
`--`	unary postfix decrement	
`typeid`	runtime type information	
`dynamic_cast < type >`	runtime type-checked cast	
`static_cast< type >`	compile-time type-checked cast	
`reinterpret_cast< type >`	cast for nonstandard conversions	
`const_cast< type >`	cast away const-ness	
`++`	unary prefix increment	right to left
`--`	unary prefix decrement	
`+`	unary plus	
`-`	unary minus	
`!`	unary logical negation	
`~`	unary bitwise complement	
`sizeof`	determine size in bytes	
`&`	address	
`*`	dereference	
`new`	dynamic memory allocation	
`new[]`	dynamic array allocation	
`delete`	dynamic memory deallocation	
`delete[]`	dynamic array deallocation	
`( type )`	C-style unary cast	right to left

Fig. A.1 | Operator precedence and associativity chart. (Part 1 of 2.)

Operator	Type	Associativity
.* ->*	pointer to member via object pointer to member via pointer	left to right
* / %	multiplication division modulus	left to right
+ -	addition subtraction	left to right
<< >>	bitwise left shift bitwise right shift	left to right
< <= > >=	relational less than relational less than opr equal to relational greater than relational greater than or equal to	left to right
== !=	relational is equal to relational is not equal to	left to right
&	bitwise AND	left to right
^	bitwise exclusive OR	left to right
|	bitwise inclusive OR	left to right
&&	logical AND	left to right
||	logical OR	left to right
?:	ternary conditional	right to left
= += -= *= /= %= &= ^= |= <<= >>=	assignment addition assignment subtraction assignment multiplication assignment division assignment modulus assignment bitwise AND assignment bitwise exclusive OR assignment bitwise inclusive OR assignment bitwise left-shift assignment bitwise right-shift assignment	right to left
,	comma	left to right

Fig. A.1 | Operator precedence and associativity chart. (Part 2 of 2.)

ASCII Character Set

ASCII Character Set

	0	1	2	3	4	5	6	7	8	9
0	nul	soh	stx	etx	eot	enq	ack	bel	bs	ht
1	nl	vt	ff	cr	so	si	dle	dc1	dc2	dc3
2	dc4	nak	syn	etb	can	em	sub	esc	fs	gs
3	rs	us	sp	!	"	#	$	%	&	'
4	(	)	*	+	,	-	.	/	0	1
5	2	3	4	5	6	7	8	9	:	;
6	<	=	>	?	@	A	B	C	D	E
7	F	G	H	I	J	K	L	M	N	O
8	P	Q	R	S	T	U	V	W	X	Y
9	Z	[	\	]	^	_	'	a	b	c
10	d	e	f	g	h	i	j	k	l	m
11	n	o	p	q	r	s	t	u	v	w
12	x	y	z	{	|	}	~	del		

Fig. B.1 | ASCII character set.

The digits at the left of the table are the left digits of the decimal equivalents (0–127) of the character codes, and the digits at the top of the table are the right digits of the character codes. For example, the character code for "F" is 70, and the character code for "&" is 38.

C

Fundamental Types

Figure C.1 lists C++'s fundamental types. The C++ Standard Document does not provide the exact number of bytes required to store variables of these types in memory. However, the C++ Standard Document does indicate how the memory requirements for fundamental types relate to one another. By order of increasing memory requirements, the signed integer types are `signed char`, `short int`, `int`, `long int` and `long long int`. This means that a `short int` must provide at least as much storage as a `signed char`; an `int` must provide at least as much storage as a `short int`; a `long int` must provide at least as much storage as an `int`; and a `long long int` must provide at least as much storage as a `long int`. Each signed integer type has a corresponding unsigned integer type that has the same memory requirements. Unsigned types cannot represent negative values, but can represent approximately twice as many positive values as their associated signed types. By order of increasing memory requirements, the floating-point types are `float`, `double` and `long double`. Like integer types, a `double` must provide at least as much storage as a `float` and a `long double` must provide at least as much storage as a `double`.

Integral types	Floating-point types
bool	float
char	double
signed char	long double
unsigned char	
short int	
unsigned short int	
int	
unsigned int	
long int	
unsigned long int	
long long int	
unsigned long long int	
char16_t	
char32_t	
wchar_t	

Fig. C.1 | C++ fundamental types.

The exact sizes and ranges of values for the fundamental types are implementation dependent. The header files <climits> (for the integral types) and <cfloat> (for the floating-point types) specify the ranges of values supported on your system.

The range of values a type supports depends on the number of bytes that are used to represent that type. For example, consider a system with 4 byte (32 bit) ints. For the signed int type, the nonnegative values are in the range 0 to 2,147,483,647 ($2^{31} - 1$). The negative values are in the range -1 to $-2,147,483,647$ ($-2^{31} - 1$). This is a total of 2^{32} possible values. An unsigned int on the same system would use the same number of bits to represent data, but would not represent any negative values. This results in values in the range 0 to 4,294,967,295 ($2^{32} - 1$). On the same system, a short int could not use more than 32 bits to represent its data and a long int must use at least 32 bits.

C++ provides the data type bool for variables that can hold only the values true and false. C++11 introduced the types long long int and unsigned long long int—typically for 64-bit integer values (though this is not required by the standard). C++11 also introduced the new character types char16_t and char32_t for representing Unicode characters.

D

Number Systems

Here are only numbers ratified.
—William Shakespeare

Objectives

In this appendix you'll learn:

- To understand basic number systems concepts, such as base, positional value and symbol value.

- To understand how to work with numbers in the binary, octal and hexadecimal number systems.

- To abbreviate binary numbers as octal numbers or hexadecimal numbers.

- To convert octal numbers and hexadecimal numbers to binary numbers.

- To convert back and forth between decimal numbers and their binary, octal and hexadecimal equivalents.

- To understand binary arithmetic and how negative binary numbers are represented using two's complement notation.

D.1 Introduction

In this appendix, we introduce the key number systems that C++ programmers use, especially when they are working on software projects that require close interaction with machine-level hardware. Projects like this include operating systems, computer networking software, compilers, database systems and applications requiring high performance.

When we write an integer such as 227 or –63 in a C++ program, the number is assumed to be in the **decimal (base 10) number system**. The **digits** in the decimal number system are 0, 1, 2, 3, 4, 5, 6, 7, 8 and 9. The lowest digit is 0 and the highest is 9—one less than the base of 10. Internally, computers use the **binary (base 2) number system**. The binary number system has only two digits, namely 0 and 1. Its lowest digit is 0 and its highest is 1—one less than the base of 2.

As we'll see, binary numbers tend to be much longer than their decimal equivalents. Programmers who work in assembly languages, and in high-level languages like C++ that enable them to reach down to the machine level, find it cumbersome to work with binary numbers. So two other number systems—the **octal number system (base 8)** and the **hexadecimal number system (base 16)**—are popular, primarily because they make it convenient to abbreviate binary numbers.

In the octal number system, the digits range from 0 to 7. Because both the binary and the octal number systems have fewer digits than the decimal number system, their digits are the same as the corresponding digits in decimal.

The hexadecimal number system poses a problem because it requires 16 digits—a lowest digit of 0 and a highest digit with a value equivalent to decimal 15 (one less than the base of 16). By convention, we use the letters A through F to represent the hexadecimal digits corresponding to decimal values 10 through 15. Thus in hexadecimal we can have numbers like 876 consisting solely of decimal-like digits, numbers like 8A55F consisting of digits and letters and numbers like FFE consisting solely of letters. Occasionally, a hexadecimal number spells a common word such as FACE or FEED—this can appear strange to programmers accustomed to working with numbers. The digits of the binary, octal, decimal and hexadecimal number systems are summarized in Figs. D.1–D.2.

Each of these number systems uses **positional notation**—each position in which a digit is written has a different **positional value**. For example, in the decimal number 937 (the 9, the 3 and the 7 are referred to as **symbol values**), we say that the 7 is written in the ones position, the 3 is written in the tens position and the 9 is written in the hundreds position. Note that each of these positions is a power of the base (base 10) and that these powers begin at 0 and increase by 1 as we move left in the number (Fig. D.3).

Binary digit	Octal digit	Decimal digit	Hexadecimal digit
0	0	0	0
1	1	1	1
	2	2	2
	3	3	3
	4	4	4
	5	5	5
	6	6	6
	7	7	7
		8	8
		9	9
			A (decimal value of 10)
			B (decimal value of 11)
			C (decimal value of 12)
			D (decimal value of 13)
			E (decimal value of 14)
			F (decimal value of 15)

Fig. D.1 | Digits of the binary, octal, decimal and hexadecimal number systems.

Attribute	Binary	Octal	Decimal	Hexadecimal
Base	2	8	10	16
Lowest digit	0	0	0	0
Highest digit	1	7	9	F

Fig. D.2 | Comparing the binary, octal, decimal and hexadecimal number systems.

Positional values in the decimal number system			
Decimal digit	9	3	7
Position name	Hundreds	Tens	Ones
Positional value	100	10	1
Positional value as a power of the base (10)	10^2	10^1	10^0

Fig. D.3 | Positional values in the decimal number system.

For longer decimal numbers, the next positions to the left would be the thousands position (10 to the 3rd power), the ten-thousands position (10 to the 4th power), the hundred-thousands position (10 to the 5th power), the millions position (10 to the 6th power), the ten-millions position (10 to the 7th power) and so on.

In the binary number 101, the rightmost 1 is written in the ones position, the 0 is written in the twos position and the leftmost 1 is written in the fours position. Note that each position is a power of the base (base 2) and that these powers begin at 0 and increase by 1 as we move left in the number (Fig. D.4). So, $101 = 2^2 + 2^0 = 4 + 1 = 5$.

Positional values in the binary number system			
Binary digit	1	0	1
Position name	Fours	Twos	Ones
Positional value	4	2	1
Positional value as a power of the base (2)	2^2	2^1	2^0

Fig. D.4 | Positional values in the binary number system.

For longer binary numbers, the next positions to the left would be the eights position (2 to the 3rd power), the sixteens position (2 to the 4th power), the thirty-twos position (2 to the 5th power), the sixty-fours position (2 to the 6th power) and so on.

In the octal number 425, we say that the 5 is written in the ones position, the 2 is written in the eights position and the 4 is written in the sixty-fours position. Note that each of these positions is a power of the base (base 8) and that these powers begin at 0 and increase by 1 as we move left in the number (Fig. D.5).

Positional values in the octal number system			
Decimal digit	4	2	5
Position name	Sixty-fours	Eights	Ones
Positional value	64	8	1
Positional value as a power of the base (8)	8^2	8^1	8^0

Fig. D.5 | Positional values in the octal number system.

For longer octal numbers, the next positions to the left would be the five-hundred-and-twelves position (8 to the 3rd power), the four-thousand-and-ninety-sixes position (8 to the 4th power), the thirty-two-thousand-seven-hundred-and-sixty-eights position (8 to the 5th power) and so on.

In the hexadecimal number 3DA, we say that the A is written in the ones position, the D is written in the sixteens position and the 3 is written in the two-hundred-and-fifty-sixes position. Note that each of these positions is a power of the base (base 16) and that these powers begin at 0 and increase by 1 as we move left in the number (Fig. D.6).

For longer hexadecimal numbers, the next positions to the left would be the four-thousand-and-ninety-sixes position (16 to the 3rd power), the sixty-five-thousand-five-hundred-and-thirty-sixes position (16 to the 4th power) and so on.

Positional values in the hexadecimal number system			
Decimal digit	3	D	A
Position name	Two-hundred-and-fifty-sixes	Sixteens	Ones
Positional value	256	16	1
Positional value as a power of the base (16)	16^2	16^1	16^0

Fig. D.6 | Positional values in the hexadecimal number system.

D.2 Abbreviating Binary Numbers as Octal and Hexadecimal Numbers

The main use for octal and hexadecimal numbers in computing is for abbreviating lengthy binary representations. Figure D.7 highlights the fact that lengthy binary numbers can be expressed concisely in number systems with higher bases than the binary number system.

Decimal number	Binary representation	Octal representation	Hexadecimal representation
0	0	0	0
1	1	1	1
2	10	2	2
3	11	3	3
4	100	4	4
5	101	5	5
6	110	6	6
7	111	7	7
8	1000	10	8
9	1001	11	9
10	1010	12	A
11	1011	13	B
12	1100	14	C
13	1101	15	D
14	1110	16	E
15	1111	17	F
16	10000	20	10

Fig. D.7 | Decimal, binary, octal and hexadecimal equivalents.

A particularly important relationship that both the octal number system and the hexadecimal number system have to the binary system is that the bases of octal and hexadecimal (8 and 16 respectively) are powers of the base of the binary number system (base 2).

Consider the following 12-digit binary number and its octal and hexadecimal equivalents. See if you can determine how this relationship makes it convenient to abbreviate binary numbers in octal or hexadecimal. The answers follow the numbers.

Binary number	Octal equivalent	Hexadecimal equivalent
100011010001	4321	8D1

To see how the binary number converts easily to octal, simply break the 12-digit binary number into groups of three consecutive bits each, starting from the right, and write those groups over the corresponding digits of the octal number as follows:

100	011	010	001
4	3	2	1

Note that the octal digit you've written under each group of three bits corresponds precisely to the octal equivalent of that 3-digit binary number, as shown in Fig. D.7.

The same kind of relationship can be observed in converting from binary to hexadecimal. Break the 12-digit binary number into groups of four consecutive bits each, starting from the right, and write those groups over the corresponding digits of the hexadecimal number as follows:

1000	1101	0001
8	D	1

Notice that the hexadecimal digit you wrote under each group of four bits corresponds precisely to the hexadecimal equivalent of that 4-digit binary number as shown in Fig. D.7.

D.3 Converting Octal and Hexadecimal Numbers to Binary Numbers

In the previous section, we saw how to convert binary numbers to their octal and hexadecimal equivalents by forming groups of binary digits and simply rewriting them as their equivalent octal digit values or hexadecimal digit values. This process may be used in reverse to produce the binary equivalent of a given octal or hexadecimal number.

For example, the octal number 653 is converted to binary simply by writing the 6 as its 3-digit binary equivalent 110, the 5 as its 3-digit binary equivalent 101 and the 3 as its 3-digit binary equivalent 011 to form the 9-digit binary number 110101011.

The hexadecimal number FAD5 is converted to binary simply by writing the F as its 4-digit binary equivalent 1111, the A as its 4-digit binary equivalent 1010, the D as its 4-digit binary equivalent 1101 and the 5 as its 4-digit binary equivalent 0101 to form the 16-digit 1111101011010101.

D.4 Converting from Binary, Octal or Hexadecimal to Decimal

We are accustomed to working in decimal, and therefore it is often convenient to convert a binary, octal, or hexadecimal number to decimal to get a sense of what the number is "really" worth. Our diagrams in Section D.1 express the positional values in decimal. To convert a number to decimal from another base, multiply the decimal equivalent of each digit by its positional value and sum these products. For example, the binary number 110101 is converted to decimal 53 as shown in Fig. D.8.

Converting a binary number to decimal					
Positional values:	32	16	8	4	2	1
Symbol values:	1	1	0	1	0	1
Products:	1*32=32	1*16=16	0*8=0	1*4=4	0*2=0	1*1=1
Sum:	= 32 + 16 + 0 + 4 + 0s + 1 = 53					

Fig. D.8 | Converting a binary number to decimal.

To convert octal 7614 to decimal 3980, we use the same technique, this time using appropriate octal positional values, as shown in Fig. D.9.

Converting an octal number to decimal			
Positional values:	512	64	8	1
Symbol values:	7	6	1	4
Products	7*512=3584	6*64=384	1*8=8	4*1=4
Sum:	= 3584 + 384 + 8 + 4 = 3980			

Fig. D.9 | Converting an octal number to decimal.

To convert hexadecimal AD3B to decimal 44347, we use the same technique, this time using appropriate hexadecimal positional values, as shown in Fig. D.10.

Converting a hexadecimal number to decimal			
Positional values:	4096	256	16	1
Symbol values:	A	D	3	B
Products	A*4096=40960	D*256=3328	3*16=48	B*1=11
Sum:	= 40960 + 3328 + 48 + 11 = 44347			

Fig. D.10 | Converting a hexadecimal number to decimal.

D.5 Converting from Decimal to Binary, Octal or Hexadecimal

The conversions in Section D.4 follow naturally from the positional notation conventions. Converting from decimal to binary, octal, or hexadecimal also follows these conventions.

Suppose we wish to convert decimal 57 to binary. We begin by writing the positional values of the columns right to left until we reach a column whose positional value is greater than the decimal number. We do not need that column, so we discard it. Thus, we first write:

Positional values: 64   32   16   8   4   2   1

Then we discard the column with positional value 64, leaving:

Positional values:	32	16	8	4	2	1

Next we work from the leftmost column to the right. We divide 32 into 57 and observe that there is one 32 in 57 with a remainder of 25, so we write 1 in the 32 column. We divide 16 into 25 and observe that there is one 16 in 25 with a remainder of 9 and write 1 in the 16 column. We divide 8 into 9 and observe that there is one 8 in 9 with a remainder of 1. The next two columns each produce quotients of 0 when their positional values are divided into 1, so we write 0s in the 4 and 2 columns. Finally, 1 into 1 is 1, so we write 1 in the 1 column. This yields:

Positional values:	32	16	8	4	2	1
Symbol values:	1	1	1	0	0	1

and thus decimal 57 is equivalent to binary 111001.

To convert decimal 103 to octal, we begin by writing the positional values of the columns until we reach a column whose positional value is greater than the decimal number. We do not need that column, so we discard it. Thus, we first write:

Positional values:	512	64	8	1

Then we discard the column with positional value 512, yielding:

Positional values:		64	8	1

Next we work from the leftmost column to the right. We divide 64 into 103 and observe that there is one 64 in 103 with a remainder of 39, so we write 1 in the 64 column. We divide 8 into 39 and observe that there are four 8s in 39 with a remainder of 7 and write 4 in the 8 column. Finally, we divide 1 into 7 and observe that there are seven 1s in 7 with no remainder, so we write 7 in the 1 column. This yields:

Positional values:	64	8	1
Symbol values:	1	4	7

and thus decimal 103 is equivalent to octal 147.

To convert decimal 375 to hexadecimal, we begin by writing the positional values of the columns until we reach a column whose positional value is greater than the decimal number. We do not need that column, so we discard it. Thus, we first write:

Positional values:	4096	256	16	1

Then we discard the column with positional value 4096, yielding:

Positional values:		256	16	1

Next we work from the leftmost column to the right. We divide 256 into 375 and observe that there is one 256 in 375 with a remainder of 119, so we write 1 in the 256 column. We divide 16 into 119 and observe that there are seven 16s in 119 with a remainder of 7 and write 7 in the 16 column. Finally, we divide 1 into 7 and observe that there are seven 1s in 7 with no remainder, so we write 7 in the 1 column. This yields:

Positional values:	256	16	1
Symbol values:	1	7	7

and thus decimal 375 is equivalent to hexadecimal 177.

D.6 Negative Binary Numbers: Two's Complement Notation

The discussion so far in this appendix has focused on positive numbers. In this section, we explain how computers represent negative numbers using two's complement notation. First we explain how the two's complement of a binary number is formed, then we show why it represents the negative value of the given binary number.

Consider a machine with 32-bit integers. Suppose

```
int value = 13;
```

The 32-bit representation of value is

```
00000000 00000000 00000000 00001101
```

To form the negative of value we first form its **one's complement** by applying C++'s bit-wise complement operator (~):

```
onesComplementOfValue = ~value;
```

Internally, ~value is now value with each of its bits reversed—ones become zeros and zeros become ones, as follows:

```
value:
00000000 00000000 00000000 00001101

~value (i.e., value's one's complement):
11111111 11111111 11111111 11110010
```

To form the two's complement of value, we simply add 1 to value's one's complement. Thus

```
Two's complement of value:
11111111 11111111 11111111 11110011
```

Now if this is in fact equal to −13, we should be able to add it to binary 13 and obtain a result of 0. Let's try this:

```
  00000000 00000000 00000000 00001101
+ 11111111 11111111 11111111 11110011
-------------------------------------
  00000000 00000000 00000000 00000000
```

The carry bit coming out of the leftmost column is discarded and we indeed get 0 as a result. If we add the one's complement of a number to the number, the result will be all 1s. The key to getting a result of all zeros is that the two's complement is one more than the one's complement. The addition of 1 causes each column to add to 0 with a carry of 1. The carry keeps moving leftward until it is discarded from the leftmost bit, and thus the resulting number is all zeros.

Computers actually perform a subtraction, such as

```
x = a - value;
```

by adding the two's complement of value to a, as follows:

```
x = a + (~value + 1);
```

Suppose a is 27 and `value` is 13 as before. If the two's complement of `value` is actually the negative of `value`, then adding the two's complement of value to a should produce the result 14. Let's try this:

```
a (i.e., 27)           00000000 00000000 00000000 00011011
+(~value + 1)         +11111111 11111111 11111111 11110011
                       ------------------------------------
                       00000000 00000000 00000000 00001110
```

which is indeed equal to 14.

Summary

- An integer such as 19 or 227 or –63 in a C++ program is assumed to be in the decimal (base 10) number system. The digits in the decimal number system are 0, 1, 2, 3, 4, 5, 6, 7, 8 and 9. The lowest digit is 0 and the highest is 9—one less than the base of 10.
- Computers use the binary (base 2) number system. The binary number system has only two digits, namely 0 and 1. Its lowest digit is 0 and its highest is 1—one less than the base of 2.
- The octal number system (base 8) and the hexadecimal number system (base 16) are popular primarily because they make it convenient to abbreviate binary numbers.
- The digits of the octal number system range from 0 to 7.
- The hexadecimal number system poses a problem because it requires 16 digits—a lowest digit of 0 and a highest digit with a value equivalent to decimal 15 (one less than the base of 16). By convention, we use the letters A through F to represent the hexadecimal digits corresponding to decimal values 10 through 15.
- Each number system uses positional notation—each position in which a digit is written has a different positional value.
- A particularly important relationship of both the octal and the hexadecimal number systems to the binary system is that their bases (8 and 16 respectively) are powers of the base of the binary number system (base 2).
- To convert from octal to binary, replace each octal digit with its three-digit binary equivalent.
- To convert a hexadecimal to a binary number, simply replace each hexadecimal digit with its four-digit binary equivalent.
- Because we are accustomed to working in decimal, it is convenient to convert a binary, octal or hexadecimal number to decimal to get a sense of the number's "real" worth.
- To convert a number to decimal from another base, multiply the decimal equivalent of each digit by its positional value and sum the products.
- Computers represent negative numbers using two's complement notation.
- To form the negative of a value in binary, first form its one's complement by applying C++'s bitwise complement operator (~). This reverses the bits of the value. To form the two's complement of a value, simply add one to the value's one's complement.

Self-Review Exercises

D.1   The bases of the decimal, binary, octal and hexadecimal number systems are _____, _____, _____ and _____ respectively.

D.2   In general, the decimal, octal and hexadecimal representations of a given binary number contain (more/fewer) digits than the binary number contains.

D.3   (*True/False*) A popular reason for using the decimal number system is that it forms a convenient notation for abbreviating binary numbers simply by substituting one decimal digit per group of four binary bits.

D.4   The [octal/hexadecimal/decimal] representation of a large binary value is the most concise (of the given alternatives).

D.5   (*True/False*) The highest digit in any base is one more than the base.

D.6   (*True/False*) The lowest digit in any base is one less than the base.

D.7   The positional value of the rightmost digit of any number in either binary, octal, decimal or hexadecimal is always _____.

D.8   The positional value of the digit to the left of the rightmost digit of any number in binary, octal, decimal or hexadecimal is always equal to _____.

D.9   Fill in the missing values in this chart of positional values for the rightmost four positions in each of the indicated number systems:

	1000	100	10	1
decimal	1000	100	10	1
hexadecimal	...	256	...	...
binary	...	...	...	...
octal	512	...	8	...

D.10   Convert binary 110101011000 to octal and to hexadecimal.

D.11   Convert hexadecimal FACE to binary.

D.12   Convert octal 7316 to binary.

D.13   Convert hexadecimal 4FEC to octal. [*Hint:* First convert 4FEC to binary, then convert that binary number to octal.]

D.14   Convert binary 1101110 to decimal.

D.15   Convert octal 317 to decimal.

D.16   Convert hexadecimal EFD4 to decimal.

D.17   Convert decimal 177 to binary, to octal and to hexadecimal.

D.18   Show the binary representation of decimal 417. Then show the one's complement of 417 and the two's complement of 417.

D.19   What's the result when a number and its two's complement are added to each other?

Answers to Self-Review Exercises

D.1   10, 2, 8, 16.

D.2   Fewer.

D.3   False. Hexadecimal does this.

D.4   Hexadecimal.

D.5   False. The highest digit in any base is one less than the base.

D.6   False. The lowest digit in any base is zero.

D.7   1 (the base raised to the zero power).

D.8   The base of the number system.

D.9   Filled in chart shown below:

decimal	1000	100	10	1
hexadecimal	4096	256	16	1
binary	8	4	2	1
octal	512	64	8	1

D.10   Octal 6530; Hexadecimal D58.

D.11   Binary 1111 1010 1100 1110.

D.12   Binary 111 011 001 110.

D.13   Binary 0 100 111 111 101 100; Octal 47754.

D.14   Decimal 2 + 4 + 8 + 32 + 64 = 110.

D.15   Decimal 7 + 1 * 8 + 3 * 64 = 7 + 8 + 192 = 207.

D.16   Decimal 4 + 13 * 16 + 15 * 256 + 14 * 4096 = 61396.

D.17   Decimal 177
to binary:

```
256 128 64 32 16 8 4 2 1
128 64 32 16 8 4 2 1
(1*128)+(0*64)+(1*32)+(1*16)+(0*8)+(0*4)+(0*2)+(1*1)
10110001
```

to octal:

```
512 64 8 1
64 8 1
(2*64)+(6*8)+(1*1)
261
```

to hexadecimal:

```
256 16 1
16 1
(11*16)+(1*1)
(B*16)+(1*1)
B1
```

D.18   Binary:

```
512 256 128 64 32 16 8 4 2 1
256 128 64 32 16 8 4 2 1
(1*256)+(1*128)+(0*64)+(1*32)+(0*16)+(0*8)+(0*4)+(0*2)+(1*1)
110100001
```

One's complement: 001011110
Two's complement: 001011111
Check: Original binary number + its two's complement

```
110100001
001011111
---------
000000000
```

D.19   Zero.

Exercises

D.20   Some people argue that many of our calculations would be easier in the base 12 than in the base 10 (decimal) number system because 12 is divisible by so many more numbers than 10. What's the lowest digit in base 12? What would be the highest symbol for the digit in base 12? What are the positional values of the rightmost four positions of any number in the base 12 number system?

D.21   Complete the following chart of positional values for the rightmost four positions in each of the indicated number systems:

	1000	100	10	1
decimal	1000	100	10	1
base 6	...	...	6	...
base 13	...	169	...	...
base 3	27	...	...	...

D.22   Convert binary 100101111010 to octal and to hexadecimal.

D.23   Convert hexadecimal 3A7D to binary.

D.24   Convert hexadecimal 765F to octal. [*Hint:* First convert 765F to binary, then convert that binary number to octal.]

D.25   Convert binary 1011110 to decimal.

D.26   Convert octal 426 to decimal.

D.27   Convert hexadecimal FFFF to decimal.

D.28   Convert decimal 299 to binary, to octal and to hexadecimal.

D.29   Show the binary representation of decimal 779. Then show the one's complement of 779 and the two's complement of 779.

D.30   Show the two's complement of integer value −1 on a machine with 32-bit integers.

Preprocessor

Hold thou the good; define it well.
—Alfred, Lord Tennyson

I have found you an argument; but I am not obliged to find you an understanding.
—Samuel Johnson

A good symbol is the best argument, and is a missionary to persuade thousands.
—Ralph Waldo Emerson

Conditions are fundamentally sound.
—Herbert Hoover [December 1929]

Objectives

In this appendix you'll learn:

- To use `#include` for developing large programs.
- To use `#define` to create macros and macros with arguments.
- To understand conditional compilation.
- To display error messages during conditional compilation.
- To use assertions to test if the values of expressions are correct.

E.1 Introduction

This chapter introduces the **preprocessor**. Preprocessing occurs before a program is compiled. Some possible actions are inclusion of other files in the file being compiled, definition of **symbolic constants** and **macros, conditional compilation** of program code and **conditional execution of preprocessing directives.** All preprocessing directives begin with #, and only whitespace characters may appear before a preprocessing directive on a line. Preprocessing directives are not C++ statements, so they do not end in a semicolon (;). Preprocessing directives are processed fully before compilation begins.

Common Programming Error E.1

Placing a semicolon at the end of a preprocessing directive can lead to a variety of errors, depending on the type of preprocessing directive.

Software Engineering Observation E.1

Many preprocessor features (especially macros) are more appropriate for C programmers than for C++ programmers. C++ programmers should familiarize themselves with the preprocessor, because they might need to work with C legacy code.

E.2 #include Preprocessing Directive

The **#include preprocessing directive** has been used throughout this text. The #include directive causes a copy of a specified file to be included in place of the directive. The two forms of the #include directive are

```
#include <filename>
#include "filename"
```

The difference between these is the location the preprocessor searches for the file to be included. If the filename is enclosed in angle brackets (< and >)—used for standard library header files—the preprocessor searches for the specified file in an implementation-dependent manner, normally through predesignated directories. If the file name is enclosed in quotes, the preprocessor searches first in the same directory as the file being compiled, then in the same implementation-dependent manner as for a file name enclosed in angle brackets. This method is normally used to include programmer-defined header files.

The #include directive is used to include standard header files such as <iostream> and <iomanip>. The #include directive is also used with programs consisting of several source files that are to be compiled together. A header file containing declarations and definitions common to the separate program files is often created and included in the file. Examples of such declarations and definitions are classes, structures, unions, enumerations, function prototypes, constants and stream objects (e.g., `cin`).

E.3 #define Preprocessing Directive: Symbolic Constants

The **#define** preprocessing directive creates symbolic constants—constants represented as symbols—and macros—operations defined as symbols. The #define preprocessing directive format is

> #define *identifier replacement-text*

When this line appears in a file, all subsequent occurrences (except those inside a string) of *identifier* in that file will be replaced by *replacement-text* before the program is compiled. For example,

> #define PI 3.14159

replaces all subsequent occurrences of the symbolic constant PI with the numeric constant 3.14159. Symbolic constants enable you to create a name for a constant and use the name throughout the program. Later, if the constant needs to be modified throughout the program, it can be modified once in the #define preprocessing directive—and when the program is recompiled, all occurrences of the constant in the program will be modified. [*Note:* Everything to the right of the symbolic constant name replaces the symbolic constant. For example, #define PI = 3.14159 causes the preprocessor to replace every occurrence of PI with = 3.14159. Such replacement is the cause of many subtle logic and syntax errors.] Redefining a symbolic constant with a new value without first undefining it is also an error. Note that const variables in C++ are preferred over symbolic constants. Constant variables have a specific data type and are visible by name to a debugger. Once a symbolic constant is replaced with its replacement text, only the replacement text is visible to a debugger. A disadvantage of const variables is that they might require a memory location of their data type size—symbolic constants do not require any additional memory.

Common Programming Error E.2
Using symbolic constants in a file other than the file in which the symbolic constants are defined is a compilation error (unless they are #included from a header file).

Good Programming Practice E.1
Using meaningful names for symbolic constants makes programs more self-documenting.

E.4 #define Preprocessing Directive: Macros

[*Note:* This section is included for the benefit of C++ programmers who will need to work with C legacy code. In C++, macros can often be replaced by templates and inline functions.] A macro is an operation defined in a #define preprocessing directive. As with symbolic constants, the *macro-identifier* is replaced with the *replacement-text* before the program is compiled. Macros may be defined with or without *arguments*. A macro without arguments is processed like a symbolic constant. In a macro with arguments, the arguments are substituted in the *replacement-text*, then the macro is expanded—i.e., the *replacement-text* replaces the macro-identifier and argument list in the program. There is no data type checking for macro arguments. A macro is used simply for text substitution.

Consider the following macro definition with one argument for the area of a circle:

```
#define CIRCLE_AREA( x ) ( PI * ( x ) * ( x ) )
```

Wherever CIRCLE_AREA(y) appears in the file, the value of y is substituted for x in the replacement text, the symbolic constant PI is replaced by its value (defined previously) and the macro is expanded in the program. For example, the statement

```
area = CIRCLE_AREA( 4 );
```

is expanded to

```
area = ( 3.14159 * ( 4 ) * ( 4 ) );
```

Because the expression consists only of constants, at compile time the value of the expression can be evaluated, and the result is assigned to area at runtime. The parentheses around each x in the replacement text and around the entire expression force the proper order of evaluation when the macro argument is an expression. For example, the statement

```
area = CIRCLE_AREA( c + 2 );
```

is expanded to

```
area = ( 3.14159 * ( c + 2 ) * ( c + 2 ) );
```

which evaluates correctly, because the parentheses force the proper order of evaluation. If the parentheses are omitted, the macro expansion is

```
area = 3.14159 * c + 2 * c + 2;
```

which evaluates incorrectly as

```
area = ( 3.14159 * c ) + ( 2 * c ) + 2;
```

because of the rules of operator precedence.

Common Programming Error E.3

Forgetting to enclose macro arguments in parentheses in the replacement text is an error.

Macro CIRCLE_AREA could be defined as a function. Function circleArea, as in

```
double circleArea( double x ) { return 3.14159 * x * x; }
```

performs the same calculation as CIRCLE_AREA, but the overhead of a function call is associated with function circleArea. The advantages of CIRCLE_AREA are that macros insert code directly in the program—avoiding function overhead—and the program remains readable because CIRCLE_AREA is defined separately and named meaningfully. A disadvantage is that its argument is evaluated twice. Also, every time a macro appears in a program, the macro is expanded. If the macro is large, this produces an increase in program size. Thus, there is a trade-off between execution speed and program size (if disk space is low).

Note that `inline` functions (see Chapter 6) are preferred to obtain the performance of macros and the software engineering benefits of functions.

Performance Tip E.1

Macros can sometimes be used to replace a function call with `inline` code prior to execution time. This eliminates the overhead of a function call. Inline functions are preferable to macros because they offer the type-checking services of functions.

The following is a macro definition with two arguments for the area of a rectangle:

```
#define RECTANGLE_AREA( x, y ) ( ( x ) * ( y ) )
```

Wherever RECTANGLE_AREA(a, b) appears in the program, the values of a and b are substituted in the macro replacement text, and the macro is expanded in place of the macro name. For example, the statement

```
rectArea = RECTANGLE_AREA( a + 4, b + 7 );
```

is expanded to

```
rectArea = ( ( a + 4 ) * ( b + 7 ) );
```

The value of the expression is evaluated and assigned to variable `rectArea`.

The replacement text for a macro or symbolic constant is normally any text on the line after the identifier in the `#define` directive. If the replacement text for a macro or symbolic constant is longer than the remainder of the line, a backslash (\) must be placed at the end of each line of the macro (except the last line), indicating that the replacement text continues on the next line.

Symbolic constants and macros can be discarded using the `#undef` preprocessing directive. Directive `#undef` "undefines" a symbolic constant or macro name. The scope of a symbolic constant or macro is from its definition until it is either undefined with `#undef` or the end of the file is reached. Once undefined, a name can be redefined with `#define`.

Note that expressions with side effects (e.g., variable values are modified) should not be passed to a macro, because macro arguments may be evaluated more than once.

Common Programming Error E.4

Macros often replace a name that wasn't intended to be a use of the macro but just happened to be spelled the same. This can lead to exceptionally mysterious compilation and syntax errors.

E.5 Conditional Compilation

Conditional compilation enables you to control the execution of preprocessing directives and the compilation of program code. Each of the conditional preprocessing directives evaluates a constant integer expression that will determine whether the code will be compiled. Cast expressions, `sizeof` expressions and enumeration constants cannot be evaluated in preprocessing directives because these are all determined by the compiler and preprocessing happens before compilation.

The conditional preprocessor construct is much like the `if` selection structure. Consider the following preprocessor code:

```
#ifndef NULL
    #define NULL 0
#endif
```

which determines whether the symbolic constant NULL is already defined. The expression #ifndef NULL includes the code up to #endif if NULL is not defined, and skips the code if NULL is defined. Every #if construct ends with **#endif**. Directives **#ifdef** and **#ifndef** are shorthand for #if defined(*name*) and #if !defined(*name*). A multiple-part conditional preprocessor construct may be tested using the #elif (the equivalent of else if in an if structure) and the #else (the equivalent of else in an if structure) directives.

During program development, programmers often find it helpful to "comment out" large portions of code to prevent it from being compiled. If the code contains C-style comments, /* and */ cannot be used to accomplish this task, because the first */ encountered would terminate the comment. Instead, you can use the following preprocessor construct:

```
#if 0
    code prevented from compiling
#endif
```

To enable the code to be compiled, simply replace the value 0 in the preceding construct with the value 1.

Conditional compilation is commonly used as a debugging aid. Output statements are often used to print variable values and to confirm the flow of control. These output statements can be enclosed in conditional preprocessing directives so that the statements are compiled only until the debugging process is completed. For example,

```
#ifdef DEBUG
    cerr << "Variable x = " << x << endl;
#endif
```

causes the cerr statement to be compiled in the program if the symbolic constant DEBUG has been defined before directive #ifdef DEBUG. This symbolic constant is normally set by a command-line compiler or by settings in the IDE (e.g., Visual Studio) and not by an explicit #define definition. When debugging is completed, the #define directive is removed from the source file, and the output statements inserted for debugging purposes are ignored during compilation. In larger programs, it might be desirable to define several different symbolic constants that control the conditional compilation in separate sections of the source file.

Common Programming Error E.5

Inserting conditionally compiled output statements for debugging purposes in locations where C++ currently expects a single statement can lead to syntax errors and logic errors. In this case, the conditionally compiled statement should be enclosed in a compound statement. Thus, when the program is compiled with debugging statements, the flow of control of the program is not altered.

E.6 #error and #pragma Preprocessing Directives

The #error directive

```
#error tokens
```

prints an implementation-dependent message including the *tokens* specified in the directive. The tokens are sequences of characters separated by spaces. For example,

```
#error 1 - Out of range error
```

contains six tokens. In one popular C++ compiler, for example, when a #error directive is processed, the tokens in the directive are displayed as an error message, preprocessing stops and the program does not compile.

The #pragma directive

```
#pragma tokens
```

causes an implementation-defined action. A pragma not recognized by the implementation is ignored. A particular C++ compiler, for example, might recognize pragmas that enable you to take advantage of that compiler's specific capabilities. For more information on #error and #pragma, see the documentation for your C++ implementation.

E.7 Operators # and

The # and ## preprocessor operators are available in C++ and ANSI/ISO C. The # operator causes a replacement-text token to be converted to a string surrounded by quotes. Consider the following macro definition:

```
#define HELLO( x ) cout << "Hello, " #x << endl;
```

When HELLO(John) appears in a program file, it is expanded to

```
cout << "Hello, " "John" << endl;
```

The string "John" replaces #x in the replacement text. Strings separated by white space are concatenated during preprocessing, so the above statement is equivalent to

```
cout << "Hello, John" << endl;
```

Note that the # operator must be used in a macro with arguments, because the operand of # refers to an argument of the macro.

The ## operator concatenates two tokens. Consider the following macro definition:

```
cout << "Hello, John" << endl;
#define TOKENCONCAT( x, y )  x ## y
```

When TOKENCONCAT appears in the program, its arguments are concatenated and used to replace the macro. For example, TOKENCONCAT(O, K) is replaced by OK in the program. The ## operator must have two operands.

E.8 Predefined Symbolic Constants

There are six predefined symbolic constants (Fig. E.1). The identifiers for each of these begin and (except for __cplusplus) end with *two* underscores. These identifiers and preprocessor operator defined (Section E.5) cannot be used in #define or #undef directives.

Symbolic constant	Description
__LINE__	The line number of the current source-code line (an integer constant).
__FILE__	The presumed name of the source file (a string).
__DATE__	The date the source file is compiled (a string of the form "Mmm dd yyyy" such as "Aug 19 2002").
__STDC__	Indicates whether the program conforms to the ANSI/ISO C standard. Contains value 1 if there is full conformance and is undefined otherwise.
__TIME__	The time the source file is compiled (a string literal of the form "hh:mm:ss").
__cplusplus	Contains the value 199711L (the date the ISO C++ standard was approved) if the file is being compiled by a C++ compiler, undefined otherwise. Allows a file to be set up to be compiled as either C or C++.

Fig. E.1 | The predefined symbolic constants.

E.9 Assertions

The **assert** macro—defined in the `<cassert>` header file—tests the value of an expression. If the value of the expression is 0 (false), then `assert` prints an error message and calls function **abort** (of the general utilities library—`<cstdlib>`) to terminate program execution. This is a useful debugging tool for testing whether a variable has a correct value. For example, suppose variable x should never be larger than 10 in a program. An assertion may be used to test the value of x and print an error message if the value of x is incorrect. The statement would be

```
assert( x <= 10 );
```

If x is greater than 10 when the preceding statement is encountered in a program, an error message containing the line number and file name is printed, and the program terminates. You may then concentrate on this area of the code to find the error. If the symbolic constant NDEBUG is defined, subsequent assertions will be ignored. Thus, when assertions are no longer needed (i.e., when debugging is complete), we insert the line

```
#define NDEBUG
```

in the program file rather than deleting each assertion manually. As with the DEBUG symbolic constant, NDEBUG is often set by compiler command-line options or through a setting in the IDE.

Most C++ compilers now include exception handling. C++ programmers prefer using exceptions rather than assertions. But assertions are still valuable for C++ programmers who work with C legacy code.

E.10 Wrap-Up

This appendix discussed the `#include` directive, which is used to develop larger programs. You also learned about the `#define` directive, which is used to create macros. We introduced conditional compilation, displaying error messages and using assertions.

Summary

Section E.2 `#include` Preprocessing Directive

- All preprocessing directives begin with # and are processed before the program is compiled.
- Only whitespace characters may appear before a preprocessing directive on a line.
- The `#include` directive includes a copy of the specified file. If the filename is enclosed in quotes, the preprocessor begins searching in the same directory as the file being compiled for the file to be included. If the filename is enclosed in angle brackets (< and >), the search is performed in an implementation-defined manner.

Section E.3 `#define` Preprocessing Directive: Symbolic Constants

- The `#define` preprocessing directive is used to create symbolic constants and macros.
- A symbolic constant is a name for a constant.

Section E.4 `#define` Preprocessing Directive: Macros

- A macro is an operation defined in a `#define` preprocessing directive. Macros may be defined with or without arguments.
- The replacement text for a macro or symbolic constant is any text remaining on the line after the identifier (and, if any, the macro argument list) in the `#define` directive. If the replacement text for a macro or symbolic constant is too long to fit on one line, a backslash (\) is placed at the end of the line, indicating that the replacement text continues on the next line.
- Symbolic constants and macros can be discarded using the `#undef` preprocessing directive. Directive `#undef` "undefines" the symbolic constant or macro name.
- The scope of a symbolic constant or macro is from its definition until it is either undefined with `#undef` or the end of the file is reached.

Section E.5 Conditional Compilation

- Conditional compilation enables you to control the execution of preprocessing directives and the compilation of program code.
- The conditional preprocessing directives evaluate constant integer expressions. Cast expressions, `sizeof` expressions and enumeration constants cannot be evaluated in preprocessing directives.
- Every `#if` construct ends with `#endif`.
- Directives `#ifdef` and `#ifndef` are provided as shorthand for `#if defined(`*name*`)` and `#if !defined(`*name*`)`.
- A multiple-part conditional preprocessor construct is tested with directives `#elif` and `#else`.

Section E.6 `#error` and `#pragma` Preprocessing Directives

- The `#error` directive prints an implementation-dependent message that includes the tokens specified in the directive and terminates preprocessing and compiling.
- The `#pragma` directive causes an implementation-defined action. If the pragma is not recognized by the implementation, the pragma is ignored.

Section E.7 Operators # and ##

- The # operator causes the following replacement text token to be converted to a string surrounded by quotes. The # operator must be used in a macro with arguments, because the operand of # must be an argument of the macro.
- The ## operator concatenates two tokens. The ## operator must have two operands.

Section E.8 Predefined Symbolic Constants

- There are six predefined symbolic constants. Constant `__LINE__` is the line number of the current source-code line (an integer). Constant `__FILE__` is the presumed name of the file (a string). Constant `__DATE__` is the date the source file is compiled (a string). Constant `__TIME__` is the time the source file is compiled (a string). Note that each of the predefined symbolic constants begins (and, with the exception of `__cplusplus`, ends) with two underscores.

Section E.9 Assertions

- The assert macro—defined in the `<cassert>` header file—tests the value of an expression. If the value of the expression is 0 (false), then `assert` prints an error message and calls function `abort` to terminate program execution.

Self-Review Exercises

E.1 Fill in the blanks in each of the following:
  a) Every preprocessing directive must begin with _____.
  b) The conditional compilation construct may be extended to test for multiple cases by using the _____ and the _____ directives.
  c) The _____ directive creates macros and symbolic constants.
  d) Only _____ characters may appear before a preprocessing directive on a line.
  e) The _____ directive discards symbolic constant and macro names.
  f) The _____ and _____ directives are provided as shorthand notation for `#if defined(name)` and `#if !defined(name)`.
  g) _____ enables you to control the execution of preprocessing directives and the compilation of program code.
  h) The _____ macro prints a message and terminates program execution if the value of the expression the macro evaluates is 0.
  i) The _____ directive inserts a file in another file.
  j) The _____ operator concatenates its two arguments.
  k) The _____ operator converts its operand to a string.
  l) The character _____ indicates that the replacement text for a symbolic constant or macro continues on the next line.

E.2 Write a program to print the values of the predefined symbolic constants `__LINE__`, `__FILE__`, `__DATE__` and `__TIME__` listed in Fig. E.1.

E.3 Write a preprocessing directive to accomplish each of the following:
  a) Define symbolic constant YES to have the value 1.
  b) Define symbolic constant NO to have the value 0.
  c) Include the header file `common.h`. The header is found in the same directory as the file being compiled.
  d) If symbolic constant TRUE is defined, undefine it, and redefine it as 1. Do not use `#ifdef`.
  e) If symbolic constant TRUE is defined, undefine it, and redefine it as 1. Use the `#ifdef` preprocessing directive.
  f) If symbolic constant ACTIVE is not equal to 0, define symbolic constant INACTIVE as 0. Otherwise, define INACTIVE as 1.
  g) Define macro CUBE_VOLUME that computes the volume of a cube (takes one argument).

Answers to Self-Review Exercises

E.1 a) #. b) #elif, #else. c) #define. d) whitespace. e) #undef. f) #ifdef, #ifndef. g) Conditional compilation. h) assert. i) #include. j) ##. k) #. l) \.

E.2   (See below.)

```
1    // exE_02.cpp
2    // Self-Review Exercise E.2 solution.
3    #include <iostream>
4    using namespace std;
5
6    int main()
7    {
8       cout << "__LINE__ = " << __LINE__ << endl
9            << "__FILE__ = " << __FILE__ << endl
10           << "__DATE__ = " << __DATE__ << endl
11           << "__TIME__ = " << __TIME__ << endl
12           << "__cplusplus = " << __cplusplus << endl;
13   } // end main
```

```
__LINE__ = 9
__FILE__ = c:\cpp4e\ch19\ex19_02.CPP
__DATE__ = Jul 17 2002
__TIME__ = 09:55:58
__cplusplus = 199711L
```

E.3   a) `#define YES 1`
        b) `#define NO 0`
        c) `#include "common.h"`
        d) `#if defined(TRUE)`

```
        #undef TRUE
        #define TRUE 1
    #endif
```
        e) `#ifdef TRUE`
```
        #undef TRUE
        #define TRUE 1
    #endif
```
        f) `#if ACTIVE`
```
        #define INACTIVE 0
    #else
        #define INACTIVE 1
    #endif
```
        g) `#define CUBE_VOLUME( x ) ( ( x ) * ( x ) * ( x ) )`

Exercises

E.4   Write a program that defines a macro with one argument to compute the volume of a sphere. The program should compute the volume for spheres of radii from 1 to 10 and print the results in tabular format. The formula for the volume of a sphere is

$$(4.0 / 3) * \pi * r^3$$

where π is 3.14159.

E.5   Write a program that produces the following output:

```
The sum of x and y is 13
```

The program should define macro SUM with two arguments, x and y, and use SUM to produce the output.

E.6   Write a program that uses macro MINIMUM2 to determine the smaller of two numeric values. Input the values from the keyboard.

E.7   Write a program that uses macro MINIMUM3 to determine the smallest of three numeric values. Macro MINIMUM3 should use macro MINIMUM2 defined in Exercise E.6 to determine the smallest number. Input the values from the keyboard.

E.8   Write a program that uses macro PRINT to print a string value.

E.9   Write a program that uses macro PRINTARRAY to print an array of integers. The macro should receive the array and the number of elements in the array as arguments.

E.10   Write a program that uses macro SUMARRAY to sum the values in a numeric array. The macro should receive the array and the number of elements in the array as arguments.

E.11   Rewrite the solutions to Exercises E.4–E.10 as inline functions.

E.12   For each of the following macros, identify the possible problems (if any) when the preprocessor expands the macros:
   a) #define SQR(x) x * x
   b) #define SQR(x) (x * x)
   c) #define SQR(x) (x) * (x)
   d) #define SQR(x) ((x) * (x))

Appendices on the Web

The following appendices are available as PDF documents from this book's Companion Website, which is accessible from www.pearsoninternationaleditions.com/deitel:

- Appendix F, C Legacy Code Topics
- Appendix G, UML 2: Additional Diagram Types
- Appendix H, Using the Visual Studio Debugger
- Appendix I, Using the GNU C++ Debugger
- Appendix J, Using the Xcode Debugger
- Appendix K, Test Driving a C++ Program on Mac OS X

These files can be viewed in Adobe® Reader® (get.adobe.com/reader).

New copies of this book come with a Companion Website access code that is located on the inside of the front cover. If the access code is already visible, you purchased a used book. If there is no access code inside the front cover, you purchased an edition that does not come with an access code. In either case, you can purchase access directly from the Companion Website.

Index